Y0-ABK-218

RULES OF DEBIT AND CREDIT

Withdrawals
(Sole Proprietorship/Partnership)

Debit	Credit
+	−
Increase	Decrease
Normal Balance	

Example: Linda Carter, Withdrawals

Revenue

Debit	Credit
−	+
Decrease	Increase
	Normal Balance

Examples: Fees Income
Sales

Contra Revenue

Debit	Credit
+	−
Increase	Decrease
Normal Balance	

Examples: Sales Discounts
Sales Returns and Allowances

Cost of Goods Sold

Debit	Credit
+	−
Increase	Decrease
Normal Balance	

Examples: Purchases
Freight In

Contra Cost of Goods Sold

Debit	Credit
−	+
Decrease	Increase
	Normal Balance

Examples: Purchases Discounts
Purchases Returns and Allowances

Expenses

Debit	Credit
+	−
Increase	Decrease
Normal Balance	

Examples: Advertising Expense
Utilities Expense
Rent Expense

College Accounting

UPDATED TENTH EDITION
CHAPTERS 1–32

John Ellis Price, Ph.D., C.P.A.
KPMG Professor of Taxation and Chair
Department of Accounting
College of Business Administration
University of North Texas
Denton, Texas

M. David Haddock, Jr., Ed.D., C.P.A.
Professor of Accounting
Chattanooga State Technical Community College
Chattanooga, Tennessee

Horace R. Brock, Ph.D., C.P.A.
Distinguished Professor of Accounting Emeritus
College of Business Administration
University of North Texas
Denton, Texas

Visit the *College Accounting* Web site at:
www.mhhe.com/price10e

 **McGraw-Hill Irwin**

Boston   Burr Ridge, IL   Dubuque, IA   Madison, WI   New York   San Francisco   St. Louis
Bangkok   Bogotá   Caracas   Kuala Lumpur   Lisbon   London   Madrid   Mexico City
Milan   Montreal   New Delhi   Santiago   Seoul   Singapore   Sydney   Taipei   Toronto

The **McGraw·Hill** Companies

 **McGraw-Hill Irwin**

COLLEGE ACCOUNTING, UPDATED TENTH EDITION
CHAPTERS 1–32
Published by McGraw-Hill/Irwin, a business unit of The McGraw-Hill Companies, Inc.,
1221 Avenue of the Americas, New York, NY, 10020. Copyright © 2003, 1999, 1996, 1990, 1986,
1981, 1974, 1969, 1963 by The McGraw-Hill Companies, Inc. All rights reserved. No part of this
publication may be reproduced or distributed in any form or by any means, or stored in a database or
retrieval system, without the prior written consent of The McGraw-Hill Companies, Inc., including,
but not limited to, in any network or other electronic storage or transmission, or broadcast for
distance learning.
Some ancillaries, including electronic and print components, may not be available to customers outside
the United States.

Peachtree, the peach logo, Peachtree Complete and Peachtree First are registered trademarks, and
Peachtree Today and Accounting Behind the Screens are trademarks of Peachtree Software, Inc.
Microsoft, Excel, PowerPoint, MS-DOS, and Windows are registered trademarks of
Microsoft Corporation.
QuickBooks is a registered trademark of Intuit Inc.

This book is printed on acid-free paper.

3 4 5 6 7 8 9 0 DOW/DOW 0 9 8 7 6 5 4

ISBN 0-07-294957-0

Editor-in-chief: *Rob Zwettler*
Editorial director: *Brent Gordon*
Editor-in-chief: *Rob Zwettler*
Publisher: *Stewart Mattson*
Executive editor: *Tim Vertovec*
Developmental editor: *Sarah Wood*
Marketing manager: *Katherine Mattison*
Project manager: *Susanne Riedell*
Senior production supervisor: *Rose Hepburn*
Coordinator freelance design: *Artemio Ortiz Jr.*
Typeface: *11/13 Giovanni Book*
Compositor: *GAC Indianapolis*
Printer: *R. R. Donnelley*

NOTICE. Information on featured companies, organizations, their products and
services is included for educational purposes only, and it does not present or imply
endorsement of the *College Accounting* program. Permission to use all business
logos has been granted by the businesses represented in this text.

www.mhhe.com

Preface

Who do you want to be? Do you hope to become a dynamic leader, one of the inspirational members of a corporate team, an innovative contributor in a new business startup? Do you want to solve tough management challenges while utilizing your business skills to the fullest extent possible? If you answered "yes" to these questions, these desires can become a reality. Career development begins by constructing a framework of necessary knowledge, work experience, and personal skills. Employers today seek candidates who can effectively communicate in a business situation, analyze financial data, work creatively with a team, and proactively find answers to difficult problems.

We wrote this text to help you construct a framework of skills and knowledge necessary for success in the business world today. You will learn the "language of business" used in boardrooms, financial newscasts, and corporate meetings every day. This language will become part of your working vocabulary. Real-world perspectives from companies such as The Home Depot, Southwest Airlines, Guess?, and Wal-Mart give you a deeper understanding of business transactions and how they affect the financial condition and performance of a company.

In the workplace, knowledge of a particular topic is not enough. You will be asked to make presentations, write reports and summaries, lead team meetings, analyze financial options, and solve new business challenges. This textbook offers countless opportunities to enhance these valuable skills as you apply and practice accounting procedures and concepts.

Features and Elements of Your Textbook

Textbook Organization

College Accounting is offered in three versions: Chapters 1–13, Chapters 1–25, and Chapters 1–32. Each chapter is divided into two or three sections. Each section is numbered, titled, and treated as a self-contained learning segment. Sections are again broken down into easy-to-digest portions of information labeled with informative headings.

Content

College Accounting, Chapters 1–32, provides a solid coverage of accounting concepts, procedures, and principles. The textbook first examines the traditional framework of a sole proprietorship accounting cycle, and then builds on these concepts with discussions of asset, liability, and equity accounts. The textbook expands its coverage of basic principles by presenting partnership, corporation, and managerial accounting concepts.

Learning Objectives. Each chapter opens with a preview of learning objectives for the material. Keep these objectives in mind as you work through the content of the chapter. Note that the running text offers an indicator in the side margin signaling that a new learning objective is being addressed.

Vocabulary. Mastery of the "language of business" is key to success in this course and in the business world. Each chapter provides the following learning aids:

- **New Terms Preview.** All new terms are previewed on chapter-opener pages. Each section within a chapter also previews the terms that will be used in that portion of learning. Before beginning each chapter, read the new terms and recall instances in which you have heard these terms used.
- **Definitions.** As each term is introduced in the running text of a chapter, it appears in boldface type and is highlighted. Take special note of these terms as they appear and make sure you understand the term before you continue reading.
- **Glossaries.** A glossary at the end of each chapter provides definitions and page number references. Use the master glossary located at the end of the textbook for a quick way to find definitions and page number references for terms you need to review.

Chapter Summary. Accounting is a subject that continually builds on learned concepts and procedures. The Chapter Summary offers you the chance to review the concepts learned within a specific chapter. It is organized by learning objective, providing further reinforcement of your learning milestones.

Exercises and Problems. Once you have studied new accounting concepts and analyzed business transactions, you will be ready to practice what you have learned. At the end of each chapter, exercises and problems challenge you to apply the techniques and procedures you have studied. Track your learning progress by noting the learning objective that each exercise or problem addresses.

Visual Learning Tools

Have you ever heard the saying "A picture is worth a thousand words"? *College Accounting* takes every opportunity to reinforce your learning experience with the effective use of color, eye-catching text treatments, and meaningful visual presentations.

In-Text Worksheet Transparencies. In Chapter 5 you will learn about a helpful tool called the *worksheet*. A special worksheet illustration using multiple overlay transparencies is bound into the chapter and highlights step-by-step procedures for its preparation.

Business Transaction Analysis Models. One of the most important concepts you will learn in this course is how to properly analyze and record business transactions. Step-by-step transaction analysis illustrations show you how to identify the appropriate general ledger accounts affected, determine debit or credit activity for each account, present the transaction in T-account form, and record the entry in the general journal.

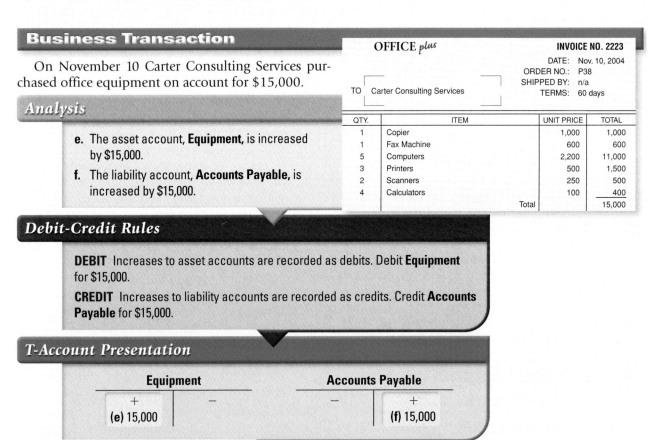

The Bottom Line. The Bottom Line visuals appear in the margins alongside select transactions and concepts in the textbook. These visuals offer a summary of the effects of these transactions—the end result—on the financial statements of a business.

T Accounts. In this course, you will learn that a T account is a visual tool used by the accountant to help analyze business transactions. T accounts are used extensively throughout the textbook. Note that the account's normal balance is indicated by shading. An increase in the account balance is represented by $(+)$ and a decrease is represented by $(-)$.

Full-Color Illustrations. Tables, flowcharts, diagrams, journals, ledgers, and financial statements are presented in full color to provide you with an understanding of the documents and reports found and used extensively in the real world of business.

Highlighting. Vocabulary terms are highlighted in yellow as they appear in the running text. Pause to absorb the meaning and the context of each term as it appears.

Boldface Text. As you progress through this textbook, you will learn that general ledger accounts are a vital part of the accounting profession. These general ledger account names are presented in boldface text to help you distinguish them from accounting concepts with similar or identical names.

Reinforcement

Most of us learn most effectively by careful review of materials and by practicing what we have learned. *College Accounting* takes every opportunity to construct concepts in an understandable way and then reinforce them at critical junctures.

Recall and Important! The **Recall** margin feature is a series of brief reinforcements that serve as reminders of material covered in *previous* chapters that are relevant to new information being presented. The **Important!** margin features draw your attention to critical materials introduced in the *current* chapter.

End-of-Chapter Review and Applications. Retention and reinforcement of concepts are further enhanced through discussion questions, exercises, problems, challenge problems, and critical thinking problems at the end of each chapter.

Business Connections. New enrichment and alternative assessment activities, collectively known as **Business Connections,** reinforce chapter materials from practical and real-world perspectives.

Section Self Reviews. Each section concludes with a Self Review that includes questions, multiple choice exercises, and an analysis assignment. You may check your work with the answers that are provided at the end of each chapter.

Section 1 — Self Review

Questions

1. Why is accounting called the "language of business"?
2. What are the names of three accounting job positions?
3. What are financial statements?

Exercises

4. One requirement for becoming a CPA is to pass the
   a. State Board Examination
   b. Uniform CPA Examination
   c. SEC Accounting Examination
   d. Final CPA Examination
5. Which organization has the final say on financial accounting issues faced by publicly owned corporations?
   a. Internal Revenue Service
   b. U.S. Treasury Department
   c. Federal Trade Commission
   d. Securities and Exchange Commission

Analysis

6. The owner of the sporting goods store where you work has decided to expand the store. She has decided to apply for a loan. What type of information will she need to give to the bank?

(Answers to Section 1 Self Review are on page 21.)

Real-World Connections

College Accounting transforms academic concepts into real-world applications and associations by integrating materials about well-known companies and organizations.

Part Opener. Each part opener presents a vignette of a real-world company like Avis, SAS Institute, or Johnson & Johnson, connecting the Part business theme to real-world issues or profiles. An evocative Thinking Critically question stimulates thought on the topics to be explored in the Part.

Chapter Opener. Setting the stage for learning, each chapter opener presents brief features about real-world companies such as Adobe Systems Incorporated, Lands' End, Inc., and The Boeing Company. You will assess a topic presented in the Thinking Critically question that concludes each feature.

Street Wise: Questions from the Real World. Excerpts from The Home Depot, Inc. annual report are presented in Appendix B of the text. In **Street Wise: Questions from the Real World,** you will be asked to research various components of the annual report and answer questions related to content, presentation, and meaning.

Financial Statement Analysis. A brief excerpt of a real-world annual report is also included at the end of each chapter in the **Financial Statement Analysis** activities. Questions presented will lead you through an analysis of the statement and conclude with an Analyze Online activity for which you will research the company's most recent financial reports on the Internet.

Internet Connections. The **Internet Connections** activity provides the opportunity to conduct online research about major companies, accounting trends, organizations, and government agencies.

Real-World Snapshots. As you read through each chapter, you will be presented with relevant news, company profiles, and facts related to real-world businesses or situations.

Career Applications

The Big Picture. Accounting plays a role in every aspect of our personal and business lives. As you learn key accounting concepts and procedures, it is important to know why these issues are relevant and what role they play in the larger picture of business. **Why It's Important** statements accompany each learning objective, highlighting practical applications for the objective.

Career Paths. Accounting skills are useful, and often critical, to landing and keeping that perfect job. **Accounting on the Job** features, found in each even-numbered chapter, highlight the benefits of accounting in various careers:

- hospitality and tourism
- legal and protective services
- information technology services
- retail/wholesale sales and service
- human services
- business and administration
- education and training
- finance
- transportation, distribution, and logistics

FINANCIAL $TATEMENT ANALYSIS Income Statement An excerpt from the Consolidated Statements of Income for Wal-Mart Stores, Inc. is presented below. Review the financial data and answer the analysis questions.

◄ **Connection 4**
WAL★MART

Amounts in millions
Fiscal years ended January 31

	2000	1999	1998
Revenues:			
Net Sales	$165,013	$137,634	$117,958
Other Income Net	1,796	1,574	1,341
Total Revenues	$166,809	$139,208	$119,299

- agriculture and natural resources
- government and public administration
- arts, audio-video technology, communications
- health science
- manufacturing
- architecture and construction
- scientific research/engineering

These fields are among the "career clusters" defined by the U.S. Department of Education. Optional Internet Application activities and Thinking Critically Questions are included.

The Business Manager. The business environment today requires managers to make strategic business decisions based on a variety of factors. Financial and accounting information, in particular, are elements that managers must be well prepared to consider. Near the end of each chapter, **Managerial Implications** summarizes the chapter's accounting concepts from the point of view of the manager. The feature ends with a Thinking Critically question that requires contemplation of chapter content from management's perspective. End-of-chapter assessment materials include **Managerial Focus** questions where you will apply accounting concepts to business situations.

Business Research and Reporting. In order to be useful, business information must be presented in a meaningful format and must be interpreted for its users. Optional end-of-chapter features such as **Street Wise: Questions from the Real World, Financial Statement Analysis, Teamwork,** and **Internet Connections** provide opportunities for you to review real-world financial data, research current trends, offer interpretations, communicate findings, and work as part of a team. Within the chapters themselves, **Accounting on the Job** and **Computers in Accounting** features provide research opportunities in the realms of careers, business technologies, and software.

The Analyst. Problem Sets A and B, Challenge Problems, and Mini-Practice Sets conclude with an **Analyze** question. You will review your work and extend your learning process with summarizations and conclusions about what you have done.

The Problem Solver. The ability to think critically, solve problems, and create solutions is one of the most sought after attributes in the workplace today.

Thinking Critically questions are incorporated in **Part Openers, Chapter Openers, Managerial Implications, Accounting on the Job,** and **Computers in Accounting.** Critical thinking skills are flexed in the **Section Self Reviews, Comprehensive Self Reviews,** and the end-of-chapter **Business Connections** activities.

The Team Player. Each chapter contains a collaborative learning activity, **Teamwork,** which will provide learning opportunities to prepare for team-oriented projects and work environments.

The Ethical Worker. Reasoning, societal norms, morals, laws, and personal judgment are factors that play critical roles in decision making in the business world. An **Ethical Dilemma** activity within each chapter provides the opportunity for you to discuss ethics in the workplace, formulate a course of action for certain scenarios, and support your opinions.

The International Professional. Accounting issues that provide connections to the global world of business are presented in an in-text feature called **International Insights.**

The Effective Communicator. Excellent communication skills are paramount to a successful career. In this course, you will write memos, reports, essays; present oral presentations; create visual presentation aids; communicate via electronic methods; and hone your interpersonal skills via **Business Communications** activities presented in each chapter.

Technology Applications

The world of business today is largely fueled and sustained by process and information technologies. In that spirit, *College Accounting* provides many opportunities to work with and learn about various software applications, communications technologies, and Web-based applications.

***College Accounting* Web Site.** From reinforcement quizzes to case studies, Internet research activities to demonstration problems, the *College Accounting* Web site features a realm of opportunities to review, reinforce, and supplement your learning. You may explore tips for completing end-of-chapter problems or use the online glossary for a quick review of vocabulary and accounting concepts.

Commercial Software. The tenth edition of *College Accounting* offers more than twice as many accounting software problems as the previous edition. Master your skills in the following software products:

 Peachtree   QuickBooks   Spreadsheets

Student Tutorial CD-ROM. Supplement your learning with this interactive CD-ROM utilizing exceptional PowerPoint presentations, chapter quizzes, and ten-key practice exercises.

Computers in Accounting. Highlighting a variety of aspects related to computer technologies in the accounting workplace, **Computers in Accounting** activities bring relevant issues to light with optional Internet Application activities and Thinking Critically questions.

The Tenth Edition at a Glance

We are excited to bring you the Tenth Edition of *College Accounting* complete with new designs, activities, reinforcement opportunities, and real-world connections developed to enhance and strengthen your learning experience.

New design
New high-interest photos and full-color illustrations
New business transaction analysis visuals
New "The Bottom Line" visuals
New part opener business vignettes
New chapter opener business vignettes
New section openers with "Why It's Important" statements for each learning objective
New exercises in Section Self Reviews
New analysis assignments in Section Self Reviews
New Comprehensive Self Review
New Recall margin features
New Important! margin features
New real-world snapshots featured in running text
New International Insights margin features
New Accounting on the Job features
New Thinking Critically questions
New Analyze questions
New Chapter Review organized by learning objectives
New Appendix B, featuring Excerpts from The Home Depot, Inc. *1999 Annual Report*

New Business Connections activities:
- Managerial Focus
- Ethical Dilemma
- Street Wise: Questions from the Real World
- Financial Statement Analysis
- Extending the Thought
- Business Communication
- Teamwork
- Internet Connection

Revised chapter structure, organized into easy-to-grasp learning segments
Revised Computers in Accounting features
Revised mini-practice sets
Revised About Accounting margin features

Content Revisions

Chapter 2 Analyzing Business Transactions: This chapter introduces an important visual tool, the Business Transaction Analysis Model. This tool is expanded on in Chapters 3 and 4, providing a step-by-step process used to analyze transactions from source document through T accounts and general journal entry.

Chapter 5 Adjustments and the Worksheet: The term *contra account* is introduced in the discussion of depreciation.

The coverage of depreciation is supplemented with the online Chapter 5 Appendix: Methods of Depreciation on the *College Accounting* Web site.

Chapter 6 Closing Entries and the Postclosing Trial Balance: The term *interpret* is introduced as a New Term to better explain the last step of the accounting cycle: interpreting the financial information.

The coverage of financial statements is supplemented with the online Chapter 6 Appendix: Statement of Cash Flows on the *College Accounting* Web site.

Chapter 7 Accounting for Sales and Accounts Receivable: The merchandising business chart of accounts separates cost of goods sold accounts from the expense accounts. Each category has a different series of account numbers: 500 for cost of goods sold accounts, and 600 for expense accounts.

This chapter introduces The Bottom Line, a visual tool that shows the effect of transactions on the income statement and the balance sheet.

Chapter 8 Accounting for Purchases and Accounts Payable: The term *cost of goods sold* is introduced as a New Term. The concept is explained in the discussion of merchandise purchases.

Chapter 10 Payroll Computations, Records, and Payment: The discussion of employees versus independent contractors is supplemented with the online Chapter 10 Appendix: Independent Contractors on the *College Accounting* Web site.

Chapter 11 Payroll Taxes, Deposits, and Reports: The Electronic Federal Tax Payment System (EFTPS) is introduced in this chapter.

Chapter 14 Accounting Principles and Reporting Standards: The term *recognition* is now treated as a New Term to further emphasize the importance of this concept. The terms *public sector* and *private sector* are introduced in the discussion of generally accepted accounting principles.

Chapter 16 Notes Payable and Notes Receivable: The terms *negotiable instrument* and *contingent liability* are now treated as New Terms to reinforce the importance of these concepts.

Chapter 17 Merchandise Inventory: The discussion of inventory cost flow assumptions now includes international considerations.

Chapter 18 Property, Plant, and Equipment: This chapter introduces the concept of asset impairment and how it affects the financial statements. The term *intangible asset* is now treated as a New Term to emphasize the importance of this concept.

Chapter 20 Corporations: Formation and Capital Stock Transactions: This chapter introduces the "hybrid" business entities S corporation, limited liability company, and limited liability partnership.

Chapter 22 Long-Term Bonds: The term *market interest rate* is now treated as a New Term to emphasize this concept's importance in the discussion of bonds issued at a premium or a discount.

Chapter 27 Departmentalized Profit and Cost Centers: The term *departmental income statement* is now treated as a New Term to emphasize the importance of segment reporting.

Chapter 32 Cost-Revenue Analysis for Decision Making: The term *capacity* is introduced as a New Term to better illustrate considerations in the decision-making process.

Supplements for the Student

Study Guide & Working Papers (1–13)
Study Guide & Working Papers (14–25)
Study Guide & Working Papers (26–32)
Practice Set 1—*Action Video Productions*
Practice Set 2—*Home Team Advantage*
Practice Set 3—*Awesome Software*
Peachtree User's Guide and Templates CD
QuickBooks User's Guide and Templates CD
Student Tutorial CD-ROM (1–32)
College Accounting Web site:
  collegeaccounting.glencoe.com

Focus on Features

Computers in Accounting

interNET CONNECTION

International INSIGHTS

Exploring the Real World of Business

The Tenth Edition focuses on a **business perspective** by using examples from the business world to illustrate accounting concepts.

Information on featured companies, organizations, their products, and services is included for educational purposes only and does not represent or imply endorsement of the *College Accounting* program. The following companies appear throughout the text:

Openers

Part 1
Avis Group Holdings, Inc.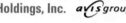

Chapter 1
Yahoo! Inc. YAHOO!

Chapter 2
Southwest Airlines Co.

Chapter 3
Guess?, Inc. GUESS?, INC.

Chapter 4
CSX Corporation **CSX** CORPORATION

Chapter 5
The Boeing Company *BOEING*

Chapter 6
Galileo International Inc. GALILEO

Part 2
The Home Depot, Inc.

Chapter 7
Wal-Mart Stores, Inc. **WAL★MART**

Chapter 8
Pier 1 Imports Pier 1 imports

Chapter 9
H&R Block, Inc. H&R BLOCK

Part 3
SAS Institute Inc. sas.

Chapter 10
Adobe Systems Incorporated Adobe

Chapter 11
Lands' End, Inc. LANDS' END DIRECT MERCHANTS

Part 4
Johnson & Johnson *Johnson&Johnson*

Chapter 12
American Eagle Outfitters, Inc. AMERICAN EAGLE OUTFITTERS

Chapter 13
Safeway Inc. SAFEWAY

Part 5
Carnival Corporation CARNIVAL CORPORATION

Chapter 14
The Goodyear Tire & Rubber Company GOODYEAR

Chapter 15
FedEx Corporation FedEx Corporation

Chapter 16
KB HOME KBHOME

Chapter 17
Circuit City Stores, Inc.

Chapter 18
The Coca-Cola Company

Part 6
Caterpillar Inc. **CATERPILLAR**®

Chapter 19
Woolpert LLP  WOOLPERT

Chapter 20
Sara Lee Corporation *SaraLee*

Chapter 21
McDonald's Corporation McDonald's

Chapter 22
3M **3M**

Part 7
International Truck and Engine Corporation

Chapter 23
Dole Food Company, Inc. Dole.

Chapter 24
The Walt Disney Company The *Walt Disney* Company ©Disney Enterprises, Inc.

Chapter 25
Eastman Kodak Company **Kodak**

Part 8
Amgen Inc. **AMGEN**

Chapter 26
Dell Computer Corporation **D∕LL**

Chapter 27
Mattel, Inc. MATTEL

Chapter 28
Goodrich Corporation GOODRICH

Acknowledgments

The authors are deeply grateful to the following accounting educators for their ongoing involvement with *College Accounting*. The efforts of these knowledgeable and dedicated instructors provide the authors with valuable assistance in meeting the changing needs of the college accounting classroom.

Ms. Deborah Abercrombie
Wallace Community College,
Sparks Campus
Euflaula, AL

Ms. Terry Aime
Delgado Community College
New Orleans, LA

Mr. Lorenza Balthazar
LTC—Lafayette
Lafayette, LA

Ms. Marilyn Beebe
Kirkwood Community College
Cedar Rapids, IA

Ms. Dianne Bridges
South Plains College
Levelland, TX

Ms. Michele Burleson
McDowell Technical
Community College
Marion, NC

Mr. George Carter
New Hampshire Community
Technical College
Berlin, NH

Mr. Michael Choma
Newport Business Institute
New Kensington, PA

Ms. Juanita Clobes
Gateway Technical College
Racine, WI

Mr. George Converse
Stone Academy
Hamden, CT

Ms. Joan Cook
Milwaukee Area Technical College
Milwaukee, WI

Ms. Karen Cortis
Dorsey Business Schools
Madison Heights, MI

Dr. Michael G. Curran, Jr.
Rider University
Lawrenceville, NJ

Mr. Mike Discello
Pittsburgh Technical Institute
Pittsburgh, PA

Mr. John Dixon
Education America, Dallas Campus
Garland, TX

Dr. Paul Doran
Jefferson State Community College
Birmingham, AL

Ms. Elsie Dubac
The Stuart School of
Business Administration
Wall, NJ

Mr. Richard Dugger
Kilgore College
Kilgore, TX

Mr. Samuel Ehie
Trenholm State Technical College
Montgomery, AL

Ms. Teresa Ferguson
Court Reporting Institute
Seattle, WA

Ms. Tanya Fontenot
LTC—Lamar Salter
Leesville, LA

Mr. Kevin Fura
Allentown Business School
Allentown, PA

Ms. Cheryl Furbee
Cabrillo College
Aptos, CA

Ms. Selena Gardner
International Academy of
Design & Technology
Pittsburgh, PA

Mr. George P. Geran
Florida Metropolitan University,
North Orlando
Orlando, FL

Ms. Deborah Hammons
Shelton State Community College
Tuscaloosa, AL

Mr. Neil Hayes
ECPI College of Technology
Virginia Beach, VA

Dr. Lynn Hogan
Calhoun Community College
Decatur, AL

Mr. Paul Hogan
Northwest Shoals Community College
Muscle Shoals, AL

Mr. Bob Horst
Western Wyoming Community College
Rock Springs, WY

Ms. Verna Mae Johnson
Brown Mackie Business College
Salina, KS

Ms. Janine Jones
Lansdale School of Business
North Wales, PA

Ms. Beverly Kibbie
International Business College
Indianapolis, IN

Ms. Judith Kizzie
Clinton Community College
Clinton, IA

Dr. Tom Land
Bessemer State Technical College
Bessemer, AL

Ms. Lynn LeBlanc
LTC—Lafayette
Lafayette, LA

Mr. Gene Lefort
LTC—Lafourche
Thibodaux, LA

Ms. Sylvia Liverman
Paul D. Camp Community College
Franklin, VA

Ms. Debbie Luna
El Paso Community College,
NW Campus
El Paso, TX

Ms. Linda R. Lyle
Nashville State Tech
Nashville, TN

Ms. Kathy Marino
ESS College of Business
Dallas, TX

Ms. Betty McClain
Mid Florida Tech
Orlando, FL

Mr. Fred McCracken
Indiana Business College
Marion, IN

Ms. Cheryl McQueen
Jones County Junior College
Ellisville, MS

Ms. Catherine Merrikin
Pearl River Junior College
Hattiesburg, MS

Ms. Wanda Metzgar
Boise State University
Boise, ID

Mr. Raymond J. Miller
Lane Community College
Eugene, OR

Ms. Margie Mixon
LTC—Delta Ouachita
West Monroe, LA

Mr. Paul Morgan
Mississippi Gulf Coast
Community College
Gautier, MS

Ms. Judy Parker
North Idaho College
Coeur d'Alene, ID

Mr. David Payne
North Metro Technical College
Acworth, GA

Ms. Linda Petraglia
The Stuart School of Business
Administration
Wall, NJ

Mr. Ellis Plowman
Churchman Business School
Easton, PA

Ms. Betsy Ray
Indiana Business College
Indianapolis, IN

Mr. Phil Reffitt
FMU/Orlando College South
Orlando, FL

Mr. Randy Rogers
Western Business College
Portland, OR

Ms. Peggy Rusek
Mountain Empire Community College
Big Stone Gap, VA

Dr. Francis Sakiey
Mercer County Community College
West Windsor, NJ

Mr. Roman Salazar
Modesto Junior College
Modesto, CA

Mr. Kyle Saunders
Bridgerland ATC
Logan, UT

Mr. Wayne Smith
Indiana Business College
Lafayette, IN

Ms. Linda Stanley
Quapaw Technical Institute
Hot Springs, AR

Ms. Verlindsey Stewart
J. F. Drake State Technical College
Huntsville, AL

Ms. Karla Stroud
Idaho State University
Pocatello, ID

Ms. Lynette Teal
Western Wisconsin Technical College
LaCrosse, WI

Mr. Thomas Tolan
Plaza Business Institute
Jackson Heights, NY

Mr. Gary Tusing
Lord Fairfax Community College
Middletown, VA

Dr. Laverne Ulmer
Jones Junior College
Ellisville, MS

Mr. Jack Verani
New Hampshire Community
Technical College
Berlin, NH

Ms. Patricia Vickers
George Stone Vocational Center
Pensacola, FL

Mr. Philip Waits
Harry M. Ayers State
Technical College
Anniston, AL

Mr. Frank Walker
Lee University
Cleveland, TN

Mr. Douglas Ward
Southwestern Community College
Sylva, NC

Ms. Naomi Ward
Northwest Kansas Technical College
Goodland, KS

Mr. Jeffrey Waybright
Spokane Falls Community College
Spokane, WA

Mr. Jim Weglin
North Seattle Community College
Seattle, WA

Ms. Linda Whitten
Skyline College
San Bruno, CA

Mr. Rick Wilson
Bowling Green Technical College
Bowling Green, KY

Ms. Dawn Wright
Rhodes College
Springfield, MO

Ms. Eileen Yadlowsky
The Cittone Institute
Mt. Laurel, NJ

Brief Contents

Contents

CHAPTER 7

CHAPTER 8

PART 4
Summarizing and Reporting Financial Information   427

PART 5
Accounting for Assets and Liabilities — 521

PART 7
Financial Reporting and Analysis
845

PART 1

The Accounting Cycle

avis group In 1999 Avis Group Holdings, Inc. expanded its focus by adding new services for corporate customers. Avis now manages leased fleets of autos by tracking fuel usage and maintaining the vehicles. All of these transportation operations amounted to annual revenues of $3.3 billion for the year ended December 31, 1999.

Thinking Critically
Why do you think the leasing services are popular with Avis's corporate clients?

1

CHAPTER 1

Learning Objectives

1. Define accounting.

2. Identify and discuss career opportunities in accounting.

3. Identify the users of financial information.

4. Compare and contrast the three types of business entities.

5. Describe the process used to develop generally accepted accounting principles.

6. Define the accounting terms new to this chapter.

Accounting: The Language of Business

YAHOO!
www.yahoo.com

*I*n the early 1990s Internet users needed an efficient way to organize and find information on the tens of thousands of computers linked to the Internet. In 1994 David Filo and Jerry Yang, the founders of Yahoo! Inc., created software and a customized database to efficiently locate, identify, and categorize material stored on the Internet.

Now a global communications, commerce, and media company, Yahoo! Inc. offers a wide range of services to more than 156 million individuals. As a publicly owned company, Yahoo! Inc. releases its financial information to investors, owners, and managers quarterly.

Thinking Critically
If you were considering becoming a stockholder in Yahoo! Inc., why would it be important for you to have a basic understanding of accounting?

For more information on Yahoo! Inc., go to: collegeaccounting.glencoe.com.

New Terms

Accounting
Accounting system
Auditing
Auditor's report
Certified public accountant (CPA)
Corporation
Creditor
Discussion memorandum
Economic entity
Entity
Exposure draft
Financial statements
Generally accepted accounting principles (GAAP)
Governmental accounting
International accounting
Management advisory services
Managerial accounting
Partnership
Public accountants
Separate entity assumption
Social entity
Sole proprietorship
Statements of Financial Accounting Standards
Stock
Stockholders
Tax accounting

Section Objectives

1 **Define accounting.**

WHY IT'S IMPORTANT
Business transactions affect many aspects of our lives.

2 **Identify and discuss career opportunities in accounting.**

WHY IT'S IMPORTANT
There's something for everyone in the field of accounting. Accounting professionals are found in every workplace from public accounting firms to government agencies, from corporations to nonprofit organizations.

3 **Identify the users of financial information.**

WHY IT'S IMPORTANT
A wide variety of individuals and businesses depend on financial information to make decisions.

Terms to Learn

accounting
accounting system
auditing
certified public accountant (CPA)
financial statements
governmental accounting
management advisory services
managerial accounting
public accountants
tax accounting

1 **Objective**

Define accounting.

What Is Accounting?

Accounting provides financial information about a business or a nonprofit organization. Owners, managers, investors, and other interested parties need financial information in order to make decisions. Because accounting is used to communicate financial information, it is often called the "language of business."

The Need for Financial Information

Suppose a relative leaves you a substantial sum of money and you decide to carry out your lifelong dream of opening a small sportswear shop. You rent space in a local shopping center, purchase fixtures and equipment, purchase goods to sell, hire salespeople, and open the store to customers. Before long you realize that, to run your business successfully, you need financial information about the business. You probably need information that provides answers to the following questions:

- How much cash does the business have?
- How much money do customers owe the business?
- What is the cost of the merchandise sold?
- What is the change in sales volume?
- How much money is owed to suppliers?
- What is the profit or loss?

As your business grows, you will need even more financial information to evaluate the firm's performance and make decisions about the future. An efficient accounting system allows owners and managers to quickly obtain a wide range of useful information. The need for timely information is one reason that businesses have an accounting system directed by a professional staff.

Accounting Defined

Accounting is the process by which financial information about a business is recorded, classified, summarized, interpreted, and communicated to owners, managers, and other interested parties. An **accounting system** is designed to accumulate data about a firm's financial affairs, classify the data in a meaningful way, and summarize it in periodic reports called **financial statements**. Owners and managers obtain a lot of information from financial statements. The accountant

- establishes the records and procedures that make up the accounting system,
- supervises the operations of the system,
- interprets the resulting financial information.

Most owners and managers rely heavily on the accountant's judgment and knowledge when making financial decisions.

Accounting Careers

Many jobs are available in the accounting profession, and they require varying amounts of education and experience. Bookkeepers and accountants are responsible for keeping records and providing financial information about the business. Generally bookkeepers are responsible for recording business transactions. In large firms bookkeepers may also supervise the work of accounting clerks. Accounting clerks are responsible for recordkeeping for a part of the accounting system—perhaps payroll, accounts receivable, or accounts payable. Accountants usually supervise bookkeepers and prepare the financial statements and reports of the business.

Newspapers and Web sites often have job listings for accounting clerks, bookkeepers, and accountants:

- Accounting clerk positions usually require one to two accounting courses and little or no experience.
- Bookkeeper positions usually require one to two years of accounting education plus experience as an accounting clerk.
- Accountant positions usually require a bachelor's degree but are sometimes filled by experienced bookkeepers or individuals with a two-year college degree. Most entry-level accountant positions do not have an experience requirement. Both the education and experience requirements for accountant positions vary according to the size of the firm.

Accountants usually choose to practice in one of three areas:

- public accounting
- managerial accounting
- governmental accounting

Public Accounting

Public accountants work for public accounting firms. Public accounting firms provide accounting services for other companies. Usually they offer three services:

- auditing
- tax accounting
- management advisory services

The largest public accounting firms in the United States are called the "Big Four." The "Big Four" are Deloitte & Touche, Ernst & Young, KPMG, and PricewaterhouseCoopers. The list formerly included Arthur Andersen and was known as the "Big Five."

Many public accountants are **certified public accountants (CPAs)**. To become a CPA, an individual must have a certain number of college credits in accounting courses, demonstrate good personal character, pass the Uniform CPA Examination, and fulfill the experience requirements of the state of practice. CPAs must follow the professional code of ethics.

Auditing is the review of financial statements to assess their fairness and adherence to generally accepted accounting principles. Accountants who are CPAs perform financial audits.

Tax accounting involves tax compliance and tax planning. *Tax compliance* deals with the preparation of tax returns and the audit of those returns. *Tax planning* involves giving advice to clients on how to structure their financial affairs in order to reduce their tax liability.

About Accounting

Accounting Services
The role of the CPA is expanding. In the past, accounting firms handled audits and taxes. Today accountants provide a wide range of services, including financial planning, investment advice, accounting and tax software advice, and profitability consulting. Accountants provide clients with information and advice on electronic business, health care performance measurement, risk assessment, business performance measurement, and information system reliability.

Management advisory services involve helping clients improve their information systems or their business performance.

Managerial Accounting

Managerial accounting, also referred to as *private accounting*, involves working for a single business in industry. Managerial accountants perform a wide range of activities, including

- establishing accounting policies,
- managing the accounting system,
- preparing financial statements,
- interpreting financial information,
- providing financial advice to management,
- preparing tax forms,
- performing tax planning services,
- preparing internal reports for management.

Governmental Accounting

Governmental accounting involves keeping financial records and preparing financial reports as part of the staff of federal, state, or local governmental units. Governmental units do not earn profits. However, governmental units receive and pay out huge amounts of money and need procedures for recording and managing this money.

Some governmental agencies hire accountants to audit the financial statements and records of the businesses under their jurisdiction and to uncover possible violations of the law. The Securities and Exchange Commission, the Internal Revenue Service, and the Federal Bureau of Investigation employ a large number of accountants.

Users of Financial Information

The results of the accounting process are communicated to many individuals and organizations. Who are these individuals and organizations, and why do they want financial information about a particular firm?

③ Objective
Identify the users of financial information.

Owners and Managers

Assume your sportswear shop is in full operation. One user of financial information about the business is you, the owner. You need information that will help you evaluate the results of your operations and plan and make decisions for the future. Questions such as the following are difficult to answer without financial information:

- Should you drop the long-sleeved pullover that is not selling well from the product line, or should you just reduce the price?
- How much should you charge for the denim jacket that you are adding to the product line?
- How much should you spend on advertising?
- How does this month's profit compare with last month's profit?
- Should you open a new store?

Suppliers

A number of other people are interested in the financial information about your business. For example, businesses that supply you with sportswear need to assess the ability of your firm to pay its bills. They also need to set a credit limit for your firm.

Banks

What if you decide to ask your bank for a loan so that you can open a new store? The bank needs to be sure that your firm will repay the loan on time. The bank will ask for financial information prepared by your accountant. Based on this information, the bank will decide whether to make the loan and the terms of the loan.

Tax Authorities

The Internal Revenue Service (IRS) and other tax authorities are interested in financial information about your firm. This information is used to determine the tax base:

- Income taxes are based on taxable income.
- Sales taxes are based on sales income.
- Property taxes are based on the assessed value of buildings, equipment, and inventory (the goods available for sale).

The accounting process provides all of this information.

Regulatory Agencies and Investors

If an industry is regulated by a governmental agency, businesses in that industry have to supply financial information to the regulating agency. For example, the Federal Communications Commission receives financial information from radio and television stations. The Securities and Exchange Commission (SEC) oversees the financial information provided by publicly owned corporations to their investors and potential investors. Publicly owned corporations trade their shares on stock exchanges and in over-the-counter markets. Congress passed the Securities Act of 1933 and the Securities Exchange Act of 1934 in order to protect those who invest in publicly owned corporations.

The SEC is responsible for reviewing the accounting methods used by publicly owned corporations. The SEC has delegated this review to the accounting profession but still has the final say on any financial accounting issue faced by publicly owned corporations. If the SEC does not agree with the reporting that results from an accounting method, the SEC can suspend trading of a company's shares on the stock exchanges.

> The SEC encourages foreign corporations to file financial data in order to provide U.S. investors protection under U.S. securities laws. More than 1,100 foreign companies from 56 countries file reports with the SEC.

Customers

Customers pay special attention to financial information about the firms with which they do business. For example, before a business spends a lot of money on a mainframe computer, the business wants to know that the computer manufacturer will be around for the next several years in order to service the computer, replace parts, and provide additional components. The business analyzes the financial information about the computer manufacturer in order to determine its economic health and the likelihood that it will remain in business.

Employees and Unions

Often employees are interested in the financial information of the business that employs them. Employees who are members of a profit-sharing plan pay close attention to the financial results because they affect employee income. Employees who are members of a labor union use financial information about the firm to negotiate wages and benefits.

Figure 1-1 illustrates different financial information users. As you learn about the accounting process, you will appreciate why financial information is so important to these individuals and organizations. You will learn how financial information meets users' needs.

FIGURE 1-1 ▶
Users of Financial Information

Inside the Business

Owners

Managers

FINANCIAL REPORTS

REPORTS

Outside the Business

Tax Authorities

Suppliers

Regulatory Agencies

Unions

Banks

Customers

Investors and Potential Investors

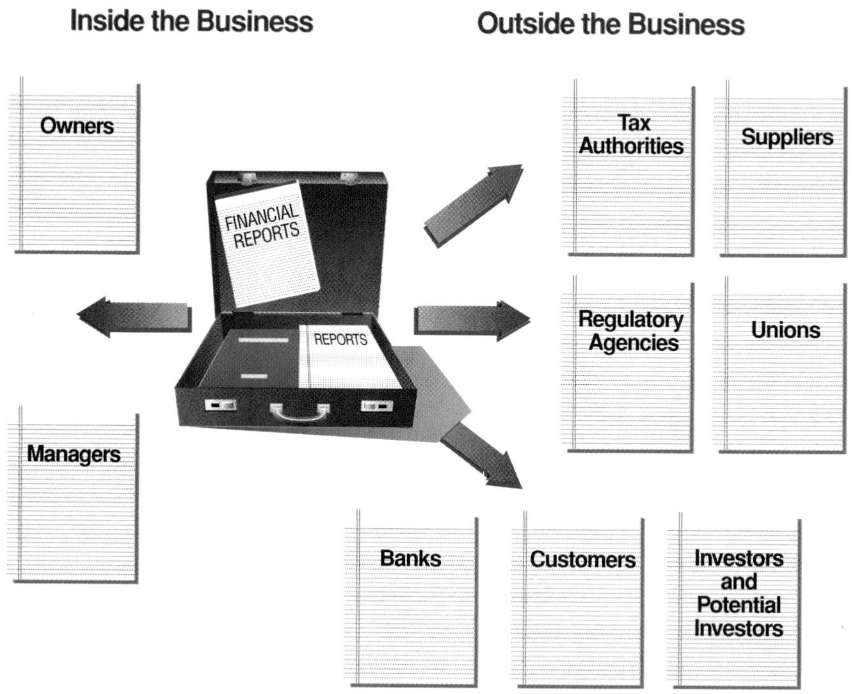

Section 1 Self Review

Questions

1. Why is accounting called the "language of business"?

2. What are the names of three accounting job positions?

3. What are financial statements?

Exercises

4. One requirement for becoming a CPA is to pass the

   a. State Board Examination

   b. Uniform CPA Examination

   c. SEC Accounting Examination

   d. Final CPA Examination

5. Which organization has the final say on financial accounting issues faced by publicly owned corporations?

   a. Internal Revenue Service

   b. U.S. Treasury Department

   c. Federal Trade Commission

   d. Securities and Exchange Commission

Analysis

6. The owner of the sporting goods store where you work has decided to expand the store. She has decided to apply for a loan. What type of information will she need to give to the bank?

(Answers to Section 1 Self Review are on page 21.)

Business and Accounting

The accounting process involves recording, classifying, summarizing, interpreting, and communicating financial information about an economic or social entity. An **entity** is recognized as having its own separate identity. An entity may be an individual, a town, a university, or a business. The term **economic entity** usually refers to a business or organization whose major purpose is to produce a profit for its owners. **Social entities** are nonprofit organizations, such as cities, public schools, and public hospitals. This book focuses on the accounting process for businesses, but keep in mind that nonprofit organizations also need financial information.

Types of Business Entities

The three major legal forms of business entity are the sole proprietorship, the partnership, and the corporation. In general the accounting process is the same for all three forms of business. Later in the book you will study the different ways certain transactions are handled depending on the type of business entity. For now, however, you will learn about the different types of business entities.

Sole Proprietorships

A **sole proprietorship** is a business entity owned by one person. The life of the business ends when the owner is no longer willing or able to keep the business going. Many small businesses are operated as sole proprietorships.

The owner of a sole proprietorship is legally responsible for the debts and taxes of the business. If the business is unable to pay its debts, the **creditors** (those people, companies, or government agencies to whom the business owes money) can turn to the owner for payment. The owner may have to pay the debts of the business from personal resources, including personal savings. When the time comes to pay income taxes, the owner's income and the income of the business are combined to compute the total tax responsibility of the owner.

It is important that the business transactions be kept separate from the owner's personal transactions. If the owner's personal transactions are mixed with those of the business, it will be difficult to measure the performance of the business. The term **separate entity assumption** describes the concept of keeping the firm's financial records separate from the owner's personal financial records.

Partnerships

A **partnership** is a business entity owned by two or more people. The partnership structure is common in businesses that offer professional services, such as law firms, accounting firms, architectural firms, medical

Section Objectives

4 Compare and contrast the three types of business entities.

WHY IT'S IMPORTANT
Each type of business entity requires unique legal and accounting considerations.

5 Describe the process used to develop generally accepted accounting principles.

WHY IT'S IMPORTANT
Accounting professionals are required to use common standards and principles in order to produce reliable financial information.

Terms to Learn

auditor's report
corporation
creditor
discussion memorandum
economic entity
entity
exposure draft
generally accepted
    accounting principles
    (GAAP)
international accounting
partnership
separate entity assumption
social entity
sole proprietorship
Statements of Financial
    Accounting Standards
stock
stockholders

4 Objective

Compare and contrast the three types of business entities.

Public Company Accounting Reform and Investor Protection Act of 2002 or Accounting Regulatory Environment Reform

Major changes are in store for the regulatory environment in the accounting profession with the passage of the Public Company Accounting Reform and Investor Protection Act of 2002 (also known as the Sarbanes-Oxley Act) that was signed into law by President Bush on August 2, 2002. The Act is the most far-reaching regulatory crackdown on corporate fraud and corruption since the creation of the Securities and Exchange Commission in 1934.

The Act was passed in response to the wave of corporate accounting scandals starting with the demise of Enron Corporation in 2001, the arrest of top executives at WorldCom and Adelphia Communications Corporation, and ultimately the demise of Arthur Andersen, an international public accounting firm formerly a member of the "Big Five." Arthur Andersen was found guilty of an obstruction of justice charge after admitting that the firm destroyed thousands of documents and electronics files related to the Enron audit engagement. As a result of the demise of Arthur Andersen, the "Big Five" are now the "Big Four."

The Act significantly tightens regulation of financial reporting by publicly held companies and their accountants and auditors. The Sarbanes-Oxley Act creates a five-member Public Company Accounting Oversight Board. The Board will have investigative and enforcement powers to oversee the accounting profession and to discipline corrupt accountants and auditors. The Securities and Exchange Commission will oversee the Board. Two members of the Board will be certified public accountants, to regulate the accountants who audit public companies, and the remaining three must not be and cannot have been CPAs. The chair of the Board may be held by one of the CPA members, provided that the individual has not been engaged as a practicing CPA for five years.

Major provisions of the bill include rules on consulting services, auditor rotation, criminal penalties, corporate governance, and securities regulation. The Act prohibits accountants from offering a broad range of consulting services to publicly traded companies that they audit and requires accounting firms to change the lead audit or coordinating partner and the reviewing partner for a company every five years. Additionally, it is a felony to "knowlingly" destroy or create documents to "impede, obstruct or influence" any existing or contemplated federal investigation. Auditors are also required to maintain all audit or review work papers for five years. Criminal penalties, up to 20 years in prison, are imposed for obstruction of justice and the Act raises the maximum sentence for defrauding pension funds to 10 years.

Chief executives and chief financial officers of publicly traded corporations are now required to certify their financial statements and these executives will face up to 20 years in prison if they "knowingly or willfully" allow materially misleading information into their financial statements. Companies must also disclose, as quickly as possible, material changes in their financial position. Wall Street investment firms are prohibited from retaliating against analysts who criticize investment-banking clients of the firm. The Act contains a provision with broad new protection for whistle blowers and lengthens the time that investors have to file lawsuits against corporations for securities fraud.

By narrowing the type of consulting services that accountants can provide to companies that they audit, requiring auditor rotation, and imposing stiff criminal penalties for violation of the Act, it appears that this new legislation will significantly help to restore public confidence in financial statements and markets and change the regulatory environment in which accountants operate.

practices, and dental practices. At the beginning of the partnership, two or more individuals enter into a contract that details the rights, obligations, and limitations of each partner, including

- the amount each partner will contribute to the business,
- each partner's percentage of ownership,
- each partner's share of the profits,
- the duties each partner will perform,
- the responsibility each partner has for the amounts owed by the business to creditors and tax authorities.

The partners choose how to share the ownership and profits of the business. They may share equally or in any proportion agreed upon in the contract. When a partner leaves, the partnership is dissolved and a new partnership may be formed with the remaining partners.

> Operating as a partnership since 1911, Woolpert LLP has 17 partners and offers engineering, architecture, and design services internationally. Since 1996 the firm has been ranked as one of the nation's top 100 design firms by *Engineering News-Record*. Woolpert LLP employs approximately 700 in-house professional and technical employees.

Partners are individually, and as a group, responsible for the debts and taxes of the partnership. If the partnership is unable to pay its debts or taxes, the partners' personal property, including personal bank accounts, may be used to provide payment. It is important that partnership transactions be kept separate from the personal financial transactions of the partners.

Corporations

A **corporation** is a business entity that is separate from its owners. A corporation has a legal right to own property and do business in its own name. Corporations are very different from sole proprietorships and partnerships.

Stock, issued in the form of stock certificates, represents the ownership of the corporation. Corporations may be *privately* or *publicly* owned. Privately owned corporations are also called *closely held* corporations. The ownership of privately owned corporations is limited to specific individuals, usually family members. Stock of closely held corporations is not traded on an exchange. In contrast, stock of publicly owned corporations is bought and sold on stock exchanges and in over-the-counter markets. Most large corporations have issued (sold) thousands of shares of stock.

An owner's share of the corporation is determined by the number of shares of stock held by the owner compared to the total number of shares issued by the corporation. Assume that Nancy Ling owns 250 shares of Sample Corporation. If Sample Corporation has issued 1,000 shares of stock, Ling owns 25 percent of the corporation (250 shares ÷ 1,000 shares = 0.25 or 25%). Some corporate decisions require a vote by the owners. For Sample Corporation, Ling has 250 votes, one for each share of stock that she owns. The other owners have 750 votes.

> The Boeing Company is the world's largest manufacturer of commercial jetliners and military aircraft. In its 1999 annual report, Boeing reported that 1,001,879,159 shares of common stock have been issued.

One of the advantages of the corporate form of business is the indefinite life of the corporation. A sole proprietorship ends when the owner dies or discontinues the business. A partnership ends on the death or withdrawal of a partner. In contrast, a corporation does not end when ownership changes. Some corporations have new owners daily because their shares are actively traded (sold) on stock exchanges.

Important!

Separate Entity Assumption
For *accounting* purposes all forms of business are considered separate entities from their owners. However, the corporation is the only form of business that is a separate *legal* entity.

Corporate owners, called **stockholders** or *shareholders*, are not personally responsible for the debts or taxes of the corporation. If the corporation is unable to pay its bills, the most stockholders can lose is their investment in the corporation. In other words, the stockholders will not lose more than the cost of the shares of stock.

The accounting process for the corporate entity, like that of the sole proprietorship and the partnership, is separate from the financial affairs of its owners. Usually this separation is easy to maintain. Most stockholders do not participate in the day-to-day operations of the business.

Table 1-1 summarizes the business characteristics for sole proprietorships, partnerships, and corporations.

TABLE 1-1 ▼
Major Characteristics
of Business Entities

Characteristic	Type of Business Entity		
	Sole Proprietorship	**Partnership**	**Corporation**
Ownership	One owner	Two or more owners	One or more owners, even thousands
Life of the business	Ends when the owner dies, is unable to carry on operations, or decides to close the firm	Ends when one or more partners withdraw, when a partner dies, or when the partners decide to close the firm	Can continue indefinitely; ends only when the business goes bankrupt or when the stockholders vote to liquidate
Responsibility for debts of the business	Owner is responsible for firm's debts when the firm is unable to pay	Partners are responsible individually and jointly for firm's debts when the firm is unable to pay	Stockholders are not responsible for firm's debts; they can lose only the amount they invested

GAAP

The SEC requires all publicly owned companies to follow generally accepted accounting principles. As new standards are developed or refined, accountants interpret the standards and adapt accounting practices to the new standards.

⑤ **Objective**

Describe the process used to develop generally accepted accounting principles.

Generally Accepted Accounting Principles

The Securities and Exchange Commission has the final say on matters of financial reporting by publicly owned corporations. The SEC has delegated the job of determining proper accounting standards to the accounting profession. However, the SEC sometimes overrides decisions the accounting profession makes. To fulfill its responsibility, the accounting profession has developed, and continues to develop, **generally accepted accounting principles (GAAP)**. Generally accepted accounting principles must be followed by publicly owned companies unless they can show that doing so would produce information that is misleading.

The Development of Generally Accepted Accounting Principles

Generally accepted accounting principles are developed by the Financial Accounting Standards Board (FASB), which is composed of seven full-time members. The FASB issues **Statements of Financial Accounting Standards**. The FASB develops these statements and, before issuing them, obtains feedback from interested people and organizations.

First, the FASB writes a **discussion memorandum** to explain the topic being considered. Then public hearings are held where interested parties can express their opinions, either orally or in writing. The groups that consistently express opinions about proposed FASB statements are the

SEC, the American Institute of Certified Public Accountants (AICPA), public accounting firms, the American Accounting Association (AAA), and businesses with a direct interest in a particular statement.

The AICPA is a national association for certified public accountants. The AAA is a group of accounting educators. AAA members research possible effects of a proposed FASB statement and offer their opinions to the FASB.

After public hearings, the FASB releases an **exposure draft**, which describes the proposed statement. Then the FASB receives and evaluates public comment about the exposure draft. Finally, FASB members vote on the statement. If at least four members approve, the statement is issued. The process used to develop GAAP is shown in Figure 1-2 on page 14.

Accounting principles vary from country to country. **International accounting** is the study of the accounting principles used by different countries. In 1973, the International Accounting Standards Committee (IASC) was formed. Recently, the IASC's name was changed to the International Accounting Standards Board (IASB). The IASB deals with issues caused by the lack of uniform accounting principles. The IASB also makes recommendations to enhance comparability of reporting practices.

The Use of Generally Accepted Accounting Principles

Every year publicly traded companies submit financial statements to the SEC. The financial statements are audited by independent certified public accountants (CPAs). The CPAs are called *independent* because they are not employees of the company being audited and they do not have a financial interest in the company. The financial statements include the auditor's report. The **auditor's report** contains the auditor's opinion

International INSIGHTS

Standards

In 1999 the FASB chairman offered the IASC three guiding principles for its work:

1. Identify a common mission or objective for all parties involved in the process.

2. Develop an accepted and trusted process for creating the standards.

3. Develop standards that achieve high quality.

Managerial

IMPLICATIONS

Financial Information

- Managers of a business make sure that the firm's accounting system produces financial information that is timely, accurate, and fair.

- Financial statements should be based on generally accepted accounting principles.

- Each year a publicly traded company must submit financial statements, including an independent auditor's report, to the SEC.

- Internal reports for management need not follow generally accepted accounting principles but should provide useful information that will aid in monitoring and controlling operations.

- Financial information can help managers to control present operations, make decisions, and plan for the future.

- The sound use of financial information is essential to good management.

Thinking Critically

If you were a manager, how would you use financial information to make decisions?

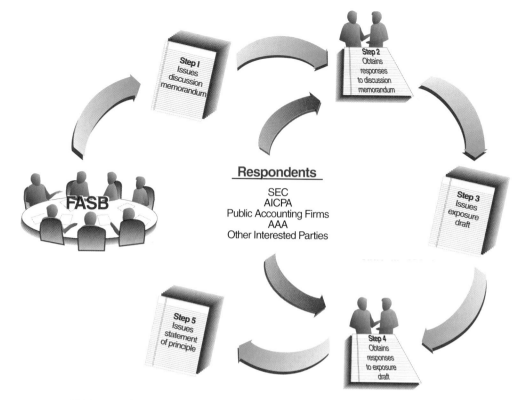

FIGURE 1-2 ▲
The Process Used by FASB to Develop Generally Accepted Accounting Principles

about the fair presentation of the operating results and financial position of the business. The auditor's report also confirms that the financial information is prepared in conformity with generally accepted accounting principles. The financial statements and the auditor's report are made available to the public, including existing and potential stockholders.

Businesses and the environment in which they operate are constantly changing. The economy, technology, and laws change. Generally accepted accounting principles are changed and refined as accountants respond to the changing environment.

Section 2 Self Review

Questions

1. What are generally accepted accounting principles?

2. Why are generally accepted accounting principles needed?

3. How are generally accepted accounting principles developed?

Exercises

4. An organization that has two or more owners who are legally responsible for the debts and taxes of the business is a

    a. corporation

    b. sole proprietorship

    c. partnership

    d. social entity

5. A nonprofit organization such as a public school is a(n)

    a. economic entity

    b. social entity

    c. economic unit

    d. social unit

Analysis

6. You plan to open a business with two of your friends. You would like to form a corporation, but your friends prefer the partnership form of business. What are some of the advantages of the corporate form of business?

(Answers to Section 2 Self Review are on page 21.)

Review

Chapter Summary

Accounting is often called the "language of business." The financial information about a business is communicated to interested parties in financial statements.

Learning Objectives

1 Define accounting.

Accounting is the process by which financial information about a business is recorded, classified, summarized, interpreted, and communicated to owners, managers, and other interested parties. Accurate accounting information is essential for making business decisions.

2 Identify and discuss career opportunities in accounting.

- There are many job opportunities in accounting.
  - Accounting clerk positions, such as accounts receivable clerk, accounts payable clerk, and payroll clerk, require the least education and experience.
  - Bookkeepers usually have experience as accounting clerks and a minimum of one to two years of accounting education.
  - Most entry-level accounting positions require a college degree or significant experience as a bookkeeper.
- Accountants usually specialize in one of three major areas.
  - Some accountants work for public accounting firms and perform auditing, tax accounting, or management advisory functions.
  - Other accountants work in private industry where they set up and supervise accounting systems, prepare financial reports, prepare internal reports, or assist in determining the prices to charge for the firm's products.
  - Still other accountants work for government agencies. They keep track of public funds and expenditures, or they audit the financial records of businesses and individuals to determine whether the records are in compliance with regulatory laws, tax laws, and other laws. The Securities and Exchange Commission, the Internal Revenue Service, and the Federal Bureau of Investigation employ many accountants.

3 Identify the users of financial information.

All types of businesses need and use financial information. Users of financial information include owners and managers, suppliers, banks, tax authorities, regulatory agencies, and investors. Nonprofit organizations need similar financial information.

4 Compare and contrast the three types of business entities.

- A sole proprietorship is owned by one person. The owner is legally responsible for the debts and taxes of the business.
- A partnership is owned by two or more people. The owners are legally responsible for the debts and taxes of the business.
- A corporation is a separate legal entity from its owners.
- Note that all three types of business entities are considered separate entities for accounting purposes.

5 Describe the process used to develop generally accepted accounting principles.

- The SEC has delegated the authority to develop generally accepted accounting principles to the accounting profession. The Financial Accounting Standards Board handles this task. A series of steps used by the FASB includes issuing a discussion memorandum, an exposure draft, and a statement of principle.
- Each year firms that sell stock on stock exchanges or in over-the-counter markets must publish audited financial reports that follow generally accepted accounting principles. They must submit their reports to the Securities and Exchange Commission. They must also make the reports available to stockholders.

6 Define the accounting terms new to this chapter.

CHAPTER 1 GLOSSARY

Accounting (p. 4) The process by which financial information about a business is recorded, classified, summarized, interpreted, and communicated to owners, managers, and other interested parties

Accounting system (p. 4) A process designed to accumulate, classify, and summarize financial data

Auditing (p. 5) The review of financial statements to assess their fairness and adherence to generally accepted accounting principles

Auditor's report (p. 13) An independent accountant's review of a firm's financial statements

Certified public accountant (CPA) (p. 5) An independent accountant who provides accounting services to the public for a fee

Corporation (p. 11) A publicly or privately owned business entity that is separate from its owners and has a legal right to own property and do business in its own name; stockholders are not responsible for the debts or taxes of the business

Creditor (p. 9) One to whom money is owed

Discussion memorandum (p. 12) An explanation of a topic under consideration by the Financial Accounting Standards Board

Economic entity (p. 9) A business or organization whose major purpose is to produce a profit for its owners

Entity (p. 9) Anything having its own separate identity, such as an individual, a town, a university, or a business

Exposure draft (p. 13) A proposed solution to a problem being considered by the Financial Accounting Standards Board

Financial statements (p. 4) Periodic reports of a firm's financial position or operating results

Generally accepted accounting principles (GAAP) (p. 12) Accounting standards developed and applied by professional accountants

Governmental accounting (p. 6) Accounting work performed for a federal, state, or local governmental unit

International accounting (p. 13) The study of accounting principles used by different countries

Management advisory services (p. 6) Services designed to help clients improve their information systems or their business performance

Managerial accounting (p. 6) Accounting work carried on by an accountant employed by a single business in industry

Partnership (p. 9) A business entity owned by two or more people who are legally responsible for the debts and taxes of the business

Public accountants (p. 5) Members of firms that perform accounting services for other companies

Separate entity assumption (p. 9) The concept of keeping a firm's financial records separate from the owner's personal financial records

Social entity (p. 9) A nonprofit organization, such as a city, public school, or public hospital

Sole proprietorship (p. 9) A business entity owned by one person who is legally responsible for the debts and taxes of the business

Statements of Financial Accounting Standards (p. 12) Accounting principles established by the Financial Accounting Standards Board

Stock (p. 11) Certificates that represent ownership of a corporation

Stockholders (p. 12) The owners of a corporation; also called shareholders

Tax accounting (p. 5) A service that involves tax compliance and tax planning

Comprehensive Self Review

1. What is the purpose of accounting?
2. What does the accounting process involve?
3. What are the three types of business entities?
4. How is the ownership of a corporation different from that of a sole proprietorship?
5. What is the purpose of the auditor's report?

(Answers to Comprehensive Self Review are on page 21.)

Discussion Questions

1. What are the three major areas of accounting?
2. What types of services do public accountants provide?
3. What is tax planning?
4. What are the major functions or activities performed by accountants in private industry?
5. What types of people or organizations are interested in financial information about a firm, and why are they interested in this information?
6. What is the function of the Securities and Exchange Commission?
7. What are the three types of business entities, and how do they differ?
8. Why is it important for business records to be separate from the records of the business's owner or owners? What is the term accountants use to describe this separation of personal and business records?
9. What is the purpose of the Financial Accounting Standards Board?
10. What groups consistently offer opinions about proposed FASB statements?

Applications

Which Type of Business Entity?

Since graduating from college five years ago, Ned Turner has worked for a national chain of men's clothing stores. Ned has held several positions with the company and is currently manager of a local branch store.

Over the past three years, Ned has observed a pattern in men who purchase suits. He believes that the majority of men's suit purchases are black, brown, blue, gray, and olive. He also notices that French cuff shirts are now fashionable, but few stores carry a wide color selection. Since he has always wanted to be in business for himself, Ned's idea is to open a shop that sells suits that are black, brown, blue, gray, and olive and to carry a wide array of colors of French cuff shirts. The store will also sell fashionable ties and cuff links. Ned already has a name for his store, The Three B's and Go Suit Shop. Ned has discussed his plan with a number of people in the industry and they believe his idea is a viable one.

A new upscale shopping mall is opening nearby and Ned has decided that now is the time to take the plunge and go into business for himself. Ned plans to open The Three B's and Go Suit Shop in the new mall.

One of the things Ned must decide in the process of transforming his idea into reality is the form of ownership for his new business. Should it be organized as a sole proprietorship, a partnership, or corporation?

What advice would you give Ned? What advantages and disadvantages are there to each choice? The following diagram will help you to organize your thoughts.

Business Entity	Advantages	Disadvantages
Sole Proprietorship		
Partnership		
Corporation		

Business Connections

MANAGERIAL FOCUS   Know Accounting

1. Why is it important for managers to have financial information?

2. Do you think a manager will obtain enough financial information to control operations effectively if the manager simply reads a set of financial statements once a year? Why or why not?

3. The owner of a small business commented to a friend that he did not see the need for an accounting system in his firm because he closely supervises day-to-day operations and knows exactly what is happening in the business. Would you agree with his statement? Why or why not?

4. This chapter listed a number of questions that the owner or manager of a firm might ask when trying to evaluate the results of the firm's operations and its financial position. If you were an owner or manager, what other questions would you ask to judge the firm's performance, control operations, make decisions, and plan for the future?

5. The major objective of most businesses is to earn a profit. What other objectives might a business have? How can financial information help management to achieve these objectives?

6. Many business owners and managers are not accountants. Why is it useful for such people to have a basic knowledge of accounting?

7. Are international accounting standards important to management? Why or why not?

8. Why is the separate entity assumption important to a manager?

Ethical DILEMMA

Attendance The professor of your *College Accounting* class requires class attendance. Students who miss three or more classes with unexcused absences will have their earned course grade reduced by one letter grade. Because the class is large, the professor's only check on attendance is to have each student sign in upon entering the class. Your roommate is also enrolled in this class and you have observed him sign in and immediately leave class on two occasions. He has indicated that he will continue this practice and intends to get the class notes from you. What would you do if you were in this ethical dilemma?

Street WISE:
Questions from the Real World

Information Refer to The Home Depot, Inc. *1999 Annual Report* in Appendix B.

1. Review the letter written by Arthur M. Blank, President and Chief Executive Officer. To what audiences is the letter directed? Describe the types of financial information presented in the letter. Why would this information be important to readers?

2. Information provided in a company's annual report can also include nonfinancial strategies for merchandising, customer service, or new ventures. Based on the letter presented from The Home Depot, Inc.'s president and CEO, describe three successful strategies that the company implemented in 1999.

FINANCIAL $TATEMENT
A N A L Y S I S   **Notes to Financial Statements** Within a company's annual report, a section called "Notes to Consolidated Financial Statements" offers general information about the company along with detailed notes related to its financial statements. An excerpt from American Eagle Outfitters, Inc.'s, "Notes to Consolidated Financial Statements," *1999 Annual Report*, is presented below.

> American Eagle Outfitters, Inc. ("the Company") is a specialty retailer of all-American casual apparel, accessories, and footwear for men and women between the ages of 16 and 34. The Company designs, markets, and sells its own brand of versatile, relaxed, and timeless classics like AE dungarees, khakis, and T-shirts, providing high-quality merchandise at affordable prices. The Company operates retail stores located primarily in regional enclosed shopping malls principally in the Midwest, Northeast, and Southeast.

Analyze:

1. Would American Eagle Outfitters, Inc., be considered an economic entity or a social entity? Why?
2. What types of merchandise does this company sell?
3. Who are the potential users of the information presented? Why would this information be helpful to these users?

Analyze Online: On the American Eagle Outfitters, Inc., Web site **(www.ae.com),** review the *Company Overview* section, under *Investment Information* within the *Corporate* link.

4. What age consumer does the company target?
5. What types of merchandise does the company offer? Has the merchandise selection changed from the merchandise described in the *1999 Annual Report*?
6. What information is offered to the shareholder on the Web site?

Extending the *Thought*   **Independent Auditor** A certified public accountant (CPA) who audits a company's financial statements must be independent. What is meant by "independent" in this sense? Why is it important? What situations or factors might affect a CPA's independence?

Business Communication   **Memo** As the manager of the accounting department, you have been asked by the human resources director to help prepare a job description for a job opening in your department. The company wishes to fill the position of bookkeeper. The heading of your memo should include the following:

    Date:
    To:
    From:
    Subject:

The body of your memo should include the job responsibilities, and the training and experience necessary for the position.

Team_Work_   **Sharing Information** You and your family own a chain of bakeries. Your employees are awarded annual bonuses based on the financial performance of the business. As a group, prepare a list of the types of information that you plan to distribute to your employees that will help them understand the financial condition of the business.

◄ **Connection 7**

inter**NET**
CONNECTION   **FASB** Visit the Financial Accounting Standards Board Web site **(www.fasb.org)** and select *FASB Facts.*

◄ **Connection 8**

- What is FASB's mission?
- What is the GASB?

Answers to Self Reviews

Answers to Section 1 Self Review

1. The results of the accounting process—financial statements—communicate essential information about a business to concerned individuals and organizations.
2. Clerk, bookkeeper, and accountant.
3. Periodic reports that summarize the financial affairs of a business.
4. **b.** Uniform CPA Examination
5. **d.** Securities and Exchange Commission
6. Current sales and expenses figures, anticipated sales and expenses, and the cost of the expansion.

Answers to Section 2 Self Review

1. Accounting standards that are changed and refined in response to changes in the environment in which businesses operate.
2. GAAP help to ensure that financial information fairly presents a firm's operating results and financial position.
3. FASB develops proposed statements and solicits feedback from interested individuals, groups, and companies. FASB evaluates the opinions received and votes on the statement.
4. **c.** partnership
5. **b.** social entity
6. The shareholders are not responsible for the debts and taxes of the corporation. Corporations can continue in existence indefinitely.

Answers to Comprehensive Self Review

1. To gather and communicate financial information about a business.
2. Recording, classifying, summarizing, interpreting, and communicating financial information about a business.
3. Sole proprietorship, partnership, and corporation.
4. A sole proprietorship is a business entity owned by one person. A corporation is a separate legal entity that has a legal right to own property and do business in its own name.
5. To obtain the objective opinion of a professional accountant from outside the company that the statements fairly present the operating results and financial position of the business and that the information was prepared according to GAAP.

CHAPTER 2

Learning Objectives

1 Record in equation form the financial effects of a business transaction.

2 Define, identify, and understand the relationship between asset, liability, and owner's equity accounts.

3 Analyze the effects of business transactions on a firm's assets, liabilities, and owner's equity and record these effects in accounting equation form.

4 Prepare an income statement.

5 Prepare a statement of owner's equity and a balance sheet.

6 Define the accounting terms new to this chapter.

Analyzing Business Transactions

www.southwest.com

*I*n addition to having low fares, fun flights, and friendly employees, Southwest Airlines Company has been profitable for 27 consecutive years. Chief Executive Officer Herb Kelleher believes an efficient all-Boeing 737 fleet designed for direct short-haul routes, effective cost controls, and a happy, productive workforce are the keys to its success. Voted as CEO of 1999 by his peers, the maverick leader is known for his good humor and creating a company culture brimming with employee chili cook-offs, paper airplane contests, and dance competitions.

Thinking Critically
In what ways do you think a happy workforce contributes to the bottom line, or net profit, of the company?

For more information on Southwest Airlines Company, go to:
collegeaccounting.glencoe.com.

New Terms

Accounts payable	Income statement
Accounts receivable	Liabilities
Assets	Net income
Balance sheet	Net loss
Break even	On account
Business transaction	Owner's equity
Capital	Revenue
Equity	Statement of owner's equity
Expense	
Fair market value	Withdrawals
Fundamental accounting equation	

Section Objectives

1 **Record in equation form the financial effects of a business transaction.**

WHY IT'S IMPORTANT
Learning the fundamental accounting equation is a basis for understanding business transactions.

2 **Define, identify, and understand the relationship between asset, liability, and owner's equity accounts.**

WHY IT'S IMPORTANT
The relationship between assets, liabilities, and owner's equity is the basis for the entire accounting system.

Terms to Learn

accounts payable
assets
balance sheet
business transaction
capital
equity
liabilities
on account
owner's equity

1 **Objective**
Record in equation form the financial effects of a business transaction.

Property and Financial Interest

The accounting process starts with the analysis of business transactions. A **business transaction** is any financial event that changes the resources of a firm. For example, purchases, sales, payments, and receipts of cash are all business transactions. The accountant analyzes each business transaction to decide what information to record and where to record it.

Beginning with Analysis

Let's analyze the transactions of Carter Consulting Services, a firm that provides a wide range of accounting and consulting services. Linda Carter, CPA, has a master's degree in accounting. She is the sole proprietor of Carter Consulting Services. Beatrice Wilson, the office manager, has an associate's degree in business and has taken 12 semester hours of accounting. The firm is located in a large office complex.

Every month Carter Consulting Services bills clients for the accounting and consulting services provided that month. Customers can also pay in cash when the services are rendered.

Starting a Business

Let's start from the beginning. Linda Carter obtained the funds to start the business by withdrawing $80,000 from her personal savings account. The first transaction of the new business was opening a checking account in the name of Carter Consulting Services. The separate bank account helps Carter keep her financial interest in the business separate from her personal funds.

When a business transaction occurs, it is analyzed to identify how it affects the equation *property equals financial interest*. This equation reflects the fact that in a free enterprise system, all property is owned by someone. In this case Carter owns the business because she supplied the property (cash).

Use these steps to analyze the effect of a business transaction:

1. Describe the financial event.
   - Identify the property.
   - Identify who owns the property.
   - Determine the amount of increase or decrease.
2. Make sure the equation is in balance.

Property	=	Financial Interest

Business Transaction

Linda Carter withdrew $80,000 from personal savings and deposited it in a new checking account in the name of Carter Consulting Services.

Analysis

a. The business received $80,000 of *property* in the form of cash.

b. Carter had an $80,000 *financial interest* in the business.

Note that the equation *property equals financial interest* remains in balance.

Property	Cash	=	Financial Interest Linda Carter, Capital
(a) Invested cash	+ **$80,000**		
(b) Increased equity			+ **$80,000**
New balances	$80,000	=	$80,000

An owner's financial interest in the business is called **equity**, or **capital**. Linda Carter has $80,000 equity in Carter Consulting Services.

Purchasing Equipment for Cash

The first priority for office manager Beatrice Wilson was to get the business ready for opening day on December 1.

Business Transaction

Carter Consulting Services issued a $20,000 check to purchase a computer and other equipment.

Analysis

c. The firm purchased new property (equipment) for $20,000.

d. The firm paid out $20,000 in cash.

The equation remains in balance.

	Property			=	Financial Interest
	Cash	+	Equipment	=	Linda Carter, Capital
Previous balances	$80,000			=	$80,000
(c) Purchased equipment		+	**$20,000**		
(d) Paid cash	**−20,000**				
New balances	$60,000	+	$20,000	=	$80,000

Notice that there is a change in the composition of the firm's property. Now the firm has cash and equipment. The equation shows that the total value of the property remains the same, $80,000. Linda Carter's financial interest, or equity, is also unchanged. Note that property (Cash and Equipment) is equal to financial interest (Linda Carter, Capital).

These activities are recorded for the business entity Carter Consulting Services. Linda Carter's personal assets, such as her personal bank account, house, furniture, and automobile, are kept separate from the property of the firm. Nonbusiness property is not included in the accounting records of the business entity.

Purchasing Equipment on Credit

Wilson purchased additional office equipment. Office Plus, the store selling the equipment, allows Carter Consulting Services 60 days to pay the bill. This arrangement is called buying **on account**. The business has a *charge account*, or *open-account credit*, with its suppliers. Amounts that a business must pay in the future are known as **accounts payable**. The companies or individuals to whom the amounts are owed are called *creditors*.

Business Transaction

Carter Consulting Services purchased office equipment on account from Office Plus for $15,000.

Analysis

e. The firm purchased new property (equipment) that cost $15,000.

f. The firm owes $15,000 to Office Plus.

The equation remains in balance.

	Property			=	Financial Interest		
	Cash	+	Equipment	=	Accounts Payable	+	Linda Carter, Capital
Previous balances	$60,000	+	$20,000	=			$80,000
(e) Purchased equip.			+**15,000**				
(f) Incurred debt					+**$15,000**		
New balances	$60,000	+	$35,000	=	$15,000	+	$80,000

Office Plus is willing to accept a claim against Carter Consulting Services until the bill is paid. Now there are two different financial interests or claims against the firm's property—the creditor's claim (Accounts Payable) and the owner's claim (Linda Carter, Capital). Notice that the total property increases to $95,000. Cash is $60,000 and equipment is $35,000. Linda Carter, Capital stays the same; but the creditor's claim increases to $15,000. After this transaction is recorded, the left side of the equation still equals the right side.

About Accounting

History

For as long as people have been involved in business, there has been a need for accounting. The system of accounting we use is based upon the works of Luca Pacioli, a Franciscan monk in Italy. In 1494, Pacioli wrote about the bookkeeping techniques in practice during his time.

When Ben Cohen and Jerry Greenfield founded Ben & Jerry's Homemade Ice Cream, Inc., in 1978, they invested $8,000 of their own funds and borrowed funds of $4,000. The equation *property equals financial interest* is expressed as

Property	=	Financial Interest
cash	=	creditors' claims
		+ owners' claims
$12,000	=	$ 4,000
		+ 8,000
		$12,000

Purchasing Supplies

Wilson purchased supplies so that Carter Consulting Services could start operations. The company that sold the items requires cash payments from companies that have been in business less than six months.

Business Transaction

Carter Consulting Services issued a check for $2,000 to Resource Supplies, Inc. to purchase office supplies.

Analysis

g. The firm purchased office supplies that cost $2,000.

h. The firm paid $2,000 in cash.

The equation remains in balance.

	Property				=	Financial Interest		
	Cash	+	Supplies	+	Equipment	=	Accounts Payable	+	Linda Carter, Capital
Previous balances	$60,000			+	$35,000	=	$15,000	+	$80,000
(g) Purchased supplies		+	$2,000						
(h) Paid cash	− 2,000								
New balances	$58,000	+	$2,000	+	$35,000	=	$15,000	+	$80,000

Notice that total property remains the same, even though the form of the property has changed. Also note that all of the property (left side) equals all of the financial interests (right side).

Paying a Creditor

Wilson decided to reduce the firm's debt to Office Plus by $3,000.

Business Transaction

Carter Consulting Services issued a check for $3,000 to Office Plus.

Analysis

i. The firm paid $3,000 in cash.

j. The claim of Office Plus against the firm decreased by $3,000.

The equation remains in balance.

	Property				=	Financial Interest		
	Cash	+	Supplies	+	Equipment	=	Accounts Payable	+	Linda Carter, Capital
Previous balances	$58,000	+	$2,000	+	$35,000	=	$15,000	+	$80,000
(i) Paid cash	− 3,000								
(j) Decreased debt							− 3,000		
New balances	$55,000	+	$2,000	+	$35,000	=	$12,000	+	$80,000

Renting Facilities

In November Carter arranged to rent facilities for $3,000 per month, beginning in December. The landlord required that rent for the first two months—December and January—be paid in advance. The firm prepaid (paid in advance) the rent for two months. As a result, the firm obtained the right to occupy facilities for a two-month period. In accounting this right is considered a form of property.

Business Transaction

Carter Consulting Services issued a check for $6,000 to pay for rent for the months of December and January.

Analysis

k. The firm prepaid the rent for the next two months in the amount of $6,000.

l. The firm decreased its cash balance by $6,000.

The equation remains in balance.

	Cash	+	Supplies	+	Prepaid Rent	+	Equipment	=	Accounts Payable	+	Linda Carter, Capital
					Property			=	**Financial Interest**		
Previous balances	$55,000	+	$2,000			+	$35,000	=	$12,000	+	$80,000
(k) Paid cash	− **6,000**										
(l) Prepaid rent					+**$6,000**						
New balances	$49,000	+	$2,000	+	$6,000	+	$35,000	=	$12,000	+	$80,000

Notice that when property values and financial interests increase or decrease, the total of the items on one side of the equation still equals the total on the other side.

Property		=	Financial Interest	
Cash	$49,000		Accounts Payable	$12,000
Supplies	2,000		Linda Carter, Capital	80,000
Prepaid Rent	6,000			
Equipment	35,000			
Total	$92,000	=	Total	$92,000

> The balance sheet is also called the *statement of financial position*. Caterpillar Inc., reported assets of $26.6 billion, liabilities of $21.2 billion, and owners' equity of $5.4 billion on its statement of financial position at December 31, 1999.

Assets, Liabilities, and Owner's Equity

❷ Objective

Define, identify, and understand the relationship between asset, liability, and owner's equity accounts.

Accountants use special accounting terms when they refer to property and financial interests. For example, they refer to the property that a business owns as **assets** and to the debts or obligations of the business as **liabilities**. The owner's financial interest is called **owner's equity**. (Sometimes owner's equity is called *proprietorship* or *net worth*. Owner's equity is

Carter Consulting Services
Balance Sheet
November 30, 2004

Assets				Liabilities			
Cash	49 0 0 0 00			Accounts Payable	12 0 0 0 00		
Supplies	2 0 0 0 00						
Prepaid Rent	6 0 0 0 00			*Owner's Equity*			
Equipment	35 0 0 0 00			Linda Carter, Capital	80 0 0 0 00		
Total Assets	92 0 0 0 00			Total Liabilities and Owner's Equity	92 0 0 0 00		

▲ **FIGURE 2-1**
Balance Sheet for Carter Consulting Services

the preferred term and is used throughout this book.) At regular intervals Carter reviews the status of the firm's assets, liabilities, and owner's equity in a financial statement called a **balance sheet**. The balance sheet shows the firm's financial position on a given date. Figure 2-1 shows the firm's balance sheet on November 30, the day before the company opened for business.

The assets are listed on the left side of the balance sheet and the liabilities and owner's equity are on the right side. This arrangement is similar to the equation *property equals financial interest*. Property is shown on the left side of the equation, and financial interest appears on the right side.

The balance sheet in Figure 2-1 shows

- the amount and types of property the business owns,
- the amount owed to creditors,
- the owner's interest.

This statement gives Linda Carter a complete picture of the financial position of her business on November 30.

Section 1 Self Review

Questions

1. What is a business transaction?
2. Describe a transaction that increases an asset and the owner's equity.
3. What does the term "accounts payable" mean?

Exercises

4. Maria Sanders purchased a computer for $2,000 on account for her business. What is the effect of this transaction?

   a. Cash decrease of $2,000 and owner's equity increase of $2,000.

   b. Equipment increase of $2,000 and cash increase of $2,000.

   c. Equipment decrease of $2,000 and accounts payable increase of $2,000.

   d. Equipment increase of $2,000 and accounts payable increase of $2,000.

5. Tara Swift began a new business by depositing $40,000 in the business bank account. She wrote two checks from the business account: $5,000 for office furniture and $1,000 for office supplies. What is her financial interest in the company?

   a. $34,000
   b. $35,000
   c. $39,000
   d. $40,000

Analysis

6. T. D. Whatley Co. has no liabilities. The asset and owner's equity balances are as follows. What is the balance of "Supplies"?

Cash	$12,000
Office Equipment	$8,000
Supplies	????
T. D. Whatley, Capital	$22,500

(Answers to Section 1 Self Review are on page 55.)

The Accounting Equation and Financial Statements

Terms to Learn

accounts receivable
break even
expense
fair market value
fundamental accounting
   equation
income statement
net income
net loss
revenue
statement of owner's equity
withdrawals

❸ Objective

Analyze the effects of business transactions on a firm's assets, liabilities, and owner's equity and record these effects in accounting equation form.

The word *balance* in the title "balance sheet" has a special meaning. It emphasizes that the total on the left side of the report must equal, or balance, the total on the right side.

The Fundamental Accounting Equation

In accounting terms the firm's assets must equal the total of its liabilities and owner's equity. This equality can be expressed in equation form, as illustrated here. The amounts are for Carter Consulting Services on November 30.

Assets	=	Liabilities	+	Owner's Equity
$92,000	=	$12,000	+	$80,000

The relationship between assets and liabilities plus owner's equity is called the **fundamental accounting equation**. The entire accounting process of analyzing, recording, and reporting business transactions is based on the fundamental accounting equation.

If any two parts of the equation are known, the third part can be determined. For example, consider the basic accounting equation for Carter Consulting Services on November 30, with some information missing.

	Assets	=	Liabilities	+	Owner's Equity
1.	?	=	$12,000	+	$80,000
2.	$92,000	=	?	+	$80,000
3.	$92,000	=	$12,000	+	?

In the first case, we can solve for assets by adding liabilities to owner's equity ($12,000 + $80,000) to determine that assets are $92,000. In the second case, we can solve for liabilities by subtracting owner's equity from assets ($92,000 − $80,000) to determine that liabilities are $12,000. In the third case, we can solve for owner's equity by subtracting liabilities from assets ($92,000 − $12,000) to determine that owner's equity is $80,000.

Earning Revenue and Incurring Expenses

Carter Consulting Services opened for business on December 1. Some of the other businesses in the office complex became the firm's first clients. Carter also used her contacts in the community to identify other clients. Providing services to clients started a stream of revenue for the business. **Revenue**, or *income*, is the inflow of money or other assets that results from the sales of goods or services or from the use of money or property. A sale on account does not increase money, but it does create a claim to money. When a sale occurs, the revenue increases assets and also increases owner's equity.

An **expense**, on the other hand, involves the outflow of money, the use of other assets, or the incurring of a liability. Expenses include the costs of any materials, labor, supplies, and services used to produce revenue. Expenses cause a decrease in owner's equity.

A firm's accounting records show increases and decreases in assets, liabilities, and owner's equity as well as details of all transactions involving revenue and expenses. Let's use the fundamental accounting equation to show how revenue and expenses affect the business.

Important!

Revenues increase owner's equity.
Expenses decrease owner's equity.

Selling Services for Cash

During the month of December, Carter Consulting Services earned a total of $21,000 in revenue from clients who paid cash for accounting and bookkeeping services. This involved several transactions throughout the month. The total effect of these transactions is analyzed below.

Analysis

m. The firm received $21,000 in cash for services provided to clients.

n. Revenues increased by $21,000, which results in a $21,000 increase in owner's equity.

The fundamental accounting equation remains in balance.

	Assets				=	Liabilities +	Owner's Equity		
	Cash	+ Supplies	+ Prepaid Rent	+ Equipment	=	Accounts Payable	+ Linda Carter, Capital	+ Revenue	
Previous balances	$49,000	+ $2,000	+ $6,000	+ $35,000	=	$12,000	+ $80,000		
(m) Received cash	+ 21,000								
(n) Increased owner's equity by earning revenue								+	$21,000
New balances	$70,000	+ $2,000	+ $6,000	+ $35,000	=	$12,000	+ $80,000	+	$21,000
	$113,000						$113,000		

Notice that revenue amounts are recorded in a separate column under owner's equity. Keeping revenue separate from the owner's equity will help the firm compute total revenue more easily when the financial statements are prepared.

Selling Services on Credit

Carter Consulting Services has some charge account clients. These clients are allowed 30 days to pay. Amounts owed by these clients are known as **accounts receivable**. This is a new form of asset for the firm—claims for future collection from customers. During December Carter Consulting Services earned $7,000 of revenue from charge account clients. The effect of these transactions is analyzed on page 32.

Analysis

o. The firm acquired a new asset, accounts receivable, of $7,000.

p. Revenues increased by $7,000, which results in a $7,000 increase in owner's equity.

The fundamental accounting equation remains in balance.

		Assets			=	Liab.	+	Owner's Equity	
		Accts.		Prepaid		Accts.		Linda Carter,	
	Cash	+ Rec.	+ Supp.	+ Rent	+ Equip.	= Pay.	+	Capital	+ Rev.
Previous balances	$70,000		+ $2,000	+ $6,000	+ $35,000	= $12,000	+	$80,000	+ $21,000
(o) Received new asset—accts. rec.		+ **$7,000**							
(p) Increased owner's equity by earning revenue									+ **7,000**
New balances	$70,000	+ $7,000	+ $2,000	+ $6,000	+ $35,000	= $12,000	+	$80,000	+ $28,000
			$120,000					$120,000	

Collecting Receivables

During December Carter Consulting Services received $3,000 on account from clients who owed money for services previously billed. The effect of these transactions is analyzed below.

Analysis

q. The firm received $3,000 in cash.

r. Accounts receivable decreased by $3,000.

The fundamental accounting equation remains in balance.

		Assets			=	Liab.	+	Owner's Equity	
		Accts.		Prepaid		Accts.		Linda Carter,	
	Cash	+ Rec.	+ Supp.	+ Rent	+ Equip.	= Pay.	+	Capital	+ Rev.
Previous balances	$70,000	+ $7,000	+ $2,000	+ $6,000	+ $35,000	= $12,000	+	$80,000	+ $28,000
(q) Received cash	+ **3,000**								
(r) Decreased accounts receivable		− **3,000**							
New balances	$73,000	+ $4,000	+ $2,000	+ $6,000	+ $35,000	= $12,000	+	$80,000	+ $28,000
			$120,000					$120,000	

In this type of transaction one asset is changed for another asset (accounts receivable for cash). Notice that revenue is not increased when cash is collected from charge account clients. The revenue was recorded when the sale on account took place (see entry (p)). Notice that the fundamental accounting equation, *assets equal liabilities plus owner's equity,* stays in balance regardless of the changes arising from individual transactions.

Paying Employees' Salaries

So far Carter has done very well. Her equity has increased by the revenues earned. However, running a business costs money, and these expenses reduce owner's equity.

During the first month of operations, Carter Consulting Services hired an accounting clerk. The salaries for the new accounting clerk and the office manager are considered an expense to the firm.

Business Transaction

In December Carter Consulting Services paid $5,000 in salaries for the accounting clerk and Beatrice Wilson.

Analysis

s. The firm decreased its cash balance by $5,000.

t. The firm paid salaries expense in the amount of $5,000, which decreased owner's equity.

The fundamental accounting equation remains in balance.

	Assets							=	Liab.	+	Owner's Equity			
	Cash	+	Accts. Rec.	+	Supp.	+	Prepaid Rent	+	Equip.	=	Accts. Pay.	+	L. Carter, Capital	+ Rev.	− Exp.
Previous balances	$73,000	+ $4,000	+ $2,000	+ $6,000	+ $35,000	= $12,000	+ $80,000	+ $28,000						
(s) Paid cash	− 5,000													
(t) Decreased owner's equity by incurring salaries exp.														− $5,000
New balances	$68,000	+ $4,000	+ $2,000	+ $6,000	+ $35,000	= $12,000	+ $80,000	+ $28,000				− $5,000		

$115,000 $115,000

Notice that expenses are recorded in a separate column under owner's equity. The separate record of expenses is kept for the same reason that the separate record of revenue is kept—to analyze operations for the period.

Paying Utilities Expense

At the end of December, the firm received a $600 utilities bill.

Business Transaction

Carter Consulting Services issued a check for $600 to pay the utilities bill.

Analysis

u. The firm decreased its cash balance by $600.

v. The firm paid utilities expense of $600, which decreased owner's equity.

The fundamental accounting equation remains in balance.

	Assets					=	Liab.	+	Owner's Equity		
	Cash +	Accts. Rec. +	Supp. +	Prepaid Rent +	Equip. =		Accts. Pay. +		L. Carter, Capital +	Rev. −	Exp.
Previous balances	$68,000 +	$4,000 +	$2,000 +	$6,000 +	$35,000 =		$12,000 +		$80,000 +	$28,000 −	$5,000
(u) Paid cash	− 600										
(v) Decreased owner's equity by utilities exp.											− 600
New balances	$67,400 +	$4,000 +	$2,000 +	$6,000 +	$35,000 =		$12,000 +		$80,000 +	$28,000 −	$5,600

$114,400 $114,400

Effect of Owner's Withdrawals

On December 30, Carter withdrew $3,000 in cash for personal expenses. **Withdrawals** are funds taken from the business by the owner for personal use. Withdrawals are not a business expense but a decrease in the owner's equity.

Business Transaction

Linda Carter wrote a check to withdraw $3,000 cash for personal use.

Analysis

w. The firm decreased its cash balance by $3,000.

x. Owner's equity decreased by $3,000.

The fundamental accounting equation remains in balance.

	Assets					=	Liab.	+	Owner's Equity		
	Cash +	Accts. Rec. +	Supp. +	Prepaid Rent +	Equip. =		Accts. Pay. +		L. Carter, Capital +	Rev. −	Exp.
Previous bal.	$67,400 +	$4,000 +	$2,000 +	$6,000 +	$35,000 =		$12,000 +		$80,000 +	$28,000 −	$5,600
(w) Withdrew cash	−3,000										
(x) Decreased owner's equity									−3,000		
New bal.	$64,400 +	$4,000 +	$2,000 +	$6,000 +	$35,000 =		$12,000 +		$77,000 +	$28,000 −	$5,600

$111,400 $111,400

Summary of Transactions

Figure 2-2 on page 35 summarizes the transactions of Carter Consulting Services through December 31. Notice that after each transaction, the fundamental accounting equation is in balance. Test your understanding by describing the nature of each transaction. Then check your results by referring to the discussion of each transaction.

④ Objective

Prepare an income statement.

The Income Statement

To be meaningful to owners, managers, and other interested parties, financial statements should provide information about revenue and expenses, assets and claims on the assets, and owner's equity.

	Assets						=	Liab.	+	Owner's Equity			
	Cash	+	Accts. Rec.	+	Supp.	+	Prepaid Rent	+	Equip.	=	Accts. Pay.	+	L. Carter, Cap.	+	Rev.	−	Exp.

	Cash	Accts. Rec.	Supp.	Prepaid Rent	Equip.	Accts. Pay.	L. Carter, Cap.	Rev.	Exp.
(a) & (b)	+80,000						80,000		
Balances	80,000					=	80,000		
(c) & (d)	−20,000				+20,000				
Balances	60,000				+20,000	=	80,000		
(e) & (f)					+15,000	= +15,000			
Balances	60,000				+35,000	= 15,000	+ 80,000		
(g) & (h)	−2,000	+2,000							
Balances	58,000	+2,000			+35,000	= 15,000	+ 80,000		
(i) & (j)	−3,000					−3,000			
Balances	55,000	+2,000			+35,000	= 12,000	+ 80,000		
(k) & (l)	−6,000		+6,000						
Balances	49,000	+2,000	+6,000		+35,000	= 12,000	+ 80,000		
(m) & (n)	+21,000							+21,000	
Balances	70,000	+2,000	+6,000		+35,000	= 12,000	+ 80,000	+ 21,000	
(o) & (p)		+7,000						+7,000	
Balances	70,000	+7,000	+2,000	+6,000	+35,000	= 12,000	+ 80,000	+ 28,000	
(q) & (r)	+3,000	−3,000							
Balances	73,000	+4,000	+2,000	+6,000	+35,000	= 12,000	+ 80,000	+ 28,000	
(s) & (t)	−5,000								− 5,000
Balances	68,000	+4,000	+2,000	+6,000	+35,000	= 12,000	+ 80,000	+ 28,000	− 5,000
(u) & (v)	−600								−600
Balances	67,400	+4,000	+2,000	+6,000	+35,000	= 12,000	+ 80,000	+ 28,000	− 5,600
(w) & (x)	−3,000						−3,000		
Balances	$64,400	+ $4,000	+ $2,000	+ $6,000	+ $35,000	= $12,000	+ $77,000	+ $28,000	− $5,600

$111,400 = $111,400

The **income statement** shows the results of business operations for a specific period of time such as a month, a quarter, or a year. The income statement shows the revenue earned and the expenses of doing business. (The income statement is sometimes called a *profit and loss statement* or a *statement of income and expenses*. The most common term, income statement, is used throughout this text.) Figure 2-3 shows the income statement for Carter Consulting Services for its first month of operation.

▲ **FIGURE 2-2**
Transactions of Carter Consulting Services Through December 31, 2004

◄ **FIGURE 2-3**
Income Statement for Carter Consulting Services

Carter Consulting Services
Income Statement
Month Ended December 31, 2004

Revenue		
Fees Income		28 000 00
Expenses		
Salaries Expense	5 000 00	
Utilities Expense	600 00	
Total Expenses		5 600 00
Net Income		22 400 00

The income statement shows the difference between income from services provided or goods sold and the amount spent to operate the business. **Net income** results when revenue is greater than the expenses for the period. When expenses are greater than revenue, the result is a **net loss**. In the rare case when revenue and expenses are equal, the firm is said to **break even**. The income statement in Figure 2-3 shows a net income; revenue is greater than expenses.

The three-line heading of the income statement shows *who, what,* and *when.*

- Who—the business name appears on the first line.
- What—the report title appears on the second line.
- When—the period covered appears on the third line.

The third line of the income statement heading in Figure 2-3 indicates that the report covers operations for the "Month Ended December 31, 2004." Review how other time periods are reported on the third line of the income statement heading.

Period Covered	Third Line of Heading
Jan., Feb., Mar.	Three-Month Period Ended March 31, 20--
Jan. to Dec.	Year Ended December 31, 20--
July 1 to June 30	Fiscal Year Ended June 30, 20--

Note the use of single and double rules in amount columns. A single line is used to show that the amounts above it are being added or subtracted. Double lines are used under the final amount in a column or section of a report to show that the amount is complete. Nothing is added to or subtracted from an amount with a double line.

> Some companies refer to the income statement as the *statement of operations.* American Eagle Outfitters, Inc. reported $832 million in sales on consolidated statements of operations for the fiscal year ended January 29, 2000. American Eagle Outfitters, Inc. was ranked as the sixteenth fastest-growing company in the United States by *Fortune* magazine in September 2000.

The income statement for Carter Consulting Services does not have dollar signs because it was prepared on accounting paper with ruled columns. However, dollar signs are used on income statements that are prepared on plain paper, that is, not on a ruled form.

The Statement of Owner's Equity and the Balance Sheet

The **statement of owner's equity** reports the changes that occurred in the owner's financial interest during the reporting period. This statement is prepared before the balance sheet so that the amount of the ending capital balance is available for presentation on the balance sheet. Figure 2-4 on page 38 shows the statement of owner's equity for Carter Consulting Services. Note that the statement of owner's equity has a three-line heading: *who, what,* and *when.*

Recall

Financial Statements

Financial statements are reports that summarize a firm's financial affairs.

Business Etiquette

In Japan, business cards are always offered with two hands. The receiver should accept the card with two hands, study it, and bow slightly before placing it into a shirt or jacket pocket. Placing the card near the heart shows respect for both the person and the company.

5 Objective

Prepare a statement of owner's equity and a balance sheet.

Accounting
On The Job

Hospitality and Tourism

Industry Overview

Hospitality is the world's largest industry, accounting for more jobs, sales, and tax revenue than any other industry. The hospitality industry, also known as the travel or tourism industry, is composed of hotels, restaurants, institutional food service, cruise lines, arenas, travel agencies, meeting and convention centers, sport complexes, resorts, parks, clubs, spas, and tourism-related transportation. In the United States, the hospitality industry's employment growth is twice that of any other industry. Hospitality is forecasted to become the nation's largest industry by the year 2010.

Career Opportunities
- State Tourism Bureau Director
- Director of Resort Contracts and Purchasing
- Executive Chef
- Travel Technology Specialist
- Tour Promotions Manager
- Vice President of Hotel Operations
- Airport Passenger Services Supervisor
- Catering Director

Preparing for a Hospitality and Tourism Career
- Gain expertise in database administration or programming. Hotels, spas, golf courses, and airlines use sophisticated computerized systems to track reservations and memberships.
- Obtain an associate's or bachelor's degree in hotel, restaurant, and institutional management or a degree in hospitality and tourism management. Core course requirements include database management, electronic spreadsheets, and accounting.
- Enroll in an advanced internship program. The Disney College Program offers specialties in marketing, hotel management, finance, and communications. Marriott International offers paid internships from 8 to 16 weeks in duration. Opportunities exist in accounting and finance, catering, front office, human resources, sales, and culinary arts.
- Receive training on the latest Worldspan computer reservation system developed by Delta, TWA, and Northwest Airlines.

Thinking Critically
What skills and education might be required for the position of hotel general manager with a major hotel chain such as Marriott International?

Internet Application
Visit the Web site of a trade organization such as the Travel Industry Association of America to learn about potential career paths within the industry. Describe the purpose of the association. What resources are offered on the site?

- The first line of the statement of owner's equity is the capital balance at the beginning of the period.
- Net income is an increase to owner's equity; net loss is a decrease to owner's equity.
- Withdrawals by the owner are a decrease to owner's equity.
- Additional investments by the owners are an increase to owner's equity.
- The total of changes in equity is reported on the line "Increase in Capital" (or "Decrease in Capital").
- The last line of the statement of owner's equity is the capital balance at the end of the period.

Carter Consulting Services
Statement of Owner's Equity
Month Ended December 31, 2004

Linda Carter, Capital, December 1, 2004		8 0 0 0 0 00
Net Income for December	2 2 4 0 0 00	
Less Withdrawals for December	3 0 0 0 00	
Increase in Capital		1 9 4 0 0 00
Linda Carter, Capital, December 31, 2004		9 9 4 0 0 00

If Linda Carter had made any additional investments during December, this would appear as a separate line on Figure 2-4. Additional investments can be cash or other assets such as equipment. If an investment is made in a form other than cash, the investment is recorded at its fair market value. **Fair market value** is the current worth of an asset or the price the asset would bring if sold on the open market.

The ending balances in the asset and liability accounts are used to prepare the balance sheet.

	Assets					=	Liab.	+	Owner's Equity		
	Cash +	Accts. Rec. +	Supp. +	Prepaid Rent +	Equip. =		Accts. Pay. +	L. Carter, Capital +	Rev.	−	Exp.
New balances	$64,400 +	$4,000 +	$2,000 +	$6,000 +	$35,000 =		$12,000 +	$77,000 +	$28,000	−	$5,600
			$111,400						$111,400		

The ending capital balance from the statement of owner's equity is also used to prepare the balance sheet. Figure 2-5 on page 39 shows the balance sheet for Carter Consulting Services on December 31, 2004.

The balance sheet shows

- Assets—the types and amounts of property that the business owns,
- Liabilities—the amounts owed to creditors,
- Owner's Equity—the owner's equity on the reporting date.

In preparing a balance sheet, remember the following.

- The three-line heading gives the firm's name (who), the title of the report (what), and the date of the report (when).
- Balance sheets prepared using the account form (as in Figure 2-5) show total assets on the same horizontal line as the total liabilities and owner's equity.
- Dollar signs are omitted when financial statements are prepared on paper with ruled columns. Statements that are prepared on plain paper, not ruled forms, show dollar signs with the first amount in each column and with each total.
- A single line shows that the amounts above it are being added or subtracted. Double lines indicate that the amount is the final amount in a column or section of a report.

Figure 2-6 on page 40 shows the connections among the financial statements. Financial statements are prepared in a specific order:

- income statement
- statement of owner's equity
- balance sheet

Important!

Financial Statements
The balance sheet is a snapshot of the firm's financial position on a specific date. The income statement, like a movie or video, shows the results of business operations over a period of time.

Carter Consulting Services
Balance Sheet
December 31, 2004

Assets							Liabilities						
Cash		6 4	4 0 0	00			Accounts Payable		1 2	0 0 0	00	
Accounts Receivable			4 0 0 0	00								
Supplies			2 0 0 0	00								
Prepaid Rent			6 0 0 0	00			Owner's Equity					
Equipment		3 5	0 0 0	00			Linda Carter, Capital		9 9	4 0 0	00	
Total Assets		1 1 1	4 0 0 0	0			Total Liabilities and Owner's Equity		1 1 1	4 0 0	00	

Net income from the income statement is used to prepare the statement of owner's equity. The ending capital balance from the statement of owner's equity is used to prepare the balance sheet.

▲ **FIGURE 2-5**
Balance Sheet for Carter Consulting Services

The Importance of Financial Statements

Preparing financial statements is one of the accountant's most important jobs. Each day millions of business decisions are made based on the information in financial statements.

Business managers and owners use the balance sheet and the income statement to control current operations and plan for the future. Creditors, prospective investors, governmental agencies, and others are interested in the profits of the business and in the asset and equity structure.

Managerial
IMPLICATIONS

Accounting Systems

- Sound financial records and statements are necessary so that business-people can make good decisions.

- Financial statements show
  - the amount of profit or loss,
  - the assets on hand,
  - the amount owed to creditors,
  - the amount of owner's equity.

- Well-run and efficiently managed businesses have good accounting systems that provide timely and useful information.

- Transactions involving revenue and expenses are recorded separately from owner's equity in order to analyze operations for the period.

Thinking Critically

If you were buying a business, what would you look for in the company's financial statements?

Step 1: Prepare the Income Statement

Carter Consulting Services
Income Statement
Month Ended December 31, 2004

Revenue		
Fees Income		28 0 0 0 00
Expenses		
Salaries Expense	5 0 0 0 00	
Utilities Expense	6 0 0 00	
Total Expenses		5 6 0 0 00
Net Income		22 4 0 0 00

Net income (or loss) is transferred to the statement of owner's equity.

Step 2: Prepare the Statement of Owner's Equity

Carter Consulting Services
Statement of Owner's Equity
Month Ended December 31, 2004

Linda Carter, Capital, December 1, 2004		80 0 0 0 00
Net Income for December	22 4 0 0 00	
Less Withdrawals for December	3 0 0 0 00	
Increase in Capital		19 4 0 0 00
Linda Carter, Capital, December 31, 2004		99 4 0 0 00

The ending capital balance is transferred to the balance sheet.

Step 3: Prepare the Balance Sheet

Carter Consulting Services
Balance Sheet
December 31, 2004

Assets		Liabilities	
Cash	64 4 0 0 00	Accounts Payable	12 0 0 0 00
Accounts Receivable	4 0 0 0 00		
Supplies	2 0 0 0 00		
Prepaid Rent	6 0 0 0 00	Owner's Equity	
Equipment	35 0 0 0 00	Linda Carter, Capital	99 4 0 0 00
Total Assets	111 4 0 0 00	Total Liabilities and Owner's Equity	111 4 0 0 00

Section 2 Self Review

Questions

1. What are withdrawals and how do they affect the basic accounting equation?

2. If an owner gives personal tools to the business, how is the transaction recorded?

3. What information is included in the financial statement headings?

Exercises

4. Hartwell Sporting Goods has assets of $50,000 and liabilities of $35,000. What is the owner's equity?
   a. $85,000   c. $35,000
   b. $20,000   d. $15,000

5. What information is contained on the income statement?
   a. revenues and expenses for a period of time
   b. revenue and expenses on a specific date

   c. assets, liabilities, and owner's equity for a period of time
   d. assets, liabilities, and owner's equity on a specific date

Analysis

6. Jensen Computers had revenues of $35,000 and expenses of $28,000. How does this affect owner's equity?

     (Answers to Section 2 Self Review are on page 55.)

CHAPTER 2 — Review and Applications

Review

Chapter Summary

Accounting begins with the analysis of business transactions. Each transaction changes the financial position of a business. In this chapter, you have learned how to analyze business transactions and how they affect assets, liabilities, and owner's equity. After transactions are analyzed and recorded, financial statements reflect the summarized changes to and results of business operations.

Learning Objectives

1 Record in equation form the financial effects of a business transaction.

The equation *property equals financial interest* reflects the fact that in a free enterprise system all property is owned by someone. This equation remains in balance after each business transaction.

2 Define, identify, and understand the relationship between asset, liability, and owner's equity accounts.

The term *assets* refers to property. The terms *liabilities* and *owner's equity* refer to financial interest. The relationship between assets, liabilities, and owner's equity is shown in equation form.

Assets   = Liabilities + Owner's Equity
Owner's Equity = Assets   − Liabilities
Liabilities   = Assets   − Owner's Equity

3 Analyze the effects of business transactions on a firm's assets, liabilities, and owner's equity and record these effects in accounting equation form.

1. Describe the financial event.
   - Identify the property.
   - Identify who owns the property.
   - Determine the amount of the increase or decrease.
2. Make sure the equation is in balance.

4 Prepare an income statement.

The income statement summarizes changes in owner's equity that result from revenue and expenses. The difference between revenue and expenses is the net income or net loss of the business for the period.

An income statement has a three-line heading:
- who
- what
- when

For the income statement, "when" refers to a period of time.

5 Prepare a statement of owner's equity and a balance sheet.

Changes in owner's equity for the period are summarized on the statement of owner's equity.
- Net income increases owner's equity.
- Added investments increase owner's equity.
- A net loss for the period decreases owner's equity.
- Withdrawals by the owner decrease owner's equity.

A statement of owner's equity has a three-line heading:
- who
- what
- when

For the statement of owner's equity, "when" refers to a period of time.

The balance sheet shows the assets, liabilities, and owner's equity on a given date.

A balance sheet has a three-line heading:
- who
- what
- when

For the balance sheet, "when" refers to a single date.

The financial statements are prepared in the following order.
1. Income Statement
2. Statement of Owner's Equity
3. Balance Sheet

6 Define the accounting terms new to this chapter.

CHAPTER 2 GLOSSARY

Accounts payable (p. 26) Amounts a business must pay in the future

Accounts receivable (p. 31) Claims for future collection from customers

Assets (p. 28) Property owned by a business

Balance sheet (p. 29) A formal report of a business's financial condition on a certain date; reports the assets, liabilities, and owner's equity of the business

Break even (p. 36) A point at which revenue equals expenses

Business transaction (p. 24) A financial event that changes the resources of a firm

Capital (p. 25) Financial investment in a business; equity

Equity (p. 25) An owner's financial interest in a business

Expense (p. 31) An outflow of cash, use of other assets, or incurring of a liability

Fair market value (p. 38) The current worth of an asset or the price the asset would bring if sold on the open market

Fundamental accounting equation (p. 30) The relationship between assets and liabilities plus owner's equity

Income statement (p. 35) A formal report of business operations covering a specific period of time; also called a profit and loss statement or a statement of income and expenses

Liabilities (p. 28) Debts or obligations of a business

Net income (p. 36) The result of an excess of revenue over expenses

Net loss (p. 36) The result of an excess of expenses over revenue

On account (p. 26) An arrangement to allow payment at a later date; also called a charge account or open-account credit

Owner's equity (p. 28) The financial interest of the owner of a business; also called proprietorship or net worth

Revenue (p. 30) An inflow of money or other assets that results from the sales of goods or services or from the use of money or property; also called income

Statement of owner's equity (p. 36) A formal report of changes that occurred in the owner's financial interest during a reporting period

Withdrawals (p. 34) Funds taken from the business by the owner for personal use

Comprehensive Self Review

1. What is the difference between buying for cash and buying on account?
2. Describe a transaction that will cause Accounts Payable and Cash to decrease by $500.
3. In what order are the financial statements prepared? Why?
4. If one side of the fundamental accounting equation is decreased, what will happen to the other side? Why?
5. What effect do revenue and expenses have on owner's equity?

(Answers to Comprehensive Self Review are on page 55.)

Discussion Questions

1. What are assets, liabilities, and owner's equity?
2. What information does the balance sheet contain?
3. What is the fundamental accounting equation?
4. What is revenue?
5. What are expenses?
6. Describe the effects of each of the following business transactions on assets, liabilities, and owner's equity.
   a. Bought equipment on credit.
   b. Paid salaries to employees.
   c. Sold services for cash.
   d. Paid cash to a creditor.
   e. Bought furniture for cash.
   f. Sold services on credit.
7. What information does the income statement contain?
8. How is net income determined?
9. What information is shown in the heading of a financial statement?
10. Why does the third line of the headings differ on the balance sheet and the income statement?
11. What information does the statement of owner's equity contain?
12. How does net income affect owner's equity?

Applications

EXERCISES

Exercise 2-1 ►
Objectives 1, 2

Completing the accounting equation.

The fundamental accounting equation for several businesses follows. Supply the missing amounts.

Assets	=	Liabilities	+	Owner's Equity
1. $43,500	=	$7,500	+	$?
2. $34,600	=	$6,750	+	$?
3. $26,000	=	$?	+	$22,950
4. $?	=	$1,750	+	$14,250
5. $12,900	=	$?	+	$ 9,350

Exercise 2-2 ►
Objectives 1, 2

Determining accounting equation amounts.

Just before Medical Supply Laboratories opened for business, Wes Rowland, the owner, had the following assets and liabilities. Determine the totals that would appear in the firm's fundamental accounting equation (Assets = Liabilities + Owner's Equity).

Cash	$17,900
Laboratory Equipment	42,500
Laboratory Supplies	2,400
Loan Payable	6,800
Accounts Payable	4,100

Exercise 2-3 ►
Objectives 1, 2, 3

Determining balance sheet amounts.

The following financial data is for the dental practice of Dr. Steve Smith when he began operations in July. Determine the amounts that would appear in Dr. Smith's balance sheet.

1. Owes $7,500 to the Jones Equipment Company.
2. Has cash balance of $2,825.
3. Has dental supplies of $1,170.
4. Owes $1,400 to the Nolen Furniture Company.
5. Has dental equipment of $11,850.
6. Has office furniture of $1,725.

Exercise 2-4 ►
Objectives 1, 2, 3

Determining the effects of transactions on the accounting equation.

Indicate the impact of each of the transactions below on the fundamental accounting equation (Assets = Liabilities + Owner's Equity) by placing a "+" to indicate an increase and a "−" to indicate a decrease. The first transaction is entered as an example.

	Assets	=	Liabilities	+	Owner's Equity
Transaction 1	+				+

TRANSACTIONS

1. Owner invested $20,000 in the business.
2. Purchased $2,000 supplies on account.

3. Purchased equipment for $10,000 cash.
4. Paid $1,400 for rent (in advance).
5. Performed services for $2,400 cash.
6. Paid $400 for utilities.
7. Performed services for $3,000 on account.
8. Received $1,500 from charge customers.
9. Paid salaries of $2,400 to employees.
10. Paid $1,000 to a creditor on account.

Determining the effects of transactions on the accounting equation.

◄ **Exercise 2-5**
Objectives 1, 2, 3

Delta Copy Shop had the transactions listed below during the month of April. Show how each transaction would be recorded in the accounting equation. Compute the totals at the end of the month. The headings to be used in the equation follow.

Assets			=	Liabilities	+	Owner's Equity		
Cash	+	Accounts Receivable + Equipment	=	Accounts Payable	+	Lacie Hodges, Capital + Revenue		− Expenses

TRANSACTIONS

1. Lacie Hodges started the business with a cash investment of $18,000.
2. Purchased equipment for $7,000 on credit.
3. Performed services for $900 in cash.
4. Purchased additional equipment for $1,500 in cash.
5. Performed services for $2,100 on credit.
6. Paid salaries of $1,600 to employees.
7. Received $700 cash from charge account customers.
8. Paid $3,500 to a creditor on account.

Identifying transactions.

◄ **Exercise 2-6**
Objectives 1, 2, 3

The following equation shows the effects of a number of transactions that took place at Auto Mart Repair Company during the month of August. Describe each transaction.

	Cash	+	Accounts Receivable	+	Equipment	=	Accounts Payable	+	Capital	+	Revenue	−	Expenses
Bal.	$30,000	+	$1,000	+	$36,000	=	$17,000	+	$50,000	+	0	−	0
1.	+4,000										+$4,000		
2.	−3,400				+3,400								
3.	−1,000						−1,000						
4.	−3,800												−$3,800
5.	+600		−600										
6.			+4,000								+4,000		
7.	−1,800												−1,800

Exercise 2-7 ►
Objective 4

Computing net income or net loss.

Millennium Computer Center had the following revenue and expenses during the month ended June 30. Did the firm earn a net income or incur a net loss for the period? What was the amount?

Fees for computer repairs	$16,400
Advertising expense	1,800
Salaries expense	8,550
Telephone expense	360
Fees for printer repairs	2,520
Utilities expense	750

Exercise 2-8 ►
Objective 4

Computing net income or net loss.

On December 1 Emilio Flores opened a speech and hearing clinic. During December his firm had the following transactions involving revenue and expenses. Did the firm earn a net income or incur a net loss for the period? What was the amount?

Paid $400 for advertising.
Provided services for $525 in cash.
Paid $75 for telephone service.
Paid salaries of $950 to employees.
Provided services for $650 on credit.
Paid $50 for office cleaning service.

Exercise 2-9 ►
Objective 4

Preparing an income statement.

At the beginning of September, Jody Seed started Seed's Investment Services, a firm that offers advice about investing and managing money. On September 30, the accounting records of the business showed the following information. Prepare an income statement for the month of September 20--.

Cash	$15,200	Fees Income	$33,400
Accounts Receivable	1,200	Advertising Expense	2,100
Office Supplies	800	Salaries Expense	6,800
Office Equipment	17,100	Telephone Expense	400
Accounts Payable	1,400	Withdrawals	2,000
Jody Seed, Capital,			
September 1, 20--	10,800		

Exercise 2-10 ►
Objective 5

Preparing a statement of owner's equity and a balance sheet.

Using the information provided in Exercise 2-9, prepare a statement of owner's equity and a balance sheet for Seed's Investment Services as of September 30, 20--.

Problems

Selected problems can be completed using:
🍑 **Peachtree**   📋 **QuickBooks**   ▦ **Spreadsheets**

PROBLEM SET A

Analyzing the effects of transactions on the accounting equation.

On July 1, Perry Aaron established Expert Opinions, a firm that specializes in providing expert witness testimony.

Analyze the following transactions. Record in equation form the changes that occur in assets, liabilities, and owner's equity. (Use plus, minus, and equals signs.)

◄ **Problem 2-1A**
Objectives 1, 2, 3

INSTRUCTIONS

TRANSACTIONS

1. The owner invested $36,000 in cash to begin the business.
2. Paid $9,180 in cash for the purchase of equipment.
3. Purchased additional equipment for $5,600 on credit.
4. Paid $4,500 in cash to creditors.
5. The owner made an additional investment of $11,200 in cash.
6. Performed services for $3,200 in cash.
7. Performed services for $1,900 on account.
8. Paid $1,300 for rent expense.
9. Received $850 in cash from credit clients.
10. Paid $2,500 in cash for office supplies.
11. The owner withdrew $2,000 in cash for personal expenses.

Analyze: What is the ending balance of cash after all transactions have been recorded?

Analyzing the effects of transactions on the accounting equation.

Don Roganne is a painting contractor who specializes in painting commercial buildings. At the beginning of June, his firm's financial records showed the following assets, liabilities, and owner's equity.

◄ **Problem 2-2A**
Objectives 1, 2, 3

Cash	$10,350	Accounts Payable	$ 3,900
Accounts Receivable	7,000	Don Roganne, Capital	45,000
Office Furniture	15,400	Revenue	18,600
Auto	26,000	Expenses	8,750

INSTRUCTIONS

Set up an accounting equation using the balances given above. Record the effects of the following transactions in the equation. (Use plus, minus, and equals signs.) Record new balances after each transaction has been entered. Prove the equality of the two sides of the final equation on a separate sheet of paper.

TRANSACTIONS

1. Performed services for $2,400 on credit.
2. Paid $500 in cash for a new office chair.
3. Received $1,500 in cash from credit clients.
4. Paid $160 in cash for telephone service.
5. Sent a check for $600 in partial payment of the amount due creditors.
6. Paid salaries of $3,700 in cash.
7. Sent a check for $250 to pay electric bill.
8. Performed services for $3,900 in cash.
9. Paid $860 in cash for auto repairs.
10. Performed services for $3,500 on account.

Analyze: What is the amount of total assets after all transactions have been recorded?

Problem 2-3A ►
Objective 5

Preparing a balance sheet.

Abalos' Equipment Repair Service is owned by Donald Abalos.

INSTRUCTIONS

Use the following figures to prepare a balance sheet dated February 28, 20--. (You will need to compute the owner's equity.)

Cash	$15,250	Equipment	$35,600
Supplies	2,780	Accounts Payable	10,400
Accounts Receivable	5,000		

Analyze: What is the net worth, or owner's equity, at February 28, 20-- for Abalos' Equipment Repair Service?

Problem 2-4A ►
Objectives 4, 5

Preparing an income statement, a statement of owner's equity, and a balance sheet.

The following equation shows the transactions of Perfection Cleaning Service during March. The business is owned by Raymond Abbey.

	Assets				=	Liab.	+	Owner's Equity		
	Cash +	Accts. Rec. +	Supp. +	Equip. =		Accts. Pay. +	R. Abbey, Capital +	Rev.	−	Exp.
Balances, March 1	3,500 +	500 +	1,200 +	8,200 =		1,500 +	11,900 +	0	−	0
Paid for utilities	−220									−220
New balances	3,280 +	500 +	1,200 +	8,200 =		1,500 +	11,900 +	0	−	220
Sold services for cash	+1,220							+1,220		
New balances	4,500 +	500 +	1,200 +	8,200 =		1,500 +	11,900 +	1,220	−	220
Paid a creditor	−400					−400				
New balances	4,100 +	500 +	1,200 +	8,200 =		1,100 +	11,900 +	1,220	−	220
Sold services on credit		+600						+600		
New balances	4,100 +	1,100 +	1,200 +	8,200 =		1,100 +	11,900 +	1,820	−	220
Paid salaries	−2,100									−2,100
New balances	2,000 +	1,100 +	1,200 +	8,200 =		1,100 +	11,900 +	1,820	−	2,320
Paid telephone bill	−76									−76
New balances	1,924 +	1,100 +	1,200 +	8,200 =		1,100 +	11,900 +	1,820	−	2,396
Withdrew cash for personal expenses	−500						−500			
New balances	1,424 +	1,100 +	1,200 +	8,200 =		1,100 +	11,400 +	1,820	−	2,396

Analyze each transaction carefully. Prepare an income statement and a statement of owner's equity for the month. Prepare a balance sheet for March 31, 20--. List the expenses in detail on the income statement.

Analyze: In order to complete the balance sheet, which amount was transferred from the statement of owner's equity?

PROBLEM SET B

Analyzing the effects of transactions on the accounting equation.

On September 1, Selena Rodriguez opened Better Grades Tutoring Service.

◄ **Problem 2-1B**
Objectives 1, 2, 3

Analyze the following transactions. Use the fundamental accounting equation form to record the changes in property, claims of creditors, and owner's equity. (Use plus, minus, and equals signs.)

INSTRUCTIONS

TRANSACTIONS

1. The owner invested $6,000 in cash to begin the business.
2. Purchased equipment for $3,500 in cash.
3. Purchased $750 of additional equipment on credit.
4. Paid $375 in cash to creditors.
5. The owner made an additional investment of $1,250 in cash.
6. Performed services for $780 in cash.
7. Performed services for $390 on account.
8. Paid $450 for rent expense.
9. Received $275 in cash from credit clients.
10. Paid $650 in cash for office supplies.
11. The owner withdrew $500 in cash for personal expenses.

Analyze: Which transactions increased the company's debt? By what amount?

Analyzing the effects of transactions on the accounting equation.

Stacy Abrams owns Abrams' Consulting Service. At the beginning of September, her firm's financial records showed the following assets, liabilities, and owner's equity.

◄ **Problem 2-2B**
Objectives 1, 2, 3

Cash	$7,750	Accounts Payable	$ 1,200
Accounts Receivable	1,500	Stacy Abrams, Capital	12,000
Supplies	1,600	Revenue	6,000
Office Furniture	5,000	Expenses	3,350

INSTRUCTIONS

Set up an equation using the balances given above. Record the effects of the following transactions in the equation. (Use plus, minus, and equals signs.) Record new balances after each transaction has been entered. Prove the equality of the two sides of the final equation on a separate sheet of paper.

TRANSACTIONS

1. Performed services for $1,000 on credit.
2. Paid $360 in cash for utilities.
3. Performed services for $1,200 in cash.
4. Paid $200 in cash for office cleaning service.
5. Sent a check for $600 to a creditor.
6. Paid $240 in cash for the telephone bill.
7. Issued checks for $2,060 to pay salaries.
8. Performed services for $1,780 in cash.
9. Purchased additional supplies for $180 on credit.
10. Received $800 in cash from credit clients.

Analyze: What is the ending balance for owner's equity after all transactions have been recorded?

Problem 2-3B ►
Objective 5

Preparing a balance sheet.

Paul Price is opening a tax preparation service on December 1, which will be called Paul's Tax Service. Paul plans to open the business by depositing $6,000 cash into a business checking account. The following assets will also be owned by the business: furniture (fair market value of $2,000), and a computer and printer (fair market value of $4,400). There are no outstanding debts of the business as it is formed.

INSTRUCTIONS

Prepare a balance sheet for December 1, 20--, for Paul's Tax Service by entering the correct balances in the appropriate accounts. (You will need to use the accounting equation to compute owner's equity.)

Analyze: If Paul's Tax Service had an outstanding debt of $2,000 when the business was formed, what amount should be reported on the balance sheet for owner's equity?

Problem 2-4B ►
Objectives 4, 5

Preparing an income statement, a statement of owner's equity, and a balance sheet.

The equation on page 51 shows the transactions of LaToya Hailey, Attorney and Counselor of Law, during August. This law firm is owned by LaToya Hailey.

INSTRUCTIONS

Analyze each transaction carefully. Prepare an income statement and a statement of owner's equity for the month. Prepare a balance sheet for August 31, 20--. List the expenses in detail on the income statement.

Analyze: In order to complete the statement of owner's equity, which amount was transferred from the income statement?

	Assets						=	Liab.	+		Owner's Equity			
	Cash	+	Accts. Rec.	+	Supp.	+	Equip.	=	Accts. Pay.	+	L. Hailey Capital	+	Rev.	−	Exp.
Balances, Aug. 1	1,800	+	450	+	1,350	+	2,500	=	300	+	5,800	+	0	−	0
Paid for utilities	−150														−150
New balances	1,650	+	450	+	1,350	+	2,500	=	300	+	5,800	+	0	−	150
Sold services for cash	+1,500												+1,500		
New balances	3,150	+	450	+	1,350	+	2,500	=	300	+	5,800	+	1,500	−	150
Paid a creditor	−150								−150						
New balances	3,000	+	450	+	1,350	+	2,500	=	150	+	5,800	+	1,500	−	150
Sold services on credit			+1,200										+1,200		
New balances	3,000	+	1,650	+	1,350	+	2,500	=	150	+	5,800	+	2,700	−	150
Paid salaries	−1,350														−1,350
New balances	1,650	+	1,650	+	1,350	+	2,500	=	150	+	5,800	+	2,700	−	1,500
Paid telephone bill	−150														−150
New balances	1,500	+	1,650	+	1,350	+	2,500	=	150	+	5,800	+	2,700	−	1,650
Withdrew cash for personal expenses	−300										−300				
New balances	1,200	+	1,650	+	1,350	+	2,500	=	150	+	5,500	+	2,700	−	1,650

CHAPTER 2 CHALLENGE PROBLEM

Financial Statements

The following account balances are for Don Adler, Certified Public Accountant, as of April 30, 20--.

Cash	$3,250
Accounts Receivable	1,410
Maintenance Expense	550
Advertising Expense	450
Fees Earned	4,750
Don Adler, Capital, April 1	?
Salaries Expense	1,500
Machinery	4,250
Accounts Payable	1,600
Don Adler, Drawing	600

INSTRUCTIONS

Using the accounting equation form, determine the balance for Don Adler, Capital, April 1, 20--. Prepare an income statement for the month of April, a statement of owner's equity, and a balance sheet as of April 30, 20--. List the expenses on the income statement in alphabetical order.

Analyze: What net change in owner's equity occurred during the month of April?

Accounting for a New Company

Melissa Branson opened a gym and fitness studio called Melissa's Body Builders Studio at the beginning of November of the current year. It is now the end of December, and Melissa is trying to determine whether she made a profit during her first month of operations. You offer to help her and ask to see her accounting records. She shows you a shoe box and tells you that every piece of paper pertaining to the business is in that box.

As you go through the material in the shoe box, you discover the following:

a. A receipt from Kekich Properties for $3,000 for November's rent on the exercise studio.

b. Bank deposit slips totaling $3,140 for money collected from customers who attended exercise classes.

c. An invoice for $24,000 for exercise equipment. The first payment is not due until December 31.

d. A bill for $900 from the maintenance service that cleans the studio. Melissa has not yet paid this bill.

e. A December 20 parking ticket for $50. Melissa says she was in a hurry that morning to get to the studio on time and forgot to put money in the parking meter.

f. A handwritten list of customers and fees for the classes they have taken. As the customers attend the classes, Melissa writes their names and the amount of each customer's fee on the list. As customers pay, Melissa crosses their names off the list. Fees not crossed off the list amount to $720.

g. A credit card receipt for $200 for printing flyers advertising the grand opening of the studio. For convenience, Melissa used her personal credit card.

h. A credit card receipt for $300 for two warm-up suits Melissa bought to wear at the studio. She also put this purchase on her personal credit card.

Use the concepts you have learned in this chapter to help Melissa.

1. Prepare an income statement for the first month of operation of Melissa's Body Builders Studio.

2. How would you evaluate the results of Melissa's first month of operation?

3. What advice would you give Melissa concerning her system of accounting?

Business Connections

MANAGERIAL FOCUS Interpreting Results

1. How does an accounting system help managers control operations and make sound decisions?

2. Why should managers be concerned with changes in the amount of creditors' claims against the business?

3. Is it reasonable to expect that all new businesses will have a net income from the first month's operations? From the first year's operations?

4. After examining financial data for a monthly period, the owner of a small business expressed surprise that the firm's cash balance had decreased during the month even though there was substantial net income. Do you think that this owner is right to expect cash to increase whenever there is a net income? Why or why not?

Ethical DILEMMA It's Only a Game! You just purchased a copy of Xandress II, the hottest computer game on the market. Xandress II is a copyrighted program that is protected under U.S. copyright law. You and some of your friends have just finished playing the game. Chris, your best friend, asks to borrow your computer disk of Xandress II to install the program on a computer at home.

1. What are the ethical issues?

2. What are your alternatives?

3. Who are the affected parties?

4. How do the alternatives affect the parties?

5. What is your decision?

6. Would your decision be different if you were the branch manager of a local bank and a friend who works for a competing bank asked to borrow a loan evaluation program developed especially for your bank?

*Street***WISE:**
Questions from the Real World **Financial Information** Refer to The Home Depot, Inc. *1999 Annual Report* in Appendix B.

1. Locate the consolidated balance sheets. Based on this financial statement, what is the fundamental accounting equation for the year ended January 30, 2000? Note: Because this company is publicly traded, owners' equity is represented as stockholders' equity.

2. Locate the consolidated statements of earnings. The statement presents the results of operations for what periods of time? What result of operation is presented for the most recent operating period?

Connection 4 ►

FINANCIAL **S**TATEMENT
A N A L Y S I S **Income Statement** Review the following excerpt from the 1999 consolidated statement of income for Southwest Airlines Co. Answer the questions that follow.

Southwest Airlines Co.			
Consolidated Statement of Income			
Years Ended December 31,			
	1999	*1998*	*1997*
Operating Revenues: (in thousands)			
Passenger	$4,499,360	$3,963,781	$3,639,193
Freight	102,990	98,500	94,758
Other	133,237	101,699	82,870
Total operating revenues	4,735,587	4,163,980	3,816,821
Net Income	$474,378	$433,431	$317,772

Analyze:

1. Although the format for the heading of an income statement can vary from company to company, the heading should contain the answers to who, what, and when. List the answers to each question for the statement presented above.

2. What three types of revenue are reflected on this statement?

3. The net income of $474,378,000 reflected on Southwest Airlines Co.'s consolidated statement of income for 1999 will be transferred to the next financial statement to be prepared. Net income is needed to complete which statement?

Analyze Online: Find the *Investor Relations* section of the Southwest Airlines Co. Web site (**www.southwest.com**) and answer the following questions.

4. What total operating revenues did Southwest Airlines Co. report for the most recent quarter?

5. Find the most recent press release posted on the Web site. Read the press release, and summarize the topic discussed. What effect, if any, do you think this will have on company earnings? Why?

Connection 5 ► *Extending* the *Thought* **Personal Financial Statements** The balance sheet for an individual is called a "statement of financial condition." What kinds of assets and liabilities would appear on a statement of financial condition?

Connection 6 ► **Business Communication** **Creating an Outline** You are a senior accountant for a mid-size apparel corporation. You have been asked to give a presentation on the basics of financial statements to the managers of the marketing, advertising, manufacturing, and sales departments. Each manager needs to understand what each financial statement presents and why each is important. Prepare an outline for your presentation. Be sure to cover the income statement, the statement of owner's equity, and the balance sheet.

TeamWork **Transaction Analysis** As a team, prepare a diagram showing four transactions for a neighborhood ice cream shop. List transactions that affect only the balance sheet. Include dollar amounts for each transaction and show the effect of the transactions on owner's equity.

◄ **Connection 7**

inter NET
CONNECTION **Careers in Accounting** How much can you expect to earn as an accountant? Visit the student page of the AICPA Web site at **www.aicpa.org** and look for salary information. List three career paths in accounting. How much can you expect to earn working for a small firm as a tax accountant if you have 1–3 years experience? How much can you expect to earn as a senior corporate accountant working for a large company? How much can you expect to earn as an entry-level (less than one year experience) cost accountant for a medium-size company?

◄ **Connection 8**

Answers to Self Reviews

Answers to Section 1 Self Review
1. A financial event that changes the resources of the firm.
2. An example is the initial investment of cash in a business by the owner.
3. Amounts that a company must pay to creditors in the future.
4. **d.** Equipment is increased by $2,000 and accounts payable is increased by $2,000.
5. **d.** $40,000
6. $2,500

Answers to Section 2 Self Review
1. Funds taken from the business to pay for personal expenses. They decrease the owner's equity in the business.
2. As an additional investment by the owner recorded on the basis of fair market value.
3. The firm's name (who), the title of the statement (what), and the time period covered by the report (when).
4. **d.** $15,000
5. **a.** revenue and expenses for a period of time
6. $7,000 increase

Answers to Comprehensive Self Review
1. Buying for cash results in an immediate decrease in cash; buying on account results in a liability recorded as accounts payable.
2. The payment of $500 to a creditor on account.
3. The income statement is prepared first because the net income or loss is needed to complete the statement of owner's equity. The statement of owner's equity is prepared next to update the change in owner's equity. The balance sheet is prepared last.
4. The opposite side of the accounting equation will decrease because a decrease in assets results in a corresponding decrease in either a liability or the owner's equity.
5. Revenue increases owner's equity. Expenses decrease owner's equity.

CHAPTER 3

Learning Objectives

1. Set up T accounts for assets, liabilities, and owner's equity.

2. Analyze business transactions and enter them in the accounts.

3. Determine the balance of an account.

4. Set up T accounts for revenue and expenses.

5. Prepare a trial balance from T accounts.

6. Prepare an income statement, a statement of owner's equity, and a balance sheet.

7. Develop a chart of accounts.

8. Define the accounting terms new to this chapter.

Analyzing Business Transactions Using T Accounts

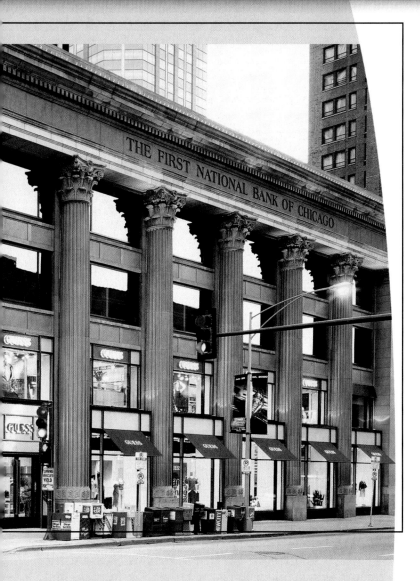

 GUESS?, INC.

www.guess.com

*T*he success of Guess?, Inc. began with a small shipment of 24 pairs of jeans to Bloomingdale's in 1981. Within hours the entire stock sold out. Today, the Guess? brand is recognized as one of the most influential and recognized names in the apparel industry. The Marciano brothers—Maurice, Paul, Armand, and Georges—created the Guess? Jeans phenomenon, building an empire with sales of $599.7 million in 1999. Guess?, Inc. designs, markets, and distributes a full collection of women's, men's, and children's apparel, as well as accessories, shoes, and home products, selling through approximately 3,000 retailers and about 180 company-owned retail and factory stores in the United States.

Thinking Critically
When accountants at Guess?, Inc. recorded the first sales transaction for the shipment of jeans to Bloomingdale's, how do you think the transaction was recorded? What effect did this transaction have on the fundamental accounting equation?

For more information on Guess?, Inc. go to: collegeaccounting.glencoe.com.

New Terms

Account balance	Footing
Accounts	Normal balance
Chart of accounts	Permanent account
Classification	Slide
Credit	T account
Debit	Temporary account
Double-entry system	Transposition
Drawing account	Trial balance

Section Objectives

1 Set up T accounts for assets, liabilities, and owner's equity.

WHY IT'S IMPORTANT
The T account is an important visual tool used as an alternative to the fundamental accounting equation.

2 Analyze business transactions and enter them in the accounts.

WHY IT'S IMPORTANT
Accountants often use T accounts to help analyze and classify business transactions.

3 Determine the balance of an account.

WHY IT'S IMPORTANT
Accurate account balances contribute to a reliable accounting system.

Terms to Learn

account balance
accounts
classification
footing
normal balance
T account

1 Objective

Set up T accounts for assets, liabilities, and owner's equity.

The Accounting Equation
Assets = Liabilities + Owner's
Equity

Transactions That Affect Assets, Liabilities, and Owner's Equity

In this chapter you will learn how to record the changes caused by business transactions. This recordkeeping is a basic part of accounting systems.

Asset, Liability, and Owner's Equity Accounts

The accounting equation is one tool for analyzing the effects of business transactions. However, businesses do not record transactions in equation form. Instead, businesses establish separate records, called **accounts**, for assets, liabilities, and owner's equity. Use of accounts helps owners and staff analyze, record, classify, summarize, and report financial information. Accounts are recognized by their **classification** as assets, liabilities, or owner's equity. Asset accounts show the property a business owns. Liability accounts show the debts of the business. Owner's equity accounts show the owner's financial interest in the business. Each account has a name that describes the type of property, the debt, or the financial interest.

Accountants use T accounts to analyze transactions. A **T account** consists of a vertical line and a horizontal line that resemble the letter **T**. The name of the account is written on the horizontal (top) line. Increases and decreases in the account are entered on either side of the vertical line.

The following are T accounts for assets, liabilities, and owner's equity.

ASSETS		=	LIABILITIES		+	OWNER'S EQUITY	
+	−		−	+		−	+
Record increases	Record decreases		Record decreases	Record increases		Record decreases	Record increases

Recording a Cash Investment

Asset accounts show items of value owned by a business. Linda Carter invested $80,000 in the business. Beatrice Wilson, the office manager for Carter Consulting Services, set up a **Cash** account. Cash is an asset. Assets appear on the left side of the accounting equation. Cash increases appear on the left side of the **Cash** T account. Decreases are shown on the right side. Wilson entered the cash investment of $80,000 **(a)** on the left side of the **Cash** account.

T accounts normally do not have plus and minus signs. We show them to help you identify increases (+) and decreases (−) in accounts.

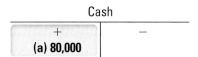

Cash

Beatrice Wilson set up an account for owner's equity called **Linda Carter, Capital.** Owner's equity appears on the right side of the accounting equation (Assets = Liabilities + Owner's Equity). Increases in owner's equity appear on the right side of the T account. Decreases in owner's equity appear on the left side. Wilson entered the investment of $80,000 **(b)** on the right side of the **Linda Carter, Capital** account.

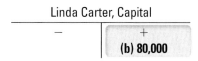

Linda Carter, Capital

❷ Objective
Analyze business transactions and enter them in the accounts.

Use these steps to analyze the effects of the business transactions:

1. Analyze the financial event.
   - Identify the accounts affected.
   - Classify the accounts affected.
   - Determine the amount of increase or decrease for each account.
2. Apply the left-right rules for each account affected.
3. Make the entry in T-account form.

Business Transaction

Linda Carter withdrew $80,000 from personal savings and deposited it in the new business checking account for Carter Consulting Services.

Analysis

a. The asset account, **Cash,** is increased by $80,000.

b. The owner's equity account, **Linda Carter, Capital,** is increased by $80,000.

Left-Right Rules

LEFT Increases to asset accounts are recorded on the left side of the T account. Record $80,000 on the left side of the **Cash** T account.

RIGHT Increases to owner's equity accounts are recorded on the right side of the T account. Record $80,000 on the right side of the **Linda Carter, Capital** T account.

T-Account Presentation

Asset Cash		Linda Carter, Capital	
+	−	−	+
(a) 80,000			(b) 80,000

Recording a Cash Purchase of Equipment

Beatrice Wilson set up an asset account, **Equipment,** to record the purchase of a computer and other equipment.

Carter Consulting Services issued a $20,000 check to purchase a computer and other equipment.

Analysis

  c. The asset account, **Equipment,** is increased by $20,000.

  d. The asset account, **Cash,** is decreased by $20,000.

Left-Right Rules

  LEFT Increases to asset accounts are recorded on the left side of the T account. Record $20,000 on the left side of the **Equipment** T account.

  RIGHT Decreases to asset accounts are recorded on the right side of the T account. Record $20,000 on the right side of the **Cash** T account.

T-Account Presentation

Equipment		Cash	
+	−	+	−
(c) 20,000			**(d) 20,000**

Let's look at the T accounts to review the effects of the transactions. Wilson entered $20,000 **(c)** on the left (increase) side of the **Equipment** account. She entered $20,000 **(d)** on the right (decrease) side of the **Cash** account. Notice that the **Cash** account shows the effects of two transactions.

Equipment		Cash	
+	−	+	−
(c) 20,000		**(a) 80,000**	**(d) 20,000**

Recording a Credit Purchase of Equipment

Liabilities are amounts a business owes its creditors. Liabilities appear on the right side of the accounting equation (Assets = Liabilities + Owner's Equity). Increases in liabilities are on the right side of liability T accounts. Decreases in liabilities are on the left side of liability T accounts.

The firm bought office equipment for $15,000 on account from Office Plus.

Analysis

  e. The asset account, **Equipment,** is increased by $15,000.

  f. The liability account, **Accounts Payable,** is increased by $15,000.

Left-Right Rules

LEFT Increases to asset accounts are recorded on the left side of the T account. Record $15,000 on the left side of the **Equipment** T account.

RIGHT Increases to liability accounts are recorded on the right side of the T account. Record $15,000 on the right side of the **Accounts Payable** T account.

T-Account Presentation

Let's look at the T accounts to review the effects of the transactions. Wilson entered $15,000 **(e)** on the left (increase) side of the **Equipment** account. It now shows two transactions. She entered $15,000 **(f)** on the right (increase) side of the **Accounts Payable** account.

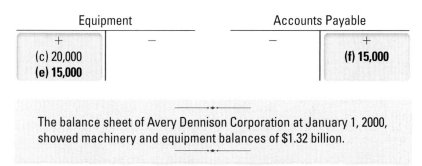

Important!

For liability T accounts
- right side shows increases,
- left side shows decreases.

The balance sheet of Avery Dennison Corporation at January 1, 2000, showed machinery and equipment balances of $1.32 billion.

Recording a Cash Purchase of Supplies

Beatrice Wilson set up an asset account called **Supplies.**

Business Transaction

Carter Consulting Services issued a check for $2,000 to Resource Supplies Inc. to purchase office supplies.

Analysis

g. The asset account, **Supplies,** is increased by $2,000.

h. The asset account, **Cash,** is decreased by $2,000.

Left-Right Rules

LEFT Increases to asset accounts are recorded on the left side of the T account. Record $2,000 on the left side of the **Supplies** T account.

RIGHT Decreases to asset accounts are recorded on the right side of the T account. Record $2,000 on the right side of the **Cash** T account.

Supplies		Cash	
+	−	+	−
(g) 2,000			(h) 2,000

Wilson entered $2,000 **(g)** on the left (increase) side of the **Supplies** account and $2,000 **(h)** on the right (decrease) side of the **Cash** account.

Supplies		Cash	
+	−	+	−
(g) 2,000		(a) 80,000	(d) 20,000
			(h) 2,000

Notice that the **Cash** account now shows three transactions: the initial investment by the owner (a), the cash purchase of equipment (d), and the cash purchase of supplies (h).

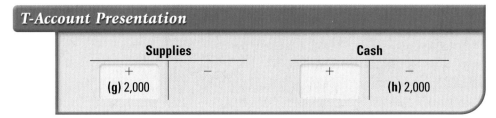

Computers in Accounting

Hardware and Software: A Working Partnership

When you arrive at work and turn on your computer, many processes happen behind the scenes. Computers are made up of hardware and software. *Hardware* includes a CPU (central processing unit), disk drives, memory, monitor, keyboard, and printer. *Software* makes computer hardware perform tasks. Without software, a computer can do nothing. Software programs come in two basic types: system software and application software.

System software controls the operation of the application software and coordinates the activities of the hardware. Think of your system software as the air-traffic controller of your computer. Popular operating systems include MacOS, Windows, Unix, and Linux.

Application software tells your computer to perform a task. A word processing application such as Microsoft Word has the tools to create, edit, and format text. Spreadsheet applications such as Microsoft Excel or Lotus 1-2-3 organize numbers and words into meaningful columns and rows. Software applications are developed to create efficient and fast ways to convert data into meaningful information. Accounting applications such as Peachtree Accounting and AccuBooks convert data into meaningful information.

Accounting software application programs range from simple and inexpensive to sophisticated and costly. These applications provide tools to enter business transactions and automatically transfer the details to the appropriate accounts. Standardized financial statements and reports can be generated using simple menus. From start to finish, these applications help the accountant maintain accurate records and provide management a wide variety of financial reports.

Thinking Critically

What software applications have you used? What suggestions would you make for improvement to these applications?

Internet Application

Use an Internet search engine to find accounting software applications. Choose two applications suitable for small businesses and write a brief review of each product. Based on your research, which product do you prefer? Why?

Recording a Payment to a Creditor

On November 30 the business paid $3,000 to Office Plus to apply against the debt of $15,000 shown in **Accounts Payable.**

Business Transaction

Carter Consulting Services issued a check in the amount of $3,000 to Office Plus.

Analysis

i. The asset account, **Cash,** is decreased by $3,000.

j. The liability account, **Accounts Payable,** is decreased by $3,000.

Left-Right Rules

LEFT Decreases to liability accounts are recorded on the left side of the T account. Record $3,000 on the left side of the **Accounts Payable** T account.

RIGHT Decreases to asset accounts are recorded on the right side of the T account. Record $3,000 on the right side of the **Cash** T account.

T-Account Presentation

Accounts Payable		Cash	
+	−	+	−
(j) 3,000			(i) 3,000

Let's look at the T accounts to review the effects of the transactions. Wilson entered $3,000 **(i)** on the right (decrease) side of the **Cash** account. She entered $3,000 **(j)** on the left (decrease) side of the **Accounts Payable** account. Notice that both accounts show the effects of several transactions.

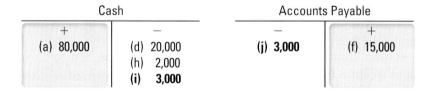

Cash		Accounts Payable	
+	−	−	+
(a) 80,000	(d) 20,000	(j) 3,000	(f) 15,000
	(h) 2,000		
	(i) 3,000		

Recording Prepaid Rent

In November Carter Consulting Services was required to pay the December and January rent in advance. Wilson set up an asset account called **Prepaid Rent.**

Business Transaction

Carter Consulting Services issued a check for $6,000 to pay rent for the months of December and January.

k. The asset account, **Prepaid Rent,** is increased by $6,000.

l. The asset account, **Cash,** is decreased by $6,000.

Left-Right Rules

LEFT Increases to asset accounts are recorded on the left side of the T account. Record $6,000 on the left side of the **Prepaid Rent** T account.

RIGHT Decreases to asset accounts are recorded on the right side of the T account. Record $6,000 on the right side of the **Cash** T account.

T-Account Presentation

Prepaid Rent			Cash	
+	−		+	−
(k) 6,000				(l) 6,000

Let's review the T accounts to see the effects of the transactions. Wilson entered $6,000 **(k)** on the left (increase) side of the **Prepaid Rent** account. She entered $6,000 **(l)** on the right (decrease) side of the **Cash** account.

Notice that the **Cash** account shows the effects of numerous transactions. It shows initial investment (a), equipment purchase (d), supplies purchase (h), payment on account (i), and advance rent payment (l).

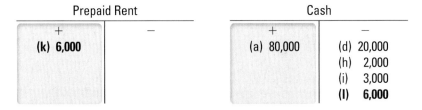

Prepaid Rent		Cash	
+	−	+	−
(k) 6,000		(a) 80,000	(d) 20,000
			(h) 2,000
			(i) 3,000
			(l) 6,000

③ Objective

Determine the balance of an account.

Account Balances

An **account balance** is the difference between the amounts on the two sides of the account. First add the figures on each side of the account. If the column has more than one figure, enter the total in small pencil figures called a **footing**. Then subtract the smaller total from the larger total. The result is the account balance.

- If the total on the right side is larger than the total on the left side, the balance is recorded on the right side.
- If the total on the left side is larger, the balance is recorded on the left side.
- If an account shows only one amount, that amount is the balance.
- If an account contains entries on only one side, the total of those entries is the account balance.

Let's look at the **Cash** account for Carter Consulting Services. The left side shows $80,000. The total of the right side is $31,000. Subtract the footing of $31,000 from $80,000. The result is the account balance of $49,000. The account balance is shown on the left side of the account.

Cash

	+		−	
(a)	80,000	(d)	20,000	
		(h)	2,000	
		(i)	3,000	
		(l)	6,000	
			31,000	◀ Footing
Bal.	49,000			

Usually account balances appear on the increase side of the account. The increase side of the account is the **normal balance** of the account.

The following is a summary of the procedures to increase or decrease accounts and shows the normal balance of accounts.

ASSETS		=	LIABILITIES		+	OWNER'S EQUITY	
+	−		−	+		−	+
Increase (Normal Balance)	Decrease		Decrease	Increase (Normal Balance)		Decrease	Increase (Normal Balance)

Figure 3-1 shows a summary of the account balances for Carter Consulting Services.

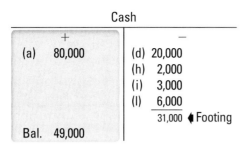

About Accounting

Law Enforcement
The FBI and other law enforcement agencies recruit accountants to investigate criminal conduct. Perhaps the most famous use of accounting by law enforcers is the conviction of Al Capone for tax evasion after he could not be jailed for his ties to organized crime.

▼ **FIGURE 3-1**
T-Account Balances for Carter Consulting Services

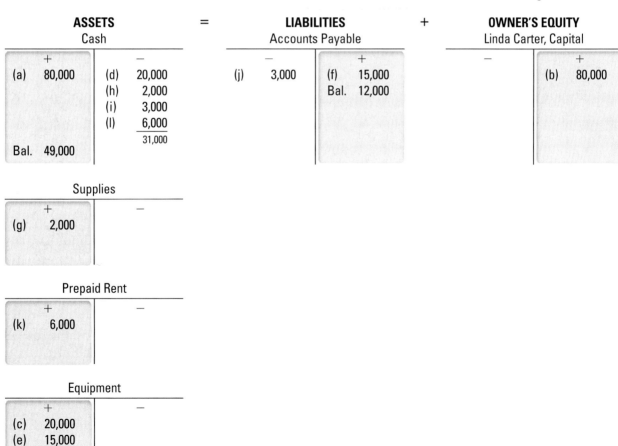

Figure 3-2 shows a balance sheet prepared for November 30, 2004.

Carter Consulting Services
Balance Sheet
November 30, 2004

Assets				Liabilities			
Cash		4 9 0 0 0	00	Accounts Payable		1 2 0 0 0	00
Supplies		2 0 0 0	00				
Prepaid Rent		6 0 0 0	00	Owner's Equity			
Equipment		3 5 0 0 0	00	Linda Carter, Capital		8 0 0 0 0	00
Total Assets		9 2 0 0 0	00	Total Liabilities and Owner's Equity		9 2 0 0 0	00

▲ **FIGURE 3-2**
Balance Sheet for
Carter Consulting Services

In equation form the firm's position after these transactions is:

Assets							=	Liabilities	+	Owner's Equity
			Prepaid					Accounts		Linda Carter,
Cash	+	Supp. +	Rent	+	Equip.	=		Payable	+	Capital
$49,000	+	$2,000 +	$6,000	+	$35,000	=		$12,000	+	$80,000

Notice how the balance sheet reflects the fundamental accounting equation.

Questions

1. Increases are recorded on which side of asset, liability, and owner's equity accounts?

2. What is a footing?

3. What is meant by the "normal balance" of an account? What is the normal balance side for asset, liability, and owner's equity accounts?

Exercises

4. Foot and find the balance of the **Cash** account.

Cash	
+	−
45,000	15,000
10,500	7,500
	3,000
	6,000

a. 55,500
b. 31,500
c. 24,000
d. 14,000

5. The Sullivan Company purchased new computers for $4,500 from Office Supplies, Inc., to be paid in 30 days. Which of the following is correct?

a. **Equipment** is increased by $4,500. **Cash** is decreased by $4,500.

b. **Equipment** is decreased by $4,500. **Accounts Payable** is increased by $4,500.

c. **Equipment** is increased by $4,500. **Accounts Payable** is increased by $4,500.

d. **Equipment** is increased by $4,500. **Accounts Payable** is decreased by $4,500.

Analysis

6. From the following accounts, show that the fundamental accounting equation is in balance. All accounts have normal balances.

Cash—$15,400
Accounts Payable—$10,000
T. R. Murphy, Capital—$30,000
Equipment—$20,000
Supplies—$4,600

(Answers to Section 1 Self Review are on page 93.)

Transactions That Affect Revenue, Expenses, and Withdrawals

Let's examine the revenue and expense transactions of Carter Consulting Services for December to see how they are recorded.

Revenue and Expense Accounts

Some owner's equity accounts are classified as revenue or expense accounts. Separate accounts are used to record revenue and expense transactions.

Recording Revenue from Services Sold for Cash

During December the business earned $21,000 in revenue from clients who paid cash for bookkeeping, accounting, and consulting services. This involved several transactions. Beatrice Wilson entered $21,000 **(m)** on the left (increase) side of the asset account **Cash.**

	Cash	
	+	−
Bal.	49,000	
(m)	21,000	

How is the increase in owner's equity recorded? One way would be to record the $21,000 on the right side of the **Linda Carter, Capital** account. However, the preferred way is to keep revenue separate from the owner's investment until the end of the accounting period. Therefore, Wilson opened a revenue account for **Fees Income.**

Wilson entered $21,000 **(n)** on the right side of the **Fees Income** account. Revenues increase owner's equity. Increases in owner's equity appear on the right side of the T account. Therefore, increases in revenue appear on the right side of revenue T accounts.

	Fees Income	
−		+
	(n)	21,000

The right side of the revenue account shows increases and the left side shows decreases. Decreases in revenue accounts are rare but might occur because of corrections or transfers.

Let's review the effects of the transactions. Wilson entered $21,000 **(m)** on the left (increase) side of the **Cash** account and $21,000 **(n)** on the right (increase) side of the **Fees Income** account.

Section Objectives

4 **Set up T accounts for revenue and expenses.**

WHY IT'S IMPORTANT
T accounts help you understand the effects of all business transactions.

5 **Prepare a trial balance from T accounts.**

WHY IT'S IMPORTANT
The trial balance is an important check of accuracy at the end of the accounting period.

6 **Prepare an income statement, a statement of owner's equity, and a balance sheet.**

WHY IT'S IMPORTANT
Financial statements summarize the financial activities and condition of the business.

7 **Develop a chart of accounts.**

WHY IT'S IMPORTANT
Businesses require a system that allows accounts to be easily identified and located.

Terms to Learn

chart of accounts
credit
debit
double-entry system
drawing account
permanent account
slide
temporary account
transposition
trial balance

Cash				Fees Income		
	+		−	−		+
Bal.	49,000				(n)	21,000
(m)	21,000					

④ Objective

Set up T accounts for revenue and expenses.

At this point the firm needs just one revenue account. Most businesses have separate accounts for different types of revenue. For example, sales of goods such as clothes are recorded in the revenue account *Sales.*

Recording Revenue from Services Sold on Credit

In December Carter Consulting Services earned $7,000 from various charge account clients. Wilson set up an asset account, **Accounts Receivable.**

Analysis

o. The asset account, **Accounts Receivable**, is increased by $7,000.

p. The revenue account, **Fees Income**, is increased by $7,000.

Left-Right Rules

LEFT Increases to asset accounts are recorded on the left side of the T account. Record $7,000 on the left side of the **Accounts Receivable** T account.

RIGHT Increases in revenue appear on the right side of the T account. Record $7,000 on the right side of the **Fees Income** T account.

T-Account Presentation

Accounts Receivable			Fees Income		
+		−	−		+
(o) 7,000					(p) 7,000

Let's review the effects of the transactions. Wilson entered $7,000 **(o)** on the left (increase) side of the **Accounts Receivable** account and $7,000 **(p)** on the right (increase) side of the **Fees Income** account.

Accounts Receivable				Fees Income		
	+		−	−		+
(o)	7,000				(n)	21,000
					(p)	7,000

Recording Collections from Accounts Receivable

Charge account clients paid $3,000, reducing the amount owed to Carter Consulting Services.

Analysis

q. The asset account, **Cash,** is increased by $3,000.

r. The asset account, **Accounts Receivable,** is decreased by $3,000.

Left-Right Rules

LEFT Increases to asset accounts are recorded on the left side of the T account. Record $3,000 on the left side of the **Cash** T account.

RIGHT Decreases to asset accounts are recorded on the right side of the T account. Record $3,000 on the right side of the **Accounts Receivable** T account.

T-Account Presentation

Cash			Accounts Receivable	
+	−		+	−
(q) 3,000				**(r)** 3,000

Let's review the effects of the transactions. Wilson entered $3,000 **(q)** on the left (increase) side of the **Cash** account and $3,000 **(r)** on the right (decrease) side of the **Accounts Receivable** account. Notice that revenue is not recorded when cash is collected from charge account clients. The revenue was recorded when the sales on credit were recorded (p).

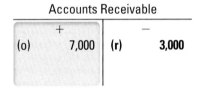

Cash			Accounts Receivable			
+		−		+		−
Bal.	49,000		(o)	7,000	(r)	**3,000**
(m)	21,000					
(q)	**3,000**					

Recording an Expense for Salaries

Expenses decrease owner's equity. Decreases in owner's equity appear on the left side of the T account. Therefore, increases in expenses (which are decreases in owner's equity) are recorded on the left side of expense T accounts. Decreases in expenses are recorded on the right side of the T accounts. Decreases in expenses are rare but may result from corrections or transfers.

Recall

Expense
An expense is an outflow of cash, the use of other assets, or the incurring of a liability.

Business Transaction

In December Carter Consulting Services paid $5,000 in salaries.

Analysis

s. The asset account, **Cash,** is decreased by $5,000.

t. The expense account, **Salaries Expense,** is increased by $5,000.

Left-Right Rules

LEFT Increases in expenses appear on the left side of the T account. Record $5,000 on the left side of the **Salaries Expense** T account.

RIGHT Decreases in asset accounts are recorded on the right side of the T account. Record $5,000 on the right side of the **Cash** T account.

T-Account Presentation

Salaries Expense		Cash	
+	–	+	–
(t) 5,000			(s) 5,000

Wilson entered $5,000 **(s)** on the right (decrease) side of the **Cash** T account.

International INSIGHTS

Electricity

Accountants who travel with laptop computers should know the voltage used at their destinations. Power in the United States is 110 volts, but in most other countries it is 220 volts.

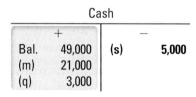

Cash			
	+	–	
Bal.	49,000	(s)	5,000
(m)	21,000		
(q)	3,000		

How is the decrease in owner's equity recorded? One way would be to record the $5,000 on the left side of the **Linda Carter, Capital** account. However, the preferred way is to keep expenses separate from owner's investment. Therefore, Wilson set up a **Salaries Expense** account.

To record the salary expense, Wilson entered $5,000 **(t)** on the left (increase) side of the **Salaries Expense** account. Notice that the plus and minus signs in the **Salaries Expense** account show the effect on the expense account, not on owner's equity.

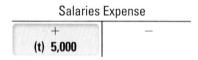

Salaries Expense	
+	–
(t) 5,000	

Most companies have numerous expense accounts. The various expense accounts appear in the Expenses section of the income statement.

Recording an Expense for Utilities

At the end of December, Carter Consulting Services received a $600 bill for utilities. Wilson set up an account for **Utilities Expense.**

Business Transaction

Carter Consulting Services issued a check for $600 to pay the utilities bill.

Analysis

  u. The asset account, **Cash,** is decreased by $600.

  v. The expense account, **Utilities Expense,** is increased by $600.

Left-Right Rules

LEFT Increases in expenses appear on the left side of the T account. Record $600 on the left side of the **Utilities Expense** T account.

RIGHT Decreases to asset accounts are recorded on the right side of the T account. Record $600 on the right side of the **Cash** T account.

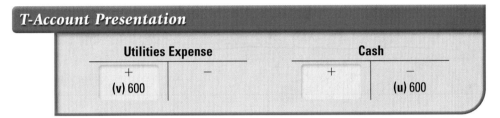

Let's review the effects of the transactions.

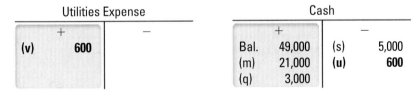

The Drawing Account

In sole proprietorships and partnerships, the owners generally do not pay themselves salaries. To obtain funds for personal living expenses, owners make withdrawals of cash. The withdrawals are against previously earned profits that have become part of capital or against profits that are expected in the future.

Since withdrawals decrease owner's equity, withdrawals could be recorded on the left side of the capital account. However, the preferred way is to keep withdrawals separate from the owner's capital account until the end of the accounting period. An owner's equity account called a **drawing account** is set up to record withdrawals. Increases in the drawing account (which are decreases in owner's equity) are recorded on the left side of the drawing T accounts.

Business Transaction

Linda Carter wrote a check to withdraw $3,000 cash for personal use.

Analysis

w. The asset account, **Cash**, is decreased by $3,000.

x. The owner's equity account, **Linda Carter, Drawing**, is increased by $3,000.

Left-Right Rules

LEFT Increases to drawing accounts are recorded on the left side of the T account. Record $3,000 on the left side of the **Linda Carter, Drawing** T account.

RIGHT Decreases to asset accounts are recorded on the right side of the T account. Record $3,000 on the right side of the **Cash** T account.

T-Account Presentation

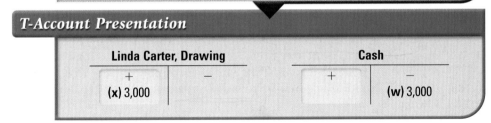

Let's review the transactions. Wilson entered $3,000 **(w)** on the right (decrease) side of the asset account, **Cash,** and $3,000 **(x)** on the left (increase) side of **Linda Carter, Drawing.** Note that the plus and minus signs show the effect on the drawing account, not on owner's equity.

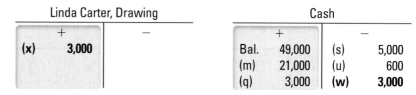

Linda Carter, Drawing		Cash			
+	−	+		−	
(x) 3,000		Bal. 49,000	(s)	5,000	
		(m) 21,000	(u)	600	
		(q) 3,000	(w)	3,000	

Figure 3-3 shows a summary of the relationship between the capital account and the revenue, expense, and drawing accounts.

FIGURE 3-3 ►
The Relationship Between
Owner's Equity and Revenue,
Expenses, and Withdrawals

Linda Carter, Capital

−	+
Decrease	Increase

Expenses

+	−
Increase	Decrease

Revenue

−	+
Decrease	Increase

Withdrawals

+	−
Increase	Decrease

Important!

Normal Balances
Debit:	*Credit:*
Asset	Liability
Expense	Revenue
Drawing	Capital

The Rules of Debit and Credit

Accountants do not use the terms *left side* and *right side* when they talk about making entries in accounts. Instead, they use the term **debit** for an entry on the left side and **credit** for an entry on the right side. Figure 3-4 summarizes the rules for debits and credits. The accounting system is called the **double-entry system**. This is because each transaction has at least two entries—a debit and a credit.

FIGURE 3-4 ▼
Rules for Debits and Credits

ASSET ACCOUNTS

Debit	Credit
+	−
Increase Side (Normal Bal.)	Decrease Side

LIABILITY ACCOUNTS

Debit	Credit
−	+
Decrease Side	Increase Side (Normal Bal.)

OWNER'S CAPITAL ACCOUNT

Debit	Credit
−	+
Decrease Side	Increase Side (Normal Bal.)

OWNER'S DRAWING ACCOUNT

Debit	Credit
+	−
Increase Side (Normal Bal.)	Decrease Side

REVENUE ACCOUNTS

Debit	Credit
−	+
Decrease Side	Increase Side (Normal Bal.)

EXPENSE ACCOUNTS

Debit	Credit
+	−
Increase Side (Normal Bal.)	Decrease Side

After the December transactions for Carter Consulting Services are recorded, the account balances are calculated. Figure 3-5 on page 73 shows the account balances at the end of December. Notice that the fundamental accounting equation remains in balance (Assets = Liabilities + Owner's Equity).

ASSETS		=	LIABILITIES	+	OWNER'S EQUITY	

Cash

Bal.	49,000	(s)	5,000
(m)	21,000	(u)	600
(q)	3,000	(w)	3,000
	73,000		8,600
Bal.	64,400		

Accounts Receivable

(o)	7,000	(r)	3,000
Bal.	4,000		

Supplies

Bal.	2,000	

Prepaid Rent

Bal.	6,000	

Equipment

Bal.	35,000	

Accounts Payable

	Bal.	12,000

Linda Carter, Capital

	Bal.	80,000

Linda Carter, Drawing

(x)	3,000	

Fees Income

	(n)	21,000
	(p)	7,000
	Bal.	28,000

Salaries Expense

(t)	5,000	

Utilities Expense

(v)	600	

▲ **FIGURE 3-5** End-of-December 2004 Account Balances

The Trial Balance

Once the account balances are computed, a trial balance is prepared. The **trial balance** is a statement that tests the accuracy of total debits and credits after transactions have been recorded. If total debits do not equal total credits, there is an error. Figure 3-6 on page 74 shows the trial balance for Carter Consulting Services. To prepare a trial balance, perform the following steps:

1. Enter the trial balance heading showing the company name, report title, and closing date for the accounting period.
2. List the account names in the same order as they appear on the financial statements.
   - Assets
   - Liabilities
   - Owner's Equity
   - Revenue
   - Expenses
3. Enter the ending balance of each account in the appropriate Debit or Credit column.

⑤ Objective

Prepare a trial balance from T accounts.

4. Total the Debit column.

5. Total the Credit column.

6. Compare the total debits with the total credits.

FIGURE 3-6 ▶
Trial Balance

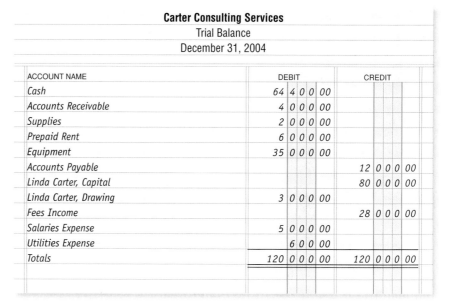

ACCOUNT NAME	DEBIT				CREDIT			
Cash	64	4	0	0	00			
Accounts Receivable	4	0	0	0	00			
Supplies	2	0	0	0	00			
Prepaid Rent	6	0	0	0	00			
Equipment	35	0	0	0	00			
Accounts Payable					12	0	0	0	00
Linda Carter, Capital					80	0	0	0	00
Linda Carter, Drawing	3	0	0	0	00			
Fees Income					28	0	0	0	00
Salaries Expense	5	0	0	0	00			
Utilities Expense		6	0	0	00			
Totals	120	0	0	0	00	120	0	0	0	00

Carter Consulting Services
Trial Balance
December 31, 2004

Recall

Financial Statement Headings
The financial statement headings answer three questions:

Who—the company name

What—the report title

When—the date of, or the period covered by, the report

Understanding Trial Balance Errors

If the totals of the Debit and Credit columns are equal, the financial records are in balance. If the totals of the Debit and Credit columns are not equal, there is an error. The error may be in the trial balance, or it may be in the financial records. Some common errors are

- adding trial balance columns incorrectly;
- recording only half a transaction—for example, recording a debit but not recording a credit, or vice versa;
- recording both halves of a transaction as debits or credits rather than recording one debit and one credit;
- recording an amount incorrectly from a transaction;
- recording a debit for one amount and a credit for a different amount;
- making an error when calculating the account balances.

Finding Trial Balance Errors

If the trial balance does not balance, try the following procedures.

1. Check the arithmetic. If the columns were originally added from top to bottom, verify the total by adding from bottom to top.

2. Check that the correct account balances were transferred to the correct trial balance columns.

3. Check the arithmetic used to compute the account balances.

4. Check that each transaction was recorded correctly in the accounts by tracing the amounts to the analysis of the transaction.

Sometimes you can determine the type of the error by the amount of the difference. Compute the difference between the debit total and the credit total. If the difference is divisible by 2, a debit might be recorded as a credit, or a credit recorded as a debit.

Managerial

IMPLICATIONS

Financial Statements

- Recording entries into accounts provides an efficient method of gathering data about the financial affairs of a business.
- A chart of accounts is usually similar from company to company; balance sheet accounts are first, followed by income statement accounts.
- A trial balance proves the financial records are in balance.
- The income statement reports the revenue and expenses for the period and shows the net income or loss.
- The statement of owner's equity shows the change in owner's equity during the period.
- The balance sheet summarizes the assets, liabilities, and owner's equity of the business on a given date.
- Owners, managers, creditors, banks, and many others use financial statements to make decisions about the business.

Thinking Critically:

What are some possible consequences of not recording financial data correctly?

If the difference is <u>divisible by 9,</u> there might be a transposition. A **transposition** occurs when the digits of a number are switched (357 for 375). The test for a transposition is

$$\begin{array}{r} 375 \\ -357 \\ \hline 18 \end{array} \qquad 18/9 = 2$$

Also check for slides. A **slide** occurs when the decimal point is misplaced (375 for 37.50). We can test for a slide in the following manner.

$$\begin{array}{r} 375.00 \\ -37.50 \\ \hline 337.50 \end{array} \qquad 337.50/9 = 37.50$$

Financial Statements

After the trial balance is prepared, the financial statements are prepared. Figure 3-7 on page 76 shows the financial statements for Carter Consulting Services. The amounts are taken from the trial balance. As you study the financial statements, note that net income from the income statement is used on the statement of owner's equity. Also note that the ending balance of the **Linda Carter, Capital** account, computed on the statement of owner's equity, is used on the balance sheet.

Chart of Accounts

A **chart of accounts** is a list of all the accounts used by a business. Figure 3-8 on page 77 shows the chart of accounts for Carter Consulting Services. Each account has a number and a name. The balance sheet accounts are listed first, followed by the income statement accounts. The account number is assigned based on the type of account.

6 Objective

Prepare an income statement, a statement of owner's equity, and a balance sheet.

7 Objective

Develop a chart of accounts.

FIGURE 3-7 ▶
Financial Statements for
Carter Consulting Services

Carter Consulting Services
Income Statement
Month Ended December 31, 2004

Revenue			
Fees Income			28 0 0 0 00
Expenses			
Salaries Expense	5 0 0 0 00		
Utilities Expense	6 0 0 00		
Total Expenses			5 6 0 0 00
Net Income			22 4 0 0 00

Carter Consulting Services
Statement of Owner's Equity
Month Ended December 31, 2004

Linda Carter, Capital, December 1, 2004		80 0 0 0 00
Net Income for December	22 4 0 0 00	
Less Withdrawals for December	3 0 0 0 00	
Increase in Capital		19 4 0 0 00
Linda Carter, Capital, December 31, 2004		99 4 0 0 00

Carter Consulting Services
Balance Sheet
December 31, 2004

Assets		Liabilities	
Cash	64 4 0 0 00	Accounts Payable	12 0 0 0 00
Accounts Receivable	4 0 0 0 00		
Supplies	2 0 0 0 00		
Prepaid Rent	6 0 0 0 00	Owner's Equity	
Equipment	35 0 0 0 00	Linda Carter, Capital	99 4 0 0 00
Total Assets	111 4 0 0 00	Total Liabilities and Owner's Equity	111 4 0 0 00

Asset Accounts	100–199	Revenue Accounts	400–499
Liability Accounts	200–299	Expense Accounts	500–599
Owner's Equity Accounts	300–399		

Notice that the accounts are not numbered consecutively. For example, asset account numbers jump from 101 to 111 and then to 121, 137, and 141. In each block of numbers, gaps are left so that additional accounts can be added when needed.

Permanent and Temporary Accounts

The asset, liability, and owner's equity accounts appear on the balance sheet at the end of an accounting period. The balances of these accounts are then carried forward to start the new period. Because they continue from one accounting period to the next, these accounts are called **permanent accounts** or *real accounts.*

CARTER CONSULTING SERVICES
Chart of Accounts

Account Number	Account Name
Balance Sheet Accounts	
100–199	**ASSETS**
101	Cash
111	Accounts Receivable
121	Supplies
137	Prepaid Rent
141	Equipment
200–299	**LIABILITIES**
202	Accounts Payable
300–399	**OWNER'S EQUITY**
301	Linda Carter, Capital
Statement of Owner's Equity Account	
302	Linda Carter, Drawing
Income Statement Accounts	
400–499	**REVENUE**
401	Fees Income
500–599	**EXPENSES**
511	Salaries Expense
514	Utilities Expense

◄ **FIGURE 3-8**
Chart of Accounts

Important!

Balance Sheet Accounts
The amounts on the balance sheet are carried forward to the next accounting period.

Important!

Income Statement Accounts
The amounts on the income statement are transferred to the capital account at the end of the accounting period.

Revenue and expense accounts appear on the income statement. The drawing account appears on the statement of owner's equity. These accounts classify and summarize changes in owner's equity during the period. They are called **temporary accounts** or *nominal accounts* because the balances in these accounts are transferred to the capital account at the end of the accounting period. In the next period, these accounts start with zero balances.

Section 2 Self Review

Questions

1. What is the increase side for **Cash; Accounts Payable;** and **Linda Carter, Capital?**

2. What is a trial balance and what is its purpose?

3. What is a transposition? A slide?

Exercises

4. Which account has a normal debit balance?

   a. Fees Income

   b. T. C., Drawing

   c. T. C., Capital

   d. Accounts Payable

5. The company owner took $1,000 cash for personal use. What is the entry for this transaction?

   a. Debit **Cash** and credit **Vijay Shah, Capital.**

   b. Debit **Vijay Shah, Capital** and credit **Cash.**

   c. Debit **Vijay Shah, Drawing** and credit **Cash.**

   d. Debit **Cash** and credit **Vijay Shah, Drawing.**

Analysis

6. Describe the errors in the Ames Interiors trial balance.

Ames Interiors
Trial Balance
December 31, 2004

	DEBIT	CREDIT
Cash	15 000 00	
Accts. Rec.	10 000 00	
Equip.	7 000 00	
Accts. Pay.		15 000 00
A. Ames, Capital		22 000 00
A. Ames, Drawing		10 000 00
Fees Income	14 000 00	
Rent Exp.	2 000 00	
Supplies Exp.	2 000 00	
Telephone Exp.	5 000 00	
Totals	55 000 00	47 000 00

CHAPTER 3 — Review and Applications

Review

Chapter Summary

In this chapter, you have learned how to use T accounts to help analyze and record business transactions. A chart of accounts can be developed to easily identify all the accounts used by a business. After determining the balance for all accounts, the trial balance is prepared to ensure that all transactions have been recorded accurately.

Learning Objectives

1 Set up T accounts for assets, liabilities, and owner's equity.

T accounts consist of two lines, one vertical and one horizontal, that resemble the letter **T**. The account name is written on the top line. Increases and decreases to the account are entered on either the left side or the right side of the vertical line.

2 Analyze business transactions and enter them in the accounts.

Each business transaction is analyzed for its effects on the fundamental accounting equation, Assets = Liabilities + Owner's Equity. Then these effects are recorded in the proper accounts. Accounts are classified as assets, liabilities, or owner's equity.

- Increases in an asset account appear on the debit, or left, side because assets are on the left side of the accounting equation. The credit, or right, side records decreases.
- An increase in a liability account is recorded on the credit, or right, side. The left, or debit, side of a liability account is used for recording decreases.
- Increases in owner's equity are shown on the credit (right) side of an account. Decreases appear on the debit (left) side.
- The drawing account is used to record the withdrawal of cash from the business by the owner. The drawing account decreases owner's equity.

3 Determine the balance of an account.

The difference between the amounts recorded on the two sides of an account is known as the balance of the account.

4 Set up T accounts for revenue and expenses.

- Revenue accounts increase owner's equity; therefore, increases are recorded on the credit side of revenue accounts.
- Expenses are recorded on the debit side of the expense accounts because expenses decrease owner's equity.

5 Prepare a trial balance from T accounts.

The trial balance is a statement to test the accuracy of the financial records. Total debits should equal total credits.

6 Prepare an income statement, a statement of owner's equity, and a balance sheet.

The income statement is prepared to report the revenue and expenses for the period. The statement of owner's equity is prepared to analyze the change in owner's equity during the period. Then the balance sheet is prepared to summarize the assets, liabilities, and owner's equity of the business at a given point in time.

7 Develop a chart of accounts.

A firm's list of accounts is called its chart of accounts. Accounts are arranged in a predetermined order and are numbered for handy reference and quick identification. Typically, accounts are numbered in the order in which they appear on the financial statements. Balance sheet accounts come first, followed by income statement accounts.

8 Define the accounting terms new to this chapter.

Account balance (p. 64) The difference between the amounts recorded on the two sides of an account

Accounts (p. 58) Written records of the assets, liabilities, and owner's equity of a business

Chart of accounts (p. 75) A list of the accounts used by a business to record its financial transactions

Classification (p. 58) A means of identifying each account as an asset, liability, or owner's equity

Credit (p. 72) An entry on the right side of an account

Debit (p. 72) An entry on the left side of an account

Double-entry system (p. 72) An accounting system that involves recording the effects of each transaction as debits and credits

Drawing account (p. 71) A special type of owner's equity account set up to record the owner's withdrawal of cash from the business

Footing (p. 64) A small pencil figure written at the base of an amount column showing the sum of the entries in the column

Normal balance (p. 65) The increase side of an account

Permanent account (p. 76) An account that is kept open from one accounting period to the next

Slide (p. 75) An accounting error involving a misplaced decimal point

T account (p. 58) A type of account, resembling a T, used to analyze the effects of a business transaction

Temporary account (p. 77) An account whose balance is transferred to another account at the end of an accounting period

Transposition (p. 75) An accounting error involving misplaced digits in a number

Trial balance (p. 73) A statement to test the accuracy of total debits and credits after transactions have been recorded

Comprehensive Self Review

1. On which side of asset, liability, and owner's equity accounts are decreases recorded?
2. What are withdrawals and how are they recorded?
3. What is a chart of accounts?
4. Your friend has prepared financial statements for her business. She has asked you to review the statements for accuracy. The trial balance debit column totals $81,000 and the credit column totals $94,000. What steps would you take to find the error?
5. What type of accounts are found on the balance sheet?

(Answers to Comprehensive Self Review are on page 93.)

Discussion Questions

1. What are accounts?
2. Why is **Prepaid Rent** considered an asset account?
3. Why is the modern system of accounting usually called the double-entry system?
4. The terms *debit* and *credit* are often used in describing the effects of transactions on different accounts. What do these terms mean?
5. Indicate whether each of the following types of accounts would normally have a debit balance or a credit balance.
    a. An asset account
    b. A liability account
    c. The owner's capital account
    d. A revenue account
    e. An expense account
6. How is the balance of an account determined?
7. What is the purpose of a chart of accounts?
8. In what order do accounts appear in the chart of accounts?
9. When a chart of accounts is created, number gaps are left within groups of accounts. Why are these number gaps necessary?
10. Accounts are classified as permanent or temporary accounts. What do these classifications mean?
11. Are the following accounts permanent or temporary accounts?
    a. Fees Income
    b. Cecil Blakeman, Drawing
    c. Accounts Payable
    d. Accounts Receivable
    e. Cecil Blakeman, Capital
    f. Prepaid Rent
    g. Cash
    h. Advertising Expense
    i. Utilities Expense
    j. Equipment
    k. Salaries Expense
    l. Prepaid Insurance

Applications

EXERCISES

Setting up T accounts.

Lake Watch and Jewelry Repair Service has the following account balances on December 31, 20--. Set up a T account for each account and enter the balance on the proper side of the account.

Cash	$4,000	Accounts Payable	$2,000
Equipment	4,000	Richard Lake, Capital	6,000

◄ **Exercise 3-1**
Objective 1

Using T accounts to analyze transactions.

Jessica Mason decided to start a dental practice. The first five transactions for the business follow. For each transaction, (1) determine which two accounts are affected, (2) set up T accounts for the affected accounts, and (3) enter the debit and credit amounts in the T accounts.

1. Jessica invested $10,000 cash in the business.
2. Paid $2,500 in cash for equipment.
3. Performed services for cash amounting to $1,000.
4. Paid $350 in cash for advertising expense.
5. Paid $250 in cash for supplies.

◄ **Exercise 3-2**
Objective 2

Identifying debits and credits.

In each of the following sentences, fill in the blanks with the word *debit* or *credit*.

1. Asset accounts normally have __?__ balances. These accounts increase on the __?__ side and decrease on the __?__ side.
2. Liability accounts normally have __?__ balances. These accounts increase on the __?__ side and decrease on the __?__ side.
3. The owner's capital account normally has a __?__ balance. This account increases on the __?__ side and decreases on the __?__ side.
4. Revenue accounts normally have __?__ balances. These accounts increase on the __?__ side and decrease on the __?__ side.
5. Expense accounts normally have __?__ balances. These accounts increase on the __?__ side and decrease on the __?__ side.

◄ **Exercise 3-3**
Objective 3

Determining debit and credit balances.

Indicate whether each of the following accounts normally has a debit balance or a credit balance.

1. Accounts Payable
2. Fees Income
3. Cash
4. Bob Childers, Capital
5. Equipment
6. Accounts Receivable
7. Salaries Expense
8. Supplies

◄ **Exercise 3-4**
Objective 3

Exercise 3-5 ►

Objective 3

Determining account balances.

The following T accounts show transactions that were recorded by Baker's Antique Repair, a firm that specializes in restoring antique furniture. The entries for the first transaction are labeled with the letter (a), the entries for the second transaction with the letter (b), and so on. Determine the balance of each account.

Cash			
(a)	40,000	(b)	10,000
(d)	5,000	(e)	150
(g)	500	(h)	2,500
		(i)	1,000

Equipment	
(c) 15,000	

Accounts Receivable			
(f)	2,000	(g)	500

Accounts Payable	
	(c) 15,000

Supplies	
(b) 10,000	

Aaron Baker, Capital	
	(a) 40,000

Fees Income			
		(d)	5,000
		(f)	2,000

Telephone Expense	
(e) 150	

Aaron Baker, Drawing	
(i) 1,000	

Salaries Expense	
(h) 2,500	

Exercise 3-6 ►

Objectives 5, 6

Preparing a trial balance and an income statement.

Using the account balances from Exercise 3-5, prepare a trial balance and an income statement for Baker's Antique Repair. The trial balance is for December 31, 20--, and the income statement is for the month ended December 31, 20--.

Exercise 3-7 ►

Objective 6

Preparing a statement of owner's equity and a balance sheet.

From the trial balance and the net income or net loss determined in Exercise 3-6, prepare a statement of owner's equity and a balance sheet for Baker's Antique Repair as of December 31, 20--.

Exercise 3-8 ►

Objective 7

Preparing a chart of accounts.

The accounts that will be used by Chastain Supply Company follow. Prepare a chart of accounts for the firm. Classify the accounts by type, arrange them in an appropriate order, and assign suitable account numbers.

Kelly Chastain, Capital	Salaries Expense
Office Supplies	Prepaid Rent
Accounts Payable	Fees Income
Cash	Accounts Receivable
Utilities Expense	Telephone Expense
Office Equipment	Kelly Chastain, Drawing

Problems

Selected problems can be completed using:
🍑 **Peachtree**   📖 **QuickBooks**   ▦ **Spreadsheets**

PROBLEM SET A

Using T accounts to record transactions involving assets, liabilities, and owner's equity.

The following transactions took place at Mill's Oil Field Equipment Service.

For each transaction, set up T accounts from the following list: **Cash; Shop Equipment; Store Equipment; Truck; Accounts Payable; Judd Mill, Capital;** and **Judd Mill, Drawing.** Analyze each transaction. Record the effects of the transactions in the T accounts. Use plus and minus signs before the amounts to show the increases and decreases.

TRANSACTIONS

1. Judd Mill invested $9,000 cash in the business.
2. Purchased shop equipment for $450 in cash.
3. Bought store fixtures for $300; payment is due in 30 days.
4. Purchased a used truck for $1,500 in cash.
5. Mill gave the firm his personal tools that have a fair market value of $500.
6. Bought a used cash register for $250; payment is due in 30 days.
7. Paid $100 in cash to apply to the amount owed for store fixtures.
8. Mill withdrew $400 in cash for personal expenses.

Analyze: Which transactions affect the **Cash** account?

◄ **Problem 3-1A**
Objectives 1, 2

INSTRUCTIONS

Using T accounts to record transactions involving assets, liabilities, and owner's equity.

The following transactions occurred at several different businesses and are not related.

Analyze each of the transactions. For each transaction, set up T accounts. Record the effects of the transaction in the T accounts. Use plus and minus signs to show the increases and decreases.

TRANSACTIONS

1. A firm purchased equipment for $4,000 in cash.
2. The owner John Cain withdrew $1,000 cash.
3. A firm sold a piece of surplus equipment for $500 in cash.
4. A firm purchased a used delivery truck for $4,000 in cash.
5. A firm paid $800 in cash to apply against an account owed.
6. A firm purchased office equipment for $900. The amount is to be paid in 60 days.
7. Holly Call, owner of the company, made an additional investment of $5,000 in cash.

◄ **Problem 3-2A**
Objectives 1, 2

INSTRUCTIONS

8. A firm paid $300 by check for office equipment that it had previously purchased on credit.

Analyze: Which transactions affect liability accounts?

Problem 3-3A ►
Objectives 2, 4

Using T accounts to record transactions involving revenue and expenses.

The following transactions took place at Factory Cleaning Service.

INSTRUCTIONS

Analyze each of the transactions. For each transaction, decide what accounts are affected and set up T accounts. Record the effects of the transaction in the T accounts. Use plus and minus signs before the amounts to show the increases and decreases.

TRANSACTIONS

1. Paid $800 for the current month's rent.
2. Performed services for $1,000 in cash.
3. Paid salaries of $1,200.
4. Performed additional services for $1,800 on credit.
5. Paid $150 for the monthly telephone bill.
6. Collected $500 from accounts receivable.
7. Received a $30 refund for an overcharge on the telephone bill.
8. Performed services for $1,200 on credit.
9. Paid $100 in cash for the monthly electric bill.
10. Paid $220 in cash for gasoline purchased for the firm's van during the month.
11. Received $900 from charge account customers.
12. Performed services for $1,800 in cash.

Analyze: What total cash was collected for accounts receivable during the month?

Problem 3-4A ►
Objectives 1, 2, 4

Using T accounts to record all business transactions.

The accounts and transactions of Justin Malone, Attorney at Law, follow.

INSTRUCTIONS

Analyze the transactions. Record each in the appropriate T accounts. Use plus and minus signs in front of the amounts to show the increases and decreases. Identify each entry in the T accounts by writing the letter of the transaction next to the entry.

ASSETS

Cash
Accounts Receivable
Office Equipment
Automobile

LIABILITIES

Accounts Payable

OWNER'S EQUITY

Justin Malone, Capital
Justin Malone, Drawing

REVENUE

Fees Income

EXPENSES

Automobile Expense
Rent Expense
Utilities Expense
Salaries Expense
Telephone Expense

TRANSACTIONS

a. Justin Malone invested $54,000 in cash to start the business.

b. Paid $1,600 for the current month's rent.

c. Bought a used automobile for the firm for $16,000 in cash.

d. Performed services for $3,000 in cash.

e. Paid $400 for automobile repairs.

f. Performed services for $3,750 on credit.

g. Purchased office chairs for $2,100 on credit.

h. Received $1,800 from credit clients.

i. Paid $1,000 to reduce the amount owed for the office chairs.

j. Issued a check for $560 to pay the monthly utility bill.

k. Purchased office equipment for $8,400 and paid half of this amount in cash immediately; the balance is due in 30 days.

l. Issued a check for $5,680 to pay salaries.

m. Performed services for $1,850 in cash.

n. Performed services for $2,600 on credit.

o. Paid $192 for the monthly telephone bill.

p. Collected $1,600 on accounts receivable from charge customers.

q. Purchased additional office equipment and received a bill for $1,360 due in 30 days.

r. Paid $300 in cash for gasoline purchased for the automobile during the month.

s. Justin Malone withdrew $2,000 in cash for personal expenses.

Analyze: What outstanding amount is owed to the company from its credit customers?

Preparing financial statements from T accounts.

The accountant for the firm owned by Justin Malone prepares financial statements at the end of each month.

◀ **Problem 3-5A**
Objectives 3, 5, 6

INSTRUCTIONS

Use the figures in the T accounts for Problem 3-4A to prepare a trial balance, an income statement, a statement of owner's equity, and a balance sheet. (The first line of the statement headings should read "Justin Malone, Attorney at Law.") Assume that the transactions took place during the month ended April 30, 20--. Determine the account balances before you start work on the financial statements.

Analyze: What net change in owner's equity occurred during the month of April?

Problem 3-1B ►
Objectives 1, 2

Using T accounts to record transactions involving assets, liabilities, and owner's equity.

The following transactions took place at the legal services business established by Jill Morris.

INSTRUCTIONS

For each transaction, set up T accounts from this list: **Cash; Office Furniture; Office Equipment; Automobile; Accounts Payable; Jill Morris, Capital;** and **Jill Morris, Drawing.** Analyze each transaction. Record the amounts in the T accounts affected by that transaction. Use plus and minus signs to show increases and decreases in each account.

TRANSACTIONS

1. Jill Morris invested $15,000 cash in the business.
2. Purchased office furniture for $4,000 in cash.
3. Bought a fax machine for $1,300; payment is due in 30 days.
4. Purchased a used car for the firm for $4,000 in cash.
5. Morris invested an additional $4,000 cash in the business.
6. Bought a new computer for $5,000; payment is due in 60 days.
7. Paid $1,300 to settle the amount owed on the fax machine.
8. Morris withdrew $1,000 in cash for personal expenses.

Analyze: Which transactions affected asset accounts?

Problem 3-2B ►
Objectives 1, 2

Using T accounts to record transactions involving assets, liabilities, and owner's equity.

The following transactions occurred at several different businesses and are not related.

INSTRUCTIONS

Analyze each of the transactions. For each, decide what accounts are affected and set up T accounts. Record the effects of the transaction in the T accounts. Use plus and minus signs before the amounts to show the increases and decreases.

TRANSACTIONS

1. Roby Black, an owner, made an additional investment of $3,000 in cash.
2. A firm purchased equipment for $1,750 in cash.
3. A firm sold some surplus office furniture for $150 in cash.
4. A firm purchased a computer for $1,300, to be paid in 60 days.
5. A firm purchased office equipment for $1,750 on credit. The amount is due in 60 days.
6. Debbie Allen, owner of Allen Travel Agency, withdrew $500 of her original cash investment.
7. A firm bought a delivery truck for $4,500 on credit; payment is due in 90 days.
8. A firm issued a check for $125 to a supplier in partial payment of an open account balance.

Analyze: List the transactions that directly affected an owner's equity account.

Using T accounts to record transactions involving revenues and expenses.

The following occurred during April at Loan Accounting Service.

Analyze each transaction. Use T accounts to record these transactions and be sure to put the name of the account on the top of each account. Record the effects of the transaction in the T accounts. Use plus and minus signs before the amounts to show the increases and decreases.

TRANSACTIONS

1. Purchased office supplies for $500.
2. Delivered monthly accounting statements, collected fee income of $350.
3. Paid the current month's office rent of $1,150.
4. Completed monthly audit, billed client for $500.
5. Client paid fee of $250 for monthly audit.
6. Paid office salary of $800.
7. Paid telephone bill of $120.
8. Billed client for $500 fee for preparing return.
9. Purchased office supplies of $250 on account.
10. Paid office salary of $800.
11. Collected $500 from client who was billed.
12. Clients paid a total of $5,000 cash in fees.

Analyze: How much cash did the business spend during the month of April?

Using T accounts to record all business transactions.

The following accounts and transactions are for Richard Wall, Consulting Engineer.

Analyze the transactions. Record each in the appropriate T accounts. Use plus and minus signs in front of the amounts to show the increases and decreases. Identify each entry in the T accounts by writing the letter of the transaction next to the entry.

ASSETS

Cash
Accounts Receivable
Office Furniture
Office Equipment

LIABILITIES

Accounts Payable

OWNER'S EQUITY

Richard Wall, Capital
Richard Wall, Drawing

◄ **Problem 3-3B**
Objectives 2, 4

INSTRUCTIONS

◄ **Problem 3-4B**
Objectives 1, 2, 4

INSTRUCTIONS

REVENUE

Fees Income

EXPENSES

Rent Expense
Utilities Expense
Salaries Expense
Telephone Expense
Miscellaneous Expense

TRANSACTIONS

a. Wall invested $90,000 in cash to start the business.

b. Paid $4,500 for the current month's rent.

c. Bought office furniture for $15,600 in cash.

d. Performed services for $6,300 in cash.

e. Paid $1,350 for the monthly telephone bill.

f. Performed services for $7,650 on credit.

g. Purchased a computer and copier for $23,700 on credit; paid $5,700 in cash immediately with the balance due in 30 days.

h. Received $4,200 from credit clients.

i. Paid $1,800 in cash for office cleaning services for the month.

j. Purchased additional office chairs for $4,800; received credit terms of 30 days.

k. Purchased office equipment for $33,000 and paid half of this amount in cash immediately; the balance is due in 30 days.

l. Issued a check for $19,500 to pay salaries.

m. Performed services for $6,150 in cash.

n. Performed services for $6,900 on credit.

o. Collected $3,600 on accounts receivable from charge customers.

p. Issued a check for $2,400 in partial payment of the amount owed for office chairs.

q. Paid $600 to a duplicating company for photocopy work performed during the month.

r. Paid $1,500 for the monthly electric bill.

s. Wall withdrew $6,000 in cash for personal expenses.

Analyze: What liabilities does the business have after all transactions have been recorded?

Problem 3-5B ▶
Objectives 3, 5, 6

SPREADSHEET

INSTRUCTIONS

Preparing financial statements from T accounts.

The accountant for the firm owned by Richard Wall prepares financial statements at the end of each month.

Use the figures in the T accounts for Problem 3-4B to prepare a trial balance, an income statement, a statement of owner's equity, and a balance sheet. (The first line of the statement headings should read "Richard Wall, Consulting Engineer.") Assume that the transactions took place during the month ended June 30, 20--. Determine the account balances before you start work on the financial statements.

Analyze: What is the change in owner's equity for the month of June?

Sole Proprietorship

Kim Chumley is an architect who operates her own business. The accounts and transactions for the business follow.

(1) Analyze the transactions for January 20--. Record each in the appropriate T accounts. Use plus and minus signs in front of the amounts to show the increases and decreases. Identify each entry in the T account by writing the letter of the transaction next to the entry.

(2) Determine the account balances. Prepare a trial balance, an income statement, a statement of owner's equity, and a balance sheet.

ASSETS

Cash
Accounts Receivable
Office Furniture
Office Equipment

LIABILITIES

Accounts Payable

OWNER'S EQUITY

Kim Chumley, Capital
Kim Chumley, Drawing

REVENUE

Fees Income

EXPENSES

Advertising Expense
Utilities Expense
Salaries Expense
Telephone Expense
Miscellaneous Expense

TRANSACTIONS

a. Kim Chumley invested $20,000 in cash to start the business.

b. Paid $1,000 for advertisements in a design magazine.

c. Purchased office furniture for $3,000 in cash.

d. Performed services for $2,400 in cash.

e. Paid $270 for the monthly telephone bill.

f. Performed services for $2,160 on credit.

g. Purchased a fax machine for $1,500; paid $600 in cash with the balance due in 30 days.

h. Paid a bill for $330 from the office cleaning service.

i. Received $1,080 from clients on account.

j. Purchased additional office chairs for $900; received credit terms of 30 days.

k. Paid $2,000 for salaries.

l. Issued a check for $550 in partial payment of the amount owed for office chairs.

m. Received $1,400 in cash for services performed.

n. Issued a check for $480 for utilities expense.

o. Performed services for $2,400 on credit.

p. Collected $400 from clients on account.

q. Kim Chumley withdrew $1,400 in cash for personal expenses.

r. Paid $300 to Kevin's Photocopy Service for photocopy work performed during the month.

Analyze: Using the basic accounting equation, what is the financial condition of Kim Chumley's business at month-end?

CHAPTER 3 CRITICAL THINKING PROBLEM

Financial Condition

At the beginning of the summer, Adam McCoy was looking for a way to earn money to pay for his college tuition in the fall. He decided to start a lawn service business in his neighborhood. To get the business started, Adam used $750 from his savings account to open a checking account for his new business, AM Lawn Care. He purchased two used power mowers and various lawn care tools for $250, and paid $450 for a second-hand truck to transport the mowers.

Several of his neighbors hired him to cut their grass on a weekly basis. He sent these customers monthly bills. By the end of the summer, they had paid him $100 in cash and owed him another $175. Adam also cut grass on an as-needed basis for other neighbors who paid him $50.

During the summer, Adam spent $50 for gasoline for the truck and mowers. He paid $125 to a friend who helped him on several occasions. An advertisement in the local paper cost $15. Now, at the end of the summer, Adam is concerned because he has only $10 left in his checking account. He says, "I worked hard all summer and have only $10 to show for it. It would have been better to leave the money in the bank."

Prepare an income statement, a statement of owner's equity, and a balance sheet for AM Lawn Care. Explain to Adam whether or not he is "better off" than he was at the beginning of the summer. (Hint: T accounts might be helpful in organizing the data.)

Business Connections

MANAGERIAL *Focus*   Informed Decisions

1. How do the income statement and the balance sheet help management make sound decisions?

2. How can management find out, at any time, whether a firm can pay its bills as they become due?

3. If a firm's expenses equal or exceed its revenue, what actions might management take?

4. In discussing a firm's latest financial statements, a manager says that it is the "results on the bottom line" that really count. What does the manager mean?

Ethical DILEMMA   Reporting Cash Sales

Joe's Quick Stop is a convenience store that sells an array of products. The store is owned by Joseph Lawson, who has offered you a job in the store as a clerk. On your first day on the job, Joseph informs you that when customers pay cash for certain items, the cash should be deposited in a cigar box that is kept under the cash register. At the end of the day, you notice that Joseph empties the cash in the cigar box into his money bag. The cash deposited in the cash register is recorded as the amount of cash received for the day and does not include the cash in the cigar box. You are concerned that Joseph is not properly recording his total amount of cash received. What would you do?

Street WISE:
Questions from the Real World   Account Categories

Refer to the *1999 Annual Report* for The Home Depot, Inc. in Appendix B.

1. To prepare financial statements, The Home Depot, Inc. summarizes general ledger account balances into summary categories for presentation on statements. List five "permanent" summarized account categories reflected in these statements. List five "temporary" summarized account categories found in the statements.

2. Locate the consolidated balance sheets for The Home Depot, Inc. If The Home Depot, Inc. purchased new store fixtures on account for $25,000, describe the effect on the company's balance sheet categories.

FINANCIAL $TATEMENT
ANALYSIS   Management Letter

Annual reports released by publicly held companies include a letter to the stockholders written by the chief executive officer, chairman of the board, or president. Excerpts from the Adobe Systems Incorporated *1999 Annual Report* "To Our Stockholders" letter are presented below. The appearance of an ellipsis (. . .) indicates that some of the text of the letter has been deleted to save space.

> For everyone at Adobe Systems, 1999 will be remembered as a year of turnaround . . . Adobe stock began a steady ascent, and by the end of fiscal year 1999, its value had increased fourfold . . . our operating profit increased by 107% year over year . . .

. . . net income reached a record level of $238 million, a 126% increase compared with fiscal 1998 . . .

. . . by improving operational efficiency, Adobe was able to enhance operations . . . by outsourcing functions such as order fulfillment and utilizing the Internet to work more efficiently with our customers . . .

Analyze:

1. Based on the excerpts above, what types of information can a company's management deliver using the letter to stockholders?
2. What net income did Adobe Systems Incorporated report for fiscal 1999?
3. What operational efficiencies are discussed for fiscal 1999?

Analyze Online: Locate the Adobe Systems Incorporated Web site **(www.adobe.com).** Within *Investor Relations* in the *About Adobe* link, find the annual report for the current year. Read the letter to the stockholders within the annual report.

4. Are the financial results presented in the current year more or less favorable than those presented for fiscal 1999?
5. What new products were introduced in the current year and mentioned in the stockholders' letter?

Connection 5 ► *Extending* the *Thought* **Systems** A company's chart of accounts is an organization system. Discuss similar organization systems in subject areas other than accounting.

Connection 6 ► Business Communication **Memo** The junior accountant in your department does not agree that a trial balance should be prepared before the financial statements are completed. As the senior accountant, write a memo to your co-worker explaining your position on the topic. Express possible ramifications that you foresee if the trial balance is not prepared.

Connection 7 ► Team*Work* **Chart of Accounts** As a team, develop a chart of accounts for a retail garden supply store. Brainstorm with your team about the types of revenue and expense accounts that would be required. List asset, liability, and owner's equity accounts. Finally, assign an organized numeric scheme to your chart of accounts. Write instructions for adding new accounts if it becomes necessary.

Connection 8 ► *inter* NET CONNECTION **SBA** The Small Business Administration (SBA) offers a wide variety of resources to the entrepreneur. Go to the Web site at **www.sba.gov.** List two counseling or resource services available through the Small Business Administration. Based on the information at the Web site, what goes into a business plan?

Answers to Section 1 Self Review

1. Increases in asset accounts are recorded on the left side. Increases in liability and owner's equity accounts are recorded on the right side.
2. The sum of several entries on either side of an account that is entered in small pencil figures.
3. The increase side of an account. The normal balance of an asset account is on the left side. The normal balance of liability and owner's equity accounts is on the right side.
4. c. $24,000
5. c. **Equipment** is increased by $4,500. **Accounts Payable** is increased by $4,500.
6. Cash + Equipment + Supplies = Accounts Payable + T. R. Murphy, Capital
   15,400 + 20,000 + 4,600 = 10,000 + 30,000
   40,000 = 40,000

Answers to Section 2 Self Review

1. The increase side of **Cash** is the left, or debit, side. The increase side of **Accounts Payable** is the right, or credit, side. The increase side of **Linda Carter, Capital** is the right, or credit, side.
2. The trial balance is a list of all the accounts and their balances. Its purpose is to prove the equality of the total debits and credits.
3. A transposition is an error in which the digits of a number are switched, for example, when 517 is recorded as 571.

   A slide is an error in which the decimal point is misplaced, for example, when 317 is written as 3.17.
4. b. **T. C., Drawing**
5. c. **Vijay Shah, Drawing** would be debited and **Cash** would be credited.
6. **A. Ames, Drawing**—10,000 should be in the Debit column.

   Fees Income—14,000 should be in the Credit column.

   The new column totals will be 51,000.

Answers to Comprehensive Self Review

1. Decreases in asset accounts are recorded on the credit side. Decreases in liability and owner's equity accounts are recorded on the debit side.
2. Cash taken from the business by the owner to obtain funds for personal living expenses. Withdrawals are recorded in a special type of owner's equity account called a drawing account.
3. A list of the numbers and names of the accounts of a business. It provides a system by which the accounts of the business can be easily identified and located.
4. • Check the math by adding the columns again.
   • Determine whether the account balances are in the correct columns.
   • Check the accounts to see whether the balances in the accounts were computed correctly.
   • Check the accuracy of transactions recorded during the period.
5. The asset, liability, and owner's equity accounts.

CHAPTER 4

Learning Objectives

1. Record transactions in the general journal.

2. Prepare compound journal entries.

3. Post journal entries to general ledger accounts.

4. Correct errors made in the journal or ledger.

5. Define the accounting terms new to this chapter.

The General Journal and the General Ledger

CSX
CORPORATION

www.csx.com

*E*conomic development in a geographic area often hinges on the transportation infrastructure of the region. No one understands this better than CSX Corporation. Founded originally as the Louisa Railroad Company in 1836, this Fortune 500 company now moves consumer products, automobiles, forest products, coal, and iron from location to location via ocean liners, barges, trucks, and trains. CSX Corporation played a key role from 1994 to 2000 helping approximately 500 companies locate and expand along its rail lines. In addition to rail services, customers contract with CSX Corporation for warehouse management, container shipping, and equipment maintenance services.

Thinking Critically
Why would CSX Corporation expand its services beyond transportation?

For more information on CSX Corporation, go to: collegeaccounting.glencoe.com.

New Terms

Accounting cycle	General journal
Audit trail	General ledger
Balance ledger form	Journal
Chronological order	Journalizing
Compound entry	Ledger
Correcting entry	Posting

The General Journal

1 **Record transactions in the general journal.**

WHY IT'S IMPORTANT
Written records for all business transactions are necessary. The general journal acts as the "diary" of the business.

2 **Prepare compound journal entries.**

WHY IT'S IMPORTANT
Compound entries contain several debits or credits for a single business transaction, creating efficiencies in journalizing.

Terms to Learn

accounting cycle
audit trail
chronological order
compound entry
general journal
journal
journalizing

1 **Objective**

Record transactions in the general journal.

The **accounting cycle** is a series of steps performed during each accounting period to classify, record, and summarize data for a business and to produce needed financial information. The first step in the accounting cycle is to analyze business transactions. You learned this skill in Chapter 3. The second step in the accounting cycle is to prepare a record of business transactions.

Journals

Business transactions are recorded in a **journal**, which is a diary of business activities. The journal lists transactions in **chronological order**, that is, in the order in which they occur. The journal is sometimes called the *record of original entry* because it is where transactions are first entered in the accounting records. There are different types of journals. This chapter will examine the general journal. You will become familiar with other journals in later chapters.

> Most corporations use accounting software to record business transactions. Texaco International uses Solomon IV accounting software.

The General Journal

The **general journal** is a financial record for entering all types of business transactions. **Journalizing** is the process of recording transactions in the general journal.

Figure 4-1 shows the general journal for Carter Consulting Services. Notice that the general journal has a page number. To record a transaction, enter the year at the top of the Date column. In the Date column, write the month and day on the first line of the first entry. After the first entry, enter the year and month only when a new page is started or when the year or the month changes. In the Date column, write the day of each transaction on the first line of each transaction.

FIGURE 4-1 ▶
General Journal Entry

Record the year first, then the month and day. ──────▶

Record the debit first. ──────▶

Indent about one-half inch and record the credit.

	DATE		DESCRIPTION	POST. REF.	DEBIT	CREDIT	
1	2004						1
2	Nov.	6	Cash		80 000 00		2
3			Linda Carter, Capital			80 000 00	3
4			Investment by owner				4
5							5

Indent again and write the description.

In the Description column, enter the account to be debited. Write the account name close to the left margin of the Description column, and enter the amount on the same line in the Debit column.

Enter the account to be credited on the line beneath the debit. Indent the account name about one-half inch from the left margin. Enter the amount on the same line in the Credit column.

Then enter a complete but concise description of the transaction in the Description column. Begin the description on the line following the credit. The description is indented about one inch from the left margin.

Write account names exactly as they appear in the chart of accounts. This will minimize errors when amounts are transferred from the general journal to the accounts.

Leave a blank line between general journal entries. Some accountants use this blank line to number each general journal entry.

When possible, the journal entry description should refer to the source of the information. For example, the journal entry to record a payment should include the check number in the description. Document numbers are part of the audit trail. The **audit trail** is a chain of references that makes it possible to trace information, locate errors, and prevent fraud. The audit trail provides a means of checking the journal entry against the original data on the documents.

Recording November Transactions in the General Journal

In Chapters 2 and 3, you learned a step-by-step method for analyzing business transactions. In this chapter you will learn how to complete the journal entry for a business transaction in the same manner. Review the following steps before you continue.

1. Analyze the financial event.
   - Identify the accounts affected.
   - Classify the accounts affected.
   - Determine the amount of increase or decrease for each account affected.
2. Apply the rules of debit and credit.
   a. Which account is debited? For what amount?
   b. Which account is credited? For what amount?
3. Make the entry in T-account form.
4. Record the complete entry in general journal form.

Important!

The Diary of a Business
The general journal is similar to a diary. The general journal details, in chronological order, the economic events of the business.

Important!

Audit Trail
To maintain the audit trail, descriptions should refer to document numbers whenever possible.

Business Transaction

On November 6 Linda Carter withdrew $80,000 from personal savings and deposited it in a new business checking account for Carter Consulting Services.

Analysis

a. The asset account, **Cash**, is increased by $80,000.

b. The owner's equity account, **Linda Carter, Capital,** is increased by $80,000.

CARTER
CONSULTING
SERVICES

MEMORANDUM 01

TO: Beatrice Wilson
FROM: Linda Carter
DATE: November 6, 2004
SUBJECT: Contributed personal funds to the business

I contributed $80,000 from my personal savings to Carter Consulting Services.

Debit-Credit Rules

DEBIT Increases to asset accounts are recorded as debits. Debit **Cash** for $80,000.

CREDIT Increases to the owner's equity account are recorded as credits. Credit **Linda Carter, Capital** for $80,000.

T-Account Presentation

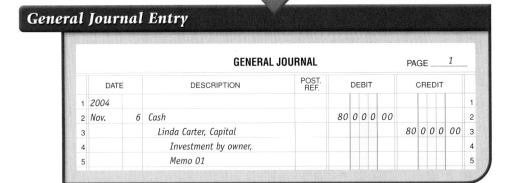

Cash		Linda Carter, Capital	
+	−	−	+
(a) 80,000			(b) 80,000

General Journal Entry

	GENERAL JOURNAL				PAGE ___1___	
DATE	DESCRIPTION	POST. REF.	DEBIT	CREDIT	
1	2004					1
2	Nov. 6 Cash		80 0 0 0 00			2
3	Linda Carter, Capital			80 0 0 0 00	3
4	Investment by owner,					4
5	Memo 01					5

Business Transaction

On November 7 Carter Consulting Services issued Check 1001 for $20,000 to purchase a computer and other equipment.

Analysis

c. The asset account, **Equipment,** is increased by $20,000.

d. The asset account, **Cash,** is decreased by $20,000.

Debit-Credit Rules

DEBIT Increases to asset accounts are recorded as debits. Debit **Equipment** for $20,000.

CREDIT Decreases to asset accounts are recorded as credits. Credit **Cash** for $20,000.

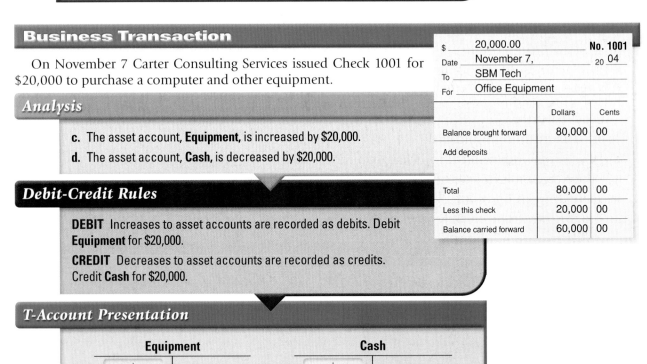

$	20,000.00		No. 1001
Date	November 7,		20 04
To	SBM Tech		
For	Office Equipment		
		Dollars	Cents
Balance brought forward		80,000	00
Add deposits			
Total		80,000	00
Less this check		20,000	00
Balance carried forward		60,000	00

T-Account Presentation

Equipment		Cash	
+	−	+	−
(c) 20,000			(d) 20,000

General Journal Entry

	DATE		DESCRIPTION	POST. REF.	DEBIT	CREDIT	
			GENERAL JOURNAL			PAGE ___1___	
6	Nov.	7	Equipment		20 0 0 0 00		6
7			Cash			20 0 0 0 00	7
8			Purchased equip., Check 1001				8

The check number appears in the description and forms part of the audit trail for the transaction.

Business Transaction

On November 10 Carter Consulting Services purchased office equipment on account for $15,000.

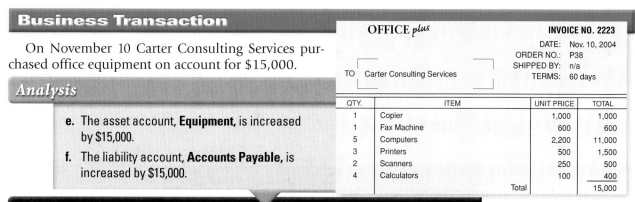

OFFICE plus			INVOICE NO. 2223
			DATE: Nov. 10, 2004
			ORDER NO.: P38
			SHIPPED BY: n/a
TO	Carter Consulting Services		TERMS: 60 days

QTY.	ITEM	UNIT PRICE	TOTAL
1	Copier	1,000	1,000
1	Fax Machine	600	600
5	Computers	2,200	11,000
3	Printers	500	1,500
2	Scanners	250	500
4	Calculators	100	400
	Total		15,000

Analysis

e. The asset account, **Equipment,** is increased by $15,000.

f. The liability account, **Accounts Payable,** is increased by $15,000.

Debit-Credit Rules

DEBIT Increases to asset accounts are recorded as debits. Debit **Equipment** for $15,000.

CREDIT Increases to liability accounts are recorded as credits. Credit **Accounts Payable** for $15,000.

T-Account Presentation

Equipment		Accounts Payable	
+	–	–	+
(e) 15,000			(f) 15,000

General Journal Entry

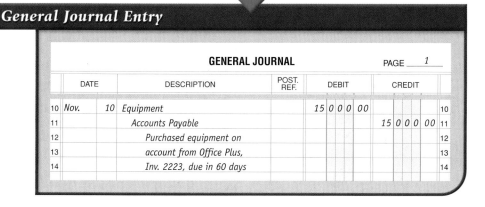

	DATE		DESCRIPTION	POST. REF.	DEBIT	CREDIT	
			GENERAL JOURNAL			PAGE ___1___	
10	Nov.	10	Equipment		15 0 0 0 00		10
11			Accounts Payable			15 0 0 0 00	11
12			Purchased equipment on				12
13			account from Office Plus,				13
14			Inv. 2223, due in 60 days				14

The supplier's name (Office Plus) and invoice number (2223) appear in the journal entry description and form part of the audit trail for the transaction. The journal entry can be checked against the data on the original document, Invoice 2223.

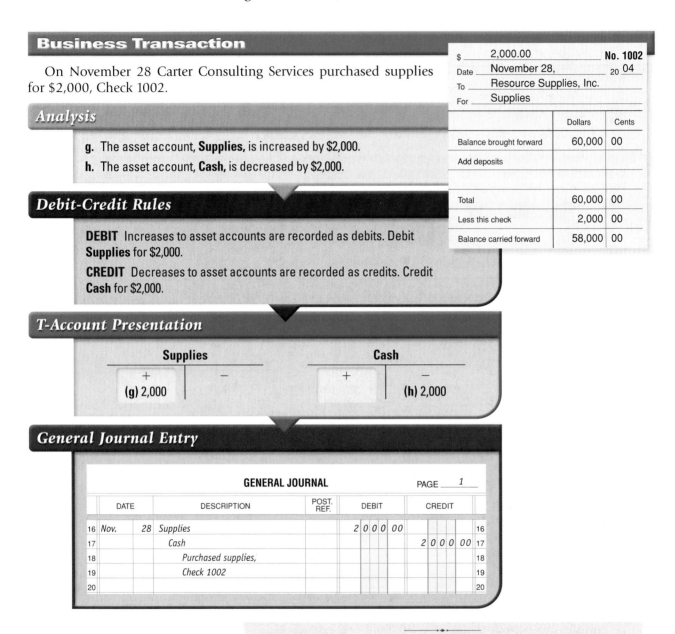

Business Transaction

On November 28 Carter Consulting Services purchased supplies for $2,000, Check 1002.

				No. 1002
$	2,000.00			
Date	November 28,		20	04
To	Resource Supplies, Inc.			
For	Supplies			

	Dollars	Cents
Balance brought forward	60,000	00
Add deposits		
Total	60,000	00
Less this check	2,000	00
Balance carried forward	58,000	00

Analysis

g. The asset account, **Supplies**, is increased by $2,000.

h. The asset account, **Cash**, is decreased by $2,000.

Debit-Credit Rules

DEBIT Increases to asset accounts are recorded as debits. Debit **Supplies** for $2,000.

CREDIT Decreases to asset accounts are recorded as credits. Credit **Cash** for $2,000.

T-Account Presentation

Supplies		Cash	
+	−	+	−
(g) 2,000			(h) 2,000

General Journal Entry

GENERAL JOURNAL   PAGE ___1___

	DATE		DESCRIPTION	POST. REF.	DEBIT	CREDIT	
16	Nov.	28	Supplies		2 0 0 0 00		16
17			Cash			2 0 0 0 00	17
18			Purchased supplies,				18
19			Check 1002				19
20							20

A few boxes of pens, pencils, highlighters, toner cartridges, several reams of paper—the cost of office supplies might not seem like much. The accountants at Duke University can attest that these costs add up. In 1999 Duke spent approximately $12.5 million for office supplies.

Beatrice Wilson decided to reduce the firm's debt to Office Plus. Recall that the firm had purchased equipment on account in the amount of

$15,000. On November 30 Carter Consulting Services issued a check to Office Plus. Beatrice Wilson analyzed the transaction and recorded the journal entry as follows.

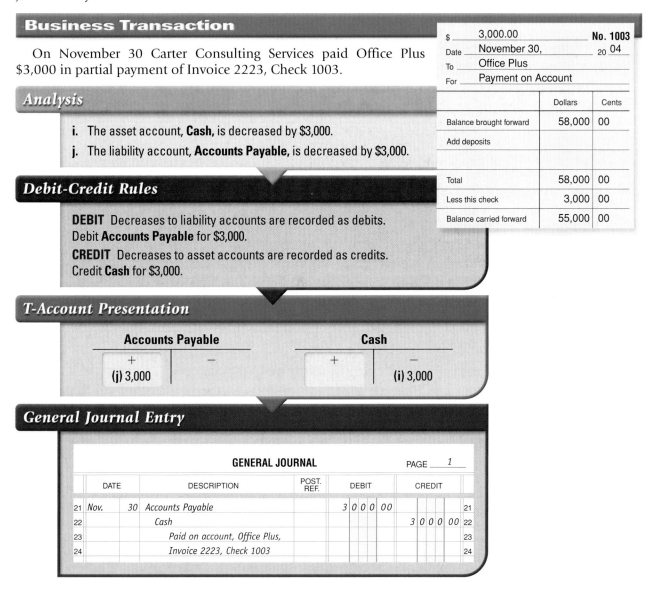

Business Transaction

On November 30 Carter Consulting Services paid Office Plus $3,000 in partial payment of Invoice 2223, Check 1003.

$ 3,000.00		No. 1003
Date November 30,		20 04
To Office Plus		
For Payment on Account		

	Dollars	Cents
Balance brought forward	58,000	00
Add deposits		
Total	58,000	00
Less this check	3,000	00
Balance carried forward	55,000	00

Analysis

i. The asset account, **Cash,** is decreased by $3,000.
j. The liability account, **Accounts Payable,** is decreased by $3,000.

Debit-Credit Rules

DEBIT Decreases to liability accounts are recorded as debits. Debit **Accounts Payable** for $3,000.

CREDIT Decreases to asset accounts are recorded as credits. Credit **Cash** for $3,000.

T-Account Presentation

Accounts Payable			Cash	
+	−		+	−
(j) 3,000				(i) 3,000

General Journal Entry

| | GENERAL JOURNAL | | | | PAGE 1 | |

	DATE	DESCRIPTION	POST. REF.	DEBIT	CREDIT	
21	Nov. 30	Accounts Payable		3 0 0 0 00		21
22		Cash			3 0 0 0 00	22
23		Paid on account, Office Plus,				23
24		Invoice 2223, Check 1003				24

Notice that the general journal Description column includes three important items for the audit trail:

- the supplier name,
- the invoice number,
- the check number.

In the general journal, always enter debits before credits. This is the case even if the credit item is considered first when mentally analyzing the transaction.

Carter Consulting Services issued a check in November to pay December and January rent in advance. Recall that the right to occupy facilities is considered a form of property. Beatrice Wilson analyzed the transaction and recorded the journal entry as follows.

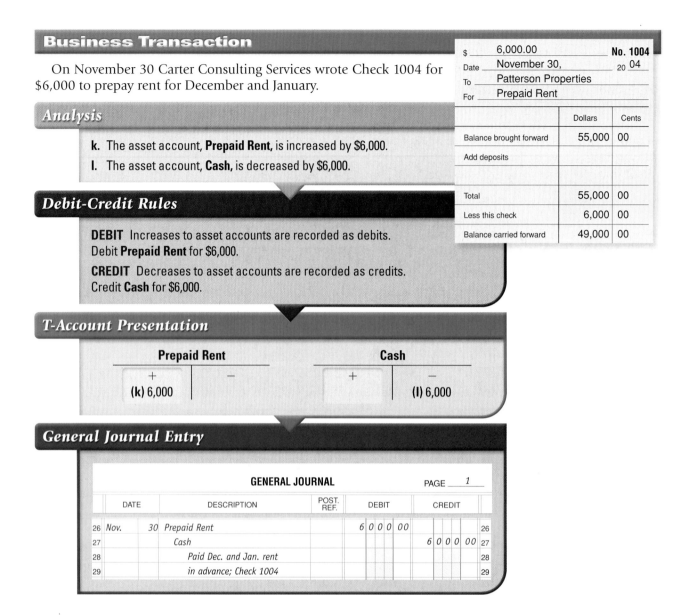

Business Transaction

On November 30 Carter Consulting Services wrote Check 1004 for $6,000 to prepay rent for December and January.

$ 6,000.00	No. 1004
Date November 30,	20 04
To Patterson Properties	
For Prepaid Rent	

	Dollars	Cents
Balance brought forward	55,000	00
Add deposits		
Total	55,000	00
Less this check	6,000	00
Balance carried forward	49,000	00

Analysis

k. The asset account, **Prepaid Rent,** is increased by $6,000.

l. The asset account, **Cash,** is decreased by $6,000.

Debit-Credit Rules

DEBIT Increases to asset accounts are recorded as debits. Debit **Prepaid Rent** for $6,000.

CREDIT Decreases to asset accounts are recorded as credits. Credit **Cash** for $6,000.

T-Account Presentation

Prepaid Rent		Cash	
+	−	+	−
(k) 6,000			(l) 6,000

General Journal Entry

GENERAL JOURNAL   PAGE ___1___

	DATE		DESCRIPTION	POST. REF.	DEBIT	CREDIT	
26	Nov.	30	Prepaid Rent		6 0 0 0 00		26
27			Cash			6 0 0 0 00	27
28			Paid Dec. and Jan. rent				28
29			in advance; Check 1004				29

Recording December Transactions in the General Journal

Carter Consulting Services opened for business on December 1. Let's review the transactions that occurred in December. Refer to items **m** through **x** in Chapter 3 for the analysis of each transaction.

1. Performed services for $21,000 in cash.

2. Performed services for $7,000 on credit.

3. Received $3,000 in cash from credit clients on their accounts.

4. Paid $5,000 for salaries.

5. Paid $600 for a utility bill.

6. The owner withdrew $3,000 for personal expenses.

Figure 4-2 shows the entries in the general journal. In an actual business, transactions involving fees income and accounts receivable occur throughout the month and are recorded when they take place. For the sake of simplicity, these transactions are summarized and recorded as of December 31 for Carter Consulting Services.

◄ **FIGURE 4-2**
General Journal Entries
for December

GENERAL JOURNAL PAGE ___2___

	DATE		DESCRIPTION	POST. REF.	DEBIT	CREDIT	
1	2004						1
2	Dec.	31	Cash		21 0 0 0 00		2
3			Fees Income			21 0 0 0 00	3
4			Performed services for cash				4
5							5
6		31	Accounts Receivable		7 0 0 0 00		6
7			Fees Income			7 0 0 0 00	7
8			Performed services on credit				8
9							9
10		31	Cash		3 0 0 0 00		10
11			Accounts Receivable			3 0 0 0 00	11
12			Received cash from credit				12
13			clients on account				13
14							14
15		31	Salaries Expense		5 0 0 0 00		15
16			Cash			5 0 0 0 00	16
17			Paid monthly salaries to				17
18			employees, Checks				18
19			1005–1006				19
20							20
21		31	Utilities Expense		6 0 0 00		21
22			Cash			6 0 0 00	22
23			Paid monthly bill for utilities,				23
24			Check 1007				24
25							25
26		31	Linda Carter, Drawing		3 0 0 0 00		26
27			Cash			3 0 0 0 00	27
28			Owner withdrew cash for				28
29			personal expenses,				29
30			Check 1008				30

Trade Agreements

The General Agreement on Tariffs and Trade (GATT) is both an organization and a set of agreements. The organization began in 1947 with 223 member nations. Its purpose is to end quotas and lower tariffs. GATT has had a beneficial effect on world trade.

Preparing Compound Entries

So far, each journal entry consists of one debit and one credit. Some transactions require a **compound entry**—a journal entry that contains more than one debit or credit. In a compound entry, record all debits first followed by the credits.

❷ **Objective**

Prepare compound journal entries.

> In 1999 Allstate purchased an insurance division of CNA Financial Corporation. Allstate paid cash and issued a 10-year note payable (a promise to pay). Detailed accounting records are not available to the public, but a compound journal entry was probably used to record this transaction.

Suppose that on November 7, when Carter Consulting Services purchased the equipment for $20,000, Linda Carter paid $10,000 in cash and agreed to pay the balance in 30 days. This transaction is analyzed on page 104.

On November 7 the firm purchased equipment for $20,000, issued Check 1001 for $10,000, and agreed to pay the balance in 30 days.

Analysis

The asset account, **Equipment,** is increased by $20,000. The asset account, **Cash,** is decreased by $10,000.

The liability account, **Accounts Payable,** is increased by $10,000.

Debit-Credit Rules

DEBIT Increases to assets are recorded as debits. Debit **Equipment** for $20,000.

CREDIT Decreases to assets are credits. Credit **Cash** for $10,000. Increases to liabilities are credits. Credit **Accounts Payable** for $10,000.

T-Account Presentation

Equipment		Cash		Accounts Payable	
+	−	+	−	−	+
20,000			10,000		10,000

General Journal Entry

GENERAL JOURNAL   PAGE ___1___

	DATE		DESCRIPTION	POST. REF.	DEBIT	CREDIT	
6	Nov.	7	Equipment		20 0 0 0 00		6
7			Cash			10 0 0 0 00	7
8			Accounts Payable			10 0 0 0 00	8
9			Bought equip. from SBM Tech,				9
10			Inv. 11, issued Ck. 1001 for				10
11			$10,000, bal. due in 30 days				11

Recall

Debits = Credits
No matter how many accounts are affected by a transaction, total debits must equal total credits.

Section 1 Self Review

Questions

1. Why are check and invoice numbers included in the journal entry description?

2. In a compound journal entry, if two accounts are debited, must two accounts be credited?

3. Why is the journal referred to as the "record of original entry"?

Exercises

4. A general journal is like a(n)
   a. address book.
   b. appointment calendar.
   c. diary.
   d. to-do list.

5. The part of the journal entry to be recorded first is the
   a. asset.
   b. credit.
   c. debit.
   d. liability.

Analysis

6. The accountant for Luxury Lawncare never includes descriptions when making journal entries. What effect will this have on the accounting system?

(Answers to Section 1 Self Review are on page 127.)

The General Ledger

You learned that a journal contains a chronological (day-by-day) record of a firm's transactions. Each journal entry shows the accounts and the amounts involved. Using the journal as a guide, you can enter transaction data in the accounts.

Ledgers

T accounts are used to analyze transactions quickly but are not used to maintain financial records. Instead, businesses keep account records on a special form that makes it possible to record all data efficiently. There is a separate form for each account. The account forms are kept in a book or binder called a **ledger**. The ledger is called the *record of final entry* because the ledger is the last place that accounting transactions are recorded.

The process of transferring data from the journal to the ledger is known as **posting**. Posting takes place after transactions are journalized. Posting is the third step of the accounting cycle.

The General Ledger

Every business has a general ledger. The **general ledger** is the master reference file for the accounting system. It provides a permanent, classified record of all accounts used in a firm's operations.

Ledger Account Forms

There are different types of general ledger account forms. Beatrice Wilson decided to use a balance ledger form. A **balance ledger form** shows the balance of the account after each entry is posted. Look at Figure 4-3 on page 106. It shows the first general journal entry, the investment by the owner. It also shows the general ledger forms for **Cash** and **Linda Carter, Capital**. On the ledger form, notice the

- account name and number;
- columns for date, description, and posting reference (post. ref.);
- columns for debit, credit, balance debit, and balance credit.

Posting to the General Ledger

Examine Figure 4-4 on page 107. On November 7 Beatrice Wilson made a general journal entry to record the purchase of equipment. To post the data from the journal to the general ledger, Wilson entered the debit amount in the Debit column in the **Equipment** account and the credit amount in the Credit column in the **Cash** account.

In the general journal, identify the first account listed. In Figure 4-4, **Equipment** is the first account. In the general ledger, find the ledger form for the first account listed. In Figure 4-4 this is the **Equipment** ledger form.

The steps to post from the general journal to the general ledger follow.

Section Objectives

3 Post journal entries to general ledger accounts.

WHY IT'S IMPORTANT
The general ledger provides a permanent, classified record for a company's accounts.

4 Correct errors made in the journal or ledger.

WHY IT'S IMPORTANT
Errors must be corrected to ensure a proper audit trail and to provide good information.

Terms to Learn

balance ledger form
correcting entry
general ledger
ledger
posting

Important!

General Journal and General Ledger
The general journal is the record of *original* entry. The general ledger is the record of *final* entry.

3 Objective
Post journal entries to general ledger accounts.

FIGURE 4-3 ▶
Posting from the General
Journal to the General Ledger

GENERAL JOURNAL   PAGE ___1___

	DATE		DESCRIPTION	POST. REF.	DEBIT	CREDIT	
1	2004						1
2	Nov.	6	Cash	101	80 0 0 0 00		2
3			Linda Carter, Capital	301		80 0 0 0 00	3
4			Investment by owner				4
5							5
6							
7							

ACCOUNT __Cash__   ACCOUNT NO. __101__

DATE		DESCRIPTION	POST. REF.	DEBIT	CREDIT	BALANCE DEBIT	BALANCE CREDIT
2004							
Nov.	6		J1	80 0 0 0 00		80 0 0 0 00	

ACCOUNT __Linda Carter, Capital__   ACCOUNT NO. __301__

DATE		DESCRIPTION	POST. REF.	DEBIT	CREDIT	BALANCE DEBIT	BALANCE CREDIT
2004							
Nov.	6		J1		80 0 0 0 00		80 0 0 0 00

About Accounting

Careers
How do you get to be the
president of a large corporation in the United States?
Probably by beginning your
career as an accountant.
More accountants have
advanced to be presidents
of large corporations than
people with any other
background.

Recall

Normal Balance
The normal balance of an account
is its increase side.

1. On the ledger form, enter the date of the transaction. Enter a description of the entry, if necessary. Usually routine entries do not require descriptions.

2. On the ledger form, enter the general journal page in the Posting Reference column. On the **Equipment** ledger form, the **J1** in the Posting Reference column indicates that the journal entry is recorded on page 1 of the general journal. The letter **J** refers to the general journal.

3. On the ledger form, enter the debit amount in the Debit column or the credit amount in the Credit column. In Figure 4-4 on the **Equipment** ledger form, $20,000 is entered in the Debit column.

4. On the ledger form, compute the balance and enter it in the Debit Balance column or the Credit Balance column. In Figure 4-4 the balance in the **Equipment** account is a $20,000 debit.

5. On the general journal, enter the ledger account number in the Posting Reference column. In Figure 4-4 the account number 141 is entered in the Posting Reference column next to "Equipment."

Repeat the process for the next account in the general journal. In Figure 4-4 Wilson posted the credit amount from the general journal to the **Cash** ledger account. Notice on the **Cash** ledger form that she entered the credit of $20,000 and then computed the account balance. After the transaction is posted, the balance of the **Cash** account is $60,000.

Be sure to enter the numbers in the Posting Reference columns. This indicates that the entry was posted and ensures against posting the same entry twice. Posting references are part of the audit trail. They allow a transaction to be traced from the ledger to the journal entry, and then to the source document.

Figure 4-5 on pages 108–109 shows the general ledger after all the entries for November and December are posted.

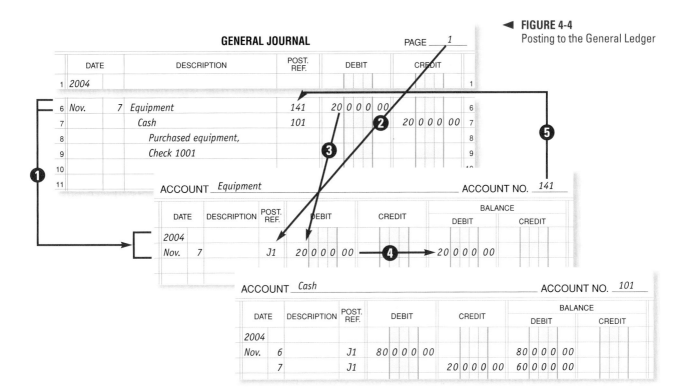

FIGURE 4-4 Posting to the General Ledger

Accounting
On The Job

Legal & Protective Services

Industry Overview

U.S. legal and protective services workers include lawyers, judicial workers, and persons trained in specialized community services like fire protection and law enforcement. The U.S. Department of Justice is the largest employer of law enforcement professionals.

Career Opportunities

- Tax Attorney
- Criminal Investigator
- Corrections Administrator
- Director of Emergency Services
- FBI Agent

Preparing for a Legal or Protective Services Career

- For a career in law:
  - Complete a four-year college degree, three years in law school, and the bar exam.
  - Develop skills in writing, speaking, researching, analyzing, and thinking logically.
  - Gain extensive accounting knowledge to specialize in tax law or corporate law.
  - Apply for a court clerkship.
- For a career in protective services:
  - Obtain a four-year degree, professional certification, or master's degree for specialized protective service careers.
  - For an entry level emergency services job, pass the Medical First Responder (MFR) certification test.

Thinking Critically

If you were a corporate attorney for an airline, what issues do you think you might be required to handle? Hint: Review news releases on companies' Web sites.

Internet Application

Use the Internet to research job responsibilities, education requirements, and recommended skills for one of the following: Paralegal, Fire Department Chief, Correctional Officer.

DATE		DESCRIPTION	POST. REF.	DEBIT	CREDIT	BALANCE	
						DEBIT	CREDIT
2004							
Nov.	6		J1	80 000 00		80 000 00	
	7		J1		20 000 00	60 000 00	
	28		J1		2 000 00	58 000 00	
	30		J1		3 000 00	55 000 00	
	30		J1		6 000 00	49 000 00	
Dec.	31		J2	21 000 00		70 000 00	
	31		J2	3 000 00		73 000 00	
	31		J2		5 000 00	68 000 00	
	31		J2		600 00	67 400 00	
	31		J2		3 000 00	64 400 00	

ACCOUNT _Accounts Receivable_   ACCOUNT NO. _111_

DATE		DESCRIPTION	POST. REF.	DEBIT	CREDIT	BALANCE	
						DEBIT	CREDIT
2004							
Dec.	31		J2	7 000 00		7 000 00	
	31		J2		3 000 00	4 000 00	

ACCOUNT _Supplies_   ACCOUNT NO. _121_

DATE		DESCRIPTION	POST. REF.	DEBIT	CREDIT	BALANCE	
						DEBIT	CREDIT
2004							
Nov.	28		J1	2 000 00		2 000 00	

ACCOUNT _Prepaid Rent_   ACCOUNT NO. _137_

DATE		DESCRIPTION	POST. REF.	DEBIT	CREDIT	BALANCE	
						DEBIT	CREDIT
2004							
Nov.	30		J1	6 000 00		6 000 00	

ACCOUNT _Equipment_   ACCOUNT NO. _141_

DATE		DESCRIPTION	POST. REF.	DEBIT	CREDIT	BALANCE	
						DEBIT	CREDIT
2004							
Nov.	7		J1	20 000 00		20 000 00	
	10		J1	15 000 00		35 000 00	

ACCOUNT _Accounts Payable_   ACCOUNT NO. _202_

DATE		DESCRIPTION	POST. REF.	DEBIT	CREDIT	BALANCE	
						DEBIT	CREDIT
2004							
Nov.	10		J1		15 000 00		15 000 00
	30		J1	3 000 00			12 000 00

FIGURE 4-5 ▶
Posted General Ledger Accounts

ACCOUNT Linda Carter, Capital   ACCOUNT NO. 301

DATE		DESCRIPTION	POST. REF.	DEBIT	CREDIT	BALANCE	
						DEBIT	CREDIT
2004							
Nov.	6		J1		80 000 00		80 000 00

ACCOUNT Linda Carter, Drawing   ACCOUNT NO. 302

DATE		DESCRIPTION	POST. REF.	DEBIT	CREDIT	BALANCE	
						DEBIT	CREDIT
2004							
Dec.	31		J2	3 000 00		3 000 00	

ACCOUNT Fees Income   ACCOUNT NO. 401

DATE		DESCRIPTION	POST. REF.	DEBIT	CREDIT	BALANCE	
						DEBIT	CREDIT
2004							
Dec.	31		J2		21 000 00		21 000 00
	31		J2		7 000 00		28 000 00

ACCOUNT Salaries Expense   ACCOUNT NO. 511

DATE		DESCRIPTION	POST. REF.	DEBIT	CREDIT	BALANCE	
						DEBIT	CREDIT
2004							
Dec.	31		J2	5 000 00		5 000 00	

ACCOUNT Utilities Expense   ACCOUNT NO. 514

DATE		DESCRIPTION	POST. REF.	DEBIT	CREDIT	BALANCE	
						DEBIT	CREDIT
2004							
Dec.	31		J2	600 00		600 00	

Each ledger account provides a complete record of the increases and decreases to that account. The balance ledger form also shows the current balance for the account.

In the general ledger accounts, the balance sheet accounts appear first and are followed by the income statement accounts. The order is:

- assets
- liabilities
- owner's equity
- revenue
- expenses

This arrangement speeds the preparation of the trial balance and the financial statements.

Order of Accounts
The general ledger lists accounts in the same order as they appear on the trial balance: assets, liabilities, owner's equity, revenue, and expenses.

Managerial IMPLICATIONS

Accounting Systems

- Business managers should be sure that their firms have efficient procedures for recording transactions.

- A well-designed accounting system allows timely and accurate posting of data to the ledger accounts.

- The information that appears in the financial statements is taken from the general ledger.

- Since management uses financial information for decision making, it is essential that the financial statements be prepared quickly at the end of each period and that they contain the correct amounts.

- The promptness and accuracy of the statements depend on the efficiency of the recording process.

- A well-designed accounting system has a strong audit trail.

- Every business should be able to trace amounts through the accounting records and back to the documents where the transactions were first recorded.

Thinking Critically

What are three situations you might encounter in which you need to "follow" the audit trail?

---

4 Objective

Correct errors made in the journal or ledger.

Correcting Journal and Ledger Errors

Sometimes errors are made when recording transactions in the journal. For example, a journal entry may show the wrong account name or amount. The method used to correct an error depends on whether or not the journal entry has been posted to the ledger:

- If the error is discovered *before* the entry is posted, neatly cross out the incorrect item and write the correct data above it. Do not erase the error. To ensure honesty and provide a clear audit trail, erasures are not made in the journal.

- If the error is discovered *after* posting, a **correcting entry**—a journal entry made to correct the erroneous entry—is journalized and posted. Do not erase or change the journal entry or the postings in the ledger accounts.

Note that erasures are never permitted in the journal or ledger.

Let's look at an example. On September 1 an automobile repair shop purchased some shop equipment for $8,000 in cash. By mistake the journal entry debited the **Office Equipment** account rather than the **Shop Equipment** account, as follows.

GENERAL JOURNAL PAGE _16_

	DATE	DESCRIPTION	POST. REF.	DEBIT	CREDIT	
1	2004					1
2	Sept.	1 Office Equipment	141	8 0 0 0 00		2
3		Cash	101		8 0 0 0 00	3
4		Purchased equipment,				4
5		Check 2141				5
6						6
7						7

The error was discovered after the entry was posted to the ledger. To correct the error, a correcting journal entry was prepared and posted. The correcting entry debits **Shop Equipment** and credits **Office Equipment** for $8,000. This entry transfers $8,000 out of the **Office Equipment** account and into the **Shop Equipment** account.

GENERAL JOURNAL PAGE _28_

	DATE	DESCRIPTION	POST. REF.	DEBIT	CREDIT	
1	2004					1
2	Oct.	1 Shop Equipment	151	8 0 0 0 00		2
3		Office Equipment	141		8 0 0 0 00	3
4		To correct error made on				4
5		Sept. 1 when a purchase				5
6		of shop equipment was				6
7		recorded as office				7
8		equipment				8
9						9

Suppose that the error was discovered before the journal entry was posted to the ledger. In that case the accountant would neatly cross out "Office Equipment" and write "Shop Equipment" above it. The correct account **(Shop Equipment)** would be posted to the ledger in the usual manner.

Section 2 Self Review

Questions

1. What is entered in the Posting Reference column of the general journal?

2. Why are posting references made in ledger accounts and in the journal?

3. Are the following statements true or false? Why?

   a. "If a journal entry that contains an error has been posted, erase the entry and change the posting in the ledger accounts."

   b. "Once an incorrect journal entry has been posted, the incorrect amounts remain in the general ledger accounts."

Exercises

4. The general ledger organizes accounting information in
   a. account order.
   b. alphabetical order.
   c. date order.

5. The general journal organizes accounting information in
   a. account order.
   b. alphabetical order.
   c. date order.

Analysis

6. Draw a diagram of the first three steps of the accounting cycle.

(Answers to Section 2 Self Review are on page 127.)

Review — Chapter Summary

In this chapter, you have studied the method for journalizing business transactions in the records of a company. The details of each transaction are then posted to the general ledger. A well-designed accounting system provides for prompt and accurate journalizing and posting of all transactions.

Learning Objectives

1 Record transactions in the general journal.
- Recording transactions in a journal is called journalizing, the second step in the accounting cycle.
  - A journal is a daily record of transactions.
  - A written analysis of each transaction is contained in a journal.
- The general journal is widely used in business. It can accommodate all kinds of business transactions. Use the following steps to record a transaction in the general journal:
  - Number each page in the general journal. The page number will be used as a posting reference.
  - Enter the year at the top of the Date column. After that, enter the year only when a new page is started or when the year changes.
  - Enter the month and day in the Date column of the first line of the first entry. After that, enter the month only when a new page is started or when the month changes. Always enter the day on the first line of a new entry.
  - Enter the name of the account to be debited in the Description column.
  - Enter the amount to be debited in the Debit column.
  - Enter the name of the account to be credited on the next line. Indent the account name about one-half inch.
  - Enter the amount to be credited in the Credit column.
  - Enter a complete but concise description on the next line. Indent the description about one inch.
- Note that the debit portion is always recorded first.
- If possible, include source document numbers in descriptions in order to create an audit trail.

2 Prepare compound journal entries.
A transaction might require a journal entry that contains several debits or credits. All debits are recorded first, followed by the credits.

3 Post journal entries to general ledger accounts.
- Posting to the general ledger is the third step in the accounting cycle. Posting is the transfer of data from journal entries to ledger accounts.
- The individual accounts together form a ledger. All the accounts needed to prepare financial statements are found in the general ledger.
- Use the following steps to post a transaction.
  - On the ledger form:
    1. Enter the date of the transaction. Enter the description, if necessary.
    2. Enter the posting reference in the Posting Reference column. When posting from the general journal, use the letter **J** followed by the general journal page number.
    3. Enter the amount in either the Debit column or the Credit column.
    4. Compute the new balance and enter it in either the Debit Balance column or the Credit Balance column.
  - On the general journal:
    5. Enter the ledger account number in the Posting Reference column.
- To summarize the steps of the accounting cycle discussed so far:
  1. Analyze transactions.
  2. Journalize transactions.
  3. Post transactions.

4 Correct errors made in the journal or ledger.
To ensure honesty and to provide a clear audit trail, erasures are not permitted in a journal. A correcting entry is journalized and posted to correct a previous mistake. Posting references in the journal and the ledger accounts cross reference the entries and form another part of the audit trail. They make it possible to trace or recheck any transaction.

5 Define the accounting terms new to this chapter.

CHAPTER 4 GLOSSARY

Accounting cycle (p. 96) A series of steps performed during each accounting period to classify, record, and summarize data for a business and to produce needed financial information

Audit trail (p. 97) A chain of references that makes it possible to trace information, locate errors, and prevent fraud

Balance ledger form (p. 105) A ledger account form that shows the balance of the account after each entry is posted

Chronological order (p. 96) Organized in the order in which the events occur

Compound entry (p. 103) A journal entry with more than one debit or credit

Correcting entry (p. 110) A journal entry made to correct an erroneous entry

General journal (p. 96) A financial record for entering all types of business transactions; a record of original entry

General ledger (p. 105) A permanent, classified record of all accounts used in a firm's operation; a record of final entry

Journal (p. 96) The record of original entry

Journalizing (p. 96) Recording transactions in a journal

Ledger (p. 105) The record of final entry

Posting (p. 105) Transferring data from a journal to a ledger

Comprehensive Self Review

1. Give examples of items that might appear in an audit trail.
2. Which of the following shows both the debits and credits of the entire transaction?
   a. An entry in the general journal
   b. A posting to a general ledger account
3. Why is the ledger called the "record of final entry"?
4. What is recorded in the Posting Reference column of a general journal?
5. How do you correct a journal entry that has not been posted?

(Answers to Comprehensive Self Review are on page 127.)

Discussion Questions

1. What is posting?
2. In what order are accounts arranged in the general ledger? Why?
3. What are posting references? Why are they used?
4. What is an audit trail? Why is it desirable to have an audit trail?
5. How should corrections be made in the general journal?
6. What is the accounting cycle?
7. What is the purpose of a journal?
8. What procedure is used to record an entry in the general journal?
9. What is the value of having a description for each general journal entry?
10. What is a compound journal entry?
11. What is a ledger?

Applications

EXERCISES

Exercise 4-1 ▶
Objective 1

Analyzing transactions.

Selected accounts from the general ledger of the Express Mail Service follow. Analyze the following transactions and indicate by number what accounts should be debited and credited for each transaction.

101 Cash
111 Accounts Receivable
121 Supplies
131 Equipment
202 Accounts Payable
301 Calvin Jefferson, Capital
401 Fees Income
511 Rent Expense
514 Salaries Expense
517 Utilities Expense

TRANSACTIONS

1. Issued a check for $1,700 to pay the monthly rent.
2. Purchased supplies for $1,000 on credit.
3. The owner made an additional investment of $16,000 in cash.
4. Collected $2,800 from credit customers.
5. Performed services for $3,900 in cash.
6. Issued a check for $1,500 to pay a creditor on account.
7. Purchased new equipment for $2,150 and paid for it immediately by check.
8. Provided services for $5,600 on credit.
9. Sent a check for $600 to the utility company to pay the monthly bill.
10. Gave a cash refund of $180 to a customer because of a lost package. (The customer had previously paid in cash.)

Exercise 4-2 ▶
Objective 1

Recording transactions in the general journal.

Selected accounts from the general ledger of Custom Decorating Company follow. Record the general journal entries that would be made to record the following transactions. Be sure to include dates and descriptions in these entries.

101 Cash
111 Accounts Receivable
121 Supplies
131 Equipment
141 Automobile
202 Accounts Payable
301 Dan Baxter, Capital
302 Dan Baxter, Drawing
401 Fees Income
511 Rent Expense
514 Salaries Expense
517 Telephone Expense

114 • **Chapter 4** *The General Journal and the General Ledger*

DATE	TRANSACTIONS
Sept. 1	Dan Baxter invested $26,000 in cash to start the firm.
4	Purchased office equipment for $5,800 on credit from Zen, Inc.; received Invoice 2398, payable in 30 days.
16	Purchased an automobile that will be used to visit clients; issued Check 1001 for $10,400 in full payment.
20	Purchased supplies for $160; paid immediately with Check 1002.
23	Returned damaged supplies for a cash refund of $50.
30	Issued Check 1003 for $2,800 to Zen, Inc., as payment on account for Invoice 2398.
30	Withdrew $1,000 in cash for personal expenses.
30	Issued Check 1004 for $600 to pay the rent for October.
30	Performed services for $850 in cash.
30	Paid $50 for monthly telephone bill, Check 1005.

Posting to the general ledger.

◀ **Exercise 4-3**
Objectives 1, 3

Post the journal entries that you prepared for Exercise 4-2 to the general ledger. Use the account names shown in Exercise 4-2.

Compound journal entries.

◀ **Exercise 4-4**
Objective 2

The following transactions took place at the Talent Search Agency during November 20--. Give the general journal entries that would be made to record these transactions. Use a compound entry for each transaction.

DATE	TRANSACTIONS
Nov. 5	Performed services for Screen Artist, Inc., for $16,000; received $6,000 in cash and the client promised to pay the balance in 60 days.
18	Purchased a graphing calculator for $150 and some supplies for $200 from Office Supply Center; issued Check 1008 for the total.
23	Received Invoice 2601 for $900 from Sam's Automotive Services for repairs to the firm's automobile; issued Check 1009 for half the amount and arranged to pay the other half in 30 days.

Recording a correcting entry.

◀ **Exercise 4-5**
Objective 4

On June 5, 20--, an employee of Harris Corporation mistakenly debited **Utilities Expense** rather than **Telephone Expense** when recording a bill of $450 for the May telephone service. The error was discovered on June 30. Prepare a general journal entry to correct the error.

Recording a correcting entry.

◀ **Exercise 4-6**
Objective 4

On August 16, 20--, an employee of Barker Company mistakenly debited the **Truck** account rather than the **Repair Expense** account when recording a bill of $345 for repairs. The error was discovered on September 1. Prepare a general journal entry to correct the error.

Problems

Selected problems can be completed using:
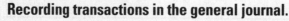
Peachtree   QuickBooks   Spreadsheets

PROBLEM SET A

Problem 4-1A ►
Objective 1

INSTRUCTIONS

Recording transactions in the general journal.

The transactions that follow took place at the Fitness Tennis Center during December 20--. This firm has indoor courts where customers can play tennis for a fee. It also rents equipment and offers tennis lessons.

Record each transaction in the general journal, using the following chart of accounts. Be sure to number the journal page 1 and to write the year at the top of the Date column. Include a description for each entry.

ASSETS

101 Cash
111 Accounts Receivable
121 Supplies
141 Equipment

LIABILITIES

202 Accounts Payable

OWNER'S EQUITY

301 Martina Garcia, Capital
302 Martina Garcia, Drawing

REVENUE

401 Fees Income

EXPENSES

511 Equipment Repair Expense
512 Rent Expense
513 Salaries Expense
514 Telephone Expense
517 Utilities Expense

DATE		TRANSACTIONS
Dec.	1	Issued Check 2169 for $1,150 to pay the December rent.
	5	Performed services for $2,200 in cash.
	6	Performed services for $1,950 on credit.
	10	Paid $120 for monthly telephone bill; issued Check 2170.
	11	Paid for equipment repairs of $105 with Check 2171.
	12	Received $600 on account from credit clients.
	15	Issued Checks 2172–2177 for $3,200 for salaries.
	18	Issued Check 2178 for $250 to purchase supplies.
	19	Purchased new tennis rackets for $1,850 on credit from The Sports Shop; received Invoice 1133, payable in 30 days.
	20	Issued Check 2179 for $490 to purchase new nets. (Equip.)
	21	Received $650 on account from credit clients.
	21	Returned a damaged net and received a cash refund of $106.
	22	Performed services for $2,980 in cash.
	23	Performed services for $3,520 on credit.
	26	Issued Check 2180 for $280 to purchase supplies.
	28	Paid the monthly electric bill of $475 with Check 2181.
		Continued

DATE	4-1A (cont.)	TRANSACTIONS
Dec. 31		Issued Checks 2182–2187 for $3,200 for salaries.
31		Issued Check 2188 for $500 cash to Martina Garcia for personal expenses.

Analyze: If the company paid a bill for supplies on January 1, what check number would be included in the journal entry description?

Journalizing and posting transactions.

On October 1, 20--, Cathy Landers opened an advertising agency. She plans to use the chart of accounts listed below.

◄ **Problem 4-2A**
Objectives 1, 2, 3

INSTRUCTIONS

1. Journalize the transactions. Number the journal page 1, write the year at the top of the Date column, and include a description for each entry.
2. Post to the ledger accounts. Before you start the posting process, open accounts by entering account names and numbers in the headings. Follow the order of the accounts in the chart of accounts.

ASSETS
101 Cash
111 Accounts Receivable
121 Supplies
141 Office Equipment
151 Art Equipment

LIABILITIES
202 Accounts Payable

OWNER'S EQUITY
301 Cathy Landers, Capital
302 Cathy Landers, Drawing

REVENUE
401 Fees Income

EXPENSES
511 Office Cleaning Expense
514 Rent Expense
517 Salaries Expense
520 Telephone Expense
523 Utilities Expense

DATE	TRANSACTIONS
Oct. 1	Cathy Landers invested $60,000 cash in the business.
2	Paid October office rent of $1,900; issued Check 1001.
5	Purchased desks and other office furniture for $12,000 from Discount Mart, Inc.; received Invoice 4767 payable in 60 days.
6	Issued Check 1002 for $3,900 to purchase art equipment.
7	Purchased supplies for $700; paid with Check 1003.
10	Issued Check 1004 for $210 for office cleaning service.
12	Performed services for $1,600 in cash and $4,300 on credit. (Use a compound entry.)
15	Returned damaged supplies for a cash refund of $150.
18	Purchased a computer for $2,100 from Discount Mart, Inc., Invoice 5003; issued Check 1005 for a $1,050 down payment, with the balance payable in 30 days. (Use one compound entry.)
	Continued

DATE	4-2A (cont.) TRANSACTIONS
Oct. 20	Issued Check 1006 for $6,000 to Discount Mart, Inc., as payment on account for Invoice 4767.
26	Performed services for $2,750 on credit.
27	Paid $230 for monthly telephone bill; issued Check 1007.
30	Received $1,600 in cash from credit customers.
30	Mailed Check 1008 to pay the monthly utility bill of $696.
30	Issued Checks 1009–1011 for $5,750 for salaries.

Analyze: What is the balance of account 202 in the general ledger?

Problem 4-3A ►
Objective 4

Recording correcting entries.

The following journal entries were prepared by an employee of ABC Company who does not have an adequate knowledge of accounting.

INSTRUCTIONS

Examine the journal entries carefully to locate the errors. Provide a brief written description of each error. Assume that **Office Equipment** and **Office Supplies** were recorded at the correct values.

GENERAL JOURNAL   PAGE ___3___

	DATE		DESCRIPTION	POST. REF.	DEBIT	CREDIT	
1	20--						1
2	Mar.	1	Accounts Payable		2 6 0 0 00		2
3			Fees Income			2 6 0 0 00	3
4			Performed services on credit				4
5							5
6		2	Cash		2 2 0 00		6
7			Telephone Expense			2 2 0 00	7
8			Paid for February telephone				8
9			service, Check 1801				9
10							10
11		3	Office Equipment		4 5 0 0 00		11
12			Office Supplies		5 0 0 00		12
13			Cash			5 2 0 0 00	13
14			Purchased file cabinet and				14
15			office supplies, Check 1802				15
16							16
17							17
18							18
19							19

Analyze: After the correcting journal entries have been posted, what effect do the corrections have on the company's reported assets?

Journalizing and posting transactions.

Four transactions for Traditions Repair Service that took place in November 20-- appear below, along with the general ledger accounts used by the company.

◀ **Problem 4-4A**
Objectives 1, 2, 3

INSTRUCTIONS

Record the transactions in the general journal and post them to the appropriate ledger accounts. Be sure to number the journal page 1 and to write the year at the top of the Date column.

Cash	101	Accounts Payable	202
Accounts Receivable	111	Barbara Doyle, Capital	301
Office Supplies	121	Fees Income	401
Tools	131		
Machinery	141		
Equipment	151		

DATE		TRANSACTIONS
Nov.	1	Barbara Doyle invested $12,500 in cash plus tools with a fair market value of $250 to start the business.
	2	Purchased equipment for $750 and supplies for $250 from Office Ready, Invoice 110; issued Check 100 for $250 as a down payment with the balance due in 30 days.
	10	Performed services for Brian Marshall for $750, who paid $250 in cash with the balance due in 30 days.
	20	Purchased machinery for $1,250 from Zant Machinery, Inc., Invoice 850; issued Check 101 for $250 in cash as a down payment with the balance due in 30 days.

Analyze: What liabilities does the business owe as of November 30?

PROBLEM SET B

Recording transactions in the general journal.

The transactions listed on page 120 took place at Chang Commercial Cleaning Service during October 20--. This firm cleans commercial buildings for a fee.

◀ **Problem 4-1B**
Objective 1

INSTRUCTIONS

Analyze and record each transaction in the general journal. Choose the account names from the chart of accounts shown below. Be sure to number the journal page 1 and to write the year at the top of the Date column.

ASSETS

101 Cash
111 Accounts Receivable
141 Equipment

LIABILITIES

202 Accounts Payable

OWNER'S EQUITY

301 Raymond Chang, Capital
302 Raymond Chang, Drawing

REVENUE

401 Fees Income

EXPENSES

501 Cleaning Supplies Expense
502 Equipment Repair Expense
503 Office Supplies Expense
511 Rent Expense
514 Salaries Expense
521 Telephone Expense
524 Utilities Expense

DATE		TRANSACTIONS
Oct.	1	Raymond Chang invested $36,000 in cash to start the business.
	5	Performed services for $2,400 in cash.
	6	Issued Check 1000 for $1,700 to pay the October rent.
	7	Performed services for $1,800 on credit.
	9	Paid $300 for monthly telephone bill; issued Check 1001.
	10	Issued Check 1002 for $240 for equipment repairs.
	12	Received $850 from credit clients.
	14	Issued Checks 1003–1004 for $7,200 to pay salaries.
	18	Issued Check 1005 for $600 for cleaning supplies.
	19	Issued Check 1006 for $500 for office supplies.
	20	Purchased equipment for $5,000 from Casey's Equipment, Inc., Invoice 2010; issued Check 1007 for $1,000 with the balance due in 30 days.
	22	Performed services for $3,950 in cash.
	24	Issued Check 1008 for $380 for the monthly electric bill.
	26	Performed services for $1,800 on account.
	30	Issued Checks 1009–1010 for $7,200 to pay salaries.
	30	Issued Check 1011 for $2,000 to Raymond Chang to pay for personal expenses.

Analyze: How many transactions affected expense accounts?

Problem 4-2B ►
Objectives 1, 2, 3

Journalizing and posting transactions.

In July 20-- Richard Hailey opened a photography studio that provides services to public and private schools. His firm's financial activities for the first month of operations are listed on page 121. The chart of accounts appears below.

INSTRUCTIONS

1. Journalize the transactions. Number the journal page 1 and write the year at the top of the Date column. Describe each entry.

2. Post to the ledger accounts. Before you start the posting process, open the accounts by entering the names and numbers in the headings. Follow the order of the accounts in the chart of accounts.

ASSETS

101 Cash
111 Accounts Receivable
121 Supplies
141 Office Equipment
151 Photographic Equipment

LIABILITIES

202 Accounts Payable

OWNER'S EQUITY

301 Richard Hailey, Capital
302 Richard Hailey, Drawing

REVENUE

401 Fees Income

EXPENSES

511 Office Cleaning Expense
514 Rent Expense
517 Salaries Expense
520 Telephone Expense
523 Utilities Expense

DATE		TRANSACTIONS
July	1	Richard Hailey invested $28,000 cash in the business.
	2	Issued Check 1001 for $800 to pay the July rent.
	5	Purchased desks and other office furniture for $6,500 from Craft, Inc.; received Invoice 4762, payable in 60 days.
	6	Issued Check 1002 for $1,600 to purchase photographic equipment.
	7	Purchased supplies for $416; paid with Check 1003.
	10	Issued Check 1004 for $110 for office cleaning service.
	12	Performed services for $600 in cash and $1,300 on credit. (Use one compound entry.)
	15	Returned damaged supplies; received a $60 cash refund.
	18	Purchased a computer for $1,050 from Brown Office Supply, Invoice 430; issued Check 1005 for a $250 down payment. The balance is payable in 30 days. (Use one compound entry.)
	20	Issued Check 1006 for $3,250 to Craft, Inc., as payment on account for office furniture, Invoice 4762.
	26	Performed services for $1,400 on credit.
	27	Paid $120 for monthly telephone bill; issued Check 1007.
	30	Received $1,100 in cash from credit clients on account.
	30	Issued Check 1008 to pay the monthly utility bill of $250.
	30	Issued Checks 1009–1011 for $4,800 for salaries.

Analyze: What was the **Cash** account balance after the transaction of July 20 was recorded?

Recording correcting entries.

All the journal entries shown on page 122 contain errors. The entries were prepared by an employee of Becknell Corporation who does not have an adequate knowledge of accounting.

Examine the journal entries carefully to locate the errors. Provide a brief written description of each error. Assume that **Office Equipment** and **Office Supplies** were recorded at the correct values.

◄ **Problem 4-3B**
Objective 4

_____

INSTRUCTIONS

GENERAL JOURNAL

PAGE ___1___

	DATE		DESCRIPTION	POST. REF.	DEBIT	CREDIT	
1	20--						1
2	Jan.	1	Accounts Payable		7 5 0 00		2
3			Fees Income			7 5 0 00	3
4			Performed services on credit				4
5							5
6		2	Cash		6 5 00		6
7			Telephone Expense			6 5 00	7
8			Paid for January telephone				8
9			service, Check 1706				9
10							10
11		3	Office Equipment		6 7 5 00		11
12			Office Supplies		8 5 00		12
13			Cash			7 0 0 00	13
14			Purchased file cabinet and				14
15			office supplies, Check 1707				15
16			*Cash*		60 00		16

add →

Analyze: After the correcting journal entries have been posted, what effect do the corrections have on the reported assets of the company?

Problem 4-4B ►
Objectives 1, 2, 3

INSTRUCTIONS

Journalizing and posting transactions.

Several transactions that occurred during December 20--, the first month of operation for Louise's Accounting Services, follow. The company uses the general ledger accounts listed below.

Record the transactions in the general journal (page 1) and post to the appropriate accounts.

Cash	101	Accounts Payable	202
Accounts Receivable	111	Louise Hodges, Capital	301
Office Supplies	121	Fees Income	401
Computers	131		
Office Equipment	141		
Furniture & Fixtures	151		

DATE		TRANSACTIONS
Dec.	3	Louise Hodges began business by depositing $20,000 cash into a business checking account.
	4	Purchased a computer for $4,400 cash.
	5	Purchased furniture and fixtures on account for $6,000.
	6	Purchased office equipment for $1,190 cash.
	10	Rendered services to client and sent bill for $1,000.
	11	Purchased office supplies for $450.
	15	Received invoice for furniture purchased on December 5 and paid it.

Analyze: Describe the activity for account 202 during the month.

Start-Up Business

On June 1, 20--, Darren McDonald opened the Dance and Voice Agency.
He plans to use the chart of accounts given below.

INSTRUCTIONS

1. Journalize the transactions. Be sure to number the journal pages and write the year at the top of the Date column. Include a description for each entry.

2. Post to the ledger accounts. Before you start the posting process, open the accounts by entering the account names and numbers in the headings. Using the list of accounts below, assign appropriate account numbers and place them in the correct order in the ledger.

3. Prepare a trial balance.

4. Prepare the income statement.

5. Prepare a statement of owner's equity.

6. Prepare the balance sheet.

ACCOUNTS

Accounts Payable	Darren McDonald, Drawing
Office Furniture	Recording Equipment
Accounts Receivable	Rent Expense
Advertising Expense	Salaries Expense
Cash	Supplies
Fees Income	Telephone Expense
Darren McDonald, Capital	Utilities Expense

DATE		TRANSACTIONS
June	1	Darren McDonald invested $40,000 cash to start the business.
	2	Issued Check 301 for $1,600 to pay the June rent for the office.
	3	Purchased desk and other office furniture for $10,000 from Lawson Office Supply, Invoice 3105; issued Check 302 for a $2,000 down payment with the balance due in 30 days.
	4	Issued Check 303 for $1,800 for supplies.
	6	Performed services for $5,000 in cash.
	7	Issued Check 304 for $1,000 to pay for advertising expense.
	8	Purchased recording equipment for $12,000 from Top Ten Dance and Sounds, Inc., Invoice 3330; issued Check 305 for a down payment of $4,000 with the balance due in 30 days.
	10	Performed services for $3,700 on account.
	11	Issued Check 306 for $2,000 to Lawson Office Supply as payment on account.
	12	Performed services for $6,000 in cash.
		Continued

DATE	(cont.)	TRANSACTIONS
15		Issued Check 307 for $4,000 to pay an employee's salary.
18		Received payments of $2,000 from credit clients on account.
20		Issued Check 308 for $3,000 to Top Ten Dance and Sounds, Inc. as payment on account.
25		Issued Check 309 in the amount of $750 for the monthly telephone bill.
27		Issued Check 310 in the amount of $900 for the monthly electric bill.
28		Issued Check 311 to Darren McDonald for $3,000 for personal living expenses.
30		Issued Check 312 for $4,000 to pay salary of an employee.

Analyze: How many postings were made to the **Cash** account?

CHAPTER 4 CRITICAL THINKING PROBLEM

Financial Statements

Jim Hall is a new staff accountant for Sutton Cleaning Chemicals. He has asked you to review the financial statements prepared for April to find and correct any errors. Review the income statement and balance sheet that follow and identify the errors Hall made (he did not prepare a statement of owner's equity). Prepare a corrected income statement and balance sheet as well as a statement of owner's equity, for Sutton Cleaning Chemicals.

Sutton Cleaning Chemicals
Income Statement
April 30, 20--

Revenue		
Fees Income		6 2 0 0 00
Expenses		
Salaries Expense	2 2 5 0 00	
Rent Expense	4 5 0 00	
Repair Expense	7 5 00	
Utilities Expense	6 5 0 00	
Drawing	1 0 0 0 00	
Total Expenses		4 4 2 5 00
Net Income		10 6 2 5 00

Sutton Cleaning Chemicals
Balance Sheet
Month Ended April 30, 20--

Assets		Liabilities	
Land	5 0 0 0 00	Accounts Receivable	2 5 0 0 00
Building	15 0 0 0 00		
Cash	6 7 7 5 00	Owner's Equity	
Accounts Payable	2 5 0 0 00	Scott Jones, Capital, April 1, 20--	25 0 0 0 00
Total Assets	29 2 7 5 00	Total Liabilities and Owner's Equity	27 5 0 0 00

Business Connections

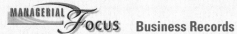

Business Records

◄ **Connection 1**

1. The owner of a new business recently questioned the accountant about the value of having both a journal and a ledger. The owner believes that it is a waste of effort to enter data about transactions in two different records. How would you explain the value of having both records?

2. Why should management insist that a firm's accounting system have a strong audit trail?

3. Why should management be concerned about the efficiency of a firm's procedures for journalizing and posting transactions?

4. How might a poor set of recording procedures affect the flow of information to management?

Ethical DILEMMA **Testing** You and your roommate are taking principles of accounting from the same professor but at different times. After the first exam, you discover that the professor gives the same exam to both sections. Your roommate has not been studying as much since this discovery and is depending on you to furnish him with the answers to questions on the second exam. What will you do?

◄ **Connection 2**

Street WISE:
Questions from the Real World **General Ledger Accounts** Refer to The Home Depot, Inc. *1999 Annual Report* in Appendix B.

◄ **Connection 3**

1. Review the report called *Selected Consolidated Statements of Earnings Data*. How many sales transactions were reported for 1999? For sales on account transactions, which accounts would be affected when the transactions are recorded?

2. Based on the financial statements, which account categories would be affected by the following transactions?
   a. Paid $5,000 cash for store rent.
   b. Paid $2,000 cash for store utility bill.
   c. Received $1,000 from a customer in payment of their account.

FINANCIAL STATEMENT ANALYSIS **Balance Sheet** Review the following excerpt taken from the Wal-Mart Stores, Inc. consolidated balance sheet as of January 31, 2000.

◄ **Connection 4**
WAL★MART

(Amounts in millions) January 31, 2000	
Property, Plant and Equipment at cost:	
Land	$ 8,785
Building and improvements	21,169
Fixtures and equipment	10,362
Transportation equipment	747

Analyze:

1. When the accountant for Wal-Mart Stores, Inc. records a purchase of transportation equipment, what type of account is debited? If Wal-Mart purchases transportation equipment on credit, what account might be credited?

2. What type of source document might be reflected in the journal entry to record the purchase of equipment?

3. If the accounting manager reviewed the **Transportation Equipment** account in the general ledger, what types of information might be listed there? What ending balance would be reflected at January 31, 2000?

Analyze Online: Locate the Web site for the Wal-Mart Stores, Inc. (**www.walmartstores.com**), which provides an online store for consumers as well as corporation information. Within the Web site, locate the consolidated balance sheet for the current year.

4. What kinds of property, plant, and equipment are listed on the balance sheet?

5. What is the balance reported for transportation equipment?

Connection 5 ▶ *Extending* the *Thought* **Getting Organized** Business transactions are recorded in a financial record called a journal. List and discuss other organizational records and devices used in everyday life. Why are these records and devices used? What similarities do these records share with the journal used in accounting?

Connection 6 ▶ **Business Communication** **Training Manual** You have been asked to teach a new accounting clerk how to journalize business transactions. Create a written step-by-step guide to give to the new accounting clerk on his first day at work. Use a sample business transaction of your choice to illustrate the process.

Connection 7 ▶ **Team***Work* **Interview** Business owners use financial information to prepare for future operations and to make business decisions. As a team, choose a local business in your area and interview the owner or manager to discover how financial data has influenced the operations of the business. First, make a list of questions to ask the business owner. Prepare a summary report of your findings.

Connection 8 ▶ *inter* **NET** **CONNECTION** **SEC** The Securities and Exchange Commission is an independent regulatory agency that administers the federal laws related to securities such as stock in corporations. Go to **www.sec.gov** and select *Investor Education*. Search terms for *Annual Report*. What information is usually contained in an annual report? What is a Form 10K? What is an IPO?

Answers to Section 1 Self Review

1. To provide an audit trail to trace information through the accounting system.
2. No. The only requirement is that the total debits must equal the total credits.
3. It is the first accounting record where transactions are entered.
4. **c.** diary.
5. **c.** debit.
6. The audit trail will not exist.

Answers to Section 2 Self Review

1. The ledger account number.
2. They indicate that the entry has been posted and ensure against posting the same entry twice.
3. Both statements are false. If an incorrect journal entry was posted, a correcting entry should be journalized and posted. To ensure honesty and provide a clear audit trail, erasures are not permitted in the journal.
4. **a.** account order.
5. **c.** date order.
6.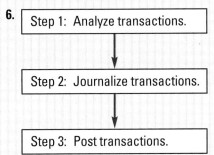

Answers to Comprehensive Self Review

1. Check number
   Invoice number for goods purchased on credit from a vendor
   Invoice number for services billed to a charge account customer
   Memorandum number
2. **a.** An entry in the general journal
3. It is the last accounting record in which a transaction is recorded.
4. The general ledger account number.
5. Neatly cross out the incorrect item and write the correct data above it.

CHAPTER 5

Learning Objectives

1. Complete a trial balance on a worksheet.

2. Prepare adjustments for unrecorded business transactions.

3. Complete the worksheet.

4. Prepare an income statement, statement of owner's equity, and balance sheet from the completed worksheet.

5. Journalize and post the adjusting entries.

6. Define the accounting terms new to this chapter.

Adjustments and the Worksheet

www.boeing.com

The construction and development of the International Space Station (ISS) has been characterized by Boeing Chairman and CEO Phil Condit as "one of the most complex and challenging projects ever undertaken."[1] Boeing is the ISS's prime contractor.

In early 2001 the Boeing-built *Destiny* laboratory was successfully installed on the ISS, providing a shirtsleeve workstation environment where science experiments can be performed in the near zero gravity of space. *Destiny* also provides command and control capabilities as well as maintenance of the proper orientation of the outpost.

Efforts in the space and communications sectors have proven successful for the company. In the first quarter of 2001, the Space and Communications division reported a 35 percent increase in revenue as compared to the first quarter of 2000.

[1] Boeing Web site: International Space Station/Boeing's Role

Thinking Critically
How do you think the company accounts for the wear and tear of its own equipment?

For more information on Boeing, go to: collegeaccounting.glencoe.com.

New Terms

Account form balance sheet
Adjusting entries
Adjustments
Book value
Contra account
Contra asset account

Depreciation
Prepaid expenses
Report form balance sheet
Salvage value
Straight-line depreciation
Worksheet

1 **Complete a trial balance on a worksheet.**

WHY IT'S IMPORTANT
Time and effort can be saved when the trial balance is prepared directly on the worksheet. Amounts can be easily transferred to other sections of the worksheet.

2 **Prepare adjustments for unrecorded business transactions.**

WHY IT'S IMPORTANT
Not all business transactions occur between separate business entities. Some financial events occur within a business and need to be recorded.

Terms to Learn

adjusting entries
adjustments
book value
contra account
contra asset account
depreciation
prepaid expenses
salvage value
straight-line depreciation
worksheet

The Worksheet

Financial statements are completed as soon as possible in order to be useful. One way to speed the preparation of financial statements is to use a worksheet. A **worksheet** is a form used to gather all data needed at the end of an accounting period to prepare the financial statements. Preparation of the worksheet is the fourth step in the accounting cycle.

Figure 5-1 shows a common type of worksheet. The heading shows the company name, report title, and period covered. In addition to the Account Name column, this worksheet contains five sections: Trial Balance, Adjustments, Adjusted Trial Balance, Income Statement, and Balance Sheet. Each section includes a Debit column and a Credit column. The worksheet has 10 columns in which to enter dollar amounts.

The Trial Balance Section

Refer to Figure 5-2 on page 132 as you read about how to prepare the Trial Balance section of the worksheet.

1. Enter the general ledger account names.
2. Transfer the general ledger account balances to the Debit and Credit columns of the Trial Balance section.
3. Total the Debit and Credit columns to prove that the trial balance is in balance.
4. Place a double rule under each Trial Balance column to show that the work in that column is complete.

Notice that the trial balance has four new accounts: **Accumulated Depreciation—Equipment, Supplies Expense, Rent Expense,** and **Depreciation Expense—Equipment.** These accounts have zero balances now, but they will be needed later as the worksheet is completed.

The Adjustments Section

Usually account balances change because of transactions with other businesses or individuals. For Carter Consulting Services, the account changes recorded in Chapter 4 were caused by transactions with the

1 **Objective**
Complete a trial balance on a worksheet.

Trial Balance
If total debits do not equal total credits, there is an error in the financial records. The error must be found and corrected.

	ACCOUNT NAME	TRIAL BALANCE		ADJUSTMENTS	
		DEBIT	CREDIT	DEBIT	CREDIT
1					
2					
3					
4					
5					

Carter Consulting Services
Worksheet
Month Ended December 31, 2004

firm's suppliers, customers, the landlord, and employees. It is easy to recognize, journalize, and post these transactions as they occur.

Some changes are not caused by transactions with other businesses or individuals. They arise from the internal operations of the firm during the accounting period. Journal entries made to update accounts for previously unrecorded items are called **adjustments** or **adjusting entries**. These changes are first entered on the worksheet at the end of each accounting period. The worksheet provides a convenient form for gathering the information and determining the effects of the changes. Let's look at the adjustments made by Carter Consulting Services on December 31, 2004.

Adjusting for Supplies Used

On November 28, 2004, Carter Consulting Services purchased $2,000 of supplies. On December 31 the trial balance shows a $2,000 balance in the **Supplies** account. This amount is too high because some of the supplies were used during December.

An adjustment must be made for the supplies used. Otherwise, the asset account, **Supplies,** is overstated because fewer supplies are actually on hand. The expense account, **Supplies Expense,** is understated. The cost of the supplies used represents an operating expense that has not been recorded.

On December 31 Beatrice Wilson counted the supplies. Remaining supplies totaled $1,500. This meant that supplies amounting to $500 were used during December ($2,000 − $1,500 = $500). At the end of December, an adjustment must be made to reflect the supplies used. The adjustment reduces the **Supplies** account to $1,500, the amount of supplies remaining. It increases the **Supplies Expense** account by $500 for the amount of supplies used. Notice that the adjustment for supplies is based on actual usage.

Refer to Figure 5-2 on page 132 to review the adjustment on the worksheet: a debit of $500 to **Supplies Expense** and a credit of $500 to **Supplies.** Both the debit and credit are labeled **(a)** to identify the two parts of the adjustment.

Supplies is a type of prepaid expense. **Prepaid expenses** are items that are acquired and paid for in advance of their use. Other common prepaid expenses are prepaid rent, prepaid insurance, and prepaid advertising. When cash is paid for these items, amounts are debited to **Prepaid Rent, Prepaid Insurance,** and **Prepaid Advertising;** all are asset accounts. As prepaid expenses are used, an adjustment is made to reduce the asset accounts and to increase the related expense accounts.

❷ Objective
Prepare adjustments for unrecorded business transactions.

Trial Balance
On the trial balance, accounts are listed in this order: assets, liabilities, owner's equity, revenue, and expenses.

About Accounting

E-business
E-commerce and e-business are not the same thing. *E-commerce* is only a small piece of e-business. *E-business* relates to automating an entire company and all its business processes, including electronic transaction workflows, online storefronts, self-service data access, and the reengineering of business processes.

◀ **FIGURE 5-1**
Ten-column Worksheet

	ADJUSTED TRIAL BALANCE		INCOME STATEMENT		BALANCE SHEET		
	DEBIT	CREDIT	DEBIT	CREDIT	DEBIT	CREDIT	
							1
							2
							3
							4
							5

	ACCOUNT NAME	TRIAL BALANCE		ADJUSTMENTS	
		DEBIT	CREDIT	DEBIT	CREDIT
1	Cash	64 4 0 0 00			
2	Accounts Receivable	4 0 0 0 00			
3	Supplies	2 0 0 0 00			(a) 5 0 0 00
4	Prepaid Rent	6 0 0 0 00			(b) 3 0 0 0 00
5	Equipment	35 0 0 0 00			
6	Accumulated Depreciation—Equipment				(c) 5 8 3 00
7	Accounts Payable		12 0 0 0 00		
8	Linda Carter, Capital		80 0 0 0 00		
9	Linda Carter, Drawing	3 0 0 0 00			
10	Fees Income		28 0 0 0 00		
11	Salaries Expense	5 0 0 0 00			
12	Utilities Expense	6 0 0 00			
13	Supplies Expense			(a) 5 0 0 00	
14	Rent Expense			(b) 3 0 0 0 00	
15	Depreciation Expense—Equipment			(c) 5 8 3 00	
16	Totals	120 0 0 0 00	120 0 0 0 00	4 0 8 3 00	4 0 8 3 00
17					

▲ **FIGURE 5-2** A Partial Worksheet

Adjustment

Record the adjustment for supplies.

Analysis

The expense account, **Supplies Expense,** is increased by $500. The asset account, **Supplies,** is decreased by $500.

Debit-Credit Rules

DEBIT Increases to expense accounts are recorded as debits. Debit **Supplies Expense** for $500.

CREDIT Decreases to asset accounts are recorded as credits. Credit **Supplies** for $500.

T-Account Presentation

Supplies Expense		Supplies	
+	−	+	−
500			500

Let's review the effect of the adjustment on the asset account, **Supplies.** Recall that the **Supplies** account already had a balance of $2,000. If no adjustment is made, the balance would remain at $2,000, even though only $1,500 of supplies are left.

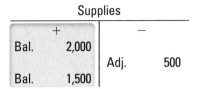

Supplies

	+		−	
Bal.	2,000			
		Adj.	500	
Bal.	1,500			

Adjusting for Expired Rent

On November 30, 2004, Carter Consulting Services paid $6,000 rent for December and January. The right to occupy facilities for the specified period is an asset. The $6,000 was debited to **Prepaid Rent,** an asset account. On December 31, 2004, the **Prepaid Rent** balance is $6,000. This is too high because one month of rent has been used. The expired rent is $3,000 ($6,000 ÷ 2 months). At the end of December, an adjustment is made to reflect the expired rent.

Adjustment

Record the adjustment for expired rent.

Analysis

The expense account, **Rent Expense,** is increased by $3,000. The asset account, **Prepaid Rent,** is decreased by $3,000.

Debit-Credit Rules

DEBIT Increases to expense accounts are recorded as debits. Debit **Rent Expense** for $3,000.

CREDIT Decreases to asset accounts are recorded as credits. Credit **Prepaid Rent** for $3,000.

T-Account Presentation

Rent Expense			Prepaid Rent	
+	−		+	−
3,000				3,000

Let's review the effect of the adjustment on the asset account, **Prepaid Rent.** The beginning balance of $6,000 represents prepaid rent for the months of December and January. By December 31, the prepaid rent for the month of December is "used up." The adjustment reducing **Prepaid Rent** recognizes the expense of occupying the facilities in December. The $3,000 ending balance represents prepaid rent for the month of January.

Prepaid Rent

	+		−	
Bal.	6,000			
		Adj.	3,000	
Bal.	3,000			

Important!

Prepaid Expense
Prepaid rent is recorded as an asset at the time it is paid. As time elapses, the asset is used up. An adjustment is made to reduce the asset and to recognize rent expense.

Computers in Accounting

Computerized Accounting Systems

Computerized systems are widely used by companies to record, summarize, and analyze large volumes of financial data. From the Disney corporate offices in Burbank, California, to the Southwest Airlines headquarters in Dallas, Texas, accountants prepare paychecks, track bank accounts, and generate financial statements using computerized applications. Accounting systems can be standard commercial packages or customized to fit the unique needs of a company. Six common types of accounting applications are available: general ledger, accounts receivable, accounts payable, sales/order processing, inventory control, and payroll.

General ledger programs are basic to any computerized accounting system and are used to record general journal entries. Posting is completed automatically by the computer. The accountant can easily generate reports such as the trial balance, income statement, balance sheet, or statement of owner's equity. At the end of the accounting period, the general ledger program will complete the closing process, preparing the records for the next accounting period.

Other programs provide tools to the accountant for managing accounts receivable, accounts payable, payroll, and inventory.

Companies may use one or more of these accounting applications, or they may build or purchase a completely integrated package of applications. An "integrated" accounting system means that each module, or application, communicates and transfers data to other modules, keeping the accounting records in balance across all programs.

Thinking Critically

What benefits can you identify to using an integrated computerized accounting system?

Internet Application

Using an Internet search engine, locate information on the general ledger module for AccuBooks accounting software. Create a summary report describing the features of the general ledger module.

Refer to Figure 5-2 to review the adjustment on the worksheet: a debit of $3,000 to **Rent Expense** and a credit of $3,000 to **Prepaid Rent.** Both parts of the adjustment are labeled **(b).**

Adjusting for Depreciation

There is one more adjustment to make at the end of December. It involves the equipment purchased in November. The cost of long-term assets such as equipment is not recorded as an expense when purchased. Instead the cost is recorded as an asset and spread over the time the assets are used for the business. **Depreciation** is the process of allocating the cost of long-term assets over their expected useful lives. There are many ways to calculate depreciation. Carter Consulting Services uses the **straight-line depreciation** method. This method results in an equal amount of depreciation being charged to each accounting period during the asset's useful life. The formula for straight-line depreciation is

$$\text{Depreciation} = \frac{\text{Cost} - \text{Salvage value}}{\text{Estimated useful life}}$$

Salvage value is an estimate of the amount that may be received by selling or disposing of an asset at the end of its useful life.

Carter Consulting Services purchased $35,000 worth of equipment. The equipment has an estimated useful life of five years and no salvage value. The depreciation for December, the first month of operations, is $583 (rounded).

$$\frac{\$35,000 - \$0}{60 \text{ months}} = \$583 \text{ (rounded)}$$

1. Convert the asset's useful life from years to months: 5 years × 12 months = 60 months.
2. Divide the total depreciation to be taken by the total number of months: $35,000 ÷ 60 = $583 (rounded).
3. Record depreciation expense of $583 each month for the next 60 months.

> Conoco Inc. depreciates property such as refinery equipment, pipelines, and deepwater drill ships on a straight-line basis over the estimated life of each asset, ranging from 15 to 25 years.

As the cost of the equipment is gradually transferred to expense, its recorded value as an asset must be reduced. This procedure cannot be carried out by directly decreasing the balance in the asset account. Generally accepted accounting principles require that the original cost of a long-term asset continue to appear in the asset account until the firm has used up or disposed of the asset.

The adjustment for depreciation is recorded in a contra account named **Accumulated Depreciation—Equipment.** A **contra account** has a normal balance that is opposite that of a related account. For example, the **Equipment** account is an asset and has a normal debit balance. **Accumulated Depreciation—Equipment** is a **contra asset account** with a normal credit balance, which is opposite the normal balance of an asset account. The adjustment to reflect depreciation for December is a $583 debit to **Depreciation Expense—Equipment** and a $583 credit to **Accumulated Depreciation—Equipment.**

The **Accumulated Depreciation—Equipment** account is a record of all depreciation taken on the equipment. The financial records show the original cost of the equipment (**Equipment,** $35,000) and all depreciation taken (**Accumulated Depreciation—Equipment,** $583). The difference between the two accounts is called book value. **Book value** is that portion of an asset's original cost that has not yet been depreciated. Three amounts are reported on the financial statements for equipment:

Important!

Contra Accounts
The normal balance for a contra account is the opposite of the related account. **Accumulated Depreciation** is a contra asset account. The normal balance of an asset account is a *debit.* The normal balance of a contra asset account is a *credit.*

Adjustment

Record the adjustment for depreciation.

Analysis

The expense account, **Depreciation Expense—Equipment,** is increased by $583. The contra asset account, **Accumulated Depreciation—Equipment,** is increased by $583.

Debit-Credit Rules

DEBIT Increases to expense accounts are recorded as debits. Debit **Depreciation Expense—Equipment** for $583.

CREDIT Increases to contra asset accounts are recorded as credits. Credit **Accumulated Depreciation—Equipment** for $583.

T-Account Presentation

Depreciation Expense— Equipment			Accumulated Depreciation— Equipment	
+	−		−	+
583				583

Equipment	$35,000
Less accumulated depreciation	− 583
Equipment at book value	$34,417

Refer to Figure 5-2 on page 132 to review the depreciation adjustment on the worksheet. The two parts of the adjustment are labeled **(c).**

If Carter Consulting Services had other kinds of long-term assets, an adjustment for depreciation would be made for each one. Long-term assets include land, buildings, equipment, trucks, automobiles, furniture, and fixtures. Depreciation is calculated on all long-term assets except land. Land is not depreciated.

Notice that each adjustment involved a balance sheet account (an asset or a contra asset) and an income statement account (an expense). When all adjustments have been entered, total and rule the Adjustments columns. Be sure that the totals of the Debit and Credit columns are equal. If they are not, locate and correct the error or errors before continuing. Figure 5-2 shows the completed Adjustments section.

Section 1 Self Review

Questions

1. Why is the worksheet prepared?

2. What are adjustments?

3. Why are prepaid expenses adjusted at the end of an accounting period?

Exercises

4. A firm paid $500 for supplies during the accounting period. At the end of the accounting period, the firm had $150 of supplies on hand. What adjustment is entered on the worksheet?
   a. **Supplies Expense** is debited for $350 and **Supplies** is credited for $350.
   b. **Supplies** is debited for $150 and **Supplies Expense** is credited for $150.
   c. **Supplies Expense** is debited for $150 and **Supplies** is credited for $150.
   d. **Supplies** is debited for $350 and **Supplies Expense** is credited for $350.

5. On January 1 a firm paid $9,000 for six months' rent, January through June. What is the adjustment for rent expense at the end of January?
   a. **Rent Expense** is debited for $9,000 and **Prepaid Rent** is credited for $9,000.
   b. **Rent Expense** is debited for $1,500 and **Prepaid Rent** is credited for $1,500.
   c. **Prepaid Rent** is debited for $1,500 and **Rent Expense** is credited for $1,500.
   d. No adjustment is made until the end of June.

Analysis

6. Three years ago T.K. Systems bought a delivery truck for $25,000. The truck has no salvage value and a five-year useful life. What is the book value of the truck at the end of three years?

Financial Statements

The worksheet is used to prepare the financial statements. Preparing financial statements is the fifth step in the accounting cycle.

The Adjusted Trial Balance Section

The next task is to prepare the Adjusted Trial Balance section.

1. Combine the figures from the Trial Balance section and the Adjustments section of the worksheet. Record the computed results in the Adjusted Trial Balance columns.
2. Total the Debit and Credit columns in the Adjusted Trial Balance section. Confirm that debits equal credits.

Figure 5-3 on pages 138–139 shows the completed Adjusted Trial Balance section of the worksheet. The accounts that do not have adjustments are simply extended from the Trial Balance section to the Adjusted Trial Balance section. For example, the **Cash** account balance of $64,400 is recorded in the Debit column of the Adjusted Trial Balance section without change.

The balances of accounts that are affected by adjustments are recomputed. Look at the **Supplies** account. It has a $2,000 debit balance in the Trial Balance section and shows a $500 credit in the Adjustments section. The new balance is $1,500 ($2,000 − $500). It is recorded in the Debit column of the Adjusted Trial Balance section.

Use the following guidelines to compute the amounts for the Adjusted Trial Balance section.

- If the account has a debit balance in the Trial Balance section and a debit entry in the Adjustments section, add the two amounts.
- If the account has a debit balance in the Trial Balance section and a credit entry in the Adjustments section, subtract the credit amount.
- If the account has a credit balance in the Trial Balance section and a credit entry in the Adjustments section, add the two amounts.
- If the account has a credit balance in the Trial Balance section and a debit entry in the Adjustments section, subtract the debit amount.

If the Trial Balance section has a:	AND if the entry in the Adjustments section is a:	Then:
Debit balance	Debit	Add the amounts.
Debit balance	Credit	Subtract the credit amount.
Credit balance	Credit	Add the amounts.
Credit balance	Debit	Subtract the debit amount.

Section Objectives

3 Complete the worksheet.

WHY IT'S IMPORTANT
The worksheet summarizes both internal and external financial events of a period.

4 Prepare an income statement, statement of owner's equity, and balance sheet from the completed worksheet.

WHY IT'S IMPORTANT
Using a worksheet saves time in preparing the financial statements.

5 Journalize and post the adjusting entries.

WHY IT'S IMPORTANT
Adjusting entries update the financial records of the business.

Terms to Learn
account form balance sheet
report form balance sheet

3 Objective
Complete the worksheet.

	ACCOUNT NAME	TRIAL BALANCE		ADJUSTMENTS	
		DEBIT	CREDIT	DEBIT	CREDIT
1	Cash	64 4 0 0 00			
2	Accounts Receivable	4 0 0 0 00			
3	Supplies	2 0 0 0 00			(a) 5 0 0 00
4	Prepaid Rent	6 0 0 0 00			(b) 3 0 0 0 00
5	Equipment	35 0 0 0 00			
6	Accumulated Depreciation—Equipment				(c) 5 8 3 00
7	Accounts Payable		12 0 0 0 00		
8	Linda Carter, Capital		80 0 0 0 00		
9	Linda Carter, Drawing	3 0 0 0 00			
10	Fees Income		28 0 0 0 00		
11	Salaries Expense	5 0 0 0 00			
12	Utilities Expense	6 0 0 00			
13	Supplies Expense			(a) 5 0 0 00	
14	Rent Expense			(b) 3 0 0 0 00	
15	Depreciation Expense—Equipment			(c) 5 8 3 00	
16	Totals	120 0 0 0 00	120 0 0 0 00	4 0 8 3 00	4 0 8 3 00
17	Net Income				

▲ **FIGURE 5-3**
Partial Worksheet

Locating Errors
If total debits do not equal total credits, find the difference between total debits and total credits. If the difference is divisible by 9, there could be a transposition error. If the difference is divisible by 2, an amount could be entered in the wrong (Debit or Credit) column.

Prepaid Rent has a Trial Balance debit of $6,000 and an Adjustments credit of $3,000. Enter $3,000 ($6,000 − $3,000) in the Adjusted Trial Balance Debit column.

Four accounts that started with zero balances in the Trial Balance section are affected by adjustments. They are **Accumulated Depreciation—Equipment, Supplies Expense, Rent Expense,** and **Depreciation Expense—Equipment.** The figures in the Adjustments section are simply extended to the Adjusted Trial Balance section. For example, **Accumulated Depreciation—Equipment** has a zero balance in the Trial Balance section and a $583 credit in the Adjustments section. Extend the $583 to the Adjusted Trial Balance Credit column.

Once all account balances are recorded in the Adjusted Trial Balance section, total and rule the Debit and Credit columns. Be sure that total debits equal total credits. If they are not equal, find and correct the error or errors.

The Income Statement and Balance Sheet Sections

The Income Statement and Balance Sheet sections of the worksheet are used to separate the amounts needed for the balance sheet and the income statement. For example, to prepare an income statement, all revenue and expense account balances must be in one place.

Starting at the top of the Adjusted Trial Balance section, examine each general ledger account. For accounts that appear on the balance sheet, enter the amount in the appropriate column of the Balance Sheet section. For accounts that appear on the income statement, enter the amount in the appropriate column of the Income Statement section. Take care to enter debit amounts in the Debit column and credit amounts in the Credit column.

| ADJUSTED TRIAL BALANCE | | INCOME STATEMENT | | BALANCE SHEET | | |
DEBIT	CREDIT	DEBIT	CREDIT	DEBIT	CREDIT	
64 4 0 0 00						1
4 0 0 0 00						2
1 5 0 0 00						3
3 0 0 0 00						4
35 0 0 0 00						5
	5 8 3 00					6
	12 0 0 0 00					7
	80 0 0 0 00					8
3 0 0 0 00						9
	28 0 0 0 00					10
5 0 0 0 00						11
6 0 0 00						12
5 0 0 00						13
3 0 0 0 00						14
5 8 3 00						15
120 5 8 3 00	120 5 8 3 00					16
						17

Preparing the Balance Sheet Section

Refer to Figure 5-4 on pages 140–141 as you learn how to complete the worksheet. Asset, liability, and owner's equity accounts appear on the balance sheet. The first five accounts that appear on the worksheet are assets. Extend the asset accounts to the Debit column of the Balance Sheet section. The next account, **Accumulated Depreciation—Equipment,** is a contra asset account. Extend it to the Credit column of the Balance Sheet section. Extend **Accounts Payable** and **Linda Carter, Capital** to the Credit column of the Balance Sheet section. Extend **Linda Carter, Drawing** to the Debit column of the Balance Sheet section.

Preparing the Income Statement Section

Revenue and expense accounts appear on the income statement. Extend the **Fees Income** account to the Credit column of the Income Statement section. The last five accounts on the worksheet are expense accounts. Extend these accounts to the Debit column of the Income Statement section.

After all account balances are transferred from the Adjusted Trial Balance section of the worksheet to the financial statement sections, total the Debit and Credit columns in the Income Statement section. For Carter Consulting Services, the debits (expenses) total $9,683 and the credits (revenue) total $28,000.

Next total the columns in the Balance Sheet section. For Carter Consulting Services the debits (assets and drawing account) total $110,900 and the credits (contra asset, liabilities, and owner's equity) total $92,583.

Return to the Income Statement section. The totals of these columns are used to determine the net income or net loss. Subtract the smaller

Proper Names

When conducting business in the international marketplace, it is important to address individuals in the proper manner. Some countries do not use the "first name-last name" style as used in the United States. For example, in Spanish-speaking Latin America, the surname is a combination of the mother's and father's last names. The father's name comes first and is the only one used in conversations.

Carter Consulting Services
Worksheet
Month Ended December 31, 2004

	ACCOUNT NAME	TRIAL BALANCE DEBIT	TRIAL BALANCE CREDIT	ADJUSTMENTS DEBIT	ADJUSTMENTS CREDIT
1	*Cash*	64 400 00			
2	*Accounts Receivable*	4 000 00			
3	*Supplies*	2 000 00			(a) 500 00
4	*Prepaid Rent*	6 000 00			(b) 3 000 00
5	*Equipment*	35 000 00			
6	*Accumulated Depreciation—Equipment*				(c) 583 00
7	*Accounts Payable*		12 000 00		
8	*Linda Carter, Capital*		80 000 00		
9	*Linda Carter, Drawing*	3 000 00			
10	*Fees Income*		28 000 00		
11	*Salaries Expense*	5 000 00			
12	*Utilities Expense*	600 00			
13	*Supplies Expense*			(a) 500 00	
14	*Rent Expense*			(b) 3 000 00	
15	*Depreciation Expense—Equipment*			(c) 583 00	
16	*Totals*	120 000 00	120 000 00	4 083 00	4 083 00
17	*Net Income*				
18					

▲ **FIGURE 5-4**
Completed Worksheet

column total from the larger one. Enter the difference on the line below the smaller total. In the Account Name column, enter "Net Income" or "Net Loss."

In this case the total of the Credit column, $28,000, exceeds the total of the Debit column, $9,683. The Credit column total represents revenue. The Debit column total represents expenses. The difference between the two amounts is a net income of $18,317. Enter $18,317 in the Debit column of the Income Statement section.

Net income causes a net increase in owner's equity. As a check on accuracy, the amount in the Balance Sheet Debit column is subtracted from the amount in the Credit column and compared to net income. In the Balance Sheet section, subtract the smaller column total from the larger one. The difference should equal the net income or net loss computed in the Income Statement section. Enter the difference on the line below the smaller total. For Carter Consulting Services, enter $18,317 in the Credit column of the Balance Sheet section.

Total the Income Statement and Balance Sheet columns. Make sure that total debits equal total credits for each section.

Carter Consulting Services had a net income. If it had a loss, the loss would be entered in the Credit column of the Income Statement section and the Debit column of the Balance Sheet section. "Net Loss" would be entered in the Account Name column on the worksheet.

Important!

Net Income

The difference between the Debit and Credit columns of the Income Statement section represents net income. The difference between the Debit and Credit columns of the Balance Sheet section should equal the net income amount.

4 Objective

Prepare an income statement, statement of owner's equity, and balance sheet from the completed worksheet.

Preparing Financial Statements

When the worksheet is complete, the next step is to prepare the financial statements, starting with the income statement. Preparation of the financial statements is the fifth step in the accounting cycle.

ADJUSTED TRIAL BALANCE		INCOME STATEMENT		BALANCE SHEET		
DEBIT	CREDIT	DEBIT	CREDIT	DEBIT	CREDIT	
64 400 00				64 400 00		1
4 000 00				4 000 00		2
1 500 00				1 500 00		3
3 000 00				3 000 00		4
35 000 00				35 000 00		5
	583 00				583 00	6
	12 000 00				12 000 00	7
	80 000 00				80 000 00	8
3 000 00				3 000 00		9
	28 000 00		28 000 00			10
5 000 00		5 000 00				11
600 00		600 00				12
500 00		500 00				13
3 000 00		3 000 00				14
583 00		583 00				15
120 583 00	120 583 00	9 683 00	28 000 00	110 900 00	92 583 00	16
		18 317 00			18 317 00	17
		28 000 00	28 000 00	110 900 00	110 900 00	18

↑ Net income
Bottom ½

Top ½

Preparing the Income Statement

Use the Income Statement section of the worksheet to prepare the income statement. Figure 5-5 shows the income statement for Carter Consulting Services. Compare it to the worksheet in Figure 5-4.

If the firm had incurred a net loss, the final amount on the income statement would be labeled "Net Loss for the Month."

◀ **FIGURE 5-5**
Income Statement

Carter Consulting Services
Income Statement
Month Ended December 31, 2004

Revenue		
Fees Income		2 8 0 0 0 00
Expenses		
Salaries Expense	5 0 0 0 00	
Utilities Expense	6 0 0 00	
Supplies Expense	5 0 0 00	
Rent Expense	3 0 0 0 00	
Depreciation Expense—Equipment	5 8 3 00	
Total Expenses		9 6 8 3 00
Net Income for the Month		1 8 3 1 7 00

Preparing the Statement of Owner's Equity

The statement of owner's equity reports the changes that have occurred in the owner's financial interest during the reporting period. Use the data in the Balance Sheet section of the worksheet, as well as the net income or net loss figure, to prepare the statement of owner's equity.

- From the Balance Sheet section of the worksheet, use the amounts for owner's capital; owner's withdrawals, if any; and owner's investments, if any.
- From the Income Statement section of the worksheet, use the amount calculated for net income or net loss.

The statement of owner's equity is prepared before the balance sheet because the ending capital balance is needed to prepare the balance sheet. The statement of owner's equity reports the change in owner's capital during the period ($15,317) as well as the ending capital ($95,317). Figure 5-6 shows the statement of owner's equity for Carter Consulting Services.

FIGURE 5-6 ▶
Statement of Owner's Equity

Carter Consulting Services
Statement of Owner's Equity
Month Ended December 31, 2004

Linda Carter, Capital, December 1, 2004		80 0 0 0 00
Net Income for December	18 3 1 7 00	
Less Withdrawals for December	3 0 0 0 00	
Increase in Capital		15 3 1 7 00
Linda Carter, Capital, December 31, 2004		95 3 1 7 00

Preparing the Balance Sheet

The accounts listed on the balance sheet are taken directly from the Balance Sheet section of the worksheet. Figure 5-7 shows the balance sheet for Carter Consulting Services.

FIGURE 5-7 ▶
Balance Sheet

Carter Consulting Services
Balance Sheet
December 31, 2004

Assets		
Cash		64 4 0 0 00
Accounts Receivable		4 0 0 0 00
Supplies		1 5 0 0 00
Prepaid Rent		3 0 0 0 00
Equipment	35 0 0 0 00	
Less Accumulated Depreciation	5 8 3 00	34 4 1 7 00
Total Assets		107 3 1 7 00
Liabilities and Owner's Equity		
Liabilities		
Accounts Payable		12 0 0 0 00
Owner's Equity		
Linda Carter, Capital		95 3 1 7 00
Total Liabilities and Owner's Equity		107 3 1 7 00

Note that the equipment's book value is reported on the balance sheet ($34,417). Do not confuse book value with market value. Book value is

Figure 5-9A Worksheet Summary

The worksheet is used to gather all the data needed at the end of an accounting period to prepare the financial statements. The worksheet heading contains the name of the company (WHO), the title of the statement being prepared (WHAT), and the period covered (WHEN). The worksheet contains ten money columns that are arranged in five sections labeled Trial Balance, Adjustments, Adjusted Trial Balance, Income Statement, and Balance Sheet. Each section includes a Debit column and a Credit column.

    The information reflected in the worksheet below is for Arrow Accounting Services for the period ended December 31, 20X5. The illustrations that follow will highlight the preparation of each part of the worksheet.

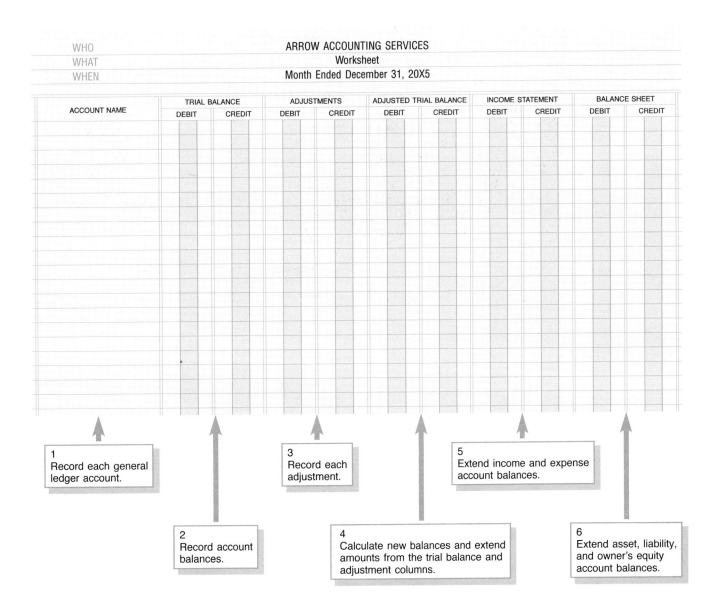

Figure 5–9B The Trial Balance Columns

The first step in preparing the worksheet for Arrow Accounting Services is to list the general ledger accounts and their balances in the Account Name and Trial Balance sections of the worksheet. The equality of total debits and credits is proved by totaling the Debit and Credit columns.

above line – Balance Sheet

ARROW ACCOUNTING SERVICES
Worksheet
Month Ended December 31, 20X5

ACCOUNT NAME	TRIAL BALANCE DEBIT	TRIAL BALANCE CREDIT	ADJUSTMENTS DEBIT	ADJUSTMENTS CREDIT	ADJUSTED TRIAL BALANCE DEBIT	ADJUSTED TRIAL BALANCE CREDIT	INCOME STATEMENT DEBIT	INCOME STATEMENT CREDIT	BALANCE SHEET DEBIT	BALANCE SHEET CREDIT
Cash	16 200 00									
Accounts Receivable	2 000 00									
Supplies	1 000 00									
Prepaid Rent	20 000 00									
Equipment	15 000 00									
Accum. Depr.—Equip.										
Accounts Payable		4 000 00								
John Arrow, Capital		40 000 00								
John Arrow, Drawing	1 000 00									
Fees Income		14 000 00								
Salaries Expense	2 500 00									
Utilities Expense	300 00									
Supplies Expense										
Rent Expense										
Depr. Expense—Equip.										
Totals	58 000 00	58 000 00								

Draw a single rule to indicate addition of a set of Debit/Credit columns.

Draw a double rule under the totals of a set of Debit/Credit columns to indicate that no further amounts are to be added.

Trial Balance totals must be equal.

Below line – Income Statement

Figure 5–9G Preparing the Financial Statements

The information needed to prepare the financial statements is obtained from the worksheet.

ARROW ACCOUNTING SERVICES
Income Statement
Month Ended December 31, 20X5

Revenue		
Fees Income		14 0 0 0 00
Expenses		
Salaries Expense	2 5 0 0 00	
Utilities Expense	3 0 0 00	
Supplies Expense	5 0 0 00	
Rent Expense	2 5 0 0 00	
Depreciation Expense—Equipment	2 5 0 00	
Total Expenses		6 0 5 0 00
Net Income		7 9 5 0 00

> When expenses for the period are less than revenue, a net income results. The net income is transferred to the statement of owner's equity.

ARROW ACCOUNTING SERVICES
Statement of Owner's Equity
Month Ended December 31, 20X5

John Arrow, Capital, December 1, 20X5		40 0 0 0 00
Net Income for December	7 9 5 0 00	
Withdrawals for December	1 0 0 0 00	
Increase in Capital		6 9 5 0 00
John Arrow, Capital, December 31, 20X5		46 9 5 0 00

> The withdrawals are subtracted from the net income for the period to determine the change in owner's equity.

ARROW ACCOUNTING SERVICES
Balance Sheet
December 31, 20X5

Assets		
Cash		16 2 0 0 00
Accounts Receivable		2 0 0 0 00
Supplies		5 0 0 00
Prepaid Rent		17 5 0 0 00
Equipment	15 0 0 0 00	
Less Accumulated Depreciation	2 5 0 00	14 7 5 0 00
Total Assets		50 9 5 0 00
Liabilities and Owner's Equity		
Liabilities		
Accounts Payable		4 0 0 0 00
Owner's Equity		
John Arrow, Capital		46 9 5 0 00
Total Liabilities and Owner's Equity		50 9 5 0 00

> The ending capital balance is transferred from the statement of owner's equity to the balance sheet.

SUMMARY OF FINANCIAL STATEMENTS

THE INCOME STATEMENT

The income statement is prepared directly from the data in the Income Statement section of the worksheet. The heading of the income statement contains the name of the firm (WHO), the name of the statement (WHAT), and the period covered by the statement (WHEN). The revenue section of the statement is prepared first. The revenue account name is obtained from the Account Name column of the worksheet. The balance of the revenue account is obtained from the Credit column of the Income Statement section of the worksheet. The expenses section of the income statement is prepared next. The expense account titles are obtained from the Account Name column of the worksheet. The balance of each expense account is obtained from the Debit column of the Income Statement section of the worksheet.

Determining the net income or net loss for the period is the last step in preparing the income statement. If the firm has more revenue than expenses, a net income is reported for the period. If the firm has more expenses than revenue, a net loss is reported. The net income or net loss reported must agree with the amount calculated on the worksheet.

THE STATEMENT OF OWNER'S EQUITY

The statement of owner's equity is prepared from the data in the Balance Sheet section of the worksheet and the general ledger capital account. The statement of owner's equity is prepared before the balance sheet so that the amount of the ending capital balance is available for presentation on the balance sheet. The heading of the statement contains the name of the firm (WHO), the name of the statement (WHAT), and the date of the statement (WHEN).

The statement begins with the capital account balance at the beginning of the period. Next, the increase or decrease in the owner's capital account is determined. The increase or decrease is computed by adding the net income (or net loss) for the period to any additional investments made by the owner during the period and subtracting withdrawals for the period. The increase or decrease is added to the beginning capital balance to obtain the ending capital balance.

THE BALANCE SHEET

The balance sheet is prepared from the data in the Balance Sheet section of the worksheet and the statement of owner's equity. The balance sheet reflects the assets, liabilities, and owner's equity of the firm on the balance sheet date. The heading of the statement contains the name of the firm (WHO), the name of the statement (WHAT), and the date of the statement (WHEN).

The assets section of the statement is prepared first. The asset account titles are obtained from the Account Name column of the worksheet. The balance of each asset account is obtained from the Debit column of the Balance Sheet section of the worksheet. The liability and owner's equity section is prepared next. The liability and owner's equity account titles are obtained from the Account Name column of the worksheet. The balance of each liability account is obtained from the Credit column of the Balance Sheet section of the worksheet. The ending balance for the owner's capital account is obtained from the statement of owner's equity. Total liabilities and owner's equity must equal total assets.

the portion of the original cost that has not been depreciated. *Market value* is what a willing buyer will pay a willing seller for the asset. Market value may be higher or lower than book value.

Notice that the amount for **Linda Carter, Capital,** $95,317, comes from the statement of owner's equity.

The balance sheet in Figure 5-7 is prepared using the report form. The **report form balance sheet** lists the asset accounts first, followed by liabilities and owner's equity. Chapters 2 and 3 illustrated the **account form balance sheet,** with assets on the left and liabilities and owner's equity on the right. The report form is widely used because it provides more space for entering account names and its format is easier to prepare.

Some companies show long-term assets at a net amount. "Net" means that accumulated depreciation has been subtracted from the original cost. For example, The Boeing Company's consolidated statement of financial position as of December 31, 1999, states:

Property, plant, and equipment, net: $8,245 million

The accumulated depreciation amount does not appear on the balance sheet.

Figure 5-8 provides a step-by-step demonstration of how to complete the worksheet and financial statements for Carter Consulting Services.

Journalizing and Posting Adjusting Entries

⑤ Objective

Journalize and post the adjusting entries.

The worksheet is a tool. It is used to determine the effects of adjustments on account balances. It is also used to prepare the financial statements. However, the worksheet is not part of the permanent accounting record.

After the financial statements are prepared, the adjustments shown on the worksheet must become part of the permanent accounting record. Each adjustment is journalized and posted to the general ledger accounts. Journalizing and posting adjusting entries is the sixth step in the accounting cycle.

For Carter Consulting Services, three adjustments are needed to provide a complete picture of the firm's operating results and its financial position. Adjustments are needed for supplies expense, rent expense, and depreciation expense.

Refer to Figure 5-4 on pages 140–141 for data needed to record the adjustments. Enter the words "Adjusting Entries" in the Description column of the general journal. Some accountants prefer to start a new page when they record the adjusting entries. Then journalize the adjustments in the order in which they appear on the worksheet.

After journalizing the adjusting entries, post them to the general ledger accounts. Figure 5-9 on page 144 shows how the adjusting entries for Carter Consulting Services on December 31, 2004 were journalized and posted. Account numbers appear in the general journal Posting Reference column because all entries have been posted. In each general ledger account, the word "Adjusting" appears in the Description column.

GENERAL JOURNAL

PAGE ___3___

	DATE		DESCRIPTION	POST. REF.	DEBIT	CREDIT	
1	2004		*Adjusting Entries*				1
2	Dec.	31	Supplies Expense	517	5 0 0 00		2
3			Supplies	121		5 0 0 00	3
4							4
5		31	Rent Expense	520	3 0 0 0 00		5
6			Prepaid Rent	137		3 0 0 0 00	6
7							7
8		31	Depr. Expense—Equipment	523	5 8 3 00		8
9			Accum. Depr.—Equipment	142		5 8 3 00	9
10							10
11							

ACCOUNT __Supplies__ ACCOUNT NO. __121__

DATE		DESCRIPTION	POST. REF.	DEBIT	CREDIT	BALANCE DEBIT	BALANCE CREDIT
2004							
Nov.	28		J1	2 0 0 0 00		2 0 0 0 00	
Dec.	31	Adjusting	J3		5 0 0 00	1 5 0 0 00	

ACCOUNT __Prepaid Rent__ ACCOUNT NO. __137__

DATE		DESCRIPTION	POST. REF.	DEBIT	CREDIT	BALANCE DEBIT	BALANCE CREDIT
2004							
Nov.	30		J1	6 0 0 0 00		6 0 0 0 00	
Dec.	31	Adjusting	J3		3 0 0 0 00	3 0 0 0 00	

ACCOUNT __Accumulated Depreciation—Equipment__ ACCOUNT NO. __142__

DATE		DESCRIPTION	POST. REF.	DEBIT	CREDIT	BALANCE DEBIT	BALANCE CREDIT
2004							
Dec.	31	Adjusting	J3		5 8 3 00		5 8 3 00

ACCOUNT __Supplies Expense__ ACCOUNT NO. __517__

DATE		DESCRIPTION	POST. REF.	DEBIT	CREDIT	BALANCE DEBIT	BALANCE CREDIT
2004							
Dec.	31	Adjusting	J3	5 0 0 00		5 0 0 00	

ACCOUNT __Rent Expense__ ACCOUNT NO. __520__

DATE		DESCRIPTION	POST. REF.	DEBIT	CREDIT	BALANCE DEBIT	BALANCE CREDIT
2004							
Dec.	31	Adjusting	J3	3 0 0 0 00		3 0 0 0 00	

ACCOUNT __Depreciation Expense—Equipment__ ACCOUNT NO. __523__

DATE		DESCRIPTION	POST. REF.	DEBIT	CREDIT	BALANCE DEBIT	BALANCE CREDIT
2004							
Dec.	31	Adjusting	J3	5 8 3 00		5 8 3 00	

Managerial IMPLICATIONS

Worksheets

- The worksheet permits quick preparation of the financial statements. Quick preparation of financial statements allows management to obtain timely information.
- Timely information allows management to
  - evaluate the results of operations,
  - evaluate the financial position of the business,
  - make decisions.
- The worksheet provides a convenient form for gathering information and determining the effects of internal changes such as
  - recording an expense for the use of a long-term asset like equipment,
  - recording the actual use of prepaid items.
- The more accounts that a firm has in its general ledger, the more useful the worksheet is in speeding the preparation of the financial statements.
- It is important to management that the appropriate adjustments are recorded in order to present a complete and accurate picture of the firm's financial affairs.

Thinking Critically

If you skip the adjustment process, how will this affect the financial statements?

Remember that the worksheet is not part of the accounting records. Adjustments that are on the worksheet must be recorded in the general journal and posted to the general ledger in order to become part of the permanent accounting records.

Self Review

Questions

1. What amounts appear on the statement of owner's equity?
2. What is the difference between a report form balance sheet and an account form balance sheet?
3. Why is it necessary to journalize and post adjusting entries even though the data is already recorded on the worksheet?

Exercises

4. On a worksheet, the adjusted balance of the **Supplies** account is extended to the
   a. Income Statement Debit column.
   b. Balance Sheet Debit column.
   c. Income Statement Credit column.
   d. Balance Sheet Credit column.
5. **Accumulated Depreciation— Equipment** is a(n)
   a. asset account.
   b. contra asset account.
   c. liability account.
   d. contra liability account.

Analysis

6. J. Cloves Repair Shop purchased equipment for $12,000. **Depreciation Expense** for the month is $120. What is the balance of the **Equipment** account after posting the depreciation entry? Why?

(Answers to Section 2 Self Review are on page 161.)

Review   Chapter Summary

At the end of the operating period, adjustments for internal events are recorded to update the accounting records. In this chapter, you have learned how the accountant uses the worksheet and adjusting entries to accomplish this task.

Learning Objectives

1 Complete a trial balance on a worksheet.

A worksheet is normally used to save time in preparing the financial statements. Preparation of the worksheet is the fourth step in the accounting cycle. The trial balance is the first section of the worksheet to be prepared.

2 Prepare adjustments for unrecorded business transactions.

Some changes arise from the internal operations of the firm itself. Adjusting entries are made to record these changes. Any adjustments to account balances should be entered in the Adjustments section of the worksheet.

- Prepaid expenses are expense items that are acquired and paid for in advance of their use. At the time of their acquisition, these items represent assets and are recorded in asset accounts. As they are used, their cost is transferred to expense by means of adjusting entries at the end of each accounting period.

Examples of general ledger asset accounts and the related expense accounts follow:

Asset Accounts	Expense Accounts
Supplies	Supplies Expense
Prepaid Rent	Rent Expense
Prepaid Insurance	Insurance Expense

- Depreciation is the process of allocating the cost of a long-term asset to operations over its expected useful life. Part of the asset's cost is charged off as an expense at the end of each accounting period during the asset's useful life. The straight-line method of depreciation is widely used. The formula for straight-line depreciation is:

$$\text{Depreciation} = \frac{\text{Cost} - \text{Salvage value}}{\text{Estimated useful life}}$$

3 Complete the worksheet.

An adjusted trial balance is prepared to prove the equality of the debits and credits after adjustments have been entered on the worksheet. Once the Debit and Credit columns have been totaled and ruled, the Income Statement and Balance Sheet columns of the worksheet are completed. The net income or net loss for the period is determined, and the worksheet is completed.

4 Prepare an income statement, statement of owner's equity, and balance sheet from the completed worksheet.

All figures needed to prepare the financial statements are properly reflected on the completed worksheet. The accounts are arranged in the order in which they must appear on the income statement and balance sheet. Preparation of the financial statements is the fifth step of the accounting cycle.

5 Journalize and post the adjusting entries.

After the financial statements have been prepared, the accountant must make permanent entries in the accounting records for the adjustments shown on the worksheet. The adjusting entries are then posted to the general ledger. Journalizing and posting the adjusting entries is the sixth step in the accounting cycle.

To summarize the steps of the accounting cycle discussed so far:

1. Analyze transactions.
2. Journalize transactions.
3. Post the journal entries.
4. Prepare a worksheet.
5. Prepare financial statements.
6. Record adjusting entries.

6 Define the accounting terms new to this chapter.

Account form balance sheet (p. 143) A balance sheet that lists assets on the left and liabilities and owner's equity on the right (see Report form balance sheet)

Adjusting entries (p. 131) Journal entries made to update accounts for items that were not recorded during the accounting period

Adjustments (p. 131) See Adjusting entries

Book value (p. 135) That portion of an asset's original cost that has not yet been depreciated

Contra account (p. 135) An account with a normal balance that is opposite that of a related account

Contra asset account (p. 135) An asset account with a credit balance, which is contrary to the normal balance of an asset account

Depreciation (p. 134) Allocation of the cost of a long-term asset to operations during its expected useful life

Prepaid expenses (p. 131) Expense items acquired, recorded, and paid for in advance of their use

Report form balance sheet (p. 143) A balance sheet that lists the asset accounts first, followed by liabilities and owner's equity

Salvage value (p. 134) An estimate of the amount that could be received by selling or disposing of an asset at the end of its useful life

Straight-line depreciation (p. 134) Allocation of an asset's cost in equal amounts to each accounting period of the asset's useful life

Worksheet (p. 130) A form used to gather all data needed at the end of an accounting period to prepare financial statements

Comprehensive Self Review

1. Why are assets depreciated?
2. Why is the net income for a period recorded in the Balance Sheet section of the worksheet as well as the Income Statement section?
3. Is the normal balance for **Accumulated Depreciation** a debit or credit balance?
4. The **Supplies** account has a debit balance of $5,000 in the Trial Balance column. The Credit column in the Adjustments section is $1,750. What is the new balance? The new balance will be extended to which column of the worksheet?
5. The **Drawing** account is extended to which column of the worksheet?

(Answers to Comprehensive Self Review are on page 161.)

Discussion Questions

1. Why is it necessary to journalize and post adjusting entries?
2. What three amounts are reported on the balance sheet for a long-term asset such as equipment?
3. How does a contra asset account differ from a regular asset account?
4. What is book value?
5. Why is an accumulated depreciation account used in making the adjustment for depreciation?
6. How does the straight-line method of depreciation work?
7. Give three examples of assets that are subject to depreciation.
8. A firm purchases machinery, which has an estimated useful life of 10 years and no salvage value, for $15,000 at the beginning of the accounting period. What is the adjusting entry for depreciation at the end of one month if the firm uses the straight-line method of depreciation?
9. What adjustment would be recorded for expired insurance?
10. What are prepaid expenses? Give four examples.
11. Why is it necessary to make an adjustment for supplies used?
12. Are the following assets depreciated? Why or why not?
    a. Prepaid Insurance
    b. Delivery Truck
    c. Land
    d. Manufacturing Equipment
    e. Prepaid Rent
    f. Furniture
    g. Store Equipment
    h. Prepaid Advertising
    i. Computers
13. What effect does each of the following items have on net income?
    a. The owner withdrew cash from the business.
    b. Credit customers paid $1,000 on outstanding balances that were past due.
    c. The business bought equipment on account that cost $10,000.
    d. The business journalized and posted an adjustment for depreciation of equipment.
14. What effect does each item in Question 13 have on owner's equity?

Applications

EXERCISES

Calculating adjustments.

Determine the necessary end-of-June adjustments for Brown Company.

1. On June 1, 20--, Brown Company, a new firm, paid $7,200 rent in advance for a six-month period. The $7,200 was debited to the **Prepaid Rent** account.

2. On June 1, 20--, the firm bought supplies for $1,950. The $1,950 was debited to the **Supplies** account. An inventory of supplies at the end of June showed that items costing $700 were on hand.

3. On June 1, 20--, the firm bought equipment costing $24,000. The equipment has an expected useful life of ten years and no salvage value. The firm will use the straight-line method of depreciation.

◀ **Exercise 5-1**
Objective 2

Calculating adjustments.

For each of the following situations, determine the necessary adjustments.

1. A firm purchased a two-year insurance policy for $4,800 on July 1, 2004. The $4,800 was debited to the **Prepaid Insurance** account. What adjustment should be made to record expired insurance on the firm's July 31, 2004, worksheet?

2. On December 1, 2004, a firm signed a contract with a local radio station for advertising that will extend over a one-year period. The firm paid $4,080 in advance and debited the amount to **Prepaid Advertising.** What adjustment should be made to record expired advertising on the firm's December 31, 2004, worksheet?

◀ **Exercise 5-2**
Objective 2

Worksheet through Adjusted Trial Balance.

On January 31, 20--, the general ledger of Ortiz Company showed the following account balances. Prepare the worksheet through the Adjusted Trial Balance section. Assume that every account has the normal debit or credit balance. The worksheet covers the month of January.

◀ **Exercise 5-3**
Objectives 1, 2

ACCOUNTS			
Cash	$ 57,000	Fees Income	90,000
Accounts Receivable	19,200	Depreciation Exp.—Equip.	0
Supplies	9,000	Insurance Expense	0
Prepaid Insurance	17,100	Rent Expense	7,200
Equipment	95,580	Salaries Expense	8,520
Accum. Depr.—Equip.	0	Supplies Expense	0
Accounts Payable	10,200		
Dennis Ortiz, Capital	113,400		

Additional information:

a. Supplies used during January totaled $4,800.

b. Expired insurance totaled $1,500.

c. Depreciation expense for the month was $1,380.

Exercise 5-4 ▶

Objectives 2, 3

Correcting net income.

Assume that a firm reports net income of $30,000 prior to making adjusting entries for the following items: expired rent, $2,000; depreciation expense, $2,400; and supplies used, $1,000.

Assume that the required adjusting entries have not been made. What effect do these errors have on the reported net income?

Exercise 5-5 ▶

Objective 5

Journalizing and posting adjustments.

Thomas Company must make three adjusting entries on December 31, 20--.

a. Supplies used, $2,000; (supplies totaling $3,000 were purchased on December 1, 20--, and debited to the **Supplies** account).

b. Expired insurance, $1,600 on December 1, 20--; the firm paid $9,600 for six months' insurance coverage in advance and debited **Prepaid Insurance** for this amount.

c. Depreciation expense for equipment, $800.

Make the journal entries for these adjustments and post the entries to the general ledger accounts. Use page 3 of the general journal for the adjusting entries. Use the following accounts and numbers.

Supplies	121	Depreciation Exp.—Equip.	517
Prepaid Insurance	131	Insurance Expense	521
Accum. Depr.—Equip.	142	Supplies Expense	523

Problems

Selected problems can be completed using:
 Peachtree   QuickBooks   Spreadsheets

PROBLEM SET A

Problem 5-1A ▶

Objectives 1, 2, 3

Completing the worksheet.

The trial balance of Dallas Company as of January 31, 20--, after the company completed the first month of operations, is shown in the partial worksheet on page 151.

INSTRUCTIONS

1. Record the trial balance in the Trial Balance section of the worksheet.

2. Complete the worksheet by making the following adjustments: supplies on hand at the end of the month, $1,500; expired insurance, $2,000; depreciation expense for the period, $200.

Analyze: How does the insurance adjustment affect **Prepaid Insurance?**

Problem 5-2A ▶

Objectives 1, 2, 3

Reconstructing a partial worksheet.

The adjusted trial balance of University Book Store as of September 30, 20--, after the firm's first month of operations, appears on page 151.

Appropriate adjustments have been made for the following items.

a. Supplies used during the month, $1,000.

b. Expired rent for the month, $1,200.

c. Depreciation expense for the month, $600.

Dallas Company
Worksheet (Partial)
Month Ended January 31, 20--

| | ACCOUNT NAME | TRIAL BALANCE | | ADJUSTMENTS | |
		DEBIT	CREDIT	DEBIT	CREDIT
1	Cash	31 0 0 0 00			
2	Accounts Receivable	2 6 0 0 00			
3	Supplies	2 9 0 0 00			
4	Prepaid Insurance	12 0 0 0 00			
5	Equipment	24 0 0 0 00			
6	Accumulated Depreciation—Equipment				
7	Accounts Payable		4 0 0 0 00		
8	J. C. Dallas, Capital		60 0 0 0 00		
9	J. C. Dallas, Drawing	2 4 0 0 00			
10	Fees Income		16 3 0 0 00		
11	Depreciation Expense—Equipment				
12	Insurance Expense				
13	Salaries Expense	4 8 0 0 00			
14	Supplies Expense				
15	Utilities Expense	6 0 0 00			
16	Totals	80 3 0 0 00	80 3 0 0 00		

INSTRUCTIONS

1. Record the Adjusted Trial Balance in the Adjusted Trial Balance columns of the worksheet.

2. Prepare the adjusting entries in the Adjustments columns.

3. Complete the Trial Balance columns of the worksheet prior to making the adjusting entries.

Analyze: What was the balance of **Prepaid Rent** prior to the adjusting entry for expired rent?

University Book Store
Adjusted Trial Balance
September 30, 20--

Account Name	Debit	Credit
Cash	19,000	
Accounts Receivable	3,000	
Supplies	2,400	
Prepaid Rent	14,400	
Equipment	24,000	
Accumulated Depreciation—Equipment		600
Accounts Payable		6,000
Chuck Keen, Capital		32,100
Chuck Keen, Drawing	2,000	
Fees Income		36,000
Depreciation Expense—Equipment	600	
Rent Expense	1,200	
Salaries Expense	6,400	
Supplies Expense	1,000	
Utilities Expense	700	
Totals	74,700	74,700

Problem 5-3A ►
Objective 4

Preparing financial statements from the worksheet.

The completed worksheet for Penn Corporation as of December 31, 20--, after the company had completed the first month of operation, appears below.

INSTRUCTIONS

1. Prepare an income statement.
2. Prepare a statement of owner's equity. The owner made no additional investments during the month.
3. Prepare a balance sheet (use the report form).

Analyze: If the adjustment to **Prepaid Advertising** had been $700 instead of $1,000, what net income would have resulted?

Problem 5-4A ►
Objectives 1, 2, 3, 4, 5

Preparing a worksheet and financial statements, journalizing adjusting entries, and posting to ledger accounts.

David Flores owns Flores Creative Designs. The trial balance of the firm for January 31, 20--, the first month of operations, is shown on page 153.

INSTRUCTIONS

1. Complete the worksheet for the month.
2. Prepare an income statement, statement of owner's equity, and balance sheet. No additional investments were made by the owner during the month.
3. Journalize and post the adjusting entries. Use 3 for the journal page number.

End-of-the-month adjustments must account for the following items:

a. Supplies were purchased on January 1, 20--; inventory of supplies on January 31, 20--, is $200.

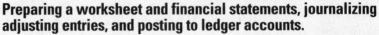

| | | TRIAL BALANCE | | | ADJUSTMENTS | | |
	ACCOUNT NAME	DEBIT	CREDIT		DEBIT		CREDIT
1	Cash	36 8 0 0 00					
2	Accounts Receivable	4 0 0 0 00					
3	Supplies	4 0 0 0 00				(a)	2 0 0 0 00
4	Prepaid Advertising	6 0 0 0 00				(b)	1 0 0 0 00
5	Equipment	20 0 0 0 00					
6	Accumulated Depreciation—Equipment					(c)	8 0 0 00
7	Accounts Payable		4 0 0 0 00				
8	Jeff Penn, Capital		50 0 0 0 00				
9	Jeff Penn, Drawing	2 8 0 0 00					
10	Fees Income		25 0 0 0 00				
11	Advertising Expense			(b)	1 0 0 0 00		
12	Depreciation Expense—Equipment			(c)	8 0 0 00		
13	Salaries Expense	4 8 0 0 00					
14	Supplies Expense			(a)	2 0 0 0 00		
15	Utilities Expense	6 0 0 00					
16	Totals	79 0 0 0 00	79 0 0 0 00		3 8 0 0 00		3 8 0 0 00
17	Net Income						
18							
19							

Penn Corporation
Worksheet
Month Ended December 31, 20--

Flores Creative Designs
Worksheet (Partial)
Month Ended January 31, 20--

	ACCOUNT NAME	TRIAL BALANCE DEBIT	TRIAL BALANCE CREDIT	ADJUSTMENTS DEBIT	ADJUSTMENTS CREDIT
1	Cash	10 2 0 0 00			
2	Accounts Receivable	3 6 0 0 00			
3	Supplies	1 1 5 0 00			
4	Prepaid Advertising	1 2 0 0 00			
5	Prepaid Rent	8 4 0 0 00			
6	Equipment	9 6 0 0 00			
7	Accumulated Depreciation—Equipment				
8	Accounts Payable		5 0 0 0 00		
9	David Flores, Capital		18 1 0 0 00		
10	David Flores, Drawing	1 5 0 0 00			
11	Fees Income		16 5 0 0 00		
12	Advertising Expense				
13	Depreciation Expense—Equipment				
14	Rent Expense				
15	Salaries Expense	3 6 0 0 00			
16	Supplies Expense				
17	Utilities Expense	3 5 0 00			
18	Totals	39 6 0 0 00	39 6 0 0 00		
19					

b. The prepaid advertising contract was signed on January 1, 20--, and covers a four-month period.

c. Rent of $700 expired during the month.

ADJUSTED TRIAL BALANCE DEBIT	ADJUSTED TRIAL BALANCE CREDIT	INCOME STATEMENT DEBIT	INCOME STATEMENT CREDIT	BALANCE SHEET DEBIT	BALANCE SHEET CREDIT	
36 8 0 0 00				36 8 0 0 00		1
4 0 0 0 00				4 0 0 0 00		2
2 0 0 0 00				2 0 0 0 00		3
5 0 0 0 00				5 0 0 0 00		4
20 0 0 0 00				20 0 0 0 00		5
	8 0 0 00				8 0 0 00	6
	4 0 0 0 00				4 0 0 0 00	7
	50 0 0 0 00				50 0 0 0 00	8
2 8 0 0 00				2 8 0 0 00		9
	25 0 0 0 00		25 0 0 0 00			10
1 0 0 0 00		1 0 0 0 00				11
8 0 0 00		8 0 0 00				12
4 8 0 0 00		4 8 0 0 00				13
2 0 0 0 00		2 0 0 0 00				14
6 0 0 00		6 0 0 00				15
79 8 0 0 00	79 8 0 0 00	9 2 0 0 00	25 0 0 0 00	70 6 0 0 00	54 8 0 0 00	16
		15 8 0 0 00			15 8 0 0 00	17
		25 0 0 0 00	25 0 0 0 00	70 6 0 0 00	70 6 0 0 00	18
						19

d. Depreciation is computed using the straight-line method. The equipment has an estimated useful life of 10 years with no salvage value.

Analyze: If the adjusting entries had not been made for the month, would net income be overstated or understated?

PROBLEM SET B

Problem 5-1B ►
Objectives 1, 2, 3

─────────────

INSTRUCTIONS

Completing the worksheet.

The trial balance of Harding Company as of February 28, 20--, appears below.

1. Record the trial balance in the Trial Balance section of the worksheet.

2. Complete the worksheet by making the following adjustments: supplies on hand at the end of the month, $1,600; expired rent, $1,800; depreciation expense for the period, $500.

Analyze: Why do you think the account **Accumulated Depreciation—Equipment** has a zero balance on the trial balance shown?

Harding Company
Worksheet (Partial)
Month Ended February 28, 20--

	ACCOUNT NAME	TRIAL BALANCE DEBIT	TRIAL BALANCE CREDIT	ADJUSTMENTS DEBIT	ADJUSTMENTS CREDIT
1	Cash	37 0 0 0 00			
2	Accounts Receivable	4 6 0 0 00			
3	Supplies	2 4 0 0 00			
4	Prepaid Rent	21 6 0 0 00			
5	Equipment	28 0 0 0 00			
6	Accumulated Depreciation—Equipment				
7	Accounts Payable		6 0 0 0 00		
8	Robert Harding, Capital		67 0 0 0 00		
9	Robert Harding, Drawing	2 0 0 0 00			
10	Fees Income		27 0 0 0 00		
11	Depreciation Expense—Equipment				
12	Rent Expense				
13	Salaries Expense	3 6 0 0 00			
14	Supplies Expense				
15	Utilities Expense	8 0 0 00			
16	Totals	100 0 0 0 00	100 0 0 0 00		
17					

Problem 5-2B ►
Objectives 1, 2, 3

Reconstructing a partial worksheet.

The adjusted trial balance of Cheryl Shore, Attorney-at-Law, as of November 30, 20--, after the company had completed the first month of operations, appears on page 155.

Appropriate adjustments have been made for the following items.

a. Supplies used during the month, $1,600.

b. Expired rent for the month, $1,800.

c. Depreciation expense for the month, $700.

─────────────

INSTRUCTIONS

1. Record the adjusted trial balance in the Adjusted Trial Balance columns of the worksheet.

2. Prepare the adjusting entries in the Adjustments columns.

3. Complete the Trial Balance columns of the worksheet prior to making the adjusting entries.

Analyze: Which contra asset account is on the adjusted trial balance?

Cheryl Shore, Attorney-at-Law Adjusted Trial Balance November 30, 20--		
ACCOUNT NAME	DEBIT	CREDIT
Cash	16,480	
Accounts Receivable	3,600	
Supplies	1,400	
Prepaid Rent	19,800	
Equipment	24,000	
Accumulated Depreciation—Equipment		700
Accounts Payable		7,000
Cheryl Shore, Capital		37,530
Cheryl Shore, Drawing	2,000	
Fees Income		31,200
Depreciation Expense—Equipment	700	
Rent Expense	1,800	
Salaries Expense	4,500	
Supplies Expense	1,600	
Utilities Expense	550	
Totals	76,430	76,430

Preparing financial statements from the worksheet.

The completed worksheet for Reliable Accounting Services for the month ended December 31, 20--, appears on pages 156–157.

1. Prepare an income statement.

2. Prepare a statement of owner's equity. The owner made no additional investments during the month.

3. Prepare a balance sheet.

Analyze: By what total amount did the value of assets reported on the balance sheet decrease due to the adjusting entries?

Preparing a worksheet and financial statements, journalizing adjusting entries, and posting to ledger accounts.

Jim Griffith owns Griffith Estate Planning and Investments. The trial balance of the firm for April 30, 20--, the first month of operations, is shown on page 156.

1. Complete the worksheet for the month.

2. Prepare an income statement, statement of owner's equity, and balance sheet. No additional investments were made by the owner during the month.

3. Journalize and post the adjusting entries. Use 3 for the journal page number.

◄ **Problem 5-3B**
Objective 4

INSTRUCTIONS

◄ **Problem 5-4B**
Objectives 1, 2, 3, 4, 5

INSTRUCTIONS

Griffith Estate Planning and Investments
Worksheet (Partial)
Month Ended April 30, 20--

	ACCOUNT NAME	TRIAL BALANCE		ADJUSTMENTS	
		DEBIT	CREDIT	DEBIT	CREDIT
1	Cash	9 4 0 0 00			
2	Accounts Receivable	2 6 0 0 00			
3	Supplies	1 2 0 0 00			
4	Prepaid Advertising	1 6 0 0 00			
5	Prepaid Rent	11 4 0 0 00			
6	Equipment	12 0 0 0 00			
7	Accumulated Depreciation—Equipment				
8	Accounts Payable		2 7 0 0 00		
9	Jim Griffith, Capital		25 2 9 0 00		
10	Jim Griffith, Drawing	1 0 0 0 00			
11	Fees Income		13 4 5 0 00		
12	Advertising Expense				
13	Depreciation Expense—Equipment				
14	Rent Expense				
15	Salaries Expense	1 9 5 0 00			
16	Supplies Expense				
17	Utilities Expense	2 9 0 00			
18	Totals	41 4 4 0 00	41 4 4 0 00		
19					

End-of-month adjustments must account for the following.

a. The supplies were purchased on April 1, 20--; inventory of supplies on April 30, 20--, showed a value of $400.

Reliable Accounting Services
Worksheet
Month Ended December 31, 20--

	ACCOUNT NAME	TRIAL BALANCE		ADJUSTMENTS	
		DEBIT	CREDIT	DEBIT	CREDIT
1	Cash	19 5 0 0 00			
2	Accounts Receivable	1 1 0 0 00			
3	Supplies	6 0 0 00			(a) 4 0 0 00
4	Prepaid Advertising	2 0 0 0 00			(b) 1 0 0 0 00
5	Fixtures	11 8 0 0 00			
6	Accumulated Depreciation—Fixtures				(c) 1 8 0 0 00
7	Accounts Payable		5 0 0 0 00		
8	Marsha Lynch, Capital		24 2 0 0 00		
9	Marsha Lynch, Drawing	2 0 0 0 00			
10	Fees Income		44 0 0 0 00		
11	Advertising Expense			(b) 1 0 0 0 00	
12	Depreciation Expense—Fixtures			(c) 1 8 0 0 00	
13	Rent Expense	7 2 0 0 00			
14	Salaries Expense	24 0 0 0 00			
15	Supplies Expense			(a) 4 0 0 00	
16	Utilities Expense	5 0 0 0 00			
17	Totals	73 2 0 0 00	73 2 0 0 00	3 2 0 0 00	3 2 0 0 00
18	Net Income				
19					
20					

b. The prepaid advertising contract was signed on April 1, 20--, and covers a four-month period.

c. Rent of $950 expired during the month.

d. Depreciation is computed using the straight-line method. The equipment has an estimated useful life of five years with no salvage value.

Analyze: Why are the costs that reduce the value of equipment not directly posted to the asset account **Equipment?**

CHAPTER 5 CHALLENGE PROBLEM

Worksheet and Financial Statements

The account balances for the Sanchez International Company on January 31, 20--, follow. The balances shown are after the first month of operations.

101	Cash	$36,950	401	Fees Income	$14,700
111	Accounts Receivable	1,700	511	Advertising Expense	1,000
121	Supplies	1,800	514	Depr. Expense—Equip.	0
131	Prepaid Insurance	10,000	517	Insurance Expense	0
141	Equipment	12,000	518	Rent Expense	1,600
142	Accum. Depr.—Equip.	0	519	Salaries Expense	8,000
202	Accounts Payable	3,000	520	Supplies Expense	0
301	Jamie Sanchez, Capital	60,000	523	Telephone Expense	750
302	Jamie Sanchez, Drawing	3,000	524	Utilities Expense	900

ADJUSTED TRIAL BALANCE		INCOME STATEMENT		BALANCE SHEET		
DEBIT	CREDIT	DEBIT	CREDIT	DEBIT	CREDIT	
19 5 0 0 00				19 5 0 0 00		1
1 1 0 0 00				1 1 0 0 00		2
2 0 0 00				2 0 0 00		3
1 0 0 0 00				1 0 0 0 00		4
11 8 0 0 00				11 8 0 0 00		5
	1 8 0 0 00				1 8 0 0 00	6
	5 0 0 0 00				5 0 0 0 00	7
	24 2 0 0 00				24 2 0 0 00	8
2 0 0 0 00				2 0 0 0 00		9
	44 0 0 0 00		44 0 0 0 00			10
1 0 0 0 00		1 0 0 0 00				11
1 8 0 0 00		1 8 0 0 00				12
7 2 0 0 00		7 2 0 0 00				13
24 0 0 0 00		24 0 0 0 00				14
4 0 0 00		4 0 0 00				15
5 0 0 0 00		5 0 0 0 00				16
75 0 0 0 00	75 0 0 0 00	39 4 0 0 00	44 0 0 0 00	35 6 0 0 00	31 0 0 0 00	17
		4 6 0 0 00			4 6 0 0 00	18
		44 0 0 0 00	44 0 0 0 00	35 6 0 0 00	35 6 0 0 00	19
						20

INSTRUCTIONS

1. Prepare the Trial Balance section of the worksheet.

2. Record the following adjustments in the Adjustments section of the worksheet.

    a. Supplies used during the month amounted to $900.

    b. The amount in the **Prepaid Insurance** account represents a payment made on January 1, 20--, for four months of insurance coverage.

    c. The equipment, purchased on January 1, 20--, has an estimated useful life of 10 years with no salvage value. The firm uses the straight-line method of depreciation.

3. Complete the worksheet.

4. Prepare an income statement, statement of owner's equity, and balance sheet (use the report form).

5. Record the balances in the general ledger accounts, then journalize and post the adjusting entries. Use 3 for the journal page number.

Analyze: If the useful life of the equipment had been 12 years instead of 10 years, how would net income have been affected?

CHAPTER 5   CRITICAL THINKING PROBLEM

The Effect of Adjustments

Assume you are the accountant for B&H Enterprises. Charles Brown, the owner of the company, is in a hurry to receive the financial statements for the year and asks you how soon they will be ready. You tell him you have just completed the trial balance and are getting ready to prepare the adjusting entries. Mr. Brown tells you not to waste time preparing adjusting entries but to complete the worksheet without them and prepare the financial statements based on the data in the trial balance. According to him, the adjusting entries will not make that much difference. The trial balance shows the following account balances:

Prepaid Insurance	$ 8,000
Supplies	16,000
Building	360,000
Accumulated Depreciation—Building	54,000

If the income statement were prepared using trial balance amounts, the net income would be $330,000.

A review of the company's records reveals the following information:

1. A two-year insurance policy was purchased three months prior to the end of the year for $8,000.

2. Purchases of supplies during the year totaled $16,000. An inventory of supplies taken at year-end showed supplies on hand of $2,000.

3. The building was purchased three years ago and has an estimated life of 20 years.

Write a memo to Mr. Brown explaining the effect on the financial statements of omitting the adjustments. Indicate the change to net income that results from the adjusting entries.

Business Connections

MANAGERIAL *FOCUS*   Understanding Adjustments   ◄ **Connection 1**

1. A building owned by Amos Company was recently valued at $425,000 by a real estate expert. The president of the company is questioning the accuracy of the firm's latest balance sheet because it shows a book value of $275,000 for the building. How would you explain this situation to the president?

2. At the beginning of the year, Wilson Company purchased a new building and some expensive new machinery. An officer of the firm has asked you whether this purchase will affect the firm's year-end income statement. What answer would you give?

3. Suppose the president of a company where you work as an accountant questions whether it is worthwhile for you to spend time making adjustments at the end of each accounting period. How would you explain the value of the adjustments?

4. How does the worksheet help provide vital information to management?

Ethical *DILEMMA*   **Depreciation Expense** One of your clients is   ◄ **Connection 2**
preparing for a bank loan and wants to show the highest income possible so that he can obtain the loan. The client uses the straight-line method for depreciating assets. Although you recommend a salvage value of $1,000 for a depreciable asset, the client insists that you use $3,000 in order to show less depreciation on the asset and consequently, a higher net income. What would you do?

Street **WISE:**
| Questions from the Real World | **Internal Changes** Refer to The Home Depot, Inc.   ◄ **Connection 3**
1999 Annual Report in Appendix B.

1. Based on the account categories listed on the consolidated statements of earnings and the consolidated balance sheets, what types of adjustments do you think the company makes each fiscal year? List three types of adjustments you believe would be necessary for this company. Describe your reasons for the adjustments you have listed.

2. By what amount has the account category "accumulated depreciation and amortization" increased from fiscal year 1998 to fiscal year 1999? Explain why you think this account has increased from 1998 to 1999.

FINANCIAL $TATEMENT
| A N A L Y S I S | **Depreciation** DuPont reported depreciation expense   ◄ **Connection 4**
of $1,444 million on its consolidated income statement for the period ended December 31, 1999. The following excerpt is taken from the company's consolidated balance sheet for the same year.

Consolidated Balance Sheet	
(Dollars in millions, except per share) December 31, 1999	
Property, Plant and Equipment (Note 16)	35,416
Less: Accumulated Depreciation	20,545
Net Property, Plant and Equipment	14,871

Analyze:

1. What percentage of the original cost of property, plant, and equipment was depreciated *during* 1999?

2. What percentage of property, plant, and equipment cost was depreciated *as of* December 31, 1999?

3. If the company continued to record depreciation expense at this level each year, how many years remain until all assets would be fully depreciated? (Assume no salvage values.)

Analyze Online: Connect to the DuPont Web site (**www.dupont.com**). Click on the *For Investor* link to find information on quarterly earnings.

4. What is the most recent quarterly earnings statement presented? What period does the statement cover?

5. For the most recent quarter, what depreciation expense was reported?

Connection 5 ▶ *Extending the Thought* **Adjusting Entries** Adjusting entries update accounts at the end of an accounting period. Items that belong to the period and were not previously recorded are recorded using an adjusting entry. Suppose that a customer owes money to your business, but you are informed that the customer plans to file bankruptcy. You believe that the customer will never pay the amount owed. Do you think that an entry should be made for this event? Why or why not?

Connection 6 ▶ **Business Communication** **Prepare for a Telephone Meeting** The owner of a sparkling water bottling business believes that it is sufficient to record depreciation only at year-end, yet financial statements are prepared at the end of every month. As the accountant for the business, you believe adjusting entries should be made to update equipment depreciation expense on a monthly basis. You plan to call the owner to discuss the issue. How will you begin the conversation? How would you suggest that the situation be handled? Prepare notes on what you plan to say before you make the call to the owner.

Connection 7 ▶ **TeamWork** **Research and Apply SFAS** Break into teams of three students. Have two team members research the Statement of Financial Accounting Standards No. 106, "Accounting for Post-Retirement Benefits Other Than Pensions," using library or Internet resources. Prepare notes on your findings. The third team member should prepare a final summary one-page report on the statement and how it relates to adjusting entries. Your report should include answers to these questions:

- When do companies record post-retirement benefits?
- Which adjusting entries are needed to record employee future benefits?

inter **NET**
CONNECTION **Big Four** Ernst & Young is one of the "Big Four" account-
ing firms. Visit their Web site at **www.ey.com.** What services does Ernst &
Young provide? What industries does the firm serve?

◄ **Connection 8**

Answers to Self Reviews

Answers to Section 1 Self Review

1. So that the financial statements can be prepared more efficiently.
2. Entries made to update accounts at the end of an accounting period to include previously unrecorded items that belong to the period.
3. To properly reflect the remaining cost to be used by the business (asset) and the amount already used by the business (expense).
4. **a. Supplies Expense** is debited for $350. **Supplies** is credited for $350.
5. **b. Rent Expense** is debited for $1,500. **Prepaid Rent** is credited for $1,500.
6. $10,000

Answers to Section 2 Self Review

1. (a) Beginning owner's equity
   (b) Net income or net loss for the period
   (c) Additional investments by the owner for the period
   (d) Withdrawals by the owner for the period
   (e) Ending balance of owner's equity
2. On a report form balance sheet, the liabilities and owner's equity are listed under the assets. On the account form, they are listed to the right of the assets.
3. The worksheet is only a tool that aids in the preparation of financial statements. Any changes in account balances recorded on the worksheet are not shown in the general journal and the general ledger until the adjusting entries have been journalized and posted.
4. **b.** Balance Sheet Debit column.
5. **b.** contra asset account.
6. $12,000. The adjustment for equipment depreciation is a debit to **Depreciation Expense** and a credit to **Accumulated Depreciation—Equipment.** The **Equipment** account is not changed.

Answers to Comprehensive Self Review

1. To allocate the cost of the asset to operations during its expected useful life.
2. Net income causes a net increase in owner's equity.
3. Credit balance.
4. $3,250. Debit column of the Balance Sheet section.
5. Debit column of the Balance Sheet section.

CHAPTER 6

Learning Objectives

1. Journalize and post closing entries.

2. Prepare a postclosing trial balance.

3. Interpret financial statements.

4. Review the steps in the accounting cycle.

5. Define the accounting terms new to this chapter.

Closing Entries and the Postclosing Trial Balance

GALILEO

www.galileo.com

*I*f you've ever used a travel agency to plan a vacation, book an airline flight, reserve a hotel room, or rent a car, chances are that your agent used a Galileo International Inc. product or service. The company provides travel agencies with the ability to access schedule and fare information, book reservations, and issue tickets for more than 500 airlines, 37 car rental companies, 47,000 hotel properties, 368 tour operators, and all major cruise lines.

Galileo International Inc. customers select from a wide array of sales, reservations, customer service, and business management products and services. Revenue is generated from electronic global distribution and information services, while expenses are incurred for operating, selling, administrative, and commission costs.

Thinking Critically
How do you think Galileo International Inc. executives and managers use financial statements to evaluate financial performance? How might these evaluations affect business policies or strategies?

For more information on Galileo International Inc., go to:
collegeaccounting.glencoe.com.

New Terms
Closing entries
Income Summary account
Interpret
Postclosing trial balance

Section Objective

1 Journalize and post closing entries.

WHY IT'S IMPORTANT
A business ends its accounting cycle at a given point in time. The closing process prepares the accounting records for the beginning of a new accounting cycle.

Terms to Learn

closing entries
Income Summary account

Closing Entries

In Chapter 5 we discussed the worksheet and the adjusting entries. In this chapter you will learn about closing entries.

The Closing Process

The seventh step in the accounting cycle is to journalize and post closing entries. **Closing entries** are journal entries that

- transfer the results of operations (net income or net loss) to owner's equity,
- reduce revenue, expense, and drawing account balances to zero.

The Income Summary Account

The **Income Summary account** is a special owner's equity account that is used only in the closing process to summarize results of operations. **Income Summary** has a zero balance after the closing process, and it remains with a zero balance until after the closing procedure for the next period.

Income Summary is classified as a temporary owner's equity account. Other names for this account are *Revenue and Expense Summary* and *Income and Expense Summary*.

FIGURE 6-1 ▼
Worksheet for Carter
Consulting Services

	ACCOUNT NAME	TRIAL BALANCE				ADJUSTMENTS			
		DEBIT		CREDIT		DEBIT		CREDIT	
1	Cash	64 4 0 0 00							
2	Accounts Receivable	4 0 0 0 00							
3	Supplies	2 0 0 0 00						(a)	5 0 0 0
4	Prepaid Rent	6 0 0 0 00						(b)	3 0 0 0 00
5	Equipment	35 0 0 0 00							
6	Accumulated Depreciation—Equipment							(c)	5 8 3 00
7	Accounts Payable			12 0 0 0 00					
8	Linda Carter, Capital			80 0 0 0 00					
9	Linda Carter, Drawing	3 0 0 0 00							
10	Fees Income			28 0 0 0 00					
11	Salaries Expense	5 0 0 0 00							
12	Utilities Expense	6 0 0 00							
13	Supplies Expense					(a)	5 0 0 00		
14	Rent Expense					(b)	3 0 0 0 00		
15	Depreciation Expense—Equipment					(c)	5 8 3 00		
16	Totals	120 0 0 0 00		120 0 0 0 00		4 0 8 3 00		4 0 8 3 00	
17	Net Income								
18									
19									

Carter Consulting Services
Worksheet
Month Ended December 31, 2004

Steps in the Closing Process

There are four steps in the closing process:

1. Transfer the balance of the revenue account to the **Income Summary** account.
2. Transfer the expense account balances to the **Income Summary** account.
3. Transfer the balance of the **Income Summary** account to the owner's capital account.
4. Transfer the balance of the drawing account to the owner's capital account.

The worksheet contains the data necessary to make the closing entries. Refer to Figure 6-1 as you study each closing entry.

Step 1: Transfer Revenue Account Balances

On December 31 the worksheet for Carter Consulting Services shows one revenue account, **Fees Income**. It has a credit balance of $28,000. To *close* an account means to reduce its balance to zero. In the general journal, enter a debit of $28,000 to close the **Fees Income** account. To balance the journal entry, enter a credit of $28,000 to the **Income Summary** account. This closing entry transfers the total revenue for the period to the **Income Summary** account and reduces the balance of the revenue account to zero.

The analysis of this closing entry is shown on page 166. In this chapter the visual analyses will show the beginning balances in all T accounts in order to illustrate closing entries.

1 Objective
Journalize and post closing entries.

Important!

Income Summary Account
The **Income Summary** account does not have an increase or decrease side and no normal balance side.

ADJUSTED TRIAL BALANCE		INCOME STATEMENT		BALANCE SHEET		
DEBIT	CREDIT	DEBIT	CREDIT	DEBIT	CREDIT	
64 4 0 0 00				64 4 0 0 00		1
4 0 0 0 00				4 0 0 0 00		2
1 5 0 0 00				1 5 0 0 00		3
3 0 0 0 00				3 0 0 0 00		4
35 0 0 0 00				35 0 0 0 00		5
	5 8 3 00				5 8 3 00	6
	12 0 0 0 00				12 0 0 0 00	7
	80 0 0 0 00				80 0 0 0 00	8
3 0 0 0 00				3 0 0 0 00		9
	28 0 0 0 00		28 0 0 0 00			10
5 0 0 0 00		5 0 0 0 00				11
6 0 0 00		6 0 0 00				12
5 0 0 00		5 0 0 00				13
3 0 0 0 00		3 0 0 0 00				14
5 8 3 00		5 8 3 00				15
120 5 8 3 00	120 5 8 3 00	9 6 8 3 00	28 0 0 0 00	110 9 0 0 00	92 5 8 3 00	16
		18 3 1 7 00			18 3 1 7 00	17
		28 0 0 0 00	28 0 0 0 00	110 9 0 0 00	110 9 0 0 00	18
						19

First Closing Entry—Close Revenue to Income Summary

Analysis

The revenue account, **Fees Income,** is decreased by $28,000 to zero. The $28,000 is transferred to the temporary owner's equity account, **Income Summary.**

Debit-Credit Rules

DEBIT Decreases in revenue accounts are recorded as debits. Debit **Fees Income** for $28,000.

CREDIT To transfer the revenue to the **Income Summary** account, credit **Income Summary** for $28,000.

T-Account Presentation

Fees Income		Income Summary
– | +		
Closing 28,000 | Balance 28,000		Closing 28,000

General Journal Entry

	DATE		DESCRIPTION	POST. REF.	DEBIT	CREDIT	
1	2004		Closing Entries				1
2	Dec.	31	Fees Income		28 0 0 0 00		2
3			Income Summary			28 0 0 0 00	3
4							4

GENERAL JOURNAL   PAGE ___4___

Write "Closing Entries" in the Description column of the general journal on the line above the first closing entry.

> Safeway Inc. reported sales of $28.8 billion for the fiscal year ended January 2, 2000. To close the revenue, the company would debit the **Sales** account and credit the **Income Summary** account.

Recall

Revenue
Revenue increases owner's equity.

Recall

Expenses
Expenses decrease owner's equity.

Step 2: Transfer Expense Account Balances

The Income Statement section of the worksheet for Carter Consulting Services lists five expense accounts. Since expense accounts have debit balances, enter a credit in each account to reduce its balance to zero. Debit the total of the expenses, $9,683, to the **Income Summary** account. This closing entry transfers total expenses to the **Income Summary** account and reduces the balances of the expense accounts to zero. This is a compound journal entry; it has more than one credit.

Second Closing Entry—Close Expenses to Income Summary

Analysis

The five expense account balances are reduced to zero. The total, $9,683, is transferred to the temporary owner's equity account, **Income Summary.**

Debit-Credit Rules

DEBIT To transfer the expenses to the **Income Summary** account, debit **Income Summary** for $9,683.

CREDIT Decreases to expense accounts are recorded as credits. Credit **Salaries Expense** for $5,000, **Utilities Expense** for $600, **Supplies Expense** for $500, **Rent Expense** for $3,000, and **Depreciation Expense—Equipment** for $583.

T-Account Presentation

Income Summary		Salaries Expense	
		+	–
Closing 9,683	Balance 28,000	Balance 5,000	Closing 5,000

Utilities Expense		Supplies Expense	
+	–	+	–
Balance 600	Closing 600	Balance 500	Closing 500

Rent Expense		Depreciation Expense—Equip.	
+	–	+	–
Balance 3,000	Closing 3,000	Balance 583	Closing 583

General Journal Entry

		GENERAL JOURNAL			PAGE 4		
	DATE	DESCRIPTION	POST. REF.	DEBIT	CREDIT		
4							4
5	Dec. 31	Income Summary		9 6 8 3 00			5
6		Salaries Expense			5 0 0 0 00		6
7		Utilities Expense			6 0 0 00		7
8		Supplies Expense			5 0 0 00		8
9		Rent Expense			3 0 0 0 00		9
10		Depreciation Expense—Equip.			5 8 3 00		10

After the second closing entry, the **Income Summary** account reflects all of the entries in the Income Statement columns of the worksheet.

Income Summary	
Dr.	Cr.
Closing 9,683	Closing 28,000
	Balance 18,317

For the three months ended March 30, 2000, operating expenses for Amazon.com totaled $326 million. At the end of the year, accountants for Amazon.com transferred the balances of all expense accounts to the **Income Summary** account.

Step 3: Transfer Net Income or Net Loss to Owner's Equity

The next step in the closing process is to transfer the balance of **Income Summary** to the owner's capital account. After the revenue and expense accounts are closed, the **Income Summary** account has a credit balance of $18,317, which is net income for the month. The journal entry to transfer net income to owner's equity is a debit to **Income Summary** and a credit to **Linda Carter, Capital** for $18,317. When this entry is posted, the balance of the **Income Summary** account is reduced to zero and the owner's capital account is increased by the amount of net income.

Closing Entry

Third Closing Entry—Close Income Summary to Capital

Analysis

The **Income Summary** account is reduced to zero. The net income amount, $18,317, is transferred to the owner's equity account. **Linda Carter, Capital** is increased by $18,317.

Debit-Credit Rules

DEBIT To reduce **Income Summary** to zero, debit **Income Summary** for $18,317.

CREDIT Net income increases owner's equity. Increases in owner's equity accounts are recorded as credits. Credit **Linda Carter, Capital** for $18,317.

T-Account Presentation

Income Summary		Linda Carter, Capital	
		−	+
Closing 18,317	Balance 18,317		Balance 80,000
			Closing 18,317

General Journal Entry

	GENERAL JOURNAL				PAGE 4	
DATE	DESCRIPTION	POST. REF.	DEBIT		CREDIT	
12 Dec. 31	Income Summary		18 3 1 7 00			12
13	Linda Carter, Capital				18 3 1 7 00	13

After the third closing entry, the **Income Summary** account has a zero balance. The summarized expenses ($9,683) and revenue ($28,000) have been transferred to the owner's equity account ($18,317 net income).

Income Summary				Linda Carter, Capital	
Dr.		**Cr.**		**Dr.**	**Cr.**
				−	+
Expenses	9,683	Revenue 28,000			Balance 80,000
Closing	18,317				Net Inc. 18,317
Balance	0				Balance 98,317

Step 4: Transfer the Drawing Account Balance to Capital

You will recall that withdrawals are funds taken from the business by the owner for personal use. Withdrawals are recorded in the drawing account. Withdrawals are not expenses of the business. They do not affect net income or net loss.

Withdrawals appear in the statement of owner's equity as a deduction from capital. Therefore, the drawing account is closed directly to the capital account.

When this entry is posted, the balance of the drawing account is reduced to zero and the owner's capital account is decreased by the amount of the withdrawals.

Withdrawals
Withdrawals decrease owner's equity.

Closing Entry

Fourth Closing Entry—Close Withdrawals to Capital

Analysis

The drawing account balance is reduced to zero. The balance of the drawing account, $3,000, is transferred to the owner's equity account.

Debit-Credit Rules

DEBIT Decreases in owner's equity accounts are recorded as debits. Debit **Linda Carter, Capital** for $3,000.

CREDIT Decreases in the drawing account are recorded as credits. Credit **Linda Carter, Drawing** for $3,000.

T-Account Presentation

Linda Carter, Capital		Linda Carter, Drawing	
−	+	+	−
Closing 3,000	Balance 98,317	Balance 3,000	Closing 3,000

General Journal Entry

GENERAL JOURNAL PAGE ___4___

	DATE		DESCRIPTION	POST. REF.	DEBIT	CREDIT	
15	Dec.	31	Linda Carter, Capital		3 0 0 0 00		15
16			Linda Carter, Drawing			3 0 0 0 00	16

The new balance of the **Linda Carter, Capital** account agrees with the amount listed in the Owner's Equity section of the balance sheet.

Linda Carter, Drawing			Linda Carter, Capital	
Dr.	Cr.		Dr.	Cr.
+	−		−	+
Balance 3,000	Closing 3,000		Drawing 3,000	Balance 80,000
				Net Inc. 18,317
Balance 0				Balance 95,317

Figure 6-2 on pages 170–172 shows the general journal and general ledger for Carter Consulting Services after the closing entries are recorded and posted. Note that

- "Closing" is entered in the Description column of the ledger accounts;
- the balance of **Linda Carter, Capital** agrees with the amount shown on the balance sheet for December 31;
- the ending balances of the drawing, revenue, and expense accounts are zero.

This example shows the closing process at the end of one month. Usually businesses make closing entries at the end of the fiscal year only.

FIGURE 6-2 ▶
Closing Process Completed: General Journal and General Ledger

Step 1
Close revenue.

Step 2
Close expense accounts.

Step 3
Close Income Summary.

Step 4
Close Drawing account.

GENERAL JOURNAL PAGE ___4___

	DATE		DESCRIPTION	POST. REF.	DEBIT	CREDIT	
1	2004		*Closing Entries*				1
2	Dec.	31	Fees Income	401	28 0 0 0 00		2
3			Income Summary	309		28 0 0 0 00	3
4							4
5		31	Income Summary	309	9 6 8 3 00		5
6			Salaries Expense	511		5 0 0 0 00	6
7			Utilities Expense	514		6 0 0 00	7
8			Supplies Expense	517		5 0 0 00	8
9			Rent Expense	520		3 0 0 0 00	9
10			Depreciation Expense—Equip.	523		5 8 3 00	10
11							11
12		31	Income Summary	309	18 3 1 7 00		12
13			Linda Carter, Capital	301		18 3 1 7 00	13
14							14
15		31	Linda Carter, Capital	301	3 0 0 0 00		15
16			Linda Carter, Drawing	302		3 0 0 0 00	16
17							17

ACCOUNT Linda Carter, Capital   ACCOUNT NO. 301

DATE		DESCRIPTION	POST. REF.	DEBIT	CREDIT	BALANCE DEBIT	BALANCE CREDIT
2004							
Nov.	6		J1		80 000 00		80 000 00
Dec.	31	Closing	J4		18 317 00		98 317 00
	31	Closing	J4	3 000 00			95 317 00

ACCOUNT Linda Carter, Drawing   ACCOUNT NO. 302

DATE		DESCRIPTION	POST. REF.	DEBIT	CREDIT	BALANCE DEBIT	BALANCE CREDIT
2004							
Dec.	31		J2	3 000 00		3 000 00	
	31	Closing	J4		3 000 00	— 0 —	

ACCOUNT Income Summary   ACCOUNT NO. 309

DATE		DESCRIPTION	POST. REF.	DEBIT	CREDIT	BALANCE DEBIT	BALANCE CREDIT
2004							
Dec.	31	Closing	J4		28 000 00		28 000 00
	31	Closing	J4	9 683 00			18 317 00
	31	Closing	J4	18 317 00			— 0 —

ACCOUNT Fees Income   ACCOUNT NO. 401

DATE		DESCRIPTION	POST. REF.	DEBIT	CREDIT	BALANCE DEBIT	BALANCE CREDIT
2004							
Dec.	31		J2		21 000 00		21 000 00
	31		J2		7 000 00		28 000 00
	31	Closing	J4	28 000 00			— 0 —

ACCOUNT Salaries Expense   ACCOUNT NO. 511

DATE		DESCRIPTION	POST. REF.	DEBIT	CREDIT	BALANCE DEBIT	BALANCE CREDIT
2004							
Dec.	31		J2	5 000 00		5 000 00	
	31	Closing	J4		5 000 00	— 0 —	

ACCOUNT Utilities Expense   ACCOUNT NO. 514

DATE		DESCRIPTION	POST. REF.	DEBIT	CREDIT	BALANCE DEBIT	BALANCE CREDIT
2004							
Dec.	31		J2	600 00		600 00	
	31	Closing	J4		600 00	— 0 —	

ACCOUNT _Supplies Expense_   ACCOUNT NO. _517_

DATE		DESCRIPTION	POST. REF.	DEBIT	CREDIT	BALANCE DEBIT	BALANCE CREDIT
2004							
Dec.	31	Adjusting	J3	5 0 0 00		5 0 0 00	
	31	Closing	J4		5 0 0 00	— 0 —	

ACCOUNT _Rent Expense_   ACCOUNT NO. _520_

DATE		DESCRIPTION	POST. REF.	DEBIT	CREDIT	BALANCE DEBIT	BALANCE CREDIT
2004							
Dec.	31	Adjusting	J3	3 0 0 0 00		3 0 0 0 00	
	31	Closing	J4		3 0 0 0 00	— 0 —	

ACCOUNT _Depreciation Expense—Equipment_   ACCOUNT NO. _523_

DATE		DESCRIPTION	POST. REF.	DEBIT	CREDIT	BALANCE DEBIT	BALANCE CREDIT
2004							
Dec.	31	Adjusting	J3	5 8 3 00		5 8 3 00	
	31	Closing	J4		5 8 3 00	— 0 —	

You have now seen seven steps of the accounting cycle. The steps we have discussed are (1) analyze transactions, (2) journalize the transactions, (3) post the transactions, (4) prepare a worksheet, (5) prepare financial statements, (6) record adjusting entries, and (7) record closing entries. Two steps remain. They are (8) prepare a postclosing trial balance, and (9) interpret the financial information.

Section 1 Self Review

Questions

1. How is the **Income Summary** account classified?

2. What are the four steps in the closing process?

3. What is the journal entry to close the drawing account?

Exercises

4. After closing, which accounts have zero balances?

   a. asset and liability accounts

   b. liability and capital accounts

   c. liability, drawing, and expense accounts

   d. revenue, drawing, and expense accounts

5. After the closing entries are posted, which account normally has a balance other than zero?

   a. **Capital**

   b. **Fees Income**

   c. **Income Summary**

   d. **Rent Expense**

Analysis

6. The business owner removes supplies that are worth $600 from the company stockroom. She intends to take them home for personal use. What effect will this have on the company's net income?

Using Accounting Information

In this section we will complete the accounting cycle for Carter Consulting Services.

Preparing the Postclosing Trial Balance

The eighth step in the accounting cycle is to prepare the postclosing trial balance, or *after-closing trial balance*. The **postclosing trial balance** is a statement that is prepared to prove the equality of total debits and credits. It is the last step in the end-of-period routine. The postclosing trial balance verifies that

- total debits equal total credits;
- revenue, expense, and drawing accounts have zero balances.

On the postclosing trial balance, the only accounts with balances are the permanent accounts:

- assets
- liabilities
- owner's equity

Figure 6-3 shows the postclosing trial balance for Carter Consulting Services.

Section Objectives

2 Prepare a postclosing trial balance.

WHY IT'S IMPORTANT
The postclosing trial balance helps the accountant identify any errors in the closing process.

3 Interpret financial statements.

WHY IT'S IMPORTANT
Financial statements contain information that can impact and drive operating decisions and plans for the future of the company.

4 Review the steps in the accounting cycle.

WHY IT'S IMPORTANT
Proper treatment of data as it flows through the accounting system ensures reliable financial reports.

Terms to Learn

interpret
postclosing trial balance

Carter Consulting Services
Postclosing Trial Balance
December 31, 2004

ACCOUNT NAME	DEBIT	CREDIT
Cash	64 4 0 0 00	
Accounts Receivable	4 0 0 0 00	
Supplies	1 5 0 0 00	
Prepaid Rent	3 0 0 0 00	
Equipment	35 0 0 0 00	
Accumulated Depreciation—Equipment		5 8 3 00
Accounts Payable		12 0 0 0 00
Linda Carter, Capital		95 3 1 7 00
Totals	107 9 0 0 00	107 9 0 0 00

◀ **FIGURE 6-3**
Postclosing Trial Balance

Finding and Correcting Errors

If the postclosing trial balance does not balance, there are errors in the accounting records. Find and correct the errors before continuing. Refer to Chapter 3 for tips on how to find common errors. Also use the audit trail to trace data through the accounting records to find errors.

2 Objective
Prepare a postclosing trial balance.

Accounting

Information Technology Services

Industry Overview

The information technology industry is projected to grow 117 percent between 1998 and 2008, making it the fastest growing industry in the United States. Products include software applications, data processing and retrieval systems, network systems, and Internet technologies.

Career Opportunities

- Financial Systems Analyst
- Database Marketing Programmer
- Data Services Manager
- Instructional Design Manager
- Accounting Technologist
- Director of Accounting Applications Development
- E-Commerce Director

Preparing for an Information Technology Services Career

- For a career as an accounting technologist or financial systems analyst, learn installation and implementation procedures for a variety of accounting applications.
- For general programming careers, obtain a bachelor's degree in computer or information science, mathematics, engineering, or the physical sciences.
- Learn current programming languages such as Java, VRML, or Visual C++.
- Gain extensive knowledge of systems and applications software packages.
- Obtain certification in database systems such as DB2, Oracle, or Sybase.
- Develop analytical and communication skills.
- Apply for a summer or co-op internship with a leading technology company like Intel.

Thinking Critically

Peachtree Software, Inc., the developer of Windows-based accounting software, frequently employs senior software engineers. What skills, experience, or education do you think would be desirable for this position?

Internet Application

Use Web sites to research information technology job opportunities in Great Plains, Peachtree, and Microsoft programs. Describe one job opportunity of interest to you. Include job title, position responsibilities, and education and skills requirements.

---

③ Objective

Interpret financial statements.

Interpreting the Financial Statements

The ninth and last step in the accounting cycle is interpreting the financial statements. Management needs timely and accurate financial information to operate the business successfully. To **interpret** the financial statements means to understand and explain the meaning and importance of information in accounting reports. Information in the financial statements provides answers to many questions:

- What is the cash balance?
- How much do customers owe the business?
- How much does the business owe suppliers?
- What is the profit or loss?

Managers of The Home Depot, Inc. use the corporation's financial statements to answer questions about the business. How much cash does our business have? What net earnings did our company report this year? For the fiscal year ended January 30, 2000, The Home Depot, Inc. reported an ending cash balance of $168 million and net earnings of $2.32 billion.

Figure 6-4 shows the financial statements for Carter Consulting Services at the end of its first accounting period. By interpreting these statements, management learns that

- the cash balance is $64,400,
- customers owe $4,000 to the business,
- the business owes $12,000 to its suppliers,
- the profit was $18,317.

◀ **FIGURE 6-4**
End-of-Month Financial
Statements

Carter Consulting Services
Income Statement
Month Ended December 31, 2004

Revenue		
Fees Income		28 000 00
Expenses		
Salaries Expense	5 000 00	
Utilities Expense	600 00	
Supplies Expense	500 00	
Rent Expense	3 000 00	
Depreciation Expense—Equipment	583 00	
Total Expenses		9 683 00
Net Income for the Month		18 317 00

Carter Consulting Services
Statement of Owner's Equity
Month Ended December 31, 2004

Linda Carter, Capital, December 1, 2004		80 000 00
Net Income for December	18 317 00	
Less Withdrawals for December	3 000 00	
Increase in Capital		15 317 00
Linda Carter, Capital, December 31, 2004		95 317 00

Carter Consulting Services
Balance Sheet
December 31, 2004

Assets		
Cash		64 400 00
Accounts Receivable		4 000 00
Supplies		1 500 00
Prepaid Rent		3 000 00
Equipment	35 000 00	
Less Accumulated Depreciation	583 00	34 417 00
Total Assets		107 317 00
Liabilities and Owner's Equity		
Liabilities		
Accounts Payable		12 000 00
Owner's Equity		
Linda Carter, Capital		95 317 00
Total Liabilities and Owner's Equity		107 317 00

About Accounting

Medical Accounting
Professionals in the health field, such as doctors and dentists, need to understand accounting so they can bill for services performed. Because patients have different insurance and payment plans, specialized software is used to manage the paperwork and keep track of the payments.

Objective

Review the steps in the accounting cycle.

The Accounting Cycle

You have learned about the entire accounting cycle as you studied the financial affairs of Carter Consulting Services during its first month of operations. Figure 6-5 summarizes the steps in the accounting cycle.

FIGURE 6-5 ▶
The Accounting Cycle

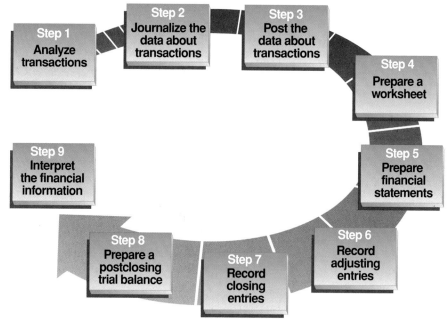

The Accounting Cycle
The accounting cycle is a series of steps performed during each period to classify, record, and summarize data to produce needed financial information.

International ‧‧‧‧‧‧‧‧‧ **INSIGHTS**

European Union

The European Economic Community was formed in 1958 to allow goods, services, workers, and money to move freely among its member countries. Now known as the European Union, the organization has developed a single currency, the *euro*. The euro is divided into one hundred cents.

Step 1. Analyze transactions. Analyze source documents to determine their effects on the basic accounting equation. The data about transactions appears on a variety of source documents such as:
- sales slips,
- purchase invoices,
- credit memorandums,
- check stubs.

Step 2. Journalize the transactions. Record the effects of the transactions in a journal.

Step 3. Post the journal entries. Transfer data from the journal to the general ledger accounts.

Step 4. Prepare a worksheet. At the end of each period, prepare a worksheet.
- Use the Trial Balance section to prove the equality of debits and credits in the general ledger.
- Use the Adjustments section to enter changes in account balances that are needed to present an accurate and complete picture of the financial affairs of the business.
- Use the Adjusted Trial Balance section to verify the equality of debits and credits after the adjustments. Extend the amounts from the Adjusted Trial Balance section to the Income Statement and Balance Sheet sections.
- Use the Income Statement and Balance Sheet sections to prepare the financial statements.

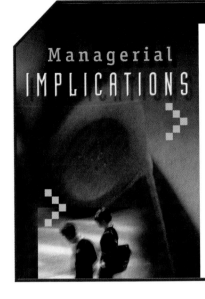

Managerial IMPLICATIONS

Financial Information

- Management needs timely and accurate financial information to control operations and make decisions.
- A well-designed and well-run accounting system provides reliable financial statements to management.
- Although management is not involved in day-to-day accounting procedures and end-of-period processes, the efficiency of the procedures affects the quality and promptness of the financial information that management receives.

Thinking Critically
If you owned or managed a business, how often would you want financial statements prepared? Why?

Step 5. Prepare financial statements. Prepare financial statements to report information to owners, managers, and other interested parties.
- The income statement shows the results of operations for the period.
- The statement of owner's equity reports the changes in the owner's financial interest during the period.
- The balance sheet shows the financial position of the business at the end of the period.

Step 6. Record adjusting entries. Use the worksheet to journalize and post adjusting entries. The adjusting entries are a permanent record of the changes in account balances shown on the worksheet.

Step 7. Record closing entries. Journalize and post the closing entries to
- transfer net income or net loss to owner's equity;
- reduce the balances of the revenue, expense, and drawing accounts to zero.

Step 8. Prepare a postclosing trial balance. The postclosing trial balance shows that the general ledger is in balance after the closing entries are posted. It is also used to verify that there are zero balances in revenue, expense, and drawing accounts.

Step 9. Interpret the financial information. Use financial statements to understand and communicate financial information and to make decisions. Accountants, owners, managers, and other interested parties interpret financial statements by comparing such things as profit, revenue, and expenses from one accounting period to the next.

In addition to financial statements, Adobe Systems Incorporated prepares a Financial Highlights report. This report lists total assets, revenue, net income, and number of worldwide employees for the past five years.

After studying the accounting cycle of Carter Consulting Services, you have an understanding of how data flows through a simple accounting system for a small business:

- Source documents are analyzed.
- Transactions are recorded in the general journal.
- Transactions are posted from the general journal to the general ledger.
- Financial information is proved, adjusted, and summarized on the worksheet.
- Financial information is reported on financial statements.

Figure 6-6 illustrates this data flow.

FIGURE 6-6 ▶
Flow of Data through a Simple Accounting System

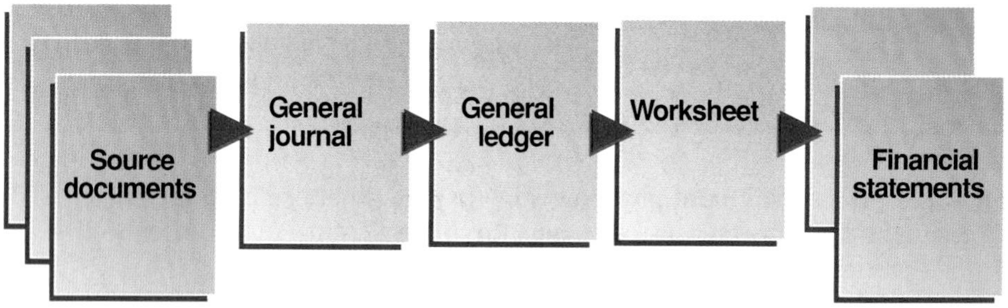

As you will learn in later chapters, some accounting systems have more complex records, procedures, and financial statements. However, the steps of the accounting cycle and the underlying accounting principles remain the same.

Section 2 Self Review

Questions

1. Why is a postclosing trial balance prepared?
2. What accounts appear on the postclosing trial balance?
3. What are the last three steps in the accounting cycle?

Exercises

4. Which of the following accounts will not appear on the postclosing trial balance?
   a. **J. T. Owens, Drawing**
   b. **Cash**
   c. **J. T. Owens, Capital**
   d. **Accounts Payable**
5. After the revenue and expense accounts are closed, **Income Summary** has a debit balance of $15,000. What does this figure represent?
   a. net profit of $15,000
   b. net loss of $15,000
   c. owner's withdrawals of $15,000
   d. increase in owner's equity of $15,000

Analysis

6. On which financial statement would you find the answer to each question?
   - What were the total fees earned this month?
   - How much money is owed to suppliers?
   - Did the business make a profit?
   - Is there enough cash to purchase new equipment?
   - What were the expenses?
   - Do customers owe money to the business?

(Answers to Section 2 Self Review are on page 195.)

Review

Chapter Summary

After the worksheet and financial statements have been completed and adjusting entries have been journalized and posted, the closing entries are recorded and a postclosing trial balance is prepared.

Learning Objectives

1 Journalize and post closing entries.

Journalizing and posting the closing entries is the seventh step in the accounting cycle. Closing entries transfer the results of operations to owner's equity and reduce the balances of the revenue and expense accounts to zero. The worksheet provides the data necessary for the closing entries. A temporary owner's equity account, **Income Summary,** is used. There are four steps in the closing process:

1. The balance of the revenue account is transferred to the **Income Summary** account.

Debit **Revenue**
  Credit **Income Summary**

2. The balances of the expense accounts are transferred to the **Income Summary** account.

Debit **Income Summary**
  Credit **Expenses**

3. The balance of the **Income Summary** account—net income or net loss—is transferred to the owner's capital account.

If **Income Summary** has a credit balance:

Debit **Income Summary**
  Credit **Owner's Capital**

If **Income Summary** has a debit balance:

Debit **Owner's Capital**
  Credit **Income Summary**

4. The drawing account is closed to the owner's capital account.

Debit **Owner's Capital**
  Credit **Drawing**

After the closing entries have been posted, the capital account reflects the results of operations for the period. The revenue and expense accounts, with zero balances, are ready to accumulate data for the next period.

2 Prepare a postclosing trial balance.

Preparing the postclosing trial balance is the eighth step in the accounting cycle. A postclosing trial balance is prepared to test the equality of total debit and credit balances in the general ledger after the adjusting and closing entries have been recorded. This report lists only permanent accounts open at the end of the period—asset, liability, and the owner's capital accounts. The temporary accounts—revenue, expenses, drawing, and **Income Summary**—apply only to one accounting period and do not appear on the postclosing trial balance.

3 Interpret financial statements.

The ninth step in the accounting cycle is interpreting the financial statements. Business decisions must be based on accurate and timely financial data.

4 Review the steps in the accounting cycle.

The accounting cycle consists of a series of steps that are repeated in each fiscal period. These steps are designed to classify, record, and summarize the data needed to produce financial information.

The steps of the accounting cycle are:
1. Analyze transactions.
2. Journalize the transactions.
3. Post the journal entries.
4. Prepare a worksheet.
5. Prepare financial statements.
6. Record adjusting entries.
7. Record closing entries.
8. Prepare a postclosing trial balance.
9. Interpret the financial information.

5 Define the accounting terms new to this chapter.

CHAPTER 6 GLOSSARY

Closing entries (p. 164) Journal entries that transfer the results of operations (net income or net loss) to owner's equity and reduce the revenue, expense, and drawing account balances to zero

Income Summary account (p. 164) A special owner's equity account that is used only in the closing process to summarize the results of operations

Interpret (p. 174) To understand and explain the meaning and importance of something (such as financial statements)

Postclosing trial balance (p. 173) A statement that is prepared to prove the equality of total debits and credits after the closing process is completed

Comprehensive Self Review

1. A firm has $25,000 in revenue for the period. Give the entry to close the **Fees Income** account.
2. A firm has the following expenses: **Rent Expense,** $1,600; **Salaries Expense,** $3,360; **Supplies Expense,** $640. Give the entry to close the expense accounts.
3. What three financial statements are prepared during the accounting cycle?
4. What is the last step in the accounting cycle?
5. Is the following statement true or false? Why? "All owner's equity accounts appear on the postclosing trial balance."

(Answers to Comprehensive Self Review are on page 195.)

Discussion Questions

1. Why is a postclosing trial balance prepared?
2. What accounts appear on a postclosing trial balance?
3. What is the accounting cycle?
4. Name the steps of the accounting cycle.
5. Briefly describe the flow of data through a simple accounting system.
6. What three procedures are performed at the end of each accounting period before the financial information is interpreted?
7. Where does the accountant obtain the data needed for the adjusting entries?
8. Why does the accountant record closing entries at the end of a period?
9. How is the **Income Summary** account used in the closing procedure?
10. Where does the accountant obtain the data needed for the closing entries?

Applications

EXERCISES

Journalize closing entries.

On December 31 the ledger of McWilliams Company contained the following account balances:

Cash	$18,000	Jerry McWilliams, Drawing	$12,000
Accounts Receivable	1,200	Fees Income	42,500
Supplies	800	Depreciation Expense	1,500
Equipment	15,000	Salaries Expense	14,000
Accumulated Depreciation	1,500	Supplies Expense	2,000
Accounts Payable	2,000	Telephone Expense	1,800
Jerry McWilliams, Capital	23,100	Utilities Expense	3,600

All the accounts have normal balances. Journalize the closing entries. Use 4 as the general journal page number.

◄ **Exercise 6-1**
Objective 1

Postclosing trial balance.

From the following list identify the accounts that will appear on the postclosing trial balance.

◄ **Exercise 6-2**
Objective 2

ACCOUNTS

1. Cash
2. Accounts Receivable
3. Supplies
4. Equipment
5. Accumulated Depreciation
6. Accounts Payable
7. Theron White, Capital
8. Theron White, Drawing
9. Fees Income
10. Depreciation Expense
11. Salaries Expense
12. Supplies Expense
13. Utilities Expense

Accounting cycle.

Following are the steps in the accounting cycle. Arrange the steps in the proper sequence.

◄ **Exercise 6-3**
Objective 4

1. Journalize the transactions.
2. Prepare a worksheet.
3. Analyze transactions.
4. Record adjusting entries.
5. Post the journal entries.
6. Prepare a postclosing trial balance.
7. Prepare financial statements.
8. Record closing entries.
9. Interpret the financial information.

Financial statements.

Managers often consult financial statements for specific types of information. Indicate whether each of the following items would appear on the income statement, statement of owner's equity, or the balance sheet. Use *I* for the income statement, *E* for the statement of owner's equity, and *B* for the balance sheet. If an item appears on more than one statement, use all letters that apply to that item.

1. Cash on hand
2. Revenue earned during the period
3. Total assets of the business
4. Net income for the period
5. Owner's capital at the end of the period
6. Supplies on hand
7. Cost of supplies used during the period
8. Accounts receivable of the business
9. Accumulated depreciation on the firm's equipment
10. Amount of depreciation charged off on the firm's equipment during the period
11. Original cost of the firm's equipment
12. Book value of the firm's equipment
13. Total expenses for the period
14. Accounts payable of the business
15. Owner's withdrawals for the period

Exercise 6-5 ►

Objective 1

Closing entries.

The **Income Summary** and **Alexis Wells, Capital** accounts for Alexis Production Company at the end of its accounting period follow.

ACCOUNT _Income Summary_   ACCOUNT NO. _399_

DATE		DESCRIPTION	POST. REF.	DEBIT	CREDIT	BALANCE DEBIT	BALANCE CREDIT
20--							
Dec.	31	Closing	J4		7 7 5 0 00		7 7 5 0 00
	31	Closing	J4	5 0 5 0 00			2 7 0 0 00
	31	Closing	J4	2 7 0 0 00			— 0 —

ACCOUNT _Alexis Wells, Capital_   ACCOUNT NO. _301_

DATE		DESCRIPTION	POST. REF.	DEBIT	CREDIT	BALANCE DEBIT	BALANCE CREDIT
20--							
Dec.	1		J1		25 0 0 0 00		25 0 0 0 00
	31	Closing	J4		2 7 0 0 00		27 7 0 0 00
	31	Closing	J4	1 4 0 0 00			26 3 0 0 00

Complete the following statements.

1. Total revenue for the period is _____.

2. Total expenses for the period are _____.

3. Net income for the period is _____.

4. Owner's withdrawals for the period are _____.

Closing entries.

◀ **Exercise 6-6**
Objective 1

The ledger accounts of Cool Streams Internet Company appear as follows on March 31, 20--.

ACCOUNT NO.	ACCOUNT	BALANCE
101	Cash	$11,500
111	Accounts Receivable	2,200
121	Supplies	1,350
131	Prepaid Insurance	3,480
141	Equipment	16,800
142	Accumulated Depreciation—Equipment	3,360
202	Accounts Payable	1,800
301	Alonzo Hernandez, Capital	19,600
302	Alonzo Hernandez, Drawing	1,000
401	Fees Income	46,000
510	Depreciation Expense—Equipment	1,680
511	Insurance Expense	1,600
514	Rent Expense	4,800
517	Salaries Expense	23,600
518	Supplies Expense	650
519	Telephone Expense	900
523	Utilities Expense	1,200

All accounts have normal balances. Journalize and post the closing entries. Use 4 as the page number for the general journal in journalizing the closing entries.

Closing entries.

◀ **Exercise 6-7**
Objective 1

On December 31 the **Income Summary** account of Hensley Company has a debit balance of $9,000 after revenue of $14,000 and expenses of $23,000 were closed to the account. **Ronnie Hensley, Drawing** has a debit balance of $1,000 and **Ronnie Hensley, Capital** has a credit balance of $28,000. Record the journal entries necessary to complete closing the accounts. What is the new balance of **Ronnie Hensley, Capital?**

Accounting cycle.

◀ **Exercise 6-8**
Objective 4

Complete a chart of the accounting cycle by writing the steps of the cycle in their proper sequence.

Problems

Selected problems can be completed using:
🕐 **Peachtree** 📖 **QuickBooks** ▦ **Spreadsheets**

PROBLEM SET A

Problem 6-1A ►
Objective 1

Adjusting and closing entries.

The Longacre Consumer Satisfaction Company, owned by Mary Longacre, is employed by large companies to test consumer reaction to new products. On January 31 the firm's worksheet showed the following adjustments data: (a) supplies used, $280; (b) expired rent, $1,500; and (c) depreciation on office equipment, $560. The balances of the revenue and expense accounts listed in the Income Statement section of the worksheet and the drawing account listed in the Balance Sheet section of the worksheet are given below.

REVENUE AND EXPENSE ACCOUNTS

401	Fees Income	$38,500 Cr.
511	Depr. Expense—Office Equipment	560 Dr.
514	Rent Expense	1,500 Dr.
517	Salaries Expense	20,600 Dr.
520	Supplies Expense	280 Dr.
523	Telephone Expense	470 Dr.
526	Travel Expense	4,460 Dr.
529	Utilities Expense	230 Dr.

DRAWING ACCOUNT

302	Mary Longacre, Drawing	2,400 Dr.

Wilson Talent Agency
Worksheet
Month Ended December 31, 20--

	ACCOUNT NAME	TRIAL BALANCE DEBIT	TRIAL BALANCE CREDIT	ADJUSTMENTS DEBIT	ADJUSTMENTS CREDIT
1	Cash	7 7 0 0 00			
2	Accounts Receivable	1 0 0 0 00			
3	Supplies	5 0 0 00			(a) 2 0 0 00
4	Prepaid Advertising	2 0 0 0 00			(b) 2 5 0 00
5	Equipment	5 0 0 0 00			
6	Accumulated Depreciation—Equipment				(c) 2 0 0 00
7	Accounts Payable		1 0 0 0 00		
8	Virginia Wilson, Capital		11 0 0 0 00		
9	Virginia Wilson, Drawing	7 0 0 00			
10	Fees Income		6 2 5 0 00		
11	Supplies Expense			(a) 2 0 0 00	
12	Advertising Expense			(b) 2 5 0 00	
13	Depreciation Expense—Equipment			(c) 2 0 0 00	
14	Salaries Expense	1 2 0 0 00			
15	Utilities Expense	1 5 0 00			
16	Totals	18 2 5 0 00	18 2 5 0 00	6 5 0 00	6 5 0 00
17	Net Income				
18					
19					

1. Record the adjusting entries in the general journal, page 3.
2. Record the closing entries in the general journal, page 4.

Analyze: What closing entry is required to close a drawing account?

Journalizing and posting adjusting and closing entries and preparing a postclosing trial balance.

A completed worksheet for Wilson Talent Agency is shown on pages 184–185.

◄ **Problem 6-2A**
Objectives 1, 2

INSTRUCTIONS

1. Record balances as of December 31, 20--, in the ledger accounts.
2. Journalize (use 3 as the page number) and post the adjusting entries.
3. Journalize (use 4 as the page number) and post the closing entries.
4. Prepare a postclosing trial balance.

Analyze: How many accounts are listed in the Adjusted Trial Balance section? How many accounts are listed on the postclosing trial balance?

Journalizing and posting closing entries.

On December 31, after adjustments, Preston Company's ledger contains the following account balances.

◄ **Problem 6-3A**
Objective 1

101	Cash	$ 9,300 Dr.
111	Accounts Receivable	4,200 Dr.
121	Supplies	750 Dr.
131	Prepaid Rent	9,900 Dr.
141	Equipment	13,500 Dr.
142	Accumulated Depreciation—Equip.	375 Cr.

ADJUSTED TRIAL BALANCE		INCOME STATEMENT		BALANCE SHEET		
DEBIT	CREDIT	DEBIT	CREDIT	DEBIT	CREDIT	
7 7 0 0 00				7 7 0 0 00		1
1 0 0 0 00				1 0 0 0 00		2
3 0 0 00				3 0 0 00		3
1 7 5 0 00				1 7 5 0 00		4
5 0 0 0 00				5 0 0 0 00		5
	2 0 0 00				2 0 0 00	6
	1 0 0 0 00				1 0 0 0 00	7
	11 0 0 0 00				11 0 0 0 00	8
7 0 0 00				7 0 0 00		9
	6 2 5 0 00		6 2 5 0 00			10
2 0 0 00		2 0 0 00				11
2 5 0 00		2 5 0 00				12
2 0 0 00		2 0 0 00				13
1 2 0 0 00		1 2 0 0 00				14
1 5 0 00		1 5 0 00				15
18 4 5 0 00	18 4 5 0 00	2 0 0 0 00	6 2 5 0 00	16 4 5 0 00	12 2 0 0 00	16
		4 2 5 0 00			4 2 5 0 00	17
		6 2 5 0 00	6 2 5 0 00	16 4 5 0 00	16 4 5 0 00	18
						19

202	Accounts Payable	1,875 Cr.
301	Sara Preston, Capital (12/1/20--)	13,905 Cr.
302	Sara Preston, Drawing	1,800 Dr.
401	Fees Income	34,500 Cr.
511	Advertising Expense	1,200 Dr.
514	Depreciation Expense—Equip.	225 Dr.
517	Rent Expense	900 Dr.
519	Salaries Expense	7,200 Dr.
523	Utilities Expense	1,680 Dr.

INSTRUCTIONS

1. Record the balances in the ledger accounts as of December 31.
2. Journalize the closing entries in the general journal, page 4.
3. Post the closing entries to the general ledger accounts.

Analyze: What is the balance of the **Salaries Expense** account after closing entries are posted?

Problem 6-4A ►
Objectives 1, 2, 4

Worksheet, journalizing and posting adjusting and closing entries, and the postclosing trial balance.

A partially completed worksheet for Bush Auto Detailing Service, a firm that details cars and vans, follows.

Bush Auto Detailing Service
Worksheet
Month Ended December 31, 20--

	ACCOUNT NAME	TRIAL BALANCE DEBIT	TRIAL BALANCE CREDIT	ADJUSTMENTS DEBIT	ADJUSTMENTS CREDIT
1	Cash	31 0 5 0 00			
2	Accounts Receivable	4 9 5 0 00			
3	Supplies	4 0 0 0 00			(a) 1 6 0 0 00
4	Prepaid Advertising	3 0 0 0 00			(b) 1 4 0 0 00
5	Equipment	20 0 0 0 00			
6	Accumulated Depreciation—Equipment				(c) 4 8 0 00
7	Accounts Payable		5 0 0 0 00		
8	Mark Bush, Capital		35 5 0 0 00		
9	Mark Bush, Drawing	2 0 0 0 00			
10	Fees Income		30 0 0 0 00		
11	Supplies Expense			(a) 1 6 0 0 00	
12	Advertising Expense			(b) 1 4 0 0 00	
13	Depreciation Expense—Equipment			(c) 4 8 0 00	
14	Salaries Expense	4 8 0 0 00			
15	Utilities Expense	7 0 0 00			
16	Totals	70 5 0 0 00	70 5 0 0 00	3 4 8 0 00	3 4 8 0 00
17					
18					
19					
20					

1. Record balances as of December 31 in the ledger accounts.

2. Prepare the worksheet.

3. Journalize (use 3 as the journal page number) and post the adjusting entries.

4. Journalize (use 4 as the journal page number) and post the closing entries.

5. Prepare a postclosing trial balance.

Analyze: What total debits were posted to the general ledger to complete all closing entries for the month of December?

PROBLEM SET B

Adjusting and closing entries.

◄ **Problem 6-1B**
Objective 1

Thrifty Maid Service, owned by Michael Turner, provides cleaning services to hotels, motels, and hospitals. On January 31 the firm's worksheet showed the following adjustment data. The balances of the revenue and expense accounts listed in the Income Statement section of the worksheet and the drawing account listed in the Balance Sheet section of the worksheet are also given.

ADJUSTMENTS

a. Supplies used, $2,860
b. Expired insurance, $370
c. Depreciation on machinery, $1,120

REVENUE AND EXPENSE ACCOUNTS

401 Fees Income	$32,800	Cr.
511 Depreciation Expense—Machinery	1,120	Dr.
514 Insurance Expense	370	Dr.
517 Rent Expense	3,000	Dr.
520 Salaries Expense	16,000	Dr.
523 Supplies Expense	2,860	Dr.
526 Telephone Expense	210	Dr.
529 Utilities Expense	640	Dr.

DRAWING ACCOUNT

302 Michael Turner, Drawing	2,400	Dr.

1. Record the adjusting entries in the general journal, page 3.

2. Record the closing entries in the general journal, page 4.

Analyze: What effect did the adjusting entry for expired insurance have on the **Insurance Expense** account?

Dave's Lawn and Garden Service
Worksheet
Month Ended December 31, 20--

	ACCOUNT NAME	TRIAL BALANCE		ADJUSTMENTS			
		DEBIT	CREDIT	DEBIT		CREDIT	
1	Cash	2 7 0 0 00					
2	Accounts Receivable	5 0 0 00					
3	Supplies	5 0 0 00			(a)	2 5 0 00	
4	Prepaid Advertising	7 5 0 00			(b)	1 0 0 00	
5	Equipment	5 0 0 0 00					
6	Accumulated Depreciation—Equipment				(c)	1 2 5 00	
7	Accounts Payable		7 5 0 00				
8	Dave Andrews, Capital		6 8 5 0 00				
9	Dave Andrews, Drawing	7 0 0 00					
10	Fees Income		3 9 0 0 00				
11	Supplies Expense			(a)	2 5 0 00		
12	Advertising Expense			(b)	1 0 0 00		
13	Depreciation Expense—Equipment			(c)	1 2 5 00		
14	Salaries Expense	1 2 0 0 00					
15	Utilities Expense	1 5 0 00					
16	Totals	11 5 0 0 00	11 5 0 0 00	4 7 5 00		4 7 5 00	
17	Net Income						
18							
19							
20							
21							

Problem 6-2B ►
Objectives 1, 2

Journalizing and posting adjusting and closing entries and preparing a postclosing trial balance.

A completed worksheet for Dave's Lawn and Garden Service is shown above.

INSTRUCTIONS

1. Record the balances as of December 31 in the ledger accounts.
2. Journalize (use 3 as the page number) and post the adjusting entries.
3. Journalize (use 4 as the page number) and post the closing entries.
4. Prepare a postclosing trial balance.

Analyze: What total credits were posted to the general ledger to complete the closing entries?

| | ADJUSTED TRIAL BALANCE | | INCOME STATEMENT | | BALANCE SHEET | | |
	DEBIT	CREDIT	DEBIT	CREDIT	DEBIT	CREDIT	
1	2 7 0 0 00				2 7 0 0 00		1
2	5 0 0 00				5 0 0 00		2
3	2 5 0 00				2 5 0 00		3
4	6 5 0 00				6 5 0 00		4
5	5 0 0 0 00				5 0 0 0 00		5
6		1 2 5 00				1 2 5 00	6
7		7 5 0 00				7 5 0 00	7
8		6 8 5 0 00				6 8 5 0 00	8
9	7 0 0 00				7 0 0 00		9
10		3 9 0 0 00		3 9 0 0 00			10
11	2 5 0 00		2 5 0 00				11
12	1 0 0 00		1 0 0 00				12
13	1 2 5 00		1 2 5 00				13
14	1 2 0 0 00		1 2 0 0 00				14
15	1 5 0 00		1 5 0 00				15
16	11 6 2 5 00	11 6 2 5 00	1 8 2 5 00	3 9 0 0 00	9 8 0 0 00	7 7 2 5 00	16
17			2 0 7 5 00			2 0 7 5 00	17
18			3 9 0 0 00	3 9 0 0 00	9 8 0 0 00	9 8 0 0 00	18
19							19
20							20
21							21

Journalizing and posting closing entries.

On December 31, after adjustments, The Green House's ledger contains the following account balances.

◄ **Problem 6-3B**
Objective 1

101	Cash	$ 9,500 Dr.
111	Accounts Receivable	2,400 Dr.
121	Supplies	1,000 Dr.
131	Prepaid Rent	7,700 Dr.
141	Equipment	12,000 Dr.
142	Accumulated Depreciation—Equip.	300 Cr.
202	Accounts Payable	3,250 Cr.
301	Shane McCoy, Capital (12/1/20--)	19,150 Cr.
302	Shane McCoy, Drawing	1,200 Dr.
401	Fees Income	18,000 Cr.
511	Advertising Expense	1,100 Dr.
514	Depreciation Expense—Equip.	300 Dr.
517	Rent Expense	700 Dr.
519	Salaries Expense	3,600 Dr.
523	Utilities Expense	1,200 Dr.

INSTRUCTIONS

1. Record the balances in the ledger accounts as of December 31.
2. Journalize the closing entries in the general journal, page 4.
3. Post the closing entries to the general ledger accounts.

Analyze: List the accounts that required closing entries for the month of December.

Problem 6-4B ►
Objectives 1, 2, 4

INSTRUCTIONS

Worksheet, journalizing and posting adjusting and closing entries, and the postclosing trial balance.

A partially completed worksheet for Lance Wallace, CPA, for the month ending June 30, 20--, is shown below.

1. Record the balances as of June 30 in the ledger accounts.
2. Prepare the worksheet.
3. Journalize (use 3 as the journal page number) and post the adjusting entries.
4. Journalize (use 4 as the journal page number) and post the closing entries.
5. Prepare a postclosing trial balance.

Analyze: What is the reported net income for the month of June for Lance Wallace, CPA?

Lance Wallace, CPA
Worksheet
Month Ended June 30, 20--

	ACCOUNT NAME	TRIAL BALANCE DEBIT	TRIAL BALANCE CREDIT	ADJUSTMENTS DEBIT		ADJUSTMENTS CREDIT	
1	Cash	3 3 0 0 00					
2	Accounts Receivable	2 7 0 0 00					
3	Supplies	2 4 0 0 00				(a)	4 5 0 00
4	Computers	10 8 0 0 00					
5	Accumulated Depreciation—Computers		9 0 0 00			(b)	1 8 0 00
6	Accounts Payable		3 6 0 0 00				
7	Lance Wallace, Capital		11 2 5 0 00				
8	Lance Wallace, Drawing	3 0 0 0 00					
9	Fees Income		17 7 0 0 00				
10	Salaries Expense	9 0 0 0 00					
11	Supplies Expense			(a)	4 5 0 00		
12	Depreciation Expense—Computers			(b)	1 8 0 00		
13	Travel Expense	1 5 0 0 00					
14	Utilities Expense	7 5 0 00					
15	Totals	33 4 5 0 00	33 4 5 0 00		6 3 0 00		6 3 0 00
16							
17							
18							
19							

CHAPTER 6 | CHALLENGE PROBLEM

The Closing Process

The Trial Balance section of the worksheet for The Car Wash for the period ended December 31, 20--, appears below. Adjustments data is also given.

ADJUSTMENTS

a. Supplies used, $1,200
b. Expired insurance, $800
c. Depreciation expense for machinery, $400

INSTRUCTIONS

1. Complete the worksheet.

2. Prepare an income statement.

3. Prepare a statement of owner's equity.

4. Prepare a balance sheet.

5. Journalize the adjusting entries in the general journal, page 3.

6. Journalize the closing entries in the general journal, page 4.

7. Prepare a postclosing trial balance.

Analyze: If the adjusting entry for expired insurance had been recorded in error as a credit to **Insurance Expense** and a debit to **Prepaid Insurance** for $800, what reported net income would have resulted?

The Car Wash
Worksheet
Month Ended December 31, 20--

	ACCOUNT NAME	TRIAL BALANCE		ADJUSTMENTS	
		DEBIT	CREDIT	DEBIT	CREDIT
1	Cash	13 6 0 0 00			
2	Accounts Receivable	3 0 0 0 00			
3	Supplies	2 4 0 0 00			(a) 1 2 0 0 00
4	Prepaid Insurance	3 6 0 0 00			(b) 8 0 0 00
5	Machinery	28 0 0 0 00			
6	Accumulated Depreciation—Machinery				(c) 4 0 0 00
7	Accounts Payable		4 5 0 0 00		
8	T. A. Watson, Capital		24 8 6 0 00		
9	T. A. Watson, Drawing	2 0 0 0 00			
10	Fees Income		27 5 0 0 00		
11	Supplies Expense			(a) 1 2 0 0 00	
12	Insurance Expense			(b) 8 0 0 00	
13	Salaries Expense	3 7 0 0 00			
14	Depreciation Expense—Machinery			(c) 4 0 0 00	
15	Utilities Expense	5 6 0 00			
16	Totals	56 8 6 0 00	56 8 6 0 00	2 4 0 0 00	2 4 0 0 00
17					
18					

Closing Entries and the Postclosing Trial Balance **Chapter 6 • 191**

Owner's Equity

Brenda Powell, the bookkeeper for Executive Home Designs Company, has just finished posting the closing entries for the year to the ledger. She is concerned about the following balances:

Capital account balance in the general ledger:	$194,200
Ending capital balance on the statement of owner's equity:	111,200

Brenda knows that these amounts should agree and asks for your assistance in reviewing her work.

Your review of the general ledger of Executive Home Designs Company reveals a beginning capital balance of $100,000. You also review the general journal for the accounting period and find the following closing entries.

GENERAL JOURNAL   PAGE ___15___

	DATE		DESCRIPTION	POST. REF.	DEBIT	CREDIT	
1	20--		*Closing Entries*				1
2	Dec.	31	Fees Income		196 0 0 0 00		2
3			Accumulated Depreciation		17 0 0 0 00		3
4			Accounts Payable		66 0 0 0 00		4
5			Income Summary			279 0 0 0 00	5
6							6
7		31	Income Summary		184 8 0 0 00		7
8			Salaries Expense			156 0 0 0 00	8
9			Supplies Expense			10 0 0 0 00	9
10			Depreciation Expense			4 8 0 0 00	10
11			Brenda Powell, Drawing			14 0 0 0 00	11
12							12
13							13
14							14

1. What errors did Ms. Powell make in preparing the closing entries for the period?

2. Prepare a general journal entry to correct the errors made.

3. Explain why the balance of the capital account in the ledger after closing entries have been posted will be the same as the ending capital balance on the statement of owner's equity.

Business Connections

 **Interpreting Financial Statements**

◀ **Connection 1**

1. An officer of Carson Company recently commented that when he receives the firm's financial statements, he looks at just the bottom line of the income statement—the line that shows the net income or net loss for the period. He said that he does not bother with the rest of the income statement because "it's only the bottom line that counts." He also does not read the balance sheet. Do you think this manager is correct in the way he uses the financial statements? Why or why not?

2. The president of Henderson Corporation is concerned about the firm's ability to pay its debts on time. What items on the balance sheet would help her to assess the firm's debt-paying ability?

3. Why is it important that a firm's financial records be kept up to date and that management receive the financial statements promptly after the end of each accounting period?

4. What kinds of operating and general policy decisions might be influenced by data on the financial statements?

Ethical **DILEMMA** **Overstated Income** You have just taken over as bookkeeper of a company and immediately discover that the firm did not make adjusting entries every year. From your conversations with other employees in the firm, you have determined that the former bookkeeper intentionally did this in order to report a higher net income to impress the owner. What will you do?

◀ **Connection 2**

Street WISE:
Questions from the Real World **Closing Process** Refer to The Home Depot, Inc. *1999 Annual Report* in Appendix B.

◀ **Connection 3**

1. Locate the consolidated balance sheets and consolidated statements of earnings. List ten permanent account categories and five temporary account categories found within these statements.

2. Based on the consolidated statements of earnings, what is the closing entry that should be made to zero out all operating expense categories?

FINANCIAL STATEMENT
A N A L Y S I S **Income Statement** In 1999 CSX Corporation reported operating expenses of $10,203 million. A partial list of the company's operating expenses follows. CSX Corporation reported revenues from external customers to be $10,811 million for the year. These revenues are divided among three operations: surface transportation, container shipping, and contract logistics.

◀ **Connection 4**

CSX
CORPORATION

Revenues from External Customers (Dollars in millions)		Operating Expenses (partial list) (Dollars in millions)	
Surface Transportation	$6,566	Labor and Fringe Benefits	$3,471
Container Shipping	3,809	Materials, Supplies, and Other	2,662
Contract Logistics	436	Conrail Operating Fee, Rent, and Services	280
		Building and Equipment Rent	1,211
		Inland Transportation	1,044
		Depreciation	595
		Fuel	484

Analyze:

1. If the given categories represent the related general ledger accounts, what journal entry would be made to close the expense accounts at year-end?

2. What journal entry would be made to close the revenue accounts?

Analyze Online: Locate the Web site for CSX Corporation **(www.csx.com).** Click on *About CSX Corporation.* Within the *Financial Information* link, find the most recent annual report.

3. On the consolidated statement of earnings, what was the amount reported for operating expenses?

4. What percentage increase or decrease does this figure represent from the operating expenses reported in 1999 of $10,203 million?

Connection 5 ► *Extending the Thought* **Worksheets** Suppose that an accountant with many years' experience suggests that you skip preparation of the worksheet. The accountant claims that the financial statements can be prepared using only the general ledger account balances. What risks can you identify if the accountant uses this procedure? Do you agree or disagree with this approach? Why?

Connection 6 ► Business Communication **Training** As the general ledger accountant for a music supply store, you have just completed the trial balance, closing entries, and postclosing trial balance for the month. Next month, you will be on vacation during the closing process. Your boss has hired a temporary employee to perform these duties while you are away. Prepare a descriptive report for your replacement explaining the differences between a postclosing trial balance and a trial balance.

Connection 7 ► **Team**Work **Job Opportunities** Using the Internet or your local newspaper, review job listings to find accounting positions that require knowledge of adjusting and closing entries. Each member of the team should contribute at least two job titles and their related description and required skills. Create a listing for all jobs.

inter NET CONNECTION GAO Visit the U.S. General Accounting Office Web site at **www.gao.gov.** When was the GAO founded? What is its purpose? Who is the head of the GAO? When does this person's term expire? What is the purpose of FraudNET? ◄ **Connection 8**

Answers to Self Reviews

Answers to Section 1 Self Review

1. A temporary owner's equity account.
2. Close the revenue account to **Income Summary.**
   Close the expense accounts to **Income Summary.**
   Close the **Income Summary** account to the capital account.
   Close the drawing account to the capital account.
3. Debit **Capital** and credit **Drawing.**
4. **d.** revenue, drawing, and expense accounts
5. **a. Capital**
6. No effect on net income.

Answers to Section 2 Self Review

1. To make sure the general ledger is in balance after the adjusting and closing entries are posted.
2. Asset, liability, and the owner's capital accounts.
3. (7) Record closing entries, (8) prepare a postclosing trial balance, (9) interpret the financial statements.
4. **a. J. T. Owens, Drawing**
5. **b.** net loss of $15,000
6. The income statement will answer questions about fees earned, expenses incurred, and profit. The balance sheet will answer questions about the cash balance, the amount owed by customers, and the amount owed to suppliers.

Answers to Comprehensive Self Review

1. Fees Income   25,000
      Income Summary   25,000

2. Income Summary   5,600
      Rent Expense   1,600
      Salaries Expense   3,360
      Supplies Expense   640

3. Income statement, statement of owner's equity, and balance sheet.
4. Interpret the financial statements.
5. False. The *temporary* owner's equity accounts do not appear on the postclosing trial balance. The temporary owner's equity accounts are the drawing account and **Income Summary.**

Service Business Accounting Cycle

Carter Consulting Services

This project will give you an opportunity to apply your knowledge of accounting principles and procedures by handling all the accounting work of Carter Consulting Services for the month of January 2005.

INTRODUCTION

Assume that you are the chief accountant for Carter Consulting Services. During January the business will use the same types of records and procedures that you learned about in Chapters 1 through 6. The chart of accounts for Carter Consulting Services has been expanded to include a few new accounts. Follow the instructions to complete the accounting records for the month of January.

Carter Consulting Services
Chart of Accounts

Assets
101 Cash
111 Accounts Receivable
121 Supplies
134 Prepaid Insurance
137 Prepaid Rent
141 Equipment
142 Accumulated Depreciation—
     Equipment

Liabilities
202 Accounts Payable

Owner's Equity
301 Linda Carter, Capital
302 Linda Carter, Drawing
309 Income Summary

Revenue
401 Fees Income

Expenses
511 Salaries Expense
514 Utilities Expense
517 Supplies Expense
520 Rent Expense
523 Depreciation Expense—
     Equipment
526 Advertising Expense
529 Maintenance Expense
532 Telephone Expense
535 Insurance Expense

INSTRUCTIONS

1. Open the general ledger accounts and enter the balances for January 1, 2005. Obtain the necessary figures from the postclosing trial balance prepared on December 31, 2004, which appears on page 173.

2. Analyze each transaction and record it in the general journal. Use page 3 to begin January's transactions.

3. Post the transactions to the general ledger accounts.

4. Prepare the Trial Balance section of the worksheet.

5. Prepare the Adjustments section of the worksheet.

   a. Compute and record the adjustment for supplies used during the month. An inventory taken on January 31 showed supplies of $1,450 on hand.

   b. Compute and record the adjustment for expired insurance for the month.

   c. Record the adjustment for one month of expired rent of $3,000.

   d. Record the adjustment for depreciation of $583 on the old equipment for the month. The first adjustment for depreciation for the new equipment will be recorded in February.

6. Complete the worksheet.

7. Prepare an income statement for the month.

8. Prepare a statement of owner's equity.

9. Prepare a balance sheet using the report form.

10. Journalize and post the adjusting entries.

11. Journalize and post the closing entries.

12. Prepare a postclosing trial balance.

DATE		TRANSACTIONS
Jan.	2	Purchased supplies for $3,000; issued Check 1015.
	2	Purchased a one-year insurance policy for $2,400; issued Check 1016.
	7	Sold services for $11,600 in cash and $1,490 on credit during the first week of January.
	12	Collected a total of $590 on account from credit customers during the first week of January.
	12	Issued Check 1017 for $790 to pay for special promotional advertising to new businesses on the local radio station during the month.
	13	Collected a total of $1,000 on account from credit customers during the second week of January.
	14	Returned supplies that were damaged for a cash refund of $80.
	15	Sold services for $17,000 in cash and $800 on credit during the second week of January.
	20	Purchased supplies for $1,600 from Partners, Inc.; received Invoice 4823, payable in 30 days. *accts pay*
	20	Sold services for $7,780 in cash and $5,120 on credit during the third week of January.
	20	Collected a total of $1,500 on account from credit customers during the third week of January.
		Continued

DATE	(cont.)	TRANSACTIONS
Jan. 21		Issued Check 1018 for $2,550 to pay for maintenance work on the office equipment.
22		Issued Check 1019 for $300 to pay for special promotional advertising to new businesses in the local newspaper.
23		Received the monthly telephone bill for $430 and paid it with Check 1020.
26		Collected a total of $3,120 on account from credit customers during the fourth week of January.
27		Issued Check 1021 for $8,000 to Office Plus, as payment on account for Invoice 2223.
28		Sent Check 1022 for $470 in payment of the monthly bill for utilities.
29		Sold services for $11,780 in cash and $1,350 on credit during the fourth week of January.
31		Issued Checks 1023–1027 for $10,800 to pay the monthly salaries of the regular employees and three part-time workers.
31		Issued Check 1028 for $4,000 for personal use.
31		Issued Check 1029 for $830 to pay for maintenance services for the month.
31		Purchased additional equipment for $12,000 from Expert Equipment Company; issued Check 1030 for $2,500 and bought the rest on credit. The equipment has a five-year life and no salvage value.
31		Sold services for $1,090 in cash and $650 on credit on January 31.

Analyze: Compare the January 31 balance sheet you prepared with the December 31 balance sheet shown in Chapter 6 on page 175.

a. What changes occurred in total assets, liabilities, and the owner's ending capital?

b. What changes occurred in the **Cash** and **Accounts Receivable** accounts?

c. Has there been an improvement in the firm's financial position? Why or why not?

PART 2

Recording Financial Data

Chapter 7

Accounting for Sales and Accounts Receivable

Chapter 8

Accounting for Purchases and Accounts Payable

Chapter 9

Cash Receipts, Cash Payments, and Banking Procedures

A large company such as The Home Depot, Inc. must account for millions of transactions each year. The Home Depot, Inc. has been named "America's Most Admired Specialty Retailer" by *Fortune* magazine for seven consecutive years.

Thinking Critically
What do you think it takes to be voted America's Most Admired Specialty Retailer?

Learning Objectives

1. Record credit sales in a sales journal.

2. Post from the sales journal to the general ledger accounts.

3. Post from the sales journal to the customers' accounts in the accounts receivable subsidiary ledger.

4. Record sales returns and allowances in the general journal.

5. Post sales returns and allowances.

6. Prepare a schedule of accounts receivable.

7. Compute trade discounts.

8. Record credit card sales in appropriate journals.

9. Prepare the state sales tax return.

10. Define the accounting terms new to this chapter.

Accounting for Sales and Accounts Receivable

WAL★MART®
www.walmartstores.com

*E*xploding from a small chain of variety stores that began in Arkansas and Missouri in 1962, Wal-Mart Stores, Inc. has grown into a powerhouse of more than 1,773 Wal-Mart stores, 780 Supercenters, and 466 Sam's Clubs. Founder Sam Walton attributed his company's phenomenal growth to its hometown identity, low prices, and friendly customer service. During store visits, Sam Walton was known to ask his employees to implement the "10-Foot Attitude":

"I want you to promise that whenever you come within 10 feet of a customer, you will look him in the eye, greet him and ask if you can help him."[1]

[1] Wal-Mart Stores, Inc. Web site, Culture Stores

Thinking Critically
What other factors besides customer service have contributed to Wal-Mart's phenomenal success?

For more information on Wal-Mart Stores, Inc., go to: collegeaccounting.glencoe.com.

New Terms

Accounts receivable ledger

Charge-account sales

Contra revenue account

Control account

Credit memorandum

Invoice

List price

Manufacturing business

Merchandise inventory

Merchandising business

Net price

Net sales

Open-account credit

Retail business

Sales allowance

Sales journal

Sales return

Schedule of accounts receivable

Service business

Special journal

Subsidiary ledger

Trade discount

Wholesale business

Section Objectives

1 Record credit sales in a sales journal.

WHY IT'S IMPORTANT
Credit sales are a major source of revenue for many businesses. The sales journal is an efficient option for recording large volumes of credit sales transactions.

2 Post from the sales journal to the general ledger accounts.

WHY IT'S IMPORTANT
A well-designed accounting system prevents repetitive tasks.

Terms to Learn

manufacturing business
merchandise inventory
merchandising business
retail business
sales journal
service business
special journal
subsidiary ledger

Merchandise Sales

When an accounting system is developed for a firm, one important consideration is the nature of the firm's operations. The three basic types of businesses are a **service business**, which sells services; a **merchandising business**, which sells goods that it purchases for resale; and a **manufacturing business**, which sells goods that it produces.

Carter Consulting Services, the firm that was described in Chapters 2 through 6, is a service business. The firm that we will examine next, The Trend Center, is a merchandising business that sells the latest fashion clothing for men, women, and children. It is a **retail business**, which sells goods and services directly to individual consumers. The Trend Center is a sole proprietorship owned and operated by Stacee Harris, who was formerly a sales manager for a major retail clothing store.

The Trend Center must account for purchases and sales of goods, and for **merchandise inventory**—the stock of goods that is kept on hand. Refer to the chart of accounts for The Trend Center on page 203. You will learn about the accounts in this and following chapters.

To allow for efficient recording of financial data, the accounting systems of most merchandising businesses include special journals and subsidiary ledgers.

Special Journals and Subsidiary Ledgers

A **special journal** is a journal that is used to record only one type of transaction. A **subsidiary ledger** is a ledger that contains accounts of a single type. Table 7-1 lists the journals and ledgers that merchandising businesses generally use in their accounting systems. In this chapter we will discuss the sales journal and the accounts receivable subsidiary ledger.

TABLE 7-1 ▶
Journals and Ledgers Used by Merchandising Businesses

JOURNALS

Type of Journal	Purpose
Sales	To record sales of merchandise on credit
Purchases	To record purchases of merchandise on credit
Cash receipts	To record cash received from all sources
Cash payments	To record all disbursements of cash
General	To record all transactions that are not recorded in another special journal and all adjusting and closing entries

LEDGERS

Type of Ledger	Content
General	Assets, liabilities, owner's equity, revenue, and expense accounts
Accounts receivable	Accounts for credit customers
Accounts payable	Accounts for creditors

THE TREND CENTER
Chart of Accounts

ASSETS
101 Cash
105 Petty Cash Fund
109 Notes Receivable
111 Accounts Receivable
112 Allowance for Doubtful Accounts
116 Interest Receivable
121 Merchandise Inventory
126 Prepaid Insurance
127 Prepaid Interest
129 Supplies
131 Store Equipment
132 Accumulated Depreciation— Store Equipment
141 Office Equipment
142 Accumulated Depreciation— Office Equipment

LIABILITIES
201 Notes Payable—Trade
202 Notes Payable—Bank
205 Accounts Payable
216 Interest Payable
221 Social Security Tax Payable
222 Medicare Tax Payable
223 Employee Income Tax Payable
225 Federal Unemployment Tax Payable
227 State Unemployment Tax Payable
229 Salaries Payable
231 Sales Tax Payable

OWNER'S EQUITY
301 Stacee Harris, Capital
302 Stacee Harris, Drawing
399 Income Summary

REVENUE
401 Sales
451 Sales Returns and Allowances
491 Interest Income
493 Miscellaneous Income

COST OF GOODS SOLD
501 Purchases
502 Freight In
503 Purchases Returns and Allowances
504 Purchases Discounts

EXPENSES
611 Salaries Expense—Sales
612 Supplies Expense
614 Advertising Expense
617 Cash Short or Over
626 Depreciation Expense—Store Equipment
634 Rent Expense
637 Salaries Expense—Office
639 Insurance Expense
641 Payroll Taxes Expense
643 Utilities Expense
649 Telephone Expense
651 Uncollectible Accounts Expense
657 Bank Fees Expense
658 Delivery Expense
659 Depreciation Expense— Office Equipment
691 Interest Expense
693 Miscellaneous Expense

The Sales Journal

The **sales journal** is used to record only sales of merchandise on credit. To understand the need for a sales journal, consider how credit sales made at The Trend Center would be entered and posted using a general journal and general ledger. Refer to Figure 7-1 on pages 204–205.

Note the word "Balance" in the ledger accounts. To record beginning balances, enter the date in the Date column, the word "Balance" in the Description column, a check mark in the Posting Reference column, and the amount in the Debit or Credit Balance column.

Most state and many local governments impose a sales tax on retail sales of certain goods and services. Businesses are required to collect this tax from their customers and send it to the proper tax agency at regular intervals. When goods or services are sold on credit, the sales tax is usually recorded at the time of the sale even though it will not be collected immediately. A liability account called **Sales Tax Payable** is credited for the sales tax charged.

As you can see, a great amount of repetition is involved in both journalizing and posting these sales. The four credit sales made on January 3, 8, 11, and 15 required four separate entries in the general journal and involved four debits to **Accounts Receivable,** four credits to **Sales Tax Payable,** four

Important!

Business Classifications
The term *merchandising* refers to the type of business operation, not the type of legal entity. The Trend Center could have been a partnership or a corporation instead of a sole proprietorship.

credits to **Sales** (the firm's revenue account), and four descriptions. The posting of twelve items to the three general ledger accounts represents still further duplication of effort. This recording procedure is not efficient for a business that has a substantial number of credit sales each month.

FIGURE 7-1 ▶

Journalizing and Posting
Credit Sales

GENERAL JOURNAL PAGE ___2___

	DATE		DESCRIPTION	POST. REF.	DEBIT	CREDIT	
1	20--						1
2	Jan.	3	Accounts Receivable	111	2 1 4 00		2
3			Sales Tax Payable	231		1 4 00	3
4			Sales	401		2 0 0 00	4
5			Sold merchandise on				5
6			credit to John Allen,				6
7			Sales Slip 1101				7
8							8
9		8	Accounts Receivable	111	5 3 5 00		9
10			Sales Tax Payable	231		3 5 00	10
11			Sales	401		5 0 0 00	11
12			Sold merchandise on				12
13			credit to Larry Bates,				13
14			Sales Slip 1102				14
15							15
16		11	Accounts Receivable	111	6 4 2 00		16
17			Sales Tax Payable	231		4 2 00	17
18			Sales	401		6 0 0 00	18
19			Sold merchandise on				19
20			credit to Blake Howard,				20
21			Sales Slip 1103				21
22							22
23		15	Accounts Receivable	111	4 2 8 00		23
24			Sales Tax Payable	231		2 8 00	24
25			Sales	401		4 0 0 00	25
26			Sold merchandise on				26
27			credit to Sarah Gomez,				27
28			Sales Slip 1104				28
29							29
30							30
31							31
32							32

ACCOUNT _Accounts Receivable_   ACCOUNT NO. _111_

DATE		DESCRIPTION	POST. REF.	DEBIT	CREDIT	BALANCE DEBIT	BALANCE CREDIT
20--							
Jan.	1	Balance	✓			3 2 1 0 00	
	3		J2	2 1 4 00		3 4 2 4 00	
	8		J2	5 3 5 00		3 9 5 9 00	
	11		J2	6 4 2 00		4 6 0 1 00	
	15		J2	4 2 8 00		5 0 2 9 00	

ACCOUNT *Sales Tax Payable*   **ACCOUNT NO.** _231_

DATE	DESCRIPTION	POST. REF.	DEBIT	CREDIT	BALANCE DEBIT	BALANCE CREDIT
20--						
Jan. 1	Balance	✓				7 4 9 00
3		J2		1 4 00		7 6 3 00
8		J2		3 5 00		7 9 8 00
11		J2		4 2 00		8 4 0 00
15		J2		2 8 00		8 6 8 00

ACCOUNT *Sales*   **ACCOUNT NO.** _401_

DATE	DESCRIPTION	POST. REF.	DEBIT	CREDIT	BALANCE DEBIT	BALANCE CREDIT
20--						
Jan. 3		J2		2 0 0 00		2 0 0 00
8		J2 ✓		5 0 0 00		7 0 0 00
11		J2		6 0 0 00		1 3 0 0 00
15		J2		4 0 0 00		1 7 0 0 00

Recording Transactions in a Sales Journal

A special journal intended only for credit sales provides a more efficient method of recording these transactions. Figure 7-2 shows the January credit sales of The Trend Center recorded in a sales journal. Since The Trend Center is located in a state that has a 7 percent sales tax on retail transactions, its sales journal includes a Sales Tax Payable Credit column. For the sake of simplicity, the sales journal shown here includes a limited number of transactions. The firm actually has many more credit sales each month.

❶ Objective

Record credit sales in a sales journal.

◀ **FIGURE 7-2**
Sales Journal

SALES JOURNAL   PAGE ___1___

	DATE	SALES SLIP NO.	CUSTOMER'S ACCOUNT DEBITED	POST. REF.	ACCOUNTS RECEIVABLE DEBIT	SALES TAX PAYABLE CREDIT	SALES CREDIT	
1	20--							1
2	Jan. 3	1101	John Allen		2 1 4 00	1 4 00	2 0 0 00	2
3	8	1102	Larry Bates		5 3 5 00	3 5 00	5 0 0 00	3
4	11	1103	Blake Howard		6 4 2 00	4 2 00	6 0 0 00	4
5	15	1104	Sarah Gomez		4 2 8 00	2 8 00	4 0 0 00	5
6	18	1105	Ed Ramirez		8 5 6 00	5 6 00	8 0 0 00	6
7	21	1106	James Walker		3 2 1 00	2 1 00	3 0 0 00	7
8	28	1107	Linda Sanchez		1 0 7 00	7 00	1 0 0 00	8
9	29	1108	Newton Wu		1 0 7 0 00	7 0 00	1 0 0 0 00	9
10	31	1109	Kim Johnson		9 6 3 00	6 3 00	9 0 0 00	10
11	31	1110	John Allen		2 6 7 50	1 7 50	2 5 0 00	11
12								12

Notice that the headings and columns in the sales journal speed up the recording process. No general ledger account names are entered. Only one line is needed to record all information for each transaction—date, sales slip number, customer's name, debit to **Accounts Receivable,** credit

Recall

Journals
A journal is a day-to-day record of a firm's transactions.

to **Sales Tax Payable,** and credit to **Sales.** Since the sales journal is used for a single purpose, there is no need to enter any descriptions. Thus a great deal of repetition is avoided.

Entries in the sales journal are usually made daily. In a retail business such as The Trend Center, the data needed for each entry is taken from a copy of the customer's sales slip, as shown in Figure 7-3.

FIGURE 7-3 ▶
Customer's Sales Slip

The Trend Center
1010 Red Bird Lane
Dallas, Texas 75268

DATE	SALESPERSON	AUTH.
1/3/--	A. Wells	

Goods Taken [X]   To Be Delivered [ ]

S e n d   t o

Special Instructions:

I authorize this purchase to be charged on my account.

John Au
Signature

SALES SLIP 1101

Qty.	Description	Unit Price	Amount
1	Sports Coat	200 00	200 00
		Sales Tax	14 00
		Amount	214 00

NAME: John Allen
ADDRESS: 1313 Broken Arrow Road
Dallas, TX 75267-6205

Many small retail firms use a sales journal similar to the one shown in Figure 7-2. However, keep in mind that special journals vary in format according to the needs of individual businesses.

Posting from a Sales Journal

A sales journal not only simplifies the initial recording of credit sales, it also eliminates a great deal of repetition in posting these transactions. With a sales journal, it is not necessary to post each credit sale individually to general ledger accounts. Instead, summary postings are made at the end of the month after the amount columns of the sales journal are totaled. See Figure 7-4 on page 207 for an illustration of posting from the sales journal to the general ledger.

In actual practice, before any posting takes place, the equality of the debits and credits recorded in the sales journal is proved by comparing the column totals. The proof for the sales journal in Figure 7-4 is given below. All multicolumn special journals should be proved in a similar manner before their totals are posted.

PROOF OF SALES JOURNAL

	Debits
Accounts Receivable Debit column	$5,403.50

	Credits
Sales Tax Payable Credit column	$ 353.50
Sales Credit column	5,050.00
	$5,403.50

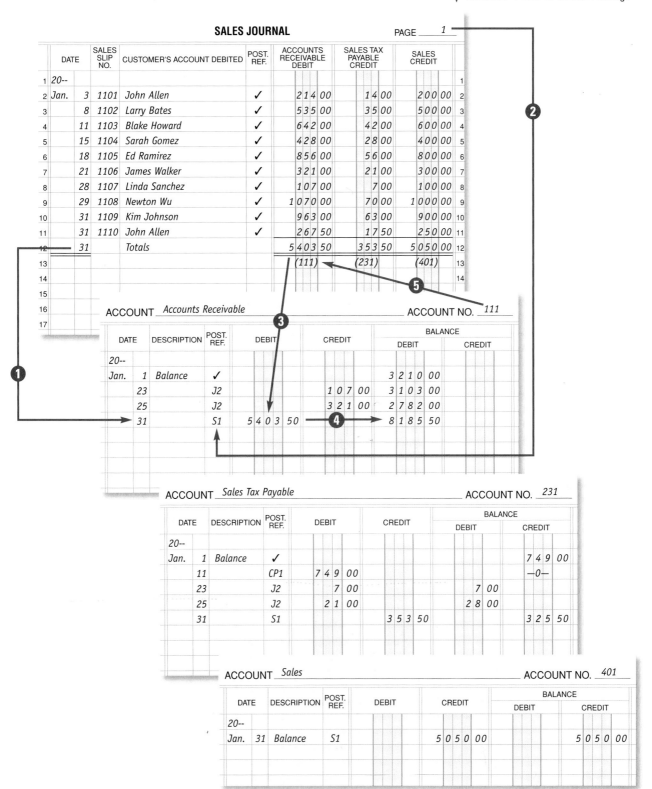

SALES JOURNAL   PAGE ____1____

	DATE		SALES SLIP NO.	CUSTOMER'S ACCOUNT DEBITED	POST. REF.	ACCOUNTS RECEIVABLE DEBIT	SALES TAX PAYABLE CREDIT	SALES CREDIT	
1	20--								1
2	Jan.	3	1101	John Allen	✓	214 00	14 00	200 00	2
3		8	1102	Larry Bates	✓	535 00	35 00	500 00	3
4		11	1103	Blake Howard	✓	642 00	42 00	600 00	4
5		15	1104	Sarah Gomez	✓	428 00	28 00	400 00	5
6		18	1105	Ed Ramirez	✓	856 00	56 00	800 00	6
7		21	1106	James Walker	✓	321 00	21 00	300 00	7
8		28	1107	Linda Sanchez	✓	107 00	7 00	100 00	8
9		29	1108	Newton Wu	✓	1 070 00	70 00	1 000 00	9
10		31	1109	Kim Johnson	✓	963 00	63 00	900 00	10
11		31	1110	John Allen	✓	267 50	17 50	250 00	11
12		31		Totals		5 403 50	353 50	5 050 00	12
13						(111)	(231)	(401)	13
14									14
15									15
16									16
17									17

ACCOUNT _Accounts Receivable_   **ACCOUNT NO.** ___111___

DATE		DESCRIPTION	POST. REF.	DEBIT	CREDIT	BALANCE DEBIT	BALANCE CREDIT
20--							
Jan.	1	Balance	✓			3 210 00	
	23		J2		107 00	3 103 00	
	25		J2		321 00	2 782 00	
	31		S1	5 403 50		8 185 50	

ACCOUNT _Sales Tax Payable_   **ACCOUNT NO.** ___231___

DATE		DESCRIPTION	POST. REF.	DEBIT	CREDIT	BALANCE DEBIT	BALANCE CREDIT
20--							
Jan.	1	Balance	✓				749 00
	11		CP1	749 00			—0—
	23		J2	7 00		7 00	
	25		J2	21 00		28 00	
	31		S1		353 50		325 50

ACCOUNT _Sales_   **ACCOUNT NO.** ___401___

DATE		DESCRIPTION	POST. REF.	DEBIT	CREDIT	BALANCE DEBIT	BALANCE CREDIT
20--							
Jan.	31	Balance	S1		5 050 00		5 050 00

Important!

Posting
When posting from the sales journal, post information moving from left to right across the ledger form.

After the equality of the debits and credits has been verified, the sales journal is ruled and the column totals are posted to the general ledger accounts involved. To indicate that the postings have been made, the general ledger account numbers are entered in parentheses under the column totals in the sales journal. The abbreviation S1 is written in the Posting Reference column of the accounts, showing that the data was posted from page 1 of the sales journal.

The check marks in the sales journal in Figure 7-4 indicate that the amounts have been posted to the individual customer accounts. Posting from the sales journal to the customer accounts in the subsidiary ledger is illustrated later in this chapter.

Advantages of a Sales Journal

Using a special journal for credit sales saves time, effort, and recording space. Both the journalizing process and the posting process become more efficient, but the advantage in the posting process is especially significant. If a business used the general journal to record 300 credit sales a month, the firm would have to make 900 postings to the general ledger—300 to **Accounts Receivable,** 300 to **Sales Tax Payable,** and 300 to **Sales.** With a sales journal, the firm makes only three summary postings to the general ledger at the end of each month no matter how many credit sales were entered.

The use of a sales journal and other special journals also allows division of work. In a business with a fairly large volume of transactions, it is essential that several employees be able to record transactions at the same time.

Finally, the sales journal improves the audit trail by bringing together all entries for credit sales in one place and listing them by source document number as well as by date. This procedure makes it easier to trace the details of such transactions.

Section 1 Self Review

Questions

1. What type of transaction is recorded in the sales journal?

2. What is a subsidiary ledger? Give two examples of subsidiary ledgers.

3. What is a special journal? Give four examples of special journals.

Exercises

4. Types of business operations are
   a. service, merchandising, corporation.
   b. sole proprietorship, merchandising, manufacturing.
   c. service, merchandising, manufacturing.

5. Which of the following is not a reason to use a sales journal?
   a. increases efficiency
   b. allows division of work
   c. increases credit sales
   d. improves audit trail

Analysis

6. All sales recorded in this sales journal were made on account and are taxable at a rate of 6 percent. What errors have been made in the entries? Assume the Sales Credit column is correct.

SALES JOURNAL   PAGE ___1___

	DATE	SALES SLIP NO.	CUSTOMER'S ACCOUNT DEBITED	POST. REF.	ACCOUNTS RECEIVABLE DEBIT	SALES TAX PAYABLE CREDIT	SALES CREDIT	
12	Apr. 25	4100	Susan Li		3 21 00	21 00	3 00 00	12
13	25	4101	James Hahn		4 27 00	27 00	4 50 00	13
14								14

Accounts Receivable

A business that extends credit to customers must manage its accounts receivable carefully. Accounts receivable represents a substantial asset for many businesses, and this asset must be converted into cash in a timely manner. Otherwise, a firm may not be able to pay its bills even though it has a large volume of sales and earns a satisfactory profit.

The Accounts Receivable Ledger

The accountant needs detailed information about the transactions with credit customers and the balances owed by such customers at all times. This information is provided by an **accounts receivable ledger** with individual accounts for all credit customers. The accounts receivable ledger is referred to as a subsidiary ledger because it is separate from and subordinate to the general ledger.

Using an accounts receivable ledger makes it possible to verify that customers are paying their balances on time and that they are within their credit limits. The accounts receivable ledger also provides a convenient way to answer questions from credit customers. Customers may ask about their current balances or about a possible billing error.

The accounts for credit customers are maintained in a balance ledger form with three money columns, as shown in Figure 7-5 on page 210. Notice that this form does not contain a column for indicating the type of account balance. The balances in the customer accounts are presumed to be debit balances since asset accounts normally have debit balances. However, occasionally there is a credit balance because a customer has overpaid an amount owed or has returned goods that were already paid for. One common procedure for dealing with this situation is to circle the balance in order to show that it is a credit amount.

For a small business such as The Trend Center, customer accounts are alphabetized in the accounts receivable ledger. Larger firms and firms that use computers assign an account number to each credit customer and arrange the customer accounts in numeric order. Postings to the accounts receivable ledger are usually made daily so that the customer accounts can be kept up to date at all times.

Posting a Credit Sale

Each credit sale recorded in the sales journal is posted to the appropriate customer's account in the accounts receivable ledger, as shown in Figure 7-5. The date, the sales slip number, and the amount that the customer owes as a result of the sale are transferred from the sales journal to the customer's account. The amount is taken from the Accounts Receivable Debit column of the journal and is entered in the Debit column of the account. Next, the new balance is determined and recorded.

Section Objectives

3 Post from the sales journal to the customers' accounts in the accounts receivable subsidiary ledger.

WHY IT'S IMPORTANT
This ledger contains individual records that reflect all transactions of each customer.

4 Record sales returns and allowances in the general journal.

WHY IT'S IMPORTANT
Companies can see how much revenue is lost due to merchandise problems.

5 Post sales returns and allowances.

WHY IT'S IMPORTANT
Accurate, up-to-date customer records contribute to overall customer satisfaction.

6 Prepare a schedule of accounts receivable.

WHY IT'S IMPORTANT
This schedule provides a snapshot of amounts due from customers.

Terms to Learn

accounts receivable ledger
contra revenue account
control account
credit memorandum
net sales
sales allowance
sales return
schedule of accounts
  receivable

❸Objective

Post from the sales journal to the customers' accounts in the accounts receivable subsidiary ledger.

To show that the posting has been completed, a check mark (✓) is entered in the sales journal and the abbreviation S1 is entered in the Posting Reference column of the customer's account. As noted before, this abbreviation identifies page 1 of the sales journal.

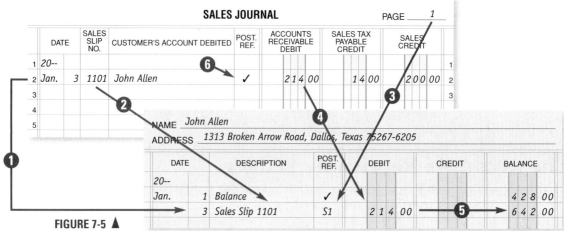

FIGURE 7-5 ▲
Posting from the Sales Journal to the Accounts Receivable Ledger

Posting Cash Received on Account

When the transaction involves cash received on account from a credit customer, the cash collected is first recorded in a cash receipts journal. (The necessary entry in the cash receipts journal is discussed in Chapter 9.) The cash is then posted to the individual customer account in the accounts receivable ledger. Figure 7-6 shows a posting for cash received on January 7 from John Allen, a credit customer of The Trend Center.

FIGURE 7-6 ▶
Posting for Cash Received on Account

NAME __John Allen__
ADDRESS __1313 Broken Arrow Road, Dallas, Texas 75267-6205__

DATE		DESCRIPTION	POST. REF.	DEBIT	CREDIT	BALANCE
20--						
Jan.	1	Balance	✓			4 2 8 00
	3	Sales Slip 1101	S1	2 1 4 00		6 4 2 00
	7		CR1		4 2 8 00	2 1 4 00

❹Objective

Record sales returns and allowances in the general journal.

Sales Returns and Allowances

A sale is entered in the accounting records when the goods are sold or the service is provided. If something is wrong with the goods or service, the firm may take back the goods, resulting in a **sales return**, or give the customer a reduction in price, resulting in a **sales allowance**.

When a return or allowance is related to a credit sale, the normal practice is to issue a document called a **credit memorandum** to the customer rather than giving a cash refund. The credit memorandum states that the customer's account is being reduced by the amount of the return or allowance plus any sales tax. A copy of the credit memorandum provides the data needed to enter the transaction in the firm's accounting records.

A debit to the **Sales Returns and Allowances** account is preferred to making a direct debit to **Sales.** This procedure gives a complete record of sales returns and allowances for each accounting period. Business managers use this record as a measure of operating efficiency. The **Sales Returns and Allowances** account is a **contra revenue account** because it has a debit balance, which is contrary, or opposite, to the normal balance for a revenue account.

Business Transaction

On January 23 The Trend Center issued Credit Memorandum 101 for a sales allowance to Ed Ramirez for merchandise purchased on account. The merchandise was damaged but still usable.

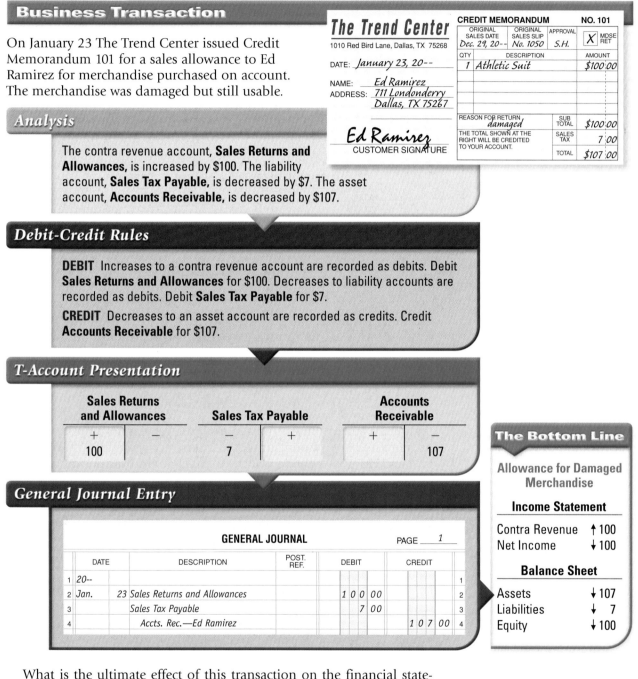

CREDIT MEMORANDUM   NO. 101

The Trend Center
1010 Red Bird Lane, Dallas, TX 75268

ORIGINAL SALES DATE	ORIGINAL SALES SLIP	APPROVAL	X MDSE RET
Dec. 29, 20--	No. 1050	S.H.	

DATE: *January 23, 20--*

NAME: *Ed Ramirez*
ADDRESS: *711 Londonderry*
Dallas, TX 75267

Ed Ramirez
CUSTOMER SIGNATURE

QTY	DESCRIPTION	AMOUNT
1	Athletic Suit	$100 00

REASON FOR RETURN *damaged*	SUB TOTAL	$100 00
THE TOTAL SHOWN AT THE RIGHT WILL BE CREDITED TO YOUR ACCOUNT.	SALES TAX	7 00
	TOTAL	$107 00

Analysis

The contra revenue account, **Sales Returns and Allowances,** is increased by $100. The liability account, **Sales Tax Payable,** is decreased by $7. The asset account, **Accounts Receivable,** is decreased by $107.

Debit-Credit Rules

DEBIT Increases to a contra revenue account are recorded as debits. Debit **Sales Returns and Allowances** for $100. Decreases to liability accounts are recorded as debits. Debit **Sales Tax Payable** for $7.

CREDIT Decreases to an asset account are recorded as credits. Credit **Accounts Receivable** for $107.

T-Account Presentation

Sales Returns and Allowances		Sales Tax Payable		Accounts Receivable	
+	–	–	+	+	–
100		7			107

General Journal Entry

GENERAL JOURNAL   PAGE __1__

	DATE	DESCRIPTION	POST. REF.	DEBIT	CREDIT	
1	20--					1
2	Jan.	23 Sales Returns and Allowances		1 0 0 00		2
3		Sales Tax Payable		7 00		3
4		Accts. Rec.—Ed Ramirez			1 0 7 00	4

The Bottom Line

Allowance for Damaged Merchandise

Income Statement

Contra Revenue	↑ 100
Net Income	↓ 100

Balance Sheet

Assets	↓ 107
Liabilities	↓ 7
Equity	↓ 100

What is the ultimate effect of this transaction on the financial statements? An increase in contra revenue causes a decrease in net income. Note that the $100 decrease in net income causes a $100 decrease in owner's equity. The asset **Accounts Receivable** is decreased, and the liability **Sales Tax Payable** is also decreased. The eventual effect of this transaction on the income statement and the balance sheet is summarized in the box titled *The Bottom Line*.

Recording Sales Returns and Allowances

Depending on the volume of sales returns and allowances, a business may use a general journal to record these transactions, or it may use a special sales returns and allowances journal.

Using the General Journal for Sales Returns and Allowances. A small firm that has a limited number of sales returns and allowances each month has no need to establish a special journal for such transactions. Instead, the required entries are made in the general journal.

Using a Sales Returns and Allowances Journal. In a business having many sales returns and allowances, it is efficient to use a special journal for these transactions. An example of a *sales returns and allowances journal* is shown in Figure 7-7.

FIGURE 7-7 ►
Sales Returns and
Allowances Journal

SALES RETURNS AND ALLOWANCES JOURNAL PAGE ___8___

	DATE	CREDIT MEMO NO.	CUSTOMER'S ACCOUNT CREDITED	POST. REF.	ACCOUNTS RECEIVABLE CREDIT	SALES TAX PAYABLE DEBIT	SALES RET. & ALLOW. DEBIT	
1	20--							1
2	Jan. 23	101	Ed Ramirez	✓	107 00	7 00	100 00	2
3	25	102	James Walker	✓	321 00	21 00	300 00	3
4								4
17	31		Totals		3210 00	210 00	3000 00	17
18					(111)	(231)	(451)	18
19								19

⑤ Objective
Post sales returns and allowances.

Posting a Sales Return or Allowance

Whether sales returns and allowances are recorded in the general journal or in a special sales returns and allowances journal, each of these transactions must be posted from the general ledger to the appropriate customer's account in the accounts receivable ledger. Figure 7-8 on page 213 shows how a return of merchandise was posted from the general journal to the account of James Walker.

Because the credit amount in the general journal entry for this transaction requires two postings, the account number 111 and a check mark are entered in the Posting Reference column of the journal. The 111 indicates that the amount was posted to the **Accounts Receivable** account in the general ledger, and the check mark indicates that the amount was posted to the customer's account in the accounts receivable ledger. Notice that a diagonal line was used to separate the two posting references.

Refer to Figure 7-7, which shows a special sales returns and allowances journal instead of a general journal. The account numbers at the bottom of each column are the posting references for the three general ledger accounts: **Accounts Receivable, Sales Tax Payable,** and **Sales Returns and Allowances.** The check marks in the Posting Reference column show that the credits were posted to individual customer accounts in the accounts receivable subsidiary ledger.

Remember that a business can use the general journal or special journals for transactions related to credit sales. A special journal is an efficient option for recording and posting large numbers of transactions.

FIGURE 7-8
Posting a Sales Return to the
Customer's Account

GENERAL JOURNAL   PAGE ___1___

	DATE	DESCRIPTION	POST. REF.	DEBIT	CREDIT	
1	20--					1
6	Jan. 25	Sales Returns and Allowances	451	3 0 0 00		6
7		Sales Tax Payable	231	2 1 00		7
8		Accounts Rec./James Walker	111 ✓		3 2 1 00	8
9		Accepted a return of				9
10		defective merchandise,				10
11		Credit Memorandum 102;				11
12		original sale made on Sales				12
13		Slip 1106 of January 21.				13
14						14
15						15
16						16
17						

NAME   James Walker
ADDRESS   5415 Stuart Road, Dallas, Texas 75267-6205

DATE	DESCRIPTION	POST. REF.	DEBIT	CREDIT	BALANCE
20--					
Jan. 1	Balance	✓			5 3 50
21	Sales Slip 1106	S1	3 2 1 00		3 7 4 50
25	CM 102	J1		3 2 1 00	5 3 50

Figure 7-9 on pages 214–215 shows the accounts receivable ledger after posting is completed.

Reporting Net Sales

At the end of each accounting period, the balance of the **Sales Returns and Allowances** account is subtracted from the balance of the **Sales** account in the Revenue section of the income statement. The resulting figure is the **net sales** for the period.

For example, suppose that the **Sales Returns and Allowances** account contains a balance of $400 at the end of January. Also suppose that the **Sales** account has a balance of $20,250 at the end of January. The Revenue section of the firm's income statement will appear as follows.

THE TREND CENTER
Income Statement (Partial)
Month Ended January 31, 20--

Revenue	
Sales	$20,250.00
Less Sales Returns and Allowances	400.00
Net Sales	$19,850.00

About Accounting

Investing in Ethics
Are ethical companies—those with a strong internal enforcement policy—really more profitable? Yes, such companies are listed among the top 100 financial performers twice as often as those without an ethics focus, according to a study by Curtis Verschoor at DePaul University.

FIGURE 7-9 ▼
Accounts Receivable Ledger

NAME _John Allen_

ADDRESS _1313 Broken Arrow Road, Dallas, Texas 75267-6205_

DATE		DESCRIPTION	POST. REF.	DEBIT	CREDIT	BALANCE
20--						
Jan.	1	Balance	✓			4 2 8 00
	3	Sales Slip 1101	S1	2 1 4 00		6 4 2 00
	7		CR1		4 2 8 00	2 1 4 00
	31	Sales Slip 1110	S1	2 6 7 50		4 8 1 50

NAME _Larry Bates_

ADDRESS _2712 Broken Arrow Road, Dallas, Texas 75267-6205_

DATE		DESCRIPTION	POST. REF.	DEBIT	CREDIT	BALANCE
20--						
Jan.	8	Sales Slip 1102	S1	5 3 5 00		5 3 5 00

NAME _Clyde Davis_

ADDRESS _1007 Woodrow Willson Lane, Dallas, Texas 75267-6502_

DATE		DESCRIPTION	POST. REF.	DEBIT	CREDIT	BALANCE
20--						
Jan.	1	Balance	✓			2 6 7 50
	11		CR1		2 6 7 50	—0—

NAME _Sarah Gomez_

ADDRESS _3111 Berry Lane, Dallas, Texas 75267-6318_

DATE		DESCRIPTION	POST. REF.	DEBIT	CREDIT	BALANCE
20--						
Jan.	1	Balance	✓			6 4 2 00
	15	Sales Slip 1104	S1	4 2 8 00		1 0 7 0 00

NAME _Blake Howard_

ADDRESS _2525 Whetstone Drive, Dallas, Texas 75267-6205_

DATE		DESCRIPTION	POST. REF.	DEBIT	CREDIT	BALANCE
20--						
Jan.	1	Balance	✓			1 0 7 0 00
	11	Sales Slip 1103	S1	6 4 2 00		1 7 1 2 00
	13		CR1		5 3 5 00	1 1 7 7 00

NAME Kim Johnson

ADDRESS 1501 Ryan Road, Dallas, Texas 75267-6318

DATE		DESCRIPTION	POST. REF.	DEBIT	CREDIT	BALANCE
20--						
Jan.	1	Balance	✓			1 0 7 00
	16		CR1		1 0 7 00	—0—
	31	Sales Slip 1109	S1	9 6 3 00		9 6 3 00

NAME Ed Ramirez

ADDRESS 711 Londonderry Lane, Dallas, Texas 75267-6318

DATE		DESCRIPTION	POST. REF.	DEBIT	CREDIT	BALANCE
20--						
Jan.	1	Balance	✓			2 1 4 00
	18	Sales Slip 1105	S1	8 5 6 00		1 0 7 0 00
	22		CR1		2 0 0 00	8 7 0 00
	23	CM 101	J1		1 0 7 00	7 6 3 00

NAME Linda Sanchez

ADDRESS 1010 Laney Road, Dallas, Texas 75267-6205

DATE		DESCRIPTION	POST. REF.	DEBIT	CREDIT	BALANCE
20--						
Jan.	1	Balance	✓			2 1 4 00
	28	Sales Slip 1107	S1	1 0 7 00		3 2 1 00
	31		CR1		1 0 7 00	2 1 4 00

NAME James Walker

ADDRESS 5415 Stuart Road, Dallas, Texas 75267-6205

DATE		DESCRIPTION	POST. REF.	DEBIT	CREDIT	BALANCE
20--						
Jan.	1	Balance	✓			5 3 50
	21	Sales Slip 1106	S1	3 2 1 00		3 7 4 50
	25	CM 102	J1		3 2 1 00	5 3 50

NAME Newton Wu

ADDRESS 9110 Stella Street, Dallas, Texas 75267-6205

DATE		DESCRIPTION	POST. REF.	DEBIT	CREDIT	BALANCE
20--						
Jan.	1	Balance	✓			2 1 4 00
	29	Sales Slip 1108	S1	1 0 7 0 00		1 2 8 4 00
	31		CR1		2 6 0 00	1 0 2 4 00

Computers in Accounting

Sales and Fulfillment Systems

One definition of "fulfill" is "to meet the requirements of a business order."[2] Department stores like Macy's and Bloomingdale's have developed sophisticated order processing systems for physical store locations and Web site operations.

When a customer places an order online using a credit card, data such as the customer's account number, the product identification number, product attributes like color and size, and the quantity ordered are transmitted to the company fulfillment and credit processing systems. These computerized systems review the data to verify item availability and to secure credit approval. Seconds later, the customer receives an onscreen confirmation, containing order total, sales tax, and shipping details. Behind the scenes, packing slips are generated at the company's fulfillment centers and the customer's order is packed and shipped per the customer's instructions.

Advanced sales and order systems can also identify sales trends by product and by geographic region, and they can pinpoint the most popular purchasing times of the day.

Thinking Critically

How might management use these reporting features to its benefit?

Internet Application

Visit the Federal Trade Commission Web site to learn more about electronic commerce. Choose an article about e-commerce under *Consumer Protection*. Write a summary of the article.

[2] *Merriam-Webster's Collegiate Dictionary*, Tenth Edition

---

6 Objective

Prepare a schedule of accounts receivable.

Schedule of Accounts Receivable

The use of an accounts receivable ledger does not eliminate the need for the **Accounts Receivable** account in the general ledger. This account remains in the general ledger and continues to appear on the balance sheet at the end of each fiscal period. However, the **Accounts Receivable** account is now considered a control account. A **control account** serves as a link between a subsidiary ledger and the general ledger. Its balance summarizes the balances of its related accounts in the subsidiary ledger.

At the end of each month, after all the postings have been made from the sales journal, the cash receipts journal, and the general journal to the accounts receivable ledger, the balances in the accounts receivable ledger must be proved against the balance of the **Accounts Receivable** general ledger account. First a **schedule of accounts receivable**, which lists the subsidiary ledger account balances, is prepared. The total of the schedule is compared with the balance of the **Accounts Receivable** account. If the two figures are not equal, errors must be located and corrected.

On January 31 the accounts receivable ledger at The Trend Center contains the accounts shown in Figure 7-9. To prepare a schedule of accounts receivable, the names of all customers with account balances are listed with the amount of their unpaid balances. Next the figures are added to find the total owed to the business by its credit customers.

Federated Department Stores, Inc. reported accounts receivable of $4.31 billion or 24.4 percent of the corporation's total assets at January 30, 2000.

A comparison of the total of the schedule of accounts receivable prepared at The Trend Center on January 31 and the balance of the **Accounts Receivable** account in the general ledger shows that the two figures are the same, as shown in Figure 7-10. The posting reference CR1 refers to the cash receipts journal, which is discussed in Chapter 9.

In addition to providing a proof of the subsidiary ledger, the schedule of accounts receivable serves another function. It reports information about the firm's accounts receivable at the end of the month. Management can review the schedule to see exactly how much each customer owes.

◀ **FIGURE 7-10**
Schedule of Accounts Receivable and Accounts Receivable Account

The Trend Center
Schedule of Accounts Receivable
January 31, 20--

John Allen	4 8 1 50
Larry Bates	5 3 5 00
Sarah Gomez	1 0 7 0 00
Blake Howard	1 1 7 7 00
Kim Johnson	9 6 3 00
Ed Ramirez	7 6 3 00
Linda Sanchez	2 1 4 00
James Walker	5 3 50
Newton Wu	1 0 2 4 00
Total	6 2 8 1 00

ACCOUNT _Accounts Receivable_   ACCOUNT NO. _111_

DATE		DESCRIPTION	POST. REF.	DEBIT	CREDIT	BALANCE DEBIT	BALANCE CREDIT
20--							
Jan.	1	Balance	✓			3 2 1 0 00	
	23		J1		1 0 7 00	3 1 0 3 00	
	25		J1		3 2 1 00	2 7 8 2 00	
	31		S1	5 4 0 3 50		8 1 8 5 50	
	31		CR1		1 9 0 4 50	6 2 8 1 00	

Section 2 — Self Review

Questions

1. Which accounts are kept in the accounts receivable ledger?

2. What are net sales?

3. What is a sales return? What is a sales allowance?

Exercises

4. Where would you report net sales?
   a. sales general ledger account
   b. general journal
   c. income statement
   d. sales journal

5. Which of the following general ledger accounts would appear in a sales returns and allowances journal?
   a. Sales Returns and Allowances, Sales Tax Payable, Accounts Receivable
   b. Sales Returns and Allowances, Sales, Accounts Receivable
   c. Sales Returns, Sales Allowances, Sales

Analysis

6. Draw a diagram showing the relationship between the accounts receivable ledger, the schedule of accounts receivable, and the general ledger.

(Answers to Section 2 Self Review are on page 250.)

Section Objectives

7 **Compute trade discounts.**

WHY IT'S IMPORTANT
Trade discounts allow for flexible pricing structures.

8 **Record credit card sales in appropriate journals.**

WHY IT'S IMPORTANT
Credit cards are widely used in merchandising transactions.

9 **Prepare the state sales tax return.**

WHY IT'S IMPORTANT
Businesses are legally responsible for accurately reporting and remitting sales taxes.

Terms to Learn

charge-account sales
invoice
list price
net price
open-account credit
trade discount
wholesale business

7 **Objective**

Compute trade discounts.

Important!

Trade Discounts
The amount of sales revenue recorded is the list price *minus* the trade discount.

Special Topics in Merchandising

Merchandisers have many accounting concerns. These include pricing, credit, and sales taxes.

Credit Sales for a Wholesale Business

The operations of The Trend Center are typical of those of many retail businesses—businesses that sell goods and services directly to individual consumers. In contrast, a **wholesale business** is a manufacturer or distributor of goods that sells to retailers or large consumers such as hotels and hospitals. The basic procedures used by wholesalers to handle sales and accounts receivable are the same as those used by retailers. However, many wholesalers offer cash discounts and trade discounts, which are not commonly found in retail operations.

The procedures used in connection with cash discounts are examined in Chapter 9. The handling of trade discounts is described here.

Computing Trade Discounts

A wholesale business offers goods to trade customers at less than retail prices. This price adjustment is based on the volume purchased by trade customers and takes the form of a **trade discount**, which is a reduction from the **list price**—the established retail price. There may be a single trade discount or a series of discounts for each type of goods. The **net price** (list price less all trade discounts) is the amount the wholesaler records in its sales journal.

The same goods may be offered to different customers at different trade discounts, depending on the size of the order and the costs of selling to the various types of customers.

Single Trade Discount. Suppose the list price of goods is $1,000 and the trade discount is 40 percent. The amount of the discount is $400, and the net price to be shown on the invoice and recorded in the sales journal is $600.

List price	$1,000
Less 40% discount ($1,000 × 0.40)	400
Invoice price	$ 600

Series of Trade Discounts. If the list price of goods is $1,000 and the trade discount is quoted in a series such as 25 and 15 percent, a different net price will result.

List price	$1,000.00
Less first discount ($1,000 × 0.25)	250.00
Difference	$ 750.00
Less second discount ($750 × 0.15)	112.50
Invoice price	$ 637.50

Using a Sales Journal for a Wholesale Business

Since sales taxes apply only to retail transactions, a wholesale business does not need to account for such taxes. Its sales journal may therefore be as simple as the one illustrated in Figure 7-11. This sales journal has a single amount column. The total of this column is posted to the general ledger at the end of the month as a debit to the **Accounts Receivable** account and a credit to the **Sales** account (Figure 7-12). During the month the individual entries in the sales journal are posted to the customer accounts in the accounts receivable ledger.

Important!

Special Journal Format
Special journals such as the sales journal can vary in format from company to company.

◄ **FIGURE 7-11**
Wholesaler's Sales Journal

SALES JOURNAL PAGE ___1___

	DATE	INVOICE NO.	CUSTOMER'S ACCOUNT DEBITED	POST. REF.	ACCOUNTS RECEIVABLE DR. SALES CR.	
1	20--					1
2	Jan.	3	9907	Discount Hardware Company		1 600 00	2
25		31	10017	Tyson's Department Store		3 800 00	25
26		31		Total		30 750 00	26
27						(111/401)	27
28							28

◄ **FIGURE 7-12**
General Ledger Accounts

ACCOUNT _Accounts Receivable_   ACCOUNT NO. _111_

DATE	DESCRIPTION	POST. REF.	DEBIT	CREDIT	BALANCE DEBIT	BALANCE CREDIT
20--						
Jan. 1	Balance	✓			45 200 00	
31		S1	30 750 00		75 950 00	

ACCOUNT _Sales_   ACCOUNT NO. _401_

DATE	DESCRIPTION	POST. REF.	DEBIT	CREDIT	BALANCE DEBIT	BALANCE CREDIT
20--						
Jan. 31		S1		30 750 00		30 750 00

Wholesale businesses issue invoices. An **invoice** is a customer billing for merchandise bought on credit. Copies of the invoices are used to enter the transactions in the sales journal.

The next merchandising topic, credit policies, applies to both wholesalers and retailers. The discussion in this textbook focuses on credit policies and accounting for retail firms.

Credit Policies

The use of credit is considered to be one of the most important factors in the rapid growth of modern economic systems. Sales on credit are made by large numbers of wholesalers and retailers of goods and by many professional people and service businesses. The assumption is that the volume of both sales and profits will increase if buyers are given a period of a month or more to pay for the goods or services they purchase.

However, the increase in profits a business expects when it grants credit will be realized only if each customer completes the transaction by paying for the goods or services purchased. If payment is not received, the expected profits become actual losses and the purpose for granting the credit is defeated. Business firms try to protect against the possibility of such losses by investigating a customer's credit record and ability to pay for purchases before allowing any credit to the customer.

Professional people, such as doctors, lawyers, and architects, and owners of small businesses like The Trend Center usually make their own decisions about granting credit. Such decisions may be based on personal judgment or on reports available from credit bureaus, information supplied by other creditors, and credit ratings supplied by national firms such as Dun & Bradstreet.

> Equifax, a leader in providing consumer and commercial credit information, was founded in Atlanta in 1899. For the fiscal year ended December 1999, 100 years later, the company reported revenues of $1.77 billion dollars.

Larger businesses maintain a credit department to determine the amounts and types of credit that should be granted to customers. In addition to using credit data supplied by institutions, the credit department may obtain financial statements and related reports from customers who have applied for credit. This information is analyzed to help determine the maximum amount of credit that may be granted and suitable credit terms for the customer. Financial statements that have been audited by certified public accountants are used extensively by credit departments.

Even though the credit investigation is thorough, some accounts receivable become uncollectible. Unexpected business developments, errors of judgment, incorrect financial data, and many other causes may lead to defaults in payments by customers. Experienced managers know that some uncollectible accounts are to be expected in normal business operations and that limited losses indicate that a firm's credit policies are sound. Provisions for such limited losses from uncollectible accounts are usually made in budgets and other financial projections.

Each business must develop credit policies that achieve maximum sales with minimum losses from uncollectible accounts:

- A credit policy that is too tight results in a low level of losses at the expense of increases in sales volume.
- A credit policy that is too lenient may result in increased sales volume accompanied by a high level of losses.

Good judgment based on knowledge and experience must be used to achieve a well balanced credit policy.

Different types of credit have evolved with the growing economy and changing technology. The different types of credit require different accounting treatments.

Accounting for Different Types of Credit Sales

The most common types of credit sales are

- open-account credit,
- business credit cards,
- bank credit cards,
- cards issued by credit card companies.

Open-Account Credit. The form of credit most commonly offered by professional people and small businesses permits the sale of services or goods to the customer with the understanding that the amount is to be paid at a later date. This type of arrangement is called **open-account credit**. It is usually granted on the basis of personal acquaintance or knowledge of the customer. However, formal credit checks may also be used. The amount involved in each transaction is usually small, and payment is expected within 30 days or on receipt of a monthly statement. Open-account sales are also referred to as **charge-account sales**.

The Trend Center uses the open-account credit arrangement. Sales transactions are recorded as debits to the **Accounts Receivable** account and credits to the **Sales** account. Collections on account are recorded as debits to the **Cash** account and credits to the **Accounts Receivable** account.

Business Credit Cards. Many retail businesses, especially large ones such as department store chains and gasoline companies, provide their own credit cards (sometimes called charge cards) to customers who have established credit. Whenever a sale is completed using a business credit card, a sales slip is prepared in the usual manner. Then the sales slip and the credit card are placed in a mechanical device that prints the customer's name, account number, and other data on all copies of the sales slip. Some companies use computerized card readers and sales registers that print out a sales slip with the customer information and a line for the customer's signature. Many businesses require that the salesclerk contact the credit department by telephone or computer terminal to verify the customer's credit status before completing the transaction.

Business credit card sales are similar to open-account credit sales. A business credit card sale is recorded as

- a debit to **Accounts Receivable,**
- a credit to a revenue account such as **Sales.**

A customer payment is recorded as

- a debit to **Cash,**
- a credit to **Accounts Receivable.**

Bank Credit Cards. Retailers can provide credit while minimizing or avoiding the risk of losses from uncollectible accounts by accepting bank credit cards. The most widely accepted bank credit cards are MasterCard and Visa. Many banks participate in one or both of these credit card programs, and other banks have their own credit cards. Bank credit cards are issued to consumers directly by banks.

A business may participate in these credit card programs by meeting the conditions set by the bank. When a sale is made to a cardholder, the business completes a special sales slip such as the one shown in Figure 7-13 on page 222. This form must be imprinted with data from the customer's bank credit card and then signed by the customer. Many businesses continue to complete their regular sales slips for internal control and other purposes.

Bank Credit Cards

Using a bank credit card is one of the best ways to acquire money when conducting business in another country because you get the bank's exchange rate.

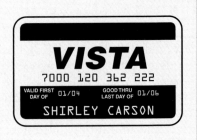

The Trend Center
    0601X3
 851 7007 763
 928 6548 421

Shirley Carson

 7000 120 362 222
    04/X7BWG

DATE 1/28/--	AUTH NO. 12	IDENTIFICATION	CLERK	REG/DEPT	☐ TAKE ☐ SEND

QTY	CLASS	DESCRIPTION	PRICE	AMOUNT
1		Sweater		80 00

The issuer of the card identified on this items authorized to pay the amount shown on TOTAL upon proper authorization. I promis to pay such TOTAL (together with any other charges due) subject to and in accordance with the agreement governing the use of such card.

	SUB TOTAL	80 00
CUSTOMER SIGNATURE *Shirley Carson*	TAX	5 60
SALES SLIP	**TOTAL**	85 60

MERCHANT RETAIN THIS COPY FOR RECORDS

VISTA
7000 120 362 222
VALID FIRST DAY OF 01/04 GOOD THRU LAST DAY OF 01/06
SHIRLEY CARSON

FIGURE 7-13 ▲
Sales Slip for a
Bank Credit Card Transaction

When a business makes a sale on a bank credit card, it acquires an asset that can be converted into cash immediately without responsibility for later collection from the customer. Periodically (preferably each day) the completed sales slips from bank credit card sales are totaled. The number of sales slips and the total amount of the sales are recorded on a special deposit form, as shown in Figure 7-14.

FIGURE 7-14 ▶
Deposit Form for
Bank Credit Card Sales

The Trend Center

851 7007 763
928 6548 421

Attach calculator tape to Bank Copy when more than one sales slip is enclosed.

x *Stacee Harris*
MERCHANT SIGNATURE

DATE _____

ITEM	NO. SLIPS	AMOUNT
Total Sales	10	1177 00
LESS: Total Credits		
NET SALES		1177 00
LESS: DISCOUNT __3__ %		35 31
NET AMOUNT		1141 69

VISTA MERCHANT
SUMMARY SLIP

The deposit form, along with the completed sales slips, is presented to the firm's bank in much the same manner as a cash deposit. Depending on the arrangements that have been made, either the bank will deduct a fee, called a *discount* (usually between 1 and 8 percent), and immediately credit the depositor's checking account with the net amount of the sales, or it will credit the depositor's checking account for the full amount of the sales and then deduct the discount at the end of the month. If the second procedure is used, the total discount for the month will appear on the bank statement.

The bank is responsible for collecting from the cardholder. If any amounts are uncollectible, the bank sustains the loss. For the retailer, bank credit card sales are like cash sales. The accounting procedures for such sales are therefore quite similar to the accounting procedures for cash sales, which will be discussed in Chapter 9. If the business is billed once each month for the bank's discount, the total amount involved in the daily deposit of the credit card sales slips is debited to **Cash** and credited to **Sales.**

Credit Card Companies. Credit cards such as American Express and Diners Club are issued by business firms or subsidiaries of business firms that are operated for the special purpose of handling credit card transactions. The potential cardholder must submit an application and pay an annual fee to the credit card company. If the credit references are satisfactory, the credit card is issued. It is normally reissued at one-year intervals so long as the company's credit experience with the cardholder remains satisfactory.

Hotels, restaurants, airline companies, many types of retail stores, and a wide variety of other businesses accept these credit cards. When making sales to cardholders, sellers usually prepare their own sales slip or bill and then complete a special sales slip required by the credit card company. As with the sales slips for bank credit cards, the forms must be imprinted with the identifying data on the customer's card and signed by the customer. Such sales slips are sometimes referred to as *sales invoices, sales drafts,* or *sales vouchers.* The term used varies from one credit card company to another.

The seller acquires an account receivable from the credit card company rather than from the customer. At approximately one-month intervals, the credit card company bills the cardholders for all sales slips it has acquired during the period. It is the responsibility of the credit card company to collect from the cardholders.

Accounting for Credit Card Sales

The procedure used to account for credit card sales is similar to the procedure for recording open-account credit sales. However, the account receivable is with the credit card company, not with the cardholders who buy the goods or services.

There are two basic methods of recording these sales. Businesses that have few transactions with credit card companies normally debit the amounts of such sales to the usual **Accounts Receivable** account in the general ledger and credit them to the same **Sales** account that is used for cash sales and other types of credit sales. An individual account for each credit card company is set up in the accounts receivable subsidiary ledger. This method of recording sales is shown in Figure 7-15.

Payment from a credit card company is recorded in the cash receipts journal, a procedure discussed in Chapter 9. Fees charged by the credit card companies for processing these sales are debited to an account called **Discount Expense on Credit Card Sales.** For example, assume that American Express charges a 7 percent discount fee on the sale charged by Richard Harris on January 3 and remits the balance to the firm.

⑧ Objective

Record credit card sales in appropriate journals.

◀ **FIGURE 7-15**
Recording Credit Card Company Sales

SALES JOURNAL PAGE ___12___

	DATE	SALES SLIP NO.	CUSTOMER'S ACCOUNT DEBITED	POST. REF.	ACCOUNTS RECEIVABLE DEBIT	SALES TAX PAYABLE CREDIT	SALES CREDIT	
1	20--							1
2	Jan. 3	335	American Express		428 00	28 00	400 00	2
3			(Richard Harris)					3
26	11	351	Diners Club		107 00	7 00	100 00	26
27			(Penny Howard)					27
28								28

This transaction would be recorded in the cash receipts journal by debiting **Cash** for $398.04, debiting **Discount Expense on Credit Card Sales** for $29.96, and crediting **Accounts Receivable** for $428.00.

Firms that do a large volume of business with credit card companies may debit all such sales to a special **Accounts Receivable from Credit Card Companies** account in the general ledger, thus separating this type of receivable from the accounts receivable resulting from open-account credit sales. A special account called **Sales—Credit Card Companies** is credited for the revenue from these transactions. Figure 7-16 shows how the necessary entries are made in the sales journal.

FIGURE 7-16 ▼
Recording Sales for
Accounts Receivable from
Credit Card Companies

SALES JOURNAL   PAGE ___7___

	DATE	SALES SLIP NO.	CUSTOMER'S ACCOUNT DEBITED	POST. REF.	ACCOUNTS RECEIVABLE DEBIT	ACCT. REC.— CREDIT CARD COMPANIES DEBIT	SALES TAX PAYABLE CREDIT	SALES CREDIT	SALES— CREDIT CARD COMPANIES CREDIT	
1	20--									1
2	Jan.	3	Summary of credit card sales/							2
3			American Express			8 560 00	560 00		8 000 00	3
16		11	Summary of credit card sales/			4 280 00	280 00		4 000 00	16
17			Diners Club							17
29		31	Totals			42 800 00	2 800 00		40 000 00	29
30						(114)	(231)		(404)	30
31										31

Sales Taxes

Many cities and states impose a tax on retail sales. Sales taxes imposed by city and state governments vary. However, the procedures used to account for these taxes are similar.

A sales tax may be levied on all retail sales, but often certain items are exempt. In most cases the amount of the sales tax is stated separately and then added to the retail price of the merchandise.

> The California State Board of Equalization collects approximately $22.9 billion dollars annually from sales tax revenues. These revenues foot the bill for state and local programs, including hospitals, social welfare efforts, transportation, schools, and housing.

The retailer is required to collect sales tax from customers, make periodic (usually monthly) reports to the taxing authority, and pay the taxes due when the reports are filed. The government may allow the retailer to retain part of the tax as compensation for collecting it.

⑨ Objective

Prepare the state sales tax return.

Preparing the State Sales Tax Return

At the end of each month, after the accounts have all been posted, The Trend Center prepares the sales tax return. The information required for the monthly return comes from the accounting data of the current month. Three accounts are involved: **Sales Tax Payable, Sales,** and **Sales**

Returns and Allowances. In some states the sales tax return is filed quarterly rather than monthly.

The procedures to file a sales tax return are similar to those used by The Trend Center on February 7 when it filed the monthly sales tax return for January with the state tax commissioner. The firm's sales are subject to a 7 percent state sales tax. To highlight the data needed, the January postings are shown in the ledger accounts in Figure 7-17.

◀ **FIGURE 7-17**
Ledger Account Postings for Sales Tax

ACCOUNT _Sales Tax Payable_   ACCOUNT NO. _231_

DATE	DESCRIPTION	POST. REF.	DEBIT	CREDIT	BALANCE DEBIT	BALANCE CREDIT
20--						
Jan. 1	Balance	✓				7 4 9 00
11		CP1	7 4 9 00			—0—
23		J1	7 00		7 00	
25		J1	2 1 00		2 8 00	
31		S1		3 5 3 50		3 2 5 50
31		CR1		1 0 6 4 00		1 3 8 9 50

ACCOUNT _Sales_   ACCOUNT NO. _401_

DATE	DESCRIPTION	POST. REF.	DEBIT	CREDIT	BALANCE DEBIT	BALANCE CREDIT
20--						
Jan. 31		S1		5 0 5 0 00		5 0 5 0 00
31		CR1		15 2 0 0 00		20 2 5 0 00

ACCOUNT _Sales Returns and Allowances_   ACCOUNT NO. _451_

DATE	DESCRIPTION	POST. REF.	DEBIT	CREDIT	BALANCE DEBIT	BALANCE CREDIT
20--						
Jan. 23		J1	1 0 0 00		1 0 0 00	
25		J1	3 0 0 00		4 0 0 00	

Using these figures as a basis, the amount of the firm's taxable gross sales for January is determined as follows:

Cash Sales	$15,200
Credit Sales	5,050
Total Sales	$20,250
Less Sales Returns and Allowances	400
Taxable Gross Sales for January	$19,850

The 7 percent sales tax on the gross sales of $19,850 amounts to $1,389.50. Note that the firm's increase in assets (**Cash** and **Accounts Receivable**) is equal to sales revenue plus the sales tax liability on that revenue.

In the state where The Trend Center is located, a retailer who files the sales tax return (see Figure 7-18 on page 226) on time and who pays the tax when it is due is entitled to a discount. The discount is intended to compensate the retailer, at least in part, for acting as a collection agent for the government. The discount rate depends on the amount of tax to be

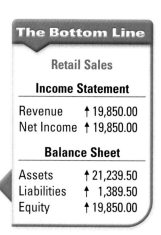

The Bottom Line

Retail Sales

Income Statement

Revenue	↑ 19,850.00
Net Income	↑ 19,850.00

Balance Sheet

Assets	↑ 21,239.50
Liabilities	↑ 1,389.50
Equity	↑ 19,850.00

SALES TAX RETURN

	LICENSE NUMBER	
ALWAYS REFER TO THIS NUMBER WHEN WRITING THE DIVISION →	217539	**STATE TAX COMMISSION**

STATE TAX COMMISSION
SALES AND USE TAX DIVISION
DRAWER 20
CAPITAL CITY, STATE 78711
RETURN REQUESTED

—IMPORTANT—
ANY CHANGE IN OWNERSHIP
REQUIRES A NEW LICENSE:
NOTIFY THIS DIVISION
IMMEDIATELY.

This return DUE on the 1st day of month following period covered by the return, and becomes DELINQUENT on the 21st day.

37-9462315
FED. E.I. NO. OR S.S NO.

January 31, 20--

—Sales for period ending—

MAKE ALL REMITTANCES
PAYABLE TO
STATE TAX COMMISSIOIN
DO NOT SEND CASH
STAMPS NOT ACCEPTED

OWNER'S NAME AND LOCATION

THE TREND CENTER
1010 Red Bird Lane
Dallas, Texas 75268-7783

COMPUTATION OF SALES TAX	For Taxpayer's Use	Do Not Use This Column
1. TOTAL Gross proceeds of sales or Gross Receipts (to include rentals)	19,850.00	
2. Add cost of personal property purchased on a RETAIL LICENSE FOR RESALE but USED BY YOU or YOUR EMPLOYEES, including GIFTS and PREMIUMS	–0–	
3. USE TAX—Add cost of personal property purchased outside of STATE for your use, storage, or consumption	–0–	
4. Total (Lines 1, 2, and 3)	19,850.00	
5. LESS ALLOWABLE DEDUCTIONS (Must be itemized on reverse side)	–0–	
6. Net taxable total (Line 4 minus Line 5)	19,850.00	
7. Sales and Use Tax Due (7% of Line 6)	1,389.50	
8. LESS TAXPAYER'S DISCOUNT—(Deductible only when amount of TAX due is not delinquent at time of payment) →	13.90	
IF LINE 7 IS LESS THAN $100.00 —DEDUCT 3% IF LINE 7 IS $100 BUT LESS THAN $1,000.00 —DEDUCT 2% IF LINE 7 IS $1,000.00 OR MORE —DEDUCT 1%		
9. NET AMOUNT OF TAX PAYABLE (Line 7 minus Line 8)	1,375.60	
Add the following penalty and interest if return or remittance is late. 10. Specific Penalty: 25% of tax _ _ _ _ _ _ _ _ _ _ _ _ _ _ _ $_____ 11. Interest: 1/2 of 1% per month from due date until paid. $_____ TOTAL PENALTY AND INTEREST →		
12. TOTAL TAX, PENALTY AND INTEREST	1,375.60	
13. Subtract credit memo No.		
14. TOTAL AMOUNT DUE (IF NO SALES MADE SO STATE)	1,375.60	

I certify that this return, including the accompanying schedules or statements, has been examined by me and to the best of my knowledge and belief, a true and complete return, made in good faith, for the period stated, pursuant to the provisions of the Code of Laws, 20--, and Acts Amendatory Thereto.

URGENT—SEE THAT LICENSE NUMBER IS ON RETURN

Stacee Harris
_____
SIGNATURE

Division Use Only

_____
Owner
Owner, partner or title

_____
February 7, 20--
Date

Return must be signed by owner or if corporation, authorized person.

State Sales Tax Return **FIGURE 7-18** ▲

paid. For amounts over $1,000, the rate is 1 percent of the total tax due. For The Trend Center, the discount for January is determined as follows:

Taxable Gross Sales for January	$19,850.00
7% Sales Tax Rate	× 0.07
Sales Tax Due	$ 1,389.50
1% Discount Rate	× 0.01
Discount	$ 13.90
Sales Tax Due	$ 1,389.50
Discount	(13.90)
Net Sales Tax Due	$ 1,375.60

The firm sends a check for the net sales tax due with the sales tax return. The accounting entry made to record this payment includes a debit to **Sales Tax Payable** and a credit to **Cash** (for $1,375.60 in this case). After the amount of the payment is posted, the balance in the **Sales Tax Payable** account should be equal to the discount, as shown in Figure 7-19. Slight differences can arise because the tax collected at the time of the sale is determined by a tax bracket method that can give results slightly more or less than the final computations on the tax return.

◀ **FIGURE 7-19**
Effect of Paying Sales Tax

ACCOUNT _Sales Tax Payable_   ACCOUNT NO. _231_

DATE		DESCRIPTION	POST. REF.	DEBIT	CREDIT	BALANCE DEBIT	BALANCE CREDIT
20--							
Jan.	1	Balance	✓				7 4 9 00
	11		CP1	7 4 9 00			—0—
	23		J1	7 00		7 00	
	25		J1	2 1 00		2 8 00	
	31		S1		3 5 3 50		3 2 5 50
	31		CR1		1 0 6 4 00		1 3 8 9 50
Feb.	6		CP1	1 3 7 5 60			1 3 90

Tax payment ⟶   Amount of discount ⟶

The Bottom Line

Discount on Sales Tax

Income Statement

Misc. Income	↑	13.90
Net Income	↑	13.90

Balance Sheet

Assets	↓1,375.60
Liabilities	↓1,389.50
Equity	↑ 13.90

If there is a balance in the **Sales Tax Payable** account after the sales tax liability is satisfied, the balance is transferred to an account called **Miscellaneous Income** by a general journal entry. This entry consists of a debit to **Sales Tax Payable** and a credit to **Miscellaneous Income.**

Recording Sales Tax in the Sales Account

In some states retailers can credit the entire sales price plus tax to the **Sales** account. At the end of each month or quarter, they must remove from the **Sales** account the amount of tax included and transfer that amount to the **Sales Tax Payable** account. Assume that during January a retailer whose sales are all taxable sells merchandise for a total price of $16,050, which includes a 7 percent tax. The entry to record these sales is summarized in general journal form on page 228.

Credit Sales

- Credit sales are a major source of revenue in many businesses, and accounts receivable represent a major asset.

- Management needs up-to-date and correct information about both sales and accounts receivable in order to monitor the financial health of the firm.

- Special journals save time and effort and reduce the cost of accounting work.

- In a retail firm that must handle sales tax, the sales journal and the cash receipts journal provide a convenient method of recording the amounts owed for sales tax.

  - When the data is posted to the Sales Tax Payable account in the general ledger, the firm has a complete and systematic record that speeds the completion of the periodic sales tax return.

  - The firm has detailed proof of its sales tax figures in the case of a tax audit.

- An accounts receivable subsidiary ledger provides management and the credit department with up-to-date information about the balances owed by all customers.

  - This information is useful in controlling credit and collections.

  - Detailed information helps in evaluating the effectiveness of credit policies.

  - Management must keep a close watch on the promptness of customer payments because much of the cash needed for day-to-day operations usually comes from payments on accounts receivable.

- A well-balanced credit policy helps increase sales volume but also keeps losses from uncollectible accounts at an acceptable level.

- Retailers are liable for any undercollection of sales taxes. This situation can be avoided with an efficient control system.

Thinking Critically
What are some possible consequences of out-of-date accounts receivable records?

	DATE		DESCRIPTION	POST. REF.	DEBIT	CREDIT	
1	20--						1
2	Jan.	31	Accounts Receivable	111	16 0 5 0 00		2
3			Sales	401		16 0 5 0 00	3
4			To record total sales and				4
5			sales tax collected during				5
6			the month				6
7							7

GENERAL JOURNAL   PAGE ___4___

At the end of the month, the retailer must transfer the sales tax from the **Sales** account to the **Sales Tax Payable** account. The first step in the transfer process is to determine the amount of tax involved. The sales tax payable is computed as follows.

Sales + tax	= $16,050
100% of sales + 7% of sales	= $16,050
107% of sales	= $16,050
Sales	= $16,050/1.07
Sales	= $15,000
Tax	= $15,000 × 0.07 = $1,050

The firm then makes the following entry to transfer the liability from the **Sales** account.

GENERAL JOURNAL   PAGE ____4____

	DATE		DESCRIPTION	POST. REF.	DEBIT	CREDIT	
1	20--						1
8	Jan.	31	Sales	401	1 0 5 0 00		8
9			Sales Tax Payable	231		1 0 5 0 00	9
10			To transfer sales tax				10
11			payable from the Sales				11
12			account to the liability				12
13			account				13
14							14
15							15

The retailer in this example originally recorded the entire sales price plus tax in the **Sales** account. The sales tax was transferred to the **Sales Tax Payable** account at the end of the month.

Section 3 Self Review

Questions

1. What are four types of credit sales?

2. What account is used to record sales tax owed by a business to a city or state?

3. What is the difference between list price and net price?

Exercises

4. If a wholesale business offers a trade discount of 35 percent on a sale of $2,400, what is the amount of the discount?

a. $84
b. $85
c. $840
d. $845

5. A company that buys $3,000 of goods from a wholesaler offering trade discounts of 20 and 10 percent will pay what amount for the goods?

a. $1,560
b. $2,100
c. $2,130
d. $2,160

Analysis

6. What factors would you consider in deciding whether or not to extend credit to a customer?

(Answers to Section 3 Self Review are on page 251.)

Review

Chapter Summary

The nature of the operations of a business, the volume of its transactions, and other factors influence the design of an accounting system. In this chapter, you have learned about the use of special journals and subsidiary ledgers suitable for a merchandising business. These additional journals and ledgers increase the efficiency of recording credit transactions and permit the division of labor.

Learning Objectives

1 Record credit sales in a sales journal.

The sales journal is used to record credit sales transactions, usually on a daily basis. For sales transactions that include sales tax, the sales tax liability is recorded at the time of the sale to ensure that company records reflect the appropriate amount of sales tax liability.

2 Post from the sales journal to the general ledger accounts.

At the end of each month, the sales journal is totaled, proved, and ruled. Column totals are then posted to the general ledger. Using a sales journal rather than a general journal to record sales saves the time and effort of posting individual entries to the general ledger during the month.

3 Post from the sales journal to the customers' accounts in the accounts receivable subsidiary ledger.

The accounts of individual credit customers are kept in a subsidiary ledger called the accounts receivable ledger. Daily postings are made to this ledger from the sales journal, the cash receipts journal, and the general journal or the sales returns and allowances journal. The current balance of a customer's account is computed after each posting so that the amount owed is known at all times.

4 Record sales returns and allowances in the general journal.

Sales returns and allowances are usually debited to a contra revenue account. A firm with relatively few sales returns and allowances could use the general journal to record these transactions.

5 Post sales returns and allowances.

Sales returns and allowances transactions must be posted to the general ledger and to the appropriate accounts receivable subsidiary ledgers. The balance of the **Sales Returns and Allowances** account is subtracted from the balance of the **Sales** account to show net sales on the income statement.

6 Prepare a schedule of accounts receivable.

Each month a schedule of accounts receivable is prepared. It is used to prove the subsidiary ledger against the **Accounts Receivable** account. It also reports the amounts due from credit customers.

7 Compute trade discounts.

Wholesale businesses often offer goods to trade customers at less than retail prices. Trade discounts are expressed as a percentage off the list price. Multiply the list price by the percentage trade discount offered to compute the dollar amount.

8 Record credit card sales in appropriate journals.

Credit sales are common, and different credit arrangements are used. Businesses that have few transactions with credit card companies normally record these transactions in the sales journal by debiting the usual **Accounts Receivable** account in the general ledger and crediting the same **Sales** account that is used for cash sales.

9 Prepare the state sales tax return.

In states and cities that have a sales tax, the retailer must prepare a sales tax return and send the total tax collected to the taxing authority.

10 Define the accounting terms new to this chapter.

CHAPTER 7 GLOSSARY

Accounts receivable ledger (p. 209) A subsidiary ledger that contains credit customer accounts

Charge-account sales (p. 221) Sales made through the use of open-account credit or one of various types of credit cards

Contra revenue account (p. 211) An account with a debit balance, which is contrary to the normal balance for a revenue account

Control account (p. 216) An account that links a subsidiary ledger and the general ledger since its balance summarizes the balances of the accounts in the subsidiary ledger

Credit memorandum (p. 210) A note verifying that a customer's account is being reduced by the amount of a sales return or sales allowance plus any sales tax that may have been involved

Invoice (p. 219) A customer billing for merchandise bought on credit

List price (p. 218) An established retail price

Manufacturing business (p. 202) A business that sells goods that it has produced

Merchandise inventory (p. 202) The stock of goods a merchandising business keeps on hand

Merchandising business (p. 202) A business that sells goods purchased for resale

Net price (p. 218) The list price less all trade discounts

Net sales (p. 213) The difference between the balance in the **Sales** account and the balance in the **Sales Returns and Allowances** account

Open-account credit (p. 221) A system that allows the sale of services or goods with the understanding that payment will be made at a later date

Retail business (p. 202) A business that sells directly to individual consumers

Sales allowance (p. 210) A reduction in the price originally charged to customers for goods or services

Sales journal (p. 203) A special journal used to record sales of merchandise on credit

Sales return (p. 210) A firm's acceptance of a return of goods from a customer

Schedule of accounts receivable (p. 216) A listing of all balances of the accounts in the accounts receivable subsidiary ledger

Service business (p. 202) A business that sells services

Special journal (p. 202) A journal used to record only one type of transaction

Subsidiary ledger (p. 202) A ledger dedicated to accounts of a single type and showing details to support a general ledger account

Trade discount (p. 218) A reduction from list price

Wholesale business (p. 218) A business that manufactures or distributes goods to retail businesses or large consumers such as hotels and hospitals

Comprehensive Self Review

1. Explain how service, merchandising, and manufacturing businesses differ from each other.
2. Why does a small merchandising business usually need a more complex set of financial records and statements than a small service business?
3. Why is it useful for a firm to have an accounts receivable ledger?
4. What is a control account?
5. Name the two different time periods usually covered in sales tax returns.

(Answers to Comprehensive Self Review are on page 251.)

Discussion Questions

1. What is a trade discount? Why do some firms offer trade discounts to their customers?
2. What is open-account credit?
3. Why are bank credit card sales similar to cash sales for a business?
4. What is the discount on credit card sales? What type of account is used to record this item?
5. When a firm makes a sale involving a credit card issued by a credit card company, does the firm have an account receivable with the cardholder or with the credit card company?
6. What procedure does a business use to collect amounts owed to it for sales on credit cards issued by credit card companies?
7. What two methods are commonly used to record sales involving credit cards issued by credit card companies?
8. In a particular state, the sales tax rate is 5 percent of sales. The retailer is allowed to record both the selling price and the tax in the same account. Explain how to compute the sales tax due when this method is used.
9. The sales tax on a credit sale is not collected from the customer immediately. When is this tax usually entered in a firm's accounting records? What account is used to record this tax?
10. How is a multicolumn special journal proved at the end of each month?
11. What kind of account is **Sales Returns and Allowances**?
12. Why is a sales return or allowance usually recorded in a special **Sales Returns and Allowances** account rather than being debited to the **Sales** account?
13. How are the net sales for an accounting period determined?
14. What purposes does the schedule of accounts receivable serve?
15. How do retail and wholesale businesses differ?

Applications

EXERCISES

Identifying the accounts used to record sales and related transactions.

◀ **Exercise 7-1**
Objective 1

The transactions below took place at Resort Camping Center, a retail business that sells outdoor clothing and camping equipment. Indicate the numbers of the general ledger accounts that would be debited and credited to record each transaction.

GENERAL LEDGER ACCOUNTS

101 Cash	401 Sales
111 Accounts Receivable	451 Sales Returns and Allowances
231 Sales Tax Payable	

DATE		TRANSACTIONS
May	1	Sold merchandise on credit; the transaction involved sales tax.
	2	Received checks from credit customers on account.
	3	Accepted a return of merchandise from a credit customer; the original sale involved sales tax.
	4	Sold merchandise for cash; the transaction involved sales tax.
	5	Gave an allowance to a credit customer for damaged merchandise; the original sale involved sales tax.
	6	Provided a cash refund to a customer who returned merchandise; the original sale was made for cash and involved sales tax.

accts Rec

Identifying the journal to record transactions.

◀ **Exercise 7-2**
Objective 1

The accounting system of Resort Camping Center includes the journals listed below. Indicate the specific journal in which each of the transactions listed below would be recorded.

JOURNALS

Cash receipts journal	Sales journal
Cash payments journal	General journal
Purchases journal	

DATE		TRANSACTIONS
May	1	Sold merchandise on credit.
	2	Accepted a return of merchandise from a credit customer.
	3	Sold merchandise for cash.
	4	Purchased merchandise on credit.
	5	Gave a $200 allowance for damaged merchandise.
	6	Collected sums on account from credit customers.
	7	Received an additional cash investment from the owner.
	8	Issued a check to pay a creditor on account.

Exercise 7-3 ►
Objective 2

Recording credit sales.

The following transactions took place at Tina's Camp Shop during May. Indicate how these transactions would be entered in a sales journal like the one shown in Figure 7-2.

DATE		TRANSACTIONS
May	1	Sold a tent and other items on credit to Brad Winkler; issued Sales Slip 1101 for $280 plus sales tax of $14.
	2	Sold a backpack, an air mattress, and other items to Mary Fuller; issued Sales Slip 1102 for $120 plus sales tax of $6.
	3	Sold a lantern, cooking utensils, and other items to James Baker; issued Sales Slip 1103 for $100 plus sales tax of $5.

Exercise 7-4 ►
Objective 2

Recording sales returns and allowances.

Record the general journal entries for the following transactions of World of Styles that occurred in May 20--.

DATE		TRANSACTIONS
May	7	Accepted a return of some damaged merchandise from Shanda Perry, a credit customer; issued Credit Memorandum 130 for $636, which includes sales tax of $36; the original sale was made on Sales Slip 1605 of May 5.
	22	Gave an allowance to Jared Lewis, a credit customer, for some merchandise that was slightly damaged but usable; issued Credit Memorandum 131 for $848, which includes sales tax of $48; the original sale was made on Sales Slip 1649 of May 19.

Exercise 7-5 ►
Objective 2

Posting from the sales journal.

The sales journal for Crocker Company is shown below. Describe how the amounts would be posted to the general ledger accounts.

			SALES JOURNAL					PAGE 1	
	DATE	SALES SLIP NO.	CUSTOMER'S ACCOUNT DEBITED	POST. REF.	ACCOUNTS RECEIVABLE DEBIT	SALES TAX PAYABLE CREDIT	SALES CREDIT		
1	20--								1
2	July 2	1101	Ned Turner		642 00	42 00	600 00		2
3	7	1102	Selena Hines		749 00	49 00	700 00		3
11	31	1110	Julie Sanders		267 50	17 50	250 00		11
12	31		Totals		4 146 25	271 25	3 875 00		12
13					(111)	(231)	(401)		13

Exercise 7-6 ►
Objective 7

Computing a trade discount.

Renquist Wholesale Company made sales using the following list prices and trade discounts. What amount will be recorded for each sale in the sales journal?

1. List price of $350 and trade discount of 40 percent
2. List price of $600 and trade discount of 40 percent

3. List price of $180 and trade discount of 30 percent

Computing a series of trade discounts.

Masonville Distributing Company, a wholesale firm, made sales using the following list prices and trade discounts. What amount will be recorded for each sale in the sales journal?

1. List price of $4,000 and trade discounts of 25 and 15 percent

2. List price of $3,600 and trade discounts of 25 and 15 percent

3. List price of $1,880 and trade discounts of 20 and 10 percent

◀ **Exercise 7-7**
Objective 7

Computing the sales tax due and recording its payment.

The balances of certain accounts of Hazelnut Corporation on February 28, 20--, were as follows:

Sales	$212,500
Sales Returns and Allowances	1,750

The firm's net sales are subject to a 6 percent sales tax. Give the general journal entry to record payment of the sales tax payable on February 28, 20--.

◀ **Exercise 7-8**
Objective 9

Preparing a schedule of accounts receivable.

The accounts receivable ledger for Style Corner follows.

1. Prepare a schedule of accounts receivable as of January 31.

2. What should the balance in the **Accounts Receivable** (control) account be?

◀ **Exercise 7-9**
Objective 6

NAME _Jim Brown_

ADDRESS _2001 5th Avenue, New York, NY 10018_

DATE		DESCRIPTION	POST. REF.	DEBIT	CREDIT	BALANCE
20--						
Jan.	1	Balance	✓			1 2 7 2 00
	2	Sales Slip 1604	S1	4 2 4 00		1 6 9 6 00

NAME _Ashley Ellis_

ADDRESS _901 Broadway, New York, NY 10018_

DATE		DESCRIPTION	POST. REF.	DEBIT	CREDIT	BALANCE
20--						
Jan.	1	Balance	✓			4 2 4 00
	27	Sales Slip 1607	S1	1 3 0 00		5 5 4 00
	31		CR1		2 1 2 00	3 4 2 00

NAME _Darren Flanagan_

ADDRESS _5021 Park Avenue, New York, NY 10018_

DATE		DESCRIPTION	POST. REF.	DEBIT	CREDIT	BALANCE
20--						
Jan.	1	Balance	✓			2 1 2 00
	15	Sales Slip 1609	CR1		2 1 2 00	—0—
	31		S1	7 4 2 00		7 4 2 00

NAME   *Maria Gonzalez*

ADDRESS   *94 Houston Street, New York, NY 10019*

DATE		DESCRIPTION	POST. REF.	DEBIT	CREDIT	BALANCE
20--						
Jan.	1	Balance	✓			4 2 4 00
	20	Sales Slip 1606	S1	2 1 2 00		6 3 6 00
	21		CR1		4 0 0 00	2 3 6 00
	22	Sales Slip 1610	S1	8 4 8 00		1 0 8 4 00

NAME   *Aaren McCord*

ADDRESS   *619 Lexington Avenue, New York, NY 10017*

DATE		DESCRIPTION	POST. REF.	DEBIT	CREDIT	BALANCE
20--						
Jan.	1	Balance	✓			5 3 0 00
	31	Sales Slip 1615	S1	2 1 2 0 00		2 6 5 0 00

NAME   *Ron Thomas*

ADDRESS   *2110 West 32nd Street, New York, NY 10027*

DATE		DESCRIPTION	POST. REF.	DEBIT	CREDIT	BALANCE
20--						
Jan.	1	Balance	✓			2 1 2 0 00
	12		CR1		1 0 6 0 00	1 0 6 0 00
	17		S1	8 4 8 00		1 9 0 8 00

Exercise 7-10 ►
Objective 5

Posting sales returns and allowances.

Post the journal entries below to the appropriate ledger accounts. Assume the following account balances:

Accounts Receivable (control account)	$901
Accounts Receivable—Marsha Cline	424
Accounts Receivable—Reba Black	477

GENERAL JOURNAL   PAGE ___42___

	DATE		DESCRIPTION	POST. REF.	DEBIT	CREDIT	
1	20--						1
2	Feb.	14	Sales Returns and Allowances		1 5 0 00		2
3			Sales Tax Payable		9 00		3
4			Accounts Rec.—Marsha Cline			1 5 9 00	4
5			Accepted return on defective				5
6			merchandise, Credit Memo				6
7			101; original sale of Jan. 12,				7
8			Sales Slip 1101				8
9							9
10		23	Sales Returns and Allowances		5 0 00		10
11			Sales Tax Payable		3 00		11
12			Accounts Rec.—Reba Black			5 3 00	12
13			Gave allowance for damaged				13
14			merchandise, Credit Memo				14
15			102; original sale Jan. 20,				15
16			Sales Slip 1150				16

Problems

Selected problems can be completed using:
🍑 **Peachtree**   📘 **QuickBooks**   ▦ **Spreadsheets**

PROBLEM SET A

Recording credit sales and posting from the sales journal.

The Metroplex Appliance Center is a retail store that sells household appliances. The firm's credit sales for June are listed below, along with the general ledger accounts used to record these sales. The balance shown for **Accounts Receivable** is for the beginning of the month.

◄ **Problem 7-1A**
Objectives 1, 2

INSTRUCTIONS

1. Open the general ledger accounts and enter the balance of **Accounts Receivable** for June 1, 20--.
2. Record the transactions in a sales journal like the one shown in Figure 7-4. Use 7 as the journal page number.
3. Total, prove, and rule the sales journal as of June 30.
4. Post the column totals from the sales journal to the proper general ledger accounts.

GENERAL LEDGER ACCOUNTS

111   Accounts Receivable, $15,700 Dr.

231   Sales Tax Payable

401   Sales

DATE	TRANSACTIONS
June 1	Sold a dishwasher to Tonya Wonders; issued Sales Slip 105 for $1,700 plus sales tax of $102.
6	Sold a washer to Denise Permenter; issued Sales Slip 106 for $1,200 plus sales tax of $72.
11	Sold a high-definition television set to Tucker Allen; issued Sales Slip 107 for $4,100 plus sales tax of $246.
17	Sold an electric dryer to Arlene Hillman; issued Sales Slip 108 for $800 plus sales tax of $48.
23	Sold a trash compactor to Mary Alvarez; issued Sales Slip 109 for $600 plus sales tax of $36.
27	Sold a color television set to Clint Lewis; issued Sales Slip 110 for $600 plus sales tax of $36.
29	Sold an electric range to Pat Ashley; issued Sales Slip 111 for $1,200 plus sales tax of $72.
30	Sold a microwave oven to Rusty Ryan; issued Sales Slip 112 for $500 plus sales tax of $30.

Analyze: What percentage of credit sales were for entertainment items?

Problem 7-2A ►

Objectives 1, 2, 4

Journalizing, posting, and reporting sales transactions.

Millennium Furniture specializes in modern living room and dining room furniture. Merchandise sales are subject to a 5 percent sales tax. The firm's credit sales and sales returns and allowances for February 20-- are reflected below, along with the general ledger accounts used to record these transactions. The balances shown are for the beginning of the month.

INSTRUCTIONS

1. Open the general ledger accounts and enter the balances for February 1.
2. Record the transactions in a sales journal and in a general journal. Use 8 as the page number for the sales journal and 24 as the page number for the general journal.
3. Post the entries from the general journal to the general ledger.
4. Total, prove, and rule the sales journal as of February 28.
5. Post the column totals from the sales journal.
6. Prepare the heading and the Revenue section of the firm's income statement for the month ended February 28, 20--.

GENERAL LEDGER ACCOUNTS

111 Accounts Receivable, $5,212 Dr.

231 Sales Tax Payable, $2,390 Cr.

401 Sales

451 Sales Returns and Allowances

DATE		TRANSACTIONS
Feb.	1	Sold a living room sofa to Barbara Evans; issued Sales Slip 1516 for $1,750 plus sales tax of $87.50.
	5	Sold three recliners to Richard Clinton; issued Sales Slip 1517 for $1,580 plus sales tax of $79.
	9	Sold a dining room set to Louise Mack; issued Sales Slip 1518 for $5,200 plus sales tax of $260.
	11	Accepted a return of one damaged recliner from Richard Clinton that was originally sold on Sales Slip 1517 of February 5; issued Credit Memorandum 207 for $556.50, which includes sales tax of $26.50.
	17	Sold living room tables and bookcases to Raymond Cheng; issued Sales Slip 1519 for $4,500 plus sales tax of $225.
	23	Sold eight dining room chairs to Anna Wallace; issued Sales Slip 1520 for $3,200 plus sales tax of $160.
	25	Gave Raymond Cheng an allowance for scratches on his bookcases; issued Credit Memorandum 208 for $105, which includes sales taxes of $5; the bookcases were originally sold on Sales Slip 1519 of February 17.
	27	Sold a living room sofa and four chairs to Victor De la Hoya; issued Sales Slip 1521 for $3,680 plus sales tax of $184.
	28	Sold a dining room table to Sue Barker; issued Sales Slip 1522 for $1,300 plus sales tax of $65.
	28	Sold a living room modular wall unit to Mack Slaughter; issued Sales Slip 1523 for $3,140 plus sales tax of $157.

Analyze: Based on the beginning balance of the **Sales Tax Payable** account, what was the amount of net sales for January? (Hint: Sales tax returns are filed and paid to the state quarterly.)

Recording sales transactions, posting to the accounts receivable ledger, and preparing a schedule of accounts receivable.

Bradford China Shop sells china, glassware, and other gift items that are subject to a 6 percent sales tax. The shop uses a general journal and a sales journal similar to those illustrated in this chapter.

1. Record the transactions for November in the proper journal. Use 5 as the page number for the sales journal and 15 as the page number for the general journal.

2. Immediately after recording each transaction, post to the accounts receivable ledger.

3. Post the amounts from the general journal daily. Post the sales journal amount as a total at the end of the month.

4. Prepare a schedule of accounts receivable. Compare the balance of the **Accounts Receivable** control account with the total of the schedule.

◄ **Problem 7-3A**
Objectives 1, 2, 3, 4, 6

INSTRUCTIONS

DATE		TRANSACTIONS
Nov.	1	Sold china to Connie Tolbert; issued Sales Slip 1401 for $1,200 plus $72 sales tax.
	5	Sold a brass serving tray to Jill Mason; issued Sales Slip 1402 for $1,800 plus $108 sales tax.
	6	Sold a vase to Durwood Cluck; issued Sales Slip 1403 for $600 plus $36 sales tax.
	10	Sold a punch bowl and glasses to Amy Sadler; issued Sales Slip 1404 for $1,500 plus $90 sales tax.
	14	Sold a set of serving bowls to Troy Dockery; issued Sales Slip 1405 for $450 plus $27 sales tax.
	17	Gave Amy Sadler an allowance because of a broken glass discovered when unpacking the punch bowl and glasses sold on November 10, Sales Slip 1404; issued Credit Memorandum 201 for $127.20, which includes sales tax of $7.20.
	21	Sold a coffee table to Jeff Marx; issued Sales Slip 1406 for $3,000 plus $180 sales tax.
	24	Sold sterling silver teaspoons to Brint Polinksi; issued Sales Slip 1407 for $600 plus $36 sales tax.
	25	Gave Jeff Marx an allowance for scratches on his coffee table sold on November 21, Sales Slip 1406; issued Credit Memorandum 202 for $318, which includes $18 in sales tax.
	30	Sold a clock to Henry Griffon; issued Sales Slip 1408 for $3,600 plus $216 sales tax

Analyze: How many postings would be made to the general ledger if the business did not use a sales journal?

Recording sales transactions, posting to the accounts receivable ledger, and preparing a schedule of accounts receivable.

Flowers & More is a wholesale shop that sells flowers, plants, and plant supplies. The transactions shown below took place during January.

INSTRUCTIONS

1. Record the transactions in the proper journal. Use 6 as the page number for the sales journal and 10 as the page number for the general journal.
2. Immediately after recording each transaction, post to the accounts receivable ledger.
3. Post the amounts from the general journal daily. Post the sales journal amount as a total at the end of the month.
4. Prepare a schedule of accounts receivable. Compare the balance of the **Accounts Receivable** control account with the total of the schedule.

DATE	TRANSACTIONS
Jan. 3	Sold a floral arrangement to Jefferson Florist; issued Invoice 1801 for $300.
8	Sold potted plants to Goree Garden Supply; issued Invoice 1802 for $751.
9	Sold floral arrangements to Henderson Flower Shop; issued Invoice 1803 for $361.50.
10	Sold corsages to Lowe's Flower Shop; issued Invoice 1804 for $530.
15	Gave Henderson Flower Shop an allowance because of withered blossoms discovered in one of the floral arrangements sold on Invoice 1803 on January 9; issued Credit Memorandum 101 for $20.
20	Sold table arrangements to Town Floral Shop; issued Invoice 1805 for $424.
22	Sold plants to Metroplex Nursery; issued Invoice 1806 for $642.50.
25	Sold roses to Lowe's Flower Shop; issued Invoice 1807 for $383.
27	Sold several floral arrangements to Jefferson Florist; issued Invoice 1808 for $860.
31	Gave Jefferson Florist an allowance because of withered blossoms discovered in one of the floral arrangements sold on Invoice 1808 on January 27; issued Credit Memorandum 102 for $106.

Analyze: Damaged goods decreased the net sales by what dollar amount? By what percentage amount?

PROBLEM SET B

Recording credit sales and posting from the sales journal.

The Appliance Mart is a retail store that sells household appliances. The firm's credit sales for July are listed below, along with the general ledger accounts used to record these sales. The balance shown for Accounts Receivable is for the beginning of the month.

◄ **Problem 7-1B**
Objectives 1, 2

INSTRUCTIONS

1. Open the general ledger accounts and enter the balance of **Accounts Receivable** for July 1.
2. Record the transactions in a sales journal like the one shown in Figure 7-4. Use 7 as the journal page number.
3. Total, prove, and rule the sales journal as of July 31.
4. Post the column totals from the sales journal to the proper general ledger accounts.

GENERAL LEDGER ACCOUNTS

111 Accounts Receivable, $36,400 Dr.

231 Sales Tax Payable

401 Sales

DATE		TRANSACTIONS
July	1	Sold a dishwasher to Ted Gates; issued Sales Slip 101 for $1,400 plus sales tax of $84.
	6	Sold a washer to Jay Robinson; issued Sales Slip 102 for $1,000 plus sales tax of $60.
	11	Sold a high-definition television set to Samuel Davis; issued Sales Slip 103 for $3,600 plus sales tax of $216.
	17	Sold an electric dryer to Angela Bush; issued Sales Slip 104 for $800 plus sales tax of $48.
	23	Sold a trash compactor to Selena Lozono; issued Sales Slip 105 for $700 plus sales tax of $42.
	27	Sold a portable color television set to Wes Reeves; issued Sales Slip 106 for $500 plus sales tax of $30.
	29	Sold an electric range to David Turner; issued Sales Slip 107 for $1,300 plus sales tax of $78.
	30	Sold a microwave oven to Lauren Ashford; issued Sales Slip 108 for $400 plus sales tax of $24.

Analyze: What percentage of credit sales were for entertainment items?

Problem 7-2B ►

Objectives 1, 2, 4

Journalizing, posting, and reporting sales transactions.

Furniture Future is a retail store that specializes in modern living room and dining room furniture. Merchandise sales are subject to a 6 percent sales tax. The firm's credit sales and sales returns and allowances for May are reflected below, along with the general ledger accounts used to record these transactions. The balances shown are for the beginning of the month.

INSTRUCTIONS

1. Open the general ledger accounts and enter the balances for May 1.
2. Record the transactions in a sales journal and a general journal. Use 8 as the page number for the sales journal and 24 as the page number for the general journal.
3. Post the entries from the general journal to the general ledger.
4. Total, prove, and rule the sales journal as of May 31.
5. Post the column totals from the sales journal.
6. Prepare the heading and the Revenue section of the firm's income statement for the month ended May 31, 20--.

GENERAL LEDGER ACCOUNTS

111 Accounts Receivable, $5,644 Dr.

231 Sales Tax Payable, $960 Cr.

401 Sales

451 Sales Returns and Allowances

DATE		TRANSACTIONS
May	1	Sold a living room sofa to Marion Cherry; issued Sales Slip 1507 for $1,800 plus sales tax of $108.
	5	Sold three recliners to Giffen Cruit; issued Sales Slip 1508 for $1,200 plus sales tax of $72.
	9	Sold a dining room set to Jennifer Ashley; issued Sales Slip 1509 for $6,000 plus sales tax of $360.
	11	Accepted a return of a damaged chair from Giffen Cruit; the chair was originally sold on Sales Slip 1508 of May 5; issued Credit Memorandum 210 for $424, which includes sales tax of $24.
	17	Sold living room tables and bookcases to Victor Salez; issued Sales Slip 1510 for $5,000 plus sales tax of $300.
	23	Sold eight dining room chairs to Nelvia Wilson; issued Sales Slip 1511 for $3,600 plus sales tax of $216.
	25	Gave Victor Salez an allowance for scratches on his bookcases; issued Credit Memorandum 211 for $159, which includes sales taxes of $9; the bookcases were originally sold on Sales Slip 1510 of May 17.
	27	Sold a living room sofa and four chairs to Henry Barker; issued Sales Slip 1512 for $3,200 plus sales tax of $192.
	29	Sold a dining room table to Jenny Lemons; issued Sales Slip 1513 for $1,350 plus sales tax of $81.
	30	Sold a living room modular wall unit to John Morris; issued Sales Slip 1514 for $2,900 plus sales tax of $174.

Analyze: Based on the beginning balance of the **Sales Tax Payable** account, what was the amount of net sales for April? (Hint: Sales tax returns are filed and paid to the state quarterly.)

Recording sales transactions, posting to the accounts receivable ledger, and preparing a schedule of accounts receivable.

Amy's Special Occasions Card Shop sells cards, supplies, and various holiday gift items. All sales are subject to a sales tax of 6 percent. The shop uses a sales journal and general journal.

1. Record the credit sale transactions for February in the proper journal. Use 5 as the page number for the sales journal and 15 as the page number for the general journal.

2. Immediately after recording each transaction, post to the accounts receivable ledger.

3. Post the entries to the appropriate accounts.

4. Prepare a schedule of accounts receivable and compare the balance due with the amount shown in the **Accounts Receivable** control account.

◄ **Problem 7-3B**
Objectives 1, 2, 3, 4, 6

_____

INSTRUCTIONS

DATE		TRANSACTIONS
Feb.	3	Sold Vicki Grey a box of holiday greeting cards for $50 plus sales tax of $3 on Sales Slip 302.
	4	Sold to Dave Dorris a Valentine's Day party pack for $100 plus sales tax of $6 on Sales Slip 303.
	5	Ken Blackmon bought 10 boxes of Valentine's Day gift packs for his office. Sales Slip 304 was issued for $50 plus sales tax of $3.
	8	Sold Misty Woodall a set of crystal glasses for $300 plus sales tax of $18 on Sales Slip 305.
	9	Adam Harris purchased two statues for $200 plus $12 sales tax on Sales Slip 306.
	9	Gave Ken Blackmon an allowance because of incomplete items in one gift pack; issued Credit Memorandum 1000 for $5.30, which includes sales tax of $0.30.
	10	Sold Darryl Wrenn a Valentine Birthday package for $150 plus $9 sales tax on Sales Slip 307.
	13	Gave Misty Woodall an allowance of $50 because of two broken glasses in the set she purchased on February 8. Credit Memorandum 1001 was issued for the allowance plus sales tax of $3.
	14	Sold Vicki Grey 12 boxes of gift candy for $150 plus sales tax of $9 on Sales Slip 308.
	15	Sold a punch serving set with glasses for $100 to Corey Lambert. Sales tax of $6 was included on Sales Slip 309.

Analyze: How many postings were made to the general ledger? How many additional postings would be needed if the business did not use a sales journal?

Recording sales transactions, posting to the accounts receivable ledger, and preparing a schedule of accounts receivable.

County Town Nursery is a wholesale shop that sells flowers, plants, and plant supplies. The transactions shown below took place during February.

INSTRUCTIONS

1. Record the transactions in the proper journal. Use 4 as the page number for the sales journal and 9 as the page number for the general journal.
2. Immediately after recording each transaction, post to the accounts receivable ledger.
3. Post the amounts from the general journal daily. Post the sales journal amount as a total at the end of the month.
4. Prepare a schedule of accounts receivable. Compare the balance of the **Accounts Receivable** control account with the total of the schedule.

DATE	TRANSACTIONS
Feb. 3	Sold a floral arrangement to Jamestown Funeral Home; issued Invoice 1101 for $500.
8	Sold potted plants to The Nursery; issued Invoice 1102 for $900.00.
9	Sold floral arrangements to Town Flower Shop; issued Invoice 1103 for $1,161.50.
10	Sold corsages to City Flower Shop; issued Invoice 1104 for $650.
15	Gave Town Flower Shop an allowance because of withered blossoms discovered in one of the floral arrangements sold on Invoice 1103 on February 9; issued Credit Memorandum 102 for $40.
20	Sold table arrangements to City Flower Shop; issued Invoice 1105 for $636.
22	Sold plants to Winter Nursery; issued Invoice 1106 for $750.50.
25	Sold roses to Lewisville Flower Shop; issued Invoice 1107 for $423.
27	Sold several floral arrangements to Jamestown Funeral Home; issued Invoice 1108 for $950.
28	Gave Jamestown Funeral Home an allowance because of withered blossoms discovered in one of the floral arrangements sold on Invoice 1108 on February 27; issued Credit Memorandum 103 for $53.

Analyze: Damaged goods decreased the net sales by what dollar amount? By what percentage amount?

CHAPTER 7 CHALLENGE PROBLEM

Wholesaler Transactions

The Play Therapy Company sells toys and games to retail stores. The firm offers a trade discount of 40 percent on toys and 30 percent on games. Its credit sales and sales returns and allowances transactions for August are shown on page 246. The general ledger accounts used to record these transactions are listed below. The balance shown for **Accounts Receivable** is as of the beginning of August.

INSTRUCTIONS

1. Open the general ledger accounts and enter the balance of **Accounts Receivable** for August 1.

2. Set up an accounts receivable subsidiary ledger. Open an account for each of the credit customers listed below and enter the balances as of August 1.

Zane's Department Store	$14,880
Variety Toy Stores	20,200
Dallas Bookstores	
Pebblebrook Toy Center	
Emporium Game Center	8,420
Hanson's Game Store	

3. Record the transactions in a sales journal and in a general journal. Use 10 as the page number for the sales journal and 30 as the page number for the general journal. Be sure to enter each sale at its net price.

4. Post the individual entries from the sales journal and the general journal.

5. Total and rule the sales journal as of August 31.

6. Post the column total from the sales journal to the proper general ledger accounts.

7. Prepare the heading and the Revenue section of the firm's income statement for the month ended August 31.

8. Prepare a schedule of accounts receivable for August 31.

9. Check the total of the schedule of accounts receivable against the balance of the **Accounts Receivable** account in the general ledger. The two amounts should be equal.

GENERAL LEDGER ACCOUNTS

111 Accounts Receivable, $43,500 Dr.

401 Sales

451 Sales Returns and Allowances

DATE	TRANSACTIONS
August 1	Sold toys to Zane's Department Store; issued Invoice 2501, which shows a list price of $17,600 and a trade discount of 40 percent.
5	Sold games to the Dallas Bookstores; issued Invoice 2502, which shows a list price of $21,300 and a trade discount of 30 percent.
9	Sold games to the Emporium Game Center; issued Invoice 2503, which shows a list price of $7,040 and a trade discount of 30 percent.
14	Sold toys to the Variety Toy Stores; issued Invoice 2504, which shows a list price of $24,400 and a trade discount of 40 percent.
18	Accepted a return of all the games shipped to the Emporium Game Center because they were damaged in transit; issued Credit Memo 162 for the original sale made on Invoice 2503 on August 9.
22	Sold toys to Hanson's Game Store; issued Invoice 2505, which shows a list price of $16,320 and a trade discount of 40 percent.
26	Sold games to the Zane's Department Store; issued Invoice 2506, which shows a list price of $20,300 and a trade discount of 30 percent.
30	Sold toys to the Pebblebrook Toy Center; issued Invoice 2507, which shows a list price of $23,400 and a trade discount of 40 percent.

Analyze: What is the effect on net sales if the company offers a series of trade discounts on toys (25 percent, 15 percent) instead of a single 40 percent discount?

Retail Store

Jim Hogan is the owner of The Linen Closet, a housewares store that sells a wide variety of items for the kitchen, bathroom, and home workshop. The Linen Closet offers a company credit card to customers.

The company has experienced an increase in sales since the credit card was introduced. Jim is considering replacing his manual system of recording sales with electronic point-of-sale cash registers that are linked to a computer.

Cash sales are now rung up by the salesclerks on a cash register that generates a tape listing total cash sales at the end of the day. For credit sales, salesclerks prepare handwritten sales slips that are forwarded to the accountant for manual entry into the sales journal and accounts receivable ledger.

The electronic register system Jim is considering would use an optical scanner to read coded labels attached to the merchandise. As the merchandise is passed over the scanner, the code is sent to the computer. The computer is programmed to read the code and identify the item being sold, record the amount of the sale, maintain a record of total sales, update the inventory record, and keep a record of cash received.

If the sale is a credit transaction, the customer's company credit card number is entered into the register. The computer updates the customer's account in the accounts receivable ledger stored in computer memory.

If this system is used, many of the accounting functions are done automatically as sales are entered into the register. At the end of the day, the computer prints a complete sales journal, along with up-to-date balances for the general ledger and the accounts receivable ledger accounts related to sales transactions.

Listed below are four situations that Jim is eager to eliminate. Would use of an electronic point-of-sale system as described above reduce or prevent these problems? Why or why not?

1. The salesclerk was not aware that the item purchased was on sale and did not give the customer the sale price.

2. The customer purchased merchandise using a stolen credit card.

3. The salesclerk did not charge a customer for an item.

4. The accountant did not post a sale to the customer's subsidiary ledger account.

Business Connections

Connection 1 ►

 **Retail Sales**

1. How does the **Sales Returns and Allowances** account provide management with a measure of operating efficiency? What problems might be indicated by a high level of returns and allowances?

2. Suppose you are the accountant for a small chain of clothing stores. Up to now the firm has offered open-account credit to qualified customers but has not allowed the use of bank credit cards. The president of the chain has asked your advice about changing the firm's credit policy. What advantages might there be in eliminating the open-account credit and accepting bank credit cards instead? Do you see any disadvantages?

3. During the past year Cravens Company has had a substantial increase in its losses from uncollectible accounts. Assume that you are the newly hired controller of this firm and that you have been asked to find the reason for the increase. What policies and procedures would you investigate?

4. Suppose a manager in your company has suggested that the firm not hire an accountant to advise it on tax matters and to file tax returns. He states that tax matters are merely procedural in nature and that anyone who can read the tax form instructions can do the necessary work. Comment on this idea.

5. Why is it usually worthwhile for a business to sell on credit even though it will have some losses from uncollectible accounts?

6. How can a firm's credit policy affect its profitability?

7. Why should management insist that all sales on credit and other transactions affecting the firm's accounts receivable be journalized and posted promptly?

8. How can efficient accounting records help management maintain sound credit and collection policies?

Connection 2 ►

Ethical DILEMMA **Working in Sales** Assume that you were just hired as a salesclerk at a clothing store. On your first day on the job, you observe the manager making a deal with a customer to sell a designer suit with "no tax." What would you do?

Connection 3 ►

*Street***WISE:**

Questions from the Real World **Revenue Growth** Refer to the *1999 Annual Report* of The Home Depot, Inc. in Appendix B.

1. Locate Management's Discussion and Analysis of Results of Operations and Financial Condition. By what percentage did net sales increase from fiscal 1998 to fiscal 1999? What factors contributed to this growth?

2. Review the Consolidated Balance Sheets. By what percentage did net accounts receivable change from fiscal 1998 to fiscal 1999? Consider your answer to Question 1 above. Describe the relationship between your answer to Question 1 and the change in net accounts receivable.

FINANCIAL $TATEMENT ANALYSIS

Income Statement An excerpt from the Consolidated Statements of Income for Wal-Mart Stores, Inc. is presented below. Review the financial data and answer the following analysis questions.

◄ **Connection 4**
WAL★MART

Amounts in millions

Fiscal years ended January 31	2000	1999	1998
Revenues:			
Net Sales	$165,013	$137,634	$117,958
Other Income Net	1,796	1,574	1,341
Total Revenues	$166,809	$139,208	$119,299

Analyze:

1. Based on the financial statement presented above, what is Wal-Mart Stores, Inc.'s fiscal year period?
2. Wal-Mart Stores, Inc.'s statement reports one figure for net sales. Name one account whose balance may have been deducted from the **Sales** account balance to determine a net sales amount.
3. The data presented demonstrates a steady increase in net sales over the three-year period. By what percentage have sales of 2000 increased over sales of 1998?

Analyze Online: Find the most recent consolidated statements of income on the Wal-Mart Stores, Inc. Web site **(www.walmartstores.com).** Click on the link *Financial Information*, then select the link for the most recent annual report.

4. What dollar amount is reported for net sales for the most recent year?
5. What is the trend in net sales over the last three years?
6. What are some possible reasons for this trend?

Extending the Thought

e-commerce Some retailers only operate online and do not have "bricks-and-mortar" physical locations where consumers can shop. What benefits and drawbacks do you see for retailers who operate entirely online?

◄ **Connection 5**

Business Communication

Memo You and your partner own three children's bookstores. Your partner comments on the separate general ledger accounts used for **Sales, Sales Tax Payable,** and **Sales Returns and Allowances,** saying this seems like unnecessary "busy work." Write a memo to your partner in response to these concerns.

◄ **Connection 6**

Accounting for Sales and Accounts Receivable **Chapter 7 • 249**

Connection 7 ▶ **Team**Work Store Policies As a team, gather information about the sales returns and allowance policies of various stores. Choose stores that sell different types of merchandise, such as

    a shoe store,
    a hardware store,
    a video store,
    a supermarket,
    a nursery.

Summarize your findings in a one-page report.

Connection 8 ▶ *inter*NET **CONNECTION** Privacy and Security Locate the Web sites for three major online retailers. Research the policy of each retailer regarding privacy and security. Prepare a report that compares the policies.

Answers to Self Reviews

Answers to Section 1 Self Review

1. Sales of merchandise on credit.
2. A ledger that contains accounts of a single type. Examples are the accounts receivable ledger and the accounts payable ledger.
3. A journal that is used to record only one type of transaction. Examples are the sales journal, the purchases journal, the cash receipts journal, and the cash payments journal.
4. **c.** service, merchandising, manufacturing.
5. **c.** increases credit sales
6. The sale to Li was recorded at a taxable rate of 7 percent instead of 6 percent. Therefore, the Sales Tax Payable column should have an entry of $18, not $21. The Accounts Receivable Debit column should have an entry of $318, not $321.

   The sale to Hahn should have an entry in the Accounts Receivable Debit column of $477, not $427.

Answers to Section 2 Self Review

1. Individual accounts for all credit customers.
2. Sales minus sales returns.
3. A sales return results when a customer returns goods and the firm takes them back. A sales allowance results when the firm gives a customer a reduction in the price of the good or service.
4. **c.** income statement
5. **a. Sales Returns and Allowances, Sales Tax Payable, Accounts Receivable**

6.

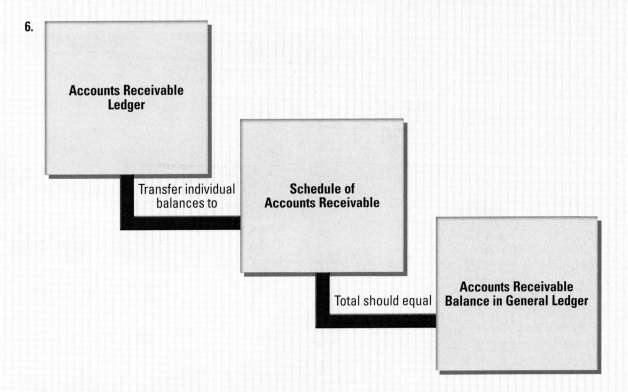

Answers to Section 3 Self Review

1. Four types of credit sales are open-account credit, business credit card sales, bank credit card sales, and credit card company sales.
2. **Sales Tax Payable** is the account used to record the liability for sales taxes to be paid in the future.
3. List price is the established retail price of an item; net price is the amount left after all trade discounts are subtracted from the list price.
4. **c.** $840
5. **d.** $2,160
6. Possible factors are payment history, amount of current debt, amount of potential debt (available credit cards), employment history, salary, references from other creditors.

Answers to Comprehensive Self Review

1. A service business sells services; a merchandising business sells goods that it has purchased for resale; and a manufacturing business sells goods that it has produced.
2. A merchandising business must account for the purchase and sale of goods and for its merchandise inventory.
3. It contains detailed information about the transactions with credit customers and shows the balances owed by credit customers at all times.
4. A control account is an account that serves as a link between a subsidiary ledger and the general ledger because its balance summarizes the balances of the accounts in the subsidiary ledger.
5. The month and the quarter.

CHAPTER 8

Learning Objectives

1. Record purchases of merchandise on credit in a three-column purchases journal.

2. Post from the three-column purchases journal to the general ledger accounts.

3. Post credit purchases from the purchases journal to the accounts payable subsidiary ledger.

4. Record purchases returns and allowances in the general journal and post them to the accounts payable subsidiary ledger.

5. Prepare a schedule of accounts payable.

6. Compute the net delivered cost of purchases.

7. Demonstrate a knowledge of the procedures for effective internal control of purchases.

8. Define the accounting terms new to this chapter.

Accounting for Purchases and Accounts Payable

Pier 1 imports®

www.pier1.com

*I*n the 1960s when the first Pier 1 Imports store opened in San Mateo, California, the company offered merchandise such as beanbag chairs, love beads, and incense. Throughout the 1970s and 1980s, the company's merchandise assortment changed along with the demands of its customer base. Pier 1 Imports reshaped its image over the years to sell quality, unique home furnishings and imaginative decorative accessories. By 1989, 500 stores offered items such as occasional tables, Jamaican wicker shelves, and bamboo birdcages. Pier 1 Imports now operates more than 800 stores worldwide, importing products from more than 50 countries.

Thinking Critically
How do you think Pier 1 Imports chooses the products that are offered for sale in its stores?

For more information on Pier 1 Imports, go to: collegeaccounting.glencoe.com.

New Terms

Accounts payable ledger	Purchases account
Cash discount	Purchases discount
Cost of goods sold	Purchases journal
Freight In account	Receiving report
Purchase allowance	Sales discount
Purchase invoice	Sales invoice
Purchase order	Schedule of accounts payable
Purchase requisition	
Purchase return	Transportation In account

Section Objectives

1 Record purchases of merchandise on credit in a three-column purchases journal.

WHY IT'S IMPORTANT
Most merchandisers purchase goods on credit, and the use of a special journal improves efficiency when recording these transactions.

2 Post from the three-column purchases journal to the general ledger accounts.

WHY IT'S IMPORTANT
Summary postings from the purchases journal minimize repetitive tasks.

Terms to Learn

cash discount
cost of goods sold
Freight In account
purchase invoice
purchase order
purchase requisition
Purchases account
purchases discount
purchases journal
receiving report
sales discount
sales invoice
Transportation In account

Merchandise Purchases

In this chapter you will learn how The Trend Center manages its purchases of goods for resale and its accounts payable.

Accounting for Purchases

Most merchandising businesses purchase goods on credit under open-account arrangements. A large firm usually has a centralized purchasing department that is responsible for locating suppliers, obtaining price quotations, negotiating credit terms, and placing orders. In small firms purchasing activities are handled by a single individual, usually the owner or manager.

Purchasing Procedures

When a sales department needs goods, it sends the purchasing department a purchase requisition (Figure 8-1 on page 255). A **purchase requisition** lists the items to be ordered. It is signed by someone with the authority to approve requests for merchandise, usually the manager of the sales department. The purchasing department selects a supplier who can furnish the goods at a competitive price and then issues a purchase order (Figure 8-2 on page 255). The **purchase order** specifies the exact items, quantity, price, and credit terms. It is signed by someone with authority to approve purchases, usually the purchasing agent.

When the goods arrive at the business, they are inspected. A **receiving report** is prepared to show the quantity and condition of the goods received. The purchasing department receives a copy of the receiving report and compares it to the purchase order. If defective goods or the wrong quantity of goods are received, the purchasing department contacts the supplier and settles the problem.

Figure 8-3 on page 255 shows the invoice, or *bill*, for items ordered and shipped. The customer, The Trend Center, calls it a **purchase invoice**. The supplier, Clothes Rack Depot, calls it a **sales invoice**. The customer's accounting department compares the invoice to copies of the purchase order and receiving report. The accounting department checks the quantities, prices, and math on the invoice and then records the purchase. It is important to record purchases in the accounting records as soon as the invoice is verified. Shortly before the due date of the invoice, the accounting department issues a check to the supplier and records the payment.

> The purchasing department for The Home Depot, Inc. purchases 40,000 to 50,000 different kinds of home improvement supplies, building materials, and lawn and garden products.

The Trend Center
1010 Red Bird Lane
Dallas, TX 75268-7783

PURCHASE REQUISITION

No. __325__

DEPARTMENT __Men's__   DATE OF REQUEST __January 2, 20--__

ADVISE ON DELIVERY __Virginia Richey__   DATE REQUIRED __January 25, 20--__

QUANTITY	DESCRIPTION
5	Assorted colors men's suits

APPROVED BY_____   REQUESTED BY _____

FOR PURCHASING DEPARTMENT USE ONLY

PURCHASE ORDER __8001__   ISSUED TO: __Clothes Rack Depot__
DATE __January 5, 20--__   __1677 Mandela Lane__
__Dallas, TX 75267-6205__

The Trend Center
1010 Red Bird Lane
Dallas, TX 75268-7783

PURCHASE ORDER

To   Clothes Rack Depot   Date: __January 5, 20--__
1677 Mandela Lane   Order No: __8001__
Dallas, TX 75267-6205   Terms: __n/30__

QUANTITY	ITEM	UNIT PRICE	TOTAL
5	Assorted colors men's suits	476.00	2,380.00

APPROVED BY _____

Clothes Rack Depot   INVOICE NO. 7985
1677 Mandela Lane
Dallas, TX 75267-6205

SOLD TO: The Trend Center   DATE: January 22, 20--
1010 Red Bird Lane   ORDER NO.: 8001
Dallas, TX 75268-7783   SHIPPED BY: City Express
    TERMS: n/30

YOUR ORDER NO.	SALESPERSON		TERMS
8001			n/30

DATE SHIPPED	SHIPPED BY		FOB
January 22, 20--	City Express		Dallas

QUANTITY	DESCRIPTION	UNIT PRICE	TOTAL
5	Assorted colors men's suits	476 00	2,380 00
	Freight		180 00
	Total		2,560 00

National Preferences

When conducting business, the customer's tastes should be considered. Consumers around the world have different preferences in product packaging. For example, in France and Italy, consumers expect stylish looks, while in Germany many consumers look for recyclable materials. Accountants who work with international clients should consider national preferences when designing letterhead, creating portfolios, or choosing paper quality.

The Purchases Account

The purchase of merchandise for resale is a cost of doing business. The purchase of merchandise is debited to the **Purchases account**. **Purchases** is a temporary account classified as a cost of goods sold account. The **cost of goods sold** is the actual cost to the business of the merchandise sold to customers.

Cost of goods sold accounts follow the debit and credit rules of expense accounts. The **Purchases** account is increased by debits and decreased by credits. Its normal balance is a debit. In the chart of accounts, the cost of goods sold accounts appear just before the expense accounts.

> Wal-Mart Stores, Inc. purchases private-label products from suppliers and markets these as Wal-Mart brands. Products such as Ol'Roy™ dog food, Spring Valley® vitamins, and EverStart® automotive batteries are purchased at lower costs than nationally known brands. Thus, Wal-Mart Stores, Inc. can sell these items at a lower price to its customers.

Freight Charges for Purchases

Sometimes the buyer pays the freight charge—the cost of shipping the goods from the seller's warehouse to the buyer's location. There are two ways to handle the freight charges paid by the buyer:

- The buyer is billed directly by the transportation company for the freight charge. The buyer issues a check directly to the freight company.
- The seller pays the freight charge and includes it on the invoice. The invoice includes the price of the goods and the freight charge.

The freight charge is debited to the **Freight In** or **Transportation In account**. This is a cost of goods sold account showing transportation charges for merchandise purchased. The buyer enters three elements in the accounting records:

Price of goods	(debit **Purchases**)	$2,380.00
Freight charge	(debit **Freight In**)	180.00
Total invoice	(credit **Accounts Payable**)	$2,560.00

Purchases		Freight In		Accounts Payable	
Dr.	Cr.	Dr.	Cr.	Dr.	Cr.
+	–	+	–	–	+
2,380		180			2,560

The Purchases Journal

For most merchandising businesses, it is not efficient to enter purchases of goods in the general journal. Instead, credit purchases of merchandise are recorded in a special journal called the **purchases journal**.

The following illustrates how credit purchases appear in a general journal. Each entry involves a debit to **Purchases** and **Freight In** and a credit to **Accounts Payable** plus a detailed explanation.

Important!

Credit Purchases
The purchases journal is used to record *only credit purchases of merchandise for resale.* Credit purchases of other items used in the business are recorded in the general journal.

GENERAL JOURNAL

PAGE _____1_____

	DATE		DESCRIPTION	POST. REF.	DEBIT	CREDIT	
1	20--						1
2	Jan.	3	Purchases	501	3 0 0 0 00		2
3			Freight In	502	2 5 0 00		3
4			Accounts Payable	205		3 2 5 0 00	4
5			Purchased merchandise from				5
6			Sebrina's Clothing Store,				6
7			Invoice 8434, dated December 29,				7
8			terms 2/10, n/30				8
9							9
10		5	Purchases	501	3 3 6 0 00		10
11			Freight In	502	2 6 0 00		11
12			Accounts Payable	205		3 6 2 0 00	12
13			Purchased merchandise from				13
14			The Style Shop, Invoice 336,				14
15			dated December 30, terms n/30				15
16							16
17		6	Purchases	501	2 7 0 0 00		17
18			Freight In	502	2 2 0 00		18
19			Accounts Payable	205		2 9 2 0 00	19
20			Purchased merchandise from				20
21			The Women's Shop, Invoice 9080,				21
22			dated December 31, terms n/30				22
23							23
24		7	Purchases	501	3 8 5 0 00		24
25			Freight In	502	4 5 0 00		25
26			Accounts Payable	205		4 3 0 0 00	26
27			Purchased merchandise from				27
28			Fashion World, Invoice 4321, dated				28
29			December 31, terms 2/10, n/30				29
30							30
31							31

These four general journal entries require twelve separate postings to general ledger accounts: four to **Purchases,** four to **Freight In,** and four to **Accounts Payable.** As you can see from the ledger accounts that follow, it takes a great deal of time and effort to post these entries.

ACCOUNT _Accounts Payable_   ACCOUNT NO. _205_

DATE		DESCRIPTION	POST. REF.	DEBIT	CREDIT	BALANCE	
						DEBIT	CREDIT
20--							
Jan.	1	Balance	✓				5 4 0 0 00
	3		J1		3 2 5 0 00		8 6 5 0 00
	5		J1		3 6 2 0 00		12 2 7 0 00
	6		J1		2 9 2 0 00		15 1 9 0 00
	7		J1		4 3 0 0 00		19 4 9 0 00

ACCOUNT _Purchases_   ACCOUNT NO. _501_

DATE	DESCRIPTION	POST. REF.	DEBIT	CREDIT	BALANCE DEBIT	BALANCE CREDIT
20--						
Jan. 3		J1	3 0 0 0 00		3 0 0 0 00	
5		J1	3 3 6 0 00		6 3 6 0 00	
6		J1	2 7 0 0 00		9 0 6 0 00	
7		J1	3 8 5 0 00		12 9 1 0 00	

ACCOUNT _Freight In_   ACCOUNT NO. _502_

DATE	DESCRIPTION	POST. REF.	DEBIT	CREDIT	BALANCE DEBIT	BALANCE CREDIT
20--						
Jan. 3		J1	2 5 0 00		2 5 0 00	
5		J1	2 6 0 00		5 1 0 00	
6		J1	2 2 0 00		7 3 0 00	
7		J1	4 5 0 00		1 1 8 0 00	

Figure 8-4 shows the purchases journal for The Trend Center. Remember that the purchases journal is only for credit purchases of merchandise for resale to customers. Notice how the columns efficiently organize the data about the credit purchases. The purchases journal makes it possible to record each purchase on a single line. In addition, there is no need to enter account names and descriptions.

FIGURE 8-4 ▼
Purchases Journal

PURCHASES JOURNAL   PAGE _1_

DATE	CREDITOR'S ACCOUNT CREDITED	INVOICE NUMBER	INVOICE DATE	TERMS	POST. REF.	ACCOUNTS PAYABLE CREDIT	PURCHASES (DEBIT)	FREIGHT IN DEBIT
20--								
Jan. 3	Sebrina's Clothing Store	8434	12/29/--	2/10, n/30		3 2 5 0 00	3 0 0 0 00	2 5 0 00
5	The Style Shop	336	12/30/--	n/30		3 6 2 0 00	3 3 6 0 00	2 6 0 00
6	The Women's Shop	9080	12/31/--	n/30		2 9 2 0 00	2 7 0 0 00	2 2 0 00
7	Fashion World	4321	12/31/--	2/10, n/30		4 3 0 0 00	3 8 5 0 00	4 5 0 00
19	Designer's Fashions	9789	01/15/--	2/10, n/30		2 1 0 0 00	1 9 3 0 00	1 7 0 00
23	Clothes Rack Depot	7985	01/22/--	n/30		2 5 6 0 00	2 3 8 0 00	1 8 0 00
31						18 7 5 0 00	17 2 2 0 00	1 5 3 0 00

❶ Objective

Record purchases of merchandise on credit in a three-column purchases journal.

Recording Transactions in a Purchases Journal

Use the information on the purchase invoice to make the entry in the purchases journal.

1. Enter the date, supplier name, invoice number, invoice date, and credit terms.
2. In the Accounts Payable Credit column, enter the total owed to the supplier.
3. In the Purchases Debit column, enter the price of the goods purchased.
4. In the Freight In Debit column, enter the freight amount.

Accounting

Retail/Wholesale Sales & Service

Industry Overview

In the United States today, retailing represents $3 trillion in annual sales. Wholesale markets fuel these sales, supplying products and services for resale in department stores, discount stores, factory outlets, catalogs, and on the Web. The retail industry alone employs more than 20 million workers in the United States.

Career Opportunities

- Store Manager
- Vice President of Acquisitions and Real Estate
- Inventory Specialist
- Manager of Logistics
- Fashion Merchandiser
- Senior Buyer
- Director of E-Commerce Distribution
- Customer Service Manager

Preparing for a Retail/Wholesale Career

- Obtain a business-related degree to open doors to management-level positions.
- Apply to corporate executive training programs for paths to senior buyer, manager of planning and distribution, or regional merchandise manager.

- Complete college courses in marketing, finance, accounting, communications, merchandising, and information systems, as recommended by the National Retail Federation.
- Complete one or two introductory accounting courses, one financial accounting course, and one managerial accounting course for degree programs in fashion merchandising and retail marketing.
- Obtain specialized certifications such as the Buyers Certification or Logistics Certification.

Thinking Critically

Describe why an understanding of credit policies and credit terms might help a retail store manager direct the operations of the store more effectively.

Internet Application

Locate a recruiting Web site for a company such as Federated Department Stores. Review the job description for store manager or buyer. In a half-page report, list the primary responsibilities for this job. What accounting or financial responsibilities does the position entail?

The total of the Purchases Debit and Freight In Debit columns must equal the amount entered in the Accounts Payable Credit column.

The invoice date and credit terms determine when payment is due. The following credit terms often appear on invoices:

- *Net 30 days* or *n/30* means that payment in full is due 30 days after the date of the invoice.
- *Net 10 days EOM,* or *n/10 EOM,* means that payment in full is due 10 days after the end of the month in which the invoice was issued.
- *2% 10 days, net 30 days,* or *2/10, n/30* means that if payment is made within 10 days of the invoice date, the customer can take a 2 percent discount. Otherwise, payment in full is due in 30 days.

The 2 percent discount is a **cash discount**; it is a discount offered by suppliers to encourage quick payment by customers. To the customer it is known as a **purchases discount**. To the supplier it is known as a **sales discount**.

Important!

Cash Discounts
In the purchases journal, record the amount shown on the invoice. The cash discount is recorded when the payment is made.

② Objective

Post from the three-column purchases journal to the general ledger accounts.

Posting to the General Ledger

The purchases journal simplifies the posting process. Summary amounts are posted at the end of the month. Refer to Figure 8-5 as you learn how to post from the purchases journal to the general ledger accounts.

Total the Accounts Payable Credit, the Purchases Debit, and the Freight In Debit columns. Before posting, prove the equality of the debits and credits recorded in the purchases journal.

PROOF OF PURCHASES JOURNAL

	Debits
Purchases Debit column	$17,220.00
Freight In Debit column	1,530.00
	$18,750.00

	Credits
Accounts Payable Credit column	$18,750.00

FIGURE 8-5 ▼
Posting to the General Ledger

PURCHASES JOURNAL

PAGE 1

DATE	CREDITOR'S ACCOUNT CREDITED	INVOICE NUMBER	INVOICE DATE	TERMS	POST. REF.	ACCOUNTS PAYABLE CREDIT	PURCHASES DEBIT	FREIGHT IN DEBIT
20--								
Jan. 3	Sebrina's Clothing Store	8434	12/29/--	2/10, n/30	✓	3 250 00	3 000 00	250 00
5	The Style Shop	336	12/30/--	n/30	✓	3 620 00	3 360 00	260 00
6	The Women's Shop	9080	12/31/--	n/30	✓	2 920 00	2 700 00	220 00
7	Fashion World	4321	12/31/--	2/10, n/30	✓	4 300 00	3 850 00	450 00
19	Designer's Fashions	9789	01/15/--	2/10, n/30	✓	2 100 00	1 930 00	170 00
23	Clothes Rack Depot	7985	01/22/--	n/30	✓	2 560 00	2 380 00	180 00
31						18 750 00	17 220 00	1 530 00
						(205)	(501)	(502)

ACCOUNT _Accounts Payable_   ACCOUNT NO. _205_

DATE	DESCRIPTION	POST. REF.	DEBIT	CREDIT	BALANCE DEBIT	BALANCE CREDIT
20--						
Jan. 1	Balance	✓				5 400 00
31		P1		18 750 00		24 150 00

ACCOUNT _Purchases_   ACCOUNT NO. _501_

DATE	DESCRIPTION	POST. REF.	DEBIT	CREDIT	BALANCE DEBIT	BALANCE CREDIT
20--						
Jan. 31		P1	17 220 00		17 220 00	

ACCOUNT _Freight In_   ACCOUNT NO. _502_

DATE	DESCRIPTION	POST. REF.	DEBIT	CREDIT	BALANCE DEBIT	BALANCE CREDIT
20--						
Jan. 31		P1	1 530 00		1 530 00	

P.267

After the equality of debits and credits is verified, rule the purchases journal. The steps to post the column totals to the general ledger follow.

1. Locate the **Accounts Payable** ledger account.

2. Enter the date.

3. Enter the posting reference, P1. The **P** is for purchases journal. The **1** is the purchases journal page number.

4. Enter the amount from the Accounts Payable Credit column in the purchases journal in the Credit column of the **Accounts Payable** ledger account.

5. Compute the new balance and enter it in the Balance Credit column.

6. In the purchases journal, enter the **Accounts Payable** ledger account number (205) under the column total.

7. Repeat the steps for the Purchases Debit and Freight In Debit columns.

During the month the individual entries in the purchases journal are posted to the creditor accounts in the accounts payable ledger. The check marks in the purchases journal in Figure 8-5 indicate that these postings have been completed. This procedure is discussed later in this chapter.

Advantages of a Purchases Journal

Every business has certain types of transactions that occur over and over again. A well-designed accounting system includes journals that permit efficient recording of such transactions. In most merchandising firms, purchases of goods on credit take place often enough to make it worthwhile to use a purchases journal.

A special journal for credit purchases of merchandise saves time and effort when recording and posting purchases. The use of a purchases journal and other special journals allows for the division of accounting work among different employees. The purchases journal strengthens the audit trail. All credit purchases are recorded in one place, and each entry refers to the number and date of the invoice.

Section 1 Self Review

Questions

1. What type of transaction is recorded in the purchases journal?

2. What are the advantages of using a purchases journal?

3. What activities does a purchasing department perform?

Exercises

4. When the sales department needs goods, what document is sent to the purchasing department?

   a. Purchase invoice
   b. Purchase order
   c. Purchase requisition
   d. Sales requisition

5. What form is sent to the supplier to order goods?

   a. Purchase invoice
   b. Purchase order
   c. Purchase requisition
   d. Sales invoice

Analysis

6. An invoice dated January 15 for $1,000 shows credit terms 2/10, n/30. What do the credit terms mean?

(Answers to Section 1 Self Review are on page 289.)

3 Post credit purchases from the purchases journal to the accounts payable subsidiary ledger.

WHY IT'S IMPORTANT
Up-to-date records allow prompt payment of invoices.

4 Record purchases returns and allowances in the general journal and post them to the accounts payable subsidiary ledger.

WHY IT'S IMPORTANT
For unsatisfactory goods received, an allowance or return is reflected in the accounting records.

5 Prepare a schedule of accounts payable.

WHY IT'S IMPORTANT
This schedule provides a snapshot of amounts owed to suppliers.

6 Compute the net delivered cost of purchases.

WHY IT'S IMPORTANT
This is an important component in measuring operational results.

7 Demonstrate a knowledge of the procedures for effective internal control of purchases.

WHY IT'S IMPORTANT
Businesses try to prevent fraud, errors, and holding excess inventory.

Terms to Learn

accounts payable ledger
purchase allowance
purchase return
schedule of accounts payable

Accounts Payable

Businesses that buy merchandise on credit can conduct more extensive operations and use financial resources more effectively than if they paid cash for all purchases. It is important to pay invoices on time so that the business maintains a good credit reputation with its suppliers.

The Accounts Payable Ledger

Businesses need detailed records in order to pay invoices promptly. The **accounts payable ledger** provides information about the individual accounts for all creditors. The accounts payable ledger is a subsidiary ledger; it is separate from and subordinate to the general ledger. The accounts payable ledger contains a separate account for each creditor. Each account shows purchases, payments, and returns and allowances. The balance of the account shows the amount owed to the creditor.

Figure 8-6 on page 263 shows the accounts payable ledger for Clothes Rack Depot. Notice that the Balance column does not indicate whether the balance is a debit or a credit. The form assumes that the balance will be a credit because the normal balance of liability accounts is a credit. A debit balance may exist if more than the amount owed was paid to the creditor or if returned goods were already paid for. If the balance is a debit, circle the amount to show that the account does not have the normal balance.

Small businesses like The Trend Center arrange the accounts payable ledger in alphabetical order. Large businesses and businesses that use computerized accounting systems assign an account number to each creditor and arrange the accounts payable ledger in numeric order.

Posting a Credit Purchase

To keep the accounting records up to date, invoices are posted to the accounts payable subsidiary ledger every day. Refer to Figure 8-6 as you learn how to post to the accounts payable ledger.

1. Locate the accounts payable ledger account for the creditor Clothes Rack Depot.
2. Enter the date
3. In the Description column, enter the invoice number and date.
4. In the Posting Reference column, enter the purchases journal page number.
5. Enter the amount from the Accounts Payable Credit column in the purchases journal in the Credit column of the accounts payable subsidiary ledger.
6. Compute and enter the new balance in the Balance column.
7. In the purchases journal (Figure 8-5 on page 260), enter a check mark (✓) in the Posting Reference column. This indicates that the transaction is posted in the accounts payable subsidiary ledger.

NAME	Clothes Rack Depot						TERMS	n/30				
ADDRESS	1677 Mandela Lane, Dallas, Texas 75267-6205											

DATE		DESCRIPTION	POST. REF.	DEBIT	CREDIT	BALANCE
20--						
Jan.	1	Balance	✓			8 0 0 00
	23	Invoice 7985, 01/22/--	P1		2 5 6 0 00	3 3 6 0 00

③ **Objective**

Post credit purchases from the purchases journal to the accounts payable subsidiary ledger.

Posting Cash Paid on Account

When the transaction involves cash paid on account to a supplier, the payment is first recorded in a cash payments journal. (The cash payments journal is discussed in Chapter 9.) The cash payment is then posted to the individual creditor's account in the accounts payable ledger. Figure 8-7 shows a posting for cash paid to a creditor on January 27.

NAME	Clothes Rack Depot						TERMS	n/30				
ADDRESS	1677 Mandela Lane, Dallas, Texas 75267-6205											

DATE		DESCRIPTION	POST. REF.	DEBIT	CREDIT	BALANCE
20--						
Jan.	1	Balance	✓			8 0 0 00
	23	Invoice 7985, 01/22/--	P1		2 5 6 0 00	3 3 6 0 00
	27		CP1	1 2 0 0 00		2 1 6 0 00

Purchases Returns and Allowances

When merchandise arrives, it is examined to confirm that it is satisfactory. Occasionally, the wrong goods are shipped, or items are damaged or defective. A **purchase return** is when the business returns the goods. A **purchase allowance** is when the purchaser keeps the goods but receives a reduction in the price of the goods. The supplier issues a credit memorandum for the return or allowance. The credit memorandum reduces the amount that the purchaser owes.

Purchases returns and allowances are entered in the **Purchases Returns and Allowances** account, not in the **Purchases** account. The **Purchases Returns and Allowances** account is a complete record of returns and allowances. Business managers analyze this account to identify problem suppliers.

Purchases Returns and Allowances is a contra cost of goods sold account. The normal balance of cost of goods sold accounts is a debit. The normal balance of **Purchases Returns and Allowances,** a contra cost of goods sold account, is a credit.

④ **Objective**

Record purchases returns and allowances in the general journal and post them to the accounts payable subsidiary ledger.

Recall

Subsidiary Ledger
The total of the accounts in the subsidiary ledger must equal the control account balance.

Recording Purchases Returns and Allowances

The Trend Center received merchandise from Clothes Rack Depot on January 23. Some goods were damaged, and the supplier granted a $500 purchase allowance. The Trend Center recorded the full amount of the invoice, $2,560, in the purchases journal. The purchase allowance was recorded separately in the general journal.

On January 30 The Trend Center received a credit memorandum for $500 from Clothes Rack Depot as an allowance for damaged merchandise.

Clothes Rack Depot
1677 Mandela Lane
Dallas, TX 75267-6205

CREDIT MEMORANDUM
NUMBER: 73
DATE: January 30, 20--

TO: The Trend Center
     1010 Red Bird Lane
     Dallas, TX 75268-7783

ORIGINAL INVOICE: 7985
INVOICE DATE: January 22, 20--
DESCRIPTION: Credit for damaged suits: $500.00

Analysis

The liability account, **Accounts Payable,** is decreased by $500. The contra cost of goods sold account, **Purchases Returns and Allowances,** is increased by $500.

Debit-Credit Rules

DEBIT Decreases to liabilities are debits. Debit **Accounts Payable** for $500.

CREDIT Increases to contra cost of goods sold accounts are recorded as credits. Credit **Purchases Returns and Allowances** for $500.

T-Account Presentation

Accounts Payable	
−	+
500	

Purchases Returns and Allowances	
−	+
	500

General Journal Entry

GENERAL JOURNAL   PAGE ___2___

	DATE		DESCRIPTION	POST. REF.	DEBIT	CREDIT	
15	Jan.	30	Accounts Payable/Clothes Rack Depot		500 00		15
16			Purchases Returns and Allowances			500 00	16
17			Received Credit Memo 73 for				17
18			an allowance for damaged				18
19			merchandise; original Invoice				19
20			7985, January 22, 20--				20

The Bottom Line

Purchase Allowance

Income Statement

Contra Cost of Goods Sold	↑500
Net Income	↑500

Balance Sheet

Liabilities	↓500
Equity	↑500

Notice that this entry includes a debit to **Accounts Payable** and a credit to **Purchases Returns and Allowances.** In addition, there is a debit to the creditor's account in the accounts payable subsidiary ledger. Businesses that have few returns and allowances use the general journal to record these transactions. Businesses with many returns and allowances use a special journal for purchases returns and allowances.

Posting a Purchases Return or Allowance

Whether recorded in the general journal or in a special journal, it is important to promptly post returns and allowances to the creditor's account in the accounts payable ledger. Refer to Figure 8-8 to learn how to post purchases returns and allowances to the supplier's account.

1. Enter the date.
2. In the Description column, enter the credit memorandum number.
3. In the Posting Reference column, enter the general journal page number.
4. Enter the amount of the return or allowance in the Debit column.
5. Compute the new balance and enter it in the Balance column.
6. In the general journal, enter a check mark (✓) to show that the transaction was posted to the creditor's account in the accounts payable subsidiary ledger.

After the transaction is posted to the general ledger, enter the **Purchases Returns and Allowances** ledger account number in the Posting Reference column.

Recall

Contra Accounts
The **Purchases Returns and Allowances** account is a contra account. Contra accounts have normal balances that are the opposite of related accounts.

◀ **FIGURE 8-8**
Posting to a Creditor's Account

GENERAL JOURNAL PAGE ___2___

	DATE		DESCRIPTION	POST. REF.	DEBIT	CREDIT	
15	Jan.	30	Accounts Payable/Clothes Rack Depot	205 ✓	5 0 0 00		15
16			Purchases Returns and Allowances	503		5 0 0 00	16
17			Received Credit Memo 73 for				17
18			an allowance for damaged				18
19			merchandise; original Invoice				19
20			7985, January 22, 20--				20
21							21
22							

NAME _Clothes Rack Depot_ TERMS _n/30_
ADDRESS _1677 Mandela Lane, Dallas, Texas 75267-6205_

DATE		DESCRIPTION	POST. REF.	DEBIT	CREDIT	BALANCE
20--						
Jan.	1	Balance	✓			8 0 0 00
	23	Invoice 7985, 01/22/--	P1		2 5 6 0 00	3 3 6 0 00
	27		CP1	1 2 0 0 00		2 1 6 0 00
	30	CM 73	J2	5 0 0 00		1 6 6 0 00

Schedule of Accounts Payable

The total of the individual creditor accounts in the subsidiary ledger must equal the balance of the **Accounts Payable** control account. To prove that the control account and the subsidiary ledger are equal, businesses prepare a **schedule of accounts payable**—a list of all balances owed to creditors. Figure 8-9 on page 266 shows the accounts payable subsidiary ledger for The Trend Center on January 31.

Figure 8-10 on page 267 shows the schedule of accounts payable for The Trend Center. Notice that the accounts payable control account balance is $10,940. This equals the total on the schedule of accounts payable. If the amounts are not equal, it is essential to locate and correct the errors.

⑤ **Objective**
Prepare a schedule of accounts payable.

NAME Clothes Rack Depot   TERMS n/30
ADDRESS 1677 Mandela Lane, Dallas, Texas 75267-6205

DATE		DESCRIPTION	POST. REF.	DEBIT	CREDIT	BALANCE
20--						
Jan.	1	Balance	✓			8 0 0 00
	23	Invoice 7985, 01/22/--	P1		2 5 6 0 00	3 3 6 0 00
	27		CP1	1 2 0 0 00		2 1 6 0 00
	30	CM 73	J2	5 0 0 00		1 6 6 0 00

NAME Designer's Fashions   TERMS 2/10, n/30
ADDRESS 7701 Holly Hill Drive, Dallas, Texas 75267-6205

DATE		DESCRIPTION	POST. REF.	DEBIT	CREDIT	BALANCE
20--						
Jan.	19	Invoice 9789, 01/15/--	P1		2 1 0 0 00	2 1 0 0 00

NAME Fashion World   TERMS 2/10, n/30
ADDRESS 2701 George Avenue, Dallas, Texas 75267-6205

DATE		DESCRIPTION	POST. REF.	DEBIT	CREDIT	BALANCE
20--						
Jan.	1	Balance	✓			1 5 0 0 00
	7	Invoice 4321, 01/03/--	P1		4 3 0 0 00	5 8 0 0 00
	11		CP1	1 0 0 0 00		4 8 0 0 00
	31		CP1	2 5 6 0 00		2 2 4 0 00

NAME Sebrina's Clothing Store   TERMS 2/10, n/30
ADDRESS 5671 Preston Road, Dallas, Texas 75267-6205

DATE		DESCRIPTION	POST. REF.	DEBIT	CREDIT	BALANCE
20--						
Jan.	1	Balance	✓			1 1 0 0 00
	3	Invoice 8434, 12/29/--	P1		3 2 5 0 00	4 3 5 0 00
	13		CP1	3 2 5 0 00		1 1 0 0 00
	30		CP1	4 0 0 00		7 0 0 00

NAME The Style Shop   TERMS n/30
ADDRESS 3123 Belt Line Road, Dallas, Texas 75267-6205

DATE		DESCRIPTION	POST. REF.	DEBIT	CREDIT	BALANCE
20--						
Jan.	1	Balance	✓			1 2 0 0 00
	5	Invoice 336, 12/30/--	P1		3 6 2 0 00	4 8 2 0 00
	17		CP1	4 3 0 0 00		5 2 0 00

NAME The Women's Shop   TERMS n/30
ADDRESS 6028 Audra Lane, Dallas, Texas 75267-6205

DATE		DESCRIPTION	POST. REF.	DEBIT	CREDIT	BALANCE
20--						
Jan.	1	Balance	✓			8 0 0 00
	6	Invoice 9080, 12/31/--	P1		2 9 2 0 00	3 7 2 0 00

The Trend Center

Schedule of Accounts Payable

January 31, 20--

Clothes Rack Depot	1 6 6 0	00
Designer's Fashions	2 1 0 0	00
Fashion World	2 2 4 0	00
Sebrina's Clothing Store	7 0 0	00
The Style Shop	5 2 0	00
The Women's Shop	3 7 2 0	00
Total	10 9 4 0	00

ACCOUNT   Accounts Payable

ACCOUNT NO. 205

DEBIT	CREDIT	BALANCE DEBIT	BALANCE CREDIT
			5 4 0 0 00
5 0 0 00			4 9 0 0 00
	18 7 5 0 00		23 6 5 0 00
2 7 1 0 00			10 9 4 0 00

X   P. 260

Cost of Purchases

...mulates the cost of merchandise bought
...t of a merchandising business contains a
...f purchases. This section combines infor-
...rchases, freight in, and purchases returns
... Assume that The Trend Center has the
...t balances at January 31:

	$28,125
	2,295
s	4,250

...rchases for The Trend Center for January is

	$28,125
	2,295
	$30,420
ances	4,250
	$26,170

6 Objective

Compute the net delivered
cost of purchases.

Lands' End, Inc. reported cost of sales as 55.1 percent of net sales
for the period ended January 28, 2000. This means that for every
dollar a consumer spent on a product, Lands' End, Inc. paid approximately 55 cents to purchase the item.

Accounting for Purchases

- Management and the accounting staff need to work together to make sure that there are good internal controls over purchasing.

- A carefully designed system of checks and balances protects the business against fraud, errors, and excessive investment in merchandise.

- The accounting staff needs to record transactions efficiently so that up-to-date information about creditors is available.

- Using the purchases journal and the accounts payable subsidiary ledger improves efficiency.

- To maintain a good credit reputation with suppliers, it is important to have an accounting system that ensures prompt payment of invoices.

- A well-run accounting system provides management with information about cash: cash required to pay suppliers, short-term loans needed to cover temporary cash shortages, and cash available for short-term investments.

- Separate accounts for recording purchases, freight charges, and purchases returns and allowances make it easy to analyze the elements in the cost of purchases.

Thinking Critically

As a manager, what internal controls would you put in your accounting system?

For firms that do not have freight charges, the amount of net purchases is calculated as follows.

Purchases	$28,125
Less Purchases Returns and Allowances	4,250
Net Purchases	$23,875

In Chapter 13 you will see how the complete income statement for a merchandising business is prepared. You will learn about the Cost of Goods Sold section and how the net delivered cost of purchases is used in calculating the results of operations.

⑦ Objective

Demonstrate a knowledge of the procedures for effective internal control of purchases.

Internal Control of Purchases

Because of the large amount of money spent to buy goods, most businesses develop careful procedures for the control of purchases and payments. Some firms have a *voucher system*, a special system used to achieve internal control. Whether the voucher system is used or not, a business should be sure that its control process includes sufficient safeguards. The objectives of the controls are to

- create written proof that purchases and payments are authorized;
- ensure that different people are involved in the process of buying goods, receiving goods, and making payments.

Separating duties among employees provides a system of checks and balances. In a small business with just a few employees, it might be difficult or impossible to separate duties. However, the business should design as effective a set of control procedures as the company's resources will allow. Effective systems have the following controls in place.

1. All purchases should be made only after proper authorization has been given in writing.

2. Goods should be carefully checked when they are received. They should then be compared with the purchase order and with the invoice received from the supplier.

3. The purchase order, receiving report, and invoice should be checked to confirm that the information on the documents is in agreement.

4. The computations on the invoice should be checked for accuracy.

5. Authorization for payment should be made by someone other than the person who ordered the goods, and this authorization should be given only after all the verifications have been made.

6. Another person should write the check for payment.

7. Prenumbered forms should be used for purchase requisitions, purchase orders, and checks. Periodically the numbers of the documents issued should be verified to make sure that all forms can be accounted for.

---•---

Lands' End, Inc. reported a 2.7 percent decrease in the cost of purchases in fiscal 2000. The company believes this decrease is the result of more efficient negotiations with its suppliers. Effective internal controls verify that the agreed price is accurately reflected on the invoice received from the supplier.

---•---

About Accounting

Employee Fraud
According to the U.S. Chamber of Commerce, businesses lose $20 to $40 billion each year to employee fraud. The best defense against fraud is to use good internal controls: Have multiple employees in contact with suppliers and screen employees and vendors to reduce fraud opportunities.

Section 2 — Self Review

Questions

1. A firm has a debit balance of $55,160 in its **Purchases** account and a credit balance of $2,520 in its **Purchases Returns and Allowances** account. Calculate net purchases for the period.

2. A firm receives an invoice that reflects the price of goods as $1,120 and the freight charge as $84. How is this transaction recorded?

3. What is the purpose of the schedule of accounts payable?

Exercises

4. The net delivered cost of purchases for the period appears on the
   a. balance sheet.
   b. income statement.
   c. schedule of accounts payable.
   d. statement of owner's equity.

5. In the accounts payable ledger, a supplier's account has a beginning balance of $2,400. A transaction of $800 is posted from the purchases journal. What is the balance of the supplier's account?

   a. $1,600 debit
   b. $1,600 credit
   c. $3,200 debit
   d. $3,200 credit

Analysis

6. In the general ledger, the **Accounts Payable** account has a balance of $12,500. The schedule of accounts payable lists accounts totaling $17,500. What could cause this error?

Review

Chapter Summary

In this chapter, you have learned about the accounting journals and ledgers required for the efficient processing of purchases for a business. Businesses with strong internal controls establish and follow procedures for approving requests for new merchandise, choosing suppliers, placing orders with suppliers, checking goods after they arrive, identifying invoices, and approving payments.

Learning Objectives

1 **Record purchases of merchandise on credit in a three-column purchases journal.**

Purchases and payments on account must be entered in the firm's accounting records promptly and accurately. Most merchandising businesses normally purchase goods on credit. The most efficient system for recording purchases on credit is the use of a special purchases journal. With this type of journal, only one line is needed to enter all the data.

The purchases journal is used only to record the credit purchase of goods for resale. General business expenses are not recorded in the purchases journal.

2 **Post from the three-column purchases journal to the general ledger accounts.**

The use of the three-column purchases journal simplifies the posting process because nothing is posted to the general ledger until the month's end. Then, summary postings are made to the **Purchases, Freight In,** and **Accounts Payable** accounts.

3 **Post purchases on credit from the purchases journal to the accounts payable subsidiary ledger.**

An accounts payable subsidiary ledger helps a firm keep track of the amounts it owes to creditors. Postings are made to this ledger on a daily basis.

- Each credit purchase is posted from the purchases journal to the accounts payable subsidiary ledger.
- Each payment on account is posted from the cash payments journal to the accounts payable subsidiary ledger.

4 **Record purchases returns and allowances in the general journal and post them to the accounts payable subsidiary ledger.**

Returns and allowances on purchases of goods are credited to an account called **Purchases Returns and Allowances.** These transactions may be recorded in the general journal or in a special purchases returns and allowances journal. Each return or allowance on a credit purchase is posted to the accounts payable subsidiary ledger.

5 **Prepare a schedule of accounts payable.**

At the month's end, a schedule of accounts payable is prepared. The schedule lists the balances owed to the firm's creditors and proves the accuracy of the subsidiary ledger. The total of the schedule of accounts payable is compared with the balance of the **Accounts Payable** account in the general ledger, which acts as a control account. The two amounts should be equal.

6 **Compute the net delivered cost of purchases.**

The net delivered cost of purchases is computed by adding the cost of purchases and freight in, then subtracting any purchases returns and allowances. Net delivered cost of purchases is reported in the Cost of Goods Sold section of the income statement.

7 **Demonstrate a knowledge of the procedures for effective internal control of purchases.**

Purchases and payments should be properly authorized and processed with appropriate documentation to provide a system of checks and balances. A division of responsibilities within the purchases process ensures strong internal controls.

8 **Define the accounting terms new to this chapter.**

CHAPTER 8 GLOSSARY

Accounts payable ledger (p. 262) A subsidiary ledger that contains a separate account for each creditor

Cash discount (p. 259) A discount offered by suppliers for payment received within a specified period of time

Cost of goods sold (p. 256) The actual cost to the business of the merchandise sold to customers

Freight In account (p. 256) An account showing transportation charges for items purchased

Purchase allowance (p. 263) A price reduction from the amount originally billed

Purchase invoice (p. 254) A bill received for goods purchased

Purchase order (p. 254) An order to the supplier of goods specifying items needed, quantity, price, and credit terms

Purchase requisition (p. 254) A list sent to the purchasing department showing the items to be ordered

Purchase return (p. 263) Return of unsatisfactory goods

Purchases account (p. 256) An account used to record cost of goods bought for resale during a period

Purchases discount (p. 259) A cash discount offered to the customer for payment within a specified period

Purchases journal (p. 256) A special journal used to record the purchase of goods on credit

Receiving report (p. 254) A form showing quantity and condition of goods received

Sales discount (p. 259) A cash discount offered by the supplier for payment within a specified period

Sales invoice (p. 254) A supplier's billing document

Schedule of accounts payable (p. 265) A list of all balances owed to creditors

Transportation In account (p. 256) See Freight In account

Comprehensive Self Review

1. What is the difference between a receiving report and an invoice?
2. What is the purpose of a purchase requisition? A purchase order?
3. What is the purpose of the **Freight In** account?
4. What is a cash discount and why is it offered?
5. What type of account is **Purchases Returns and Allowances?**

(Answers to Comprehensive Self Review are on page 289.)

Discussion Questions

1. How is the net delivered cost of purchases computed?
2. Why is it useful for a business to have an accounts payable ledger?
3. What type of accounts are kept in the accounts payable ledger?
4. What is the relationship of the **Accounts Payable** account in the general ledger to the accounts payable subsidiary ledger?
5. What is a schedule of accounts payable? Why is it prepared?
6. What is a purchase return?
7. What is a purchase allowance?
8. What is the purpose of a credit memorandum?
9. What major safeguards should be built into a system of internal control for purchases of goods?
10. Why are the invoice date and terms recorded in the purchases journal?
11. A business has purchased some new equipment for use in its operations, not for resale to customers. The terms of the invoice are n/30. Should this transaction be entered in the purchases journal? If not, where should it be recorded?
12. What do the following credit terms mean?
    a. n/30
    b. 2/10, n/30
    c. n/10 EOM
    d. n/20
    e. 1/10, n/20
    f. 3/5, n/30
    g. n/15 EOM
13. Why is the use of a **Purchases Returns and Allowances** account preferred to crediting these transactions to **Purchases?**
14. On what financial statement do the accounts related to purchases of merchandise appear? In which section of this statement are they reported?
15. What is the normal balance of the **Purchases** account?
16. What is the difference between a purchase invoice and a sales invoice?
17. What journals can be used to enter various merchandise purchase transactions?

Applications

EXERCISES

Identifying journals used to record purchases and related transactions.

The following transactions took place at Mountain Hike and Bike Shop. Indicate the general ledger account numbers that would be debited and credited to record each transaction.

GENERAL LEDGER ACCOUNTS
101 Cash
205 Accounts Payable
501 Purchases
502 Freight In
503 Purchases Returns and Allowances

TRANSACTIONS

1. Purchased merchandise for $1,000; the terms are 2/10, n/30. *P. 256*
2. Returned damaged merchandise to a supplier and received a credit memorandum for $200.
3. Issued a check for $400 to a supplier as a payment on account.
4. Purchased merchandise for $1,200 plus a freight charge of $130; the supplier's invoice is payable in 30 days.
5. Received an allowance for merchandise that was damaged but can be sold at a reduced price; the supplier's credit memorandum is for $300.
6. Purchased merchandise for $2,100 in cash.

◄ **Exercise 8-1**
Objective 1

Identifying the journals used to record purchases and related transactions.

The accounting system of Discount Rack includes the following journals. Indicate which journal is used to record each transaction.

JOURNALS
Cash receipts journal
Cash payments journal
Purchases journal
Sales journal
General journal

TRANSACTIONS

1. Purchased merchandise for $1,500; the terms are 2/10, n/30.
2. Returned damaged merchandise to a supplier and received a credit memorandum for $700.
3. Issued a check for $1,800 to a supplier as a payment on account.
4. Purchased merchandise for $1,000 plus a freight charge of $70; the supplier's invoice is payable in 30 days.
5. Received an allowance for merchandise that was damaged but can be sold at a reduced price; the supplier's credit memorandum is for $360.
6. Purchased merchandise for $1,750 in cash.

◄ **Exercise 8-2**
Objective 1

Exercise 8-3 ►
Objective 1

Recording credit purchases.

The following transactions took place at Metroplex Auto Parts and Detailing Center during the first week of July. Indicate how these transactions would be entered in a purchases journal like the one shown in this chapter.

DATE		TRANSACTIONS
July	1	Purchased batteries for $3,900 plus a freight charge of $64 from Car Parts Corporation; received Invoice 2168, dated June 27, which has terms of n/30.
	3	Purchased mufflers for $1,560 plus a freight charge of $40 from Sharpe Company; received Invoice 144, dated June 30, which has terms of 1/10, n/60.
	5	Purchased car radios for $4,900 plus freight of $50 from Sounds From Above, Inc.; received Invoice 1056, dated July 1, which has terms of 2/10, n/30.
	10	Purchased truck tires for $3,900 from Big Wheel Tire Company; received Invoice 2011, dated July 8, which has terms of 2/10, n/30.

Exercise 8-4 ►
Objective 4

Recording a purchase return.

On February 9, 20--, City Appliance Center, a retail store, received Credit Memorandum 442 for $1,960 from Broken Bow Corporation. The credit memorandum covered a return of damaged trash compactors originally purchased on Invoice 1041 dated January 3. Prepare the general journal entry that City Appliance Center would make for this transaction.

Exercise 8-5 ►
Objective 4

Recording a purchase allowance.

On March 15, 20--, The Ides of March Company was given an allowance of $500 by City Appliance Center, which issued Credit Memorandum 333. The allowance was for scratches on stoves that were originally purchased on Invoice 686 dated February 20. Prepare the general journal entry that The Ides of March Company would make for this transaction.

Exercise 8-6 ►
Objective 4

Determining the cost of purchases.

On June 30 the general ledger of Fashion World, a clothing store, showed a balance of $35,360 in the **Purchases** account, a balance of $1,156 in the **Freight In** account, and a balance of $3,620 in the **Purchases Returns and Allowances** account. What was the delivered cost of the purchases made during June? What was the net delivered cost of these purchases?

Exercise 8-7 ►
Objectives 1, 4

Errors in recording purchase transactions.

The following errors were made in recording transactions in posting from the purchases journal. How will these errors be detected?

a. A credit of $1,000 to Zant Furniture Company account in the accounts payable ledger was posted as $100.

b. The Accounts Payable column total of the purchases journal was understated by $100.

c. An invoice of $840 for merchandise from Davis Company was recorded as having been received from Darrin Company, another supplier.

d. A $500 payment to Darrin Company was debited to Davis Company.

Determining the cost of purchases.

Complete the following schedule by supplying the missing information.

◄ **Exercise 8-8**
Objective 4

Net Delivered Cost of Purchases	Case A	Case B
Purchases	(a)	83,600
Freight In	3,000	(c)
Delivered Cost of Purchases	93,600	(d)
Less Purchases Returns and Allowances	(b)	3,600
Net Delivered Cost of Purchases	88,640	93,100

Problems

Selected problems can be completed using:
🍑 **Peachtree**　📘 **QuickBooks**　▦ **Spreadsheets**

PROBLEM SET A

Journalizing credit purchases and purchases returns and allowances and posting to the general ledger.

◄ **Problem 8-1A**
Objectives 1, 2, 3

Picture Perfect Photo Mart is a retail store that sells cameras and photography supplies. The firm's credit purchases and purchases returns and allowances transactions for June 20-- appear below and on page 276, along with the general ledger accounts used to record these transactions. The balance shown in **Accounts Payable** is for the beginning of June.

INSTRUCTIONS

1. Open the general ledger accounts and enter the balance of **Accounts Payable** for June 1, 20--.

2. Record the transactions in a three-column purchases journal and in a general journal. Use 13 as the page number for the purchases journal and 37 as the page number for the general journal.

3. Post entries from the general journal to the general ledger accounts.

4. Total and rule the purchases journal as of June 30.

5. Post the column total from the purchases journal to the proper general ledger accounts.

6. Compute the net purchases of the firm for the month of June.

GENERAL LEDGER ACCOUNTS
205　Accounts Payable, $6,952 Cr.
501　Purchases
502　Freight In
503　Purchases Returns and Allowances

DATE		TRANSACTIONS
June	1	Purchased instant cameras for $3,990 plus a freight charge of $90 from Jarvis Company, Invoice 1442, dated May 26; the terms are 60 days net.
	8	Purchased film for $695 from Photographic Products, Invoice 2101, dated June 3, net payable in 45 days.
	12	Purchased lenses for $453 from The Optical Mart, Invoice 3872, dated June 9; the terms are 1/10, n/60.
		Continued

DATE	(8-1A cont.) TRANSACTIONS
June 18	Received Credit Memorandum 112 for $450 from Jarvis Company for defective cameras that were returned; they were originally purchased on Invoice 1442, dated May 26.
20	Purchased color film for $2,100 plus freight of $50 from Photographic Products, Invoice 2151, dated June 15, net payable in 45 days.
23	Purchased camera cases for $970 from Dallas Case Company, Invoice 8310, dated June 18, net due and payable in 45 days.
28	Purchased disk cameras for $4,940 plus freight of $60 from Penn Corporation, Invoice 2750, dated June 24; the terms are 2/10, n/30.
30	Received Credit Memorandum 1120 for $120 from Dallas Case Company; the amount is an allowance for damaged but usable goods purchased on Invoice 8310, dated June 18.

(**Note:** Save your working papers for use in Problem 8-2A.)

Analyze: What total purchases were posted to the **Purchases** general ledger account for June?

Problem 8-2A ►
Objectives 4, 6

Posting to the accounts payable ledger and preparing a schedule of accounts payable.

This problem is a continuation of Problem 8-1A.

INSTRUCTIONS

1. Set up an accounts payable subsidiary ledger for Picture Perfect Photo Mart. Open an account for each of the creditors listed below and enter the balances as of June 1, 20--.

2. Post the individual entries from the purchases journal and the general journal prepared in Problem 8-1A.

3. Prepare a schedule of accounts payable for June 30.

4. Check the total of the schedule of accounts payable against the balance of the **Accounts Payable** account in the general ledger. The two amounts should be equal.

Creditors		
Name	Terms	Balance
Dallas Case Company	n/45	$ 600
Jarvis Company	n/60	
The Optical Mart	1/10, n/60	1,112
Penn Corporation	2/10, n/30	
Photographic Products	n/45	5,240

Analyze: What amount is owed to The Optical Mart on June 30?

Problem 8-3A ►
Objectives 1, 2, 3, 4, 5, 6

Journalizing credit purchases and purchases returns and allowances, computing the net delivered cost of goods, posting to the general ledger, posting to the accounts payable ledger, and preparing a schedule of accounts payable.

The Garden Center is a retail store that sells garden equipment, furniture, and supplies. Its credit purchases and purchases returns and allowances for July are listed below. The general ledger accounts used to record these transactions are also provided. The balance shown is for the beginning of July 20--.

Part I

1. Open the general ledger accounts and enter the balance of **Accounts Payable** for July 1.

2. Record the transactions in a three-column purchases journal and in a general journal. Use 7 as the page number for the purchases journal and 19 as the page number for the general journal.

3. Post the entries from the general journal to the proper general ledger accounts.

4. Total, prove, and rule the purchases journal as of July 31.

5. Post the column totals from the purchases journal to the proper general ledger accounts.

6. Compute the net delivered cost of the firm's purchases for the month of July.

GENERAL LEDGER ACCOUNTS

205 Accounts Payable, $17,940 Cr.	502 Freight In
501 Purchases	503 Purchases Returns and Allowances

DATE		TRANSACTIONS
July	1	Purchased lawn mowers for $9,400 plus a freight charge of $260 from Bronze Corporation, Invoice 1077, dated June 26, net due and payable in 60 days.
	5	Purchased outdoor chairs and tables for $8,740 plus a freight charge of $276 from Bailey Garden Furniture Company, Invoice 936, dated July 2, net due and payable in 45 days.
	9	Purchased grass seed for $1,900 from Parks and Gardens Lawn Products, Invoice 4681, dated July 5; the terms are 30 days net.
	16	Received Credit Memorandum 110 for $400 from Bailey Garden Furniture Company; the amount is an allowance for scratches on some of the chairs and tables originally purchased on Invoice 936, dated July 2.
	19	Purchased fertilizer for $2,400 plus a freight charge of $128 from Parks and Garden Lawn Products, Invoice 5139, dated July 15; the terms are 30 days net.
	21	Purchased hoses from Bush Rubber Company for $1,840 plus a freight charge of $112, Invoice 5817, dated July 17; terms are 1/15, n/60.
	28	Received Credit Memorandum 322 for $600 from Bush Rubber Company for damaged hoses that were returned; the goods were purchased on Invoice 5817, dated July 17.
	31	Purchased lawn sprinkler systems for $11,400 plus a freight charge of $320 from Woods Industrial Products, Invoice 5889, dated July 26; the terms are 2/10, n/30.

INSTRUCTIONS

Part II

1. Set up an accounts payable subsidiary ledger for The Garden Center. Open an account for each of the creditors listed below and enter the balances as of July 1.

2. Post the individual entries from the purchases journal and the general journal prepared in Part I.

3. Prepare a schedule of accounts payable for July 31, 20--.

4. Check the total of the schedule of accounts payable against the balance of the **Accounts Payable** account in the general ledger. The two amounts should be equal.

Creditors		
Name	Terms	Balance
Bailey Garden Furniture Company	n/45	$5,560
Bronze Corporation	n/60	9,060
Bush Rubber Company	1/15, n/60	1,952
Parks and Garden Lawn Products	n/30	3,320
Woods Industrial Products	2/10, n/30	

Analyze: What total freight charges were posted to the general ledger for the month of July?

Problem 8-4A ►
Objectives 1, 2, 3, 4, 5, 6

Journalizing credit purchases and purchases returns and allowances, posting to the general ledger, posting to the accounts payable ledger, and preparing a schedule of accounts payable.

Essential Office Products Center is a retail business that sells office equipment, furniture, and supplies. Its credit purchases and purchases returns and allowances for September are shown on page 279. The general ledger accounts and the creditors' accounts in the accounts payable subsidiary ledger used to record these transactions are also provided. All balances shown are for the beginning of September.

INSTRUCTIONS

1. Open the general ledger accounts and enter the balance of **Accounts Payable** for September 1, 20--.

2. Open the creditors' accounts in the accounts payable ledger and enter the balances for September 1.

3. Record the transactions in a three-column purchases journal and in a general journal. Use 5 as the page number for the purchases journal and 14 as the page number for the general journal.

4. Post to the accounts payable ledger daily.

5. Post the entries from the general journal to the proper general ledger accounts at the end of the month.

6. Total and rule the purchases journal as of September 30.

7. Post the column totals from the purchases journal to the proper general ledger accounts.

8. Prepare a schedule of accounts payable and compare the balance of the **Accounts Payable** control account with the schedule of accounts payable.

GENERAL LEDGER ACCOUNTS

205 Accounts Payable, $14,128 Cr.
501 Purchases
502 Freight In
503 Purchases Returns and Allowances

Creditors		
Name	Terms	Balance
American Office Machines, Inc.	n/60	$5,480
Badge Paper Company	1/10, n/30	1,060
Brint Corporation	n/30	
City Office Furniture Company	n/30	4,788
Depot Furniture, Inc.	2/10, n/30	2,800

DATE	TRANSACTIONS
Sept. 3	Purchased desks for $3,960 plus a freight charge of $106 from City Office Furniture Company, Invoice 1342, dated August 29; the terms are 30 days net.
7	Purchased computers for $5,650 from American Office Machines, Inc., Invoice 1792, dated September 2, net due and payable in 60 days.
10	Received Credit Memorandum 561 for $300 from City Office Furniture Company; the amount is an allowance for damaged but usable desks purchased on Invoice 1342, dated August 29.
16	Purchased file cabinets for $1,278 plus a freight charge of $62 from Brint Corporation, Invoice 6680, dated September 11; the terms are 30 days net.
20	Purchased electronic desk calculators for $500 from American Office Machines, Inc., Invoice 6556, dated September 15, net due and payable in 60 days.
23	Purchased bond paper and copy machine paper for $3,750 plus a freight charge of $50 from Badge Paper Company, Invoice 9864, dated September 18; the terms are 1/10, n/30.
28	Received Credit Memorandum 296 for $440 from American Office Machines, Inc., for defective calculators that were returned; the calculators were originally purchased on Invoice 6556, dated September 15.
30	Purchased office chairs for $1,920 plus a freight charge of $80 from Depot Furniture, Inc., Invoice 966, dated September 25, the terms are 2/10, n/30.

Analyze: What total amount was recorded for purchases returns and allowances in the month of September? What percentage of total purchases does this represent?

Problem 8-1B ►
Objectives 1, 2, 3

Journalizing credit purchases and purchases returns and allowances and posting to the general ledger.

Colorado Ski Shop is a retail store that sells ski equipment and clothing. The firm's credit purchases and purchases returns and allowances during May 20-- follow, along with the general ledger accounts used to record these transactions. The balance shown in **Accounts Payable** is for the beginning of May.

INSTRUCTIONS

1. Open the general ledger accounts and enter the balance of **Accounts Payable** for May 1, 20--.

2. Record the transactions in a three-column purchases journal and in a general journal. Use 14 as the page number for the purchases journal and 37 as the page number for the general journal.

3. Post the entries from the general journal to the proper general ledger accounts.

4. Total and rule the purchases journal as of May 30.

5. Post the column total from the purchases journal to the proper general ledger accounts.

6. Compute the net purchases of the firm for the month of May.

GENERAL LEDGER ACCOUNTS
205 Accounts Payable, $10,804 Cr.
501 Purchases
502 Freight In
503 Purchases Returns and Allowances

DATE		TRANSACTIONS
May	1	Purchased ski boots for $3,300 plus a freight charge of $110 from Denver Shop for Skiers, Invoice 7265, dated April 28; the terms are 45 days net.
	8	Purchased skis for $5,550 from Andover Industries, Invoice 1649, dated May 2; the terms are net payable in 30 days.
	9	Received Credit Memorandum 551 for $800 from Denver Shop for Skiers for damaged ski boots that were returned; the boots were originally purchased on Invoice 7265, dated April 28.
	12	Purchased ski jackets for $2,500 from Chilly Winter Fashions, Inc., Invoice 869, dated May 11, net due and payable in 60 days.
	16	Purchased ski poles for $1,580 from Andover Industries, Invoice 1766, dated May 15; the terms are n/30.
	22	Purchased ski pants for $1,120 from Chilton Clothing Company, Invoice 1940, dated May 16; the terms are 1/10, n/60.
		Continued

DATE	(8-1B cont.) TRANSACTIONS
May 28	Received Credit Memorandum 83 for $210 from Andover Industries for defective ski poles that were returned; the items were originally purchased on Invoice 1766, dated May 15.
31	Purchased sweaters for $1,650 plus a freight charge of $50 from Knit Ski Goods, Invoice 5483, dated May 27; the terms are 2/10, n/30.

(**Note:** Save your working papers for use in Problem 8-2B.)

Analyze: What total accounts payable were posted from the purchases journal to the general ledger for the month?

Posting to the accounts payable ledger and preparing a schedule of accounts payable.

◀ **Problem 8-2B**
Objectives 4, 6

This problem is a continuation of Problem 8-1B.

INSTRUCTIONS

1. Set up an accounts payable subsidiary ledger for Colorado Ski Shop. Open an account for each of the creditors listed and enter the balances as of May 1, 20--.

2. Post the individual entries from the purchases journal and the general journal prepared in Problem 8-1B.

3. Prepare a schedule of accounts payable for May 31.

4. Check the total of the schedule of accounts payable against the balance of the **Accounts Payable** account in the general ledger. The two amounts should be equal.

Creditors		
Name	Terms	Balance
Andover Industries	n/30	$ 850
Chilly Winter Fashions, Inc.	n/60	4,360
Chilton Clothing Company	1/10, n/60	2,500
Denver Shop for Skiers	n/45	3,094
Knit Ski Goods	2/10, n/30	

Analyze: What amount did Colorado Ski Shop owe to its supplier, Denver Shop for Skiers, on May 31?

Journalizing credit purchases and purchases returns and allowances, computing the net delivered cost of goods, posting to the general ledger, posting to the accounts payable ledger, and preparing a schedule of accounts payable.

◀ **Problem 8-3B**
Objectives 1, 2, 3, 4, 5, 6

The Flower and Garden Nursery is a retail store that sells garden equipment, furniture, and supplies. Its credit purchases and purchases returns and allowances for December are shown on page 282. The general ledger accounts used to record these transactions are also provided. The balance shown is for the beginning of December 20--.

Part I

1. Open the general ledger accounts and enter the balance of **Accounts Payable** for December 1.

2. Record the transactions in a three-column purchases journal and in a general journal. Use 7 as the page number for the purchases journal and 19 as the page number for the general journal.

3. Post the entries from the general journal to the proper general ledger accounts.

4. Total, prove, and rule the purchases journal as of December 31.

5. Post the column totals from the purchases journal to the proper general ledger accounts.

6. Compute the net delivered cost of the firm's purchases for the month of December.

GENERAL LEDGER ACCOUNTS
205 Accounts Payable, $6,745 Cr.
501 Purchases
502 Freight In
503 Purchases Returns and Allowances

DATE		TRANSACTIONS
Dec.	1	Purchased lawn mowers for $2,890 plus a freight charge of $78 from River Corporation, Invoice 1021, dated November 26, net due and payable in 45 days.
	5	Purchased outdoor chairs and tables for $2,850 plus a freight charge of $50 from Garden Furniture Shop, Invoice 363, dated December 2; the terms are 1/15, n/60.
	9	Purchased grass seed for $574 from Springtime Lawn Center, Invoice 2711, dated December 4; the terms are 30 days net.
	16	Received Credit Memorandum 101 for $200 from Garden Furniture Shop; the amount is an allowance for scratches on some of the chairs and tables originally purchased on Invoice 363, dated December 2.
	19	Purchased fertilizer for $800 plus a freight charge of $78 from Springtime Lawn Center, Invoice 3157, dated December 15; the terms are 30 days net.
	21	Purchased garden hoses for $380 plus a freight charge of $38 from City Rubber Company, Invoice 1785, dated December 17; the terms are n/60.
	28	Received Credit Memorandum 209 for $75 from City Rubber Company for damaged hoses that were returned; the goods were purchased on Invoice 1785, dated December 17.
	31	Purchased lawn sprinkler systems for $1,850 plus a freight charge of $40 from Carlton Industries, Invoice 1988, dated December 26; the terms are 2/10, n/30.

Part II

1. Set up an accounts payable subsidiary ledger for The Flower and Garden Nursery. Open an account for each of the following creditors and enter the balances as of December 1.

2. Post the individual entries from the purchases journal and the general journal prepared in Part I.

3. Prepare a schedule of accounts payable for December 31.

4. Check the total of the schedule of accounts payable against the balance of the **Accounts Payable** account in the general ledger. The two amounts should be equal.

CREDITORS

Name	Terms	Balance
Carlton Industries	2/10, n/30	$1,075
City Rubber Company	n/60	1,925
Garden Furniture Shop	1/15, n/60	
River Corporation	n/45	2,421
Springtime Lawn Center	n/30	1,324

Analyze: By what amount did **Accounts Payable** increase during the month of December?

Journalizing credit purchases and purchases returns and allowances, posting to the general ledger, posting to the accounts payable ledger, and preparing a schedule of accounts payable.

Rochelle's Cards and Stuff is a retail card, novelty, and business supply store. Its credit purchases and purchases returns and allowances for February 20-- appear on page 284. The general ledger accounts and the creditors' accounts in the accounts payable subsidiary ledger used to record these transactions are also provided. The balance shown is for the beginning of February.

◄ **Problem 8-4B**
Objectives 1, 2, 3, 4, 5, 6

1. Open the general ledger accounts and enter the balance of **Accounts Payable** for February.

2. Open the creditors' accounts in the accounts payable ledger and enter the balances for February 1, 20--.

3. Record each transaction in the appropriate journal, purchases or general. Use page 3 in the purchases journal and page 11 in the general journal.

4. Post entries to the accounts payable ledger daily.

5. Post entries in the general journal to the proper general ledger accounts at the end of the month.

6. Total and rule the purchases journal as of February 28.

7. Post the totals to the appropriate general ledger accounts.

8. Calculate the net delivered cost of purchases.

9. Prepare a schedule of accounts payable and compare the balance of the **Accounts Payable** control account with the schedule of accounts payable.

GENERAL LEDGER ACCOUNTS
203 Accounts Payable, $7,600 credit balance
501 Purchases
502 Freight In
503 Purchases Returns and Allowances

Creditors		
Name Terms Balance		
Cards & Gifts for Holidays	2/10, n/30	$2,000
Forms for Business, Inc.	n/30	4,000
Office Supplies, Packing & Mailing, Inc.	2/10, n/30	1,600
Unique Business Cards	1/10, n/45	

DATE	TRANSACTIONS
Feb. 5	Purchased copy paper from Office Supplies, Packing & Mailing, Inc., for $1,000 plus $50 shipping charges on Invoice 502, dated February 2.
8	Purchased assorted holiday cards from Cards & Gifts for Holidays on Invoice 8028, $950, dated February 5.
12	Purchased five boxes of novelty items from Cards & Gifts for Holidays for a total cost of $600, Invoice 9032, dated February 8.
13	Purchased tray of cards from Unique Business Cards on Invoice 1320 for $550, dated February 9.
19	Purchased supply of forms from Forms for Business, Inc., for $990 plus shipping charges of $30 on Invoice 1920, dated February 16.
20	One box of cards purchased on February 8 from Cards & Gifts for Holidays was water damaged. Received Credit Memorandum 1002 for $100.
21	Toner supplies are purchased from Unique Business Cards for $1,800 plus shipping charges of $100, Invoice 1420, dated February 19.
27	Received Credit Memorandum 1022 for $120 from Cards & Gifts for Holidays as an allowance for damaged novelty items purchased on February 12.

Analyze: What total amount did Rochelle's Cards and Stuff pay in freight charges during the month of February? What percentage of delivered cost of purchases does this represent?

Merchandising: Sales and Purchases

Casual Fashions is a retail clothing store. Sales of merchandise and purchases of goods on account for January 20--, the first month of operations, appear on pages 285–286.

INSTRUCTIONS

1. Record the purchases of goods on account on page 5 of a three-column purchases journal.

2. Record the sales of merchandise on account on page 1 of a sales journal.

3. Post the entries from the purchases journal and the sales journal to the individual accounts in the accounts payable and accounts receivable subsidiary ledgers.

4. Total, prove, and rule the journals as of January 31.

5. Post the column totals from the special journals to the proper general ledger accounts.

6. Prepare a schedule of accounts payable for January 31.

7. Prepare a schedule of accounts receivable for January 31.

		PURCHASES OF GOODS ON ACCOUNT
Jan.	3	Purchased dresses for $2,500 plus a freight charge of $50 from Fashion World, Invoice 101, dated December 26; the terms are net 30 days.
	5	Purchased handbags for $1,740 plus a freight charge of $40 from Modern Handbags, Invoice 322, dated December 28; the terms are 2/10, n/30.
	7	Purchased blouses for $1,950 plus a freight charge of $30 from Trendsetters, Inc., Invoice 655, dated January 3; the terms are 2/10, n/30.
	9	Purchased casual pants for $1,180 from The Trousers Company, Invoice 109, dated January 5; terms are n/30.
	12	Purchased business suits for $2,700 plus a freight charge of $50 from Suits for Executives, Invoice 104, dated January 9; the terms are 2/10, n/30.
	18	Purchased shoes for $1,560 plus freight of $40 from Larry's Shoes, Invoice 111, dated January 14; the terms are n/60.
	25	Purchased hosiery for $700 from Socks Warehouse, Invoice 1211, dated January 20; the terms are 2/10, n/30.
	29	Purchased scarves and gloves for $800 from The Trousers Company, Invoice 809, dated January 26; the terms are n/30.
	31	Purchased party dresses for $2,500 plus a freight charge of $50 from Carolyn's Wholesale Shop, Invoice 1033, dated January 27; the terms are 2/10, n/30.

		SALES OF MERCHANDISE ON ACCOUNT
Jan.	4	Sold two dresses to Selena Ramirez; issued Sales Slip 101 for $400 plus $24 sales tax.
	5	Sold a handbag to Ruby Darbandi; issued Sales Slip 102 for $200 plus $12 sales tax.
	6	Sold four blouses to Gloria Hughes; issued Sales Slip 103 for $200 plus $12 sales tax.
	10	Sold casual pants and a blouse to Brenda Davis; issued Sales Slip 104 for $500 plus $30 sales tax.
	14	Sold a business suit to Linda Washington; issued Sales Slip 105 for $400 plus $24 sales tax.
	17	Sold hosiery, shoes, and gloves to Lisa Mariani; issued Sales Slip 106 for $600 plus $36 sales tax.
	21	Sold dresses and scarves to Rosa Maria Vasquez; issued Sales Slip 107 for $1,000 plus $60 sales tax.
	24	Sold a business suit to Emily Adams; issued Sales Slip 108 for $200 plus $12 sales tax.
	25	Sold shoes to Natasha Wells; issued Sales Slip 109 for $150 plus $9 sales tax.
	29	Sold a casual pants set to Melissa Anderson; issued Sales Slip 110 for $200 plus $12 sales tax.
	31	Sold a dress and handbag to Denise Cooper; issued Sales Slip 111 for $300 plus $18 sales tax.

Analyze: What is the net delivered cost of purchases for the month of January?

CHAPTER 8 CRITICAL THINKING PROBLEM

Internal Control

Kim Coda, owner of The Linen Shop, was preparing checks for payment of the current month's purchase invoices when she realized that there were two invoices from Romantic Towel Company, each for the purchase of 100 red, heart-imprinted bath towels. Coda thinks that Romantic Towel Company must have billed The Linen Shop twice for the same shipment because she knows the shop would not have needed two orders for 100 red bath towels within a month.

1. How can Coda determine whether Romantic Towel Company billed The Linen Shop in error or whether The Linen Shop placed two identical orders for red, heart-imprinted bath towels?

2. If two orders were placed, how can Coda prevent duplicate purchases from happening in the future?

Business Connections

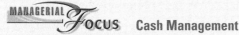

MANAGERIAL FOCUS   Cash Management   ◄ **Connection 1**

1. Why should management be concerned about the timely payment of invoices?

2. Why is it important for a firm to maintain a satisfactory credit rating?

3. Suppose you are the new controller of a small but growing company and you find that the firm has a policy of paying cash for all purchases of goods even though it could obtain credit. The president of the company does not like the idea of having debts, but the vice president thinks this is a poor business policy that will hurt the firm in the future. The president has asked your opinion. Would you agree with the president or the vice president? Why?

4. Why should management be concerned about the internal control of purchases?

5. How can good internal control of purchases protect a firm from fraud and errors and from excessive investment in merchandise?

6. In what ways would excessive investment in merchandise harm a business?

Ethical DILEMMA   Favor for a Friend   Assume that you are a sales   ◄ **Connection 2**
clerk in a retail clothing store. One of your friends regularly shops at this store and has asked you to ring some items at a price substantially below their marked price. Would you do this for your friend?

*Street***WISE:** Questions from the Real World   Accounts Payable and Cost of Merchandise   Refer to   ◄ **Connection 3**
the *1999 Annual Report* for The Home Depot, Inc. in Appendix B.

1. Locate the consolidated balance sheets. What is the reported amount of accounts payable at January 30, 2000? Has this balance increased or decreased since the prior fiscal year-end? By what amount?

2. Review Management's Discussion and Analysis of Results of Operations and Financial Condition for The Home Depot, Inc. What factors contributed to the lower cost of merchandise for the operating period?

FINANCIAL STATEMENT ANALYSIS   Income Statement   The following financial state-   ◄ **Connection 4**
ment excerpt is taken from the *2000 Annual Report* for Lands' End, Inc.

Consolidated Statements of Operations		
	For the period ended	
	January 28, 2000	January 29, 1999
(In thousands, except per share data)		
Net Sales	$ 1,319,823	$ 1,371,375
Cost of Sales	727,271	754,661
Gross Profit	$ 592,552	$ 616,714

1. The Cost of Sales amount on Lands' End, Inc. consolidated statements of operations represents the net cost of the goods that were sold for the period. For fiscal 2000, what percentage of net sales was the cost of sales? For fiscal 1999?

2. What factors might affect a merchandising company's cost of sales from one period to another?

Analyze Online: On the Lands' End, Inc. Web site **(www.landsend.com)**, locate the investor information section.

3. Review the consolidated statements of operations found in the current year's annual report.

4. What amount is reported for cost of sales?

5. What amount is reported for net sales?

Connection 5 ▶ *Extending the Thought* **Timing** A purchase order expresses an authorized intent to buy a particular item at a specific price from a supplier. Some companies record a debit to **Purchases** and a credit to **Accounts Payable** at the time the purchase order is issued. Other companies wait until the invoice for the merchandise arrives and then record the purchase. Which method do you think is better? Why?

Connection 6 ▶ Business Communication **Memo** You own a retail gourmet cooking supply store. As the owner of the business, you have noticed that your manager, bookkeeper, and sales clerk all place orders with suppliers, sometimes resulting in duplicate orders and confusion in processing invoices. You need to strengthen your internal controls in regard to the purchase of goods for resale. Prepare a memo to your staff that outlines proper procedures for placement of merchandise orders, receipt of goods, and payment of invoices.

Connection 7 ▶ **Team**Work **System Design** Form teams of three to four individuals. Create an idea for a merchandising business needed in your community. Then, design an automated purchasing system that will support strong internal controls over order placement and invoice payment for this business. The system should use current technologies that will free managers or store clerks from the necessity of calling suppliers when merchandise is needed. In a presentation to the class, describe the automated system that you have designed. Use a visual flowchart to demonstrate the flow of purchasing tasks including who will complete each task, how merchandise orders should be placed, what merchandise is needed, when orders are placed, and how invoices are processed.

inter **NET**
CONNECTION **AIPB** The Web site address of the American Institute of
Professional Bookkeepers (AIPB) is **www.aipb.com.** List two of the goals
of the Certified Bookkeeper Program. What are the eligibility requirements to become a certified bookkeeper? List some of the benefits of
becoming a certified bookkeeper.

◄ **Connection 8**

Answers to Self Reviews

Answers to Section 1 Self Review

1. Merchandise purchased on credit for resale.
2. It saves time and effort, and it strengthens the audit trail.
3. Locating suitable suppliers, obtaining price quotations and credit terms, and placing orders.
4. **c.** Purchase requisition
5. **b.** Purchase order
6. The business will receive a 2 percent discount if the invoice is paid within 10 days. If the invoice is not paid within 10 days, the total amount is due within 30 days.

Answers to Section 2 Self Review

1. $52,640
2.
Purchases	1,120.00	
Freight In	84.00	
Accounts Payable		1,204.00
3. It lists all of the creditors to whom money is owed.
4. **b.** income statement.
5. **d.** $3,200 credit
6. A payment was made and recorded in the general ledger account, but was not recorded in the creditor's subsidiary ledger account.

Answers to Comprehensive Self Review

1. The receiving report shows the quantity of goods received and the condition of the goods. The invoice shows quantities and prices; it is the document from which checks are prepared in payment of purchases.
2. The purchase requisition is used by a sales department to notify the purchasing department of the items wanted. The purchase order is prepared by the purchasing department to order the necessary goods at an appropriate price from the selected supplier.
3. To accumulate freight charges paid for purchases.
4. A price reduction offered to encourage quick payment of invoices by customers.
5. A contra cost of goods sold account.

CHAPTER 9

Learning Objectives

1. Record cash receipts in a cash receipts journal.

2. Account for cash short or over.

3. Post from the cash receipts journal to subsidiary and general ledgers.

4. Record cash payments in a cash payments journal.

5. Post from the cash payments journal to subsidiary and general ledgers.

6. Demonstrate a knowledge of procedures for a petty cash fund.

7. Demonstrate a knowledge of internal control routines for cash.

8. Write a check, endorse checks, prepare a bank deposit slip, and maintain a checkbook balance.

9. Reconcile the monthly bank statement.

10. Record any adjusting entries required from the bank reconciliation.

11. Define the accounting terms new to this chapter.

Cash Receipts, Cash Payments, and Banking Procedures

H&R BLOCK

www.hrblock.com

*I*n 1955 the founders of H&R Block made a decision to shift the focus of services away from bookkeeping to tax return preparation. A small ad purchased in *The Kansas City Star* newspaper pictured a man behind an eight ball and a simple headline, "Taxes, $5." The office was flooded with new customers and the strategy proved successful—business tripled over the previous year's volume.

Today, in more than 9,000 U.S. tax offices, the company handles approximately one in every seven regular returns and nearly one-half of all electronic returns filed with the Internal Revenue Service. Receipts for services, products, and royalties totaled $2.5 billion in 2000. Payments for expenses, which included items such as employee compensation, office rent, supplies, and postage, totaled $2.1 billion.

Thinking Critically
What types of daily receipts and payments do you think occur in a single H&R Block office location?

For more information on H&R Block, go to: collegeaccounting.glencoe.com.

New Terms

Bank reconciliation statement
Blank endorsement
Bonding
Canceled check
Cash
Cash payments journal
Cash receipts journal
Cash register proof
Cash Short or Over account
Check
Credit memorandum
Debit memorandum
Deposit in transit
Deposit slip
Dishonored (NSF) check

Drawee
Drawer
Endorsement
Full endorsement
Negotiable
Outstanding checks
Payee
Petty cash analysis sheet
Petty cash fund
Petty cash voucher
Postdated check
Promissory note
Restrictive endorsement
Service charge
Statement of account

Cash Receipts

Section Objectives

1. **Record cash receipts in a cash receipts journal.**

   WHY IT'S IMPORTANT
   The cash receipts journal is an efficient option for recording incoming cash.

2. **Account for cash short or over.**

   WHY IT'S IMPORTANT
   Discrepancies in cash are a possible indication that cash is mismanaged.

3. **Post from the cash receipts journal to subsidiary and general ledgers.**

   WHY IT'S IMPORTANT
   The subsidiary and general ledgers must hold accurate, up-to-date information about cash transactions.

Terms to Learn

cash
cash receipts journal
cash register proof
Cash Short or Over account
petty cash fund
promissory note
statement of account

1 Objective

Record cash receipts in a cash receipts journal.

Cash is the business asset that is most easily lost, mishandled, or even stolen. A well-managed business has careful procedures for controlling cash and recording cash transactions.

Cash Transactions

In accounting, the term **cash** is used for currency, coins, checks, money orders, and funds on deposit in a bank. Most cash transactions involve checks.

Cash Receipts

The type of cash receipts depends on the nature of the business. Supermarkets receive checks as well as currency and coins. Department stores receive checks in the mail from charge account customers. Cash received by wholesalers is usually in the form of checks.

Cash Payments

For safety and convenience, most businesses make payments by check. Sometimes a limited number of transactions are paid with currency and coins. The **petty cash fund** is used to handle payments involving small amounts of money, such as postage stamps, delivery charges, and minor purchases of office supplies. Some businesses maintain a fund to provide cash for business-related travel and entertainment expenses.

The Cash Receipts Journal

To improve the recordkeeping of cash receipts, many businesses use a special **cash receipts journal**. The cash receipts journal simplifies the recording of transactions and eliminates repetition in posting.

Recording Transactions in the Cash Receipts Journal

The format of the cash receipts journal varies according to the needs of each business. Figure 9-1 on page 293 shows the cash receipts journal for The Trend Center. The Trend Center has two major sources of cash receipts: checks from credit customers who are making payments on account, and currency and coins from cash sales.

The cash receipts journal has separate columns for the accounts frequently used when recording cash receipts. There are columns for

- debits to **Cash,**
- credits to **Accounts Receivable** for payments received on account,
- credits to **Sales** and **Sales Tax Payable** for cash sales.

At the end of the month, the totals of these columns are posted to the general ledger.

CASH RECEIPTS JOURNAL PAGE __1__

DATE	DESCRIPTION	POST. REF.	ACCOUNTS RECEIVABLE CREDIT	SALES TAX PAYABLE CREDIT	SALES CREDIT	OTHER ACCOUNTS CREDIT — ACCOUNT NAME	POST. REF.	AMOUNT	CASH DEBIT
20--									
Jan. 7	John Allen		428 00						428 00
8	Cash Sales			212 80	3040 00				3252 80
11	Clyde Davis		267 50						267 50
12	Investment					S. Harris, Capital		10000 00	10000 00
13	Blake Howard		535 00						535 00
15	Cash Sales			275 10	3930 00	Cash Short/Over		9 00	4196 10
16	Kim Johnson		107 00						107 00
17	Cash Refund					Supplies		50 00	50 00
22	Ed Ramirez		200 00						200 00
22	Cash Sales			295 40	4220 00				4515 40
29	Cash Sales			49 00	700 00	Cash Short/Over		7 00	756 00
31	Linda Sanchez		107 00						107 00
31	Newton Wu		260 00						260 00
31	Cash Sales			231 70	3310 00				3541 70
31	Collection of					Notes Receivable		4000 00	
	note/Jeff Wells					Interest Income		18 00	4018 00

▲ **FIGURE 9-1**
Cash Receipts Journal

Notice the Other Accounts Credit section, which is for entries that do not fit into one of the special columns. Entries in the Other Accounts Credit section are individually posted to the general ledger.

Cash Sales and Sales Taxes. The Trend Center uses a cash register to record cash sales and to store currency and coins. As each transaction is entered, the cash register prints a receipt for the customer. It also records the sale and the sales tax on an audit tape locked inside the machine. At the end of the day, when the machine is cleared, the cash register prints the transaction totals on the audit tape. The manager of the store removes the audit tape, and a cash register proof is prepared. The **cash register proof** is a verification that the amount in the cash register agrees with the amount shown on the audit tape. The cash register proof is used to record cash sales and sales tax in the cash receipts journal. The currency and coins are deposited in the firm's bank.

Refer to Figure 9-1, the cash receipts journal for The Trend Center. To keep it simple, it shows weekly, rather than daily, cash sales entries. Look at the January 8 entry. The steps to record the January 8 sales follow.

1. Enter the sales tax collected, $212.80, in the Sales Tax Payable Credit column.
2. Enter the sales, $3,040.00, in the Sales Credit column.
3. Enter the cash received, $3,252.80, in the Cash Debit column.
4. Confirm that total credits equal total debits ($212.80 + $3,040.00 = $3,252.80).

Cash Short or Over. Occasionally errors occur when making change. When errors happen, the cash in the cash register is either more than or less than the cash listed on the audit tape. When cash in the register is more than the audit tape, cash is *over*. When cash in the register is less than the

About **Accounting**

Automated Teller Machines
The banking industry paved the way for the Internet's self-service applications (such as ordering products online) with ATMs.

② Objective
Account for cash short or over.

audit tape, cash is *short*. Cash tends to be short more often than over because customers are more likely to notice and complain if they receive too little change.

Record short or over amounts in the **Cash Short or Over account**. If the account has a credit balance, there is an overage, which is treated as revenue. If the account has a debit balance, there is a shortage, which is treated as an expense.

Figure 9-1 shows how cash overages and shortages appear in the cash receipts journal. Look at the January 29 entry. Cash sales were $700. Sales tax collected was $49. The cash drawer was over $7. Overages are recorded as credits. Notice that the account name and the overage are entered in the Other Accounts Credit section.

Now look at the January 15 entry. This time the cash register was short. Shortages are recorded as debits. Debits are not the normal balance of the Other Accounts Credit column, so the debit entry is circled.

Businesses that have frequent entries for cash shortages and overages add a Cash Short or Over column to the cash receipts journal.

Cash Received on Account. The Trend Center makes sales on account and bills customers once a month. It sends a **statement of account** that shows the transactions during the month and the balance owed. Customers are asked to pay within 30 days of receiving the statement. Checks from credit customers are entered in the cash receipts journal, and then the checks are deposited in the bank.

Figure 9-1 shows how cash received on account is recorded. Look at the January 7 entry for John Allen. The check amount is entered in the Accounts Receivable Credit and the Cash Debit columns.

Cash Discounts on Sales. The Trend Center, like most retail businesses, does not offer cash discounts. However, many wholesale businesses offer cash discounts to customers who pay within a certain time period. For example, a wholesaler may offer a 1 percent discount if the customer pays within 10 days. To the wholesaler this is a *sales discount*. Sales discounts are recorded when the payment is received. Sales discounts are recorded in a contra revenue account, **Sales Discounts.** Businesses with many sales discounts add a Sales Discounts Debit column to the cash receipts journal.

Additional Investment by the Owner. Figure 9-1 shows that on January 12, the owner Stacee Harris invested an additional $10,000 in The Trend Center. She intends to use the money to expand the product line. The account name and amount are entered in the Other Accounts Credit section. The debit is entered in the Cash Debit column.

Receipt of a Cash Refund. Sometimes a business receives a cash refund for supplies, equipment, or other assets that are returned to the supplier. Figure 9-1 shows that on January 17, The Trend Center received a $50 cash refund for supplies that were returned to the seller. The account name and amount are entered in the Other Accounts Credit section. The debit is entered in the Cash Debit column.

Collection of a Promissory Note and Interest. A **promissory note** is a written promise to pay a specified amount of money on a certain date. Most notes require that interest is paid at a specified rate. Businesses use promissory notes to extend credit for some sales transactions.

Sometimes promissory notes are used to replace an accounts receivable balance when the account is overdue. For example, on July 31 The Trend Center accepted a six-month promissory note from Jeff Wells, who owed $400 on account (see Figure 9-2). Wells had asked for more time to pay his balance. The Trend Center agreed to grant more time if Wells signed a promissory note with 9 percent annual interest. The note provides more legal protection than an account receivable. The interest is compensation for the delay in receiving payment.

◀ **FIGURE 9-2**
A Promissory Note

$ 400.00	July 31, 20--
Six Months	AFTER DATE _I_ PROMISE TO PAY
TO THE ORDER OF	The Trend Center
Four Hundred and no/100	DOLLARS
PAYABLE AT	First Security National Bank
VALUE RECEIVED	with interest at 9%
NO. 30 DUE January 31, 20--	Jeff Wells

On the date of the transaction, July 31, The Trend Center recorded a general journal entry to increase notes receivable and to decrease accounts receivable for $400. The asset account, **Notes Receivable,** was debited and **Accounts Receivable** was credited.

GENERAL JOURNAL PAGE _16_

	DATE	DESCRIPTION	POST. REF.	DEBIT	CREDIT	
1	20--					1
2	July 31	Notes Receivable	109	4 0 0 00		2
3		Accounts Receivable/Jeff Wells	111 ✓		4 0 0 00	3
4		Received a 6-month, 9% note from				4
5		Jeff Wells to replace open account				5

On January 31, the due date of the note, The Trend Center received a check for $418 from Wells. This sum covered the amount of the note ($400) and the interest owed for the six-month period ($18). Figure 9-1 shows the entry in the cash receipts journal. The account names, **Notes Receivable** and **Interest Income,** and the amounts are entered on two lines in the Other Accounts Credit section. The debit is in the Cash Debit column.

Posting from the Cash Receipts Journal

During the month the amounts recorded in the Accounts Receivable Credit column are posted to individual accounts in the accounts receivable subsidiary ledger. Similarly, the amounts that appear in the Other Accounts Credit column are posted individually to the general ledger accounts during the month. The "CR1" posting references in the **Cash Short or Over** general ledger account on page 296 show that the entries appear on the first page of the cash receipts journal.

❸ Objective

Post from the cash receipts journal to subsidiary and general ledgers.

ACCOUNT	Cash Short or Over						ACCOUNT NO.	617	

DATE		DESCRIPTION	POST. REF.	DEBIT	CREDIT	BALANCE DEBIT	BALANCE CREDIT
20--							
Jan.	15		CR1	9 00		9 00	
	29		CR1		7 00	2 00	

Posting the Column Totals. At the end of the month, the cash receipts journal is totaled and the equality of debits and credits is proved.

PROOF OF CASH RECEIPTS JOURNAL

	Debits
Cash Debit column	$28,634.50

	Credits
Accounts Receivable Credit column	$ 1,904.50
Sales Tax Payable Credit column	1,064.00
Sales Credit column	15,200.00
Other Accounts Credit column	10,466.00
Total Credits	$28,634.50

FIGURE 9-3 ▼
Posted Cash Receipts Journal

Figure 9-3 shows The Trend Center's cash receipts journal after all posting is completed.

CASH RECEIPTS JOURNAL   PAGE 1

DATE		DESCRIPTION	POST. REF.	ACCOUNTS RECEIVABLE CREDIT	SALES TAX PAYABLE CREDIT	SALES CREDIT	OTHER ACCOUNTS CREDIT ACCOUNT NAME	POST. REF.	AMOUNT	CASH DEBIT
20--										
Jan.	7	John Allen	✓	4 2 8 00						4 2 8 00
	8	Cash Sales			2 1 2 80	3 0 4 0 00				3 2 5 2 80
	11	Clyde Davis	✓	2 6 7 50						2 6 7 50
	12	Investment					S. Harris, Capital	301	10 0 0 0 00	10 0 0 0 00
	13	Blake Howard	✓	5 3 5 00						5 3 5 00
	15	Cash Sales			2 7 5 10	3 9 3 0 00	Cash Short/Over	617	9 00	4 1 9 6 10
	16	Kim Johnson	✓	1 0 7 00						1 0 7 00
	17	Cash Refund					Supplies	129	5 0 00	5 0 00
	22	Ed Ramirez	✓	2 0 0 00						2 0 0 00
	22	Cash Sales			2 9 5 40	4 2 2 0 00				4 5 1 5 40
	29	Cash Sales			4 9 00	7 0 0 00	Cash Short/Over	617	7 00	7 5 6 00
	31	Linda Sanchez	✓	1 0 7 00						1 0 7 00
	31	Newton Wu	✓	2 6 0 00						2 6 0 00
	31	Cash Sales			2 3 1 70	3 3 1 0 00				3 5 4 1 70
	31	Collection of					Notes Receivable	109	4 0 0 00	
		note/Jeff Wells					Interest Income	491	1 8 00	4 1 8 00
	31	Totals		1 9 0 4 50	1 0 6 4 00	15 2 0 0 00			10 4 6 6 00	28 6 3 4 50
				(1 1 1)	(2 3 1)	(4 0 1)			(X)	(1 0 1)

When the cash receipts journal has been proved, rule the columns and post the totals to the general ledger. Figure 9-4 on page 297 shows how to post from the cash receipts journal to the general ledger accounts.

FIGURE 9-4 ▼
Posting from the Cash Receipts Journal

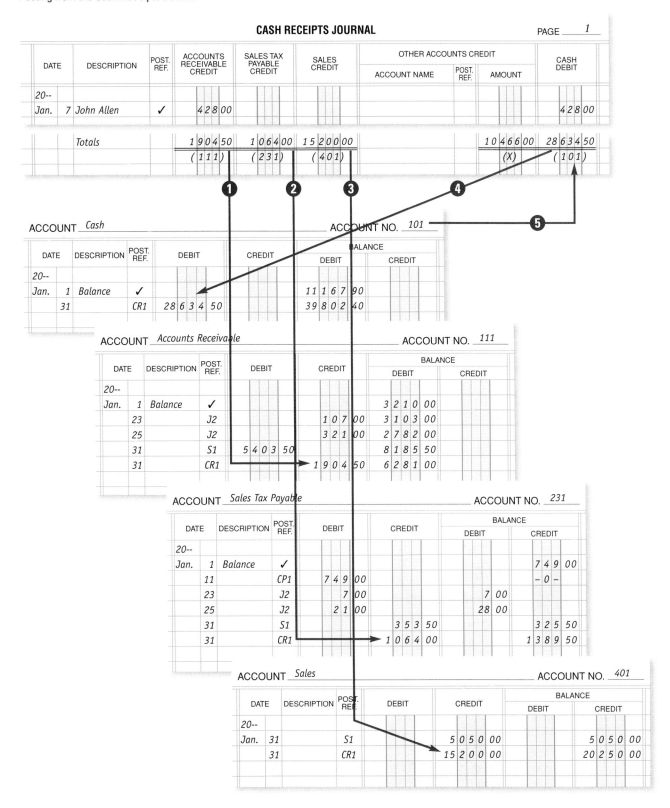

CASH RECEIPTS JOURNAL

PAGE _1_

DATE	DESCRIPTION	POST. REF.	ACCOUNTS RECEIVABLE CREDIT	SALES TAX PAYABLE CREDIT	SALES CREDIT	OTHER ACCOUNTS CREDIT			CASH DEBIT
						ACCOUNT NAME	POST. REF.	AMOUNT	
20--									
Jan. 7	John Allen	✓	4 2 8 00						4 2 8 00
	Totals		1 9 0 4 50	1 0 6 4 00	15 2 0 0 00			1 0 4 6 6 00	28 6 3 4 50
			(1 1 1)	(2 3 1)	(4 0 1)			(X)	(1 0 1)

① ② ③ ④ ⑤

ACCOUNT _Cash_ ACCOUNT NO. _101_

DATE	DESCRIPTION	POST. REF.	DEBIT	CREDIT	BALANCE	
					DEBIT	CREDIT
20--						
Jan. 1	Balance	✓			11 1 6 7 90	
31		CR1	28 6 3 4 50		39 8 0 2 40	

ACCOUNT _Accounts Receivable_ ACCOUNT NO. _111_

DATE	DESCRIPTION	POST. REF.	DEBIT	CREDIT	BALANCE	
					DEBIT	CREDIT
20--						
Jan. 1	Balance	✓			3 2 1 0 00	
23		J2		1 0 7 00	3 1 0 3 00	
25		J2		3 2 1 00	2 7 8 2 00	
31		S1	5 4 0 3 50		8 1 8 5 50	
31		CR1		1 9 0 4 50	6 2 8 1 00	

ACCOUNT _Sales Tax Payable_ ACCOUNT NO. _231_

DATE	DESCRIPTION	POST. REF.	DEBIT	CREDIT	BALANCE	
					DEBIT	CREDIT
20--						
Jan. 1	Balance	✓				7 4 9 00
11		CP1	7 4 9 00			- 0 -
23		J2		7 00	7 00	
25		J2		2 1 00	28 00	
31		S1		3 5 3 50		3 2 5 50
31		CR1		1 0 6 4 00		1 3 8 9 50

ACCOUNT _Sales_ ACCOUNT NO. _401_

DATE	DESCRIPTION	POST. REF.	DEBIT	CREDIT	BALANCE	
					DEBIT	CREDIT
20--						
Jan. 31		S1		5 0 5 0 00		5 0 5 0 00
31		CR1		15 2 0 0 00		20 2 5 0 00

To post a column total to a general ledger account, enter "CR1" in the Posting Reference column to show that the entry is from the first page of the cash receipts journal. Enter the column total in the general ledger account Debit or Credit column. Figure 9-4 shows the entries to **Accounts Receivable** (1), **Sales Tax Payable** (2), **Sales** (3), and **Cash** (4). Compute the new balance for each account and enter it in the Balance Debit or Balance Credit column.

Enter the general ledger account numbers under the column totals on the cash receipts journal. The (X) in the Other Accounts Credit Amount column indicates that the individual amounts were posted, not the total.

Posting to the Accounts Receivable Ledger. To keep customer balances current, accountants post entries from the Accounts Receivable Credit column to the customers' accounts in the accounts receivable subsidiary ledger daily. For example, on January 7, $428 was posted to John Allen's account in the subsidiary ledger. The "CR1" in the Posting Reference column indicates that the transaction appears on page 1 of the cash receipts journal. The check mark (✓) in the Posting Reference column in the cash receipts journal (Figure 9-4 on page 297) shows that the amount was posted to John Allen's account in the accounts receivable subsidiary ledger.

NAME __John Allen__

ADDRESS __1313 Broken Arrow Road, Dallas, Texas 75267-6205__

DATE		DESCRIPTION	POST. REF.	DEBIT	CREDIT	BALANCE
20--						
Jan.	1	Balance	✓			4 2 8 00
	3	Sales Slip 1101	S1	2 1 4 00		6 4 2 00
	7		CR1		4 2 8 00	2 1 4 00
	31	Sales Slip 1110	S1	2 6 7 50		4 8 1 50

Advantages of the Cash Receipts Journal

The cash receipts journal
- saves time and effort when recording and posting cash receipts,
- allows for the division of work among the accounting staff,
- strengthens the audit trail by recording all cash receipts transactions in one place.

Section 1 Self Review

Questions

1. What is a promissory note? In what situation would a business accept a promissory note?

2. How and when are the amounts in the Accounts Receivable Credit column posted?

3. What is a cash shortage? A cash overage? How are they recorded?

Exercises

4. Which items are considered cash?
   a. Currency
   b. Funds on deposit in the bank
   c. Money orders
   d. All of the above

5. Collection of a note receivable is recorded in the
   a. accounts receivable journal.
   b. cash receipts journal.
   c. general journal.
   d. promissory note journal.

Analysis

6. You notice that the **Cash Short or Over** account has 15 entries during the month. The ending balance is a $5 shortage for the month. Is this a problem? Why or why not?

Cash Payments

A good system of internal control requires that payments be made by check. In a good internal control system one employee approves payments, another employee prepares the checks, and another employee records the transactions.

The Cash Payments Journal

Unless a business has just a few cash payments each month, the process of recording these transactions in the general journal is time consuming. The **cash payments journal** is a special journal used to record transactions involving the payment of cash.

Recording Transactions in the Cash Payments Journal

Refer to Figure 9-5 on page 300 for The Trend Center's cash payments journal. Notice that there are separate columns for the accounts frequently used when recording cash payments—**Cash, Accounts Payable,** and **Purchases Discounts.** At the end of the month, the totals of these columns are posted to the general ledger.

The Other Accounts Debit section is for entries that do not fit into one of the special columns. Entries in the Other Accounts Debit section are individually posted to the general ledger.

Payments for Expenses. Businesses write checks for a variety of expenses each month. In January The Trend Center issued checks for rent, electricity, telephone service, advertising, and salaries. Refer to the January 3 entry for rent expense in Figure 9-5. Notice that the account name and amount are entered in the Other Accounts Debit section. The credit is in the Cash Credit column.

> In 1999 JC Penney Company, Inc. spent $1.05 billion for newspaper, catalog, television, and radio advertising. Payment of these expenses is recorded in the cash payments journal.

Payments on Account. Merchandising businesses usually make numerous payments on account for goods that were purchased on credit. If there is no cash discount, the entry in the cash payments journal is a debit to **Accounts Payable** and a credit to **Cash.** For an example of a payment without a discount, refer to the January 27 entry for Clothes Rack Depot in Figure 9-5.

Purchases Discounts is a contra cost of goods sold account that appears in the Cost of Goods Sold section of the income statement. Purchases discounts are subtracted from purchases to obtain net purchases.

For an example of a payment with a discount, refer to the January 13 entry for Sebrina's Clothing Store in Figure 9-5. The Trend Center takes a

Section Objectives

4 **Record cash payments in a cash payments journal.**

WHY IT'S IMPORTANT
The cash payments journal is an efficient option for recording payments by check.

5 **Post from the cash payments journal to subsidiary and general ledgers.**

WHY IT'S IMPORTANT
The subsidiary and general ledgers must hold accurate, up-to-date information about cash transactions.

6 **Demonstrate a knowledge of procedures for a petty cash fund.**

WHY IT'S IMPORTANT
Businesses use the petty cash fund to pay for small operating expenditures.

7 **Demonstrate a knowledge of internal control routines for cash.**

WHY IT'S IMPORTANT
Internal controls safeguard business assets.

Terms to Learn

bonding
cash payments journal
petty cash analysis sheet
petty cash voucher

4 Objective

Record cash payments in a cash payments journal.

CASH PAYMENTS JOURNAL

PAGE 1

DATE	CK. NO.	DESCRIPTION	POST. REF.	ACCOUNTS PAYABLE DEBIT	ACCOUNT NAME	POST. REF.	AMOUNT	PURCHASES DISCOUNT CREDIT	CASH CREDIT
20--									
Jan. 3	111	January rent			Rent Expense		1 400 00		1 400 00
10	112	Store fixtures			Store Equipment		1 200 00		1 200 00
11	113	Tax remittance			Sales Tax Payable		749 00		749 00
11	114	Fashion World		1 000 00					1 000 00
13	115	Sebrina's Clothing Store		3 250 00				65 00	3 185 00
14	116	Store supplies			Supplies		750 00		750 00
15	117	Withdrawal			Stacee Harris, Drawing		2 400 00		2 400 00
17	118	Electric bill			Utilities Expense		300 00		300 00
17	119	The Style Shop		4 300 00					4 300 00
21	120	Telephone bill			Telephone Expense		250 00		250 00
25	121	Newspaper ad			Advertising Expense		420 00		420 00
27	122	Clothes Rack Depot		1 200 00					1 200 00
30	123	Sebrina's Clothing Store		400 00					400 00
31	124	Fashion World		2 560 00				51 20	2 508 80
31	125	January payroll			Salaries Expense		4 200 00		4 200 00
31	126	Purchase of goods			Purchases		2 400 00		2 400 00
31	127	Freight charge			Freight In		150 00		150 00
31	128	Cash refund			Sales Returns & Allow.		80 00		
					Sales Tax Payable		5 60		85 60
31	129	Note paid to Dallas			Notes Payable		3 000 00		
		Equipment Company			Interest Expense		150 00		3 150 00
31	130	Establish petty cash fund			Petty Cash Fund		200 00		200 00

▲ **FIGURE 9-5**
Cash Payments Journal

Discount Terms
The terms 2/10, n/30 mean that if payment is made within 10 days, the customer can take a 2 percent discount. Otherwise, payment in full is due in 30 days.

2 percent discount for paying within the discount period ($3,250 × 0.02 = $65). When there is a cash discount, three elements must be recorded.

- Debit **Accounts Payable** for the invoice amount, $3,250.
- Credit **Purchases Discounts** for the amount of the discount, $65.
- Credit **Cash** for the amount of cash paid, $3,185.

> Kroger Corporation reported accounts payable of $2.87 billion at January 29, 2000.

Cash Purchases of Equipment and Supplies. Businesses use cash to purchase equipment, supplies, and other assets. These transactions are recorded in the cash payments journal. In January The Trend Center issued checks for store fixtures and store supplies. Refer to the entries on January 10 and 14 in Figure 9-5. Notice that the account names and amounts appear in the Other Accounts Debit section. The credits are recorded in the Cash Credit column.

Payment of Taxes. Retail businesses collect sales tax from their customers. Periodically the sales tax is remitted to the taxing authority. Refer to the entry on January 11 in Figure 9-5. The Trend Center issued a check for $749 to pay the December sales tax. Notice that the account name and amount appear in the Other Accounts Debit section. The credit is in the Cash Credit column.

Cash Purchases of Merchandise. Most merchandising businesses buy their goods on credit. Occasionally purchases are made for cash. These purchases are recorded in the cash payments journal. Refer to the January 31 entry for the purchase of goods in Figure 9-5.

Payment of Freight Charges. Freight charges on purchases of goods are handled in two ways. In some cases, the seller pays the freight charge and then includes it on the invoice. This method was covered in Chapter 8. The other method is for the buyer to pay the transportation company when the goods arrive. The buyer issues a check for the freight charge and records it in the cash payments journal. Refer to the entry on January 31 in Figure 9-5. The account name and amount appear in the Other Accounts Debit section. The credit is in the Cash Credit column.

Payment of a Cash Refund. When a customer purchases goods for cash and later returns them or receives an allowance, the customer is usually given a cash refund. Refer to the January 31 entry in Figure 9-5. The Trend Center issued a check for $85.60 to a customer who returned a defective item. When there is a cash refund, three elements are recorded.

- Debit **Sales Returns and Allowances** for the amount of the purchase, $80.00.
- Debit **Sales Tax Payable** for the sales tax, $5.60.
- Credit **Cash** for the amount of cash paid, $85.60.

Notice that the debits in the Other Accounts Debit section appear on two lines because two general ledger accounts are debited.

Payment of a Promissory Note and Interest. A promissory note can be issued to settle an overdue account or to obtain goods, equipment, or other property. For example, on August 2 The Trend Center issued a six-month promissory note for $3,000 to purchase store fixtures from Dallas Equipment Company. The note had an interest rate of 10 percent. The Trend Center recorded this transaction in the general journal by debiting **Store Equipment** and crediting **Notes Payable,** a liability account.

Currency

If an American business buys a product from a French company and promises to pay in 90 days, does the business pay in euros or dollars? The accountant reads the terms of the invoice before making payment. If the invoice is in euros, the accountant uses the exchange rate to calculate the amount of the payment.

	DATE		DESCRIPTION	POST. REF.	DEBIT	CREDIT	
1	20--						1
2	Aug.	2	Store Equipment	131	3 0 0 0 00		2
3			Notes Payable	201		3 0 0 0 00	3
4			Issued a 6-month, 10% note to Dallas				4
5			Equipment Company for purchase of				5
6			new store fixtures				6
7							7

GENERAL JOURNAL   PAGE ___16___

On January 31 The Trend Center issued a check for $3,150 in payment of the note, $3,000, and the interest, $150. This transaction was recorded in the cash payments journal in Figure 9-5.

- Debit **Notes Payable,** $3,000.
- Debit **Interest Expense,** $150.
- Credit **Cash,** $3,150.

Notice that the debits in the Other Accounts Debit section appear on two lines.

⑤ Objective

Post from the cash payments journal to subsidiary and general ledgers.

Posting from the Cash Payments Journal

During the month the amounts recorded in the Accounts Payable Debit column are posted to individual accounts in the accounts payable subsidiary ledger. The amounts in the Other Accounts Debit column are also posted individually to the general ledger accounts during the month. For example, the January 3 entry in the cash payments journal was posted to the **Rent Expense** account. The "CP1" indicates that the entry is recorded on page 1 of the cash payments journal.

ACCOUNT Rent Expense					ACCOUNT NO. 634	
DATE	DESCRIPTION	POST. REF.	DEBIT	CREDIT	BALANCE DEBIT	BALANCE CREDIT
20--						
Jan. 3		CP1	1 4 0 0 00		1 4 0 0 00	

Posting the Column Totals. At the end of the month, the cash payments journal is totaled and proved. The total debits must equal total credits.

PROOF OF CASH PAYMENTS JOURNAL

	Debits
Accounts Payable Debit column	$12,710.00
Other Accounts Debit column	17,654.60
Total Debits	$30,364.60

	Credits
Purchases Discount Credit column	$ 116.20
Cash Credit column	30,248.40
Total Credits	$30,364.60

Figure 9-6 on page 303 shows the January cash payments journal after posting for The Trend Center. Notice that the account numbers appear in the Posting Reference column of the Other Accounts Debit section to show that the amounts were posted.

When the cash payments journal has been proved, rule the columns and post the totals to the general ledger. Figure 9-7 on page 304 shows how to post from the cash payments journal to the general ledger accounts.

To post a column total to a general ledger account, enter "CP1" in the Posting Reference column to show that the entry is from page 1 of the cash payments journal.

Enter the column total in the general ledger account Debit or Credit column. Figure 9-7 shows the entries to **Accounts Payable** (1), **Purchases Discounts** (2), and **Cash** (3). Compute the new balance and enter it in the Balance Debit or Balance Credit column.

Enter the general ledger account numbers under the column totals on the cash payments journal. The (X) in the Other Accounts Debit column indicates that the individual accounts were posted, not the total.

Posting to the Accounts Payable Ledger. To keep balances current, accountants post entries from the Accounts Payable Debit column of the cash payments journal to the vendor accounts in the accounts payable subsidiary ledger daily. For example, on January 13, $3,250 was posted to Sebrina's Clothing Store account in the subsidiary ledger. The "CP1" in

CASH PAYMENTS JOURNAL

PAGE 1

DATE	CK. NO.	DESCRIPTION	POST. REF.	ACCOUNTS PAYABLE DEBIT	ACCOUNT NAME	POST. REF.	AMOUNT	PURCHASES DISCOUNT CREDIT	CASH CREDIT
20--									
Jan. 3	111	January rent			Rent Expense	634	1 400 00		1 400 00
10	112	Store fixtures			Store Equipment	131	1 200 00		1 200 00
11	113	Tax remittance			Sales Tax Payable	231	749 00		749 00
11	114	Fashion World	✓	1 000 00					1 000 00
13	115	Sebrina's Clothing Store	✓	3 250 00				65 00	3 185 00
14	116	Store supplies			Supplies	129	750 00		750 00
15	117	Withdrawal			Stacee Harris, Drawing	302	2 400 00		2 400 00
17	118	Electric bill			Utilities Expense	643	300 00		300 00
17	119	The Style Shop	✓	4 300 00					4 300 00
21	120	Telephone bill			Telephone Expense	649	250 00		250 00
25	121	Newspaper ad			Advertising Expense	614	420 00		420 00
27	122	Clothes Rack Depot	✓	1 200 00					1 200 00
30	123	Sebrina's Clothing Store	✓	400 00					400 00
31	124	Fashion World	✓	2 560 00				51 20	2 508 80
31	125	January payroll			Salaries Expense	637	4 200 00		4 200 00
31	126	Purchase of goods			Purchases	501	2 400 00		2 400 00
31	127	Freight charge			Freight In	502	150 00		150 00
31	128	Cash refund			Sales Returns & Allow.	451	80 00		
					Sales Tax Payable	231	5 60		85 60
31	129	Note paid to Dallas			Notes Payable	201	3 000 00		
		Equipment Company			Interest Expense	691	150 00		3 150 00
31	130	Establish petty cash fund			Petty Cash Fund	105	200 00		200 00
31		Totals		12 710 00			17 654 60	116 20	30 248 40
				(205)			(X)	(504)	(101)

the Posting Reference column indicates that the entry is recorded on page 1 of the cash payments journal. The check mark (✓) in the Posting Reference column of the cash payments journal (Figure 9-7 on page 304) shows that the amount was posted to the supplier's account in the accounts payable subsidiary ledger.

▲ **FIGURE 9-6**
Posted Cash Payments Journal

NAME _Sebrina's Clothing Store_ TERMS _2/10, n/30_
ADDRESS _5671 Preston Road, Dallas, Texas 75267-6205_

DATE	DESCRIPTION	POST. REF.	DEBIT	CREDIT	BALANCE
20--					
Jan. 1	Balance	✓			1 100 00
3	Invoice 8434, 12/29/--	P1		3 250 00	4 350 00
13		CP1	3 250 00		1 100 00
30		CP1	400 00		700 00

Advantages of the Cash Payments Journal

The cash payments journal

- saves time and effort when recording and posting cash payments,
- allows for a division of labor among the accounting staff,
- improves the audit trail because all cash payments are recorded in one place and listed by check number.

FIGURE 9-7 ▼
Posting from the Cash Payments Journal

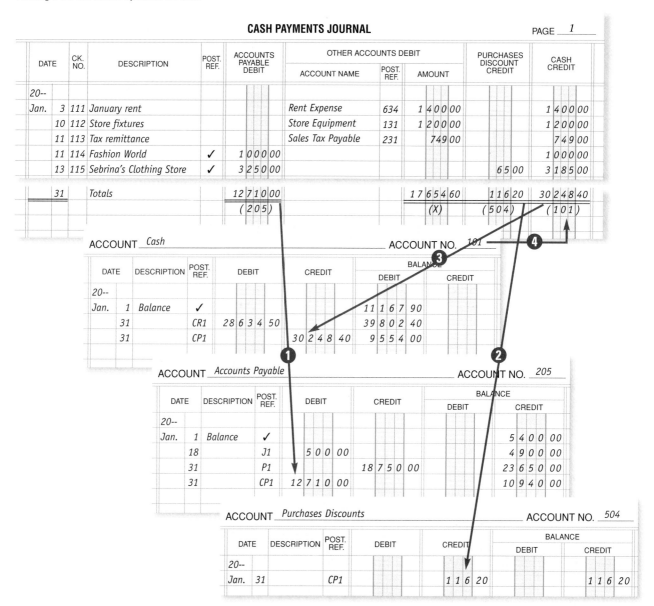

The Petty Cash Fund

6 Objective

Demonstrate a knowledge of procedures for a petty cash fund.

In a well-managed business, most bills are paid by check. However, there are times when small expenditures are made with currency and coins. Most businesses use a petty cash fund to pay for small expenditures. Suppose that in the next two hours the office manager needs a $3 folder for a customer. It is not practical to obtain an approval and write a check for $3 in the time available. Instead, the office manager takes $3 from the petty cash fund to purchase the folder.

Establishing the Fund

The amount of the petty cash fund depends on the needs of the business. Usually the office manager, cashier, or assistant is in charge of the petty cash fund. The Trend Center's cashier is responsible for petty cash. To set up the petty cash fund, The Trend Center wrote a $200 check to the cashier. She cashed the check and put the currency in a locked cash box.

The establishment of the petty cash fund should be recorded in the cash payments journal. Debit **Petty Cash Fund** in the Other Accounts Debit section of the journal, and enter the credit in the Cash Credit column.

Making Payments from the Fund

Petty cash fund payments are limited to small amounts. A **petty cash voucher** is used to record the payments made from the petty cash fund. The petty cash voucher shows the voucher number, amount, purpose of the expenditure, and account to debit. The person receiving the funds signs the voucher, and the person who controls the petty cash fund initials the voucher. Figure 9-8 shows a petty cash voucher for $17.50 for office supplies.

Important!

Petty Cash
Only one person controls the petty cash fund. That person keeps receipts for all expenditures.

◀ **FIGURE 9-8**
Petty Cash Voucher

PETTY CASH VOUCHER 1

NOTE: This form must be computer processed or filled out in black ink.

DESCRIPTION OF EXPENDITURE	ACCOUNTS TO BE CHARGED	AMOUNT	
Office supplies	Supplies 129	17	50
	Total	17	50

RECEIVED
THE SUM OF _Seventeen_ ------------------------------- DOLLARS AND __50/100__ CENTS
SIGNED _A.C. Abbot_ _____ DATE _2/3/--_ APPROVED BY __D.W.__ DATE _2/3/--_
Delta Office Supply Co.

The Petty Cash Analysis Sheet

Most businesses use a **petty cash analysis sheet** to record transactions involving petty cash. The Receipts column shows cash put in the fund, and the Payments column shows the cash paid out. There are special columns for accounts that are used frequently, such as **Supplies, Freight In,** and **Miscellaneous Expense.** There is an Other Accounts Debit column for entries that do not fit in a special column. Figure 9-9 on page 306 shows the petty cash analysis sheet for The Trend Center for February.

Replenishing the Fund. The total vouchers plus the cash on hand should always equal the amount of the fund—$200 for The Trend Center. Replenish the petty cash fund at the end of each month or sooner if the fund is low. Refer to Figures 9-9 and 9-10 on page 306 as you learn how to replenish the petty cash fund.

1. Total the columns on the petty cash analysis sheet.

2. Prove the petty cash fund by adding cash on hand and total payments. This should equal the petty fund balance ($33 + $167 = $200).

3. Write a check to restore the petty cash fund to its original balance.

4. Record the check in the cash payments journal. Refer to the petty cash analysis sheet for the accounts and amounts to debit. Notice that the debits appear on four lines of the Other Accounts Debit section. The credit appears in the Cash Credit column.

FIGURE 9-9 ▼
Petty Cash Analysis Sheet

PETTY CASH ANALYSIS

PAGE _____ 1

DATE	VOU. NO.	DESCRIPTION	RECEIPTS	PAYMENTS	SUPPLIES DEBIT	DELIVERY EXPENSE DEBIT	MISC. EXPENSE DEBIT	OTHER ACCOUNTS DEBIT	
								ACCOUNT NAME	AMOUNT
20--									
Feb. 1		Establish fund	200 00						
4	1	Office supplies		17 50	17 50				
6	2	Delivery service		25 00		25 00			
11	3	Withdrawal		30 00				S. Harris, Drawing	30 00
15	4	Postage stamps		33 00			33 00		
20	5	Delivery service		18 50		18 50			
26	6	Window washing		28 00			28 00		
28	7	Store supplies		15 00	15 00				
28		Totals	200 00	167 00	32 50	43 50	61 00		30 00
28		Balance on hand		33 00					
			200 00	200 00					
28		Balance on hand	33 00						
28		Replenish fund	167 00						
28		Carried forward	200 00						

CASH PAYMENTS JOURNAL

PAGE _____ 1

DATE	CK. NO.	DESCRIPTION	POST. REF.	ACCOUNTS PAYABLE DEBIT	OTHER ACCOUNTS DEBIT			PURCHASES DISCOUNT CREDIT	CASH CREDIT
					ACCOUNT NAME	POST. REF.	AMOUNT		
20--									
Feb. 28	191	Replenish petty cash fund			Supplies	129	32 50		
					S. Harris, Drawing	302	30 00		
					Delivery Expense	658	43 50		
					Miscellaneous Expense	693	61 00		167 00

FIGURE 9-10 ▲
Reimbursing the Petty Cash Fund

Internal Control of the Petty Cash Fund

Whenever there is valuable property or cash to protect, appropriate safeguards must be established. Petty cash is no exception. The following internal control procedures apply to petty cash.

1. Use the petty cash fund only for small payments that cannot conveniently be made by check.

2. Limit the amount set aside for petty cash to the approximate amount needed to cover one month's payments from the fund.

3. Write petty cash fund checks to the person in charge of the fund, not to the order of "Cash."

4. Assign one person to control the petty cash fund. This person has sole control of the money and is the only one authorized to make payments from the fund.

5. Keep petty cash in a safe, a locked cash box, or a locked drawer.

6. Obtain a petty cash voucher for each payment. The voucher should be signed by the person who receives the money and should show the payment details. This provides an audit trail for the fund.

Internal Control over Cash

⑦ Objective

Demonstrate a knowledge of internal control routines for cash.

In a well-managed business, there are internal control procedures for handling and recording cash receipts and cash payments. The internal control over cash should be tailored to the needs of the business. Accountants play a vital role in designing, establishing, and monitoring the cash control system. In developing internal control procedures for cash, certain basic principles must be followed.

Control of Cash Receipts

As noted already, cash is the asset that is most easily stolen, lost, or mishandled. Yet cash is essential to carrying on business operations. It is important to protect all cash receipts to make sure that funds are available to pay expenses and take care of other business obligations. The following are essential cash receipt controls.

1. Have only designated employees receive and handle cash whether it consists of checks and money orders, or currency and coins. These employees should be carefully chosen for reliability and accuracy and should be carefully trained. In some businesses employees who handle cash are bonded. **Bonding** is the process by which employees are investigated by an insurance company. Employees who pass the background check can be bonded; that is, the employer can purchase insurance on the employees. If the bonded employees steal or mishandle cash, the business is insured against the loss.

2. Keep cash receipts in a cash register, a locked cash drawer, or a safe while they are on the premises.

3. Make a record of all cash receipts as the funds come into the business. For currency and coins, this record is the audit tape in a cash register or duplicate copies of numbered sales slips. The use of a cash register provides an especially effective means of control because the machine automatically produces a tape showing the amounts entered. This tape is locked inside the cash register until it is removed by a supervisor.

4. Before a bank deposit is made, check the funds to be deposited against the record made when the cash was received. The employee who checks the deposit is someone other than the one who receives or records the cash.

5. Deposit cash receipts in the bank promptly—every day or several times a day. Deposit the funds intact—do not make payments directly from the cash receipts. The person who makes the bank deposit is someone other than the one who receives and records the funds.

6. Enter cash receipts transactions in the accounting records promptly. The person who records cash receipts is not the one who receives or deposits the funds.

7. Have the monthly bank statement sent to and reconciled by someone other than the employees who handle, record, and deposit the funds.

One of the advantages of efficient procedures for handling and recording cash receipts is that the funds reach the bank sooner. Cash receipts are not kept on the premises for more than a short time, which means that the funds are safer and are readily available for paying bills owed by the firm.

Control of Cash Payments

It is important to control cash payments so that the payments are made only for authorized business purposes. The following are essential cash payment controls.

1. Make all payments by check except for payments from special-purpose cash funds such as a petty cash fund or a travel and entertainment fund.

2. Issue checks only with an approved bill, invoice, or other document that describes the reason for the payment.

3. Have only designated personnel, who are experienced and reliable, approve bills and invoices.

4. Have checks prepared and recorded in the checkbook or check register by someone other than the person who approves the payments.

5. Have still another person sign and mail the checks to creditors.

6. Use prenumbered check forms. Periodically the numbers of the checks that were issued and the numbers of the blank check forms remaining should be verified to make sure that all check numbers are accounted for.

7. During the bank reconciliation process, compare the canceled checks to the checkbook or check register. The person who does the bank reconciliation should be someone other than the person who prepares or records the checks.

8. Enter promptly in the accounting records all cash payment transactions. The person who records cash payments should not be the one who approves payments or the one who writes the checks.

Small businesses usually cannot achieve the division of responsibility recommended for cash receipts and cash payments. However, no matter what size the firm, efforts should be made to set up effective control procedures for cash.

Section 2 Self Review

Questions

1. Why does a business use a petty cash fund?

2. What cash payments journal entry records a cash withdrawal by the owner of a sole proprietorship?

3. How and when are amounts in the Other Accounts Debit column of the cash payments journal posted?

Exercises

4. Cash purchases of merchandise are recorded in the
   a. cash payments journal.
   b. general journal.
   c. merchandise journal.
   d. purchases journal.

5. To take the discount, what is the payment date for an invoice dated January 20 with terms 3/15, n/30?
   a. February 3

   b. February 4
   c. February 5
   d. February 6

Analysis

6. Your employer keeps a $50 petty cash fund. She asked you to replenish the fund. She is missing a receipt for $6.60, which she says she spent on postage. How should you handle this?

Banking Procedures

Businesses with good internal control systems safeguard cash. Many businesses make a daily bank deposit, and some make two or three deposits a day. Keeping excess cash is a dangerous practice. Also, frequent bank deposits provide a steady flow of funds for the payment of expenses.

Writing Checks

A **check** is a written order signed by an authorized person, the **drawer**, instructing a bank, the **drawee**, to pay a specific sum of money to a designated person or business, the **payee**. The checks in Figure 9-11 on page 310 are **negotiable**, which means that ownership of the checks can be transferred to another person or business.

Before writing the check, complete the check stub. In Figure 9-11, the check stub for Check 111 shows

- Balance brought forward: $11,167.90
- Check amount: $1,400
- Balance: $9,767.90
- Date: January 3, 20--
- Payee: Turner Real Estate Associates
- Purpose: January rent

Once the stub has been completed, fill in the check. Carefully enter the date, the payee, and the amount in figures and words. Draw a line to fill any empty space after the payee's name and after the amount in words. To be valid, checks need an authorized signature. For The Trend Center only Stacee Harris, the owner, is authorized to sign checks.

Figure 9-11 shows the check stub for Check 112, a cash purchase from The Merchandising Equipment Center for $1,200. After Check 112, the account balance is $8,567.90 ($9,767.90 − $1,200.00).

Endorsing Checks

Each check needs an endorsement to be deposited. The **endorsement** is a written authorization that transfers ownership of a check. After the payee transfers ownership to the bank by an endorsement, the bank has a legal right to collect payment from the drawer, the person or business that issued the check. If the check cannot be collected, the payee guarantees payment to all subsequent holders.

Several forms of endorsement are shown in Figure 9-12 on page 310. Endorsements are placed on the back of the check, on the left, near the perforated edge where the check was separated from the stub.

A **blank endorsement** is the signature of the payee that transfers ownership of the check without specifying to whom or for what purpose. Checks with a blank endorsement can be further endorsed by anyone who has the check, even if the check is lost or stolen.

Section Objectives

8 Write a check, endorse checks, prepare a bank deposit slip, and maintain a checkbook balance.

WHY IT'S IMPORTANT
Banking tasks are basic practices in every business.

9 Reconcile the monthly bank statement.

WHY IT'S IMPORTANT
Reconciliation of the bank statement provides a good control of cash.

10 Record any adjusting entries required from the bank reconciliation.

WHY IT'S IMPORTANT
Certain items are not recorded in the accounting records during the month.

Terms to Learn

bank reconciliation statement
blank endorsement
canceled check
check
credit memorandum
debit memorandum
deposit in transit
deposit slip
dishonored (NSF) check
drawee
drawer
endorsement
full endorsement
negotiable
outstanding checks
payee
postdated check
restrictive endorsement
service charge

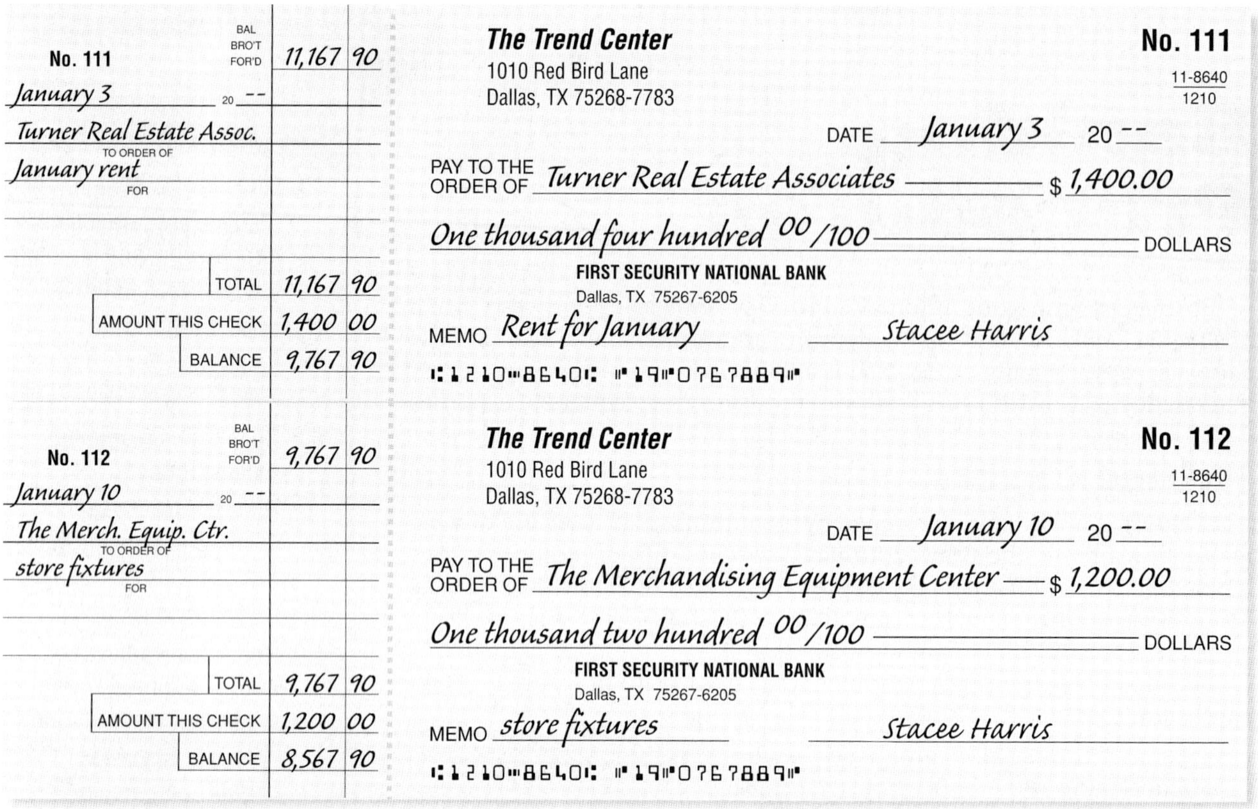

Check Stubs (left column)

		BAL BRO'T FOR'D	11,167	90
No. 111				
January 3	20 --			
Turner Real Estate Assoc.				
TO ORDER OF				
January rent				
FOR				
	TOTAL		11,167	90
	AMOUNT THIS CHECK		1,400	00
	BALANCE		9,767	90

		BAL BRO'T FOR'D	9,767	90
No. 112				
January 10	20 --			
The Merch. Equip. Ctr.				
TO ORDER OF				
store fixtures				
FOR				
	TOTAL		9,767	90
	AMOUNT THIS CHECK		1,200	00
	BALANCE		8,567	90

Check No. 111

The Trend Center
1010 Red Bird Lane
Dallas, TX 75268-7783

No. 111
11-8640 / 1210

DATE _January 3_ 20 --

PAY TO THE ORDER OF _Turner Real Estate Associates_ $ _1,400.00_

One thousand four hundred 00/100 DOLLARS

FIRST SECURITY NATIONAL BANK
Dallas, TX 75267-6205

MEMO _Rent for January_   _Stacee Harris_

⑈1210⑈8640⑈ ⑈19⑈0767889⑈

Check No. 112

The Trend Center
1010 Red Bird Lane
Dallas, TX 75268-7783

No. 112
11-8640 / 1210

DATE _January 10_ 20 --

PAY TO THE ORDER OF _The Merchandising Equipment Center_ $ _1,200.00_

One thousand two hundred 00/100 DOLLARS

FIRST SECURITY NATIONAL BANK
Dallas, TX 75267-6205

MEMO _store fixtures_   _Stacee Harris_

⑈1210⑈8640⑈ ⑈19⑈0767889⑈

▲ **FIGURE 9-11**
Checks and Check Stubs

A **full endorsement** is a signature transferring a check to a specific person, business, or bank. Only the person, business, or bank named in the full endorsement can transfer it to someone else.

The safest endorsement is the **restrictive endorsement**. A restrictive endorsement is a signature that transfers the check to a specific party for a specific purpose, usually for deposit to a bank account. Most businesses restrictively endorse the checks they receive using a rubber stamp.

FIGURE 9-12 ▶
Types of Check Endorsement

Full Endorsement

PAY TO THE ORDER OF
FIRST SECURITY NATIONAL BANK
THE TREND CENTER
19-07-67889

Blank Endorsement

Stacee Harris
19-07-67889

Restrictive Endorsement

PAY TO THE ORDER OF
FIRST SECURITY NATIONAL BANK
FOR DEPOSIT ONLY
THE TREND CENTER
19-07-67889

❽ Objective

Write a check, endorse checks, prepare a bank deposit slip, and maintain a checkbook balance.

Preparing the Deposit Slip

Businesses prepare a **deposit slip** to record each deposit of cash or checks to a bank account. Usually the bank provides deposit slips preprinted with the account name and number. Figure 9-13 on page 311 shows the deposit slip for the January 8 deposit for The Trend Center.

CHECKING ACCOUNT DEPOSIT

DATE *January 8, 20--*

THE TREND CENTER
1010 Red Bird Lane
Dallas, TX 75268-7783

FIRST SECURITY NATIONAL BANK
Dallas, TX 75267-6205

ENTER ADDITIONAL CHECKS ON OTHER SIDE

CURRENCY	DOLLARS	CENTS
	1350	00
COIN	109	90
1 11-8182	240	80
2 11-8182	230	00
3 11-5216	171	20
4 11-5216	280	00
5 11-7450	460	50
6 11-7450	410	40
7		
8		
9		
10		
11		
12		
TOTAL FROM OTHER SIDE		
OR ATTACHED LIST		
TOTAL	3,252.80	

Checks and other items are received for deposit subject to the terms and conditions of this bank's collection agreement.

⑆1210⑈8640⑆ ⑆19⑈07 67889⑈

Notice the printed numbers on the lower edge of the deposit slip. These are the same numbers on the bottom of the checks, Figure 9-11. The numbers are printed using a special *magnetic ink character recognition (MICR)* type that can be "read" by machine. Deposit slips and checks encoded with MICR are rapidly and efficiently processed by machine.

- The 12 indicates that the bank is in the 12th Federal Reserve District.
- The 10 is the routing number used in processing the document.
- The 8640 identifies First Security National Bank.
- The 19 07 67889 is The Trend Center account number.

The deposit slip for The Trend Center shows the date, January 8. *Currency* is the paper money, $1,350.00. *Coin* is the amount in coins, $109.90. The checks and money orders are individually listed. Some banks ask that the *American Bankers Association (ABA) transit number* for each check be entered on the deposit slip. The transit number appears on the top part of the fraction that appears in the upper right corner of the check. In Figure 9-11, the transit number is 11-8640.

Handling Postdated Checks

Occasionally a business will receive a postdated check. A **postdated check** is dated some time in the future. If the business receives a postdated check, it should not deposit it before the date on the check. Otherwise, the check could be refused by the drawer's bank. Postdated checks are written by drawers who do not have sufficient funds to cover the check. The drawer expects to have adequate funds in the bank by the date on the check. Issuing or accepting postdated checks is not a proper business practice.

Reconciling the Bank Statement

Once a month the bank sends a statement of the deposits received and the checks paid for each account. Figure 9-14 on page 313 shows the bank statement for The Trend Center. It shows a day-to-day listing of all transactions during the month. A code, explained at the bottom,

⑨ Objective
Reconcile the monthly bank statement.

Computers in Accounting

Banking on Computer Technologies

The banking industry has long been a major user of computer technologies to process and maintain accurate records for internal operations and customer accounts. As early as 1950, the banking industry adopted magnetic ink character recognition (MICR) type to be printed along the bottom edge of checks and deposit slips. Using MICR readers, banks process millions of checks and deposit slips annually. MICR readers are also used in retail stores where checks are accepted.

Bank computer systems use real-time processing. Every banking transaction is recorded immediately in the bank's accounting records, and customer account balances are instantly updated.

Banking consumers today rely heavily on automated teller machines (ATMs). The banking industry has invested billions of dollars to maintain and upgrade teller machines to offer the services that their customers demand. Newer ATMs allow customers to cash checks, purchase stamps, and withdraw money in bills and coins.

Online banking is a service now offered by most financial institutions. Password-protected Web sites offer customers an easy-to-use interface where many banking transactions are completed. Consumers now pay bills, transfer funds, purchase IRAs, download bank statements, and review their account activity using home or office computers. Some consumers have abandoned the bricks-and-mortar bank altogether. Again, the banking industry has responded quickly with investment in Internet technologies and security software applications necessary to serve the needs of customers.

Thinking Critically

As a banking customer, what concerns do you have about online banking? What benefits and disadvantages can you identify?

Internet Application

Locate the Web site for your banking institution. What online banking services are offered? What costs are associated with these services?

identifies transactions that do not involve checks or deposits. For example, *SC* indicates a service charge. The last column of the bank statement shows the account balance at the beginning of the period, after each day's transactions, and at the end of the period.

Often the bank encloses canceled checks with the bank statement. **Canceled checks** are checks paid by the bank during the month. The bank stamps the word *PAID* across the face of each check. Canceled checks are proof of payment. They are filed after the bank reconciliation is complete.

Usually there is a difference between the ending balance shown on the bank statement and the balance shown in the checkbook. A bank reconciliation determines why the difference exists and brings the records into agreement.

Changes in the Checking Account Balance

A **credit memorandum** explains any addition, other than a deposit, to the checking account. For example, when a note receivable is due, the bank may collect the note from the maker and place the proceeds in the checking account. The amount collected appears on the bank statement, and the credit memorandum showing the details of the transaction is enclosed with the bank statement.

FIRST SECURITY NATIONAL BANK

THE TREND CENTER
1010 Red Bird Lane
Dallas, TX 75268-7783

Account Number: 19-07-67889

Period Ending   January, 31, 20--

CHECKS		DEPOSITS	DATE	BALANCE
Beginning Balance			December 31	11,167.90
1,400.00-		428.00+	January 7	10,195.90
1,200.00-		3,252.80+	January 8	12,248.70
749.00-		267.50+	January 11	11,767.20
1,000.00-		10,000.00+	January 12	20,767.20
3,185.00-		535.00+	January 13	18,117.20
750.00-		4,196.10+	January 15	21,563.30
2,400.00-		107.00+	January 16	19,270.30
250.00-	300.00-	50.00+	January 17	18,770.30
420.00-	4,300.00-	200.00+	January 22	14,250.30
800.00-	1,200.00-	4,515.40+	January 22	16,765.70
250.00- DM		756.00+	January 29	17,271.70
20.00- SC		107.00+	January 31	17,358.70
400.00-		260.00+	January 31	17,218.70
		418.00+	January 31	17,636.70

LAST AMOUNT IN THIS
COLUMN IS YOUR BALANCE

Codes:	CC	Certified Check	EC	Error Correction
	CM	Credit Memorandum	OD	Overdrawn
	DM	Debit Memorandum	SC	Service Charge

PLEASE EXAMINE THIS STATEMENT UPON RECEIPT AND REPORT ANY ERRORS WITHIN TEN DAYS.

A **debit memorandum** explains any deduction, other than a check, to the checking account. Service charges and dishonored checks appear as debit memorandums.

Bank **service charges** are fees charged by banks to cover the costs of maintaining accounts and providing services, such as the use of the night deposit box and the collection of promissory notes. The debit memorandum shows the type and amount of each service charge.

Figure 9-15 on page 314 shows a debit memorandum for a $250 dishonored check. A **dishonored check** is one that is returned to the depositor unpaid. Normally, checks are dishonored because there are insufficient funds in the drawer's account to cover the check. The bank usually stamps the letters *NSF* for *Not Sufficient Funds* on the check. The business records a journal entry to create an account receivable from the drawer for the amount of the dishonored check.

When a check is dishonored, the business contacts the drawer to arrange for collection. The drawer can ask the business to redeposit the check because the funds are now in the account. If so, the business records the check deposit again. Sometimes, the business requests a cash payment.

FIGURE 9-15 ▶
Debit Memorandum

DEBIT: **THE TREND CENTER**
1010 Red Bird Lane
Dallas, TX 75268-7783

FIRST SECURITY NATIONAL BANK

19-07-67889

DATE: *January 31, 20--*

NSF Check - Bridgette Wilson	250	00

APPROVED: *DCP*

The Bank Reconciliation Process: An Illustration

When the bank statement is received, it is reconciled with the financial records of the business. On February 5 The Trend Center received the bank statement shown in Figure 9-14. The ending cash balance according to the bank is $17,636.70. On January 31 the **Cash** account, called the *book balance of cash,* is $9,554.00. The same amount appears on the check stub at the end of January.

Sometimes the difference between the bank balance and the book balance is due to errors. The bank might make an arithmetic error, give credit to the wrong depositor, or charge a check against the wrong account. Many banks require that errors in the bank statement be reported within a short period of time, usually 10 days. The errors made by businesses include not recording a check or deposit, or recording a check or deposit for the wrong amount.

Other than errors, there are four reasons why the book balance of cash may not agree with the balance on the bank statement.

1. **Outstanding checks** are checks that are recorded in the cash payments journal but have not been paid by the bank.

2. **Deposit in transit** is a deposit that is recorded in the cash receipts journal but that reaches the bank too late to be shown on the monthly bank statement.

3. **Service charges and other deductions** are not recorded in the business records.

4. **Deposits,** such as the collection of promissory notes, are not recorded in the business records.

Figure 9-16 on page 315 shows a **bank reconciliation statement** that accounts for the differences between the balance on the bank statement and the book balance of cash. The bank reconciliation statement format is:

First Section		**Second Section**	
	Bank statement balance		Book balance
+	deposits in transit	+	deposits not recorded
−	outstanding checks	−	deductions
+ or −	bank errors	+ or −	errors in the books
	Adjusted bank balance		Adjusted book balance

When the bank reconciliation statement is complete, the adjusted bank balance must equal the adjusted book balance.

FIGURE 9-16
Bank Reconciliation Statement

The Trend Center
Bank Reconciliation Statement
January 31, 20--

Bank statement balance		17 6 3 6 70
Additions:		
Deposits of January 31 in transit	3 5 4 1 70	
Check incorrectly charged to account	8 0 0 00	4 3 4 1 70
		21 9 7 8 40
Deductions for outstanding checks:		
Check 124 of January 31	2 5 0 8 80	
Check 125 of January 31	4 2 0 0 00	
Check 126 of January 31	2 4 0 0 00	
Check 127 of January 31	1 5 0 00	
Check 128 of January 31	8 5 60	
Check 129 of January 31	3 1 5 0 00	
Check 130 of January 31	2 0 0 00	
Total outstanding checks		12 6 9 4 40
Adjusted bank balance		9 2 8 4 00
Book balance		9 5 5 4 00
Deductions:		
NSF Check	2 5 0 00	
Bank service charge	2 0 00	2 7 0 00
Adjusted book balance		9 2 8 4 00

Use the following steps to prepare the bank reconciliation statement:

First Section

1. Enter the balance on the bank statement, $17,636.70.

2. Compare the deposits in the checkbook with the deposits on the bank statement. The Trend Center had one deposit in transit. On January 31 receipts of $3,541.70 were placed in the bank's night deposit box. The bank recorded the deposit on February 1. The deposit will appear on the February bank statement.

3. List the outstanding checks.
   - Put the canceled checks in numeric order.
   - Compare the canceled checks to the check stubs, verifying the check numbers and amounts.
   - Examine the endorsements to make sure that they agree with the names of the payees.
   - List the checks that have not cleared the bank.
   - The Trend Center has seven outstanding checks totaling $12,694.40.

4. While reviewing the canceled checks for The Trend Center, Stacee Harris found an $800 check issued by Trudie's Dress Barn. The $800 was deducted from The Trend Center's account; it should have been deducted from the account for Trudie's Dress Barn. This is a bank error. Stacee Harris contacted the bank about the error. The correction will appear on the next bank statement. The bank error amount is added to the bank statement balance on the bank reconciliation statement.

5. The adjusted bank balance is $9,284.

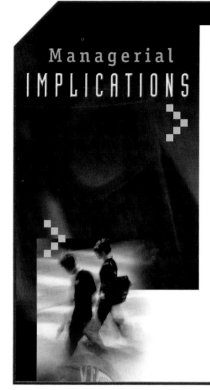

Managerial

IMPLICATIONS

Cash

- It is important to safeguard cash against loss and theft.
- Management and the accountant need to work together
  - to make sure that there are effective controls for cash receipts and cash payments,
  - to monitor the internal control system to make sure that it functions properly,
  - to develop procedures that ensure the quick and efficient recording of cash transactions.
- To make decisions, management needs up-to-date information about the cash position so that it can anticipate cash shortages and arrange loans or arrange for the temporary investment of excess funds.
- Management and the accountant need to establish controls over the banking activities—depositing funds, issuing checks, recording checking account transactions, and reconciling the monthly bank statement.

Thinking Critically

How would you determine how much cash to keep in the business checking account, as opposed to in a short-term investment?

Important!

Adjusted Book Balance
Make journal entries to record additions and deductions that appear on the bank statement but that have not been recorded in the general ledger.

⑩ Objective
Record any adjusting entries required from the bank reconciliation.

Second Section

1. Enter the balance in books from the **Cash** account, $9,554.
2. Record any deposits made by the bank that have not been recorded in the accounting records. The Trend Center did not have any.
3. Record deductions made by the bank. There are two items:
   - the NSF check for $250,
   - the bank service charge for $20.
4. Record any errors in the accounting records that were discovered during the reconciliation process. The Trend Center did not have any errors in January.
5. The adjusted book balance is $9,284.

Notice that the adjusted bank balance and the adjusted book balance agree.

Adjusting the Financial Records

Items in the second section of the bank reconciliation statement include additions and deductions made by the bank that do not appear in the accounting records. Businesses prepare journal entries to record these items in the books.

For The Trend Center, two entries must be made. The first entry is for the NSF check from Bridgette Wilson, a credit customer. The second entry is for the bank service charge. The effect of the two items is a decrease in the **Cash** account balance.

The January bank reconciliation statement (Figure 9-16 on page 315) shows an NSF check of $250 and a bank service charge of $20.

Analysis

The asset account, **Accounts Receivable**, is increased by $250 for the returned check. The expense account, **Bank Fees Expense**, is increased by $20 for the service charge. The asset account, **Cash**, is decreased by $270 ($250 + $20).

Debit-Credit Rules

DEBIT Increases to assets are debits. Debit **Accounts Receivable** for $250. Increases to expenses are debits. Debit **Bank Fees Expense** for $20.

CREDIT Decreases to assets are credits. Credit **Cash** for $270.

T-Account Presentation

Accounts Receivable		Bank Fees Expense		Cash	
+	−	+	−	+	−
250		20			270

General Journal Entry

GENERAL JOURNAL PAGE _16_

	DATE		DESCRIPTION	POST. REF.	DEBIT	CREDIT	
29	Jan.	31	Accounts Receivable/ Bridgette Wilson		250 00		29
30			Bank Fees Expense		20 00		30
31			Cash			270 00	31
32			To record NSF check and service charge				32

The Bottom Line

Adjusting Entries

Income Statement

Expenses	↑ 20
Net Income	↓ 20

Balance Sheet

Assets	↓ 20
Equity	↓ 20

After these entries are posted, the **Cash** account appears as follows.

ACCOUNT _Cash_   ACCOUNT NO. _101_

DATE		DESCRIPTION	POST. REF.	DEBIT	CREDIT	BALANCE DEBIT	BALANCE CREDIT
20--							
Jan.	1	Balance	✓			11 1 6 7 90	
	31		CR1	28 6 3 4 50		39 8 0 2 40	
	31		CP1		30 2 4 8 40	9 5 5 4 00	
	31		J16		2 7 0 00	9 2 8 4 00	

Notice that $9,284 is the adjusted bank balance, the adjusted book balance, and the general ledger **Cash** balance. A notation is made on the latest check stub to deduct the amounts ($250 and $20). The notation includes the reasons for the deductions.

Sometimes the bank reconciliation reveals an error in the firm's financial records. For example, the February bank reconciliation for The Trend Center found that Check 151 was written for $355. The amount on the bank statement is $355. However, the check was recorded in the accounting records as $345. The business made a $10 error when recording the check. The Trend Center prepared the following journal entry to correct the error. The $10 is also deducted on the check stub.

GENERAL JOURNAL   PAGE _17_

	DATE		DESCRIPTION	POST. REF.	DEBIT	CREDIT	
1	20--						1
2	Feb.	28	Advertising Expense	614	10 00		2
3			Cash	101		10 00	3
4			To correct error for Check 151 of				4
5			Feb. 21				5

Internal Control of Banking Activities

Well-run businesses put the following internal controls in place.

1. Limit access to the checkbook to designated employees. When the checkbook is not in use, keep it in a locked drawer or cabinet.
2. Use prenumbered check forms. Periodically, verify and account for all checks. Examine checks before signing them. Match each check to an approved invoice or other payment authorization.
3. Separate duties.
   - The person who writes the check should not sign or mail the check.
   - The person who performs the bank reconciliation should not handle or deposit cash receipts or write, record, sign, or mail checks.
4. File all deposit receipts, canceled checks, voided checks, and bank statements for future reference. These documents provide a strong audit trail for the checking account.

Section 3 Self Review

Questions

1. What is a postdated check? When should postdated checks be deposited?
2. Which bank reconciliation items require journal entries?
3. Why does a payee endorse a check before depositing it?

Exercises

4. On the bank reconciliation statement, you would not find a list of
   a. canceled checks.
   b. deposits in transit.
   c. outstanding checks.
   d. NSF checks.
5. Which of the following does not require an adjustment to the financial records?
   a. NSF check
   b. Bank service charge
   c. Check that was incorrectly recorded at $65, but was written and paid by the bank as $56
   d. Deposits in transit

Analysis

6. James is one of several accounting clerks at Avery Beverage Company. His job duties include recording invoices as they are received, filing the invoices, and writing the checks for accounts payable. He is a fast and efficient clerk and usually has some time available each day to help other clerks. It has been suggested that reconciling the bank statement should be added to his job duties. Do you agree or disagree? Why or why not?

     (Answers to Section 3 Self Review are on page 348.)

CHAPTER 9

Review and Applications

Review

Chapter Summary

In this chapter, you have learned the basic principles of accounting for cash payments and cash receipts.

Learning Objectives

1 Record cash receipts in a cash receipts journal.
Use of special journals leads to an efficient recording process for cash transactions. The cash receipts journal has separate columns for the accounts used most often for cash receipt transactions.

2 Account for cash short or over.
Errors can occur when making change. Cash register discrepancies should be recorded using the expense account **Cash Short or Over.**

3 Post from the cash receipts journal to subsidiary and general ledgers.
Individual accounts receivable amounts are posted to the subsidiary ledger daily. Figures in the Other Accounts Credit column are posted individually to the general ledger during the month. All other postings are done on a summary basis at month-end.

4 Record cash payments in a cash payments journal.
The cash payments journal has separate columns for the accounts used most often, eliminating the need to record the same account names repeatedly.

5 Post from the cash payments journal to subsidiary and general ledgers.
Individual accounts payable amounts are posted daily to the accounts payable subsidiary ledger. Amounts listed in the Other Accounts Debit column are posted individually to the general ledger during the month. All other postings are completed on a summary basis at the end of the month.

6 Demonstrate a knowledge of procedures for a petty cash fund.
Although most payments are made by check, small payments are often made through a petty cash fund. A petty cash voucher is prepared for each payment and signed by the person receiving the money. The person in charge of the fund records expenditures on a petty cash analysis sheet. The fund is replenished with a check for the sum spent. An entry is made in the cash payments journal to debit the accounts involved.

7 Demonstrate a knowledge of internal control routines for cash.
All businesses need a system of internal controls to protect cash from theft and mishandling and to ensure accurate records of cash transactions. A checking account is essential to store cash safely and to make cash payments efficiently. For maximum control over outgoing cash, all payments should be made by check except those from carefully controlled special-purpose cash funds such as a petty cash fund.

8 Write a check, endorse checks, prepare a bank deposit slip, and maintain a checkbook balance.
Check writing requires careful attention to details. If a standard checkbook is used, the stub should be completed before the check so that it will not be forgotten. The stub gives the data needed to journalize the payment.

9 Reconcile the monthly bank statement.
A bank statement should be immediately reconciled with the cash balance in the firm's financial records. Usually, differences are due to deposits in transit, outstanding checks, and bank service charges, but many factors can cause lack of agreement between the bank balance and the book balance.

10 Record any adjusting entries required from the bank reconciliation.
Some differences between the bank balance and the book balance may require that the firm's records be adjusted after the bank statement is reconciled. Journal entries are recorded and then posted to correct the **Cash** account balance and the checkbook balance.

11 Define the accounting terms new to this chapter.

CHAPTER 9 GLOSSARY

Bank reconciliation statement (p. 314) A statement that accounts for all differences between the balance on the bank statement and the book balance of cash

Blank endorsement (p. 309) A signature of the payee written on the back of the check that transfers ownership of the check without specifying to whom or for what purpose

Bonding (p. 307) The process by which employees are investigated by an insurance company that will insure the business against losses through employee theft or mishandling of funds

Canceled check (p. 312) A check paid by the bank on which it was drawn

Cash (p. 292) In accounting, currency, coins, checks, money orders, and funds on deposit in a bank

Cash payments journal (p. 299) A special journal used to record transactions involving the payment of cash

Cash receipts journal (p. 292) A special journal used to record and post transactions involving the receipt of cash

Cash register proof (p. 293) A verification that the amount of currency and coins in a cash register agrees with the amount shown on the cash register audit tape

Cash Short or Over account (p. 294) An account used to record any discrepancies between the amount of currency and coins in the cash register and the amount shown on the audit tape

Check (p. 309) A written order signed by an authorized person instructing a bank to pay a specific sum of money to a designated person or business

Credit memorandum (p. 312) A form that explains any addition, other than a deposit, to a checking account

Debit memorandum (p. 313) A form that explains any deduction, other than a check, from a checking account

Deposit in transit (p. 314) A deposit that is recorded in the cash receipts journal but that reaches the bank too late to be shown on the monthly bank statement

Deposit slip (p. 310) A form prepared to record the deposit of cash or checks to a bank account

Dishonored check (p. 313) A check returned to the depositor unpaid because of insufficient funds in the drawer's account; also called an NSF check

Drawee (p. 309) The bank on which a check is written

Drawer (p. 309) The person or firm issuing a check

Endorsement (p. 309) A written authorization that transfers ownership of a check

Full endorsement (p. 310) A signature transferring a check to a specific person, firm, or bank

Negotiable (p. 309) A financial instrument whose ownership can be transferred to another person or business

Outstanding checks (p. 314) Checks that have been recorded in the cash payments journal but have not yet been paid by the bank

Payee (p. 309) The person or firm to whom a check is payable

Petty cash analysis sheet (p. 305) A form used to record transactions involving petty cash

Petty cash fund (p. 292) A special-purpose fund used to handle payments involving small amounts of money

Petty cash voucher (p. 305) A form used to record the payments made from a petty cash fund

Postdated check (p. 311) A check dated some time in the future

Promissory note (p. 294) A written promise to pay a specified amount of money on a specific date

Restrictive endorsement (p. 310) A signature that transfers a check to a specific party for a stated purpose

Service charge (p. 313) A fee charged by a bank to cover the costs of maintaining accounts and providing services

Statement of account (p. 294) A form sent to a firm's customers showing transactions during the month and the balance owed

Comprehensive Self Review

1. What does the term *cash* mean in business?
2. What are the advantages of using special journals for cash receipts and cash payments?
3. Describe a full endorsement.
4. What is a petty cash voucher?
5. When is the petty cash fund replenished?

(Answers to Comprehensive Self Review are on page 348.)

Discussion Questions

1. Why are MICR numbers printed on deposit slips and checks?
2. What is a check?
3. What type of information is entered on a check stub? Why should a check stub be prepared before the check is written?
4. What information is shown on the bank statement?
5. Why is a bank reconciliation prepared?
6. What is the book balance of cash?
7. Give some reasons why the bank balance and the book balance of cash might differ.
8. Why are journal entries sometimes needed after the bank reconciliation statement is prepared?
9. What procedures are used to achieve internal control over banking activities?

10. Explain the meaning of the following terms.
    a. Canceled check
    b. Outstanding check
    c. Deposit in transit
    d. Debit memorandum
    e. Credit memorandum
    f. Dishonored check
    g. Blank endorsement
    h. Deposit slip
    i. Drawee
    j. Restrictive endorsement
    k. Payee
    l. Drawer
    m. Service charge
11. Describe the major controls for cash receipts.
12. Explain what *bonding* means. How does bonding relate to safeguarding cash?
13. Describe the major controls for cash payments.
14. What is a promissory note? What entry is made to record the collection of a promissory note and interest? Which journal is used?
15. Why do some wholesale businesses offer cash discounts to their customers?
16. How does a wholesale business record a check received on account from a customer when a cash discount is involved? Which journal is used?
17. How does a firm record a payment on account to a creditor when a cash discount is involved? Which journal is used?
18. What type of account is **Purchases Discounts?** How is this account presented on the income statement?
19. When are petty cash expenditures entered in a firm's accounting records?
20. Describe the major controls for petty cash.
21. How are cash shortages and overages recorded?
22. Which type of endorsement is most appropriate for a business to use?

Applications

EXERCISES

Recording cash receipts.

The following transactions took place at Comfort Zone Shoe Store during the first week of September 20--. Indicate how these transactions would be entered in a cash receipts journal.

◄ **Exercise 9-1**
Objective 1

DATE		TRANSACTIONS
Sept.	1	Had cash sales of $2,800 plus sales tax of $112; there was a cash overage of $4.
	2	Collected $360 on account from Brenda Joy, a credit customer.
	3	Had cash sales of $2,500 plus sales tax of $100.
	4	Angela Sadler, the owner, made an additional cash investment of $14,000.
	5	Had cash sales of $3,200 plus sales tax of $128; there was a cash shortage of $10.

Recording cash payments.

The following transactions took place at Comfort Zone Shoe Store during the first week of September 20--. Indicate how these transactions would be entered in a cash payments journal.

◄ **Exercise 9-2**
Objective 4

DATE		TRANSACTIONS
Sept.	1	Issued Check 5038 for $1,200 to pay the monthly rent.
	1	Issued Check 5039 for $2,440 to Amos Company, a creditor, on account.
	2	Issued Check 5040 for $5,120 to purchase new equipment.
	2	Issued Check 5041 for $992 to remit sales tax to the state sales tax authority.
	3	Issued Check 5042 for $1,372 to Nathan Company, a creditor, on account for invoice of $1,400 less cash discount of $28.
	4	Issued Check 5043 for $1,180 to purchase merchandise.
	5	Issued Check 5044 for $1,500 as a cash withdrawal for personal use by Angela Sadler, the owner.

Recording the establishment of a petty cash fund.

On January 2 Davis Insurance Company issued Check 7921 for $150 to establish a petty cash fund. Indicate how this transaction would be recorded in a cash payments journal.

◄ **Exercise 9-3**
Objective 6

Recording the replenishment of a petty cash fund.

On January 31 Fox Inc. issued Check 4431 to replenish its petty cash fund. An analysis of payments from the fund showed these totals: **Supplies,** $84; **Delivery Expense,** $72; and **Miscellaneous Expense,** $60. Indicate how this transaction would be recorded in a cash payments journal.

◄ **Exercise 9-4**
Objective 6

Analyzing bank reconciliation items.

At Marshall Security Company the following items were found to cause a difference between the bank statement and the firm's records. Indicate whether each item will affect the bank balance or the book balance when the bank reconciliation statement is prepared. Also indicate which items will require an accounting entry after the bank reconciliation is completed.

1. A deposit in transit.

2. A debit memorandum for a dishonored check.

3. A credit memorandum for a promissory note that the bank collected for Marshall.

4. An error found in Marshall's records, which involves the amount of a check. The firm's checkbook and cash payments journal indicate $404 as the amount, but the canceled check itself and the listing on the bank statement show that $440 was the actual sum.

5. An outstanding check.

6. A bank service charge.

7. A check issued by another firm that was charged to Marshall's account by mistake.

Determining an adjusted bank balance.

Gagliardi Corporation received a bank statement showing a balance of $29,840 as of October 31, 20--. The firm's records showed a book balance of $28,724 on October 31. The difference between the two balances was caused by the following items. Prepare the adjusted bank balance section and the adjusted book balance section of the bank reconciliation statement. Also prepare the necessary journal entry.

1. A debit memorandum for an NSF check from Jim Night for $600.

2. Three outstanding checks: Check 7107 for $258, Check 7125 for $130 and Check 7147 for $3,066.

3. A bank service charge of $24.

4. A deposit in transit of $1,714.

Preparing a bank reconciliation statement.

Wilner Building Supply Company received a bank statement showing a balance of $135,810 as of March 31, 20--. The firm's records showed a book balance of $138,774 on March 31. The difference between the two balances was caused by the following items. Prepare a bank reconciliation statement for the firm as of March 31 and the necessary journal entries from the statement.

1. A debit memorandum for $42, which covers the bank's collection fee for the note.

2. A deposit in transit of $7,440.

3. A check for $534 issued by another firm that was mistakenly charged to Wilner's account.

4. A debit memorandum for an NSF check of $11,550 issued by Ames Construction Company, a credit customer.

5. Outstanding checks: Check 8237 for $4,260; Check 8244 for $342.

6. A credit memorandum for a $12,000 noninterest-bearing note receivable that the bank collected for the firm.

Problems

Selected problems can be completed using:
🍎 **Peachtree**   📘 **QuickBooks**   ▦ **Spreadsheets**

PROBLEM SET A

Journalizing cash receipts and posting to the general ledger.

Movies To Go is a retail store that rents movies and sells blank and prerecorded videocassettes. The firm's cash receipts for February are listed below and on page 326. The general ledger accounts used to record these transactions appear below.

◄ **Problem 9-1A**
Objectives 1, 2, 3

INSTRUCTIONS

1. Open the general ledger accounts and enter the balances as of February 1, 20--.

2. Record the transactions in a cash receipts journal. Use 3 as the page number.

3. Post the individual entries from the Other Accounts Credit section of the cash receipts journal to the proper general ledger accounts.

4. Total, prove, and rule the cash receipts journal as of February 28, 20--.

5. Post the column totals from the cash receipts journal to the proper general ledger accounts.

GENERAL LEDGER ACCOUNTS

101	Cash	$ 9,920 Dr.	401	Sales
109	Notes Receivable	700 Dr.	491	Interest Income
111	Accounts Receivable	2,050 Dr.	620	Cash Short or Over
129	Supplies	1,220 Dr.		
231	Sales Tax Payable	590 Cr.		
301	Durwood McGrew, Capital	68,000 Cr.		

DATE		TRANSACTIONS
Feb.	3	Received $250 from Kirk Walker, a credit customer, on account.
	5	Received a cash refund of $60 for damaged supplies.
	7	Had cash sales of $4,280 plus sales tax of $214 during the first week of February; there was a cash shortage of $10.
	9	Durwood McGrew, the owner, invested an additional $10,000 cash in the business.
	12	Received $190 from Kim Reno, a credit customer, in payment of her account.
	14	Had cash sales of $3,520 plus sales tax of $176 during the second week of February; there was an overage of $4.
	16	Received $420 from Kelly Rock, a credit customer, to apply toward her account.
	19	Received a check from Michael Lane to pay his $700 promissory note plus interest of $14.
	21	Had cash sales of $3,240 plus sales tax of $162 during the third week of February.
		Continued

DATE	(9-1A cont.)	TRANSACTIONS
Feb. 25	Jason Bolima, a credit customer, sent a check for $290 to pay the balance he owes.	
28	Had cash sales of $3,960 plus sales tax of $198 during the fourth week of February; there was a cash shortage of $6.	

Analyze: What total accounts receivable were collected in February?

Problem 9-2A ►
Objectives 4, 5, 6

Journalizing cash payments, recording petty cash, and posting to the general ledger.

The cash payments of Crown Jewelry Store, a retail business, for June are listed below and on page 327. The general ledger accounts used to record these transactions appear below.

INSTRUCTIONS

1. Open the general ledger accounts and enter the balances as of June 1.
2. Record all payments by check in a cash payments journal; use 8 as the page number.
3. Record all payments from the petty cash fund on a petty cash analysis sheet; use 8 as the sheet number.
4. Post the individual entries from the Other Accounts Debit section of the cash payments journal to the proper general ledger accounts.
5. Total, prove, and rule the petty cash analysis sheet as of June 30. Record the replenishment of the fund and the final balance on the sheet.
6. Total, prove, and rule the cash payments journal as of June 30.
7. Post the column totals from the cash payments journal to the proper general ledger accounts.

GENERAL LEDGER ACCOUNTS

101	Cash	$48,960 Dr.
105	Petty Cash Fund	
129	Supplies	2,120 Dr.
201	Notes Payable	2,800 Cr.
205	Accounts Payable	17,840 Cr.
231	Sales Tax Payable	3,920 Cr.
302	Lenny Jefferson, Drawing	
451	Sales Returns and Allowances	
504	Purchases Discounts	
611	Delivery Expense	
620	Rent Expense	
623	Salaries Expense	
626	Telephone Expense	
634	Interest Expense	
635	Miscellaneous Expense	

DATE	TRANSACTIONS
June 1	Issued Check 1241 for $2,400 to pay the monthly rent.
2	Issued Check 1242 for $3,920 to remit the state sales tax.
3	Issued Check 1243 for $2,300 to Digital Watch Company, a creditor, in payment of Invoice 8086, dated May 5.
	Continued

DATE	(9-2A cont.)	TRANSACTIONS
June 4		Issued Check 1244 for $400 to establish a petty cash fund. (After journalizing this transaction, be sure to enter it on the first line of the petty cash analysis sheet.)
	5	Paid $60 from the petty cash fund for office supplies, Petty Cash Voucher 1.
	7	Issued Check 1245 for $2,884 to Evergreen Corporation in payment of a $2,800 promissory note and interest of $84.
	8	Paid $40 from the petty cash fund for postage stamps, Petty Cash Voucher 2.
	10	Issued Check 1246 for $520 to a customer as a cash refund for a defective watch that was returned; the original sale was made for cash.
	12	Issued Check 1247 for $312 to pay the telephone bill.
	14	Issued Check 1248 for $4,900 to Rudy Importers, a creditor, in payment of Invoice 2986, dated May 6 ($5,000), less a cash discount ($100).
	15	Paid $37 from the petty cash fund for delivery service, Petty Cash Voucher 3.
	17	Issued Check 1249 for $700 to purchase store supplies.
	20	Issued Check 1250 for $2,744 to Flashy Chains, Inc., a creditor, in payment of Invoice 3115, dated June 12 ($2,800), less a cash discount ($56).
	22	Paid $48 from the petty cash fund for a personal withdrawal by Lenny Jefferson, the owner, Petty Cash Voucher 4.
	25	Paid $60 from the petty cash fund to have the store windows washed and repaired, Petty Cash Voucher 5.
	27	Issued Check 1251 for $3,560 to Emerald Creations, a creditor, in payment of Invoice 566, dated May 30.
	30	Paid $47 from the petty cash fund for delivery service, Petty Cash Voucher 6.
	30	Issued Check 1252 for $7,000 to pay the monthly salaries.
	30	Issued Check 1253 for $6,000 to Lenny Jefferson, the owner, as a withdrawal for personal use.
	30	Issued Check 1254 for $292 to replenish the petty cash fund. (Foot the columns of the petty cash analysis sheet in order to determine the accounts that should be debited and the amounts involved.)

Analyze: What total payments were made from the petty cash fund for the month?

Journalizing sales and cash receipts and posting to the general ledger.

◄ **Problem 9-3A**
Objectives 1, 2, 3

Sounds Unlimited is a wholesale business that sells musical instruments. Transactions involving sales and cash receipts for the firm during April 20-- follow, along with the general ledger accounts used to record these transactions.

1. Open the general ledger accounts and enter the balances as of April 1, 20--.

2. Record the transactions in a sales journal, a cash receipts journal, and a general journal. Use 6 as the page number for each of the special journals and 16 as the page number for the general journal.

3. Post the entries from the general journal to the general ledger.

4. Total, prove, and rule the special journals as of April 30, 20--.

5. Post the column totals from the special journals to the proper general ledger accounts.

6. Prepare the heading and the Revenue section of the firm's income statement for the month ended April 30.

GENERAL LEDGER ACCOUNTS

101	Cash	$ 8,200 Dr.
109	Notes Receivable	
111	Accounts Receivable	10,500 Dr.
401	Sales	
451	Sales Returns and Allowances	
452	Sales Discounts	

DATE	TRANSACTIONS
April 1	Sold merchandise for $3,700 to Alto Music Center; issued Invoice 1239 with terms of 2/10, n/30.
3	Received a check for $1,430.80 from Band Shop in payment of Invoice 1237 of March 24 ($1,460), less a cash discount ($29.20).
5	Sold merchandise for $1,270 in cash to a new customer who has not yet established credit.
8	Sold merchandise for $4,840 to The Music Store; issued Invoice 1240 with terms of 2/10, n/30.
10	Alto Music Center sent a check for $3,626 in payment of Invoice 1239 of April 1 ($3,700), less a cash discount ($74).
15	Accepted a return of damaged merchandise from The Music Store; issued Credit Memorandum 108 for $700; the original sale was made on Invoice 1240 of April 8.
19	Sold merchandise for $10,340 to Emporium Music Center; issued Invoice 1241 with terms of 2/10, n/30.
23	Collected $2,960 from Golden Oldies Shop for Invoice 1232 of March 25.
26	Accepted a two-month promissory note for $5,200 from Webster's Country Music Store in settlement of its overdue account; the note has an interest rate of 12 percent.
28	Received a check for $10,133.20 from Emporium Music Center in payment of Invoice 1241, dated April 19 ($10,340), less a cash discount ($206.80).
30	Sold merchandise for $8,990 to Jam Sounds, Inc.; issued Invoice 1242 with terms of 2/10, n/30.

Analyze: What total sales on account were made in the month of April prior to any returns or allowances?

Journalizing purchases, cash payments, and purchases discounts; posting to the general ledger.

◀ **Problem 9-4A**
Objectives 4, 5

The Joggers Outlet Center is a retail store. Transactions involving purchases and cash payments for the firm during June 20-- are listed below and on page 330. The general ledger accounts used to record these transactions appear below.

INSTRUCTIONS

1. Open the general ledger accounts and enter the balances as of June 1, 20--.

2. Record the transactions in a purchases journal, a cash payments journal, and a general journal. Use 7 as the page number for each of the special journals and 18 as the page number for the general journal.

3. Post the entries from the general journal and from the Other Accounts Debit section of the cash payments journal to the proper general ledger accounts.

4. Total, prove, and rule the special journals as of June 30.

5. Post the column totals from the special journals to the general ledger.

6. Show how the firm's net cost of purchases would be reported on its income statement for the month ended June 30.

GENERAL LEDGER ACCOUNTS

101	Cash	$19,660 Dr.	
131	Equipment	28,000 Dr.	
201	Notes Payable		
205	Accounts Payable	2,440 Cr.	
501	Purchases		

503 Purchases Ret. and Allow.
504 Purchases Discounts
611 Rent Expense
614 Salaries Expense
617 Telephone Expense

DATE	TRANSACTIONS
June 1	Issued Check 1580 for $1,450 to pay the monthly rent.
3	Purchased merchandise for $2,200 from Variety Shoe Shop, Invoice 476, dated May 30; the terms are 2/10, n/30.
5	Purchased new store equipment for $3,000 from Wilson Company, Invoice 6790 dated June 4, net payable in 30 days.
7	Issued Check 1581 for $1,380 to Hikers and Bikers Clothing Company, a creditor, in payment of Invoice 4233 of May 9.
8	Issued Check 1582 for $2,156 to Variety Shoe Shop, a creditor, in payment of Invoice 476 dated May 30 ($2,200), less a cash discount ($44).
12	Purchased merchandise for $1,700 from Mundy's Coat Shop, Invoice 2992, dated June 9, net due and payable in 30 days.
15	Issued Check 1583 for $190 to pay the monthly telephone bill.
	Continued

DATE	(9-4A cont.)	TRANSACTIONS
June 18		Received Credit Memorandum 423 for $530 from Mundy's Coat Shop for defective goods that were returned; the original purchase was made on Invoice 2992 dated June 9.
21		Purchased new store equipment for $8,000 from Smith Company; issued a three-month promissory note with interest at 11 percent.
23		Purchased merchandise for $4,500 from Racing Products, Invoice 7219, dated June 20; terms of 2/10, n/30.
25		Issued Check 1584 for $1,060 to Mundy's Coat Shop, a creditor, in payment of Invoice 1674 dated May 28.
28		Issued Check 1585 for $4,410 to Racing Products, a creditor, in payment of Invoice 7219 of June 20 ($4,500), less a cash discount ($90).
30		Purchased merchandise for $1,820 from Running Shoes Store, Invoice 1347, dated June 26; the terms are 1/10, n/30.
30		Issued Check 1586 for $3,600 to pay the monthly salaries of the employees.

Analyze: What total liabilities does the company have at month-end?

Problem 9-5A ►
Objectives 9, 10

SPREADSHEET

Preparing a bank reconciliation statement and journalizing entries to adjust the cash balance.

On May 2, 20--, Dream Vacations received its April bank statement from First State Bank. Enclosed with the bank statement, which appears on page 331, was a debit memorandum for $80 that covered an NSF check issued by Porter Watson, a credit customer. The firm's checkbook contained the following information about deposits made and checks issued during April. The balance of the **Cash** account and the checkbook on April 30, 20--, was $7,944.

DATE	TRANSACTIONS	
April 1	Balance	$12,178
1	Check 1144	200
3	Check 1145	600
5	Deposit	700
5	Check 1146	550
10	Check 1147	4,000
17	Check 1148	100
19	Deposit	300
22	Check 1149	18
23	Deposit	300
26	Check 1150	400
28	Check 1151	36
30	Check 1152	30
30	Deposit	400

FIRST STATE BANK

Dream Vacations
895 Martin Luther King Drive
Atlanta, GA 30305

Account Number: 56-7874-09

Period Ending April 30, 20--

CHECKS		DEPOSITS	DATE	BALANCE
			Beginning Balance	
			March 31	12,178.00
200.00-		700.00+	April 6	12,678.00
550.00-	600.00-		April 10	11,528.00
4,000.00-			April 13	7,528.00
3.30- SC			April 14	7,524.70
		300.00+	April 20	7,824.70
100.00-			April 22	7,724.70
		300.00+	April 25	8,024.70
			April 26	8,006.70
18.00-			April 29	7,526.70
400.00-	80.00- DM			

1. Prepare a bank reconciliation statement for the firm as of April 30, 20--.

2. Record general journal entries for any items on the bank reconciliation statement that must be journalized. Date the entries May 2, 20--.

Analyze: What checks remain outstanding after the bank statement has been reconciled?

Preparing a bank reconciliation statement and journalizing entries to adjust the cash balance.

◄ **Problem 9-6A**
Objectives 9, 10

On August 31, 20--, the balance in the checkbook and the **Cash** account of the Jefferson Inn was $23,098. The balance shown on the bank statement on the same date was $23,564.10.

Notes

a. The firm's records indicate that a $1,759.20 deposit dated August 30 and a $953.60 deposit dated August 31 do not appear on the bank statement.

b. A service charge of $9 and a debit memorandum of $160 covering an NSF check have not yet been entered in the firm's records. (The check was issued by Don Grant, a credit customer.)

c. The following checks were issued but have not yet been paid by the bank.

Check 684, $221.00
Check 685, $23.20
Check 688, $476.40
Check 708, $1,152.60
Check 711, $154.70
Check 713, $290.00

d. A credit memorandum shows that the bank collected a $1,000 note receivable and interest of $30 for the firm. These amounts have not yet been entered in the firm's records.

INSTRUCTIONS

1. Prepare a bank reconciliation statement for the firm as of August 31.

2. Record general journal entries for items on the bank reconciliation statement that must be journalized. Date the entries September 4, 20--.

Analyze: What effect did the journal entries recorded as a result of the bank reconciliation have on the fundamental accounting equation?

Problem 9-7A ▶
Objectives 9, 10

Correcting errors revealed by a bank reconciliation.

During the bank reconciliation process at Teel Company on May 2, 20--, the following two errors were discovered in the firm's records.

a. The checkbook and the cash payments journal indicated that Check 4021 dated April 10 was issued for $700 to make a cash purchase of supplies. However, examination of the canceled check and the listing on the bank statement showed that the actual amount of the check was $70.

b. The checkbook and the cash payments journal indicated that Check 4712 dated April 18 was issued for $332 to pay a utility bill. However, examination of the canceled check and the listing on the bank statement showed that the actual amount of the check was $372.

INSTRUCTIONS

1. Prepare the adjusted book balance section of the firm's bank reconciliation statement. The book balance as of April 30 was $17,126. The errors listed above are the only two items that affect the book balance.

2. Prepare general journal entries to correct the errors. Date the entries May 2, 20--. Check 4021 was debited to **Supplies** on April 10, and Check 4712 was debited to **Utilities Expense** on April 18.

Analyze: If the errors described had not been corrected, would net income for the period be overstated or understated? By what amount?

PROBLEM SET B

Problem 9-1B ▶
Objectives 1, 2, 3

Journalizing cash receipts and posting to the general ledger.

The Reading Den is a retail store that sells books, cards, business supplies, and novelties. The firm's cash receipts during June 20-- are shown on page 333. The general ledger accounts used to record these transactions appear below.

INSTRUCTIONS

1. Open the general ledger accounts and enter the balances as of June 1.

2. Record the transactions in a cash receipts journal. (Use page 12.)

3. Post the individual entries from the Other Accounts Credit section of the cash receipts journal to the proper general ledger accounts.

4. Total, prove, and rule the cash receipts journal as of June 30.

5. From the cash receipts journal, post the totals to the general ledger.

GENERAL LEDGER ACCOUNTS

102	Cash	$ 600	231	Sales Tax Payable	$ 200
111	Accounts Receivable	4,200	302	James Walker, Capital	3,800
115	Notes Receivable	1,400	401	Sales	
129	Office Supplies	500	791	Interest Income	

DATE		TRANSACTIONS
June	3	Received $200 from Night Hawk Copy Center, a credit customer.
	4	Received a check for $1,500 from Juan Gonzo to pay his note receivable; the total included $100 of interest.
	5	Received a $180 refund for damaged supplies purchased from Cards-R-Us.
	7	Recorded cash sales of $1,400 plus sales tax payable of $84.
	10	Received $700 from Vicky Neal, a credit customer.
	13	James Walker, the owner, contributed additional capital of $5,000 to the business.
	14	Recorded cash sales of $800 plus sales tax of $48.
	18	Received $580 from David Jackson, a credit customer.
	19	Received $600 from Jane Todd, a credit customer.
	21	Recorded cash sales of $1,300 plus sales tax of $78.
	27	Received $400 from Richard Sneed, a credit customer.

Analyze: What are total assets for The Reading Den at June 30, 20--?

Journalizing cash payments and recording petty cash; posting to the general ledger.

◄ **Problem 9-2B**
Objectives 4, 5, 6

The cash payments of International Gift Shop, a retail business, for September are listed below and on pages 334–335. The general ledger accounts used to record these transactions appear below and on page 334.

INSTRUCTIONS

1. Open the general ledger accounts and enter the balances as of September 1, 20--.

2. Record all payments by check in a cash payments journal. Use 10 as the page number.

3. Record all payments from the petty cash fund on a petty cash analysis sheet with special columns for **Delivery Expense** and **Miscellaneous Expense.** Use 10 as the sheet number.

4. Post the individual entries from the Other Accounts Debit section of the cash payments journal to the proper general ledger accounts.

5. Total, prove, and rule the petty cash analysis sheet as of September 30, then record the replenishment of the fund and the final balance on the sheet.

6. Total, prove, and rule the cash payments journal as of September 30.

7. Post the column totals from the cash payments journal to the proper general ledger accounts.

GENERAL LEDGER ACCOUNTS

101	Cash	$10,765	Dr.
105	Petty Cash Fund		
141	Equipment	21,500	Dr.
201	Notes Payable	840	Cr.
205	Accounts Payable	3,985	Cr.
231	Sales Tax Payable	672	Cr.

GENERAL LEDGER ACCOUNTS (cont.)

302 Peter Chen, Drawing
451 Sales Ret. and Allow.
504 Purchases Discounts
511 Delivery Expense
611 Interest Expense
614 Miscellaneous Expense
620 Rent Expense
623 Salaries Expense
626 Telephone Expense

DATE		TRANSACTIONS
Sept.	1	Issued Check 394 for $672 to remit sales tax to the state tax commission.
	2	Issued Check 395 for $850 to pay the monthly rent.
	4	Issued Check 396 for $75 to establish a petty cash fund. (After journalizing this transaction, be sure to enter it on the first line of the petty cash analysis sheet.)
	5	Issued Check 397 for $1,176 to Crystal Glassware, a creditor, in payment of Invoice 9367, dated August 28 ($1,200), less a cash discount ($24).
	6	Paid $10.50 from the petty cash fund for delivery service, Petty Cash Voucher 1.
	9	Purchased store equipment for $500; issued Check 398.
	11	Paid $8 from the petty cash fund for office supplies, Petty Cash Voucher 2 (charge to **Miscellaneous Expense**).
	13	Issued Check 399 for $485 to Scott Company, a creditor, in payment of Invoice 2579, dated August 15.
	14	Issued Check 400 for $57 to a customer as a cash refund for a defective watch that was returned; the original sale was made for cash.
	16	Paid $15 from the petty cash fund for a personal withdrawal by Peter Chen, the owner, Petty Cash Voucher 3.
	18	Issued Check 401 for $92 to pay the monthly telephone bill.
	21	Issued Check 402 for $735 to European Imports, a creditor, in payment of Invoice 2218, dated September 13 ($750), less a cash discount ($15).
	23	Paid $12 from the petty cash fund for postage stamps, Petty Cash Voucher 4.
	24	Issued Check 403 for $854 to Simpson Corporation in payment of an $840 promissory note and interest of $14.
	26	Issued Check 404 for $620 to Pacific Ceramics, a creditor, in payment of Invoice 1035, dated August 29.
	27	Paid $9 from the petty cash fund for delivery service, Petty Cash Voucher 5.
	28	Issued Check 405 for $1,200 to Peter Chen, the owner, as a withdrawal for personal use.
		Continued

DATE	(9-2B cont.) TRANSACTIONS
Sept. 30	Issued Check 406 for $1,900 to pay the monthly salaries of the employees.
30	Issued Check 407 for $68 to replenish the petty cash fund. (Foot the columns of the petty cash analysis sheet in order to determine the accounts that should be debited and the amounts involved.)

Analyze: What was the amount of total debits to general ledger liability accounts during the month of September?

Journalizing sales and cash receipts and posting to the general ledger.

◄ **Problem 9-3B**
Objectives 1, 2, 3

Thomas Construction Company is a wholesale business. The transactions involving sales and cash receipts for the firm during August 20-- are listed below and on page 336. The general ledger accounts used to record these transactions are listed below.

INSTRUCTIONS

1. Open the general ledger accounts and enter the balances as of August 1, 20--.
2. Record the transactions in a sales journal, a cash receipts journal, and a general journal. Use 9 as the page number for each of the special journals and 25 as the page number for the general journal.
3. Post the entries from the general journal to the proper general ledger accounts.
4. Total, prove, and rule the special journals as of August 31, 20--.
5. Post the column totals from the special journals to the proper general ledger accounts.
6. Prepare the heading and the Revenue section of the firm's income statement for the month ended August 31, 20--.

GENERAL LEDGER ACCOUNTS

101 Cash	$12,680 Dr.	401 Sales	
109 Notes Receivable		451 Sales Returns and Allowances	
111 Accounts Receivable	20,200 Dr.	452 Sales Discounts	

DATE	TRANSACTIONS
Aug. 1	Received a check for $5,390 from Builders Supply Company in payment of Invoice 7782 dated July 21 ($5,500), less a cash discount ($110).
2	Sold merchandise for $14,960 to Wilson Builders; issued Invoice 7928 with terms of 2/10, n/30.
4	Accepted a three-month promissory note for $9,000 from Henderson Homes to settle its overdue account; the note has an interest rate of 11 percent.
7	Sold merchandise for $18,690 to Colonial Construction Company; issued Invoice 7929 with terms of 2/10, n/30.
11	Collected $14,660.80 from Wilson Builders for Invoice 7928 dated August 2 ($14,960), less a cash discount ($299.20).
	Continued

DATE	(9-3B cont.) TRANSACTIONS
Aug. 14	Sold merchandise for $3,500 in cash to a new customer who has not yet established credit.
16	Colonial Construction Company sent a check for $18,316.20 in payment of Invoice 7929 dated August 7 ($18,690), less a cash discount ($373.80).
22	Sold merchandise for $6,260 to Modern Homes; issued Invoice 7930 with terms of 2/10, n/30.
24	Received a check for $5,000 from Harrison Homes Center to pay Invoice 7778, dated July 23.
26	Accepted a return of damaged merchandise from Modern Homes; issued Credit Memorandum 311 for $420; the original sale was made on Invoice 7930, dated August 22.
31	Sold merchandise for $12,740 to Warren County Builders; issued Invoice 7931 with terms of 2/10, n/30.

Analyze: What total sales on account were made in August? Include sales returns and allowances in your computation.

Problem 9-4B ▶
Objectives 4, 5

Journalizing purchases, cash payments, and purchase discounts; posting to the general ledger.

Best Value Center is a retail store that sells a variety of household appliances. Transactions involving purchases and cash payments for the firm during December 20-- are listed on page 337. The general ledger accounts used to record these transactions appear below.

INSTRUCTIONS

1. Open the general ledger accounts and enter the balances in these accounts as of December 1, 20--.
2. Record the transactions in a purchases journal, a cash payments journal, and a general journal. Use 11 as the page number for each of the special journals and 32 as the page number for the general journal.
3. Post the entries from the general journal and from the Other Accounts Debit section of the cash payments journal to the proper accounts in the general ledger.
4. Total, prove, and rule the special journals as of December 31, 20--.
5. Post the column totals from the special journals to the general ledger accounts.
6. Show how the firm's cost of purchases would be reported on its income statement for the month ended December 31, 20--.

GENERAL LEDGER ACCOUNTS

101	Cash	$45,700	Dr.
131	Equipment	62,000	Dr.
201	Notes Payable		
205	Accounts Payable	3,800	Cr.
501	Purchases		
503	Purchases Returns and Allowances		
504	Purchases Discounts		
611	Rent Expense		
614	Salaries Expense		
617	Telephone Expense		

DATE		TRANSACTIONS
Dec.	1	Purchased merchandise for $6,400 from Axis Products for Homes, Invoice 5965, dated November 28; the terms are 2/10, n/30.
	2	Issued Check 1506 for $2,800 to pay the monthly rent.
	4	Purchased new store equipment for $13,000 from Blaine Company; issued a two-month promissory note with interest at 10 percent.
	6	Issued Check 1507 for $6,272 to Axis Products for Homes, a creditor, in payment of Invoice 5965, dated November 28 ($6,400), less a cash discount ($128).
	10	Purchased merchandise for $8,900 from the Parr Corporation, Invoice 9115, dated December 7; terms of 2/10, n/30.
	13	Issued Check 1508 for $240 to pay the monthly telephone bill.
	15	Issued Check 1509 for $8,722 to Parr Corporation, a creditor, in payment of Invoice 9115, dated December 7 ($8,900), less a cash discount ($178).
	18	Purchased merchandise for $11,800 from Appliance Center, Invoice 8372, dated December 16; terms of 3/10, n/30.
	20	Purchased new store equipment for $4,000 from Security Systems Inc., Invoice 635, dated December 17, net payable in 45 days.
	21	Issued Check 1510 for $3,800 to Hogan Lighting and Appliances, a creditor, in payment of Invoice 1378, dated November 23.
	22	Purchased merchandise for $5,300 from Davis Corporation, Invoice 6131, dated December 19, net due in 30 days.
	24	Issued Check 1511 for $11,446 to Appliance Center, a creditor, in payment of Invoice 8372, dated December 16 ($11,800), less a cash discount ($354).
	28	Received Credit Memorandum 128 for $900 from Security Systems Inc. for damaged goods that were returned; the original purchase was made on Invoice 635, dated December 17.
	31	Issued Check 1512 for $5,400 to pay the monthly salaries of the employees.

Analyze: List the dates for transactions in December that would be categorized as expenses of the business.

Preparing a bank reconciliation statement and journalizing entries to adjust the cash balance.

◄ **Problem 9-5B**
Objectives 9, 10

On October 5, 20--, Sam Yao, Attorney at Law, received his September bank statement from First Security National Bank. Enclosed with the bank statement, which appears on page 338, was a debit memorandum for $112 that covered an NSF check issued by Julia Anderson, a credit customer. The firm's checkbook contained the following information about deposits made and checks issued during September. The balance of the **Cash** account and the checkbook on September 30 was $16,622.

DATE		TRANSACTIONS	
Sept.	1	Balance	$13,000
	1	Check 124	200
	3	Check 125	20
	3	Deposit	1,000
	6	Check 126	450
	10	Deposit	820
	11	Check 127	400
	15	Check 128	150
	21	Check 129	120
	22	Deposit	1,460
	25	Check 130	8
	25	Check 131	40
	27	Check 132	70
	28	Deposit	1,800

FIRST SECURITY NATIONAL BANK

Sam Yao, Attorney-at-Law
2222 Sam Houston Lane
Columbus, OH 44106

Account Number: 11-4568-03

Period Ending September 30, 20--

CHECKS	DEPOSITS	DATE	BALANCE
Beginning Balance		August 31	13,000.00
	1,000.00+	September 3	14,000.00
200.00-		September 6	13,800.00
400.00-	20.00-	820.00+	September 11	14,200.00
450.00-		September 15	13,750.00
120.00-		September 19	13,630.00
	1,460.00+	September 23	15,090.00
40.00-	8.00-	September 25	15,042.00
7.50- SC	112.00- DM	September 28	14,922.50

INSTRUCTIONS

1. Prepare a bank reconciliation statement for the firm as of September 30, 20--.

2. Record general journal entries for any items on the bank reconciliation statement that must be journalized. Date the entries October 5, 20--.

Analyze: How many checks were paid (cleared the bank) according to the September 30 bank statement?

Preparing a bank reconciliation statement and journalizing entries to adjust the cash balance.

◀ **Problem 9-6B**
Objectives 9, 10

On June 30, 20--, the balance in Wilson Builder's checkbook and **Cash** account was $12,837.18. The balance shown on the bank statement on the same date was $15,084.06.

Notes

a. The following checks were issued but have not yet been paid by the bank: Check 335 for $297.90, Check 337 for $195, and Check 339 for $850.80.

b. A credit memorandum shows that the bank has collected a $3,000 note receivable and interest of $60 for the firm. These amounts have not yet been entered in the firm's records.

c. The firm's records indicate that a deposit of $1,888.14 made on June 30 does not appear on the bank statement.

d. A service charge of $28.68 and a debit memorandum of $240 covering an NSF check have not yet been entered in the firm's records. (The check was issued by Alan Hutchins, a credit customer.)

INSTRUCTIONS

1. Prepare a bank reconciliation statement for the firm as of June 30, 20--.

2. Record general journal entries for any items on the bank reconciliation statement that must be journalized. Date the entries July 3, 20--.

Analyze: After all journal entries have been recorded and posted, what is the balance in the **Cash** account?

Correcting errors revealed by a bank reconciliation.

◀ **Problem 9-7B**
Objectives 9, 10

During the bank reconciliation process at ABC Liquidators Corporation on March 3, 20--, the following errors were discovered in the firm's records.

a. The checkbook and the cash payments journal indicated that Check 1285 dated February 7 was issued for $158 to pay for hauling expenses. However, examination of the canceled check and the listing on the bank statement showed that the actual amount of the check was $154.

b. The checkbook and the cash payments journal indicated that Check 1292 dated February 23 was issued for $202 to pay a telephone bill. However, examination of the canceled check and the listing on the bank statement showed that the actual amount of the check was $220.

INSTRUCTIONS

1. Prepare the adjusted book balance section of the firm's bank reconciliation statement. The book balance as of February 28, 20--, was $38,902. The errors listed are the only two items that affect the book balance.

2. Prepare general journal entries to correct the errors. Date the entries March 3, 20--. Check 1285 was debited to **Hauling Expense** on February 7, and Check 1292 was debited to **Telephone Expense** on February 23.

Analyze: What net change to the **Cash** account occurred as a result of the correcting journal entries?

Special Journals

During September 20-- Jo's Specialty Shop, a retail store, had the transactions listed on pages 342–343. The general ledger accounts used to record these transactions are provided on page 341.

INSTRUCTIONS

1. Open the general ledger accounts and enter the balances as of September 1, 20--.

2. Record the transactions in a sales journal, a cash receipts journal, a purchases journal, a cash payments journal, and a general journal. Use page 11 as the page number for each of the special journals and page 31 as the page number for the general journal.

3. Post the entries from the general journal to the proper general ledger accounts.

4. Post the entries from the Other Accounts Credit section of the cash receipts journal to the proper general ledger accounts.

5. Post the entries from the Other Accounts Debit section of the cash payments journal to the proper general ledger accounts.

6. Total, prove, and rule the special journals as of September 30.

7. Post the column totals from the special journals to the proper general ledger accounts.

8. Set up an accounts receivable ledger for Jo's Specialty Shop. Open an account for each of the customers listed below, and enter the balances as of September 1. All of these customers have terms of n/30.

Credit Customers	
Name	Balance 9/01/--
Marty Cooper	
Theresa Den	$ 630.00
Kevin Kaylor	865.20
Lacie Lawson	
George Polk	525.00
Michael Turner	
Ralph Wall	1,050.00

9. Post the individual entries from the sales journal, cash receipts journal, and the general journal to the accounts receivable subsidiary ledger.

10. Prepare a schedule of accounts receivable for September 30, 20--.

11. Check the total of the schedule of accounts receivable against the balance of the **Accounts Receivable** account in the general ledger. The two amounts should be the same.

Creditors		
Name	Balance 9/01/--	Terms
Baker Mills		n/45
McDavid Corporation	$11,000	1/10, n/30
Northern Craft Products		2/10, n/30
Reed Company		n/30
Robertson Mills		2/10, n/30
Sadie's Floor Coverings	3,880	n/30
Wilson Products	4,240	n/30

12. Set up an accounts payable subsidiary ledger for Jo's Specialty Shop. Open an account for each of the creditors listed above, and enter the balances as of September 1, 20--.

13. Post the individual entries from the purchases journal, the cash payments journal, and the general journal to the accounts payable subsidiary ledger.

14. Prepare a schedule of accounts payable for September 1, 20--.

15. Check the total of the schedule of accounts payable against the balance of the **Accounts Payable** account in the general ledger. The two amounts should be the same.

GENERAL LEDGER ACCOUNTS

101	Cash	$37,890.00	Dr.
109	Notes Receivable		
111	Accounts Receivable	3,070.20	Dr.
121	Supplies	1,420.00	Dr.
201	Notes Payable		
205	Accounts Payable	19,120.00	Cr.
231	Sales Tax Payable		
301	Eric Flores, Capital	91,200.00	Cr.
401	Sales		
451	Sales Returns and Allowances		
501	Purchases		
502	Freight In		
503	Purchases Returns and Allowances		
504	Purchases Discounts		
611	Cash Short or Over		
614	Rent Expense		
617	Salaries Expense		
619	Utilities Expense		

DATE	TRANSACTIONS
Sept. 1	Received a check for $525.00 from George Polk to pay his account.
1	Issued Check 1372 for $3,880 to Sadie's Floor Coverings, a creditor, in payment of Invoice 5236 dated August 3.
2	Issued Check 1373 for $2,400 to pay the monthly rent.
3	Sold a table on credit for $1,330 plus sales tax of $66.50 to Lacie Lawson, Sales Slip 1972.
5	Eric Flores, the owner, invested an additional $14,000 cash in the business in order to expand operations.
6	Had cash sales of $3,560 plus sales tax of $178 during the period September 1–6; there was a cash shortage of $10.
6	Purchased carpeting for $8,900 from Robertson Mills, Invoice 728, dated September 3; terms of 2/10, n/30.
6	Issued Check 1374 for $122 to City Trucking Company to pay the freight charge on goods received from Robertson Mills.
8	Purchased store supplies for $740 from Reed Company, Invoice 0442, dated September 6, net amount due in 30 days.
8	Sold chairs on credit for $1,860 plus sales tax of $93.00 to Michael Turner, Sales Slip 1973.
11	Accepted a two-month promissory note for $1,050 from Ralph Wall to settle his overdue account; the note has an interest rate of 10 percent.
11	Issued Check 1375 for $8,722 to Robertson Mills, a creditor, in payment of Invoice 728 dated September 3 ($8,900) less a cash discount ($178).
13	Had cash sales of $3,920 plus sales tax of $196 during the period September 8–13.
14	Purchased carpeting for $7,400 plus a freight charge of $84 from Wilson Products, Invoice 3594, dated September 11, net due and payable in 30 days.
15	Collected $630 on account from Theresa Den.
17	Gave a two-month promissory note for $11,000 to McDavid Corporation, a creditor, to settle an overdue balance; the note bears interest at 12 percent.
19	Sold a lamp on credit to Marty Cooper for $480 plus sales tax of $24, Sales Slip 1974.
20	Had cash sales of $3,300 plus sales tax of $165 during the period September 15–20; there was a cash shortage of $4.50.
21	Purchased area rugs for $5,600 from Northern Craft Products, Invoice 776, dated September 18; the terms are 2/10, n/30.

Continued

DATE	(cont.)	TRANSACTIONS
Sept. 22		Issued Check 1376 for $360 to pay the monthly utility bill.
23		Granted an allowance to Marty Cooper for scratches on the lamp that she bought on Sales Slip 1974 of September 19; issued Credit Memorandum 651 for $42, which includes a price reduction of $40 and sales tax of $2.
24		Received Credit Memorandum 14 for $600 from Northern Craft Products for a damaged rug that was returned; the original purchase was made on Invoice 776 dated September 18.
24		Kevin Kaylor sent a check for $865.20 to pay the balance he owes.
25		Issued Check 1377 for $3,300 to make a cash purchase of merchandise.
26		Issued Check 1378 for $4,900 to Northern Craft Products, a creditor, in payment of Invoice 776 of September 18 ($5,600), less a return ($600) and a cash discount ($100).
27		Purchased hooked rugs for $8,200 plus a freight charge of $112 from Baker Mills, Invoice 1368, dated September 23, net payable in 45 days.
27		Had cash sales of $4,310 plus sales tax of $215.50 during the period September 22–27.
28		Issued Check 1379 for $4,240 to Wilson Products, a creditor, in payment of Invoice 1184 dated August 30.
29		Sold a cabinet on credit to Theresa Den for $1,180 plus sales tax of $59, Sales Slip 1975.
30		Had cash sales of $1,440 plus sales tax of $72 for September 29–30; there was a cash overage of $2.20.
30		Issued Check 1380 for $5,200 to pay the monthly salaries of the employees.

Analyze: What were the total cash payments for September?

CHAPTER 9 CRITICAL THINKING PROBLEM

Cash Controls

James Wilson is the owner of a successful small construction company. He spends most of his time out of the office supervising work at various construction sites, leaving the operation of the office to the company's cashier/bookkeeper, Roberta Smith. Roberta makes bank deposits, pays the company's bills, maintains the accounting records, and prepares monthly bank reconciliations.

Recently a friend told James that while he was at a party he overheard Roberta bragging that she paid for her new dress with money from the company's cash receipts. She said her boss would never know because he never checks the cash records.

James admits that he does not check on Roberta's work. He now wants to know if Roberta is stealing from him. He asks you to examine the company's cash records to determine whether Roberta has stolen cash from the business and, if so, how much.

Your examination of the company's cash records reveals the following information.

1. Roberta prepared the following August 31, 20--, bank reconciliation.

Balance in books, August 31, 20--		$37,572
Additions:		
Outstanding checks		
Check 2778	$1,584	
Check 2792	3,638	
Check 2814	768	5,390
		$42,962
Deductions:		
Deposit in transit, August 28, 20--	$9,764	
Bank service charge	20	9,784
Balance on bank statement, July 31, 20--		$33,178

2. An examination of the general ledger shows the **Cash** account with a balance of $37,572 on August 31, 20--.

3. The August 31 bank statement shows a balance of $33,178.

4. The August 28 deposit of $9,764 does not appear on the August 31 bank statement.

5. A comparison of canceled checks returned with the August 31 bank statement with the cash payments journal reveals the following checks as outstanding:

Check 2419	$ 526
Check 2508	2,436
Check 2724	972
Check 2778	1,584
Check 2792	3,638
Check 2814	768

Prepare a bank statement using the format presented in this chapter for the month of August. Assume there were no bank or bookkeeping errors in August. Did Roberta take cash from the company? If so, how much and how did she try to conceal the theft? What changes would you recommend to James to provide better internal control over cash?

Business Connections

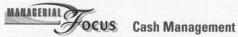
1. The new accountant for Asheville Hardware Center, a large retail store, found the following weaknesses in the firm's cash-handling procedures. How would you explain to management why each of these procedures should be changed?
   a. No cash register proof is prepared at the end of each day. The amount of money in the register is considered the amount of cash sales for the day.
   b. Small payments are sometimes made from the currency and coins in the cash register. (The store has no petty cash fund.)
   c. During busy periods for the firm, cash receipts are sometimes kept on the premises for several days before a bank deposit is made.
   d. When funds are removed from the cash register at the end of each day, they are placed in an unlocked office cabinet until they are deposited.
   e. The person who makes the bank deposits also records them in the checkbook, journalizes cash receipts, and reconciles the bank statement.

2. Why should management be concerned about having accurate information about the firm's cash position available at all times?

3. Many banks now offer a variety of computer services to clients. Why is it not advisable for a firm to pay its bank to complete the reconciliation procedure at the end of each month?

4. Assume that you are the newly hired controller at Norton Company and that you have observed the following banking procedures in use at the firm. Would you change any of these procedures? Why or why not?
   a. A blank endorsement is made on all checks to be deposited.
   b. The checkbook is kept on the top of a desk so that it will be handy.
   c. The same person prepares bank deposits, issues checks, and reconciles the bank statement.
   d. The reconciliation process usually takes place two or three weeks after the bank statement is received.
   e. The bank statement and the canceled checks are thrown away after the reconciliation process is completed.
   f. As a shortcut in the reconciliation process, there is no attempt to compare the endorsements on the back of the canceled checks with the names of the payees shown on the face of these checks.

5. Why should management be concerned about achieving effective internal control over cash receipts and cash payments?

6. How does management benefit when cash transactions are recorded quickly and efficiently?

7. Why do some companies require that all employees who handle cash be bonded?

8. Why is it a good practice for a business to make all payments by check except for minor payments from a petty cash fund?

Connection 2 ▶

Ethical DILEMMA   **Out of Balance** Assume that you are a sales clerk in a retail clothing store. The owner of the business frequently takes cash out of your cash register without explanation and provides you with an IOU slip so that you can reconcile the cash intake with the cash register tape. When you questioned the owner about the use of the funds, he replied, "It's my store, I can take whatever I want."

What do you think of the owner's actions? Is he being ethical?

Connection 3 ▶

*Street***WISE:**

Questions from the Real World   **Cash** Refer to the *1999 Annual Report* of The Home Depot, Inc. in Appendix B.

1. Review the consolidated balance sheet. Store operations provide the company with a significant source of cash. What amount is reported for "Cash and Cash Equivalents" for January 30, 2000? For January 31, 1999? By what percentage has this figure increased?

2. Locate the report named "Selected Consolidated Statements of Earnings Data." How many sales transactions were reported for 1999? What is the average sale per transaction? If 40 percent of these sales were comprised of cash transactions (as opposed to credit transactions), what total cash receipts would have been recorded in 1999?

Connection 4 ▶

Armstrong

FINANCIAL $TATEMENT
ANALYSIS   **Balance Sheet** Armstrong Holdings, Inc. is a global leader in the design, innovation, and manufacture of floors and ceilings. In 1999 Armstrong's net sales totaled more than $3.4 billion. The following excerpt was taken from the company's *1999 Annual Report.*

Consolidated Balance Sheets		
	As of December 31	
Millions except for numbers of shares and per-share data	1999	1998
ASSETS		
Current Assets:		
Cash and cash equivalents*	$ 35.6	$ 38.2
Accounts and notes receivable	436.0	440.4
Total current assets	$1,029.9	$1,121.1
* Cash and Cash Equivalents: Short-term investments that have		
maturities of three months or less when purchased are considered		
to be cash equivalents.		

Analyze:

1. What percentage of total current assets is made up of cash and cash equivalents for fiscal 1999?

2. Cash receipt and cash payment transactions affect the total value of a company's assets. By what amount did the category "Cash and cash equivalents" change from 1998 to 1999?

3. If accountants at Armstrong failed to record cash receipts of $125,000 on the final day of fiscal 1999, what impact would this error have on the balance sheet category "Cash and cash equivalents"?

Analyze Online: Find the *Corporate Information* link on the Web site for Armstrong Holdings, Inc. (**www.armstrong.com**). Review the most recent annual report.

4. What amount is reported for the balance sheet line item "Cash and cash equivalents"?

5. Does this amount represent an increase or decrease from the amount reported in fiscal 1999? By what amount has this figure changed?

Extending **the** *Thought*   **E-commerce** A small gift shop has just launched a new Web site where customers can purchase products. The Web site's e-commerce software systems automatically generate daily sales reports and forward the reports to the gift shop's accountant. The gift shop uses an online e-cash processing company, which deposits cash receipts to the gift shop's bank account automatically. What strategies should the gift shop implement to ensure proper accounting for cash receipts generated from online sales?   ◄ **Connection 5**

Business Communication   **Agenda** You have just been hired as the chief financial officer for a software development company. In an effort to familiarize yourself with the processes of the accounting office, you have requested a meeting with the accounting manager to discuss the company's internal control procedures. To prepare for the meeting, create a list of questions and topics that you would like to discuss. Your list should include questions that will help you verify that the department is enforcing the appropriate controls over cash payments and cash receipts.   ◄ **Connection 6**

Team*Work*   **Petty Cash** Your photo supply store has established a petty cash fund of $200. Form two teams to enact five petty cash transactions.   ◄ **Connection 7**

1. Team 1 should create five receipts that will represent payments from the petty cash fund. Present each receipt individually to Team 2 to receive cash from the fund.

2. Team 2 will act as the manager of the petty cash fund and should prepare the appropriate vouchers as payments are made.

3. After all five payments are made, Team 2 should prepare a petty cash analysis sheet so that the petty cash fund can be replenished to its original balance.

inter **NET**
CONNECTION   "The Fed" The Federal Reserve System is the central bank of the United States. Go to the Web site at **www.federalreserve.gov.** From the *Board of Governors* site, access the related Web site for the *National Information Center of Banking.* Name the three largest banks and the total assets of each bank. From the *Board of Governors* site, access the site for *Federal Reserve Banks.* In which of the 12 Federal Reserve Districts do you live?   ◄ **Connection 8**

Answers to Self Reviews

Answers to Section 1 Self Review

1. A written promise to pay a specified amount of money on a specified date. To grant credit in certain sales transactions or to replace open-account credit when a customer has an overdue balance.
2. Amounts from the Accounts Receivable Credit column are posted as credits to the individual customers' accounts in the accounts receivable subsidiary ledger daily. The total of the Accounts Receivable Credit column is posted as a credit to the **Accounts Receivable** control account in the general ledger at the end of the accounting period.
3. A cash shortage occurs when cash in the register is less than the audit tape; an overage occurs when cash is more than the audit tape. Debit shortages and credit overages in the **Cash Short or Over** account.
4. **d.** all of the above
5. **b.** cash receipts journal
6. The frequency of cash discrepancies indicates that a problem exists in the handling of the cash.

Answers to Section 2 Self Review

1. To make small expenditures that require currency and coins.
2. Record the name of the owner's drawing account and the amount in the Other Accounts Debit section of the cash payments journal, and record the amount in the Cash Credit column.
3. Amounts in the Other Accounts Debit section are posted individually to the general ledger accounts daily. The total of the Other Accounts Debit column is not posted because the individual amounts were previously posted to the general ledger.
4. **a.** cash payments journal
5. **b.** February 4
6. You should explain to your employer that she must keep all receipts regardless of the amount. Ask your employer to complete a voucher for that amount, then record the entry in the proper account.

Answers to Section 3 Self Review

1. A check that is dated in the future. It should not be deposited before its date because the drawer of the check may not have sufficient funds in the bank to cover the check at the current time.
2. Items in the second section of the bank reconciliation statement require entries in the firm's financial records to correct the **Cash** account balance and make it equal to the checkbook balance. These may include bank fees, debit memorandums, NSF checks, and interest income.
3. Endorsement is the legal process by which the payee transfers ownership of the check to the bank.
4. **a.** canceled checks
5. **d.** Deposits in transit
6. Disagree. Good internal control requires separation of duties.

Answers to Comprehensive Self Review

1. Checks, money orders, and funds on deposit in a bank as well as currency and coins.
2. They eliminate repetition in postings; the initial recording of transactions is faster.
3. A full endorsement contains the name of the payee plus the name of the firm or bank to whom the check is payable.
4. A record of when a payment is made from petty cash, the amount and purpose of the expenditure, and the account to be charged.
5. Petty cash can be replenished at any time if the fund runs low, but it should be replenished at the end of each month so that all expenses for the month are recorded.

PART 3

Payroll Records and Procedures

Chapter 10

Payroll Computations, Records, and Payment

Chapter 11

Payroll Taxes, Deposits, and Reports

SAS e-Intelligence

Executives at SAS Institute Inc., a leading provider of business intelligence software and services, believe that happy employees are productive ones. The software leader's award-winning culture earned a No. 2 ranking in *Fortune* magazine's "100 Best Companies to Work For in America" in 2000.

Thinking Critically

What types of benefits, philosophies, or company policies contribute to a happy workforce?

CHAPTER 10

Learning Objectives

1. Explain the major federal laws relating to employee earnings and withholding.

2. Compute gross earnings of employees.

3. Determine employee deductions for social security tax.

4. Determine employee deductions for Medicare tax.

5. Determine employee deductions for income tax.

6. Enter gross earnings, deductions, and net pay in the payroll register.

7. Journalize payroll transactions in the general journal.

8. Maintain an earnings record for each employee.

9. Define the accounting terms new to this chapter.

Payroll Computations, Records, and Payment

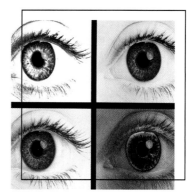

Adobe
www.adobe.com

"*H* ire the best and treat them well." Adobe Systems Incorporated is committed to providing rewarding work experiences for its employees. The company was recognized by *Inter@ctive Week* magazine as one of the "Top 10 Companies to Work For"[1] and placed number 30 in *Fortune* magazine's "100 Best Companies to Work for in America".[2]

Adobe Systems Incorporated distributes paychecks for a workforce of 2,800 employees worldwide. Salaried and hourly wages are computed. Calculations for federal, state, and social security taxes are made and employee payroll records must be updated after each payroll period.

[1] Adobe Press Release, April 12, 2000

[2] Adobe Press Release, December 20, 2000

Thinking Critically
What types of benefits would be important to you if you worked for a company like Adobe Systems Incorporated?

For more information on Adobe Systems Incorporated, go to: collegeaccounting.glencoe.com.

New Terms

Commission basis

Compensation record

Employee

Employee's Withholding Allowance Certificate (Form W-4)

Exempt employees

Federal unemployment taxes

Hourly rate basis

Independent contractor

Individual earnings record

Medicare tax

Payroll register

Piece-rate basis

Salary basis

Social Security Act

Social security (FICA) tax

State unemployment taxes

Tax-exempt wages

Time and a half

Wage-bracket table method

Workers' compensation insurance

Payroll Laws and Taxes

Section Objective

1 Explain the major federal laws relating to employee earnings and withholding.

WHY IT'S IMPORTANT
Tax and labor laws protect the rights of both the employee and the employer. Income tax withholding laws ensure continued funding of certain federal and state programs.

Terms to Learn

employee
federal unemployment taxes
independent contractor
Medicare tax
Social Security Act
social security (FICA) tax
state unemployment taxes
time and a half
workers' compensation
  insurance

A large component of the activity of any business is concerned with payroll work. Payroll accounting is so important that it requires special consideration.

Who Is an Employee?

Payroll accounting relates only to earnings of those individuals classified as employees. An **employee** is hired by and works under the control and direction of the employer. Usually the employer provides the tools or equipment used by the employee, sets the employee's working hours, and determines how the employee completes the job. Examples of employees are the company president, the bookkeeper, the sales clerk, and the warehouse worker.

In contrast to an employee, an **independent contractor** is paid by the company to carry out a specific task or job, but is not under the direct supervision or control of the company. The independent contractor is told what needs to be done, but the means of doing the job is left to the independent contractor. Examples of independent contractors are the accountant who performs the independent audit, the outside attorney who renders legal advice, and the consultant who installs a new accounting system.

This text addresses issues related to employees but not to independent contractors. When dealing with independent contractors, businesses do not have to follow federal labor laws regulating minimum rates of pay and maximum hours of employment. The business is not required to withhold or match payroll taxes on amounts paid to independent contractors.

Federal Employee Earnings and Withholding Laws

Since the 1930s many federal and state laws have affected the relationship between employers and employees. Some of these laws deal with working conditions, including hours and earnings. Others relate to income tax withholding. Some concern taxes that are levied against the employer to provide specific employee benefits.

The Fair Labor Standards Act

The *Fair Labor Standards Act* of 1938, often referred to as the Wage and Hour Law, applies only to firms engaged directly or indirectly in interstate commerce. It sets a minimum hourly rate of pay and maximum hours of work per week to be performed at the regular rate of pay. When this book

1 Objective

Explain the major federal laws relating to employee earnings and withholding.

was printed, the minimum hourly rate of pay was $5.15, and the maximum number of hours at the regular pay rate was 40 hours per week. When an employee works more than 40 hours in a week, the employee earns at least one and one-half times the regular hourly rate of pay. This overtime rate is called **time and a half**. Even if the federal law does not apply to them, many employers pay time and a half for overtime because of union contracts or simply as good business practice.

Social Security Tax

The *Federal Insurance Contributions Act (FICA)* is commonly referred to as the **Social Security Act**. The act, first passed in the 1930s, has been amended frequently. The Social Security Act provides the following benefits:

- Retirement benefits, or pension, when a worker reaches age 62.
- Benefits for the dependents of the retired worker.
- Benefits for the worker and the worker's dependents when the worker is disabled.

These retirement and disability benefits are paid by the **social security tax**, sometimes called the **FICA tax**. Both the employer and the employee pay an equal amount of social security tax. The employer is required to withhold social security tax from the employee's pay. Periodically the employer sends the social security tax withheld to the federal government.

The rate of the social security tax and the calendar year earnings base to which it applies are frequently changed by Congress. In recent years, the social security tax rate has remained constant at 6.2 percent. The earnings base to which the tax applies has increased yearly. In 2000 the social security tax rate was 6.2 percent of the first $76,200 of salary or wages paid to each employee. In examples and problems, this text uses a social security tax rate of 6.2 percent of the first $76,200 of salary or wages.

Medicare Tax

The Medicare tax is closely related to the social security tax. Prior to 1992 it was a part of the social security tax. The **Medicare tax** is a tax levied equally on employees and employers to provide medical care for the employee and the employee's spouse after each has reached age 65.

In recent years, the Medicare tax rate has remained constant at 1.45 percent. The Medicare tax applies to all salaries and wages paid during the year. The employer is required to withhold the Medicare tax from the employee's pay and periodically send it to the federal government.

Note that the social security tax has an earnings base limit. The Medicare tax does not have an earnings base limit. The Medicare tax applies to *all* earnings paid during the year.

Important!

Wage Base Limit
The social security tax has a wage base limit. There is no wage base limit for the Medicare tax. All salaries and wages are subject to the Medicare tax.

Federal Income Tax

Employers are required to withhold from employees' earnings an estimated amount of income tax that will be payable by the employee on the earnings. The amount depends on several factors. Later in this chapter you will learn how to determine the amount to withhold from an employee's paycheck.

State and Local Taxes

Most states, and many local governments, require employers to withhold income taxes from employees' earnings to prepay the employees' state and local income taxes. These rules are generally almost identical to those governing federal income tax withholding, but they require separate general ledger accounts in the firm's accounting system.

Employer's Payroll Taxes and Insurance Costs

Remember that employers withhold social security and Medicare taxes from employees' earnings. In addition, employers pay social security and Medicare taxes on their employees' earnings. Employers are also required to pay federal and state taxes for unemployment benefits and to carry workers' compensation insurance.

Social Security Tax

The employer's share of the social security tax is 6.2 percent up to the earnings base. (In this text, the social security tax is 6.2 percent of the first $76,200 of earnings.) Periodically the employer pays to the federal government the social security tax withheld plus the employer's share of the social security tax.

	FICA
Employee (withheld)	6.2%
Employer (match)	6.2
Total	12.4%

Medicare Tax

The employer's share of Medicare tax is 1.45 percent of earnings. Periodically the employer pays to the federal government the Medicare tax withheld plus the employer's share of the Medicare tax.

The total social security and Medicare taxes the employer remits to the federal government are shown below.

	Medicare
Employee (withheld)	1.45%
Employer (match)	1.45
Total	2.90%

Federal Unemployment Tax

The *Federal Unemployment Tax Act (FUTA)* provides benefits for employees who become unemployed. Taxes levied by the federal government against employers to benefit unemployed workers are called **federal unemployment taxes (FUTA)**. Employers pay the entire amount of these taxes. In this text we assume that the taxable earnings base is $7,000. That is, the tax applies to the first $7,000 of each employee's earnings for the year. The FUTA tax rate is 6.2 percent.

Accounting

Human Services

Industry Overview

The human services field provides essential services to those who are not fully equipped to help themselves. Social disabilities, economic disadvantage, employment difficulties, food and housing hardships, and alcohol and drug dependencies are issues addressed by professionals in this field.

Career Opportunities
- Child Support Payment Specialist
- Social Worker
- Senior Accounting Supervisor—Human Services
- Income Maintenance Program Advisor
- Social Services Grant Administrator
- Budget Analyst—U.S. Administration on Aging

Preparing for a Human Services Career
- Demonstrate an understanding of and sensitivity to individual, ethnic, and cultural differences among individuals and families.
- Complete governmental accounting courses to prepare for administration of human service department budgets and funds.
- Develop proficiencies in electronic spreadsheets and database applications to manage client files, administer benefits, and track human services programs.
- Obtain certification or an associate's degree in social work or human services for middle management or entry-level positions.
- Secure a bachelor's degree for supervisory or managerial positions with an emphasis in human services management, social work, behavioral science, math, science, child development, world languages, computer science, or consumer science.
- Apply to participate in a Presidential Management Internship Program with the U.S. Department of Health and Human Services.

Thinking Critically

Social worker planners and policymakers develop programs to address issues such as homelessness, poverty, and violence. What skills or proficiencies do you think might be beneficial to these professionals as they identify specific problems, create plans of action, and suggest solutions?

Internet Application

Locate the Web site for the U.S. Department of Health and Human Services. Describe the purpose of this human services agency. What is the department's budget for the current year? How many individuals does this agency employ?

State Unemployment Tax

The federal and state unemployment programs work together to provide benefits for employees who become unemployed. Employers pay all of the **state unemployment taxes (SUTA)**. Usually the earnings base for the federal and state unemployment taxes are the same, the first $7,000 of each employee's earnings for the year. For many states the SUTA tax rate is 5.4 percent.

The federal tax rate (6.2 percent) can be reduced by the rate charged by the state (5.4 percent in this example), so the FUTA rate can be as low as 0.8 percent (6.2% − 5.4%).

SUTA tax		5.4%
FUTA tax rate	6.2%	
Less SUTA tax	(5.4)	
Net FUTA tax		0.8
Total federal and state unemployment tax		6.2%

Workers' Compensation Insurance

Workers' compensation insurance protects employees against losses from job-related injuries or illnesses, or compensates their families if death occurs in the course of the employment. Workers' compensation requirements are defined by each state. Most states mandate workers' compensation insurance.

Employee Records Required by Law

> Some companies outsource payroll duties to professional payroll companies. ADP, Inc., is the world's largest provider of payroll services and employee information systems.

Federal laws require that certain payroll records be maintained. For each employee the employer must keep a record of

- the employee's name, address, social security number, and date of birth;
- hours worked each day and week, and wages paid at the regular and overtime rates (certain exceptions exist for employees who earn salaries);
- cumulative wages paid throughout the year;
- amount of income tax, social security tax, and Medicare tax withheld for each pay period;
- proof that the employee is a United States citizen or has a valid work permit.

Section 1 Self Review

Questions

1. What is "time and a half"?
2. How are social security benefits financed?
3. How are unemployment insurance benefits financed?

Exercises

4. The earnings base limit for Medicare
   a. is the same as the earnings base limit for social security.
   b. is lower than the earnings base limit for social security.
   c. is higher than the earnings base limit for social security.
   d. does not exist.
5. The purpose of FUTA is to provide benefits for
   a. employees who become unemployed.
   b. employees who become injured while on the job.
   c. retired workers.
   d. disabled employees.

Analysis

6. Julie Kerns was hired by Jacob's Architects to create three oil paintings for the president's office. Is Kerns an employee? Why or why not?

(Answers to Section 1 Self Review are on page 387.)

Calculating Earnings and Taxes

On Line Furnishings is a sole proprietorship owned and managed by Roberta Rosario. On Line Furnishings imports furniture and novelty items to sell over the Internet. It has five employees. The three shipping clerks and the shipping supervisor are paid on an hourly basis. The office clerk is paid a weekly salary. Payday is each Monday; it covers the wages and salaries earned the previous week. The employees are subject to withholding of social security, Medicare, and federal income taxes. The business pays social security and Medicare taxes, and federal and state unemployment insurance taxes. The business is required by state law to carry workers' compensation insurance. Since it is involved in interstate commerce, On Line Furnishings is subject to the Fair Labor Standards Act.

From time to time, Roberta Rosario, the owner, makes cash withdrawals to cover her personal expenses. The withdrawals of the owner of a sole proprietorship are not treated as salaries or wages.

Computing Total Earnings of Employees

The first step in preparing payroll is to compute the gross wages or salary for each employee. There are several ways to compute earnings.

- **Hourly rate basis** workers earn a stated rate per hour. Gross pay depends on the number of hours worked.
- **Salary basis** workers earn an agreed-upon amount for each week, month, or other period.
- **Commission basis** workers, usually salespeople, earn a percentage of net sales.
- **Piece-rate basis** manufacturing workers are paid based on the number of units produced.

> Wal-Mart Stores, Inc., has approximately 889,000 employees in its U.S. operations, which include Wal-Mart Discount Stores, SAM's Clubs, the distribution centers, and the home office. The company reports that 65 percent of Wal-Mart managers, who are compensated on a salary basis, first entered the company as hourly rate basis employees.

Determining Pay for Hourly Employees

Two pieces of data are needed to compute gross pay for hourly rate basis employees: the number of hours worked during the payroll period, and the rate of pay.

Section 2

Section Objectives

2 Compute gross earnings of employees.

WHY IT'S IMPORTANT
Payroll is a large part of business activity.

3 Determine employee deductions for social security tax.

WHY IT'S IMPORTANT
Employers are legally responsible for collecting and remitting this tax.

4 Determine employee deductions for Medicare tax.

WHY IT'S IMPORTANT
Employers have legal responsibility.

5 Determine employee deductions for income tax.

WHY IT'S IMPORTANT
Employers are legally responsible.

6 Enter gross earnings, deductions, and net pay in the payroll register.

WHY IT'S IMPORTANT
The payroll register provides information needed to prepare paychecks.

Terms to Learn

commission basis
Employee's Withholding
    Allowance Certificate
    (Form W-4)
exempt employees
hourly rate basis
payroll register
piece-rate basis
salary basis
tax-exempt wages
wage-bracket table method

2 Objective

Compute gross earnings of employees.

Owner Withdrawals

Withdrawals by the owner of a sole proprietorship are debited to a temporary owner's equity account (in this case, **Roberta Rosario, Drawing**). Withdrawals are not treated as salary or wages.

Salaries

More than three million Americans live and work overseas. One of the reasons may be the salary. Americans working abroad can earn up to 300 percent more than the same job pays in the United States.

Hours Worked

At On Line Furnishings, the shipping supervisor keeps a weekly time sheet. Each day she enters the hours worked by each shipping clerk. At the end of the week, the office clerk uses the time sheet to compute the total hours worked and to prepare the payroll.

Many businesses use time clocks for hourly employees. Each employee has a time card and inserts it in the time clock to record the times of arrival and departure. The payroll clerk collects the cards at the end of the week, determines the hours worked by each employee, and multiplies the number of hours by the pay rate to compute the *gross pay*. Some time cards are machine readable. A computer determines the hours worked and makes the earnings calculations.

Gross Pay

Cindy Taylor, Edward Gallegos, and Bill Turner are shipping clerks at On Line Furnishings. They are hourly employees. Their gross pay for the week ended January 6 is determined as follows:

- Taylor worked 40 hours. She earns $9 an hour. Her gross pay is $360 (40 hours × $9).
- Turner worked 40 hours. He earns $7.50 an hour. His gross pay is $300 (40 × $7.50).
- Gallegos earns $8 per hour. He worked 45 hours. He is paid 40 hours at regular pay and 5 hours at time and a half. There are two ways to compute Gallegos' gross pay:

  1. The Wage and Hour Law method identifies the *overtime premium,* the amount the firm could have saved if all the hours were paid at the regular rate. The overtime premium rate is $4, one-half of the regular rate ($8 × ½ = $4).

Total hours × regular rate:	
45 hours × $8	$360.00
Overtime premium:	
5 hours × $4	20.00
Gross pay	$380.00

  2. The second method identifies how much the employee earned by working overtime.

Regular earnings:	
40 hours × $8	$320.00
Overtime earnings:	
5 hours × $12 ($8 × 1½)	60.00
Gross pay	$380.00

Cecilia Lin is the shipping supervisor at On Line Furnishings. She is an hourly employee. She earns $13 an hour, and she worked 40 hours. Her gross pay is $520 (40 × $13).

Withholdings for Hourly Employees Required by Law

Recall that three deductions from employees' gross pay are required by federal law. They are FICA (social security) tax, Medicare tax, and federal income tax withholding.

Social Security Tax. The social security tax is levied on both the employer and the employee. This text calculates social security tax using a 6.2 percent tax rate on the first $76,200 of wages paid during the calendar year. **Tax-exempt wages** are earnings in excess of the base amount set by the Social Security Act ($76,200). Tax-exempt wages are not subject to FICA withholding.

❸ Objective
Determine employee deductions for social security tax.

If an employee works for more than one employer during the year, the FICA tax is deducted and matched by each employer. When the employee files a federal income tax return, any excess FICA tax withheld from the employee's earnings is refunded by the government or applied to payment of the employee's federal income taxes.

To determine the amount of social security tax to withhold from an employee's pay, multiply the taxable wages by the social security tax rate. Round the result to the nearest cent.

The following shows the social security tax deductions for On Line Furnishings' hourly employees.

Employee	Gross Pay	Tax Rate	Tax
Cindy Taylor	$360.00	6.2%	$22.32
Edward Gallegos	380.00	6.2	23.56
Bill Turner	300.00	6.2	18.60
Cecilia Lin	520.00	6.2	32.24
Total social security tax			$96.72

❹ Objective
Determine employee deductions for Medicare tax.

Medicare Tax. The Medicare tax is levied on both the employee and the employer. To compute the Medicare tax to withhold from the employee's paycheck, multiply the wages by the Medicare tax rate, 1.45 percent. The following shows the Medicare tax deduction for hourly employees.

Employee	Gross Pay	Tax Rate	Tax
Cindy Taylor	$360.00	1.45%	$ 5.22
Edward Gallegos	380.00	1.45	5.51
Bill Turner	300.00	1.45	4.35
Cecilia Lin	520.00	1.45	7.54
Total Medicare tax			$22.62

❺ Objective
Determine employee deductions for income tax.

Federal Income Tax. A substantial portion of the federal government's revenue comes from the income tax on individuals. Employers are required to withhold federal income tax from employees' pay. Periodically the employer pays the federal income tax withheld to the federal government. After the end of the year, the employee files an income tax return. If the amount of federal income tax withheld does not cover the amount of income tax due, the employee pays the balance. If too much federal income tax has been withheld, the employee receives a refund.

According to tax collection statistics reported by the IRS for 1997, employers withheld more than $580 billion from the paychecks of their employees for income taxes.

Important!

Pay-As-You-Go
Employee income tax withholding is designed to place employees on a pay-as-you-go basis in paying their federal income tax.

Important!

Get It in Writing
Employers need a signed Form W-4 in order to change the employee's federal income tax withholding.

FIGURE 10-1 ▼
Form W-4 (Partial)

Withholding Allowances. The amount of federal income tax to withhold from an employee's earnings depends on the

- earnings during the pay period,
- length of the pay period,
- marital status,
- number of withholding allowances.

Determining the number of withholding allowances for some taxpayers is complex. In the simplest circumstances, a taxpayer claims a withholding allowance for

- the taxpayer,
- a spouse who does not also claim an allowance,
- each dependent for whom the taxpayer provides more than half the support during the year.

As the number of withholding allowances increases, the amount of federal income tax withheld decreases. The goal is to claim the number of withholding allowances so that the federal income tax withheld is about the same as the employee's tax liability.

To claim withholding allowances, employees complete **Employee's Withholding Allowance Certificate, Form W-4**. The employee gives the completed Form W-4 to the employer. If the number of exemption allowances decreases, the employee must file a new Form W-4 within 10 days. If the number of exemption allowances increases, the employee may, but is not required to, file another Form W-4. If an employee does not file a Form W-4, the employer withholds federal income tax based on zero withholding allowances.

Figure 10-1 shows Form W-4 for Cindy Taylor. Notice that on Line 5, Taylor claims one withholding allowance.

- - - - - - - - - - - - - - - Cut here and give the certificate to your employer. Keep the top portion for your records. - - - - - - - - - - - - - -

Form **W-4** Department of the Treasury Internal Revenue Service	**Employee's Withholding Allowance Certificate** ► **For Privacy Act and Paperwork Reduction Act Notice, see page 2.**	OMB No. 1545-0010 **20--**

1 Type or print your first name and middle initial | Last Name | **2** Your social security number

Cindy   M.   Taylor   123 XX XXXX

Home address (number and street or rural route)
6480 Oak Tree Drive

3 ☐ Single ☑ Married ☐ Married, but withhold at higher Single rate
Note: *If married, but legally separated, or spouse is a nonresident alien, check the Single box.*

City or town, state, and ZIP code
Denton, TX 76209-6789

4 If your last name differs from that on your social security card,
check here. You must call 1-800-772-1213 for a new card. ► ☐

5 Total number of allowances you are claiming (from line **H** above **or** from the applicable worksheet on page 2) . . . **5** | 1

6 Additional amount, if any, you want deducted from each paycheck . . . . **6** | $

7 I claim exemption from withholding for 20--, and I certify that I meet **both** of the following conditions for exemption:
- Last year I had a right to a refund of **all** Federal income tax withheld because I had **no** tax liability **and**
- This year I expect a refund of **all** Federal income tax withheld because I expect to have **no** tax liability.
If you meet both conditions, write "Exempt" here . . . . ► | **7**

Under penalty of perjury, I certify that I am entitled to the number of withholding allowances claimed on this certificate, or I am entitled to claim exempt status.

Employee's signature
(Form is not valid unless you sign it.) ► *Cindy Taylor*   Date ► *December 1,* 20 --

8 Employer's name and address (Employer: Complete lines 8 and 10 only if sending to IRS.) | **9** Office code (optional) | **10** Employer identification number

Cat. No. 10220Q

Computing Federal Income Tax Withholding. Although there are several ways to compute the federal income tax to withhold from an employee's earnings, the **wage-bracket table method** is almost universally used. The wage-bracket tables are in *Publication 15, Circular E*. This publication contains withholding tables for weekly, biweekly, semimonthly, monthly, and daily or miscellaneous payroll periods for single and married persons. Figure 10-2 on pages 362–363 shows partial tables for single and married persons who are paid weekly.

Use the following steps to determine the amount to withhold:

1. Choose the table for the pay period and the employee's marital status.

2. Find the row in the table that matches the wages earned. Find the column that matches the number of withholding allowances claimed on Form W-4. The income tax to withhold is the intersection of the row and the column.

As an example, let's determine the amount to withhold from Cecilia Lin's gross pay. Lin is married, claims two withholding allowances, and earned $520 for the week.

1. Go to the table for married persons paid weekly, Figure 10-2b.

2. Find the line covering wages between $520 and $530. Find the column for two withholding allowances. The tax to withhold is $44; this is where the row and the column intersect.

Using the wage-bracket tables, can you find the federal income tax amounts to withhold for Taylor, Gallegos, and Turner?

Employee	Gross Pay	Marital Status	Withholding Allowances	Income Tax Withholding
Cindy Taylor	$360.00	Married	1	$ 28.00
Edward Gallegos	380.00	Single	1	42.00
Bill Turner	300.00	Single	3	14.00
Cecilia Lin	520.00	Married	2	44.00
				$128.00

Other Deductions Required by Law. Most states and some local governments require employers to withhold state and local income taxes from earnings. In some states employers are also required to withhold unemployment tax or disability tax. The procedures are similar to those for federal income tax withholding. Apply the tax rate to the earnings, or use withholding tables.

Withholdings Not Required by Law

There are many payroll deductions not required by law but made by agreement between the employee and the employer. Some examples are

- group life insurance,
- group medical insurance,
- company retirement plans,
- bank or credit union savings plans or loan repayments,
- United States saving bonds purchase plans,
- stocks and other investment purchase plans,
- employer loan repayments,
- union dues.

SINGLE Persons—WEEKLY Payroll Period

(For Wages Paid in 20--)

If the wages are –		And the number of withholding allowances claimed is –										
At least	But less than	0	1	2	3	4	5	6	7	8	9	10
		The amount of income tax to be withheld is –										
$0	$55	0	0	0	0	0	0	0	0	0	0	0
55	60	1	0	0	0	0	0	0	0	0	0	0
60	65	2	0	0	0	0	0	0	0	0	0	0
65	70	2	0	0	0	0	0	0	0	0	0	0
70	75	3	0	0	0	0	0	0	0	0	0	0
75	80	4	0	0	0	0	0	0	0	0	0	0
80	85	5	0	0	0	0	0	0	0	0	0	0
85	90	5	0	0	0	0	0	0	0	0	0	0
90	95	6	0	0	0	0	0	0	0	0	0	0
95	100	7	0	0	0	0	0	0	0	0	0	0
100	105	8	0	0	0	0	0	0	0	0	0	0
105	110	8	0	0	0	0	0	0	0	0	0	0
110	115	9	1	0	0	0	0	0	0	0	0	0
115	120	10	2	0	0	0	0	0	0	0	0	0
120	125	11	3	0	0	0	0	0	0	0	0	0
125	130	11	3	0	0	0	0	0	0	0	0	0
130	135	12	4	0	0	0	0	0	0	0	0	0
135	140	13	5	0	0	0	0	0	0	0	0	0
140	145	14	6	0	0	0	0	0	0	0	0	0
145	150	14	6	0	0	0	0	0	0	0	0	0
150	155	15	7	0	0	0	0	0	0	0	0	0
155	160	16	8	0	0	0	0	0	0	0	0	0
160	165	17	9	1	0	0	0	0	0	0	0	0
165	170	17	9	1	0	0	0	0	0	0	0	0
170	175	18	10	2	0	0	0	0	0	0	0	0
175	180	19	11	3	0	0	0	0	0	0	0	0
180	185	20	12	4	0	0	0	0	0	0	0	0
185	190	20	12	4	0	0	0	0	0	0	0	0
190	195	21	13	5	0	0	0	0	0	0	0	0
195	200	22	14	6	0	0	0	0	0	0	0	0
200	210	23	15	7	0	0	0	0	0	0	0	0
210	220	25	17	8	0	0	0	0	0	0	0	0
220	230	26	18	10	2	0	0	0	0	0	0	0
230	240	28	20	11	3	0	0	0	0	0	0	0
240	250	29	21	13	5	0	0	0	0	0	0	0
250	260	31	23	14	6	0	0	0	0	0	0	0
260	270	32	24	16	8	0	0	0	0	0	0	0
270	280	34	26	17	9	1	0	0	0	0	0	0
280	290	35	27	19	11	3	0	0	0	0	0	0
290	300	37	29	20	12	4	0	0	0	0	0	0
300	310	38	30	22	14	6	0	0	0	0	0	0
310	320	40	32	23	15	7	0	0	0	0	0	0
320	330	41	33	25	17	9	1	0	0	0	0	0
330	340	43	35	26	18	10	2	0	0	0	0	0
340	350	44	36	28	20	12	4	0	0	0	0	0
350	360	46	38	29	21	13	5	0	0	0	0	0
360	370	47	39	31	23	15	7	0	0	0	0	0
370	380	49	41	32	24	16	8	0	0	0	0	0
380	390	50	42	34	26	18	10	2	0	0	0	0
390	400	52	44	35	27	19	11	3	0	0	0	0
400	410	53	45	37	29	21	13	5	0	0	0	0
410	420	55	47	38	30	22	14	6	0	0	0	0
420	430	56	48	40	32	24	16	8	0	0	0	0
430	440	58	50	41	33	25	17	9	1	0	0	0
440	450	59	51	43	35	27	19	11	3	0	0	0
450	460	61	53	44	36	28	20	12	4	0	0	0
460	470	62	54	46	38	30	22	14	6	0	0	0
470	480	64	56	47	39	31	23	15	7	0	0	0
480	490	65	57	49	41	33	25	17	9	0	0	0
490	500	67	59	50	42	34	26	18	10	2	0	0
500	510	68	60	52	44	36	28	20	12	3	0	0
510	520	70	62	53	45	37	29	21	13	5	0	0
520	530	71	63	55	47	39	31	23	15	6	0	0
530	540	73	65	56	48	40	32	24	16	8	0	0
540	550	75	66	58	50	42	34	26	18	9	1	0
550	560	78	68	59	51	43	35	27	19	11	3	0
560	570	81	69	61	53	45	37	28	21	12	4	0
570	580	84	71	62	54	46	38	30	22	14	6	0
580	590	87	72	64	56	48	40	32	24	16	7	0
590	600	89	74	65	57	49	41	33	25	17	9	1

MARRIED Persons—WEEKLY Payroll Period

(For Wages Paid in 20--)

If the wages are –		And the number of withholding allowances claimed is –										
At least	But less than	0	1	2	3	4	5	6	7	8	9	10
		The amount of income tax to be withheld is –										
$0	$125	0	0	0	0	0	0	0	0	0	0	0
125	130	1	0	0	0	0	0	0	0	0	0	0
130	135	1	0	0	0	0	0	0	0	0	0	0
135	140	2	0	0	0	0	0	0	0	0	0	0
140	145	3	0	0	0	0	0	0	0	0	0	0
145	150	4	0	0	0	0	0	0	0	0	0	0
150	155	4	0	0	0	0	0	0	0	0	0	0
155	160	5	0	0	0	0	0	0	0	0	0	0
160	165	6	0	0	0	0	0	0	0	0	0	0
165	170	7	0	0	0	0	0	0	0	0	0	0
170	175	7	0	0	0	0	0	0	0	0	0	0
175	180	8	0	0	0	0	0	0	0	0	0	0
180	185	9	1	0	0	0	0	0	0	0	0	0
185	190	10	1	0	0	0	0	0	0	0	0	0
190	195	10	2	0	0	0	0	0	0	0	0	0
195	200	11	3	0	0	0	0	0	0	0	0	0
200	210	12	4	0	0	0	0	0	0	0	0	0
210	220	14	6	0	0	0	0	0	0	0	0	0
220	230	15	7	0	0	0	0	0	0	0	0	0
230	240	17	9	0	0	0	0	0	0	0	0	0
240	250	18	10	2	0	0	0	0	0	0	0	0
250	260	20	12	3	0	0	0	0	0	0	0	0
260	270	21	13	5	0	0	0	0	0	0	0	0
270	280	23	15	6	0	0	0	0	0	0	0	0
280	290	24	16	8	0	0	0	0	0	0	0	0
290	300	26	18	9	1	0	0	0	0	0	0	0
300	310	27	19	11	3	0	0	0	0	0	0	0
310	320	29	21	12	4	0	0	0	0	0	0	0
320	330	30	23	14	6	0	0	0	0	0	0	0
330	340	32	24	15	7	0	0	0	0	0	0	0
340	350	33	25	17	9	1	0	0	0	0	0	0
350	360	35	27	18	10	2	0	0	0	0	0	0
360	370	36	28	20	12	4	0	0	0	0	0	0
370	380	38	30	21	13	5	0	0	0	0	0	0
380	390	39	31	23	15	7	0	0	0	0	0	0
390	400	41	33	24	16	8	0	0	0	0	0	0
400	410	42	34	26	18	10	2	0	0	0	0	0
410	420	44	36	27	19	11	3	0	0	0	0	0
420	430	45	37	29	21	13	5	0	0	0	0	0
430	440	47	39	30	22	14	6	0	0	0	0	0
440	450	48	40	32	24	16	8	0	0	0	0	0
450	460	50	42	33	25	17	9	1	0	0	0	0
460	470	51	43	35	27	19	11	3	0	0	0	0
470	480	53	45	36	28	20	12	4	0	0	0	0
480	490	54	46	38	30	22	14	6	0	0	0	0
490	500	56	48	39	31	23	15	7	0	0	0	0
500	510	57	49	41	33	25	17	9	1	0	0	0
510	520	59	51	42	34	26	18	10	2	0	0	0
520	530	60	52	44	36	28	20	12	4	0	0	0
530	540	62	54	45	37	29	21	13	5	0	0	0
540	550	63	55	47	39	31	23	15	7	0	0	0
550	560	65	57	48	40	32	24	16	8	0	0	0
560	570	66	58	50	42	34	26	18	10	2	0	0
570	580	68	60	51	43	35	27	19	11	3	0	0
580	590	69	61	53	45	37	29	21	13	5	0	0
590	600	71	63	54	46	38	30	22	14	6	0	0
600	610	72	64	56	48	40	32	24	16	8	0	0
610	620	74	66	57	49	41	33	25	17	9	1	0
620	630	75	67	59	51	43	35	27	19	11	2	0
630	640	77	69	60	52	44	36	28	20	12	4	0
640	650	78	70	62	54	46	38	30	22	14	5	0
650	660	80	72	63	55	47	39	31	23	15	7	0
660	670	81	73	65	57	49	41	33	25	17	8	0
670	680	83	75	66	58	50	42	34	26	18	10	2
680	690	84	76	68	60	52	44	36	28	20	11	3
690	700	86	78	69	61	53	45	37	29	21	13	5
700	710	87	79	71	63	55	47	39	31	23	14	6
710	720	89	81	72	64	56	48	40	32	24	16	8
720	730	90	82	74	66	58	50	42	34	26	17	9
730	740	92	84	75	67	59	51	43	35	27	19	11

These and other payroll deductions increase the payroll recordkeeping work but do not involve any new principles or procedures. They are handled in the same way as the deductions for social security, Medicare, and federal income taxes.

On Line Furnishings pays all medical insurance premiums for each employee. If the employee chooses to have medical coverage for a spouse or dependent, On Line Furnishings deducts $20 per week for coverage for the spouse and each dependent. Turner and Lin each have $20 per week deducted to obtain the medical coverage.

Determining Pay for Salaried Employees

A salaried employee earns a specific sum of money for each payroll period. The office clerk at On Line Furnishings earns a weekly salary.

Hours Worked

Salaried workers who do not hold supervisory jobs are covered by the provisions of the Wage and Hour Law that deal with maximum hours and overtime premium pay. Employers keep time records for all non-supervisory salaried workers to make sure that their hourly earnings meet the legal requirements.

Salaried employees who hold supervisory or managerial positions are called **exempt employees**. They are not subject to the maximum hour and overtime premium pay provisions of the Wage and Hour Law.

Gross Earnings

Selena Anderson is the office clerk at On Line Furnishings. During the first week of January, she worked 40 hours, her regular schedule. There are no overtime earnings because she did not work more than 40 hours during the week. Her salary of $400 is her gross pay for the week.

Withholdings for Salaried Employees Required by Law

The procedures for withholding taxes for salaried employees is the same as withholding for hourly rate employees. Apply the tax rate to the earnings, or use withholding tables.

FIGURE 10-3 ▼
Payroll Register

PAYROLL REGISTER   **WEEK BEGINNING** _January 1, 20--_

NAME	NO. OF ALLOW.	MARITAL STATUS	CUMULATIVE EARNINGS	NO. OF HRS.	RATE/ SALARY	EARNINGS			CUMULATIVE EARNINGS
						REGULAR	OVERTIME	GROSS AMOUNT	
Taylor, Cindy	1	M		40	9.00	360 00		360 00	360 00
Gallegos, Edward	1	S		45	8.00	320 00	60 00	380 00	380 00
Turner, Bill	3	S		40	7.50	300 00		300 00	300 00
Lin, Cecilia	2	M		40	13.00	520 00		520 00	520 00
Anderson, Selena	1	S		40	400.00	400 00		400 00	400 00
						1 900 00	60 00	1 960 00	1 960 00
(A)	(B)		(C)	(D)	(E)	(F)	(G)	(H)	(I)

Recording Payroll Information for Employees

A payroll register is prepared for each pay period. The **payroll register** shows all the payroll information for the pay period.

⑥ **Objective**

Enter gross earnings, deductions, and net pay in the payroll register.

The Payroll Register

Figure 10-3 on pages 364–365 shows the payroll register for On Line Furnishings for the week ended January 6. Note that all employees were paid for eight hours on January 1, a holiday. To learn how to complete the payroll register, refer to Figure 10-3 and follow these steps.

1. *Columns A, B, and E.* Enter the employee's name (Column A), number of withholding allowances and marital status (Column B), and rate of pay (Column E). In a computerized payroll system, this information is entered once and is automatically retrieved each time payroll is prepared.

2. *Column C.* The Cumulative Earnings column (Column C) shows the total earnings for the calendar year before the current pay period. This figure is needed to determine whether the employee has exceeded the earnings limit for the FICA and FUTA taxes. Since this is the first payroll period of the year, there are no cumulative earnings prior to the current pay period.

3. *Column D.* In Column D enter the total number of hours worked in the current period. This data comes from the weekly time sheet.

4. *Columns F, G, and H.* Using the hours worked and the pay rate, calculate regular pay (Column F), the overtime earnings (Column G), and gross pay (Column H).

5. *Column I.* Calculate the cumulative earnings after this pay period (Column I) by adding the beginning cumulative earnings (Column C) and the current period's gross pay (Column H).

6. *Columns J, K, and L.* The Taxable Wages columns show the earnings subject to taxes for social security (Column J), Medicare (Column K), and FUTA (Column L). Only the earnings at or under the earnings limit are included in these columns.

AND ENDING _January 6, 20--_   **PAID** _January 8, 20--_

TAXABLE WAGES			DEDUCTIONS				DISTRIBUTION			
SOCIAL SECURITY	MEDICARE	FUTA	SOCIAL SECURITY	MEDICARE	INCOME TAX	HEALTH INSURANCE	NET AMOUNT	CHECK NO.	OFFICE SALARIES	SHIPPING WAGES
360 00	360 00	360 00	22 32	5 22	28 00		304 46	1725		360 00
380 00	380 00	380 00	23 56	5 51	42 00		308 93	1726		380 00
300 00	300 00	300 00	18 60	4 35	14 00	20 00	243 05	1727		300 00
520 00	520 00	520 00	32 24	7 54	44 00	20 00	416 22	1728		520 00
400 00	400 00	400 00	24 80	5 80	45 00		324 40	1729	400 00	
1 960 00	1 960 00	1 960 00	121 52	28 42	173 00	40 00	1 597 06		400 00	1 560 00
(J)	(K)	(L)	(M)	(N)	(O)	(P)	(Q)	(R)	(S)	(T)

7. *Columns M, N, O, and P.* The Deductions columns show the withholding for social security tax (Column M), Medicare tax (Column N), federal income tax (Column O), and medical insurance (Column P).

8. *Column Q.* Subtract the deductions (Columns M, N, O, and P) from the gross earnings (Column H). Enter the results in the Net Amount column (Column Q). This is the amount paid to each employee.

9. *Column R.* Enter the check number in Column R.

10. *Columns S and T.* The payroll register's last two columns classify employee earnings as office salaries (Column S) or shipping wages (Column T).

When the payroll data for all employees has been entered in the payroll register, total the columns. Check the balances of the following columns:

- Total regular earnings plus total overtime earnings must equal the gross amount (Columns F + G = Column H).
- The total gross amount less total deductions must equal the total net amount.

Gross amount		$1,960.00
Less deductions:		
Social security tax	$121.52	
Medicare tax	28.42	
Income tax	173.00	
Health insurance	40.00	
Total deductions		362.94
Net amount		$1,597.06

- The office salaries and the shipping wages must equal gross earnings (Columns S + T = Column H).

The payroll register supplies all the information to make the journal entry to record the payroll. Journalizing the payroll is discussed in Section 3.

Section 2 Self Review

Questions

1. What three payroll deductions does federal law require?

2. List four payroll deductions that are not required by law but can be made by agreement between the employee and the employer.

3. What factors determine the amount of federal income tax to be withheld from an employee's earnings?

Exercises

4. Casey Klein worked 46 hours during the week ending October 19. His regular rate is $8 per hour. Calculate his gross earnings for the week.

   a. $320
   b. $392
   c. $368
   d. $344

5. Which of the following affects the amount of Medicare tax to be withheld from an hourly rate employee's pay?

   a. medical insurance premium
   b. marital status
   c. withholding allowances claimed on Form W-4
   d. hours worked

Analysis

6. Maria Sanchez left a voice mail asking you to withhold an additional $20 of federal income tax from her wages each pay period, starting May 1. When should you begin withholding the extra amount?

(Answers to Section 2 Self Review are on page 387.)

Recording Payroll Information

In this section you will learn how to prepare paychecks and journalize and post payroll transactions by following the January payroll activity for On Line Furnishings.

Recording Payroll

Recording payroll involves two separate entries: one to record the payroll expense and another to pay the employees. The general journal entry to record the payroll expense is based on the payroll register. The gross pay is debited to **Shipping Wages Expense** for the shipping clerks and supervisor and to **Office Salaries Expense** for the office clerk. Each type of deduction is credited to a separate liability account **(Social Security Tax Payable, Medicare Tax Payable, Employee Income Tax Payable, Health Insurance Premiums Payable).** Net pay is credited to the liability account, **Salaries and Wages Payable.**

Refer to Figure 10-3 on pages 364–365 to see how the data on the payroll register is used to prepare the January 8 payroll journal entry for On Line Furnishings. Following is an analysis of the entry.

Section Objectives

7 Journalize payroll transactions in the general journal.

WHY IT'S IMPORTANT
Payroll cost is an operating expense.

8 Maintain an earnings record for each employee.

WHY IT'S IMPORTANT
Federal law requires that employers maintain records.

Terms to Learn

compensation record
individual earnings record

7 Objective

Journalize payroll transactions in the general journal.

Business Transaction

The information in the payroll register (Figure 10-3) is used to record the payroll expense.

Analysis

The expense account, **Office Salaries Expense,** is increased by $400.00. The expense account, **Shipping Wages Expense,** is increased by $1,560.00. The liability account for each deduction is increased: **Social Security Tax Payable,** $121.52; **Medicare Tax Payable,** $28.42; **Employee Income Tax Payable,** $173.00; **Health Insurance Premiums Payable,** $40.00. The liability account, **Salaries and Wages Payable,** is increased by the net amount of the payroll, $1,597.06.

Debit-Credit Rules

DEBIT Increases in expenses are recorded as debits. Debit **Office Salaries Expense** for $400.00. Debit **Shipping Wages Expense** for $1,560.00.

CREDIT Increases in liability accounts are recorded as credits. Credit **Social Security Tax Payable** for $121.52. Credit **Medicare Tax Payable** for $28.42. Credit **Employee Income Tax Payable** for $173.00. Credit **Health Insurance Premiums Payable** for $40.00. Credit **Salaries and Wages Payable** for $1,597.06

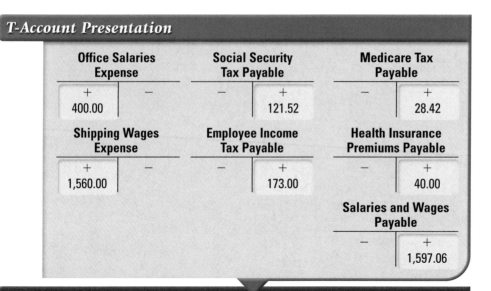

Office Salaries Expense	
+	−
400.00	

Social Security Tax Payable	
−	+
	121.52

Medicare Tax Payable	
−	+
	28.42

Shipping Wages Expense	
+	−
1,560.00	

Employee Income Tax Payable	
−	+
	173.00

Health Insurance Premiums Payable	
−	+
	40.00

Salaries and Wages Payable	
−	+
	1,597.06

General Journal Entry

	DATE	DESCRIPTION	POST. REF.	DEBIT	CREDIT	
1	20--					1
2	Jan. 8	Office Salaries Expense		400 00		2
3		Shipping Wages Expense		1 560 00		3
4		Social Security Tax Payable			121 52	4
5		Medicare Tax Payable			28 42	5
6		Employee Income Tax Payable			173 00	6
7		Health Insurance Premiums Payable			40 00	7
8		Salaries and Wages Payable			1 597 06	8
9		Payroll for week ending Jan. 6				9

GENERAL JOURNAL PAGE 1

The Bottom Line

Record Payroll

Income Statement

Expenses	↑ 1,960
Net Income	↓ 1,960

Balance Sheet

Liabilities	↑ 1,960
Equity	↓ 1,960

Southwest Airlines Co. recorded salaries, wages, and benefits of more than $1.4 billion for the year ended December 31, 1999.

Paying Employees

Most businesses pay their employees by check or by direct deposit. By using these methods, the business avoids the inconvenience and risk involved in dealing with currency.

Paying by Check

Paychecks may be written on the firm's regular checking account or on a payroll bank account. The check stub shows information about the employee's gross earnings, deductions, and net pay. Employees detach the stubs and keep them as a record of their payroll data. The check number is entered in the Check Number column of the payroll register (Figure 10-3, Column R). The canceled check provides a record of the payment, and the employee's endorsement serves as a receipt. Following is an analysis of the transaction to pay On Line Furnishings' employees.

Important!

Payroll Liabilities
Deductions from employee paychecks are liabilities for the employer.

On January 8 On Line Furnishings wrote five checks for payroll, Check numbers 1725–1729.

Analysis

The liability account, **Salaries and Wages Payable,** is decreased by $1,597.06. The asset account, **Cash,** is decreased by $1,597.06.

Debit-Credit Rules

DEBIT Decreases to liability accounts are recorded as debits. Debit **Salaries and Wages Payable** for $1,597.06.

CREDIT Decreases to assets are credits. Credit **Cash** for $1,597.06.

T-Account Presentation

Salaries and Wages Payable		Cash	
−	+	+	−
1,597.06			1,597.06

General Journal Entry

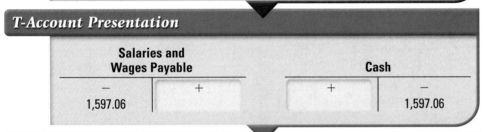

	DATE		DESCRIPTION	POST. REF.	DEBIT	CREDIT	
11	Jan.	8	Salaries and Wages Payable		1 5 9 7 06		11
12			Cash			1 5 9 7 06	12
13			To record payment of salaries and wages				13
14			for week ended Jan. 6				14

GENERAL JOURNAL   PAGE ___1___

The Bottom Line

Issue Paychecks

Income Statement

No effect on net income

Balance Sheet

| Assets | ↓1,597.06 |
| Liabilities | ↓1,597.06 |

No effect on equity

Checks Written on Regular Checking Account. The above entry is shown in general journal form for illustration purposes only. When paychecks are written on the regular checking account, the entries are recorded in the cash payments journal. Figure 10-4 on page 370 shows the January 8 entries to pay employees. Notice that there is a separate Salaries and Wages Payable Debit column.

Checks Written on a Separate Payroll Account. Many businesses write payroll checks from a separate payroll bank account. This is a two-step process.

1. A check is drawn on the regular bank account for the total amount of net pay and deposited in the payroll bank account.

2. Individual payroll checks are issued from the payroll bank account.

Using a separate payroll account simplifies the bank reconciliation of the regular checking account and makes it easier to identify outstanding payroll checks.

Important!

Separate Payroll Account
Using a separate payroll account facilitates the bank reconciliation and provides better internal control.

FIGURE 10-4 ▶
Cash Payments Journal

CASH PAYMENTS JOURNAL   PAGE _____1_____

DATE	CK. NO.	DESCRIPTION	POST. REF.	ACCOUNTS PAYABLE DEBIT	SALARIES AND WAGES PAYABLE DEBIT	PURCHASES DISCOUNT CREDIT	CASH CREDIT
Jan. 2	1711	Discount Furniture Company		1 2 0 0 00		2 4 00	1 1 7 6 00
8	1725	Cindy Taylor			3 0 4 46		3 0 4 46
8	1726	Edward Gallegos			3 0 8 93		3 0 8 93
8	1727	Bill Turner			2 4 3 05		2 4 3 05
8	1728	Cecilia Lin			4 1 6 22		4 1 6 22
8	1729	Selena Anderson			3 2 4 40		3 2 4 40
31		Totals		XX X X X XX	6 3 8 8 24	XX X X X XX	XX X X X XX

Paying by Direct Deposit

A popular method of paying employees is the direct deposit method. The bank electronically transfers net pay from the employer's account to the personal account of the employee. On payday the employee receives a statement showing gross earnings, deductions, and net pay.

Individual Earnings Records

An **individual earnings record**, also called a **compensation record**, is created for each employee. This record contains the employee's name, address, social security number, date of birth, number of withholding allowances claimed, rate of pay, and any other information needed to compute earnings and complete tax reports.

The payroll register provides the details that are entered on the employee's individual earnings record for each pay period. Figure 10-5 on page 371 shows the earnings record for Cindy Taylor.

Managerial
IMPLICATIONS

Laws and Controls

- It is management's responsibility to ensure that the payroll procedures and records comply with federal, state, and local laws.
- For most businesses, wages and salaries are a large part of operating expenses. Payroll records help management to keep track of and control expenses.
- Management should investigate large or frequent overtime expenditures.
- To prevent errors and fraud, management periodically should have the payroll records audited and payroll procedures evaluated.
- Two common payroll frauds are the overstatement of hours worked and the issuance of checks to nonexistent employees.

Thinking Critically

What controls would you put in place to prevent payroll fraud?

NAME _Cindy Taylor_   **RATE** _$9 per hour_   **SOCIAL SECURITY NO.** _123-XX-XXXX_

ADDRESS _6480 Oak Tree Drive, Denton, TX 76209-6789_   **DATE OF BIRTH** _November 23, 1979_

WITHHOLDING ALLOWANCES _1_   **MARITAL STATUS** _M_

PAYROLL NO.	DATE WK. END.	DATE PAID	HOURS RG	HOURS OT	EARNINGS REGULAR	EARNINGS OVERTIME	EARNINGS TOTAL	EARNINGS CUMULATIVE	DEDUCTIONS SOCIAL SECURITY	DEDUCTIONS MEDICARE	DEDUCTIONS INCOME TAX	DEDUCTIONS OTHER	NET PAY
1	1/06	1/08	40		360 00		360 00	360 00	22 32	5 22	28 00		304 46
2	1/13	1/15	40		360 00		360 00	720 00	22 32	5 22	28 00		304 46
3	1/20	1/22	40		360 00		360 00	1080 00	22 32	5 22	28 00		304 46
4	1/27	1/29	40		360 00		360 00	1440 00	22 32	5 22	28 00		304 46
	January		1440 00				1440 00	1440 00	89 28	20 88	112 00		1217 84

▲ **FIGURE 10-5**
An Individual Earnings Record

The earnings record shows the payroll period, the date paid, the regular and overtime hours, the regular and overtime earnings, the deductions, and the net pay. The cumulative earnings on the earnings record agrees with Column I of the payroll register (Figure 10-3). The earnings records are totaled monthly and at the end of each calendar quarter. This provides information needed to make tax payments and file tax returns.

Completing January Payrolls

Figure 10-6 on pages 371–372 shows the entire cycle of computing, paying, journalizing, and posting payroll data. In order to complete the

▼ **FIGURE 10-6** Journalizing and Posting Payroll Data

AND ENDING _January 6, 20--_   **PAID** _January 8, 20--_

TAXABLE WAGES SOCIAL SECURITY	TAXABLE WAGES MEDICARE	TAXABLE WAGES FUTA	DEDUCTIONS SOCIAL SECURITY	DEDUCTIONS MEDICARE	DEDUCTIONS INCOME TAX	DEDUCTIONS HEALTH INSURANCE	DISTRIBUTION NET AMOUNT	DISTRIBUTION CHECK NO.	DISTRIBUTION OFFICE SALARIES	DISTRIBUTION SHIPPING WAGES
360 00	360 00	360 00	22 32	5 22	28 00		304 46	1725		360 00
380 00	380 00	380 00	23 56	5 51	42 00		308 93	1726		380 00
300 00	300 00	300 00	18 60	4 35	14 00	20 00	243 05	1727		300 00
520 00	520 00	520 00	32 24	7 54	44 00	20 00	416 22	1728		520 00
400 00	400 00	400 00	24 80	5 80	45 00		324 40	1729	400 00	
1960 00	1960 00	1960 00	121 52	28 42	173 00	40 00	1597 06		400 00	1560 00
(J)	(K)	(L)	(M)	(N)	(O)	(P)	(Q)	(R)	(S)	(T)

1	20--					1
2	Jan.	8	Office Salaries Expense	641	400 00	2
3			Shipping Wages Expense	642	1560 00	3
4			Social Security Tax Payable	221	121 52	4
5			Medicare Tax Payable	222	28 42	5
6			Employee Income Tax Payable	223	173 00	6
7			Health Insurance Premiums Payable	224	40 00	7
8			Salaries and Wages Payable	229	1597 06	8
9			Payroll for week ending Jan. 6			9

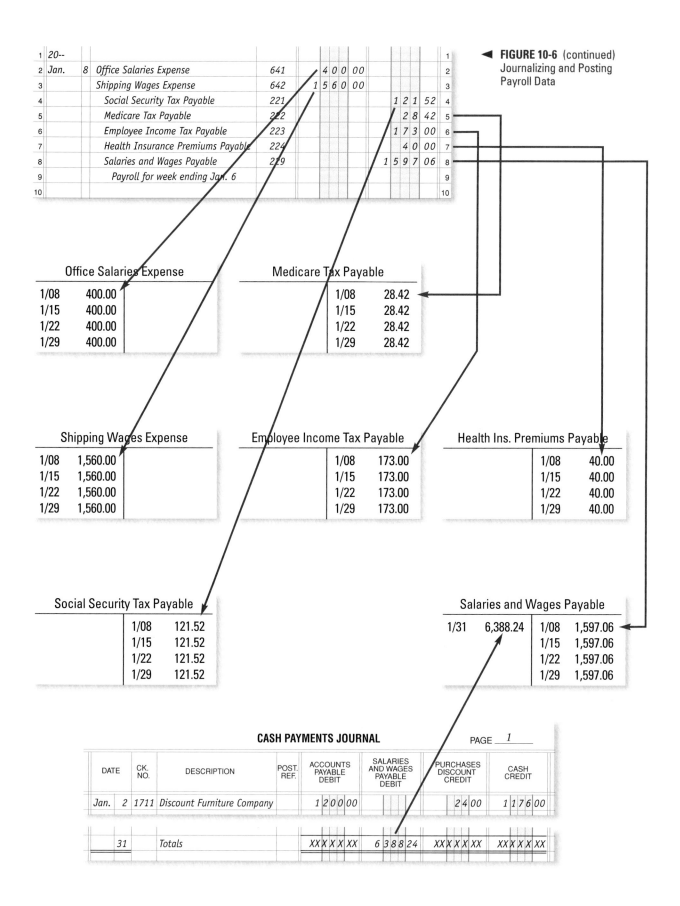

1	20--														1
2	Jan.	8	Office Salaries Expense	641		4 0 0	00								2
3			Shipping Wages Expense	642	1 5 6 0	00									3
4			Social Security Tax Payable	221				1 2 1	52		4
5			Medicare Tax Payable	222				2 8	42		5
6			Employee Income Tax Payable	223				1 7 3	00		6
7			Health Insurance Premiums Payable	224				4 0	00		7
8			Salaries and Wages Payable	229				1 5 9 7	06		8
9			Payroll for week ending Jan. 6								9
10											10

◀ **FIGURE 10-6** (continued) Journalizing and Posting Payroll Data

Office Salaries Expense

1/08	400.00
1/15	400.00
1/22	400.00
1/29	400.00

Medicare Tax Payable

1/08	28.42
1/15	28.42
1/22	28.42
1/29	28.42

Shipping Wages Expense

1/08	1,560.00
1/15	1,560.00
1/22	1,560.00
1/29	1,560.00

Employee Income Tax Payable

1/08	173.00
1/15	173.00
1/22	173.00
1/29	173.00

Health Ins. Premiums Payable

1/08	40.00
1/15	40.00
1/22	40.00
1/29	40.00

Social Security Tax Payable

1/08	121.52
1/15	121.52
1/22	121.52
1/29	121.52

Salaries and Wages Payable

1/31	6,388.24	1/08	1,597.06
		1/15	1,597.06
		1/22	1,597.06
		1/29	1,597.06

CASH PAYMENTS JOURNAL   PAGE 1

DATE	CK. NO.	DESCRIPTION	POST. REF.	ACCOUNTS PAYABLE DEBIT	SALARIES AND WAGES PAYABLE DEBIT	PURCHASES DISCOUNT CREDIT	CASH CREDIT
Jan. 2	1711	Discount Furniture Company		1 2 0 0 00		2 4 00	1 1 7 6 00
31		Totals		XX XXX XX	6 388 24	XX XXX XX	XX XXX XX

372 • **Chapter 10** *Payroll Computations, Records, and Payment*

January payroll for On Line Furnishings, assume that all employees worked the same number of hours each week of the month as they did the first week. Thus they had the same earnings, deductions, and net pay each week.

Entry to Record Payroll

As illustrated earlier in this section, one general journal entry is made to record the weekly payroll for all employees of On Line Furnishings. This general journal entry records the payroll expense and liability, but not the payments to employees. Since we are assuming an identical payroll for each week of the month, each of the four weekly payrolls requires general journal entries identical to the one shown in Figure 10-6. Notice how the payroll register column totals are recorded in the general journal.

Entry to Record Payment of Payroll

The weekly entries in the cash payments journal to record payments to employees are the same as the January 8 entries in Figure 10-4 on page 370. At the end of January, the columns in the cash payments journal are totaled, including the Salaries and Wages Payable Debit column.

Postings to Ledger Accounts

The entries to record the weekly payroll expense and liability amounts are posted from the general journal to the accounts in the general ledger. The total of the Salaries and Wages Payable Debit column in the cash payments journal is posted to the **Salaries and Wages Payable** general ledger account.

About Accounting

Tax Returns
Research conducted by the Tax Foundation found that Americans spend 5.4 billion hours each year completing their tax returns.

Section 3 Self Review

Questions

1. What accounts are debited and credited when individual payroll checks are written on the regular checking account?

2. What is the purpose of a payroll bank account?

3. What appears on an individual earnings record?

Exercises

4. Payroll deductions are recorded in a separate
   a. asset account.
   b. expense account.
   c. liability account.
   d. revenue account.

5. Details related to all employees' gross earnings, deductions, and net pay for a period are found in the
   a. payroll register.
   b. individual earnings record.
   c. general journal.
   d. cash payments journal.

Analysis

6. This general journal entry was made to record the payroll liability.

Ofc. Salaries Exp.	300.00	
Shipping Wages Exp.	1,292.00	
Health Ins. Prem. Exp.	20.00	
Soc. Sec. Taxes Exp.		103.48
Medicare Taxes Pay.		23.88
Employee Income Tax Payable		133.00
Cash		1,311.64

What corrections should be made to this journal entry?

Review   Chapter Summary

The main goal of payroll work is to compute the gross wages or salaries earned by each employee, the amounts to be deducted for various taxes and other purposes, and the net amount payable.

Learning Objectives

1 Explain the major federal laws relating to employee earnings and withholding.

Several federal laws affect payroll.

- The federal Wage and Hour Law limits to 40 the number of hours per week an employee can work at the regular rate of pay. For more than 40 hours of work a week, an employer involved in interstate commerce must pay one and one-half times the regular rate.
- Federal laws require that the employer withhold at least three taxes from the employee's pay: the employee's share of social security tax, the employee's share of Medicare tax, and federal income tax. Instructions for computing these taxes are provided by the government.
- If they are required, state and city income taxes can also be deducted. Some states require the employer to withhold contributions to an unemployment fund from the employee's paycheck.
- Voluntary deductions can also be made.

2 Compute gross earnings of employees.

To compute gross earnings for an employee, it is necessary to know whether the employee is paid using an hourly rate basis, a salary basis, a commission basis, or a piece-rate basis.

3 Determine employee deductions for social security tax.

The social security tax is levied in an equal amount on both the employer and the employee. The tax is a percentage of the employee's gross wages during a calendar year up to a wage base limit.

4 Determine employee deductions for Medicare tax.

The Medicare tax is levied in an equal amount on both the employer and the employee. There is no wage base limit for Medicare taxes.

5 Determine employee deductions for income tax.

Income taxes are deducted from an employee's paycheck by the employer and then are paid to the government periodically. Although several methods can be used to compute the amount of federal income tax to be withheld from employee earnings, the wage-bracket table method is most often used. The wage-bracket tables are in *Publication 15, Circular E, Employer's Tax Guide*. Withholding tables for various pay periods for single and married persons are contained in *Circular E*.

6 Enter gross earnings, deductions, and net pay in the payroll register.

Daily records of the hours worked by each nonsupervisory employee are kept. Using these hourly time sheets, the payroll clerk computes the employees' earnings, deductions, and net pay for each payroll period and records the data in a payroll register.

7 Journalize payroll transactions in the general journal.

The payroll register is used to prepare a general journal entry to record payroll expense and liability amounts. A separate journal entry is made to record payments to employees.

8 Maintain an earnings record for each employee.

At the beginning of each year, the employer sets up an individual earnings record for each employee. The amounts in the payroll register are posted to the individual earnings records throughout the year so that the firm has detailed payroll information for each employee. At the end of the year, employers provide reports that show gross earnings and total deductions to each employee.

9 Define the accounting terms new to this chapter.

Commission basis (p. 357) A method of paying employees according to a percentage of net sales

Compensation record (p. 370) See Individual earnings record

Employee (p. 352) A person who is hired by and works under the control and direction of the employer

Employee's Withholding Allowance Certificate, Form W-4 (p. 360) A form used to claim exemption (withholding) allowances

Exempt employees (p. 364) Salaried employees who hold supervisory or managerial positions who are not subject to the maximum hour and overtime pay provisions of the Wage and Hour Law

Federal unemployment taxes (FUTA) (p. 354) Taxes levied by the federal government against employers to benefit unemployed workers

Hourly rate basis (p. 357) A method of paying employees according to a stated rate per hour

Independent contractor (p. 352) One who is paid by a company to carry out a specific task or job but is not under the direct supervision or control of the company

Individual earnings record (p. 370) An employee record that contains information needed to compute earnings and complete tax reports

Medicare tax (p. 353) A tax levied on employees and employers to provide medical care for the employee and the employee's spouse after each has reached age 65

Payroll register (p. 365) A record of payroll information for each employee for the pay period

Piece-rate basis (p. 357) A method of paying employees according to the number of units produced

Salary basis (p. 357) A method of paying employees according to an agreed-upon amount for each week or month

Social Security Act (p. 353) A federal act providing certain benefits for employees and their families; officially the Federal Insurance Contributions Act

Social security (FICA) tax (p. 353) A tax imposed by the Federal Insurance Contributions Act and collected on employee earnings to provide retirement and disability benefits

State unemployment taxes (SUTA) (p. 355) Taxes levied by a state government against employers to benefit unemployed workers

Tax-exempt wages (p. 359) Earnings in excess of the base amount set by the Social Security Act

Time and a half (p. 353) Rate of pay for an employee's work in excess of 40 hours a week

Wage-bracket table method (p. 361) A simple method to determine the amount of federal income tax to be withheld using a table provided by the government

Workers' compensation insurance (p. 356) Insurance that protects employees against losses from job-related injuries or illnesses, or compensates their families if death occurs in the course of the employment

Comprehensive Self Review

1. What is the purpose of workers' compensation insurance?
2. How is the amount of social security tax to be withheld from an employee's earnings determined?
3. What is the purpose of the payroll register?
4. From an accounting and internal control viewpoint, would it be preferable to pay employees by check or cash? Explain.
5. How does an independent contractor differ from an employee?

(Answers to Comprehensive Self Review are on page 387.)

Discussion Questions

1. How does the salary basis differ from the hourly rate basis of paying employees?
2. What publication of the Internal Revenue Service provides information about the current federal income tax rates and the procedures that employers should use to withhold federal income tax from an employee's earnings?
3. What is the simplest method for finding the amount of federal income tax to be deducted from an employee's gross pay?
4. What are the four bases for determining employee gross earnings?
5. How does the direct deposit method of paying employees operate?
6. What is the purpose of the social security tax?
7. What is the purpose of the Medicare tax?
8. How are earnings determined when employees are paid on the hourly rate basis?
9. Does the employer bear any part of the SUTA tax? Explain.
10. How are the federal and state unemployment taxes related?
11. What is an exempt employee?
12. Give two examples of common payroll fraud.
13. What aspects of employment are regulated by the Fair Labor Standards Act? What is another commonly used name for this act?
14. How does the Fair Labor Standards Act affect the wages paid by many firms? What types of firms are regulated by the act?
15. What factors affect how much federal income tax must be withheld from an employee's earnings?

Applications

`EXERCISES`

Computing gross earnings.

The hourly rates of four employees of High Water Company follow, along with the hours that these employees worked during one week. Determine the gross earnings of each employee.

◄ **Exercise 10-1**
Objective 2

Employee No.	Hourly Rate	Hours Worked
1	$8.20	38
2	8.25	40
3	6.90	40
4	9.15	35

Computing regular earnings, overtime earnings, and gross pay.

During one week four production employees of Costal Manufacturing Company worked the hours shown below. All these employees receive overtime pay at one and one-half times their regular hourly rate for any hours worked beyond 40 in a week. Determine the regular earnings, overtime earnings, and gross earnings for each employee.

◄ **Exercise 10-2**
Objective 2

Employee No.	Hourly Rate	Hours Worked
1	$8.75	44
2	8.50	48
3	9.00	33
4	9.25	45

Determining social security withholding.

The monthly salaries for December and the year-to-date earnings of the employees of Seattle Broadcasting Company as of November 30 follow.

◄ **Exercise 10-3**
Objective 3

Employee No.	December Salary	Year-to-Date Earnings through November 30
1	$9,000	$85,800
2	5,000	71,500
3	8,800	80,860
4	4,000	57,200

Determine the amount of social security tax to be withheld from each employee's gross pay for December. Assume a 6.2 percent social security tax rate and an earnings base of $76,200 for the calendar year.

Determining deduction for Medicare tax.

Using the earnings data given in Exercise 10-3, determine the amount of Medicare tax to be withheld from each employee's gross pay for December. Assume a 1.45 percent Medicare tax rate and that all salaries and wages are subject to the tax.

◄ **Exercise 10-4**
Objective 4

Exercise 10-5 ►
Objective 5

Determining federal income tax withholding.

Data about the marital status, withholding allowances, and weekly salaries of the four office workers at Taylor Publishing Company follow. Use the tax tables in Figure 10-2 on pages 362–363 to find the amount of federal income tax to be deducted from each employee's gross pay.

Employee No.	Marital Status	Withholding Allowances	Weekly Salary
1	S	1	$550
2	M	3	675
3	S	2	480
4	M	1	420

Exercise 10-6 ►
Objective 7

Recording payroll transactions in the general journal.

Jackson Corporation has two office employees. A summary of their earnings and the related taxes withheld from their pay for the week ending June 6, 20--, follows.

	Scott Barkley	Jill Wrenn
Gross earnings	$780.00	$875.00
Social security deduction	(48.36)	(54.25)
Medicare deduction	(11.31)	(12.69)
Income tax withholding	(83.00)	(96.00)
Net pay for week	$637.33	$712.06

1. Give the general journal entry to record the company's payroll for the week. Use the account names given in this chapter.

2. Give the general journal entry to summarize the checks to pay the weekly payroll.

Exercise 10-7 ►
Objective 7

Journalizing payroll transactions.

On June 30, 20--, the payroll register of Food Products Wholesale Company showed the following totals for the month: gross earnings, $19,200; social security tax, $1,190; Medicare tax, $278; income tax, $1,520; and net amount due, $16,212. Of the total earnings, $15,200 was for sales salaries and $4,000 was for office salaries. Prepare a general journal entry to record the monthly payroll of the firm on June 30, 20--.

Problems

Selected problems can be completed using:
🍑 **Peachtree**   QB **QuickBooks**   ▦ **Spreadsheets**

PROBLEM SET A

Problem 10-1A ►
Objectives 2, 3, 4, 5, 6, 7

Computing gross earnings, determining deductions, preparing payroll register, journalizing payroll transactions.

Movie Time Theaters has four employees and pays them on an hourly basis. During the week beginning June 1 and ending June 7, 20--, these employees worked the hours shown below. Information about hourly rates, marital status, withholding allowances, and cumulative earnings prior to the current pay period also appears below.

Employee	Hours Worked	Hourly Rate	Marital Status	Withholding Allowances	Cumulative Earnings
Gary Smith	45	$9.25	M	4	$ 9,620
Ben Lewis	43	9.75	S	1	10,140
Shawn Jones	37	8.90	S	2	9,256
Debbie Watson	47	9.00	M	1	9,360

INSTRUCTIONS

1. Enter the basic payroll information for each employee in a payroll register. Record the employee's name, number of withholding allowances, marital status, total and overtime hours, and hourly rate. Consider any hours worked more than 40 in the week as overtime hours.

2. Compute the regular, overtime, and gross earnings for each employee. Enter the figures in the payroll register.

3. Compute the amount of social security tax to be withheld from each employee's earnings. Assume a 6.2 percent social security rate on the first $76,200 earned by the employee during the year. Enter the figures in the payroll register.

4. Compute the amount of Medicare tax to be withheld from each employee's earnings. Assume a 1.45 percent Medicare tax rate on all salaries and wages earned by the employee during the year. Enter the figures in the payroll register.

5. Determine the amount of federal income tax to be withheld from each employee's total earnings. Use the tax tables in Figure 10-2 on pages 362–363. Enter the figures in the payroll register.

6. Compute the net pay of each employee and enter the figures in the payroll register.

7. Total and prove the payroll register. Watson is an office worker. All other employees work in the theater.

8. Prepare a general journal entry to record the payroll for the week ended June 7, 20--.

9. Record the general journal entry to summarize payment of the payroll on June 10, 20--.

Analyze: What are Gary Smith's cumulative earnings on June 7?

Computing gross earnings, determining deductions, preparing payroll register, journalizing payroll transactions.

◄ **Problem 10-2A**
Objectives 2, 3, 4, 5, 6, 7

Tom Phillips operates Same Day Delivery Service. He has four employees who are paid on an hourly basis. During the work week beginning December 12 and ending December 18, 20--, his employees worked the following number of hours. Information about their hourly rates, marital status, and withholding allowances also follows, along with their cumulative earnings for the year prior to the December 12–18 payroll period.

Employee	Hours Worked	Hourly Rate	Marital Status	Withholding Allowances	Cumulative Earnings
Jason Knight	44	$ 9.85	M	3	$19,700
Aaron Fuller	39	26.50	S	1	55,120
Jon Perot	46	22.75	M	2	47,320
Kelly Aikman	43	10.50	S	0	21,840

INSTRUCTIONS

1. Enter the basic payroll information for each employee in a payroll register. Record the employee's name, number of withholding allowances, marital status, total and overtime hours, and hourly rate. Consider any hours worked more than 40 in the week as overtime hours.

2. Compute the regular, overtime, and gross earnings for each employee. Enter the figures in the payroll register.

3. Compute the amount of social security tax to be withheld from each employee's gross earnings. Assume a 6.2 percent social security rate on the first $76,200 earned by the employee during the year. Enter the figures in the payroll register.

4. Compute the amount of Medicare tax to be withheld from each employee's gross earnings. Assume a 1.45 percent Medicare tax rate on all salaries and wages earned by the employee during the year. Enter the figures in the payroll register.

5. Determine the amount of federal income tax to be withheld from each employee's total earnings. Fuller's withholding is $197, and Perot's is $142. Use the tax tables in Figure 10-2 on pages 362–363 to determine the withholding for Knight and Aikman. Enter the figures in the payroll register.

6. Compute the net amount due each employee and enter the figures in the payroll register.

7. Total and prove the payroll register. Knight and Aikman are office workers. Fuller and Perot are delivery workers.

8. Prepare a general journal entry to record the payroll for the week ended December 18, 20--.

9. Give the entry in general journal form on December 20, 20--, to summarize payment of wages for the week.

Analyze: What percentage of total taxable wages was delivery wages?

PROBLEM SET B

Problem 10-1B ►
Objectives 2, 3, 4, 5, 6, 7

Computing earnings, determining deductions and net amount due, preparing payroll register, journalizing payroll transactions.

The four employees of Swan's Ice Cream Parlor are paid on an hourly basis. During the week March 6–12, 20--, these employees worked the following number of hours. Information about their hourly rates, marital status, withholding allowances, and cumulative earnings prior to the current pay period also follows.

Employee	Hours Worked	Hourly Rate	Marital Status	Withholding Allowances	Cumulative Earnings
Corey Hunter	45	$8.75	M	4	$2,800.00
Peter Black	26	7.50	M	1	2,400.00
Latoya Snow	43	7.75	S	0	2,480.00
Haven England	13	7.25	S	2	0.00

1. Enter the basic payroll information for each employee in a payroll register. Record the employee's name, number of withholding allowances, marital status, total number of hours worked, overtime hours, and hourly rate. Consider any hours worked beyond 40 in the week as overtime hours.

2. Compute the regular earnings, overtime earnings, and gross earnings for each employee. Enter the figures in the payroll register.

3. Compute the amount of social security tax to be withheld from each employee's gross earnings. Assume a 6.2 percent social security tax rate on the first $76,200 earned by each employee during the year. Enter the figures in the payroll register.

4. Compute the amount of Medicare tax to be withheld from each employee's gross earnings. Assume a 1.45 percent Medicare tax rate on all earnings for each employee during the year. Enter the figure on the payroll register.

5. Determine the amount of federal income tax to be withheld from each employee's gross earnings. Use the tax tables in Figure 10-2 on pages 362–363. Enter the amounts in the payroll register.

6. Compute the net amount due each employee and enter the figures in the payroll register.

7. Complete the payroll register. All employees are classified as store employees.

8. Prepare a general journal entry to record the payroll for the week ended March 12, 20--.

9. Record the general journal entry to summarize the payment on March 14, 20-- of the net amount due employees.

Analyze: What is the difference between the amount credited to the **Cash** account on March 14 for the payroll week ended March 12 and the amount debited to **Store Wages Expenses** for the same payroll period? What causes the difference between these two figures?

Computing earnings, determining deductions and net amount due, preparing payroll register, journalizing payroll transactions.

◄ **Problem 10-2B**
Objectives 2, 3, 4, 5, 6, 7

David Flores operates Flores Consulting Service. He has four employees and pays them on an hourly basis. During the week November 6–12, 20--, his employees worked the following number of hours. Information about their hourly rates, marital status, withholding allowances, and cumulative earnings for the year prior to the current pay period also follows.

Employee	Hours Worked	Hourly Rate	Marital Status	Withholding Allowances	Cumulative Earnings
Barbara Cain	43	$ 8.50	M	2	$15,640
Casey Bryant	36	8.25	S	1	15,180
Linda Hogan	45	28.00	M	3	51,520
Leona Stewart	41	33.00	S	1	77,500

INSTRUCTIONS

1. Enter the basic payroll information for each employee in a payroll register. Record the employee's name, number of withholding allowances, marital status, total hours, overtime hours, and hourly rate. Consider any hours worked beyond 40 in the week as overtime hours.

2. Compute the regular earnings, overtime earnings, and gross earnings for each employee. Enter the figures in the payroll register.

3. Compute the amount of social security tax to be withheld from each employee's gross earnings. Assume a 6.2 percent social security rate on the first $76,200 earned by the employee during the year. Enter the figures in the payroll register.

4. Compute the amount of Medicare tax to be withheld from each employee's gross earnings. Assume a 1.45 percent Medicare tax rate on all earnings paid during the year. Enter the figures in the payroll register.

5. Determine the amount of federal income tax to be withheld from each employee's earnings. Federal income tax to be withheld from Hogan's pay is $189 and from Stewart's pay is $296. Use the tax tables in Figure 10-2 on pages 362–363 to determine the withholding for Cain and Bryant. Enter the figures in the payroll register.

6. Compute the net amount due each employee and enter the figures in the payroll register.

7. Complete the payroll register. Cain and Bryant are office workers. Earnings for Hogan and Stewart are charged to consulting wages.

8. Prepare a general journal entry to record the payroll for the week ended November 12, 20--. Use the account names given in this chapter.

9. Give the general journal entry to summarize payment of amounts due employees on November 15, 20--.

Analyze: What total deductions were taken from employee paychecks for the pay period ended November 12?

Payroll Accounting

Bueno Company pays salaries and wages on the last day of each month. Payments made on November 30, 20--, for amounts incurred during November are shown below. Cumulative amounts paid prior to November 30 to the persons named are also shown.

a. Jason Jackson, president, gross monthly salary $14,000; gross earnings paid prior to November 30, $140,000.

b. Laura Peters, vice president, gross monthly salary $11,000; gross earnings paid prior to November 30, $55,000.

c. Martha Spiller, independent accountant who audits the company's accounts and performs certain consulting services, $13,000; gross amount paid prior to November 30, $5,000.

d. Pat Hammon, treasurer, gross monthly salary $5,000; gross earnings paid prior to November 30, $50,000.

e. Payment to Anderson Security Services for Neal Black, a security guard who is on duty on Saturdays and Sundays, $900; amount paid to Anderson Security prior to November 30, $10,500.

INSTRUCTIONS

1. Using the tax rates and earnings bases given in this chapter, prepare a schedule showing this information:

    a. Each employee's cumulative earnings prior to November 30, 20--.

    b. Each employee's gross earnings for November.

    c. The amounts to be withheld for each payroll tax from each employee's earnings (employee income tax withholdings for Jackson are $3,700; for Peters, $3,200; and for Hammon, $875).

    d. The net amount due each employee.

    e. The total gross earnings, the total of each payroll tax deduction, and the total net amount payable to employees.

2. Record the general journal entry for the company's payroll on November 30, 20--.

3. Record the general journal entry for payments to employees on November 30, 20--.

Analyze: What is the balance of the **Salaries Payable** account after all payroll entries have been posted for the month?

Payroll Internal Controls

Several years ago, Hector Martinez opened the Fajita Grill, a restaurant specializing in homemade Mexican food. The restaurant was so successful that Martinez was able to expand, and his company now operates seven restaurants in the local area.

Martinez tells you that when he first started, he handled all aspects of the business himself. Now that there are seven Fajita Grills, he depends on the managers of each restaurant to make decisions and oversee day-to-day operations. Hector oversees operations at the company's headquarters, which is located at the first Fajita Grill.

Each manager interviews and hires new employees for a restaurant. The new employee is required to complete a Form W-4, which is sent by the manager to the headquarters office. Each restaurant has a time clock, and employees are required to clock in as they arrive or depart. Blank time cards are kept in a box under the time clock. At the beginning of each week, employees complete the top of the card they will use during the week. The manager collects the cards at the end of the week and sends them to headquarters.

Hector hired his cousin Rosa Maria to prepare the payroll instead of assigning this task to the accounting staff. Since she is a relative, Hector trusts her and has confidence that confidential payroll information will not be divulged to other employees.

When Rosa Maria receives a Form W-4 for a new employee, she sets up an individual earnings record for the employee. Each week, using the time cards sent by each restaurant's manager, she computes the gross pay, deductions, and net pay for all employees. She then posts details to the employees' earnings records and prepares and signs the payroll checks. The checks are sent to the managers, who distribute them to the employees.

As long as Rosa Maria receives a time card for an employee, she prepares a paycheck. If she fails to get a time card for an employee, she checks with the manager to see if the employee was terminated or has quit. At the end of the month, Rosa Maria reconciles the payroll bank account. She also prepares quarterly and annual payroll tax returns.

1. Identify any weaknesses in Fajita Grill's payroll system.

2. Identify one way a manager could defraud Fajita Grill under the present payroll system.

3. What internal control procedures would you recommend to Hector to protect against the fraud you identified above?

Business Connections

◄ Connection 1

MANAGERIAL FOCUS   **Cash Management**

1. Why should managers check the amount spent for overtime?
2. The new controller for Ellis Company, a manufacturing firm, has suggested to management that the business change from paying the factory employees in cash to paying them by check. What reasons would you offer to support this suggestion?
3. Why should management make sure that a firm has an adequate set of payroll records?
4. How can detailed payroll records help managers to control expenses?

◄ Connection 2

Ethical DILEMMA   **Clocking Out** You are employed by a firm that uses a time clock for employees to punch in when they arrive at work and punch out at quitting time. One employee asks you to punch out for him on a day that he plans to leave work two hours early. What will you do?

◄ Connection 3

Street WISE:
Questions from the Real World   **Human Resources** Refer to the *1999 Annual Report* of The Home Depot in Appendix B.

1. Locate the letter written by the president and chief executive officer to the stockholders, customers, and associates. Describe the goals and company vision in regard to the employees of The Home Depot. Based on your knowledge of The Home Depot stores and the financial information presented in Appendix B, what types of positions do you think the company hires? Describe whether you think each job position listed is paid on hourly rate, commission, or salary basis.
2. Locate the financial discussion titled "Fiscal year ended January 30, 2000 compared to January 31, 1999." Describe the financial data regarding payroll expenses. What factors contributed to increases in payroll expenses?

◄ Connection 4

FINANCIAL STATEMENT ANALYSIS   **Income Statement** Southwest Airlines Co. reported the following data on its consolidated statement of income for the years ended December 31, 1999, 1998, and 1997.

Southwest Airlines Co.			
Consolidated Statement of Income			
(in thousands except per share amounts)	Years Ended December 31		
	1999	*1998*	*1997*
Operating expenses:			
Salaries, wages, and benefits	1,455,237	1,285,942	1,136,542
Total operating expenses	3,954,011	3,480,369	3,292,582

Analyze:

1. The amounts reported for the line item "Salaries, wages, and benefits" include expenses for company retirement plans and profit-sharing plans. If Southwest Airlines Co. spent approximately $1,263,237,000 on wages and salaries alone, compute the employer's Medicare tax expense for 1999. Use a rate of 1.45 percent.

2. What percentage of total operating expenses was spent on salaries, wages, and benefits in 1999?

3. By what amount did salaries, wages, and benefits increase from 1997 to 1999?

Analyze Online: Go to the company Web site for Southwest Airlines Co. **(www.southwest.com).** Locate the company fact sheet within the *About SWA* section of the site.

4. How many employees does Southwest Airlines Co. employ?

5. How many resumes were submitted to the company for consideration in the current year?

Connection 5 ►

Extending the *Thought*   **Exempt Employees** Salaried exempt employees generally work for a predetermined annual rate regardless of the actual number of hours they work. In many cases, supervisors and managers work considerably more than 40 hours per week. What do you think of this practice from the employee's perspective? From the employer's perspective?

Connection 6 ►

Business Communication   **Pie Chart** Employees should understand how take-home, or net, pay is computed. As the payroll manager, you have been asked to make a presentation to the employees of Broad Street Bakery on how their gross earnings are allocated to taxes and net pay. You decide that a visual representation of the allocation would be most effective. Create a pie chart for the following information.

Employee: Carol Blakley		Federal income tax:	$ 35.00
Gross earnings:	$312.00	State income tax:	6.71
Social security tax:	20.79	Medical insurance:	4.10
Medicare tax:	4.86	Net pay:	240.54

Connection 7 ►

Team*Work*   **Career Research** ADP, Inc., provides payroll services to clients worldwide. The company processes paychecks for 29 million workers each payday. As a team, research career opportunities found on the ADP Web site **(www.adp.com).** Identify one job title of interest to each member of your team and prepare a report comparing the jobs.

Connection 8 ►

inter **NET**
CONNECTION   **U.S. Department of Labor** The federal government makes a great deal of information available related to wages and earnings. Visit the Department of Labor Web site at **www.dol.gov.** What is the current minimum wage? Give three examples of employees who are exempt from both minimum wage and overtime pay requirements. When both the federal and state laws apply, which standard of laws must be observed?

Answers to Section 1 Self Review

1. The federal requirement that covered employees be paid at a rate equal to one and one-half times their normal hourly rate for each hour worked in excess of 40 hours per week.

2. By a tax levied equally on both employers and employees. The tax amount is based on the earnings.

3. By state and federal taxes levied on the employer.

4. **d.** does not exist.

5. **a.** employees who become unemployed.

6. She is not an employee. She is an independent contractor because she has been hired to complete a specific job and is not under the control of the employer.

Answers to Section 2 Self Review

1. Social security tax, Medicare tax, and federal income tax

2. Health insurance premiums, life insurance premiums, union dues, retirement plans

3. Amount of earnings, period covered by the payment, employee's marital status, and the number of withholding allowances

4. **b.** $392

5. **d.** hours worked

6. When you receive a signed Form W-4 for the change in withholding.

Answers to Section 3 Self Review

1. Debit **Salaries and Wages Payable** and credit **Cash.**

2. Using a separate payroll account simplifies the bank reconciliation procedure and makes it easier to identify outstanding payroll checks.

3. Employee's name, address, social security number, date of birth, number of withholding allowances claimed, rate of pay, and any other information needed to compute earnings and complete tax reports.

4. **c.** liability account.

5. **a.** payroll register.

6. **Health Insurance Premiums Expense** Dr. 20.00 should be **Health Insurance Premiums Payable** Cr. 20.00; **Social Security Taxes Expense** Cr. 103.48 should be **Social Security Tax Payable** Cr. 103.48; **Cash** Cr. 1,311.64 should be **Salaries and Wages Payable** Cr. 1,311.64

Answers to Comprehensive Self Review

1. To compensate workers for losses suffered from job-related injuries or to compensate their families if the employee's death occurs in the course of employment.

2. Social security taxes are determined by multiplying the amount of taxable earnings by the social security tax rate.

3. To record in one place all information about an employee's earnings and withholdings for the period.

4. By check because there is far less possibility of mistake, lost money, or fraud. The check serves as a receipt and permanent record of the transaction.

5. An employee is one who is hired by the employer and who is under the control and direction of the employer. An independent contractor is paid by the company to carry out a specific task or job and is not under the direct supervision and control of the employer.

CHAPTER 11

Learning Objectives

1. Explain how and when payroll taxes are paid to the government.

2. Compute and record the employer's social security and Medicare taxes.

3. Record deposit of social security, Medicare, and employee income taxes.

4. Prepare an Employer's Quarterly Federal Tax Return, Form 941.

5. Prepare Wage and Tax Statement (Form W-2) and Annual Transmittal of Wage and Tax Statements (Form W-3).

6. Compute and record liability for federal and state unemployment taxes and record payment of the taxes.

7. Prepare an Employer's Federal Unemployment Tax Return, Form 940 or 940-EZ.

8. Compute and record workers' compensation insurance premiums.

9. Define the accounting terms new to this chapter.

Payroll Taxes, Deposits, and Reports

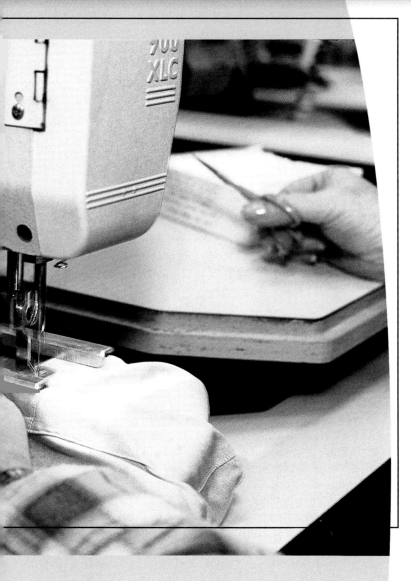

© Lands' End, Inc. Used with permission.

www.landsend.com

*I*n 1963 the first Lands' End store opened in the old tannery district of Chicago. It started with catalog sales of sailing equipment, duffel bags, and clothing suitable for sailing. Now the company operates 16 outlet stores in the United States and two outlet stores in the United Kingdom and Japan. Lands' End is also on the Internet.

In 1999 the company employed approximately 7,200 individuals. During the peak holiday season (September to December), the employee count increases to 9,700. Keeping accurate payroll records for a workforce of this size requires an effective payroll system and a knowledgeable accounting staff.

Thinking Critically
Lands' End hires a large number of seasonal employees. What challenges does this present to the payroll accounting department?

For more information on Lands' End, go to: collegeaccounting.glencoe.com.

New Terms

Employer's Annual Federal Unemployment Tax Return, Form 940 or Form 940-EZ

Employer's Quarterly Federal Tax Return, Form 941

Experience rating system

Merit rating system

Transmittal of Wage and Tax Statements, Form W-3

Unemployment insurance program

Wage and Tax Statement, Form W-2

Withholding statement

Section Objectives

1 **Explain how and when payroll taxes are paid to the government.**

WHY IT'S IMPORTANT
Employers are required by law to deposit payroll taxes.

2 **Compute and record the employer's social security and Medicare taxes.**

WHY IT'S IMPORTANT
Accounting records should reflect all liabilities.

3 **Record deposit of social security, Medicare, and employee income taxes.**

WHY IT'S IMPORTANT
Payments decrease the payroll tax liability.

4 **Prepare an Employer's Quarterly Federal Tax Return, Form 941.**

WHY IT'S IMPORTANT
Completing a federal tax return is part of the employer's legal obligation.

5 **Prepare Wage and Tax Statement (Form W-2) and Annual Transmittal of Wage and Tax Statements (Form W-3).**

WHY IT'S IMPORTANT
Employers are legally required to provide end-of-year payroll information.

Terms to Learn

Employer's Quarterly Federal Tax Return, Form 941
Transmittal of Wage and Tax Statements, Form W-3
Wage and Tax Statement, Form W-2
withholding statement

Social Security, Medicare, and Employee Income Tax

In Chapter 10 you learned that the law requires employers to act as collection agents for certain taxes due from employees. In this chapter you will learn how to compute the employer's taxes, make tax payments, and file the required tax returns and reports.

Payment of Payroll Taxes

The payroll register provides information about wages subject to payroll taxes. Figure 11-1 on page 391 shows a portion of the payroll register for On Line Furnishings for the week ending January 6.

Employers make tax deposits for federal income tax withheld from employee earnings, the employees' share of social security and Medicare taxes withheld from earnings, and the employer's share of social security and Medicare taxes. The deposits are made in a Federal Reserve Bank or other authorized financial institution. Businesses usually make payroll tax deposits at their own bank. There are two ways to deposit payroll taxes: by electronic deposit or with a tax deposit coupon.

The *Electronic Federal Tax Payment System (EFTPS)* is a system for electronically depositing employment taxes using a telephone or a computer. Any employer can use EFTPS. An employer *must* use EFTPS if the annual federal tax deposits are more than $200,000. Employers who are required to make electronic deposits and do not do so can be subject to a 10 percent penalty.

Employers who are not required to use EFTPS may deposit payroll taxes using a *Federal Tax Deposit Coupon, Form 8109*. The employer's name, tax identification number, and address are preprinted on Form 8109. The employer enters the deposit amount on the form and makes the payment with a check, money order, or cash.

In some cases an employer may use Form 8109-B. *Form 8109-B is a coupon that is not preprinted.* Form 8109-B may be used if a new employer has been assigned an identification number but has not yet received a supply of Forms 8109, or an employer has not received a resupply of Forms 8109. Figure 11-2 on page 391 shows the completed Form 8109-B for On Line Furnishings.

The frequency of deposits depends on the amount of tax liability. The amount currently owed is compared to the tax liability threshold. For simplicity this textbook uses $1,000 as the tax liability threshold.

The deposit schedules are not related to how often employees are paid. The deposit schedules are based on the amount currently owed and the amount reported in the lookback period. The *lookback period* is a four-quarter period ending on June 30 of the preceding year.

| AND ENDING _January 6, 20--_ | | | | | | | | PAID _January 8, 20--_ | | | |

TAXABLE WAGES			DEDUCTIONS				DISTRIBUTION			
SOCIAL SECURITY	MEDICARE	FUTA	SOCIAL SECURITY	MEDICARE	INCOME TAX	HEALTH INSURANCE	NET AMOUNT	CHECK NO.	OFFICE SALARIES	SHIPPING WAGES
360 00	360 00	360 00	22 32	5 22	28 00		304 46	1725		360 00
380 00	380 00	380 00	23 56	5 51	42 00		308 93	1726		380 00
300 00	300 00	300 00	18 60	4 35	14 00	20 00	243 05	1727		300 00
520 00	520 00	520 00	32 24	7 54	44 00	20 00	416 22	1728		520 00
400 00	400 00	400 00	24 80	5 80	45 00		324 40	1729	400 00	
1 960 00	1 960 00	1 960 00	121 52	28 42	173 00	40 00	1 597 06		400 00	1 560 00

1. If the amount owed is less than $1,000, payment is due quarterly with the payroll tax return (Form 941).

    Example. An employer's tax liability is as follows:

January	$290
February	320
March	310
	$920

    Since at no time during the quarter is the accumulated tax liability $1,000 or more, no deposit is required during the quarter. The employer may pay the amount with the payroll tax returns.

2. If the amount owed is $1,000 or more, the schedule is determined from the total taxes reported on Form 941 during the lookback period.

    a. If the amount reported in the lookback period was $50,000 or less, the employer is subject to the *Monthly Deposit Schedule Rule*. Monthly payments are due on the 15th day of the following month. For example, the January payment is due by February 15.

    b. If the amount reported in the lookback period was more than $50,000, the employer is subject to the *Semiweekly Deposit Schedule Rule*. "Semiweekly" refers to the fact that deposits are due on either Wednesdays or Fridays, depending on the employer's payday.

▲ **FIGURE 11-1**
Portion of a Payroll Register

① Objective
Explain how and when payroll taxes are paid to the government.

▼ **FIGURE 11-2**
Federal Tax Deposit Coupon, Form 8109-B

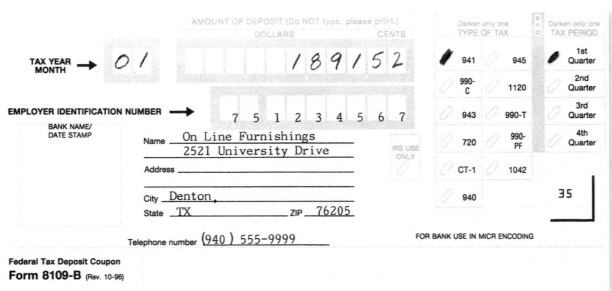

- If payday is a Wednesday, Thursday, or Friday, the deposit is due on the following Wednesday.
- If payday is a Saturday, Sunday, Monday, or Tuesday, the deposit is due on the following Friday.

   c. For new employers with no lookback period, if the amount owed is $1,000 or more, payments are due under the Monthly Deposit Schedule Rule.

3. If the total accumulated tax liability reaches $100,000 or more on any day, a deposit is due on the next banking day. This applies even if the employer is on a monthly or a semiweekly deposit schedule.

Employer's Social Security and Medicare Tax Expenses

② Objective
Compute and record the employer's social security and Medicare taxes.

Tax Liability
The employer's tax liability is the amount owed for
- employee withholdings (income tax, social security tax, Medicare tax);
- employer's share of social security and Medicare taxes.

Remember that both employers and employees pay social security and Medicare taxes. Figure 11-1 shows the *employee's* share of these payroll taxes. The *employer* pays the same amount of payroll taxes. At the assumed rate of 6.2 percent for social security and 1.45 percent for Medicare tax, the employer's tax liability is $299.88.

	Employee (Withheld)	Employer (Matched)
Social security	$121.52	$121.52
Medicare	28.42	28.42
	$149.94	$149.94
Total	$299.88	

In Chapter 10 you learned how to record employee payroll deductions. The entry to record the employer's share of social security and Medicare taxes is made at the end of each payroll period. The debit is to the **Payroll Taxes Expense** account. The credits are to the same liability accounts used to record the employee's share of payroll taxes.

Business Transaction

On January 8 On Line Furnishings recorded the employer's share of social security and Medicare taxes. The information on the payroll register (Figure 11-1 on page 391) is used to record the payroll taxes expense.

Analysis

The expense account, **Payroll Taxes Expense,** is increased by the employer's share of social security and Medicare taxes, $149.94. The liability account, **Social Security Tax Payable,** is increased by $121.52. The liability account, **Medicare Tax Payable,** is increased by $28.42.

Debit-Credit Rules

DEBIT Increases to expense accounts are recorded as debits. Debit **Payroll Taxes Expense** for $149.94.

CREDIT Increases to liability accounts are recorded as credits. Credit **Social Security Tax Payable** for $121.52. Credit **Medicare Tax Payable** for $28.42.

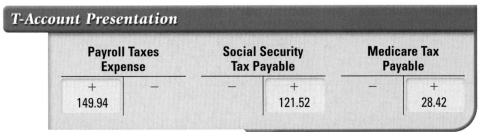

T-Account Presentation

Payroll Taxes Expense	Social Security Tax Payable	Medicare Tax Payable
+ | –	– | +	– | +
149.94	121.52	28.42

General Journal Entry

	DATE	DESCRIPTION	POST. REF.	DEBIT	CREDIT	
1	20--					1
2	Jan. 8	Payroll Taxes Expense		1 4 9 94		2
3		Social Security Tax Payable			1 2 1 52	3
4		Medicare Tax Payable			2 8 42	4
5		To record social security and				5
6		Medicare taxes for Jan. 8 payroll				6

GENERAL JOURNAL   PAGE 1

The Bottom Line

Employer's Payroll Taxes

Income Statement

Expenses	↑ 149.94
Net Income	↓ 149.94

Balance Sheet

Liabilities	↑ 149.94
Equity	↓ 149.94

According to the American Payroll Association, the Social Security Administration provides benefits to approximately 44 million men, women, and children. It is essential that earnings are correctly reported so that future benefits can be calculated accurately.

Recording the Payment of Taxes Withheld

At the end of January, the accounting records for On Line Furnishings contained the following information.

	Employee (Withheld)	Employer (Matched)	Total
Social security	$ 486.08	$486.08	$ 972.16
Medicare	113.68	113.68	227.36
Federal income tax	692.00	–	692.00
Total	$1,291.76	$599.76	$1,891.52

On Line Furnishings is on a monthly payment schedule. The amount reported in the lookback period is less than $50,000. The current payroll tax liability is more than $1,000. (Recall that this textbook uses $1,000 as the tax liability threshold.) A tax payment is due on the 15th day of the following month, February 15.

Figure 11-2 on page 391 shows the Federal Tax Deposit Coupon for On Line Furnishings. Notice that the type of tax (Form 941) and the tax period (first quarter) are indicated on the form. The coupon is accompanied by a check from On Line Furnishings for $1,891.52 written to First State Bank, an authorized financial institution.

The entry to record the tax deposit is shown on page 394. The entry is shown in general journal form for illustration purposes only. (On Line Furnishings actually uses a cash payments journal.)

③ Objective

Record deposit of social security, Medicare, and employee income taxes.

GENERAL JOURNAL   PAGE _2_

	DATE		DESCRIPTION	POST. REF.	DEBIT	CREDIT	
1	20--						1
22	Feb.	15	Social Security Tax Payable		9 7 2 16		22
23			Medicare Tax Payable		2 2 7 36		23
24			Employee Income Tax Payable		6 9 2 00		24
25			Cash			1 8 9 1 52	25
26			Deposit of payroll taxes withholding				26
27			at First State Bank				27

February Payroll Records

There were four weekly payroll periods in February. Each hourly employee worked the same number of hours each week and had the same gross pay and deductions as in January. The office clerk earned her regular salary and had the same deductions as in January. At the end of the month

- the individual earnings records were updated;
- Form 8109, Federal Tax Deposit Coupon, was prepared, and the taxes were deposited before March 15;
- the tax deposit was recorded in the cash payments journal.

March Payroll Records

There were five weekly payroll periods in March. Assume that the payroll period ended on March 31, and the payday was on March 31. Also assume that the earnings and deductions of the employees were the same for each week as in January and February. At the end of the month the individual earnings records were updated, the taxes were deposited, and the tax deposit was recorded in the cash payments journal.

Quarterly Summary of Earnings Records

At the end of each quarter, the individual earnings records are totaled. This involves adding the columns in the Earnings, Deductions, and Net Pay sections. Figure 11-3 on page 395 shows the earnings record, posted and summarized, for Cindy Taylor for the first quarter.

Table 11-1 below shows the quarterly totals for each employee of On Line Furnishings. This information is taken from the individual earnings records. Through the end of the first quarter, no employee has exceeded the social security earnings limit ($76,200) or the FUTA/SUTA limit ($7,000).

TABLE 11-1 ▼
Summary of Earnings

	Summary of Earnings, Quarter Ended March 31, 20--						
	Taxable Earnings				**Deductions**		
Employee	**Total Earnings**	**Social Security**	**Medicare**	**SUTA & FUTA**	**Social Security**	**Medicare Tax**	**Income Tax**
Cindy Taylor	4,680	4,680	4,680	4,680	290.16	67.86	364.00
Edward Gallegos	4,940	4,940	4,940	4,940	306.28	71.63	546.00
Bill Turner	3,900	3,900	3,900	3,900	241.80	56.55	182.00
Cecilia Lin	6,760	6,760	6,760	6,760	419.12	98.02	572.00
Selena Anderson	5,200	5,200	5,200	5,200	322.40	75.40	585.00
Totals	25,480	25,480	25,480	25,480	1,579.76	369.46	2,249.00

EARNINGS RECORD FOR ___ 20-- ___

NAME _Cindy Taylor_   RATE _$9 per hour_   SOCIAL SECURITY NO. _123-XX-XXXX_
ADDRESS _6480 Oak Tree Drive, Denton, TX 76209-6789_   DATE OF BIRTH _November 23, 1979_
WITHHOLDING ALLOWANCES _1_   MARITAL STATUS _M_

PAYROLL NO.	WK. END.	PAID	RG	OT	REGULAR	OVERTIME	TOTAL	CUMULATIVE	SOCIAL SECURITY	MEDICARE	INCOME TAX	OTHER	NET PAY
1	1/06	1/08	40		360 00		360 00	360 00	22 32	5 22	28 00		304 46
2	1/13	1/15	40		360 00		360 00	720 00	22 32	5 22	28 00		304 46
3	1/20	1/22	40		360 00		360 00	1080 00	22 32	5 22	28 00		304 46
4	1/27	1/29	40		360 00		360 00	1440 00	22 32	5 22	28 00		304 46
	January				1440 00		1440 00	1440 00	89 28	20 88	112 00		1217 84
1	2/03	2/05	40		360 00		360 00	360 00	22 32	5 22	28 00		304 46
2	2/10	2/12	40		360 00		360 00	720 00	22 32	5 22	28 00		304 46
3	2/17	2/19	40		360 00		360 00	1080 00	22 32	5 22	28 00		304 46
4	2/24	2/25	40		360 00		360 00	1440 00	22 32	5 22	28 00		304 46
	February				1440 00		1440 00	1440 00	89 28	20 88	112 00		1217 84
1	3/03	3/05	40		360 00		360 00	360 00	22 32	5 22	28 00		304 46
2	3/10	3/12	40		360 00		360 00	720 00	22 32	5 22	28 00		304 46
3	3/17	3/19	40		360 00		360 00	1080 00	22 32	5 22	28 00		304 46
4	3/24	3/26	40		360 00		360 00	1440 00	22 32	5 22	28 00		304 46
5	3/31	3/31	40		360 00		360 00	1800 00	22 32	5 22	28 00		304 46
					1800 00		1800 00	1800 00	111 60	26 10	140 00		1522 30
	March												
					4680 00		4680 00	4680 00	290 16	67 86	364 00		3957 98
	First Quarter												

▲ FIGURE 11-3
Individual Earnings Record

Employer's Quarterly Federal Tax Return

Each quarter an employer files an **Employer's Quarterly Federal Tax Return, Form 941** with the Internal Revenue Service. Form 941 must be filed by all employers subject to federal income tax withholding, social security tax, or Medicare tax, with certain exceptions as specified in *Publication 15, Circular E*. This tax return provides information about employee earnings, the tax liability for each month in the quarter, and the deposits made.

> The Social Security Administration administers the Old Age and Survivors, Disability Insurance, and Supplemental Security Income Programs. These programs are funded by the social security taxes collected from employees and matched by employers. In 1999 more than $462 billion of social security taxes were collected by the Social Security Administration.

When to File Form 941. The due date for Form 941 is the last day of the month following the end of each calendar quarter. If the taxes for the quarter were deposited when due, the due date is extended by 10 days.

❹ Objective

Prepare an Employer's Quarterly Federal Tax Return, Form 941.

Important!

Quarters
A quarter is a three-month period. There are four quarters in a year:
- 1st quarter: January, February, March
- 2nd quarter: April, May, June
- 3rd quarter: July, August, September
- 4th quarter: October, November, December

Working Abroad

The IRS has tax treaties with more than 50 countries including Canada, Germany, and France. These tax treaties spell out exactly how income taxes are handled for U.S. citizens working abroad.

Tax Calculations
Social security and Medicare taxes are calculated by multiplying the taxable wages by the tax rate.

Completing Form 941. Figure 11-4 on page 397 shows Form 941 for On Line Furnishings. Form 941 is prepared using the data on the quarterly summary of earnings records, Table 11-1. Let's examine Form 941.

- Use the preprinted form if it is available. Otherwise, enter the employer's name, address, and identification number at the top of Form 941. Enter the date the quarter ended.
- *Line 1* is completed for the first quarter only. Enter the number of employees in the pay period that includes March 12.
- *Line 2* shows total wages and tips subject to withholding. For On Line Furnishings, the total subject to withholding is $25,480.
- *Line 3* shows the total employee income tax withheld during the quarter, $2,249.
- *Line 4* shows adjustments of income tax withheld in prior quarters of the year. This line would be used to show corrections of errors made in previous withholdings.
- *Line 5* shows the adjusted income tax withheld. Since there were no adjustments on Line 4, the amount on Line 5 is the same as on Line 3, $2,249.
- *Line 6a* shows the total amount of wages that are subject to social security taxes, $25,480. The amount is multiplied by the combined social security tax rate, 12.4 percent.

Social security tax:

Employee's share	6.2%
Employer's share	6.2
Total	12.4%

- *Line 6b* shows the amount of social security taxes, $3,159.52.
- *Line 6c* is for reporting social security tips. It is blank for On Line Furnishings.
- *Line 7a* shows the amount of wages and tips that are subject to Medicare taxes, $25,480. The amount is multiplied by the combined Medicare tax rate, 2.9 percent.

Medicare tax:

Employee's share	1.45%
Employer's share	1.45
Total	2.90%

- *Line 7b* shows the amount of Medicare taxes, $738.92.
- *Line 8* shows the total social security and Medicare taxes, $3,898.44 ($3,159.52 + $738.92).
- *Line 9* is blank. There were no adjustments.
- *Line 10* shows the adjusted social security and Medicare taxes, $3,898.44. It is the same as Line 8 because there were no adjustments on Line 9.
- *Line 11* shows the total tax liability for employee income tax withheld plus social security and Medicare taxes, $6,147.44 ($2,249.00 + $3,898.44).

Don't be surprised if there is a small difference between the tax withheld that is computed on Form 941 and the tax withheld that is computed on the sum of the payroll registers. Any small difference that is due to rounding is settled on Form 941.

Form 941
(Rev. October 2000)
Department of the Treasury
Internal Revenue Service

Employer's Quarterly Federal Tax Return
▶ See separate instructions for information on completing this return.
Please type or print.

OMB No. 1545-0029

Enter state code for state in which deposits were made **only** if different from state in address to the right ▶ ☐ : (see page 2 of instructions).

Name (as distinguished from trade name)	Date quarter ended
Roberta Rosario	*March 31, 20--*
Trade name, if any	Employer identification number
On Line Furnishings	*75-1234567*
Address (number and street)	City, state, and ZIP code
2521 University Drive	*Denton, TX 76205*

T	
FF	
FD	
FP	
I	
T	

If address is different from prior return, check here ▶ ☐

IRS Use

1 1 1 1 1 1 1 1 1 1   2   3 3 3 3 3 3 3 3   4 4 4   5 5 5

6   7   8 8 8 8 8 8 8   9 9 9 9 9   10 10 10 10 10 10 10 10 10 10

If you do not have to file returns in the future, check here ▶ ☐ and enter date final wages paid ▶
If you are a seasonal employer, see **Seasonal employers** on page 1 of the instructions and check here ▶ ☐

1	Number of employees in the pay period that includes March 12th ▶ 5	
2	Total wages and tips, plus other compensation	**2** 25,480 00
3	Total income tax withheld from wages, tips, and sick pay	**3** 2,249 00
4	Adjustment of withheld income tax for preceding quarters of calendar year	**4**
5	Adjusted total of income tax withheld (line 3 as adjusted by line 4—see instructions) .	**5** 2,249 00
6	Taxable social security wages . . . . . **6a** 25,480 00 × 12.4% (.124) =	**6b** 3,159 52
	Taxable social security tips . . . . . **6c** × 12.4% (.124) =	**6d**
7	Taxable Medicare wages and tips . . **7a** 25,480 00 × 2.9% (.029) =	**7b** 738 92
8	Total social security and Medicare taxes (add lines 6b, 6d, and 7b). Check here if wages are not subject to social security and/or Medicare tax . . . . ▶ ☐	**8** 3,898 44
9	Adjustment of social security and Medicare taxes (see instructions for required explanation) Sick Pay $ _____ ± Fractions of Cents $ _____ ± Other $ _____ =	**9**
10	Adjusted total of social security and Medicare taxes (line 8 as adjusted by line 9—see instructions)	**10** 3,898 44
11	**Total taxes** (add lines 5 and 10)	**11** 6,147 44
12	Advance earned income credit (EIC) payments made to employees	**12**
13	Net taxes (subtract line 12 from line 11). **If $1,000 or more, this must equal line 17, column (d) below (or line D of Schedule B (Form 941))**	**13** 6,147 44
14	Total deposits for quarter, including overpayment applied from a prior quarter	**14** 6,147 44
15	**Balance due** (subtract line 14 from line 13). See instructions	**15** 0 00
16	**Overpayment.** If line 14 is more than line 13, enter excess here ▶ $ _____ and check if to be: ☐ Applied to next return **or** ☐ Refunded.	

All filers: If line 13 is less than $1,000, you need not complete line 17 or Schedule B (Form 941).
Semiweekly schedule depositors: Complete Schedule B (Form 941) and check here . . . . ▶ ☐
Monthly schedule depositors: Complete line 17, columns (a) through (d), and check here . . . . ▶ ☒

17	**Monthly Summary of Federal Tax Liability.** Do not complete if you were a semiweekly schedule depositor		
(a) First month liability	**(b)** Second month liability	**(c)** Third month liability	**(d)** Total liability for quarter
1,891.52	*1,891.52*	*2,364.40*	*6,147.44*

Sign Here

Under penalties of perjury, I declare that I have examined this return, including accompanying schedules and statements, and to the best of my knowledge and belief, it is true, correct, and complete.

Signature ▶ *Roberta Rosario*   Print Your Name and Title ▶ *Roberta Rosario, Owner*   Date ▶ *April 30, 20--*

For Privacy Act and Paperwork Reduction Act Notice, see back of Payment Voucher.   Cat. No. 17001Z   Form **941** (Rev. 10-2000)

▲ **FIGURE 11-4** Employer's Quarterly Federal Tax Return, Form 941

- *Line 12* is blank. There were no advance earned income credit payments.
- *Line 13* shows total net taxes for the quarter, $6,147.44.
- *Line 14* shows total deposits for the quarter, $6,147.44. On Line Furnishings deposited all the taxes during the quarter.
- *Line 15* and *Line 16* are blank. There is no balance due and no overpayment.

Read Line 13 carefully. The taxes for On Line Furnishings were more than $1,000, so Line 17 is completed. This section shows the taxes for each month during the quarter. Line 17(d) and Line 13 must be equal.

If the employer did not make sufficient deposits, a check for the balance due is mailed to the Internal Revenue Service with Form 941. An employer may instead make a deposit at an authorized financial institution.

If the employer did not deduct enough taxes from an employee's earnings, the business pays the difference. The deficiency is debited to **Payroll Taxes Expense.**

Wage and Tax Statement, Form W-2

Employers provide a **Wage and Tax Statement, Form W-2**, to each employee by January 31 of the following year. Form W-2 is sometimes called a **withholding statement**. Form W-2 contains information about the employee's earnings and tax withholdings for the year. The information for Form W-2 comes from the employee's earnings record.

Employees who stop working for the business during the year may ask that a Form W-2 be issued early. The Form W-2 must be issued within 30 days after the request or after the final wage payment, whichever is later.

Figure 11-5 on page 399 shows Form W-2 for Cindy Taylor. This is the standard form provided by the Internal Revenue Service (IRS). Some employers use a "substitute" Form W-2 that is approved by the IRS. The substitute form permits the employer to list total deductions and to reconcile the gross earnings, the deductions, and the net pay. If the firm issues 250 or more Forms W-2, the returns must be filed electronically or on magnetic media (tape or disk).

At least four copies of each of Form W-2 are prepared:

1. One copy for the employer to send to the Social Security Administration, which shares the information with the IRS.

2. One copy for the employee to attach to the federal income tax return.

3. One copy for the employee's records.

4. One copy for the employer's records.

If there is a state income tax, two more copies of Form W-2 are prepared:

5. One copy for the employer to send to the state tax department.

6. One copy for the employee to attach to the state income tax return.

Additional copies are prepared if there is a city or county income tax.

> FedEx Corporation prepared and distributed 106,300 Forms W-2 to its employees for 1998.

⑤ Objective

Prepare Wage and Tax Statement (Form W-2) and Annual Transmittal of Wage and Tax Statements (Form W-3).

Important!

Form W-2

The employer must provide each employee with a Wage and Tax Statement, Form W-2, by January 31 of the following year.

a Control number		Void ☐	For Official Use Only ▶ OMB No. 1545-0008	

b Employer identification number 75-1234567	1 Wages, tips, other compensation 18,720.00	2 Federal income tax withheld 1,456.00

c Employer's name, address, and ZIP code On Line Furnishings 2521 University Drive Denton, TX 76205	3 Social security wages 18,720.00	4 Social security tax withheld 1,160.64
	5 Medicare wages and tips 18,720.00	6 Medicare tax withheld 271.44
	7 Social security tips	8 Allocated tips

d Employee's social security number 123-XX-XXXX	9 Advance EIC payment	10 Dependent care benefits

e Employee's name (first, middle initial, last) Cindy Taylor 6480 Oak Tree Drive Denton, TX 76209–6789	11 Nonqualified plans	12 Benefits included in box 1
	13 See instrs. for box 13	14 Other

15 Statutory employee ☐   Deceased ☐   Pension plan ☐   Legal rep. ☐   Deferred compensation ☐

f Employee's address and ZIP code

16 State TX	Employer's state I.D. no. 12-98765	17 State wages, tips, etc. 18,720.00	18 State income tax	19 Locality name	20 Local wages, tips, etc.	21 Local income tax

Form **W-2** Wage and Tax Statement   **20 - -**

Copy A For Social Security Administration—Send this entire page with Form W-3 to the Social Security Administration; photocopies are **not** acceptable.

Cat. No. 10134D

Department of the Treasury—Internal Revenue Service

For Privacy Act and Paperwork Reduction Act Notice, see separate instructions.

▲ **FIGURE 11-5**
Wage and Tax Statement, Form W-2

Annual Transmittal of Wage and Tax Statements, Form W-3

The **Transmittal of Wage and Tax Statements, Form W-3**, is submitted with Forms W-2 to the Social Security Administration. Form W-3 reports the total social security wages; total Medicare wages; total social security tax withheld; total Medicare tax withheld; total wages, tips, and other compensation; total federal income tax withheld; and other information.

A copy of Form W-2 for each employee is attached to Form W-3. Form W-3 is due by the last day of February following the end of the calendar year. The Social Security Administration shares the tax information on Forms W-2 with the Internal Revenue Service. Figure 11-6 on page 400 shows the completed Form W-3 for On Line Furnishings.

The amounts on Form W-3 must equal the sums of the amounts on the attached Forms W-2. For example, the amount entered in Box 1 of Form W-3 must equal the sum of the amounts entered in Box 1 of all the Forms W-2.

About Accounting

IRS Electronic Filing

More than 19 million taxpayers have filed their tax returns electronically. Returns that are filed electronically are more accurate than paper returns. Electronic filing means refunds in half the time, especially if the taxpayer chooses direct deposit of the refund.

FIGURE 11-6 ▶
Transmittal of
Wage and Tax
Statements,
Form W-3

a Control number	33333	For Official Use Only ▶ OMB No. 1545-0008		
b **Kind of Payer** ▶	941 ☒ Military ☐ 943 ☐ CT-1 ☐ Hshld. emp. ☐ Medicare govt. emp. ☐	1 Wages, tips, other compensation 101,920.00	2 Federal income tax withheld 8,996.00	
		3 Social security wages 101,920.00	4 Social security tax withheld 6,319.04	
c Total number of Forms W-2 5	d Establishment number	5 Medicare wages and tips 101,920.00	6 Medicare tax withheld 1,477.84	
e Employer identification number 75-1234567		7 Social security tips	8 Allocated tips	
f Employer's name Roberta Rosario		9 Advance EIC payments	10 Dependent care benefits	
On Line Furnishings 2521 University Drive Denton, TX 76205		11 Nonqualified plans	12 Deferred compensation	
		13		
		14		
g Employer's address and ZIP code				
h Other EIN used this year		15 Income tax withheld by third-party payer		
i Employer's state I.D. no. 12-98765				
Contact person Roberta Rosario	Telephone number (940) 555-9999	Fax number (940) 555-8018	E-mail address	

Under penalties of perjury, I declare that I have examined this return and accompanying documents, and, to the best of my knowledge and belief, they are true, correct, and complete.

Signature ▶ *Roberta Rosario*   Title ▶ *Owner*   Date ▶ *February 10, 20--*

Form **W-3** Transmittal of Wage and Tax Statements **20 - -**   Department of the Treasury
Internal Revenue Service

The amounts on Form W-3 also must equal the sums of the amounts reported on the Forms 941 during the year. For example, the social security wages reported on the Form W-3 must equal the sum of the social security wages reported on the four Forms 941.

The filing of Form W-3 marks the end of the routine procedures needed to account for payrolls and for payroll tax withholdings.

Section 1 Self Review

Questions

1. Where does a business deposit federal payroll taxes?

2. What is the purpose of Form 941?

3. What is the purpose of Form W-2?

Exercises

4. Employers usually record social security taxes in the accounting records at the end of

   a. each payroll period.

   b. each month.

   c. each quarter.

   d the year.

5. Which tax is shared equally by the employee and employer?

   a. Federal income tax

   b. State income tax

   c. Social security tax

   d. Federal unemployment tax

Analysis

6. Your business currently owes $2,550 in payroll taxes. During the lookback period, your business paid $10,000 in payroll taxes. How often does your business need to make payroll tax deposits?

(Answers to Section 1 Self Review are on page 426.)

Unemployment Tax and Workers' Compensation

Section 2

In Section 1 we discussed taxes that are withheld from employees' earnings and in some cases matched by the employer. In this section we will discuss payroll related expenses that are paid solely by the employer.

Unemployment Compensation Insurance Taxes

The unemployment compensation tax program, often called the **unemployment insurance program**, provides unemployment compensation through a tax levied on employers.

Coordination of Federal and State Unemployment Rates

The unemployment insurance program is a federal program that encourages states to provide unemployment insurance for employees working in the state. The federal government allows a credit—or reduction—in the federal unemployment tax for amounts charged by the state for unemployment taxes.

This text assumes that the federal unemployment tax rate is 6.2 percent less a state unemployment tax credit of 5.4 percent; thus the federal tax rate is reduced to 0.8 percent (6.2% − 5.4%). The earnings limits for the federal and the state unemployment tax are usually the same, $7,000.

A few states levy an unemployment tax on the employee. The tax is withheld from employee pay and remitted by the employer to the state.

For businesses that provide steady employment, the state unemployment tax rate may be lowered based on an **experience rating system**, or a **merit rating system**. Under the experience rating system, the state tax rate may be reduced to less than 1 percent for businesses that provide steady employment. In contrast, some states levy penalty rates as high as 10 percent for employers with poor records of providing steady employment.

The reduction of state unemployment taxes because of favorable experience ratings does not affect the credit allowable against the federal tax. An employer may take a credit against the federal unemployment tax as though it were paid at the normal state rate even though the employer actually pays the state a lower rate.

Because of its experience rating, On Line Furnishings pays state unemployment tax of 4.0 percent, which is less than the standard rate of 5.4 percent. Note that the business may take the credit for the full amount of the state rate (5.4%) against the federal rate, even though the business actually pays a state rate of 4.0%.

Section Objectives

6 Compute and record liability for federal and state unemployment taxes and record payment of the taxes.

WHY IT'S IMPORTANT
Businesses need to record all payroll tax liabilities.

7 Prepare an Employer's Federal Unemployment Tax Return, Form 940 or 940-EZ.

WHY IT'S IMPORTANT
The unemployment insurance programs provide support to individuals during temporary periods of unemployment.

8 Compute and record workers' compensation insurance premiums.

WHY IT'S IMPORTANT
Businesses need insurance to cover workplace injury claims.

Terms to Learn

Employer's Annual Federal Unemployment Tax Return, Form 940 or Form 940-EZ
experience rating system
merit rating system
unemployment insurance program

6 Objective

Compute and record liability for federal and state unemployment taxes and record payment of the taxes.

Computing and Recording Unemployment Taxes

On Line Furnishings records its state and federal unemployment tax expense at the end of each payroll period. The unemployment taxes for the payroll period ending January 6 are as follows.

Federal unemployment tax	($1,960 × 0.008) =	$15.68
State unemployment tax	($1,960 × 0.040) =	78.40
Total unemployment taxes	=	$94.08

The entry to record the employer's unemployment payroll taxes follows.

GENERAL JOURNAL   PAGE ___1___

	DATE		DESCRIPTION	POST. REF.	DEBIT	CREDIT	
8	Jan.	8	Payroll Taxes Expense		94 08		8
9			Federal Unemployment Tax Payable			15 68	9
10			State Unemployment Tax Payable			78 40	10
11			Unemployment taxes on				11
12			weekly payroll				12

Reporting and Paying State Unemployment Taxes

In most states the due date for the unemployment tax return is the last day of the month following the end of the quarter. Generally the tax is paid with the return.

Employer's Quarterly Report. Figure 11-7 on page 403 shows the Employer's Quarterly Report for the State of Texas filed by On Line Furnishings in April for the first quarter. The report for Texas is similar to the tax forms of other states. The top of the form contains information about the company.

- *Block 4* at the top of the form shows the tax rate assigned by the state based on the experience rating. The tax rate for On Line Furnishings is 4.0 percent.
- *Block 10* (3 boxes) shows the number of employees in the state on the 12th day of each month of the quarter.
- *Line 13* shows the total wages paid during the quarter to employees in the state, $25,480.
- *Line 14* shows the total *taxable* wages paid during the quarter, $25,480. Note that the limit on taxable wages is $7,000. Table 11-1 on page 394 shows that at the end of the first quarter, no employee earned more than $7,000. All wages and salaries are taxable for state unemployment. Actually, the base in Texas was changed to $9,000 for 1989 and later years. We use a base of $7,000 for the sake of simplicity and because the increase to $9,000 was intended to be "temporary."
- *Line 15* shows the total tax for the quarter. Taxable wages are multiplied by the tax rate ($25,480 × 0.04 = $1,019.20).
- *Lines 16a* and *b* are a breakdown of the amount on Line 15. In Texas, part of the 4 percent tax is set aside for job training and other incentive programs. Box 4a contains the tax rate for the unemployment tax (3.9%). Box 4b contains the tax rate for training incentives or *Smart Jobs Assessment* (0.1%).

TEXAS WORKFORCE COMMISSION
AUSTIN, TEXAS 78714-9037
(512)-463-2222

EMPLOYER'S QUARTERLY REPORT

11111

1. ACCOUNT NUMBER	2. COUNTY CODE	3. TAX AREA	4. TAX RATE	5. SIC CODE	6. FEDERAL I.D. NUMBER	7. QTR. YR.
12-98765	121	2	4.0 %	59	75-1234567	1st/20--

8. EMPLOYER NAME AND ADDRESS (SEE ITEM 25 FOR CHANGES TO NAME, ADDRESS, ETC.)

9. TELEPHONE NUMBER
(940) 555-9999

Roberta Rosario, DBA

On Line Furnishings

2521 University Drive

Denton, TX 76205

4a. UI TAX RATE	4b. SMART JOBS ASSESSMENT
3.9 %	.1 %

ALIGNMENT

9A. QUARTER ENDING

9B. PENALTIES WILL BE ASSESSED IF REPORT IS NOT POSTMARKED BY

1st Month	2nd Month	3rd Month
5	5	5

10. Enter in the boxes above the number of employees both full-time and part-time, in pay periods that include 12th day of the calendar month. (ENTER NUMERALS ONLY)

11. SHOW THE COUNTY CODE (see list on the back of this form) in which you had the greatest number of employees. **121**

12. IF you have employees in more than one county in TEXAS, how many are outside the county shown in Item 11?

	DOLLARS	CENTS
13. Total (Gross) Wages Paid During this Quarter to Texas Employees	25,480	00
14. Taxable Wages paid this quarter to each employee up to $7000, the annual maximum amount. (If none, enter "0")	25,480	00
15. Tax Due (Multiply Taxable Wages By Tax Rate, Item 4 Above)	1,019	20

You must FILE this return even though you had no payroll this quarter. If you had no payroll show '0' in item 13 and sign the declaration (item 26) on this form.

14a. ☐ Mark box with an 'X' if reporting wages to another state during the year for employees listed in Item 22.

16a. UI TAX	993	72		
b. Smart Jobs Assessment	25	48		
17. Interest, If Tax is Past Due				
18. Penalty, If Report Is Past Due				
19. Balance Due From Prior Periods (Subtract Credit Or Add Debit)				
20. Total Due - Make Remittance Payable To TEXAS WORKFORCE COMMISSION	1,019	20		

FOR TWC USE ONLY

	MONTH	DAY	YEAR
POSTMARK DATE C3			
POSTMARK DATE S			
EX DATE C3			
EX DATE S			

☐ Est

DOLLARS	CENTS	INITIALS

AMOUNT RECEIVED

21. SOCIAL SECURITY NUMBER	1ST INIT	2ND INIT	22. EMPLOYEE NAME LAST NAME	23. TOTAL WAGES PAID THIS QUARTER	
1 587-XX-XXXX			S. Anderson	5,200	00
2 427-XX-XXXX			E. Gallegos	4,940	00
3 687-XX-XXXX			C. Lin	6,760	00
4 123-XX-XXXX			C. Taylor	4,680	00
5 587-XX-XXXX			B. Turner	3,900	00
6					
7					
8					
9					
10					
24. PAGE TOTAL				25,480	00

26. I DECLARE that the information herein is true and correct to the best of my knowledge and belief.

SIGNATURE _Roberta Rosario_

TITLE _Owner_ DATE 4/29/20--

PREPARERS NAME _Roberta Rosario_

PREPARERS PHONE NUMBER _(940) 555-9999_

For assistance in completing form call,

MAIL REPORT AND REMITTANCE TO:
CASHIER
TEXAS WORKFORCE COMMISSION
P.O. BOX 149037
AUSTIN, TEXAS 78714-9037

DO NOT STAPLE REPORT
(Write Account No. On Check)

FORM C - 3 (6/99)
SCANC3

25. MAKE CHANGES TO EMPLOYER INFORMATION USING C-3 **INSTRUCTION SHEET.** CHANGES NOTED ON THIS FORM MAY NOT BE CAPTURED DURING PROCESSING.

▲ **FIGURE 11-7** Employer's Quarterly Report Form for State Unemployment Taxes

- *Lines 17* and *18* are blank. There are no penalties or interest because no taxes or reports are past due.
- *Line 19* is blank. There is no balance due from prior periods.
- *Line 20* shows the tax due.

On Line Furnishings submits the report and issues a check payable to the state tax authority for the amount shown on Line 20. The entry is recorded in the cash payments journal. The transaction is shown here in general journal form for purposes of illustration.

1	20--					1
2	Apr.	29	State Unemployment Tax Payable	1 0 1 9 20		2
3			Cash		1 0 1 9 20	3
4			Paid SUTA taxes for quarter			4
5			ending March 31			5
6						6

Earnings in Excess of Base Amount. State unemployment tax is paid on the first $7,000 of annual earnings for each employee. Earnings over $7,000 are not subject to state unemployment tax.

For example, suppose Cindy Taylor earns $360 every week of the year. Table 11-1 on page 394 shows that she earned $4,680 at the end of the first quarter. In the four weeks of April, she earned $1,440 ($360 × 4). She earned $360 in the first week and in the second week of May. So far, all of Taylor's earnings are subject to state unemployment tax.

	Earnings	Cumulative Earnings
First quarter	$4,680	$4,680
April	1,440	6,120
May, week 1	360	6,480
May, week 2	360	6,840

In the third week of May, Taylor earned $360, but only $160 of it is subject to state unemployment tax ($7,000 earnings limit − $6,840 cumulative earnings = $160). For the rest of the calendar year, Taylor's earnings are not subject to state unemployment tax.

Reporting and Paying Federal Unemployment Taxes

The rules for reporting and depositing federal unemployment taxes differ from those used for social security and Medicare taxes.

Depositing Federal Unemployment Taxes. There are two ways to make federal unemployment tax deposits: with electronic deposits using EFTPS or with a Federal Tax Deposit Coupon, Form 8109, at an authorized financial institution. Deposits are made quarterly and are due on the last day of the month following the end of the quarter.

The federal unemployment tax is calculated at the end of each quarter. It is computed by multiplying the first $7,000 of each employee's wages by 0.008. A deposit is required when more than $100 of federal unemployment tax is owed. If $100 or less is owed, no deposit is due.

For example, suppose that a business calculates its federal unemployment tax to be $80 at the end of the first quarter. Since it is not more than $100, no deposit is due. At the end of the second quarter, it calculates its federal unemployment taxes on second quarter wages to be $65. The total undeposited unemployment tax now is more than $100, so a deposit is required.

First quarter undeposited tax	$ 80
Second quarter undeposited tax	65
Total deposit due	$145

In the case of On Line Furnishings, the company owed $203.84 in federal unemployment tax at the end of March. Since this is more than $100, a deposit of $203.84 is due by April 30.

Month	Taxable Earnings Paid	Rate	Tax Due	Deposit Due Date
January	$ 7,840	0.008	$ 62.72	April 30
February	7,840	0.008	62.72	April 30
March	9,800	0.008	78.40	April 30
Total	$25,480		$203.84	

On April 30 On Line Furnishings records the payment of federal unemployment tax in the cash payments journal. The transaction is shown here in general journal form for illustration purposes.

8	Apr.	30	Federal Unemployment Tax Payable		203 84		8
9			Cash			203 84	9
10			Deposit FUTA due				10
11							11

Reporting Federal Unemployment Tax, Form 940 or 940-EZ. Tax returns are not due quarterly for the federal unemployment tax. The employer submits an annual return. The **Employer's Annual Federal Unemployment Tax Return, Form 940 or 940-EZ**, is a preprinted government form used to report unemployment taxes for the calendar year. It is due by January 31 of the following year. The due date is extended to February 10 if all tax deposits were made on time. Instead of using Form 940, businesses can use Form 940-EZ if

- they paid unemployment tax to only one state,
- they paid all federal unemployment taxes by January 31 of the following year,
- all wages that were taxable for federal unemployment were also taxable for state unemployment.

On Line Furnishings prepares Form 940-EZ. The information needed to complete Form 940-EZ comes from the annual summary of individual earnings records and from the state unemployment tax returns filed during the year.

Figure 11-8 on page 406 shows Form 940-EZ prepared for On Line Furnishings. Refer to it as you learn how to complete Form 940-EZ.

- *Line A* shows the total state unemployment tax paid. All five employees of On Line Furnishings reached the earnings limit during the year. Wages subject to state unemployment tax are $35,000 ($7,000 × 5 employees). The state rate is 4 percent. On Line Furnishings paid state unemployment tax of $1,400 ($35,000 × 0.04).

⑦ Objective

Prepare an Employer's Federal Unemployment Tax Return, Form 940 or 940-EZ.

Form 940-EZ

Department of the Treasury
Internal Revenue Service (99)

Employer's Annual Federal Unemployment (FUTA) Tax Return

See separate Instructions for Form 940-EZ for information on completing this form.

OMB No. 1545-1110

20--

T	
FF	
FD	
FP	
I	
T	

Name (as distinguished from trade name)
Roberta Rosario

Trade name, if any
On Line Furnishings

Address and ZIP code
2521 University Drive, Denton, TX 76205

Calendar year
20--

Employer identification number
75:1234567

Answer the questions under **Who May Use Form 940-EZ** on page 2. If you cannot use Form 940-EZ, you must use Form 940.

A Enter the amount of contributions paid to your state unemployment fund. (See separate instructions.) ▶ $ **1,400|00**

B (1) Enter the name of the state where you have to pay contributions ▶ **TX**
   (2) Enter your state reporting number as shown on your state unemployment tax return ▶ **12-98765**

If you will not have to file returns in the future, check here (see **Who Must File** in separate instructions), **and complete and sign the return.** ▶ ☐

If this is an Amended Return, check here . . . . ▶ ☐

Part I Taxable Wages and FUTA Tax

1	Total payments (including payments shown on lines 2 and 3) during the calendar year for services of employees		1	101,920|00
2	Exempt payments. (Explain all exempt payments, attaching additional sheets if necessary.) ▶ -------------------------------- --------------------------------	2		
3	Payments of more than $7,000 for services. Enter only amounts over the first $7,000 paid to each employee. Do not include any exempt payments from line 2. (See separate instructions.) The $7,000 amount is the Federal wage base. Your state wage base may be different. **Do not use your state wage limitation**	3	66,920|00	
4	Total exempt payments (add lines 2 and 3)		4	66,920|00
5	**Total taxable wages** (subtract line 4 from line 1) . . . . ▶		5	35,000|00
6	**FUTA tax.** Multiply the wages on line 5 by .008 and enter here. **(If the result is over $100, also complete Part II.)**		6	280|00
7	Total FUTA tax deposited for the year, including any overpayment applied from a prior year		7	280|00
8	**Balance due** (subtract line 7 from line 6). Pay to the **"United States Treasury"** . . . . ▶		8	0|00
	If you owe more than $100, see **Depositing FUTA tax** in separate instructions.			
9	**Overpayment** (subtract line 6 from line 7). Check if it is to be: ☐ Applied to next return or ☐ Refunded ▶		9	

Part II Record of Quarterly Federal Unemployment Tax Liability (Do not include state liability.) **Complete only if line 6 is over $100.**

Quarter	First (Jan. 1 – Mar. 31)	Second (Apr. 1 – June 30)	Third (July 1 – Sept. 30)	Fourth (Oct. 1 – Dec. 31)	Total for year
Liability for quarter	203.84	76.16	-0-	-0-	280.00

Under penalties of perjury, I declare that I have examined this return, including accompanying schedules and statements, and, to the best of my knowledge and belief, it is true, correct, and complete, and that no part of any payment made to a state unemployment fund claimed as a credit was, or is to be, deducted from the payments to employees.

Signature ▶ *Roberta Rosario*   Title (Owner, etc.) ▶ **Owner**   Date ▶ January 31, 20--

For Privacy Act and Paperwork Reduction Act Notice, see separate instructions.   Cat. No. 10983G   Form **940-EZ** (20--)

DETACH HERE

- -

Form 940-EZ(V)

Department of the Treasury
Internal Revenue Service

Form 940-EZ Payment Voucher

Use this voucher only when making a payment with your return.

OMB No. 1545-1110

20--

Complete boxes 1, 2, 3, and 4. Do not send cash, and do not staple your payment to this voucher. Make your check or money order payable to the **"United States Treasury."** Be sure to enter your employer identification number, "Form 940-EZ," and "20--" on your payment.

1 Enter the first four letters of your last name (business name if partnership or corporation).	2 Enter your employer identification number.	3 Enter the amount of your payment.
		$.

Instructions for Box 1

—Individuals (sole proprietors, trusts, and estates)— Enter the first four letters of your last name.

—Corporations and partnerships—Enter the first four characters of your business name (omit "The" if followed by more than one word).

4 Enter your business name (individual name for sole proprietors)

Enter your address

Enter your city, state, and ZIP code

▲ **FIGURE 11-8** Employer's Annual Federal Unemployment Tax Return, Form 940-EZ

PART I: Taxable Wages and FUTA Tax

- *Line 1* shows the total compensation paid to employees, $101,920.
- *Line 2* is blank because there were no exempt payments for On Line Furnishings.
- *Line 3* shows the compensation that exceeds the $7,000 earnings limit, $66,920 ($101,920 − $35,000).
- *Line 4* shows the wages not subject to federal unemployment tax, $66,920.
- *Line 5* shows the taxable wages for the year, $35,000. This amount must agree with the total taxable FUTA wages shown on the individual employee earnings records for the year.
- *Line 6* shows the FUTA tax, $280 ($35,000 × 0.008).
- *Line 7* shows the FUTA tax deposited during the year, $280.
- *Line 8* shows the balance due. On Line Furnishings deposited $280, so there is no balance due.
- *Line 9* is blank because there is no overpayment.

PART II: Record of Quarterly Federal Unemployment Tax Liability shows the FUTA tax due for each quarter. The total for the year must equal Line 6.

Computers in Accounting

Payroll Applications

Southwest Airlines processes more than 29,000 paychecks every pay period. It would be impossible to manually prepare this many checks every two weeks. Instead, companies with large numbers of employees use computerized payroll systems to process payroll. Computerized payroll applications can access current tax laws and tax forms using Internet connections.

Setting up a computerized payroll system begins by creating a master file for the employer. The employer's name, address, and federal employer identification number are entered. A master file is then prepared for each employee.

At the end of each pay period, the accountant enters the hours worked for hourly employees and any bonuses or commissions. The software calculates gross earnings, tax deductions, voluntary deductions, and net pay for all employees. A payroll proof report is printed and reviewed by the accountant. Once the payroll proof report is approved, the system automatically updates the earnings records for each employee. Paycheck forms are inserted into the printer, and paychecks are printed.

If the payroll module is integrated with a general ledger system, the payroll entries are posted to the general ledger accounts. Sophisticated payroll applications send reminders to the accountant when payroll tax deposits are due.

At the end of each calendar quarter and year, the payroll system generates summary reports to use in preparing Forms 940 and 941, as well as state unemployment returns. At year-end, Forms W-2 are generated using the payroll application.

Thinking Critically

When an accountant reviews the payroll proof report, what types of information do you think the accountant checks?

Internet Application

Go to the Web site for the American Payroll Association. What resources does the site offer on selecting a payroll system?

Workers' Compensation Insurance

Workers' compensation provides benefits for employees who are injured on the job. The insurance premium, which is paid by the employer, depends on the risk involved with the work performed. It is important to classify earnings according to the type of work the employees perform and to summarize labor costs according to the insurance premium classifications.

There are two ways to handle workers' compensation insurance. The method a business uses depends on the number of its employees.

Estimated Annual Premium in Advance. Employers who have few employees pay an estimated premium in advance. At the end of the year, the employer calculates the actual premium. If the actual premium is more than the estimated premium paid, the employer pays the balance due. If the actual premium is less than the estimated premium paid, the employer receives a refund.

On Line Furnishings has two work classifications: office work and shipping work. The workers' compensation premium rates are

Office workers $0.40 per $100 of labor costs
Shipping workers   1.20 per $100 of labor costs

The insurance premium rates recognize that injuries are more likely to occur to shipping workers than to office workers. Based on employee earnings for the previous year, On Line Furnishings paid an estimated premium of $1,000 for the new year. The payment was made on January 15.

1	20--				1
14	Jan.	15 Workers' Compensation Insurance Expense	1 000 00		14
15		Cash		1 000 00	15
16		*Estimated workers' compensation*			16
17		*insurance for 20--*			17
18					18

At the end of the year, the actual premium was computed, $1,056.64. The actual premium was computed by applying the proper rates to the payroll data for the year:

- The office wages were $20,800.
  ($20,800 ÷ $100) × $0.40 =
  $$208 \times \$0.40 = \$ \quad 83.20$$
- The shipping wages were $81,120.
  ($81,120 ÷ $100) × $1.20 =
  $$811.2 \times \$1.20 = \underline{\$ \quad 973.44}$$
  Total premium for year   = $1,056.64

Classification	Payroll	Rate	Premium
Office work	$20,800	$0.40 per $100	$ 83.20
Shipping work	81,120	1.20 per $100	973.44
Total premium for year			$1,056.64
Less estimated premium paid			1,000.00
Balance of premium due			$ 56.64

Payroll Taxes

Managerial IMPLICATIONS

- Management must ensure that payroll taxes are computed properly and paid on time.
- In order to avoid penalties, it is essential that a business prepares its payroll tax returns accurately and files the returns and required forms promptly.
- The payroll system should ensure that payroll reports are prepared in an efficient manner.
- Managers need to be familiar with all payroll taxes and how they impact operating expenses.
- Managers must be knowledgeable about unemployment tax regulations in their state because favorable experience ratings can reduce unemployment tax expense.
- Management is responsible for developing effective internal control procedures over payroll operations and ensuring that they are followed.

Thinking Critically
What accounting records are used to prepare Form 941?

On December 31 the balance due to the insurance company is recorded as a liability by an adjusting entry. On Line Furnishings owes $56.64 ($1,056.64 − $1,000.00) for the workers' compensation insurance.

	20--				
2	Dec.	31	Workers' Compensation Insurance Expense	56 64	
3			Workers' Compensation Insurance Payable		56 64
4					

Suppose that on January 15 On Line Furnishings had paid an estimated premium of $1,200 instead of $1,000. The actual premium at the end of the year was $1,056.64. On Line Furnishings would be due a refund from the insurance company for the amount overpaid, $143.36 ($1,200.00 − $1,056.64).

	20--				
2	Dec.	31	Workers' Compensation Refund Receivable	143 36	
3			Workers' Compensation Insurance Expense		143 36
4					

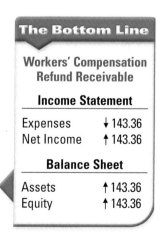

The Bottom Line

Workers' Compensation Refund Receivable

Income Statement

Expenses	↓ 143.36
Net Income	↑ 143.36

Balance Sheet

Assets	↑ 143.36
Equity	↑ 143.36

Deposit and Monthly Premium Payments. Employers with many employees use a different method to handle workers' compensation insurance. At the beginning of the year, they make large deposits, often 25 percent of the estimated annual premium. From January through November, they pay the actual premium due based on an audit of the month's wages. The premium for the last month is deducted from the deposit. Any balance is refunded or applied toward the following year's deposit.

Internal Control over Payroll Operations

Now that we have examined the basic accounting procedures used for payrolls and payroll taxes, let's look at some internal control procedures that are recommended to protect payroll operations.

1. Assign only highly responsible, well-trained employees to work in payroll operations.

2. Keep payroll records in locked files. Train payroll employees to maintain confidentiality about pay rates and other information in the payroll records.

3. Add new employees to the payroll system and make all changes in employee pay rates only with proper written authorization from management.

4. Make changes to an employee's withholding allowances based only on a Form W-4 properly completed and signed by the employee.

5. Make voluntary deductions from employee earnings based only on a signed authorization from the employee.

6. Have the payroll checks examined by someone other than the person who prepares them. Compare each check to the entry for the employee in the payroll register.

7. Have payroll checks distributed to the employees by someone other than the person who prepares them.

8. Have the monthly payroll bank account statement received and reconciled by someone other than the person who prepares the payroll checks.

9. Use prenumbered forms for the payroll checks. Periodically the numbers of the checks issued and the numbers of the unused checks should be verified to make sure that all checks can be accounted for.

10. Maintain files of all authorization forms for adding new employees, changing pay rates, and making voluntary deductions. Also retain all Forms W-4.

 **Section 2 Self Review**

Questions

1. How does a favorable experience rating affect the state unemployment tax rate?

2. Why is it important for workers' compensation wages to be classified according to the type of work performed?

3. Who pays the federal unemployment tax? The state unemployment tax?

Exercises

4. State unemployment taxes are filed
   a. monthly.
   b. quarterly.
   c. yearly.
   d. at the end of each pay period.

5. The federal unemployment taxes are reported on
   a. Form 941.
   b. Form 8109.
   c. Form W-3.
   d. Form 940.

Analysis

6. At the end of the year, the business has a balance due for workers' compensation insurance. If no adjusting entry is made, will the amount of net income reported be correct? If not, how will it be wrong?

Review and Applications

Review

Chapter Summary

Employers must pay social security, SUTA, FUTA, and Medicare taxes. They must also collect federal and state taxes from their employees and then remit those taxes to the appropriate taxing authorities. In this chapter, you have learned how to compute the employer's taxes and how to file the required tax returns and reports.

Learning Objectives

1 Explain how and when payroll taxes are paid to the government.

Employers act as collection agents for social security, Medicare, and federal income taxes withheld from employee earnings. Employers must remit these sums, with their own share of social security and Medicare taxes, to the government. The taxes must be deposited in an authorized depository, usually a commercial bank. The methods and schedules for deposits vary according to the sums involved.

2 Compute and record the employer's social security and Medicare taxes.

Employers should multiply the social security and Medicare tax rates by taxable wages to compute the employer's portion of taxes due.

3 Record deposit of social security, Medicare, and employee income taxes.

As taxes are paid to the government, the accounting records should be updated to reflect the payment, thereby reducing tax liability accounts.

4 Prepare an Employer's Quarterly Federal Tax Return, Form 941.

The Form 941 reports wages paid, federal employee income tax withheld, and applicable social security and Medicare taxes.

5 Prepare Wage and Tax Statement (Form W-2) and Annual Transmittal of Wage and Tax Statements (Form W-3).

By the end of January each employee must be given a Wage and Tax Statement, Form W-2, showing the previous year's earnings and withholdings for social security, Medicare, and employee income tax. The employer files a Transmittal of Wage and Tax Statements, Form W-3, with copies of employees' Forms W-2. Form W-3 is due by the last day of February following the end of the calendar year.

6 Compute and record liability for federal and state unemployment taxes and record payment of the taxes.

Unemployment insurance taxes are paid by the employer to both state and federal governments. State unemployment tax returns differ from state to state but usually require a list of employees, their social security numbers, and taxable wages paid. The rate of state unemployment tax depends on the employer's experience rating. The net federal unemployment tax rate can be as low as 0.8 percent.

7 Prepare an Employer's Federal Unemployment Tax Return, Form 940 or 940-EZ.

An Employer's Annual Federal Unemployment Tax Return, Form 940 or 940-EZ, must be filed in January for the preceding calendar year. The form shows the total wages paid, the amount of wages subject to unemployment tax, and the federal unemployment tax owed for the year. A credit is allowed against gross federal tax for unemployment tax charged under state plans, up to 5.4 percent of wages subject to the federal tax.

8 Compute and record workers' compensation insurance premiums.

By state law, employers might be required to carry workers' compensation insurance. For companies with a few employees, an estimated premium is paid at the start of the year. A final settlement is made with the insurance company on the basis of an audit of the payroll after the end of the year. Premiums vary according to the type of work performed by each employee. Other premium payment plans can be used for larger employers.

9 Define the accounting terms new to this chapter.

CHAPTER 11 GLOSSARY

Employer's Annual Federal Unemployment Tax Return, Form 940 (p. 405) Preprinted government form used by the employer to report unemployment taxes for the calendar year

Employer's Annual Federal Unemployment Tax Return, Form 940-EZ (p. 405) See Employer's Annual Federal Unemployment Tax Return, Form 940

Employer's Quarterly Federal Tax Return, Form 941 (p. 395) Preprinted government form used by the employer to report payroll tax information relating to social security, Medicare, and employee income tax withholding to the Internal Revenue Service

Experience rating system (p. 401) A system that rewards an employer for maintaining steady employment conditions by reducing the firm's state unemployment tax rate

Merit rating system (p. 401) See Experience rating system

Transmittal of Wage and Tax Statements, Form W-3 (p. 399) Preprinted government form submitted with Forms W-2 to the Social Security Administration

Unemployment insurance program (p. 401) A program that provides unemployment compensation through a tax levied on employers

Wage and Tax Statement, Form W-2 (p. 398) Preprinted government form that contains information about an employee's earnings and tax withholdings for the year

Withholding statement (p. 398) See Wage and Tax Statement, Form W-2

Comprehensive Self Review

1. Which of the following factors determine the frequency of deposits of social security, Medicare, and income tax withholdings?
   a. Experience rating.
   b. Amount of taxes reported in the lookback period.
   c. Company's net income.
   d. Amount of taxes currently owed.
   e. How often employees are paid.

2. Under the monthly deposit schedule rule, when must deposits for employee income tax and other withheld taxes be made?

3. Is the ceiling on earnings subject to unemployment taxes larger than or smaller than the ceiling on earnings subject to the social security tax?

4. How do the FUTA and SUTA taxes relate to each other?

5. What is Form W-3?

(Answers to Comprehensive Self Review are on page 426.)

Discussion Questions

1. Why was the unemployment insurance system established?

2. What is the purpose of allowing a credit against the FUTA for state unemployment taxes?

3. What is the purpose of Form 940? How often is it filed?

4. A state charges a basic SUTA tax rate of 5.4 percent. Because of an excellent experience rating, an employer in the state has to pay only 1.0 percent of the taxable payroll as state tax. What is the percentage to be used in computing the credit against the federal unemployment tax?

5. Is the employer required to deposit the federal unemployment tax during the year? Explain.

6. What is Form 941? How often is the form filed?

7. Who pays for workers' compensation insurance?

8. When is the premium for workers' compensation insurance usually paid?

9. How can an employer keep informed about changes in the rates and bases for the social security, Medicare, and FUTA taxes?

10. What government form is prepared to accompany deposits of federal taxes?

11. What happens if the employer fails to deduct enough employee income tax or FICA tax from employee earnings?

12. When must Form W-2 be issued? To whom is it sent?

13. What is the purpose of Form W-3? When must it be issued? To whom is it sent?

14. What is the lookback period?

15. What are the four taxes levied on employers?

16. What is a business tax identification number?

17. When is the use of Form 8109-B permitted?

18. What is EFTPS? When is EFTPS required?

19. What does "semiweekly" refer to in the Semiweekly Deposit Schedule Rule?

20. What does "monthly" refer to in the Monthly Deposit Schedule Rule?

21. Which of the following are withheld from employees' earnings?

    a. FUTA

    b. income tax

    c. Medicare

    d. social security

    e. SUTA

    f. workers' compensation

Applications

EXERCISES

Exercise 11-1 ►
Objective 1

Depositing payroll taxes.

The amounts of employee income tax withheld and social security and Medicare taxes (both employee and employer shares) shown below were owed by different businesses on the specified dates. In each case decide whether the firm is required to deposit the sum in an authorized financial institution. If a deposit is necessary, give the date by which it should be made. The employers are monthly depositors.

1. Total taxes of $4,375 owed on February 28, 20--.
2. Total taxes of $600 owed on March 31, 20--.
3. Total taxes of $825 owed on April 30, 20--.
4. Total taxes of $275 owed on July 31, 20--.

Exercise 11-2 ►
Objective 3

Recording deposit of social security, Medicare, and income taxes.

After Elite Corporation paid its employees on July 15, 20--, and recorded the corporation's share of payroll taxes for the payroll paid that date, the firm's general ledger showed a balance of $10,080 in the **Social Security Tax Payable** account, a balance of $2,322 in the **Medicare Tax Payable** account, and a balance of $9,180 in the **Employee Income Tax Payable** account. On July 16 the business issued a check to deposit the taxes owed in the Northstar National Bank. Record this transaction in general journal form.

Exercise 11-3 ►
Objectives 2, 6

Computing employer's payroll taxes.

At the end of the weekly payroll period on June 30, 20--, the payroll register of Tanaka Professional Consultants Company showed employee earnings of $65,400. Determine the firm's payroll taxes for the period. Use a social security rate of 6.2 percent, Medicare rate of 1.45 percent, FUTA rate of 0.8 percent, and SUTA rate of 5.4 percent. Consider all earnings subject to social security tax and Medicare tax and $33,000 subject to FUTA and SUTA taxes.

Exercise 11-4 ►
Objective 6

Depositing federal unemployment tax.

On March 31, 20--, the **Federal Unemployment Tax Payable** account in the general ledger of The Boston Trading Company showed a balance of $576. This represents the FUTA tax owed for the first quarter of the year. On April 30, 20--, the firm issued a check to deposit the amount owed in the Provident National Bank. Record this transaction in general journal form.

Exercise 11-5 ►
Objective 6

Computing SUTA tax.

On April 29, 20--, Thompson Furniture Company prepared its state unemployment tax return for the first quarter of the year. The firm had taxable wages of $90,600. Because of a favorable experience rating, Thompson pays SUTA tax at a rate of 1.6 percent. How much SUTA tax did the firm owe for the quarter?

Exercise 11-6 ►
Objective 6

Paying SUTA tax.

On June 30, 20--, the **State Unemployment Tax Payable** account in the general ledger of Gulf Shore Sea Food Company showed a balance of

$1,368. This represents the SUTA tax owed for the second quarter of the year. On July 31, 20--, the business issued a check to the state unemployment insurance fund for the amount due. Record this payment in general journal form.

Computing FUTA tax.

On January 31 Simply Beautiful Salon prepared its Employer's Annual Federal Unemployment Tax Return, Form 940. During the previous year, the business paid total wages of $374,400 to its eight employees. Of this amount, $112,000 was subject to FUTA tax. Using a rate of 0.8 percent, determine the FUTA tax owed and the balance due on January 31, 20--, when Form 940 was filed. A deposit of $748.80 was made during the year.

◀ **Exercise 11-7**
Objective 6

Computing workers' compensation insurance premiums.

Electronic Computer Services Company estimates that its office employees will earn $160,000 next year and its factory employees will earn $840,000. The firm pays the following rates for workers' compensation insurance: $0.30 per $100 of wages for the office employees and $6.00 per $100 of wages for the factory employees. Determine the estimated premium for each group of employees and the total estimated premium for next year.

◀ **Exercise 11-8**
Objective 8

Problems

Selected problems can be completed using:
🍑 **Peachtree**　📘 **QuickBooks**　🪟 **Spreadsheets**

PROBLEM SET A

Computing and recording employer's payroll tax expense.

The payroll register of Goree Lawn Equipment Company showed total employee earnings of $2,400 for the payroll period ended June 14, 20--.

◀ **Problem 11-1A**
Objectives 2, 6

INSTRUCTIONS

1. Compute the employer's payroll taxes for the period. Use rates of 6.2 percent for the employer's share of the social security tax, 1.45 percent for Medicare tax, 0.8 percent for FUTA tax, and 5.4 percent for SUTA tax. All earnings are taxable.

2. Prepare a general journal entry to record the employer's payroll taxes for the period.

Analyze: Which of the above taxes are paid by the employee and matched by the employer?

Computing employer's social security tax, Medicare tax, and unemployment taxes and recording payment of taxes; preparing employer's quarterly federal tax return.

A payroll summary for Nelson Sullivan, who owns and operates Sullivan Broadcasting Company, for the quarter ending June 30, 20--, appears on page 416. The firm prepared the required tax deposit forms and issued checks as follows.

◀ **Problem 11-2A**
Objectives 2, 3, 4, 6

a. Federal Tax Deposit Coupon, Form 8109, check for April taxes, paid on May 15.

b. Federal Tax Deposit Coupon, Form 8109, check for May taxes, paid on June 17.

Date Wages Paid		Total Earnings	Social Security Tax Deducted	Medicare Tax Deducted	Income Tax Withheld
April	8	$ 2,120.00	$ 131.44	$ 30.74	$ 210.00
	15	2,200.00	136.40	31.90	216.00
	22	2,120.00	131.44	30.74	210.00
	29	2,160.00	133.92	31.32	214.00
		$ 8,600.00	$ 533.20	$124.70	$ 850.00
May	5	$ 2,080.00	$ 128.96	$ 30.16	206.00
	12	2,120.00	131.44	30.74	210.00
	19	2,120.00	131.44	30.74	210.00
	26	2,160.00	133.92	31.32	214.00
		$ 8,480.00	$ 525.76	$122.96	$ 840.00
June	2	$ 2,200.00	$ 136.40	$ 31.90	$ 216.00
	9	2,120.00	131.44	30.74	210.00
	16	2,160.00	133.92	31.32	214.00
	23	2,120.00	131.44	30.74	210.00
	30	2,080.00	128.96	30.16	206.00
		$10,680.00	$ 662.16	$154.86	$1,056.00
Total		$27,760.00	$1,721.12	$402.52	$2,746.00

INSTRUCTIONS

1. Using the tax rates given below, and assuming that all earnings are taxable, make the general journal entry on April 8, 20--, to record the employer's payroll tax expense on the payroll ending that date.

Social security	6.2 percent
Medicare	1.45
FUTA	0.8
SUTA	5.4

2. Give the entries in general journal form to record deposit of the employee income tax withheld and the social security and Medicare taxes (employee and employer shares) on May 15 for April taxes and on June 17 for May taxes.

3. On July 15, the firm issued a check to deposit the employee income tax withheld and the FICA tax (both employee and employer shares) for the third month (June). In general journal form, record issuance of the check.

4. Complete Form 941 in accordance with the discussions in this chapter. Use a 12.4 percent social security rate and a 2.9 percent Medicare rate in computations. Use the following address for the company: 3465 Merit Drive, Dallas, TX 75201. Use 75-3333333 as the employer identification number. Date the return July 31, 20--.

Analyze: Based on the entries you have recorded, what is the balance of the **Employee Income Tax Payable** account at July 15?

Problem 11-3A ►
Objectives 6, 7

Computing and recording unemployment taxes; completing Form 940.

Certain transactions and procedures relating to federal and state unemployment taxes follow for The Fashion Center, a retail store owned by

Debra Jones. The firm's address is 1112 Misty Mountain Drive, Denton, TX 76209. The employer's federal and state identification numbers are 75-4444444 and 12-44444, respectively. Carry out the procedures as instructed in each of the following steps.

1. Compute the state unemployment insurance tax owed on the employees' wages for the quarter ended March 31, 2004. This information will be shown on the employer's quarterly report to the state agency that collects SUTA tax. The employer has recorded the tax on each payroll date. Although the state charges a 5.4 percent unemployment tax rate, The Fashion Center's rate is only 1.7 percent because of its experience rating. The employee earnings for the first quarter are shown below. All earnings are subject to SUTA tax.

Name of Employee	Total Earnings
Gus Salvage	$ 4,020
Marvel Turner	3,720
Sadie Judge	4,030
Paul Torres	4,000
Nelsy Li	3,800
Nita Williams	4,200
Steven Holmes	4,450
Total	$28,220

2. On April 30, 2004, the firm issued a check to the state employment commission for the amount computed above. In general journal form, record the issuance of the check.

3. Complete Form 940-EZ, the Employer's Annual Federal Unemployment Tax Return, on January 15, 2005. Assume that all wages have been paid and that all quarterly payments have been submitted to the state as required. The payroll information appears below. The required federal tax deposit forms and checks were submitted as follows: a deposit of $225.76 on April 21, a deposit of $211.92 on July 22, and a deposit of $72.00 on October 21. Date the unemployment tax return January 28, 2005. A check for the balance due will be sent with Form 940-EZ.

Quarter Ended	Total Wages Paid	Wages Paid in Excess of $7,000	State Unemployment Tax Paid
Mar. 31	$ 28,220.00	–0–	$ 479.74
June 30	29,520.00	$ 3,030.00	450.33
Sept. 30	29,720.00	20,720.00	153.00
Dec. 31	30,820.00	27,700.00	53.04
Totals	$118,280.00	$51,450.00	$1,136.11

4. In general journal form, record the issuance of a check on January 28, 2005, for the balance of FUTA tax due.

Analyze: What total debits were made to liability accounts for the entries you have recorded?

Problem 11-4A ►
Objective 8

Computing and recording workers' compensation insurance premiums.

The following information relates to Mason Manufacturing Company's workers' compensation insurance premiums for 2004. On January 15, 2004, the company estimated its premium for workers' compensation insurance for the year on the basis of that data.

Work Classification	Amount of Estimated Wages	Insurance Rates
Office work	$ 66,000	$0.30/$100
Shop work	300,000	$4.00/$100

INSTRUCTIONS

1. Compute the estimated premiums.
2. Record in general journal form payment of the estimated premium on January 15, 2004.
3. On January 4, 2005, an audit of the firm's payroll records showed that it had actually paid wages of $76,000 to its office employees and wages of $302,000 to its shop employees. Compute the actual premium for the year and the balance due the insurance company or the credit due the firm.
4. Give the general journal entry to adjust the **Workers' Compensation Insurance Expense** account as of the end of 2004. Date the entry December 31, 2004.

Analyze: If all wages were attributable to shop employees, what premium estimate would have been calculated and recorded on January 15, 2004?

PROBLEM SET B

Problem 11-1B ►
Objectives 2, 6

Computing and recording employer's payroll tax expense.

The payroll register of Kline Automotive Repair Shop showed total employee earnings of $2,160 for the week ended April 8, 20--.

INSTRUCTIONS

1. Compute the employer's payroll taxes for the period. The tax rates are as follows:

Social security	6.2 percent
Medicare	1.45
FUTA	0.8
SUTA	2.2

2. Prepare a general journal entry to record the employer's payroll taxes for the period.

Analyze: If the FUTA tax rate had been 1.2 percent, what total employer payroll taxes would have been recorded?

Computing employer's social security tax, Medicare tax, and unemployment taxes and recording payment of taxes; preparing employer's quarterly federal tax return.

A payroll summary for Jenny Schwartz, who owns and operates The Dress Shop, for the quarter ending September 30, 20--, appears below. The business prepared the tax deposit forms and issued checks as follows during the quarter.

a. Federal Tax Deposit Coupon, Form 8109, check for July taxes, paid on August 15.

b. Federal Tax Deposit Coupon, Form 8109, check for August taxes, paid on September 15.

Date Wages Paid	Total Earnings	Social Security Tax Withheld	Medicare Tax Withheld	Income Tax Withheld
July 7	$ 1,800.00	$ 111.60	$ 26.10	$ 175.00
14	1,800.00	111.60	26.10	175.00
21	2,100.00	130.20	30.45	205.00
28	1,800.00	111.60	26.10	175.00
	$ 7,500.00	$ 465.00	$108.75	$ 730.00
Aug. 4	$ 2,100.00	$ 130.20	$ 30.45	205.00
11	2,700.00	167.40	39.15	265.00
18	2,700.00	167.40	39.15	265.00
25	2,400.00	148.80	34.80	235.00
	$ 9,900.00	$ 613.80	$143.55	$ 970.00
Sept. 3	$ 1,800.00	$ 111.60	$ 26.10	$ 175.00
10	2,100.00	130.20	30.45	205.00
17	2,100.00	130.20	30.45	205.00
24	2,100.00	130.20	30.45	205.00
30	1,800.00	111.60	26.10	175.00
	$ 9,900.00	$ 613.80	$143.55	$ 965.00
Total	$27,300.00	$1,692.60	$395.85	$2,665.00

INSTRUCTIONS

1. Prepare the general journal entry on July 7, 20--, to record the employer's payroll tax expense on the payroll ending that date. All earnings are subject to the following taxes:

Social security	6.2 percent
Medicare	1.45
FUTA	0.8
SUTA	2.2

2. Make the entries in general journal form to record deposit of the employee income tax withheld and the social security and Medicare taxes (both employees' withholding and employer's matching portion) on August 15 for July taxes and on September 15 for the August taxes.

3. On October 15 the firm issued a check to deposit the employee income tax withheld and the social security and Medicare taxes for September (both employees' withholding and employer's matching portion). Record the issuance of this check in your general journal.

4. Complete Form 941 in accordance with the discussions in this chapter and the instructions on the form itself. Use the tax rates of 12.4 percent for social security and 2.9 percent for Medicare in computations. Use the following company information: The Dress Shop, 2001 University Drive, Waco, TX 76706. Use the following employer identification number, 75-89023920. Date the return October 31, 20--.

Analyze: What total taxes were deposited with the IRS for the quarter ended September 30, 20--?

Problem 11-3B ►

Objectives 6, 7

Computing and recording unemployment taxes; completing Form 940.

Certain transactions and procedures relating to federal and state unemployment taxes are given below for The Saddle Shop, a retail store owned by Guy Gagliardi. The firm's address is 4560 LBJ Freeway, Dallas, TX 75201. The employer's federal and state identification numbers are 75-7777777 and 12-12345, respectively. Carry out the procedures as instructed in each step.

INSTRUCTIONS

1. Compute the state unemployment insurance tax owed for the quarter ended March 31, 2004. This information will be shown on the employer's quarterly report to the state agency that collects SUTA tax. The employer has recorded the tax expense and liability on each payroll date. Although the state charges a 5.4 percent unemployment tax rate, The Saddle Shop has received a favorable experience rating and therefore pays only a 2.3 percent state tax rate. The employee earnings for the first quarter are given below. All earnings are subject to SUTA tax.

Name of Employee	Total Earnings
Susan Benson	$ 3,275
Emma Johnson	3,500
John Alexander	3,100
Selena Ramos	3,250
Patricia Reed	2,975
Melvin Miller	2,980
Total	$19,080

2. On April 30, 2004, the firm issued a check for the amount computed above. Record the transaction in general journal form.

3. Complete Form 940-EZ, the Employer's Annual Federal Unemployment Tax Return. Assume that all wages have been paid and that all quarterly payments have been submitted to the state as required. The FUTA deposits made during the year were $152.64 on April 12, $159.80 on July 14, and $74.40 on October 12. Date the unemployment tax return January 22, 2005. A check for the balance due will be sent with Form 940. The payroll information is given in the following table.

Quarter Ended	Total Wages Paid	Wages Paid in Excess of $7,000	State Unemployment Tax Paid
Mar. 31	$19,080.00	–0–	$ 438.84
June 30	19,975.00	–0–	459.43
Sept. 30	17,245.00	$ 8,200.00	208.04
Dec. 31	20,400.00	19,700.00	16.10
Totals	$76,700.00	$27,900.00	$1,122.41

4. On January 25, 2005, the firm issued a check for the amount shown on line 8, Part I, of Form 940-EZ. In general journal form, record issuance of the check.

Analyze: What is the balance of the **Federal Unemployment Tax Payable** account on January 26, 2005?

Computing and recording premiums on workers' compensation insurance.

◄ **Problem 11-4B**
Objective 8

The following information is for Taylor's Office Supply workers' compensation insurance premiums. On January 15, 2004, the company estimated its premium for workers' compensation insurance for the year on the basis of the following data.

Work Classification	Amount of Estimated Wages	Insurance Rates
Office work	$ 76,000	$0.40/$100
Factory work	370,000	$8.00/$100

INSTRUCTIONS

1. Use the information to compute the estimated premium for the year.

2. A check was issued to pay the estimated premium on January 15, 2004. Record the transaction in general journal form.

3. On January 17, 2005, an audit of the firm's payroll records showed that it had actually paid wages of $72,800 to its office employees and wages of $357,000 to its factory employees. Compute the actual premium for the year and the balance due the insurance company or the credit due the firm.

4. Give the general journal entry to adjust the **Workers' Compensation Insurance Expense** account. Date the entry December 31, 2004.

Analyze: What is the balance of the **Workers' Compensation Insurance Expense** account at December 31, 2004, after all journal entries have been posted?

CHAPTER 11 CHALLENGE PROBLEM

Determining Employee Status

In each of the following independent situations, decide whether the business organization should treat the person being paid as an employee and should withhold social security, Medicare, and employee income taxes from the payment made.

1. Munich Corporation carries on very little business activity. It merely holds land and certain assets. The board of directors has concluded that they need no employees. They have decided instead to pay Harry White, one of the shareholders, a consulting fee of $12,000 per year to serve as president, secretary, and treasurer and to manage all the affairs of the company. White spends an average of one hour per week on the corporation's business affairs. However, his fee is fixed regardless of how few or how many hours he works.

2. Patrick Hicks owns and operates a crafts shop, using the sole proprietorship form of business. Each week a check for $1,000 is written on the crafts shop's bank account as a salary payment to Hicks.

3. Clare Parks is a public stenographer, or court reporter. She has an office at the Trenton Court Reporting Center but pays no rent. The manager of the center receives requests from attorneys for public stenographers to take depositions at legal hearings. The manager then chooses a stenographer who best meets the needs of the client and contacts the stenographer chosen. The stenographer has the right to refuse to take on the job, and the stenographer controls his or her working hours and days. Clients make payments to the center, which deducts a 25 percent fee for providing facilities and rendering services to support the stenographer. The balance is paid to the stenographer. During the current month, the center collected fees of $20,000 for Clare, deducted $5,000 for the center's fee, and remitted the proper amount to Clare.

4. David, a registered nurse, has retired from full-time work. However, because of his experience and special skills, on each Monday, Wednesday, and Thursday afternoon he assists Dr. Nancy Heart, a dermatologist. David is paid an hourly fee by Dr. Heart. During the current week, his hourly fees totaled $800.

5. After working several years as an editor for a magazine publisher, Leola quit her job to stay at home with her two small children. Later the publisher asked her to work in her home performing editorial work as needed. Leola is paid an hourly fee for the work she performs. In some cases she goes to the publishing company's offices to pick up or return a manuscript, and in other cases the firm sends a manuscript to her or she returns one by mail. During the current month Leola's hourly earnings totaled $1,800.

Analyze: What characteristics do the persons you identified as "employees" have in common?

CHAPTER 11 CRITICAL THINKING PROBLEM

Comparing Employees and Independent Contractors

The *City Record Chronicle* is a local newspaper that is published Monday through Friday. It sells 90,000 copies daily. The paper is currently in a profit squeeze, and the publisher, Amanda Lewis, is looking for ways to reduce expenses.

A review of current distribution procedures reveals that the *City Record Chronicle* employs 100 truck drivers to drop off bundles of newspapers to 1,200 teenagers who deliver papers to individual homes. The drivers are paid an hourly wage while the teenagers receive 3 cents for each paper they deliver.

Lewis is considering an alternative method of distributing the papers, which she says has worked in other cities the size of Denton (where the *City Record Chronicle* is published). Under the new system, the newspaper would retain 25 truck drivers to transport papers to four distribution centers around the city. The distribution centers are operated by independent contractors who would be responsible for making their own arrangements to deliver papers to subscribers' homes. The 25 drivers retained by the *City Record Chronicle* would receive the same hourly rate as they currently earn, and the independent contractors would receive 15 cents for each paper delivered.

1. What payroll information does Lewis need in order to make a decision about adopting the alternative distribution method?

2. Assume the following information:
   a. The average driver earns $44,000 per year.
   b. Average employee income tax withholding is 17 percent.
   c. The social security tax is 6.2 percent of the first $76,200 of earnings.
   d. The Medicare tax is 1.45 percent of all earnings.
   e. The state unemployment tax is 4 percent, and the federal unemployment tax is 0.8 percent of the first $7,000 of earnings.
   f. Workers' compensation insurance is 90 cents per $100 of wages.
   g. The paper pays $290 per month for health insurance for each driver and contributes $220 per month to each driver's pension plan.
   h. The paper has liability insurance coverage for all teenage carriers that costs $120,000 per year.

   Prepare a schedule showing the costs of distributing the newspapers under the current system and the proposed new system. Based on your analysis, which system would you recommend to Lewis?

3. What other factors, monetary and nonmonetary, might influence your decision?

Business Connections

Connection 1 ▶ MANAGERIAL *FOCUS* **Payroll**

1. Davis Company recently discovered that a payroll clerk had issued checks to nonexistent employees for several years and cashed the checks himself. The firm does not have any internal control procedures for its payroll operations. What specific controls might have led to the discovery of this fraud more quickly or discouraged the payroll clerk from even attempting the fraud?

2. Johnson Company has 20 employees. Some employees work in the office, others in the warehouse, and still others in the retail store. In the company's records, all employees are simply referred to as "general employees." Explain to management why this is not an acceptable practice.

3. Why should management be concerned about the accuracy and promptness of payroll tax deposits and payroll tax returns?

4. What is the significance to management of the experience rating system used to determine the employer's tax under the state unemployment insurance laws?

Connection 2 ▶ Ethical *DILEMMA* **Personal Expenses** You work in the payroll department of State University where you attend college. You use the copy machine, fax, and telephone to make personal copies, fax letters to family and friends, and call family and friends out of town. State University prohibits personal use of these items and requires employees to sign a statement at the end of each month certifying that all copies, calls, and faxes were made for business use. You sign the statement each month. Are your actions ethical? Why or why not?

Connection 3 ▶ Street**WISE:**

Questions from the Real World   **Payroll and Promotions** Refer to The Home Depot, Inc. *1999 Annual Report* in Appendix B.

1. Locate the consolidated balance sheets. When The Home Depot, Inc. records payroll tax liabilities, which category reflected on the balance sheet most likely contains these obligations?

2. The Home Depot, Inc. employed 201,400 associates at the close of fiscal 1999. According to the company's employment strategies, store managers are rarely recruited externally. Most store managers are promoted from within the organization. Discuss why you think The Home Depot, Inc. employs this strategy. What advantages and disadvantages do you think the company experiences as a result of this procedure?

Connection 4 ▶ FINANCIAL $TATEMENT **A N A L Y S I S** **Income Statement** The following excerpt was taken from H&R Block, Inc.'s consolidated statements of earnings for the year ended April 30, 2000.

H&R BLOCK

H&R Block
Consolidated Statements of Earnings
(Amounts in thousands, except per share amounts)

| | Year Ended April 30 | | |
	2000	1999	1998
Expenses:			
Employee compensation and benefits	963,536	610,866	483,951
Occupancy and equipment	253,171	182,701	157,995
Interest	153,500	69,338	38,899
Depreciation and amortization	147,218	74,605	54,972
Marketing and advertising	140,683	90,056	71,594
Supplies, freight and postage	64,599	57,157	51,705
Bad debt	51,719	71,662	53,736
Other	273,902	133,206	85,612
Total Operating Expenses	2,048,328	1,289,591	998,464

Analyze:

1. What percentage of total operating expenses was spent on employee compensation and benefits in the year ended April 30, 2000?

2. Assume that FICA (social security) wages for the first quarter of 2000 were $251,694,000. What deposit did H&R Block send to the federal government for FICA taxes for the quarter? (Assume FICA rate of 6.2%.)

3. By what percentage did employee compensation and benefits increase from the years ended April 30, 1998 to 1999; and 1999 to 2000?

Analyze Online: Find the H&R Block Web site **(www.hrblock.com).** Locate *Investor Relations* within the *About* section of the Web site. Find the most recent annual report.

4. What percentage of total operating expenses was spent on employee compensation and benefits?

5. Which expense line had the highest percentage increase in the last two years?

Extending (the) *Thought* **Unemployment Insurance** Businesses must pay unemployment insurance taxes required by federal and state agencies. The program provides benefits to unemployed workers. Your business has never fired or laid off an employee, yet you are required to pay the minimum tax rate on gross salaries. Do you agree or disagree with this system? Why?

◀ **Connection 5**

Business Communication **Memo—Payroll Forms** You have opened a new office supply store and plan to hire 10 employees to help with sales, inventory maintenance, and advertising. You would like your payroll clerk to set up his office to prepare for the year's payroll duties. Write a memo to your payroll clerk requesting that he gather all the necessary employee forms, payroll tax return forms, and accounting forms that will be needed for payroll. Include a detailed list of the items that should be gathered.

◀ **Connection 6**

Connection 7 ▶

TeamWork   **Taxation** Taxation can be based on a progressive, regressive, or proportional basis. As a team, research the definitions of each type of taxation. Create index cards for each type of taxation with arguments that support or refute the taxation basis. Use these cards for a class discussion on the topic.

Connection 8 ▶

*inter*NET
CONNECTION   **IRS** The Internal Revenue Service (IRS) processes approximately 205 million tax returns a year while assisting 99 million taxpayers by telephone and 6.3 million taxpayers at walk-in offices throughout the country. Go to its Web site at **www.irs.gov.** What is an ITIN? Can you receive an ITIN if you have a social security number? What is Revenue Procedure 96-13?

Answers to Self Reviews

Answers to Section 1 Self Review

1. Federal Reserve Bank or a commercial bank that is designated as a federal depository.
2. Form 941 shows income taxes withheld, social security and Medicare taxes due for the quarter, and tax deposits. The form is due on the last day of the month following the end of the quarter.
3. Form W-2 provides information to enable the employees to complete their federal income tax return. Copies are given to the employee and to the federal government (and to other governmental units that levy an income tax).
4. **a.** each payroll period.
5. **c.** Social security tax
6. Monthly

Answers to Section 2 Self Review

1. It reduces the rate of SUTA tax that must actually be paid.
2. The amount of the premium depends on the type of work the employee performs.
3. The employer pays FUTA. Usually the employer pays SUTA, although a few states also levy SUTA on employees.
4. **b.** quarterly.
5. **d.** Form 940.
6. Expenses will be understated. Net income will be overstated.

Answers to Comprehensive Self Review

1. **b.** Amount of taxes reported in the lookback period.
   d. Amount of taxes currently owed.
2. By the 15th day of the following month.
3. Smaller
4. A credit, with limits, is allowed against the federal tax for unemployment tax charged by the state.
5. Form W-3 is sent to the Social Security Administration. It reports the total social security wages; total Medicare wages; total social security and Medicare taxes withheld; total wages, tips, and other compensation; total employee income tax withheld; and other information.

PART 4

Summarizing and Reporting Financial Information

Johnson & Johnson In January 2001 Johnson & Johnson announced worldwide pharmaceutical segment sales of $12 billion in 2000, an 11.8 percent increase over 1999 sales. The company recorded and summarized millions of transactions to arrive at the sales figure for 2000.

Thinking Critically
What importance do you think financial measurements hold for a company like Johnson & Johnson? What implications do these milestones carry in the investment community and within the organization?

CHAPTER 12

Learning Objectives

1. Determine the adjustment for merchandise inventory, and enter the adjustment on the worksheet.

2. Compute adjustments for accrued and prepaid expense items, and enter the adjustments on the worksheet.

3. Compute adjustments for accrued and deferred income items, and enter the adjustments on the worksheet.

4. Complete a ten-column worksheet.

5. Define the accounting terms new to this chapter.

Accruals, Deferrals, and the Worksheet

AMERICAN EAGLE
OUTFITTERS
www.ae.com

C lothing from American Eagle Outfitters, Inc. is hip, fun, and youthful. The company designs, markets, and sells its own brand of casual classics including AE khakis, jeans, accessories, footwear, and T-shirts. The company targets men and women between the ages of 16 and 34. The prices are affordable, and the styles hit the mark. Apparently U.S. consumers like the mix. Sales have increased at an average annual rate of 37 percent since 1996. AE styles have been seen on television shows such as *Dawson's Creek,* in major Hollywood films, and in national newspapers and magazines, resulting in exposure to more than 1.5 billion viewers in 1999.

Thinking Critically
American Eagle Outfitters, Inc.'s plans for 2000 included opening 90 new stores and remodeling more than 40 existing stores. What types of adjustments do you think the accountants at American Eagle Outfitters, Inc. recorded as a result of this expansion activity?

For more information on American Eagle Outfitters, Inc., go to: collegeaccounting.glencoe.com.

New Terms

Accrual basis

Accrued expenses

Accrued income

Deferred expenses

Deferred income

Inventory sheet

Net income line

Prepaid expenses

Property, plant, and equipment

Unearned income

Updated account balances

Section Objectives

1 Determine the adjustment for merchandise inventory, and enter the adjustment on the worksheet.

WHY IT'S IMPORTANT
The change in merchandise inventory affects the financial statements.

2 Compute adjustments for accrued and prepaid expense items, and enter the adjustments on the worksheet.

WHY IT'S IMPORTANT
Each expense item needs to be assigned to the accounting period in which it helped to earn revenue.

3 Compute adjustments for accrued and deferred income items, and enter the adjustments on the worksheet.

WHY IT'S IMPORTANT
The accrual basis of accounting states that income is recognized in the period it is earned.

Terms to Learn

accrual basis
accrued expenses
accrued income
deferred expenses
deferred income
inventory sheet
prepaid expenses
property, plant, and
   equipment
unearned income

Calculating and Recording Adjustments

In Chapter 5 you learned how to make adjustments so that all revenue and expenses that apply to a fiscal period appear on the income statement for that period. In this chapter you will learn more about adjustments and how they affect Modern Casuals, a retail merchandising business.

The Accrual Basis of Accounting

Financial statements usually are prepared using the **accrual basis** of accounting because it most nearly attains the goal of matching expenses and revenue in an accounting period.

- *Revenue is recognized when earned, not necessarily when the cash is received.* Revenue is recognized when the sale is complete. A sale is complete when title to the goods passes to the customer or when the service is provided. For sales on account, revenue is recognized when the sale occurs even though the cash is not collected immediately.
- *Expenses are recognized when incurred or used, not necessarily when cash is paid.* Each expense is assigned to the accounting period in which it helped to earn revenue for the business, even if cash is not paid at that time. This is often referred to as *matching revenues and expenses.*

Sometimes cash changes hands before the revenue or expense is recognized. For example, insurance premiums are normally paid in advance, and the coverage extends over several accounting periods. In other cases cash changes hands after the revenue or expense has been recognized. For example, employees might work during December but be paid in January of the following year. Because of these timing differences, adjustments are made to ensure that revenue and expenses are recognized in the appropriate period.

Using the Worksheet to Record Adjustments

The worksheet is used to assemble data about adjustments and to organize the information for the financial statements. Figure 12-1 on pages 432–433 shows the first two sections of the worksheet for Modern Casuals. Let's review how to prepare the worksheet.

- Enter the trial balance in the Trial Balance section. Total the columns. Be sure that total debits equal total credits.
- Enter the adjustments in the Adjustments section. Use the same letter to identify the debit part and the credit part of each adjustment. Total the columns. Be sure that total debits equal total credits.

- For each account, combine the amounts in the Trial Balance section and the Adjustments section. Enter the results in the Adjusted Trial Balance section, total the columns, and make sure that total debits equal total credits.
- Extend account balances to the Income Statement and Balance Sheet sections and complete the worksheet.

Adjustment for Merchandise Inventory

Merchandise inventory consists of the goods that a business has on hand for sale to customers. An asset account for merchandise inventory is maintained in the general ledger. During the accounting period, all purchases of merchandise are debited to the **Purchases** account. All sales of merchandise are credited to the revenue account **Sales.**

Notice that no entries are made directly to the **Merchandise Inventory** account during the accounting period. Consequently, when the trial balance is prepared at the end of the period, the **Merchandise Inventory** account still shows the *beginning* inventory for the period. At the end of each period a business determines the *ending* balance of the **Merchandise Inventory** account. The first step in determining the ending inventory is to count the number of units of each type of item on hand. As the merchandise is counted, the quantity on hand is entered on an inventory sheet. The **inventory sheet** lists the quantity of each type of goods a firm has in stock. For each item the quantity is multiplied by the unit cost to find the totals per item. The totals for all items are added to compute the total cost of merchandise inventory.

The trial balance for Modern Casuals shows **Merchandise Inventory** of $51,500. Based on a count taken on December 31, merchandise inventory at the end of the year actually totaled $46,000. Modern Casuals needs to adjust the **Merchandise Inventory** account to reflect the balance at the end of the year.

The adjustment is made in two steps, using the accounts **Merchandise Inventory** and **Income Summary.**

1. The beginning inventory ($51,500) is taken off the books by transferring the account balance to the **Income Summary** account. This entry is labeled **(a)** on the worksheet in Figure 12-1 and is illustrated in T-account form below.

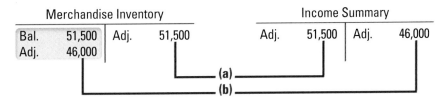

2. The ending inventory ($46,000) is placed on the books by debiting **Merchandise Inventory** and crediting **Income Summary.** This entry is labeled **(b)** on the worksheet in Figure 12-1.

Recognize
The word "recognize" means to record in the accounting records.

1 Objective
Determine the adjustment for merchandise inventory, and enter the adjustment on the worksheet.

Recall
Income Summary
The **Income Summary** account is a temporary owner's equity account used in the closing process.

Modern Casuals

Worksheet

Year Ended December 31, 2004

	ACCOUNT NAME	TRIAL BALANCE DEBIT	TRIAL BALANCE CREDIT	ADJUSTMENTS DEBIT	ADJUSTMENTS CREDIT
1	Cash	21 1 3 6 00			
2	Petty Cash Fund	1 0 0 00			
3	Notes Receivable	1 2 0 0 00			
4	Accounts Receivable	32 0 0 0 00			
5	Allowance for Doubtful Accounts		1 0 0 00		(c) 7 5 0 00
6	Interest Receivable			(m) 2 4 00	
7	Merchandise Inventory	51 5 0 0 00		(b) 46 0 0 0 00	(a) 51 5 0 0 00
8	Prepaid Insurance	7 2 0 0 00			(k) 3 6 0 0 00
9	Prepaid Interest	2 2 5 00			(l) 1 5 0 00
10	Supplies	6 3 0 0 00			(j) 4 9 7 5 00
11	Store Equipment	20 0 0 0 00			
12	Accumulated Depreciation—Store Equipment				(d) 2 2 5 0 00
13	Office Equipment	7 0 0 0 00			
14	Accumulated Depreciation—Office Equipment				(e) 1 2 0 0 00
15	Notes Payable—Trade		2 0 0 0 00		
16	Notes Payable—Bank		9 0 0 0 00		
17	Accounts Payable		24 1 2 9 00		
18	Interest Payable				(i) 2 0 00
19	Social Security Tax Payable		1 0 8 4 00		(g) 9 3 00
20	Medicare Tax Payable		2 5 0 00		(g) 2 1 75
21	Employee Income Taxes Payable		9 9 0 00		
22	Federal Unemployment Tax Payable				(h) 1 2 00
23	State Unemployment Tax Payable				(h) 8 1 00
24	Salaries Payable				(f) 1 5 0 0 00
25	Sales Tax Payable		7 2 0 0 00	(n) 1 4 4 00	
26	Sonia Sanchez, Capital		61 2 2 1 00		
27	Sonia Sanchez, Drawing	27 6 0 0 00			
28	Income Summary			(a) 51 5 0 0 00	(b) 46 0 0 0 00
29	Sales		559 6 5 0 00		
30	Sales Returns and Allowances	13 0 0 0 00			
31	Interest Income		1 3 6 00		(m) 2 4 00
32	Miscellaneous Income		3 6 6 00		(n) 1 4 4 00
33	Purchases	320 5 0 0 00			
34	Freight In	8 8 0 0 00			
35	Purchases Returns and Allowances		3 0 5 0 00		
36	Purchase Discounts		3 1 3 0 00		
37	Salaries Expense—Sales	78 4 9 0 00		(f) 1 5 0 0 00	
38	Advertising Expense	7 4 2 5 00			
39	Cash Short or Over	1 2 5 00			
40	Supplies Expense			(j) 4 9 7 5 00	

▲ FIGURE 12-1
10-Column Worksheet—Partial

| | TRIAL BALANCE | | ADJUSTMENTS | |
ACCOUNT NAME	DEBIT	CREDIT	DEBIT	CREDIT
41 Depreciation Expense—Store Equipment			(d) 2 2 5 0 00	
42 Rent Expense	27 6 0 0 00			
43 Salaries Expense—Office	26 5 0 0 00			
44 Insurance Expense			(k) 3 6 0 0 00	
45 Payroll Taxes Expense	7 2 0 5 00		(g) 1 1 4 75	
46			(h) 9 3 00	
47 Telephone Expense	1 8 7 5 00			
48 Uncollectible Accounts Expense			(c) 7 5 0 00	
49 Utilities Expense	5 9 2 5 00			
50 Depreciation Expense—Office Equipment			(e) 1 2 0 0 00	
51 Interest Expense	6 0 0 00		(i) 2 0 00	
52			(l) 1 5 0 00	
53 Totals	672 3 0 6 00	672 3 0 6 00	112 3 2 0 75	112 3 2 0 75
54				

▲ FIGURE 12-1 (continued)
10-Column Worksheet—Partial

The effect of this adjustment is to remove the beginning merchandise inventory balance and replace it with the ending merchandise inventory balance. Merchandise inventory is adjusted in two steps on the worksheet because both the beginning and the ending inventory figures appear on the income statement, which is prepared directly from the worksheet.

Adjustment for Loss from Uncollectible Accounts

Credit sales are made with the expectation that the customers will pay the amount due later. Sometimes the account receivable is never collected. Losses from uncollectible accounts are classified as operating expenses.

Under accrual accounting, the expense for uncollectible accounts is recorded in the same period as the related sale. The expense is estimated because the actual amount of uncollectible accounts is not known until later periods. To match the expense for uncollectible accounts with the sales revenue for the same period, the estimated expense is debited to an account named **Uncollectible Accounts Expense.**

Several methods exist for estimating the expense for uncollectible accounts. Modern Casuals uses the *percentage of net credit sales* method. The rate used is based on the company's past experience with uncollectible accounts and management's assessment of current business conditions. Modern Casuals estimates that three-fourths of 1 percent (0.75 percent) of net credit sales will be uncollectible. Net credit sales for the year were $100,000. The estimated expense for uncollectible accounts is $750 ($100,000 × 0.0075).

The entry to record the expense for uncollectible accounts includes a credit to a contra asset account, **Allowance for Doubtful Accounts.** This account appears on the balance sheet as follows.

Accounts Receivable	$32,000
Allowance for Doubtful Accounts	(750)
Net Accounts Receivable	$31,250

Adjustment **(c)** appears on the worksheet in Figure 12-1 for the expense for uncollectible accounts.

② Objective

Compute adjustments for accrued and prepaid expense items, and enter the adjustments on the worksheet.

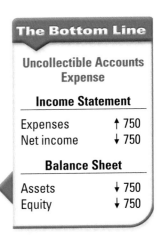

The Bottom Line

Uncollectible Accounts Expense

Income Statement

Expenses	↑ 750
Net income	↓ 750

Balance Sheet

Assets	↓ 750
Equity	↓ 750

Uncollectible Accounts Expense				Allowance for Doubtful Accounts	
Adj.	750			Bal.	100
				Adj.	750

└────────────────────────── (c) ──────────────────────────┘

When a specific account becomes uncollectible, it is written off.

- The entry is a debit to **Allowance for Doubtful Accounts** and a credit to **Accounts Receivable.**
- The customer's account in the accounts receivable subsidiary ledger is also reduced.

Uncollectible Accounts Expense is not affected by the write-off of individual accounts identified as uncollectible. It is used only when the end-of-period adjustment is recorded.

Notice that net income is decreased at the end of the period when the adjustment for *estimated* expense for uncollectible accounts is made. When a specific customer account is written off, net income is *not* affected. The write-off of a specific account affects only the balance sheet accounts **Accounts Receivable** (asset) and **Allowance for Doubtful Accounts** (contra asset).

The balance of **Allowance for Doubtful Accounts** is reduced throughout the year as customer accounts are written off. Notice that **Allowance for Doubtful Accounts** already has a credit balance of $100 in the Trial Balance section of the worksheet. When the estimate of uncollectible accounts expense is based on sales, any remaining balance from previous periods is not considered when recording the adjustment.

Adjustments for Depreciation

Most businesses have long-term assets that are used in the operation of the business. These are often referred to as **property, plant, and equipment**. Property, plant, and equipment includes buildings, trucks, automobiles, machinery, furniture, fixtures, office equipment, and land.

Property, plant, and equipment costs are not charged to expense accounts when purchased. Instead, the cost of a long-term asset is allocated over the asset's expected useful life by depreciation. This process involves the gradual transfer of acquisition cost to expense. There is one exception. Land is not depreciated.

There are many ways to calculate depreciation. Modern Casuals uses the straight-line method, so an equal amount of depreciation is taken in each year of the asset's useful life. The formula for straight-line depreciation is

$$\frac{\text{Cost} - \text{Salvage Value}}{\text{Estimated Useful Life}} = \text{Depreciation}$$

Important!

Depreciation
To calculate monthly straight-line depreciation, divide the depreciable base by the number of months in the useful life.

Salvage value is an estimate of the amount that could be obtained from the sale or disposition of an asset at the end of its useful life. Cost minus salvage value is called the *depreciable base*.

Depreciation of Store Equipment. The trial balance shows that Modern Casuals has $20,000 of store equipment. What is the amount of annual depreciation expense using the straight-line method?

Cost of store equipment	$20,000
Salvage value	(2,000)
Depreciable base	$18,000
Expected useful life	8 years

$$\frac{\$20,000 - \$2,000}{8 \text{ years}} = \$2,250 \text{ Per year}$$

The annual depreciation expense is $2,250. Adjustment **(d)** appears on the worksheet in Figure 12-1 for the depreciation expense for store equipment.

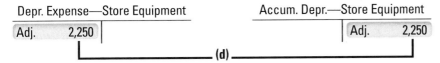

Depreciation of Office Equipment. Modern Casuals reports $7,000 of office equipment on the trial balance. What is the amount of annual depreciation expense using the straight-line method?

Cost of office equipment	$7,000
Salvage value	(1,000)
Depreciable base	$6,000
Expected useful life	5 years

$$\frac{\$7,000 - \$1,000}{5 \text{ Years}} = \$1,200 \text{ Per year}$$

Annual depreciation expense is $1,200. Adjustment **(e)** appears on the worksheet in Figure 12-1 for depreciation expense for office equipment.

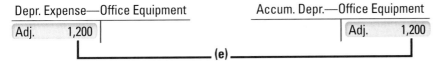

Adjustments for Accrued Expenses

Many expense items are paid for, recorded, and used in the same accounting period. However, some expense items are paid for and recorded in one period but used in a later period. Other expense items are used in one period and paid for in a later period. In these situations adjustments are made so that the financial statements show all expenses in the appropriate period.

Accrued expenses are expenses that relate to (are used in) the current period but have not yet been paid and do not yet appear in the accounting records. Modern Casuals makes adjustments for three types of accrued expenses:

- accrued salaries
- accrued payroll taxes
- accrued interest on notes payable

Because accrued expenses involve amounts that must be paid in the future, the adjustment for each item is a debit to an expense account and a credit to a liability account.

Accrued Salaries. At Modern Casuals all full-time sales and office employees are paid semimonthly—on the 15th and the last day of the month. The trial balance in Figure 12-1 shows the correct salaries expense for the full-time employees for the year. From December 28 to January 3, the firm hired several part-time sales clerks for the year-end sale. Through December 31, 2004, these employees earned $1,500. The part-time salaries expense has not yet been recorded because the employees will

About *Accounting*

Electronic Payments
Congress ordered the U.S. Treasury Department to begin electronic payments for all checks except taxpayer refunds by January 2, 1999. The initiative saves taxpayers an estimated $100 million per year.

not be paid until January 3, 2005. An adjustment is made to record the amount owed, but not yet paid, as of the end of December.

Adjustment **(f)** appears on the worksheet in Figure 12-1 for accrued salaries.

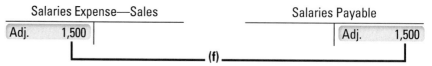

Accrued Payroll Taxes. Payroll taxes are not legally owed until the salaries are paid. Businesses that want to match revenue and expenses in the appropriate period make adjustments to accrue the employer's payroll taxes even though the taxes are technically not yet due. Modern Casuals makes adjustments for accrued employer's payroll taxes.

The payroll taxes related to the full-time employees of Modern Casuals have been recorded and appear on the trial balance. However, the payroll taxes for the part-time sales clerks have not been recorded. None of the part-time clerks have reached the social security wage base limit. The entire $1,500 of accrued salaries is subject to the employer's share of social security and Medicare taxes. The accrued employer's payroll taxes are

Social security tax	$1,500 × 0.0620 =	$ 93.00
Medicare tax	1,500 × 0.0145 =	21.75
Total accrued payroll taxes		$114.75

Adjustment **(g)** appears on the worksheet in Figure 12-1 for accrued payroll taxes.

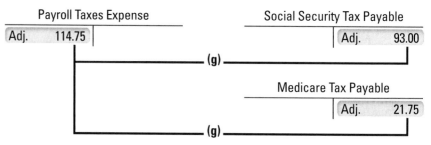

The entire $1,500 of accrued salaries is also subject to unemployment taxes. The unemployment tax rates for Modern Casuals are 0.8 percent for federal and 5.4 percent for state.

Federal unemployment tax	$1,500 × 0.008 =	$12.00
State unemployment tax	1,500 × 0.054 =	81.00
Total accrued taxes		$93.00

Adjustment **(h)** appears on the worksheet in Figure 12-1 for accrued unemployment taxes.

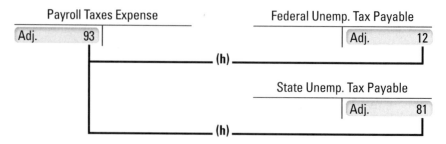

Matching
Adjustments for accrued expenses match the expense to the period in which the expense was used.

Accrued Interest on Notes Payable. On December 1, 2004, Modern Casuals issued a two-month note for $2,000, with annual interest of 12 percent. The note was recorded in the **Notes Payable—Trade** account. Modern Casuals will pay the interest when the note matures on February 1, 2005. However, the interest expense is incurred day by day and should be allocated to each fiscal period involved in order to obtain a complete and accurate picture of expenses. The accrued interest amount is determined by using the interest formula *Principal × Rate × Time.*

Principal	×	Rate	×	Time		
$2,000	×	0.12	×	1/12	=	$20

The fraction 1/12 represents one month, which is 1/12 of a year.

Adjustment **(i)** appears on the worksheet in Figure 12-1 for the accrued interest expense.

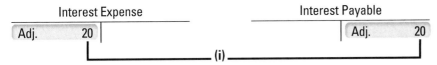

Other Accrued Expenses. Many businesses pay property taxes to state and local governments. They accrue these taxes at the end of the accounting period. Adjustments might also be necessary for commissions, professional services, and many other accrued expenses.

Adjustments for Prepaid Expenses

Prepaid expenses, or **deferred expenses**, are expenses that are paid for and recorded before they are used. Often a portion of a prepaid item remains unused at the end of the period; it is applicable to future periods. When paid for, these items are recorded as assets. At the end of the period, an adjustment is made to recognize as an expense the portion used during the period. Modern Casuals makes adjustments for three types of prepaid expenses:

- prepaid supplies
- prepaid insurance
- prepaid interest on notes payable

> Avery Dennison Corporation reported prepaid expenses of $23.7 million at January 1, 2000. Adjustments are made to these accounts to allocate expenses to the appropriate period.

Supplies Used. When supplies are purchased, they are debited to the asset account **Supplies.** On the trial balance in Figure 12-1, **Supplies** has a balance of $6,300. A physical count on December 31 showed $1,325 of supplies on hand. This means that $4,975 ($6,300 − $1,325) of supplies were used during the year. An adjustment is made to charge the cost of supplies used to the current year's operations and to reflect the value of the supplies on hand.

Adjustment **(j)** appears on the worksheet in Figure 12-1 for supplies expense.

Expired Insurance. On January 1, 2004, Modern Casuals wrote a check for $7,200 for a two-year insurance policy. The asset account **Prepaid Insurance** was debited for $7,200. On December 31, 2004, one year of insurance had expired. An adjustment for $3,600 ($7,200 × 1/2) was made to charge the cost of the expired insurance to operations and to decrease **Prepaid Insurance** to reflect the prepaid insurance premium that remains.

Adjustment **(k)** appears on the worksheet in Figure 12-1 for the insurance.

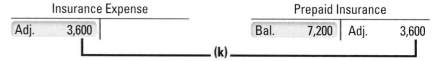

Prepaid Interest on Notes Payable. On November 1, 2004, Modern Casuals borrowed $9,000 from its bank and signed a three-month note at an annual interest rate of 10 percent. The bank deducted the entire amount of interest in advance. The interest for three months is $225.

Principal	×	Rate	×	Time		
$9,000	×	0.10	×	3/12	=	$225

Modern Casuals received $8,775 ($9,000 − $225). The transaction was recorded as a debit to **Cash** for $8,775, a debit to **Prepaid Interest** for $225, and a credit to **Notes Payable—Bank** for $9,000.

On December 31 two months of prepaid interest ($225 × 2/3 = $150) had been incurred and needed to be recorded as an expense. The adjustment consists of a debit to **Interest Expense** and a credit to **Prepaid Interest.**

Adjustment **(l)** appears on the worksheet in Figure 12-1 for the interest expense.

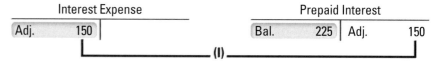

Other Prepaid Expenses. Other common prepaid expenses are prepaid rent, prepaid advertising, and prepaid taxes. When paid, the amounts are debited to the asset accounts **Prepaid Rent, Prepaid Advertising,** and **Prepaid Taxes.** At the end of each period, an adjustment is made to transfer the portion used from the asset account to an expense account. For example, the adjustment for expired rent would be a debit to **Rent Expense** and a credit to **Prepaid Rent.**

Alternative Method. Some businesses use a different method for prepaid expenses. At the time cash is paid, they debit an expense account (not an asset account). At the end of each period, they make an adjustment to transfer the portion that is not used from the expense account to an asset account.

Suppose that Modern Casuals used this alternative method when it purchased the two-year insurance policy. On January 1, 2004, the transaction would have been recorded as a debit to **Insurance Expense** for $7,200 and

Accounting

On The Job

Business & Administration

Industry Overview

Business and administration services extend into every sector of the economy. The coordination and support of business operations is required in organizations ranging from insurance firms to government offices, steel manufacturers to retail stores.

Career Opportunities

- Account Executive
- Cost Accountant
- Payroll Supervisor
- Human Resources Manager
- Facility Manager
- Contract Administrator
- Chief Financial Officer

Preparing for a Career in Business & Administration

- Develop solid communication and analytical skills. Be flexible, decisive, and capable of coordinating many activities at once. Develop strategies to cope with deadlines.

- Attain certification specific to your area of interest. For example, the Certified Administrative Manager (CAM) is offered by the Institute of Certified Professional Managers.

- Complete a bachelor's degree with a major in accounting, finance, management, manage-ment information systems, marketing, or production and operations management.

- Become proficient in database, spreadsheet, and word processing applications.

- Complete a degree in engineering, architecture, business administration, or facility management for a career as a facility manager.

- Become familiar with basic office equipment such as fax machines, telephone systems, and personal computers.

- Gain a solid understanding of standard business forms such as purchase orders, invoices, contracts, and packing slips.

- Be prepared to interpret and analyze financial statements to effectively contribute to business discussions and decisions.

Thinking Critically

Describe 10 business tasks or responsibilities involved in the operation of Southwest Airlines Co. or a similar company.

Internet Application

The Internet contains a wealth of information provided to help individuals as they launch new businesses. Using an Internet search engine, list five resources that offer entrepreneurs guidance on their new endeavors. Describe the information or resources offered at each Web site.

---

a credit to **Cash** for $7,200. On December 31, 2004, after the insurance coverage for one year had expired, coverage for one year remained. The adjustment would be recorded as a debit to **Prepaid Insurance** for $3,600 ($7,200 × 1/2) and a credit to **Insurance Expense** for $3,600.

Identical amounts appear on the financial statements at the end of each fiscal period no matter which method is used to handle prepaid expenses.

Adjustments for Accrued Income

Accrued income is income that has been earned but not yet received and recorded. On December 31, 2004, Modern Casuals had two types of accrued income: accrued interest on notes receivable and accrued commission on sales tax.

3 Objective

Compute adjustments for accrued and deferred income items, and enter the adjustments on the worksheet.

Accruals, Deferrals, and the Worksheet **Chapter 12 • 439**

Accrued Interest on Notes Receivable. Interest-bearing notes receivable are recorded at face value and are carried in the accounting records at this value until they are collected. The interest income is recorded when it is received, which is normally when the note matures. However, interest income is earned day by day. At the end of the period, an adjustment is made to recognize interest income earned but not yet received or recorded.

On November 1, 2004, Modern Casuals accepted from a customer a four-month, 12 percent note for $1,200. The note and interest are due on March 1, 2005. As of December 31, 2004, two months (November and December) of interest income was earned but not received. The amount of earned interest income is $24.

Principal	×	Rate	×	Time		
$1,200	×	0.12	×	2/12	=	$24

Adjustment **(m)** appears on the worksheet in Figure 12-1 for the interest income. To record the interest income of $24 earned, but not yet received, an adjustment debiting the asset account **Interest Receivable** and crediting a revenue account called **Interest Income** is made.

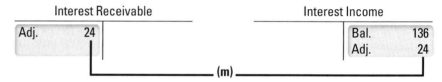

Accrued Commission on Sales Tax. Modern Casuals collects sales tax on retail sales. It sends the tax to the state agency on a quarterly basis. The state sales tax law allows firms that file the quarterly tax returns and pay the tax promptly to keep 2 percent of the tax. On December 31, 2004, Modern Casuals owed $7,200 of sales tax. In January the tax will be paid less the permitted commission of $144 ($7,200 × 0.02). The commission represents income earned and is recorded in the **Miscellaneous Income** account.

Adjustment **(n)** appears on the worksheet in Figure 12-1. The adjustment decreases the sales tax liability.

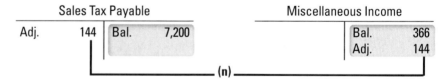

Adjustments for Unearned Income

Unearned income, or **deferred income**, exists when income is received before it is earned. Under the accrual basis of accounting, only income that has been earned appears on the income statement. Modern Casuals has no unearned income. The following is an example of unearned income for another business.

Unearned Subscription Income for a Publisher. Magazine publishers receive cash in advance for subscriptions. When the publisher receives the cash, it is unearned income and is a liability. It is a liability because the publisher has an obligation to provide magazines during the subscription period. As the magazines are sent to the subscribers, income is earned and the liability decreases.

Hitech Publishing Corporation publishes *Computer Trends and Techniques*. When subscriptions are received, **Cash** is debited and **Unearned Subscription Income,** a liability account, is credited. At the end of the year, **Unearned Subscription Income** had a balance of $450,000. During the year $184,000 of magazines were delivered; income was earned in the amount of $184,000. The adjustment to recognize income is a debit to **Unearned Subscription Income** for $184,000 and a credit to **Subscription Income** for $184,000.

After the adjustment the **Unearned Subscription Income** account has a balance of $266,000, which represents subscriptions for future periods.

Unearned Subscription Income

12/31 Adj. 184,000	12/31 Bal. 450,000
	12/31 Bal. 266,000

Other Unearned Income Items. Other types of unearned income include management fees, rental income, legal fees, architectural fees, construction fees, and advertising income. The cash received in advance is recorded as unearned income. As the income is earned, the amount is transferred from the liability account to a revenue account.

Alternative Method. Some businesses use a different method to handle unearned income. At the time the cash is received, a credit is made to a revenue account (not a liability account). At the end of each period, the adjustment transfers the portion that is not earned to a liability account. For example, suppose Hitech Publishing Corporation uses this method. When cash for subscriptions is received, it is credited to **Subscription Income.** At the end of the period, an adjustment is made to transfer the unearned income to a liability account. The entry is a debit to **Subscription Income** and a credit to **Unearned Subscription Income.**

Identical amounts appear on the financial statements at the end of each fiscal period no matter which method is used to handle unearned income.

Section 1 Self Review

Questions

1. Under the accrual basis of accounting, when is revenue recognized?

2. Under the accrual basis of accounting, when are the costs of merchandise inventory normally recorded?

3. Under the accrual basis of accounting, when are operating expenses recognized?

Exercises

4. Under the accrual basis of accounting, it is appropriate to recognize

revenue from a credit sale

  a. on the date of the sale.

  b. on the date that the account is collected in full.

  c. each time a customer payment is received.

  d. on the date the monthly statement is sent to the customer.

5. Accrued income is income that has been

  a. received but not earned.

  b. earned but not received.

  c. earned and received.

  d. expected to be received within the next accounting period.

Analysis

6. A company makes an end-of-period adjustment for uncollectible accounts expense. Does net accounts receivable change when a specific customer's account is later identified as being uncollectible and is written off? Why or why not?

Section Objective

4 Complete a ten-column worksheet.

WHY IT'S IMPORTANT
Using the worksheet is a convenient way to gather the information needed for the financial statements.

Terms to Learn

net income line
updated account balances

4 Objective

Complete a ten-column worksheet.

Completing the Worksheet

After all adjustments have been entered on the worksheet, total the Adjustments Debit and Credit columns and verify that debits and credits are equal. The next step in the process is to prepare the Adjusted Trial Balance section.

Preparing the Adjusted Trial Balance Section

Figure 12-2 on pages 444–447 shows the completed worksheet for Modern Casuals. The Adjusted Trial Balance section of the worksheet is completed as follows.

1. Combine the amount in the Trial Balance section and the Adjustments section for each account.

2. Enter the results in the Adjusted Trial Balance section. The accounts that do not have adjustments are simply extended from the Trial Balance section to the Adjusted Trial Balance section. For example, the balance of the **Cash** account is recorded in the Debit column of the Adjusted Trial Balance section without change.

3. The accounts that are affected by adjustments are recomputed. Follow these rules to combine amounts on the worksheet.

Trial Balance Section	Adjustments Section	Action
Debit	Debit	Add
Debit	Credit	Subtract
Credit	Credit	Add
Credit	Debit	Subtract

- If the account has a debit balance in the Trial Balance section and a debit entry in the Adjustments section, add the two amounts. Look at the **Salaries Expense—Sales** account. It has a $78,490 debit balance in the Trial Balance section and a $1,500 debit entry in the Adjustments section. The new balance is $79,990 ($78,490 + $1,500). It is entered in the Debit column of the Adjusted Trial Balance section.

- If the account has a debit balance in the Trial Balance section and a credit entry in the Adjustments section, subtract the credit amount. Look at the **Supplies** account. It has a $6,300 debit balance in the Trial Balance section and a $4,975 credit entry in the Adjustments section. The new balance is $1,325 ($6,300 − $4,975). It is entered in the Debit column of the Adjusted Trial Balance section.

- If the account has a credit balance in the Trial Balance section and a credit entry in the Adjustments section, add the two amounts. Look at **Allowance for Doubtful Accounts.** It has a $100 credit balance in the Trial Balance section and a $750 credit entry in the Adjustments section. The new balance is $850 ($100 + $750). It is entered in the Credit column of the Adjusted Trial Balance section.

- If the account has a credit balance in the Trial Balance section and a debit entry in the Adjustments section, subtract the debit amount. Look at the **Sales Tax Payable** account. It has a $7,200 Credit balance in the Trial Balance section and a $144 debit entry in the Adjustments section. The new balance is $7,056 ($7,200 − $144). It is entered in the Credit column of the Adjusted Trial Balance section.

The Adjusted Trial Balance section now contains the **updated account balances**.

Look at the **Income Summary** account. Recall that the debit entry removed the *beginning* balance from **Merchandise Inventory** and the credit entry added the *ending* balance to **Merchandise Inventory.** (See pages 444–447.) Notice that the debit and credit amounts in **Income Summary** are not combined in the Adjusted Trial Balance section.

Once all the updated account balances have been entered in the Adjusted Trial Balance section, total and rule the columns. Confirm that total debits equal total credits.

Preparing the Balance Sheet and Income Statement Sections

To complete the Income Statement and Balance Sheet sections of the worksheet, identify the accounts that appear on the balance sheet. On Figure 12-2 the accounts from **Cash** through **Sonia Sanchez, Drawing** appear on the balance sheet. For each account enter the amount in the appropriate Debit or Credit column of the Balance Sheet section of the worksheet.

For accounts that appear on the income statement, **Sales** through **Interest Expense,** enter the amounts in the appropriate Debit or Credit column of the Income Statement section. The **Income Summary** debit and credit amounts are also entered in the Income Statement section of the worksheet. Notice that the debit and credit amounts in **Income Summary** are not combined in the Income Statement section.

Calculating Net Income or Net Loss

Once all account balances have been entered in the financial statement sections of the worksheet, the net income or net loss for the period is determined.

1. Total the Debit and Credit columns in the Income Statement section. For Modern Casuals, the debits total $564,197.75 and the credits total $612,500.00. Since the credits exceed the debits, the difference represents net income of $48,302.25.

2. To balance the Debit and the Credit columns in the Income Statement section, enter $48,302.25 in the Debit column of the Income Statement section. Total each column again and record the final total of each column ($612,500.00) on the worksheet.

3. Total the columns in the Balance Sheet section. Total debits are $160,060.00 and total credits are $111,757.75. The difference must equal the net income for the year, $48,302.25.

Two Sets of Books

A Russian company called Inotec sells computers, supports innovations in international accounting, and distributes software made by other companies. Inotec distributes Microsoft's Solution Provider software. The software allows companies to comply with separate accounting requirements, such as U.S. generally accepted accounting principles and the accounting standards of other countries.

	ACCOUNT NAME	TRIAL BALANCE DEBIT	TRIAL BALANCE CREDIT	ADJUSTMENTS DEBIT	ADJUSTMENTS CREDIT
1	Cash	21 136 00			
2	Petty Cash Fund	100 00			
3	Notes Receivable	1200 00			
4	Accounts Receivable	32000 00			
5	Allowance for Doubtful Accounts		100 00		(c) 750 00
6	Interest Receivable			(m) 24 00	
7	Merchandise Inventory	51500 00		(b) 46000 00	(a) 51500 00
8	Prepaid Insurance	7200 00			(k) 3600 00
9	Prepaid Interest	225 00			(l) 150 00
10	Supplies	6300 00			(j) 4975 00
11	Store Equipment	20000 00			
12	Accumulated Depreciation—Store Equipment				(d) 2250 00
13	Office Equipment	7000 00			
14	Accumulated Depreciation—Office Equipment				(e) 1200 00
15	Notes Payable—Trade		2000 00		
16	Notes Payable—Bank		9000 00		
17	Accounts Payable		24129 00		
18	Interest Payable				(i) 20 00
19	Social Security Tax Payable		1084 00		(g) 93 00
20	Medicare Tax Payable		250 00		(g) 21 75
21	Employee Income Taxes Payable		990 00		
22	Federal Unemployment Tax Payable				(h) 12 00
23	State Unemployment Tax Payable				(h) 81 00
24	Salaries Payable				(f) 1500 00
25	Sales Tax Payable		7200 00	(n) 144 00	
26	Sonia Sanchez, Capital		61221 00		
27	Sonia Sanchez, Drawing	27600 00			
28	Income Summary			(a) 51500 00	(b) 46000 00
29	Sales		559650 00		
30	Sales Returns and Allowances	13000 00			
31	Interest Income		136 00		(m) 24 00
32	Miscellaneous Income		366 00		(n) 144 00
33	Purchases	320500 00			
34	Freight In	8800 00			
35	Purchases Returns and Allowances		3050 00		
36	Purchase Discounts		3130 00		
37	Salaries Expense—Sales	78490 00		(f) 1500 00	
38	Advertising Expense	7425 00			
39	Cash Short or Over	125 00			
40	Supplies Expense			(j) 4975 00	

▲ FIGURE 12-2 10-Column Worksheet—Complete

ADJUSTED TRIAL BALANCE		INCOME STATEMENT		BALANCE SHEET		
DEBIT	CREDIT	DEBIT	CREDIT	DEBIT	CREDIT	
21 136 00				21 136 00		1
100 00				100 00		2
1 200 00				1 200 00		3
32 000 00				32 000 00		4
	850 00				850 00	5
	24 00				24 00	6
46 000 00				46 000 00		7
3 600 00				3 600 00		8
	75 00				75 00	9
1 325 00				1 325 00		10
20 000 00				20 000 00		11
	2 250 00				2 250 00	12
7 000 00				7 000 00		13
	1 200 00				1 200 00	14
	2 000 00				2 000 00	15
	9 000 00				9 000 00	16
	24 129 00				24 129 00	17
	20 00				20 00	18
	1 177 00				1 177 00	19
	271 75				271 75	20
	990 00				990 00	21
	12 00				12 00	22
	81 00				81 00	23
	1 500 00				1 500 00	24
	7 056 00				7 056 00	25
	61 221 00				61 221 00	26
27 600 00				27 600 00		27
51 500 00	46 000 00	51 500 00	46 000 00			28
	559 650 00		559 650 00			29
13 000 00		13 000 00				30
	160 00		160 00			31
	510 00		510 00			32
320 500 00		320 500 00				33
8 800 00		8 800 00				34
	3 050 00		3 050 00			35
	3 130 00		3 130 00			36
79 990 00		79 990 00				37
7 425 00		7 425 00				38
125 00		125 00				39
4 975 00		4 975 00				40

▲ FIGURE 12-2 (continued) 10-Column Worksheet—Complete

ACCOUNT NAME	TRIAL BALANCE		ADJUSTMENTS	
	DEBIT	CREDIT	DEBIT	CREDIT
41 Depreciation Expense—Store Equipment			(d) 2 2 5 0 00	
42 Rent Expense	27 6 0 0 00			
43 Salaries Expense—Office	26 5 0 0 00			
44 Insurance Expense				(k) 3 6 0 0 00
45 Payroll Taxes Expense	7 2 0 5 00		(g) 1 1 4 75	
46			(h) 9 3 00	
47 Telephone Expense	1 8 7 5 00			
48 Uncollectible Accounts Expense			(c) 7 5 0 00	
49 Utilities Expense	5 9 2 5 00			
50 Depreciation Expense—Office Equipment			(e) 1 2 0 0 00	
51 Interest Expense	6 0 0 00		(i) 2 0 00	
52			(l) 1 5 0 00	
53 Totals	672 3 0 6 00	672 3 0 6 00	112 3 2 0 75	112 3 2 0 75
54 Net Income				
55				
56				

▲ **FIGURE 12-2 (continued)** 10-Column Worksheet—Complete

Managerial
IMPLICATIONS

Effect of Adjustments on Financial Statements

- If managers are to know the true revenue, expenses, and net income or net loss for a period, the matching process is necessary.
- If accounts are not adjusted, the financial statements will be incomplete, misleading, and of little help in evaluating operations.
- Managers need to be familiar with the procedures and underlying assumptions used by the accountant to make adjustments because adjustments increase or decrease net income.
- Managers need information about uncollectible accounts expense in order to review the firm's credit policy. If losses are too high, management might tighten the requirements for obtaining credit. If losses are very low, management might investigate whether easing credit requirements would increase net income.
- The worksheet is a useful device for gathering data about adjustments and for preparing the financial statements.
- Managers are keenly interested in receiving timely financial statements, especially the income statement, which shows the results of operations.
- Managers are also interested in the prompt preparation of the balance sheet because it shows the financial position of the business at the end of the period.

Thinking Critically
What are some possible consequences of not making adjusting entries?

ADJUSTED TRIAL BALANCE		INCOME STATEMENT		BALANCE SHEET		
DEBIT	CREDIT	DEBIT	CREDIT	DEBIT	CREDIT	
2 2 5 0 00		2 2 5 0 00				41
27 6 0 0 00		27 6 0 0 00				42
26 5 0 0 00		26 5 0 0 00				43
3 6 0 0 00		3 6 0 0 00				44
7 4 1 2 75		7 4 1 2 75				45
						46
1 8 7 5 00		1 8 7 5 00				47
7 5 0 00		7 5 0 00				48
5 9 2 5 00		5 9 2 5 00				49
1 2 0 0 00		1 2 0 0 00				50
7 7 0 00		7 7 0 00				51
						52
724 2 5 7 75	724 2 5 7 75	564 1 9 7 75	612 5 0 0 00	160 0 6 0 00	111 7 5 7 75	53
		48 3 0 2 25			48 3 0 2 25	54
		612 5 0 0 00	612 5 0 0 00	160 0 6 0 00	160 0 6 0 00	55
						56

▲ FIGURE 12-2 (continued)
10-Column Worksheet—
Complete

4. Enter $48,302.25 in the Credit column of the Balance Sheet section. Total each column again and record the final total in each column ($160,060.00).

5. Rule the Debit and Credit columns in all sections to show that the worksheet is complete.

Notice that the net income is recorded in two places on the **net income line** of the worksheet. It is recorded in the Credit column of the Balance Sheet section because net income *increases* owner's equity. It is recorded in the Debit column of the Income Statement section to balance the two columns in that section.

Section 2 Self Review

Questions

1. What is merchandise inventory?
2. How is the amount of ending merchandise inventory determined?
3. How many entries are made to adjust **Merchandise Inventory** on the worksheet? What are the entries?

Exercises

4. **Allowance for Doubtful Accounts** is reported in the

   a. Assets section of the balance sheet.
   b. Operating Expenses section of the income statement.
   c. Liabilities section of the balance sheet.
   d. Owner's Equity section of the balance sheet.

5. The amount of net income appears on the worksheet in the

   a. Income Statement Debit column only.
   b. Income Statement Debit and the Balance Sheet Credit columns.
   c. Income Statement Credit and the Balance Sheet Debit Columns.
   d. Balance Sheet Credit column only.

Analysis

6. If the accountant does not adjust **Merchandise Inventory,** how is the balance sheet affected?

(Answers to Section 2 Self Review are on page 469.)

CHAPTER 12 Review and Applications

Review

Chapter Summary

Accrual basis accounting requires that all revenue and expenses for a fiscal period to be matched and reported on the income statement to determine net income or net loss for the period. In this chapter, you have learned the techniques used to adjust accounts so that they accurately reflect the operations of the period.

Learning Objectives

1 Determine the adjustment for merchandise inventory, and enter the adjustment on the worksheet.

Merchandise inventory consists of goods that a business has on hand for sale to customers. When the trial balance is prepared at the end of the period, the **Merchandise Inventory** account still reflects the beginning inventory. Before the financial statements can be prepared, **Merchandise Inventory** must be updated to reflect the ending inventory for the period. The actual quantity of the goods on hand at the end of the period must be counted. Then the adjustment is completed in two steps:

1. Remove the beginning inventory balance from the **Merchandise Inventory** account. Debit **Income Summary**; credit **Merchandise Inventory.**

2. Add the ending inventory to the **Merchandise Inventory** account. Debit **Merchandise Inventory**; credit **Income Summary.**

2 Compute adjustments for accrued and prepaid expense items, and enter the adjustments on the worksheet.

Expense accounts are adjusted at the end of the period so that they correctly reflect the current period. Examples of adjustments include provision for uncollectible accounts and depreciation. Other typical adjustments of expense accounts involve accrued expenses and prepaid expenses.

- Accrued expenses are expense items that have been incurred or used but not yet paid or recorded. They include salaries, payroll taxes, interest on notes payable, and property taxes.

- Prepaid expenses are expense items that a business pays for and records before it actually uses the items. Rent, insurance, and advertising paid in advance are examples.

3 Compute adjustments for accrued and deferred income items, and enter the adjustments on the worksheet.

Revenue accounts are adjusted at the end of the period so that they correctly reflect the current period.

- Adjustments can affect either accrued income or deferred income.

- Accrued income is income that has been earned but not yet received and recorded.

- Deferred, or unearned, income is income that has not yet been earned but has been received.

4 Complete a ten-column worksheet.

When all adjustments have been entered on the worksheet, the worksheet is completed so that the financial statements can be prepared easily.

1. Figures in the Trial Balance section are combined with the adjustments to obtain an adjusted trial balance.

2. Each item in the Adjusted Trial Balance section is extended to the Income Statement and Balance Sheet sections of the worksheet.

3. The Income Statement columns are totaled and the net income or net loss is determined and entered in the net income line.

4. The amount of net income or net loss is entered in the net income line in the Balance Sheet section. After net income or net loss is added, the total debits must equal the total credits in the Balance Sheet section columns.

5 Define the accounting terms new to this chapter.

CHAPTER 12 GLOSSARY

Accrual basis (p. 430) A system of accounting by which all revenues and expenses are matched and reported on financial statements for the applicable period, regardless of when the cash related to the transaction is received or paid

Accrued expenses (p. 435) Expense items that relate to the current period but have not yet been paid and do not yet appear in the accounting records

Accrued income (p. 439) Income that has been earned but not yet received and recorded

Deferred expenses (p. 437) See Prepaid expenses

Deferred income (p. 440) See Unearned income

Inventory sheet (p. 431) A form used to list the volume and type of goods a firm has in stock

Net income line (p. 447) The worksheet line immediately following the column totals on which net income (or net loss) is recorded in two places: the Income Statement section and the Balance Sheet section

Prepaid expenses (p. 437) Expenses that are paid for and recorded before they are used, such as rent or insurance

Property, plant, and equipment (p. 434) Long-term assets that are used in the operation of a business and that are subject to depreciation (except for land, which is not depreciated)

Unearned income (p. 440) Income received before it is earned

Updated account balances (p. 443) The amounts entered in the Adjusted Trial Balance section of the worksheet

Comprehensive Self Review

1. What is the purpose of the accrual basis of accounting?
2. Why must the accounts be examined carefully at the end of a fiscal period before financial statements are prepared?
3. What types of accounts appear in the Income Statement section of the worksheet?
4. What types of accounts appear in the Balance Sheet section of the worksheet?
5. What are accrued expenses?

(Answers to Comprehensive Self Review are on page 469.)

Discussion Questions

1. What are the advantages of preparing a worksheet?

2. Should the estimated expense for uncollectible accounts be recorded at the time each of these accounts actually becomes worthless or before the losses from individual accounts actually occur?

3. What adjustment is made to record the estimated expense for uncollectible accounts?

4. Why is depreciation recorded?

5. What types of assets are subject to depreciation? Give three examples of such assets.

6. Explain the meaning of the following terms that relate to depreciation.
   a. Salvage value
   b. Depreciable base
   c. Useful life
   d. Straight-line method

7. What adjustment is made for depreciation on office equipment?

8. What is an accrued expense? Give three examples of items that often become accrued expenses.

9. What adjustment is made to record accrued salaries?

10. What is a prepaid expense? Give three examples of prepaid expense items.

11. How is the cost of an insurance policy recorded when the policy is purchased?

12. What adjustment is made to record expired insurance?

13. What is the alternative method of handling prepaid expenses?

14. What is accrued income? Give an example of an item that might produce accrued income.

15. What adjustment is made for accrued interest on a note receivable?

16. What is unearned income? Give two examples of items that would be classified as unearned income.

17. How is unearned income recorded when it is received?

18. What adjustment is made to record income earned during a period?

19. What is the alternative method of handling unearned income?

20. How does the worksheet help the accountant to prepare financial statements more efficiently?

21. **Unearned Fees Income** is classified as which type of account?

Applications

EXERCISES

Determining the adjustments for inventory.

The beginning inventory of a merchandising business was $126,000, and the ending inventory is $112,000. What entries are needed at the end of the fiscal period to adjust **Merchandise Inventory?**

◀ Exercise 12-1
Objective 1

Determining the adjustments for inventory.

The Income Statement section of the worksheet of Bryan Company for the year ended December 31, 20--, has $144,000 recorded in the Debit column and $168,000 in the Credit column on the line for the **Income Summary** account. What were the beginning and ending balances for **Merchandise Inventory?**

◀ Exercise 12-2
Objective 1

Computing adjustments for accrued and prepaid expense items.

For each of the following independent situations, indicate the adjusting entry that must be made on the December 31, 20--, worksheet. Omit descriptions.

◀ Exercise 12-3
Objective 2

a. During the year 20--, Janus Company had net credit sales of $850,000. Past experience shows that 0.9 percent of the firm's net credit sales result in uncollectible accounts.

b. Equipment purchased by Quick Burger Center for $26,000 on January 2, 20--, has an estimated useful life of five years and an estimated salvage value of $3,500. What adjustment for depreciation should be recorded on the firm's worksheet for the year ended December 31, 20--?

c. On December 31, 20--, Lawson Metal Company owed wages of $5,200 to its factory employees, who are paid weekly.

d. On December 31, 20--, Lawson Metal Company owed the employer's social security (6.2%) and Medicare (1.45%) taxes on the entire $5,200 of accrued wages for its factory employees.

e. On December 31, 20--, Lawson Metal Company owed federal (0.8%) and state (5.4%) unemployment taxes on the entire $5,200 of accrued wages for its factory employees.

Computing adjustments for accrued and prepaid expense items.

For each of the following independent situations, indicate the adjusting entry that must be made on the December 31, 20--, worksheet. Omit descriptions.

◀ Exercise 12-4
Objective 2

a. On December 31, 20--, the **Notes Payable** account at Mercado Manufacturing Company had a balance of $9,000. This balance represented a three-month, 12 percent note issued on November 1.

b. On January 2, 20--, Valdez Word Processing Service purchased floppy disks, paper, and other supplies for $4,800 in cash. On December 31, 20--, an inventory of supplies showed that items costing $1,140 were on hand. The **Supplies** account has a balance of $4,800.

c. On August 1, 20--, Homegrown Company paid a premium of $9,720 in cash for a one-year insurance policy. On December 31, 20--, an examination of the insurance records showed that coverage for a period of five months had expired.

d. On April 1, 20--, Capside Restaurant signed a one-year advertising contract with a local radio station and issued a check for $11,520 to pay the total amount owed. On December 31, 20--, the **Prepaid Advertising** account has a balance of $11,520.

Exercise 12-5 ►
Objective 2

Recording adjustments for accrued and prepaid expense items.

On December 1, 20--, Clear Camera Center borrowed $20,000 from its bank in order to expand its operations. The firm issued a four-month, 12 percent note for $20,000 to the bank and received $19,200 in cash because the bank deducted the interest for the entire period in advance. In general journal form, show the entry that would be made to record this transaction and the adjustment for prepaid interest that should be recorded on the firm's worksheet for the year ended December 31, 20--. Omit descriptions.

Exercise 12-6 ►
Objective 2

Recording adjustments for accrued and prepaid expense items.

On December 31, 20--, the **Notes Payable** account at McNear's Antique Shop had a balance of $40,000. This amount represented funds borrowed on a four-month, 12 percent note from the firm's bank on December 1. Record the journal entry for interest expense on this note that should be recorded on the firm's worksheet for the year ended December 31, 20--. Omit descriptions.

Exercise 12-7 ►
Objective 3

Recording adjustments for accrued and deferred income items.

For each of the following independent situations, indicate the adjusting entry that must be made on the December 31, 20--, worksheet. Omit descriptions.

a. On December 31, 20--, the **Notes Receivable** account at Denton Company had a balance of $9,600, which represented a six-month, 10 percent note received from a customer on August 1.

b. On December 31, 20--, the **Sales Tax Payable** account at Lane Shoe Store had a balance of $1,290. This balance represented the sales tax owed for the fourth quarter. The firm is scheduled to send the amount to the state sales tax agency on January 15. At that time the firm will deduct a commission of 2 percent of the tax due, as allowed by state law.

c. During the week ended January 7, 20--, Jordan Magazines Company received $24,000 from customers for subscriptions to its magazine *Modern Business*. On December 31, 20--, an analysis of the **Unearned Subscription Revenue** account showed that $12,000 of the subscriptions were earned in 20--.

d. On September 1, 20--, Eaton Realty Company rented a commercial building to a new tenant and received $30,000 in advance to cover the rent for six months.

Exercise 12-8 ►
Objective 4

Completing a ten-column worksheet.

Indicate whether each of the following accounts would appear in the Income Statement Debit or Credit column or the Balance Sheet Debit or Credit column of the worksheet.

ACCOUNTS

Purchases
Purchases Returns and Allowances
Purchases Discounts
Unearned Rent
Subscription Revenue

Jerome Newton, Capital
Income Summary
Accumulated Depreciation—Equipment
Sales Discounts

Problems

Selected problems can be completed using:
🍑 **Peachtree**　📘 **QuickBooks**　▥ **Spreadsheets**

PROBLEM SET A

Recording adjustments for accrued and prepaid expense items and unearned income.

◄ **Problem 12-1A**
Objectives 2, 3

On July 1, 20--, David Watson established his own accounting practice. Selected transactions for the first few days of July follow.

INSTRUCTIONS

1. Record the transactions on page 1 of the general journal. Omit descriptions. Assume that the firm initially records prepaid expenses as assets and unearned income as a liability.

2. Record the adjusting journal entries that must be made on July 31, 20--, on page 2 of the general journal. Omit descriptions.

DATE		TRANSACTIONS
July	1	Signed a lease for an office and issued Check 101 for $12,000 to pay the rent in advance for six months.
	1	Borrowed money from First National Bank by issuing a four-month, 12 percent note for $18,000; received $17,280 because the bank deducted the interest in advance.
	1	Signed an agreement with Young Company to provide accounting and tax services for one year at $4,000 per month; received the entire fee of $48,000 in advance.
	1	Purchased office equipment for $15,600 from Office Supplies; issued a two-month, 12 percent note in payment. The equipment is estimated to have a useful life of six years and a $1,200 salvage value. The equipment will be depreciated using the straight-line method.
	1	Purchased a one-year insurance policy and issued Check 102 for $1,920 to pay the entire premium.
	3	Purchased office furniture for $16,800 from Office Warehouse; issued Check 103 for $8,400 and agreed to pay the balance in 60 days. The equipment has an estimated useful life of five years and a $1,200 salvage value. The office furniture will be depreciated using the straight-line method.
	5	Purchased office supplies for $2,160 with Check 104. Assume $800 of supplies are on hand July 31, 20--.

Analyze: What balance should be reflected in **Unearned Accounting Fees** at July 31, 20--?

Problem 12-2A ►
Objectives 2, 3

Recording adjustments for accrued and prepaid expense items and earned income.

On July 31, 20--, after one month of operation, the general ledger of Hillary Rao, Consultant, contained the accounts and balances given below.

INSTRUCTIONS

1. Prepare a partial worksheet with the following sections: Trial Balance, Adjustments, and Adjusted Trial Balance. Use the data about the firm's accounts and balances to complete the Trial Balance section.

2. Enter the adjustments described below in the Adjustments section. Identify each adjustment with the appropriate letter.

3. Complete the Adjusted Trial Balance section.

ACCOUNTS AND BALANCES

Cash	$22,200	Dr.
Accounts Receivable	1,300	Dr.
Supplies	860	Dr.
Prepaid Rent	9,000	Dr.
Prepaid Insurance	1,680	Dr.
Prepaid Interest	400	Dr.
Furniture	11,800	Dr.
Accumulated Depreciation—Furniture		
Equipment	6,400	Dr.
Accumulated Depreciation—Equipment		
Notes Payable	18,400	Cr.
Accounts Payable	4,000	Cr.
Interest Payable		
Unearned Consulting Fees	3,600	Cr.
Hillary Rao, Capital	25,220	Cr.
Hillary Rao, Drawing	2,000	Dr.
Consulting Fees	8,000	Cr.
Salaries Expense	3,200	Dr.
Utilities Expense	220	Dr.
Telephone Expense	160	Dr.
Supplies Expense		
Rent Expense		
Insurance Expense		
Depreciation Expense—Furniture		
Depreciation Expense—Equipment		
Interest Expense		

ADJUSTMENTS

a. On July 31 an inventory of the supplies showed that items costing $760 were on hand.

b. On July 1 the firm paid $9,000 in advance for six months of rent.

c. On July 1 the firm purchased a one-year insurance policy for $1,680.

d. On July 1 the firm paid $400 interest in advance on a four-month note that it issued to the bank.

e. On July 1 the firm purchased office furniture for $11,800. The furniture is expected to have a useful life of five years and a salvage value of $1,000.

f. On July 1 the firm purchased office equipment for $6,400. The equipment is expected to have a useful life of five years and a salvage value of $1,600.

g. On July 1 the firm issued a two-month, 12 percent note for $6,400.

h. On July 1 the firm received a consulting fee of $3,600 in advance for a one-year period.

Analyze: By what total amount were the expense accounts of the business adjusted?

Recording adjustments and completing the worksheet.

The Garden House is a retail store that sells plants, soil, and decorative pots. On December 31, 2005, the firm's general ledger contained the accounts and balances that appear below and on page 456.

◀ **Problem 12-3A**
Objectives 1, 2, 3, 4

INSTRUCTIONS

1. Prepare the Trial Balance section of a ten-column worksheet. The worksheet covers the year ended December 31, 2005.

2. Enter the adjustments below in the Adjustments section of the worksheet. Identify each adjustment with the appropriate letter.

3. Complete the worksheet.

ACCOUNTS AND BALANCES

Cash	$ 4,700	Dr.
Accounts Receivable	3,100	Dr.
Allowance for Doubtful Accounts	52	Cr.
Merchandise Inventory	11,800	Dr.
Supplies	1,200	Dr.
Prepaid Advertising	960	Dr.
Store Equipment	7,000	Dr.
Accumulated Depreciation—Store Equipment	1,300	Cr.
Office Equipment	1,600	Dr.
Accumulated Depreciation—Office Equipment	280	Cr.
Accounts Payable	1,750	Cr.
Social Security Tax Payable	430	Cr.
Medicare Tax Payable	98	Cr.
Federal Unemployment Tax Payable		
State Unemployment Tax Payable		
Salaries Payable		
Tony Rowe, Capital	25,712	Cr.
Tony Rowe, Drawing	20,000	Dr.
Sales	89,768	Cr.
Sales Returns and Allowances	1,100	Dr.
Purchases	46,400	Dr.
Purchases Returns and Allowances	430	Cr.
Rent Expense	6,000	Dr.
Telephone Expense	590	Dr.
Salaries Expense	14,100	Dr.
Payroll Taxes Expense	1,270	Dr.
Income Summary		
Supplies Expense		

ACCOUNTS AND BALANCES (cont.)

Advertising Expense
Depreciation Expense—Store Equipment
Depreciation Expense—Office Equipment
Uncollectible Accounts Expense

ADJUSTMENTS

a.–b. Merchandise inventory on December 31, 2005, is $13,000.

c. During 2005 the firm had net credit sales of $35,000; the firm estimates that 0.6 percent of these sales will result in uncollectible accounts.

d. On December 31, 2005, an inventory of the supplies showed that items costing $350 were on hand.

e. On October 1, 2005, the firm signed a six-month advertising contract for $960 with a local newspaper and paid the full amount in advance.

f. On January 2, 2004, the firm purchased store equipment for $7,000. At that time, the equipment was estimated to have a useful life of five years and a salvage value of $500.

g. On January 2, 2004, the firm purchased office equipment for $1,600. At that time the equipment was estimated to have a useful life of five years and a salvage value of $200.

h. On December 31, 2005, the firm owed salaries of $1,500 that will not be paid until 2006.

i. On December 31, 2005, the firm owed the employer's social security tax (assume 6.2 percent) and Medicare tax (assume 1.45 percent) on the entire $1,500 of accrued wages.

j. On December 31, 2005, the firm owed federal unemployment tax (assume 0.8 percent) and state unemployment tax (assume 5.4 percent) on the entire $1,500 of accrued wages.

Analyze: By what total amount were the net assets of the business affected by adjustments?

Problem 12-4A ►
Objectives 1, 2, 3, 4

Recording adjustments and completing the worksheet.

Fitness Foods Company is a distributor of nutritious snack foods such as granola bars. On December 31, 2005, the firm's general ledger contained the accounts and balances that follow.

INSTRUCTIONS

1. Prepare the Trial Balance section of a ten-column worksheet. The worksheet covers the year ended December 31, 2005.

2. Enter the adjustments in the Adjustments section of the worksheet. Identify each adjustment with the appropriate letter.

3. Complete the worksheet.

Note: This problem will be required to complete Problem 13-3A in Chapter 13.

ACCOUNTS AND BALANCES

Cash	$30,600	Dr.
Accounts Receivable	35,200	Dr.
Allowance for Doubtful Accounts	420	Cr.
Merchandise Inventory	86,000	Dr.

ACCOUNTS AND BALANCES (cont.)

Supplies	$ 10,400	Dr.
Prepaid Insurance	5,400	Dr.
Office Equipment	7,800	Dr.
Accum. Depreciation—Office Equipment	2,800	Cr.
Warehouse Equipment	28,000	Dr.
Accum. Depreciation—Warehouse Equipment	9,600	Cr.
Notes Payable—Bank	30,000	Cr.
Accounts Payable	12,200	Cr.
Interest Payable		
Social Security Tax Payable	1,680	Cr.
Medicare Tax Payable	388	Cr.
Federal Unemployment Tax Payable		
State Unemployment Tax Payable		
Salaries Payable		
Warren Jones, Capital	110,534	Cr.
Warren Jones, Drawing	56,000	Dr.
Sales	653,778	Cr.
Sales Returns and Allowances	10,000	Dr.
Purchases	350,000	Dr.
Purchases Returns and Allowances	9,200	Cr.
Income Summary		
Rent Expense	36,000	Dr.
Telephone Expense	2,200	Dr.
Salaries Expense	160,000	Dr.
Payroll Taxes Expense	13,000	Dr.
Supplies Expense		
Insurance Expense		
Depreciation Expense—Office Equip.		
Depreciation Expense—Warehouse Equip.		
Uncollectible Accounts Expense		
Interest Expense		

ADJUSTMENTS

a.–b. Merchandise inventory on December 31, 2005, is $84,000.

c. During 2005 the firm had net credit sales of $560,000; past experience indicates that 0.5 percent of these sales should result in uncollectible accounts.

d. On December 31, 2005, an inventory of supplies showed that items costing $1,200 were on hand.

e. On May 1, 2005, the firm purchased a one-year insurance policy for $5,400.

f. On January 2, 2003, the firm purchased office equipment for $7,800. At that time the equipment was estimated to have a useful life of five years and a salvage value of $800.

g. On January 2, 2003, the firm purchased warehouse equipment for $28,000. At that time the equipment was estimated to have a useful life of five years and a salvage value of $4,000.

h. On November 1, 2005, the firm issued a four-month, 11 percent note for $30,000.

i. On December 31, 2005, the firm owed salaries of $5,000 that will not be paid until 2006.

j. On December 31, 2005, the firm owed the employer's social security tax (assume 6.2 percent) and Medicare tax (assume 1.45 percent) on the entire $5,000 of accrued wages.

k. On December 31, 2005, the firm owed the federal unemployment tax (assume 0.8 percent) and the state unemployment tax (assume 5.4 percent) on the entire $5,000 of accrued wages.

Analyze: When the financial statements for Fitness Foods Company are prepared, what net income will be reported for the period ended December 31, 2005?

PROBLEM SET B

Problem 12-1B ▶
Objectives 2, 3

Recording adjustments for accrued and prepaid expense items and unearned income.

On June 1, 20--, Jane Sadler established her own advertising firm. Selected transactions for the first few days of June follow.

INSTRUCTIONS

1. Record the transactions on page 1 of the general journal. Omit descriptions. Assume that the firm initially records prepaid expenses as assets and unearned income as a liability.

2. Record the adjusting journal entries that must be made on June 30, 20--, on page 2 of the general journal. Omit descriptions.

DATE		TRANSACTIONS
June	1	Signed a lease for an office and issued Check 101 for $14,400 to pay the rent in advance for six months.
	1	Borrowed money from National Trust Bank by issuing a three-month, 10 percent note for $16,000; received $15,600 because the bank deducted interest in advance.
	1	Signed an agreement with Universe of Fashion Clothing Store to provide advertising consulting for one year at $5,000 per month; received the entire fee of $60,000 in advance.
	1	Purchased office equipment for $21,600 from The Furniture Store; issued a three-month, 12 percent note in payment. The equipment is estimated to have a useful life of five years and a $1,200 salvage value and will be depreciated using the straight-line method.
	1	Purchased a one-year insurance policy and issued Check 102 for $2,160 to pay the entire premium.
	3	Purchased office furniture for $19,200 from Office Furniture Mart; issued Check 103 for $9,600 and agreed to pay the balance in 60 days. The equipment is estimated to have a useful life of five years and a $1,200 salvage value and will be depreciated using the straight-line method.
	5	Purchased office supplies for $2,800 with Check 104; assume $1,200 of supplies are on hand June 30, 20--.

Analyze: At the end of the year, what total rent expense should have been recorded?

Recording adjustments for accrued and prepaid expense items and unearned income.

On September 30, 20--, after one month of operation, the general ledger of Professional Skills Company contained the accounts and balances shown below.

◀ **Problem 12-2B**
Objectives 2, 3

INSTRUCTIONS

1. Prepare a partial worksheet with the following sections: Trial Balance, Adjustments, and Adjusted Trial Balance. Use the data about the firm's accounts and balances to complete the Trial Balance section.

2. Enter the adjustments described below in the Adjustments section. Identify each adjustment with the appropriate letter.

3. Complete the Adjusted Trial Balance section.

ACCOUNTS AND BALANCES

Cash	$27,000	Dr.
Supplies	740	Dr.
Prepaid Rent	4,200	Dr.
Prepaid Advertising	2,400	Dr.
Prepaid Interest	450	Dr.
Furniture	5,600	Dr.
Accumulated Depreciation—Furniture		
Equipment	9,000	Dr.
Accumulated Depreciation—Equipment		
Notes Payable	20,600	Cr.
Accounts Payable	4,000	Cr.
Interest Payable		
Unearned Course Fees	22,000	Cr.
Durwood Becknell, Capital	6,730	Cr.
Durwood Becknell, Drawing	2,000	Dr.
Course Fees		
Salaries Expense	1,600	Dr.
Telephone Expense	120	Dr.
Entertainment Expense	220	Dr.
Supplies Expense		
Rent Expense		
Advertising Expense		
Depreciation Expense—Furniture		
Depreciation Expense—Equipment		
Interest Expense		

ADJUSTMENTS

a. On September 30 an inventory of the supplies showed that items costing $640 were on hand.

b. On September 1 the firm paid $4,200 in advance for six months of rent.

c. On September 1 the firm signed a six-month advertising contract for $2,400 and paid the full amount in advance.

d. On September 1 the firm paid $450 interest in advance on a three-month note that it issued to the bank.

e. On September 1 the firm purchased office furniture for $5,600. The furniture is expected to have a useful life of five years and a salvage value of $800.

f. On September 3 the firm purchased equipment for $9,000. The equipment is expected to have a useful life of five years and a salvage value of $1,200.

g. On September 1 the firm issued a two-month, 9 percent note for $5,600.

h. During September the firm received $22,000 fees in advance. An analysis of the firm's records shows that $7,000 applies to services provided in September and the rest pertains to future months.

Analyze: What was the net dollar effect of the adjustments to the accounting records of the business?

Problem 12-3B ▶
Objectives 1, 2, 3, 4

Recording adjustments and completing the worksheet.

Eastwood Toys is a retail store that sells toys, games, and bicycles. On December 31, 2005, the firm's general ledger contained the following accounts and balances.

INSTRUCTIONS

1. Prepare the Trial Balance section of a ten-column worksheet. The worksheet covers the year ended December 31, 2005.

2. Enter the adjustments below in the Adjustments section of the worksheet. Identify each adjustment with the appropriate letter.

3. Complete the worksheet.

ACCOUNTS AND BALANCES

Cash	$ 27,600	Dr.
Accounts Receivable	21,200	Dr.
Allowance for Doubtful Accounts	320	Cr.
Merchandise Inventory	138,000	Dr.
Supplies	11,600	Dr.
Prepaid Advertising	5,280	Dr.
Store Equipment	32,800	Dr.
Accumulated Depreciation—Store Equipment	5,760	Cr.
Office Equipment	8,400	Dr.
Accumulated Depreciation—Office Equipment	1,440	Cr.
Accounts Payable	8,600	Cr.
Social Security Tax Payable	5,920	Cr.
Medicare Tax Payable	1,368	Cr.
Federal Unemployment Tax Payable		
State Unemployment Tax Payable		
Salaries Payable		
Ross Moss, Capital	113,520	Cr.
Ross Moss, Drawing	100,000	Dr.
Sales	1,042,392	Cr.
Sales Returns and Allowances	17,200	Dr.
Purchases	507,600	Dr.
Purchases Returns and Allowances	5,040	Cr.
Rent Expense	120,000	Dr.
Telephone Expense	4,280	Dr.

ACCOUNTS AND BALANCES (cont.)

Salaries Expense	$ 169,200 Dr.
Payroll Taxes Expense	15,200 Dr.
Income Summary	
Supplies Expense	
Advertising Expense	6,000 Dr.
Depreciation Expense—Store Equipment	
Depreciation Expense—Office Equipment	
Uncollectible Accounts Expense	

ADJUSTMENTS

a.–b. Merchandise inventory on December 31, 2005, is $144,000.

c. During 2005 the firm had net credit sales of $440,000. The firm estimates that 0.7 percent of these sales will result in uncollectible accounts.

d. On December 31, 2005, an inventory of the supplies showed that items costing $2,800 were on hand.

e. On September 1, 2005, the firm signed a six-month advertising contract for $5,280 with a local newspaper and paid the full amount in advance.

f. On January 2, 2004, the firm purchased store equipment for $32,800. At that time the equipment was estimated to have a useful life of five years and a salvage value of $4,000.

g. On January 2, 2004, the firm purchased office equipment for $8,400. At that time the equipment was estimated to have a useful life of five years and a salvage value of $1,200.

h. On December 31, 2005, the firm owed salaries of $6,000 that will not be paid until 2006.

i. On December 31, 2005, the firm owed the employer's social security tax (assume 6.2 percent) and Medicare tax (assume 1.45 percent) on the entire $6,000 of accrued wages.

j. On December 31, 2005, the firm owed federal unemployment tax (assume 0.8 percent) and state unemployment tax (assume 5.4 percent) on the entire $6,000 of accrued wages.

Analyze: If the adjustment for advertising had not been recorded, what would the reported net income have been?

Recording adjustments and completing the worksheet.

Village Novelties is a retail seller of cards, novelty items, and business products. On December 31, 2005, the firm's general ledger contained the following accounts and balances.

◄ **Problem 12-4B**
Objectives 1, 2, 3, 4

INSTRUCTIONS

1. Prepare the Trial Balance section of a ten-column worksheet. The worksheet covers the year ended December 31, 2005.

2. Enter the adjustments in the Adjustments section of the worksheet. Identify each adjustment with the appropriate letter.

3. Complete the worksheet.

Note: This problem will be required to complete Problem 13-3B in Chapter 13.

ACCOUNTS AND BALANCES

Cash	$ 1,180	Dr.
Accounts Receivable	2,200	Dr.
Allowance for Doubtful Accounts	600	Cr.
Merchandise Inventory	17,600	Dr.
Supplies	600	Dr.
Prepaid Insurance	2,400	Dr.
Store Equipment	6,000	Dr.
Accumulated Depreciation—Store Equip.		
Store Fixtures	15,000	Dr.
Accumulated Depreciation—Store Fixtures		
Notes Payable	4,000	Cr.
Accounts Payable	600	Cr.
Interest Payable		
Social Security Tax Payable		
Medicare Tax Payable		
Federal Unemployment Tax Payable		
State Unemployment Tax Payable		
Salaries Payable		
Jordi Riker, Capital	39,780	Cr.
Jordi Riker, Drawing	8,000	Dr.
Sales	235,600	Cr.
Sales Returns and Allowances	6,000	Dr.
Purchases	160,000	Dr.
Purchases Returns and Allowances	2,000	Cr.
Income Summary		
Rent Expense	18,000	Dr.
Telephone Expense	2,400	Dr.
Salaries Expense	40,000	Dr.
Payroll Tax Expense	3,200	Dr.
Supplies Expense		
Insurance Expense		
Depreciation Expense—Store Equipment		
Depreciation Expense—Store Fixtures		
Uncollectible Accounts Expense		
Interest Expense		

ADJUSTMENTS

a.–b. Merchandise inventory on hand on December 31, 2005, is $16,000.

c. During 2005 the firm had net credit sales of $160,000. Past experience indicates that 0.8 percent of these sales should result in uncollectible accounts.

d. On December 31, 2005, an inventory of supplies showed that items costing $200 were on hand.

e. On July 1, 2005, the firm purchased a one-year insurance policy for $2,400.

f. On January 2, 2003, the firm purchased store equipment for $6,000. The equipment was estimated to have a five-year useful life and a salvage value of $1,000.

g. On January 4, 2003, the firm purchased store fixtures for $15,000. At the time of the purchase, the fixtures were assumed to have a useful life of seven years and a salvage value of $1,000.

h. On October 1, 2005, the firm issued a six-month, $4,000 note payable at 9 percent interest with a local bank.

i. At year-end (December 31, 2005), the firm owed salaries of $1,200 that will not be paid until January 2006.

j. On December 31, 2005, the firm owed the employer's social security tax (assume 6.2 percent) and Medicare tax (assume 1.45 percent) on the entire $1,200 of accrued wages.

k. On December 31, 2005, the firm owed federal unemployment tax (assume 1.0 percent) and state unemployment tax (assume 5.0 percent) on the entire $1,200 of accrued wages.

Analyze: After all adjustments have been recorded, what is the total value of the company's assets?

CHAPTER 12 CHALLENGE PROBLEM

Completing the Worksheet

The unadjusted trial balance of Quick Stop Discount Store on December 31, 20--, the end of its accounting period, appears on page 464.

1. Copy the unadjusted trial balance onto a worksheet and complete the worksheet using the following information.

    a.–b. Ending merchandise inventory, $99,360.

    c. Uncollectible accounts expense, $1,000.

    d. Store supplies on hand December 31, 20--, $550.

    e. Office supplies on hand December 31, 20--, $380.

    f. Depreciation on store equipment, $11,000.

    g. Depreciation on office equipment, $3,000.

    h. Accrued sales salaries, $4,000, and accrued office salaries, $1,000.

    i. Social security tax on accrued salaries, $326; Medicare tax on accrued salaries, $76.

    j. Federal unemployment tax on accrued salaries, $56; state unemployment tax on accrued salaries, $270.

2. Journalize the adjusting entries on page 30 of the general journal. Omit descriptions.

3. Journalize the closing entries on page 32 of the general journal. Omit descriptions.

4. Compute the following:

    a. net sales

    b. net delivered cost of purchases

    c. cost of goods sold

    d. net income or net loss

    e. balance of **Don Black, Capital** on December 31, 20--.

Analyze: What change(s) to **Don Black, Capital** will be reported on the statement of owner's equity?

QUICK STOP DISCOUNT STORE
Trial Balance
December 31, 20--

Cash	$ 12,950	Dr
Accounts Receivable	50,000	Dr.
Allowance for Doubtful Accounts	2,000	Cr.
Merchandise Inventory	106,630	Dr.
Store Supplies	3,840	Dr.
Office Supplies	2,950	Dr.
Store Equipment	113,590	Dr.
Accumulated Depreciation—Store Equipment	12,620	Cr.
Office Equipment	27,320	Dr.
Accumulated Depreciation—Office Equipment	4,770	Cr.
Accounts Payable	4,390	Cr.
Salaries Payable		
Social Security Tax Payable		
Medicare Tax Payable		
Federal Unemployment Tax Payable		
State Unemployment Tax Payable		
Don Black, Capital	168,000	Cr.
Don Black, Drawing	30,000	Dr.
Income Summary		
Sales	862,230	Cr.
Sales Returns and Allowances	7,580	Dr.
Purchases	505,430	Dr.
Purchases Returns and Allowances	4,240	Cr.
Purchases Discounts	10,770	Cr.
Freight In	7,000	Dr.
Salaries Expense—Sales	75,950	Dr.
Rent Expense	36,000	Dr.
Advertising Expense	12,300	Dr.
Store Supplies Expense		
Depreciation Expense—Store Equipment		
Salaries Expense—Office	77,480	Dr.
Payroll Taxes Expense		
Uncollectible Accounts Expense		
Office Supplies Expense		
Depreciation Expense—Office Equipment		

Net Profit

When Reuben Van Gogh's father became seriously ill and had to go to the hospital, Reuben stepped in to run the family business, Van Gogh's Cab Company. Under his father's direction, the cab company was a successful operation and provided ample money to meet the family's needs, including Reuben's college tuition.

Reuben was majoring in psychology in college and knew little about business or accounting, but he was eager to do a good job of running the business in his father's absence. Since all the service performed by the cab company was for cash, Reuben figured that he would do all right as long as the **Cash** account increased. Thus he was delighted to watch the cash balance increase from $31,642 at the beginning of the first month to $70,850 at the end of the second month—an increase of $39,208. Reuben assumed that the company had made $39,208 during the two months he was in charge. He did not understand why the income statement prepared by the company's bookkeeper did not show that amount as income but instead reported a lower amount as net income.

Knowing that you are taking an accounting class, Reuben brings the income statement, shown below, to you and asks if you can explain the difference.

VAN GOGH'S CAB COMPANY Income Statement For the Past Two Months		
Operating Revenue		
Fares Income		$192,934
Operating Expenses		
Salaries Expense	$120,000	
Gasoline and Oil Expense	26,000	
Repairs Expense	5,570	
Supplies Expense	2,268	
Insurance Expense	3,166	
Depreciation Expense	17,000	
Total Operating Expense		174,004
Net Income		$ 18,930

In addition, Reuben permits you to examine the accounting records, which show that **Salaries Payable** were $2,680 at the beginning of the first month but had increased to $3,240 at the end of the second month. Most of the **Insurance Expense** account reflects monthly insurance payments covering only one month. However, the **Prepaid Insurance** account had decreased $450 during the two months, and all supplies had been purchased before Reuben took over. The balances of the company's other asset and liability accounts showed no changes.

1. Explain the cause of the difference between the increase in the **Cash** account balance and the net income for the two months.

2. Prepare a schedule that accounts for this difference.

Business Connections

Connection 1 ▶  MANAGERIAL *Focus* Adjustments

1. Assume that you are the newly hired controller for Timmons Company, a wholesale firm that sells most of its goods on credit. You have found that the business does not make an adjustment for estimated uncollectible accounts at the end of each year. Instead, the expense for uncollectible accounts is recorded during the year as individual accounts are identified as bad debts. Would you recommend that the firm continue its present accounting treatment of uncollectible accounts? Why or why not?

2. On July 1, 20--, Secrist Company rented a portion of its warehouse to another business for a one-year period and received the full amount of $4,200 in advance. At the end of Secrist's fiscal year on December 31, 20--, the firm's income statement showed $2,100 as rental income. The other $2,100 appeared in the liabilities section of the firm's balance sheet as unearned rental income. The owner, Omer Secrist, felt that the entire sum should have been reported on the income statement as income because all the cash was received in 20--. How would you explain to Omer why the accountant's treatment of the $4,200 was correct?

3. Some firms initially record the cost of an insurance policy as an expense and then make an adjustment at the end of the fiscal year to transfer the unexpired amount to an asset account. Does this method produce financial results different from the method used by Modern Casuals? Explain.

4. Why is it important for management to understand the accounting methods used to report data on the firm's financial statements?

Connection 2 ▶ **Ethical** DILEMMA **Out of Balance** As the accountant of a company, you were overwhelmed with work at the end of March and could not begin the process of closing the accounts and preparing the quarterly financial statements until almost mid-April. You are under pressure to have the financial statements ready for a meeting of the company's management on April 14.

To your distress, you discovered that the March 31 trial balance does not balance. The debits exceed the credits by $4,800. After spending several hours trying to find the reason for the error, you have concluded that the $4,800 is not a critical error. You are considering simply adding $4,800 to the **Sales** account in order to bring the accounts into balance and to enable you to complete the statements on time. You believe that if you do this, you will have time to find the reason for the trial balance error after the meeting of the management. At that time you can correct the $4,800 adjustment.

Will you "force" the accounts to balance? Discuss your decision from an ethical perspective.

StreetWISE:
Questions from the Real World

Balance Sheet Accounts Refer to the *1999 Annual Report* for The Home Depot, Inc. found in Appendix B.

◄ **Connection 3**

1. Review the balance sheet. Based only on the asset account categories shown, list two types of adjusting entries you think are required each fiscal period. Which accounts are affected?

2. Based on the account categories found in the Liabilities section, describe two types of adjusting entries that may be recorded by The Home Depot, Inc. in an effort to match revenues with expenses.

FINANCIAL STATEMENT ANALYSIS

Balance Sheet The following financial data was reported in the DuPont *1999 Annual Report*.

◄ **Connection 4**

Consolidated Balance Sheet		
As of December 31		
(Dollars in millions, except per share)	*1999*	*1998*
Assets		
Current Assets		
Cash and Cash Equivalents	$ 1,466	$ 1,059
Marketable Securities	116	10
Accounts and Notes Receivable	5,318	4,201
Inventories	5,057	3,129
Prepaid Expenses	202	192
Deferred Income Taxes	494	645
Total Current Assets	12,653	9,236
Property, Plant and Equipment	35,416	34,728
Less: Accumulated Depreciation	20,545	20,597
Net Property, Plant and Equipment	14,871	14,131

Analyze:

1. Based on the information presented above, which categories do you think might require adjustments at the end of an operating period?

2. List the potential adjusting entries that would be necessary. Do not worry about the dollar amounts.

3. By what percentage did DuPont's inventories increase from 1998 to 1999?

Analyze Online: Log on to the DuPont Web site **(www.dupont.com).** Review the current annual report and answer the following questions.

4. What method is used to depreciate property, plant, and equipment at DuPont?

5. What is the company's policy for revenue recognition?

Connection 5 ► *Extending* **the** *Thought* **Catalog Sales** JC Penney Company, Inc., records sales for in-store purchases, catalog, and Internet transactions. For catalog orders, sales are not recorded in the accounting records until customers pick up the merchandise they have ordered. Other retailers record catalog or Internet sales at the point that an order is placed and credit card information has been submitted. Do you agree or disagree with the method that JC Penney, Inc., uses to record catalog sales? Prepare a statement supporting your opinion.

Connection 6 ► **Business Communication** **Memo** You are the owner of a raw furniture company that sells products via two channels of distribution: the Internet and catalogs. Your accounting clerk has prepared a ten-column worksheet for the month ended September 30, 20--. As you review the worksheet, you notice the following errors.

1. The balances of the **Depreciation Expense** account and the **Insurance Expense** account were carried over into the Balance Sheet Debit columns in error.

2. There were no adjustments recorded for **Merchandise Inventory.**

Prepare a memo to the accounting clerk outlining the errors you have noticed. Explain the impact of the errors on the financial statements. Be sure to explain the importance of the adjustment to the **Merchandise Inventory** account.

Connection 7 ► **Team**Work **Gift Certificates** Have you ever purchased a gift card or gift certificate from a retail business? How do these companies recognize gift certificate revenue? As a team, research the revenue recognition practices for retail businesses of your choice. Publicly traded companies often provide financial statements online where you find a discussion of revenue recognition with the notes that accompany the statements. Write a report on your findings.

Connection 8 ► *inter* NET **CONNECTION** **E-commerce** The United States has developed a framework for dealing with electronic commerce. Go to **www.ecommerce.gov** to see the *United States Electronic Commerce Policy*. What are two other sites that you can link to from this site? Click on *International Sites*. What does the acronym APEC mean? What does the abbreviation EU stand for?

Answers to Section 1 Self Review

1. When a sale of goods is completed or when the service is provided, regardless of when payment is received.
2. When the purchases are made, regardless of when payment is received.
3. They are normally recognized for the period in which they help to earn revenue.
4. **a.** on the date of the sale.
5. **b.** earned but not received.
6. Net accounts receivable does not change because the entry is a debit to **Allowance For Doubtful Accounts** (contra asset) and a credit to **Accounts Receivable** (asset).

Answers to Section 2 Self Review

1. The stock of goods that a business has on hand for sale to customers.
2. **a.** The quantity of each type of goods in stock is listed on the inventory sheet.
   b. The quantity is multiplied by the unit cost to find the total cost of the item.
   c. The totals for all the different items on hand are added to find the cost of the entire inventory.
3. Two entries are made.
   - The beginning inventory is taken off the books by transferring the beginning inventory balance to the **Income Summary** account. This is accomplished by debiting the **Income Summary** account and crediting the **Merchandise Inventory** account.
   - The ending inventory is placed on the books by debiting the **Merchandise Inventory** account and crediting the **Income Summary** account.
4. **a.** Assets section of the balance sheet.
5. **b.** Income Statement Debit and the Balance Sheet Credit columns.
6. The assets would be overstated if inventory is less than the account balance or understated if inventory is more than the account balance.

Answers to Comprehensive Self Review

1. To match revenues and expenses of specific fiscal periods.
2. To see if each account contains amounts of revenue or expense that should be allocated to other periods.
3. The revenue, expense, and cost of goods sold accounts. **Purchases** is an example of a cost of goods sold account. The figures for the beginning and ending inventory accounts also appear in the Income Statement section in the **Income Summary** account.
4. Assets, liabilities, and owner's equity (including drawing) accounts.
5. Expenses that relate to the current period but have not yet been paid.

CHAPTER 13

Learning Objectives

1. **Prepare a classified income statement from the worksheet.**

2. **Prepare a statement of owner's equity from the worksheet.**

3. **Prepare a classified balance sheet from the worksheet.**

4. **Journalize and post the adjusting entries.**

5. **Journalize and post the closing entries.**

6. **Prepare a postclosing trial balance.**

7. **Journalize and post reversing entries.**

8. **Define the accounting terms new to this chapter.**

Financial Statements and Closing Procedures

SAFEWAY

www.safeway.com

Safeway Inc. is one of the largest food and drug retailers in North America, operating 1,754 stores in the United States and western Canada. For many consumers, a trip to the grocery story is synonymous with a trip to Safeway. Even pop culture has embraced the Safeway name. Marge Simpson shops at Safeway for pacifiers and Fred Flintstone tried to sell Wilma's gravelberry pies to the "Safestone" Market.

As Safeway stores spread across the United States from 1926 to the present, a network of supporting distribution, manufacturing, and food processing facilities emerged. Safeway owns and operates 41 milk, ice cream, soft drink bottling, bread-baking plants, and other food processing facilities.

Thinking Critically
If you owned stock in Safeway Inc., what types of financial information would be most important to you?

For more information on Safeway Inc., go to:
collegeaccounting.glencoe.com.

New Terms

Classified financial statement

Current assets

Current liabilities

Current ratio

Gross profit

Gross profit percentage

Inventory turnover

Liquidity

Long-term liabilities

Multiple-step income statement

Plant and equipment

Reversing entries

Single-step income statement

Section Objectives

① Prepare a classified income statement from the worksheet.

WHY IT'S IMPORTANT
To help decision-makers, financial information needs to be presented in a meaningful and easy-to-use way.

② Prepare a statement of owner's equity from the worksheet.

WHY IT'S IMPORTANT
The statement of owner's equity reports changes to and balances of the owner's equity account.

③ Prepare a classified balance sheet from the worksheet.

WHY IT'S IMPORTANT
Grouping accounts helps financial statement users to identify total assets, equity, and financial obligations of the business.

Terms to Learn

classified financial statement
current assets
current liabilities
gross profit
liquidity
long-term liabilities
multiple-step income
  statement
plant and equipment
single-step income
  statement

① Objective

Prepare a classified income statement from the worksheet.

Preparing the Financial Statements

The information needed to prepare the financial statements is on the worksheet in the Income Statement and Balance Sheet sections. At the end of the period, Modern Casuals prepares three financial statements: income statement, statement of owner's equity, and balance sheet. The income statement and the balance sheet are arranged in a classified format. On **classified financial statements**, revenues, expenses, assets, and liabilities are divided into groups of similar accounts and a subtotal is given for each group. This makes the financial statements more useful to the readers.

> The annual report of The Coca-Cola Company includes Consolidated Balance Sheets, Consolidated Statements of Income, and Consolidated Statements of Share-Owners' Equity. The annual report also contains a statement of Selected Financial Data that reports 11 consecutive years of summarized financial information.

The Classified Income Statement

A classified income statement is sometimes called a **multiple-step income statement** because several subtotals are computed before net income is calculated. The simpler income statement you learned about in previous chapters is called a **single-step income statement**. It lists all revenues in one section and all expenses in another section. Only one computation is necessary to determine the net income (Total Revenue − Total Expenses = Net Income).

Figure 13-1 on page 474 shows the classified income statement for Modern Casuals. Refer to it as you learn how to prepare a multiple-step income statement.

Operating Revenue

The first section of the classified income statement contains the revenue from operations. This is the revenue earned from normal business activities. Other income is presented separately near the bottom of the statement. For Modern Casuals all operating revenue comes from sales of merchandise.

Because Modern Casuals is a retail firm, it does not offer sales discounts to its customers. If it did, the sales discounts would be deducted from total sales in order to compute net sales. The net sales amount is computed as follows.

```
          Sales
         (Sales Returns and Allowances)
         (Sales Discounts)
          Net Sales
```

The parentheses indicate that the amount is subtracted. Net sales for Modern Casuals is $546,650.

Cost of Goods Sold

The Cost of Goods Sold section contains information about the cost of the merchandise that was sold during the period. Three elements are needed to compute the cost of goods sold: beginning inventory, net delivered cost of purchases, and ending inventory. The format is

```
          Purchases
      +   Freight In
         (Purchases Returns and Allowances)
         (Purchases Discounts)
          Net Delivered Cost of Purchases

          Beginning Merchandise Inventory
      +   Net Delivered Cost of Purchases
          Total Merchandise Available for Sale
         (Ending Merchandise Inventory)
          Cost of Goods Sold
```

For Modern Casuals the net delivered cost of purchases is $323,120 and the cost of goods sold is $328,620. **Merchandise Inventory** is the one account that appears on both the income statement and the balance sheet. Beginning and ending merchandise inventory balances appear on the income statement. Ending merchandise inventory also appears on the balance sheet in the Assets section.

Gross Profit on Sales

The **gross profit** on sales is the difference between the net sales and the cost of goods sold. For Modern Casuals net sales is the revenue earned from selling clothes. Cost of goods sold is what Modern Casuals paid for the clothes that were sold during the fiscal period. Gross profit is what is left to cover operating expenses and provide a profit. The format is

```
          Net Sales
         (Cost of Goods Sold)
          Gross Profit on Sales
```

For Modern Casuals gross profit on sales is $218,030.

Operating Expenses

Operating expenses are expenses that arise from normal business activities. Modern Casuals separates operating expenses into two categories: *Selling Expenses* and *General and Administrative Expenses.* The selling expenses relate directly to the sale and delivery of goods. The general and administrative expenses are necessary for business operations but are not directly connected with the sales function. Rent, utilities, and salaries for office employees are examples of general and administrative expenses.

Modern Casuals
Income Statement
Year Ended December 31, 2004

Operating Revenue				
Sales				559 650 00
Less Sales Returns and Allowances				13 000 00
Net Sales				546 650 00
Cost of Goods Sold				
Merchandise Inventory, Jan. 1, 2004			51 500 00	
Purchases		320 500 00		
Freight In		8 800 00		
Delivered Cost of Purchases		329 300 00		
Less Purchases Returns and Allowances	3 050 00			
Purchases Discounts	3 130 00	6 180 00		
Net Delivered Cost of Purchases			323 120 00	
Total Merchandise Available for Sale			374 620 00	
Less Merchandise Inventory, Dec. 31, 2004			46 000 00	
Cost of Goods Sold				328 620 00
Gross Profit on Sales				218 030 00
Operating Expenses				
Selling Expenses				
Salaries Expense—Sales		79 990 00		
Advertising Expense		7 425 00		
Cash Short or Over		125 00		
Supplies Expense		4 975 00		
Depreciation Expense—Store Equipment		2 250 00		
Total Selling Expenses			94 765 00	
General and Administrative Expenses				
Rent Expense		27 600 00		
Salaries Expense—Office		26 500 00		
Insurance Expense		3 600 00		
Payroll Taxes Expense		7 412 75		
Telephone Expense		1 875 00		
Uncollectible Accounts Expense		750 00		
Utilities Expense		5 925 00		
Depreciation Expense—Office Equipment		1 200 00		
Total General and Administrative Expenses			74 862 75	
Total Operating Expenses				169 627 75
Net Income from Operations				48 402 25
Other Income				
Interest Income		160 00		
Miscellaneous Income		510 00		
Total Other Income			670 00	
Other Expenses				
Interest Expense			770 00	
Net Nonoperating Expense				100 00
Net Income for Year				48 302 25

▲ FIGURE 13-1 Classified Income Statement

Net Income or Net Loss from Operations

Keeping operating and nonoperating income separate helps financial statement users learn about the operating efficiency of the firm. The format for determining net income (or net loss) from operations is

Gross Profit on Sales
(Total Operating Expenses)
Net Income (or Net Loss) from Operations

For Modern Casuals net income from operations is $48,402.25.

Other Income and Other Expenses

Income that is earned from sources other than normal business activities appears in the Other Income section. For Modern Casuals other income includes interest on notes receivable and one miscellaneous income item.

Expenses that are not directly connected with business operations appear in the Other Expenses section. The only other expense for Modern Casuals is interest expense.

Net Income or Net Loss

Net income is all the revenue minus all the expenses. For Modern Casuals net income is $48,302.25. If there is a net loss, it appears in parentheses. Net income or net loss is used to prepare the statement of owner's equity.

The Statement of Owner's Equity

The statement of owner's equity reports the changes that occurred in the owner's financial interest during the period. Figure 13-2 shows the statement of owner's equity for Modern Casuals. The ending capital balance for Sonia Sanchez, $81,923.25, is used to prepare the balance sheet.

❷ Objective
Prepare a statement of owner's equity from the worksheet.

◀ **FIGURE 13-2**
Statement of Owner's Equity

Modern Casuals					
Statement of Owner's Equity					
Year Ended December 31, 2004					
Sonia Sanchez, Capital, January 1, 2004			61 2 2 1 00	
Net Income for Year	48 3 0 2 25			
Less Withdrawals for the Year	27 6 0 0 00			
Increase in Capital			20 7 0 2 25	
Sonia Sanchez, Capital, December 31, 2004			81 9 2 3 25	

The Classified Balance Sheet

The classified balance sheet divides the various assets and liabilities into groups. Figure 13-3 on page 476 shows the balance sheet for Modern Casuals. Refer to it as you learn how to prepare a classified balance sheet.

❸ Objective
Prepare a classified balance sheet from the worksheet.

Current Assets

Current assets consist of cash, items that will normally be converted into cash within one year, and items that will be used up within one year.

Current assets are usually listed in order of liquidity. **Liquidity** is the ease with which an item can be converted into cash. Current assets are vital to the survival of a business because they provide the funds needed to pay bills and meet expenses. The current assets for Modern Casuals total $104,610.

FIGURE 13-3 ▶
Classified Balance Sheet

Modern Casuals
Balance Sheet
December 31, 2004

Assets				
Current Assets				
Cash			21 1 3 6 00	
Petty Cash Fund			1 0 0 00	
Notes Receivable			1 2 0 0 00	
Accounts Receivable		32 0 0 0 00		
Less Allowance for Doubtful Accounts		8 5 0 00	31 1 5 0 00	
Interest Receivable			2 4 00	
Merchandise Inventory			46 0 0 0 00	
Prepaid Expenses				
Supplies		1 3 2 5 00		
Prepaid Insurance		3 6 0 0 00		
Prepaid Interest		7 5 00	5 0 0 0 00	
Total Current Assets			104 6 1 0 00	
Plant and Equipment				
Store Equipment	20 0 0 0 00			
Less Accumulated Depreciation	2 2 5 0 00	17 7 5 0 00		
Office Equipment	7 0 0 0 00			
Less Accumulated Depreciation	1 2 0 0 00	5 8 0 0 00		
Total Plant and Equipment			23 5 5 0 00	
Total Assets			128 1 6 0 00	
Liabilities and Owner's Equity				
Current Liabilities				
Notes Payable—Trade			2 0 0 0 00	
Notes Payable—Bank			9 0 0 0 00	
Accounts Payable			24 1 2 9 00	
Interest Payable			2 0 00	
Social Security Tax Payable			1 1 7 7 00	
Medicare Tax Payable			2 7 1 75	
Employee Income Tax Payable			9 9 0 00	
Federal Unemployment Tax Payable			1 2 00	
State Unemployment Tax Payable			8 1 00	
Salaries Payable			1 5 0 0 00	
Sales Tax Payable			7 0 5 6 00	
Total Current Liabilities			46 2 3 6 75	
Owner's Equity				
Sonia Sanchez, Capital			81 9 2 3 25	
Total Liabilities and Owner's Equity			128 1 6 0 00	

Plant and Equipment

Noncurrent assets are called *long-term assets.* An important category of long-term assets is plant and equipment. **Plant and equipment** consists of property that will be used in the business for longer than one year. For many businesses plant and equipment represents a sizable investment. The balance sheet shows three amounts for each category of plant and equipment:

Asset
(Accumulated depreciation)
Book value

For Modern Casuals total plant and equipment is $23,550.

Current Liabilities

Current liabilities are the debts that must be paid within one year. They are usually listed in order of priority of payment. Management must ensure that funds are available to pay current liabilities when they become due in order to maintain the firm's good credit reputation. For Modern Casuals total current liabilities are $46,236.75.

Long-Term Liabilities

Long-term liabilities are debts of the business that are due more than one year in the future. Although repayment of long-term liabilities might not be due for several years, management must make sure that periodic interest is paid promptly. Long-term liabilities include mortgages, notes payable, and loans payable. Modern Casuals had no long-term liabilities on December 31, 2004.

Owner's Equity

Modern Casuals prepares a separate statement of owner's equity that reports all information about changes that occurred in the owner's financial interest during the period. The ending balance from that statement is transferred to the Owner's Equity section of the balance sheet.

Recall

Book Value
Book value is the portion of the original cost that has not been depreciated. Often book value bears no relation to the market value of the asset.

International **INSIGHTS**

Paying Bills
According to a payment survey conducted by Dun & Bradstreet, businesses in Germany are more likely to pay their bills on time; only 20 percent of invoices were paid more than 15 days after their due date. In contrast, the European average was 35 percent.

Section 1 Self Review

Questions

1. What are classified financial statements?

2. What is the purpose of the income statement?

3. What is gross profit on sales?

Exercises

4. Which of the following is not a current asset?

   a. Equipment

   b. Prepaid Insurance

   c. Merchandise Inventory

   d. Accounts Receivable

5. Purchases are shown in the

   a. Current Assets section of the balance sheet.

   b. Plant and Equipment section of the balance sheet.

   c. Cost of Goods Sold section of the income statement.

   d. Operating Expenses section of the income statement.

Analysis

6. Assume that a business listed the **Freight In** account in the Operating Expense section of the income statement. What is the effect on net purchases? On total operating expenses? On net income from operations?

Section Objectives

4 **Journalize and post the adjusting entries.**

WHY IT'S IMPORTANT
Adjusting entries match revenue and expenses to the proper periods.

5 **Journalize and post the closing entries.**

WHY IT'S IMPORTANT
The temporary accounts are closed in order to prepare for the next accounting period.

6 **Prepare a postclosing trial balance.**

WHY IT'S IMPORTANT
The general ledger must remain in balance.

7 **Journalize and post reversing entries.**

WHY IT'S IMPORTANT
Reversing entries are made so that transactions can be recorded in the usual way in the next accounting period.

Terms to Learn

current ratio
gross profit percentage
inventory turnover
reversing entries

Completing the Accounting Cycle

The complete accounting cycle was presented in Chapter 6 (pages 176–177). In this section we will complete the accounting cycle for Modern Casuals.

Journalizing and Posting the Adjusting Entries

All adjustments are shown on the worksheet. After the financial statements have been prepared, the adjustments are made a permanent part of the accounting records. They are recorded in the general journal as adjusting journal entries and are posted to the general ledger.

Journalizing the Adjusting Entries

Figure 13-4 on pages 479–481 shows the adjusting journal entries for Modern Casuals. Each adjusting entry shows how the adjustment was calculated. Supervisors and auditors need to understand, without additional explanation, why the adjustment was made.

Let's review the types of adjusting entries made by Modern Casuals:

Type of Adjustment	Worksheet Reference	Purpose
Inventory	(a–b)	Removes beginning inventory and adds ending inventory to the accounting records.
Expense	(c–e)	Matches expense to revenue for the period; the credit is to a contra asset account.
Accrued Expense	(f–i)	Matches expense to revenue for the period; the credit is to a liability account.
Prepaid Expense	(j–l)	Matches expense to revenue for the period; the credit is to an asset account.
Accrued Income	(m–n)	Recognizes income earned in the period. The debit is to an asset account (**Interest Receivable**) or a liability account (**Sales Tax Payable**).

4 **Objective**

Journalize and post the adjusting entries.

Posting the Adjusting Entries

After the adjustments have been recorded in the general journal, they are promptly posted to the general ledger. The word *Adjusting* is entered in the Description column of the general ledger account. This distinguishes it from entries for transactions that occurred during that period. After the adjusting entries have been posted, the general ledger account balances match the amounts shown in the Adjusted Trial Balance section of the worksheet in Figure 12-2.

GENERAL JOURNAL

PAGE __25__

	DATE		DESCRIPTION	POST. REF.	DEBIT	CREDIT	
1			*Adjusting Entries*				1
2	2004		*(Adjustment a)*				2
3	Dec.	31	Income Summary	399	51 5 0 0 00		3
4			Merchandise Inventory	121		51 5 0 0 00	4
5			To transfer beginning inventory				5
6			to Income Summary				6
7							7
8			*(Adjustment b)*				8
9		31	Merchandise Inventory	121	46 0 0 0 00		9
10			Income Summary	399		46 0 0 0 00	10
11			To record ending inventory				11
12							12
13			*(Adjustment c)*				13
14		31	Uncollectible Accounts Expense	685	7 5 0 00		14
15			Allowance For Doubtful Accounts	112		7 5 0 00	15
16			To record estimated loss				16
17			from uncollectible accounts				17
18			based on 0.75% of net				18
19			credit sales of $100,000				19
20							20
21			*(Adjustment d)*				21
22		31	Depreciation Expense—Store Equip.	620	2 2 5 0 00		22
23			Accum. Depreciation—Store Equip.	132		2 2 5 0 00	23
24			To record depreciation				24
25			for 2004 as shown by				25
26			schedule on file				26
27							27
28			*(Adjustment e)*				28
29		31	Depreciation Expense—Office Equip.	689	1 2 0 0 00		29
30			Accum. Depreciation—Office Equip.	142		1 2 0 0 00	30
31			To record depreciation				31
32			for 2004 as shown by				32
33			schedule on file				33
34							34
35			*(Adjustment f)*				35
36		31	Salaries Expense—Sales	602	1 5 0 0 00		36
37			Salaries Payable	229		1 5 0 0 00	37
38			To record accrued salaries				38
39			of part-time sales clerks				39
40			for Dec. 28–31				40
41							41

▲ **FIGURE 13-4** Adjusting Entries in the General Journal

GENERAL JOURNAL

PAGE __26__

	DATE		DESCRIPTION	POST. REF.	DEBIT	CREDIT	
1			*Adjusting Entries*				1
2	2004		*(Adjustment g)*				2
3	Dec.	31	Payroll Taxes Expense	665	1 1 4 75		3
4			Social Security Tax Payable	221		9 3 00	4
5			Medicare Tax Payable	223		2 1 75	5
6			To record accrued payroll				6
7			taxes on accrued salaries				7
8			for Dec. 28–31				8
9							9
10			*(Adjustment h)*				10
11		31	Payroll Taxes Expense	665	9 3 00		11
12			Fed. Unemployment Tax Payable	225		1 2 00	12
13			State Unemployment Tax Payable	227		8 1 00	13
14			To record accrued payroll				14
15			taxes on accrued salaries				15
16			for Dec. 28–31				16
17							17
18			*(Adjustment i)*				18
19		31	Interest Expense	695	2 0 00		19
20			Interest Payable	216		2 0 00	20
21			To record interest on a				21
22			2-month, $2,000, 12%				22
23			note payable dated				23
24			Dec. 1, 2004				24
25							25
26			*(Adjustment j)*				26
27		31	Supplies Expense	615	4 9 7 5 00		27
28			Supplies	129		4 9 7 5 00	28
29			To record supplies used				29
30							30
31			*(Adjustment k)*				31
32		31	Insurance Expense	660	3 6 0 0 00		32
33			Prepaid Insurance	126		3 6 0 0 00	33
34			To record expired				34
35			insurance on 2-year				35
36			policy purchased for				36
37			$7,200 on Jan. 1, 2004				37
38							38
39							39
40							40

▲ **FIGURE 13-4 (continued)** Adjusting Entries in the General Journal

GENERAL JOURNAL

	DATE		DESCRIPTION	POST. REF.	DEBIT	CREDIT	
1	2004		(Adjustment l)				1
2	Dec.	31	Interest Expense	695	1 5 0 00		2
3			Prepaid Interest	127		1 5 0 00	3
4			To record transfer of 2/3				4
5			of prepaid interest of				5
6			$225 for a 3-month,				6
7			10% note payable issued				7
8			to bank on Nov. 1, 2004				8
9							9
10			(Adjustment m)				10
11		31	Interest Receivable	116	2 4 00		11
12			Interest Income	491		2 4 00	12
13			To record accrued interest				13
14			earned on a 4-month,				14
15			12% note receivable				15
16			dated Nov. 1, 2004				16
17			($1,200 x 0.12 x 2/12)				17
18							18
19			(Adjustment n)				19
20		31	Sales Tax Payable	231	1 4 4 00		20
21			Miscellaneous Income	493		1 4 4 00	21
22			To record accrued				22
23			commission earned on				23
24			sales tax owed for fourth				24
25			quarter of 2004:				25
26			Sales Tax Payable $7,200				26
27			Commission rate x 0.02				27
28			Commission due $ 144				28
29							29

▲ FIGURE 13-4 (continued)
Adjusting Entries in the
General Journal

Journalizing and Posting the Closing Entries

At the end of the period, the temporary accounts are closed. The temporary accounts are the revenue, cost of goods sold, expense, and drawing accounts.

Journalizing the Closing Entries

The Income Statement section of the worksheet in Figure 12-2 on pages 444–447 provides the data needed to prepare closing entries. There are four steps in the closing process.

1. Close revenue accounts and cost of goods sold accounts with credit balances to **Income Summary.**

5 Objective

Journalize and post the closing entries.

2. Close expense accounts and cost of goods sold accounts with debit balances to **Income Summary.**

3. Close **Income Summary,** which now reflects the net income or loss for the period, to owner's capital.

4. Close the drawing account to owner's capital.

Step 1: Closing the Revenue Accounts and the Cost of Goods Sold Accounts with Credit Balances. The first entry closes the revenue accounts and other temporary income statement accounts with credit balances. Look at the Income Statement section of the worksheet in Figure 12-2. There are five items listed in the Credit column, not including **Income Summary.** Debit each account, *except* **Income Summary,** for its balance. Credit **Income Summary** for the total, $566,500.

	DATE		DESCRIPTION	POST. REF.	DEBIT	CREDIT	
1	2004		*Closing Entries*				1
2	Dec.	31	Sales	401	559 650 00		2
3			Interest Income	491	160 00		3
4			Miscellaneous Income	493	510 00		4
5			Purchases Returns and Allowances	503	3 050 00		5
6			Purchases Discounts	504	3 130 00		6
7			Income Summary			566 500 00	7

GENERAL JOURNAL · PAGE 28

Step 2: Closing the Expense Accounts and the Cost of Goods Sold Accounts with Debit Balances. The Debit column of the Income Statement section of the worksheet in Figure 12-2 shows the expense accounts and the cost of goods sold accounts with debit balances. Credit each account, *except* **Income Summary,** for its balance. Debit **Income Summary** for the total, $512,697.75.

GENERAL JOURNAL · PAGE 28

	DATE		DESCRIPTION	POST. REF.	DEBIT	CREDIT	
9	Dec.	31	Income Summary	399	512 697 75		9
10			Sales Returns and Allowances	451		13 000 00	10
11			Purchases	501		320 500 00	11
12			Freight In	502		8 800 00	12
13			Salaries Expense—Sales	602		79 990 00	13
14			Advertising Expense	605		7 425 00	14
15			Cash Short or Over	610		125 00	15
16			Supplies Expense	615		4 975 00	16
17			Depreciation Expense—Store Equip.	620		2 250 00	17
18			Rent Expense	640		27 600 00	18
19			Salaries Expense—Office	645		26 500 00	19
20			Insurance Expense	660		3 600 00	20
21			Payroll Taxes Expense	665		7 412 75	21
22			Telephone Expense	680		1 875 00	22
23			Uncollectible Accounts Expense	685		750 00	23
24			Utilities Expense	687		5 925 00	24
25			Depreciation Expense—Office Equip.	689		1 200 00	25
26			Interest Expense	695		770 00	26

Step 3: Closing the Income Summary Account. After the first two closing entries have been posted, the balance of the **Income Summary** account is net income or net loss for the period. The third closing entry transfers the **Income Summary** balance to the owner's capital account. **Income Summary** after the second closing entry has a balance of $48,302.25.

		Income Summary		
Adjusting Entries (a–b)	12/31	51,500.00	12/31	46,000.00
Closing Entries	12/31	512,697.75	12/31	566,500.00
		564,197.75		612,500.00
			Bal.	48,302.25

For Modern Casuals the third closing entry is as follows. This closes the **Income Summary** account, which remains closed until it is used in the end-of-period process for the next year.

GENERAL JOURNAL   PAGE _28_

	DATE		DESCRIPTION	POST. REF.	DEBIT	CREDIT	
28	Dec.	31	Income Summary	399	48 30 2 25		28
29			Sonia Sanchez, Capital	301		48 30 2 25	29

Step 4: Closing the Drawing Account. This entry closes the drawing account and updates the capital account so that its balance agrees with the ending capital reported on the statement of owner's equity and on the balance sheet.

GENERAL JOURNAL   PAGE _28_

	DATE		DESCRIPTION	POST. REF.	DEBIT	CREDIT	
31	Dec.	31	Sonia Sanchez, Capital	301	27 60 0 00		31
32			Sonia Sanchez, Drawing	302		27 60 0 00	32

Posting the Closing Entries

The closing entries are posted from the general journal to the general ledger. This process brings the temporary account balances to zero. The word *Closing* is entered in the Description column. After the closing entry is posted, the account balance is zero.

Preparing a Postclosing Trial Balance

❻ Objective

Prepare a postclosing trial balance.

After the closing entries have been posted, prepare a postclosing trial balance to confirm that the general ledger is in balance. Only the accounts that have balances—the asset, liability and owner's capital accounts—appear on the postclosing trial balance. The postclosing trial balance matches the amounts reported on the balance sheet. To verify this, compare the postclosing trial balance, Figure 13-5 on page 484, with the balance sheet, Figure 13-3 on page 476.

If the postclosing trial balance shows that the general ledger is out of balance, find and correct the error or errors immediately. Any necessary correcting entries must be journalized and posted so that the general ledger is in balance before any transactions can be recorded for the new period.

FIGURE 13-5 ▶
Postclosing Trial Balance

Modern Casuals
Postclosing Trial Balance
December 31, 2004

ACCOUNT NAME	DEBIT	CREDIT
Cash	21 1 3 6 00	
Petty Cash Fund	1 0 0 00	
Notes Receivable	1 2 0 0 00	
Accounts Receivable	32 0 0 0 00	
Allowance for Doubtful Accounts		8 5 0 00
Interest Receivable	2 4 00	
Merchandise Inventory	46 0 0 0 00	
Supplies	1 3 2 5 00	
Prepaid Insurance	3 6 0 0 00	
Prepaid Interest	7 5 00	
Store Equipment	20 0 0 0 00	
Accumulated Depreciation—Store Equipment		2 2 5 0 00
Office Equipment	7 0 0 0 00	
Accumulated Depreciation—Office Equipment		1 2 0 0 00
Notes Payable—Trade		2 0 0 0 00
Notes Payable—Bank		9 0 0 0 00
Accounts Payable		24 1 2 9 00
Interest Payable		2 0 00
Social Security Tax Payable		1 1 7 7 00
Medicare Tax Payable		2 7 1 75
Employee Income Taxes Payable		9 9 0 00
Federal Unemployment Tax Payable		1 2 00
State Unemployment Tax Payable		8 1 00
Salaries Payable		1 5 0 0 00
Sales Tax Payable		7 0 5 6 00
Sonia Sanchez, Capital		81 9 2 3 25
Totals	132 4 6 0 00	132 4 6 0 00

Interpreting the Financial Statements

Interested parties analyze the financial statements to evaluate the results of operations and to make decisions. Interpreting financial statements requires an understanding of the business and the environment in which it operates as well as the nature and limitations of accounting information. Ratios and other measurements are used to analyze and interpret financial statements. Three such measurements are used by Modern Casuals.

The **gross profit percentage** reveals the amount of gross profit from each sales dollar. The gross profit percentage is calculated by dividing gross profit by net sales. For Modern Casuals, for every dollar of net sales, gross profit was almost 40 cents.

$$\frac{\text{Gross profit}}{\text{Net sales}} = \frac{\$218,030}{\$546,650} = 0.399 = 39.9\%$$

Important!

Current Ratio
Banks and other lenders look closely at the current ratio of each loan applicant.

The **current ratio** is a relationship between current assets and current liabilities that provides a measure of a firm's ability to pay its current debts. Modern Casuals has $2.26 in current assets for every dollar of current liabilities. The current ratio is calculated in the following manner.

$$\frac{\text{Current assets}}{\text{Current liabilities}} = \frac{\$104,610.00}{\$ 46,236.75} = 2.26 \text{ to } 1$$

Caterpillar Inc. reported current assets of $11.7 billion and current liabilities of $8.2 billion on December 31, 1999. The current ratio shows that the business has $1.43 of current assets for every dollar of current liabilities.

Inventory turnover shows the number of times inventory is replaced during the accounting period. Inventory turnover is calculated in the following manner.

$$\text{Inventory turnover} = \frac{\text{Cost of goods sold}}{\text{Average inventory}}$$

$$\text{Average inventory} = \frac{\text{Beginning inventory} + \text{Ending inventory}}{2}$$

$$\text{Average inventory} = \frac{\$51,500 + \$46,000}{2} = \$48,750$$

$$\text{Inventory turnover} = \frac{\$328,620}{\$48,750} = 6.74 \text{ times}$$

For Modern Casuals the average inventory for the year was $48,750. The inventory turnover was 6.74; that is, inventory was replaced about seven times during the year.

Journalizing and Posting Reversing Entries

Some adjustments made at the end of one period can cause problems in the next period. **Reversing entries** are made to reverse the effect of certain adjustments. This helps prevent errors in recording payments or cash receipts in the new accounting period.

Let's use adjustment **(f)** as an illustration of how reversing entries are helpful. On December 31 Modern Casuals owed $1,500 of salaries to its part-time sales clerks. The salaries will be paid in January. To recognize the salaries expense in December, adjustment **(f)** was made to debit **Salaries Expense—Sales** for $1,500 and credit **Salaries Payable** for $1,500. The adjustment was recorded and posted in the accounting records.

By payday on January 3, the part-time sales clerks have earned $2,000:

$1,500 earned in December
$ 500 earned in January

The entry to record the January 3 payment of the salaries is a debit to **Salaries Expense—Sales** for $500, a debit to **Salaries Payable** for $1,500, and a credit to **Cash** for $2,000. This entry recognizes the salary expense for January and reduces the **Salaries Payable** account to zero.

7 Objective
Journalize and post reversing entries.

Accrual Basis
Revenues are recognized when earned, and expenses are recognized when incurred or used, regardless of when cash is received or paid.

Salaries Expense—Sales	
1/3 500	

Cash			
12/31 21,136	1/3	2,000
Bal. 19,136		

Salaries Payable			
1/3 1,500	12/31	1,500
	Bal.	0

To record this transaction, the accountant had to review the adjustment in the end-of-period records and divide the amount paid between the expense and liability accounts. This review is time consuming, can cause errors, and is sometimes forgotten.

Reversing entries provide a way to guard against oversights, eliminate the review of accounting records, and simplify the entry made in the new period. As an example of a reversing entry, we will analyze the same transaction (January 3 payroll of $2,000) if reversing entries are made.

First, record the adjustment on December 31. Then record the reversing entry on January 1. Note that the reversing entry is the exact opposite (the reverse) of the adjustment. After the reversing entry is posted, the **Salaries Payable** account shows a zero balance and the **Salaries Expense—Sales** account has a credit balance. This is unusual because the normal balance of an expense account is a debit.

Computers in Accounting

Tools for Success: Decision Support Systems

Executives and managers use financial statements to make decisions about the future. Transportation of goods might be moved from trucking vendors to air vendors. Staff reductions or increases might be in order. These managerial decisions are made while keeping in mind the goals of the company.

Computerized decision support systems help managers make the best possible decisions. *Decision support system (DSS)* is a term used to describe computer software designed to assemble, arrange, and analyze data in order to find the most profitable plan of action. For example, an automobile manufacturing company might use the software to determine the most cost-efficient manufacturing method. In this case the decision support system would extract information from the manufacturing, engineering, accounting information, and production planning systems. The various costs associated with different techniques for body formation, engineering models, and assembly processes would be assembled and combined in potential groupings.

Then the DSS would make projections based on "what-if" scenarios, calculating outcome on profits or operational costs. For example, would costs decrease if manufacturing of glass components were completed by an outside firm? Would profits increase if steel fabrication contained different composite

materials? A DSS can provide executives a vision of the integrated relationships between manufacturing processes and the bottom line.

A computerized decision support system, however, cannot integrate the human elements into decisions. For example, a DSS might reveal a change in the production process that positively affects the bottom line, but doesn't reveal its impact on employees. How will the change affect job satisfaction or stress levels? Is retraining required? A business that uses DSS in combination with human element considerations will have the information to make decisions that positively impact not only the bottom line, but also the entire organization.

Thinking Critically

Companies select among a variety of transportation methods when moving goods from suppliers to warehouses or to retail locations. Describe how you think a decision support system could be used to evaluate the various shipping methods.

Internet Application

Using a search engine on the Internet, find a decision support system used in the farming, aviation, robotics, or natural or biological resources management industry. Write a one-page report on the decision support system. Describe the goal of the software, the types of data needed, and the benefits provided.

GENERAL JOURNAL PAGE 25

	DATE	DESCRIPTION	POST. REF.	DEBIT	CREDIT	
1	2004	Adjusting Entries				1
35		(Adjustment f)				35
36	Dec. 31	Salaries Expense—Sales	602	1 5 0 0 00		36
37		Salaries Payable	229		1 5 0 0 00	37

GENERAL JOURNAL PAGE 29

	DATE	DESCRIPTION	POST. REF.	DEBIT	CREDIT	
1	2005	Reversing Entries				1
2	Jan. 1	Salaries Payable	229	1 5 0 0 00		2
3		Salaries Expense—Sales	602		1 5 0 0 00	3

ACCOUNT Salaries Payable ACCOUNT NO. 229

DATE	DESCRIPTION	POST. REF.	DEBIT	CREDIT	BALANCE DEBIT	BALANCE CREDIT
2004						
Dec. 31	Adjusting	J25		1 5 0 0 00		1 5 0 0 00
2005						
Jan. 1	Reversing	J29	1 5 0 0 00			—0—

ACCOUNT Salaries Expense—Sales ACCOUNT NO. 602

DATE	DESCRIPTION	POST. REF.	DEBIT	CREDIT	BALANCE DEBIT	BALANCE CREDIT
2004						
Dec. 31	Balance				78 4 9 0 00	
31	Adjusting	J25	1 5 0 0 00		79 9 9 0 00	
31	Closing	J28		79 9 9 0 00	—0—	
2005						
Jan. 1	Reversing	J29		1 5 0 0 00		1 5 0 0 00

On January 3 the payment of $2,000 of salaries is recorded in the normal manner. Notice that this entry reduces cash and increases the expense account for the entire $2,000. It does not allocate the $2,000 between the expense and liability accounts.

GENERAL JOURNAL PAGE 30

	DATE	DESCRIPTION	POST. REF.	DEBIT	CREDIT	
1	2005					1
2	Jan. 3	Salaries Expense—Sales	602	2 0 0 0 00		2
3		Cash	101		2 0 0 0 00	3

After this entry is posted, the expenses are properly divided between the two periods: $1,500 in December and $500 in January. The **Salaries Payable** account has a zero balance. The accountant did not have to review the previous records or allocate the payment between two accounts.

ACCOUNT _Salaries Expense—Sales_   ACCOUNT NO. _602_

| DATE | | DESCRIPTION | POST. REF. | DEBIT | CREDIT | BALANCE | |
						DEBIT	CREDIT
2004							
Dec.	31	Balance				78 4 9 0 00	
	31	Adjusting	J25	1 5 0 0 00		79 9 9 0 00	
	31	Closing	J28		79 9 9 0 00	—0—	
2005							
Jan.	1	Reversing	J29		1 5 0 0 00		1 5 0 0 00
	3		J30	2 0 0 0 00		5 0 0 00	

Identifying Items for Reversal

Not all adjustments need to be reversed. Normally, reversing entries are made for accrued items that involve future payments or receipts of cash. Reversing entries are not made for uncollectible accounts, depreciation, and prepaid expenses—if they are initially recorded as assets. However, when prepaid expenses are initially recorded as expenses (the alternative method), the end-of-period adjustment needs to be reversed.

Modern Casuals makes reversing entries for:

- accrued salaries—adjustment **(f),**
- accrued payroll taxes—adjustments **(g)** and **(h),**
- interest payable—adjustment **(i),**
- interest receivable—adjustment **(m).**

Journalizing Reversing Entries

We just analyzed the reversing entry for accrued salaries, adjustment **(f).** The next two reversing entries are for accrued payroll taxes. Making these reversing entries means that the accountant does not have to review the year-end adjustments before recording the payment of payroll taxes in the next year.

GENERAL JOURNAL   PAGE _29_

	DATE		DESCRIPTION	POST. REF.	DEBIT	CREDIT	
6	Jan.	1	Social Security Tax Payable	221	9 3 00		6
7			Medicare Tax Payable	223	2 1 75		7
8			Payroll Taxes Expense	665		1 1 4 75	8
9			To reverse adjusting entry				9
10			(g) made Dec. 31, 2004				10
11							11
12		1	Federal Unemployment Tax Payable	225	1 2 00		12
13			State Unemployment Tax Payable	227	8 1 00		13
14			Payroll Taxes Expense	665		9 3 00	14
15			To reverse adjusting entry				15
16			(h) made Dec. 31, 2004				16

The next reversing entry is for accrued interest expense. The reversing entry that follows prevents recording difficulties when the note is paid on February 1.

GENERAL JOURNAL   PAGE ___29___

	DATE		DESCRIPTION	POST. REF.	DEBIT	CREDIT	
18	Jan.	1	Interest Payable	216	2 0 00		18
19			Interest Expense	695		2 0 00	19
20			To reverse adjusting entry				20
21			(i) made Dec. 31, 2004				21
22							22

In addition to adjustments for accrued expenses, Modern Casuals made two adjustments for accrued income items. The next reversing entry is for accrued interest income on the note receivable. Modern Casuals will receive cash for the note and the interest on March 1. The reversing entry eliminates any difficulties in recording the interest income when the note is paid on March 1.

GENERAL JOURNAL   PAGE ___29___

	DATE		DESCRIPTION	POST. REF.	DEBIT	CREDIT	
23	Jan.	1	Interest Income	491	2 4 00		23
24			Interest Receivable	116		2 4 00	24
25			To reverse adjusting entry				25
26			(m) made Dec. 31, 2004				26
27							27

After the reversing entry has been posted, the **Interest Receivable** account has a zero balance and the **Interest Income** account has a debit balance of $24. This is unusual because the normal balance of **Interest Income** is a credit.

On March 1 Modern Casuals received a check for $1,248 in payment of the note ($1,200) and the interest ($48). The transaction is recorded in the normal manner as a debit to **Cash** for $1,248, a credit to **Notes Receivable** for $1,200, and a credit to **Interest Income** for $48.

Refer to the **Interest Income** general ledger account on page 490. After this entry has been posted, note that interest income is properly divided between the two periods, $24 in the previous year and $24 in the current year. The balance of **Interest Receivable** is zero. The accountant does not have to review the year-end adjustments before recording the receipt of the principal and interest relating to the note receivable.

ACCOUNT ___Interest Receivable___   ACCOUNT NO. ___116___

	DATE		DESCRIPTION	POST. REF.	DEBIT	CREDIT	BALANCE DEBIT	BALANCE CREDIT
	2004							
	Dec.	31	Adjusting	J27	2 4 00		2 4 00	
	2005							
	Jan.	1	Reversing	J29		2 4 00	—0—	

ACCOUNT _Interest Income_   ACCOUNT NO. _491_

DATE		DESCRIPTION	POST. REF.	DEBIT	CREDIT	BALANCE DEBIT	BALANCE CREDIT
2004							
Dec.	31	Balance					1 3 6 00
	31	Adjusting	J27		2 4 00		1 6 0 00
	31	Closing	J28	1 6 0 00			—0—
2005							
Jan.	1	Reversing	J29	2 4 00		2 4 00	
Mar.	1		CR3		4 8 00		2 4 00

Notice that the adjustment for sales tax commission, adjustment **(n),** is not reversed. Since no cash will be received in the new year when the sales tax return is filed, there is no need to reverse the adjustment.

Review of the Accounting Cycle

In Chapters 7, 8, and 9, The Trend Center was used to introduce accounting procedures, records, and statements for merchandising businesses. In Chapters 12 and 13, Modern Casuals was used to illustrate the end-of-period activities for merchandising businesses. Underlying the various procedures described were the steps in the accounting cycle. Let's review the accounting cycle.

1. **Analyze transactions.** Transaction data comes into an accounting system from a variety of source documents—sales slips, purchase invoices, credit memorandums, check stubs, and so on. Each document is analyzed to determine the accounts and amounts affected.

2. **Journalize the data about transactions.** Each transaction is recorded in either a special journal or the general journal.

3. **Post the data about transactions.** Each transaction is transferred from the journal to the ledger accounts. Merchandising businesses typically maintain several subsidiary ledgers in addition to the general ledger.

4. **Prepare a worksheet.** At the end of each period, a worksheet is prepared. The Trial Balance section of the worksheet is used to prove the equality of the debits and credits in the general ledger. Adjustments are entered in the Adjustments section so that the financial statements will be prepared using the accrual basis of accounting. The Adjusted Trial Balance section is used to prove the equality of the debit and credits of the updated account balances. The Income Statement and Balance Sheet sections are used to arrange data in an orderly manner.

5. **Prepare financial statements.** A formal set of financial statements is prepared to report information to interested parties.

6. **Journalize and post adjusting entries.** Adjusting entries are journalized and posted in the accounting records. This creates a permanent record of the changes shown on the worksheet.

7. **Journalize and post closing entries.** Closing entries are journalized and posted in order to transfer the results of operations to owner's equity and to prepare the temporary accounts for the next period. The closing entries reduce the temporary account balances to zero.

About Accounting

Professional Conduct

In September 1998 the Securities and Exchange Commission (SEC) defined improper professional conduct by accountants. The new rule allows the SEC to censure, suspend, or bar accountants who violate it. The American Institute of Certified Public Accountants (AICPA) supported the rule.

8. **Prepare a postclosing trial balance.** The postclosing trial balance confirms that the general ledger is still in balance and that the temporary accounts have zero balances.

9. **Interpret the financial information.** The accountant, owners, managers, and other interested parties interpret the information shown on the financial statements and other less formal financial reports that might be prepared. This information is used to evaluate the results of operations and the financial position of the business and to make decisions.

In addition to the nine steps listed here, some firms record reversing entries. Reversing entries simplify the recording of cash payments for accrued expenses and cash receipts for accrued income.

Figure 13-6 on page 492 shows the flow of data through an accounting system that uses special journals and subsidiary ledgers. The system is composed of subsystems that perform specialized functions.

The accounts receivable area records transactions involving sales and cash receipts and maintains the individual accounts for credit customers. This area also handles billing for credit customers.

The accounts payable area records transactions involving purchases and cash payments and maintains the individual accounts for creditors.

Managerial IMPLICATIONS

Financial Statements

- Managers carefully study the financial statements to evaluate the operating efficiency and financial strength of the business.

- A common analysis technique is to compare the data on current statements with the data from previous statements. This can reveal developing trends.

- In large businesses, financial statements are compared with the published financial reports of other companies in the same industry.

- In order to evaluate information on classified financial statements, managers need to understand the nature and significance of the groupings.

- Management ensures that closing entries are promptly made so that transactions for the new period can be recorded. Any significant delay means that valuable information, such as the firm's cash position, will not be available or up to date.

- The efficiency and effectiveness of the adjusting and closing procedures can have a positive effect on the annual independent audit. For example, detailed descriptions in the general journal make it easy for the auditor to understand the adjusting entries.

Thinking Critically

How can managers use the financial statements to learn about a company's operating efficiency?

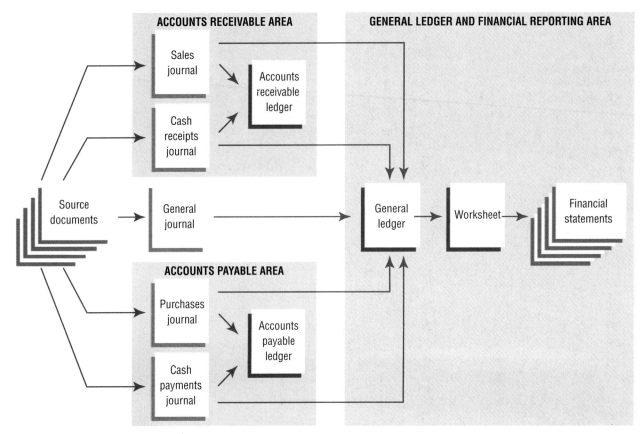

FIGURE 13-6 ▲
Flow of Financial Data through
an Accounting System

The general ledger and financial reporting area records transactions in the general journal, maintains the general ledger accounts, performs the end-of-period procedures, and prepares financial statements. This area is the focal point for the accounting system because all transactions eventually flow into the general ledger. In turn, the general ledger provides the data that appears on the financial statements.

Section 2 Self Review

Questions

1. Since adjustments already appear on the worksheet, why is it necessary to journalize and post them?

2. Why do adjusting entries need detailed explanations in the general journal?

3. What do the four steps in the closing process accomplish?

Exercises

4. A reversing entry is made for an end-of-period adjustment that recorded

a. depreciation.

b. an accrued expense that involves future cash payments.

c. a transfer of an amount from a prepaid asset account to an expense account.

d. the change in merchandise inventory.

5. The current ratio is

a. current liabilities divided by current assets.

b. total assets divided by total current liabilities.

c. total assets divided by total liabilities.

d. current assets divided by current liabilities.

Analysis

6. At the end of the previous accounting period, an adjusting entry to record accrued employer payroll taxes was made. Reversing entries were not made for the current accounting period. What effect will this have on the current financial statements?

(Answers to Section 2 Self Review are on page 514.)

Review

Chapter Summary

In this chapter, you have learned how to prepare classified financial statements from the worksheet and how to close the accounting records for the period.

Learning Objectives

1 Prepare a classified income statement from the worksheet.

- A classified income statement for a merchandising business usually includes these sections: Operating Revenue, Cost of Goods Sold, Gross Profit on Sales, Operating Expenses, and Net Income.

- To make the income statement even more useful, operating expenses may be broken down into categories, such as selling expenses and general and administrative expenses.

2 Prepare a statement of owner's equity from the worksheet.

A statement of owner's equity is prepared to provide detailed information about the changes in the owner's financial interest during the period. The ending owner's capital balance is used to prepare the balance sheet.

3 Prepare a classified balance sheet from the worksheet.

- Assets are usually presented in two groups—current assets, and plant and equipment. Current assets consist of cash, items to be converted into cash within one year, and items to be used up within one year. Plant and equipment consists of property that will be used for a long time in the operations of the business.

- Liabilities are also divided into two groups—current liabilities and long-term liabilities. Current liabilities will normally be paid within one year. Long-term liabilities are due in more than one year.

4 Journalize and post the adjusting entries.

When the year-end worksheet and financial statements have been completed, adjusting entries are recorded in the general journal and posted to the general ledger. The data comes from the worksheet Adjustments section.

5 Journalize and post the closing entries.

After the adjusting entries have been journalized and posted, the closing entries should be recorded in the records of the business. The data in the Income Statement section of the worksheet can be used to journalize the closing entries.

6 Prepare a postclosing trial balance.

To confirm that the general ledger is still in balance after the adjusting and closing entries have been posted, a postclosing trial balance is prepared.

7 Journalize and post reversing entries.

At the start of each new period, many firms follow the practice of reversing certain adjustments that were made in the previous period.

- This is done to avoid recording problems with transactions that will occur in the new period.

- Usually, only adjusting entries for accrued expenses and accrued income need be considered for reversing. Of these, usually only accrued expense and income items involving future payments and receipts of cash can cause difficulties later and should therefore be reversed.

- The use of reversing entries is optional. Reversing entries save time, promote efficiency, and help to achieve a proper matching of revenue and expenses in each period.

- With reversing entries, there is no need to examine each transaction to see whether a portion applies to the past period and then divide the amount of the transaction between the two periods.

8 Define the accounting terms new to this chapter.

Classified financial statement (p. 472) A format by which revenues and expenses on the income statement, and assets and liabilities on the balance sheet, are divided into groups of similar accounts and a subtotal is given for each group

Current assets (p. 475) Assets consisting of cash, items that normally will be converted into cash within one year, or items that will be used up within one year

Current liabilities (p. 477) Debts that must be paid within one year

Current ratio (p. 484) A relationship between current assets and current liabilities that provides a measure of a firm's ability to pay its current debts (current ratio = current assets ÷ current liabilities)

Gross profit (p. 473) The difference between net sales and the cost of goods sold (gross profit = net sales − cost of goods sold)

Gross profit percentage (p. 484) The amount of gross profit from each dollar of sales (gross profit percentage = gross profit ÷ net sales)

Inventory turnover (p. 485) The number of times inventory is purchased and sold during the accounting period (inventory turnover = cost of good sold ÷ average inventory)

Liquidity (p. 476) The ease with which an item can be converted into cash

Long-term liabilities (p. 477) Debts of a business that are due more than one year in the future

Multiple-step income statement (p. 472) A type of income statement on which several subtotals are computed before the net income is calculated

Plant and equipment (p. 477) Property that will be used in the business for longer than one year

Reversing entries (p. 485) Journal entries made to reverse the effect of certain adjusting entries involving accrued income or accrued expenses to avoid problems in recording future payments or receipts of cash in a new accounting period

Single-step income statement (p. 472) A type of income statement where only one computation is needed to determine the net income (total revenue − total expenses = net income)

Comprehensive Self Review

1. Explain the difference between a single-step income statement and a multiple-step income statement.

2. How is net income from operations determined?

3. Why would a factory machine not be considered a current asset?

4. After closing entries are posted, which of the following types of accounts will have zero balances?

   a. asset accounts

   b. revenue accounts

   c. owner's drawing account

   d. liability accounts

e. Income Summary account

f. expense accounts

g. owner's capital account

h. cost of goods sold accounts

5. Describe the entry that would be made to close the **Income Summary** account in each of the following cases. The owner of the firm is Harold Hicks.

   a. There is a net income of $62,000.

   b. There is a net loss of $28,000.

(Answers to Comprehensive Self Review are on page 514.)

Discussion Questions

1. What is the difference between operating revenue and other revenues or income?

2. What are operating expenses?

3. Which section of the income statement contains information about the purchases made during the period and the beginning and ending merchandise inventory?

4. What is the purpose of the balance sheet?

5. What are current assets? Give four examples of items that would be considered current assets.

6. What is plant and equipment? Give two examples of items that would be considered plant and equipment.

7. How do current liabilities and long-term liabilities differ?

8. What information is provided by the statement of owner's equity?

9. What is the purpose of the postclosing trial balance?

10. What types of accounts appear on the postclosing trial balance?

11. Why are reversing entries helpful?

12. What types of adjustments are reversed?

13. On December 31 Chan Company made an adjusting entry debiting **Interest Receivable** and crediting **Interest Income** for $30 of accrued interest. What reversing entry would be recorded for this item as of January 1?

14. Various adjustments made at Smith Company are listed below. Which ones should normally be reversed?

   a. An adjustment for the estimated loss from uncollectible accounts

   b. An adjustment for depreciation on equipment

   c. An adjustment for accrued salaries expense

   d. An adjustment for accrued payroll taxes expense

   e. An adjustment for accrued interest expense

   f. An adjustment for supplies used

   g. An adjustment for expired insurance

   h. An adjustment for accrued interest income

15. Name the steps of the accounting cycle.

Applications

Exercise 13-1 ►
Objective 1

Classifying income statement items.

The following accounts appear on the worksheet of Huntsville Variety Store. Indicate the section of the classified income statement in which each account will be reported.

SECTIONS OF CLASSIFIED INCOME STATEMENT

 a. Operating Revenue

 b. Cost of Goods Sold

 c. Operating Expenses

 d. Other Income

 e. Other Expenses

ACCOUNTS

 1. Purchases

 2. Salaries Expense—Sales

 3. Sales

 4. Interest Expense

 5. Merchandise Inventory

 6. Interest Income

 7. Freight In

 8. Sales Returns and Allowances

 9. Utilities Expense

 10. Purchases Discounts

Exercise 13-2 ►
Objective 3

Classifying balance sheet items.

The following accounts appear on the worksheet of Huntsville Record Store. Indicate the section of the classified balance sheet in which each account will be reported.

SECTIONS OF CLASSIFIED BALANCE SHEET

 a. Current Assets

 b. Plant and Equipment

 c. Current Liabilities

 d. Long-Term Liabilities

 e. Owner's Equity

ACCOUNTS

 1. Sales Tax Payable

 2. Cash

 3. Mike Valdez, Capital

 4. Building

 5. Accounts Payable

 6. Store Supplies

 7. Mortgage Payable

8. Prepaid Insurance

9. Delivery Van

10. Accounts Receivable

Preparing a classified income statement.

The worksheet of Village Auto Supply contains the following revenue, cost, and expense accounts. Prepare a classified income statement for this firm for the year ended December 31, 20--. The merchandise inventory amounted to $54,000 on January 1, 20--, and $50,400 on December 31, 20--. The expense accounts numbered 611 through 617 represent selling expenses, and those numbered 631 through 646 represent general and administrative expenses.

◄ **Exercise 13-3**
Objective 1

ACCOUNTS

401	Sales	$247,000	Cr.
451	Sales Returns and Allowances	5,200	Dr.
491	Miscellaneous Income	220	Cr.
501	Purchases	102,000	Dr.
502	Freight In	1,800	Dr.
503	Purchases Returns and Allowances	3,000	Cr.
504	Purchases Discounts	1,600	Cr.
611	Salaries Expense—Sales	44,000	Dr.
614	Store Supplies Expense	2,200	Dr.
617	Depreciation Expense—Store Equipment	1,600	Dr.
631	Rent Expense	12,000	Dr.
634	Utilities Expense	2,800	Dr.
637	Salaries Expense—Office	20,000	Dr.
640	Payroll Taxes Expense	5,000	Dr.
643	Depreciation Expense—Office Equipment	400	Dr.
646	Uncollectible Accounts Expense	640	Dr.
691	Interest Expense	520	Dr.

Preparing a statement of owner's equity.

The worksheet of Village Auto Supply contains the following owner's equity accounts. Use this data and the net income determined in Exercise 13-3 to prepare a statement of owner's equity for the year ended December 31, 20--. No additional investments were made during the period.

◄ **Exercise 13-4**
Objective 2

ACCOUNTS

301	Sue Davis, Capital	$60,120	Cr.
302	Sue Davis, Drawing	42,000	Dr.

Preparing a classified balance sheet.

The worksheet of Village Auto Supply contains the following asset and liability accounts. The balance of the **Notes Payable** account consists of notes that are due within a year. Prepare a balance sheet dated December 31, 20--. Obtain the ending capital for the period from the statement of owner's equity completed in Exercise 13-4.

◄ **Exercise 13-5**
Objective 3

ACCOUNTS

101	Cash	$10,800	Dr.
107	Change Fund	400	Dr.
111	Accounts Receivable	5,400	Dr.
112	Allowance for Doubtful Accounts	760	Cr.

ACCOUNTS (cont.)

121	Merchandise Inventory	$50,400	Dr.
131	Store Supplies	2,000	Dr.
133	Prepaid Interest	80	Dr.
141	Store Equipment	10,200	Dr.
142	Accum. Depreciation—Store Equipment	1,600	Cr.
151	Office Equipment	3,200	Dr.
152	Accum. Depreciation—Office Equipment	400	Cr.
201	Notes Payable	5,400	Cr.
203	Accounts Payable	3,600	Cr.
216	Interest Payable	60	Cr.
231	Sales Tax Payable	2,480	Cr.

Exercise 13-6 ►
Objective 5

Recording closing entries.

On December 31, 20--, the Income Statement section of the worksheet for Lozozo Company contained the following information. Give the entries that should be made in the general journal to close the revenue, cost of goods sold, expense, and other temporary accounts.

INCOME STATEMENT SECTION

	Debit	Credit
Income Summary	$ 38,000	$ 40,000
Sales		245,000
Sales Returns and Allowances	3,100	
Sales Discounts	2,300	
Interest Income		100
Purchases	125,000	
Freight In	1,700	
Purchases Returns and Allowances		1,900
Purchases Discounts		2,200
Rent Expense	8,400	
Utilities Expense	2,100	
Telephone Expense	1,300	
Salaries Expense	65,000	
Payroll Taxes Expense	5,150	
Supplies Expense	1,600	
Depreciation Expense	2,400	
Interest Expense	350	
Totals	$256,400	$289,200

Assume further that the owner of the firm is Lexi Lozozo and that the **Lexi Lozozo, Drawing** account had a balance of $26,000 on December 31, 20--.

Exercise 13-7 ►
Objective 7

Journalizing reversing entries.

Examine the following adjusting entries and determine which ones should be reversed. Show the reversing entries that should be recorded in the general journal as of January 1, 2005. Include appropriate descriptions.

2004	(Adjustment a)		
Dec. 31	Uncollectible Accounts Expense	3,600.00	
	Allowance for Doubtful Accounts		3,600.00
	To record estimated loss from uncollectible accounts based on 0.5% of net credit sales, $720,000		

(Adjustment b)

		Debit	Credit
Dec. 31	Supplies Expense	4,640.00	
	Supplies		4,640.00
	To record supplies used during the year		

(Adjustment c)

31	Insurance Expense	1,800.00	
	Prepaid Insurance		1,800.00
	To record expired insurance on 1-year $5,400 policy purchased on Sept. 1		

(Adjustment d)

31	Depreciation. Exp.—Store Equipment	15,400.00	
	Accum. Depreciation—Store Equip.		15,400.00
	To record depreciation		

(Adjustment e)

31	Salaries Expense—Office	2,360.00	
	Salaries Payable		2,360.00
	To record accrued salaries for Dec. 29–31		

(Adjustment f)

31	Payroll Tax Expense	180.54	
	Social Security Tax Payable		146.32
	Medicare Tax Payable		34.22
	To record accrued payroll taxes on accrued salaries: social security, 6.2% × 2,360 = $146.32; Medicare, 1.45% × 2,360 = $34.22		

(Adjustment g)

31	Interest Expense	660.00	
	Interest Payable		660.00
	To record accrued interest on a 4-month, 11% trade note payable dated Oct. 1: $24,000 × 0.11 × 3/12 = $660		

(Adjustment h)

31	Interest Receivable	100.00	
	Interest Income		100.00
	To record interest earned on 6-month, 10% note receivable dated Nov. 1: $6,000 × 0.10 × 2/12 = $100		

Preparing a postclosing trial balance.

◄ **Exercise 13-8**
Objective 6

The Adjusted Trial Balance section of the worksheet for Lucas Implement Company follows. The owner made no additional investments during the year. Prepare a postclosing trial balance for the firm on December 31, 20--.

ACCOUNTS	Debit	Credit
Cash	$ 20,400	
Accounts Receivable	40,800	
Allowance for Doubtful Accounts		$ 120
Merchandise Inventory	189,000	
Supplies	7,140	

ACCOUNTS (cont.)	Debit	Credit
Prepaid Insurance	$ 3,060	
Equipment	51,000	
Accumulated Depreciation—Equipment		$ 16,800
Notes Payable		10,500
Accounts Payable		8,700
Social Security Tax Payable		1,392
Medicare Tax Payable		324
Don Lucas, Capital		233,430
Don Lucas, Drawing	84,000	
Income Summary	180,000	189,000
Sales		768,000
Sales Returns and Allowances	14,400	
Purchases	477,000	
Freight In	5,400	
Purchases Returns and Allowances		10,500
Purchases Discounts		6,900
Rent Expense	21,600	
Telephone Expense	3,246	
Salaries Expense	124,140	
Payroll Taxes Expense	11,100	
Supplies Expense	3,600	
Insurance Expense	660	
Depreciation Expense—Equipment	9,000	
Uncollectible Accounts Expense	120	
Totals	$1,245,666	$1,245,666

Problems

Selected problems can be completed using:
    Peachtree   QuickBooks   **Spreadsheets**

PROBLEM SET A

Problem 13-1A ►
Objectives 1, 2, 3
SPREADSHEET

Preparing classified financial statements.

Mayfair Company distributes electronic components to small manufacturers. The adjusted trial balance data given below is from the firm's worksheet for the year ended December 31, 20--.

INSTRUCTIONS

1. Prepare a classified income statement for the year ended December 31, 20--. The expense accounts represent warehouse expenses, selling expenses, and general and administrative expenses.

2. Prepare a statement of owner's equity for the year ended December 31, 20--. No additional investments were made during the period.

3. Prepare a classified balance sheet as of December 31, 20--. The mortgage and the loans extend for more than a year.

ACCOUNTS	Debit	Credit
Cash	$27,100	
Petty Cash Fund	400	
Notes Receivable	10,800	
Accounts Receivable	54,500	
Allowance for Doubtful Accounts		$5,000

ACCOUNTS (cont.)	Debit	Credit
Merchandise Inventory	$ 224,000	
Warehouse Supplies	2,760	
Office Supplies	1,320	
Prepaid Insurance	7,200	
Land	36,000	
Building	168,000	
Accumulated Depreciation—Building		$ 48,000
Warehouse Equipment	32,000	
Accumulated Depreciation—Warehouse Equipment		14,400
Delivery Equipment	46,000	
Accumulated Depreciation—Delivery Equipment		17,600
Office Equipment	20,000	
Accumulated Depreciation—Office Equipment		9,000
Notes Payable		19,200
Accounts Payable		42,000
Interest Payable		480
Mortgage Payable		56,000
Loans Payable		12,000
Jeff London, Capital (Jan. 1)		397,640
Jeff London, Drawing	126,000	
Income Summary	234,000	224,000
Sales		1,673,600
Sales Returns and Allowances	17,200	
Interest Income		1,480
Purchases	770,400	
Freight In	12,800	
Purchases Returns and Allowances		7,440
Purchases Discounts		10,160
Warehouse Wages Expense	189,600	
Warehouse Supplies Expense	6,100	
Depreciation Expense—Warehouse Equipment	4,800	
Salaries Expense—Sales	259,200	
Travel and Entertainment Expense	20,500	
Delivery Wages Expense	84,000	
Depreciation Expense—Delivery Equipment	8,800	
Salaries Expense—Office	69,600	
Office Supplies Expense	3,000	
Insurance Expense	5,200	
Utilities Expense	9,600	
Telephone Expense	5,520	
Payroll Taxes Expense	54,000	
Property Taxes Expense	4,600	
Uncollectible Accounts Expense	4,800	
Depreciation Expense—Building	8,000	
Depreciation Expense—Office Equipment	3,000	
Interest Expense	7,200	
Totals	$2,538,000	$2,538,000

Analyze: What is the current ratio for this business?

Preparing classified financial statements.

Superior Auto Products distributes automobile parts to service stations and repair shops. The adjusted trial balance data that follows is from the firm's worksheet for the year ended December 31, 20--.

◄ **Problem 13-2A**
Objectives 1, 2, 3

INSTRUCTIONS

1. Prepare a classified income statement for the year ended December 31, 20--. The expense accounts represent warehouse expenses, selling expenses, and general and administrative expenses.

2. Prepare a statement of owner's equity for the year ended December 31, 20--. No additional investments were made during the period.

3. Prepare a classified balance sheet as of December 31, 20--. The mortgage and the long-term notes extend for more than one year.

ACCOUNTS	Debit	Credit
Cash	$ 86,000	
Petty Cash Fund	400	
Notes Receivable	10,000	
Accounts Receivable	101,200	
Allowance for Doubtful Accounts		$ 2,800
Interest Receivable	200	
Merchandise Inventory	124,000	
Warehouse Supplies	2,300	
Office Supplies	600	
Prepaid Insurance	3,640	
Land	15,000	
Building	92,000	
Accumulated Depreciation—Building		14,400
Warehouse Equipment	18,800	
Accumulated Depreciation—Warehouse Equipment		9,600
Office Equipment	8,400	
Accumulated Depreciation—Office Equipment		3,040
Notes Payable—Short-Term		14,000
Accounts Payable		59,000
Interest Payable		300
Notes Payable—Long-Term		10,000
Mortgage Payable		20,000
Luis Garcia, Capital (Jan. 1)		327,020
Luis Garcia, Drawing	64,000	
Income Summary	130,400	124,000
Sales		990,200
Sales Returns and Allowances	7,400	
Interest Income		480
Purchases	438,000	
Freight In	8,800	
Purchases Returns and Allowances		11,560
Purchases Discounts		8,240
Warehouse Wages Expense	107,200	
Warehouse Supplies Expense	4,800	
Depreciation Expense—Warehouse Equipment	2,400	
Salaries Expense—Sales	150,200	
Travel Expense	23,000	
Delivery Expense	36,400	
Salaries Expense—Office	84,000	
Office Supplies Expense	1,120	
Insurance Expense	8,800	
Utilities Expense	6,000	
Telephone Expense	3,180	
Payroll Taxes Expense	30,600	

ACCOUNTS (cont.)	Debit	Credit
Building Repairs Expense	$ 2,700	
Property Taxes Expense	12,400	
Uncollectible Accounts Expense	2,580	
Depreciation Expense—Building	3,600	
Depreciation Expense—Office Equipment	1,520	
Interest Expense	3,000	
Totals	$1,594,640	$1,594,640

Analyze: What percentage of total operating expenses is attributable to warehouse expenses?

Journalizing adjusting, closing, and reversing entries.

Obtain all data that is necessary from the worksheet prepared for Fitness Foods Company in Problem 12-4A. Then follow the instructions to complete this problem.

◄ **Problem 13-3A**
Objectives 4, 5, 7

INSTRUCTIONS

1. Record adjusting entries in the general journal as of December 31, 2005. Use 25 as the first journal page number. Include descriptions for the entries.

2. Record closing entries in the general journal as of December 31, 2005. Include descriptions.

3. Record reversing entries in the general journal as of January 1, 2006. Include descriptions.

Analyze: Assuming that the firm did not record a reversing entry for salaries payable, what entry is required when salaries of $5,000 are paid in January?

Journalizing adjusting and reversing entries.

The data below concerns adjustments to be made at Lakers Company.

◄ **Problem 13-4A**
Objectives 4, 7

INSTRUCTIONS

1. Record the adjusting entries in the general journal as of December 31, 2004. Use 25 as the first journal page number. Include descriptions.

2. Record reversing entries in the general journal as of January 1, 2005. Include descriptions.

ADJUSTMENTS

a. On September 1, 2004, the firm signed a lease for a warehouse and paid rent of $16,800 in advance for a six-month period.

b. On December 31, 2004, an inventory of supplies showed that items costing $1,840 were on hand. The balance of the **Supplies** account was $11,120.

c. A depreciation schedule for the firm's equipment shows that a total of $7,800 should be charged off as depreciation for 2004.

d. On December 31, 2004, the firm owed salaries of $4,400 that will not be paid until January 2005.

e. On December 31, 2004, the firm owed the employer's social security (6.2 percent) and Medicare (1.45 percent) taxes on all accrued salaries.

f. On November 1, 2004, the firm received a four-month, 10 percent note for $5,400 from a customer with an overdue balance.

Analyze: After the adjusting entries have been posted, what is the balance of the **Prepaid Rent** account on January 1?

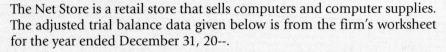

PROBLEM SET B

Problem 13-1B ►
Objectives 1, 2, 3

SPREADSHEET

Preparing classified financial statements.

The Net Store is a retail store that sells computers and computer supplies. The adjusted trial balance data given below is from the firm's worksheet for the year ended December 31, 20--.

INSTRUCTIONS

1. Prepare a classified income statement for the year ended December 31, 20--. The expense accounts represent warehouse expenses, selling expenses, and general and administrative expenses.

2. Prepare a statement of owner's equity for the year ended December 31, 20--. No additional investments were made during the period.

3. Prepare a classified balance sheet as of December 31, 20--. The mortgage and the loans extend for more than one year.

ACCOUNTS	Debit	Credit
Cash	$ 8,924	
Petty Cash Fund	100	
Notes Receivable	3,200	
Accounts Receivable	16,326	
Allowance for Doubtful Accounts		$ 2,250
Merchandise Inventory	36,000	
Warehouse Supplies	750	
Office Supplies	730	
Prepaid Insurance	2,200	
Land	7,000	
Building	48,000	
Accum. Depr.—Building		12,000
Warehouse Equipment	9,000	
Accumulated Depreciation—Warehouse Equipment		2,600
Delivery Equipment	14,000	
Accumulated Depreciation—Delivery Equipment		3,600
Office Equipment	6,000	
Accumulated Depreciation—Office Equipment		2,500
Notes Payable		5,000
Accounts Payable		12,800
Interest Payable		240
Mortgage Payable		16,000
Loans Payable		4,000
Carol Hall, Capital (Jan. 1)		60,490
Carol Hall, Drawing	24,000	
Income Summary	34,000	36,000
Sales		430,500
Sales Returns and Allowances	3,150	
Interest Income		420
Purchases	185,550	
Freight In	2,200	
Purchases Returns and Allowances		1,920
Purchases Discounts		2,350
Warehouse Wages Expense	39,400	
Warehouse Supplies Expense	1,790	
Depreciation Expense—Warehouse Equipment	1,400	

504 • **Chapter 13** *Financial Statements and Closing Procedures*

ACCOUNTS (cont.)	Debit	Credit
Salaries Expense—Sales	$ 70,200	
Travel and Entertainment Expense	6,300	
Delivery Wages Expense	24,000	
Depreciation Expense—Delivery Equipment	2,400	
Salaries Expense—Office	15,900	
Office Supplies Expense	950	
Insurance Expense	1,500	
Utilities Expense	2,800	
Telephone Expense	1,380	
Payroll Taxes Expense	15,100	
Property Taxes Expense	1,750	
Uncollectible Accounts Expense	1,050	
Depreciation Expense—Building	3,000	
Depreciation Expense—Office Equipment	1,020	
Interest Expense	1,600	
Totals	$592,670	$592,670

Analyze: What is the gross profit percentage for the period ended December 31, 20--?

Preparing classified financial statements.

Motor Center is a retail firm that sells motorcycles, parts, and accessories. The adjusted trial balance data given below is from the firm's worksheet for the year ended December 31, 20--.

1. Prepare a classified income statement for the year ended December 31, 20--. The expense accounts represent warehouse expenses, selling expenses, and general and administrative expenses.

2. Prepare a statement of owner's equity for the year ended December 31, 20--. No additional investments were made during the period.

3. Prepare a classified balance sheet as of December 31, 20--. The mortgage and the long-term notes extend for more than one year.

◄ **Problem 13-2B**
Objectives 1, 2, 3

INSTRUCTIONS

ACCOUNTS	Debit	Credit
Cash	$ 13,200	
Petty Cash Fund	200	
Notes Receivable	6,000	
Accounts Receivable	55,000	
Allowance for Doubtful Accounts		$ 5,000
Interest Receivable	200	
Merchandise Inventory	85,000	
Warehouse Supplies	3,700	
Office Supplies	1,800	
Prepaid Insurance	7,200	
Land	18,000	
Building	54,000	
Accumulated Depreciation—Building		8,400
Warehouse Equipment	24,000	
Accumulated Depreciation—Warehouse Equipment		4,000
Office Equipment	12,800	
Accumulated Depreciation—Office Equipment		1,800
Notes Payable—Short-Term		8,000
Accounts Payable		32,500

ACCOUNTS (cont.)	Debit	Credit
Interest Payable		$ 600
Notes Payable—Long-Term		6,000
Mortgage Payable		32,000
Ruby Mitchell, Capital (Jan. 1)		200,170
Ruby Mitchell, Drawing	$ 56,000	
Income Summary	89,000	85,000
Sales		602,902
Sales Returns and Allowances	9,400	
Interest Income		720
Purchases	225,000	
Freight In	9,600	
Purchases Returns and Allowances		6,200
Purchases Discounts		4,340
Warehouse Wages Expense	63,500	
Warehouse Supplies Expense	4,300	
Depreciation Expense—Warehouse Equipment	2,400	
Salaries Expense—Sales	79,100	
Travel Expense	21,000	
Delivery Expense	35,400	
Salaries Expense—Office	46,000	
Office Supplies Expense	1,360	
Insurance Expense	9,120	
Utilities Expense	6,912	
Telephone Expense	3,740	
Payroll Taxes Expense	28,800	
Building Repairs Expense	3,100	
Property Taxes Expense	11,700	
Uncollectible Accounts Expense	2,620	
Depreciation Expense—Building	3,200	
Depreciation Expense—Office Equipment	1,680	
Interest Expense	3,600	
Totals	$997,632	$997,632

Analyze: What is the inventory turnover for Motor Center?

Problem 13-3B ▶
Objectives 4, 5, 7

Journalizing adjusting, closing, and reversing entries.

Obtain all data that is necessary from the worksheet prepared for Village Novelties in Problem 12-4B. Then follow the instructions to complete this problem.

INSTRUCTIONS

1. Record adjusting entries in the general journal as of December 31, 2005. Use 29 as the first journal page number. Include descriptions for the entries.

2. Record closing entries in the general journal as of December 31, 2005. Include descriptions.

3. Record reversing entries in the general journal as of January 1, 2006. Include descriptions.

Analyze: Assuming that the company did not record a reversing entry for salaries payable, what entry is required when salaries of $1,200 are paid in January?

Journalizing adjusting and reversing entries.

The data below concerns adjustments to be made at Najar Company.

◄ **Problem 13-4B**
Objectives 4, 7

INSTRUCTIONS

1. Record the adjusting entries in the general journal as of December 31, 2005. Use 25 as the first journal page number. Include descriptions.

2. Record reversing entries in the general journal as of January 1, 2006. Include descriptions.

ADJUSTMENTS

a. On August 1, 2005, the firm signed a one-year advertising contract with a trade magazine and paid the entire amount, $6,000, in advance. **Prepaid Advertising** has a balance of $6,000.

b. On December 31, 2005, an inventory of supplies showed that items costing $1,500 were on hand. The balance of the **Supplies** account was $6,980.

c. A depreciation schedule for the firm's equipment shows that a total of $5,260 should be charged off as depreciation for 2005.

d. On December 31, 2005, the firm owed salaries of $3,200 that will not be paid until January 2006.

e. On December 31, 2005, the firm owed the employer's social security (6.2 percent) and Medicare (1.45 percent) taxes on all accrued salaries.

f. On October 1, 2005, the firm received a six-month, 12 percent note for $4,400 from a customer with an overdue balance.

Analyze: Assuming that the company did not make a reversing entry for salaries payable, what entry would be required to record the payment of salaries of $3,500 in January?

CHAPTER 13 CHALLENGE PROBLEM

Year-End Processing

Software Center is a retail firm that sells computer programs for home and business use. On December 31, 2005, its general ledger contained the accounts and balances shown below.

ACCOUNTS	BALANCES	
Cash	$ 13,600	Dr.
Accounts Receivable	27,200	Dr.
Allowance for Doubtful Accounts	80	Cr.
Merchandise Inventory	62,000	Dr.
Supplies	4,760	Dr.
Prepaid Insurance	2,040	Dr.
Equipment	34,000	Dr.
Accumulated Depreciation—Equipment	11,200	Cr.
Notes Payable	7,000	Cr.
Accounts Payable	5,800	Cr.
Social Security Tax Payable	560	Cr.
Medicare Tax Payable	130	Cr.
Matt Alexi, Capital	92,246	Cr.
Matt Alexi, Drawing	50,000	Dr.
Sales	512,348	Cr.
Sales Returns and Allowances	9,600	Dr.
Purchases	318,000	Dr.
Freight In	3,600	Dr.
Purchases Returns and Allowances	7,000	Cr.
Purchases Discounts	4,600	Cr.
Rent Expense	14,400	Dr.
Telephone Expense	2,164	Dr.
Salaries Expense	92,000	Dr.
Payroll Taxes Expense	7,400	Dr.
Interest Expense	200	Dr.

The following accounts had zero balances:

Interest Payable
Salaries Payable
Income Summary
Supplies Expense
Insurance Expense
Depreciation Expense—Equipment
Uncollectible Accounts Expense

The data needed for the adjustments on December 31 are as follows:

a.–b. Ending merchandise inventory, $68,000.

c. Uncollectible accounts, 0.6 percent of net credit sales of $230,000.

d. Supplies on hand December 31, $1,100.

e. Expired insurance, $1,190.

f. **Depreciation Expense—Equipment,** $5,600.

g. Accrued interest expense on notes payable, $280.

h. Accrued salaries, $1,600.

i. **Social Security Tax Payable** (6.2 percent) and **Medicare Tax Payable** (1.45 percent) of accrued salaries.

1. Prepare a worksheet for the year ended December 31, 2005.

2. Prepare a classified income statement. The firm does not divide its operating expenses into selling and administrative expenses.

3. Prepare a statement of owner's equity. No additional investments were made during the period.

4. Prepare a classified balance sheet. All notes payable are due within one year.

5. Journalize the adjusting entries.

6. Journalize the closing entries.

7. Journalize the reversing entries.

Analyze: By what percentage did the owner's capital account change in the period from January 1, 2005, to December 31, 2005?

Classified Balance Sheet

Tommie Jones is the owner of Clothing Galore, a store specializing in women's and children's sweaters. During the past year, in response to increased demand, Tommie doubled her selling space by expanding into the vacant store next to Clothing Galore. This expansion has been expensive because of the need to increase inventory and to purchase new store fixtures and equipment. Tommie notes that the company's cash position has gone down, and she is worried about paying for the expansion. Tommie shows you balance sheet data for the current year and last year and asks your opinion on the company's ability to pay for the recent expansion.

	December 31, 2004		December 31, 2005	
Assets				
Cash	100,000		20,000	
Accounts Receivable	30,000		61,000	
Inventory	70,000		156,000	
Prepaid Expenses	4,000		6,000	
Store Fixtures and Equipment	120,000		260,000	
Total Assets		324,000		503,000
Liabilities and Owner's Equity				
Liabilities				
Notes Payable (due in 5 years)	60,000		160,000	
Accounts Payable	88,000		114,000	
Salaries Payable	12,000		13,000	
Total Liabilities		160,000		287,000
Owner's Equity				
Tommie Jones, Capital		164,000		216,000
Total Liabilities and Owner's Equity		324,000		503,000

INSTRUCTIONS

1. Prepare classified balance sheets for Clothing Galore for the years 2004 and 2005.

2. Based on the information that is presented in the classified balance sheets, what is your opinion of Clothing Galore's ability to pay its current bills in a timely manner?

3. What is the advantage of a classified balance sheet over a balance sheet that is not classified?

Business Connections

◄ Connection 1

MANAGERIAL _FOCUS_   **Understanding Financial Statements**

1. Why should management be concerned about the efficiency of the end-of-period procedures?

2. Spector Company had an increase in sales and net income during its last fiscal year, but cash decreased and the firm was having difficulty paying its bills by the end of the year. What factors might cause a shortage of cash even though a firm is profitable?

3. For the last three years, the balance sheet of Desai Hardware Center, a large retail store, has shown a substantial increase in merchandise inventory. Why might management be concerned about this development?

4. Why is it important to compare the financial statements of the current year with those of prior years?

5. Should a manager be concerned if the balance sheet shows a large increase in current liabilities and a large decrease in current assets? Explain your answer.

6. The latest income statement prepared at Wilkes Company shows that net sales increased by 10 percent over the previous year and selling expenses increased by 25 percent. Do you think that management should investigate the reasons for the increase in selling expenses? Why or why not?

7. Why is it useful for management to compare a firm's financial statements with financial information from other companies in the same industry?

◄ Connection 2

Ethical DILEMMA   **Current or Long-Term?** The owner of the health and beauty aids store where you are employed has received a bank loan of $50,000 that requires her to maintain a current ratio of at least 1.3 to 1. On December 31 the business also owes $135,000 on a mortgage on the company's land and building. Of the $135,000, $15,000 falls due within the next 12 months. The current assets on December 31 are $125,000, and other current liabilities are $94,000. Sue, the owner, suggests that you include the entire $135,000 mortgage balance as long-term so that the bank loan covenant will be met ($125,000/$94,000 = 1.33 to 1). What will you do in response to this suggestion?

◄ Connection 3

Street**WISE:**   Questions from the Real World   **Financial Performance** Refer to The Home Depot, Inc. _1999 Annual Report_ in Appendix B.

1. Locate the consolidated statements of earnings. What gross profit was reported for the year ended January 30, 2000? For January 31,1999? If the company had targeted a 25 percent increase in gross profit between fiscal 1999 and fiscal 2000, was the goal achieved?

2. Using the financial statements, calculate the following measurements of financial performance and condition for The Home Depot, Inc. as of January 30, 2000.

a. Gross profit percentage

b. Current ratio

Connection 4 ►

FINANCIAL **S**TATEMENT
A N A L Y S I S   **Balance Sheet** The following excerpts were taken from the Mattel, Inc. *1999 Annual Report.*

Consolidated Balance Sheets		
	December 31	
(in thousands)	*1999*	*1998*
Assets		
Current Assets		
Cash and short-term investments	$ 275,024	$ 469,213
Accounts receivable, less allowances of $229.2 million at December 31, 1999, and $125.1 million at December 31, 1998	1,270,005	1,150,051
Inventories	544,296	644,270
Prepaid expenses and other current assets	330,702	371,772
Total current assets	2,420,027	2,635,306
Liabilities and Stockholders' Equity		
Current Liabilities		
Short-term borrowings	$ 369,549	$ 199,006
Current portion of long-term liabilities	3,173	33,666
Accounts payable	360,609	362,467
Accrued liabilities	825,874	748,837
Income taxes payable	258,319	299,058
Total current liabilities	1,817,524	1,643,034

Analyze:

1. What is the current ratio for 1999? For 1998?

2. Has the ratio improved from 1998 to 1999? Why or why not?

3. The company reported net sales of $5,514,950,000 and gross profit of $2,601,040,000 for the period ended December 31, 1999. What is the gross profit percentage for this period?

Analyze Online: On the Mattel, Inc. Web site **(www.mattel.com),** find the investor relations section. Locate the consolidated statements of operations and the consolidated balance sheets within the most recent annual report. Answer the following questions.

4. What is the current ratio?

5. What is the gross profit percentage?

6. Compare these calculations with your calculations for 1999. Based on these two measurements, do you think the company is in a better financial position than it was in 1999? Why or why not?

Extending **the** *Thought* **Annual Report** Once the year-end finan- ◄ **Connection 5**
cial statements have been prepared, companies often publish an annual
report, containing both financial and nonfinancial information about
the company's operation over the past fiscal year.

In addition to the financial statements for the period, the report frequently includes

- a letter to its shareholders,
- management's discussion and analysis of the company's performance,
- notes that accompany the financial statements.

Although there is no comprehensive list of items that should be disclosed
in an annual report, the accountants of the business must use their best
professional judgement when deciding what information to include.
What types of information do you think should be included in a company's annual report? Why?

Business Communication **Memo** You have been placed in charge of the ◄ **Connection 6**
closing process for Magnolia Tree Services for the period ending December
31. Time is short, and you must delegate the closing tasks to three accountants in your department: Brenda Calhoun, Sean Miele, and Cassandra
Wilson. Write an e-mail to your co-workers, assigning each of them specific tasks to complete by the end of the week. In the e-mail, list the
required closing tasks and identify which employee is responsible for each
task. Make sure that your co-workers understand the order of the tasks that
they are to perform.

TeamWork **Interpreting Financial Statements** Locate the Web ◄ **Connection 7**
site for a major corporation such as Sara Lee Corporation or McDonald's
Corporation. Then do the following:

- Locate the most recent annual report found in the company's investor
  relations section of the site.
- Review the balance sheet and statement of earnings for the corporation.
- Compute the gross profit percentage and the current ratio for the
  current year and the previous year.
- Write a report about the trends you discover based on these computations.

inter NET
CONNECTION **Credit Counseling** The National Foundation for Credit ◄ **Connection 8**
Counseling is a national nonprofit agency that provides counseling for
credit problems. Go to the organization's Web site at **www.nfcc.org.** How
often do they recommend checking your credit report? Under what circumstances are you able to obtain a free report?

Answers to Section 1 Self Review

1. Statements on which the revenues, expenses, assets, and liabilities are divided into groups of similar accounts with a subtotal given for each group.
2. To show the results of operations for a specific period of time.
3. The difference between the net sales and the cost of goods sold.
4. **a.** Equipment
5. **c.** Cost of Goods Sold section of the income statement.
6. Net delivered cost of purchases are understated. Operating expenses are overstated. The net income from operations is unchanged.

Answers to Section 2 Self Review

1. To complete the financial records for the accounting period.
2. To show how the adjustments were determined.
3. **a.** Debit the revenue accounts and other temporary accounts with credit balances. Credit **Income Summary** for the total.
   b. Debit the **Income Summary** account for the total of the balances of the expense accounts and other temporary accounts with debit balances. Credit each account balance listed.
   c. Transfer the balance of the **Income Summary** account to the owner's capital account.
   d. Transfer the balance of the owner's drawing account to the owner's capital account.
4. **b.** an accrued expense that involves future cash payments.
5. **d.** current assets divided by current liabilities.
6. If the accountant correctly allocates the payment between the payroll taxes expense account and the liability account, there will be no effect on financial statements in the current period.

   If the accountant records the entire payment in the payroll taxes expense account, payroll taxes expense will be overstated for the period, net income will be understated, and payroll tax liabilities will be overstated.

Answers to Comprehensive Self Review

1. Single-step: all revenues are listed in one section and all expenses in another section. Multiple step: various sections in which subtotals and totals are computed before the net income is presented.
2. Deduct the total of the operating expenses from the gross profit on sales.
3. Long-term asset, classified as plant and equipment.
4. **b.** revenue accounts
   c. owner's drawing account
   e. Income Summary account
   f. expense accounts
   h. cost of goods sold accounts
5. **a.** Debit **Income Summary** and credit **Harold Hicks, Capital** for $62,000.
   b. Debit **Harold Hicks, Capital** and credit **Income Summary** for $28,000.

MINI-PRACTICE SET 2

Merchandising Business Accounting Cycle

Best for Less

Best for Less is a retail merchandising business that sells brand-name cloth-ing at discount prices. The firm is owned and managed by Peg Rezak, who started the business on May 1, 2004. This project will give you an opportu-nity to put your knowledge of accounting into practice as you handle the accounting work of Best for Less during the month of October 2004.

INTRODUCTION

Best for Less has a monthly accounting period. The firm's chart of accounts is shown on page 516. The journals used to record transactions are the sales journal, purchases journal, cash receipts journal, cash payments journal, and general journal. Postings are made from the journals to the accounts receivable ledger, accounts payable ledger, and general ledger. The employees are paid at the end of the month. A computerized payroll service prepares all payroll records and checks.

INSTRUCTIONS

1. Open the general ledger accounts and enter the balances for October 1, 2004. Obtain the necessary figures from the postclosing trial balance prepared on September 30, 2004, which is shown on page 520. (If you are using the *Study Guide & Working Papers*, you will find that the gen-eral ledger accounts are already open.)

2. Open the subsidiary ledger accounts and enter the balances for October 1, 2004. Obtain the necessary figures from the schedule of accounts payable and schedule of accounts receivable prepared on September 30, 2004, which appear on page 520. (If you are using the *Study Guide & Working Papers*, you will find that the subsidiary ledger accounts are already open.)

3. Analyze the transactions for October and record each transaction in the proper journal. (Use 10 as the number for the first page of each special journal and 16 as the number for the first page of the general journal.)

4. Post the individual entries that involve customer and creditor accounts from the journals to the subsidiary ledgers on a daily basis. Post the individual entries that appear in the general journal and in the Other Accounts sections of the cash receipts and cash payments journals to the general ledger on a daily basis.

5. Total, prove, and rule the special journals as of October 31, 2004.

6. Post the column totals from the special journals to the general ledger accounts.

Best for Less
Chart of Accounts

Assets
101 Cash
111 Accounts Receivable
112 Allowance for Doubtful Accounts
121 Merchandise Inventory
131 Supplies
133 Prepaid Insurance
135 Prepaid Advertising
141 Equipment
142 Accumulated Depreciation—
Equipment

Liabilities
203 Accounts Payable
221 Social Security Tax Payable
222 Medicare Tax Payable
223 Employee Income Tax Payable
225 Federal Unemployment Tax
Payable
227 State Unemployment Tax Payable
229 Salaries Payable
231 Sales Tax Payable

Owner's Equity
301 Peg Rezak, Capital
302 Peg Rezak, Drawing
399 Income Summary

Revenue
401 Sales
402 Sales Returns and Allowances

Cost of Goods Sold
501 Purchases
502 Freight In
503 Purchases Returns and
Allowances
504 Purchases Discounts

Expenses
611 Advertising Expense
614 Depreciation Expense—
Equipment
617 Insurance Expense
620 Uncollectible Accounts Expense
623 Payroll Processing Expense
626 Payroll Taxes Expense
629 Rent Expense
632 Salaries Expense
635 Supplies Expense
638 Telephone Expense
644 Utilities Expense

7. Check the accuracy of the subsidiary ledgers by preparing a schedule of accounts receivable and a schedule of accounts payable as of October 31, 2004. Compare the totals with the balances of the **Accounts Receivable** account and the **Accounts Payable** account in the general ledger.

8. Check the accuracy of the general ledger by preparing a trial balance in the first two columns of a 10-column worksheet. Make sure that the total debits and the total credits are equal.

9. Complete the Adjustments section of the worksheet. Use the following data. Identify each adjustment with the appropriate letter.

   a. During October the firm had net credit sales of $9,240. From experience with similar businesses, the previous accountant had estimated that 0.8 percent of the firm's net credit sales would result in uncollectible accounts. Record an adjustment for the expected loss from uncollectible accounts for the month of October.

b. On October 31 an inventory of the supplies showed that items costing $2,840 were on hand. Record an adjustment for the supplies used in October.

c. On September 30, 2004, the firm purchased a one-year insurance policy for $8,100. Record an adjustment for the expired insurance for October.

d. On October 1 the firm signed a four-month advertising contract for $2,800 with a local radio station and paid the full amount in advance. Record an adjustment for the expired advertising for October.

e. On May 1, 2004, the firm purchased equipment for $83,000. The equipment was estimated to have a useful life of five years and a salvage value of $8,600. Record an adjustment for depreciation on the equipment for October.

f.–g. Based on a physical count, ending merchandise inventory was determined to be $80,200.

10. Complete the Adjusted Trial Balance section of the worksheet.

11. Determine the net income or net loss for October and complete the worksheet.

12. Prepare a classified income statement for the month ended October 31, 2004. (The firm does not divide its operating expenses into selling and administrative expenses.)

13. Prepare a statement of owner's equity for the month ended October 31, 2004.

14. Prepare a classified balance sheet as of October 31, 2004.

15. Journalize and post the adjusting entries using general journal page 17.

16. Prepare and post the closing entries using general journal page 18.

17. Prepare a postclosing trial balance.

DATE		TRANSACTIONS
Oct.	1	Issued Check 601 for $3,200 to pay the monthly rent.
	1	Signed a four-month radio advertising contract for $2,800; issued Check 602 to pay the full amount in advance.
	2	Received $470 from Carol Damus, a credit customer, in payment of her account.
	2	Issued Check 603 for $17,820 to remit the sales tax owed for July through September to the state sales tax agency.
	2	Issued Check 604 for $6,701.24 to Able Fashions, a creditor, in payment of Invoice 9387 ($6,838.00), less a cash discount ($136.76).
	3	Sold merchandise on credit for $2,480 plus sales tax of $124 to Vince Ramos, Sales Slip 241.
		Continued

DATE		(cont.)	TRANSACTIONS
Oct.	4		Issued Check 605 for $1,000 to purchase supplies.
	4		Issued Check 606 for $8,547.56 to Young Togs, a creditor, in payment of Invoice 5671 ($8,722.00), less a cash discount ($174.44).
	5		Collected $1,220 on account from Sharon Scott, a credit customer.
	5		Accepted a return of merchandise from Vince Ramos. The merchandise was originally sold on Sales Slip 241, dated October 3; issued Credit Memorandum 18 for $630, which includes sales tax of $30.
	5		Issued Check 607 for $1,470 to Classic Styles Inc., a creditor, in payment of Invoice 3292 ($1,500), less a cash discount ($30).
	6		Had cash sales of $17,200 plus sales tax of $860 during October 1–6.
	8		Keith Larson, a credit customer, sent a check for $832 to pay the balance he owes.
	8		Issued Check 608 for $1,884 to deposit social security tax ($702), Medicare tax ($162), and federal income tax withholding ($1,020) from the September payroll.
	9		Sold merchandise on credit for $1,840 plus sales tax of $92 to Diane Nichols, Sales Slip 242.
	10		Issued Check 609 for $2,000 to pay for a newspaper advertisement that appeared in October.
	11		Purchased merchandise for $4,820 from Able Fashions, Invoice 9422, dated October 8; the terms are 2/10, n/30.
	12		Issued Check 610 for $300 to pay freight charges to the trucking company that delivered merchandise from Able Fashions on September 27 and October 11.
	13		Had cash sales of $11,520 plus sales tax of $576 during October 8–13.
	15		Sold merchandise on credit for $1,940 plus sales tax of $97 to Keith Larson, Sales Slip 243.
	16		Made a purchase of discontinued merchandise; paid for it immediately with Check 611 for $4,600.
	16		Received $486 on account from Vince Ramos, a credit customer.
	16		Issued Check 612 for $4,723.60 to Able Fashions, a creditor, in payment of Invoice 9422 ($4,820.00), less a cash discount ($96.40).
			Continued

DATE	(cont.)	TRANSACTIONS
Oct.	18	Issued Check 613 for $6,000 to Peg Rezak as a withdrawal for personal use.
	20	Had cash sales of $12,800 plus sales tax of $640 during October 15–20.
	22	Issued Check 614 for $760 to pay the monthly electric bill.
	24	Sold merchandise on credit for $820 plus sales tax of $41 to Carol Damus, Sales Slip 244.
	25	Purchased merchandise for $3,120 from Classic Styles Inc., Invoice 3418, dated October 23; the terms are 2/10, n/30.
	26	Issued Check 615 for $480 to pay the monthly telephone bill.
	27	Had cash sales of $12,240 plus sales tax of $612 during October 22–27.
	29	Received Credit Memorandum 175 for $430 from Classic Styles Inc. for defective goods that were returned. The original purchase was made on Invoice 3418, dated October 23.
	29	Sold merchandise on credit for $2,760 plus sales tax of $138 to Sharon Scott, Sales Slip 245.
	29	Recorded the October payroll. The records prepared by the payroll service show the following totals: earnings, $10,800; social security, $702; Medicare, $162; income tax, $1,020; and net pay, $8,916.
	29	Recorded the employer's payroll taxes, which were calculated by the payroll service: social security, $702; Medicare, $162; federal unemployment tax, $118; and state unemployment tax, $584.
	30	Purchased merchandise for $2,300 from Young Togs, Invoice 5821, dated October 26; the terms are 1/10, n/30.
	31	Issued Check 616 for $8,916 to pay the October payroll.
	31	Issued Check 617 for $200 to pay the fee owed to the payroll service for processing the October payroll.
	31	Had cash sales of $1,440 plus sales tax of $72 for October 29–31.

Analyze: Compare the end-of-period accounting procedures of Best for Less to the end-of-period procedures for Carter Consulting Services in Chapters 2–6. How do the procedures for a merchandising business differ from the procedures for a service business? How are they similar?

Best for Less
Postclosing Trial Balance
September 30, 2004

ACCOUNT NAME	DEBIT	CREDIT
Cash	60 7 0 0 00	
Accounts Receivable	5 1 8 8 00	
Allowance for Doubtful Accounts		2 3 4 00
Merchandise Inventory	87 4 0 0 00	
Supplies	4 4 0 0 00	
Prepaid Insurance	8 1 0 0 00	
Equipment	83 0 0 0 00	
Accumulated Depreciation—Equipment		6 0 6 0 00
Accounts Payable		17 0 6 0 00
Social Security Tax Payable		7 0 2 00
Medicare Tax Payable		1 6 2 00
Employee Income Tax Payable		1 0 2 0 00
Federal Unemployment Tax Payable		5 1 2 00
State Unemployment Tax Payable		1 2 6 8 00
Sales Tax Payable		17 8 2 0 00
Peg Rezak, Capital		203 9 5 0 00
Totals	248 7 8 8 00	248 7 8 8 00

Best for Less
Schedule of Accounts Payable
September 30, 2004

Able Fashions	6 8 3 8 00
Classic Styles Inc.	1 5 0 0 00
Young Togs	8 7 2 2 00
Total	17 0 6 0 00

Best for Less
Schedule of Accounts Receivable
September 30, 2004

Jan Adams	8 2 0 00
Carol Damus	4 7 0 00
Keith Larson	8 3 2 00
Diane Nichols	2 2 4 00
Michael O'Mara	1 1 3 6 00
Vince Ramos	4 8 6 00
Sharon Scott	1 2 2 0 00
Total	5 1 8 8 00

PART 5

Accounting for Assets and Liabilities

CARNIVAL
CORPORATION

Carnival Corporation is known for its "Fun Ships" where passengers of all ages enjoy great food, games, movies, musical reviews, and lots of sunshine. As of 2000 the company operated 15 cruise ships. Six new ships are slated for delivery by 2004, bringing the total number of vessels in the fleet to 21.

Thinking Critically
Describe the methods Carnival might choose to fund the purchase of a cruise ship. What effect would these methods have on the accounting records of the business?

521

CHAPTER 14

Learning Objectives

1. Describe the process used to develop generally accepted accounting principles.

2. Identify, assess, and apply the assumptions that underlie current accounting principles and procedures and the modifying conventions that can alter their application.

3. Define the accounting terms new to this chapter.

Accounting Principles and Reporting Standards

New Terms

Conservatism

Consistency principle

Cost basis principle

Full disclosure principle

Going concern
assumption

Historical cost principle

Matching principle

Materiality

Objectivity assumption

Periodicity of income
assumption

Private sector

Public sector

Qualitative
characteristics

Realization principle

Recognition

Separate entity
assumption

Stable monetary unit
assumption

www.goodyear.com

*T*he Goodyear Tire & Rubber Company manufactures and markets tires, belts, hoses, and other rubber products. In early 2000 Goodyear released its *1999 Annual Report* containing financial statements, a letter to stockholders, operating highlights and goals, management's discussion and analysis of financial condition, and notes on standard accounting practices and procedures. The financial notes that accompany a company's financial statements describe significant accounting policies used in the preparation of the statements. Topics like revenue recognition, inventory pricing, property and plant costing, and accounts payable and accounts receivable are covered, helping users of financial reports understand how the statements were prepared. For example, Goodyear accounting practices dictate that revenues are recognized when finished goods are shipped to customers or services have been rendered.

Thinking Critically

If Goodyear changes the way it recognizes revenues, why do you think it would be important to include this information in its annual report?

For more information on Goodyear, go to:
collegeaccounting.glencoe.com.

Section Objective

1 Describe the process used to develop generally accepted accounting principles.

WHY IT'S IMPORTANT
Users of financial statements must have confidence in the accounting principles underlying the statements.

Terms to Learn

private sector
public sector

Generally Accepted Accounting Principles

In previous chapters you learned how to record business transactions and summarize them in financial statements. Financial statements are prepared using accounting rules and principles. In this chapter you will learn about these rules and principles.

The Need for Generally Accepted Accounting Principles

In order to ensure that they are meaningful and useful, financial statements are prepared using generally accepted accounting principles (GAAP). GAAP is used whether the business is a sole proprietorship managed by the owner or a large company such as Goodyear. GAAP allows the financial statements of different companies to be compared. It also allows a company to compare its own financial statements from period to period.

The Development of Generally Accepted Accounting Principles

1 Objective

Describe the process used to develop generally accepted accounting principles.

Accounting principles are developed in several ways in the United States. Sometimes an accounting procedure becomes widely used over time by professional accountants. The organizations responsible for developing accounting principles might recognize the procedure and include it in GAAP.

In other cases accounting standards result from a decision by the rule-making organization to adopt one alternative among several methods in practice. Sometimes the rule-making bodies develop standards based on logic or deductive reasoning because no clearly defined practices are being used to account for certain transactions or events.

In the United States, accounting principles are developed through a cooperative effort between the **private sector** (business) and the **public sector** (government). The Securities and Exchange Commission (SEC) represents the public sector, and the Financial Accounting Standards Board (FASB) represents the private sector.

The Securities and Exchange Commission

In 1934 the Congress of the United States established the Securities and Exchange Commission (SEC) to administer the Securities Act of

1933 and the Securities Exchange Act of 1934. Among its powers, the SEC has authority to define accounting terms and to prescribe accounting principles for companies under its jurisdiction. The SEC also determines the form and content of accounting reports that are required to be filed with the SEC. The SEC regulates the financial reporting of publicly held corporations (companies whose stock is traded in the securities exchanges and in over-the-counter markets). The SEC is a dominant force in accounting. Historically, however, the SEC has used its powers sparingly, preferring to let the accounting profession develop accounting principles and financial reporting standards.

The Financial Accounting Standards Board

For many years, accepted accounting principles were developed by committees within the American Institute of Certified Public Accountants (AICPA). However, many statement users and preparers felt that a broader representation was needed. In 1972 the AICPA, the American Accounting Association, the National Association of Accountants (now the Institute of Management Accountants), the Financial Executives Institute, and the Financial Analysts Federation jointly established the Financial Accounting Standards Board (FASB). The FASB is responsible for developing financial accounting standards and principles. By having so many groups involved, the organizers hoped that the FASB rulings would have wide support.

The FASB receives its funding from the Financial Accounting Foundation, whose trustees are chosen by the member organizations. These trustees are responsible for general oversight of the foundation and for securing financial support through contributions from the private sector. No governmental funds are used. The trustees select the seven members of the Financial Accounting Standards Board. The FASB members are full-time employees who generally have distinguished accounting backgrounds. They develop and issue accounting pronouncements.

The authoritative pronouncements of the FASB are known as *Statements of Financial Accounting Standards*. To date the FASB has issued about 140 Statements. The pronouncements of the FASB automatically become generally accepted accounting principles. The SEC recognizes these pronouncements as authoritative. The AICPA gives these statements additional support by requiring that its members make sure the companies being audited follow the accounting and reporting standards specified in the FASB statements.

In the 1970s the FASB started the "conceptual framework project." The goal is to provide a cohesive set of closely related objectives and concepts to use in developing accounting and reporting standards. The FASB has issued several *Statements of Financial Accounting Concepts*. The concepts covered in these Statements are as follows:

- Define the objectives of accounting.
- Identify users of financial reports and the uses made of these reports.
- Define the financial elements such as assets, liabilities, revenues, and expenses.
- Establish the form and content of financial statements.
- Develop measurement standards for income and other financial statement items.

To some extent, the conceptual framework project reflects the suggestion by many accountants that accounting principles should be arrived at *deductively*. This means that rules should be based on observations of the general needs and uses of financial accounting. The deductive process might use the following steps.

Step 1: Identify the users of financial reports.

Step 2: Describe how the financial reports are used.

Step 3: Determine the accounting information that best serves these uses.

Step 4: Define basic assumptions about the society in which business exists and about the nature of business activities and functions.

Step 5: Based on the assumptions, develop broad principles, standards, or guides for providing the information needed.

Step 6: Develop detailed rules and procedures for implementing the broad principles.

Other Organizations

Other organizations have also played an important role in developing accounting principles. The American Accounting Association (AAA) is one such group. About half of its members teach accounting. Many of them have written textbooks and articles dealing with accounting principles. Thus in a variety of ways the Association has been able to stimulate the acceptance of the principles it has developed and perfected over the years.

As early as 1900, the New York Stock Exchange (NYSE) required corporations listed on it to publish annual reports. Later, quarterly reports were required. In 1933 the Exchange insisted upon independent audits for all corporations that applied to have their securities (stocks and bonds) listed.

Federal and state regulatory agencies have prescribed detailed systems of accounting for public utilities, including the railroad and the electric power industries. These agencies are concerned with regulation more than with the development of accounting principles. As a result, the accounting and reporting requirements imposed on regulated industries frequently do not reflect GAAP.

Similarly, federal income tax requirements have had an impact on financial accounting. Businesses are not required to use the same financial accounting and tax accounting practices. However, some taxpayers adopt tax accounting rules to avoid keeping two sets of records. This is possible if the tax requirements do not conflict with authoritative financial accounting principles.

Recall that accounting principles vary from country to country. The lack of uniform accounting principles creates a challenge for users of financial statements.

The International Accounting Standards Board (IASB) was formed to develop accounting standards that can be adopted throughout the world. The organization has issued about 40 international accounting standards that provide a body of accounting principles. It is developing standards covering more complicated areas of accounting and specific industries. Many countries have adopted the IASB standards as their own accounting guides. The United States has been reluctant to adopt the international standards, but the SEC and the FASB are studying this issue.

Users and Uses of Financial Reports

The FASB has concluded that financial reporting rules should concentrate on providing information that is helpful to current and potential investors and creditors in order to make investment and credit decisions. The focus is not on providing information to management, tax authorities, or regulatory agencies because they have access to specific information from the firm's records not available to the public.

In its conceptual framework project, the FASB has also concluded that the information needed by investors and creditors should help them assess the likelihood of receiving a future cash flow, the amount of such a cash flow, and the time when the cash flow may be received. This conclusion is based on the idea that investors and creditors expect to receive a cash flow directly or indirectly from the business entity:

- *directly* from the distribution of the company's earnings,
- *indirectly* through the disposal of their interests for cash.

Thus, financial report users need information about

- profits,
- economic resources (assets),
- claims against the assets (liabilities and owner's equity),
- changes in assets and in the claims against assets.

Information about profits appears in the income statement. Information about assets, liabilities, and owner's equity is provided primarily by the balance sheet.

The statement of cash flows provides information about the cash received from major sources during the period and the uses made of that cash. The statement of cash flows is discussed in Chapter 25.

Certain analyses of the financial statements also supply meaningful information about the results of operations and the financial condition of a business. The analysis of financial statements is discussed in Chapters 23 and 24.

Section 1 — Self Review

Questions

1. How does an accounting principle originate?

2. Coffee-to-Go is a large privately held corporation. Is it required to file its financial statements with the SEC? Why or why not?

3. What are *Statements of Financial Accounting Standards?*

Exercises

4. The Financial Accounting Standards Board is
   a. a branch of the AICPA.
   b. a branch of the IRS.
   c. a branch of the American Accounting Association.
   d. an independent organization.

5. Which organization has the "final say" in prescribing accounting principles?
   a. IRS
   b. SEC
   c. FASB
   d. AICPA

Analysis

6. The financial statements for Premier Photo have an auditor's notation that the statements are "not in conformity with GAAP." What does this mean to you as an investor?

Section Objective

2 **Identify, assess, and apply the assumptions that underlie current accounting principles and procedures and the modifying conventions that can alter their application.**

WHY IT'S IMPORTANT
Reliable financial information depends on a common framework of assumptions and concepts.

Terms to Learn

conservatism
consistency principle
cost basis principle
full disclosure principle
going concern assumption
historical cost principle
matching principle
materiality
objectivity assumption
periodicity of income
   assumption
qualitative characteristics
realization principle
recognition
separate entity assumption
stable monetary unit
   assumption

2 **Objective**

Identify, assess, and apply the assumptions that underlie current accounting principles and procedures and the modifying conventions that can alter their application.

Understanding Accounting Principles

The rules of accounting that you are learning in this textbook are based on a number of concepts.

The Present Framework of Accounting Principles

Let's discuss accounting concepts by separating them into four categories: qualitative characteristics, underlying assumptions, general principles, and modifying conventions.

Qualitative Characteristics of Financial Reports

The FASB has concluded that the information given in financial statements should have several **qualitative characteristics**.

Qualitative Characteristics

Usefulness	Understandability
Relevance	Timeliness
Reliability	Comparability
Verifiability	Completeness
Neutrality	

Usefulness
The information should be useful to decision makers. Usefulness is a rather broad term and embraces most of the other qualitative characteristics.

Relevance
The information should be appropriate for and have a bearing on decisions to be made by the users.

Reliability
The information should be dependable, that is, free from error and also free from any bias on the part of the preparer.

Verifiability
If individuals outside the company review the financial information, they should arrive at the same conclusions as the preparers of the statements. Verifiability implies that supporting documents such as checks, invoices, and contracts are available for examination.

Neutrality
The information should not favor one group of users (management, owners, creditors, employees, etc.) over another group. The information should be prepared in such a way that it is helpful to all groups.

Understandability

The information should be presented in a clear and understandable manner. However, it is assumed that financial statement users have a basic knowledge of business and economics and that they will devote an appropriate amount of time to studying and analyzing the statements.

Timeliness

The information should be reported promptly so that it is useful in making decisions. "Old" information can be irrelevant.

Comparability

The information should be presented so that it can be compared with the financial statements of other businesses and with the firm's own statements from one period to the next.

Completeness

The information should present all items that would have a material impact on the decisions of users. The key word is "material" since financial statements cannot include every item of information about a company.

Underlying Assumptions

Accountants make several assumptions about the economy, business enterprises, and business activities when applying accounting principles.

Assumptions

Separate Entity
Going Concern
Stable Monetary Unit
Objectivity
Periodicity of Income

Separate Entity Assumption

Accounting records are kept for a particular business organization or activity. The **separate entity assumption** assumes that the business is separate from its owners. Transactions are recorded in relation to the business entity only.

It is easy to understand the separate entity assumption for a corporation such as Microsoft because Microsoft is legally separate from its owners. However, the separate entity concept applies equally to sole proprietorships and partnerships, even though the owners may be legally liable for all debts of the business and for actions carried out on behalf of the business.

Going Concern Assumption

When financial statements are prepared, it is assumed that the business is a **going concern**—that is, it will continue to operate indefinitely. This assumption permits businesses to record property and equipment as assets that will provide benefits in future periods.

Stable Monetary Unit Assumption

Accounting records are kept in terms of money, or a **stable monetary unit**. It is convenient for accountants to assume that the value of money is stable. It allows the costs of assets purchased many years ago to be added to the costs of recently purchased assets and a total dollar amount is reported on the financial statements.

About Accounting

IRS
In 1999 the IRS flunked an audit conducted by the General Accounting Office (the government's watchdog agency). The GAO reported that the IRS displayed "pervasive weaknesses" in several key areas, including financial management systems, accounting procedures, recordkeeping, and computer security controls.

However, the purchasing power of money is not stable; it changes substantially over the years. For this reason many people question the validity of the stable monetary unit assumption. In the past three decades, research committees of various accounting organizations have suggested that changing price levels should be reflected in the financial statements or in supplementary statements. In addition, the FASB and the SEC have suggested that certain companies disclose the impact that price-level changes would have on their financial statements.

Accountants continue to support the stable monetary unit assumption and are reluctant to recognize changes in the value of the dollar for the following reasons:

- Recorded costs are objective and verifiable and reflect actual transactions.
- Much analysis and many adjustments are required to record amounts in dollars of current purchasing power.
- Not all assets and liabilities are affected equally by changes in the purchasing power of the dollar. If all assets and liabilities were adjusted to reflect dollars of constant purchasing power, some of the amounts changed would result in new asset and liability amounts that reflect neither current values nor historical costs.

Objectivity Assumption

The financial statements should be **objective**—unbiased and fair to all parties. They should be based on verifiable evidence rather than on the opinions of the preparers or others. This means that two competent accountants who look at the same evidence should arrive at the same conclusion. However, objectivity and verifiability do not eliminate judgment. For example, accountants use judgment to estimate the useful lives of plant and equipment, select depreciation methods, and estimate salvage value to calculate depreciation expense.

Periodicity of Income Assumption

The income statement covers certain time periods. This concept is called the **periodicity of income**. In reality the final results of a business are known only when the business ceases to exist. When all assets are sold and all liabilities paid, the owners can determine whether they have a profit or loss. Because this does not provide any interim results, accountants have developed techniques, including the accrual basis of accounting, to prepare financial statements at regular intervals.

Although the fiscal year is generally perceived as the standard accounting period, the SEC and FASB require the same accounting rules be applied in measuring income for each quarter as for the year.

General Principles

Several basic accounting principles or concepts serve as guides to preparing financial statements.

International INSIGHTS

Chief Risk Officer

The volatile nature of operating in a global economy has caused some firms to create a new executive position—the chief risk officer. Other companies, including Microsoft, don't see a need for a chief risk officer because they believe that the CEO is already performing the job.

Principles

Cost Basis	Accrual
Realization	Consistency
Recognition	Full Disclosure
Matching	

Cost Basis Principle

Business transactions are, almost without exception, recorded on a **cost basis**, which is the amount of money determined through dealings in the market between the business and outsiders. Assets are carried at "historical cost" until they are used. **Historical cost** is the cost at the time the asset is acquired or the liability incurred. Historical cost is preferred to some possible alternatives because cost, when determined in an "arm's length" transaction (with independent outsiders) is an objective, verifiable measure of economic value.

Other cost bases are appraisal value, current cost, fair value, and present value of discounted cash flows. Following are examples of when a business may use a cost basis other than historical cost:

- Inventory is reported at the "lower of cost or market" when the inventory is worth less than it cost.
- Stocks and bonds to be sold in the near future are often reported at current market values.
- Fixed assets may, in some cases, be reported at their current value when their historical cost is higher than their current value.

Realization Principle and Recognition

One of the greatest challenges an accountant faces is the **recognition** of revenue; that is, determining the period in which to record revenue and report it on the income statement. Revenue represents the inflow of new assets resulting from the sale of goods or services. As a general rule, revenue is recognized in the accounts when a sale is made or a service is provided to an outsider. The **realization** of revenue occurs at the time new assets are created in the form of money or in claims against others (usually accounts receivable). The realization principle provides objective, verifiable evidence for the accounting records. Accounting principles state that revenue should be recognized (reported on the income statement) only in the period in which it has been earned and only if it has been realized.

However, the realization principle is the subject of much criticism. For example, if a company owns stock in another publicly traded corporation, some accountants believe an increase in the market value of the stock should be recognized as income. This violates the realization principle, which states gain should not be recognized until the stock is sold. Accountants who support the realization principle are concerned that the gain might be eliminated by a decrease in stock price before the stock is sold.

Historical Cost
Property, plant, and equipment assets are recorded at historical, or original, cost. Depreciation is recorded in a separate accumulated depreciation account.

> Appropriate recognition of revenue can be a controversial issue in the world of accounting. Penske Motorsports, owner of racetracks, was criticized in 1997 when it recognized revenue from the sale of lifetime licenses for stadium seats over only two years. Others in the stadium industry recognize revenue for lifetime licenses over the life of the stadium. Industry analysts felt that Penske had overstated income as a result of this practice.

There are some exceptions to the realization principle for reporting revenue. For example, contractors who build long-term projects often report income on a "percentage-of-completion" basis. If a bridge takes three years to complete, the contractor can recognize a portion of the estimated profit each year.

In contrast, some businesses, especially service firms operated by physicians, attorneys, and accountants, record revenue only when they receive cash, not when it is earned. This is because of high losses that occur on the outstanding bills owed by patients or clients.

Matching Principle

To properly measure income, revenue must be matched against the expired costs incurred in earning the revenue. This concept is called the **matching principle**. Many of the controversial questions in accounting involve determining when a cost should be charged as an expense. Accountants seek systematic, rational approaches for determining when to recognize revenue and which costs should be charged against the revenue.

There are numerous ways to match revenue and expenses:

- Office salaries do not clearly benefit future periods and are charged as expenses when they are incurred.
- Manufacturing costs identified with specific products are charged to cost of goods sold when the products are sold.
- The cost of a building is recorded as an asset. Depreciation expense is recognized over the period the building helps to earn revenue for the business.

> The Coca-Cola Company charges the costs to produce radio, television, and print advertising to expense accounts on the first day the advertisements appear. The company "matches" the production costs to the period in which the advertisements are likely to produce revenue.

Accrual Principle

Accruals help to properly measure a firm's profit or loss for the period and to reflect its liabilities and assets on the balance sheet. Accruals involve recognizing revenue or expenses in the period to which they apply, rather than some later period when the cash is received or paid. Examples of accruals are for wages earned in one period and paid in the next and for rent received in one period and earned in the next.

Consistency Principle

The **consistency principle** requires that the business apply an accounting principle the same way from one period to the next. Lack of consistency means that financial reports cannot be compared across accounting periods.

It is possible to make changes in accounting principles or methods if the change provides a fairer presentation of earnings or financial position. However, businesses are not allowed to switch accounting principles frequently. If a change is made, the accounting principle or method is binding unless it can be shown that another method is superior.

Full Disclosure Principle

The **full disclosure principle** requires that all information that might affect the user's interpretation of the profitability and financial position of a business must be disclosed in the financial statements or in the footnotes to the statements. The SEC has long maintained that the key element of financial reporting is full disclosure of all facts that might materially impact the users' interpretations of the statements. In recent years there

Recall

Adjustments
End-of-period adjustments are made to record income and expenses in the appropriate accounting period. The goal of adjustments is to match revenue and expenses.

Important!

Auditor's Letter
The auditor's letter states that the auditor has reviewed the financial statements and, unless otherwise stated, attests that the statements are in conformity with generally accepted accounting principles.

Accounting

Education and Training

Industry Overview

The education and training of adults and children occurs in a variety of environments—universities, corporations, museums, and public and private schools. Teachers alone held approximately 3.4 million jobs in 1999. Training specialists conduct corporate training programs, guide employees into life enrichment activities, and introduce individuals to new technologies.

Career Opportunities
- Corporate Trainer
- Public School Budget Administrator
- Accounting Instructor
- Instructional Media Specialist
- Museum Curator
- Student Financial Aid Coordinator

Preparing for an Education and Training Career
- Join the National Education Association (NEA) Student Program.
- Research your career area of interest and volunteer in public educational outreach programs, tours, lectures, or classes.
- Obtain a bachelor's degree and state teaching credential for a career as a teacher. Achieve National Board Certification from the NEA.
- Develop proficiencies in budget creation and administration for educational institutions.
- Develop proficiency with computer software such as spreadsheet and database applications for teaching tools, lesson plans, and archival of student records.
- Complete coursework in human resources, business, technical, or liberal arts subjects for a career in corporate training.
- Sharpen communication and motivational skills for a successful career as a trainer.

Thinking Critically
What personal attributes do you think are most essential for those in the teaching or training career field? Explain your answer.

Internet Application
Use the Web site of an organization such as Education World to research technology issues faced in the classroom today. Select one article and write a one-page report on the topic.

have been numerous lawsuits charging that the financial statements did not disclose facts that would have influenced investor decisions. As a result, accountants are careful to include sufficient information so that the informed reader can obtain a complete understanding of the financial position of the business.

Modifying Conventions

The accounting principles and underlying assumptions provide a framework for analyzing business transactions. However, a number of practical considerations are accepted as limiting or modifying the application of the general principles. The most important modifying conventions are materiality, conservatism, and industry practice.

Modifying Conventions
Materiality
Conservatism
Industry Practice

Managerial
IMPLICATIONS

Financial Statements

- Management relies on the information in financial statements to make decisions.

- Management needs to understand the underlying principles used to prepare financial statements.

- Managers of large businesses compare their financial statements with those of their competitors. The universal application of accounting assumptions, principles, and modifying conventions allows financial statements to be compared.

- Proper accounting using generally accepted accounting principles can help prevent lawsuits by financial statement users.

- Full disclosure of pertinent information in financial statements and accompanying footnotes can reduce the possibility of lawsuits.

Thinking Critically

What are some income statement and balance sheet items that could mislead investors?

Cash Short or Over
Each business establishes standards to determine what amount of cash short or over is considered "material" and should be investigated.

Materiality

Materiality is the significance of an item in relation to a particular situation. The accounting treatment depends on whether or not the item is considered material. Suppose that a small business purchases a $200 piece of equipment that will last three years. Because $200 is material to a small business, the equipment is recorded as an asset and depreciated over its useful life. In contrast, Intel might charge the equipment to expense because $200 is immaterial to a large corporation.

There are no hard-and-fast rules for judging materiality. Some methods include comparing the cost of the item to net income or to owner's equity.

Conservatism

Accountants have long followed a doctrine of **conservatism**. If alternative presentations are allowed under GAAP, revenue and assets should be understated rather than overstated. Similarly, expenses and liabilities should be overstated rather than understated, if any question exists. Recognition of income is deferred until it is realized, and losses and expenses are recognized as soon as they occur.

Some accountants feel that valuation and timing may be more important than conservatism. They believe that aggressive conservatism today can result in a lack of conservatism in the future. For example, charging excess depreciation today will conservatively state expenses and the book value of the asset. However, in future years, depreciation expense will be understated and net income will be overstated.

Industry Practice

Sometimes accounting practices have become acceptable in certain industries although not acceptable in other industries. These exceptions occur because of tax laws, regulatory requirements, the high risk involved, or the absence of clearly defined standards.

Sometimes industry-specific rules evolve into generally accepted accounting principles. For many decades in the public utility industry, interest incurred on money borrowed to build a power plant was treated as a cost of the plant, just like the cost of cement and steel. The interest was included in the cost of the plant asset, rather than charged to an interest expense account. Now this accounting practice is required by the FASB for all construction projects regardless of the industry.

In December 1999 the Securities and Exchange Commission began careful scrutiny of the aggressive accounting practices of many dot-com firms. New guidelines were released to ensure that revenue is not inflated. The SEC required some companies to restate financial results. For example, MicroStrategy Inc. was required to prepare new financial statements. The reported $12.8 million profit was restated to an estimated loss of between $33.6 million and $39.9 million. Prior to restatement the company had recognized contract revenue before the work was completed.

The Impact of Generally Accepted Accounting Principles

This book contains many references to accounting principles, assumptions, and modifying conventions. Being familiar with these concepts will help you to understand how individual transactions are accounted for and why they are handled in a specific way. Often businesses encounter new or unusual transactions that give rise to accounting questions that do not appear to have simple solutions. Almost invariably, the solutions to these questions will fall back on the concepts discussed in this chapter. Thus, an understanding of these concepts is essential to an understanding of complex accounting issues.

 **Section 2 Self Review**

Questions

1. What is the stable monetary unit assumption? What is the weakness of this assumption?

2. Why is historical cost used to record long-term assets?

3. According to the consistency principle, when is a change in an accounting method allowed?

Exercises

4. Recording land at its cost rather than its appraisal value illustrates the
   a. full disclosure principle.
   b. cost basis principle.
   c. realization principle.
   d. conservatism principle.

5. Depreciating equipment over its useful life is an example of the
   a. objectivity assumption.
   b. matching principle.
   c. realization principle.
   d. periodicity of income assumption.

Analysis

6. The **Accounts Receivable** control account balance is $2,000,000 and the schedule of accounts receivable has a total of $2,000,700. Is this difference material? Why or why not?

Review and Applications

Review

Chapter Summary

The increasing interest of a large and diverse group—government, owners, analysts, creditors, and economists—in financial reports ensures continuing progress in the search for accounting principles that will make the reports more meaningful and reliable. In this chapter, you have learned how generally accepted accounting principles (GAAP) are developed.

Learning Objectives

1 **Describe the process used to develop generally accepted accounting principles.**

In the United States, generally accepted accounting principles are developed cooperatively by the public and private sectors.

- The Securities and Exchange Commission (SEC) is the agency responsible for the reporting standards of publicly held corporations. Historically, the SEC has preferred to let the private sector develop accounting principles and accounting reporting standards.

- The Financial Accounting Standards Board (FASB), a private-sector group, has been assigned the specific task of developing accounting principles and financial reporting standards. The FASB's *Statements of Financial Accounting Standards* automatically become generally accepted accounting principles.

- Other organizations have also played an important role in developing and supporting generally accepted accounting principles:
  - American Institute of Certified Public Accountants (AICPA)
  - American Accounting Association (AAA)
  - New York Stock Exchange (NYSE)
  - Federal and state regulatory agencies
  - Federal income tax requirements
  - International Accounting Standards Board (IASB)

2 **Identify, assess, and apply the assumptions that underlie current accounting principles and procedures and the modifying conventions that can alter their application.**

- Information given in financial statements should have several qualitative characteristics:
  - *usefulness*
  - *relevance*
  - *reliability*
  - *verifiability*
  - *neutrality*
  - *understandability*
  - *timeliness*
  - *comparability*
  - *completeness*

- Important ideas or principles underlie accounting:
  - *cost basis principle*
  - *recognition*
  - *realization principle*
  - *matching principle*
  - *accrual principle*
  - *consistency principle*
  - *full disclosure principle*

- Certain assumptions influence accounting:
  - *separate entity assumption*
  - *going concern assumption*
  - *stable monetary unit assumption*
  - *objectivity assumption*
  - *periodicity of income assumption*

- Modifying conventions limit, or modify, accounting principles:
  - *materiality*
  - *conservatism*
  - *industry practice*

3 **Define the accounting terms new to this chapter.**

CHAPTER 14 GLOSSARY

Conservatism (p. 534) The concept that revenue and assets should be understated rather than overstated if GAAP allows alternatives. Similarly, expenses and liabilities should be overstated rather than understated.

Consistency principle (p. 532) The concept that requires a business to apply an accounting principle the same way from one period to the next

Cost basis principle (p. 531) The principle that requires assets to be recorded at their cost at the time they are acquired

Full disclosure principle (p. 532) The requirement that all information that might affect the user's interpretation of the profitability and financial position of a business be disclosed in the financial statements or in footnotes to the statements

Going concern assumption (p. 529) The assumption that a firm will continue to operate indefinitely

Historical cost principle (p. 531) See Cost basis principle

Matching principle (p. 532) The concept that revenue and the costs incurred in earning the revenue should be matched in the appropriate accounting periods

Materiality (p. 534) The significance of an item in relation to a particular situation or set of facts

Objectivity assumption (p. 530) The idea that financial reports are unbiased and fair to all parties

Periodicity of income assumption (p. 530) The concept that income should be reported in certain time periods

Private sector (p. 524) The business sector, which is represented in developing accounting principles by the Financial Accounting Standards Board (FASB)

Public sector (p. 524) The government sector, which is represented in developing accounting principles by the Securities and Exchange Commission (SEC)

Qualitative characteristics (p. 528) Traits necessary for credible financial statements: usefulness, relevance, reliability, verifiability, neutrality, understandability, timeliness, comparability, and completeness

Realization principle (p. 531) The concept that revenue occurs when goods or services, merchandise, or other assets are exchanged for cash or claims to cash

Recognition (p. 531) The determination of the period in which to record a business transaction

Separate entity assumption (p. 529) The concept that a business is separate from its owners

Stable monetary unit assumption (p. 529) The concept that accounting records are kept in terms of money and the assumption that the value of money is stable

Comprehensive Self Review

1. Explain the role of the U.S. Securities and Exchange Commission (SEC) in developing accounting principles.
2. Give two major reasons that the Standards issued by the FASB have a major influence on accounting in this country.
3. Under the conservatism convention, if any question exists, should revenue recognition be delayed or immediate? Likewise, should expense recognition be delayed or immediate?
4. Why is reliability important?
5. Explain the matching principle. How does the matching principle relate to the accrual principle?

(Answers to Comprehensive Self Review are on page 553.)

Discussion Questions

1. What are the two most important bodies or organizations involved in developing generally accepted accounting principles in the United States?
2. What is the major strength of, or argument for, the cost basis of accounting?
3. Name one alternative to the cost basis of accounting. Why is it not widely used?
4. Define realization. Why is the realization concept used?
5. What are the two tests that must be met in order for revenue to be recognized?
6. Explain the matching concept.
7. Why is the accrual basis generally used?
8. Explain the separate entity assumption.
9. What is the going concern assumption? Explain how this assumption is important to the cost basis of accounting.
10. What is meant by "full disclosure"?
11. How does the materiality convention affect day-to-day accounting?
12. What does periodicity of income mean?
13. What does the American Institute of Certified Public Accountants require of its members who conduct independent audits?
14. What is a potential problem of using the conservatism convention?

Applications

EXERCISES

Applying accounting principles and concepts.

◀ **Exercise 14-1**
Objective 2

For each of the following cases, respond to the question and indicate the accounting principle or concept that applies.

1. Taylor Company paid insurance premiums of $14,400 on December 1, 2004. These premiums covered a two-year period beginning on that date. What amount should the corporation show as insurance expense for the year 2004? What accounting principles, conventions, or assumptions support your answer?

2. Yucatan Construction Company signed a contract with a customer on October 1, 2005. The contract called for construction of a building to begin by December 31, 2005, and to be completed by December 31, 2007. The contract price was $4.8 million. Yucatan estimated that the building would cost $4.0 million. On October 15, 2005, the customer was required to make an advance payment of $480,000. No work was done on the project until January 2006. How much income from the project should Yucatan report in 2005? Why?

3. Rick Salazar buys and sells real estate. On December 31, 2004, his inventory of property included a tract of undeveloped land for which he had paid $600,000. The fair market value of the land was $1,200,000 at that date. How much income should Salazar report for 2004 in connection with this land? Why?

Applying accounting principles and concepts.

◀ **Exercise 14-2**
Objective 2

For each of the following cases, respond to the question asked and indicate the accounting principle or concept that applies.

1. Richards Company purchased many small tools during 2004 at a total cost of $4,200. Some tools were expected to last for a few weeks, some for several months, and some for several years. Richards' income for 2004 will be about $4 million. How should Richards account for the small tools in order to be theoretically correct? As a practical matter, how should Richards account for these tools? Why?

2. Fred Wu is the sole proprietor of Wu Video Store. Wu's accountant insists that he keep a detailed record of money and merchandise that he takes out of the business for his personal use. Why?

3. At the end of each fiscal period, the accountant for Midlothian Company requires that a careful inventory be made of the office supplies and that the amount on hand be reported as an asset and the amount used during the period be reported as an expense. Why?

Applying accounting principles and concepts.

◀ **Exercise 14-3**
Objective 2

For each of the following cases, respond to the question asked and indicate the accounting principle or concept that applies.

1. Three years ago Sienna Company purchased a machine for $440,000. The machine is expected to have no salvage value. Nevertheless, Sienna continues to keep the asset's cost in its accounting records and to depreciate the asset over its eight-year useful life, which will include the next five years. Is this correct or incorrect accounting? Why?

2. On January 14 of last year, Thornton Company purchased land for $200,000, on which it planned to construct an office building. At the end of the year, the land had increased in value to $255,000. Nevertheless, Thornton recognized no income as a result of the increase in value. Is this correct or incorrect accounting? Why?

3. Mitchell Company has decided to charge off as a loss a portion of its accounts receivable that it estimates will be uncollectible. The accounts involved resulted from the current year's sales. Is this correct or incorrect accounting? Why?

Exercise 14-4 ▶
Objective 2

Applying accounting principles and concepts.

For each of the following cases, respond to the question asked and indicate the accounting principle or concept that applies.

1. Lake Company charges off the cost of all Internet advertising in the year it is incurred even though the advertising probably results in some sales in later years. Why?

2. Pankuk Company's net income is about $2.5 million a year. Pankuk charges to expense all property insurance premiums when paid. Last year approximately $2,400 of these premiums represented amounts applicable to future years. Is this proper? Why or why not?

3. Delgado Corporation charges all of its research and development costs to expense when incurred. Why?

Exercise 14-5 ▶
Objective 2

Applying accounting principles and concepts.

Thom Company sells computer equipment. It grants all customers a 12-month warranty, agreeing to make necessary repairs within the following 12-month period free of charge. At the end of each year, the company estimates the total cost to be incurred during the next period under the warranties for equipment sold during the current period and charges that amount to expense, crediting a liability account. Is this appropriate accounting? Why or why not?

Exercise 14-6 ▶
Objective 2

Applying accounting principles and concepts.

At the end of last year, Wrenn Corporation was engaged in defending itself against several major lawsuits. The loss of any of these lawsuits will cause a major financial hardship for the corporation. The auditors insisted that the corporation include some discussion of the lawsuits in footnotes to its financial reports. Why?

Problems

PROBLEM SET A

Selected problems can be completed using:
☕ **Peachtree** 🔲 **QuickBooks** ▦ **Spreadsheets**

Problem 14-1A ▶
Objective 2

Applying accounting principles and concepts.

The accounting treatment or statement presentation of various items is discussed on the next page. The items pertain to unrelated businesses.

Indicate in each case whether the item has been handled in accordance with generally accepted accounting principles. If so, indicate the key basic concept that has been followed. If not, indicate which concept has been violated and tell how the item should have been recorded or presented.

1. At the beginning of 2005, Elmwood Company bought a building for $120,000. At the end of 2005, the building's value was appraised at $135,000. Since there was an increase in value, the company did not record depreciation on the building and also did not increase the $120,000 recorded in the building account at time of purchase.

2. Argo Company manufactured machinery for its own use at a cost of $45,000. The lowest bid from an outsider was $52,000. Nevertheless, the company recorded the machinery at $45,000.

3. On December 31, 2005, the balance sheet of Campus Sporting Goods Store reported prepaid insurance at $600, the cash value of the policy on the date when the statement was prepared. The prepaid insurance consists of the last year of a three-year fire insurance policy that originally cost $3,000 on January 1, 2004.

4. The assets listed in the accounting records of Rapid Cycle Company include a savings account of Peter Grimes, owner of the business. Grimes has established the savings account so that if he needs to invest more cash in Rapid Cycle Company, it will be readily available.

5. On December 31, 2005, an account receivable of $2,500 due from Lee Jones, who is in the county jail on charges of passing bad checks, is not included in the balance sheet. The owner of Decatur Company has written off the amount because he feels certain that the debt will not be paid, even though Jones insists that he will pay after he gets out of jail and finds a job.

6. The equipment of Whole Foods Manufacturing Company has a book value (cost less accumulated depreciation) of $60,000. However, the equipment could not be sold for more than $25,000 today. The company's owner thinks that the machinery should nevertheless be reported on the balance sheet at $60,000 because the equipment is being used regularly in the business, and it is expected to be used for the next five years—the remaining useful life that is being used for depreciation purposes.

Analyze: If Elmwood Company uses the accounting treatment described in Item 1, is net income overstated or understated for 2005?

Reconstructing an income statement to reflect proper accounting principles.

◄ **Problem 14-2A**
Objective 2

SPREADSHEET

The income statement shown on page 542 was sent by Steve Saliba, owner of Saliba Stereo Center, to several of his creditors who had asked for financial statements. The business is a sole proprietorship that sells audio and other electronic equipment. An accountant for one of the creditors looked over the income statement and reported that it did not conform to generally accepted accounting principles.

Prepare an income statement in accordance with generally accepted accounting principles.

Saliba Stereo Center
Income Statement
December 31, 20--

Cash Collected from Customers		$940,000
Cost of Goods Sold		
Merchandise Inventory, Jan. 1	$120,000	
Payments to Suppliers	580,000	
	$700,000	
Less Merchandise Inventory, Dec. 31	110,000	
Cost of Goods Sold		590,000
Gross Profit on Sales		$350,000
Operating Expenses		
Salaries of Employees	$108,000	
Salary of Owner	36,000	
Office Expense	36,000	
Depreciation Expense	35,000	
Income Tax of Owner	24,400	
Payroll Taxes Expense	13,600	
Advertising and Other Selling Expenses	34,000	
Repairs Expense	18,000	
Insurance Expense	6,000	
Interest Expense	12,000	
Utility and Telephone Expense	16,000	
Legal and Audit Expense	4,000	
Miscellaneous Expense	32,000	
Total Expenses		$375,000
Net Income from Operations		(25,000)
Increase in Appraised Value of Land during Year		20,000
Net Loss		$ (5,000)

The following additional information was made available by Saliba.

a. On January 1, 20--, accounts receivable from customers totaled $44,000. On December 31, 20--, the receivables totaled $36,000.

b. No effort has been made to charge off worthless accounts. An analysis shows that $1,800 of the accounts receivable on December 31, 20--, will never be collected.

c. The beginning and ending merchandise inventories were valued at their estimated selling price. The cost of the ending inventory is estimated to be $66,000, and the cost of the beginning inventory is estimated at $60,000.

d. On January 1, 20--, suppliers of merchandise were owed $52,000, while on December 31, 20--, these debts were $58,000.

e. The owner paid himself a salary of $3,000 per month from the funds of the business and charged this amount to an account called **Salary of Owner.**

f. The owner also withdrew cash from the firm's bank account to pay himself $10,000 interest on his capital investment. This amount was charged to **Interest Expense.**

g. A check for $24,400 to cover the owner's personal income tax for the previous year was issued from the firm's bank account. This was charged to **Income Tax of Owner.**

h. Depreciation on assets was computed at 10 percent of the gross profit. An analysis of assets showed that the original cost of the equipment and fixtures was $80,000. Their estimated useful life is 10 years with no salvage value. The building cost $150,000. Its useful life is expected to be 25 years with no salvage value.

i. Included in **Repairs Expense** was a $9,000 payment on December 22 for a new parking lot.

j. The increase in land value was based on an appraisal by a qualified real estate appraiser.

Analyze: What is the gross profit percentage based on the income statement you prepared?

Reconstructing a balance sheet to reflect proper accounting principles.

Andre Rheault owns a clothing store. He recently approached the local bank for a loan to finance a planned expansion of his store. Rheault prepared and submitted the balance sheet shown below to one of the bank's loan officers in support of his loan application.

1. Identify any errors in the balance sheet, and explain why they should be considered errors.

2. Prepare a corrected balance sheet in accordance with generally accepted accounting principles.

◀ **Problem 14-3A**
Objective 2

INSTRUCTIONS

Rheault's Jeans 'n' Things Balance Sheet December 31, 20--	
Assets	
Cash	$ 14,000
Accounts Receivable	16,000
Inventory	72,000
Equipment (cost)	40,000
Personal Residence	240,000
Supplies	6,000
Family Auto	28,000
Total Assets	$416,000
Liabilities and Owner's Equity	
Accounts Payable	$ 16,000
Note Payable on Family Car	24,000
Mortgage on House	200,000
Andre Rheault, Capital	176,000
Total Liabilities and Owner's Equity	$416,000

The following additional information was made available by Rheault.

a. The inventory has an original cost of $68,000. It is listed on the balance sheet at what it would cost to purchase today.

b. The cash listed on the balance sheet includes $2,400 in Andre Rheault's personal account. The remainder of the cash is in the store's account.

c. The store recently purchased a delivery truck for $30,000, financed through a bank loan. The bank has legal title to the truck. To date, the store has paid $6,000 on the loan. Of the remaining $24,000 liability, $9,600 is current and the remainder long-term. Andre did not include the truck or the liability on the balance sheet because neither he nor the business owns it.

d. Depreciation allowable to date is $8,000 on the equipment and $2,800 on the truck.

Analyze: If Rheault knew that $500 of accounts receivable was not collectible, what should be done to reflect this fact on the records of the business? On the balance sheet?

Problem 14-4A ►
Objective 2

Applying accounting principles and concepts.

For each of the unrelated situations below, identify the accounting principle or concept violated (if a violation exists), and explain the nature of the violation. If you believe that the treatment is in accordance with GAAP, state this as your position and defend it.

INSTRUCTIONS

1. Al Schmitz formed a new company in January 2004 and planned to pay himself a salary of $10,000 per month. Because the company was short of cash, Schmitz was paid only one-half of the annual salary during 2004. At December 31, 2004, the unpaid amount for 2004 (totaling $60,000) is expected to be paid on July 1, 2005. In its income statement for 2004, the company showed salary expense of $60,000. No mention was made in the balance sheet of the unpaid balance.

2. Penn Company does not have sufficient current assets to meet the requirements to obtain a much needed loan. Therefore, the company included among its current assets the personal savings account of its owner, William Penn, since the owner is willing to invest additional cash in the business if necessary.

3. Each year E–Supply Company has a large number of uncollectible accounts receivable from businesses engaging in "e-commerce." E–Supply charges off uncollectible accounts as they become uncollectible. On the average, this is about two years after the due date of the account.

4. A well-known Broadway play has sold out in advance for the next two years. These advance ticket sales were recognized as revenue at the time cash was received from the customers.

5. A company that offers investment services has been sued by clients for engaging in illegal securities transactions. If the lawsuit is resolved in favor of the plaintiffs, it will severely impair the company's chances of survival. No mention of this lawsuit is included in the company's financial statements on December 31, 20--, since the suit has not been settled and the company cannot objectively estimate the extent of its liability.

6. At the end of the current year, Shane Company owned land that had been purchased on January 1 for $75,000. On December 22, the company received an offer of $220,000 for the land. As a result, the company restated the land account to reflect market value.

Analyze: Based on your answer to item 6, what is the correct entry to record the purchase of land on January 1? To record the December 22 offer on the land?

PROBLEM SET B

Applying accounting principles and concepts.

The accounting treatment or statement presentation of various items is discussed below. The items pertain to unrelated businesses.

Indicate in each case whether the item has been handled in accordance with generally accepted accounting principles. If so, indicate which of the basic concepts has been followed. If not, indicate which concept has been violated and tell how the item should have been recorded or presented.

1. Included on the balance sheet of Better Reading Book Store is the personal automobile of Zeke Ankers, the owner.

2. Kowliski Manufacturing Company makes furniture. The cost of manufacturing a particular chair is $135. However, when the inventory amounts are computed for the balance sheet, the amount used for this chair is $219, the normal selling price.

3. On August 8, 2004, Pro Mining Company purchased some highly specialized, custom-made equipment for $900,000. Since the equipment is of no use to anyone else and has no resale value, it is shown on the December 31, 2004, balance sheet at $1. The equipment is projected to be used regularly in the business until the equipment wears out, approximately eight years from the date of its purchase.

4. On December 31, 2003, Cowlingshaw Corporation valued its inventory according to an acceptable accounting method. On December 31, 2004, the inventory was valued by a different but also acceptable method, and on December 31, 2005, the inventory was valued by the method that was used in 2003.

5. Each year Allen Company values its investments in land at the current market price.

6. In 2004 Showtime Corporation had sales of $16 million, all on credit. Statistics of the company for prior years show that losses from uncollectible accounts are equal to about 1 percent of sales each year. However, Showtime Corporation charges off a loss from uncollectible accounts only when a specific account is found to be uncollectible.

◄ **Problem 14-1B**
Objective 2

INSTRUCTIONS

Analyze: If the equipment described in item 3 is depreciated using the straight-line method and has a salvage value of $12,000, what amount should be charged to expense annually?

Problem 14-2B ►
Objective 2

SPREADSHEET

Reconstructing an income statement to reflect proper accounting principles.

The income statement shown below was prepared by Michelle Moore, owner of Moore's Sportswear Shoppe. The business is a sole proprietorship that sells sportswear. An accountant who looked at the income statement told Moore that the statement does not conform to generally accepted accounting principles.

INSTRUCTIONS

Prepare an income statement for Moore's Sportswear Shoppe in accordance with generally accepted accounting principles.

Moore's Sportswear Shoppe Income Statement Year Ended December 31, 20--		
Cash Receipts from Customers		$530,000
Cost of Goods Sold		
Merchandise Inventory, Jan. 1	$ 48,000	
Payments to Creditors	400,000	
	$448,000	
Less Merchandise Inventory, Dec. 31	60,000	
Cost of Goods Sold		388,000
Gross Profit on Sales		$142,000
Expenses		
Salaries Expense	$ 84,000	
Insurance Expense	2,800	
Payroll Taxes Expense	9,200	
Repairs Expense	2,000	
Supplies and Other Office Expenses	12,000	
Advertising and Other Selling Expenses	20,000	
Utilities Expense	4,000	
Interest Expense	6,000	
Total Expenses		140,000
Net Income from Operations		$ 2,000
Increase in Market Value of Store Equipment		6,400
Net Income for Year		$ 8,400

The following additional information was made available by Moore.

a. On January 1, 20--, accounts receivable from customers totaled $40,000. On December 31, 20--, receivables totaled $31,000.

b. On December 31, 20--, accounts receivable amounting to $1,600 were expected to be uncollectible.

c. On January 1, 20--, accounts payable owed to merchandise suppliers were $24,000. On December 31, 20--, the outstanding accounts payable were $42,000.

d. Included in **Salaries Expense** is $12,000 that Moore withdrew for her personal use.

e. Included in **Interest Expense** is $2,400 that Moore withdrew as interest on her capital investment.

f. Miscellaneous repairs of $1,000 were charged to **Store Equipment** during the year. No new equipment was purchased.

g. Moore explains that since the estimated value of her store equipment has increased by $6,400 during the year, no depreciation expense was recorded. The store equipment cost $66,000 and has an estimated useful life of 10 years with no salvage value.

Analyze: The entries required to correct situations a.–g. affected several permanent accounts for Moore's Sportswear Shoppe. List the permanent accounts affected.

Reconstructing a balance sheet to reflect proper accounting principles.

Clara's Hand-Made Linens is a retail shop owned by Clara Hopkins. She wants to expand her business and has submitted the following balance sheet to her bank as part of the business loan application.

◀ **Problem 14-3B**
Objective 2

INSTRUCTIONS

1. Identify any errors in the balance sheet and explain why they should be considered errors.

2. Prepare a corrected balance sheet in accordance with generally accepted accounting principles.

Clara's Hand-Made Linens Balance Sheet December 31, 20--	
Assets	
Cash	$ 26,000
Accounts Receivable	6,000
Inventory	48,000
Store Fixtures	28,000
Store Equipment	12,000
Personal Residence	260,000
Personal Automobile	36,000
Total Assets	$416,000
Liabilities and Owner's Equity	
Accounts Payable	$ 28,000
Note Payable on Personal Automobile	28,000
Mortgage Payable on Personal Residence	204,000
Clara Hopkins, Capital	156,000
Total Liabilities and Owner's Equity	$416,000

The following additional information is provided by Hopkins.

a. The inventory has an original cost of $40,000. Hopkins has valued it on the balance sheet at what it would cost today.

b. Hopkins has counted $12,000 in her personal savings account in the business cash account.

c. The store fixtures, shown at original cost, were purchased two years ago. No depreciation has been taken on them. Depreciation for the two years, based on their estimated life of 10 years, would be $5,600.

d. The store equipment cost $18,000. No depreciation has been computed on the equipment, but it has been written down to its estimated replacement cost by a charge to expense. Depreciation on the equipment's original cost for the 26 months since its purchase would be $3,250.

e. Both the personal residence and personal automobile are only occasionally used for business purposes.

Analyze: Based on the new balance sheet that you have prepared, what are the total assets for Clara's Hand-Made Linens?

Problem 14-4B ►
Objective 2

Applying accounting principles and concepts.

For each of the unrelated situations below, identify the accounting principle or concept violated (if a violation exists) and explain the nature of the violation. If you believe that the treatment is in accordance with GAAP, state this as your position and defend it.

INSTRUCTIONS

1. Osage Manufacturing Company follows the practice of charging the purchase of tools with a unit cost of less than $50 to an expense account rather than to an asset account. The average life of the tools is three years.

2. An auto rental company does not record depreciation on its fleet of autos because the company's excellent maintenance program keeps the autos in "as good as new" condition. Additionally, the autos are kept for only two years and are then sold and new autos purchased.

3. A real estate developer carries an unsold inventory of houses in its accounting records at estimated sales value rather than cost because the developer believes estimated sales value has more relevance than cost. The company rarely sells a house for less than its cost.

4. A lawsuit against a company is described in footnotes to the company's financial statements even though the lawsuit was filed with the court shortly after the company's balance sheet date.

5. Nelson Company sold for $500,000 land that was purchased 15 years ago for $150,000. Even though the general price level had doubled during this period, Nelson Company reported a gain of $350,000 on the sale of the land.

6. In recent years e-books.com has enjoyed increased profits due to customer loyalty because of its excellent reputation of putting the needs of the customer first. The company recently recorded an account called **Goodwill** in its assets to make its financial statements more reflective of its success in the industry and to reflect the true worth of the business. The offsetting credit was made to the owner's equity account.

Analyze: Review item 1. Describe the different effects to net income or loss for the company depending on whether the tools are charged to an asset account or to an expense account upon purchase.

CHAPTER 14   CHALLENGE PROBLEM

Applying GAAP

Assume that you are an independent CPA performing audits of financial statements. In the course of your work you encounter the following independent situations. Review each of the situations. If you consider the treatment to be in conformity with generally accepted accounting principles and concepts, explain why. If you do not, explain which principle or concept has been violated and how the situation should have been reported.

1. National Oil and Gas Company produces oil and gas from the ground. It drills wells to attempt to find the oil and gas and to produce any minerals found. On the average, about one out of six wells that the company drills produces oil and gas. Drilling costs range from $150,000 to $1,500,000 for each well. The company has adopted a rule that if the well results in finding oil and gas that can be produced profitably, the drilling costs will be recorded as an asset. If a dry hole results, the drilling costs are charged to expense.

2. Luxury Holiday Suites recognizes room rental revenue on the date that a reservation is made. For the summer season, many guests make reservations as far as a year in advance of their intended visit.

3. The Pleasure Shopping Department Store spends a large sum on advertising for various sales promotions during the year. The advertising includes "institutional" ads designed to bring in customers in future years. The owner is sure that the advertising will generate revenue in future periods, but she has no idea of how much revenue will be produced or over what period of time it will be earned. In the current year, $600,000 was paid for advertising, and all of this amount was charged as an expense in the current period.

4. Computer Technical Supply Company has constructed special-purpose equipment designed to manufacture other equipment that will be sold to computer chip manufacturers. Due to the special nature of this equipment, it has virtually no resale value to any other company. Therefore, Computer Technical Supply has charged the entire cost to construct the equipment, $120 million, to expense in the current period.

5. Prosper Company prepares financial statements four times each year. For convenience, these statements are prepared when business is slow and the accounting staff is less busy with other matters. Last year financial statements were prepared for the 3-month period ended March 31, the 5-month period ended May 31, the 10-month period ended October 31, and the 12-month period ended December 31.

6. In its national office, World-Wide Systems purchases at least 100 wastepaper baskets each year. These baskets cost approximately $8 each and have useful lives ranging from 3 to 10 years. They are depreciated over a period of 5 years, the estimated average life. One of the company's accountants has suggested that the costs of the baskets should be charged to expense at the time they are purchased.

Analyze: If item 2 were recorded as described, what possible implications would this have for stockholders in the company?

Judgment Call

Schnelling Products Distribution Center receives a number of different products in its warehouse. Schnelling distributes these products by truck to customers within a radius of 100 miles. The company is located near the Central City Airport, which is owned and operated by the city of Central City. Most of the products are received by rail or truck, but some are received by air.

The city and the local Chamber of Commerce have announced a joint undertaking to build a new divided highway to connect the airport with the interstate highway approximately three miles away. The Chamber of Commerce has undertaken an attempt to raise $2,500,000 as its contribution to the new highway's cost. The Chamber has asked the 10 largest enterprises in the city to make substantial contributions. Schnelling has been asked to contribute $300,000 of the total amount.

At a meeting of Schnelling's board of directors, the request has been considered. It was pointed out that although Schnelling is not located on the route of the proposed new road, the road's construction would speed up access of trucks to the warehouse and should substantially increase the value of Schnelling's property. It is difficult to measure the benefits of either of these factors. The company's president suggested that a major reason for making the contribution was to get good publicity and to improve the company's image in the community. "It is good advertising," he said.

The company's controller is asked how the contribution would be accounted for in the company's accounts. A major question is whether the $300,000 should be

- charged to expense when the contribution is made (thus reducing income of that period),
- capitalized as part of the cost of the land owned by the company in the area (increasing assets and not affecting income),
- recorded as an asset and charged to expense over a period of five years (thus increasing assets in the short run and spreading out the effects of the contribution on income).

What answer would you give if you were the controller? In your answer, consider the principles, assumptions, and concepts that you have studied in this chapter.

Business Connections

MANAGERIAL FOCUS   Judgment and Objectivity   ◀ **Connection 1**

1. How can the element of personal judgment, which is involved in such matters as estimates of salvage value and useful life, be minimized to preserve the objectivity of an accounting system?

2. What arguments can be given that the historical cost framework should be abandoned?

3. In what situations would the going concern assumption *not* be useful to management?

4. A new manager of a retail company suggests that the company should prepare its income statement on the basis of cash receipts and cash expenditures (except for the acquisition of fixed assets, such as plant and equipment). He argues that managers, investors, creditors, and others are more interested in cash receipts and disbursements than in accrual-based accounting. Do you think he is correct? Explain.

Ethical DILEMMA   **Asset or Expense?** GAAP permits a petroleum   ◀ **Connection 2**
exploration and production company to record as assets all costs incurred in searching for petroleum reserves in the ground and the costs of producing the oil found. GAAP allows two methods for recording costs that do *not* lead directly to finding and developing reserves.

1. They can be recorded as assets, just like the searching costs that lead to reserves.

2. They can be recorded as expenses. This is the preferred method.

Clearly, if the first method is followed, the assets will be greater and the expenses less than if the second method is used because a large part of such expenditures do not lead to finding oil and gas.

     In the current year, Southcentral Oil Company spent $600,000 searching for oil reserves in the ground. Of that amount, $400,000 applied to efforts that clearly will not lead to finding reserves. The owner will use the first method, so all $600,000 incurred in the first year is carried as an asset at year-end. Do you think this is unethical? Why or why not?

StreetWISE:
Questions from the Real World   **Accounting Principles** Refer to the *1999 Annual*   ◀ **Connection 3**
Report for The Home Depot, Inc. in Appendix B.

1. Discuss the qualitative characteristics of comparability and understandability in relation to the financial statements presented. In your opinion, do the statements satisfy these two criteria required by the FASB for financial reporting?

2. "Notes to Consolidated Financial Statements" are published along with the financial statements of a fiscal period, offering detailed information on significant accounting policies and financial data. Review the consolidated balance sheets and excerpts from "Notes to Consolidated Financial Statements." How are the company's "Commitments and Contingencies" represented on the balance sheet? Describe the discussion found in Note 9 and the principle addressed by it.

Connection 4 ►

AVERY DENNISON

FINANCIAL $ TATEMENT
A N A L Y S I S **Notes to Financial Statements** The following excerpts were taken from the Avery Dennison *1999 Annual Report*. The Notes to Consolidated Financial Statements contain the following details regarding significant accounting policies.

> **Use of Estimates** Preparing financial statements in conformity with GAAP requires management to make estimates and assumptions for the reporting period as of the financial statement date. These estimates and assumptions affect the reported amounts of assets and liabilities, the disclosure of contingent liabilities, and the reported amounts of revenues and expenses. Actual results could differ from those estimates.

> **Revenue Recognition** Sales, provisions for estimated sales returns, and the cost of products sold are recorded at the time of shipment.

Analyze:

1. Name one type of estimate that might affect the company's assets. What type of estimate might affect the company's liabilities?

2. What accounting principle does the *Revenue Recognition* text above address?

Analyze Online: At Avery Dennison's Web site **(www.averydennison.com),** review the most recent annual report found within the *Investor Relations* section.

3. The Notes to Consolidated Financial Statements contain summaries of significant accounting policies. What categories or topics are presented?

4. Has the company's revenue recognition policy changed since 1999? If so, describe the change.

Connection 5 ►

Extending the Thought **The Big Four** The Big Four accounting firms perform many functions for their clients. In 2000 the Chairman of the Securities and Exchange Commission became concerned that a conflict of interest exists between the accountants' role as auditor and the role they sometimes play as consultant to the same business. Do you agree or disagree? Explain. What underlying accounting assumption could be compromised by this practice? If accountants perform inadequately as auditors, what implications exist for the investor?

Connection 6 ►

Business Communication **Memo** You are an accountant for a privately owned company. The owner believes that only publicly traded companies need to be audited and follow GAAP. The previous accountant kept the company's books according to income tax requirements. Write a one-page memo to the owner containing benefits of following GAAP.

Connection 7 ►

TeamWork **Presentation** As a group, prepare a brief presentation to explain the benefits of belonging to a professional accounting organization. Address how membership contributes to the effectiveness of a CPA. Include how participation in a professional organization might contribute to ongoing development of generally accepted accounting principles.

inter **NET**
CONNECTION **FTC** Visit **www.ftc.gov,** the Federal Trade Commission ◄ **Connection 8**
Web site. The FTC enforces various federal antitrust and consumer protec-
tion laws. What is the purpose of the Bureau of Consumer Protection?
What is the Bureau of Economics?

Answers to Self Reviews

Answers to Section 1 Self Review

1. When a procedure that is devised to solve a particular problem becomes widely used in the accounting profession or from a decision by a rule-making body.
2. No. Only public companies must file with the SEC.
3. Authoritative guidelines for financial accounting and reporting. The Statements are issued by the FASB.
4. **d.** an independent organization.
5. **b.** SEC
6. The statements did not follow generally accepted accounting principles and cannot be compared to similar statements that were prepared according to GAAP.

Answers to Section 2 Self Review

1. The concept that accounting records are kept in terms of money that does not fluctuate in value. Its weakness is that the purchasing power of money is not stable; it changes substantially over the years.
2. Historical cost (the cost of assets at the time they are purchased) is objective and verifiable.
3. Only if the change gives a fairer presentation of earnings or financial position.
4. **b.** cost basis principle.
5. **b.** matching principle.
6. The difference of $700 may not be considered material because the balance of the account is $2,000,000. If the balance of the account were $2,000, the $700 would be considered material.

Answers to Comprehensive Self Review

1. The SEC has the authority to prescribe accounting principles and financial reporting requirements for companies whose stock is traded in the stock exchanges and over-the-counter markets in this country. However, the SEC also has the authority to adopt accounting and reporting requirements developed by the FASB as generally accepted accounting principles and almost always accepts the FASB standards as authoritative.
2. The SEC has generally accepted the FASB standards as the accounting rules required of companies under the SEC's jurisdiction. In addition, the AICPA requires its members, who include almost all auditing firms in the nation, to follow the standards developed by the FASB in determining whether the companies audited have followed GAAP.
3. Revenue recognition should be delayed. Expense recognition should be immediate.
4. If the information in the report is not reliable, it cannot be used to make sound decisions.
5. The matching principle states that to properly measure income in an accounting period, the costs expired during the period must be matched against that period's revenue. It is necessary to accrue revenue that has been earned in that period but not yet been received in cash or billed to customers. Similarly, expenses that have been incurred but not yet paid for must be accrued so that revenues and expenses are properly matched.

CHAPTER 15

Learning Objectives

1. Record the losses from uncollectible accounts receivable using the direct charge-off and allowance methods.

2. Write off uncollectible accounts after estimated losses have been recorded.

3. Record the collection of accounts previously written off using the direct charge-off and allowance methods.

4. Properly classify accounts receivable on the financial statements.

5. Define the accounting terms new to this chapter.

Accounts Receivable and Uncollectible Accounts

New Terms

Aging the accounts receivable

Allowance method

Direct charge-off method

Net value of accounts receivable

Reinstate

Valuation account

Corporation

www.fedex.com

C ompanies who extend credit to their customers understand that there is a big difference between making a sale and collecting cash. Every day a company waits for payment of an account, that company loses opportunities for growth and investment.

For FedEx Corporation, converting accounts receivable into cash is paramount. For the fiscal year ended May 31, 2000, net accounts receivables of $2.547 billion were reported.

Most companies realize that 100% of their receivables will not be collected. An allowance, or estimate for uncollectibles, is then established. FedEx Corporation accountants deducted estimated uncollectible accounts of approximately $86 million from total accounts receivable of $2.633 billion to yield net receivables of $2.547 billion.

Thinking Critically
How do you think companies like FedEx estimate uncollectible accounts?

For more information on FedEx Corporation, go to:
collegeaccounting.glencoe.com.

Section Objective

1 Record the losses from uncollectible accounts receivable using the direct charge-off and allowance methods.

WHY IT'S IMPORTANT
In accordance with the conservatism convention, assets should not be overstated on the balance sheet. In accordance with the matching principle, bad debt losses are matched with the related sales revenue.

Terms to Learn

aging the accounts receivable
allowance method
direct charge-off method
valuation account

1 Objective
Record the losses from uncollectible accounts receivable using the direct charge-off and allowance methods.

Important!

Subsidiary Records
When an account is written off, both the **Accounts Receivable** control account and the individual account in the subsidiary ledger are credited.

Determining Losses from Uncollectible Accounts

Most businesses extend credit to their customers. There are always customers who do not pay their bills no matter how careful the business is in granting credit and collecting accounts. Losses from uncollectible accounts are a normal cost of doing business.

A firm that extends credit to a customer expects to collect the amount owed. If a customer does not pay the account when due, a loss has occurred. The firm may carry the account in its financial records until the account has definitely become uncollectible. At that time, the firm must remove the balance owed from the accounts receivable account.

In this chapter you will learn about losses from uncollectible accounts by studying Trilli's Office Supply, a retail office supply business. Victor Trilli is the owner. He purchased the business on January 1 from his former employer. Trilli's Office Supply offers charge accounts to customers who meet its credit standards.

There are two possible methods that Trilli's Office Supply can use to recognize losses from uncollectible accounts—the direct charge-off method and the allowance method.

The Direct Charge-Off Method

Tony Peterson was a customer of Trilli's Office Supply. He left town without paying his account balance of $380. Trilli tried various ways to find Peterson and collect the money from him, but was not successful. On January 5 of the following year, Peterson's account was written off.

In this example Trilli's Office Supply uses the **direct charge-off method**. It records uncollectible account losses as they occur. The debit is to the **Uncollectible Accounts Expense** account, which is sometimes called **Bad Debts Expense** or **Loss from Uncollectible Accounts.** The credit is to **Accounts Receivable** and to Peterson's account in the accounts receivable subsidiary ledger.

	GENERAL JOURNAL				PAGE 1	

	DATE		DESCRIPTION	POST. REF.	DEBIT	CREDIT	
1	20--						1
2	Jan.	5	Uncollectible Accounts Expense		380 00		2
3			Accounts Receivable/Tony Peterson			380 00	3
4			To write off an uncollectible account				4
5			using the direct charge-off method				5

There are several important points to understand about the direct charge-off method.

- It does not match revenue and expenses. Peterson purchased the supplies, and revenue was recognized, in the previous year. The bad debt expense, however, is recorded, in the current year.
- It can overstate accounts receivable. The **Accounts Receivable** balance represents all accounts to be collected. No estimate is made for the accounts that might be uncollectible in the future.
- It is the only method allowed for income tax purposes.

The Allowance Method

The allowance method is the preferred way to account for uncollectible accounts. The **allowance method** estimates losses from uncollectible accounts and charges them to expense in the period when the sales are recorded. This matches the estimated expense for uncollectible accounts to the period when the revenue is recognized. Under the allowance method, the amount of net accounts receivable reflects the amount that the business thinks will be collected.

The estimate for losses from uncollectible accounts is credited to a contra asset account called **Allowance for Doubtful Accounts.** This account is also known as **Allowance for Bad Debts.** The **Allowance for Doubtful Accounts** is called a **valuation account** because it revalues or reappraises the balance in light of reasonable expectations. **Allowance for Doubtful Accounts** appears on the balance sheet as a reduction of **Accounts Receivable.**

There are three ways to estimate the losses from uncollectible accounts:

- percentage of net credit sales
- aging the accounts receivable
- percentage of total accounts receivable

> At the end of 1999, Avis Group Holdings, Inc. reported accounts receivable of $1.120 billion for vehicle leasing, vehicle rentals, and damage claims. The **Allowance for Doubtful Accounts** was almost $8 million. Net accounts receivable was $1.112 billion.

Percentage of Net Credit Sales

One way to estimate the uncollectible accounts expense is to multiply the net credit sales by a percentage. The percentage is based on the company's previous experience with losses from uncollectible accounts. New businesses base the percentage on the experience of other businesses in the same industry. The percentage is calculated as follows:

$$\frac{\text{Losses from Uncollectible Accounts}}{\text{Net Credit Sales}}$$

Net credit sales is calculated as total credit sales minus the sales returns and allowances on credit sales.

Trilli's Office Supply estimates that four-tenths of one percent (0.004) of the net credit sales will be uncollectible. If net credit sales are $200,000, the estimated loss from uncollectible accounts is $800 (0.004 × $200,000).

Important!

Direct Charge-Off Method
The direct charge-off method is the only method allowable for income tax purposes.

Important!

Matching Principle
The allowance method of accounting for uncollectible accounts matches the uncollectible accounts expense to the period when the sales are recorded.

Uncollectible Accounts Adjustment

Income Statement

Expense	↑ 800
Net Income	↓ 800

Balance Sheet

Assets	↓ 800
Equity	↓ 800

The entry is an adjustment. It is entered on the worksheet and is later recorded in the general journal, along with other adjusting entries.

1	20--		*Adjusting Entries*					1
22	Dec.	31	Uncollectible Accounts Expense		8 0 0 00			22
23			Allowance for Doubtful Accounts			8 0 0 00		23
24			*To record estimated uncollectible*					24
25			*accounts based on 0.4 percent of*					25
26			*net credit sales of $200,000*					26

Aging the Accounts Receivable

Another way to estimate uncollectible accounts is a procedure called **aging the accounts receivable** . This procedure involves classifying accounts receivable according to how long they have been outstanding. The first step is to prepare an aging schedule. Figure 15-1 shows the aging schedule for Trilli's Office Supply. Each account is listed by name and balance. Each invoice is classified as current (within the credit period), 1–30 days past due, 31–60 days past due, or over 60 days past due. Notice that Martin Zellner owes $98. Of this amount, $38 is over 60 days past due and $60 is between 31 and 60 days past due.

FIGURE 15-1 ▶
Trilli's Office Supply
Aged Accounts
Receivable Schedule

TRILLI'S OFFICE SUPPLY					
Schedule of Accounts Receivable by Age					
December 31, 2004					
			Past Due—Days		
Customer	**Balance**	**Current**	**1–30**	**31–60**	**Over 60**
Aliguar, Piralto	100.00		100.00		
Aston, Thomas	120.00	100.00			20.00
Beard, Hal	80.00	80.00			
Zellner, Martin	98.00			60.00	38.00
Totals	18,400.00	16,000.00	1,400.00	600.00	400.00

Important!

Aging the Accounts Receivable
The aged accounts receivable schedule serves several purposes:

- It proves that the accounts receivable subsidiary ledger is equal to the accounts receivable control account.
- It identifies slow-paying customers.
- It is used to estimate the amount of accounts that will become uncollectible.

The longer an account is past due, the less likely it is to be collected. Following are uncollectible account estimates for each category.

Category	Percentage Uncollectible
Current accounts	3%
1–30 days past due	5%
31–60 days past due	10%
Over 60 days past due	40%

Based on these percentages, the estimated uncollectible accounts on December 31 total $770.

Current	0.03	× $16,000	=	$480
1–30 days past due	0.05	× $ 1,400	=	70
31–60 days past due	0.10	× $ 600	=	60
Over 60 days past due	0.40	× $ 400	=	160
Totals		$18,400		$770

Allowance for Doubtful Accounts is adjusted so that its ending balance is a $770 credit. On December 31 **Allowance for Doubtful Accounts** has a credit balance of $88. An adjustment for $682 ($770 − $88) will bring the account to the desired balance of $770.

Allowance for Doubtful Accounts

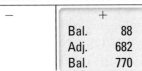

−	+	
	Bal.	88
	Adj.	682
	Bal.	770

The adjustment is recorded in the general journal as follows.

1	20--		Adjusting Entries					1
22	Dec.	31	Uncollectible Accounts Expense	682 00				22
23			Allowance for Doubtful Accounts		682 00			23
24			To adjust allowance account to $770,					24
25			based on aging of accounts receivable					25

Percentage of Total Accounts Receivable

Another way to estimate uncollectible accounts is to multiply the total amount of accounts receivable by a single percentage. The records of Trilli Office Supply show the following activity.

	Accounts Receivable	Uncollectible Accounts
12/31/01	$12,200	$ 620
12/31/02	13,800	660
12/31/03	15,900	814
Total	$41,900	$2,094
Average	$13,967	$ 698

The average loss over the three-year period is 5 percent.

$$\frac{\text{Average Uncollectible Accounts}}{\text{Average Accounts Receivable}} = \frac{\$698}{\$13,967} = 0.05 = 5 \text{ percent}$$

If the balance of **Accounts Receivable** is $18,400, estimated uncollectible accounts is $920 ($18,400 × 0.05). After the adjustment is posted, the ending balance of **Allowance for Doubtful Accounts** is $920.

If **Allowance for Doubtful Accounts** has a credit balance of $88, the adjustment for uncollectible accounts expense is $832 ($920 − $88).

Allowance for Doubtful Accounts

−	+	
	Bal.	88
	Adj.	832
	Bal.	920

1	20--		Adjusting Entries					1
22	Dec.	31	Uncollectible Accounts Expense	832 00				22
23			Allowance for Doubtful Accounts		832 00			23
24			To adjust allowance account to $920,					24
25			based on 5% of accounts receivable					25

International INSIGHTS

The World Bank

The World Bank is a development institution founded in 1944. It consists of five institutions including the International Finance Corporation and the International Development Association. The World Bank's dream is a world free of poverty.

Comparing the Methods

When the estimate of uncollectible accounts expense is based on the percentage of net credit sales, the focus is on the income statement.

- The emphasis is on the matching principle and the expense that appears on the income statement. The amount reported on the balance sheet—the net accounts receivable balance—is important but of less significance.
- The number calculated is used as the amount of the adjustment.

When the estimate of uncollectible accounts is based on the aging method or a percentage of total accounts receivable, the focus is on the balance sheet.

- The primary emphasis is on the valuation of accounts receivable—the amount that appears on the balance sheet. The expense reported on the income statement is important but of less significance.
- The number calculated is the ending balance of **Allowance for Doubtful Accounts.** The adjustment is the amount needed to bring **Allowance for Doubtful Accounts** to a credit balance for the amount calculated.

The normal balance of **Allowance for Doubtful Accounts** is a credit balance. However, it is possible for it to have a debit balance. If it does, make the adjustment so that the ending balance of **Allowance for Doubtful Accounts** is a credit balance for the amount calculated. Suppose that **Allowance for Doubtful Accounts** has a debit balance of $70 and the ending balance should be a credit of $920. The adjustment would be for $990 ($920 + $70).

Allowance for Doubtful Accounts

−		+	
Bal.	70		
		Adj.	990
		Bal.	920

Section 1 Self Review

Questions

1. Under the direct charge-off method, when a specific account is written off, what is the effect on net income and current assets?

2. Losses from uncollectible accounts are estimated to be 0.6 percent of net credit sales. Net credit sales are $500,000. **Allowance for Doubtful Accounts** has a credit balance of $300. What is the adjustment to recognize uncollectible accounts expense?

3. What is an aged accounts receivable schedule?

Exercises

4. Under the direct charge-off method, the entry to write off an uncollectible account includes a debit to
   a. **Allowance for Doubtful Accounts.**
   b. **Uncollectible Accounts Expense.**
   c. **Accounts Receivable.**
   d. **Accounts Receivable Expense.**

5. Before adjustments, **Accounts Receivable** is $100,000, and the **Allowance for Doubtful Accounts** has a $100 credit balance. It is estimated that 1 percent of accounts receivable will be uncollectible.

What amount is debited to **Uncollectible Accounts Expense?**
   a. $9,900
   b. $900
   c. $1,000
   d. $10,000

Analysis

6. Kumar Company started business 12 months ago. How can the owner estimate uncollectible accounts? If Kumar does not make an adjustment for uncollectible accounts, how will it affect the financial statements?

Accounting for Uncollectible Accounts

Under the allowance method, at the end of a period, the estimate for uncollectible accounts expense is recorded as a debit to **Uncollectible Accounts Expense** and a credit to **Allowance for Doubtful Accounts.** This entry reduces net income. **Accounts Receivable** is not affected because the business does not know which specific accounts will be uncollectible.

Recording Actual Uncollectible Accounts Under the Allowance Method

During the year when a particular account proves uncollectible, it is written off. The amount owed is debited to **Allowance for Doubtful Accounts.** The offsetting credit is to the **Accounts Receivable** control account and to the customer's account in the subsidiary ledger.

Note that when losses are provided for in advance, the write-off of a particular customer's account does not involve an entry to **Uncollectible Account Expense.** The expense has already been recorded by the adjustment for estimated uncollectible accounts made in the prior period, when the sale occurred. Consequently, net income is not affected when the particular account is written off.

Let's see how a specific account is written off under the allowance method. On February 8 Victor Trilli determined that the account of Martin Zellner for $98 was uncollectible.

			Adjusting Entries					
1	20--		Adjusting Entries					1
2	Feb.	8	Allowance for Doubtful Accounts		9 8 00			2
3			Accounts Receivable/Martin Zellner			9 8 00		3
4			To write off account of Martin Zellner,					4
5			determined to be uncollectible					5

Let's review how the write-off of a specific account under the allowance method affects net accounts receivable. Suppose that before the write-off, **Accounts Receivable** was $18,400 and **Allowance for Doubtful Accounts** was $800. Zellner's $98 account is written off. Net accounts receivable is $17,600 both before and after the write-off.

	Before	After
Accounts Receivable	$18,400	$18,302
Less Allowance for Doubtful Accounts	800	702
Net Accounts Receivable	$17,600	$17,600

Section Objectives

2 Write off uncollectible accounts after estimated losses have been recorded.

WHY IT'S IMPORTANT
The accounts receivable ledger should contain complete and accurate information so that future credit decisions are sound.

3 Record the collection of accounts previously written off using the direct charge-off and allowance methods.

WHY IT'S IMPORTANT
Customers' accounts should reflect actual payment histories.

4 Properly classify accounts receivable on the financial statements.

WHY IT'S IMPORTANT
Uncollectible accounts affect the earnings and assets of a business.

Terms to Learn

net value of accounts receivable
reinstate

2 Objective
Write off uncollectible accounts after estimated losses have been recorded.

Sometimes firms use professional collection agencies. In 1998 the American Collectors Association estimated that $170.4 billion in bad debt was placed for collection with professional debt collectors. Approximately $23.8 billion, almost 14 percent, was recovered.

Collecting an Account That Was Written Off

③ Objective

Record the collection of accounts previously written off using the direct charge-off and allowance methods.

Occasionally an account that was written off is later collected, in whole or in part. The method used to record this transaction depends on whether the business uses the direct charge-off or the allowance method.

The Direct Charge-Off Method

In section 1 Tony Peterson's account of $380 was written off under the direct charge-off method by a debit to **Uncollectible Accounts Expense** and a credit to **Accounts Receivable.** On January 2 of the following year, Trilli's Office Supply received $380 from Tony Peterson in full payment of his account. It takes two entries to record this transaction. The first entry is to **reinstate** the account receivable, which means to put back or restore the balance due from the customer.

The Bottom Line

Reinstating an Account Using the Direct Charge-Off Method

Income Statement

Expenses	↓ 380
Net Income	↑ 380

Balance Sheet

Assets	↑ 380
Equity	↑ 380

1	20--						1
2	Jan.	2	Accounts Receivable/Tony Peterson	3 8 0 00			2
3			Uncollectible Accounts Expense			3 8 0 00	3
4			To reinstate the account receivable				4
5			for Tony Peterson that was written				5
6			off and then collected in full				6

The second entry records the customer's payment in the cash receipts journal as a debit to **Cash** and a credit to **Accounts Receivable** and to the customer's account.

When the payment occurs in a period after the one in which the write-off was made, some accountants record the credit in an account called **Uncollectible Accounts Recovered** instead of **Uncollectible Accounts Expense.** The **Uncollectible Accounts Recovered** account appears on the income statement in the Other Income section.

The Allowance Method

Under the allowance method, when cash is received for an account that was previously written off, two entries are required to record the transaction. The first entry reinstates the account receivable, and the second entry records the receipt of cash. On February 8 the $98 owed by Martin Zellner was written off. On August 19 Zellner paid the $98.

The Bottom Line

Reinstating an Account Using the Allowance Method

Income Statement

No effect on net income

Balance Sheet

No effect on assets
No effect on equity

1	20--						1
20	Aug.	19	Accounts Receivable/Martin Zellner	9 8 00			20
21			Allowance for Doubtful Accounts			9 8 00	21
22			To reinstate the account receivable				22
23			for Martin Zellner that was written				23
24			off and then collected in full				24

Computers in Accounting

Computerized Accounts Receivable

Credit sales are often the majority of total sales for a company. Businesses use computerized accounts receivable systems to maintain accurate customer balances, to process sales and cash receipts transactions, and to generate invoices and statements. When sales and payments on account are entered, the general ledger and subsidiary ledger accounts are automatically updated.

Although applications vary, most computerized accounts receivable systems allow businesses to:

- Create a master file for each customer, containing the customer's name, account number, address, telephone number, credit terms, and credit limits.
- Enter sales on account using the order-entry screen. The customer account number, items and quantities ordered, shipping charges, sales tax, and discounts are recorded. The software then creates a sales transaction file, posts the sale to the customer's subsidiary ledger account, and updates the merchandise inventory accounts.
- Enter merchandise returns. The software prepares credit memorandums and posts the information to the customer's account.
- Generate the sales invoice and packing slip. The sales invoice is mailed to the customer, and the packing slip is forwarded to the warehouse.

- Enter cash receipts from credit customers using the cash receipts screen. The software creates a cash receipts transaction file and posts the transactions to the customer's subsidiary account.

Computerized accounts receivable systems provide many management reports. Aging reports, cash receipts reports, and schedules of accounts receivable help management analyze sales trends, customer payment histories, and the effectiveness of credit policies. Sophisticated systems can project cash flows based on receivables' past collection patterns.

Thinking Critically
How do you think the accounts receivable system contributes to the overall success of a business? What impact do you think the accounts receivable system has on cash flows and on customer service?

Internet Application
Using an Internet search engine, locate two commercial accounts receivable software applications. Create a report reviewing the features offered by both systems. Include details on cost, product features, and system requirements. Identify which product you prefer and explain why.

The second entry is recorded in the cash receipts journal as a debit to **Cash** and a credit to **Accounts Receivable** and to the customer's account.

If the amount recovered represents part of the balance written off, the entry reinstates *only the amount actually collected* unless the firm is almost certain that the remainder will be received. For example, if Martin Zellner pays $60, the entry to reinstate Zellner's account will be for $60 only, unless the business is reasonably sure the additional $38 will be received.

Accounting for Other Receivables and Bad Debt Losses

As with accounts receivable, notes receivable and other receivables can prove uncollectible. Losses from uncollectible notes receivable and other receivables can be handled by the direct charge-off method or the allowance method. **Uncollectible Accounts Expense** and **Allowance for Doubtful Accounts** can be used for losses from all types of receivables.

About Accounting

Delinquent Invoices
Dun & Bradstreet worldwide statistics reveal that 74 percent of invoices that remain delinquent beyond one year are never paid.

Managerial
IMPLICATIONS

Managing Credit

- It is essential that managers establish formal procedures for granting credit to customers, for tracking accounts receivable, for ensuring that customers are paying promptly, and for collecting past-due accounts.

- Management needs to be informed about the losses from uncollectible accounts so they can

  - establish effective credit policies,

    - weigh the cost of uncollectible account losses against the reduced sales volume caused by tight credit policies.

- Managers should use the allowance method for uncollectible accounts in order to match revenue and expenses.

- Managers are responsible for developing procedures to handle payments from customers whose accounts have been written off.

Thinking Critically

What reports would provide information to managers about how well the accounts receivable function is being managed?

Classifying Accounts Receivable on Financial Statements

④ Objective
Properly classify accounts receivable on the financial statements.

There are several ways to report accounts receivable and uncollectible accounts expense on the financial statements.

The Balance Sheet

Allowance for Doubtful Accounts represents the amount of accounts receivable estimated to be uncollectible. On the balance sheet, **Allowance for Doubtful Accounts** is deducted from **Accounts Receivable.** The difference is the **net value of accounts receivable**. Alternatively, some companies just show net accounts receivable on the balance sheet.

Recall

Contra Asset Account
Allowance for Doubtful Accounts is a contra asset account. Its normal balance is a credit. It is reported on the balance sheet as a deduction from **Accounts Receivable.**

Trilli's Office Supply Balance Sheet (partial) December 31, 20--		
Assets		
Current Assets		
Cash in Bank		$10,875
Accounts Receivable	$18,400	
Less Allowance for Doubtful Accounts	920	17,480

The Income Statement

Uncollectible accounts expense is an operating expense that appears on the income statement. Its classification generally depends on the department responsible for granting credit. It is usually classified as a general or administrative expense because the credit function is separate from sales. Less often the credit function reports to sales, and uncollectible accounts expense is classified as a selling expense or as a deduction from sales revenue.

Internal Control of Accounts Receivable

Internal control of the accounts receivable process is very important because accounts receivable represents one of the largest assets on the balance sheet for many companies. Common internal controls for accounts receivable include the following:

- Authorizing all credit sales.
- Developing procedures that ensure that all credit sales are recorded and customers' accounts are debited.
- Separating the following duties:
  - authorizing credit sales,
  - recording the accounts receivable transactions,
  - preparing bills or statements for customers,
  - mailing the bills or statements,
  - processing payments received from customers.
- Sending invoices and monthly statements.
- Aging the accounts receivable to allow management to identify and monitor slow-paying accounts.
- Investigating and taking appropriate action on past due accounts.
- Approving the write-off of accounts by authorized individuals only, and making the approvals in writing.
- Trying to collect past due accounts even if they have been written off.

 **Section 2 Self Review**

Questions

1. Under the allowance method, what is the journal entry to write off a specific uncollectible account?

2. In May The Lock Shop wrote off the $500 balance of Mike Michelob. The following year he sent $250 to The Lock Shop along with a note stating, "This is all I can pay." If the company uses the direct charge-off method, what is the journal entry to record the $250 receipt?

3. How is uncollectible accounts expense classified on the income statement?

Exercises

4. **Allowance for Doubtful Accounts** is reported as
   a. a liability on the balance sheet.
   b. a deduction from **Sales** on the income statement.
   c. a deduction from **Accounts Receivable** on the balance sheet.
   d. an expense on the income statement.

5. A business uses the allowance method for losses from uncollectible accounts. It collected cash from a customer whose account was previously written off. The entry to reinstate the customer's account would include a credit to

   a. Sales.
   b. Accounts Receivable.
   c. Allowance for Doubtful Accounts.
   d. Uncollectible Accounts Expense.

Analysis

6. ZippyLocks hired a collections manager who believes she might be able to collect some additional payments on accounts that had been written off. Should the accounts be reinstated in full?

CHAPTER 15 · Review and Applications

Review

Chapter Summary

When credit is extended, uncollectible accounts inevitably occur. Before receivables can be accurately presented on the balance sheet and net income can be properly measured, the accounts must be studied for possible adjustment to reflect such losses. In this chapter, you have learned how to adjust the value of receivables to account for uncollectible accounts.

Learning Objectives

1 Record the losses from uncollectible accounts receivable using the direct charge-off and allowance methods.

In the direct charge-off method, losses are recorded as specific accounts become uncollectible. In the allowance method, an estimate is made. The allowance method matches bad debt losses for a period against revenue received in the same period. It is consistent with generally accepted accounting principles and is the preferred method.

- The estimate of losses from uncollectible accounts can be based on a certain percentage of credit sales. The percentage is usually based on past experience. The estimated amount is debited to **Uncollectible Accounts Expense** and credited to **Allowance for Doubtful Accounts.**

- The estimate can also be based on the age of accounts receivable. A different percentage for credit losses is applied to each age group, and the resulting amounts are added together. Then **Allowance for Doubtful Accounts** is adjusted to the proper balance, and the same amount is charged to **Uncollectible Accounts Expense.**

- The adjustment is made the same way when losses are estimated with a single rate to all accounts receivable.

2 Write off uncollectible accounts after estimated losses have been recorded.

Under the allowance method, an account that proves uncollectible is written off by a debit to **Allowance for Doubtful Accounts** and a credit to both **Accounts Receivable** and the customer's account in the subsidiary ledger.

3 Record the collection of accounts previously written off using the direct charge-off and allowance methods.

- If a company uses the direct charge-off method, a journal entry is recorded to reverse the write-off. **Accounts Receivable** and the customer's account in the subsidiary ledger are debited, and **Uncollectible Accounts Expense** is credited.

- If a company uses the allowance method, a different journal entry is recorded to reverse the write-off. **Accounts Receivable** and the customer's account in the subsidiary ledger are debited, and **Allowance for Doubtful Accounts** is credited.

For both methods, the cash received is recorded in the cash receipts journal by debiting **Cash** and crediting **Accounts Receivable** and the customer's account in the subsidiary ledger.

4 Properly classify accounts receivable on the financial statements.

Businesses report accounts related to accounts receivable in different ways depending on the type of business and the method used to account for uncollectible accounts.

- **Uncollectible Accounts Expense** can appear as a general or administrative expense or as a deduction from **Sales.**

- **Allowance for Doubtful Accounts** appears as a deduction from the balance of **Accounts Receivable** on the balance sheet. Alternatively, net accounts receivable can appear on the balance sheet as **Accounts Receivable** less **Allowance for Doubtful Accounts.**

5 Define the accounting terms new to this chapter.

CHAPTER 15 GLOSSARY

Aging the accounts receivable (p. 558) Classifying accounts receivable balances according to how long they have been outstanding

Allowance method (p. 557) A method of recording uncollectible accounts that estimates losses from uncollectible accounts and charges them to expense in the period when the sales are recorded

Direct charge-off method (p. 556) A method of recording uncollectible account losses as they occur

Net value of accounts receivable (p. 564) The difference between the **Accounts Receivable** account and the **Allowance for Doubtful Accounts** account

Reinstate (p. 562) To put back or restore an accounts receivable amount that was previously written off

Valuation account (p. 557) An account, such as **Allowance for Doubtful Accounts,** whose balance is revalued or reappraised in light of reasonable expectations

Comprehensive Self Review

1. If the direct charge-off method is used, what account is credited when an account is determined uncollectible?
   a. **Accounts Receivable**
   b. **Allowance for Doubtful Accounts**
   c. **Sales**
   d. **Uncollectible Accounts Expense**
   e. **Uncollectible Accounts Recovered**

2. Which method of accounting for uncollectible accounts, the direct charge-off or the allowance method, is considered preferable?

3. Which method of accounting for uncollectible accounts, the direct charge-off or the allowance method, must be used for tax purposes?

4. How is the aging of accounts receivable used when making adjustments for uncollectible accounts?

5. When a specific account is written off under the allowance method, does net accounts receivable increase or decrease? Why?

(Answers to Comprehensive Self Review are on page 581.)

Discussion Questions

1. Explain the direct charge-off method for recording uncollectible accounts expense.

2. Under what condition would the direct charge-off method be appropriate?

3. What is the major weakness of the direct charge-off method?

4. Name three approaches to measuring uncollectible accounts when the allowance method is used.

5. What is meant by aging the accounts receivable?

6. Explain the purpose of estimating losses from uncollectible accounts and using the allowance method for recording uncollectible accounts.

7. Under the allowance method, what entry is made when a specific customer's account becomes uncollectible?

8. Under the direct charge-off method, what entry is made when a firm collects an account that was previously written off?

9. Explain how to treat the collection of an account receivable that was previously written off if the allowance method is used.

10. When is it logical to base the estimate of uncollectible accounts on gross credit sales rather than on net credit sales?

11. Why is **Allowance for Doubtful Accounts** sometimes referred to as a valuation account?

12. If a company is primarily interested in matching expenses and revenues each period, would it base its estimate of uncollectible accounts on sales or on accounts receivable? Explain.

13. Suppose that the estimate of uncollectible accounts is based on credit sales and that **Allowance for Doubtful Accounts** has a debit balance before the adjustment is made. Explain how this situation is handled.

14. How would an accountant show **Uncollectible Accounts Expense** on the income statement? Explain.

15. Describe two alternative methods of presenting accounts receivable on the balance sheet.

16. List some common internal controls for accounts receivable.

17. What duties should routinely be separated as part of an internal control procedure for accounts receivable?

Applications

EXERCISES

Recording losses under the direct charge-off method.

Amelia Company uses the direct charge-off method to record uncollectible accounts. On August 30, 20--, the company learned that Barbara Simms, a customer who owed $1,200, had moved and had left no forwarding address. Amelia Company concluded that no part of the debt was collectible. Give the general journal entry to write off the account.

◄ **Exercise 15-1**
Objective 1

Estimating and recording uncollectible accounts on the basis of total sales.

On December 31, 20--, certain account balances at Moreno Company were as follows before end-of-year adjustments.

◄ **Exercise 15-2**
Objective 1

Accounts Receivable	$ 1,000,000
Allowance for Doubtful Accounts (credit)	4,000
Sales	24,000,000
Sales Returns and Allowances	100,000

A further examination of the records showed that cash sales during the year were $2.4 million and credit sales were $21.6 million. Of the sales returns and allowances, $20,000 came from cash sales and $80,000 came from credit sales. Assume that Moreno Company bases its estimate of losses from uncollectible accounts on 0.3 percent of total net sales. Compute the estimated amount of **Uncollectible Accounts Expense** for 20--, and give the general journal entry to record the provision for uncollectible accounts.

Estimating and recording uncollectible accounts on the basis of net credit sales.

Assume that Moreno Company (Exercise 15-2) bases its estimate of uncollectible accounts expense on 0.4 percent of net credit sales. Compute the estimated amount of uncollectible accounts expense for 20-- and give the general journal entry to record the provision for uncollectible accounts. Obtain any data that you need for the computation from Exercise 15-2.

◄ **Exercise 15-3**
Objective 1

Estimating and recording uncollectible accounts on the basis of accounts receivable with credit balance in Allowance for Doubtful Accounts.

Assume that Moreno Company (Exercise 15-2) makes its estimate of uncollectible accounts on December 31 as 1.1 percent of total accounts receivable. Compute the estimated amount of losses for 20-- and give the general journal entry to record the provision for uncollectible accounts. Obtain any data that you need for the computation from Exercise 15-2.

◄ **Exercise 15-4**
Objective 1

Estimating and recording uncollectible accounts on the basis of accounts receivable with debit balance in Allowance for Doubtful Accounts.

On December 31, 20--, before adjusting entries, the balances of selected accounts of the Portland Motorcycle Company were as follows:

◄ **Exercise 15-5**
Objective 1

Accounts Receivable	$420,000
Allowance for Doubtful Accounts (debit)	1,000

The company has determined that historically about 2.4 percent of accounts receivable are never collected and uses this basis to determine and record its bad debts provision. Give the journal entry to record the company's estimated loss from uncollectible accounts on December 31.

Exercise 15-6 ▶
Objective 2

Recording actual uncollectible amounts under the allowance method.

On February 8, 20--, Pilgrim Remodeling Company decided that the $1,600 account of Janna McWilliams was worthless and should be written off. Give the general journal entry to record the write-off.

Exercise 15-7 ▶
Objective 3

Recording the partial collection of an account previously written off under the direct charge-off method.

On December 8, 20--, Amelia Company received a check for $400 and a letter from Barbara Simms, whose $1,200 account was written off on August 30 (Exercise 15-1). The letter was an apology from Simms and a statement that she could not pay the remaining $800. Give the general journal entry to reverse part of the write-off recorded in Exercise 15-1.

Exercise 15-8 ▶
Objective 3

Recording the collection of an account previously written off under the allowance method.

On July 10, 20--, after a threatened lawsuit by Pilgrim Remodeling Company, Janna McWilliams paid the $1,600 account charged off on February 8, 20-- (Exercise 15-6). Give the entries in general journal form to reverse the previous write-off of McWilliams' account and to record the receipt of her check.

Problems

PROBLEM SET A

Selected problems can be completed using:
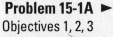 **Peachtree**   **QuickBooks**   ▦ **Spreadsheets**

Problem 15-1A ▶
Objectives 1, 2, 3

Recording uncollectible account transactions under the direct charge-off method.

Rammer Company records uncollectible accounts expense as they occur. Selected transactions for 20-- are described below. The accounts involved in these transactions are **Notes Receivable, Accounts Receivable,** and **Uncollectible Accounts Expense.** Record each transaction in general journal form.

DATE	TRANSACTIONS
Jan. 21	The $148 account receivable of Ronnie Den is determined to be uncollectible and is to be written off.
Feb. 20	Because of the death of Dorothy Fuller, her note receivable of $1,600 is considered uncollectible and is to be written off.
June 4	Received $100 from Ronnie Den in partial payment of his account, which had been written off on January 21. The cash obtained has already been recorded in the cash receipts journal. There is doubt that the balance of Den's account will be collected.
	Continued

DATE	(15-1A cont.) TRANSACTIONS
July 9	Received $48 from Ronnie Den to complete payment of his account, which had been written off on January 21. The cash obtained has already been recorded in the cash receipts journal.
Aug. 14	The $424 account receivable of Jose Garcia is determined to be uncollectible and is to be written off.
Sept. 18	Received $400 from the estate of Dorothy Fuller as part of the settlement of affairs. This amount is applicable to the note receivable written off on February 20. The cash obtained has already been recorded in the cash receipts journal.

Analyze: Based on these transactions, what total uncollectible accounts expense was recorded for the year?

Estimating and recording uncollectible accounts transactions on the basis of sales.

◄ **Problem 15-2A**
Objectives 1, 2, 3, 4

Xeno Auto Parts sells auto parts at both wholesale and retail. The company has found that there is a higher rate of uncollectible accounts from retail credit sales than from wholesale credit sales. Xeno computes its estimated loss from uncollectible accounts at the end of each year. The amount is based on the rates of loss that the firm has developed from experience for each division. A separate computation is made for each of the two types of sales. The firm uses the percentage of credit sales method.

As of December 31, 2004, **Accounts Receivable** has a balance of $373,400, and **Allowance for Doubtful Accounts** has a debit balance of $72.40. The following table provides a breakdown of the credit sales for the year 2004 and the estimated rates of loss.

CATEGORY	AMOUNT	ESTIMATED RATE OF LOSS
Wholesale	$1,816,000	0.6%
Retail	548,600	1.1%

INSTRUCTIONS

1. Compute the estimated amount of uncollectible accounts expense for each of the two categories of credit sales for the year.

2. Prepare an adjusting entry in general journal form to provide for the estimated uncollectible accounts on December 31, 2004. **Use Uncollectible Accounts Expense.**

3. Show how **Accounts Receivable** and **Allowance for Doubtful Accounts** should appear on the balance sheet of Xeno Auto Parts as of December 31, 2004.

4. On January 20, 2005, the account receivable of Russ Oates, amounting to $566, is determined to be uncollectible and is to be written off. Record this transaction in the general journal.

5. On July 13, 2005, the attorneys for Xeno Auto Parts turned over a check for $566 that they obtained from Russ Oates in settlement of his account, which had been written off on January 20. The money has already been recorded in the cash receipts journal. Give the general journal entry to reverse the original write-off.

Analyze: When the financial statements are prepared for the year ended December 31, 2004, what net accounts receivable should be reported?

Problem 15-3A ►

Objectives 1, 2, 3

Estimating and recording uncollectible account transactions on the basis of accounts receivable.

The aged accounts receivable schedule that appears below was prepared for Flores Company for its fiscal year ending December 31, 2004.

FLORES COMPANY
Aged Accounts Receivable Schedule
December 31, 2004

Account	Balance	Current	Days Past Due 1–30	Days Past Due 31–60	Days Past Due Over 60
Aaron, Ashley	360.00	360.00			
Able, John	420.00		300.00	120.00	
Anderson, Dan	208.00				208.00
Bacon, Jason	160.00	160.00			
Barker, Kelsie	124.00	84.00	40.00		
Benson, Marcie	450.00	170.00	200.00	80.00	
Black, Herman	96.00			64.00	32.00
(All other accts.)	21,496.00	18,150.00	2,100.00	720.00	526.00
Totals	23,314.00	18,924.00	2,640.00	984.00	766.00

INSTRUCTIONS

1. Compute the estimated uncollectible accounts at the end of the year using the following rates.

Current	1%
1–30 days past due	3%
31–60 days past due	8%
Over 60 days past due	20%

2. As of December 31, 2004, there is a debit balance of $128.24 in **Allowance for Doubtful Accounts.** Compute the amount of the adjustment for uncollectible accounts expense that must be made as part of the adjusting entries.

3. In general journal form, record the adjustment for the estimated losses. Use **Uncollectible Accounts Expense** and **Allowance for Doubtful Accounts.**

4. On February 10, 2005, the $216 account receivable of Sara Robin was recognized as uncollectible. Record this entry.

5. On June 12, 2005, a check for $100 was received from Mike Griffis to apply on his account, which had been written off on November 8, 2004, as uncollectible. Record the reversal of the previous write-off in the general journal. The cash obtained has already been entered in the cash receipts journal.

6. Suppose that instead of aging the accounts receivable, the company estimated the uncollectible accounts to be 3 percent of the total accounts receivable on December 31, 2004. Give the general journal entry to record the adjustment for estimated losses from uncollectible accounts. Assume that **Allowance for Doubtful Accounts** has a debit balance of $128.24 before the adjusting entry.

Analyze: What impact would the change in estimation method described in Instruction 6 have on the net income for fiscal 2004?

Using different methods to estimate uncollectible accounts.

The balances of selected accounts of Lin Company on December 31, 20--, follow. Credit sales were $5,620,000. Returns and allowances on these sales were $120,000.

Accounts Receivable	$ 633,000
Allowance for Doubtful Accounts (credit)	760
Total Sales	6,900,000
Sales Returns and Allowances	150,000

◀ **Problem 15-4A**
Objectives 1, 2, 3

INSTRUCTIONS

1. Compute the amount to be charged to **Uncollectible Accounts Expense** under each of the following different assumptions.

   a. Uncollectible accounts are estimated to be 0.4 percent of net credit sales.

   b. Uncollectible accounts are estimated to be 0.3 percent of total net sales.

   c. Experience has shown that 2.5 percent of the accounts receivable will prove worthless.

2. Suppose **Allowance for Doubtful Accounts** has a debit balance of $760 instead of a credit balance, but all other account balances remain the same. Compute the amount to be charged to **Uncollectible Accounts Expense** under each assumption in Instruction 1.

Analyze: If you were the owner of Lin Company and wished to maximize profits, which method would you use?

PROBLEM SET B

Recording transactions related to uncollectible accounts using direct charge-off method.

Half-Price Software uses the direct charge-off method to account for uncollectible accounts expenses as they occur. Selected transactions for 20-- follow. The accounts involved are **Accounts Receivable, Notes Receivable,** and **Uncollectible Accounts Expense.** Record each transaction in general journal form.

◀ **Problem 15-1B**
Objectives 1, 2, 3

DATE	TRANSACTIONS
Feb. 15	Scott Tucker, a credit customer, dies owing the firm $1,600. The account is written off.
April 2	Rosto Greer, a customer who had signed a note receivable of $1,800 to the firm, declares bankruptcy. The amount is considered uncollectible and written off.
May 30	The executor of the estate of Scott Tucker sends the firm $400 in partial settlement of account written off on February 15. The cash obtained has already been recorded in the cash receipts journal.
July 3	The bankruptcy court sends the firm $800 in settlement of the note receivable of Rosto Greer, which was written off in April (See entry of April 2). The cash obtained has already been recorded in the cash receipts journal.
	Continued

DATE	(15-1B cont.)　　　TRANSACTIONS
Sept. 16	The account owed by a customer, Payless Company, in the amount of $1,300 is determined worthless and is written off.
Oct. 18	Rosto Greer pays the remainder of the note receivable that had previously been written off. (See transactions of April 2 and July 3). The cash obtained has already been recorded in the cash receipts journal.

Analyze: When the worksheet is prepared at the end of 20--, what balance should be listed for **Uncollectible Accounts Expense?** Assume the transactions given are the only transactions that affected the account.

Problem 15-2B ►
Objectives 1, 2, 3, 4

Estimating and recording uncollectible account transactions on the basis of sales.

Build-It-Rite Company sells building materials on credit and records sales in three separate revenue accounts. The company's experience has been that each type of sale has a different rate of losses from uncollectible accounts. Thus the total that the company charges off for these losses at the end of each accounting period is based on three computations (one computation for each sales account). The firm uses the percentage of credit sales method.

As of December 31, 2004, **Accounts Receivable** has a balance of $469,100, and **Allowance for Doubtful Accounts** has a credit balance of $5,720. The following table provides a breakdown of the credit sales by division for the year 2004 and the estimated rates of loss.

DIVISION	AMOUNT	RATE OF LOSS
Siding	$1,250,000	0.9%
Flooring	940,000	1.4%
Plumbing	276,000	2.0%

INSTRUCTIONS

1. Compute the estimated amount of losses in uncollectible accounts expense for each of the three types of sales for the year.

2. Prepare an adjusting entry in general journal form to provide for the estimated losses from uncollectible accounts. Use **Uncollectible Accounts Expense** and **Allowance for Doubtful Accounts.**

3. Show how **Accounts Receivable** and **Allowance for Doubtful Accounts** should appear on the balance sheet of Build-It-Rite Company as of December 31, 2004.

4. On February 17, 2005, the account receivable of Carla Fannin, amounting to $688, is determined to be uncollectible and is to be written off. Record the transaction in general journal form.

5. On May 15, 2005, the attorneys for Build-It-Rite Company turned over a check for $688 that they obtained from Carla Fannin in settlement of her account, which had been written off on February 17, 2005. The money has already been entered in the cash receipts journal. Give the general journal entry to reverse the original write-off and reinstate Fannin's account.

Analyze: Assume Build-It-Rite uses a predetermined percentage rate on total accounts receivable to estimate uncollectibles. Use 7 percent to compute the estimated amount of uncollectible accounts receivable.

Estimating and recording uncollectible account transactions on the basis of accounts receivable.

◄ **Problem 15-3B**
Objectives 1, 2, 3

The following aged accounts receivable schedule was prepared for the Custom Blind Shop at the end of the firm's fiscal year on July 31, 2005.

CUSTOM BLIND SHOP
Schedule of Accounts Receivable by Age
July 31, 2005

Account	Balance	Current	Days Past Due 1–30	Days Past Due 31–60	Days Past Due Over 60
Aguirre, Mike	254.00	126.00	128.00		
Baker, Jeff	472.00	222.00	180.00	70.00	
Cook, Steven	196.00	196.00			
David, James	38.00	38.00			
Evans, Brad	632.00			416.00	216.00
Ivan, Tim	264.00		264.00		
(All Other Accts.)	12,438.00	6,286.00	4,152.00	1,170.00	830.00
Totals	14,294.00	6,868.00	4,724.00	1,656.00	1,046.00

INSTRUCTIONS

1. Compute the estimated uncollectible accounts at the end of the year using these rates.

Current	1%
1–30 days past due	4%
31–60 days past due	10%
Over 60 days past due	20%

2. As of July 31, 2005, there is a debit balance of $227.00 in **Allowance for Doubtful Accounts.** Compute the amount of the adjustment for uncollectible accounts expense that must be made as part of the adjusting entries.

3. In general journal form, record the adjustment for the estimated losses. Use **Uncollectible Accounts Expense** and **Allowance for Doubtful Accounts.**

4. On August 18, 2005, the account receivable of Tim Ivan, amounting to $264, was recognized as uncollectible. Record this write-off in the general journal.

5. On September 2, 2005, a check for $200 was received from Jimmy Robinson to apply on his $602 account, which had been written off as uncollectible on December 19, 2004. Record the reversal of the previous write-off in the general journal. The cash obtained has already been entered in the cash receipts journal.

6. Suppose that instead of aging the accounts receivable, the company estimated the uncollectible accounts to be 5 percent of the total accounts receivable on July 31. Assume also that **Allowance for Doubtful Accounts** has a credit balance of $125.00 before the adjusting entry. Give the general journal entry to record the adjustment for estimated losses from uncollectible accounts.

Analyze: Based on the percentages presented in Item 1, what is the average uncollectible rate for all accounts receivable?

Problem 15-4B ►
Objectives 1, 2, 3

Using different methods to estimate uncollectible accounts.

The balances of selected accounts of Sporting Goods Distributors on December 31, 20--, follow. Credit sales amounted to $26,200,000. The returns and allowances on these sales totaled $138,400.

Accounts Receivable	$ 2,960,000
Allowance for Doubtful Accounts (credit)	8,400
Total Sales	33,400,000
Sales Returns and Allowances	180,800

INSTRUCTIONS

1. Compute the amount to be charged to **Uncollectible Accounts Expense** under each of the following different sets of assumptions. Round computations to the nearest whole dollar.

   a. Bad debt losses are estimated to be 0.25 percent of net credit sales.

   b. Uncollectible accounts are estimated to be 0.2 percent of total net sales.

   c. Experience has shown that about 1.75 percent of the accounts receivable are uncollectible.

2. Suppose that **Allowance for Doubtful Accounts** has a debit balance of $8,400 instead of a credit balance, but all other account balances remain the same. Compute the amount to be charged to **Uncollectible Accounts Expense** under each of the assumptions listed in the first instruction.

Analyze: Which method results in the highest uncollectible expense for the period?

CHAPTER 15 CHALLENGE PROBLEM

Managing Uncollectible Accounts

Appliance Outlets, Inc., is a small chain of appliance stores. The company's year-end trial balance on December 31, 20--, included the following information.

Accounts Receivable	$3,500,600
Allowance for Doubtful Accounts (credit)	37,500

Net credit sales for 20-- were $10,666,000; no accounts have been previously written off during the year; and **Allowance for Doubtful Accounts** has not yet been adjusted.

INSTRUCTIONS

1. At the end of 20--, the following accounts receivable are deemed uncollectible:

Larry Canyon	$11,600
Trisha Lawson	5,000
Jefferson Moon	16,400
John Newman	3,780
Casey Perry	5,000
Heather Zachary	2,100
Total	$43,880

Of the accounts to be written off, $38,880 are more than 60 days past due and $5,000 are from 31 to 60 days past due. Prepare the December 31, 20--, journal entry to write off the above accounts.

2. Assume that the company uses the percentage of sales method to estimate uncollectible accounts expense. After analyzing the prior year's activities, management determined that losses from uncollectible accounts for 20-- should be 1.8 percent of net credit sales. Prepare the necessary adjusting journal entry.

3. Assume that the company uses the aging of accounts receivable method. The following information was furnished by the credit manager for use in calculating the estimated loss from uncollectible accounts. The balances of accounts were computed prior to the charge-offs in Instruction 1.

Receivable Category	Estimated Loss Rate	Balances of Accounts (before write-offs)
Current	1%	$2,400,000
1–30 days past due	4%	600,000
31–60 days past due	9%	250,600
Over 60 days past due	18%	250,000
Total		$3,500,600

Compute the estimate of uncollectible accounts as of December 31, 20--, rounded to the nearest dollar.

4. Prepare the necessary adjusting journal entry to record the estimated **Uncollectible Accounts Expense** on December 31.

5. Describe both the direct charge-off method and the allowance method of accounting for uncollectible accounts. Explain why one of these methods is preferable to the other and why the other method is usually not consistent with generally accepted accounting principles.

Analyze: If a company has used three different methods for estimating uncollectibles for the past three years, which basic accounting principle has been violated? Why?

CHAPTER 15 CRITICAL THINKING PROBLEM

Credit Decisions and Consequences

Jill Calvin is president of Calvin & Company, a manufacturer of decorative art objects. For the past ten years, the company has sold its product both to wholesale and to retail dealers of art objects in the north-central United States. Over the years the company has come to know its customers well. While all sales are made on credit, few credit losses have occurred. The company's experience has shown that an annual provision for uncollectible accounts of one quarter of 1 percent of sales is adequate.

Early in 20--, Calvin & Company decided to expand and develop a new sales base in the southeastern United States. Jill was pleased when credit sales of $800,000 were achieved in the new territory during the year. To achieve this level of sales and get a foothold in the new territory, though, credit was granted to some customers with lower credit ratings than had been granted in the past. Jill estimated that during the initial period of development, losses from uncollectible accounts would be 4 percent of sales in the new territory.

The credit losses connected with sales in the southeast became apparent by the end of 20--. The following losses from new territory customers were identified.

1. Old American Art Distributors, which owed Calvin $16,200, filed for bankruptcy. It was determined that nothing could be collected from the bankrupt firm.

2. Another new customer, Miami Choice Antiques, which owed Calvin $44,000, entered receivership. The receiver sent Calvin a check for $32,000 and indicated that nothing else could be paid.

3. Antiques on the Square went out of business and no collection of the $7,400 owed was possible.

The following information was also available:

- Sales in the old territory totaled $5,250,000 for 20--.
- Accounts receivable of $12,656 attributed to customers in the old sales territory were determined to be uncollectible and were written off during 20--.

INSTRUCTIONS

1. Record in general journal form all of Calvin & Company transactions that were described above. Include both territories in journal entries.

2. Compute the estimated amount of losses from uncollectible accounts for 20--. Prepare an adjusting entry in general journal form to record the provision for uncollectible accounts. Include both territories in the adjusting entry.

3. Assume that **Allowance for Doubtful Accounts** had a beginning credit balance of $6,200 before the adjustment in Instruction 2.

Was Calvin's provision for losses from uncollectible accounts adequate? To help with your analysis, set up and post amounts to a T account for **Allowance for Doubtful Accounts.**

Business Connections

◀ Connection 1

MANAGERIAL *Focus* **Uncollectible Accounts**

1. Why would managers use the allowance method for recording uncollectible accounts instead of the direct charge-off method?

2. Should the sales department be given final authority for approving credit applications? Why?

3. Why is an account receivable that was written off as uncollectible reinstated if it is later collected?

4. Why does management separate the authority to charge off uncollectible accounts from the authority to receive customers' cash?

◀ Connection 2

Ethical DILEMMA **Credit Reporting** Martyn is in charge of Big Town Store's accounts receivable. His responsibilities include filing credit rating reports of customers' payment records with a national credit agency. The agency provides this credit information to other businesses.

Martyn has several friends who are Big Town Store customers and who regularly pay their accounts late. However, they always pay the balance. Martyn knows they are good credit risks so his reports to the credit agency indicate that his friends pay promptly. This has caused no problem for the employer, nor is it likely to do so. Is this ethical? What should Martyn do?

◀ Connection 3

*Street***WISE:** Questions from the Real World **Accounts Receivable** Refer to The Home Depot, Inc. *1999 Annual Report* in Appendix B.

1. Find the consolidated balance sheets. What amount is reported for "Receivables, net" as of January 30, 2000? What deduction do you think was made to arrive at this figure?

2. What percentage of total current assets is net accounts receivable as of January 30, 2000?

FINANCIAL $TATEMENT ANALYSIS **Balance Sheet** The following excerpts were taken from the Pier 1 Imports, Inc. *Annual Report.*

◀ Connection 4

Consolidated Balance Sheets		
(in thousands except per share data)	*2000*	*1999*
ASSETS		
Current Assets		
Accounts receivable, net of allowance for doubtful	$ 5,637	$ 9,060
accounts of $44 and $230, respectively		
Total Assets	$670,710	$653,991

Analyze:

1. Compute the total accounts receivable for Pier 1 Imports in 2000 prior to allowance for doubtful accounts. What percentage of total accounts receivable was estimated to be uncollectible?

2. By what percentage did net accounts receivable decrease from 1999 to 2000?

3. What percentage of total assets are made up of net accounts receivable in 1999? In 2000?

Analyze Online: On the Pier 1 Imports Web site **(www.pier1.com),** locate the *About Us* section. Click on the *Pier 1 Credit Card* link.

4. What credit options are available to customers of Pier 1 Imports?

5. What fees or limits are applicable to each credit option?

Connection 5 ► *Extending* the *Thought* **Cash Flow** The chief financial officers of many companies believe they should wait as long as possible to pay their debts. Since cash flow is considered the lifeblood of a company, payments of trade accounts are delayed in order to maximize their float. As a supplier to these companies, this practice translates to outstanding receivables and additional costs related to collection. What do you think the phrase "maximizing float" means? How do you think this practice of delaying payment affects the business economy as a whole?

Connection 6 ► Business Communication **Memo** You are the senior accountant for Big Reef Dive Shops. The peak season for the chain of stores is June through August. In November and December, the shops do very little business. You prepare financial statements on a quarterly basis and have chosen to estimate uncollectible accounts using a percentage of net credit sales. The firm's previous accountant used the direct charge-off method. In a memo to the owner, describe your reasons for using an allowance method. Explain the implications this has for the quarterly income statements.

Connection 7 ► **Team***Work* **Collection Practices** Companies often employ collection agencies to help collect past due accounts. The activities and practices of collection agencies are governed by the Fair Debt Collection Practices Act.

1. As a team, investigate the provisions of this Federal Trade Commission law. Use resources found on the Internet or at your library.

2. Prepare a report that includes details on fair and unfair collection practices.

3. What recourse is provided to consumers who believe that a collection agency has practiced unfair collection methods?

Credit Cards Go to the VISA Web site at **www.visa.com.** ◄ **Connection 8**
How many financial institution members does VISA have? How many
Visa cards have been issued? Click on *Consumer Tips.* Select *About the Euro.*
Can you use VISA cards in countries that use the Euro?

Answers to Self Reviews

Answers to Section 1 Self Review

1. Net income and current assets both decrease by the amount that is written off.
2. Debit **Uncollectible Accounts Expense** account and credit **Allowance for Doubtful Accounts** for $3,000.
3. A list showing accounts receivable classified by how long each account has been due.
4. **b. Uncollectible Accounts Expense.**
5. **b.** $900 (0.01 × $100,000) − $100 = $900
6. The owner can base an estimate on the experience of similar firms. If Kumar does not make an adjustment for uncollectible accounts, the expenses will be understated and assets will be overstated on the financial statements.

Answers to Section 2 Self Review

1. Debit **Allowance for Doubtful Accounts.** Credit **Accounts Receivable** and the individual account in the subsidiary ledger.
2. Debit **Accounts Receivable** and the customer's subsidiary account for the amount collected, $250. Credit **Uncollectible Accounts Expense** or **Uncollectible Accounts Recovered** for that amount. The cash payment is entered in the cash receipts journal in the usual way.
3. It is usually classified as a general or administrative expense, but can be shown as a selling expense or deduction from sales revenue.
4. **c.** a deduction from **Accounts Receivable** on the balance sheet.
5. **c. Allowance for Doubtful Accounts.**
6. No. The accounts should only be reinstated in full if the firm is almost certain that the amounts will be paid.

Answers to Comprehensive Self Review

1. **a. Accounts Receivable.** The customer's account in the subsidiary ledger is also credited.
2. The allowance method because it is consistent with the matching principle. It matches bad debt losses during a period against revenue of the same period.
3. Except for certain financial institutions, the direct charge-off method must be used for tax purposes.
4. The aging is used to classify the accounts. Estimates are made based on experience of the likelihood of collecting the balance due in each age category.
5. It does not change. The journal entry to write off a specific account is a debit to **Allowance for Doubtful Accounts** and a credit to **Accounts Receivable**.

CHAPTER 16

Learning Objectives

1. Determine whether an instrument meets all the requirements of negotiability.

2. Calculate the interest on a note.

3. Determine the maturity date of a note.

4. Record routine notes payable transactions.

5. Record discounted notes payable transactions.

6. Record routine notes receivable transactions.

7. Compute the proceeds from a discounted note receivable, and record transactions related to discounting of notes receivable.

8. Understand how to use bank drafts and trade acceptances and how to record transactions related to those instruments.

9. Define the accounting terms new to this chapter.

Notes Payable and Notes Receivable

New Terms

Bank draft	Interest
Banker's year	Maturity value
Bill of lading	Negotiable instrument
Cashier's check	Note payable
Commercial draft	Note receivable
Contingent liability	Principal
Discounting	Sight draft
Draft	Time draft
Face value	Trade acceptance

kbhome.com

KB Home is one of the largest home builders in the United States and Paris, France. In 2000 the company delivered 22,847 homes and reported revenues of $3.9 billion. The company has grown rapidly in recent years, achieving impressive five-year compound annual growth rates of 24 percent and 42 percent in deliveries and net income, respectively. KB Home attributes its success to KB2000—an innovative operating model, adopted in 1996, emphasizing efficiencies of a process-driven, systematic approach to homebuilding. KB Home has leveraged KB2000 benefits through a strategy designed to achieve leading market positions among first-time homebuyers in high-growth areas. The company has expanded its existing operations and completed several acquisitions, securing the number one or number two positions in all of its markets. While experiencing tremendous growth, the company has been able to improve its gross margins and increase net income by adhering to KB2000 principles. It has also carefully managed its inventory and debt levels to maintain a strong financial position.

Thinking Critically
How has maintaining a strong financial position allowed KB Home to achieve its growth?

For more information on KB Home, go to:
collegeaccounting.glencoe.com.

Section Objectives

① **Determine whether an instrument meets all the requirements of negotiability.**

WHY IT'S IMPORTANT
Companies use financial documents prepared according to legal standards.

② **Calculate the interest on a note.**

WHY IT'S IMPORTANT
Interest represents revenue or expense.

③ **Determine the maturity date of a note.**

WHY IT'S IMPORTANT
Funds must be available to pay the note when due.

④ **Record routine notes payable transactions.**

WHY IT'S IMPORTANT
The accounting records must reflect all the firm's financial obligations.

⑤ **Record discounted notes payable transactions.**

WHY IT'S IMPORTANT
Interest is sometimes deducted in advance, not paid at maturity.

Terms to Learn

banker's year
discounting
face value
interest
maturity value
negotiable instrument
note payable
principal

Accounting for Notes Payable

In this chapter you will learn about negotiable instruments and, in particular, promissory notes.

Negotiable Instruments

The law covering negotiable instruments is a part of the Uniform Commercial Code (UCC). The UCC has been adopted by all of the states. A **negotiable instrument** is a financial document, containing a promise or order to pay, that meets all the requirements of the UCC in order to be transferable to another party. The UCC requirements specify that to be negotiable an instrument must

- be in writing and signed by the maker or *drawer*,
- contain an unconditional promise or order to pay a definite amount of money,
- be payable either on demand or at a future time that is fixed or that can be determined,
- be payable to the order of a specific person or to the bearer,
- clearly name or identify the drawee if addressed to a drawee.

Checks are negotiable instruments. Another important negotiable instrument is the promissory note.

Notes Payable

On March 18 Trilli's Office Supply purchased store equipment for $2,500 from Electronics Supply Company. The supplier agreed to accept payment in 90 days if Victor Trilli signed the promissory note shown in Figure 16-1. A promissory note is a written promise to pay a certain amount of money at a specific future time. For Electronics Supply Company, the promissory note provides more legal protection than an accounts payable.

The promissory note is a negotiable instrument. It is in writing and signed by Victor Trilli, owner of Trilli's Office Supply. It is an unconditional promise to pay a definite sum, $2,500. It is payable on a date that can be determined exactly, 90 days after March 18. It is payable to a specific party, Electronics Supply Company. Although not necessary for negotiability, the note specifies a rate of interest, 12 percent.

Calculating the Interest on a Note

Interest is the fee charged for the use of money. Interest is calculated using the following formula:

$$\text{Interest} = \text{Principal} \times \text{Rate} \times \text{Time}$$

The time period is indicated in fractions of a year. A 360-day period used to calculate interest on a note is called a **banker's year**. Interest on the note in Figure 16-1 is $75 ($2,500 × 0.12 × 90/360).

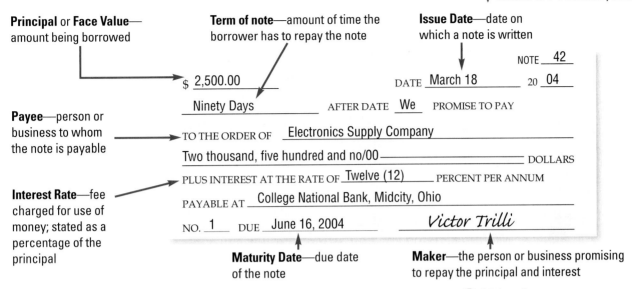

Principal or **Face Value**— amount being borrowed

Term of note—amount of time the borrower has to repay the note

Issue Date—date on which a note is written

NOTE __42__

DATE __March 18__ 20 __04__

$ __2,500.00__

__Ninety Days__ AFTER DATE __We__ PROMISE TO PAY

Payee—person or business to whom the note is payable

TO THE ORDER OF __Electronics Supply Company__

__Two thousand, five hundred and no/00__ ———————————— DOLLARS

PLUS INTEREST AT THE RATE OF __Twelve (12)__ PERCENT PER ANNUM

Interest Rate—fee charged for use of money; stated as a percentage of the principal

PAYABLE AT __College National Bank, Midcity, Ohio__

NO. __1__ DUE __June 16, 2004__ _Victor Trilli_

Maturity Date—due date of the note

Maker—the person or business promising to repay the principal and interest

① Objective
Determine whether an instrument meets all the requirements of negotiability.

The note in Figure 16-1 shows a $2,500 amount, called the **principal**, **face value**, or *face amount*. The **maturity value** is the total amount (principal plus interest) that must be paid when a note comes due. For the note in Figure 16-1, the maturity value is $2,575 ($2,500 + $75).

Calculating the Maturity Date of a Note

A note's maturity date is the number of days from the date of issue until it is due. The issue date itself is not counted. For example, a 30-day note issued on January 1 matures on January 31, 30 days after January 1. Let's find the maturity date for the note in Figure 16-1.

② Objective
Calculate the interest on a note.

Step 1.	Determine the number of days remaining in the month in which the note is issued. Do not count the issue date.	31 days in March −18 days issue date 13 days
Step 2.	Determine the number of days remaining after the first month. To do this, subtract the days calculated in Step 1 from the term of the note.	90 days term of note −13 days March days 77 days remaining
Step 3.	Subtract the number of days in the next month (April) from the number of days remaining after Step 2.	77 days −30 days in April 47 days remaining
Step 4.	Subtract the number of days in the next month (May) from the days remaining after Step 3.	47 days −31 days in May 16 days remaining
Step 5.	Since there are only 16 days remaining, the due date is 16 days into the next month (June).	The due date is June 16. Proof: March 13 days April 30 days May 31 days June 16 days Total 90 days
Step 6.	Prove the calculation. Add the days together to see if they equal the period of the note.	

③ Objective
Determine the maturity date of a note.

Sometimes the term of a note is described in months instead of days. In this case the maturity date is determined by counting ahead to the same date of the following month or months. For example, a three-month note issued on March 18 is due on June 18, regardless of the number of days in the period. If a note is issued at the end of a month, and there is no corresponding date in the month due, then the note is due on the first day of the following month. For example, a six-month note issued on August 30 should mature on February 30. Since there is no February 30, the note matures on March 1.

Recording the Issuance of a Note Payable

A **note payable** is a liability that represents a written promise by the maker of the note (the debtor) to pay another party (the creditor) a specified amount at a specified future date. The following shows how Trilli's Office Supply records the March 18 transaction to issue a 90-day, $2,500 note payable at 12 percent annual interest to purchase store equipment.

Objective

Record routine notes payable transactions.

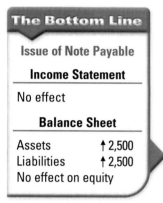

The Bottom Line

Issue of Note Payable

Income Statement

No effect

Balance Sheet

Assets	↑ 2,500
Liabilities	↑ 2,500
No effect on equity	

		GENERAL JOURNAL			PAGE ___3___	
	DATE	DESCRIPTION	POST. REF.	DEBIT	CREDIT	
1	2004					1
6	Mar. 18	Store Equipment		2 50 0 00		6
7		Notes Payable—Trade			2 50 0 00	7
8		Issued note payable to Electronics Supply				8
9		Company for purchase of store equipment				9

Recording Payment of a Note and Interest

On the maturity date, June 16, Trilli's Office Supply pays the $2,500 principal plus the $75 in interest. This transaction is recorded as follows.

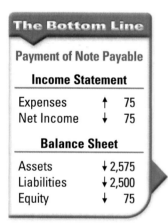

The Bottom Line

Payment of Note Payable

Income Statement

| Expenses | ↑ 75 |
| Net Income | ↓ 75 |

Balance Sheet

Assets	↓ 2,575
Liabilities	↓ 2,500
Equity	↓ 75

		GENERAL JOURNAL			PAGE ___6___	
	DATE	DESCRIPTION	POST. REF.	DEBIT	CREDIT	
1	2004					1
11	June 16	Notes Payable—Trade		2 50 0 00		11
12		Interest Expense		7 5 00		12
13		Cash			2 57 5 00	13
14		Payment of March 18 note to				14
15		Electronics Supply Company				15

Renewing or Making a Partial Payment on a Note

If the issuer of a note asks and receives an extension to the maturity date, no additional accounting entries are required. On the extended maturity date, an entry is made to record payment of the note and interest for the entire period of the debt.

Sometimes at the maturity date only part of the note is paid. The partial payment is shown on the existing note, or the existing note is canceled and a new note is issued for the balance.

Recording the Issuance of a Discounted Note Payable

Businesses often borrow money from banks and sign notes payable as evidence of the debts. Banks always charge interest on loans. For some promissory notes, such as the one to Electronics Supply Company in Figure 16-1, interest is paid on the maturity date. The interest on a bank loan may be paid at maturity. Often, however, the bank deducts the interest in advance, and the borrower receives only the difference between the face amount of the note and the interest on it to maturity. This practice of deducting the interest in advance from the principal on a note payable is called **discounting**.

On May 1 Trilli's Office Supply signed a $6,000, 10 percent, 60-day note payable with the bank. The note was issued at a discount. The interest is $100.

$$\text{Interest} = \text{Principal} \times \text{Rate} \times \text{Time}$$
$$\$100 = \$6,000 \times 0.10 \times (60/360)$$

The bank deducted the $100 interest from the face amount of the note, and Trilli's Office Supply received $5,900 ($6,000 − $100).

Trilli's Office Supply uses two note payable accounts—one for notes to vendors and the other for notes to the bank. The transaction is recorded as follows.

⑤ **Objective**
Record discounted notes payable transactions.

GENERAL JOURNAL   PAGE 5

	DATE		DESCRIPTION	POST. REF.	DEBIT	CREDIT	
1	2004						1
2	May	1	Cash		5 9 0 0 00		2
3			Interest Expense		1 0 0 00		3
4			Notes Payable—Bank			6 0 0 0 00	4
5			To record note payable issued at				5
6			a discount				6
7							7

The Bottom Line

Issue of Discounted Note Payable

Income Statement

Expenses	↑ 100
Net Income	↓ 100

Balance Sheet

Assets	↑ 5,900
Liabilities	↑ 6,000
Equity	↓ 100

Recording the Payment of a Discounted Note Payable

At maturity, June 30, Trilli's Office Supply prepares a check for $6,000 to pay the note. There is no entry for interest expense because interest was paid and recorded when the note was issued. The entry is recorded as follows.

GENERAL JOURNAL   PAGE 6

	DATE		DESCRIPTION	POST. REF.	DEBIT	CREDIT	
1	2004						1
33	June	30	Notes Payable—Bank		6 0 0 0 00		33
34			Cash			6 0 0 0 00	34
35			Record payment of note				35
36							36
37							37

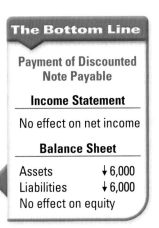

The Bottom Line

Payment of Discounted Note Payable

Income Statement

No effect on net income

Balance Sheet

Assets	↓ 6,000
Liabilities	↓ 6,000

No effect on equity

Accounting

On The Job

Finance

Industry Overview

By the year 2008, approximately 8.3 million people will be employed in the field of finance. Insurance, banking, real estate, and securities sectors provide investment, money management, and financial security products and services. Corporate finance employees implement and monitor financial policies and financing programs and manage cash resources.

Career Opportunities

- Equities Analyst
- Insurance Agent
- Financial Planner
- Tax Examiner
- Loan Officer
- Bank Auditor
- Investor Relations Officer
- Controller

Preparing for a Finance Career

- Develop advanced proficiencies in spreadsheet applications. Be prepared to write macros, link spreadsheets, and perform data imports and exports into other applications.

- Gain an understanding of accounting principles, practices, financial data analysis techniques, and accounting software applications.

- Become literate with software presentation packages, data conferencing technologies, and securities trading services.

- Join the student division of professional organizations such as the American Institute of Certified Public Accountants (AICPA) or the American Institute of Banking.

- Gain an understanding of loan applications, credit policies, and state and federal banking regulations for positions such as bank auditor or loan officer. Complete banking courses accredited by the American Institute of Banking or the Mortgage Bankers Association.

- Obtain a bachelor's degree with a major in business administration, finance, accounting, marketing, or economics.

- Obtain certification in your field of expertise: certified public accountant (CPA), certified financial planner (CFP), chartered financial consultant (ChFC), or certified management accountant (CMA).

- Obtain certification from the National Association of Securities Dealers if you plan to sell securities, mutual funds, or insurance products.

- Gain knowledge of the technical aspects of insurance policies. Complete prelicensing insurance courses and pass the state examination.

Thinking Critically
What skills or proficiencies do you currently possess that contribute to your readiness for a career in a sector of the finance industry?

Internet Application
Use an Internet search engine to research and compare the requirements to become a certified financial planner (CFP) and a certified management accountant (CMA).

Using a Notes Payable Register

If a business issues many notes payable, it is convenient to maintain a notes payable register. The notes payable register shows the important information about each note payable on a single line.

At the end of each accounting period, a schedule of notes payable is prepared from the information in the notes payable register. The schedule of notes payable must agree with the **Notes Payable** account in the general ledger.

For each note payable, the notes payable register shows the following information:

- the issue date,
- the payee,
- where the note is payable,
- the term of the note,
- the maturity date,
- the face amount,
- the interest rate,
- the interest amount, if any.

Reporting Notes Payable and Interest Expense

Notes payable represent financial obligations of the business. They appear on the balance sheet as liabilities.

- Notes due within one year are classified as current liabilities.
- Notes due in more than one year are classified as long-term liabilities.

The notes presented in this chapter are current liabilities. Long-term liabilities are discussed in Chapter 22.

Interest expense appears on the income statement as a nonoperating expense. It is listed in the Other Income and Expenses section and is deducted from Income from Operations as follows.

Sales	$50,000
Cost of Goods Sold	(35,000)
Gross Profit on Sales	$15,000
Operating Expenses	(8,000)
Income from Operations	$ 7,000
Other Income and Expenses	
Interest Expense	(900)
Net Income	$ 6,100

Section **Self Review**

Question

1. What is the maturity date of a 90-day note issued on March 17?

2. What is the interest due on a note for $12,000 at 10 percent for 30 days?

3. How much cash will the business receive for an $8,000, 60-day, noninterest-bearing note discounted at 9 percent?

Exercises

4. The total to be paid when a note payable is due is known as the
   a. face value.
   b. interest.
   c. maturity value.
   d. principal.

5. Which of the following is not required for an instrument to be negotiable?
   a. It must be in writing.
   b. It must be payable on demand or at a fixed or determinable date.
   c. It must state a rate of interest.
   d. It must contain an unconditional promise or order to pay a definite amount.

Analysis

6. Express the relationship between issue date and maturity date as a mathematical equation.

(Answers to Section 1 Self Review are on page 609.)

Accounting for Notes Receivable

Section Objectives

6 Record routine notes receivable transactions.

WHY IT'S IMPORTANT
Many businesses accept notes receivable from customers to purchase goods or to replace existing accounts receivable.

7 Compute the proceeds from a discounted note receivable, and record transactions related to discounting of notes receivable.

WHY IT'S IMPORTANT
Businesses can raise cash by discounting notes receivable at the bank.

8 Understand how to use bank drafts and trade acceptances and how to record transactions related to those instruments.

WHY IT'S IMPORTANT
Various financial instruments provide flexibility in cash management.

Terms to Learn

bank draft
bill of lading
cashier's check
commercial draft
contingent liability
draft
note receivable
sight draft
time draft
trade acceptance

Section 1 discussed promissory notes from the debtor's perspective. This section considers the creditor's perspective.

Notes Receivable

Some businesses allow customers to issue a promissory note to finance the purchase of goods. Sometimes a business requires a customer with an overdue account to sign a promissory note for the account balance. In these cases the promissory note is classified as a **note receivable**, which is an asset that represents a creditor's written promise to pay a specified amount at a specified future date. There are many similarities between notes payable and notes receivable. Of course, the journal entries are different.

Noninterest-Bearing Notes Receivable

Customer Thiu Huang owes $800 to Trilli's Office Supply. The account is overdue, and Huang needs more time to pay. On April 8 Huang signs a 30-day, noninterest-bearing note for $800. In the event legal action becomes necessary, the note provides additional protection to Trilli's Office Supply.

1	2004					1
2	Apr.	8	Notes Receivable	800 00		2
3			Accounts Receivable/Thiu Huang		800 00	3
4			To record 30-day note receivable to			4
5			replace overdue accounts receivable			5

The maturity date of the note is May 8.

Days note is issued in April (30 − 8)	22 days
Days in May	8 days
Duration of note (proof)	30 days

At maturity when Huang pays the note, the entry in the cash receipts journal is a debit to **Cash** and a credit to **Notes Receivable.** Huang's note is marked "Paid" and returned to him.

Cat Financial, a division of Caterpillar Inc., extends long-term credit to its customers to purchase Caterpillar equipment. At December 31, 1999, Cat Financial's total notes receivable of $3,483 million were listed on the balance sheet of Caterpillar Inc. Amounts of $1,564 million, $663 million, $468 million, and $788 million are due in 2000, 2001, 2002, and 2003 and after, respectively.

Interest-Bearing Notes Receivable

6 Objective

Record routine notes receivable transactions.

Customers who do not pay their bills when due are expected to pay interest. Normally, promissory notes issued to replace overdue accounts are interest bearing. Interest on notes is generally paid at the maturity date. On April 14 Trilli's Office Supply accepted a 60-day, 12 percent note for $900 from Eli Nagy to replace his past-due account. The transaction is recorded as follows.

1	2004				1
2	Apr.	14	Notes Receivable	9 0 0 00	2
3			Accounts Receivable/Eli Nagy		9 0 0 00	3
4			To record 60-day note receivable to		4
5			replace an overdue account receivable		5

The maturity date of the note is June 13.

Days note is issued in April (30 − 14)	16 days
Days in May	31 days
Total days to the end of May	47 days
Days in June to maturity (60 − 47 = 13)	13 days
Duration of note (proof)	60 days

The interest on $900 for 60 days at 12 percent is $18 ($900 × 0.12 × 60/360). Nagy's payment of the note on the maturity date will include the $900 face amount of the note plus $18 interest. The payment would be recorded as follows.

1	2004				1
2	June	13	Cash	9 1 8 00	2
3			Notes Receivable		9 0 0 00	3
4			Interest Income		1 8 00	4
5			Collection of Eli Nagy's note receivable		5

Notes Receivable—Special Situations

Accountants must know how to record notes receivable for special situations.

Accounting for Partial Collection of a Note. On June 13 Trilli's Office Supply learned that Eli Nagy could pay only half of the note receivable. Trilli's Office Supply agreed to extend the due date for another 30 days for half of the principal, $450. Trilli's Office Supply accepted payment of $18 interest and $450 principal. Partial payments are applied first to interest and then to principal. The journal entry to record the transaction is as follows.

1	2004				1
2	June	13	Cash	4 6 8 00	2
3			Notes Receivable		4 5 0 00	3
4			Interest Income		1 8 00	4
5			Collection of interest and one-half		5
6			of Eli Nagy's note; balance renewed		6
7			for 30 days		7

The original note can be endorsed to reflect the partial payment and the new maturity date, or Trilli's Office Supply can cancel the original note and ask Eli Nagy to sign a new note for $450.

Note Receivable Not Collected at Maturity. If a note is not paid at maturity and there are no arrangements for renewal, the note is said to be "dishonored." Dishonored notes do not belong in the **Notes Receivable** account. If Eli Nagy dishonored the original $900 note, the entry to transfer the balance out of **Notes Receivable** and back to **Accounts Receivable** would be as follows.

1	2004						1
2	June	13	Accounts Receivable/Eli Nagy	9 1 8 00			2
3			Notes Receivable			9 0 0 00	3
4			Interest Income			1 8 00	4
5			To charge back Nagy dishonored				5
6			note plus interest to maturity				6

Note that Nagy now owes the original balance of $900 plus $18 interest on the note. After a note is dishonored, interest continues to accrue on the note. The interest rate is usually specified by law. In most cases it is higher than the rate shown on the note, although the parties may agree on a rate different from the statutory rate. Promissory notes usually require the maker to pay attorney's fees and all other costs incurred by the holder for efforts to collect the note.

Notes Received at the Time of a Sale. Sometimes Trilli's Office Supply asks a customer to sign a promissory note at the time of sale. The transaction is recorded in the general journal as follows.

1	2004						1
2	June	5	Notes Receivable	1 2 0 0 00			2
3			Sales			1 2 0 0 00	3
4			Received 90-day, 10% note from				4
5			Sylvia Madeo on sale of goods				5

If a business routinely receives notes from customers at the time of sale, the transactions are recorded in a special Notes Receivable column of the sales journal.

Discounting a Note Receivable

A note receivable is an asset. At maturity date the holder will receive cash for the note receivable. If the holder wants cash before the maturity date, the note can be discounted (sold) at the bank. The bank pays the holder the maturity value (principal plus any interest) minus the discount charge.

Noninterest-Bearing Note Receivable Discounted. On September 4 Trilli's Office Supply needed cash to pay some bills. Victor Trilli decided to discount a 90-day, noninterest-bearing note receivable for $1,000 that the business received from Peter Ellis on July 6. The maturity date of the note is October 4.

Days note is issued in July (31 − 6)	25 days
Days in August	31 days
Days in September	30 days
Total days to the end of September	86 days
Days in October to maturity (90 − 86)	4 days
Duration of note (proof)	90 days

About Accounting

Annual Percentage Rate (APR)

Some lenders charge lower interest rates but add high fees; others do the reverse. The APR allows you to compare them on equal terms. It combines the fees and interest charges to give you the true annual interest rate.

On September 4 Trilli's Office Supply discounts the note at Midcity National Bank. The bank's discount rate is 12 percent.

Calculating the Discount and the Proceeds. The steps to determine the discount and the proceeds on notes receivable follow.

Step 1: *Determine the maturity value of the note.* Since the note from Ellis is noninterest-bearing, its maturity value and face amount are the same, $1,000.

Step 2: *Calculate the number of days in the discount period.* The discount period is the number of days from the discount date to the maturity date. The discount period is 30 days.

Days note is discounted in September (30 − 4)	26 days
Days in October until maturity	4 days
Total days in discount period	30 days

Step 3: *Compute the discount charged by the bank.* The discount formula is similar to the interest formula. The time is the number of days in the discount period. The discount is $10.

Discount = Maturity Value × Discount Rate × Discount Period
$10 = $1,000 × 0.12 × (30/360)

Step 4: *Calculate the proceeds,* the amount received from the bank. This is the maturity value of the note less the discount, $990 ($1,000 − $10).

Trilli's Office Supply received cash for the note 30 days before the note matured in exchange for a discount fee of $10.

The discount is debited to **Interest Expense.** The credit is to **Notes Receivable—Discounted,** a contra asset account. The following is the journal entry to record the discounting of the note receivable.

1	2004			1
2	Sept.	5	Cash	9 9 0 00		2
3			Interest Expense	1 0 00		3
4			Notes Receivable—Discounted		1 0 0 0 00	4
5			To record discounting of			5
6			Peter Ellis note			6
7						7

Contingent Liability for a Discounted Note. When a note receivable is discounted, the party discounting the note endorses it. If the maker (Ellis) does not pay the note at maturity, the bank can obtain payment from the endorser (Trilli's Office Supply). Hence the endorser has a contingent liability of $1,000. A **contingent liability** can become a liability if certain things happen. Contingent liabilities are shown on the financial statements so that the users are aware that the business might have a liability in the future. The contingent liability for discounted notes receivable appears on the balance sheet as follows.

Notes Receivable	$2,100
Notes Receivable—Discounted	(1,000)
Net Notes Receivable	$1,100

Another common way to show contingent liabilities is to present the net notes receivable on the balance sheet and to include a footnote with the information about the discounted notes receivable.

Discounted Noninterest-Bearing Note Receivable at Maturity. If on October 4, the maturity date, Ellis pays the note, Trilli's Office Supply is no longer contingently liable for the note. The following journal entry removes the asset and the contingent liability.

	2004					
1						1
2	Oct.	4	Notes Receivable—Discounted	1 0 0 0 00		2
3			Notes Receivable		1 0 0 0 00	3
4			Record payment of discounted note			4
5			of Peter Ellis			5

Suppose on October 4 Ellis dishonored the note by not paying it. The bank filed a formal protest. Trilli's Office Supply became liable to the bank for the maturity value of the note plus a protest fee. Midcity National Bank deducted the note ($1,000) and the protest fee ($20) from the checking account for Trilli's Office Supply. The bank sent a debit memorandum with the dishonored note and the protest form to Trilli's Office Supply. The journal entries to record this transaction are as follows:

- Record the amount owed by Ellis including the protest fee. Debit **Accounts Receivable/Peter Ellis** for $1,020 and credit **Cash** for $1,020.
- Debit **Notes Receivable—Discounted** for $1,000 and credit **Notes Receivable** for $1,000.

Trilli's Office Supply contacted Ellis and asked for payment of the note. Payment was not received, so Trilli's Office Supply turned the note over to an attorney for collection.

Interest-Bearing Note Receivable Discounted. Victor Trilli discounted another note receivable in order to meet cash needs. The $900, 60-day, 10 percent note was received from Rhonda Green on September 24. The maturity date of the note is November 23.

Days note is issued in September (30 − 24)	6 days
Days in October	31 days
Total days to the end of October	37 days
Days in November to maturity (60 − 37)	23 days
Duration of note (proof)	60 days

Calculating the Discount and the Proceeds. On October 29 Trilli's Office Supply discounted Green's note at the bank at 12 percent. The steps to compute the discount and the proceeds on the note receivable follow.

Step 1: *Determine the maturity value of the note.* The interest is $15 ($900 × 0.10 × 60/360). The maturity value is the principal and interest, $915 ($900 + $15).

Step 2: *Calculate the number of days in the discount period.* The discount period is 25 days.

Days note is discounted in October (31 − 29)	2 days
Days in November until maturity	23 days
Total days in discount period	25 days

Step 3: *Compute the discount charged by the bank.* The bank charges $7.63, 12 percent of the maturity value for the discount period ($915 × 0.12 × 25/360).

Step 4: *Calculate the proceeds.* The proceeds are $907.37, the maturity value minus the discount ($915.00 − $7.63).

International INSIGHTS

Document Dating

When dating documents for international use, writing out the month can eliminate confusion or misinterpretation. For example, in the United States, the month is followed by the day and year: November 1, 2004, or 11/1/04. In other countries the day is often followed by the month and then the year: 1 November 2004 or 1/11/04.

Interest income of $7.37 is recorded. This represents the total interest used to compute the maturity value, minus the discount charged by the bank ($15.00 − $7.63 = $7.37). If the discount charged by the bank is higher than the interest earned on the note, the difference is recorded as interest expense. The following is the journal entry to record the discount of the note receivable.

		GENERAL JOURNAL			PAGE 10	
	DATE	DESCRIPTION	POST. REF.	DEBIT	CREDIT	
1	2004					1
32	Oct. 29	Cash		907 37		32
33		Notes Receivable—Discounted			900 00	33
34		Interest Income			7 37	34
35		To record discounting of Rhonda				35
36		Green note				36

Discounted Interest-Bearing Note Receivable at Maturity. On November 23, the maturity date, Green pays the note. Trilli's Office Supply is no longer contingently liable for the note. A journal entry is made to debit **Notes Receivable—Discounted** for $900 and credit **Notes Receivable** for $900.

Suppose on November 23 Green dishonored the note. Trilli's Office Supply is liable to pay the maturity value and protest fee to the bank. Journal entries are made to

- debit **Accounts Receivable/Rhonda Green** and credit **Cash** for the maturity value and protest fee,
- debit **Notes Receivable—Discounted** and credit **Notes Receivable** for the face amount of the note.

The Notes Receivable Register

If a firm has many notes receivable, it is convenient to maintain a notes receivable register. For each note, the notes receivable register shows the date of the note, the maker, where the note is payable, the duration, the maturity date, the face amount, the rate of interest, and the amount of interest. For each discounted note, the register also shows the discount date and the bank holding the note.

Reporting Notes Receivable and Interest Income

Notes receivable appear on the balance sheet as assets.
- Notes that mature within one year are classified as current assets.
- Notes that mature in more than one year are classified as long-term assets.

The contra asset account **Notes Receivable—Discounted** appears as a deduction from **Notes Receivable.**

> Presentation of notes receivable can vary from company to company. The Goodyear Tire & Rubber Company combines notes receivable with accounts receivable and presents one line item called "Accounts and notes receivable" on the balance sheet.

Interest income is classified as nonoperating income. It is listed in the Other Income and Expenses section of the income statement and is added to income from operations. The discount charged for discounting notes is shown as interest expense in the Other Income and Expenses section and is deducted from Income from Operations. The income statement for a business that received and paid interest follows.

Sales		$150,000
Cost of Goods Sold		(105,000)
Gross Profit on Sales		$ 45,000
Operating Expenses		(24,000)
Income from Operations		$ 21,000
Other Income and Expenses		
Interest Income	$375	
Interest Expense	(600)	(225)
Net Income		$ 20,775

Drafts and Acceptances

Negotiable instruments include drafts and acceptances.

Drafts

A **draft** is a written order that requires one party (a person or business) to pay a stated sum of money to another party. A check is one type of draft. Other types are bank drafts and commercial drafts.

Bank Drafts. A **bank draft** is a check written by a bank that orders another bank to pay the stated amount to a specific party. A bank draft is more readily accepted than a personal or business check. Bank drafts are used to pay debts to suppliers with whom credit has not been established.

A **cashier's check** is a draft on the issuing bank's own funds. Cashier's checks are sometimes used to pay bills. For the creditor a cashier's check offers more protection than a business or personal check.

The business pays for the bank draft or cashier's check by issuing a business check to cover the amount of the draft or cashier's check plus the service charge.

On April 10 Trilli's Office Supply sent a $750 bank draft to CashWays Supply. The service charge for the bank draft was $12. The journal entry to record the transaction is as follows.

1	2004				1
2	Apr.	10	Accounts Payable/CashWays Supply	750 00	2
3			Miscellaneous Bank Expenses	12 00	3
4			Cash	762 00	4
5			Paid CashWays Supply bill with		5
6			bank draft		6

Commercial Drafts. A **commercial draft** is a note issued by one party that orders another party to pay a specified amount on a specified date. Commercial drafts are used for special shipment and collection situations. Commercial drafts may be either sight drafts or time drafts.

A **sight draft** is a commercial draft that is payable on presentation. When a sight draft is issued, no journal entry is made. When a sight draft is honored, the transaction is recorded as a cash receipt.

8 Objective

Understand how to use bank drafts and trade acceptances and how to record transactions related to those instruments.

Managerial

IMPLICATIONS

Negotiable Instruments

- Because notes payable and notes receivable are negotiable instruments, they fall under the rules and regulations of the Uniform Commercial Code. Management needs to understand the rights, responsibilities, and obligations of the business for negotiable instruments.

- Management should carefully control and limit borrowing to minimize the interest charged for the use of funds.

- In a well-run business, managers ensure the prompt payment of debts to minimize interest expense and to maintain the company's credit rating.

- Management authorizes specific individuals to approve the use of debt.

- When cash is needed for current operations, managers need to know that notes receivable can be discounted.

- Good managers ensure that past due accounts receivable are converted into notes receivable because notes provide more legal protection and are more likely to be collected.

- Because notes and drafts are negotiable, management ensures that internal control procedures are in place.

Thinking Critically

Why might managers use outside sources of funds for their business operations? How do they acquire these funds?

Sight drafts are used to collect past-due accounts receivable. Customers are more likely to honor a sight draft than a collection letter. The sight draft is sent to the customer's bank. If the customer does not honor the draft, the customer's credit reputation at the bank can be injured.

Sight drafts are also used to obtain cash on delivery when shipments are made to customers with poor credit or to new customers with no credit established. The sight draft is attached to a **bill of lading**, which is a business document that lists the goods accepted for transportation by a carrier. The bill of lading is sent to a bank near the customer. The customer pays the draft in order to get the bill of lading. The customer needs the bill of lading in order to obtain the goods. The collecting bank sends the money, less a collection fee, to the business issuing the draft. When the funds arrive, the business records the transaction as a cash sale and debits an expense account for the collection fee.

A **time draft** is a commercial draft that is payable during a period of time. The time period may be a specific date, or a specific number of days either after the date of the draft or after acceptance of the draft.

No journal entry is made when a time draft is issued. If the business honors (pays) the draft, the word "Accepted" is written on the draft and it is signed and dated. The business records the acceptance of a draft as a note payable. It is returned to the drawer, who records it as a note receivable.

Trade Acceptances

A **trade acceptance** is a form of commercial time draft used in transactions involving the sale of goods. The original transaction is recorded as a sale on credit. When the draft is accepted, it is accounted for as a promissory note. Merchants have fewer credit losses on trade acceptances than on accounts receivable. Trade acceptances can be discounted.

Internal Control of Notes Payable, Notes Receivable, and Drafts

The following are internal controls for notes payable, notes receivable, and drafts:

- Limit the number of people who can sign notes for the firm.
- Record all notes payable immediately.
- Identify a specific person or department to be responsible for prompt payment of interest and principal for notes payable.
- When paid, mark the note payable "Canceled" or "Paid" and file the note.
- Handle drafts as carefully as checks.
- Authorize certain persons only to accept notes.
- Record all notes receivable in the accounting records.
- Store notes receivable securely in a safe or fireproof vault to which access is limited.
- Verify and compare the actual notes receivable to the notes receivable register.
- Near the maturity date, inform the issuer of the approaching due date and the amount owed.
- If payment is not received on the due date, contact the issuer immediately.
- Review all past-due notes promptly and take necessary steps, including legal action, to ensure payment.

 **Section 2 Self Review**

Questions

1. When should a business ask a customer to sign a promissory note?

2. What does it mean to dishonor a note?

3. A note receivable with a maturity value of $5,200 is discounted at 12 percent, with 90 days remaining until the maturity date. What are the proceeds from discounting the note?

Exercises

4. Kendra Company accepted an interest-bearing note to settle a past-due account. When it is collected, the interest is credited to
   a. **Allowance for Uncollectible Accounts.**
   b. **Interest Income.**
   c. **Notes Receivable.**
   d. **Sales.**

5. The **Notes Receivable—Discounted** account

a. is a liability account.
b. is deducted from **Notes Receivable** on the balance sheet.
c. has a debit balance.
d. is used to record the amounts due on dishonored notes.

Analysis

6. When a sale is made for a note receivable instead of cash, what is the effect on cash receipts?

     (Answers to Section 2 Self Review are on page 609.)

Review and Applications

Review | Chapter Summary

In this chapter, you have learned how businesses use promissory notes, drafts, or trade acceptances to pay large amounts over a period of time. You have learned about negotiable instruments and how to record common notes payable and notes receivable.

Learning Objectives

1 Determine whether an instrument meets all the requirements of negotiability.

A negotiable instrument is a financial document that
- contains an order or promise to pay,
- meets all the requirements of the Uniform Commercial Code (UCC) to be transferable to another party.

The UCC requirements are as follows.
- It must be in writing.
- It must be signed by the maker.
- It must define the amount due and payment terms.
- It must list the payee.
- If addressed to a drawee, it must clearly name the person.

2 Calculate the interest on a note.

The borrower who signs a note payable usually pays interest on the amount borrowed. To determine the interest amount for any time period, use the formula Interest = Principal × Interest Rate × Time (years).

3 Determine the maturity date of a note.

The note's maturity date is determined at the time the note is issued, excluding the issue date itself.

4 Record routine notes payable transactions.

When purchasing an asset with a note, debit the asset account and credit **Notes Payable**. When paying the note payable, debit **Notes Payable** for the face amount of the note, debit **Interest Expense** for the interest, and credit **Cash** for the total paid (principal plus interest). **Interest Expense** appears on the income statement below Net Income from Operations in Other Income/Other Expense.

5 Record discounted notes payable transactions.

When money is borrowed on a note payable, the bank can deduct its interest charge immediately, called *discounting*. The borrower discounting a note payable receives the difference between the discount and the principal.

6 Record routine notes receivable transactions.

Notes receivable can be noninterest- or interest-bearing. Most firms charge interest.
- If the note receivable is issued at the time of a sale, record the transaction by debiting **Notes Receivable** and crediting **Sales**.
- If the note receivable results from a customer's failure to pay an accounts receivable, debit **Notes Receivable,** and credit **Accounts Receivable**.
- The recipient credits **Interest Income** for interest received when the note is paid.

7 Compute the proceeds from a discounted note receivable, and record transactions related to discounting of notes receivable.

A firm with an immediate need for cash can discount a note receivable. Debit **Cash** for the proceeds, credit **Notes Receivable—Discounted** for the face value, and either debit **Interest Expense** (if the proceeds are less than the principal) or credit **Interest Income** (if the proceeds exceed the principal). **Notes Receivable—Discounted** represent a contingent liability. If the note's maker fails to pay at maturity, the business must pay the bank.

8 Understand how to use bank drafts and trade acceptances and how to record transactions related to those instruments.

Bank drafts, commercial drafts, and trade acceptances are negotiable instruments used in business.
- Bank drafts are checks written by a bank ordering another bank in which it has funds to pay the indicated amount to a specific person or business.
- Businesses issue commercial drafts to order a person or firm to pay a sum of money at a specific time.
- Trade acceptances arise from the sale of goods. The original transaction is recorded in the same way as a sale on credit. When the draft has been accepted, it is accounted for as a promissory note.

9 Define the accounting terms new to this chapter.

CHAPTER 16 GLOSSARY

Bank draft (p. 596) A check written by a bank that orders another bank to pay the stated amount to a specific party

Banker's year (p. 584) A 360-day period used to calculate interest on a note

Bill of lading (p. 597) A business document that lists goods accepted for transportation

Cashier's check (p. 596) A draft on the issuing bank's own funds

Commercial draft (p. 596) A note issued by one party that orders another party to pay a specified sum on a specified date

Contingent liability (p. 593) An item that can become a liability if certain things happen

Discounting (p. 587) Deducting the interest from the principal on a note payable or receivable in advance

Draft (p. 596) A written order that requires one party (a person or business) to pay a stated sum of money to another party

Face value (p. 585) An amount of money indicated to be paid, exclusive of interest or discounts

Interest (p. 584) The fee charged for the use of money

Maturity value (p. 585) The total amount (principal plus interest) that must be paid when a note comes due

Negotiable instrument (p. 584) A financial document containing a promise or order to pay that meets all requirements of the Uniform Commercial Code in order to be transferable to another party

Note payable (p. 586) A liability representing a written promise by the maker of the note (the debtor) to pay another party (the creditor) a specified amount at a specified future date

Note receivable (p. 590) An asset representing a written promise by another party (the debtor) to pay the note holder (the creditor) a specified amount at a specified future date

Principal (p. 585) The amount shown on the face of a note

Sight draft (p. 596) A commercial draft that is payable on presentation

Time draft (p. 597) A commercial draft that is payable during a specified period of time

Trade acceptance (p. 598) A form of commercial time draft used in transactions involving the sale of goods

Comprehensive Self Review

1. List the elements of a negotiable instrument.
2. Of what value is a notes payable register?
3. What type of account is **Notes Receivable—Discounted?**
4. What is the most common type of draft?
5. Which account(s) will be debited and which account(s) will be credited when an interest-bearing note receivable that has been discounted is dishonored at the time of maturity?

(Answers to Comprehensive Self Review are on page 609.)

Discussion Questions

1. What are the requirements that must be met in order for a document to be negotiable?
2. What is the face amount of a note? The principal?
3. What is the maturity value of a $10,000 note, bearing interest at 10 percent, and due 180 days after date of issue of the note?
4. What is meant by "discounting a note payable"?
5. If a note dated March 31 has a three-month term, on what date must the note be paid?
6. How are notes payable maturing less than one year from the balance sheet date shown on the balance sheet?
7. Are notes payable likely to be given in the purchase of merchandise? The purchase of equipment? The borrowing of money? Why?
8. Explain why a business must keep records of the due dates of all notes payable.
9. How does a note receivable differ from an account receivable?
10. How, if at all, does computation of the maturity value of an interest-bearing note receivable differ from that for an interest-bearing note payable?
11. What is a dishonored note receivable?
12. What is meant by "discounting a note receivable"?
13. Explain how to compute the proceeds from discounting a note receivable.
14. Under what circumstances is a discounted note receivable considered to be a contingent liability?
15. What is a cashier's check?

Applications

EXERCISES

Exercise 16-1 ►
Objective 3

Determining the due dates of notes.

Find the due date of each of the following notes.

1. A note dated February 12, 2004, due one year from that date
2. A note dated May 1, 2004, due in 120 days
3. A note dated October 28, 2004, due three months from that date

Exercise 16-2 ►
Objectives 2, 3

Determining the maturity value of notes.

Compute the maturity value for each of the following notes.

1. A note payable with a face amount of $30,000, dated August 3, 2004, due in 90 days, bearing interest at 8 percent
2. A note payable with a face amount of $4,000, dated June 15, 2004, due in three months, bearing interest at 10 percent

Exercise 16-3 ►
Objectives 4, 5

Recording the issuance of notes payable.

During 2004 Horizon Company borrowed money at Second National Bank on two occasions. On June 3 the company borrowed $12,000, giving a 90-day, 8 percent note, and on December 12 the company discounted at 10 percent a $20,000, 90-day note payable.

1. Record the issuance of each of these notes in general journal form.
2. Record the issuance of checks to pay each note in general journal form.

Exercise 16-4 ►
Objective 4

Recording a note given for a purchase of equipment.

On July 1, 2004, Regan Company purchased a computer (office equipment) for $4,400, signing a 90-day, 12 percent note for the entire purchase price. Give the entry in general journal form to record this transaction.

Exercise 16-5 ►
Objectives 6, 7

Recording the receipt of a note for a past-due account.

On March 3, 2004, United Company received a 90-day, 8 percent note receivable for $8,000 from Jay Wesley, whose account was past due.

1. Record receipt of the note in general journal form.
2. Give the entry in general journal form to record the discounting of this note receivable on April 6 at College State Bank. The bank charged a discount rate of 12 percent.

Exercise 16-6 ►
Objective 7

Recording the payment of a discounted note receivable.

In general journal form, give the entry required when a discounted note receivable is paid on the maturity date.

Exercise 16-7 ►
Objective 7

Recording a dishonored note receivable.

Give the general journal entry required when a maker dishonors a note receivable that you have endorsed and discounted to the bank.

Exercise 16-8 ►
Objectives 2, 3

Computing the maturity value of notes receivable.

Find the maturity value of each of the following notes receivable.

1. A 90-day note, dated February 15, 2004, with a face value of $24,000, bearing interest at 10 percent

2. A six-month note, dated March 10, 2004, with a face value of $4,000, bearing interest at 12 percent

Computing the proceeds from a discounted note receivable.

Assume that the 90-day note described in item 1 of Exercise 16-8 was discounted at a bank on March 17, 2004. The bank charged a discount rate of 12 percent. Compute the net proceeds.

◀ **Exercise 16-9**
Objective 7

Computing the proceeds from a discounted note receivable.

Assume that the six-month note described in item 2 of Exercise 16-8 was discounted at a bank on April 10, 2004. The bank charged a discount rate of 12 percent. Compute the net proceeds.

◀ **Exercise 16-10**
Objective 7

Problems

Selected problems can be completed using:
🍑 **Peachtree**   📒 **QuickBooks**   ▦ **Spreadsheets**

PROBLEM SET A

Computing interest on notes payable.

Horatio Company issued and paid the following notes during 2004. Find the interest due on each of the following notes using the interest formula method. Show all calculations.

1. A $2,000 note at 12 percent for 180 days

2. A $4,000 note at 9 percent for four months

3. A $100,000 note at 10 percent for 90 days

Analyze: What total interest was attributable to these notes?

◀ **Problem 16-1A**
Objective 2
SPREADSHEET

Recording transactions involving notes payable.

Give the general journal entry to record each of the following transactions for Greenville Company.

1. Issued a 120-day, 12 percent note for $48,000 to purchase a small truck on April 10, 2004. (Debit **Delivery Equipment**)

2. Discounted its own 180-day, noninterest-bearing note with a principal amount of $12,000 at Merchant's National Bank on June 8, 2004. The bank charged a discount rate of 10 percent.

3. Paid the April 10 note on its due date.

4. Paid the note discounted on June 8 on its due date.

Analyze: Based on transactions 1 and 2, what total debts are owed by the Greenville Company on June 9, 2004?

◀ **Problem 16-2A**
Objectives 2, 3, 4, 5

Computing interest and maturity value.

The following notes were received by Connell Manufacturing Company during 2004.

◀ **Problem 16-3A**
Objectives 2, 3

Note No.	Date	Face Amount	Period	Interest Rate
6	Jan. 2	$10,000	2 months	12%
10	May 18	4,000	90 days	13%
15	Oct. 10	2,400	4 months	10%

Compute the maturity value of each note. Show all computations.

Analyze: What total interest was attributable to these notes transactions?

Problem 16-4A ►
Objective 7

Computing the proceeds from discounted notes receivable.

The notes receivable held by ALTA Company on July 2, 2005, are summarized below. On July 3, 2005, ALTA discounted all these notes at Guaranty State Bank at a discount rate of 13 percent. Compute the net proceeds received from discounting each note.

Note No.	Date	Face Amount	Period	Interest Rate
18	Mar. 3, 2005	$30,000	6 months	12%
15	Feb. 2, 2005	8,000	1 year	10%
20	June 1, 2005	3,600	60 days	13%

Analyze: What total debits should be posted to the **Interest Expense** account for these three note transactions?

Problem 16-5A ►
Objectives 2, 3, 4, 6, 7

Recording the receipt, discounting, and payment of notes receivable.

On July 16, 2004, Selma Corporation received a 90-day, 12 percent, interest-bearing note from ABC Company to settle ABC's $4,400 past due account. On July 31 Selma discounted this note at Midcity Bank, which charged a discount rate of 14 percent. On October 15, Selma received a notice that ABC had paid the note and the interest on the due date. Give the general journal entries required to record these transactions.

Analyze: If the company prepared a balance sheet on July 31, 2004, how should **Notes Receivable** be presented on the statement?

Problem 16-6A ►
Objective 1

Determining elements of a negotiable instrument.

Draft a note receivable that has all elements of a negotiable instrument.

Analyze: Suppose that you excluded one of the elements of a negotiable instrument. Choose an element to exclude and explain why the instrument is no longer negotiable.

PROBLEM SET B

Problem 16-1B ►
Objective 2

Computing interest on notes payable.

Alliance Company issued these notes during 2004. Find the interest due on each note using the interest formula method. Show all calculations.

1. A $2,600 note at 12 percent for 90 days
2. A $6,000 note at 8 percent for six months
3. A $40,000 note at 11.5 percent for 75 days

Analyze: If each note were issued and recorded on January 1, 2004, what would the balance of the **Notes Payable** account be on January 31, 2004?

Problem 16-2B ►
Objectives 2, 3, 4, 5

Recording transactions involving notes payable.

Give the general journal entry to record each of these transactions.

1. On May 5, 2004, Lucky Company issued a 120-day, 10 percent note for $16,000 to purchase new store equipment.
2. Lucky Company paid the May 5 note when it became due.

3. On September 18, 2004, Lucky Company borrowed money from Ames State Bank by discounting its own $20,000 note payable at a discount rate of 10 percent. This noninterest-bearing note matures in 120 days.

4. Lucky Company paid the September 18 note when it became due.

Analyze: If First National Bank offered a discount rate of 8 percent for Lucky Company's note payable of $20,000, what proceeds would be available? Assume the note would mature in 90 days.

Computing interest and maturity value.

Ling Merchandise Company received the notes below during 2004. Find the total interest and the maturity value of each note. Show all computations.

◀ **Problem 16-3B**
Objectives 2, 3

Note No.	Date	Face Amount	Period	Interest Rate
21	Feb. 22	$2,000	30 days	12.00%
27	July 8	4,000	60 days	11.25%
29	Aug. 15	6,400	3 months	12.00%

Analyze: If Ling Merchandise received these notes from customers to settle their existing accounts receivable, what total amount should be credited to the **Accounts Receivable** control account?

Computing the proceeds from discounted notes receivable.

The following notes receivable are held by Tinker Company on January 1, 2005. On January 2, 2005, Tinker discounted all these notes at First National Bank at a discount rate of 14 percent. Find the net proceeds that the firm received from discounting each note.

◀ **Problem 16-4B**
Objective 7

Note No.	Date	Face Amount	Period	Interest Rate
36	July 1, 2004	$24,000	1 year	12%
42	Sept. 1, 2004	16,000	6 months	11%
48	Dec. 1, 2004	15,000	1 year	13%

Analyze: What is the maturity date for Note 42?

Recording the receipt, discounting, and payment of notes receivable.

On March 1, 2004, Eagle Printing Company received a 120-day, 10 percent, interest-bearing note from Monroe Hall in settlement of a past due account receivable of $6,000. On March 31 Eagle discounted this note at Tennessee State Bank. The bank charged a discount rate of 12 percent. On June 29 Eagle received word that the note and interest had been paid in full.

◀ **Problem 16-5B**
Objectives 2, 3, 4, 6, 7

INSTRUCTIONS

1. Give the general journal entries to record these events, including Monroe Hall paying the note in full.

2. Assume that Hall fails to pay the note and that the bank charges Eagle with the note and a $50 protest fee. Give the general journal entry.

Analyze: On April 30, 2004, what is the balance of the **Notes Receivable** account? Eagle Printing accepted no other notes receivable.

Drawing up a negotiable instrument.

Draft a promissory note for $20,000 that will meet all requirements for a negotiable instrument.

◀ **Problem 16-6B**
Objective 1

Analyze: How does each feature of your note make it "negotiable"?

Notes Payable and Notes Receivable

Scott Ross owns Scott's Lawn and Garden Equipment. He periodically borrows money from Boise National Bank. He allows some customers to sign short-term notes receivable, which he usually discounts at the bank. Selected transactions that occurred in January 2004 follow.

INSTRUCTIONS

1. Record each of the January transactions in the general journal.
2. Record the additional data for Scott's Lawn and Garden Equipment in the general journal using the appropriate dates.

DATE		TRANSACTIONS
Jan.	15	Borrowed $6,000 from the bank on a note payable for the business at 12 percent interest for 45 days.
	22	Discounted a $9,000 note payable to the bank. Bank terms on it are 10 percent interest and a 90-day due date.
	23	Sold lawn equipment to Jennifer Donaldson for $1,800 on a note receivable. The terms of this note are 12 percent interest and a 60-day due date.
	23	Discounted the Donaldson note with the bank. The bank charges a discount rate of 15 percent.
	24	Sold $4,000 of equipment to Jeff Slaughter, who paid $2,000 cash and signed a 14 percent, 30-day note for the balance.
	25	Required Clyde Little, who is late paying his $6,000 account receivable due this day, to sign a 14 percent, 90-day note.

Additional Data

a. Ross pays all of the company's notes payable on time.
b. Jennifer Donaldson defaults on her $1,800 note loan and the bank makes a charge to the company's bank account.
c. Jeff Slaughter pays his note on time.
d. Clyde Little pays his note on time.

Analyze: What is the **Notes Payable** account balance on January 24?

CHAPTER 16 **CRITICAL THINKING PROBLEM**

Notes Receivable Discounted

Tucker Country Best, a wholesale dealer of country-style home furniture, frequently accepts promissory notes from its customers at the time of sale. Since Tucker regularly needs cash to meet its own obligations, it frequently discounts these notes at the bank.

Tucker's bookkeeper tells you that she does not bother to credit discounted notes to a **Notes Receivable—Discounted** account. Instead, she makes an entry to debit **Cash** and **Interest Expense** and to credit **Notes Receivable** (and **Interest Income** when necessary). She says that using a **Notes Receivable—Discounted** account just makes extra work, and, anyway, once the note is discounted, it becomes the bank's problem.

What is your opinion of the bookkeeper's comments?

Business Connections

MANAGERIAL FOCUS   Cash Management

1. How can management use notes receivable as a way to acquire cash?

2. You are a member of Signal Company's internal audit staff. A review of office practices indicates that an accounting assistant routinely makes arrangements with the bank for short-term notes payable and signs the notes. Evaluate this practice. Would you recommend any changes?

3. As a manager would you consider a note received at the time of sale of merchandise to be as collectible as a note received in exchange for a further extension of credit? Explain.

4. As a manager, why would you insist that dishonored notes receivable be charged back to the **Accounts Receivable** control account and the maker's subsidiary ledger account?

5. Under what circumstances would management insist on having a notes receivable register and/or a notes payable register?

◄ **Connection 1**

Ethical DILEMMA   **Payment Due** In January, Rose's employer purchased merchandise for the first time from Zinn Supply for $4,200. Rose noticed in April that Zinn had not sent a statement. She checked each month and, in August, reported this to her employer, asking if she should contact Zinn about the obvious error. Her employer said: "Do what you think best." Rose remembered that she was a participant in her employer's profit-sharing plan. She also noted that the employer did not tell her to contact Zinn. She decided not to tell the supplier of the error, concluding that the supplier should maintain better records. Comment on Rose's decision.

◄ **Connection 2**

Street WISE:
Questions from the Real World   **Long-Term Debt** Refer to the *1999 Annual Report* for The Home Depot, Inc. in Appendix B.

1. The Notes to Consolidated Financial Statements offer details about the company's financial condition. Describe the types of outstanding long-term debt listed in Note 2 for the period ending January 30, 2000.

2. Based on the information presented in Note 2, what portion of long-term debt is considered a current liability as of January 30, 2000?

◄ **Connection 3**

FINANCIAL STATEMENT ANALYSIS   **Balance Sheet** The following excerpt was taken from the Dole Food Company, Inc., *1999 Annual Report*. The Notes to Consolidated Financial Statements contained the following details on the company's long-term debt.

◄ **Connection 4**

Note 7—Debt
Long-term debt consisted of the following amounts:

(in thousands)	1999	1998
Unsecured debt		
Notes payable to banks at an average interest rate of		
6.6% (5.5% in 1998)	$ 234,000	$ 63,500
6.75% notes due 2000	225,000	225,000
7% notes due 2003	300,000	300,000
6.375% notes due 2005	300,000	300,000
7.875% debentures due 2013	175,000	175,000
Various other notes due 2000–2005 at an average		
interest rate of 7.6% (5.8% in 1998)	43,649	38,064
Secured debt		
Mortgages, contracts and notes due 2000–2012,		
at an average interest rate of 6.0% (6.4% in 1998)	19,661	23,824
Unamortized debt discount and issuance costs	(2,048)	(2,515)
	$1,295,262	$1,122,873
Current maturities	(9,546)	(6,451)
	$1,285,716	$1,116,422

Analyze:

1. What percentage of total debt matured in 1999? In 1998?

2. Which categories of notes increased from 1998 to 1999? By what amount?

3. Interest payments totaled $90 million in 1999. What average interest rate was paid on total debt?

Analyze Online: Find Dole Food Company, Inc. Web site

(www.dole.com). Recent financial reports are found within the *Company Information* link.

4. What is the fiscal period for the most recent annual report presented?

5. What long-term debt amount is reported on the balance sheet?

6. What amount of long-term debt matured in this fiscal period?

Connection 5 ► *Extending* the *Thought* **Lenders** Firms sometimes negotiate a note payable to fund expansion or to purchase equipment. If a company does not have sufficient funds to execute expansion plans or to buy equipment, why would a lending institution extend a loan? What are the risks for the borrower and for the lender? What agreements between the lender and borrower can increase the lender's confidence in the borrower?

Connection 6 ► Business Communication **Memo** The owner of Kinder Space wants to expand the parking lot. As the firm's accountant, you have been asked to compare interest-bearing notes available from two banks. The owner believes $18,000 will be needed. He assumes that the note carrying a lower interest rate is the preferred note. One note is for 90 days, 12% interest, and the other is for 120 days, 10% interest. Prepare a memo to the owner, recommending which note to secure. Explain your reasoning and include any computations you make.

TeamWork **Research** Banks and financial institutions are the largest issuers of notes and loans. As a team, select a bank and investigate the types of loans it issues. Use the bank's Web site and annual report to write a report describing the types of loans it offers. Include the total amount reported for loans receivable for the current year and any provision the bank makes for uncollectible loans. Print any financial statements or notes to financial statements to support your report.

◄ **Connection 7**

*inter*NET
CONNECTION **Buy or Lease?** Web sites such as the Smart Money site have calculators to help you make decisions about everything from investing to buying a car. Go to **www.smartmoney.com.** Select the *Leasing Calculator.* What does it recommend for a car loan with these assumptions: price, $17,000; down payment, $1,500; lease term, 36 months; rate of return, 7%; value of car at end of lease, $8,000; and monthly payment, $250. What underlying assumption is made by the calculator?

◄ **Connection 8**

Answers to Self Reviews

Answers to Section 1 Self Review

1. June 15
2. Interest = $12,000 × 0.10 × (30/360) = $100
3. Proceeds − Face Amount − Discount
   Discount = $8,000 × 0.09 × (60/360) = $120
   Proceeds = $8,000 − $120 = $7,880
4. **c.** maturity value.
5. **c.** It must state a rate of interest.
6. Maturity date = Issue date + Term

Answers to Section 2 Self Review

1. When a customer cannot pay a currently due account receivable, it is wise to have a note receivable signed.
2. The maker of the note does not pay it when it is due.
3. $5,044 ($5,200 − $156 discount)
4. **b. Interest Income.**
5. **b.** is deducted from **Notes Receivable** on the balance sheet.
6. It lowers the amount of cash initially received, but the business receives interest income from the note.

Answers to Comprehensive Self Review

1. (a) must be in writing and signed by the maker, (b) contain an unconditional promise or order to pay a definite amount of money, (c) be payable on demand or at another time that can be determined, (d) be payable to the order of the bearer, and (e) if addressed to a drawee, be clearly identified.
2. A notes payable register is valuable in keeping up with payments, interest, and due dates of liabilities.
3. A contra asset account. It is shown on the balance sheet as a reduction of **Notes Receivable.**
4. The most common type of draft is the check written from an ordinary checking account.
5. **Notes Receivable—Discounted** will be debited and **Notes Receivable** will be credited. Also, **Accounts Receivable** and the customer's account will be debited and **Cash** will be credited.

CHAPTER 17

Learning Objectives

1. Compute inventory cost by applying four commonly used costing methods.

2. Compare the different methods of inventory costing.

3. Compute inventory value under the lower of cost or market rule.

4. Estimate inventory cost using the gross profit method.

5. Estimate inventory cost using the retail method.

6. Define the accounting terms new to this chapter.

Merchandise Inventory

www.circuitcity.com

*F*or Circuit City, customer service and product availability are critical. This national retailer has made it a priority to help customers find the products they want, when they want them. In July 1999 the company launched CircuitCity.com, a Web site which is fully integrated with the chain's brick-and-mortar stores nationwide. Online customers may check inventories in Web site warehouses and in stores in real time. Products purchased online can be shipped or reserved for Express Pickup in one of Circuit City's Superstores. Not only do customers get superior service, Circuit City can measure product demand in real time, thus effectively managing inventory levels.

Thinking Critically
What operational benefits do you think Circuit City has gained since the Express Pickup feature was launched?

For more information on Circuit City, go to: collegeaccounting.glencoe.com.

New Terms

Average cost method

First in, first out (FIFO) method

Gross profit method

Last in, first out (LIFO) method

Lower of cost or market rule

Markdown

Market price

Markon

Markup

Periodic inventory

Perpetual inventory

Physical inventory

Replacement cost

Retail method

Specific identification method

Weighted average method

Inventory Costing Methods

Section Objectives

1. **Compute inventory cost by applying four commonly used costing methods.**

   WHY IT'S IMPORTANT
   Factors such as industry practices, merchandise types, and business operations affect how a business assigns costs to inventories.

2. **Compare the different methods of inventory costing.**

   WHY IT'S IMPORTANT
   Inventory valuation affects the net income or net loss of a business.

Terms to Learn

average cost method
first in, first out (FIFO) method
last in, first out (LIFO) method
periodic inventory
perpetual inventory
physical inventory
specific identification method
weighted average method

Businesses report information about merchandise inventory on the financial statements. This section covers four methods used to compute the value of merchandise inventory based on original cost.

Importance of Inventory Valuation

Assigning an appropriate value to merchandise inventory is important because the **Merchandise Inventory** account appears on both the balance sheet and the income statement. Often inventory represents the largest current asset on the balance sheet. Inventory valuation also affects the net income or net loss reported on the income statement.

A higher ending inventory value results in a lower cost of goods sold, which results in higher income from operations. On the other hand, a lower ending inventory value results in a higher cost of goods sold, which results in a lower income from operations.

> On its consolidated balance sheet on December 31, 1999, Avon Products, Inc. reported inventories valued at $523.5 million. Inventory represented 40 percent of total company assets.

We learned in Chapter 12 that many firms value merchandise inventory at the original cost of the items on hand. Merchandise inventory is counted at the end of the accounting period. The inventory value is calculated by multiplying the number of units on hand by the cost per item. Taking an actual count of the number of units of each type of good on hand is known as taking a **physical inventory**. An inventory system in which the amount of goods on hand is determined by periodic counts is called a **periodic inventory** system. It is the method that we use in this chapter.

Some businesses, especially manufacturing firms, need to know the number of units and the unit cost for the inventory on hand at all times. These businesses use a **perpetual inventory** system, in which inventory is based on a running total number of units. Electronic equipment, such as point-of-sale cash registers and scanners helps track all of the items as they are purchased and sold. Perpetual inventory records are discussed in a later chapter.

1. **Objective**

   Compute inventory cost by applying four commonly used costing methods.

Assigning Costs to Inventory

The cost of sold merchandise is transferred from the balance sheet (current assets) to the income statement (cost of goods sold). The amount of cost that is transferred depends on the method used to value inventory. Four methods are commonly used to value inventory. Accountants choose the method that works best for the industry and the company.

Specific Identification Method

The **specific identification method** of inventory valuation is based on the actual cost of each item of merchandise. Cost of goods sold is the exact cost of the specific merchandise sold, and the ending inventory balance is the exact cost of the specific inventory items on hand. Businesses that sell high-priced or one-of-a-kind items, such as art and automobile dealers, use the specific identification method. However, this method is not practical for a business where hundreds of similar items of relatively small unit value are carried in inventory. In addition, the purchase cost of many types of items may change during the accounting period.

Average Cost Method

The **average cost method** uses the average cost of units of an item available for sale during the period to arrive at the value of ending inventory. It is advantageous to use the average cost method when a company's inventory is composed of many similar items that are not subject to significant price and style changes. Table 17-1 provides an example of the average cost method.

- There were 50 units in beginning inventory valued at $8 each.
- There were three purchases during the year, at different costs.
- The beginning inventory and purchases are added together to determine that during the year 340 units were available for sale at a total cost of $3,230.
- The average cost per unit is $9.50 ($3,230 ÷ 340).
- A physical inventory count showed 48 units on hand.
- During the year 292 units were sold (340 − 48).
- Under the average cost method, the total cost of units available for sale ($3,230) is divided between the financial statements as follows:
  - Balance sheet—ending inventory is $456.
  - Income statement—cost of goods sold is $2,774.

Important!

Physical Inventory

Whether a perpetual or periodic inventory system is used, a physical inventory should be taken at least once a year.

Recall

Cost of Goods Sold

The formula for cost of goods sold is

    Beginning inventory
+ Purchases
− Ending inventory
= Cost of goods sold

◀ **TABLE 17-1**
Average Cost Method of Inventory Valuation

Explanation	Number of Units	Unit Cost	Total Cost
Beginning inventory, January 1	50	$ 8.00	$ 400.00
Purchases			
March 19	150	9.00	1,350.00
May 15	100	10.00	1,000.00
October 5	40	12.00	480.00
Total merchandise available for sale	340		$3,230.00
Average cost ($3,230 ÷ 340) = $9.50			
Ending inventory	48	9.50	456.00
Cost of goods sold ($3,230 − $456)	292	9.50	$2,774.00

This method is sometimes referred to as the **weighted average method** because it considers the number of units in each purchase and the unit purchase price to compute a "weighted average" cost per unit.

The average cost method of inventory valuation is relatively simple to use, but it reflects the limitations of any procedure that involves average figures. The average unit cost is not related to any specific unit, and it does not clearly reveal price changes. In highly competitive businesses that are subject to considerable model or style upgrades and price fluctuations, it is desirable to have a more specific and revealing method of cost determination.

> The Coca-Cola Company values inventory using the average cost or first-in, first out methods.

First In, First Out Method

Recall

Disclosure

The method of inventory valuation must be disclosed in the financial reports.

For most businesses the physical flow of inventory is "the first item purchased is the first item sold." This certainly makes sense for perishable items. Some businesses assign inventory costs using this flow. The **first in, first out method** of inventory valuation, usually referred to as **FIFO,** assumes that the oldest merchandise is sold first.

Let's calculate ending inventory under FIFO using the information in Table 17-1. During the period 292 units were sold. Under FIFO the "first cost in is the first cost transferred out" to cost of goods sold. This matches the earliest costs with the revenue from the units sold. So the cost of the ending inventory is computed by using the cost of the most recent purchases.

Table 17-2 shows that the cost assigned to the 48 units in ending inventory is $560: 40 units purchased in October at $12 and 8 units purchased in May at $10, for a total of 48 units. During the period there was $3,230 of inventory available for sale. Under the FIFO method, the cost is divided between the financial statements as follows:

- Balance sheet—ending inventory is $560.
- Income statement—cost of goods sold is $2,670 ($3,230 − $560).

TABLE 17-2 ▶
FIFO Method of Inventory Valuation

Explanation	Number of Units	Unit Cost	Total Cost
From purchase of October 5	40	$12.00	$480.00
From purchase of May 15	8	10.00	80.00
Ending inventory	48		$560.00

> A company can use several inventory valuation methods. Most inventory costs for Dole Food Company, Inc. are determined principally on a first in, first out basis. However, specific identification and average cost methods are used for certain packing material and operating inventories.

Last In, First Out Method

Important!

Inventory Costing and Net Income

Gross profit on sales and net income are affected by the inventory costing method.

The **last in, first out (LIFO) method** assumes that the most recently purchased merchandise is sold first, and thus assigns the most recent costs to cost of goods sold. The "last cost in is the first cost transferred out" to cost of goods sold. Thus the cost of ending inventory is computed using the cost of the oldest merchandise on hand during the period.

Using the figures from Table 17-1 but applying the LIFO method, Table 17-3 shows that the cost assigned to the 48 units in ending inventory is $8 per unit. This is the same cost assigned to the units in beginning inventory. During the period there was $3,230 of inventory available for sale. Under the LIFO method, the cost is divided between the financial statements as follows:

- Balance sheet—ending inventory is $384.
- Income statement—cost of goods sold is $2,846 ($3,230 − $384).

Under the LIFO method, the balance sheet reflects the earliest costs. The cost of goods sold reflects the costs applicable to the most recent purchases.

Explanation	Number of Units	Unit Cost	Total Cost
Beginning inventory, January 1	50	$8.00	$400.00
Ending inventory, December 31	48	$8.00	$384.00

◀ **TABLE 17-3**
LIFO Method of Inventory Valuation

Comparing Results of Inventory Costing Methods

Table 17-4 shows the results obtained for the average cost, FIFO, and LIFO inventory methods. The ending inventory is highest under FIFO and lowest under LIFO. The cost of goods sold is highest under LIFO and lowest under FIFO.

②Objective

Compare the different methods of inventory costing.

Explanation	Units	Unit Cost	Total Cost	Ending Inventory Valuation	Cost of Goods Sold
Beginning inventory, January 1	50	$ 8.00	$ 400.00		
Purchases					
March 19	150	9.00	1,350.00		
May 15	100	10.00	1,000.00		
October 5	40	12.00	480.00		
Total merchandise available for sale	340		$3,230.00		
1. Average cost method	48	$ 9.50		$456.00	$2,774.00
2. FIFO	40	$12.00	$ 480.00		
	8	10.00	80.00		
	48		$ 560.00	$560.00	$2,670.00
3. LIFO	48	$ 8.00	$ 384.00	$384.00	$2,846.00

▲ **TABLE 17-4**
Comparison of Results of Inventory Costing Methods

Remember the following important points about inventory valuation methods:

- Except for specific identification, the physical flow of inventory and the costs assigned to inventory are not specifically matched. Average, FIFO, and LIFO cost methods *assign* costs to inventory but do not track the cost to the specific inventory item.
- Businesses can use separate inventory valuation methods for different classes of inventory.
- Following the consistency principle, once a business adopts an inventory valuation method, it uses that method consistently from one period to the next. A business cannot change its inventory valuation method at will.
- A business can use one inventory costing method for financial accounting purposes and another for federal income tax

purposes, with one exception. Businesses that use the LIFO method for tax purposes must also use LIFO for financial accounting.

- FIFO focuses on the balance sheet. The most current costs are in ending inventory.
- LIFO focuses on the income statement and the matching principle. The most recent costs are matched to revenue. LIFO is considered the most conservative costing method.

Since price trends represent a vital element in any inventory valuation, remember these basic rules:

- When prices are rising, cost of goods sold is highest and net income is lowest under LIFO. Therefore, in periods of inflation, LIFO results in the lowest income tax expense.
- When prices are falling, cost of goods sold is lower and net income is higher under LIFO.
- Whatever direction prices take, the average cost method almost always results in net income between the amounts obtained with FIFO and LIFO.

LIFO Use Internationally

Most of the major industrialized countries use the methods of accounting for inventories discussed in this chapter. In some countries, however, LIFO is not generally accepted. Countries that prohibit its use or in which it is rarely used include:

- England
- Australia
- Hong Kong
- Ireland

LIFO can be used in Singapore only if the difference between it and FIFO is reported.

Clearly, differences in use can result in comparability problems when users of financial statements attempt to compare companies across international boundaries.

Section 1 Self Review

Questions

1. What does FIFO mean, and what is the FIFO cost flow method?
2. Under LIFO, which costs are assigned to the goods sold during the period?
3. In a period of inflation, which inventory method (LIFO, FIFO, average cost) results in the lowest income tax expense?

Exercises

4. In periods of rising prices, which inventory valuation method results in the highest ending inventory?
   a. FIFO method
   b. LIFO method
   c. Average cost method
   d. None of the above
5. During periods of changing prices, which method does the best job of matching revenues and expenses?

a. FIFO method
b. LIFO method
c. Average cost method
d. All of the above

Analysis

6. Before recommending an inventory valuation method, what questions would you ask the manager about the business and its inventory?

(Answers to Section 1 Self Review are on page 635.)

Inventory Valuation and Control

According to the historical cost principle, assets are reported on the balance sheet at their historical cost. The conservatism convention, however, states that assets should not be overstated. This section discusses how to report the value of inventory when the cost is above the market price.

Lower of Cost or Market Rule

Market price or **replacement cost** is the price the business would have to pay to buy an item of inventory through usual channels in usual quantities. To determine market price, businesses contact their suppliers, read trade publications, or review recent purchases. If the current market price is lower than the original cost, the business uses the **lower of cost or market rule**. That is, inventory is reported at its original cost or its replacement cost, whichever is lower. There are three ways to apply the lower of cost or market rule: by item, in total, or by group.

Lower of Cost or Market Rule by Item

Table 17-5 illustrates the lower of cost or market rule by item. Inventory consists of two groups of two stock items each. The report shows the quantity, cost, and market price of each item. Cost is determined using one of the acceptable methods—specific identification, average cost, FIFO, or LIFO. Each item's valuation basis (cost or market, whichever is lower) is determined; for item 1234 it is cost, $2, and for item 2765 it is market, $4.40. The quantity is multiplied by valuation basis and the amounts are totaled. The inventory balance reported on the balance sheet is $958.

Description	Quantity	Unit Price Cost	Unit Price Market	Lower of Cost or Market Valuation Basis	Lower of Cost or Market Amount
Group 1					
Stock 1234	75	$2.00	$2.20	Cost	$150.00
Stock 2765	100	5.00	4.40	Market	440.00
Total, Group 1					$590.00
Group 2					
Stock 3124	40	$3.40	$3.20	Market	$128.00
Stock 4532	75	3.20	3.60	Cost	240.00
Total, Group 2					$368.00
Inventory valuation (lower of cost or market by item)					$958.00

◀ **TABLE 17-5**
Establishing Lower of Cost or Market Valuation by Item

Section Objectives

3 Compute inventory value under the lower of cost or market rule.

WHY IT'S IMPORTANT
The conservatism convention is important when determining the cost of inventory.

4 Estimate inventory cost using the gross profit method.

WHY IT'S IMPORTANT
Often businesses need to determine the cost of inventory without taking a physical count.

5 Estimate inventory cost using the retail method.

WHY IT'S IMPORTANT
The retail method provides an easy and quick estimation of the cost of the inventory.

Terms to Learn

gross profit method
lower of cost or market rule
markdown
market price
markon
markup
replacement cost
retail method

③ Objective

Compute inventory value under the lower of cost or market rule.

Lower of Total Cost or Total Market

Table 17-6 illustrates the lower of cost or market rule applied to total inventory, not to individual items. The cost of inventory is computed using both cost and market and then are compared. Inventory is valued on the balance sheet at the lower amount, $1,003.

TABLE 17-6 ▶

Establishing Lower of Total Cost or Total Market Valuation

Description	Quantity	Unit Price Cost	Unit Price Market	Total Cost	Total Market
Group 1					
Stock 1234	75	$2.00	$2.20	$ 150.00	$ 165.00
Stock 2765	100	5.00	4.40	500.00	440.00
Totals, Group 1				$ 650.00	$ 605.00
Group 2					
Stock 3124	40	$3.40	$3.20	$ 136.00	$ 128.00
Stock 4532	75	3.20	3.60	240.00	270.00
Total, Group 2				$ 376.00	$ 398.00
Total Inventory				$1,026.00	$1,003.00
Inventory valuation (lower of total cost or total market)					$1,003.00

Conservatism

According to the modifying convention of conservatism, if GAAP allows alternatives, assets on the balance sheet should be understated rather than overstated.

> The inventories of Pier 1 Imports, Inc., are stated at the lower of average cost or market. Cost is determined using the weighted average method.

Lower of Cost or Market Rule by Groups

Another way to apply the lower of cost or market rule is by groups. The lower figure (cost or market) for each group is added to the lower figures for the other groups to obtain the total inventory valuation. As shown in Table 17-7, the valuation basis of Group 1 is market and of Group 2 is cost. Inventory is valued on the balance sheet at $981.

TABLE 17-7 ▶

Establishing the Lower of Total Cost or Total Market by Groups

Lower of cost or market valuation by <u>group</u> (as shown in Table 17-6)	
Group 1 Market	$605.00
Group 2 Cost	376.00
Total inventory valuation	$981.00

Depending on the method used, inventory could appear on the balance sheet as one of the following amounts.

Lower of Cost or Market
By Item	$ 958
By Total	1,003
By Group	981

Important!

Lower of Cost or Market Rule

If the replacement cost is less than the historical cost, the inventory is reported at replacement cost.

Accountants select the method based on the size and variety of inventory, the margin of profit, industry practices, and plans for expansion.

- Some accountants believe that the total method should be used. They think that conservatism should apply to the total inventory, not item by item. If market value of the inventory as a whole has not declined below cost, they believe inventory should be presented at historical cost.

Computers in Accounting

Inventory Control

Whether a business sells a few products or offers thousands of items, managing merchandise flow is essential in order to respond quickly to customer preferences. The Home Depot stocks between 40,000 and 50,000 different kinds of building materials, garden supplies, and home improvement products. Tracking and managing inventories at this level requires the use of a computerized inventory system.

A computerized inventory system helps to
- fill orders faster and more efficiently,
- reduce overstocked or back-ordered items,
- obtain inventory valuations quickly,
- improve inventory planning and control,
- monitor the in-store transactions.

A computerized inventory system accommodates both sales and purchase transactions. Small retail stores use software developed for microcomputers, while large stores like Wal-Mart or Kmart need more sophisticated software. As sales transactions are processed using a terminal or a scanner, data about the quantity sold and the number of units on hand is instantly updated.

Store managers can generate reports to analyze buying trends and to determine which items to reorder. A physical count is not needed in order to identify the items to reorder. Using specialized software, orders are transmitted from the stores to a central distribution center. Within a few days, the merchandise arrives at the store, and the database is updated to adjust the quantity-on-hand data for each item. Handheld scanning devices are used to facilitate the restocking process.

Thinking Critically
If you have purchased a product at a store such as The Home Depot or Wal-Mart, what computerized processes did you notice that could be part of a computerized inventory system?

Internet Application
Locate the Web site for the American Production and Inventory Control Society (APICS). Describe its mission. What certification programs does the APICS offer?

- Other accountants prefer the group method because it does not reflect individual fluctuations as does the item method, and it does not lump together all types of items as does the total method.
- Some accountants choose the item method because it is the most conservative method. Almost without exception the item method results in the lowest inventory amount.

Inventory Estimation Procedures

Occasionally managers need to know the inventory cost and cannot or do not want to take a physical count. For example, after a fire the business cannot count the items destroyed. However, for insurance and income tax purposes, the business must determine the cost of the goods destroyed. Two common techniques to estimate the cost of inventory are the gross profit method and the retail method.

Gross Profit Method of Inventory Valuation

The **gross profit method** assumes that the rate of gross profit on sales and the ratio of cost of goods sold to net sales are relatively constant from period to period.

4 Objective
Estimate inventory cost using the gross profit method.

Net sales	$100		
Cost of goods sold	(60)		
Gross profit on sales	$ 40		
Gross profit rate		40 ÷ 100 = 40%	
Cost of goods sold to net sales ratio		60 ÷ 100 = 60%	

The following example illustrates the gross profit method. On June 10 a retail store lost its entire merchandise inventory in a fire. The accounting records show that for the two preceding years, gross profit was 40 percent of net sales and cost of goods sold was 60 percent of net sales. The accounting records for the current year show

Inventory (at cost), January 1	$100,000
Net purchases, January 1 to June 10	260,000
Net sales, January 1 to June 10	440,000

Use the following steps to estimate the cost of inventory on hand on June 10:

Step 1: *Estimate the cost of goods sold.* Sales were $440,000 and the ratio of cost of goods sold to net sales is 60 percent. The estimated cost of goods sold is $264,000 ($440,000 × 0.60).

Step 2: *Determine the cost of goods available for sale.* Include in the computation freight in charges and purchases returns.

Beginning inventory	$100,000
Net purchases	260,000
Cost of goods available for sale	$360,000

Step 3: *Compute the ending (destroyed) inventory.* Subtract the estimated cost of goods sold from the cost of goods available for sale.

Cost of goods available for sale	$360,000
Estimated cost of goods sold	(264,000)
Estimated cost of ending inventory	$ 96,000

The cost of inventory destroyed in the fire is estimated to be $96,000.

International INSIGHTS

International Trade

The Bureau of Economic Analysis tracks U.S. trade with other nations in goods and services. The trade deficit continued its upward trend, reaching $89.3 billion in the second quarter of 2000.

⑤ Objective

Estimate inventory cost using the retail method.

Retail Method of Inventory Valuation

The **retail method** estimates inventory cost by applying the ratio of cost to selling price in the current accounting period to the retail price of the inventory. This widely used method permits businesses to determine the approximate cost of ending inventory from the financial records. It makes it possible for the business to prepare financial statements easily and often without taking a physical inventory count.

Using the retail method, inventory is classified into groups of items that have about the same rate of markon. **Markon** is the difference between the cost and the initial retail price of merchandise. The following steps use assumed figures to estimate the cost of inventory using the retail method.

Step 1: List the beginning inventory at both cost ($11,700) and retail ($19,500).

Step 2: When merchandise is purchased, record it at cost ($183,300 including $300 freight) and determine its retail value ($273,000).

Step 3: Compute merchandise available for sale at cost ($195,000) and at retail ($292,500).

Step 4: Record sales at retail ($238,500).

Managerial IMPLICATIONS

Inventory

- Good managers carefully control inventory because it may represent a large part of the assets of the business.

- Management should help select an inventory costing method that is practical, reliable, and as simple as possible to apply.

- Management needs to understand how the inventory valuation method affects net income and income taxes.

- Based on the gross profit method of estimating inventory, managers can prepare budgets and financial statements when a physical inventory count is not practical or possible.

- Retail managers use the retail method of inventory valuation to estimate the cost of goods on hand. Department managers, who are not permitted to exceed their inventory budgets, use this method as often as every week.

Thinking Critically
Should the gross profit method or the retail method of calculating inventory replace the physical count of inventory?

Step 5: Subtract retail sales from the retail merchandise available for sale. The difference is the ending inventory at retail ($292,500 − $238,500 = $54,000).

Step 6: Compute the cost ratio.

$$\frac{\text{Merchandise Available for Sale at Cost}}{\text{Merchandise Available for Sale at Retail}} = \frac{\$195,000}{\$292,500} = 66.67 \text{ percent}$$

Step 7: Multiply the ending inventory at retail by the cost ratio. The result is an estimate of the ending inventory cost, $36,000 ($54,000 × 0.6667).

Step 8: Estimate the cost of goods sold by subtracting the ending inventory at cost from the merchandise available for sale at cost, $159,000 ($195,000 − $36,000).

The calculations for each step are shown below.

		Cost	Retail
Step 1:	Beginning inventory	$ 11,700	$ 19,500
Step 2:	Purchases	183,000	273,000
	Freight in	300	
Step 3:	Total merchandise available for sale	$195,000	$292,500
Step 4:	Less sales		238,500
Step 5:	Ending inventory priced at retail		$ 54,000
Step 6:	Cost ratio = ($195,000 ÷ $292,500) = 66.67%		
Step 7:	Conversion to approximate cost:		
	Ending inventory at retail × Cost ratio = $54,000 × 0.6667		
	Ending inventory at cost = $36,000		
Step 8:	Cost of goods sold = $195,000 − $36,000 = $159,000		

The benefit of the retail method is that without counting inventory the business is able to estimate the ending inventory balance at cost.

The retail method is not as simple as this example suggests. Adjustments must be made for **markups**, price increases above the original markons, and markup cancelations. Adjustments are also made for **markdowns**, price reductions below the original markon, and for markdown cancelations. These details are not covered in this text.

A more accurate application of the retail method involves taking a physical inventory, which is facilitated by using scanning devices to capture the sales price marked on the merchandise. The physical inventory at retail is converted to cost by applying the cost ratio. For example, if the physical inventory count shows retail cost of $60,000 and the cost ratio is 66.67 percent, the cost of the inventory is estimated to be $40,000 ($60,000 × 0.667).

Internal Control of Inventories

The internal controls over inventory depend on the nature of the inventory. For example, controls for expensive jewelry are more elaborate than controls over lumber. Typical inventory controls are as follows:

- Limit access to inventory.
- Require documents, such as approved shipping orders, before allowing items to leave the warehouse.
- Take a physical inventory count at least annually to verify that the goods on hand match the amounts in the accounting records. Use spot checks to verify the counting techniques and the item costs. Have an independent auditor observe the count.

About Accounting

Inventory Financing
Many businesses obtain credit based on their merchandise inventory. Inventory financing uses the inventory on hand as collateral for the credit line.

Good inventory management can result in better customer service. Haggar Clothing Company's new inventory system has slashed the time it takes to fill an order from a week to about 48 hours. This has boosted cash flows and improved the customer's experience.

Section 2 Self Review

Questions

1. What does the lower of cost or market mean?

2. Which method of applying the lower of cost or market (by item, group, or total) yields the lowest inventory valuation?

3. Why would a business use the gross profit method to estimate inventory?

Exercises

4. Conservatism requires that inventory be presented on the balance sheet at
   a. cost.
   b. market value.
   c. cost or market value, whichever is lower.
   d. cost or market value, whichever is higher.

5. Which of the following inventory costing procedures does not require a physical count of merchandise?
   a. Cost or market value
   b. Specific identification method
   c. Gross profit method
   d. Average cost method

Analysis

6. When would a business use the gross profit method instead of the retail method to estimate the cost of ending inventory?

(Answers to Section 2 Self Review are on page 635.)

CHAPTER 17 — Review and Applications

Review

Chapter Summary

It is important to account for merchandise inventory because the information appears on both the balance sheet and the income statement. Industry practices, merchandise unit costs, and merchandise price fluctuations affect how costs are assigned to inventory.

Learning Objectives

1 Compute inventory cost by applying four commonly used costing methods.

There are four common inventory cost flow assumptions.

- The specific identification method uses the actual purchase price of the specific items in inventory.
- The average cost method averages the cost of all like items for sale during the period to value the ending inventory.
- The FIFO method develops the cost of the ending inventory from the cost of latest purchases.
- The LIFO method develops the cost of the ending inventory from the cost of earlier purchases.

2 Compare the different methods of inventory costing.

The method used affects the net income reported.

- With rising prices, LIFO gives a lower reported net income than FIFO, as well as lower income taxes payable.
- With falling prices, LIFO gives a higher reported net income than FIFO.
- The average cost method almost always gives a result between these.

3 Compute inventory value under the lower of cost or market rule.

- Assets are reported on financial statements at their historical cost. However, under the conservatism convention, assets should not be overstated.
- If the replacement cost of an inventory item is below its original purchase cost, it is necessary to value the inventory at the lower current value in the firm's financial records.
- Consequently, inventory is valued at either its original cost, or its replacement cost, whichever is lower. This is called the lower of cost or market.
- Cost refers to the historical cost.
- Market refers to the replacement cost.
- The lower of cost or market can be applied to individual items in the inventory, to groups of items, or to the inventory as a whole.

4 Estimate inventory cost using the gross profit method.

The gross profit method of estimating inventory assumes that the rate of gross profit on sales and the ratio of cost of goods sold to net sales are relatively constant from period to period. Ending inventory can be estimated using three steps:

1) Estimate the cost of goods sold by multiplying net sales by the ratio of cost of goods sold to net sales.
2) Determine goods available for sale by adding beginning inventory and net purchases.
3) Compute ending inventory by subtracting the estimated cost of goods sold (in step 1) from goods available for sale (in step 2).

5 Estimate inventory cost using the retail method.

The retail method uses the retail selling price of items remaining. The retail value is multiplied by the cost ratio of the current period to determine the approximate cost. This method entails a full consideration of markups, markup cancelations, markdowns, and markdown cancelations.

6 Define the accounting terms new to this chapter.

CHAPTER 17 GLOSSARY

Average cost method (p. 613) A method of inventory costing using the average cost of units of an item available for sale during the period to arrive at cost of the ending inventory

First in, first out (FIFO) method (p. 614) A method of inventory costing that assumes the oldest merchandise is sold first

Gross profit method (p. 619) A method of estimating inventory cost based on the assumption that the rate of gross profit on sales and the ratio of cost of goods sold to net sales are relatively constant from period to period

Last in, first out (LIFO) method (p. 614) A method of inventory costing that assumes that the most recently purchased merchandise is sold first

Lower of cost or market rule (p. 617) The principle by which inventory is reported at either its original cost or its replacement cost, whichever is lower

Markdown (p. 622) Price reduction below the original markon

Market price (p. 617) The price the business would pay to buy an item of inventory through usual channels in usual quantities

Markon (p. 620) The difference between the cost and the initial retail price of merchandise

Markup (p. 622) A price increase above the original markon

Periodic inventory (p. 612) Inventory based on a periodic count of goods on hand

Perpetual inventory (p. 612) Inventory based on a running total of number of units

Physical inventory (p. 612) An actual count of the number of units of each type of good on hand

Replacement cost (p. 617) See Market price

Retail method (p. 620) A method of estimating inventory cost by applying the ratio of cost to selling price in the current accounting period to the retail price of the inventory

Specific identification method (p. 613) A method of inventory costing based on the actual cost of each item of merchandise

Weighted average method (p. 613) See Average cost method

Comprehensive Self Review

1. Name four commonly used methods for determining the cost of inventory.

2. Under what circumstances would it be logical to use specific identification in determining the ending inventory?

3. What two methods of estimating inventory may be available to a business where a fire has destroyed most of the inventory?

4. What is the formula for the cost ratio used in the retail method of estimating inventory?

5. How often should a physical inventory be taken?

(Answers to Comprehensive Self Review are on page 635.)

Discussion Questions

1. Where does the ending merchandise inventory amount appear on the balance sheet? On the income statement?

2. What is a physical inventory?

3. What is a perpetual inventory?

4. Explain the specific identification method of inventory valuation.

5. Is the specific identification method of inventory valuation suitable for a retail grocery store? Why or why not?

6. Is it logical for an automobile dealer to use the average cost method? Explain.

7. A gravel dealer uses the LIFO method. Give a circumstance under which this method would match physical flow of the gravel.

8. What is meant by the term *market* as it is used in the lower of cost or market rule?

9. If a business uses the lower of cost or market method of inventory valuation, how is cost determined?

10. Explain how the lower of cost or market method is applied on a group basis.

11. Is the value of inventory likely to be lower if the lower of cost or market method is applied on an item-by-item basis, on a group basis, or to the inventory as a whole?

12. Explain the gross profit method of estimating inventories.

13. Suggest two situations in which it might be desirable to estimate inventories without a physical count.

14. Describe how the cost of an ending inventory is estimated under the retail method.

15. What is a periodic inventory?

16. Explain the relationship between inventory valuation and income.

17. Describe how electronic devices can be used in the inventory process.

18. What are some specific controls that management must provide over inventory in a business that sells diamonds?

Applications

Exercise 17-1 ►
Objective 1

Using the various costing methods of inventory valuation.

Information about Joseph Company's inventory of one item follows. Compute the cost of the ending inventory under (1) the average cost method, (2) the FIFO method, and (3) the LIFO method.

Explanation	Number of Units	Unit Cost
Beginning inventory, January 1	80	$300
Purchases:		
April	120	310
July	128	320
October	80	330
Ending inventory, December 31	84	

Exercise 17-2 ►
Objective 2

Choosing the method of inventory valuation and the effect on income.

Given the choice between average cost, FIFO, and LIFO, which method will give the lowest net income and which will give the highest net income?

Exercise 17-3 ►
Objective 3

Using the lower of cost or market method.

The following information concerns four items that Delphi Company has in its ending inventory on December 31. Two of these items are in the hardware department, and two are in the household goods department.

	Quantity	Unit Cost	Market Value
Hardware			
Item 101	200	$16	$18
Item 120	120	60	56
Household goods			
Item 220	90	84	90
Item 229	150	34	32

1. What is the valuation of ending inventory if the firm uses the lower of cost or market method and applies it on an item-by-item basis?

2. If the company applies the lower of cost or market method on the basis of total cost or total market, what is the value of ending inventory?

3. If the company elects to apply the lower of cost or market method to inventory groups, what is the value of the ending inventory?

Exercise 17-4 ►
Objective 4

Estimating inventory cost under the gross profit method.

Use the following data to compute the estimated inventory cost for Cortez Company under the gross profit method.

Average gross profit rate: 30% of sales
Inventory on January 1 (at cost): $200,000
Purchases from January 1 to date of inventory estimate: $1,436,000
Net sales for period: $2,000,000

Estimating inventory cost under the retail method.

Based on the following data, compute the estimated cost of the ending inventory at Merrick Company. Use the retail method.

◀ **Exercise 17-5**
Objective 5

	Cost	Retail
Beginning inventory	$100,000	$150,000
Purchases	360,000	778,000
Freight in	4,000	
Sales		800,000

Problems

Selected problems can be completed using:
 Peachtree   QuickBooks   Spreadsheets

PROBLEM SET A

Computing inventory costs under different valuation methods.

The following data concerns inventory and purchases at Americus Company.

Inventory, July 1	120 units at $36.00
Purchases:	
July 6	60 units at $35.60
July 14	30 units at $35.50
July 23	40 units at $35.40
Inventory, July 31	115 units

◀ **Problem 17-1A**
Objective 1

INSTRUCTIONS

Determine the cost of the ending inventory on July 31 under each of the following methods: (a) average cost method; (b) first in, first out (FIFO) method; and (c) last in, first out (LIFO) method. When using the average cost method, compute the unit cost to four decimal places.

Analyze: Which inventory valuation method resulted in the highest dollar amount for ending inventory?

Computing inventory costs under different valuation methods and applying the lower of cost or market rule.

The following data pertains to Good Investment Accounting software packages in the inventory of Computer Program Bonanza Outlets.

◀ **Problem 17-2A**
Objectives 1, 3

Inventory, January 1	80 units at $48.00
Purchases:	
January 10	50 units at $49.00
July 18	85 units at $50.00
August 12	80 units at $50.60
Inventory, December 31	82 units

INSTRUCTIONS

1. Determine the cost of the inventory on December 31 and the cost of goods sold for the year ending on that date under each of the following valuation methods: (a) FIFO, (b) LIFO, and (c) average cost. When using the average cost method, compute the unit cost to the nearest cent.

2. Assume that the replacement cost of each unit on December 31 is $47.80. Using the lower of cost or market rule, find the inventory amount under each of the methods given in instruction 1.

Analyze: What is the difference between the cost and market value of the inventory using the FIFO method?

Problem 17-3A ►
Objective 3

Applying the lower of cost or market rule by different methods.

This data is for selected inventory items at Suburban Electronics Supply.

	Quantity	Unit Cost	Market Value
Handheld Calculators			
Item 101	100	$ 12.00	$ 12.80
Item 102	150	17.60	16.80
Item 103	250	8.00	8.40
Printers			
Item 401	10	280.00	328.00
Item 402	4	1,640.00	1,600.00
Item 403	2	1,812.00	1,800.00

INSTRUCTIONS

Determine the amount to be reported as the inventory valuation at cost or market, whichever is lower, under each of these methods.

1. Lower of cost or market for each item separately.

2. Lower of total cost or total market.

3. Lower of total cost or total market by group.

Analyze: Which valuation method will yield the highest net income?

Problem 17-4A ►
Objective 4

Estimating inventory by the gross profit method.

Over the past several years, Columbia Company has had an average gross profit of 30 percent. At the end of 20--, the income statement of the company included the following information.

Sales		$3,500,000
Cost of Goods		
Inventory, January 1, 20--	$ 240,000	
Purchases	2,416,000	
Total Merchandise Available for Sale	2,656,000	
Less Inventory, December 31, 20--	156,000	
Cost of Goods Sold		2,500,000
Gross Profit on Sales		$1,000,000

Investigation revealed that employees of the company had not taken an actual physical count of the inventory on December 31. Instead, they had merely estimated the inventory.

INSTRUCTIONS

Using the gross profit method of inventory estimation, verify the reasonableness (or lack of reasonableness) of the ending inventory shown on the income statement.

Analyze: If a physical inventory count on December 31, 20--, revealed an ending inventory of 210,000, calculate the gross profit percentage.

Estimating inventory by the retail method.

The September 1 inventory of Big Apple Company had a cost of $70,000 and a retail value of $105,000. During September merchandise was purchased for $160,000 and marked to sell for $240,000. September sales totaled $300,000.

1. Compute the retail value of the ending inventory as of September 30.
2. Compute the approximate cost of the ending inventory.
3. Compute the cost of goods sold during September.

Analyze: What is the amount of estimated gross profit on sales for the period ending September 30?

◀ **Problem 17-5A**
Objective 5

─────────────
INSTRUCTIONS

Applying the correct method of evaluating inventory.

Schneider Company sells expensive jewelry. Data for selected items are given below. The beginning inventory on July 1 was composed of the following items:

◀ **Problem 17-6A**
Objectives 1, 2

	Cost	Retail
Item 1001 diamond necklace	$18,000	$45,000
Item 1012 diamond earrings	10,000	25,000
Item 1013 diamond ring	10,000	30,000
Item 2300 emerald set	19,000	44,000
Item 2311 emerald ring	4,000	10,000

─────────────
INSTRUCTIONS

Sales during the month included items 1001 and 1012, sold at the retail values shown on July 1.

1. What is the best method of valuing the ending inventory?
2. Determine the value of Schneider Company's ending inventory of items that were brought over from the beginning inventory using this method. Assume that the company's retail values had not changed.
3. Determine the cost of goods sold during July.

Analyze: What is gross profit on sales for June?

PROBLEM SET B

Computing inventory costs under different valuation methods.

The following data relates to the inventory and purchases of item 124A for Cochran Distributing Company during June.

Inventory, June 1	120 units at $40.40
Purchases:	
June 10	80 units at $40.10
June 19	60 units at $40.20
June 25	70 units at $40.00
Inventory, June 30	100 units

◀ **Problem 17-1B**
Objective 1

Determine the cost of the ending inventory on June 30 under each of the following methods: (a) average cost method; (b) first in, first out (FIFO) method; and, (c) last in, first out (LIFO) method. When using the average cost method, compute the unit cost to three decimal places.

Analyze: Which inventory amount will result in the highest income for the period?

Problem 17-2B ►
Objectives 1, 3

Computing inventory costs under different valuation methods and applying the lower of cost or market rule.

The following data pertains to Model S motorized bicycles in the inventory of Western Trail Bike Company during the first six months of 20--.

Inventory, January 1	22 units at $5,000
Purchases:	
January 31	16 units at $4,400
March 10	20 units at $4,300
May 19	20 units at $4,000
Inventory, June 30	18 units

INSTRUCTIONS

1. Determine the cost of the inventory on June 30 and the cost of goods sold for the six-month period ending on that date under each of the following valuation methods: (a) FIFO, (b) LIFO, and (c) average cost. When using the average cost method, compute the unit cost to the nearest cent.

2. Assume that the replacement cost of each unit on June 30 is $3,940. Using the lower of cost or market rule, find the inventory amount under each of the methods given in instruction 1.

Analyze: Which inventory amount will result in the highest net income for the period?

Problem 17-3B ►
Objective 3

Applying the lower of cost or market rule by different methods.

The following data concerns inventory at Recreational Products, Inc.

	Quantity	Unit Cost	Market Value
Camper Department			
Model 201	12	$19,000	$18,400
Model 205	9	22,000	23,500
Model 210	8	24,800	26,000
Boat Department			
Model 110	6	2,580	2,700
Model 150	3	3,550	3,500
Model 130	4	2,550	2,700

INSTRUCTIONS

Determine the amount that the company should report as the inventory valuation at cost or market, whichever is lower. Use each of the following three valuation methods:

1. Lower of cost or market for each item separately.

2. Lower of total cost or total market.

3. Lower of total cost or total market by group.

Analyze: Which valuation method will yield the highest net income?

Estimating inventory by the gross profit method.

◀ **Problem 17-4B**
Objective 4

Over the last three years, Veracruz Company has averaged 30 percent gross profit. At the end of 20--, the auditor found the following data in the records of the company.

Sales		$4,000,000
Cost of goods sold:		
Inventory, January 1, 20--	$ 480,000	
Purchases	2,400,000	
Total merchandise available for sale	$2,880,000	
Less inventory, December 31, 20--	600,000	
Cost of goods sold		2,280,000
Gross profit on sales		$1,720,000

Inquiry by the auditor revealed that employees of Veracruz Company had estimated the inventory on December 31, 20--, instead of taking a complete physical count.

INSTRUCTIONS

Using the gross profit method of inventory estimation, verify the reasonableness (or lack of reasonableness) of the inventory estimate made by the company's employees.

Analyze: If a physical inventory count on December 31, 20--, revealed an ending inventory of $200,000, calculate the gross profit percentage.

Estimating inventory by the retail method.

◀ **Problem 17-5B**
Objective 5

The January 1 inventory of Blue Goose Company had a cost of $90,200 and a retail value of $132,000. During January merchandise was purchased for $106,400 and marked to sell for $165,300. Freight In was $1,600. January sales totaled $212,000.

INSTRUCTIONS

1. Compute the retail value of the ending inventory as of January 31.
2. Compute the approximate cost of the ending inventory.
3. Compute the cost of goods sold during January.

Analyze: What is the gross profit on sales for the period ending January 31?

Using the correct inventory valuation method.

◀ **Problem 17-6B**
Objectives 1, 2

Walt Arthur Construction Company had two completed unsold houses on hand on January 1.

Unit 04-84: Cost, $76,200; retail price, $97,000
Unit 04-86: Cost, $89,000; retail price, $120,000

During the period January 1 through March 31, the company completed the following construction jobs.

	Cost	Sales Price
Unit 05-01	$ 90,500	$110,000
Unit 05-02	96,800	126,000
Unit 05-04	79,000	90,000
Unit 05-06	112,500	133,000

All the units except 04-86 and 05-06 were sold in the quarter ending March 31.

INSTRUCTIONS

1. Determine the appropriate costing method for inventory in this construction business.

2. What value should be reported on the balance sheet for the company for the unsold units on March 31? Assume that it is firmly believed that the two houses will be sold for the retail price shown.

3. Determine the cost of goods sold in the first quarter, assuming that all houses sold were sold for the retail prices listed.

Analyze: What is gross profit on sales for the quarter ending March 31?

CHAPTER 17 CHALLENGE PROBLEM

Inventory Estimation

One of Madrid Company's retail outlets was destroyed by fire on April 10. All merchandise was burned. The company has fire insurance on its merchandise inventory. It must therefore file a claim for recovery of cost of the lost inventory. Clearly, a physical inventory cannot be taken because the inventory has been destroyed. The branch's records were kept by the home office, and you have been asked to examine the records to determine an estimate of the cost of the lost merchandise. As of April 10, the firm's records disclosed the following figures about the beginning inventory for the year, the merchandise purchases made during the period, and total sales during the period.

	Actual Cost	Retail Sales Price
Beginning inventory, January 1	$ 36,000	$ 55,800
Merchandise purchases, January 1–April 10	400,000	744,200
Freight on purchases	4,000	
Total sales, January 1–April 10		725,000

INSTRUCTIONS

Determine the approximate cost of the inventory destroyed on April 10.

Analyze: Based on the cost you have computed for merchandise inventory, calculate the cost of goods sold for the period.

CHAPTER 17 CRITICAL THINKING PROBLEM

Inventory Estimation

Gonzales Auto Parts Company has just been destroyed by fire. Fortunately, however, the computerized accounting records had been "backed up" and were in a remote computer location so that the records were not destroyed. The company does not use the retail method of accounting, so although beginning inventory at cost, purchases at cost, purchases returns and allowances, freight in, sales, sales returns and allowances, and other accounting information is available, the retail method of estimating inventory destroyed cannot be used.

What suggestion can you give for determining the estimated cost of the inventory destroyed? What information is needed, and where would this information be found?

Business Connections

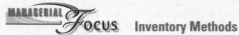 **Inventory Methods**

◄ **Connection 1**

1. What are two specific managerial reasons for using the LIFO method of inventory valuation during a period of rising prices?

2. In order to achieve better control over its investment in inventory, the management of a retail store wishes to get an estimate of the cost of inventory at the close of business each week. Outline a procedure to obtain this estimate without actually taking a physical count.

3. Explain briefly how computers and other electronic devices, such as scanners, have made perpetual inventories more practical.

4. The purchasing manager of a retail store has suggested that the company should maintain a perpetual inventory. The controller opposes this suggestion. In your opinion, on what basis does the controller probably oppose the idea?

5. In what special situations are inventory estimation procedures extremely useful?

6. The manager of a retail store has become concerned about the time taken to count the merchandise on hand each quarter. She argues that too much time is spent on this activity with a resulting high cost of labor. She suggests that the company need not take a physical inventory at all but could rely on the retail inventory estimation procedure to arrive at the cost of the inventory. Respond to this argument.

Ethical DILEMMA **Inventory Shortage** You are the accountant of North Limits Auto Supply, a retailer of auto parts, accessories, and supplies. For two or three years, you have suspected that Al Pocane, one of the firms' employees and one of your best friends, has been stealing small inventory items and selling them to an auto salvage parts dealer. Your suspicions are based in part on an apparent inventory shortage of several items with a sales price of about $14–$20 each and the fact that Pocane is a friend of the salvage parts dealer and frequently visits him. You nevertheless find it difficult to believe that your good friend is a thief. What are you going to do about your suspicions?

◄ **Connection 2**

*Street***WISE:**
Questions from the Real World   **Inventory Costs** Refer to the *1999 Annual Report* of The Home Depot, Inc. in Appendix B.

◄ **Connection 3**

1. In the Notes to Consolidated Financial Statements, review Note 1, Summary of Significant Accounting Policies. What method is used to value merchandise inventories?

2. Find the Consolidated Balance Sheets for The Home Depot, Inc. in Appendix B. What is the value of merchandise inventories at January 30, 2000? At January 31, 1999? By what percentage has this figure increased?

Connection 4 ▶
AMERICAN EAGLE
OUTFITTERS

FINANCIAL **S**TATEMENT
A N A L Y S I S   **Balance Sheet** The following excerpt was taken from the American Eagle Outfitters, Inc. *1999 Annual Report.*

Consolidated Balance Sheets			
(Dollars in thousands)	*Jan. 29, 2000*	*Jan. 30, 1999*	*Jan. 31, 1998*
Assets			
Current Assets:			
Cash and cash equivalents	$ 76,581	$ 71,940	$ 48,359
Short-term investments	91,911	13,360	--
Merchandise inventory	60,375	49,688	36,278
Total Current Assets	$262,562	$154,504	$102,473

Analyze:

1. By what amount has merchandise inventory increased from January 31, 1998, to January 29, 2000?

2. What percentage of current assets is attributable to inventories for the period ended January 29, 2000?

Analyze Online: Locate the American Eagle Outfitters, Inc. Web site **(www.ae.com),** and click on the *Corporate* link. Navigate to the *Investment Information* section.

3. Find the most recent annual report. What method is used to assign cost to the merchandise inventory? (Hint: See the Notes to Consolidated Financial Statements.)

4. What is the stated value of the most recent year's merchandise inventory?

Connection 5 ▶

Extending the *Thought* **Inventory Levels** Tykes 'N Toys, a retail toy store, records peak sales in December. The store operates on a fiscal period ending December 31. As the fourth quarter begins, the store manager is worried that the store is carrying too much merchandise. Discuss the implications that a business faces if inventories are carried at excess levels. What inventory-related costs might the company face? What effects might this have on net profits for the business year?

Connection 6 ▶

Business Communication   **List of Questions** You are considering purchasing a retail pet supply store. The inventory is valued at $225,000. Since the inventory makes up 40 percent of the cost of the business, you want to verify that the merchandise is valued properly. Make a list of questions that you plan to ask the current accountant of the pet store about the methods used for inventory valuation. What inventory records would you review?

Team_Work_ **Inventory Valuation Methods** Companies that compete in the same industry often value their inventories using the same methods. As a team, research the inventory valuation methods used by Kmart, Wal-Mart, and Target. Find the Web site for each company. Using the financial information presented in each company's annual report, create a spreadsheet that lists the valuation methods, types of inventories, and inventory dollar values at the most recent fiscal year-end for each corporation.

◄ **Connection 7**

inter **NET**
CONNECTION **Inventory Management** Many inventory management consulting firms have Web sites with links to articles and discussion about ways to control inventory costs. Visit the Inventory Management and Systems Consulting Web site at **http://freenet.edmonton.ab.ca/imasc/** and answer the following questions. What is inventory management? What services does Inventory Management and Systems Consulting provide?

◄ **Connection 8**

Answers to Self Reviews

Answers to Section 1 Self Review

1. FIFO stands for first in, first out. This method assumes that the merchandise is sold in the order in which it was acquired.
2. LIFO assumes that the last items purchased were the first sold during this period.
3. LIFO will produce the highest cost of goods sold, the lowest net income, and thus the lowest income tax expense in a period of rising prices.
4. **a.** FIFO method
5. **b.** LIFO method
6. You will want current and future economic outlook for the industry—how the cost of merchandise and the demand for the company's products are likely to change.

Answers to Section 2 Self Review

1. The principle by which inventory is valued at either its original or replacement cost, whichever is lower.
2. By item.
3. In case of fire or other inventory loss, where a physical count cannot be taken.
4. **c.** cost or market value, whichever is lower.
5. **c.** Gross profit method.
6. When the retail prices of beginning inventory and net purchases are not available.

Answers to Comprehensive Self Review

1. Specific identification, average costing, FIFO, and LIFO.
2. When there are relatively few items and each item has a high cost.
3. The retail method and the gross profit method.
4. Cost ratio = Merchandise available for sale at cost ÷ Merchandise available for sale at retail.
5. At least once a year.

CHAPTER 18

Learning Objectives

1 Determine the amount to record as an asset's cost.

2 Compute and record depreciation of property, plant, and equipment by commonly used methods.

3 Classify assets according to Modified Accelerated Cost Recovery System (MACRS) classes for federal income tax purposes.

4 Record sales of plant and equipment.

5 Record asset trade-ins using the income tax method and the fair market value method.

6 Compute and record depletion of natural resources.

7 Compute and record amortization of intangible assets.

8 Recognize asset impairment and understand the general concepts of accounting for impairment.

9 Define the accounting terms new to this chapter.

Property, Plant, and Equipment

www.cocacola.com

*I*n 1910 The Coca-Cola Company first introduced soft drink vending machines with an icebox that held 12 bottles and took nickels. Now plans are underway to link more than one-half million vending machines worldwide using innovative telecommunications technologies. The new vending machines encourage cashless vending. Consumers use cell phones to "Dial-a-Coke" or debit or credit cards to make purchases. Audio, video, and touch screens allow consumer interaction. As of August 2000, nearly 60,000 of these vending machines were operating online throughout the world. The Coca-Cola Company and the Coca-Cola bottling system expect to invest $100 million in online vending technology.

Thinking Critically
Why do you think The Coca-Cola Company is willing to invest such substantial funds in new vending machines and technologies?

For more information on The Coca-Cola Company, go to:
collegeaccounting.glencoe.com.

New Terms

Accelerated method of depreciation

Amortization

Brand name

Capitalized costs

Computer software

Copyright

Declining-balance method

Depletion

Double-declining-balance method

Fair market value method

Franchise

Gain

Goodwill

Impairment

Income tax method

Intangible assets

Loss

Net book value

Net salvage value

Patent

Real property

Recoverability test

Residual value

Scrap value

Sum-of-the-years'-digits method

Tangible personal property

Trade name

Trademark

Units-of-output method

Units-of-production method

Section Objectives

1 Determine the amount to record as an asset's cost.

WHY IT'S IMPORTANT
An asset's cost is used to compute depreciation and gain or loss on disposition.

2 Compute and record depreciation of property, plant, and equipment by commonly used methods.

WHY IT'S IMPORTANT
Business expenses include allocations of the costs of long-term assets.

3 Classify assets according to Modified Accelerated Cost Recovery System (MACRS) classes for federal income tax purposes.

WHY IT'S IMPORTANT
The IRS has special rules for cost recovery of long-term assets.

Terms **to** *Learn*

accelerated method of depreciation
capitalized costs
declining-balance method
double-declining-balance method
net book value
net salvage value
real property
residual value
scrap value
sum-of-the-years'-digits method
tangible personal property
units-of-output method
units-of-production method

Acquisition and Depreciation

Setting up and maintaining a business often requires a large investment in property, plant, and equipment—assets often referred to as *fixed assets* or *capital assets*. In this section two aspects of accounting for property, plant, and equipment are discussed:

- The costs of acquiring the assets.
- The transfer of the costs of these assets to expense through depreciation.

Property, Plant, and Equipment Classifications

As discussed in Chapter 12, *property, plant, and equipment* includes real property and tangible personal property purchased for use in the business and having a life of more than one year. **Real property** consists of land, land improvements (such as sidewalks and parking lots), buildings, and other structures attached to the land. **Tangible personal property** includes machinery, equipment, furniture, and fixtures that can be removed and used elsewhere.

The property, plant, and equipment classification does not include assets purchased for investment reasons. For example, land purchased for investment purposes is classified as other assets or investments.

Acquisition of Property, Plant, and Equipment

An important issue in accounting for property, plant, and equipment is determining which costs should be capitalized. **Capitalized costs** are all costs recorded as part of the asset's cost.

Costs of Equipment and Other Tangible Personal Property

The total cost of an asset can consist of several elements. Each element is debited to the account for that asset. The acquisition cost of an asset includes

- gross purchase price less discounts, including cash discounts for prompt payment;
- transportation costs;
- installation costs;
- costs of adjustments or modifications needed to prepare the asset for use.

Trilli's Office Supply purchased store equipment for $4,500 and paid state and local sales taxes of $270. Transportation costs were $250. When the equipment arrived, extra features were installed at a cost of $200. The **Store Equipment** account is debited for $5,220.

Purchase price	$4,500
Sales taxes	270
Transportation costs	250
Modification and installation costs	200
Total acquisition cost of machine	$5,220

Cost of Land and Building

The cost of land includes its purchase price, legal costs in connection with the acquisition, abstracts, title insurance, recording fees, and any other costs paid by the purchaser that are related to the acquisition.

The acquisition cost of land purchased for a building site should include the net costs (less salvage) of removing unwanted buildings and grading and draining the land. Remember that land is not depreciated.

Land improvements include the cost of installing permanent walks or roadways, curbing, gutters, and drainage facilities. These costs are debited to the asset account **Land Improvements.** Land improvements are depreciated.

If land and a building are purchased together for a single price, the purchase price is allocated between the **Land** and **Building** accounts. The amount allocated to the building is depreciated. The amount allocated to land is not depreciated.

Assets Constructed by or for the Business

When a building or other property, plant, and equipment is constructed and used by the business, the capitalized costs include all costs of labor, materials, permits and fees, insurance, measurable direct overhead, and other reasonable and necessary costs of construction. Interest costs incurred on borrowed funds during the construction period are capitalized as part of the asset.

Depreciation of Property, Plant, and Equipment

Buildings, machinery, equipment, furniture, and fixtures are depreciated because they have a limited life and will get used up or deteriorate over time. Depreciation is the allocation of the cost of the asset over the asset's useful life. Depreciation does not refer to a decrease in the market value of the asset.

Recording Depreciation

Assets that are used for more than one year are capitalized. Asset account names are descriptive, for example, **Office Equipment, Store Equipment, Vehicles,** or **Buildings.** At the end of each accounting period, depreciation for the period is debited to **Depreciation Expense** and credited to a contra asset account, **Accumulated Depreciation. Accumulated Depreciation** shows all depreciation that has been taken during the asset's life.

For example, a business purchased a building for $200,000. At the end of the first year, annual depreciation expense of $10,000 was entered on the worksheet as an adjustment. It was recorded as an adjusting entry in the general journal as follows.

1 Objective

Determine the amount to record as an asset's cost.

Important!

Tangible Personal Property
The term "personal" means that the property has a physical substance and is something other than real estate. Personal property is owned by the business, not by the individual owners.

Fixed Assets
According to Asset Advisors, a Florida consulting firm, fixed assets represent 35 to 50 percent of the typical Fortune 500 company's assets.

Land
Land is not depreciated. Land has an indefinite life. Land does not deteriorate or get used up.

2 Objective

Compute and record depreciation of property, plant, and equipment by commonly used methods.

11	Dec.	31	Depreciation Expense—Buildings		10 0 0 0 00			11
12			Accumulated Depreciation—Buildings			10 0 0 0 00		12
13			To record depreciation for the year					13

The balance sheet shows a long-term asset's cost minus its accumulated depreciation. The difference is *book value,* also known as **net book value**. Book value is rarely the same as fair market value, which is the asset's price on the open market. After two years of depreciation, the balance sheet presentation for the building is as follows:

Property, Plant, and Equipment
Building	$200,000.00
Less Accumulated Depreciation	20,000.00
	$180,000.00

International INSIGHTS

Advertising

When promoting your accounting practice in the international marketplace, it's important to be aware of how businesses are promoted there. Studying the details of the marketplace will help you to promote knowledgeably.

In fiscal 1999 Dole Food Company, Inc. recorded depreciation expense of $109 million. Adjusting entries affected numerous **Depreciation Expense** and **Accumulated Depreciation** accounts. On January 1, 2000, the book value of the company's property, plant, and equipment was reported at $1,125 million.

Depreciation information shown on the financial statements or in notes accompanying the financial statements includes

- depreciation expense for the period;
- balances in the depreciable asset accounts, classified according to their nature or their function;
- accumulated depreciation;
- description of the method(s) used to compute depreciation.

Depreciation Methods

Several methods are used to compute depreciation. Some of them use salvage value in the calculation. Under these methods assets are not depreciated below salvage value. *Salvage value,* **residual value**, or **scrap value** is an estimate of the amount that could be obtained from an asset's sale or disposition at the end of its useful life. The **net salvage value** is the salvage value of the asset less any costs to remove or sell it.

Straight-Line Method. The *straight-line method* introduced in Chapter 5 is the most widely used method of computing depreciation expense for financial statement purposes. Under the straight-line method, an equal amount of depreciation is recorded for each period over the useful life of the asset. Figure 18-1 shows straight-line depreciation of $216 per year.

Determining Annual Depreciation
The asset cost, the estimated salvage value, and the estimated useful life are needed in order to determine the annual depreciation.

FIGURE 18-1 ▶
Straight-Line Depreciation

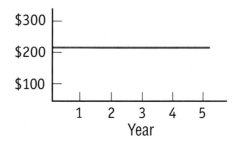

The formula for straight-line depreciation is as follows:

$$\text{Depreciation} = \frac{\text{Cost} - \text{Salvage Value}}{\text{Estimated Useful Life}}$$

On January 2 Trilli's Office Supply purchased office equipment for $1,200. The equipment has an estimated useful life of five years with a net salvage value of $120. The annual depreciation using the straight-line method is $216 [($1,200 − $120) ÷ 5]. **Depreciation Expense—Office Equipment** is debited for $216 and **Accumulated Depreciation—Office Equipment** is credited for $216.

When an asset is acquired during the year, depreciation is calculated to the nearest month. If the asset is acquired during the first 15 days of the month, depreciation is taken for the full month. If the asset is acquired after the 15th, depreciation starts in the following month. Suppose that Trilli's Office Supply purchased the office equipment on September 5. The monthly depreciation is $18 ($216 ÷ 12). Depreciation for the first year is $72 (4 months × $18). The journal entry is as follows:

11	Dec.	31	Depreciation Expense—Office Equip.		72 00		11
12			Accumulated Depreciation—Office Equip.			72 00	12
13			To record depreciation for four				13
14			months on equipment acquired				14
15			September 5				15

Declining-Balance Method. Under the **declining-balance method** of depreciation, the book value of an asset at the beginning of the year is multiplied by a percentage to determine depreciation for the year. The declining-balance method is an **accelerated method of depreciation**, which allocates greater amounts of depreciation to an asset's early years of useful life. The declining-balance method ignores salvage value. Figure 18-2 illustrates the declining-balance method in graphical form.

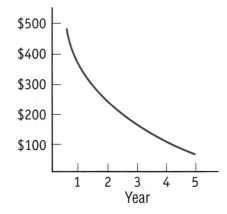

◄ **FIGURE 18-2**
Declining-Balance Depreciation

Trilli's Office Supply uses the **double-declining-balance method**, which uses a rate equal to twice the straight-line rate and applies that rate to the book value of the asset at the beginning of the year. Follow these steps to calculate double-declining-balance depreciation on the office equipment.

Step 1: *Calculate the straight-line rate.*

$$\frac{100 \text{ Percent}}{\text{Useful Life}} = \frac{100 \text{ Percent}}{5 \text{ Years}} = 20 \text{ Percent}$$

Step 2: *Calculate the double-declining rate.* The double-declining rate is the straight-line rate multiplied by 2, or 40 percent (20 percent × 2).

Step 3: *Compute depreciation for the period by multiplying the book value by the double-declining rate.* Repeat this step each year during the asset's useful life.

- In the first year, the depreciation is $480 ($1,200 × 40%).
- In the second year, the book value is $720 ($1,200 − $480). Depreciation is $288 ($720 × 40%).

At the end of the fifth year, the book value is $93.31 ($1,200 − $1,106.69). This is just less than the estimated salvage value of $120. Table 18-1 illustrates the double-declining balance method.

TABLE 18-1 ▶
Depreciation Under Double-Declining-Balance Method

Year	Beginning Book Value	Percentage	Depreciation for Year	Accumulated Depreciation
1	$1,200.00	40%	$480.00	$ 480.00
2	720.00	40	288.00	768.00
3	432.00	40	172.80	940.80
4	259.20	40	103.68	1,044.48
5	155.52	40	62.21	1,106.69

Book value at the end of five years is $93.31 ($1,200.00 − $1,106.69).

> Hasbro, the maker of games, toys, and entertainment products, depreciates tools, dies, and molds over a three-year period or their useful lives, whichever is less. An accelerated method is used. Land improvements, buildings, equipment, and machinery are depreciated using straight-line methods.

Sum-of-the-Years'-Digits Method. Another accelerated method of depreciation is the **sum-of-the-years'-digits method**. Under this method a fractional part of the asset cost is charged to expense each year. The denominator (the bottom part) of the fraction is always the "sum of the years' digits." This number is the sum of the numbers in the asset's useful life. For a machine with an expected useful life of five years, the denominator is 15 (1 + 2 + 3 + 4 + 5). The numerator (the top part) of the fraction is the number of years remaining in the useful life of the asset. For the first year the fraction is 5/15, for the second year it is 4/15, and so on. This fraction is multiplied by the acquisition cost minus the net salvage value of the asset.

Table 18-2 shows the sum-of-the-years'-digits method for the office equipment purchased by Trilli's Office Supply. Depreciation in the first year is $360 ($1,080 × 5/15) and in the second year is $288 ($1,080 × 4/15).

Suppose that the equipment was purchased on September 5. Depreciation for the first year would be $120 ($1,080 × 5/15 × 4/12). This is depreciation for four months at the first-year fraction (5/15). Depreciation for the remaining years would be calculated using 8/12 of one year's fraction and 4/12 of the next year's fraction.

$1,080 × 8/12 (8 months) × 5/15 (1st year fraction)	$240
$1,080 × 4/12 (4 months) × 4/15 (2nd year fraction)	96
Second year's depreciation	$336

Comparison of Depreciation Methods. When choosing a depreciation method, much consideration is given to the matching principle. The goal is to match the cost of the asset to the periods when the asset provides benefits to the business. Review Table 18-2. Notice that during the early years, the sum-of-the-years'-digits and declining-balance methods result in a larger depreciation expense than the straight-line method.

Accountants who adopt the straight-line method believe that the asset provides equal benefits over its useful life. Accountants who use an accelerated method think that the asset provides more benefit in the early years of its useful life and less benefit towards the end of its useful life.

	Sum-of-Years'-Digits Method			Other Methods	
Year	Fraction	Cost Minus Salvage	Depreciation for Year	Declining-Balance	Straight-Line
1	5/15	$1,080.00	$ 360.00	$ 480.00	$ 216.00
2	4/15	1,080.00	288.00	288.00	216.00
3	3/15	1,080.00	216.00	172.80	216.00
4	2/15	1,080.00	144.00	103.68	216.00
5	1/15	1,080.00	72.00	62.21	216.00
Total depreciation, 5 years			$1,080.00	$1,106.69	$1,080.00

◀ **TABLE 18-2**
Comparison of Depreciation Methods

Units-of-Output Method. Under the straight-line and accelerated methods, depreciation is computed as a function of time. For some assets depreciation is more directly related to the units of work produced. The **units-of-output method**, also known as the **units-of-production method**, calculates depreciation at the same rate for each unit produced. The unit of production may be measured in terms of the

- physical quantities of production,
- number of hours the asset is used,
- other measures.

This method is often used to depreciate the cost of cars, trucks, and other motor vehicles, using miles as a measure of production.

Suppose that a business purchased a $66,000 metal stamping press that is expected to have a salvage value of $6,000. The machine has the potential to make 1,000,000 stamping impressions. During the first year of operation, the press made 50,000 stamping impressions.

Follow these steps to calculate depreciation under the units-of-output method.

Step 1: *Determine the depreciation per unit.* Divide the cost less the estimated salvage value by the number of units that are expected to be produced.

$$\frac{\$66,000 - \$6,000}{1,000,000} = 6 \text{ cents for each stamping}$$

Step 2: *Compute depreciation.* Multiply the number of units produced by the rate for each unit.

$$50,000 \times \$0.06 = \$3,000$$

In its first year of operation, the press would have depreciation expense of $3,000.

③ Objective

Classify assets according to Modified Accelerated Cost Recovery System (MACRS) classes for federal income tax purposes.

Depreciation for Federal Income Tax Purposes

The straight-line, declining-balance, sum-of-the-years'-digits, and units-of-output methods are used by businesses to prepare their financial statements. There is a separate set of rules for calculating depreciation for income tax purposes. These rules are called the Modified Accelerated Cost Recovery System (MACRS). MACRS applies to assets purchased after December 31, 1986. Note that under MACRS the term "cost recovery" is used instead of "depreciation."

MACRS was designed to encourage companies to invest in business property. Under MACRS a company's expenses are higher in the early years of an asset's life and lower in the later years. This results in lower taxable income and tax savings in the early years. MACRS is not acceptable, however, for financial statement preparation.

Under MACRS property is separated into classes. For tangible personal property, the classes and assets that they pertain to are as follows:

Important!

Different Depreciation Methods Used

Most businesses use straight-line depreciation when preparing financial statements and MACRS when preparing tax returns.

- 3-year class—racehorses more than two years old and other horses more than 12 years old.
- 5-year class—automobiles, lightweight trucks, computers, and certain special-purpose property.
- 7-year class—office furniture and fixtures and most manufacturing equipment.
- 10-year class—special-purpose property, such as equipment used in the manufacture of food and tobacco products.
- 15-year class—telephone distribution plants, sewage treatment plants, and certain types of equipment used in the communications industry.
- 20-year class—certain types of farm buildings and municipal sewer systems.

Under MACRS the recovery periods for real property are

- residential rental buildings—27.5 years,
- nonresidential buildings (office buildings) placed in service after May 12, 1993—39 years,
- nonresidential buildings placed in service on or before May 12, 1993—31.5 years.

Each MACRS class has a table of percentages. To determine the cost recovery (depreciation) under MACRS, multiply the asset cost by the MACRS percentage. Salvage value is ignored. The following shows the MACRS cost recovery for a $10,000 five-year asset.

Year	Percent	Original Cost	Cost Recovery
1	20.00%	$10,000	$ 2,000
2	32.00	10,000	3,200
3	19.20	10,000	1,920
4	11.52	10,000	1,152
5	11.52	10,000	1,152
6	5.76	10,000	576
Totals	100.00%		$10,000

Note that it takes six years to recover the entire cost of five-year property. That is because MACRS uses the *half-year convention*. Regardless of purchase date, MACRS calculates six months of depreciation in the first year of the asset's life. The remaining six months of depreciation is taken in the year after the end of the class life (in the sixth year for five-year property).

There is an exception to the half-year convention. The *mid-quarter convention* is applied if more than 40 percent of assets purchased in a year are placed in service in the fourth quarter of a year. There is a separate set of MACRS tables if the mid-quarter convention applies. A full discussion of determining which convention to follow—half-year or mid-quarter—is beyond the scope of this text. These conventions are discussed in income tax courses.

If appropriate, a business can use the units-of-output method for income tax purposes instead of MACRS.

MACRS revised the IRS's earlier Accelerated Cost Recovery System (ACRS) by extending the recovery period (useful life) for most assets. MACRS and the original ACRS rules were designed to encourage companies to invest in productive business property by permitting a rapid charge-off of costs, with a resulting tax saving, in the early years of each asset's life.

Neither ACRS nor MACRS is suitable as a means of matching the costs of assets with the revenues produced by those assets. Thus they are not acceptable for financial accounting purposes.

Section 1 — Self Review

Questions

1. What is net salvage value?

2. An asset has a useful life of 10 years. In the ninth year of the asset's life, is depreciation higher under the declining-balance method or straight-line method? Why?

3. What does MACRS mean? When does a business use MACRS?

Exercises

4. A company purchased equipment for $20,000 cash. In addition, the company paid $2,000 to have the equipment delivered and $750 to have it installed. The cost of the asset is

   a. $20,000.
   b. $22,000.
   c. $20,750.
   d. $22,750.

5. The method of depreciation that results in the same amount of depreciation expense each year is the

   a. units-of-output method.
   b. straight-line method.
   c. MACRS.
   d. declining-balance method.

Analysis

6. Which method of depreciation, straight-line or double-declining-balance, will result in a higher net income during the first year the asset is in use? Why?

(Answers to Section 1 Self Review are on page 673.)

Disposition of Assets

The disposition of assets involves removing the asset's cost and its accumulated depreciation from the firm's accounting records. This section discusses the accounting treatment for three asset disposal methods: scrapping, sale, and trade-in.

Method of Disposition

Most business assets are eventually disposed of. They are either scrapped because they are worn out and have no value, sold because they are no longer needed by the business, or traded in on the purchase of new assets.

When assets are disposed of, the business often incurs a gain or a loss. A **gain** is the disposition of an asset for more than its book value. A **loss** is the disposition of an asset for less than its book value. The formula is

Proceeds − Book value = Gain or loss

There is a gain when proceeds are higher than book value. There is a loss when proceeds are lower than book value.

A gain results from a peripheral activity of the business. In contrast, revenue involves the routine activities of the business such as selling goods and rendering services. A loss also results from a peripheral activity of the business. In contrast, expenses involve the day-to-day activities of the business.

The rules of debit and credit for gain accounts are the same as for revenue accounts. Similarly, expense accounts and loss accounts follow the same rules of debit and credit.

Loss		Gain	
+	−	−	+
Increase	Decrease	Decrease	Increase

Disposal by Scrapping or Discarding

When an asset is worn out, often it is simply discarded. For example, the computer used by Atlanta Antiques cost $4,000 and is fully depreciated. On August 31 the computer crashed and could not be repaired for a reasonable fee. It was worthless. The business put the computer in the trash. There were no proceeds from the disposal and no costs were incurred in the disposal. There is no gain or loss from the disposition.

Proceeds	$0
(Book value)	(0)
Gain or loss	$0

The following journal entry records the asset's disposal.

11	Aug.	31	Accum. Depreciation—Office Equipment	4 0 0 0 00		11
12			Office Equipment		4 0 0 0 00	12
13			Discarded computer			13

Section Objectives

④ **Record sales of plant and equipment.**

WHY IT'S IMPORTANT
Businesses routinely sell or dispose of plant assets that are no longer useful to the business.

⑤ **Record asset trade-ins using the income tax method and the fair market value method.**

WHY IT'S IMPORTANT
The method used determines whether a gain or loss is recognized.

Terms to Learn

fair market value method
gain
income tax method
loss

If the discarded asset is not fully depreciated, depreciation is recorded up to the date of disposal. Suppose that the computer used by Atlanta Antiques cost $4,000. Accumulated depreciation through December 31 was $3,200. On August 31 the computer crashed. The depreciation for the period January 1 through August 31 is $450. The depreciation is recorded through August 31 as follows: debit **Depreciation Expense** for $450, and credit **Accumulated Depreciation** for $450. After this entry the **Accumulated Depreciation** account balance is $3,650 ($3,200 + $450). The book value of the computer is $350 ($4,000 − $3,650). There are no proceeds and no costs incurred for the disposal. There is a loss of $350 on the disposition.

Proceeds	$ 0
(Book value)	(350)
Loss	$350

The entry to record the disposal of the computer removes the cost of the asset and its accumulated depreciation from the accounting records. The difference, book value, is recorded as a loss.

Aug.	31	Accum. Depreciation—Office Equipment		3 6 5 0 00	
		Loss on Disposal of Fixed Assets		3 5 0 00	
		Office Equipment			4 0 0 0 00
		Discarded computer			

Disposal by Sale

Sometimes useful assets are sold so the company can purchase better assets or because the assets are no longer needed. When an asset is sold, follow these steps to record the transaction.

Step 1: *Record depreciation to the date of disposition.*

Step 2: *Remove the cost of the asset.*

Step 3: *Remove the accumulated depreciation.*

Step 4: *Record the proceeds.*

Step 5: *Determine and record the gain or loss, if any.*

Several years ago Atlanta Antiques purchased office equipment for $1,200. The accumulated depreciation is $648. On July 1 the equipment was sold. The first step is to record depreciation expense up to the date of sale. Annual depreciation is $216. Depreciation for one-half year is $108 ($216 ÷ 2). The entry is a debit to **Depreciation Expense—Office Equipment** for $108 and a credit to **Accumulated Depreciation—Office Equipment** for $108. After this entry the accumulated depreciation account has a balance of $756 ($648 + $108). The book value of the office equipment is $444 ($1,200 − $756).

Sale for an Amount Equal to Book Value. Suppose that the equipment was sold on account for book value, $444. Step 1, record depreciation to the date of disposition, has been illustrated. Steps 2–5 are as follows:

Step 2: *Remove the cost of the asset.* Credit **Office Equipment** for $1,200.

Step 3: *Remove the accumulated depreciation.* Debit **Accumulated Depreciation—Office Equipment** for $756.

Step 4: *Record the proceeds.* Debit **Accounts Receivable** for $444.

④ Objective

Record sales of plant and equipment.

Step 5: *Determine and record the gain or loss, if any.*

Proceeds	$444
(Book value)	(444)
Gain or loss	$ 0

The Bottom Line

Sale at Book Value

Income Statement

No change in net income

Balance Sheet

No change in equity

GENERAL JOURNAL PAGE 7

	DATE	DESCRIPTION	POST. REF.	DEBIT	CREDIT	
1	20--					1
22	July 1	Accounts Receivable		44400		22
23		Accum. Depreciation—Office Equipment		75600		23
24		Office Equipment			120000	24
25		Sold office equipment at book value				25

Sale for More Than Book Value. Suppose the equipment was sold on account for $498. The equipment was sold at a gain of $54.

Proceeds	$498
(Book value)	(444)
Gain	$ 54

The gain is recorded in the **Gain on Sale of Equipment** account. The gain is shown on the income statement in the Other Income section.

The Bottom Line

Sale Above Book Value

Income Statement

Gain	↑ 54
Net Income	↑ 54

Balance Sheet

Assets	↑ 54
Equity	↑ 54

GENERAL JOURNAL PAGE 7

	DATE	DESCRIPTION	POST. REF.	DEBIT	CREDIT	
1	20--					1
22	July 1	Accounts Receivable		49800		22
23		Accum. Depreciation—Office Equipment		75600		23
24		Office Equipment			120000	24
25		Gain on Sale of Equipment			5400	25
26		Sale of office equipment at a gain				26

Sale for Less Than Book Value. Suppose the equipment was sold on account for $398. The equipment was sold at a loss of $46.

Proceeds	$398
(Book value)	(444)
Loss	$ (46)

The loss is recorded in the **Loss on Sale of Equipment** account. The loss appears on the income statement in the Other Expenses section.

The Bottom Line

Sale Below Book Value

Income Statement

Loss	↑ 46
Net Income	↓ 46

Balance Sheet

Assets	↓ 46
Equity	↓ 46

GENERAL JOURNAL PAGE 7

	DATE	DESCRIPTION	POST. REF.	DEBIT	CREDIT	
1	20--					1
22	July 1	Accounts Receivable		39800		22
23		Accum. Depreciation—Office Equipment		75600		23
24		Loss on Sale of Equipment		4600		24
25		Office Equipment			120000	25
26		Sale of office equipment at a loss				26

Some companies use a single account to record both gains and losses on sales of assets. The account is called **Gains and Losses on Sales of**

Assets. It appears on the income statement in the Other Income section (if net gain) or Other Expenses section (if net loss).

Disposal by Trade-In

Businesses often trade in old equipment when they purchase new equipment. Trade-in transactions are recorded in two steps.

Step 1: *Record the depreciation up to the date of trade-in.*

Step 2: *Record the trade-in of the old asset and the purchase of the new asset.*

The details of the second step depend on whether the company is using the income tax method or the fair market value method. Businesses use the income tax method to prepare tax returns and the fair market value method to prepare financial statements.

The Income Tax Method. Under the **income tax method**, when a business asset is traded in for a similar business asset, no gain or loss is recorded. The cost or *tax basis* of the new asset is the book value of the old asset plus the amount paid for the new asset. To record a trade-in under the income tax method, follow these steps.

Step 1: *Remove the cost of the old asset.*

Step 2: *Remove the accumulated depreciation for the old asset.*

Step 3: *Record the payment.*

Step 4: *Determine and record the cost of the new asset.* The formula for the new asset is

	Book value of the old asset
+	Payment for the new asset
=	Cost of the new asset

Atlanta Antiques traded in a printer that it purchased several years ago for $950. The accumulated depreciation at the date of trade-in was $500. The book value was $450. On July 1 the printer was traded for a newer model with a list price and fair market value of $1,200. The seller offered a trade-in allowance of $500 on the old printer against the list price of the new printer. With the trade-in, Atlanta Antiques paid $700 ($1,200 − $500). The trade-in results in an *unrecognized gain* of $50, calculated as follows.

	Trade-in allowance	$500
−	(Book value)	(450)
=	Gain (unrecognized)	$ 50

Although there is a gain, the gain is not recognized under the income tax method. The gain simply reduces the cost of the new printer. Follow these steps to record the trade-in under the income tax method.

Step 1: *Remove the cost of the old asset,* $950.

Step 2: *Remove the accumulated depreciation for the old asset,* $500.

Step 3: *Record the payment,* $700.

Step 4: *Determine and record the cost of the new printer,* $1,150.

	Book value of old printer	$ 450
+	Payment	700
=	Cost of new printer	$1,150

⑤ **Objective**

Record asset trade-ins using the income tax method and the fair market value method.

GENERAL JOURNAL

PAGE 7

	DATE		DESCRIPTION	POST. REF.	DEBIT	CREDIT	
1	20--						1
2	July	1	Office Equipment (new)		1 1 5 0 00		2
3			Accum. Depreciation—Office Equipment		5 0 0 00		3
4			Office Equipment (old)			9 5 0 00	4
5			Accounts Payable			7 0 0 00	5
6			Trade-in of printer				6

Conservatism

According to the modifying convention of conservatism, accountants record transactions using the alternative that is least likely to overstate income.

Suppose that the trade-in allowance was $400. Atlanta Antiques would pay $800 ($1,200 − $400). There would be an unrecognized loss of $50:

	Trade-in allowance	$400
−	(Book value)	(450)
=	Loss (unrecognized)	$ 50

Under GAAP, this type of loss must be recorded. However, for income tax purposes, no loss would be recorded. The new equipment would have a "tax basis" of $1,250.

	Book value of old printer	$ 450
+	Payment	800
=	Cost of new printer	$1,250

Some argue that it is acceptable to use the income tax method (under which no loss is recognized) in recording the transaction if the loss is immaterial. If the income tax method is used to record this transaction, the following journal entry would be made.

GENERAL JOURNAL

PAGE 7

	DATE		DESCRIPTION	POST. REF.	DEBIT	CREDIT	
1	20--						1
2	July	1	Office Equipment (new)		1 2 5 0 00		2
3			Accum. Depreciation—Office Equipment		5 0 0 00		3
4			Office Equipment (old)			9 5 0 00	4
5			Accounts Payable			8 0 0 00	5
6			Trade-in of printer				6

The Fair Market Value Method

Loss on Trade-In. Under the GAAP modifying convention of conservatism, if the book value of the old asset exceeds the amount of trade-in allowance received, there is a loss on the disposal of the old asset. That loss should be recognized. The new asset is recorded at its fair market value and the loss is recorded in the accounting records. To record a trade-in under the **fair market value method**, follow these steps.

Step 1: *Remove the cost of the old asset.*

Step 2: *Remove the accumulated depreciation for the old asset.*

Step 3: *Record the payment.*

Step 4: *Record the new asset at its fair market value.*

Step 5: *Determine and record the loss.* The formula for the loss is

Trade-in − Book value = Loss if book value exceeds trade-in

On July 1 Atlanta Antiques trades in a printer for which it paid $950 several years ago. Accumulated depreciation at the date of trade-in was $500. The new printer has a list price of $1,200. Its fair market value is also $1,200. The seller offers a trade-in allowance of $400. Atlanta Antiques will pay $800 on account. The trade-in of the old printer results in a loss:

	Trade-in allowance	$400
−	(Book value)	(450)
=	Loss	$ 50

GENERAL JOURNAL   PAGE ___7___

	DATE	DESCRIPTION	POST. REF.	DEBIT	CREDIT	
1	20--					1
14	July	1 Office Equipment (new)		1 2 0 0 00		14
15		Accum. Depreciation—Office Equipment		5 0 0 00		15
16		Loss on Sale of Equipment		5 0 00		16
17		Office Equipment (old)			9 5 0 00	17
18		Accounts Payable			8 0 0 00	18
19		Trade-in of printer				19

The Bottom Line

Trade-In of an Asset
(Loss)
Fair Market Value
Method

Income Statement

Loss	↑ 50
Net Income	↓ 50

Balance Sheet

Assets	↑ 750
Liabilities	↑ 800
Equity	↓ 50

Gain on Trade-In. Under the fair market value method, if the trade-in allowance is greater than the book value of the old asset, the purchaser recognizes no gain. The transaction is recorded on the company's books using the income tax method. The gain is not recognized due to the generally accepted accounting principle modifying convention of conservatism.

Section 2 Self Review

Questions

1. What are three ways a business might dispose of an asset?

2. For financial statement purposes, in what circumstances is a loss on the sale of a long-term asset recognized?

3. When a long-lived asset is scrapped, how is the transaction recorded?

Exercises

4. An asset that cost $16,000 was sold for $10,000 cash. Accumulated depreciation on the asset was $8,000. The entry to record this transaction includes the recognition of
   a. $6,000 gain.   c. $2,000 gain.
   b. $6,000 loss.   d. $2,000 loss.

5. The entry to record the sale of business equipment might include a debit to
   a. Gain on Sale of Equipment.
   b. Equipment.

   c. Accumulated Depreciation—Equipment.
   d. Accounts Payable.

Analysis

6. If a company's fully depreciated asset was scrapped but not removed from the accounting records, what would be the effect on the company's financial statements? Assume there is no salvage value.

(Answers to Section 2 Self Review are on page 674.)   *Property, Plant, and Equipment*   **Chapter 18 • 651**

Special Topics in Long-Term Assets

Terms to Learn

amortization
brand names
computer software
copyright
depletion
franchises
goodwill
impairment
intangible assets
patent
recoverability test
trade names
trademarks

In addition to the acquisition and disposition of long-term assets, accountants should be familiar with several other topics. This section discusses depletion, intangible assets, asset impairment, and internal control of property, plant, and equipment.

Depletion

Natural resources, such as iron ore, oil, gold, and coal are physically removed from the land in the production process. Businesses must know how to allocate the cost of natural resources as they are taken from their source. As the resources are extracted, part of their cost is charged to expense. **Depletion** is the term used to describe allocating the cost of the natural resource to expense over the period in which the resource produces revenue.

There are two ways to compute depletion. For financial statement purposes, the depletion amount for property such as oil, minerals, or metals is based on cost. For federal income tax purposes, the depletion can also be computed as a percentage of gross income from the product sold, based on sales price. Both methods are discussed in this section.

Depletion for Financial Statement Purposes

Depletion of natural resources for financial statement preparation is called *cost depletion*. It is similar to the units-of-output method of depreciation. The formula is

$$\frac{\text{Cost of natural resource}}{\text{Estimated units of the resource}} = \text{Depletion per unit}$$

A business purchased a clay pit for $50,000. The clay pit is estimated to contain 500,000 tons of extractable clay suitable for making bricks. The depletion cost for each ton of clay is $0.10 ($50,000 ÷ 500,000 tons). During the year the business extracted 60,000 tons of clay. The depletion is $6,000 (60,000 × $0.10). The adjusting entry to record depletion follows.

11	Dec.	31	Depletion Expense		6 0 0 0 00			11
12			Accumulated Depletion			6 0 0 0 00		12
13			To record the extraction of					13
14			60,000 tons of clay					14

After the first year, the natural resource appears on the balance sheet as follows. The net book value of the natural resource is $44,000.

Property, Plant, and Equipment	
Clay Deposits	$50,000
Less Accumulated Depletion	6,000
Net Clay Deposits	$44,000

Oil and gas production and mining operations use long-lived assets such as oil pumps and mining equipment. These assets are depreciated, often using the units-of-output method.

Depletion for Federal Income Tax Purposes

6 Objective
Compute and record depletion of natural resources.

Depletion for federal income tax purposes is the larger of cost depletion or percentage depletion. Cost depletion for tax purposes is computed in the same way as it is for financial statement preparation. However, the amount of cost depletion may be different because the cost (the numerator) for financial purposes may be different than the cost for tax purposes. If percentage depletion is taken on the tax return, the amount taken in year 1 will reduce the cost on which cost depletion is based in future years.

Percentage depletion is calculated by multiplying the gross income from the sale of the natural resource by a percentage. The percentage depends on the specific natural resource. The amount of percentage depletion allowed is limited. Because the rules are complex, the computation of depletion for federal tax purposes is beyond the scope of this text.

Intangible Assets

In addition to property, plant, and equipment, many businesses have intangible assets. **Intangible assets** are assets that lack a physical substance. The major types of intangible assets are patents, copyrights, franchises, trademarks, brand names, organizational costs, computer software, and goodwill. With the exception of computer software, intangible assets usually do not have any physical attributes.

Classifying Intangible Assets

A **patent** is an exclusive right given by the U.S. Patent Office to manufacture and sell an invention for a period of 17 years from the date the patent is granted. A patent may not be renewed; however, a new patent may be obtained if significant improvements in the original idea can be demonstrated. The right to the patent may be sold, assigned, or otherwise controlled by the owner.

A **copyright** is the exclusive right granted by the federal government to produce, publish, and sell a literary or artistic work for a period equal to the creator's life plus 70 years.

There are two types of **franchises**. The first type is a right granted by a governmental unit for the business to provide a service to the governmental unit (such as cable television). The second type is an exclusive dealership or an exclusive arrangement between a manufacturer and a dealer or distributor.

Trademarks, **trade names**, and **brand names** are used to build consumer confidence and loyalty. They can be registered with the U.S. Patent Office. They can be sold, traded, or otherwise controlled by the owner.

Organizational costs are the costs incurred when organizing a business. Organizational costs include attorneys' fees, accountants' fees, legal filing fees, and other costs of beginning a business.

Computer software consists of written programs that instruct a computer's hardware to do certain tasks. Software can be developed by the company's employees or purchased outside the company. For some firms, computer software is the most important (and most costly) asset owned.

Goodwill represents the value of a business in excess of the value of its identifiable assets. Goodwill is recorded only at the time of the purchase of a business. It usually occurs when a business being purchased has extraordinary earnings or earnings potential.

> On December 26, 1999, Hasbro reported goodwill of $806 million. Almost one-half of Hasbro's goodwill resulted from two acquisitions: Milton Bradley Company in 1984, including the Playskool unit; and Tonka Corporation in 1991, including the Kenner and Parker Brothers units. The remaining goodwill resulted from the 1998 acquisitions of Tiger Electronics, Inc., MicroProse, Inc., and Galoob Toys, Inc., and the 1999 acquisition of Wizards of the Coast, Inc.

Acquiring Intangible Assets

There are two ways to acquire intangible assets: (1) produce or develop them or (2) purchase them. The general rule is that an intangible asset is recorded in the books of the firm only if it is purchased from another party. Costs to develop intangible assets internally are expensed in the year incurred to the **Research and Development Expense** account. Similarly, costs related to software development by a company are expensed in the year incurred. However, there are special rules if the software is to be sold, leased, or otherwise marketed:

1. Costs are expensed as incurred when creating the software product until technological feasibility is established for the product. *Technological feasibility* is deemed to occur when a detailed program design or a working model of the product has been developed.

2. Costs are capitalized to an asset account once a product is deemed to be technologically feasible.

7 Objective

Compute and record amortization of intangible assets.

Amortizing the Costs of Intangible Assets

Most intangible assets have limited legal and economic (useful) lives, and the life for each purpose might not be the same. Acquisition costs are charged to expense over the shorter of the legal life or economic life. **Amortization** is the process of periodically transferring the acquisition cost of an intangible asset to an expense account. Most intangible assets are amortized using the straight-line or units-of-output methods. Intangible assets are amortized for a period not to exceed 40 years.

The periodic amortization is debited to **Amortization Expense** and credited directly to the intangible asset account, not to a contra asset account. The intangible asset balance is its book value. Suppose that a firm purchased a patent for $800,000. The patent has a remaining legal life of 12 years and an economic life of 10 years. The economic life is the shorter life and is therefore the number used for the calculation. Amortization per year is $80,000 ($800,000 ÷ 10 years). The adjusting entry to record amortization for the year follows.

11	Dec.	31	Amortization Expense—Patent	80 0 0 0 00		11
12			Patent		80 0 0 0 00	12
13			To record annual amortization			13
14			of patent			14

Transportation, Distribution, and Logistics

Industry Overview

The transportation, distribution, and logistics industry includes the planning, management, and movement of materials, people, and products by air, road, water, and rail. It also includes support services such as transportation infrastructure planning and management, logistics services, mobile equipment, and facility maintenance.

Career Opportunities

- Air Transportation Operations Manager
- Urban Planner
- Inventory Specialist
- Distribution Technology Coordinator
- Sales Manager—Passenger Air
- Logistics Planner
- Federal Highway Administration Administrator
- Transit Authority Contracts Accountant

Preparing for a Transportation, Distribution, and Logistics Career

- Develop strong computer, data entry, bookkeeping, and calculator skills.

- Obtain a bachelor's degree in marketing, accounting, business administration, industrial relations, logistics, or economics for managerial jobs.

- Develop good communication, problem solving, and analytical skills.

- Gain an understanding of inventory control techniques, various inventory costing methods, receiving and shipping functions, productivity analysis, expense control, industrial safety, and order fulfillment services.

- Obtain training or work experience in distribution technologies like radio frequency based scanning systems, direct thermal label printing, light directed distribution systems, and high-speed sheet-fed laser printing systems.

- Demonstrate proficiencies in the creation and maintenance of fiscal budgets.

- Demonstrate the ability to prepare and comprehend statistical reports.

Thinking Critically

As the manager of a company that grows and markets fresh flowers and green plants to retail florists, grocery stores, and nurseries, what potential distribution channels do you think are available to you? What considerations should you weigh when you select vendors to distribute your product?

Internet Application

Corporations such as Wal-Mart Stores, Pier 1 Imports, or Ford Motor Company hire professionals to manage and operate their logistics, transportation, and supply chain divisions. Explore the careers or jobs section of each company's Web site. Select one transportation, distribution, or logistics job opportunity from each company. List the job title, responsibilities, and educational and work background required for each position.

Impairment of Property, Plant, and Equipment

Accountants have spent considerable time trying to develop guidelines for asset impairment. **Impairment** of long-term assets occurs when the asset is determined to have a market value or a value in use less than its book value.

The procedures to measure and record impairment are quite complex and covered in advanced accounting courses. The topic is introduced in this text, however, to provide a basic understanding because impairment is frequently encountered on financial statements.

8 Objective

Recognize asset impairment and understand the general concepts of accounting for impairment.

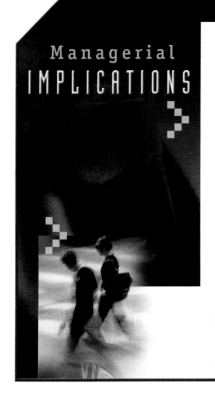

Property, Plant, and Equipment

Managerial IMPLICATIONS

- Property, plant, and equipment often represent the largest cash investment by the owners of a business.
- Managers are responsible for establishing strong internal controls over property, plant, and equipment.
- Managers should understand the different depreciation methods and how they impact the financial statements and income tax returns of the business.
- Management should ensure that procedures are in place to monitor repairs, power consumed, and other operating costs to make sure that assets are functioning efficiently.
- Managers must understand the methods used to record asset sales and trade-ins because the different methods have different results that impact the financial statements of the business.

Thinking Critically
How does the choice of depreciation method impact the financial statements?

- The going concern assumption and the historical cost principle assume that if the asset continues to be used for its intended purpose, it will generate future cash revenues, and the value of those revenues will exceed the asset's book value. Therefore, the asset should stay on the books at historical cost.
- In contrast, the conservatism convention suggests that impaired assets should be written down to their market value.

Financial Accounting Statement 121, "Accounting for Impairment of Long-Lived Assets," lists three steps to use to determine whether an asset is impaired.

Step 1: *Review circumstances that suggest impairment may have occurred.* Circumstances can include a large decrease in the market value of the asset or a major change in the extent of use or the way in which the asset is used.

Step 2: *Apply the recoverability test.* The **recoverability test** compares the asset's net book value with the estimated net cash flows from the asset's future use. If the asset's estimated net future cash flows are less than its book value, the asset might be impaired. In making impairment calculations, the unit of measurement is not a single asset, but the smallest unit of the business for which net cash flows can be determined from the assets used.

Step 3: *Compute the amount of the impairment.* It is the amount by which the asset's book value exceeds its market value. Typically market value is the present value of the stream of future net cash flows from the use of the assets.

If impairment has occurred, the difference between book value and market value is charged to expense, and the assets are written down. Once impairment has been recorded, the book value of the asset is not increased even if the market value of the asset subsequently increases.

> According to its 1999 Annual Report, Southwest Airlines Co. records impairment losses on long-lived assets used in operations when events and circumstances indicate that the assets might be impaired and the undiscounted cash flows to be generated by those assets are less than the book value of those assets.

Internal Control of Property, Plant, and Equipment

The internal control of property, plant, and equipment involves physical safeguards to prevent theft. The following are standard internal control procedures for fixed assets:

- Authorize and justify the purchase of all long-lived assets.
- Assign and, if possible, engrave an identification number on each asset.
- Maintain an asset register listing all capital assets, their costs, acquisition dates, location, and any other useful information.
- Assign responsibility for safekeeping, maintaining, and operating each asset to a specific person.
- Take a physical inventory periodically. Compare the physical inventory with the asset register and investigate any differences.
- Establish procedures to authorize asset retirement, sale, or other disposition.

The internal control of intangible assets consists primarily of the safe storage of documents and protection of the storage location. Businesses need to be alert to copyright and trademark infringements. Legal action is required when an infringement of an intangible asset occurs.

Section 3 Self Review

Questions

1. How is depletion computed on assets used in a gold mine? Why do you think this method is preferred?

2. How is depletion computed for a mineral resource for financial accounting purposes?

3. What is meant by impairment of an asset?

Exercises

4. The amortization of an intangible asset is
   a. credited to accumulated amortization.
   b. credited to the asset account.
   c. debited to the asset account.
   d. debited to accumulated amortization.

5. The acquisition cost of an intangible asset is amortized over
   a. its legal life.
   b. its economic life up to a maximum of 40 years.
   c. the longer of its legal life or its economic life, not to exceed 40 years.
   d. the shorter of its legal life or its economic life, not to exceed 40 years.

Analysis

6. How are depreciation, depletion, and amortization different? How are they similar?

(Answers to Section 3 Self Review are on page 674.)

Review

Chapter Summary

Property, plant, and equipment are those tangible assets used in carrying out the company's business operations. In this chapter, you have learned how to record transactions for the purchase, use, and disposition of these assets. You have also studied the accounting methods required to record the acquisition of intangible assets such as copyrights and patents, as well as the costs of amortization.

Learning Objectives

1 Determine the amount to record as an asset's cost.
The cost of an asset is its net purchase price, plus costs of transportation, installation, and all other costs necessary to put the asset into normal operation.

2 Compute and record depreciation of property, plant, and equipment by commonly used methods.
Costs of the asset should be charged to expense over its useful life through systematic depreciation charges. Depreciation is recorded by a debit to **Depreciation Expense** and a credit to **Accumulated Depreciation.** Four widely used methods of computing depreciation for financial accounting purposes are the
- straight-line method,
- declining-balance method,
- sum-of-the-years'-digits method,
- units-of-production method.

3 Classify assets according to Modified Accelerated Cost Recovery System (MACRS) classes for federal income tax purposes.
Under the federal income tax laws, new assets must be depreciated under the Modified Accelerated Cost Recovery System (MACRS) with minor exceptions. Under MACRS, each type of asset is assigned to a MACRS class. Each class is assigned a different depreciable life.

4 Record sales of plant and equipment.
Property, plant, and equipment are disposed of in various ways; most commonly, they are sold or scrapped. At an asset's sale, its depreciation is brought up to date. Gain or loss at the time of disposal is computed by comparing the asset's net book value with the proceeds, if any, received on its disposal. For financial accounting purposes, a gain or loss may be recorded from the sale, retirement, or scrapping of an asset.

5 Record asset trade-ins using the income tax method and the fair market value method.
If a business trades old equipment when purchasing new equipment, two transactions must be recorded. The depreciation on the used equipment must be brought up to date. Then, the trade and purchase are recorded. Using the income tax method, no gain or loss is recorded on the trade-in of an asset on a new similar asset. Using the fair market value method, a gain is not recognized, but a loss is recognized.

6 Compute and record depletion of natural resources.
The costs of natural resources such as mineral deposits are charged to expense on a per-unit-of-production basis for financial accounting and reporting purposes.

7 Compute and record amortization of intangible assets.
Except for software, intangibles have no physical characteristics. If they are bought from outside parties, intangibles are recorded at cost. Costs incurred by firms who produce their own intangible assets are not capitalized but are charged to **Research and Development Expense** in the year incurred.

8 Recognize asset impairment and understand the general concepts of accounting for impairment.
If an asset's expected future net cash flows are less than the asset's book value, impairment may need to be recognized. The amount of impairment is the amount by which the book value exceeds the asset's fair value—usually defined as the discounted value of the future net cash flows.

9 Define the accounting terms new to this chapter.

CHAPTER 18 GLOSSARY

Accelerated method of depreciation (p. 641) A method of depreciating asset cost that allocates greater amounts of depreciation to an asset's early years of useful life

Amortization (p. 654) The process of periodically transferring the acquisition cost of an intangible asset to an expense account

Brand name (p. 653) See Trade name

Capitalized costs (p. 638) All costs recorded as part of an asset's costs

Computer software (p. 653) An intangible asset; written programs that instruct a computer's hardware to do certain tasks

Copyright (p. 653) An intangible asset; an exclusive right granted by the federal government to produce, publish, and sell a literary or artistic work for a period equal to the creator's life plus 70 years

Declining-balance method (p. 641) An accelerated method of depreciation in which an asset's book value at the beginning of a year is multiplied by a percentage to determine depreciation for the year

Depletion (p. 652) Allocating the cost of a natural resource to expense over the period in which the resource produces revenue

Double-declining-balance method (p. 641) A method of depreciation that uses a rate equal to twice the straight-line rate and applies that rate to the book value of the asset at the beginning of the year

Fair market value method (p. 650) A method of recording the trade-in of an asset that allows a loss to be recognized on the transaction if the book value exceeds the trade-in allowance

Franchise (p. 653) An intangible asset; a right to exclusive dealership granted by a governmental unit or a business entity

Gain (p. 646) The disposition of an asset for more than its book value

Goodwill (p. 654) An intangible asset; the value of a business in excess of the value of its identifiable assets

Impairment (p. 655) A situation that occurs when the asset is determined to have a market value or a value in use less than its book value

Income tax method (p. 649) A method of recording the trade-in of an asset according to tax rules that do not permit a gain or loss to be recognized on the transaction

Intangible assets (p. 653) Assets that lack a physical substance, such as goodwill, patents, copyrights, and computer software, although software has, in a sense, a physical attribute

Loss (p. 646) The disposition of an asset for less than its book value

Net book value (p. 640) The cost of an asset minus its accumulated depreciation, depletion, or amortization, also known as book value

Net salvage value (p. 640) The salvage value of an asset less any costs to remove or sell the asset

Patent (p. 653) An intangible asset; an exclusive right given by the U.S. Patent Office to manufacture and sell an invention for a period of 17 years from the date the patent is granted

Real property (p. 638) Assets such as land, land improvements, buildings, and other structures attached to the land

Recoverability test (p. 656) Test for possible impairment that compares the asset's net book value with the estimated net cash flows from future use of the asset

Residual value (p. 640) The estimate of the amount that could be obtained from the sale or disposition of an asset at the end of its useful life; also called salvage or scrap value

Scrap value (p. 640) See Residual value

Sum-of-the-years'-digits method (p. 642) A method of depreciating asset costs by allocating as expense each year a fractional part of the asset's depreciable cost, based on the sum of the digits of the number of years in the asset's useful life

Tangible personal property (p. 638) Assets such as machinery, equipment, furniture, and fixtures that can be removed and used elsewhere

Trade name (p. 653) An intangible asset; an exclusive business name registered with the U.S. Patent Office; also called brand name

Trademark (p. 653) An intangible asset; an exclusive business symbol registered with the U.S. Patent Office

Units-of-output method (p. 643) See Units-of-production method

Units-of-production method (p. 643) A method of depreciating asset cost at the same rate for each unit produced during each period

Comprehensive Self Review

1. What is the denominator of the fraction used in the sum-of-the-years'-digits method of depreciation for an asset with a seven-year useful life?

2. What is the denominator of the fraction used in the calculation of annual depreciation using the straight-line method of depreciation for an asset with a useful life of seven years?

3. How is gain or loss computed for financial accounting purposes on the sale of an asset?

4. Assume that an asset with a five-year life is acquired on September 1, 2005, for $2,500. It is in the five-year class of assets for MACRS purposes. Assume that the asset is sold on December 18, 2006. Using the schedule on page 644, what would be the accumulated depreciation for federal income tax purposes?

5. What GAAP principle or convention supports the writing down of impaired assets to their fair market value?

(Answers to Comprehensive Self Review are on page 674.)

Discussion Questions

1. What is meant by "capitalized costs"?

2. How does real property differ from personal property?

3. Which of the following costs would not be included in the capitalized cost of factory equipment?

a. Net purchase price

b. Sales tax paid on purchase of asset

c. Costs of transporting equipment from seller's warehouse to purchaser's factory

d. Insurance during transportation

e. Costs of installing equipment in factory

f. "Trial run" to make adjustments and prepare equipment to produce

g. Fire and casualty insurance after installation

h. Penalty paid to the city for failure to prepare permission to install the equipment

4. A company purchases some land on which several old buildings are located. The land is bought as the location for a new factory, so the existing buildings must be torn down. Explain how to account for the purchase price and the cost of razing the old buildings.

5. Explain how straight-line depreciation is computed.

6. What is meant by the term "accelerated depreciation"?

7. Which of the depreciation methods illustrated in this chapter are accelerated methods?

8. Explain how double-declining-balance depreciation is computed on an asset with a life of six years.

9. What account is debited and what account is credited to record depreciation on office equipment?

10. Explain how the sum-of-years'-digits method would be applied to an asset with a useful life of six years.

11. Is depreciation for federal income tax purposes the same as depreciation for financial statement purposes? Explain.

12. Which method will give you a higher amount of depreciation expense in the later years of an asset's life, straight-line or declining-balance? Explain.

13. Explain when and how salvage value is considered when computing depreciation under the following methods: straight-line, declining-balance, and sum-of-the-years'-digits.

14. What information related to the company's property, plant, and equipment must be presented in the financial statements and in the notes to the financial statements?

15. What method is used to compute depletion expense for financial statement purposes for a coal mine operation?

16. What is an intangible asset?

17. Distinguish between the legal life and the economic life of an intangible asset. Which is used in computing amortization?

18. Under the income tax method, what will be the amount assigned to a new asset acquired through a trade-in of an old asset?

19. Depletion of natural resources is computed by a method similar to one of the depreciation methods discussed in this chapter. What depreciation method is that?

20. Suggest some factors (including some not specifically mentioned in this chapter) that suggest impairment of an asset may exist.

Applications

EXERCISES

Exercise 18-1 ▶
Objective 1

Determining the elements that make up the cost of an asset.

The following costs were incurred by Darin and David Co. in connection with the construction of a warehouse.

Cost of land	$ 300,000
Cost to demolish old warehouse	10,000
Cost to construct warehouse	1,500,000

1. What is the capitalized cost of the land?
2. What is the capitalized cost of the new warehouse?

Exercise 18-2 ▶
Objective 1

Determining the elements that make up the cost of an asset.

CAP Bearings incurred the costs below related to a new bearing machine.

Invoice price of bearing machine	$48,000
Cash discount for prompt payment	480
Transportation costs	1,624
Installation costs	950

What is the capitalized cost of the new bearing machine?

Exercise 18-3 ▶
Objective 2

Recording depreciation.

For the year ending December 31, 20--, the office equipment of Steve Coe Corporation had $8,000 depreciation. Journalize this adjusting entry.

Exercise 18-4 ▶
Objective 2

Computing depreciation under various methods.

Angel Company acquired an asset on January 1, 20--, that cost $110,000. It had a five-year life and a $10,000 salvage value. Compute the first two years of depreciation expense using the straight-line method, the double-declining-balance method, and the sum-of-the-years'-digits method.

Exercise 18-5 ▶
Objective 2

Computing depreciation under the units-of-production method.

Martin Company purchased a "hi-tech" machine to assemble certain electronic parts on January 6, 2004, for $440,000. It is expected to produce 500,000 units during its life and to have a salvage value of $40,000. The company will use the units-of-production method of depreciation. During 2004, it produced 125,000 units. Compute the 2004 depreciation expense using the units-of-production method. During 2005, 195,000 units were produced. Compute the amount of the 2005 depreciation expense.

Exercise 18-6 ▶
Objective 7

Computing amortization of patent costs.

Janus Company purchased a patent on July 8, 20--, for $84,000. The patent's remaining legal life is 14 years but the company believes its economic life is only 10 years. Compute its amortization for the year.

Exercise 18-7 ▶
Objective 6

Computing depletion of ore property cost.

Mountain Mining Company purchased a mine. Capitalized costs were $1,800,000. It is estimated that 1.8 million tons of ore will be mined. The company mined 250,000 tons during the first year. Compute the amount of depletion for the year.

Recording the sale of an asset.

Gomez Company owns a truck that cost $70,000. Depreciation totaling $50,000 had been taken on the truck up to the date of its sale on January 8, 20--, when it was sold for $18,000.

1. Give the journal entry to record the sale.

2. Assume that the truck is sold for $24,000. Give the journal entry to record the sale.

◀ Exercise 18-8
Objective 4

Recording the trade-in of an asset for a similar asset.

On January 5, 2001, Corker Construction Company purchased construction equipment for $600,000 with a useful life of eight years and salvage value of $40,000. The company uses the straight-line method of depreciation. On July 3, 2005, this equipment is traded for new construction equipment priced at $800,000. The company pays $600,000 cash and is given a trade-in allowance of $200,000 on the old equipment.

1. Give the general journal entry needed on July 3, 2005, to record the trade under the income tax method.

2. Give the general journal entry needed on July 3, 2005, to record the trade under the fair market value method.

◀ Exercise 18-9
Objective 5

Classifying assets using the MACRS system.

Give the class life each of the following assets would be assigned under the MACRS requirement.

1. Desks for an office
2. Auto for the president of the company
3. Computer
4. Apartment building
5. Mall

◀ Exercise 18-10
Objective 3

Problems

Selected problems can be completed using:
🕰 **Peachtree**   📖 **QuickBooks**   ▦ **Spreadsheets**

PROBLEM SET A

Determining the cost to be capitalized for acquisition of assets.

On January 10, 20--, Presley Corporation purchased a site for a new storage facility for $1,800,000. At a cost of $17,000, it razed an existing facility (fair market value of $100,000) and received $6,000 from its salvage. The firm also paid $1,500 attorney fees, $580 inspection fees, and $300 for a permit to raze the facility. After it was razed, the firm incurred these costs:

$16,000 for fill dirt for the site
$10,000 for leveling the site
$64,000 for paving sidewalks and curbs
$70,000 for paving a parking lot
$2,400,000 for building costs of new facility.

◀ Problem 18-1A
Objective 1

Compute the capitalized costs of (1) the storage facility, (2) the land, and (3) the land improvements.

INSTRUCTIONS

Analyze: For the transactions described, list the debits recorded in each of these asset accounts: **Storage Facility, Land, Land Improvements.**

Problem 18-2A ►
Objective 2
SPREADSHEET

Using different depreciation methods and comparing the results.

On January 2, 20--, Local Company purchased new equipment for $102,000 that had a useful life of four years and a salvage value of $10,000.

INSTRUCTIONS

Prepare a schedule showing the annual depreciation for the first three years of the asset's life under (1) the straight-line method, (2) the sum-of-the-years'-digits method, and (3) the double-declining-balance method.

Analyze: If the sum-of-the-years'-digits method is used to compute depreciation, what would be the balance in the **Accumulated Depreciation** account at the end of the second year?

Problem 18-3A ►
Objective 2

Using the straight-line and units-of-production methods of depreciation.

On January 3, 2005, Memphis Corporation purchased equipment with a five-year estimated useful life or 80,000 units of product for $84,000. The estimated salvage value was $2,000. Actual production for the first three years was 2005, 20,000 units; 2006, 24,000 units; and 2007, 22,000 units.

INSTRUCTIONS

Compute each year's depreciation under (1) the straight-line method and (2) the units-of-production method.

Analyze: Assume the equipment has an estimated useful life of 10 years instead of 5 years. Does this result in a higher or lower annual depreciation expense using the straight-line method?

Problem 18-4A ►
Objective 6

Computing depletion for financial accounting.

Commons Coal Company had total depletable costs of $1,000,000 for a mine purchased on July 1, 2004. It is estimated that 650,000 tons of coal are to be mined. During 2004, 98,000 tons were mined; 150,000 tons were mined in 2005.

INSTRUCTIONS

Compute the amount of depletion expense for 2004 and 2005 and give the general journal entry to record each year's depletion.

Analyze: What is the net book value of the mine on December 31, 2005?

Problem 18-5A ►
Objectives 4, 5

Recording asset trade-ins and sales.

The following transactions occurred at Reeves Company during 2005.

INSTRUCTIONS

Note: In each case assume that straight-line depreciation is used and that depreciation was last recorded on December 31, 2004. Compute depreciation to the nearest whole dollar.

1. Give the entries in general journal form to record the two exchange transactions using (a) the income tax method and (b) the fair market value method.

2. Give the entries in general journal form to record the sale of the truck, assuming (a) the sales price was $16,000 and (b) the sales price was $20,000.

DATE	TRANSACTIONS
Mar. 29	Exchanged a folding machine (Factory Equipment) that had an original cost of $2,200 when purchased on March 5, 2003, two years earlier. The useful life of the old asset was originally estimated at eight years and the salvage value at $200. The new folding machine had a sales price of $3,600. Reeves gave up the old machine and paid $2,000 cash. The new machine is estimated to have a useful life of five years and a salvage value of $600.
July 23	Exchanged a truck (Vehicles) for a new one that had a sales price of $36,800. Received a trade-in allowance of $13,600 on the old truck, which had been purchased for $31,200 on May 27, 2003, two years earlier. The life of the old truck was originally estimated at four years and the salvage value at $9,200. The life of the new truck is estimated to be four years and it is estimated to have a salvage value of $8,800.
Aug. 27	Sold a truck for cash. The truck was purchased on January 5, 2003, for $39,000. It had an estimated life of four years and an estimated salvage value of $7,000.

Analyze: Prior to its sale, what was the book value of the truck sold on August 27?

Recording asset trade-ins and sales.

Wren Shop purchased four identical machines on January 2, 2002, paying $1,500 for each. The useful life of each machine is expected to be six years, with a salvage value of $300 each. The company uses the straight-line method of depreciation. Selected transactions involving the machines follow. The accounts for recording these transactions are also given.

◀ **Problem 18-6A**
Objectives 4, 5

INSTRUCTIONS

1. Record the transactions in general journal form.

2. Assume that the income tax method is to be used, and record the trade-in of machine 4 on August 29, 2005. Round all calculations to the nearest whole dollar.

ACCOUNTS
Cash
Machinery
Accumulated Depreciation—Machinery
Gain on Sale of Machinery

Depreciation Expense—Machinery
Loss on Sale of Machinery
Loss on Stolen Machinery

DATE	TRANSACTIONS FOR 2002
Jan. 2	Paid $1,500 each, in cash, for four machines.
Dec. 31	Recorded depreciation for the year on the four machines.

DATE	TRANSACTIONS FOR 2003
Mar. 31	Machine 1 was stolen; no insurance was carried.
Dec. 31	Recorded depreciation for the year for the three remaining machines.

DATE	TRANSACTIONS FOR 2004
Sept. 30	Sold machine 2 for $1,200 cash.
Dec. 31	Recorded annual depreciation on the two remaining machines.

DATE	TRANSACTIONS FOR 2005
June 4	Traded in machine 3 for a similar machine with a $1,950 list price and fair market value. A trade-in allowance of $800 was received. The balance was paid in cash.
Aug. 29	Traded in machine 4 for a similar machine with a $2,000 list price and fair market value. A trade-in allowance of $1,000 was received. The balance was paid in cash.

Analyze: What is the balance of the **Accumulated Depreciation** account on December 31, 2003?

Problem 18-7A ►
Objective 7

Recording intangible assets and research and development costs.

Selected accounts of Fortune Company are listed below. Several transactions and events that took place at the company during 20-- are also given.

INSTRUCTIONS

1. Record the transactions for 20-- in general journal form.
2. Record amortization of the intangible assets for the year ended December 31, 20--.

ACCOUNTS

Cash	Research and Development Expense
Patent	Amortization Expense—Product Formulas
Product Formulas	Amortization Expense—Computer Software
Computer Software	Amortization Expense—Patent

DATE	TRANSACTIONS
July 1	Paid $72,000 to purchase a product formula. The formula is expected to have a useful life of five years.
Sept. 30	Paid $200,000 for a patent having a useful life of 10 years.
Oct. 4	Purchased a unique computer program for $120,000. This software has an estimated useful life of five years.

During the year the company recorded various cash expenditures of $300,000 for labor and supplies used in its research department.

Analyze: Based on the transactions above, what is the net value of Fortune Company's total intangible assets on December 31, 20--?

PROBLEM SET B

Problem 18-1B ►
Objective 1

Determining the costs to be capitalized for acquisition of assets.

On July 2, 20--, Hodges Company purchased a site for its new headquarters for $400,000. Two existing houses, with a total appraised value of $120,000, had to be torn down at a cost of $32,000. Salvage proceeds from these two houses were $14,000. Other costs incurred to develop the site included $2,000 in legal fees, $12,000 to pave the sidewalks, $2,400,000 to build the headquarters, and $28,000 to pave the parking area. Compute the capitalized costs of (1) the headquarters, (2) the land, and (3) the land improvements.

Analyze: What net effects did these transactions have on the total owner's equity of Hodges Company?

Using different depreciation methods and comparing the results.

◄ **Problem 18-2B**
Objective 2

On January 3, 20--, Randy Corporation purchased a new $140,000 machine with a five-year useful life and an estimated $8,000 salvage value.

INSTRUCTIONS

Prepare a schedule showing the annual depreciation and accumulated depreciation for each of the first three years of the asset's life under (1) the straight-line method, (2) the sum-of-the-years'-digits method, and (3) the double-declining-balance method.

Analyze: If the double-declining-balance method were used to record depreciation, what would be the balance of the **Accumulated Depreciation** account at the end of the third year?

Using the straight-line and units-of-production methods of depreciation.

◄ **Problem 18-3B**
Objective 2

SPV Company purchased a large delivery truck for $110,000 on January 5, 2004. The truck's salvage value is estimated at $10,000, and its useful life is five years or 300,000 miles. During 2004, the truck was driven 45,000 miles and in 2005, 62,500 miles.

INSTRUCTIONS

Compute the depreciation expense for 2004 and 2005 under (1) the straight-line method and (2) the units-of-production method.

Analyze: What is the book value of the delivery truck on December 31, 2005, using the straight-line method?

Computing depletion for financial accounting.

◄ **Problem 18-4B**
Objective 6

Superior Mining Company paid $500,000 for mining rights in 20--. An estimated total of 125,000 tons of ore are expected to be extracted. During 20--, 10,000 tons were mined.

INSTRUCTIONS

Compute the amount of depletion taken for income statement purposes in 20--, and record the amount in the general journal.

Analyze: If the company failed to record depletion expenses, what impact would this oversight have on earnings?

Recording asset trade-ins and sales.

◄ **Problem 18-5B**
Objectives 4, 5

The transactions that follow occurred at Odo Corporation during 2005.

Note: In each case assume that straight-line depreciation is used and that depreciation was last recorded on December 31, 2004. Compute depreciation to the nearest whole dollar.

INSTRUCTIONS

1. Record in general journal form the two exchange transactions, using (a) the income tax method and (b) the fair market value method.

2. Record the sale of the display fixture in general journal form, assuming (a) the sales price was $18,000 and (b) the sales price was $22,000.

DATE	TRANSACTIONS
Apr. 2	Exchanged a printer (Office Equipment) that had been purchased for $2,400 on January 3, 2004. The useful life of the old printer was estimated at five years, with a salvage value of $400. The new printer had a sales price of $3,000. Odo gave up the old printer and $2,000. The new printer has a useful life of four years and a salvage value of $600.
June 30	Exchanged a delivery truck (Vehicles) for a new one with a list price of $38,000. A trade-in allowance of $4,000 was received on the old truck, which had been purchased on July 1, 2004, for $32,000. The old truck had an estimated $2,000 salvage value and a five-year life.
Oct. 1	Sold a display fixture (Fixtures) for cash. The fixture was purchased on April 1, 2004, for $30,000 and was depreciated on the straight-line basis, using an estimated life of seven years and a salvage value of $2,000.

Analyze: What effect does the June 30 exchange transaction have on earnings if the income tax method is used? If the fair market value is used?

Problem 18-6B ▶
Objectives 4, 5

Recording asset trade-ins and sales.

Santana Company purchased four identical machines on January 2, 2002, for $4,000 each. Each machine's useful life is five years; no salvage value is expected. The company uses the straight-line method of depreciation. Selected transactions involving the machines are listed below. The necessary accounts for recording these transactions are also given.

INSTRUCTIONS

1. Record the transactions in general journal form.

2. Assume that the income tax method is to be used, and record the trade-in of machine 4 on August 29, 2005.

ACCOUNTS
Cash
Machinery
Accumulated Depreciation—Machinery
Gain on Sale of Machinery
Depreciation Expense—Machinery
Loss on Sale of Machinery
Fire Loss on Machinery

DATE	TRANSACTIONS FOR 2002
Jan. 2	Paid $4,000 each for four machines.
Dec. 31	Recorded depreciation for the year for the four machines.

DATE	TRANSACTIONS FOR 2003
Apr. 1	Machine 1 was destroyed by fire; no insurance was carried.
Dec. 31	Recorded annual depreciation for the three remaining machines.

DATE	TRANSACTIONS FOR 2004
Sept. 30	Sold machine 2 for $2,000 cash.
Dec. 31	Recorded annual depreciation for the two remaining machines.

DATE	TRANSACTIONS FOR 2005
June 4	Traded machine 3 for a similar machine with a $4,400 list price and fair market value. A trade-in allowance of $1,200 was received. The balance was paid in cash.
Aug. 29	Traded in machine 4 for a similar machine with a list price of $4,600. A trade-in allowance of $1,000 was received. The balance was paid in cash.

Analyze: What is the balance of the **Accumulated Depreciation** account on December 31, 2004?

Recording intangible assets and research and development costs.

◀ **Problem 18-7B**
Objective 7

Listed below are selected accounts and transactions for Saleh Company during 20--. The company cannot accurately estimate the useful life of its computer software, so it adopted the arbitrary policy of amortizing all such costs over a 36-month period, beginning with the month of acquisition. The company has also adopted the practice of amortizing all patents over a 60-month period, beginning with the month of acquisition.

INSTRUCTIONS

1. Record the transactions in general journal form.
2. Record amortization of the intangible assets for the year ending December 31, 20--.

ACCOUNTS
Cash
Patents
Computer Software
Research and Development Expense
Amortization Expense—Patents
Amortization Expense—Computer Software

DATE	TRANSACTIONS
Mar. 31	Made cash expenditures of $300,000 for research and development costs related to a new patent. This patent was developed in the company's laboratory.
Apr. 1	Purchased a patent for $120,000 in cash. The patent is to be used in the company's operations.
June 30	Made cash expenditures of $130,000 for company personnel to develop computer programs that are to be used in the company's research activities.
Sept. 1	Purchased a software program for $28,800 in cash from a computer software supply firm. The software program is to be used in the company's inventory control system.

Analyze: What is the net book value of computer software on December 31?

Building and Land Improvements

Keagens Company, Inc., develops and sells computer hardware and software. Below are several transactions that occurred during 2004 and 2005.

INSTRUCTIONS

Give the December 31, 2005, adjusting entries to record all depreciation costs for Keagens Company, Inc. assets. No depreciation was taken on the building or land improvements in 2004.

TRANSACTIONS

The company purchased a building site for $50,000 on July 3, 2004, and built a new office building on the site for $200,000. Construction was completed on January 3, 2005. Various other costs included grading and preparing the site, $10,000; paving the parking lot and sidewalks, $40,000; and fencing the back of the property, $10,000. The useful life of the building was estimated at 20 years while the land improvements were estimated at 10 years.

On January 3, 2005, Keagens moved into the building. A telephone system costing $6,000 was installed on that date, with an estimated useful life of five years. Office furniture costing $14,000 and having a useful life of seven years was purchased and delivered to the business on January 5, 2005. The company elected the double-declining-balance method to recover the costs of the telephone system and the furniture.

Analyze: How would the assets of Keagens Company be reflected on the balance sheet on December 31, 2005?

Depreciation Expense

In a review of the annual reports of Norwalk Corporation and Nobel Corporation, you note that Norwalk Corporation uses straight-line depreciation and Nobel Corporation uses the declining-balance method.

Are these companies violating the generally accepted accounting principle of consistency by using different depreciation methods?

If you examined the federal income tax returns of these companies, would you expect the depreciation expense shown on their federal income tax returns to be the same as the depreciation expense shown on their financial statements? Why or why not?

Assume that these companies are similar in all respects except for the difference in computing depreciation. Which company would you expect to report the lower net income for financial reporting purposes?

Who is responsible for determining the depreciation method used by the company for financial reporting purposes?

Business Connections

◄ Connection 1

 **MANAGERIAL FOCUS**   Plant Asset Procedures

1. Suggest three key procedures involving internal control of property, plant, and equipment that relate to accounting records.

2. Suggest three key procedures involving internal control of property, plant, and equipment that do not relate specifically to accounting records.

3. Assume that you are the accountant at a fabricating plant. One of the vice presidents has asked you why one of the pieces of equipment used in the plant is shown at its original cost in the asset accounts. Respond to the question.

4. Suppose you are on the controller's staff at a large company. You have suggested assigning responsibility for the company's equipment to specific individuals. One supervisor has objected, saying it is a waste of time. Defend your suggestion to the controller and to the supervisor.

5. Generally accepted accounting principles require that all research and development costs be expensed in the year they are incurred. An officer of the company wants to amortize these costs. What can you say to explain why this accounting requirement exists?

◄ Connection 2

Ethical DILEMMA   Changing Depreciation Method Pomgranite opened a new business in 2005. Because equipment of the type purchased decreases in value rapidly after purchase, Pomgranite decided to use declining-balance depreciation. At the end of the first year, the company reported a substantial loss and Pomgranite realized that the company is likely to report a loss for the next three of four years. In addition, there will be large equipment purchases each year, resulting in even higher depreciation charges, adding to the probability of substantial losses. The reported losses could make it difficult to borrow money or secure investments in the business. As a result, Pomgranite told you, the accountant for the company, to change the depreciation method from the declining-balance method to the straight-line method. This resulted in a substantial decrease in depreciation during the second year. You are concerned whether you have become a party to an unethical action. What are the factors you should consider?

◄ Connection 3

Street **WISE:** Questions from the Real World   Depreciation Amounts and Method Refer to the *1999 Annual Report* for The Home Depot, Inc. in Appendix B.

1. Locate the Notes to Consolidated Financial Statements. Review Note 1, Summary of Significant Accounting Policies. What method is used to depreciate the company's furniture, fixtures and equipment? What estimated useful life is assigned to buildings?

2. Find the Consolidated Balance Sheets. What was the amount of accumulated depreciation and amortization for the year ended January 30, 2000? What net value is reported for Property and Equipment?

FINANCIAL $TATEMENT
A N A L Y S I S   **Annual Report** The following excerpts were taken from the Pier 1 Imports, Inc., *1999 Annual Report.*

Notes to Consolidated Financial Statements

Properties; maintenance and repairs—buildings, equipment, furniture and fixtures; and leasehold interests and improvements are carried at cost less accumulated depreciation. Depreciation is computed using the straight-line method over estimated remaining useful lives of the assets ranging from three to thirty years. Expenditures for maintenance, repairs, and renewals that do not materially prolong the useful lives of the assets are charged to expense as incurred.

Note 3—Properties

Properties are summarized as follows as of February 26, 2000 and February 27, 1999 (in thousands):

	2000	1999
Land	$ 22,384	$ 31,620
Buildings	59,761	67,253
Equipment, furniture and fixtures	183,313	166,460
Leasehold interests and improvements	157,801	144,153
	423,259	409,486
Less accumulated depreciation and amortization	210,227	183,224
Properties, net	$213,032	$226,262

Analyze:

1. Based on the information presented above, what is the historical cost of the assets reflected on the consolidated balance sheet for Pier 1 Imports, Inc., for fiscal 2000?

2. What journal entry would be necessary to record a repair to equipment that did not materially extend the useful life of the equipment? Assume Pier 1 paid $250 for the repair with Check 13389 on March 28, 2002.

3. What percentage of total property costs has been depreciated on February 26, 2000?

Analyze Online: Locate the Pier 1 Imports Web site **(www.pier1.com)**. Review the most recent annual report provided on the site and answer the following questions.

4. What net book value of "Properties" is reflected on the consolidated balance sheets?

5. What percentage of total property costs has been depreciated at the fiscal year-end?

Extending **the** *Thought*   **Employees as Assets** A company's employees are often referred to as valuable assets of the company, yet the balance sheet makes no reference to employees. Do you agree with this? Why or why not?

Business Communication **Short Speech** You have owned and operated Gailery's Automotive Repair Shop for 20 years. As a business owner and accountant, you have been invited to speak at the next Small Business Administration luncheon for new business owners. "Accounting for Plant Assets" is the topic. Prepare a five-minute speech on plant assets and depreciation. It might be helpful to use note cards containing three or four major points that you plan to discuss. Remember that you will be speaking to new business owners who need to understand how assets should be recorded in their accounting records and why depreciation of those assets is important.

◄ **Connection 6**

Team*Work* **IRS** The Internal Revenue Service offers business owners guidance on tax laws concerning the depreciation of property. As a team, locate information on the IRS Web site **(www.irs.gov)** on depreciation of property and answer the following questions:

◄ **Connection 7**

1. What is the IRS definition of "depreciation"?
2. List three items that cannot be depreciated. Why?
3. What three requirements must property meet in order to be depreciated?
4. List three types of assets that can be depreciated that were not mentioned in this chapter.

   Hint: Locate *Publication 946, How to Depreciate Property.*

inter **NET**
CONNECTION **Copyrights** Visit the Library of Congress Web site at **www.loc.gov** and select *Copyright Office.* What is a work made for hire? Can your work be submitted on a computer disk? Can you copyright a recipe?

◄ **Connection 8**

Answers to Self Reviews

Answers to Section 1 Self Review

1. Salvage value less any costs expected to be incurred in removing and disposing of the asset at the time of its retirement.
2. Straight-line method because the declining-balance method is an accelerated method; it gives higher depreciation charges in early years and lower depreciation charges in later years.
3. MACRS stands for Modified Accelerated Cost Recovery System. MACRS provides the useful lives of different types of assets for purposes of computing depreciation for tax purposes and also provides the percent of cost to be charged off each year for each class of assets.
4. **d.** $22,750.
5. **b.** straight-line method.
6. Straight-line depreciation results in lower depreciation expense for the first year, and therefore in higher net income.

Answers to Section 2 Self Review

1. Sale, trade-in, and discarding.
2. A loss will be recognized when the cash or the value of other consideration received is less than the net book value of the asset.
3. Its cost and accumulated depreciation should be removed. If the net proceeds resulting from salvage exceed book value, a gain on retirement is recognized. If the net salvage proceeds are less than book value, a loss is recognized.
4. **c.** $2,000 gain.
5. **c. Accumulated Depreciation—Equipment.**
6. Both the asset and its accumulated depreciation would be overstated. However, since the asset is fully depreciated, net book value is zero. There would be no effect on income.

Answers to Section 3 Self Review

1. The units-of-production method is preferred because it more closely matches the capitalized costs with the benefits received.
2. Divide the capitalized mineral costs by the estimated units of resource to be produced and then multiply this per-unit rate by the number of units produced during the period.
3. Impairment means that the market value or expected future net cash flow from an asset is less than the asset's book value.
4. **b.** credited to the asset account.
5. **d.** the shorter of its legal life or its economic life, not to exceed 40 years.
6. Personal property and real property except land are depreciated. Mineral rights are depleted. Intangible assets are amortized.

Answers to Comprehensive Self Review

1. The sum of 7 + 6 + 5 + 4 + 3 + 2 + 1, or 28.
2. 7 years.
3. To compute gain or loss on the sale of an asset, the book value (cost less accumulated depreciation) is compared with the selling price.
4. $1,300. (0.52 × $2,500 = $1,300).
5. The modifying convention of conservatism.

PART 6

Accounting for Partnerships and Corporations

CATERPILLAR Caterpillar Inc. has proven that diversity and innovation are key building blocks to financial strength. In October 2000, the company and its joint venture partners were awarded almost $19 million by The Department of Commerce's National Institute of Science & Technology for two research and development projects. The goals of the projects include development of new high-powered manufacturing lasers and lighter, more efficient power transmission gears and machine components.

Thinking Critically
What other concepts or business strategies might be considered key to financial strength?

CHAPTER 19

Learning Objectives

1. Explain the major advantages and disadvantages of a partnership.

2. State the important provisions that should be included in every partnership agreement.

3. Account for the formation of a partnership.

4. Compute and record the division of net income or net loss between partners in accordance with the partnership agreement.

5. Prepare a statement of partners' equities.

6. Account for the revaluation of assets and liabilities prior to the dissolution of a partnership.

7. Account for the sale of a partnership interest.

8. Account for the investment of a new partner in an existing partnership.

9. Account for the withdrawal of a partner from a partnership.

10. Define the accounting terms new to this chapter.

Accounting For Partnerships

New Terms

Articles of partnership

Dissolution

Distributive share

General partner

Limited partner

Limited partnership

Liquidation

Memorandum entry

Mutual agency

Partnership

Partnership agreement

Statement of partners'
   equities

Unlimited liability

WOOLPERT

www.woolpert.com

Since its founding in 1911, as a surveying and civil engineering firm, Woolpert has consistently grown to offer professional services and partnered solutions, including Facilities Planning and Design, GIS/IT, Photogrammetry, Site/Civil Design, Surveying/GPS, Transportation, and Water Management within both the private and public sectors. Operating as a privately held, limited liability partnership of 19 partners, the company employs over 700 individuals.

From topographic surveys to facilities planning, there's never a dull moment in the Woolpert offices. An inspection contract for the 2,710-foot William S. Ritchie Bridge in West Virginia required installation of cable and steel bracket rigging, hydraulic snoopers, and movable platforms that extended to the bridge's upper truss. In another Woolpert project office, the engineering team plans boundary surveys, zoning reviews, and electrical designs for a new Home Depot store.

Thinking Critically
If you were one of the partners of Woolpert LLP, what responsibilities or liabilities do you think you would carry?

For more information on Woolpert LLP, go to:
collegeaccounting.glencoe.com.

Forming a Partnership

Section Objectives

1. Explain the major advantages and disadvantages of a partnership.

   WHY IT'S IMPORTANT
   Selecting the most advantageous form of business organization contributes to the overall success of a company.

2. State the important provisions that should be included in every partnership agreement.

   WHY IT'S IMPORTANT
   A partnership agreement is a legal document that dictates the operating structure and terms of the business entity.

3. Account for the formation of a partnership.

   WHY IT'S IMPORTANT
   Assets, liabilities, and owners' capital must all be correctly stated from the partnership's start.

Terms to Learn

articles of partnership
general partner
limited partner
limited partnership
memorandum entry
mutual agency
partnership
partnership agreement
unlimited liability

1 Objective

Explain the major advantages and disadvantages of a partnership.

Accounting procedures for a sole proprietorship have been covered in previous chapters. This chapter discusses accounting for partnerships.

The Characteristics of a Partnership

The *Uniform Partnership Act,* adopted by all 50 states, defines a **partnership** as "an association of two or more persons who carry on, as co-owners, a business for profit." The partnership form of organization is widely used in small service, merchandising, and manufacturing businesses. Historically, professionals such as accountants, lawyers, and physicians have formed partnerships to pool their talents and abilities.

Woolpert LLP began operations in 1911. Charlton Putnam, a surveyor and landscape engineer, joined forces with Edward Deeds and Charles Kettering, inventors of the self-starting automobile ignition system. In 1916 Ralph L. Woolpert, a civil engineer, joined the company as a partner. Throughout the years the company extended partner status to others who contributed their expertise.

Advantages of the Partnership

A partnership has three important advantages. It pools the skills, abilities, and financial resources of two or more individuals. It is easy and inexpensive to form, especially when compared with a corporation. A partnership does not pay income tax. The partners report their shares of the partnership's income or loss on their individual income tax returns.

Disadvantages of the Partnership

Certain characteristics of partnerships are clearly disadvantages. Each partner has **unlimited liability** for the partnership's debts. Thus a partner's personal assets as well as the partnership's assets can be required in payment of the firm's debts. This characteristic enhances the credit standing of the business, but it can be a danger to the individual partners.

In most states it is possible for some partners to have limited liability. A **limited partnership** is a partnership with one or more limited partners. **Limited partners** are liable only for their investment in the partnership. State laws generally require that limited partnerships have at least one **general partner**, a partner who has unlimited liability. Limited partners are prohibited from taking an active management role and from having their names in the partnership's name.

The partnership is a **mutual agency**; each partner is empowered to act as an agent for the partnership, binding the firm by those acts so long as they are within the normal scope of the partnership's activities.

A partnership lacks continuity; it has a limited life. When a partner dies or is incapacitated, the partnership is dissolved.

Partnership interest is not freely transferable; other partners must approve the sale of a partner's interest to a new partner. Upon a transfer of interest, the existing partnership is dissolved and a new partnership must be formed.

Partnership Agreements

It is easy to form a partnership. Two or more partners agree to form the business entity by entering into an oral or written contract. An oral agreement is binding on the partners, but a written contract is preferred. To avoid any future misunderstandings, an attorney prepares a legal contract forming a partnership and specifying certain details of the operation, called a **partnership agreement**. This is legally known as the **articles of partnership**. The partnership agreement can be simple, or complex and detailed. Every partnership agreement should contain the

- names of the partners;
- name, location, and nature of the business;
- starting date of the agreement;
- life of the partnership;
- rights and duties of each partner;
- amount of capital to be contributed by each partner;
- drawings by the partners;
- fiscal year and accounting method;
- method of allocating income or loss to the partners;
- procedures to be followed if the partnership is dissolved or the business is liquidated.

Partnerships dissolve upon a partner's death, incapacity, or withdrawal.

❷ Objective
State the important provisions that should be included in every partnership agreement.

Accounting for the Formation of a Partnership

Partnerships and sole proprietorships use the same types of journals and ledgers as well as asset, liability, revenue, and expense accounts. The only difference is that in a partnership, each partner has a capital account and a drawing account.

There are many ways to form a partnership. Partnerships are often formed when a sole proprietorship "takes in" a partner or partners to continue an existing business. Usually the new partners invest cash, and the sole proprietor contributes noncash assets and liabilities of the existing business. Sometimes two sole proprietors combine their operations into a partnership. Often partners start a completely new business with initial investments of cash.

When noncash assets are transferred to a partnership, they are recorded at their fair market value, as agreed to by the partners, on the transfer date. Liabilities are stated at their correct balances on the transfer date.

❸ Objective
Account for the formation of a partnership.

Sometimes two existing companies form a partnership with a new objective or mission in mind. In 1998 Weirton Steel Corporation formed a limited partnership with LTV Steel and Steel Dynamics to offer a new Web site (**www.metalsite.com**) where metal products can be purchased from various U.S. suppliers.

Let's look at a partnership formed by Tanya Ross and Don Wright. Ross operates The Jean Shop, a small clothing store that sells T-shirts, jeans, and other casual clothing. Wright works in another store selling athletic shoes. To get additional capital and to obtain Wright's talents, Ross offered to make Wright a partner in the business. Ross agreed to transfer the assets (except cash) and the liabilities of The Jean Shop to the new partnership. Wright agreed to invest cash of $30,000 in the business. Figure 19-1 shows the balance sheet of The Jean Shop on December 31.

FIGURE 19-1 ▶
Balance Sheet for a
Sole Proprietor

The Jean Shop
Balance Sheet
December 31, 20--

Assets			
Cash			1 400 00
Accounts Receivable	21 600 00		
Less Allowance for Doubtful Accounts	600 00	21 000 00	
Merchandise Inventory		119 000 00	
Store Equipment	10 000 00		
Less Accumulated Depreciation	8 000 00	2 000 00	
Total Assets		143 400 00	
Liabilities and Owner's Equity			
Liabilities			
Notes Payable—Bank	40 000 00		
Accounts Payable	36 000 00		
Total Liabilities		76 000 00	
Owner's Equity			
Tanya Ross		67 400 00	
Total Liabilities and Owner's Equity		143 400 00	

Recall

Allowance Method
Under the allowance method for uncollectible accounts, an estimate is made before actual losses occur.

After examining The Jean Shop's assets, Ross and Wright agreed that

• Net accounts receivable is $18,600.

Accounts receivable on balance sheet	$21,600
Definitely uncollectible	(1,600)
Accounts receivable, adjusted	$20,000
Likely to be uncollectible	(1,400)
Net accounts receivable	$18,600

• The value of merchandise inventory is $104,400.
• The store equipment's value is $3,000 based on an appraisal.
• Accrued interest payable on the note payable is $400. This liability was not recorded as of December 31.
• Accounts payable total is $35,600.

Thus, Ross and Wright have agreed that the net assets Ross transferred are $50,000:

Accounts receivable	$ 18,600
Merchandise inventory	104,400
Store equipment	3,000
Notes payable	(40,000)
Interest payable	(400)
Accounts payable	(35,600)
Total	$ 50,000

Memorandum Entry to Record Formation of Partnership

The first entry in the general journal of the new partnership is a **memorandum entry**, which is an informational entry. It indicates the name of the business, the partners' names, and other pertinent information. Note that the memorandum entry references the partnership agreement, which provides information about the capital contributed by each partner and the division of income.

1	20--						1
2	Jan.	1	On this date a partnership was formed				2
3			between Tanya Ross and Don Wright to				3
4			carry on a retail clothing business under				4
5			the name of The Jean Shop, according to				5
6			the terms of the partnership agreement				6
7			effective this date.				7
8							8

Investment of Assets and Liabilities by Sole Proprietor

The first journal entry records the transfer of Ross' assets and liabilities to the partnership.

9	Jan.	1	Accounts Receivable	111	20 0 0 0 00			9
10			Merchandise Inventory	121	104 4 0 0 00			10
11			Store Equipment	131	3 0 0 0 00			11
12			Allowance for Doubtful Accounts	112		1 4 0 0 00		12
13			Notes Payable—Bank	201		40 0 0 0 00		13
14			Accounts Payable	205		35 6 0 0 00		14
15			Interest Payable	215		4 0 0 00		15
16			Tanya Ross, Capital	301		50 0 0 0 00		16
17			Investment of Ross					17
18								18

Note that the entry includes **Accounts Receivable** of $20,000 and **Allowance for Doubtful Accounts** of $1,400. All individual customers' balances, except for those that were definitely uncollectible, were transferred to the partnership. Consequently, the **Accounts Receivable** control account agrees with the total of the accounts receivable subsidiary ledger. Note that **Store Equipment** is transferred at fair market value. No accumulated depreciation is transferred. Depreciation on plant and equipment that was recorded by the previous owner is irrelevant. Depreciation will be recorded by the partnership based on the asset's value at the date of transfer.

Investment of Cash by Partner

The next journal entry records the investment of cash by Wright.

19	Jan.	1	Cash	101	30 0 0 0 00			19
20			Don Wright, Capital	311		30 0 0 0 00		20
21			Investment of cash by Wright					21
22								22

About Accounting

Family Partnerships
Family partnerships are frequently designed to facilitate transfers of property, business interests, and investments between family members in a tax-efficient manner. These partnerships permit family members to pool funds for investment purposes.

Computers in Accounting

Information Security and Computer Viruses

Computer viruses and their threat to information security have long been a concern to the business community. In November 1988 a computer virus called Morris Worm crippled approximately 10 percent of all computers connected to the Internet. In response, the CERT® Coordination Center was created by the U.S. Department of Defense at Carnegie Mellon University. In 1999 CERT handled almost 9,900 virus and Internet security issues.

A computer virus is a program designed to spread itself throughout a computer system by infecting executable files or program files on the hard drive or floppy disks. Word or Excel documents can carry viruses. HTML documents that contain JavaScript or other executable code can also contain these damaging programs. Infectious codes not only attach to other programs on the computer, but will spread to other computers connected to a network.

Some viruses are designed to damage or delete files or otherwise interfere with a computer's operation.

Simply downloading a file won't activate a virus. An infected program file must be executed to trigger the virus. Viruses cannot damage hardware. They will not burn out a hard drive or cause the CPU to explode.

Follow these general guidelines to avoid virus infections and protect computer files:

- Obtain and install anti-virus software from a reputable company. Use and update it regularly.
- Scan new programs or other files that may contain executable code before opening them, no matter where they were obtained.
- Disable any e-mail or news software that has the ability to automatically execute JavaScript, Word macros, or other executable code contained in or attached to a message.
- Be extremely careful about accepting programs or other files during online chat sessions.
- Make regular backups of files.

Thinking Critically

If your home or office computer has been infected with a virus, how did you discover it? How did you rid your system of the virus? What anti-virus practices do you follow now? How did the virus impact your ability to use your computer?

Internet Application

Use a search engine to find a recent article about computer viruses and answer the following questions. What was the name and origin of the virus? How did it spread? What effect did it have on computer files or systems? What effect did it have on global commerce or communications?

Subsequent Investments and Permanent Withdrawals

During the life of the partnership, additional investments are recorded in the same manner as the initial investments. When partners make cash withdrawals that are intended to be permanent reductions of capital, the withdrawals are recorded as debits to the partners' capital accounts.

Drawing Accounts

Partners need funds with which to pay their living expenses. Partners can obtain funds by making withdrawals against anticipated income. Each partner has a drawing account to record withdrawals.

The partnership agreement of The Jean Shop specifies that Ross can withdraw up to $2,400 each month and that Wright can withdraw up to $2,000 each month. The withdrawals are recorded in the cash payments journal. The entry is a credit to **Cash** and a debit to the partners' drawing accounts. At the end of 12 months, on December 31, Ross' drawing account has a debit balance of $28,800 ($2,400 × 12), and Wright's drawing account has a debit balance of $24,000 ($2,000 × 12).

Partners sometimes pay their personal bills with partnership funds. This practice is not sound because it leads to confusion between business and personal transactions. If the business pays a partner's personal expense, however, the debit in the cash payments journal is to the partner's drawing account, not an expense account.

It is common for partners to take merchandise from the business for their personal use. The cost of merchandise is debited to the partner's drawing account. The credit is to the **Purchases** account. Note that the inventory account is not involved—beginning inventory in the current period's cost of goods sold should agree with ending inventory of the prior period. Ross withdrew merchandise that cost $160 and had a retail sales price of $220. The transaction is recorded as follows.

Recall

Separate Entity
The separate entity assumption states that the business is separate from its owners. This explains why personal expenses paid by the business are charged to the partner's drawing account rather than to a business expense account.

1	20--						1
2	June	14	Tanya Ross, Drawing	302	1 6 0 00		2
3			Purchases	501		1 6 0 00	3
4			Cost of merchandise withdrawn by Ross				4
5							5
6							6
7							7
8							8

Section 1 Self Review

Questions

1. What are the major advantages of the partnership form of business?

2. When a sole proprietorship transfers assets to a partnership, at what amount are the assets recorded?

3. How do the ledger accounts of a partnership differ from those of a sole proprietorship?

Exercises

4. The entry to record the investment of cash in a partnership consists of a

  a. debit to **Cash** and a credit to **Partners' Equities.**

  b. debit to **Partners' Equities** and a credit to **Cash.**

  c. debit to **Cash** and a credit to the individual partner's capital account.

  d. debit to individual partner's account and a credit to **Cash.**

5. The entry to record merchandise taken by a partner for personal use is recorded as a

  a. debit to the individual partner's drawing account and a credit to **Partners' Equities.**

  b. debit to the individual partner's capital account and a credit to **Purchases.**

  c. debit to **Purchases** and a credit to the individual partner's drawing account.

  d. debit to the individual partner's drawing account and a credit to **Purchases.**

Analysis

6. Lisa Garcia and Ritchie Rogers are combining their businesses to form a new partnership. Garcia invests merchandise inventory valued at $26,100 and store equipment appraised at $1,750. In addition, her business has accounts receivable of $5,000 of which $350 is assumed to be uncollectible. Garcia's business owed $10,000 to creditors. After the entry to record her investment is posted, what is the balance in Garcia's capital account?

Allocating Income or Loss

Section Objectives

4 Compute and record the division of net income or net loss between partners in accordance with the partnership agreement.

WHY IT'S IMPORTANT
The records must reflect the partnership agreement's allocation of profit and loss.

5 Prepare a statement of partners' equities.

WHY IT'S IMPORTANT
The statement of partners' equities summarizes the changes that have occurred in each partner's equity account. The ending balance appears on the balance sheet.

Terms to Learn

distributive share
statement of partners' equities

Important!

Distribution of Income
Income allocation or division is frequently referred to as the distribution of income. This does not mean that cash is distributed to the partners.

Important!

Income Allocation
Unless the partnership agreement provides otherwise, net income or net loss is allocated equally to the partners.

Recall that a partnership does not pay income tax. The net income or net loss "flows through" to the partners, who report their share of the partnership income on their individual tax returns.

Allocating Partnership Income or Loss

At the end of a period, the closing procedures for a partnership are similar to those used for a sole proprietorship.

Step 1: *Close revenue to* **Income Summary.**

Step 2: *Close expenses to* **Income Summary.**

Step 3: *Close* **Income Summary** *to the partners' capital accounts.*

Step 4: *Close each partner's drawing account to the partner's capital account.*

In step 3 the business needs to determine the **distributive share**, which is the amount of net income or net loss allocated to each partner. Distributive share refers solely to the division of net income or net loss among partners, not to cash distributions.

Partners may agree to divide or allocate the income in any manner they desire. Typical considerations for each partner include the

- amount of time spent in the business,
- skills, expertise, and experience,
- amount of capital invested.

The partnership agreement should clearly and carefully spell out the basis for allocation so that there will be no misunderstanding among the partners. *In the absence of an agreement to the contrary, partners share income and losses equally.* Typical allocations are based on a fixed ratio or on capital account balances. Some agreements call for salary allowances and interest allowances.

Let's examine the end-of-year procedures for the partnership of Ross and Wright. The following T accounts show the capital and drawing accounts for Ross and Wright at the end of the first year of business.

Tanya Ross, Capital 301	
	Dec. 31
	Bal. 50,000

Don Wright, Capital 311	
	Dec. 31
	Bal. 30,000

Tanya Ross, Drawing 302	
Dec. 31	
Bal. 28,800	

Don Wright, Drawing 312	
Dec. 31	
Bal. 24,000	

To illustrate the most common allocation methods, the allocation of income or loss is shown under four different arrangements.

Agreed Upon Ratio

Assume that Ross and Wright agreed that net income will be split in the ratio of 3:2 (3 to 2) to Ross and Wright, respectively. Follow these steps to convert the ratios to decimals.

Step 1: *Add the figures given in the ratio.*

Ross	3
Wright	2
Total	5

Step 2: *Express each figure as a fraction of the total.*

Ross' share	3/5
Wright's share	2/5

Step 3: *Convert each fraction into a percentage by dividing the numerator by the denominator.*

Ross' share	3/5 =	0.60 or 60 percent
Wright's share	2/5 =	0.40 or 40 percent

Allocating Net Income. Assume that **Income Summary** has a credit balance of $100,000 (net income) after closing the revenue and expense accounts. Net income is allocated as follows.

Ross	$100,000 × 0.60 =	$60,000
Wright	$100,000 × 0.40 =	$40,000

Step 3 of the closing process is to close **Income Summary** to the partners' capital accounts as follows.

1	20--					1
2	Dec.	31	Income Summary	399	100 00 0 00	2
3			Tanya Ross, Capital	301	60 00 0 00	3
4			Don Wright, Capital	311	40 00 0 00	4
5			To record allocation of net income in			5
6			ratio of 3:2			6

The partners' drawing accounts are then closed to their capital accounts.

1	20--					1
8	Dec.	31	Tanya Ross, Capital	301	28 80 0 00	8
9			Tanya Ross, Drawing	302	28 80 0 00	9
10						10
11		31	Don Wright, Capital	311	24 00 0 00	11
12			Don Wright, Drawing	312	24 00 0 00	12

After posting the closing entries, the T accounts appear as follows.

Income Summary		399	
Dec. 31		Dec. 31	
Clos.	100,000	Net Inc.	100,000
		Bal.	0

④ Objective

Compute and record the division of net income or net loss between partners in accordance with the partnership agreement.

Tanya Ross, Capital   301

Dec. 31 Draw.	28,800	Dec. 31 Bal.	50,000
		Dec. 31 Net Inc.	60,000
		Bal.	81,200

Don Wright, Capital   311

Dec. 31 Draw.	24,000	Dec. 31 Bal.	30,000
		Dec. 31 Net Inc.	40,000
		Bal.	46,000

Tanya Ross, Drawing   302

| Dec. 31 Bal. | 28,800 | Dec. 31 Clos. | 28,800 |
| Bal. | 0 | | |

Don Wright, Drawing   312

| Dec. 31 Bal. | 24,000 | Dec. 31 Clos. | 24,000 |
| Bal. | 0 | | |

Allocating Net Loss. Assume that **Income Summary** has a debit balance of $30,000 (net loss). After closing revenue and expense accounts, net loss is allocated as follows.

$$\text{Ross} \quad \$30,000 \times 0.60 = \$18,000$$
$$\text{Wright} \quad \$30,000 \times 0.40 = \$12,000$$

Steps 3 and 4 of the closing process are recorded as follows.

1	20--					1
14	Dec.	31	Tanya Ross, Capital	301	18 000 00		14
15			Don Wright, Capital	311	12 000 00		15
16			Income Summary	399		30 000 00	16
17							17
18		31	Tanya Ross, Capital	301	28 800 00		18
19			Tanya Ross, Drawing	302		28 800 00	19
20							20
21		31	Don Wright, Capital	311	24 000 00		21
22			Don Wright, Drawing	312		24 000 00	22

Capital Account Balances

Allocating net income or net loss on the basis of capital account balances is quite logical when capital is extremely important in the income-earning process. For example, partnerships that own and rent real estate often allocate income or loss based on capital account balances.

Ross and Wright agreed that net income or net loss will be allocated based on the ratio of capital account balances at the beginning of the year. The beginning balances for Ross and Wright were $50,000 and $30,000, respectively. Follow the steps below to convert the capital account ratio to decimals.

Step 1: *Add the capital account balances.*

Ross	$50,000
Wright	30,000
Total	$80,000

Step 2: *Express each balance as a fraction and convert it to a decimal.*

Ross $50,000/$80,000 = 0.625 or 62.5 percent
Wright $30,000/$80,000 = 0.375 or 37.5 percent

Using these percentages, net income of $100,000 is allocated as follows.

$$\text{Ross} \quad \$100{,}000 \times 0.625 = \$62{,}500$$
$$\text{Wright} \quad \$100{,}000 \times 0.375 = \$37{,}500$$

Assuming withdrawals of $28,800 for Ross and $24,000 for Wright, the steps 3 and 4 closing entries are as follows.

1	20--					1
2	Dec.	31 Income Summary	399	100 0 0 0 00		2
3		Tanya Ross, Capital	301		62 5 0 0 00	3
4		Don Wright, Capital	311		37 5 0 0 00	4
5						5
6		31 Tanya Ross, Capital	301	28 8 0 0 00		6
7		Tanya Ross, Drawing	302		28 8 0 0 00	7
8						8
9		31 Don Wright, Capital	311	24 0 0 0 00		9
10		Don Wright, Drawing	312		24 0 0 0 00	10

A net loss would be allocated in the same ratio as net income. **Income Summary** would be credited to close the debit balance to the capital accounts.

Salary Allowances

Salary allowances are intended to reward the partners for the time they spend in the business and for the expertise and talents they bring to it. Ross and Wright agreed that each would work full-time in the business. Both partners recognize Ross' long experience in retail trade, her superior skill and ability, and her good reputation and established clientele.

Ross and Wright agreed that each will receive a salary allowance equal to the monthly withdrawals permitted in the partnership agreement. After considering the salary allowance, the balance of net income or net loss will be divided between Ross and Wright in the ratio of 3:2.

Salary allowances are withdrawals. They do not represent salary expense. They do not appear in the expense section of the income statement. Salary allowances are not subject to payroll taxes or withholdings.

When salary allowances are included in the income or loss distribution formula, step 3 of the closing process has two parts:

a. *Record the salary allowances; debit* **Income Summary** *and credit the partners' capital accounts.*

b. *Close* **Income Summary** *to the partners' capital accounts based on the partnership agreement.*

Allocating Net Income. Assume that the net income of The Jean Shop is $112,800.

Step 3a: Record the salary allowances of $28,800 to Ross and $24,000 to Wright as follows.

1	20--					1
2	Dec.	31 Income Summary	399	52 8 0 0 00		2
3		Tanya Ross, Capital	301		28 8 0 0 00	3
4		Don Wright, Capital	311		24 0 0 0 00	4

After recording the salary allowances, **Income Summary** has a credit balance of $60,000.

Important!

Salary Withdrawals
A salary withdrawal is a cash payment to a partner and is debited to the partner's drawing account. It does not represent an expense of the partnership.

Important!

Partnership Income
Partnership income is not taxed. Instead, partners include their share of the net income or net loss on their individual income tax returns.

```
                        Income Summary        399
           Dec. 31              │  Dec. 31
           Sal. All.    52,800  │  Net Inc.  112,800
                                │  Bal.        60,000
```

The balance of **Income Summary** is allocated as follows.

   Ross $60,000 × 0.60 = $36,000
   Wright $60,000 × 0.40 = $24,000

Step 3b: Record the entry to close the credit balance of **Income Summary** as follows.

1	20--					1
6	Dec.	31 Income Summary	399	60 00 0 00		6
7		Tanya Ross, Capital	301		36 00 0 00	7
8		Don Wright, Capital	311		24 00 0 00	8

The partners' drawing accounts are closed to the capital accounts in the usual manner.

Allocating Net Loss. Assume net loss for The Jean Shop is $30,000. Entries to record the loss distribution follow.

Step 3a: Record the salary allowances of $28,800 to Ross and $24,000 to Wright:

1	20--					1
2	Dec.	31 Income Summary	399	52 80 0 00		2
3		Tanya Ross, Capital	301		28 80 0 00	3
4		Don Wright, Capital	311		24 00 0 00	4

After this entry is posted, **Income Summary** has a debit balance of $82,800.

```
                        Income Summary        399
           Dec. 31              │
           Net Loss    30,000   │
           Dec. 31              │
           Sal. All.   52,800   │
           Bal.        82,800   │
```

The balance of **Income Summary** is allocated as follows.

   Ross $82,800 × 0.60 = $49,680
   Wright $82,800 × 0.40 = $33,120

Step 3b: Record the entry to close **Income Summary** as follows.

1	20--					1
6	Dec.	31 Tanya Ross, Capital	301	49 68 0 00		6
7		Don Wright, Capital	311	33 12 0 00		7
8		Income Summary	399		82 80 0 00	8

The partners' drawing accounts are closed to the capital accounts in the usual way.

688 • Chapter 19 *Accounting for Partnerships*

	20--							1
10	Dec.	31	Tanya Ross, Capital	301	28 80 0 00			10
11			Tanya Ross, Drawing	302		28 80 0 00		11
12								12
13		31	Don Wright, Capital	311	24 00 0 00			13
14			Don Wright, Drawing	312		24 00 0 00		14

After the closing entries are posted, the T accounts appear as follows.

```
              Income Summary        399
   ─────────────────────┬─────────────────────
   Dec. 31              │ Dec. 31
   Net Loss   30,000    │ Clos.      82,800
                        │
   Dec. 31              │
   Sal. All.  52,800    │
             ────────   │
              82,800    │
                        │ Bal.          0
```

```
      Tanya Ross, Capital    301                    Don Wright, Capital    311
 ───────────────────┬─────────────────       ───────────────────┬─────────────────
 Dec. 31            │ Dec. 31                 Dec. 31            │ Dec. 31
 Net Loss  49,680   │ Bal.     50,000         Net Loss  33,120   │ Bal.     30,000
                    │                                            │
 Dec. 31            │ Dec. 31                 Dec. 31            │ Dec. 31
 Draw.     28,800   │ Sal. All. 28,800        Draw.     24,000   │ Sal. All. 24,000
           78,480   │          78,800                   57,120   │          54,000
                    │ Bal.        320                            │
                    │                         Bal.      3,120    │
```

```
      Tanya Ross, Drawing   302                    Don Wright, Drawing   312
 ───────────────────┬─────────────────       ───────────────────┬─────────────────
 Dec. 31            │ Dec. 31                 Dec. 31            │ Dec. 31
 Bal.      28,800   │ Clos.    28,800         Bal.      24,000   │ Clos.    24,000
 Bal.          0    │                         Bal.          0    │
```

Salary and Interest Allowances

Assume that Ross and Wright want to reward themselves for their time and skills through salary allowances of $28,800 to Ross and $24,000 to Wright. They also wish to recognize their capital investments by allowing each partner 10 percent interest on their capital balance at the start of the period.

The partnership agreement does not specify how the remaining income or loss is to be allocated. Remember that if the partnership agreement is silent on this matter, the remaining net income or net loss is divided equally.

Step 3 of the closing process has three parts:

a. Record the salary allowances.

b. Record the interest allowances. Credit each partner's capital account for the interest allowed, and debit **Income Summary** for the total interest.

c. Close **Income Summary** to the partners' capital accounts.

Allocation When Net Income Is Adequate to Cover Allowances. Assume net income of $100,000.

Step 3a: Record the salary allowances of $28,800 to Ross and $24,000 to Wright as follows.

1	20--						1
2	Dec.	31 Income Summary	399	52 80 0 00			2
3		Tanya Ross, Capital	301		28 80 0 00		3
4		Don Wright, Capital	311		24 00 0 00		4

Step 3b: Record the interest allowances. The interest allowed is 10 percent of the beginning capital balance.

$$\text{Ross} \quad \$50,000 \times 0.10 \times 1 \text{ year} = \$5,000$$
$$\text{Wright} \quad \$30,000 \times 0.10 \times 1 \text{ year} = \$3,000$$

The journal entry to record the interest allowances is as follows.

1	20--						1
6	Dec.	31 Income Summary	399	8 00 0 00			6
7		Tanya Ross, Capital	301		5 00 0 00		7
8		Don Wright, Capital	311		3 00 0 00		8
9		To record 10% interest allowance on					9
10		beginning investments					10

After recording the salary and interest allowances, **Income Summary** has a credit balance of $39,200.

Income Summary		399	
Dec. 31		Dec. 31	
Sal. All.	52,800	Net Inc.	100,000
Dec. 31			
Int. All.	8,000		
	60,800		
		Bal.	39,200

Step 3c: Close **Income Summary** to the partners' capital accounts. The balance is divided equally between Ross and Wright. The entry to close the credit balance of **Income Summary** is as follows.

1	20--						1
11	Dec.	31 Income Summary	399	39 20 0 00			11
12		Tanya Ross, Capital	301		19 60 0 00		12
13		Don Wright, Capital	311		19 60 0 00		13

Allocation of Net Loss. Assume that The Jean Shop had a $30,000 net loss for the year.

Step 3a: Record the salary allowances of $28,800 to Ross and $24,000 to Wright.

Step 3b: Record the interest allowances of $5,000 to Ross and $3,000 to Wright.

After these steps **Income Summary** has a debit balance of $90,800.

```
            Income Summary      399
      Net Loss  30,000
      Dec. 31
      Sal. All.  52,800
      Dec. 31
      Int. All.   8,000
      Bal.       90,800
```

The debit balance of $90,800 is divided equally between Ross and Wright.

Step 3c: Record the entry to close **Income Summary.** Debit each partner's capital account $45,400; credit **Income Summary;** $90,800.

After the closing entries are posted, the T accounts appear as follows.

```
            Income Summary      399
      Net Loss  30,000 | Dec. 31
                       | Closing  90,800
      Dec. 31
      Sal. All.  52,800
      Dec. 31
      Int. All.   8,000
                 90,800
                       | Bal.        0
```

```
   Tanya Ross, Capital   301              Don Wright, Capital   311
              | Bal.       50,000                   | Bal.       30,000
  Dec. 31     | Dec. 31               Dec. 31       | Dec. 31
  Net Loss 45,400 | Sal. All. 28,800  Net Loss 45,400 | Sal. All. 24,000
              | Dec. 31                             | Dec. 31
              | Int. All.   5,000                   | Int. All.   3,000
              |            83,800                    |            57,000
              | Bal.       38,400                    | Bal.       11,600
```

The partners' drawing accounts are closed to the capital accounts in the usual manner.

Income Less Than Difference Between Partners' Allocations. Assume that The Jean Shop had net income of $4,000.

Step 3a: Record the salary allowances of $28,800 to Ross and $24,000 to Wright.

Step 3b: Record the interest allowances of $5,000 to Ross and $3,000 to Wright.

After recording the salary and interest allowances, **Income Summary** has a debit balance of $56,800. The balance of **Income Summary** is divided equally between Ross and Wright.

Step 3c: Record the entry to close **Income Summary.**

After the closing entries are posted, the T accounts appear as follows.

Income Summary 399

Dec. 31		Dec. 31	
Sal. All.	52,800	Net Inc.	4,000
Dec. 31		Dec. 31	
Int. All.	8,000	Closing	56,800
	60,800		60,800
		Bal.	0

Tanya Ross, Capital 301

Dec. 31		Dec. 31	
Loss	28,400	Bal.	50,000
		Dec. 31	
		Sal. All.	28,800
		Dec. 31	
		Int. All.	5,000
			83,800
		Bal.	55,400

Don Wright, Capital 311

Dec. 31		Dec. 31	
Loss	28,400	Bal.	30,000
		Dec. 31	
		Sal. All.	24,000
		Dec. 31	
		Int. All.	3,000
			57,000
		Bal.	28,600

Notice that at this point, prior to closing the drawing accounts, the capital account balance for Ross increased by $5,400 and for Wright decreased by $1,400. This is due to the relationships between the income-sharing agreements and the amount of net income reported.

	Ross	Wright
Beginning capital balance	$50,000	$30,000
Ending capital balance	55,400	28,600
Difference	$ 5,400	($1,400)

Export-Import Bank

The Export-Import Bank of the United States (Ex-Im Bank) is an independent U.S. government agency that helps finance the overseas sales of U.S. goods and services. In 65 years Ex-Im Bank has supported more than $300 billion in U.S. exports.

Partnership Financial Statements

Once the net income or net loss distribution is complete, the financial statements are prepared.

Income Statement Presentation

With one exception, the income statements for a partnership and a sole proprietorship are identical. On a partnership's income statement, it is customary to show the division of net income or net loss among partners. The salary allowances, interest allowances, and other allocation factors are shown.

The Jean Shop's income statement for the most recent example follows. Revenue and expense details are omitted.

Net Income for Year			$ 4,000
Allocation of Net Income	Ross	Wright	Total
Salary Allowance	$28,800	$24,000	$52,800
Interest Allowance	5,000	3,000	8,000
Balance Equally	(28,400)	(28,400)	(56,800)
Totals	$ 5,400	($ 1,400)	$ 4,000

⑤ Objective

Prepare a statement of partners' equities.

Balance Sheet Presentation

The balance sheet shows the ending balance of the partners' capital accounts. The capital account for each partner appears in the Partners' Equity section of the balance sheet.

The **statement of partners' equities** summarizes the changes in the partners' capital accounts during an accounting period. It includes the following:

- beginning capital,
- additional investments,
- share of net income or net loss,
- withdrawals,
- ending capital.

Figure 19-2 shows the statement of partners' equities for The Jean Shop.

The Jean Shop
Statement of Partners' Equities
Year Ended December 31, 20--

	Ross Capital	Wright Capital	Total Capital
Capital Balances, Jan. 1, 20--	0 00	0 00	0 00
Investment During Year	50 0 0 0 00	30 0 0 0 00	80 0 0 0 00
Net Income (Loss) for Year	5 4 0 0 00	(1 4 0 0 00)	4 0 0 0 00
Totals	55 4 0 0 00	28 6 0 0 00	84 0 0 0 00
Less Withdrawals During Year	28 8 0 0 00	24 0 0 0 00	52 8 0 0 00
Capital Balances, Dec. 31, 20--	26 6 0 0 00	4 6 0 0 00	31 2 0 0 00

◄ **FIGURE 19-2**
Statement of Partners' Equities

Section 2 Self Review

Questions

1. In the absence of an agreement to the contrary, how are partnership income and losses allocated among the partners?

2. What two allowances are commonly used in allocating net income or net loss to partners?

3. If both salary and interest allowances are made to the partners, what are the three steps in closing the **Income Summary** account to the partners' capital accounts?

Exercises

4. The amount that each partner withdraws from a partnership

   a. should be specified in the partnership agreement.

   b. is the base on which federal income taxes are levied on the partnership income.

   c. cannot exceed the net income reported by the partnership.

   d. is always divided evenly among the partners.

5. The entry to record the equal distribution of net income between two partners consists of a

   a. debit to **Income Summary** and a credit to each partner's capital account.

   b. debit to each partner's capital account and a credit to **Cash.**

   c. debit to **Income Summary** and a credit to each partner's drawing account.

   d. debit to **Income Summary** and a credit to **Cash.**

Analysis

6. Ellen Riggs and Peter Olson formed a partnership. Riggs invested $35,000. Olson invested $15,000. Net income for the year is $44,000. If net income is allocated based on the capital account balances at the beginning of the year, what is the income allocation for Riggs and Olson?

(Answers to Section 2 Self Review are on page 721.)

Partnership Changes

Terms to Learn

dissolution
liquidation

6 Objective

Account for the revaluation of assets and liabilities prior to the dissolution of a partnership.

The partners in an existing business can change. Former partners might withdraw, sell their interests, or die. New partners may be admitted.

Changes in Partners

A partnership has a limited life. Whenever a partner dies or withdraws, or when a new partner is admitted, a dissolution of the old partnership occurs, and a new partnership is formed. A **dissolution** is the legal termination of a partnership. It has little impact on the business activities of the partnership. On the other hand, when the business is completely terminated, it is called a **liquidation**. The business ceases to exist, and the partnership agreement is void.

When a partnership is dissolved, two steps are taken.

Step 1: *The accounting records are closed and the net income or net loss on the date of dissolution is recorded and transferred to the partners' capital accounts.*

Step 2: *Assets and liabilities are revalued at fair market value. The partners, including any newly admitted partners, agree on the amounts.*

Recording Revaluation of Assets

The partnership agreement usually provides that when a partnership is dissolved and the business is to be continued as a new partnership, the assets and liabilities are revalued. The revaluation may require the services of a professional appraiser. The revaluation is made because the difference between the fair market value and the book value is a gain or loss resulting from events that occurred during the old partnership. The new partner does not share the gain or loss.

Based on the revaluation, the assets and liabilities are written up or down, and the difference between the book and fair market values is allocated to the original partners' capital accounts. The allocation of gains and losses is made in accordance with the formula used for sharing net income or net loss.

The partners of The Music Source agreed to admit a new partner, effective April 1. The assets and liabilities will be revalued following the close of business on March 31. Figure 19-3 shows the balance sheet of The Music Source after the closing entries are made and net income or net loss is transferred to the partners' capital accounts.

The partners agree that

- **Allowance for Doubtful Accounts** should be increased to $4,000,
- **Value of Merchandise Inventory** is $80,000,
- **Land** is worth $22,000 according to an appraisal,
- Liabilities are properly stated.

FIGURE 19-3
Partnership Balance Sheet

The Music Source
Balance Sheet
March 31, 20--

Assets						
Cash				62 0 0 0 00	
Accounts Receivable	38 0 0 0 00				
Less Allowance for Doubtful Accounts	2 0 0 0 00			36 0 0 0 00	
Merchandise Inventory				70 0 0 0 00	
Land				22 0 0 0 00	
Total Assets				190 0 0 0 00	
Liabilities and Partners' Equity					
Liabilities					
Notes Payable—Bank	18 0 0 0 00				
Accounts Payable	24 0 0 0 00				
Total Liabilities				42 0 0 0 00	
Partners' Equity					
Popo Gonzales, Capital	36 0 0 0 00				
Tom Laney, Capital	60 0 0 0 00				
Ahmed Safa, Capital	52 0 0 0 00				
Total Partners' Equity				148 0 0 0 00	
Total Liabilities and Partners' Equity				190 0 0 0 00	

Important!

Asset Revaluation
When transferred from one partnership to another, assets are revalued to their fair market value. The new value will not necessarily agree with the book value carried by the old firm.

The result is an $8,000 net increase in assets:

Merchandise inventory	$10,000
Accounts receivable/Allowance for doubtful accounts	(2,000)
Net increase in assets	$ 8,000

Assume that the partners share income and losses as follows.

Gonzales	40 percent
Laney	40 percent
Safa	20 percent

The gain on revaluation of the assets is allocated as follows.

Gonzales	$8,000 × 0.40 = $3,200
Laney	$8,000 × 0.40 = $3,200
Safa	$8,000 × 0.20 = $1,600

Revaluation of the assets is recorded as follows.

GENERAL JOURNAL   PAGE ___4___

	DATE	DESCRIPTION	POST. REF.	DEBIT	CREDIT	
1	20--					1
2	April	1 Merchandise Inventory		10 0 0 0 00		2
3		Allowance for Doubtful Accounts			2 0 0 0 00	3
4		Popo Gonzales, Capital			3 2 0 0 00	4
5		Tom Laney, Capital			3 2 0 0 00	5
6		Ahmed Safa, Capital			1 6 0 0 00	6
7		To record revaluation of assets and				7
8		allocations of gain to partners.				8

The Bottom Line

Revaluation of Assets

Income Statement

No effect on net income

Balance Sheet

Assets	↑ 8,000
Equity	↑ 8,000

After the entry is posted, the capital accounts contain the following balances.

Gonzales	($36,000 + $3,200)	$ 39,200
Laney	($60,000 + $3,200)	63,200
Safa	($52,000 + $1,600)	53,600
Total		$156,000

Admission of a New Partner

There are two ways to admit a new partner.

1. The new partner may purchase all or part of the interest of an existing partner, making payment directly to the selling partner. In this case, no cash or other asset is transferred to the partnership.

2. The new partner may invest cash or other assets directly in the existing partnership.

Objective 7

Account for the sale of a partnership interest.

Purchase of an Interest. One way to join an existing partnership is to buy a portion of a partner's share of capital. The prospective partner must have the approval of the existing partners. The money or other consideration passes directly from the new partner to the selling partner and does not appear in the accounting records of the partnership.

Suppose The Music Source's books are closed and the assets revalued as described. Gonzales sells half of his interest in the business to Ted West for $30,000. West pays $30,000 directly to Gonzales. The partnership's records do not reflect this cash transaction. In the partnership's accounting records, the transfer is recorded by a debit to **Popo Gonzales, Capital** for $19,600 and a credit to **Ted West, Capital** for $19,600. The $19,600 is one-half of Gonzales' capital account balance after revaluation (0.50 × $39,200).

Frequently the amount paid by the new partner is not the same as the amount credited to the new partner's capital account. The value of the partner's interest is a matter for bargaining between the two parties. West paid $30,000 in order to obtain a capital account of $19,600. The difference between the two amounts does not affect the partnership's accounting records.

With the admission of the new partner, the current partnership comes to an end and a new partnership is established. The partners should draw up a new partnership agreement.

Objective 8

Account for the investment of a new partner in an existing partnership.

Investment of Assets by a New Partner. A new partner may invest money or other property to obtain admission to the partnership while the existing partners remain as partners in the business. The new partner's investment, share of ownership in capital, and share of the net income or net loss are agreed upon among the partners and specified in the partnership agreement for the new partnership. The new partner may receive credit for the amount invested or for a higher or lower amount.

New Partner Given Credit for Amount Invested. Suppose the four parties involved in The Music Source agree that West will receive a one-fourth interest in the capital of the business for cash equal to one-fourth of the total capital in the new partnership. After revaluation, the capital accounts of the three existing partners total $156,000. The investment for West to own one-fourth of the capital of the new partnership is $52,000.

- The three existing partners, whose capital accounts total $156,000 after the revaluation, will own three-fourths of the business. The $156,000 is three-fourths (or 75 percent) of the new partnership capital.
- The new partnership capital is $208,000 ($156,000/0.75).
- West is purchasing one-fourth (or 25 percent) of the new partnership capital, $52,000 ($208,000 × 0.25).

The entry to record West's investment is as follows.

1	20--						1
10	April	1 Cash	101	52 000 00			10
11		Ted West, Capital	331		52 000 00		11
12		To record investment of West for					12
13		one-fourth interest in partnership					13

New Partner Given Credit for More Than Amount Invested. The new partner can be given credit for more capital than the amount invested. This is done if the new partner brings to the business skills that the existing partners are eager to have. Suppose West agreed to invest $44,000 for a one-fourth interest in the partnership. It takes two steps to record the investment: record the cash investment and adjust the capital account balances.

The cash investment is recorded as a debit to **Cash** for $44,000 and a credit to **Ted West, Capital** for $44,000. After this entry is posted, the capital account balances are $200,000.

Gonzales	$ 39,200
Laney	63,200
Safa	53,600
West	44,000
Total	$200,000

According to the capital account balances, West owns 22 percent of the partnership ($44,000/$200,000). However, West paid $44,000 to purchase a one-fourth interest in the partnership. West's capital account balance should be $50,000 ($200,000 × 1/4). The $6,000 ($50,000 − $44,000) increase necessary to bring West's account to $50,000 is referred to as a "bonus to the new partner." The $6,000 is credited to West's capital account. The debit is deducted from the original partners' capital accounts on the basis of the former partnership income and loss ratio. The amounts deducted from the original partners' accounts are as follows.

Gonzales	$6,000 × 0.40 = $2,400
Laney	$6,000 × 0.40 = $2,400
Safa	$6,000 × 0.20 = $1,200

The general journal entry to record the bonus is as follows.

1	20--						1
10	April	1 Popo Gonzales, Capital	301	2 400 00			10
11		Tom Laney, Capital	311	2 400 00			11
12		Ahmed Safa, Capital	321	1 200 00			12
13		Ted West, Capital	331		6 000 00		13
14		To record bonus allowed new partner					14

The partners' capital accounts after posting the entry for the bonus appear as follows.

Popo Gonzales, Capital 301		
April 1	April 1	
West bonus 2,400	Bal.	39,200
	Bal.	36,800

Tom Laney, Capital 311		
April 1	April 1	
West bonus 2,400	Bal.	63,200
	Bal.	60,800

Ahmed Safa, Capital 321		
April 1	April 1	
West bonus 1,200	Bal.	53,600
	Bal.	52,400

Ted West, Capital 331		
	April 1	
	Invest.	44,000
	April 1	
	Bonus	6,000
	Bal.	50,000

New Partner Given Credit for Less Than Amount Invested. Suppose that West agreed to invest $44,000 for a one-fifth interest in the capital of the partnership. The $44,000 investment is recorded as a debit to **Cash** for $44,000 and a credit **Ted West, Capital** for $44,000.

After this entry is posted, the capital account balances are $200,000.

Gonzales	$ 39,200
Laney	63,200
Safa	53,600
West	44,000
Total	$200,000

According to the capital account balances, West owns 22 percent of the partnership ($44,000/$200,000). However, he paid $44,000 for a one-fifth (or 20 percent) interest in the partnership. West's capital account balance should be $40,000 ($200,000 × 0.20). The $4,000 ($40,000 − $44,000) decrease necessary to bring West's capital account to $40,000 is referred to as "bonus allowed the original partners." The $4,000 is debited to West's capital account and credited to the original partners' capital accounts on the basis of the former partnership income and loss ratio. The amounts credited to the original partners' capital accounts are as follows.

Gonzales	$4,000 × 0.40	= $1,600
Laney	$4,000 × 0.40	= $1,600
Safa	$4,000 × 0.20	= $ 800

1	20--				1
10	April	1	Ted West, Capital	331	4 0 0 0 00		10
11			Popo Gonzales, Capital	301		1 6 0 0 00	11
12			Tom Laney, Capital	311		1 6 0 0 00	12
13			Ahmed Safa, Capital	321		8 0 0 00	13
14			To record bonus to original partners				14
15							15

After this entry is posted, West's capital account balance will be $40,000, or one-fifth of the total partnership capital of $200,000.

Managerial
IMPLICATIONS

Partnership Considerations

- Management and owners need to understand the advantages the partnership form of business offers to sole proprietors who need more capital, managerial assistance, or technical help.
- The partnership does not pay taxes. The partnership's taxable income "flows through" to the individual partners.
- It is essential that individuals who enter into a partnership have a clear understanding of the duties, obligations, rights, and responsibilities of each partner.
- There should be a written partnership agreement drafted by a lawyer and reviewed by the partners' accountants.
- The partnership agreement should be very specific about the income and loss allocation formula.
- Upon dissolution, the partnership assets and liabilities should be revalued.

Thinking Critically

In forming a partnership, what nonfinancial considerations might you want to address?

Withdrawal of a Partner

⑨ Objective

Account for the withdrawal of a partner from a partnership.

The partnership agreement should contain provisions specifying the procedures to be followed for the withdrawal of a partner. The partnership agreement for The Music Source provides that, upon withdrawal of a partner, the assets are to be revalued and the retiring partner is to be paid an amount equal to that partner's capital account after revaluation. Suppose that the partners of The Music Source agree that Ahmed Safa is to withdraw from the partnership after the close of business on March 31. He is to receive cash in an amount equal to the balance of his capital account after revaluation of the assets.

The revalued assets result in the following capital account balances.

Gonzales	$ 39,200
Laney	63,200
Safa	53,600
Total	$156,000

The entry to record the withdrawal of Safa from the partnership is as follows.

1	20--				1
2	Mar.	31	Ahmed Safa, Capital	321	53 6 0 0 00		2
3			Cash	101		53 6 0 0 00	3
4			To record cash payment made to Safa				4
5			on withdrawal from partnership				5
6							6
7							7

The parties might agree that the withdrawing partner is to receive either more or less than the balance of that partner's capital account at the time of withdrawal. In this event, the withdrawing partner's capital account is debited for the balance of the account.

- If the amount paid is higher than the withdrawing partner's capital account balance, the excess is debited to the capital accounts of the remaining partners according to their income and loss ratio.
- If the amount paid is less than the withdrawing partner's capital account balance, the difference is credited to the remaining partners' capital accounts based on their income and loss ratio.

After the assets of The Music Source are revalued, Safa's capital account balance is $53,600. Safa wishes to withdraw, and the partners agree to pay him $61,600 from partnership funds. The $8,000 ($61,600 − $53,600) bonus paid to the withdrawing partner is divided between the remaining partners according to their income and loss ratio of 40:40 (equally). The general journal entry to record the withdrawal of Safa is as follows.

1	20--					1
2	Mar.	31	Ahmed Safa, Capital	321	53 600 00	2
3			Popo Gonzales, Capital	301	4 000 00	3
4			Tom Laney, Capital	311	4 000 00	4
5			Cash	101		61 600 00	5
6			To record cash payment made to Safa			6
7			on withdrawal from partnership			7
8						8
9						9

Section 3 Self Review

Questions

1. An existing partner sells one-third of her capital interest to a new partner. What are the accounting entries to record this transaction?

2. A new partner invests more cash than the fractional share of the total capital being purchased. What are the accounting entries to record this transaction?

3. If a withdrawing partner is paid more than her capital account balance, how is the excess accounted for?

Exercises

4. The entry to record the investment of cash by a new partner includes a

a. debit to **Cash** and a credit to the new partner's capital account.

b. debit to the new partner's capital account and a credit to **Cash.**

c. debit to **Cash** and a credit to each of the current partners' capital accounts.

d. debit to the current partner's capital account and a credit to the new partner's capital account.

5. When a partner withdraws, the amount of credit given to the remaining partners is determined by

a. provisions in the partnership agreement.

b. dividing the assets evenly among the partners.

c. the partner's capital account balance.

d. subtracting the capital account from the total assets and dividing the result by the number of partners.

Analysis

6. Michelle Kim paid $30,000 to James Rosenfeld for one-half of his interest in the partnership of Rosenfeld and Murcheson. Rosenfeld's capital account prior to the purchase is $75,000. What is the journal entry in the partnership books?

(Answers to Section 3 Self Review are on page 721.)

Review

Chapter Summary

A partnership is the joining together of two or more persons under a written or oral contract as co-owners of a business. You have learned about the advantages and disadvantages of the partnership form of business. In addition, you have studied the accounting methods and procedures unique to partnerships.

Learning Objectives

1 Explain the major advantages and disadvantages of a partnership.

There are advantages to a partnership:

- It is relatively easy and inexpensive to form.
- It permits pooling of skills and resources.
- No income tax is paid on its profits, although partners report their share of income or loss on their tax returns.

There are disadvantages to a partnership:

- Partners have unlimited liability.
- Any partner can bind the other partners.
- The business lacks continuity.
- Ownership rights are not freely transferable.

2 State the important provisions that should be included in every partnership agreement.

A written agreement details the partnership specifics: amount of initial investment, partners' duties, fiscal year, accounting method, division of gains or losses (including any allowances for salaries and interest), policy for withdrawals, and length of partnership life.

3 Account for the formation of a partnership.

Assets and liabilities may be exchanged for a partnership interest.

- Assets are appraised and recorded at the agreed-upon fair market value at the transfer date.
- Each partner's capital account is credited for the amount of the investment.

4 Compute and record the division of net income or net loss between partners in accordance with the partnership agreement.

Division of partnership income and losses can be made in any manner. If no agreement has been made, income and losses are divided equally.

5 Prepare a statement of partners' equities.

A statement of partners' equities summarizes the changes in the capital accounts during the period.

6 Account for the revaluation of assets and liabilities prior to the dissolution of a partnership.

Before a partnership is dissolved, the business assets are revalued and the income or loss allocated according to the original agreement.

7 Account for the sale of a partnership interest.

A new partner may purchase a partnership interest from a current partner. The portion of ownership sold is transferred from the existing partner's capital account to the new partner's capital account.

8 Account for the investment of a new partner in an existing partnership.

A new partner may invest more or less than the proportionate part of total capital that the new partner will own after the investment.

- If more is invested, a bonus is recorded to the current partners (the new partner's capital account is debited and the current partners' capital accounts are credited).
- If less is invested, a bonus is recorded to the new partner (the new partner's capital account is credited and the current partners' capital accounts are debited).

9 Account for the withdrawal of a partner from a partnership.

When a partner withdraws, the assets and liabilities are revalued and the income or loss allocated according to the original agreement.

10 Define the accounting terms new to this chapter.

Articles of partnership (p. 679) See Partnership agreement

Dissolution (p. 694) The legal termination of a partnership

Distributive share (p. 684) The amount of net income or net loss allocated to each partner

General partner (p. 678) A member of a partnership who has unlimited liability

Limited partner (p. 678) A member of a partnership whose liability is limited to his or her investment in the partnership

Limited partnership (p. 678) A partnership having one or more limited partners

Liquidation (p. 694) Termination of a business by distributing all assets and discontinuing the business

Memorandum entry (p. 681) An informational entry in the general journal

Mutual agency (p. 678) The characteristic of a partnership by which each partner is empowered to act as an agent for the partnership, binding the firm by his or her acts

Partnership (p. 678) An association of two or more persons who carry on, as co-owners, a business for profit

Partnership agreement (p. 679) A legal contract forming a partnership and specifying certain details of operation

Statement of partners' equities (p. 693) A financial statement prepared to summarize the changes in partners' capital accounts during an accounting period

Unlimited liability (p. 678) The implication that a creditor can look to all partners' personal assets as well as the assets of the partnership for payment of the firm's debts

Comprehensive Self Review

1. Name eight major information items, other than the names of the partners, that should be included in a partnership agreement.

2. What are the major disadvantages of the partnership form of business enterprise?

3. Explain the difference between the accounting treatment of "salary withdrawals" and "salary allowances" in allocating income or loss.

4. Explain how one partner might receive a profit allocation even though the partnership has a loss for the period.

5. Why are the assets and liabilities revalued prior to a dissolution?

(Answers to Comprehensive Self Review are on page 721.)

Discussion Questions

1. Explain the liability that a limited partner has for the debts of a partnership.

2. What is a general partner?

3. Does a partnership continue to exist after the death of a partner? Explain.

4. Does a partnership pay federal income tax? Explain.

5. Why are assets of an existing proprietorship revalued when they are transferred to a partnership?

6. Is **Allowance for Doubtful Accounts** brought forward from the general ledger of a sole proprietorship when the firm's assets and liabilities are being transferred to the partnership? Why?

7. How does the balance sheet of a partnership differ from that of a sole proprietorship?

8. What is the advantage of a limited partnership?

9. Are partners' salaries considered to be expenses of the partnership? Explain.

10. Explain how the net income of a partnership is allocated if it is less than the salary and interest allowances.

11. What information appears on a statement of partners' equities?

12. The two partners in a business often pay personal bills by writing checks on the business's bank account. Is this a good business practice? Explain. How should such payments be recorded?

13. Why does the sale of one partner's capital interest not affect the capital accounts of any of the other original partners?

14. What is the difference between a dissolution and liquidation?

15. List the steps required to dissolve a partnership.

16. What are typical considerations that affect the way income is allocated among partners?

17. Explain the use of a drawing account in a partnership.

18. What are the steps involved in an income or loss allocation based on an agreed upon ratio?

19. Explain what the term "mutual agency" means in regard to a partnership.

Applications

EXERCISES

Exercise 19-1 ►
Objective 3

Recording cash investment in a partnership.

Rama Bing invests cash of $165,980 in a newly formed partnership that will operate The Tennis Center. In return, Bing receives a one-third interest in the capital of the partnership. In general journal form, record Bing's investment in the partnership.

Exercise 19-2 ►
Objective 3

Recording investment of assets and liabilities in a partnership.

Adalia Willis operates a sole proprietorship business that sells hiking equipment. Willis has agreed to transfer her assets and liabilities to a partnership that will operate The LMN Co. Willis will own a two-thirds interest in the capital of the partnership. The agreed upon values of assets and liabilities to be transferred follow.

> Total Accounts receivable of $62,300 will be transferred and approximately $1,000 of these accounts may be uncollectible
> Merchandise inventory, $85,680
> Furniture and fixtures, $33,000
> Accounts payable, $14,000

Record the receipt of the assets and liabilities by the partnership in the general journal.

Exercise 19-3 ►
Objective 3

Preparing a balance sheet for a partnership.

On May 1, 20--, Jennifer Black and Lexi Rahman formed the Exercise Center. The two partners invested cash and other assets and liabilities with the following agreed upon values.

> Jennifer: Cash, $2,800; Merchandise inventory, $8,000; Equipment, $36,000; Accounts payable, $4,800.
> Lexi: Furniture, $8,000; Cash, $13,000.

Jennifer is to own two-thirds of the capital, and Lexi is to own one-third of the capital, but they will split profits and losses equally. Prepare a balance sheet for the partnership just after the assets and liabilities have been transferred to it.

Exercise 19-4 ►
Objective 4

Computing the division of net income of a partnership.

The partnership agreement of Selena Flores and Norman Mason does not indicate how the profits and losses will be shared. Before dividing the net income, Selena's capital account balance was $160,000, and Norman's capital balance was $40,000. The net income of their firm for the year that just ended was $120,000. How much income will be allocated to Selena and how much to Norman?

Exercise 19-5 ►
Objective 4

Computing and recording division of net income based on fixed ratio.

The net income for the new partnership known as The Patch Store for the year ended December 31, 20--, was $12,000. The partners, Ray Griffis and Cody Britton, share profits in the ratio of 60 and 40 percent, respectively. Record the general journal entry (or entries) to close the **Income Summary** account.

Computing and recording division of net loss, with no partnership agreement on method of allocation.

◄ **Exercise 19-6**
Objective 4

After revenue and expense accounts of The Corner Store were closed on December 31, 20--, **Income Summary** contained a credit balance of $45,200. The drawing accounts of the two partners, Leonard Tate and Aaron Landers, showed debit balances of $36,000 and $90,000, respectively. Profits and losses are to be shared equally. Record the general journal entries to close the **Income Summary** account and the partners' drawing accounts.

Computing and recording division of net income, with salaries allowed.

◄ **Exercise 19-7**
Objective 4

Alfonso Garcia and Ali Fouad are partners who share profits and losses in the ratio of 60 and 40 percent, respectively. Their partnership agreement provides that each will be paid a yearly salary of $40,000. The salaries were paid to the partners during 20-- and were charged to the partners' drawing accounts. The **Income Summary** account has a credit balance of $164,000 after revenue and expense accounts are closed at the end of the year. What amount of net income or net loss will be allocated to each?

Computing and recording allocation of net income with interest allowed.

◄ **Exercise 19-8**
Objective 4

Gonzalez and Clinton are partners. Their partnership agreement provides that, in dividing profits, each is to be allocated interest at 10 percent of her beginning capital balance. The balance of net income or loss after the interest allowances is to be split in the ratio of 60:40 to Gonzalez and Clinton, respectively. The beginning capital balances were Gonzalez, $60,000 and Clinton, $12,000. Net income for the year was $120,000. Compute the amount of net income to be allocated to each partner.

Computing and recording allocation of net income with salaries and interest allowed.

◄ **Exercise 19-9**
Objective 4

Preston Davis and Connie Tolbert are partners who share profits and losses in the following manner. Davis receives a salary of $48,000, and Tolbert receives a salary of $70,000. These amounts were paid to the partners and charged to their drawing accounts. Both partners also receive 10 percent interest on their capital balances at the beginning of the year. The balance of any remaining profits or losses is divided equally. The beginning capital accounts for 20-- were Davis, $204,000 and Tolbert, $254,000. At the end of the year, the partnership had a net income of $144,000.

1. How much net income or loss will be allocated to each partner?
2. Prepare a statement of partners' equities for the partnership of Davis and Tolbert for the year 20--.

Recording revaluation of assets prior to dissolution of a partnership.

◄ **Exercise 19-10**
Objective 6

Stephanie Hendricks and Charles Little are partners who share profits and losses in the ratio of 60:40, respectively. On December 31, 20--, they decide that Little will sell one-half of his interest to Vernon Mullicer. At that time, the balances of the capital accounts are $250,000 for Hendricks and $350,000 for Little. The partners agree that before the new partner is admitted, certain assets should be revalued. These assets include merchandise inventory carried at $208,000 revalued at $200,000, and a building with a book value of $120,000 revalued at $240,000.

1. Record the revaluations in the general journal.
2. What will the capital balances of the two existing partners be after the revaluation is made?

Exercise 19-11 ►
Objective 7

Recording sale of a part interest.

Mary Hodge and Pat Walker are partners who share profits and losses in the ratio of 60 and 40 percent respectively. The balances of their capital accounts are Hodge, $180,000 and Walker, $220,000. With Walker's agreement, Hodge sells one-half of her interest in the partnership to Melvin Doyle for $160,000. What will the capital account balances for each of the three partners be after this sale?

Exercise 19-12 ►
Objective 9

Recording withdrawal of a partner.

Smith, Jones, and Davis are partners, sharing profits and losses in the ratio of 30, 40, and 30 percent respectively. Their partnership agreement provides that if one of them withdraws from the partnership, the assets and liabilities are to be revalued, the gain or loss allocated to the partners, and the retiring partner paid the balance of his account. Davis withdraws from the partnership on December 31, 20--. The capital account balances before recording revaluation are Smith, $120,000; Jones $120,000; and Davis $100,000. The effect of the revaluation is to increase **Merchandise Inventory** by $18,000 and the **Building** account balance by $10,000. How much cash will be paid to Davis?

Problems

Selected problems can be completed using:
 Peachtree **QuickBooks** ▦ **Spreadsheets**

PROBLEM SET A

Problem 19-1A ►
Objective 3

Accounting for formation of a partnership.

Jeremy Landon operates a small shop that sells fishing equipment. His postclosing trial balance on December 31, 2004, is as follows:

ACCOUNT NAME	DEBIT	CREDIT
Landon's Fishing Center		
Postclosing Trial Balance		
December 31, 2004		
Cash	3 6 0 0 00	
Accounts Receivable	15 0 0 0 00	
Allowance for Doubtful Accounts		1 6 0 0 00
Merchandise Inventory	44 0 0 0 00	
Furniture and Equipment	27 0 0 0 00	
Accumulated Depreciation		21 0 0 0 00
Accounts Payable		3 0 0 0 00
Capital		64 0 0 0 00
Totals	89 6 0 0 00	89 6 0 0 00

Landon plans to enter into a partnership with Kate Nolen effective January 1, 2005. Profits and losses will be shared equally. Landon is to transfer all assets and liabilities of his store to the partnership after revaluation as agreed. Nolen will invest cash equal to Landon's investment after revaluation. The agreed values are **Accounts Receivable** (net) $14,000; **Merchandise Inventory,** $46,000; and **Furniture and Equipment,** $12,400. The partnership will operate as Landon and Nolen Supply House.

INSTRUCTIONS

1. In general journal form, give the entries to record
   a. The receipt of Landon's investment of assets and liabilities.
   b. The receipt of Nolen's investment of cash.
2. Prepare a balance sheet for Landon and Nolen Supply House just after the investments.

Analyze: By what net amount were the net assets of Landon's fishing center adjusted before they were transferred to the partnership?

Accounting for formation of a partnership.

◄ **Problem 19-2A**
Objective 3

Jenny Cook operates a store that sells computer software. Cook has agreed to enter into a partnership with Corey Greer effective January 1, 20--. The new firm will be called the Efficient Computer Center. Cook is to transfer all assets and liabilities of her firm to the partnership at the values agreed on. Greer will invest cash that is equal to 80 percent of Cook's investment after revaluation. The accounts shown on Cook's books and the agreed on value of assets and liabilities are shown below.

		Balances Shown in Cook's Records	Value Agreed to by Partners
Assets Transferred			
Cash		$ 7,000	$ 7,000
Accounts Receivable	$29,000		
Allowance for Doubtful Accounts	1,000	28,000	26,800
Merchandise Inventory		168,000	174,000
Furniture and Equipment	56,000		
Accumulated Depreciation	23,000	33,000	35,800
Total Assets		236,000	243,600
Liabilities and Owner's Equity Transferred			
Accounts Payable		20,000	20,000
Jenny Cook, Capital		$216,000	$223,600

INSTRUCTIONS

1. Give the general journal entries to record the following transactions in the books of the partnership on January 1, 20--.
   a. Receipt of Cook's investment of assets and liabilities.
   b. Receipt of Greer's investment of cash.
2. Prepare a balance sheet for the partnership as of the beginning of its operations on January 1, 20--.

Analyze: Based on the balance sheet you have prepared, what percentage of total equity is owned by Jenny Cook?

Problem 19-3A ►
Objective 4

Computing and recording the division of net income or loss between partners.

Tammie Jones and Trisha Fuller own Mall Flower Shop. The partnership agreement provides that Jones can withdraw $2,800 a month and Fuller $3,600 a month in anticipation of profits. The withdrawals, which are not considered to be salaries, were made each month. Net income and net losses are to be allocated 60 percent to Jones and 40 percent to Fuller. For the year ended December 31, 20--, the partnership earned a net income of $60,000.

INSTRUCTIONS

1. Prepare general journal entries to
   a. Close the **Income Summary** account.
   b. Close the partners' drawing accounts.
2. Assume that there was a net loss of $20,000 for the year instead of a profit of $60,000. Give the general journal entries to
   a. Close the **Income Summary** account.
   b. Close the partners' drawing accounts.

Analyze: Assume the business earned net income of $60,000. If 20-- was the first year of operation for the Mall Flower Shop, what balance should be reflected for the **Tammie Jones, Capital** account at the end of the year?

Problem 19-4A ►
Objectives 4, 5

Computing and recording the division of net income or loss between partners; preparing a statement of partners' equities.

Wilma Klink and Theron Gray own Dallas Antique Shop. Their partnership agreement provides for annual salary allowances of $44,000 for Klink and $36,000 for Gray, and interest of 10 percent on each partner's invested capital at the beginning of the year. The remainder of the net income or loss is to be distributed 40 percent to Klink and 60 percent to Gray. On January 1, 20--, the Capital account balances were Klink, $170,000, and Gray, $210,000. On December 12, 20--, Gray made a permanent withdrawal of $40,000. The net income for 20-- was $144,000.

INSTRUCTIONS

1. Prepare the general journal entry on December 12, 20--, to record the permanent withdrawal by Gray.
2. Prepare the general journal entries on December 31, 20--, to
   a. Record the salary allowances for the year.
   b. Record the interest allowances for the year.
   c. Record the division of the balance of net income.
   d. Close the drawing accounts into the capital accounts, assuming that Klink and Gray have withdrawn their full salary allowances.
3. Prepare a schedule showing the division of net income to the partners as it would appear on the income statement for 20--.
4. Prepare a statement of partners' equities showing the changes that took place in the partners' capital accounts during 20--.

Analyze: By what percentage did Klink's capital account increase in the fiscal year 20--?

Accounting for revaluation of assets and liabilities of a partnership, investment of a new partner, and withdrawal of a partner.

◀ **Problem 19-5A**
Objectives 6, 8, 9

The balance sheet of Leonard Pharmacy after the revenue, expense, and partners' drawing accounts have been closed on December 31, 20--, follows:

Leonard Pharmacy			
Balance Sheet			
December 31, 20--			
Assets			
Cash			42 000 00
Accounts Receivable			8 000 00
Merchandise Inventory			208 000 00
Equipment	80 000 00		
Allowance for Depreciation—Equipment	48 000 00		32 000 00
Building	200 000 00		
Allowance for Depreciation—Building	160 000 00		40 000 00
Land			18 000 00
Total Assets			348 000 00
Liabilities and Partners' Equity			
Liabilities			
Accounts Payable			198 000 00
Taxes Payable			10 000 00
Total Liabilities			208 000 00
Partners' Equity			
Barbara Hodge, Capital	80 000 00		
Eugene Doyle, Capital	30 000 00		
Connie Tolbert, Capital	30 000 00		
Total Partners' Equity			140 000 00
Total Liabilities and Partners' Equity			348 000 00

On that date, Hodge, Doyle, and Tolbert agree to admit Emily Krauss to the partnership. The partnership agreement among Hodge, Doyle, and Tolbert provides that, in case of dissolution of the partnership, all assets and liabilities should be revalued. Profits and losses are shared in the ratio of 50:25:25, to Hodge, Doyle, and Tolbert, respectively. The agreed upon values of the assets are as follows:

Accounts receivable	$ 7,400	Building	$62,000
Merchandise inventory	199,200	Land	44,000
Equipment	34,000		

All liabilities are properly recorded.

INSTRUCTIONS

1. Give the general journal entries to record revaluation of the assets.
2. Give the general journal entry (or entries) to record Krauss' investment of $60,000, assuming that she is to receive capital equal to the amount invested.
3. Give the general journal entry (or entries) to record Krauss' investment of $60,000, assuming that she is to receive one-fifth of the capital of the partnership.

4. Give the general journal entry (or entries) to record Krauss' investment of $60,000, assuming that she is to receive one-third of the capital of the partnership.

5. Assume that after the revaluation had been recorded, the existing partners and Krauss decided that their previous agreement should be canceled and that Krauss should not become a partner. Instead, the partners agreed that Doyle would withdraw from the partnership and be paid cash by the partnership.

   a. Give the general journal entry to record the payment to Doyle if he is paid an amount equal to his capital account balance after the revaluation.

   b. Give the general journal entry to record the payment to Doyle if he is paid an amount equal to $6,000 less than his capital account balance after revaluation.

   c. Give the general journal entry to record the payment to Doyle if he is paid an amount equal to $4,800 more than his capital account balance after revaluation.

Analyze: Assume that items 1, 3, and 5(a) have been recorded in the records of the partnership. What is the balance of Connie Tolbert's capital account at December 31, 20--?

Problem 19-6A ▶
Objectives 7, 8

Accounting for sale of a partnership interest and investment of a new partner.

Enrique Peña and Dan Egemo, attorneys, operate a law practice. They would like to expand the expertise of their firm. In anticipation of this, they have agreed to admit April Kent to the partnership on January 1, 20--. The capital account balances on January 1, 20--, after revaluation of assets, are Peña, $180,000, and Egemo, $140,000. Net income or net loss is shared equally.

INSTRUCTIONS

Give the entries in general journal form to record the admission of Kent to the partnership on January 1, 20--, under each of the following independent conditions.

1. Peña sells a one-half interest in the partnership to Kent for $138,000 cash.

2. Peña sells a one-half interest in the partnership to Kent for $84,000 cash.

3. Kent invests $120,000 in the business for a 25 percent interest in the partnership.

4. Kent invests $124,000 in the business for a 30 percent interest in the partnership.

Analyze: Based only on item 3, what percentage of total equity does each partner own?

PROBLEM SET B

Accounting for the formation of a partnership.

Marie Renshaw operates the National Widget Store. Her postclosing trial balance on December 31, 2004, is as follows:

National Widget Store
Postclosing Trial Balance
December 31, 2004

ACCOUNT NAME	DEBIT	CREDIT
Cash	2 6 0 0 00	
Accounts Receivable	3 0 0 0 00	
Allowance for Doubtful Accounts		6 0 0 00
Merchandise Inventory	23 0 0 0 00	
Fixtures and Store Equipment	30 0 0 0 00	
Accumulated Depreciation		20 0 0 0 00
Accounts Payable		1 0 0 0 00
Marie Renshaw, Capital		37 0 0 0 00
Totals	58 6 0 0 00	58 6 0 0 00

Renshaw agrees to enter into a partnership with Hanna Orion effective January 1, 2005. Profits and losses will be shared equally. Renshaw is to transfer the assets and liabilities of her store to the partnership after revaluation as agreed. Orion will invest cash equal to one-half of Renshaw's investment after revaluation. The agreed upon values are **Accounts Receivable** (net), $1,000; **Merchandise Inventory,** $20,000; and **Fixtures and Store Equipment** (net), $22,000. The partnership will operate as the O&R Widget Company.

1. In general journal form, give the entries to record the following on the books of the partnership:

    a. The receipt of Renshaw's investment of assets and liabilities in the partnership.

    b. The receipt of Orion's investment of cash.

2. Prepare a balance sheet for O&R Widget Company.

Analyze: By what net amount were the assets of the National Widget Store adjusted before the partnership was formed?

Accounting for formation of a partnership.

Casey Justin operates a store that sells paintings and portraits by local artists. Justin has agreed to enter into a partnership with Debbie Griffitt, effective January 1, 20--. The new firm will be called Artist's Emporium. Justin is to transfer the assets and liabilities of his business to the partnership at the values agreed on. Griffitt will invest cash that is equal to Justin's investment after revaluation. The accounts shown on Justin's books and the agreed on value of assets and liabilities follow.

◄ **Problem 19-1B**
Objective 3

◄ **Problem 19-2B**
Objective 3

INSTRUCTIONS

	Balances Shown in Justin's Records	Value Agreed to by Partners
Assets Transferred			
Cash		$ 7,000	$ 7,000
Accounts Receivable	$ 9,000		
Allowance for Doubtful Accounts	1,000	8,000	6,800
Merchandise Inventory		96,000	84,000
Furniture and Equipment	54,000		
Accumulated Depreciation	41,000	13,000	23,800
Total Assets		124,000	121,600
Liabilities and Owner's Equity Transferred			
Accounts Payable		0	6,000
Casey Justin, Capital		$124,000	$115,600

INSTRUCTIONS

1. Give the general journal entries to record the following transactions on the books of the partnership on January 1, 20--.

   a. Receipt of Justin's investment of assets and liabilities.

   b. Receipt of Griffitt's investment of cash.

2. Prepare a balance sheet for the partnership as of the beginning of its operations on January 1, 20--.

Analyze: If Debbie Griffitt agreed to a cash investment equal to 80 percent of the value of Casey Justin's investment, what would the balance of Debbie Griffitt's capital account be after the formation of the partnership?

Problem 19-3B ►
Objective 4

Computing and recording the division of net income or loss between partners.

Bryan Hardaway and Linda Li operate a retail furniture store. Under the terms of the partnership agreement, Hardaway is authorized to withdraw $3,200 a month and Li $2,400 a month. The withdrawals, which are not considered to be salaries, were made each month and charged to the drawing accounts. The partners have agreed that net income or loss is to be allocated 35 percent to Hardaway and 65 percent to Li. For the year ended December 31, 20--, the partnership earned a net income of $93,200.

INSTRUCTIONS

1. Prepare general journal entries to

   a. Close the **Income Summary** account.

   b. Close the partners' drawing accounts.

2. Assume that there had been a net loss of $32,000 instead of net income of $93,200. Give the general journal entries to

   a. Close the **Income Summary** account.

   b. Close the partners' drawing accounts.

Analyze: Assume the business earned $93,200. If 20-- was the first year of operation for the business, what is the balance of **Linda Li, Capital** at December 31, 20--?

Computing and recording the division of net income or loss between partners; preparing a statement of partners' equities.

◄ **Problem 19-4B**
Objectives 4, 5

Leith Barker and Abbie Dodson operate City Apartments. Their partnership agreement provides for salaries of $60,000 a year for Barker and $48,000 for Dodson and for an interest allowance of 10 percent on each partner's invested capital at the beginning of the year. The remainder of the net income or loss is to be distributed equally to the two partners. On January 1, 20--, the capital account balances were $104,000 for Barker and $224,000 for Dodson. On July 15, 20--, Dodson made a permanent withdrawal of capital of $60,000 for a down payment on a yacht. The net income for 20-- was $192,800.

INSTRUCTIONS

1. Prepare the general journal entry on July 15, 20--, to record the permanent withdrawal by Dodson.

2. Prepare the general journal entries on December 31, 20--, to

   a. Record the salary allowances for the year.

   b. Record the interest allowances for the year.

   c. Record the division of the balance of net income.

   d. Close the drawing accounts into the capital accounts, assuming that the partners had withdrawn the full amount of their salary allowances.

3. Prepare a schedule showing the division of net income to the partners as it would appear on the income statement for 20--.

4. Prepare a statement of partners' equities showing the changes that took place in the partners' capital accounts during the year 20--.

Analyze: If the partnership realized a net loss of $10,000 instead of a net profit for the year, what balance would each partner's equity account reflect at December 31, 20--?

Accounting for revaluation of assets and liabilities of a partnership, investment of a new partner, and withdrawal of a partner.

◄ **Problem 19-5B**
Objectives 6, 8, 9

The balance sheet of Card Shop after the revenue, expense, and partners' drawing accounts have been closed on December 31, 20--, is provided on page 714.

On that date, Smith, Jeffry, and Jay agree to admit Don Sutter to the partnership. The partnership agreement among Smith, Jeffry, and Jay provides that in case of dissolution of the partnership, all assets and liabilities should be revalued. Profits and losses are shared in the ratio of 50:20:30 to Smith, Jeffry, and Jay, respectively. The agreed upon values of the assets are given below.

Accounts receivable	$ 3,400
Merchandise inventory	99,600
Equipment	15,000
Building	29,000
Land	22,000

All liabilities are properly recorded.

Card Shop
Balance Sheet
December 31, 20--

Assets				
Cash			21 0 0 0 00	
Accounts Receivable			4 0 0 0 00	
Merchandise Inventory			104 0 0 0 00	
Equipment	40 0 0 0 00			
Allowance for Depreciation—Equipment	24 0 0 0 00		16 0 0 0 00	
Building	100 0 0 0 00			
Allowance for Depreciation—Building	80 0 0 0 00		20 0 0 0 00	
Land			9 0 0 0 00	
Total Assets			174 0 0 0 00	
Liabilities and Partners' Equity				
Liabilities				
Accounts Payable			109 0 0 0 00	
Taxes Payable			5 0 0 0 00	
Total Liabilities			114 0 0 0 00	
Partners' Equity				
Jeff Smith, Capital	30 0 0 0 00			
Shane Jeffry, Capital	15 0 0 0 00			
Zane Jay, Capital	15 0 0 0 00			
Total Partners' Equity			60 0 0 0 00	
Total Liabilities and Partners' Equity			174 0 0 0 00	

INSTRUCTIONS

1. Give the general journal entries to record revaluation of the partnership's assets.

2. Give the general journal entry (or entries) to record Sutter's investment of $30,000, assuming that he is to receive credit for the amount invested.

3. Give the general journal entry (or entries) to record Sutter's investment of $30,000, assuming that he is to receive one-fifth of the capital of the entity.

4. Give the general journal entry (or entries) to record Sutter's investment of $30,000, assuming that he is to receive 40 percent of the capital of the entity.

5. Assume that after the revaluation had been recorded, the existing partners and Sutter decided that their previous agreement should be canceled and that Sutter should not become a partner. Instead, the partners agreed that Jay would withdraw from the partnership.

   a. Give the general journal entry to record the payment to Jay if he is paid an amount equal to his capital account balance after the revaluation.

b. Give the general journal entry to record the payment to Jay if he is paid an amount equal to $2,800 less than his capital account balance after the revaluation.

c. Give the general journal entry to record the payment to Jay if he is paid an amount equal to $4,200 more than his capital account balance after the revaluation.

Analyze: Assume only items 1, 3, and 5(b) occurred. What is the balance of the **Shane Jeffry, Capital** account at December 31, 20--?

Accounting for sale of partnership interest and investment of a new partner.

◄ **Problem 19-6B**
Objectives 7, 8

Bobby Jordan and Julia Ludwig are partners in Information Systems Agency. The balances of their capital accounts on January 2, 20--, after revaluation of assets were Jordan, $120,000, and Ludwig, $160,000. Profits and losses are shared in the ratio of 55:45 between Jordan and Ludwig. The partners agree to admit Cathy Su to the partnership effective January 3, 20--.

INSTRUCTIONS

Give the entries in general journal form to record the admission of Su under each of the following independent conditions.

1. Jordan sells one-half of his interest in the partnership to Su for $88,000 in cash.

2. Ludwig sells one-half of her interest in the partnership to Su for $64,000 in cash.

3. Su invests $120,000 in the business for a one-fourth interest in the partnership.

4. Su invests $120,000 in the business for a 35 percent interest in the partnership.

Analyze: What percentage of partnership equity was owned by Jordan after asset revaluation?

CHAPTER 19 CHALLENGE PROBLEM

From Sole Proprietor to Partner

For several years, Selea Paine had operated Selea Curio Shop as its sole proprietor. On January 1, 2005, she agreed to form a partnership with David Wilks to operate the shop under the name College Gift Shop. Pertinent terms of the partnership agreement are as follows.

1. Paine was to transfer to the partnership the accounts receivable, merchandise inventory, furniture and equipment, and all liabilities of the sole proprietorship in return for a partnership interest of 60 percent of the partnership capital. Assets were appraised and transferred to the partnership at the appraised values.

Balances in the relevant accounts of Paine's sole proprietorship at the close of business on December 31, 2004, are shown below.

Accounts Receivable	$61,000	Dr.
Allowance for Doubtful Accounts	3,000	Cr.
Merchandise Inventory	88,000	Dr.
Furniture and Equipment	60,000	Dr.
Allowance for Depreciation—Furniture & Equipment	40,000	Cr.
Accounts Payable	12,000	Cr.

The two parties agreed to the following:

- There were unrecorded accounts payable of $800.
- Unrecorded accrued expenses totaled $400.
- Accounts receivable of $1,000 were definitely uncollectible and should not be transferred to the partnership.
- The value of **Allowance for Doubtful Accounts** should be $2,800.
- The appraised value of **Merchandise Inventory** was $78,000.
- The appraised value of **Furniture and Equipment** was $16,000.

2. In return for a 40 percent interest in partnership capital, Wilks invested cash in an amount equal to two-thirds of Paine's net investment in the business.

3. Each partner was allowed a salary payable on the 15th day of each month. Paine's salary was to be $4,000 per month, and Wilks' salary was to be $3,000 per month.

4. The partners were to be allowed interest of 10 percent of their beginning capital balances.

5. No provision was made for profit division except for the salaries and interest previously discussed.

6. The partnership's revenues for the year 2005 were $800,000, and expenses were $728,000. Payments for salary allowances were charged to the partners' drawing accounts.

INSTRUCTIONS

1. Record the following information in general journal form in the partnership's records.

   a. Receipt of assets and liabilities from Paine.

   b. Investment of cash by Wilks.

   c. Summary of cash withdrawals for salaries by the two partners during the year.

   d. Profit or loss division including salary and interest allowances and the closing balance of the **Income Summary** account determined on an appropriate basis.

2. Record the journal entry to close the partners' drawing accounts into the capital accounts.

3. Open general ledger accounts for the partners' capital accounts. The account numbers are: **Selea Paine, Capital** 301, and **David Wilks, Capital** 311. Post the journal entries from instructions 1 and 2 to the capital accounts.

4. Prepare a schedule showing the division of net income to the partners as it would appear on the income statement for 2005.

5. Prepare a statement of partners' equities for the year.

6. On January 1, 2006, the partners agreed to admit Jerome Hailey as a partner. Hailey is to invest cash of $60,000 for a one-fourth interest in the capital of the partnership. The three parties agree that the book value of assets and liabilities properly reflects their values. Give the general journal entry to record Hailey's investment.

Analyze: What percentage of Wilks' total investment on January 1 was composed of cash?

New Partnership

Richard Delay has operated a successful motorcycle repair business for the past several years. Delay thinks his business is almost too successful because he has very little time for himself. Delay and Karen Danner, who is also a motorcycle enthusiast, have had a number of discussions about her joining him in the business. Finally, they agree to form a partnership that will operate under the name DD Motorcycle Repair Shop. They have asked you to provide assistance, particularly with help in establishing terms for dividing partnership profits and losses.

The partners give you the following information about their plans for the business:

a. Delay plans to contribute to the partnership the assets of his sole proprietorship. They have been appraised to have a fair market value of $176,000.

b. Danner will invest $240,000 in cash.

c. Delay will work full-time in the business while Danner will work part-time and continue to attend the class she is taking in pursuit of a college degree.

Assume that DD Motorcycle Repair earned a net income of $112,000 during its first year of operation.

INSTRUCTIONS

1. What division of profits and losses would you suggest for Delay and Danner?

2. Using your proposed plan of profit sharing, prepare a schedule showing the distribution of the first year's net income to the partners.

Business Connections

Connection 1 ►

 **MANAGERIAL FOCUS** Forming a Partnership

1. The owner of an accounting practice is considering establishing a partnership with two other persons to carry on the business. What are the major disadvantages of the partnership form of organization that she should consider in making her decision?

2. Your employer is planning to form a partnership with one of his close friends. He explains to you that because he is well acquainted with the prospective partner, there is no need to have a written partnership agreement. He asks your advice. Give him your recommendation and the reasons for it.

3. Your employer is considering investing $25,000 in a partnership. In discussing the advantages and disadvantages of the arrangement, the employer informs you that a friend has told him that his potential loss is limited to the amount invested, $25,000. Is his information regarding this arrangement correct?

4. Two individuals who are forming a partnership ask you how they should divide the income and losses of the business. What factors should you consider in making a recommendation?

5. You work for a partnership. The partnership agreement between the two partners specifies that one partner is allowed a monthly drawing of $1,500 and the other a monthly drawing of $1,000. The agreement does not mention salary allowances for the partners. At the end of the year, one partner maintains that a drawing is the same as a salary allowance. They ask your opinion. What do you tell them?

6. One of the partners in a partnership that employs you is retiring from the business. Her capital account has a balance of $128,000. She tells you that she expects to receive a check for $128,000 from the partnership. Explain to her the proper procedure for determining the amount she will be paid.

Connection 2 ►

Ethical DILEMMA **Truth or Cover-up?** Thompson is an accountant for Hastings and Poirot, a partnership. The partners are critical of employees when they make mistakes. Thompson had made several minor errors in the past three years and had been chastised by the partners. Both partners are permitted to make withdrawals from the partnership, but in some years they do not make any withdrawals and in others they make frequent withdrawals. They depend on Thompson to keep accurate records of the withdrawals. In 2006 Thompson discovered that in 2004 he had recorded a withdrawal of $10,000 by Ben Hastings by debiting **Purchases** in error. Apparently neither of the partners had noticed the error because neither had mentioned it to Thompson. He is considering three courses of action:

a. Do nothing about the error.

b. Tell the partners exactly what happened. However, Thompson fears that if he tells the partners about the error he will be severely reprimanded and perhaps lose his job.

c. Make some sort of offsetting error if possible, perhaps debiting Hastings' drawing account and crediting **Purchases** in 2006.

Which of these courses of action (or what other course of action) should he take?

◀ **Connection 3**

Street **WISE:**
Questions from the Real World | **Consolidated Financial Statements** Refer to The Home

Depot, Inc. *1999 Annual Report* in Appendix B.

1. In a partnership, two or more persons contract as co-owners of a business. For a corporation such as The Home Depot, Inc., many stockholders jointly participate as its owners. Review the consolidated balance sheets. How many shares of common stock were issued and outstanding at January 30, 2000?

2. The financial statements of a corporation often reflect consolidated, or combined, financial data from various holdings of the company. Locate Note 1 and review the "Basis of Presentation" section. What entities or holdings are included in the consolidated statements of The Home Depot, Inc.?

FINANCIAL $TATEMENT
A N A L Y S I S | Partners' Equity

◀ **Connection 4**

The following excerpts were taken from the 10-Q Quarterly Report filed by Marina Limited Partnership on May 15, 2000, with the SEC.

Balance Sheets
March 31, 2000, and December 31, 1999

(Unaudited)	2000	1999
Partners' equity:		
General partner	$8,513,834	$8,511,679
Limited partners	13,713,268	13,709,784
Total partners' equity	$22,227,102	$22,221,463

Statements of Earnings
Three Months Ended March 31, 2000, and 1999

(Unaudited)	2000	1999
Net earnings	$5,638	$1,858
Net earnings attributable to general partner	$2,155	$ 710
Net earnings attributable to limited partners	$3,483	$1,148

Analyze:

1. On March 31, 2000, what percentage of total equity belongs to the general partner of Marina LP?

2. By what amount has the equity of the limited partners increased from December 31, 1999, to March 31, 2000?

3. Based on the net earnings allocation reflected on the statements of earnings, what percentage of earnings is allocated to the general partner? To the limited partners?

Analyze Online: Locate Hoover's Web site **(www.hoovers.com).** Using the site search capability, find the most recent 10-Q SEC filing for Marina LP.

4. What is the operating period covered by the 10-Q filing?

5. What partners' equity is reported for the general partner? For the limited partners?

6. What was the earnings allocation to the general partner? To the limited partners?

Connection 5 ► *Extending the Thought* **Limited Liability Companies** Between 1997 and 2000, approximately 1.9 million businesses organized as a limited liability company or LLC. Considered a hybrid form of organization, the LLC offers the flexibility and tax advantages of a partnership while maintaining the limited liability benefits of a corporation. Partners in an LLC are not personally liable for any debts or obligations that the business incurs. Based on these provisions, members of an LLC may execute contracts or make operating decisions that they are not personally liable for. Do you agree or disagree with this practice? Why?

Connection 6 ► **Business Communication** **Pitching a Partnership Idea** You possess more than 10 years' experience in corporate accounting, and a professional colleague of yours has practiced law in the community for 7 years. Your city has become a hotbed for Internet startups, and there is a strong demand for consulting services. You would like to propose a partnership with your friend to provide consultation services for financial and legal matters. Draft a letter to your colleague containing tentative provisions of the partnership. Use the new terms introduced in this chapter in your letter. Be sure to include your proposed name for the new partnership.

Connection 7 ► **Team***Work* **Drafting a Partnership Agreement** Partnership agreements are most often customized to fit the needs of the business entity it describes. Standardized partnership agreement forms are available on legal resource Web sites as well as business marketplace sites.

1. As a team, use the Internet to find examples of partnership agreements. Print two sample partnership agreements.

2. With your team members, create an idea for a partnership. Brainstorm with the group on what skills each member will contribute to the business. Using one of the sample partnership agreements you printed, draft the partnership agreement for your new company.

Connection 8 ► *inter* **NET** **CONNECTION** **SBA** Go to the Web site of the U.S. Small Business Administration **(www.sba.gov/oit/export).** Research the following question. Is it possible for a small partnership to export to other countries? What are three advantages of exporting? What assistance, if any, does the SBA provide if your partnership decides to go international?

Answers to Self Reviews

Answers to Section 1 Self Review

1. Ease of formation, pooling of skills and financial resources, and no federal income tax on the entity itself.
2. At their fair market values, as agreed upon by the partners.
3. The accounts are essentially the same, except that there is a drawing and a capital account for each partner.
4. **c.** debit to **Cash** and a credit to the individual partner's capital account.
5. **d.** debit to the individual partner's drawing account and a credit to **Purchases.**
6. $22,500

Answers to Section 2 Self Review

1. Equally between the partners.
2. Salary and interest.
3. **(a)** Record salary allowances.
   (b) Record interest allowances.
   (c) Close balance of **Income Summary.**
4. **a.** should be specified in the partnership agreement.
5. **a.** debit to **Income Summary** and a credit to each partner's capital account.
6. Riggs will receive $30,800. Olson will receive $13,200.

Answers to Section 3 Self Review

1. The only entry is to transfer one-third of the existing partner's capital account to the new partner's capital account.
2. The excess represents a bonus to the existing partners to be credited to their capital accounts according to the original agreement.
3. The excess is charged to the other partners' capital accounts, allocated according to the agreed upon ratio.
4. **a.** debit to **Cash** and a credit to the new partner's capital account.
5. **a.** provisions in the partnership agreement.
6. Debit **James Rosenfeld, Capital** for $37,500, and credit **Michelle Kim, Capital** for $37,500.

Answers to Comprehensive Self Review

1. Name, location, and nature of business; starting date of the agreement; life of the partnership; rights and duties of each partner; amount of capital to be contributed by each partner; drawings by the partners; fiscal year and accounting method; method of allocating income or loss; and dissolution and liquidation procedures.
2. The disadvantages of a partnership stem from its inherent characteristics; that is, it brings unlimited liability, mutual agency, lack of continuity, and lack of transferability.
3. Salary withdrawals are cash payments to be charged to the partners' drawing accounts. Salary allowances are part of the income or loss allocation and are charged to **Income Summary** and credited to the partners' capital accounts.
4. One partner may receive an interest and/or salary allowance considerably larger than the other partner receives. Allowances must be made even if there is a loss.
5. The value changes represent income or loss that should be shared by the existing partners, not by the new partnership.

CHAPTER 20

Learning Objectives

1. Explain the characteristics of a corporation.

2. Describe special "hybrid" organizations that have some characteristics of partnerships and some characteristics of corporations.

3. Describe the different types of stock.

4. Compute the number of shares of common stock to be issued on the conversion of convertible preferred stock.

5. Compute dividends payable on stock.

6. Record the issuance of capital stock at par value.

7. Record organization costs.

8. Prepare a balance sheet for a corporation.

9. Record stock issued at a premium and stock with no par value.

10. Record transactions for stock subscriptions.

11. Describe the capital stock records for a corporation.

12. Define the accounting terms new to this chapter.

Corporations: Formation and Capital Stock Transactions

www.saralee.com

W hen you hear the name Sara Lee, what do you think of? Cheesecake? Dessert? Think again. You'll find dozens of Sara Lee brands at your local grocery store—Ball Park, Hillshire Farm, Jimmy Dean. From body care products to apparel lines like L'eggs, Hanes, and Playtex, Sara Lee strategically invests in new businesses to expand product lines and extend global presence.

What's in a name? Since its founding in 1939, executives, stockholders, and successive boards of directors have recreated the corporation's name four times. The company name last changed in 1985 from Consolidated Foods Corporation to Sara Lee Corporation.

Thinking Critically
What kinds of corporate issues do you think stockholders have the right to vote on?

For more information on Sara Lee, go to: collegeaccounting.glencoe.com.

New Terms

Authorized capital stock
Bylaws
Callable preferred stock
Capital stock ledger
Capital stock transfer journal
Common stock
Convertible preferred stock
Corporate charter
Cumulative preferred stock
Dividends
Limited liability company (LLC)

Limited liability partnership (LLP)
Liquidation value
Market value
Minute book
Noncumulative preferred stock
Nonparticipating preferred stock
No-par-value stock
Organization costs
Par value
Participating preferred stock
Preemptive right
Preference dividend

Preferred stock
Registrar
Shareholder
Stated value
Stock certificate
Stockholders' equity
Stockholders' ledger
Subchapter S corporation (S Corporation)
Subscribers' ledger
Subscription book
Transfer agent

Section Objectives

① **Explain the characteristics of a corporation.**

WHY IT'S IMPORTANT
The corporate form of business is widely used in the national and international marketplace.

② **Describe special "hybrid" organizations that have some characteristics of partnerships and some characteristics of corporations.**

WHY IT'S IMPORTANT
"Hybrid" organizations are becoming increasingly popular for the tax advantages and limited liability features they offer.

Terms to Learn

bylaws
corporate charter
limited liability company (LLC)
limited liability partnership (LLP)
shareholder
stockholders' equity
subchapter S corporation (S corporation)

① **Objective**

Explain the characteristics of a corporation.

Forming a Corporation

Previous chapters focused on sole proprietorships and partnerships. Now we consider the third form of business organization, the corporation.

Characteristics of a Corporation

Corporate enterprises account for a majority of business transactions, even though there are more sole proprietorships and partnerships than corporations. Most large national and international businesses use the corporate business form.

In 1818 Chief Justice John Marshall of the U.S. Supreme Court defined the *corporation* as "an artificial being, invisible, intangible, and existing only in contemplation of the law." The corporation is a legal entity, completely separate and apart from its owners. It is created by a **corporate charter** issued by the state government. Since it is a legal entity, a corporation can enter into contracts, can own property, and has almost all of the rights and privileges of a sole proprietorship or a partnership.

Corporations can have few or many owners. A *privately held* corporation is one that is owned by one or more persons and whose stock is not traded on an organized stock exchange. A *publicly held* corporation has many owners and its stock is traded on an organized stock exchange.

A **shareholder** or *stockholder* is a person who owns shares of stock in a corporation and is thus one of the owners of the corporation.

Advantages of the Corporate Form

The corporate form offers some major advantages:

- *Limited Liability.* Sole proprietors and general partners have unlimited liability; they are personally liable for all debts of the business. Shareholders have no personal liability for the corporation's debts. The corporation's creditors must look to the assets of the business to satisfy their claims, not to the owners' personal property, even in the event of liquidation. It is not unusual, however, for major shareholders of small corporations to give personal guarantees to repay its loans.
- *Restricted Agency.* A shareholder has no right to act on behalf of the business. Instead, the board of directors controls the corporation, and the corporate officers are in direct charge of operations. For example, a person who owns 10,000 shares of Microsoft Corporation has no greater power to act on behalf of Microsoft than a person who has no ownership interest at all.
- *Continuous Existence.* The death, disability, or withdrawal of a shareholder has no effect on the life of a corporation.
- *Transferability of Ownership Rights.* Generally, shareholders can sell their stock without consulting or obtaining the consent of the

other owners. Shareholders are free to shift their investments at any time, provided they can find buyers for their stock. Organized stock markets, such as the New York Stock Exchange, make it easy to sell or buy interests in corporations whose stocks are traded.

Small companies often sell shares of stock with a contract that gives the corporation or the existing shareholders "the right of first refusal" to repurchase the shares when the shareholder wishes to sell them.

- *Ease of Raising Capital.* A corporation can have an unlimited number of shareholders. Some corporations have more than a million shareholders, making available a vast pool of capital.

Disadvantages of the Corporate Form

Although the advantages are impressive, the corporate form of operation also has certain disadvantages:

- *Corporate Income Tax.* Corporate profits are subject to federal income tax. Profits distributed to shareholders in the form of dividends are taxed a second time as part of the personal income of the stockholder. The taxation of profits at the corporate level and at the shareholder level is known as *double taxation*.

  State and local governments can also levy income taxes on corporations. In addition, most states require corporations to pay an annual franchise tax for the privilege of carrying on business in the state. In some states, especially those that have no corporate income tax, the franchise tax can be quite burdensome.

- *Governmental Regulation.* Corporations are subject to laws and regulations imposed by the state. In general, the state regulatory bodies exercise closer supervision and control over corporations than they do over sole proprietorships or partnerships. State laws may prohibit corporations from entering into particular types of transactions or from owning specific types of property. Special reports are frequently required of corporations.

Entities Having Attributes of Both Partnerships and Corporations

Some business entities have characteristics of partnerships and of corporations. Three of these special entities are Subchapter S corporations, limited liability partnerships, and limited liability companies.

Subchapter S Corporations. **Subchapter S corporations**, also known as *S corporations*, are entities formed as corporations which meet the requirements of Subchapter S of the Internal Revenue Code to be treated essentially as a partnership so the corporation pays no income tax. Instead, shareholders include their share of corporate profits, and any items that require special tax treatment, on their individual income tax returns. Otherwise S corporations have all the characteristics of regular corporations. The advantage of S corporations is that the owners have limited liability and avoid double taxation.

Limited Liability Partnerships. The **limited liability partnership (LLP)** is a general partnership that provides some limited liability for all partners. LLP partners are responsible and have liability for their own actions and the actions of those under their control or supervision. They are not

Mutual Funds
Mutual funds allow small investors to pool their funds with other small investors. There are many types of mutual funds. Each fund concentrates on a particular type of stock. Index funds invest in the S&P 500. Growth funds invest in companies that are growing quickly. International funds buy stocks from European and Pacific Rim companies. Bond funds invest in the bond market.

2 Objective
Describe special "hybrid" organizations that have some characteristics of partnerships and some characteristics of corporations.

liable for the actions or malfeasance of another partner. LLPs must have more than one owner, so a sole proprietorship cannot be treated as one. In some states LLPs are for the service professions only, such as law, accounting, medicine, and engineering.

Except for the limited liability aspect, LLPs generally have the same characteristics, advantages, and disadvantages as any other partnership.

Limited Liability Companies. **Limited liability companies (LLCs)** provide limited liability to the owners, who can elect to have the profits taxed at the LLC level or on their individual income tax returns. The profits and losses can be allocated to the owners other than in proportion to the ownership interests. In most states one individual can form an LLC. Its ownership interests are not freely transferable; other owners must approve a transfer of ownership interest. When transferring ownership, the existing LLC is terminated and a new one formed. Unlike the limited partners discussed in Chapter 19, LLC owners can take part in policy and operating decisions.

Formation of a Corporation

To understand why and how a corporation is formed, place yourself in the shoes of Khalid Flemmer. Flemmer is the sole proprietor of Flemmer's College Supply Store, a retail business selling college supplies. Flemmer wants to expand the number of textbooks he sells and add cosmetics.

To expand his operations, Flemmer needs more money to remodel the store and buy new fixtures, to acquire more inventory, and to extend more credit to customers. Several of Flemmer's friends are willing to invest as partners in his business, but he has some doubts about this. Although he needs the extra funds, he does not want to share operating control with people who know nothing about the business. Also, he does not wish to go further in debt.

Flemmer's prospective backers have some doubts, too. They do not mind risking the money they invest, but they do not want to be responsible for the debts of the business. Although they do not mind letting Flemmer run the business, they do want to have some voice in general policy. They would also like to be assured of a reasonable and regular return on their money.

Flemmer and his friends consulted an attorney who specializes in business law and taxation. The lawyer suggested that a corporation offers the best solution to their needs. She explained the necessary steps to form a corporation. Requirements differ from state to state, but typically the process is as follows.

One or more persons, the "organizers" or "promoters," apply to a state officer, usually the secretary of state, for a charter permitting the proposed corporation to do business. The state charges a fee for the charter.

When issued, the charter specifies the exact name, length of life (usually unlimited), rights and duties, and scope of operations of the corporation. Most corporate charters grant the corporation a broad sphere of operation. The charter also sets forth the classes of stock and number of shares in each class that can be issued in exchange for money, property, or services.

Shortly after the charter is issued, the organizers meet to elect an acting board of directors. The corporation proceeds to issue shares of stock to individuals who have paid the full purchase price of the stock. The shareholders then elect permanent directors, usually the same individuals as the

Accounting

Agriculture and Natural Resources

Industry Overview

The agriculture and natural resources industry encompasses a variety of activities such as food and fiber production, farm and ranch management, and natural resource management. Technological developments and international competition over the past three decades have negatively impacted employment trends within farming, mining, and oil extraction industries. Today agriculture and natural resources professionals are called upon to find innovative and cost-effective techniques for production, protection, and extraction.

Career Opportunities
- Loan Officer—Farm Credit Services
- International Development Specialist
- Veterinarian Assistant
- Environmental Engineer
- Genetic Food Scientist
- Emissions Analyst
- Farm Manager
- Petroleum Geologist

Preparing for an Agriculture or Natural Resources Career
- Obtain a bachelor's or associate's degree in business with a concentration in agriculture for a career as a farm or ranch manager. Complete general courses in liberal arts, basic sciences, and mathematics as well as specialized courses in natural resources, food science, horticulture, agricultural economics, plant science, animal science, wildlife management, and forestry.
- Complete introductory accounting and business law courses to develop general business management skills.
- Develop proficiencies with basic computer software applications such as Word, Excel, and Access.
- Join an agency such as the Peace Corps to gain on-the-job experience in crop production, farm management, or livestock health care.
- Stay abreast of current developments in agricultural production including new cost-cutting procedures and marketing strategies.
- Secure designation as an Accredited Manager through the American Society of Farm Managers and Rural Appraisers.
- Become an adult leader volunteer for an agricultural youth organization such as the 4-H.
- Join the local chapter of the National Future Farmers of America organization for networking and learning opportunities.

Thinking Critically
Agricultural educators support a "whole-system" approach to the industry. This view examines factors such as economic, social, financial, and human, and how these factors relate to each other and work as a whole. In other words, a farm or ranch must efficiently operate as a part of a larger community in order to be successful. If you were the manager of a chain of dairy farms, what community factors might play a role in your operational decisions?

Internet Application
Find the AgriBiz Web site and review the articles found in the Daily News section. Select one article and prepare an oral report for presentation to the class. Include pertinent technological innovations, market trends, or public health care concerns discussed in the article.

acting directors. The directors or shareholders approve the corporation's **bylaws**, which are the guidelines for conducting the corporation's business affairs. The board then selects officers, who hire employees and begin operating the business.

The amount received for the capital stock issued by the corporation appears on the balance sheet. The corporate equivalent of owner's equity is called **stockholders' equity** or shareholders' equity.

Structure of a Corporation

Stockholders can participate in stockholders' meetings, elect a board of directors, and vote on basic corporate policy.

The board of directors formulates general operating policies and is responsible for seeing that the corporation's activities are conducted. The board selects officers and other top management personnel to direct everyday operations. The officers hire managers who hire other employees. Officers and managers make the day-to-day decisions necessary to operate the business.

A corporation's officers include the president, one or more vice presidents, a corporate secretary, and a treasurer. The top accounting official is called the *controller* or *chief financial officer.* Large firms might have several layers of management, including division managers, department heads, and supervisors. The levels depend on the nature and complexity of the operations.

Table 20-1 shows the flow of authority and responsibility in a corporate entity.

TABLE 20-1 ▶
Flow of Corporate
Authority and
Responsibility

Stockholders	• Elect directors
Directors	• Make policies
	• Appoint officers
Officers	• Carry out policies
	• Hire managers
Managers	• Oversee and supervise operations
Other employees	• Perform assigned tasks

Section 1 Self Review

Questions

1. What are some of the advantages of the corporate form of business?

2. If a shareholder in a corporation dies, will the corporation continue to exist? Explain.

3. How does an S corporation differ from a limited liability partnership?

Exercises

4. A corporation is owned by
   a. its board of directors.
   b. the president of the corporation.
   c. the partners in the corporation.
   d. its stockholders.

5. The stockholders of a corporation
   a. have no personal liability for the debts of the corporation.
   b. are agents of the corporation empowered to act for the business.
   c. cannot sell their shares of stock without obtaining the agreement of other stockholders.
   d. are responsible for any debts owed by the corporation.

Analysis

6. The Chicago Staple Corporation earned $2 million in taxable income for the year but paid no dividends. How will this affect the shareholders' individual income tax returns?

Types of Capital Stock

Decisions about the classes of stock to be offered and the number of shares of each class must be made before the charter application is filed.

Capital Stock

The **authorized capital stock** is the number of shares authorized for issue by the corporate charter. Usually the authorized stock is more than the number of shares the corporation plans to issue in the foreseeable future. This gives the corporation flexibility to issue stock in the future without having to amend the corporate charter.

When a corporation *issues* stock, the stock is sold (transferred to stockholders). *Outstanding* stock is stock that has been issued and is still in circulation, meaning it is still in the hands of stockholders.

Capital Stock Values

There are three terms commonly used to describe stock values.

- *Par Value.* **Par value** is an amount assigned by the corporate charter to each share of stock for accounting purposes. It is usually $100 or less; it can be $25, $5, or even less than $1 per share. Stock can be issued for more than par value. State laws prohibit the issuance of par-value stock for less than the par value.
- *Stated Value.* State laws permit stock to be issued without par value. This type of stock is called *no-par-value stock*. The value that can be assigned to no-par-value stock by a board of directors for accounting purposes is called the **stated value**.
- *Market Value.* **Market value** is the price per share at which stock is bought and sold. After the corporation issues stock, it can be resold for any price that can be agreed on between the shareholder and purchaser. Usually a stock's market value has little relation to its par or stated value.

Classes of Capital Stock

Each type, or class, of stock has different rights and privileges.

Common Stock. If there is only one class of stock, the stock is called **common stock**. Each share of common stock conveys to the owner the same rights and privileges as every other share including the right to

- attend stockholders' meetings,
- vote in the election of directors and on other matters (each share entitles the owner to one vote),
- receive dividends as declared by the board of directors,
- purchase a proportionate amount of any new stock issued at a later date, referred to as the **preemptive right**.

Section Objectives

3 **Describe the different types of stock.**

WHY IT'S IMPORTANT
Shareholders and others must understand the rights and limitations of each class of stock.

4 **Compute the number of shares of common stock to be issued on the conversion of convertible preferred stock.**

WHY IT'S IMPORTANT
Conversion of stock changes the allocation of stockholders' equity between classes of stock.

5 **Compute dividends payable on stock.**

WHY IT'S IMPORTANT
Dividends are a major benefit of stock ownership.

Terms to Learn

authorized capital stock
callable preferred stock
common stock
convertible preferred stock
cumulative preferred stock
dividends
liquidation value
market value
noncumulative preferred stock
nonparticipating preferred stock
par value
participating preferred stock
preemptive right
preference dividend
preferred stock
stated value

If a corporation has two or more classes of stock, one class is common. The other class or classes of stock have certain preferences over the common shares.

> As of July 3, 1999, Sara Lee Corporation had authorized 1.2 billion shares at a par value of one cent.

Preferred Stock. Preferred stock has special claims on the corporate profits or, in case of liquidation, on corporate assets. In receiving special preferences, the owners of preferred stock might lose some of their general rights, such as the right to vote. Unless the charter specifies otherwise, however, preferred stock has voting rights.

Liquidation Preferences on Preferred Stock. In case of liquidation, preferred stockholders have a claim on assets before that of common stockholders. A **liquidation value** (usually par value or an amount higher than par value) is assigned to the preferred stock. After the creditors are paid, the preferred stockholders are paid the liquidation value for each share of preferred stock before any assets are distributed to common stockholders. The liquidation value of preferred stock includes any cumulative dividends that have not been paid. (Cumulative dividends are explained later in this chapter.) The liquidation preference on preferred stock is disclosed in the Stockholders' Equity section of the balance sheet.

Assume that a corporation is going out of business. It has paid all of its liabilities. There remains $1,400,000 to distribute to the shareholders. The company has outstanding 20,000 shares of $50 preferred stock, with a liquidation value of $52 per share, and 50,000 shares of $20 par-value common stock. The preferred stockholders will receive $1,040,000 (20,000 shares × $52 per share). The common stockholders will receive what's left, $360,000 ($1,400,000 − $1,040,000).

4 Objective

Compute the number of shares of common stock to be issued on the conversion of convertible preferred stock.

Convertible Preferred Stock. Convertible preferred stock is preferred stock that conveys the right to convert that stock to common stock after a specified date or during a period of time. The conversion ratio is the number of shares of common stock that will be issued for each share of preferred stock surrendered. The conversion ratio is indicated on the preferred stock certificate.

Some investors are reluctant to purchase preferred stock because its market price does not increase significantly even if the corporation is quite profitable. The ability to convert preferred stock to common stock can make the preferred stock more attractive to investors. The decision to convert the preferred stock to common stock depends on the market prices, the relative dividends paid on the common and the preferred stock, and the degree of risk involved.

Assume that a corporation has outstanding 100,000 shares of 12 percent, $25 par-value preferred stock that can be converted into common stock. (The term "12 percent" refers to the dividend rate and will be discussed on page 731.) The conversion ratio is three shares of common stock for each share of preferred stock surrendered. The conversion privilege is exercisable on or after January 1, 20--. A stockholder can convert 600 shares of preferred stock into 1,800 (600 × 3) shares of common stock.

Callable Preferred Stock. **Callable preferred stock** gives the issuing corporation the right to repurchase the preferred shares from the stockholders at a specific price. The call price is usually substantially greater than the original issue price. The rights are effective after some specified date. Callable stock gives the corporation flexibility in controlling its capital structure.

The following example illustrates the call feature. Assume a corporation issued 50,000 shares of 11 percent, $40 par-value preferred stock at $40 per share. The corporation has the right to call any part of the preferred stock any time after December 31, 20--, for $56 per share. If the corporation has funds available, or if money can be borrowed at substantially less than 11 percent, the corporation may call the preferred stock and retire it.

Dividends on Stock

Dividends are distributions of the profits of a corporation to its shareholders. The right to receive a dividend is one of the major incentives for buying stock. The board of directors declares dividends. The board of directors has complete discretion, subject to certain legal restrictions or contractual restrictions, in deciding whether to declare a dividend and the amount of the dividend. The amount of the dividend depends on the corporation's earnings and on the need to keep profits for use in the business. Dividends are usually paid on a quarterly basis.

⑤ Objective

Compute dividends payable on stock.

Dividends on Preferred Stock

Preferred stock has a priority with respect to dividends. The priority is specified in the corporate charter. Preferred stock bears a basic or stated dividend rate, called the **preference dividend**, that must be paid before dividends can be paid on common stock. The *dividend rate* is expressed in dollars-per-share per year or as a percentage. When the dividend is expressed as a percentage, the dividend amount is par value of the stock multiplied by the percentage. For example, the annual dividend on 10 percent preferred stock with a par value of $50 is $5 per share ($50 × 0.10).

Special dividend rights can improve the market demand for preferred shares of stock.

- **Cumulative preferred stock** conveys to its owners the right to receive the preference dividend for the current year and any prior years in which the preference dividend was not paid before common stockholders receive any dividends.

- **Noncumulative preferred stock** conveys to its owners the stated preference dividend for the current year, but stockholders have no rights to dividends for years in which none were declared.

- **Nonparticipating preferred stock** conveys to its owners the right to only the preference dividend amount specified on the stock certificate.

- **Participating preferred stock** conveys the right not only to the preference dividend amount but also to a share of other dividends paid.

Dividends on Common Stock

Common stock dividends are paid only after preferred dividend requirements have been met. The fewer the dividend privileges enjoyed by preferred stockholders, the higher the dividends that common stockholders can receive, especially in prosperous years.

> In fiscal 1999, Hasbro, Inc., declared cash dividends of 24 cents per share of common stock, an increase of 3 cents per share over 1998 cash dividends.

Comparison of Dividend Provisions

Let's analyze several dividend plans.

Only Common Stock Issued. Suppose that a corporation has only one class of stock—common stock. Assume that 5,000 shares of $50 par-value common stock are authorized, issued, and outstanding.

- *Situation 1.* The board of directors declared a 6 percent dividend for the year. Total dividends are $15,000 (5,000 shares $\times$ $50 par $\times$ 0.06).
- *Situation 2.* The board of directors decides to *pass* the dividend (not pay it).

There is no guarantee that the corporation will pay dividends. The uncertainty of dividends is a risk of owning common stock.

Common and Noncumulative Nonparticipating Preferred Stock Issued. Preferred stock reduces the uncertainty of dividends. Assume that a corporation has issued preferred stock and common stock as follows.

Preferred stock, 12% noncumulative, nonparticipating, ($50 par value, 1,000 shares)	$ 50,000
Common stock ($25 par value, 8,000 shares)	200,000
Total capital stock	$250,000

- *Situation 1.* The board of directors declares dividends of $20,000. The preferred stockholders get first consideration. They receive the preference dividend of $6,000 (1,000 shares $\times$ $50 par $\times$ 0.12). There is $14,000 ($20,000 − $6,000) to distribute to the common stockholders. The dividend per share for common stock is $1.75 ($14,000 ÷ 8,000 shares).
- *Situation 2.* The board of directors declares dividends of $10,000. The preferred stockholders receive the preference dividend of $6,000. There is $4,000 ($10,000 − $6,000) to distribute to the common stockholders. The dividend per share of common stock is $0.50 ($4,000 ÷ 8,000 shares).
- *Situation 3.* The board of directors declares dividends of $4,000. The preferred stockholders receive all of it. The portion of the preference dividend not paid this year will never be paid since the stock is noncumulative. The common stockholders receive no dividends.

Common and Cumulative Nonparticipating Preferred Stock Issued. When business conditions are poor, preferred stockholders have a better chance of receiving a dividend than do common stockholders. In turn, cumulative preferred stockholders have a better chance of receiving a dividend than do noncumulative preferred stockholders. The dividends not paid on cumulative preferred stock are carried forward as a continuing claim into future periods. Cumulative preferred dividends not previously paid are shown on the balance sheet or in the footnotes to the financial statements.

When dividends are paid, they are paid in the following order.

1. To preferred stockholders for prior year dividends not paid.

2. To preferred stockholders for the preference dividend for the current year.

3. To common stockholders.

Assume that a corporation has issued preferred and common stock as follows.

Preferred stock, 12% cumulative, nonparticipating,	
($50 par value, 1,000 shares)	$ 50,000
Common stock ($25 par value, 8,000 shares)	200,000
Total capital stock	$250,000

- *Situation 1.* Last year $2,000 of preferred dividends were not paid. This year the board of directors declared dividends of $9,000. The dividends are distributed as follows.

  1. To preferred stockholders for prior year dividends $2,000

  2. To preferred stockholders for this year's preference dividend (1,000 shares × $50 par value × 0.12) $6,000

  3. To common stockholders ($9,000 − $2,000 − $6,000) $1,000

- *Situation 2.* The board of directors declares dividends of $38,000. In previous years all preferred dividends were paid. The preferred stockholders will receive the preference dividend of $6,000. There is $32,000 ($38,000 − $6,000) to distribute to common shareholders. The dividend per share of common stock is $4 ($32,000 ÷ 8,000 shares).

Common and Cumulative Participating Preferred Stock Issued. When cumulative participating preferred stock is issued, dividend distributions are allocated to preferred and common stock as follows.

1. Preferred stockholders receive any prior year dividends not paid plus the preference dividend for the current year.

2. A specific rate of dividend is paid to common stockholders.

3. The dividends that remain are shared between preferred and common stockholders. The participation terms determine how the dividends are shared.

Since almost all preferred stock is nonparticipating, this textbook provides examples of nonparticipating preferred stock only.

Table 20-2 on page 734 summarizes the dividend rights of the different classes of stock.

Capital Stock on the Balance Sheet

Owner's equity for a corporation is known as stockholders' equity. The Stockholders' Equity section of the balance sheet includes the following information for each class of stock: the number of shares authorized and issued, the par value, and any special privileges carried by the stock. The following illustrates a typical balance sheet presentation for a corporation.

Stockholders' Equity

Preferred Stock (12% noncumulative, $50 par value,
  5,000 shares authorized)
  At Par Value (1,000 shares issued) $ 50,000
Common Stock ($25 par value, 10,000 shares authorized)
  At Par Value (8,000 shares issued)   200,000
Total Stockholders' Equity $250,000

TABLE 20-2 ▼
Dividend Rights of Different
Classes of Stock

Type of Stock	Dividend Rights
Noncumulative, nonparticipating preferred stock	• Has right to receive preference dividend each year before any dividend can be paid on common stock • If dividend is passed (not paid) in one year, the amount not paid is not cumulative and does not affect dividend payments in future years
Cumulative preferred stock	• Has right to receive preference dividend each year before any dividend can be paid on common stock • If dividend is passed in one year, the amount not paid carries over and must be paid in subsequent year before any dividend can be paid on common stock
Participating preferred stock	• Has right to receive preference dividend each year before any dividend can be paid on common stock • After preference dividend is paid, any additional dividend up to specified amount is paid to common stockholders • After common shareholders have received the specified dividend, preferred and common stock share in remaining dividends
Common stock	• Receives dividends after preferred stock dividends are paid in accordance with contractual obligation

Section 2 Self Review

Questions

1. How do preferred and common stock differ?

2. What does "liquidation preference" mean?

3. What is convertible preferred stock?

Exercises

4. Stock that requires a preference dividend that was not paid in a prior year to be paid in the future before any other dividends are paid is
   a. noncumulative preferred stock.
   b. cumulative preferred stock.
   c. common stock.
   d. participating preferred stock.

5. If the corporation has the right to repurchase the preferred shares from stockholders at a specified rate, the stock is
   a. cumulative.
   b. preferred.
   c. callable.
   d. participating.

Analysis

6. Seabre Corporation has outstanding 10,000 shares of 12 percent, $50 par-value, cumulative, nonparticipating preferred stock and 80,000 shares of $10 par-value common stock. The board of directors voted to distribute $45,000 as dividends. What are the total dividends to be paid to common stockholders?

Recording Capital Stock Transactions

In this section you will learn about the entries necessary to record the issuance of capital stock and the records needed to manage capital stock.

Recording the Issuance of Stock

Stock is issued after the purchaser has paid for it in full with one of the following:

- cash
- noncash assets
- services rendered

Stock Issued at Par Value

Assume that Khalid Flemmer and his associates determine that their new corporation, College Supply Center, Inc., will ultimately have capital requirements of $1,400,000. The incorporators decide to issue two classes of stock, preferred and common.

Preferred stock (12%, $100 par value, noncumulative and nonparticipating, 4,000 shares)	$ 400,000
Common stock ($50 par value, 20,000 shares)	1,000,000
Total capital stock	$1,400,000

Flemmer transferred the noncash assets and the liabilities of his existing business to the new corporation at the close of business on December 31, 20--. Flemmer also invested cash for shares of common stock in the new corporation. Flemmer's friends invested cash for common and preferred stock.

When the corporate charter was received, the accounting records were established. The following memorandum entry provides the details of the authorized capital stock.

1	20--				1
2	Dec.	31	College Supply Center, Inc., was formed to		2
3			sell books and supplies to college students		3
4			and to carry on all necessary and related		4
5			activities. It is authorized to issue 20,000		5
6			shares of $50 par-value common stock and		6
7			4,000 shares of $100 par-value, 12%		7
8			preferred stock that is noncumulative		8
9			and nonparticipating.		9

Section Objectives

6 Record the issuance of capital stock at par value.
WHY IT'S IMPORTANT
Stock sales affect equity.

7 Record organization costs.
WHY IT'S IMPORTANT
The startup of a corporation involves a variety of costs.

8 Prepare a balance sheet for a corporation.
WHY IT'S IMPORTANT
The balance sheet must show the classes and values of stock.

9 Record stock issued at a premium and stock with no par value.
WHY IT'S IMPORTANT
Stockholders' equity must be reported accurately.

10 Record transactions for stock subscriptions.
WHY IT'S IMPORTANT
Stock subscriptions increase assets.

11 Describe the capital stock records for a corporation.
WHY IT'S IMPORTANT
Records are legally required.

Terms to Learn

capital stock ledger
capital stock transfer journal
minute book
no-par-value stock
organization costs
registrar
stock certificate
stockholders' ledger
subscribers' ledger
subscription book
transfer agent

Data relating to each class of stock is entered on ledger sheets.

ACCOUNT _Common Stock ($50 Par Value; 20,000 Shares Authorized)_ ACCOUNT NO. _301_

DATE	DESCRIPTION	POST. REF.	DEBIT	CREDIT	BALANCE	
					DEBIT	CREDIT

ACCOUNT _Preferred Stock (12% Noncumulative, Nonparticipating; $100 Par Value; 4,000 Shares Authorized)_ ACCOUNT NO. _311_

DATE	DESCRIPTION	POST. REF.	DEBIT	CREDIT	BALANCE	
					DEBIT	CREDIT

Stock Issued at Par Value for Cash.

When stock is issued for cash equal to the par value of the shares, cash proceeds are credited to the capital stock account. Flemmer and his colleagues purchased the following number of shares at par value for cash.

	Common Stock Shares	Preferred Stock Shares
Khalid Flemmer	264	
Kena Cochran	400	400
Wibb Kamp	400	400
Jill Carrell	200	
Ramon Hill	100	

The receipt of cash was recorded in the cash receipts journal. To simplify the illustration, the entry is shown for Kena Cochran only in general journal form.

Important!

Capital Stock Account
The amount credited to the capital stock account is the par value of the stock issued.

1	20--					1
11	Dec.	31	Cash ($20,000 + $40,000)		60 00 0 00		11
12			Common Stock (400 x $50)			20 00 0 00	12
13			Preferred Stock (400 x $100)			40 00 0 00	13
14			Issuance of stock to Kena Cochran:				14
15			400 shares of common at par ($50 per				15
16			share) and 400 shares of preferred at				16
17			par ($100 per share)				17

Stock Issued at Par Value for Noncash Assets.

The following are the assets and liabilities transferred by Flemmer to the corporation.

Assets
Accounts receivable	$ 18,000
Allowance for doubtful accounts	(2,000)
Merchandise inventory	40,000
Land	30,000
Building	72,000
Equipment and fixtures	8,000
Total assets	$166,000

Liabilities
Accounts payable	19,200
Net value of assets transferred	$146,800

Flemmer and the other shareholders agreed that Flemmer would be issued 800 shares of the $100 par value preferred stock, to be recorded at par value ($80,000). In addition, shares of the $50 par-value common stock are to be issued to Flemmer for the difference between the net value of the noncash assets received by the corporation and the par value of the 800 shares of preferred stock. Thus 1,336 shares of common stock are also issued.

Net value of assets transferred	$146,800
Par value of preferred stock issued (800 shares × $100/share)	80,000
Par value of common stock to be issued	$ 66,800

Number of common shares to be issued:
$66,800 ÷ $50 per share = 1,336 shares

The transaction is recorded as follows.

1	20--					1
18	Dec.	31	Accounts Receivable	18 000 00		18
19			Merchandise Inventory	40 000 00		19
20			Land	30 000 00		20
21			Building	72 000 00		21
22			Equipment and Fixtures	8 000 00		22
23			Allowance for Doubtful Accounts		2 000 00	23
24			Accounts Payable		19 200 00	24
25			Common Stock (1,336 x $50)		66 800 00	25
26			Preferred Stock (800 x $100)		80 000 00	26
27			Issuance of stock in payment for net			27
28			noncash assets of College Supply			28
29			Store, 1,336 shares of $50 par			29
30			common stock at $50 per share and			30
31			800 shares of $100 par preferred			31
32			stock at $100 per share			32

The assets and liability are recorded at fair market value. **Accounts Receivable** and **Allowance for Doubtful Accounts** are recorded separately. The $18,000 balance in the **Accounts Receivable** control account agrees with the total of the accounts receivable subsidiary ledger.

Recording Organization Costs. A variety of costs are incurred when a business is incorporated, including legal fees, attorneys' fees, charter fees paid to the state, and the cost of the organizational meeting of the directors. These costs are debited to an intangible asset account called **Organization Costs** . Organization costs are amortized over a period of up to 40 years. For tax purposes organization costs are amortized over a period of not less than 60 months.

College Supply Center, Inc., paid $2,000 of organization costs to its attorney. The amount includes reimbursement for the charter fee and the cost of drafting and printing the stock certificates. The general journal entry to record the organization costs follows.

1	20--					1
34	Dec.	31	Organization Costs	2 000 00		34
35			Cash		2 000 00	35
36			Payment of legal fees, charter fee,			36
37			and cost of printing stock certificates			37

Recall

Owner's Investment
Common and preferred stock are owners' (stockholders') equity accounts. Increases to owners' equity accounts are recorded as credits.

7 Objective
Record organization costs.

Preparing a Balance Sheet for a Corporation. Figure 20-1 shows the balance sheet for College Supply Center, Inc., immediately following the organization of the corporation. The balance sheet reflects the acquisition of the assets and liabilities of Flemmer's College Supply Store by the issuance of stock, the issuance of stock for cash, and the payment of organization costs.

FIGURE 20-1 ▶
Corporate Balance Sheet
Prepared After Organization

College Supply Center, Inc.			
Balance Sheet			
December 31, 20--			
Assets			
Current Assets			
Cash			146 2 0 0 00
Accounts Receivable	18 0 0 0 00		
Less Allowance for Doubtful Accounts	2 0 0 0 00	16 0 0 0 00	
Merchandise Inventory		40 0 0 0 00	
Total Current Assets		202 2 0 0 00	
Property, Plant, and Equipment			
Land	30 0 0 0 00		
Building	72 0 0 0 00		
Equipment and Fixtures	8 0 0 0 00		
Total Property, Plant, and Equipment		110 0 0 0 00	
Intangible Assets			
Organization Costs		2 0 0 0 00	
Total Assets		314 2 0 0 00	
Liabilities and Stockholders' Equity			
Current Liabilities			
Accounts Payable		19 2 0 0 00	
Stockholders' Equity			
Preferred Stock (12%, $100 par value,			
4,000 shares authorized)			
At Par Value (1,600 shares issued)	160 0 0 0 00		
Common Stock ($50 par value, 20,000			
shares authorized)			
At Par Value (2,700 shares issued)	135 0 0 0 00		
Total Stockholders' Equity		295 0 0 0 00	
Total Liabilities and Stockholders' Equity		314 2 0 0 00	

⑨ **Objective**

Record stock issued at a premium and stock with no par value.

Stock Issued at a Premium

If the corporation has the potential for earning very attractive profits, investors are willing to pay more than par value to become stockholders. Likewise, if the preferred stock dividend is more attractive than other investments with similar risk, investors are willing to pay more than par value. The amount received by a corporation that is in excess of the par value is called a *premium*. A premium on preferred stock is credited to an account called **Paid-in Capital in Excess of Par Value—Preferred Stock.**

Suppose that Mai Nguyen, a new shareholder, agreed to pay $110 per share for 400 shares of preferred stock of College Supply Center, Inc. She paid a premium of $10 per share ($110 price − $100 par). The general journal entry for this transaction is below.

1	20--							1
2	Mar.	2	Cash	44 000 00				2
3			Preferred Stock			40 000 00		3
4			Paid-in Capital in Excess of Par					4
5			Value—Preferred Stock			4 000 00		5
6			Issuance of 400 shares for $110					6
7			per share					7

In the Stockholders' Equity section of the balance sheet shown below, the amount of the new account, **Paid-in Capital in Excess of Par Value—Preferred Stock,** is added to the par value of the shares issued to show the total paid in by that class of stockholder. (The account title might also be **Premium on Preferred Stock** or a similar name.)

<u>Stockholders' Equity</u>

Preferred Stock (12%, $100 par value, 4,000 shares authorized)
    At Par Value (2,000 shares issued) $200,000
    Paid-in Capital in Excess of Par Value   4,000 $204,000

Issuance of No-Par-Value Stock

No-par-value stock is not assigned a par value in the corporate charter. No-par-value stock has theoretical advantages over par-value stock.

- No-par-value stock can be issued at any price. Par-value stock cannot be issued for less than its par value.
- If there is no par value, investors cannot confuse par value and market value.

No-Par-Value Stock Without Stated Value. Some states require no-par-value stock to be assigned a stated value. Even if it is not required, the board of directors can assign a stated value. If no-par-value stock does not have a stated value, the proceeds from the issue of shares are credited to the **Common Stock** account. For example, suppose that Today's Personal Communications Corporation is authorized to issue no-par-value common stock. A stated value has not been assigned the shares. On January 4 the corporation issued 2,000 shares for $10 per share, and on January 5 it issued 1,200 shares for $11 per share. The two stock issues are recorded as follows.

1	20--							1
2	Jan.	4	Cash	20 000 00				2
3			Common Stock			20 000 00		3
4			Issue of 2,000 shares of no-par-value					4
5			common stock at $10 per share					5
6								6
7		5	Cash	13 200 00				7
8			Common Stock			13 200 00		8
9			Issue of 1,200 shares of no-par-value					9
10			common stock at $11 per share					10

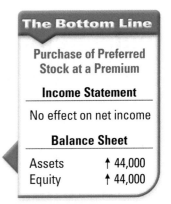

The Bottom Line

Purchase of Preferred Stock at a Premium

Income Statement

No effect on net income

Balance Sheet

Assets   ↑ 44,000
Equity   ↑ 44,000

Important!

In Excess of Par
The amount credited to the **Paid-In Capital in Excess of Par Value** account is the price paid by the stockholder minus the par value of the stock multiplied by the number of shares issued.

Corporation Considerations

- New business owners should have a clear idea of the nature of a corporation, its rights and limitations, and how the corporation differs from other forms of business organization.
- Management and stockholders need to realize that the corporation is a separate legal entity apart from its owners and that regardless of changes in ownership, the corporation continues to exist.
- New business owners need to understand the disadvantages of the corporate form of business including double taxation and government regulation.
- In order to select the most beneficial capital structure, management needs to be familiar with the various classes of stock. Management is responsible for ensuring the following:
  - Assets acquired through the issue of stock are recorded at fair market value so that the corporation's profitability can be properly computed and evaluated.
  - Capital stock issues are properly recorded and tracked.
  - Stock subscriptions are in conformity with state laws and the accounting records fully reflect all information relating to stock subscriptions.
  - The corporation has adequate records to comply with legal requirements and to track stockholder transactions.
  - Officers act within the limitations set by the board of directors and the shareholders.
  - The bylaws and charter provisions of the corporation are carefully followed, and minutes are kept of all meetings of directors and stockholders.
- Management needs to be aware that state laws prohibit the issuance of stock at less than par value.
- Management must be aware that actions of the board of directors, as reported in the corporate minutes, often have accounting effects.

Thinking Critically
Why must the management and directors of a corporation be fully informed about laws and regulations affecting corporations? How can they find out what they need to know?

No-Par-Value Stock with Stated Value. Most no-par-value stock is assigned a stated value by the board of directors. The stated value is treated like par value. If no-par-value common stock with a stated value is issued at a price higher than the stated value, the stated value is credited to the **Common Stock** account. Any excess received over stated value is treated as a premium and credited to **Paid-in Capital in Excess of Stated Value.**

For example, City Fast Food Corporation is authorized to issue no-par-value common stock. The board of directors assigned $25 as the stated value of the stock. On April 1 the corporation issued 1,600 shares at $26 per share. The stock issuance is recorded as shown on page 741.

	20--							
1	20--							1
2	Apr.	1	Cash	41 60 00				2
3			Common Stock		40 00 00			3
4			Paid-in Capital in Excess of Stated					4
5			Value		1 60 00			5
6			Issue of 1,600 shares of common					6
7			stock at $26 per share					7

The credit to the **Paid-in Capital in Excess of Stated Value** account is $1,600 [($26 price − $25 stated value) × 1,600 shares]. On the balance sheet, the premium is added to the common stock to show the total paid by common stockholders.

Summary of Recording Rules for Par-Value and No-Par-Value Stock

Table 20-3 summarizes the effects on the capital accounts of issuing stock with and without a par value.

Par-Value Stock	No-Par-Value Stock	
	Stated Value	No Stated Value
Par value is specified in corporate charter.	Stated value is assigned by directors. Corporate charter indicates that stock is no-par-value stock.	Corporate charter indicates that stock is no-par-value stock.
Stock certificate indicates par value.	Stock certificate generally does not show stated value.	Stock certificate shows that stock is no-par-value stock.
Change in par value requires revision of charter.	Stated value can be changed by directors.	
On issue of stock, par value is credited to capital stock account.	On issue of stock, stated value is credited to capital stock account.	On issue of stock, entire proceeds are credited to capital stock account.

▲ TABLE 20-3
Comparison of Rules for Par-Value and No-Par-Value Stock

Subscriptions for Capital Stock

Some prospective stockholders want to buy stock and pay for it later. They sign a subscription contract that states the stock price and describes the payment plan. They receive the stock when payment is made. A stock subscription is recorded as a receivable from the subscriber. The corporation must have stock available to issue when the subscription is paid in full.

Receipt of Subscriptions

On May 1 College Supply Center, Inc., received a subscription from Thomas Ming to purchase 400 shares of common stock at $50 per share. Ming is to pay for the stock in full on June 1. The corporation also

🔟 Objective

Record transactions for stock subscriptions.

received a subscription from Ali Bell to purchase 400 shares of preferred stock at $110 per share. Bell is to pay for the stock in two equal installments, on June 1 and July 1. These subscriptions are recorded as follows.

1	20--					1
2	May	1	Subscriptions Receivable—Common	20 000 00		2
3			Common Stock Subscribed		20 000 00	3
4			Subscription from Thomas Ming to buy			4
5			400 shares of common stock at par			5
6			value of $50 per share			6
7						7
8		1	Subscriptions Receivable—Preferred	44 000 00		8
9			Preferred Stock Subscribed		40 000 00	9
10			Paid-in Capital in Excess of Par Value—			10
11			Preferred Stock		4 000 00	11
12			Subscription from Ali Bell to buy			12
13			400 shares of $100 par preferred stock			13
14			at $110 per share			14

A separate **Subscriptions Receivable** account is used for each class of stock. There are also separate **Stock Subscribed** accounts. When the subscriptions are paid in full, the stock is issued. Until then, the **Stock Subscribed** accounts appear in the Stockholders' Equity section of the balance sheet as additions to the class of stock issued.

For example, immediately after the receipt of Bell's stock subscription, the preferred stock in the Stockholders' Equity section of the balance sheet appears as follows.

Stockholders' Equity

Preferred Stock (12%, $100 par value, 4,000 shares authorized)

At Par Value (2,000 shares issued)	$200,000
Subscribed (400 shares)	40,000
Paid-in Capital in Excess of Par Value	8,000
	$248,000

Collection of Subscriptions and Issuance of Stock

When Ming pays his $20,000 subscription in full on June 1, the corporation issues 400 shares of common stock to him. The $20,000 is recorded in the cash receipts journal. To simplify the illustration, the transaction is shown in general journal form, followed by an entry to record the issuance of the stock.

Important!

Stock Subscriptions
Stock subscribed accounts are presented in the Stockholders' Equity section of the balance sheet. Subscriptions receivable accounts are presented in the asset section.

1	20--					1
2	June	1	Cash	20 000 00		2
3			Subscriptions Receivable—Common		20 000 00	3
4			Received Thomas Ming's subscription			4
5			in full			5
6						6
7		1	Common Stock Subscribed	20 000 00		7
8			Common Stock		20 000 00	8
9			Issued 400 shares of common stock to			9
10			Thomas Ming			10

When these entries are posted, the **Subscriptions Receivable—Common** and **Common Stock Subscribed** accounts are closed. Both **Cash** and **Common Stock** are increased by $20,000.

Subscriptions Receivable—Common		
May 1 20,000	June 1 20,000

Cash	
June 1 20,000	

Common Stock Subscribed		
June 1 20,000	May 1 20,000

Common Stock	
	June 1 20,000

Bell paid his preferred stock subscription in two monthly installments of $22,000 each. The company debits each payment to **Cash** and credits **Subscriptions Receivable—Preferred.**

After Bell makes the second payment, the corporation issues the stock to him. The collection of the final installment and the issuance of the stock are recorded in the general journal as shown.

1	20--				1
2	July	1	Cash	22 0 0 0 00	2
3			Subscriptions Receivable—Preferred	22 0 0 0 00	3
4			Receipt of final installment from		4
5			Ali Bell on his stock subscription		5
6					6
7		1	Preferred Stock Subscribed	40 0 0 0 00	7
8			Preferred Stock	40 0 0 0 00	8
9			Issuance of 400 shares of preferred		9
10			stock to Ali Bell		10

This stock subscription transaction resulted in a $44,000 increase in **Cash,** a $40,000 increase in **Preferred Stock,** and a $4,000 increase in **Paid-in Capital in Excess of Par Value—Preferred Stock.**

Cash	
June 1 22,000	
July 1 22,000	

Subscriptions Receivable—Preferred		
May 1 44,000	June 1 22,000
	July 1 22,000

Preferred Stock Subscribed		
July 1 40,000	May 1 40,000

Preferred Stock	
	July 1 40,000

Paid-In Capital in Excess of Par Value—Preferred Stock	
	May 1 4,000

Special Corporation Records and Agents

11 Objective

Describe the capital stock records for a corporation.

Corporations keep detailed records of stockholders' equity. They maintain special corporate records such as

- minutes of meetings of stockholders and directors,
- corporate bylaws,
- stock certificate books,

FIGURE 20-2 ▶
Stock Certificate

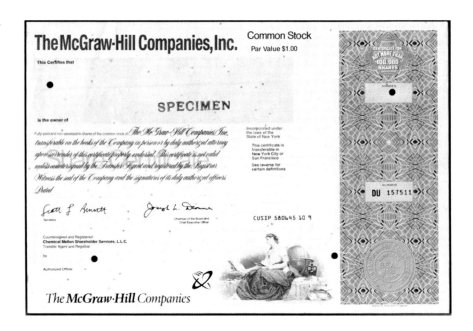

• stock ledgers,
• stock transfer records.

Minute Book

A **minute book** keeps accurate and complete records of all meetings of stockholders and directors. The minute book formally reports actions taken, directives issued, directors elected, officers elected, and other matters.

Stock Certificate Books

Capital stock is usually issued by a corporation in the form of a **stock certificate**. A separate series of stock certificates is prepared for each class of stock. A corporation that expects to issue few stock certificates can have them prepared in books. Each certificate is numbered consecutively and attached to a stub from which it is separated at the time of issuance. The certificate indicates the

Stock Certificates

In Japan as well as in other countries, stock certificates are no longer issued to shareholders. Accounting records indicate ownership.

• name of the corporation,
• name of the stockholder to whom the certificate was issued,
• class of stock,
• number of shares.

Certificates are valid when they are properly signed by corporate officers and have the corporate seal affixed to them.

Figure 20-2 shows a common stock certificate for The McGraw-Hill Companies, Inc. Certificates for preferred stock are similar to those for common stock and include the details of the preferred stock.

Capital Stock Ledger. It is essential for corporations to keep accurate records of the shares of stock issued and the names and addresses of the stockholders. This information is needed to mail dividend checks and official notices about stockholders' meetings and votes.

To keep the required information, corporations set up a **capital stock ledger**, or **stockholders' ledger**, for each class of stock issued. There is a sheet for each stockholder with the following information:

- stockholder's name and address,
- dates of transactions affecting stock holdings,
- certificate numbers,
- number of shares for each transaction.

The balance shows the number of shares held. The ledger sheets can also include a record of dividends. For each class of stock, the stockholders' ledger is a subsidiary to the capital stock account. The total shares shown in the stockholders' ledger must agree with the number of shares in the capital stock account for that class.

After the corporation issues stock, new stockholders purchase shares from existing stockholders. The process is as follows:

- The buyer pays the seller.
- The seller surrenders the stock certificate to the corporation.
- The corporation issues a new certificate to the buyer.

The **capital stock transfer journal** is a record of stock transfers used for posting to the stockholders' ledger. There is a capital stock transfer journal for each class of stock issued by the corporation.

Records of Stock Subscriptions

The corporation tracks stock subscriptions using the subscription book and the subscribers' ledger. The **subscription book**

- is a listing of the stock subscriptions received,
- shows the names and addresses of the subscribers,
- shows the number of shares subscribed,
- contains the amounts and times of payment.

A subscription book can contain the actual stock subscription contracts.

The **subscribers' ledger** contains an account receivable for each stock subscriber. The account is debited for the total subscription and credited when the subscriber makes payments. The subscribers' ledger is a subsidiary ledger. The balances of the individual subscriber accounts must agree with the **Subscriptions Receivable** control account in the general ledger.

Summary of Stock Control Accounts and Subsidiary Ledgers

Table 20-4 on page 746 shows the relationship between control accounts and subsidiary ledgers for corporate stock recordkeeping.

Special Agents

Corporations whose stock is widely held and actively traded do not keep their own stockholder records. Instead, they turn the responsibility over to a transfer agent and a registrar. The **transfer agent** receives the stock certificates surrendered. A bank that serves as a transfer agent is often chosen for its proximity to the stock exchange or market where the corporation's stock is expected to trade. The same bank may also be appointed registrar.

An assignment form on the certificate indicates to whom a new certificate should be issued. The agent

- cancels the old certificates,
- issues the new ones,

TABLE 20-4 ▶
Subsidiary Stock Ledgers

Control Account	Subsidiary Ledger
Common Stock	Common Stockholders' Ledger Contains an account for each owner of common stock and shows shares bought or transferred and the balance of shares owned
Preferred Stock	Preferred Stockholders' Ledger Contains an account for each owner of preferred stock and shows shares bought or transferred and the balance of shares owned
Subscriptions Receivable—Common Stock	Subscribers' Ledger—Common Contains the account receivable for each subscriber to common stock
Subscriptions Receivable—Preferred Stock	Subscribers' Ledger—Preferred Contains an account receivable for each subscriber to preferred stock

Recall

Subsidiary Ledgers
The total of the individual accounts must agree with the control account in the general ledger.

- makes the necessary entries in the capital stock ledger,
- prepares lists of stockholders who should receive dividend payments and notices.

The agent might also prepare and mail the dividend checks.

The **registrar** accounts for all the stock issued by the corporation and makes sure that the corporation does not issue more shares than are authorized. The registrar receives from the transfer agent all the canceled certificates and all the new certificates issued. The registrar must counter-sign the new certificates before they are valid.

Section 3 Self Review

Questions

1. What is a premium on stock?
2. How do par value and stated value differ?
3. What are organization costs?

Exercises

4. A person who buys stock under a subscription contract receives the stock when
   a. the contract is signed.
   b. the subscription is posted to the general ledger.
   c. the first payment is made.
   d. the subscription is paid in full.

5. The transfer of stock between shareholders is recorded in the
   a. general journal.
   b. stock transfer journal.
   c. minute book.
   d. subscription book.

Analysis

6. A corporation issues 100 shares of common stock for $50 per share. Par value of the stock is $4 per share. How is the transaction recorded?

(Answers to Section 3 Self Review are on page 765.)

Review

Chapter Summary

In this chapter, you have learned about the basic characteristics of a corporation and the accounting procedures unique to its formation and operation. You have learned about capital stock transactions, dividends declarations, and reporting of stockholders' equity on the balance sheet.

Learning Objectives

1 Explain the characteristics of a corporation.

A corporation is organized under state law to carry on activities permitted by its charter.

- Ownership is indicated by shares of stock.
- Stockholders owning voting stock elect a board of directors.
- The board selects officers to run the business.
- The corporate charter specifies the types and amounts of capital stock authorized.
- The bylaws guide the firm's general operation, which must be consistent with charter provisions.
- The corporation is subject to federal income tax.

2 Describe special "hybrid" organizations that have some characteristics of partnerships and some characteristics of corporations.

A corporation formed as an S corporation is taxed as a partnership. The limited liability partnership and limited liability company avoid federal corporate income tax and also provide limited liability.

3 Describe the different types of stock.

If a corporation issues only one type of stock, it is called *common stock.* Common stockholders vote on corporate matters and receive dividends as declared by the board of directors.

Corporations can issue a second class of stock that carries special preferences, called *preferred stock.* Preferred stockholders are often given priority in the distribution of dividends. Liquidation value is usually assigned to preferred stock; this stock class may be convertible to common stock.

4 Compute the number of shares of common stock to be issued on the conversion of convertible preferred stock.

Convertible preferred stock gives its owners the right to convert their shares into common stock after a specified date by using the stated conversion ratio.

5 Compute dividends payable on stock.

The board of directors declares dividends based on corporate earnings. Dividends are first allocated to preferred stockholders, then to common stockholders.

6 Record the issuance of capital stock at par value.

The entire amount of stock issued in return for a cash investment is credited to the appropriate capital stock account. Noncash assets traded for capital stock are recorded at their fair market value.

7 Record organization costs.

Organizational costs are charged initially to an intangible asset account. They can be amortized up to 40 years, but often a 60-month period is used.

8 Prepare a balance sheet for a corporation.

The Stockholders' Equity section identifies the classes, values, and number of stock authorized and issued.

9 Record stock issued at a premium and stock with no par value.

A premium on stock is recorded in a **Paid-in Capital in Excess of Par Value** account. Stock without a par value is called *no-par-value stock.* Some states require it to be assigned a stated value, similar to par value for accounting purposes.

10 Record transactions for stock subscriptions.

Stock can be subscribed to and paid for and issued later. It is recorded in a subsidiary ledger with a separate account receivable for each subscriber. Individual accounts receivable are controlled by a **Subscriptions Receivable** account in the general ledger.

11 Describe the capital stock records for a corporation.

Corporate records must include minute books, stockholders' ledgers, stock certificate books, and stock transfer records.

12 Define the accounting terms new to this chapter.

Authorized capital stock (p. 729) The number of shares authorized for issue by the corporate charter

Bylaws (p. 727) The guidelines for conducting a corporation's business affairs

Callable preferred stock (p. 731) Stock that gives the issuing corporation the right to repurchase the preferred shares from the stockholders at a specific price

Capital stock ledger (p. 745) A subsidiary ledger that contains a record of each stockholder's purchases, transfers, and current balance of shares owned; also called stockholders' ledger

Capital stock transfer journal (p. 745) A record of stock transfers used for posting to the stockholders' ledger

Common stock (p. 729) The general class of stock issued when no other class of stock is authorized; each share carries the same rights and privileges as every other share. Even if preferred stock is issued, common stock will also be issued

Convertible preferred stock (p. 730) Preferred stock that conveys the right to convert that stock to common stock after a specified date or during a period of time

Corporate charter (p. 724) A document issued by a state government that establishes a corporation

Cumulative preferred stock (p. 731) Stock that conveys to its owners the right to receive the preference dividend for the current year and any prior years in which the preference dividend was not paid before common stockholders receive any dividends

Dividends (p. 731) Distributions of the profits of a corporation to its shareholders

Limited liability company (LLC) (p. 726) Provides limited liability to the owners, who can elect to have the profits taxed at the LLC level or on their individual tax returns

Limited liability partnership (LLP) (p. 725) A partnership that provides limited liability for all partners

Liquidation value (p. 730) Value of assets to be applied to preferred stock, usually par value or an amount in excess of par value, if the corporation is liquidated

Market value (p. 729) The price per share at which stock is bought and sold

Minute book (p. 744) A book in which accurate and complete records of all meetings of stockholders and directors are kept

Noncumulative preferred stock (p. 731) Stock that conveys to its owners the stated preference dividend for the current year but no rights to dividends for years in which none were declared

Nonparticipating preferred stock (p. 731) Stock that conveys to its owners the right to only the preference dividend amount specified on the stock certificate

No-par-value stock (p. 739) Stock that is not assigned a par value in the corporate charter

Organization costs (p. 737) The costs associated with establishing a corporation; an intangible asset account

Par value (p. 729) An amount assigned by the corporate charter to each share of stock for accounting purposes

Participating preferred stock (p. 731) Stock that conveys the right not only to the preference dividend amount but also to a share of other dividends paid

Preemptive right (p. 729) A shareholder's right to purchase a proportionate amount of any new stock issued at a later date

Preference dividend (p. 731) A basic or stated dividend rate for preferred stock that must be paid before dividends can be paid on common stock

Preferred stock (p. 730) A class of stock that has special claims on the corporate profits or, in case of liquidation, on corporate assets

Registrar (p. 746) A person or institution in charge of the issuance and transfer of a corporation's stock

Shareholder (p. 724) A person who owns shares of stock in a corporation; also called a stockholder

Stated value (p. 729) The value that can be assigned to no-par-value stock by a board of directors for accounting purposes

Stock certificate (p. 744) The form by which capital stock is issued; the certificate indicates the name of the corporation, the name of the stockholder to whom the certificate was issued, the class of stock, and the number of shares

Stockholders' equity (p. 728) The corporate equivalent of owners' equity; also called shareholders' equity

Stockholders' ledger (p. 745) See Capital stock ledger

Subchapter S corporation (S corporation) (p. 725) An entity formed as a corporation that meets the requirements of Subchapter S of the Internal Revenue Code to be treated essentially as a partnership, so that the corporation pays no income tax

Subscribers' ledger (p. 745) A subsidiary ledger that contains an account receivable for each stock subscriber

Subscription book (p. 745) A list of the stock subscriptions received

Transfer agent (p. 745) A person or institution that handles all stock transfers and transfer records for a corporation

Comprehensive Self Review

1. Compare the transferability of shares of stock in a corporation with the transferability of a partner's interest in a partnership.
2. How are the **Stock Subscribed** accounts reported on the financial statements?
3. What does "market value" of a stock mean?
4. Explain the nature of a capital stock ledger.
5. Describe the information contained in a capital stock transfer journal.

(Answers to Comprehensive Self Review are on page 765.)

Discussion Questions

1. What is the difference between privately held and publicly held corporations?

2. What are the bylaws of a corporation?

3. What is the major benefit of forming a limited liability company instead of a regular corporation?

4. If there is only one class of stock, what is it called?

5. How does par value differ from stated value?

6. What is participating preferred stock?

7. What is cumulative preferred stock?

8. What is convertible preferred stock?

9. When common stock without a par value or a stated value is issued, what amount is credited to the capital stock account when the stock is issued?

10. What is the difference between the **Common Stock Subscribed** account and the **Subscriptions Receivable—Common Stock** account?

11. What is a stock subscription?

12. How are organization costs classified on the balance sheet?

13. What disposition is made of organization costs in the accounting records?

14. What role does the registrar serve?

15. What is the control account for the individual shareholder accounts in the common stockholders' ledger?

16. How does a corporation obtain a charter?

17. Selling stock on a subscription basis involves considerable record-keeping. Why does a corporation sell its shares in this way?

18. How are the members of a corporation's board of directors selected?

19. What is the purpose of a minute book?

20. Define par-value stock.

21. What is the role of the transfer agent?

22. What does the term "restricted agency" mean?

23. Who makes the day-to-day decisions necessary for a corporation to operate?

24. Describe the flow of authority and responsibility in a corporate entity.

Applications

EXERCISES

Computing dividends payable.

Herald Corporation has only one class of stock. There are 100,000 shares outstanding. During 20-- the corporation's net income after taxes was $580,000. The policy of the corporation is to declare dividends equal to 40 percent of its net income. Harold Hall owns 2,240 shares of the stock. How much will Hall receive as a dividend on his shares?

◀ **Exercise 20-1**
Objective 5

Computing dividends payable.

Zenith Corporation has outstanding 20,000 shares of noncumulative, 12 percent, $100 par-value preferred stock and 100,000 shares of no-par-value common stock.

During 2004 the corporation paid dividends of $160,000. What amount will be paid on each share of preferred stock? What amount will be paid on each share of common stock?

During 2005 the Zenith Corporation paid dividends of $680,000. How much will be paid on each share of preferred stock? How much will be paid on each share of common stock?

◀ **Exercise 20-2**
Objective 5

Computing dividends payable.

Agiba Corporation has outstanding 60,000 shares of 14 percent, $50 par-value cumulative preferred stock and 200,000 shares of no-par-value common stock.

During 2004 the corporation distributed dividends of $450,000. What amount will be paid on each share of preferred stock? What amount will be paid on each share of common stock?

During 2005 the corporation distributed dividends of $960,000. What amount will be paid on each share of preferred stock?

◀ **Exercise 20-3**
Objective 5

Converting preferred stock.

Amelio Corporation has outstanding 50,000 shares of $50 par-value preferred stock, issued at an average price of $52 per share. The preferred stock is convertible into common stock at the rate of one-half share of common stock for each share of preferred stock. Louise Jackson owns 400 shares of preferred stock. During the current year she decides to convert 200 shares into common stock. How many shares of common stock will she receive?

◀ **Exercise 20-4**
Objective 4

Issuing stock for assets.

Jay Aikman, the owner of a sole proprietorship, is planning to incorporate his business. His capital account has a balance of $360,000 after revaluation of the assets. His cash account totals $44,000. He will receive 10 percent, $25 par-value preferred stock with a total par value equal to the cash transferred. The balance of his capital is to be exchanged for shares of $50 par-value common stock with a total par value equal to the remaining capital. How many shares of preferred stock should be issued to Aikman? How many shares of common stock should be issued to Aikman?

◀ **Exercise 20-5**
Objective 6

Exercise 20-6 ►
Objective 7

Amortizing organization costs.

Tristen Corporation was formed in January 20-- with organization costs of $5,600.

1. What is the least amount of organization costs to be amortized for the year 20--?

Exercise 20-7 ►
Objective 6

Issuing stock at par value for cash.

Young Corporation issued 2,000 shares of $25 par-value common stock and 300 shares of 13 percent, $50 par-value preferred stock for cash at par value. Record in general journal form the issuance of the stock.

Exercise 20-8 ►
Objective 9

Issuing par-value stock at premium.

Beasley Corporation issued 1,000 shares of its $10 par-value common stock for cash at $11 per share. Give the entry in general journal form to record the issuance of the stock.

Exercise 20-9 ►
Objective 10

Issuing no-par-value stock for cash.

Ahmad Corporation issued 600 shares of its no-par-value common stock (stated value, $4) for cash at $5 per share. Give the entry in general journal form to record the issuance of the stock.

Exercise 20-10 ►
Objective 11

Recording transactions for stock subscriptions.

On March 1, 20--, Columbus Corporation received a subscription from Mark Coomes for 2,000 shares of its $25 par-value common stock at a price of $30 per share.

Coomes made a payment of $15 per share on the stock at the time of the subscription. Record the entries in general journal form to record the receipt of the subscription and the cash payment.

Give the entries on April 1, 20--, to record payment of the balance of Coomes' subscription and issuance of the stock.

Problems

Selected problems can be completed using:
 Peachtree   QuickBooks   Spreadsheets

PROBLEM SET A

Problem 20-1A ►
Objective 5

Computing dividends payable.

Mohair Corporation issued and has outstanding 20,000 shares of $50 par-value common stock and 2,000 shares of $100 par-value 12 percent preferred stock. The board of directors votes to distribute $10,000 as dividends in 2004, $24,000 in 2005, and $162,000 in 2006.

INSTRUCTIONS

Compute the total dividend and the dividend for each share paid to preferred stockholders and common stockholders each year under the following assumed situations.

Case A: The preferred stock is nonparticipating and noncumulative.

Case B: The preferred stock is cumulative and nonparticipating.

Analyze: If a stockholder purchased 500 shares of cumulative participating preferred stock in 2004, what total dividends should be paid to this stockholder for the fiscal year 2006?

Computing dividends payable.

This problem consists of two parts.

◄ **Problem 20-2A**
Objective 5

Part I

A portion of the Stockholders' Equity section of Cole Corporation's balance sheet as of December 31, 2005, appears below. Dividends have not been paid for the years 2003 and 2004. There has been no change in the number of shares of stock issued and outstanding during these years. Assume that the board of directors of Cole Corporation declares a dividend of $28,000 after completing operations for the year 2005.

<u>Stockholders' Equity</u>

Preferred Stock (11% cumulative, $100 par value, 2,000 shares authorized)	
At Par Value (1,400 shares issued)	$140,000
Common Stock (no-par value, with stated value of $50, 10,000 shares authorized)	
At Stated Value (6,000 shares issued)	300,000

INSTRUCTIONS

1. Compute the total amount of the dividend to be distributed to preferred stockholders.
2. Compute the amount of the dividend to be paid on each share of preferred stock.
3. Compute the total amount of the dividend available to be distributed to common stockholders.
4. Compute the amount of the dividend to be paid on each share of common stock.
5. Compute the amount of dividends in arrears (if any) that preferred stockholders may expect from future declarations of dividends.

Part II

Use the information given in Part I to solve this part of the problem. Assume that the board of directors of Cole Corporation has declared a dividend of $85,800 instead of $28,000 after operations for 2005 are completed.

INSTRUCTIONS

1. Compute the total amount of the dividend to be distributed to preferred stockholders.
2. Compute the amount of the dividend to be paid on each share of preferred stock.
3. Compute the total amount of the dividend available to be distributed to common stockholders.
4. Compute the amount of the dividend to be paid on each share of common stock.
5. Compute the amount of dividends in arrears (if any) that preferred stockholders may expect from future declarations of dividends.

Analyze: Assume only Part 1 has transpired. If, in 2006, the board of directors declared a dividend of $40,000, what amount would be paid to preferred stockholders?

Problem 20-3A ►
Objective 6

Issuing stock for cash and noncash assets at par.

Stella Smith and Clarence Parish are equal partners in S & P Audio Center, which sells audio equipment and operates a sound equipment repair service. Smith and Parish have decided to incorporate the business. The new corporation will be known as S & P Audio Corporation.

The corporation is authorized to issue 2,000 shares of $100 par-value, 10 percent preferred stock that is noncumulative and nonparticipating, and 40,000 shares of no-par-value common stock with a stated value of $50 per share. It is mutually agreed that the accounting records of S & P Audio Center will be closed on December 31, 2004, and that certain assets will be revalued. S & P Audio Corporation will then take over all assets and assume all liabilities of the partnership. In payment for the business, the corporation will issue 400 shares of preferred stock to Smith and 400 shares of preferred stock to Parish, plus a sufficient number of shares of common stock to each partner to equal the balance of the partners' capital accounts. After the partners have recorded the revaluation of their assets immediately prior to the dissolution of their partnership and withdrawn the amounts of cash agreed on, the trial balance of S & P Audio Center as of December 31, 2004, appears as shown.

S & P Audio Center
Trial Balance
December 31, 2004

ACCOUNT NAME	DEBIT	CREDIT
Cash	8 0 2 0 00	
Accounts Receivable	25 4 4 0 00	
Allowance for Doubtful Accounts		8 2 4 0 00
Merchandise Inventory	325 4 0 0 00	
Parts Inventory	21 9 0 0 00	
Land	40 0 0 0 00	
Building	275 7 4 0 00	
Allowance for Depreciation—Building		27 7 4 0 00
Furniture and Equipment	58 7 0 0 00	
Accumulated Depreciation—Furn. and Equip.		4 3 0 0 00
Accounts Payable		39 7 2 0 00
Stella Smith, Capital		337 6 0 0 00
Clarence Parish, Capital		337 6 0 0 00
Totals	755 2 0 0 00	755 2 0 0 00

INSTRUCTIONS

1. In the corporation's general journal, record a memorandum entry describing the corporation's formation on December 31, 2004.

2. Record general journal entries as of December 31 to show the takeover of the assets and liabilities of the partnership and the issuance of stock in payment to Smith and Parish. Use the same account titles that the partnership used for assets and liabilities. Also use two new accounts: **Common Stock** and **Preferred Stock**.

Analyze: What percentage of authorized common stock has been issued as of January 1, 2005?

Issuing stock at par and no-par value, recording organization costs, and preparing a balance sheet.

◄ **Problem 20-4A**
Objectives 6, 7, 8, 10

Clay Corporation, a new corporation, took over the assets and liabilities of Clay Antiques on January 2, 20--. The assets and liabilities, after appropriate revaluation by Clay, are as follows.

Cash	$ 23,600
Accounts Receivable	177,400
Allowance for Doubtful Accounts	(4,800)
Merchandise Inventory	300,000
Accounts Payable	(176,000)
Accrued Expenses Payable	(9,600)

The corporation is authorized to issue 600,000 shares of $20 par-value common stock and 400,000 shares of $10 par-value preferred stock. The preferred stock bears a stated yearly dividend rate of $1 per share. The transactions that follow were entered into at the time the corporation was formed.

INSTRUCTIONS

1. Make general journal entries to record the transactions.
2. Prepare the opening balance sheet as of January 2, 20--, for Clay Corporation.

DATE		TRANSACTIONS
Jan.	2	The corporation issued 15,530 shares of common stock to Ray Clay for his equity in the sole proprietorship business, and the corporation took over Clay's assets and liabilities.
	2	Issued 200 shares of preferred stock to Clay for his services in organizing the corporation. The agreed-upon value of these services was $2,000.
	2	Issued 2,000 shares of common stock to Scott Reese. He paid $40,000 in cash for the stock.
	2	Issued 2,000 shares of preferred stock to Juan Silver. He paid $20,000 in cash for the stock.
	2	Paid $2,000 to C. P. May, the attorney who prepared the corporate charter and the bylaws, for his services.

Analyze: What is the current ratio for the corporation at January 2, 20--?

Issuing stock at par and at premium, preparing Stockholders' Equity section of balance sheet, and recording stock subscriptions.

◄ **Problem 20-5A**
Objectives 6, 8, 9, 11

Golf Corporation was organized on July 1, 20--, to operate a taxi service. The firm is authorized to issue 50,000 shares of no-par-value common stock with a stated value of $100 per share and 20,000 shares of $100 par-value, 12 percent preferred stock that is nonparticipating and noncumulative. Selected transactions that took place during July 20-- follow.

INSTRUCTIONS

1. Set up the following general ledger accounts.

101 Cash
114 Subscriptions Receivable—Common Stock
115 Subscriptions Receivable—Preferred Stock
301 Common Stock
302 Common Stock Subscribed
305 Paid-in Capital in Excess of Stated Value—Common
311 Preferred Stock
312 Preferred Stock Subscribed
315 Paid-in Capital in Excess of Par Value—Preferred

Record in general journal form the transactions listed below, and post them to the general ledger accounts.

2. Prepare the Stockholders' Equity section of a balance sheet for Golf Corporation, as of July 31, 20--.

DATE		TRANSACTIONS
July	1	The corporation received its charter. (Make a memorandum entry.)
	1	Issued 300 shares of common stock for cash at $100 per share to Natasha Redman.
	2	Issued 250 shares of preferred stock for cash at par value to Hank Leggett.
	5	Issued 150 shares of common stock for cash at $104 to Rudy Cabrales.
	10	Received a subscription for 200 shares of common stock at $106 per share from Betty Hayes, payable in two installments due in 10 and 20 days.
	12	Received a subscription for 100 shares of preferred stock at $104 per share from Jim Baker, payable in two installments due in 15 and 30 days.
	20	Received payment of a stock subscription installment due from Betty Hayes (one-half of the purchase price—see July 10 transaction).
	27	Received payment of a stock subscription installment due from Jim Baker (one-half of the purchase price—see July 12 transaction).
	30	Received the balance due on the stock subscription of July 10 from Betty Hayes; issued the stock.

Analyze: What percentage of total stockholders' equity is held by common stockholders?

PROBLEM SET B

Problem 20-1B ►
Objective 5

Computing dividends payable.

Tremont Corporation issued and has outstanding 4,000 shares of $75 par-value common stock and 4,000 shares of $50 par-value, 10 percent preferred stock. The board of directors votes to distribute $12,000 as dividends in 2004, $20,000 in 2005, and $102,000 in 2006.

Compute the total dividend and the dividend for each share to be paid to preferred stockholders and common stockholders each year under the following assumed situations.

Case A: The preferred stock is nonparticipating and noncumulative.

Case B: The preferred stock is cumulative and nonparticipating.

Analyze: If a stockholder owned 200 shares of preferred stock throughout 2004–2006, what total dividends did he receive for Case B?

Computing dividends payable.

◄ **Problem 20-2B**
Objective 5

This problem consists of two parts.

Part I

A portion of the Stockholders' Equity section of Marino Corporation's balance sheet as of December 31, 2005, appears below. Dividends have not been paid for the year 2004. There has been no change in the number of shares of stock issued and outstanding during 2004 or 2005. Assume that the board of directors of the corporation declared a dividend of $30,000 after completing operations for the year 2005.

Stockholders' Equity

Preferred Stock (10% cumulative, $100 par value, 20,000 shares authorized)	
At Par Value (4,000 shares issued)	$400,000
Common Stock ($25 par value, 70,000 shares authorized)	
At Par Value (20,000 shares issued)	500,000

INSTRUCTIONS

1. Compute the total amount of the dividend to be distributed to preferred stockholders.

2. Compute the amount of the dividend to be paid on each share of preferred stock.

3. Compute the total amount of the dividend available to be distributed to common stockholders.

4. Compute the amount of the dividend to be paid on each share of common stock.

5. Compute the amount of dividends in arrears (if any) that preferred stockholders can expect from future declarations of dividends.

INSTRUCTIONS

Part II

Assume that after operations for 2005 were completed, the board of directors declares a dividend of $168,000 instead of $30,000. Use the information given in Part I to answer questions 1 through 5 above under these new assumptions.

Analyze: In regard to Part I, if dividends of $70,000 were declared in 2006, what per-share amount would be paid to preferred stockholders?

Issuing stock at par for cash and noncash assets.

◄ **Problem 20-3B**
Objective 6

Latasha Moore and Ray Nell Massey are equal partners in All Occasions Gift Center. Moore and Massey have decided to form New Century Corporation to take over the operation of All Occasions Gift Center on December 31, 20--. The corporation is authorized to issue 4,000 shares of no-par-value common stock with a stated value of $50 per share and 2,000 shares of $100 par-value, 12 percent preferred stock that is noncumulative and nonparticipating. Certain assets are revalued so that the accounts will reflect current values. Moore and Massey will each receive 200 shares of New Century Corporation preferred stock at par value ($50) and sufficient $100 par-value shares of common stock to cover the partners' adjusted net investment in the partnership.

The trial balance shown below was prepared after the firm's accounting records were closed at the end of its fiscal year on December 31, 20--, and the assets were revalued as agreed on.

All Occasions Gift Center
Adjusted Trial Balance
December 31, 20--

ACCOUNT NAME	DEBIT	CREDIT
Cash	12 000 00	
Accounts Receivable	29 500 00	
Allowance for Doubtful Accounts		5 00 00
Merchandise Inventory	102 000 00	
Furniture and Equipment	45 800 00	
Accumulated Depreciation—Equipment		2 200 00
Accounts Payable		26 600 00
Latasha Moore, Capital		80 000 00
Ray Nell Massey, Capital		80 000 00
Totals	189 300 00	189 300 00

INSTRUCTIONS

1. In the corporation's general journal, record a memorandum entry describing its formation on December 31, 20--.

2. Make general journal entries as of December 31 to show the takeover of the assets and liabilities of the partnership and the issuance of stock in payment to Latasha Moore and Ray Nell Massey. Use the same account names that the partnership used for assets and liabilities. Also use the following new account titles: **Common Stock** and **Preferred Stock.**

Analyze: After the corporation's formation, what is the fundamental accounting equation for New Century Corporation?

Problem 20-4B ▶
Objectives 6, 7, 8, 9

Issuing stock at par for cash and noncash assets, issuing stock at premium, recording organization costs, and preparing corporate balance sheet.

Central Florida Corporation, a new corporation, took over the assets and liabilities of Jay's Clothier on January 5, 20--. The assets and liabilities assumed, after appropriate revaluation by Jay's, are as follows.

Cash	$20,000	Merchandise Inventory	$66,000
Accounts Receivable	28,000	Accounts Payable	(5,000)
Allowance for Doubtful Accounts	(1,000)	Accrued Expenses Payable	(5,600)

The corporation is authorized to issue 100,000 shares of no-par-value common stock with a stated value of $10 per share and 10,000 shares of $20 par-value preferred stock. The preferred stock bears a dividend of $2 per share per year. The transactions entered into at the time the corporation was formed follow.

INSTRUCTIONS

1. Prepare the general journal entries to record the transactions.
2. Prepare the opening balance sheet as of January 5, 20--, for Central Florida Corporation.

DATE		TRANSACTIONS
Jan.	5	The corporation issued to Jay Stanislaw common stock with a stated value equal to his net equity in the sole proprietorship business, and the corporation took over Jay's assets and liabilities.
	5	Issued 120 shares of preferred stock to Stanislaw for his help in organizing the corporation. The agreed-upon value of these services was $2,400.
	5	Issued 1,000 shares of common stock to Lena Larson for $10,000 cash.
	5	Issued 200 shares of preferred stock to Angus Rhodes. He paid $4,000 in cash for the stock.
	5	Paid $2,000 to Selena Mays, the attorney who prepared the corporate charter and the bylaws, for her services.

Analyze: What is the amount of total stockholders' equity as of January 5, 20--?

Issuing stock at par, issuing stock at a premium, preparing Stockholders' Equity section of balance sheet, and recording stock subscriptions.

◄ **Problem 20-5B**
Objectives 6, 8, 9, 11

Party Place Corporation was organized on January 2, 20--, to operate a chain of party supply stores. The firm is authorized to issue 40,000 shares of $40 par-value common stock and 18,000 shares of $50 par-value, 11 percent preferred stock. The preferred stock is noncumulative and nonparticipating. Selected transactions that took place during January 20-- are given below.

INSTRUCTIONS

1. Set up the following general ledger accounts.

101 Cash
114 Subscriptions Receivable—
　　Common Stock
115 Subscriptions Receivable—
　　Preferred Stock
301 Common Stock
302 Common Stock Subscribed

305 Paid-in Capital in Excess
　　of Par Value—Common
311 Preferred Stock
312 Preferred Stock Subscribed
315 Paid-in Capital in Excess
　　of Par Value—Preferred

Record the transactions listed below in general journal form and post them to the general ledger accounts.

2. Prepare the Stockholders' Equity section of a balance sheet for Party Place Corporation as of January 31, 20--.

DATE		TRANSACTIONS
Jan.	2	The corporation received its corporate charter. (Make a memorandum entry.)
		Continued

DATE	(20-5B cont.)	TRANSACTIONS
Jan. 3		Issued 1,000 shares of common stock for cash at $40 per share to Anicia Trevor.
3		Issued 1,000 shares of preferred stock for cash at $50 per share to Madeline Gibbons.
10		Issued 200 shares of common stock for cash at $42 per share to Mark Merki.
10		Received a subscription for 500 shares of common stock at $42 per share from Nora Barnett, payable in two installments due in 5 and 15 days.
14		Received a subscription for 800 shares of preferred stock at $52 per share from Jim Lane, payable in two installments due in 10 and 20 days.
15		Received payment of a stock subscription installment due from Nora Barnett (one-half of purchase price—see January 10 transaction).
24		Received payment of a stock subscription installment due from Jim Lane (one-half of purchase price—see January 14 transaction).
25		Received the balance due from Nora Barnett; issued the stock.

Analyze: What percentage of authorized common stock has been issued at January 25, 20--?

CHAPTER 20 CHALLENGE PROBLEM

Understanding Stockholders' Equity

Just after its formation on July 1, 2004, the ledger accounts of the Fashion Costume Jewelry Corporation contained the following balances.

Accrued Expenses Payable	$ 10,000
Accounts Payable	80,000
Accounts Receivable	44,000
Allowance for Doubtful Accounts	4,000
Building	200,000
Cash	32,000
Common Stock ($25 par)	302,600
Common Stock Subscribed	16,000
Furniture and Fixtures	50,000
Merchandise Inventory	182,600
Notes Payable—Short Term	50,000
Organization Costs	6,000
Paid-in Capital in Excess of Par Value—Common	12,000
Paid-in Capital in Excess of Par Value—Preferred	6,000
Preferred Stock (10%, $50 par)	50,000
Preferred Stock Subscribed (10%, $50 par)	20,000
Subscriptions Receivable—Common Stock	8,200
Subscriptions Receivable—Preferred Stock	10,400

The corporation is authorized to issue 50,000 shares of $25 par-value common stock and 10,000 shares of 10 percent, $50 par-value preferred stock (noncumulative and nonparticipating).

1. Answer the following questions:
   a. How many shares of common stock are outstanding?
   b. How many shares of common stock are subscribed?
   c. How many shares of preferred stock are outstanding?
   d. How many shares of preferred stock are subscribed?
   e. At what average price has common stock been subscribed or issued?
   f. Assume that no dividends are paid in the first year of the corporation's existence. What are the rights of the preferred stockholders?
   g. Assuming that all of the **Paid-in Capital in Excess of Par Value— Common** was applicable to the shares of common stock that have been subscribed but not yet issued, what was the subscription price per share of the common stock subscribed?
   h. Assuming that the board of directors declared no dividends in 2004, what amount would have to be paid the preferred stockholders in 2005 before any dividend could be paid to the common stockholders?
2. Prepare a classified balance sheet for the corporation just after its formation on July 1, 2004.

Analyze: What is the current ratio for the corporation at July 1, 2004?

CHAPTER 20 CRITICAL THINKING PROBLEM

Interpreting the Balance Sheet

The Stockholders' Equity section of Big Town Corporation's balance sheet at the close of the current year follows.

Stockholders' Equity

Preferred stock (8%, $100 par value, 30,000 shares authorized)	
At Par Value (20,000 shares issued)	$ 2,000,000
Paid-in Capital in Excess of Par Value	260,000
Common Stock (no-par value, stated value of $10, 500,000 shares authorized)	
At Stated Value	1,500,000
Paid-in Capital in Excess of Stated Value	6,600,000
Retained Earnings	2,800,000
Total Stockholders' Equity	$13,160,000

1. What is the amount of the annual dividend on the preferred stock? Per share? In total?
2. How many shares of common stock have been issued?
3. What was the average price paid by the stockholders for the preferred stock?
4. What was the average price paid by the stockholders for the common stock?
5. How many shares of common stock are currently outstanding (held by stockholders)?
6. If total dividends of $574,400 were paid to stockholders in the current year, how much was paid to the common stockholders in total? Per share? Assume that no preferred dividends are in arrears.

Business Connections

Connection 1 ▶ MANAGERIAL *Focus*   Forming a Corporation

1. Ankers and Baker are establishing a new restaurant and discussing whether to organize as a partnership or a corporation. What are some of the most important characteristics of these two types of organizations that they should weigh in making the decision?

2. Ankers and Baker are considering organizing as a Subchapter S corporation. What are the advantages and disadvantages they should consider?

3. Ankers and Baker decide to form a regular corporation for conducting their restaurant business. They are considering whether to issue preferred stock or to borrow funds on a long-term basis. Suggest some factors they should consider. How can they make the preferred stock more attractive to investors?

4. A group of individuals is planning to form a corporation. Explain in general terms the usual steps necessary to do this.

5. Why should the management of a corporation be concerned about the realistic valuation of assets transferred to the firm?

Connection 2 ▶ Ethical **DILEMMA**   **Employee Discounts** Employees of Hancock Grocery Corporation are entitled to purchase all food items at a 15 percent discount. Tony Ricco often purchases items for his friends, taking the discount and passing it on to his friends. Ricco also sometimes purchases food for a charitable organization on whose board of directors he serves. Ricco receives no reimbursement for items given the charitable organization. Discuss the ethical aspects of Ricco's generosity.

Connection 3 ▶ Street**WISE:**   Questions from the Real World   **Common Stock** Refer to the consolidated balance sheets for The Home Depot, Inc. in its *1999 Annual Report* in Appendix B.

1. How many shares of common stock have been authorized as of January 30, 2000? What percentage of authorized shares have been issued as of January 30, 2000?

2. Review the Stockholders' Equity section. What is the par value of the company's common stock? What total amount has been paid for common stock in excess of par value as of January 30, 2000?

Connection 4 ▶ FINANCIAL **$**TATEMENT ANALYSIS   **Balance Sheet** The excerpt on page 763 was taken from the Conoco Inc. *1999 Annual Report.* Use it to answer the following questions.

Analyze:

1. What percentage of Class A Common Stock authorized has been issued at December 31, 1999?

(in millions)	December 31	
	1999	*1998*
Stockholders' Equity (Note 20)		
Preferred Stock, $.01 par value		
250,000,000 shares authorized, none issued	--	--
Class A Common Stock, $.01 par value		
3,000,000,000 shares authorized,		
191,497,821 shares issued	2	2
Class B Common Stock, $.01 par value		
1,600,000,000 shares authorized,		
436,543,573 shares issued and outstanding	4	4

2. What journal entry was made on the books of Conoco when the company authorized 250,000,000 shares of preferred stock on December 31, 1999?

3. If all the common stock that Conoco authorized was issued at par, how much capital would be raised?

Analyze Online: Log on to the Conoco Web site at **www.conoco.com.** Locate the most recent annual report.

4. How many shares of Class A Common Stock and Class B Common Stock have been issued?

5. Have any shares of preferred stock been issued? If so, how many?

6. What is the current market price for a share of Conoco stock?

Extending the *Thought* **Selective Disclosure** Stock prices hinge on a variety of market factors, including corporate earnings, new product announcements, and revenue projections. Until October 2000, it was common practice for corporations to disclose information selectively to analysts before an announcement was made to the general public. A new SEC ruling prohibits the "selective disclosure" of important information. How do you think this ruling will impact the way or frequency in which a corporation communicates to the investment community? What types of investors stand to benefit from selective disclosure? How might the ruling affect the rate of increases or decreases in stock prices when, for example, poor earnings are reported by a corporation?

◄ **Connection 5**

Business Communication **Visual Presentation** As the controller for E-Wise Internet Solutions, Inc., a publicly traded corporation, you have been asked to prepare a presentation for the annual stockholders' meeting to be held on January 31, 2005. Provide visual charts for your audience using the following data:

◄ **Connection 6**

- Fiscal 2004 quarterly stock prices: at March 31: $53.00; at June 30: $54.67; at August 31: $66.33; at December 31: $52.00
- On August 20, 2004, the company announced plans to release a new plug-n-play e-commerce software bundle. An article appeared in *Fast Company* about the new release. Due to programming delays, the software release will not happen until the first quarter of 2005.

- Quarterly dividends were declared as follows.

2003		2004	
1st Q:	$0.06	1st Q:	$0.07
2nd Q:	$0.06	2nd Q:	$0.08
3rd Q:	$0.06	3rd Q:	$0.10
4th Q:	$0.06	4th Q:	$0.09

Connection 7 ▶

Team*Work* **Stock Trends** As a team, research the current stock prices for the four corporations listed below or select four companies of interest to you. The stock symbol for each company is found in parentheses next to the company name. Use the business section of your local newspaper or an Internet site such as Hoover's Online (**www.hoovers.com**) or Forbes (**www.forbes.com**) for current stock quotes. Keep a record of the stock prices every day for five consecutive business days. What trends do you notice for each stock? What news stories, if any, were released about these firms during the week? Did the stories impact stock prices? Prepare a report of your findings.

Target (TGT)	Boeing (BA)	Hewlett Packard (HWP)	Sara Lee (SLE)

Connection 8 ▶

inter **NET** **CONNECTION** **Employee Stock Ownership** The National Center for Employee Ownership, a nonprofit membership and research organization, provides information on employee stock ownership. Go to their Web site at **www.nceo.org,** and click *Library* to answer the following questions.

- What does "employee ownership" mean?
- Approximately how many U.S. companies share ownership with their employees?
- What does the acronym "ESOP" stand for?
- What advantage, if any, does the employer gain from an ESOP?

Answers to Self Reviews

Answers to Section 1 Self Review

1. The major advantages include limited liability, restricted agency, continuous existence, transferability of ownership rights, and the ease of raising capital.

2. Yes. A corporation is a separate entity with a continuous existence. It is not affected by the death, disability, or withdrawal of individual shareholders.

3. An S corporation is organized like any other corporation under state laws, while a limited liability partnership is organized as a partnership. The S corporation is taxed essentially in the same way as a partnership, but that is the only partnership attribute it has. The limited liability partnership enables partners to be exempt from liability due to malfeasance of other partners or of employees not under the individual's supervision, but essentially possesses the other partnership attributes.

4. d. its stockholders.

5. a. have no personal liability for the debts of the corporation.

6. This has no effect on shareholders' individual income tax returns since no dividends were paid.

Answers to Section 2 Self Review

1. Preferred stock can carry certain preferred claims on the corporation's profits or on its assets in case of liquidation, and it can carry other special preferences that set it apart from common stock. Preferred stockholders may also give up certain rights, such as the right to vote on certain corporate matters; common stock has voting rights.

2. Liquidation preference refers to the right to be paid a specified liquidation value after creditors have been paid but before any assets are distributed to common stockholders.

3. Preferred stock that can be converted at the option of the owner into common stock under specified conditions.

4. b. cumulative preferred stock.

5. c. callable.

6. None. All of the dividends will be payable to preferred stockholders.

Answers to Section 3 Self Review

1. A premium on stock arises when the cash or noncash assets received for the stock exceeds its par (or stated) value.

2. Par value is established in the corporate charter; to change the par value it is necessary to change the charter. Stated value can be established by the board of directors for no-par-value stock and can be changed by the board at any time. For accounting purposes, they are treated in the same manner.

3. The costs incurred in organizing the corporation such as charter fees, attorneys' fees, costs of the organization meeting, and expenses of promoters. When incurred these costs are recorded in an intangible asset account, **Organization Costs.** Subsequently they are then charged off as an expense over a period of time.

4. d. the subscription is paid in full.

5. b. stock transfer journal.

6. Debit **Cash** for $5,000, credit **Common Stock** for $400, credit **Paid-in Capital in Excess of Par Value** for $4,600.

Answers to Comprehensive Self Review

1. Shareholders generally are free to sell any stock they own at any time and need no consent of other shareholders. Partners must obtain the consent of other partners to transfer an ownership interest.

2. As additions to the class of stock issued in the Stockholders' Equity section of the balance sheet.

3. The price per share at which the stock is bought and sold.

4. It contains the names of shareholders surrendering and receiving shares, the number of shares being surrendered and received, and the certificate number.

5. It contains a separate record for each shareholder, showing the number of shares of stock issued, the name and address of the stockholder, and information about transactions affecting the stockholder's shares.

CHAPTER 21

Learning Objectives

1. Estimate the federal corporate income tax and prepare related journal entries.

2. Compute and record amortization of organization costs.

3. Complete a worksheet for a corporation.

4. Record corporate adjusting and closing entries.

5. Prepare an income statement for a corporation.

6. Record the declaration and payment of cash dividends.

7. Record the declaration and issuance of stock dividends.

8. Record stock splits.

9. Record appropriations of retained earnings.

10. Record a corporation's receipt of donated assets.

11. Record treasury stock transactions.

12. Prepare financial statements for a corporation.

13. Define the accounting terms new to this chapter.

Corporate Earnings and Capital Transactions

![McDonald's](McDonald's logo)

www.mcdonalds.com

Each day McDonald's serves more than 43 million people in 119 countries around the world. McDonald's not only serves up favorites like Big Mac® sandwiches and fries, but also delivers steadily increasing returns to hungry stockholders. Over the past 10 years, common stockholders have seen earnings increase from $0.49 to $1.44 per share. From 1989 to 1999, dividends have steadily risen from $0.08 to $0.20 per share.

McDonald's went public in 1965, offering common stock at $22.50 per share. An investment of $2,250 then would now be worth over $2.8 million.

Thinking Critically

What financial and nonfinancial factors would you consider in deciding whether to purchase stock of a company that is going public?

For more information on McDonald's, go to: collegeaccounting.glencoe.com.

New Terms

Appropriation of retained earnings

Book value (stock)

Common Stock Dividend Distributable account

Declaration date

Deferred income taxes

Donated capital

Extraordinary, nonrecurring items

Paid-in capital

Payment date

Record date

Retained earnings

Statement of retained earnings

Statement of stockholders' equity

Stock dividend

Stock split

Stockholders of record

Treasury stock

Section Objectives

1 Estimate the federal corporate income tax and prepare related journal entries.

WHY IT'S IMPORTANT
Corporations are required to pay federal, state, and local income taxes.

2 Compute and record amortization of organization costs.

WHY IT'S IMPORTANT
Amortizing organization costs helps minimize their impact on operating income.

3 Complete a worksheet for a corporation.

WHY IT'S IMPORTANT
The worksheet is a tool used to prepare financial statements.

4 Record corporate adjusting and closing entries.

WHY IT'S IMPORTANT
Adjusting and closing entries ensure that revenues are matched with expenses and prepare temporary accounts for the next period.

5 Prepare an income statement for a corporation.

WHY IT'S IMPORTANT
Corporations must report accurate financial results.

Terms to Learn

deferred income taxes
extraordinary, nonrecurring items

Accounting for Corporate Earnings

Chapter 21 will continue Chapter 20's focus on transactions that are unique to the corporate form. We will look at transactions that affect the statement of retained earnings and the Stockholders' Equity section of the balance sheet.

Corporate Income Tax

One of the disadvantages of the corporate form of business is that corporations must pay income taxes on their profits. Taxable income can be calculated differently for federal, state, and local purposes; however, the procedures to record these taxes are identical. For the sake of simplicity, we will cover federal taxes only.

Federal Income Tax Rates

Periodically Congress changes corporate income tax rates. As of this writing, the current federal rates are as follows:

Taxable Income	Tax Rate
First $50,000	15 percent
Next $25,000	25 percent
Next $25,000	34 percent
Next $235,000	39 percent
Over $335,000*	

*See Internal Revenue Service publications for taxable incomes of more than $335,000.

Quarterly Tax Estimates

Corporations estimate their income taxes for the year and make estimated tax payments four times during the year. To avoid a penalty, the tax deposits at the end of the year must be equal to or higher than the tax liability for the year. For calendar year corporations, the estimated tax payments are due on April 15, June 15, September 15, and December 15. To record an estimated tax payment, debit **Income Tax Expense** and credit **Cash.**

County Shoe Corporation estimated its tax liability for 2004 to be $33,536. During the year it made four tax deposits of $8,384 ($33,536 ÷ 4). The journal entry to record the first deposit (April 15) is as follows.

1	2004					1
2	Apr.	15	Income Tax Expense	8 3 8 4 00		2
3			Cash		8 3 8 4 00	3
4			Quarterly income tax deposit			4

At the end of the year, the **Income Tax Expense** account has a balance of $33,536.

Year-End Adjustment of Tax Liability

At the end of the year, the tentative tax expense for the year is computed. Usually there is a difference between the tentative tax expense and the tax deposits made during the year. An adjustment is recorded to reconcile the difference.

At the end of 2004, County Shoe Corporation computed its tentative tax expense as $34,180. The corporation had underpaid its taxes by $644.

Tax liability for the year	$34,180
Quarterly payments	33,536
Additional tax due	$ 644

The amount owed is recorded in the **Income Tax Payable** account.

	2004		Adjusting Entries			1
10	Dec.	31	Income Tax Expense	6 4 4 00		10
11			Income Tax Payable		6 4 4 00	11
12			Estimate of additional tax due			12

Now suppose that County Shoe Corporation computed its tentative tax expense as $32,136. In this case the corporation would have overpaid its taxes by $1,400.

Tax liability for the year	$32,136
Quarterly payments	33,536
Overpaid tax	$(1,400)

The overpayment would be recorded in a receivable account as follows.

	2004		Adjusting Entries			1
10	Dec.	31	Income Tax Refund Receivable	1 4 0 0 00		10
11			Income Tax Expense		1 4 0 0 00	11
12			Estimate of tax overpayment			12

Note that the adjustment is made at the time the worksheet is completed and the financial statements are prepared. Because the tax return is complex and differences exist between *taxable income* and *financial income*, this computation can also be described as an estimate. The tentative tax expense computed at the end of the year usually differs from the actual tax expense shown on the tax return. The difference is recorded in the **Income Tax Expense** account.

Suppose that Sanaray Corporation made quarterly tax deposits totaling $32,000 in 2004. When the worksheet was prepared, tentative tax expense was computed at $33,600. The following adjustment was made.

	2004		Adjusting Entries			1
2	Dec.	31	Income Tax Expense	1 6 0 0 00		2
3			Income Tax Payable		1 6 0 0 00	3
4			Estimate of additional tax due			4

When the tax return was prepared, the actual tax for the year was $33,200. Sanaray Corporation sent a check for $1,200 to the Internal

Subchapter S Corporations
Subchapter S corporations do not pay taxes on corporate profits. Instead, corporate income is taxed on the shareholders' individual tax returns.

Revenue Service for the difference between the tax for the year and the tax deposits ($33,200 − $32,000). The entry is recorded as follows.

	2005						1
1	2005						1
2	Mar.	15	Income Tax Payable	1 6 0 0 00			2
3			Cash		1 2 0 0 00		3
4			Income Tax Expense		4 0 0 00		4
5			Pay balance of federal income tax				5

This entry reduces to zero the **Income Tax Payable** account. It records the check sent to the Internal Revenue Service and credits **Income Tax Expense.** Notice that the difference between the tentative tax expense and the actual tax expense, $400, is recorded in the year following the tax year. This violates the matching principle. It does not match income tax expense to taxable income. However, these differences are usually minor and do not result in a material misstatement of income.

Reporting Income Tax Expense on the Income Statement

There are two ways to show income tax expense on the income statement:

1. As a deduction at the bottom of the income statement, after Net Income Before Income Tax. To see this presentation, refer to Figure 21-3 on page 776.

2. As an operating expense, to emphasize that taxes represent a cost of doing business.

> Caterpillar Inc. treats income tax expense as a deduction from "Consolidated profit before taxes." For the year ended December 31, 1999, the company reported income tax expense, called "Provision for income taxes," of $455 million. The income tax was 32 percent of profit before taxes and consisted of U.S. federal tax, non-U.S. tax, and state tax.

Deferred Income Taxes

Usually net income reported on the financial statements does not match taxable income reported on the tax return because tax laws do not always follow generally accepted accounting principles.

- Income can be included in taxable income this year and appear on the financial statements in later years, or vice versa.
- Income can be included on the financial statements but never appear in taxable income.
- Expenses can be included in taxable income this year and appear on the financial statements in later years, or vice versa.
- Expenses can be included on the financial statements and never be deducted from taxable income.

Accountants use the concept of deferred income taxes to match income tax on the financial statements to the related net income.

Deferred income taxes represent the amount of taxes that will be payable in the future as a result of the difference between taxable income and income for financial statement purposes in the current and past years. Let's use depreciation to illustrate the concept.

Suppose that this year tax depreciation (MACRS) is higher than depreciation on the financial statements (straight-line). In the future, then, tax depreciation should be less than depreciation on the financial statements. As a result, in the future, when taxable income is higher because depreciation is lower, the company will owe more taxes. Those future taxes really apply to the income reported on the financial statement in prior years.

Each year the accountant estimates the amount of future taxes that will be paid as a result of the MACRS depreciation taken in this and prior years. An adjustment for the future taxes is made to **Tax Expense** and to the liability account, **Deferred Income Tax Liability.**

Sometimes the cumulative taxable income is higher than that reported on the financial statements. This gives rise to a *deferred tax asset* because some of the taxes that have been paid apply to future financial statement income. Deferred taxes are complex and are not covered in this text. This book assumes that income on the income statement and on the tax return are the same. Therefore, the deferred tax adjustment is not necessary.

Amortization of Organization Costs

② Objective
Compute and record amortization of organization costs.

In Chapter 20 you learned that organization costs include attorneys' fees, expenses of the organizers, and the charter fee. For financial statement purposes, organization costs can be amortized over a period of up to 40 years. For tax purposes, organization costs are amortized over a period of not less than 60 months.

County Shoe Corporation incurred organization costs of $2,000. The costs were recorded in **Organization Costs,** an intangible asset account. The costs are amortized over a 60-month period. As part of the adjustment process, $400 (12/60 × $2,000) was charged to **Amortization of Organization Costs,** an expense account. The amortization of intangibles is credited directly to the intangible asset account, not to an accumulated amortization account. For an example, refer to Figure 21-1 on page 772. In the Trial Balance section of the worksheet, **Organization Costs** of $1,600 reflect the original cost of $2,000 less the amortization of $400 taken at the end of the previous year.

Amortization of organization costs appears on the income statement as part of operating expenses or in the Other Expenses section. Organization costs appear on the balance sheet in the Intangible Assets section.

Completing the Corporate Worksheet

③ Objective
Complete a worksheet for a corporation.

The worksheet for a corporation and a sole proprietorship are almost identical. The major difference is the income tax adjustment. Figure 21-1 shows the worksheet for County Shoe Corporation for 2004. This worksheet omits the Adjusted Trial Balance columns. It is common for the experienced accountant to enter the adjusted amounts directly in the Income Statement and Balance Sheet sections. However, when the Adjusted Trial Balance section is omitted, errors in adding and subtracting adjustments are more difficult to detect.

Study the worksheet carefully as you follow the steps to complete the worksheet for County Shoe Corporation.

	ACCOUNT NAME	TRIAL BALANCE DEBIT	TRIAL BALANCE CREDIT	ADJUSTMENTS DEBIT	ADJUSTMENTS CREDIT
1	Cash	19 9 5 0 00			
2	Accounts Receivable	172 0 0 0 00			
3	Allowance for Doubtful Accounts		3 6 0 00		(c) 8 8 0 00
4	Merchandise Inventory	200 0 0 0 00		(b)262 0 0 0 00	(a)200 0 0 0 00
5	Prepaid Insurance	5 6 0 0 00			(d) 2 8 0 0 00
6	Land	60 0 0 0 00			
7	Buildings	72 0 0 0 00			
8	Accumulated Depreciation—Buildings		2 4 0 0 00		(e) 2 4 0 0 00
9	Equipment and Fixtures	72 0 0 0 00			
10	Accumulated Depreciation—Equip. and Fixtures		4 0 0 0 00		(f) 4 0 0 0 00
11	Organization Costs	1 6 0 0 00			(h) 4 0 0 00
12	Accounts Payable		69 1 3 6 00		
13	Dividends Payable—Preferred		21 6 0 0 00		
14	Dividends Payable—Common		16 0 0 0 00		
15	Accrued Expenses Payable				(g) 8 2 0 0 00
16	Income Tax Payable				(i) 6 4 4 00
17	Preferred Stock—12%, $100 Par		180 0 0 0 00		
18	Paid-in Cap. in Excess of Par—Preferred		12 0 0 0 00		
19	Common Stock, $50 Par		200 0 0 0 00		
20	Paid-in Cap. in Excess of Par—Common		1 6 0 0 00		
21	Retained Earnings		34 4 0 0 00		
22	Sales		1,840 0 0 0 00		
23	Purchases	1,256 0 0 0 00			
24	Selling Expenses (control)	314 6 0 0 00		(c) 8 8 0 00	
25				(d) 2 0 0 00	
26				(e) 2 0 0 00	
27				(f) 3 0 0 00	
28	General and Admin. Expenses (control)	174 2 1 0 00		(d) 8 0 0 00	
29				(e) 4 0 0 00	
30				(f) 1 0 0 0 00	
31				(g) 8 2 0 0 00	
32	Amortization of Organization Costs			(h) 4 0 0 00	
33	Income Tax Expense	33 5 3 6 00		(i) 6 4 4 00	
34	Income Summary			(a)200 0 0 0 00	(b)262 0 0 0 00
35		2,381 4 9 6 00	2,381 4 9 6 00	489 2 4 4 00	489 2 4 4 00
36	Net Income After Income Tax				
37					
38					
39					

▲ **FIGURE 21-1**
A Completed, Eight-Column
Worksheet

INCOME STATEMENT		BALANCE SHEET		
DEBIT	CREDIT	DEBIT	CREDIT	
		19 9 5 0 00		1
		172 0 0 0 00		2
			9 1 6 0 00	3
		262 0 0 0 00		4
		2 8 0 0 00		5
		60 0 0 0 00		6
		72 0 0 0 00		7
			4 8 0 0 00	8
		72 0 0 0 00		9
			8 0 0 0 00	10
		1 2 0 0 00		11
			69 1 3 6 00	12
			21 6 0 0 00	13
			16 0 0 0 00	14
			8 2 0 0 00	15
			6 4 4 00	16
			180 0 0 0 00	17
			12 0 0 0 00	18
			200 0 0 0 00	19
			1 6 0 0 00	20
			34 4 0 0 00	21
	1,840 0 0 0 00			22
1,256 0 0 0 00				23
				24
				25
				26
330 4 0 0 00				27
				28
				29
				30
184 6 1 0 00				31
4 0 0 00				32
34 1 8 0 00				33
200 0 0 0 00	262 0 0 0 00			34
2,005 5 9 0 00	2,102 0 0 0 00	661 9 5 0 00	565 5 4 0 00	35
96 4 1 0 00			96 4 1 0 00	36
2,102 0 0 0 00	2,102 0 0 0 00	661 9 5 0 00	661 9 5 0 00	37
				38
				39

Step 1. *Enter the trial balance in the Trial Balance section.* To simplify the example, control accounts for general expenses and selling expenses are used instead of individual expense accounts. There are a few unfamiliar accounts on the worksheet; they will be explained later.

Step 2. *Enter the adjustments (except the adjustment to income tax expense) in the Adjustments section of the worksheet.*

Step 3. *Extend the balances of all income and expense amounts (except income tax expense) to the Income Statement section of the worksheet.* Total the Debit and Credit columns of the Income Statement section. Write the totals on a separate paper. The difference between the totals represents the income or loss before income taxes. At this point, the Income Statement columns of the worksheet contain the following information.

	Income Statement	
	Debit	Credit
Sales		1,840,000
Purchases	1,256,000	
Selling Expenses	330,400	
General and Administrative Expenses	184,610	
Amortization of Organization Costs	400	
Income Summary	200,000	262,000
Totals	1,971,410	2,102,000

Worksheet
Asset, liability, and equity accounts are extended to the Balance Sheet columns. Revenue and expense accounts are extended to the Income Statement columns.

The difference between the Credit and Debit column totals is $130,590 ($2,102,000 − $1,971,410). This is income before income tax.

Step 4. *Compute income tax based on income before tax.* Assume there is no difference between financial and taxable income.

First $50,000 × 15%	$ 7,500
Next $25,000 × 25%	6,250
Next $25,000 × 34%	8,500
Last $30,590 × 39% (rounded)	11,930
Total tax on $130,590	$34,180

County Shoe Corporation made tax deposits of $33,536. The difference between the tax deposits and the total tax is $644 ($34,180 − $33,536). An adjustment is made to debit **Income Tax Expense** for $644 and to credit **Income Tax Payable** for $644.

Step 5. *Total the columns in the Adjustments section.* Extend the balance of **Income Tax Expense** to the Debit column of the Income Statement section of the worksheet.

Step 6. *Total the Debit and Credit columns of the Income Statement section.* The difference between the totals is net income after tax.

Step 7. *Extend the adjusted balances of the asset, liability, and stockholders' equity accounts to the Balance Sheet columns.* Enter net income after income tax to the Credit column of the Balance Sheet section. Complete the worksheet in the usual manner.

④ Objective
Record corporate adjusting and closing entries.

Adjusting and Closing Entries

The closing process for a corporation is similar to that of a sole proprietorship. First close revenue to **Income Summary.** Then close expenses to **Income Summary.** Finally close **Income Summary** (net income or net loss) to **Retained Earnings.** The **Retained Earnings** account accumulates the profits and losses of the business.

Figure 21-2 shows the adjusting and closing entries for County Shoe Corporation. Compare the journal entries to the worksheet to see how the journal entries are prepared.

> Corporate tax planning strategies can reduce the effective income tax paid on earnings. J.C. Penney Company, Inc., reported a decline in its income tax rate from 1997 to 1999. In 1999 the company's effective tax rate was 34.3 percent, down from 38.8 percent in 1997.

◀ **FIGURE 21-2**
Adjusting and Closing Entries

GENERAL JOURNAL　　　　　　　　　　　　　　　　PAGE ___38___

	DATE		DESCRIPTION	POST. REF.	DEBIT	CREDIT	
1	2004						1
2			*Adjusting Entries*				2
3			*(Entry a)*				3
4	Dec.	31	Income Summary		200 000 00		4
5			Merchandise Inventory			200 000 00	5
6							6
7			*(Entry b)*				7
8		31	Merchandise Inventory		262 000 00		8
9			Income Summary			262 000 00	9
10							10
11			*(Entry c)*				11
12		31	Selling Expense (control)		8 800 00		12
13			Allowance for Doubtful Accounts			8 800 00	13
14							14
15			*(Entry d)*				15
16		31	Selling Expenses (control)		2 000 00		16
17			General and Admin. Expenses (control)		800 00		17
18			Prepaid Insurance			2 800 00	18
19							19
20			*(Entry e)*				20
21		31	Selling Expenses (control)		2 000 00		21
22			General and Admin. Expenses (control)		400 00		22
23			Accumulated Depreciation—Buildings			2 400 00	23
24							24
25			*(Entry f)*				25
26		31	Selling Expenses (control)		3 000 00		26
27			General and Admin. Expenses (control)		1 000 00		27
28			Accum. Depr.—Equip. and Fixtures			4 000 00	28
29							29
30			*(Entry g)*				30
31		31	General and Admin. Expenses (control)		8 200 00		31
32			Accrued Expenses Payable			8 200 00	32
33							33
34			*(Entry h)*				34
35		31	Amortization of Organization Costs		400 00		35
36			Organization Costs			400 00	36
37							37
38			*(Entry i)*				38
39		31	Income Tax Expense		644 00		39
40			Income Tax Payable			644 00	40
41							41

FIGURE 21-2 (continued) ▶
Adjusting and Closing Entries

GENERAL JOURNAL PAGE ___39___

	DATE		DESCRIPTION	POST. REF.	DEBIT	CREDIT	
1	2004						1
2			*Closing Entries*				2
3	Dec.	31	Sales		1,840 0 0 0 00		3
4			Income Summary			1,840 0 0 0 00	4
5							5
6		31	Income Summary		1,805 5 9 0 00		6
7			Purchases			1,256 0 0 0 00	7
8			Selling Expenses (control)			330 4 0 0 00	8
9			Gen. and Admin. Expenses (control)			184 6 1 0 00	9
10			Amortization of Organization Costs			4 0 0 00	10
11			Income Tax Expense			34 1 8 0 00	11
12							12
13		31	Income Summary		96 4 1 0 00		13
14			Retained Earnings			96 4 1 0 00	14
15			Close Income Summary				15

The Corporate Income Statement

After the worksheet is complete, the financial statements are prepared. The income statement of a sole proprietorship and a corporation are similar. The major difference is income taxes. The corporate income statement contains a deduction for income tax expense.

Figure 21-3 shows the income statement for County Shoe Corporation for 2004. It is prepared from the information on the worksheet in Figure 21-1. Note that income tax expense is deducted from the Net Income Before Income Tax line to arrive at net income after income tax.

FIGURE 21-3 ▶
Corporate Income Statement

County Shoe Corporation
Income Statement
Year Ended December 31, 2004

Sales		1,840 0 0 0 00
Cost of Goods Sold		
Inventory, January 1, 2004	200 0 0 0 00	
Purchases	1,256 0 0 0 00	
Goods Available for Sale	1,456 0 0 0 00	
Less Inventory, December 31, 2004	262 0 0 0 00	
Costs of Goods Sold		1,194 0 0 0 00
Gross Profit on Sales		646 0 0 0 00
Expenses		
Selling Expenses	330 4 0 0 00	
General and Administrative Expenses	184 6 1 0 00	
Amortization of Organization Costs	4 0 0 00	515 4 1 0 00
Net Income Before Income Tax		130 5 9 0 00
Income Tax Expense		34 1 8 0 00
Net Income After Income Tax		96 4 1 0 00

Variations in Income Statement Presentation

Corporations use a variety of formats for the income statement. Some common variations are summarized as follows.

- Some corporations include cost of goods sold with the operating expenses. They do not show gross profit on sales. This text uses the traditional income statement with a separate Gross Profit section.
- Some corporations show income tax expense as an operating expense rather than as a deduction from net income before income tax. This presentation can be used to emphasize that income taxes are a cost of doing business like any other expense.
- If a gain or loss results from a transaction that is highly unusual, is clearly unrelated to routine operations, and is not expected to occur again in the near future, the gain or loss is shown in a separate section called **Extraordinary, Nonrecurring Items**.

Extraordinary items include gains or losses from fires, floods, other casualties, and retirement of bonds payable (discussed in Chapter 22).

◀ **FIGURE 21-4**
Income Statement Showing
Extraordinary Items

Thames Corporation
Partial Income Statement
Year Ended December 31, 2004

Income from Operations			
Before Income Taxes			556 4 4 0 00
Income Taxes Applicable to Operating Income			183 5 1 2 00
Net Income from Operations, After			
Income Taxes			372 9 2 8 00
Extraordinary Gains and Losses			
Add Gain on Condemnation of Land by City	20 0 0 0 00		
Less Federal Taxes on Gain	7 8 0 0 00	12 2 0 0 00	
Deduct Tornado Loss on Building	16 0 0 0 00		
Less Federal Tax Reduction	6 2 4 0 00	9 7 6 0 00	
Excess of Extraordinary Gains over Losses			2 4 4 0 00
Net Income for Year			375 3 6 8 00

Figure 21-4 shows an income statement containing extraordinary items. The tax effect of each extraordinary item is offset against each gain or loss to show the gain or loss "net of taxes."

Section 1 Self Review

Questions

1. What is the federal income tax on corporate taxable income of $280,000? (Use the tax rates in the chapter.)

2. Why is the adjustment for income tax expense entered after all the other adjustments?

3. What are deferred income taxes?

Exercises

4. The entry to record an income tax refund due to the corporation at the end of the period includes a

   a. debit to **Income Tax Refund Expense.**

   b. credit to **Income Tax Refund Expense.**

   c. debit to **Income Tax Refund Receivable.**

   d. debit to **Income Tax Payable.**

5. Organization costs are

   a. an intangible asset.

   b. an operating expense.

   c. an administrative expense.

   d. a contra asset.

Analysis

6. On the worksheet, column totals in the Income Statement section are debit, $187,000, and credit, $237,000. If the corporation paid estimated taxes of $7,000, what is the adjusting entry for income taxes?

(Answers to Section 1 Self Review are on page 809.)

Section Objectives

6 Record the declaration and payment of cash dividends.

WHY IT'S IMPORTANT
Corporate profits are distributed to stockholders through cash dividends.

7 Record the declaration and issuance of stock dividends.

WHY IT'S IMPORTANT
Corporations may declare and issue stock dividends to reward their shareholders.

8 Record stock splits.

WHY IT'S IMPORTANT
Corporations use stock splits to lower market share prices in an effort to attract new investors.

9 Record appropriations of retained earnings.

WHY IT'S IMPORTANT
One way to identify specific future transactions and related cash requirements is by appropriating retained earnings.

Terms to Learn

appropriation of retained earnings
book value (stock)
Common Stock Dividend Distributable account
declaration date
paid-in capital
payment date
record date
retained earnings
stock dividend
stock split
stockholders of record

Accounting for Retained Earnings

The fundamental accounting equation for corporations can be restated as Assets = Liabilities + (Paid-in Capital + Retained Earnings).

- **Paid-in capital** represents the amount of capital acquired from capital stock transactions.
- **Retained earnings** represents the cumulative profits and losses of the corporation not distributed as dividends. Dividends reduce retained earnings.

Retained Earnings

There are legal and financial distinctions between paid-in capital and retained earnings. This is why profits and losses are accumulated in retained earnings, separate from the capital paid in by the stockholders.

It is important to remember that retained earnings does not represent a cash fund. Retained earnings are reinvested in inventory, plant and equipment, and various other types of assets. A corporation can have a large cash balance but no retained earnings. Conversely, it can have a large balance in the **Retained Earnings** account but no cash.

Cash Dividends

Stockholders receive a share of the profits of the corporation through cash dividends. Most corporations pay dividends quarterly. In some corporations the board of directors establishes a policy of making regular cash dividends at the same or an increasing amount. A regular dividend policy tends to make a stock more attractive to investors and may help avoid sharp fluctuations in the stock's market price. Many corporations, however, retain their earnings to finance growth and do not pay cash dividends. This is especially true in the first several years of a corporation's existence.

Dividend Policy. Before declaring a dividend, the board of directors considers two issues: legality and financial feasibility.

1. *Legality.* State laws differ, but in general the corporation must have retained earnings in order to declare dividends. These laws are intended to protect the corporation's creditors. The restriction prevents an *impairment of capital*. Capital is impaired when dividends are paid that reduce total stockholders' equity to less than the paid-in capital accounts.

2. *Financial Feasibility.* The corporation must have the cash to pay the dividend. The board of directors does not declare dividends that lead to a cash shortage or other financial difficulties.

Dates Relevant to Dividends. Three dates are involved in declaring and paying dividends.

- The **declaration date** is the date on which the board of directors declares the dividend. The dividend declaration is recorded in the corporation's minute book. Once a dividend is declared, the firm has a liability to the stockholders for the amount of the declared dividend.
- The **record date** is the date used to determine who will receive the dividend. The capital stock ledger is used to prepare a list of the **stockholders of record**, that is, the stockholders who will receive the declared dividend.
- The **payment date** is the date on which the dividend is paid.

6 Objective

Record the declaration and payment of cash dividends.

Important!

Journal Entries for Dividends

A journal entry is recorded on the date of declaration and the date of payment. A journal entry is not made on the date of record.

Declaration of a Cash Dividend. County Shoe Corporation's board of directors met on December 1, 2004, and declared cash dividends of $12 per share on preferred stock and $4 per share on common stock. The dividends are payable on January 15 to stockholders of record on December 31. On the declaration date, the firm had outstanding 1,800 shares of preferred stock and 4,000 shares of common stock. The dividend declaration is recorded as shown below.

1	2004						1
2	Dec.	1	Retained Earnings	21 6 0 0 00			2
3			Dividends Payable—Preferred		21 6 0 0 00		3
4			Dividend declaration of $12				4
5			per share on 1,800 shares,				5
6			payable Jan. 15 to holders				6
7			of record Dec. 31				7
8							8
9		1	Retained Earnings	16 0 0 0 00			9
10			Dividends Payable—Common		16 0 0 0 00		10
11			Dividend declaration of $4				11
12			per share on 4,000 shares,				12
13			payable on Jan. 15 to				13
14			holders of record Dec. 31				14

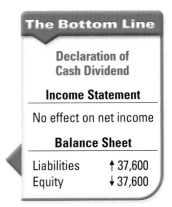

The Bottom Line

Declaration of Cash Dividend

Income Statement

No effect on net income

Balance Sheet

Liabilities	↑ 37,600
Equity	↓ 37,600

Dividends payable appears on the balance sheet as a current liability. An example is shown in the balance sheet presented later in this chapter (Figure 21-6, pages 788–789).

Payment of a Cash Dividend. The capital stock ledger is used to prepare a list of the stockholders and the number of shares owned on the record date. The list is used to determine the dividend due each shareholder. On January 15, 2005, the payment date, the dividend checks are issued to the stockholders on the list. The payment is recorded as follows.

1	2005						1
2	Jan.	15	Dividends Payable—Preferred	21 6 0 0 00			2
3			Dividends Payable—Common	16 0 0 0 00			3
4			Cash		37 6 0 0 00		4
5			Payment of cash dividends				5

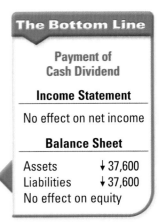

The Bottom Line

Payment of Cash Dividend

Income Statement

No effect on net income

Balance Sheet

Assets	↓ 37,600
Liabilities	↓ 37,600
No effect on equity	

Stock Dividends

A corporation may have retained earnings but be short of cash and unable to pay a cash dividend. Or the board of directors may want to transfer part of retained earnings to a paid-in capital account. In these cases the board of directors may declare a stock dividend. A **stock**

dividend is a distribution of the corporation's own stock on a pro rata basis that results in conversion of a portion of the firm's retained earnings to permanent capital.

On December 3, 2004, the board of directors of County Shoe Corporation declared a stock dividend payable the following January 20 to common stockholders of record on December 28. The stock dividend is for one new share of common stock for each 10 shares held. On the declaration date, there were 4,000 shares outstanding, so 400 (4,000 ÷ 10) additional shares will be issued.

When a stock dividend is declared, the total amount charged to the **Retained Earnings** account is the estimated market value of the shares to be issued. Assume that each share of County Shoe Corporation's stock is expected to have a market value of $52. A total of $20,800 (400 shares × $52 market value) is debited to **Retained Earnings.** The par value of the shares, $20,000 (400 shares × $50 par), is credited to **Common Stock Dividend Distributable**, an equity account used to record par or stated value of shares to be issued as the result of the declaration of a stock dividend. The excess of the market value over the par value, $800 ($20,800 − $20,000), is credited to **Paid-in Capital in Excess of Par Value—Common Stock** or to **Paid-in Capital from Common Stock Dividends.** Let's see how the declaration of a stock dividend is recorded.

<table>
<tr><td>1</td><td colspan="2">2004</td><td></td><td></td><td>1</td></tr>
<tr><td>2</td><td>Dec.</td><td>3 Retained Earnings</td><td>20 800 00</td><td></td><td>2</td></tr>
<tr><td>3</td><td></td><td>Common Stock Dividend Distributable</td><td></td><td>20 000 00</td><td>3</td></tr>
<tr><td>4</td><td></td><td>Paid-in Capital in Excess of Par</td><td></td><td></td><td>4</td></tr>
<tr><td>5</td><td></td><td>Value—Common Stock</td><td></td><td>800 00</td><td>5</td></tr>
<tr><td>6</td><td></td><td>Declaration of 10% stock dividend,</td><td></td><td></td><td>6</td></tr>
<tr><td>7</td><td></td><td>distributable on Jan. 20 to holders</td><td></td><td></td><td>7</td></tr>
<tr><td>8</td><td></td><td>of record on Dec. 28</td><td></td><td></td><td>8</td></tr>
</table>

The Bottom Line

Declaration of Stock Dividend

Income Statement

No effect on net income

Balance Sheet

No effect on equity

The **Common Stock Dividend Distributable** account appears on the balance sheet in the Stockholders' Equity section as a part of paid-in capital. One possible balance sheet presentation follows.

Common Stock ($50 par value, 10,000 shares authorized)	
Issued and outstanding, 4,000 shares	$200,000
Distributable as stock dividend, 400 shares	20,000
Paid-in Capital in Excess of Par	800
	$220,800

On December 28 a list is made of the stockholders' names, number of shares owned, and number of new shares to issue. For example, Samantha Wang owns 200 shares of common stock. She will receive 20 (200 ÷ 10) new shares as a stock dividend. On January 20 the 400 shares are distributed. This issuance of stock is recorded as follows.

<table>
<tr><td>1</td><td colspan="2">2005</td><td></td><td></td><td>1</td></tr>
<tr><td>2</td><td>Jan.</td><td>20 Common Stock Dividend Distributable</td><td>20 000 00</td><td></td><td>2</td></tr>
<tr><td>3</td><td></td><td>Common Stock</td><td></td><td>20 000 00</td><td>3</td></tr>
<tr><td>4</td><td></td><td>Distribution of stock dividend</td><td></td><td></td><td>4</td></tr>
</table>

Book value for each share of stock is the total equity applicable to the class of stock divided by the number of shares outstanding. The total book value is the same before and after a stock dividend, but each shareholder owns more shares of stock with a proportionately smaller book value per share.

Before the stock dividend, Wang owned 200 shares, or 5 percent (200 ÷ 4,000 shares), of the stock of the corporation. After the stock dividend, Wang still owned 5 percent (220 ÷ 4,400 shares) of the corporation's stock.

	Wang	Total
Shares before	200	4,000
Stock dividend	20	400
Shares after	220	4,400

In theory, a stock dividend should result in a proportionate reduction in each share's market value. Sometimes the market price declines less than it should in theory because a lower price per share can result in a wider market for the shares and because investors associate stock dividends with successful corporations. Thus after a stock dividend, the total market value of a stockholder's shares can increase slightly.

Stock Splits

A **stock split** occurs when a corporation issues two or more shares of new stock to replace each share outstanding without making any changes in the capital accounts. Stock splits are often declared when the stock is relatively difficult to sell because the market price is too high. If par-value stock is split, the corporation's charter is amended to reduce the par value.

Llano Corporation is authorized to issue 500,000 shares of no-par-value stock, with a stated value of $100 per share. There are 40,000 shares issued and outstanding. On December 1 the market price of the stock is $300 per share. The board of directors believes that if the price of the stock were lower, the shares would have a wider market. Accordingly, the board declared a 4-for-1 split and reduced the stated value to $25 ($100 ÷ 4) per share. Three new shares will be issued for each share outstanding. The shares will be issued on December 31 to holders of record on December 15. A stockholder who owned one share of stock with a stated value of $100 before the split will own four shares of stock with a stated value of $25 per share after the split. Stockholders realize no income from the stock split, and the corporation's capital balances are not affected.

Theoretically, the market price will decrease to one-fourth of the original market value, or to $75 per share ($300 × 1/4). If the price per share does not decrease to its theoretical level, the total market value of a stockholder's shares will be higher.

On the date of declaration of the stock split, a memorandum notation is made in the general journal of Llano Company.

Important!

Stock Dividends
A stock dividend does not change the total stockholders' equity, nor does it change the percentage of ownership of any stockholder.

8 Objective
Record stock splits.

Online Trading
A recent study by information technology analysts ICS Asia/Pacific concludes that by 2004, 40 percent of Asia's stock trades will be executed over the Internet.

1	2004					1
2	Dec.	1	On this date the board of directors declared a			2
3			4-for-1 stock split and reduced the stated value			3
4			of common stock from $100 to $25 per share.			4
5			Total outstanding shares will be 160,000			5

On December 31 a similar memorandum entry is made in the general journal to note issuance of the new shares.

An entry is made in the **Common Stock** account in the general ledger to indicate that the stated value is now $25 per share, and 160,000 shares are outstanding. The stockholders' records are changed to reflect the number of shares now held by each stockholder.

The Digital Language of Business: eXtensible Business Reporting Language (XBRL)

The presentation and timely exchange of financial reports is paramount to the global marketplace. Corporations face two major obstacles as they strive to deliver financial data. First, companies preparing electronic SEC filings, print statements, and Web html or pdf formats are faced with organizing and formatting the same data three or more times. Second, extracting data from a published financial statement is a manual process. Customized queries cannot be executed against an html document found on the Web or an electronic SEC filing.

In 1999 the accounting industry mobilized to find solutions to these problems. The AICPA, the Big Five accounting firms, and six information technology companies announced the development of a freely available XML-based specification to be used for digital preparation and exchange of financial reports and data.

This new digital language of business, called "eXtensible Business Reporting Language" (XBRL) is used to prepare and publish financial statements using one process, so that reports can be used on the Web, in print form, or as electronic filings for the SEC. The format will allow exchange, analysis, and reliable extraction of selected components of the statements.

The technology change will be nearly invisible to the preparer of financial statements. Accounting software vendors will place XBRL tags in their accounting systems.

Thinking Critically
What other types of financial data or reports might benefit from the use of XBRL? Explain.

Internet Application
Locate the XBRL Web site and click on the *Press Room* link to find the status of XBRL development. Select one news release and write a half-page summary of it.

Objective

9 Record appropriations of retained earnings.

Appropriations of Retained Earnings

Most corporations pay out only a portion of retained earnings as dividends. They restrict dividend payments in order to reinvest in plant assets or working capital. Sometimes dividends are restricted by contract, such as the requirements of a bond issue. A footnote to the financial statements can be used to indicate how management's plans or contractual obligations will affect (restrict) the dividends. A more formal way for the board of directors to show an intention to restrict dividends is to make an **appropriation of retained earnings** by resolution. Dividends cannot be declared from appropriated retained earnings.

County Shoe Corporation's directors foresee the need to build a $300,000 warehouse within the next five years. They want to notify the stockholders that the new storage facility will be built and that dividends will be restricted. A resolution is passed at a board meeting on November 5, 2005, to transfer $60,000 from **Retained Earnings** to a **Retained Earnings Appropriated for Warehouse Construction** account. The resolution is recorded in the minutes and the general journal entry is recorded. Similar appropriations and entries are made in each of the next four years.

The balance sheet presentation shows appropriated and unappropriated retained earnings. Assume that **Retained Earnings** had a balance of $132,742 before the first appropriation. The following is the balance sheet presentation immediately after the appropriation. Notice that total retained earnings stays the same, but it now has two parts.

Retained Earnings		
Appropriated		
Appropriated for Warehouse Construction		$ 60,000
Unappropriated		72,742
Total Retained Earnings		$132,742

1	2005					1
2	Nov.	5	Retained Earnings	60 000 00		2
3			Retained Earnings Appropriated for			3
4			Warehouse Construction		60 000 00	4
5			Appropriation made by board of			5
6			directors on Nov. 5			6

The Bottom Line

Appropriation of Retained Earnings

Income Statement

No effect on net income

Balance Sheet

No effect on equity

Remember that retained earnings does not represent cash, nor does appropriating retained earnings provide cash. The appropriation simply restricts the amount of retained earnings available for dividends, thus making it more likely that cash will be available to build the warehouse.

Assume that in six years cash was available and the warehouse construction project was completed at a cost of $342,000, which is $42,000 more than appropriated. The accounting records reflect an increase to **Building** of $342,000 and a decrease to **Cash** of $342,000. The balance of the **Retained Earnings Appropriated for Warehouse Construction** account has not been affected. When the purpose for which retained earnings was appropriated has been attained, the board can direct that the balance be transferred back to **Retained Earnings,** as follows.

1	2011					1
2	Aug.	7	Retained Earnings Appropriated for			2
3			Warehouse Construction	300 000 00		3
4			Retained Earnings		300 000 00	4

Section **Self Review**

Questions

1. Under what condition might a corporation declare a stock split?

2. Compare date of record and declaration date.

3. Does an appropriation of retained earnings include a transfer of cash to a restricted account? Explain.

Exercises

4. The balance of an appropriated retained earnings account is reduced

   a. as payments are made.

   b. as expenses are accrued.

   c. when the board declares the appropriation's purpose is completed.

   d. when the board passes a resolution to return the amount to unappropriated retained earnings.

5. Which of the following will decrease total stockholders' equity?

   a. stock split

   b. appropriation of retained earnings

   c. stock dividend

   d. cash dividend

Analysis

6. On November 21 the board of directors of Dade Corporation declared a 10 percent stock dividend payable the following January 15 to common stockholders of record on December 10. The market value is expected to be $35 per share. On the declaration date, there are 3,000 shares outstanding. The par value of the shares is $25. What amount is credited to the **Paid-in Capital in Excess of Par Value—Common Stock** account?

(Answers to Section 2 Self Review are on page 809.)   *Corporate Earnings and Capital Transactions*   **Chapter 21** • **783**

Section Objective

10 **Record a corporation's receipt of donated assets.**

WHY IT'S IMPORTANT
Corporations may receive donated property as an incentive to locate in a community.

11 **Record treasury stock transactions.**

WHY IT'S IMPORTANT
The impact of treasury stock purchases must be made clear to statement users.

12 **Prepare financial statements for a corporation.**

WHY IT'S IMPORTANT
Shareholders, analysts, and management use financial statements prepared by corporations.

Terms to Learn

donated capital
statement of retained earnings
statement of stockholders'
   equity
treasury stock

10 **Objective**

Record a corporation's receipt of donated assets.

Other Capital Transactions and Financial Statements

Many other transactions affect the stockholders' equity. Two types of transactions that occur often are donations of capital and purchase of treasury stock.

Other Capital Transactions

Transactions that affect stockholders' equity include the donation of assets to a corporation and a corporation's purchase of its own stock.

Donations of Capital

Property can be given to a corporation. This often occurs when a community that wishes to attract new industry gives a corporation land or a building for a plant site. **Donated capital** is capital resulting from the receipt of gifts by a corporation. An asset received as a gift is recorded in the accounting records at the asset's fair market value. The credit is to **Donated Capital,** a paid-in capital account. The following general journal entry indicates how a gift of a plant site valued at $100,000 is recorded.

1	2005				1
2	Jan.	2	Land	100 00 0 00	2
3			Donated Capital	100 00 0 00	3
4			Appraised value of plant site donated		4
5			by city		5

On the balance sheet, the **Donated Capital** account is shown as a new category under paid-in capital, following the preferred and common stock accounts.

Treasury Stock

Treasury stock is a corporation's own capital stock that has been issued and reacquired. To be considered treasury stock, the stock must have been previously paid for in full and issued to a stockholder. Any class or type of stock can be reacquired as treasury stock. No dividends, voting rights, or liquidation preferences apply to treasury stock.

Stockholders benefit when the corporation repurchases common stock because there are fewer shares of outstanding stock to share the profits and dividends. If preferred stock is reacquired, the dividends on the stock are no longer payable, thus increasing the dividends available to owners of common stock.

Corporations purchase their own stock for many reasons:

- The corporation has extra cash, and the board of directors thinks that the corporation's own stock is a better investment than other potential investments.
- The corporation wishes to transfer treasury stock to officers and key employees in connection with incentive plans. If unissued shares instead of treasury stock were used, it would be necessary to ask stockholders to give up their preemptive rights. However, preemptive rights do not apply to treasury stock.
- The corporation wants to create a demand for the stock and thus increase its market value.
- In privately held corporations with few owners, the board of directors can vote to purchase the shares of a stockholder who needs cash or wishes to retire.

In fiscal 2000 Wal-Mart Stores, Inc. repurchased more than 2 million shares of its common stock for $101 million. In fiscal 1999, Wal-Mart Stores, Inc. repurchased 21 million shares for $1,202 million.

Recording the Purchase of Treasury Stock. When treasury stock is purchased, the **Treasury Stock** account is debited for the entire amount paid. There is a separate treasury stock account for each class of stock. For example, in 2005 County Shoe Corporation repurchased 200 shares of $100 par preferred stock for $105 per share. The transaction is recorded as follows.

1	2005					1
7	Jan.	10	Treasury Stock—Preferred	21 0 0 0 00		7
8			Cash		21 0 0 0 00	8
9			Purchased 200 shares of treasury stock			9

Appropriation of Retained Earnings for Treasury Stock. The purchase of treasury stock reflects a payment to a shareholder and thus reduces capital. Stockholder withdrawals could be disguised as treasury stock purchases. In order to protect creditors, some states require that retained earnings be appropriated in an amount equal to the cost of treasury stock. If a corporation does not have retained earnings with a value higher than the purchase price, it cannot purchase treasury stock. If County Shoe Corporation is required to appropriate retained earnings equal to the cost of treasury stock, the following entry would be made.

1	2005					1
11	Jan.	10	Retained Earnings	21 0 0 0 00		11
12			Retained Earnings Appropriated—			12
13			Treasury Stock		21 0 0 0 00	13
14			To appropriate retained earnings equal			14
15			to purchase price of preferred treasury			15
16			stock			16

About
Accounting

Initial Public Offerings
An initial public offering (IPO) is a company's first sale of stock to the public.
   Not all companies are prepared for the rigorous scrutiny thrust upon public entities, according to a study conducted by Ernst & Young. Twenty-eight percent of executives surveyed would have made additional preparations for their IPOs.

Managerial

IMPLICATIONS

Capital Transactions

- In order to make prudent decisions, managers need to understand how net income is calculated.

- Managers need to develop a dividend policy that gives appropriate consideration to legal restrictions and to financial feasibility.

- Stock dividends offer management an opportunity to make distributions to shareholders while limiting the distribution of cash.

- Stock dividends provide a means for transforming a part of retained earnings into paid-in capital.

- Both stock dividends and stock splits reduce the price per share of the company's stock, which may make the stock more marketable.

- Prudent managers inform stockholders about restrictions on dividends by appropriating retained earnings.

- Treasury stock purchases can enhance the value of the stock held by other shareholders.

- Treasury stock can be used to offer stock incentives to officers and key employees and to obtain stock for employee stock-purchase plans.

Thinking Critically
What factors should be considered before a company declares a cash dividend?

On the balance sheet, treasury stock is deducted from the sum of all items in the Stockholders' Equity section. To see how treasury stock and retained earnings appropriated for treasury stock appear on the balance sheet, refer to Figure 21-6 on pages 788–789.

⑫ Objective

Prepare financial statements for a corporation.

Financial Statements for a Corporation

Four financial statements are usually prepared for a corporation:

- income statement,
- statement of retained earnings,
- balance sheet,
- statement of cash flows.

Figure 21-3 on page 776 shows the income statement of County Shoe Corporation. Let's move ahead two years to 2006 and examine the statement of retained earnings and the balance sheet. These statements will reflect some of the transactions that you have studied in this chapter. The statement of cash flows is explained in Chapter 25.

The Statement of Retained Earnings

The **statement of retained earnings** shows all changes that have occurred in retained earnings during the period. The statement shows the beginning balance, the changes, and the ending balance for the unappropriated and appropriated **Retained Earnings** accounts. Because of the importance of retained earnings to the corporation and the stockholders, a statement of retained earnings should be presented as part of the financial statements.

Figure 21-5 shows the statement of retained earnings of County Shoe Corporation. The unappropriated retained earnings are

- increased by net income,
- decreased by dividends and appropriations.

County Shoe Corporation has two appropriation accounts—one for warehouse construction and another for treasury stock.

Some corporations combine the statement of retained earnings with the income statement. In the combined statement of income and retained earnings, the beginning balance of **Retained Earnings** is added to the net income after taxes for the period. All other amounts are shown in the same way they are shown on the separate statement of retained earnings.

▼ FIGURE 21-5
Statement of Retained Earnings

County Shoe Corporation
Statement of Retained Earnings
Year Ended December 31, 2006

Unappropriated Retained Earnings			
Balance, January 1, 2006	187 1 4 2 00		
Add: Net Income After Taxes for 2006	192 0 0 0 00	379 1 4 2 00	
Deductions			
Dividends on Preferred Stock	19 2 0 0 00		
Dividends on Common Stock	22 0 0 0 00		
Transfer to Appropriation for Warehouse Construction	60 0 0 0 00		
Transfer to Appropriation for Treasury Stock	21 0 0 0 00	122 2 0 0 00	
Total Unappropriated Retained Earnings, December 31, 2006			256 9 4 2 00
Appropriated Retained Earnings			
Appropriated for Warehouse Construction			
Balance, January 1, 2006	60 0 0 0 00		
Add Appropriation for the Year	60 0 0 0 00		
Balance, December 31, 2006		120 0 0 0 00	
Appropriated for Treasury Stock			
Balance, January 1, 2006	— 0 —		
Add Appropriation for the Year	21 0 0 0 00		
Balance, December 31, 2006		21 0 0 0 00	
Total Appropriated Retained Earnings, December 31, 2006			141 0 0 0 00
Total Retained Earnings, December 31, 2006			397 9 4 2 00

The Securities and Exchange Commission requires publicly held corporations to disclose the reasons for major changes in equity. Corporations find that the most convenient way to make the required disclosures is to prepare a **statement of stockholders' equity** (often referred to as an *analysis of changes in stockholders' equity*). It provides an analysis reconciling the beginning and ending balance of each of the stockholders' equity accounts. There is, however, no specified form for the statement, and various types of schedules are used.

The Corporate Balance Sheet

Figure 21-6 shows the balance sheet of County Shoe Corporation. Since the statement of retained earnings shows changes in each account, only the ending balances of each appropriated retained earnings account and of the unappropriated retained earnings account are shown on the balance sheet. Note that

- income tax payable and dividends payable appear in the Current Liabilities section,
- treasury stock is subtracted from the Stockholders' Equity section.

FIGURE 21-6 ▼
An End-of-Year Balance Sheet

County Shoe Corporation			
Balance Sheet			
December 31, 2006			

Assets			
Current Assets			
Cash		96 4 0 0 00	
Accounts Receivable	246 0 0 0 00		
Less Allowance for Doubtful Accounts	8 6 0 0 00	237 4 0 0 00	
Merchandise Inventory		418 7 4 2 00	
Prepaid Insurance		6 0 0 0 00	
Total Current Assets			758 5 4 2 00
Property, Plant, and Equipment			
Land		6 0 0 0 0 00	
Buildings	72 0 0 0 00		
Less Accumulated Depreciation—Buildings	12 0 0 0 00	60 0 0 0 00	
Equipment and Fixtures	72 0 0 0 00		
Less Accumulated Depreciation—Equipment and Fixtures	16 0 0 0 00	56 0 0 0 00	
Total Property, Plant, and Equipment			176 0 0 0 00
Intangible Assets			
Organization Costs			4 0 0 00
Total Assets			934 9 4 2 00
Liabilities and Stockholders' Equity			
Current Liabilities			
Accounts Payable		88 0 0 0 00	
Dividends Payable—Preferred		19 2 0 0 00	
Dividends Payable—Common		22 0 0 0 00	
Accrued Expenses Payable		9 6 0 0 00	
Income Tax Payable		2 4 0 0 00	
Total Current Liabilities			141 2 0 0 00

(continued)

Stockholders' Equity					
Paid-in Capital					
Preferred Stock (12%, $100 par value,10,000 shares authorized)					
Issued 1,800 shares (of which 200 shares are held as treasury stock)	180 000 00				
Paid-in Capital in Excess of Par Value—Preferred	13 600 00	193 600 00			
Common Stock ($50 par value, 20,000 shares authorized)					
Issued and Outstanding, 4,400 shares	220 000 00				
Paid-in Capital in Excess of Par Value—Common	3 200 00	223 200 00			
Total Paid-in Capital		416 800 00			
Retained Earnings					
Appropriated					
For Treasury Stock Purchase	21 000 00				
For Warehouse Construction	120 000 00				
Total Appropriated	141 000 00				
Unappropriated	256 942 00				
Total Retained Earnings		397 942 00			
		814 742 00			
Deduct Treasury Stock, Preferred (200 shares at cost)		21 000 00			
Total Stockholders' Equity				793 742 00	
Total Liabilities and Stockholders' Equity				934 942 00	

▲ FIGURE 21-6 (continued)
An End-of-Year Balance Sheet

Section 3   Self Review

Questions

1. What is donated capital?

2. Is treasury stock an asset of the corporation? Explain.

3. What accounts are affected when treasury stock is purchased above par value?

Exercises

4. Treasury stock is shown on the balance sheet as

  a. an asset.

  b. an addition to common stock in the Stockholders' Equity section.

  c. a deduction from the sum of all other items in the Stockholders' Equity section.

  d. an addition to preferred stock in the Stockholders' Equity section.

5. Which of the following would not be found on the statement of retained earnings?

  a. Dividends on preferred stock.

  b. Common stock.

  c. Appropriation for treasury stock.

  d. Appropriation for construction of an office building.

Analysis

6. The balance of the **Retained Earnings** account on December 1 is $250,000. During the month dividends of $10,000 on common stock and $20,000 on preferred stock were declared. Appropriations for the purchase of treasury stock for $30,000 were made. Net income after taxes is $92,000. What is the balance of unappropriated retained earnings on December 31?

(Answers to Section 3 Self Review are on page 809.)

Review

Chapter Summary

A corporation has two major classifications of corporate capital: paid-in capital from capital stock transactions and retained earnings from its profits and losses. In this chapter you learned to account for corporate income taxes and organization costs and to record capital transactions affecting total stockholders' equity: dividends, stock splits, appropriation of retained earnings, and treasury stock.

Learning Objectives

1 **Estimate the federal corporate income tax and prepare related journal entries.**
Debit **Income Tax Expense,** and credit **Cash.** Amounts owed or overpaid are recorded as adjustments.

2 **Compute and record amortization of organization costs.**
Organization costs are amortized over a predetermined period. The IRS allows 60 months. **Amortization of Organizational Costs** is an expense account.

3 **Complete a worksheet for a corporation.**
Enter the trial balance in the Trial Balance section and the adjustments, except income tax expense, in the Adjustments section. Extend balances of all income and expense amounts except income tax expense to the Income Statement section; total its Debit and Credit columns. The difference is the income or loss before income taxes; compute income tax based on it. After entering the income tax adjustment, total the columns in the Adjustments section. Extend Income Tax Expense to the Debit column of the Income Statement section. Total the Debit and Credit columns of the Income Statement section; the difference is net income after tax. Extend the adjusted balances of the asset, liability, and stockholders' equity accounts to the Balance Sheet columns. Enter net income after income tax to the Credit column of the Balance Sheet section. Complete the worksheet in the usual manner.

4 **Record corporate adjusting and closing entries.**
Close revenues and expenses to the **Income Summary** account; close **Income Summary** to **Retained Earnings.**

5 **Prepare an income statement for a corporation.**
The corporation income statement is similar to that of a sole proprietorship, except for the inclusion of an income tax expense deduction. Extraordinary or nonrecurring items are shown in a separate section.

6 **Record the declaration and payment of cash dividends.**
Recording cash dividends involves the following: on the declaration date, debit **Retained Earnings** and credit **Dividends Payable.** No journal entry is made on the record date. On the payment date, record the outgoing cash and the reduction of the **Dividends Payable** liability established on the declaration date.

7 **Record the declaration and issuance of stock dividends.**
Issuance of stock dividends above par value price involves a debit to **Retained Earnings,** a credit to **Common Stock Dividend Distributable,** and a credit to **Paid-in Capital in Excess of Par Value.** Upon distribution **Common Stock Dividend Distributable** is debited, and **Common Stock** is credited.

8 **Record stock splits.**
A memorandum entry records it on the date of declaration, and another is made on the date of issuance.

9 **Record appropriations of retained earnings.**
Debit **Retained Earnings;** credit the **Appropriated Retained Earnings** account for the appropriation amount.

10 **Record a corporation's receipt of donated assets.**
Property given to a corporation is recorded at fair market value and is credited to **Donated Capital.**

11 **Record treasury stock transactions.**
Treasury stock purchase is recorded as a debit to **Treasury Stock** and a credit to **Cash.**

12 **Prepare financial statements for a corporation.**
The major corporation financial statements are the income statement, statement of retained earnings, balance sheet, and the statement of cash flows.

13 **Define the accounting terms new to this chapter.**

CHAPTER 21 GLOSSARY

Appropriation of retained earnings (p. 782) A formal declaration of an intention to restrict dividends

Book value (p. 780) The total equity applicable to a class of stock divided by the number of shares outstanding

Common Stock Dividend Distributable account (p. 780) Equity account used to record par, or stated, value of shares to be issued as the result of the declaration of a stock dividend

Declaration date (p. 779) The date on which the board of directors declares a dividend

Deferred income taxes (p. 770) The amount of taxes that will be payable in the future as a result of the difference between taxable income and income for financial statement purposes in the current year and in past years

Donated capital (p. 784) Capital resulting from the receipt of gifts by a corporation

Extraordinary, nonrecurring items (p. 777) Transactions that are highly unusual, clearly unrelated to routine operations, and that do not frequently occur

Paid-in capital (p. 778) Capital acquired from capital stock transactions

Payment date (p. 779) The date that dividends are paid

Record date (p. 779) The date on which the specific stockholders to receive a dividend are determined

Retained earnings (p. 778) The cumulative profits and losses of the corporation not distributed as dividends

Statement of retained earnings (p. 786) A financial statement that shows all changes that have occurred in retained earnings during the period

Statement of stockholders' equity (p. 788) A financial statement that provides an analysis reconciling the beginning and ending balance of each of the stockholders' equity accounts

Stock dividend (p. 779) Distribution of the corporation's own stock on a pro rata basis that results in conversion of a portion of the firm's retained earnings to permanent capital

Stock split (p. 781) When a corporation issues two or more shares of new stock to replace each share outstanding without making any changes in the capital accounts

Stockholders of record (p. 779) Stockholders in whose name shares are held on date of record and who will receive a declared dividend

Treasury stock (p. 784) A corporation's own capital stock that has been issued and reacquired; the stock must have been previously paid in full and issued to a stockholder

Comprehensive Self Review

1. Explain the two major classifications of stockholders' equity.

2. What are extraordinary gains and losses?

3. Does an appropriation of retained earnings represent a cash fund? Explain.

4. What is the relationship between the statement of retained earnings of a corporation and the corporation's balance sheet?

5. What effect does a stock dividend have on an individual shareholder's share of ownership in a corporation? What effect does it have on the market value of the shares owned by that shareholder?

(Answers to Comprehensive Self Review are on page 809.)

Discussion Questions

1. At the end of the year, what entries are necessary if the quarterly tax deposits are more than the income tax as computed at the time the worksheet is completed and the financial statements prepared?

2. Explain the three dates related to declaration and payment of a cash dividend. On which of these dates must journal entries be made?

3. Compare the effects on stockholders' equity of a cash dividend and a stock dividend.

4. When a stock dividend is declared, what journal entry is made? How is the amount of the dividend measured?

5. How is the **Common Stock Dividend Distributable** account classified on the balance sheet?

6. What effect does a stock split have on retained earnings? Explain.

7. What effect does an appropriation have on total retained earnings?

8. Several years ago a corporation made an appropriation of retained earnings because of a building project. The building project was completed in the current year. What accounting entry will probably be made with respect to the appropriation?

9. As an inducement for Conrad Corporation to locate in Centerville, the local Industrial Development Fund gave the corporation a tract of land with a fair market value of $250,000. How should the gift be accounted for?

10. At what amount is treasury stock shown on the balance sheet? How is it classified on the balance sheet?

11. What information is shown on the statement of retained earnings?

12. What is the purpose of the statement of stockholders' equity?

13. What is the major difference between the balance sheet of a partnership and that of a corporation?

14. How is income tax expense classified in the corporation's income statement?

Applications

EXERCISES

Estimating corporation income tax.

After all revenue and expense accounts, other than **Income Tax Expense,** have been extended to the Income Statement section of the worksheet of Atkins Corporation, the net income is determined to be $374,000. Using the tax rates given in this chapter, compute the corporation's federal income taxes payable. (Assume that the firm's taxable income is the same as its income for financial accounting purposes.)

◄ **Exercise 21-1**
Objective 1

Recording journal entries related to taxes.

A corporation has paid estimated income taxes of $44,000 during the year 20--. At the end of the year, the corporation's tax bill is computed to be $39,600. Give the general journal entry to adjust the **Income Tax Expense** account.

◄ **Exercise 21-2**
Objective 1

Amortizing organization costs.

Akim Corporation was formed and began business in June 20--. Organization costs of $6,000 were incurred in forming the corporation. The board of directors wishes to amortize the costs over the same period as used on the federal income tax return. Give the journal entry on December 31, 20--, to record amortization for the year.

◄ **Exercise 21-3**
Objective 2

Recording closing of Income Summary.

After the revenue and expense accounts were closed into **Income Summary** on December 31, 20--, the **Income Summary** account showed a net loss for the year of $68,000. Give the general journal entry to close the **Income Summary** account.

◄ **Exercise 21-4**
Objective 4

Recording cash dividends.

On September 15, 20--, the board of directors of Widget Corporation declared a cash dividend of $1 per share on its 800,000 outstanding shares of common stock. The dividend is payable on October 12 to stockholders of record on September 30. Give any general journal entries necessary on September 15, September 30, and October 12, 20--.

◄ **Exercise 21-5**
Objective 6

Recording a stock dividend.

Cooper Corporation had outstanding 200,000 shares of $20 par-value common stock on November 13, 20--. On that date, it declared a 5 percent common stock dividend distributable on December 15 to stockholders of record on December 1. The estimated market value of the shares at the time of their issue was $25 per share. Give any general journal entries necessary on November 13, December 1, and December 15, 20--.

◄ **Exercise 21-6**
Objective 7

Recording a stock split.

North Lake Corporation had outstanding 200,000 shares of no-par-value common stock, with a stated value of $10, on December 1, 20--. The directors voted to split the stock on a 2-for-1 basis, issuing one new share to stockholders for each share presently owned. The estimated market value of the new shares will be $14.50. Give any general journal entry required on December 1.

◄ **Exercise 21-7**
Objective 8

Exercise 21-8 ►
Objective 9

Recording appropriation of retained earnings.

On December 31, 20--, the board of directors of Zeman Corporation voted to appropriate $100,000 of retained earnings each year for five years to establish a reserve for contingencies. Give the general journal entry on December 31, 20--, to record the appropriation.

Exercise 21-9 ►
Objective 9

Closing appropriation of retained earnings.

Because of fears about the outcome of several lawsuits in progress during the years 2002 through 2004, Stars Corporation had appropriated retained earnings of $198,000, and transferred that amount from the **Retained Earnings** account to **Retained Earnings Appropriated for Contingencies.** In October 2005 the lawsuits were settled, and Stars Corporation paid $132,000 to settle them. The board of directors breathed a sigh of relief and on November 1, 2005, passed a resolution that the appropriation was no longer needed. Give the necessary journal entry on November 1 to close the appropriation account.

Exercise 21-10 ►
Objective 10

Recording receipt of property as gift.

The city of Cottonwood contributed to Altmos Corporation a tract of land on which to build a plant. When the contribution was made on May 10, 20--, the land's fair market value was $160,000. Give the general journal entry, if any, necessary to record the receipt of the contribution.

Exercise 21-11 ►
Objective 11

Purchasing treasury stock.

On August 31, 20--, San Diego Corporation had outstanding 200,000 shares of 10 percent preferred stock with a par value of $10. The stock was originally issued for $10.40 per share. On that date the corporation repurchased 8,000 shares of the preferred stock, paying cash of $10.30 per share for the stock. Give the general journal entry to record repurchase of the treasury stock.

Exercise 21-12 ►
Objective 12

Preparing Stockholders' Equity section of balance sheet.

The following are selected accounts from the general ledger of Joe's Hamburger Barns on December 31, 20--. Show how the corporation's Stockholders' Equity section would appear on the December 31, 20--, balance sheet.

Common Stock, $25 par, authorized 8,000 shares, issued and outstanding 8,000 shares	$200,000
Paid-in Capital in Excess of Par Value—Common	8,000
Retained Earnings (debit balance)	(34,000)

Problems

Selected problems can be completed using:
🍑 **Peachtree**   ⓆⒷ **QuickBooks**   ▦ **Spreadsheets**

PROBLEM SET A

Problem 21-1A ►
Objectives 1, 6

🍑 ⓆⒷ

Recording federal income tax transactions and cash dividend transactions.

Selected transactions of Captain Corporation during 2005 follow. Record them in the general journal.

DATE		TRANSACTIONS
Mar.	15	Filed the federal income tax return for 2004. The total tax for the year was $124,000. During 2004 quarterly deposits of estimated tax totaling $122,400 had been made. The additional tax of $1,600 was paid with the return. On December 31, 2004, the accountant had estimated the total tax for 2004 to be $123,600 and had recorded a liability of $1,200 for federal income tax payable.
Apr.	15	Paid first quarterly installment of $32,000 on 2005 estimated federal income tax.
May	5	Declared dividend of $0.55 per share on the 40,000 shares of common stock outstanding. The dividend is payable on June 5 to stockholders of record as of May 22, 2005.
June	5	Paid dividend declared on May 5.
	15	Paid second quarterly installment of $32,000 on 2005 estimated federal income tax.
Sept.	15	Paid third quarterly installment of $32,000 on 2005 estimated federal income tax.
Nov.	5	Declared dividend of $0.55 per share on 40,000 shares of common stock outstanding. The dividend is payable on December 10 to holders of record on November 30.
Dec.	10	Paid dividend declared on November 5.
	15	Paid fourth quarterly installment of $32,000 on 2005 estimated income tax.
	31	Total income tax for 2005 was $129,440. Recorded as an adjustment the difference between this amount and the total quarterly deposits.

Analyze: What annual per share dividend was paid to common stockholders in 2005?

Amortizing organization costs, completing a corporate worksheet, recording adjusting and closing entries, preparing an income statement and balance sheet.

◄ **Problem 21-2A**
Objectives 2, 3, 4, 5, 12

Hester Corporation has been authorized to issue 6,000 shares of 13 percent noncumulative, nonparticipating preferred stock with a par value of $100 per share and 400,000 shares of common stock with a par value of $10 per share. As of December 31, 2004, 1,600 shares of preferred stock and 36,000 shares of common stock had been issued. A condensed trial balance as of December 31, 2004, is provided on page 797.

INSTRUCTIONS

1. Enter the December 31, 2004, trial balance on an eight-column worksheet. Provide three lines for the **Selling Expenses** control account and three lines for the **General Expenses** control account. Total and rule the Trial Balance columns.

2. Record the following transactions in general journal form, using page number 6.

   a. Ending merchandise inventory is $110,000. Close the beginning inventory and set up the ending inventory.

b. Depreciation of buildings is $12,500 ($10,000 is selling expense; $2,500 is general expense).

c. Depreciation of equipment is $25,000 ($18,000 is selling expense; $7,000 is general expense).

d. Accrued expenses are $6,000 ($4,000 is selling expense; $2,000 is general expense).

e. Amortization of organization costs is $400.

f. The balance in **Allowance for Doubtful Accounts** is adequate.

g. The $68,000 balance in **Income Tax Expense** represents the quarterly tax deposits. Adjust the **Income Tax Expense** account using the following procedure.

> **(1)** Extend the adjusted income and expense items to the Income Statement columns. Using this data, compute the net income before taxes.
>
> **(2)** Assuming that taxable income is the same as net income before income taxes, use the tax rates given in this chapter to compute the federal income tax. Round the computed tax to the nearest whole dollar. Ignore state and local income taxes.

3. Complete the worksheet as shown in the text.

4. Prepare a condensed income statement for the year.

5. Prepare a balance sheet as of December 31, 2004. The balance of **Retained Earnings** on January 1, 2004, was $158,800. All dividends for the year were declared on December 5, 2004, and are payable January 4, 2005.

6. Journalize the adjusting and closing entries on December 31. Explanations are not required.

Analyze: Assume that dividends were declared in equal amounts over the four quarters of 2004. What percentage of Hester Corporation's annual income before tax was spent on dividends to stockholders?

Problem 21-3A ▶
Objectives 6, 7, 9, 12

SPREADSHEET

Recording cash dividends, stock dividends, and appropriation of retained earnings; preparing statement of retained earnings.

The stockholders' equity accounts of Raiders Corporation on January 1, 2004, contained the following balances.

Preferred Stock (10%, $50 par value,		
4,000 shares authorized)		
Issued and Outstanding, 1,200 Shares	$60,000	
Paid-in Capital in Excess of Par Value—Preferred	2,400	$ 62,400
Common Stock ($20 par value, 20,000 shares authorized)		
Issued and Outstanding, 10,000 Shares		200,000
Retained Earnings		196,000
Total Stockholders' Equity		$458,400

Transactions affecting stockholders' equity during 2004 follows.

INSTRUCTIONS

1. Set up a ledger account (381) for **Retained Earnings** and record the January 1, 2004, balance.

2. Record the transactions in general journal form and post them to the **Retained Earnings** account only. Use the account titles in the chapter.

3. Prepare a statement of retained earnings for the year 2004.

Hester Corporation
Trial Balance (Condensed)
December 31, 2004

ACCOUNT NAME	DEBIT	CREDIT
Cash	68 4 9 0 00	
Accounts Receivable	167 8 0 0 00	
Allowance for Doubtful Accounts		2 0 0 0 00
Income Tax Refund Receivable		
Inventory	100 0 0 0 00	
Land	100 0 0 0 00	
Buildings	400 0 0 0 00	
Accumulated Depreciation—Buildings		37 5 0 0 00
Equipment	250 0 0 0 00	
Accumulated Depreciation—Equipment		25 0 0 0 00
Organization Costs	1 2 8 0 00	
Accounts Payable		115 2 2 0 00
Dividends Payable—Preferred		20 8 0 0 00
Dividends Payable—Common		10 0 0 0 00
Accrued Expenses Payable		
Income Tax Payable		
Preferred Stock, 13%		160 0 0 0 00
Paid-in Capital in Excess of Par Value—Preferred		16 0 0 0 00
Common Stock		360 0 0 0 00
Retained Earnings		128 0 0 0 00
Sales (Net)		1,120 5 5 0 00
Purchases	600 0 0 0 00	
Selling Expenses Control	162 8 0 0 00	
General Expenses Control	76 7 0 0 00	
Amortization of Organization Costs		
Income Tax Expense	68 0 0 0 00	
Income Summary		
Totals	1,995 0 7 0 00	1,995 0 7 0 00

DATE	TRANSACTIONS
June 20	Declared a semiannual dividend of 5 percent on preferred stock, payable on July 18 to stockholders of record on June 30.
July 18	Paid the dividend on preferred stock.
Dec. 15	Declared a semiannual dividend of 5 percent on preferred stock, payable on January 8, 2005, to stockholders of record on December 31, 2004, and a cash dividend of $3 per share on common stock, payable on January 8, 2005, to stockholders of record on December 31, 2004. Make separate entries.
15	Declared a 5 percent common stock dividend to common stockholders of record on December 31, 2004. The new shares are to be issued on January 15, 2005. A market price of $52 per share is expected for the new shares of common stock.
	Continued

DATE	(21-3A cont.) TRANSACTIONS
Dec. 31	Created an "appropriation of retained earnings for contingencies" of $80,000 because of the poor economic outlook.
31	The **Income Summary** account contained a debit balance of 12,000. The board had anticipated a net loss for the year and no quarterly deposits of estimated income taxes were made, so income taxes may be ignored.

Analyze: If Raiders Corporation had not declared and paid dividends for common stockholders, what balance would be found in the unappropriated **Retained Earnings** account at December 31, 2004?

Problem 21-4A ►
Objectives 6, 8, 9, 10, 12

Recording cash dividends, stock splits, appropriations of retained earnings, and donated assets; preparing the Stockholders' Equity section of the balance sheet.

The Stockholders' Equity section of the balance sheet of Vickers Corporation on January 1, 20--, is shown below; selected transactions for the year follow.

Stockholders' Equity

Preferred Stock (14% cumulative, $20 par value,
    200,000 shares authorized)

Issued and Outstanding, 4,000 Shares	$ 80,000	
Paid-in Capital in Excess of Par Value	8,000	$ 88,000
Common Stock (no-par value, $25 stated value, 200,000 shares authorized)		
Issued and Outstanding, 2,000 Shares	50,000	
Paid-in Capital in Excess of Stated Value	10,000	60,000
Total Paid-in Capital		$148,000
Retained Earnings		180,000
Total Stockholders' Equity		$328,000

INSTRUCTIONS

1. Open the stockholders' equity accounts in the general ledger, and enter the beginning balances. In addition to the accounts listed, open the following accounts:

   Donated Capital
   Treasury Stock—Preferred
   Retained Earnings—Appropriated for Treasury Stock

2. Record the transactions in general journal form.

3. Post the transactions to the stockholders' equity accounts.

4. Prepare the Stockholders' Equity section of the balance sheet.

DATE	TRANSACTIONS
Jan. 18	Repurchased 2,000 shares of the outstanding preferred stock for $46,000 in cash. The stock is to be held as treasury stock. State law requires that an amount of retained earnings equal to the cost of treasury stock held must be appropriated. Record the purchase and the appropriation of retained earnings.
	Continued

DATE	(21-4A cont.) TRANSACTIONS
Mar. 1	Declared a 2-for-1 stock split of common stock. Each shareholder is to receive one new share for each share held. Stated value is reduced to $12.50 per share. Date of record is March 15. Date of issue of new shares is April 1.
April 1	Issued new shares called for by split.
June 15	Declared semiannual dividend of 7 percent on preferred stock, to be paid on July 10 to holders of record on June 28.
July 10	Paid cash dividend on preferred stock.
Aug. 25	Purchased 400 shares of outstanding preferred stock at $22 per share to be held as treasury stock. Appropriated retained earnings equal to cost of the treasury stock.
Dec. 15	Declared semiannual cash dividend of 7 percent on preferred stock to be paid on January 8 to holders of record on December 28.
15	Declared cash dividend of $1 per share on common stock to be paid on January 8 to holders of record on December 28.
15	Accepted title to a tract of land with a fair market value of $190,000 from the City of Greenville. The tract is to be used as a building site for the corporation's new factory.
31	Had net income after taxes for the year of $68,000. Give the entry to close the **Income Summary** account.

Analyze: If Vickers Corporation had not repurchased preferred stock to place in treasury, what total stockholders' equity would be reported on December 31, 20--?

PROBLEM SET B

Recording federal income tax and cash dividend transactions.

◄ **Problem 21-1B**
Objectives 1, 6

Selected transactions of The Whit Corporation during 2005 are given below. Record them in the general journal.

DATE	TRANSACTIONS
Mar. 15	Filed the federal tax return for 2004. The total tax for the year was $164,000. Estimated tax deposits of $160,000 had been made during 2004, and on December 31, 2004, the accountant had accrued an additional liability of $3,500. Paid the additional tax due of $4,000.
Apr. 15	Paid first quarterly installment of $42,000 on 2005 estimated federal income tax.
May 19	Declared dividend of $0.60 per share on the 32,000 shares of common stock outstanding. The dividend is payable on June 20 to holders of record on June 1.
June 15	Paid second quarterly installment of $42,000 on 2005 estimated federal income tax.
20	Paid the dividend declared on May 19.
Sept. 15	Paid third quarterly installment of $42,000 on 2005 estimated federal income tax.
	Continued

DATE	(21-1 B cont.) TRANSACTIONS
Nov. 19	Declared cash dividend of $0.60 per share on the 32,000 shares of common stock outstanding. The dividend is payable on December 13 to holders of record on November 30.
Dec. 13	Paid dividend declared on November 19.
15	Paid fourth quarterly installment of $42,000 on 2005 estimated federal income tax.
31	In completing the worksheet at the end of the year, the accountant determined that the total income tax for 2007 was $172,400. The difference between this amount and the quarterly deposits is to be recorded as an adjustment.

Analyze: If the dividends declared on November 19 were to be paid on January 15, what balance would be reflected in the **Dividends Payable** account on December 31, 2005?

Problem 21-2B ►
Objectives 2, 3, 4, 5, 12

Amortizing organization costs; completing a corporate worksheet; recording adjusting and closing entries; preparing an income statement and balance sheet.

Packers Corporation has been authorized to issue 10,000 shares of 12 percent noncumulative, nonparticipating preferred stock with a par value of $100 per share and 10,000 shares of common stock with a stated value of $100 per share. As of December 31, 20--, 800 shares of preferred stock and 400 shares of common stock have been issued and are outstanding. Dividends are paid quarterly on the preferred stock. A condensed trial balance as of December 31, 20--, follows on page 801.

INSTRUCTIONS

1. Enter the December 31 trial balance on an eight-column worksheet. Provide four lines for the **Selling Expenses** control account and three lines for the **General Expenses** control account. Total and rule the Trial Balance columns.

2. Enter the necessary adjustments on the worksheet, based on the following data for December 31.
   a. Ending merchandise inventory is $80,000. Close the beginning inventory, and set up the ending inventory.
   b. **Allowance for Doubtful Accounts** should be adjusted to a balance of $1,500 (debit **Selling Expenses**).
   c. Depreciation of buildings is $4,000 ($3,600 is selling expense; $400 is general expense).
   d. Depreciation of equipment is $6,000 ($3,000 is selling expense; $3,000 is general expense).
   e. Accrued expenses are $3,600 ($1,000 is selling expense; $2,600 is general expense).
   f. Amortization of organization costs is $160.
   g. The $13,200 balance in **Income Tax Expense** represents the quarterly tax deposits. Adjust the **Income Tax Expense** account using the following procedure.
      (1) Extend the adjusted income and expense items to the Income Statement columns. Using this data, compute the net income before income taxes.

(2) Assuming that taxable income is the same as net income before income taxes, use the tax rates given in this chapter to compute the federal income tax. Round the computed tax to the nearest whole dollar. Ignore state and local income taxes.

3. Complete the worksheet as shown in the text.

4. Prepare a condensed income statement for the year.

5. Prepare a balance sheet as of December 31, 20--. The balance of **Retained Earnings** on January 1 was $90,970. The only dividends declared during the year were dividends on preferred stock.

6. Journalize the adjusting and closing entries on December 31, 20--. Descriptions are not required.

Packers Corporation
Trial Balance (Condensed)
December 31, 20--

ACCOUNT NAME	DEBIT	CREDIT
Cash	20 5 3 0 00	
Accounts Receivable	54 8 0 0 00	
Allowance for Doubtful Accounts		2 6 0 00
Merchandise Inventory	74 9 2 0 00	
Land	36 0 0 0 00	
Buildings	88 0 0 0 00	
Accumulated Depreciation—Buildings		8 0 0 0 00
Equipment	78 0 0 0 00	
Accumulated Depreciation—Equipment		22 0 0 0 00
Organization Costs	2 4 0 00	
Accounts Payable		22 6 5 0 00
Dividends Payable—Preferred		2 4 0 0 00
Accrued Expenses Payable		
Income Tax Payable		
Preferred Stock, 12%		80 0 0 0 00
Paid-in Capital in Excess of Par Value—Preferred		6 0 0 0 00
Common Stock		40 0 0 0 00
Retained Earnings		86 1 7 0 00
Sales (Net)		444 5 8 0 00
Purchases	220 0 0 0 00	
Selling Expenses Control	86 3 7 0 00	
General Expenses Control	40 0 0 0 00	
Amortization of Organization Costs		
Income Tax Expense	13 2 0 0 00	
Income Summary		
Totals	712 0 6 0 00	712 0 6 0 00

Analyze: Assume that dividends were declared in equal amounts over the four quarters of fiscal 20--. What percentage of Packers Corporation's annual income before tax was spent on dividends to stockholders?

Recording cash dividends, stock dividends, appropriation of retained earnings; preparing statement of retained earnings.

◄ **Problem 21-3B**
Objectives 6, 7, 9, 12

SPREADSHEET

The stockholders' equity accounts of Guyton's Pizza Corporation on January 1, 20--, contained the following balances.

Preferred Stock (12%, $100 par value,
    2,000 shares authorized)
        Issued and Outstanding, 1,000 Shares $100,000
Common Stock (no-par, $50 stated value,
    10,000 shares authorized)
        Issued and Outstanding, 4,000 Shares $200,000
        Paid-in Capital in Excess of Stated Value   8,000   208,000
Retained Earnings   190,000
    Total Stockholders' Equity $498,000

The transactions affecting stockholders' equity during 20-- are given below. The worksheet at the end of 20-- showed a net loss of $16,000.

INSTRUCTIONS

1. Set up a ledger account (381) for **Retained Earnings,** and record the January 1, 20-- balance.

2. Record the following transactions in general journal form using page 6. Use the account titles used in the text. No descriptions are required. Post these entries to the **Retained Earnings** account only.

3. Prepare a statement of retained earnings for the year 20--.

DATE	TRANSACTIONS
June 15	Declared a semiannual 6 percent cash dividend on preferred stock and a cash dividend of $3 per share on common stock. Both are payable July 15 to stockholders of record on July 1. (Make a compound entry.)
July 15	Paid the cash dividends.
Aug. 15	Declared a 10 percent common stock dividend to be distributed on September 12 to common stockholders of record on September 1. The stock is expected to have a market value of $58 per share when issued.
Sept. 12	Distributed the common stock dividend.
Dec. 15	Declared a semiannual 6 percent cash dividend on preferred stock and a cash dividend of $2 per share on common stock. Both dividends are payable January 15 to stockholders of record on December 31. (Make a compound entry.)
15	Directed that retained earnings of $40,000 be appropriated each year for the next four years to purchase a new computer system. Title the account Retained Earnings Appropriated for Equipment Acquisition. Record the appropriation for 20--.
31	Close the debit balance of $16,000 in **Income Summary.**

Analyze: What balances should be reflected in the **Dividends Payable—Preferred** account on December 31, 20--?

Problem 21-4B ►
Objectives 6, 8, 9, 10, 12

Recording cash dividends, stock splits, appropriation of retained earnings, and donated assets; preparing the Stockholders' Equity section of the balance sheet.

The Stockholders' Equity section of Jason Corporation's balance sheet on January 1, 20--, follows, along with selected transactions for the year.

Stockholders' Equity
Preferred Stock (10%, $50 par value,
   20,000 shares authorized)
   Issued and Outstanding, 1,000 Shares $50,000
   Paid-in Capital in Excess of Par Value   4,000 $ 54,000
Common Stock (no-par value,
   $50 Stated value, 20,000 shares authorized)
   Issued and Outstanding, 1,800 Shares $90,000
   Paid-in Capital in Excess of Stated Value   3,000   93,000
Retained Earnings   164,950
Total Stockholders' Equity $311,950

1. Set up general ledger accounts for the stockholders' equity items and enter the given balances. In addition to the accounts listed, open the accounts **Donated Capital, Treasury Stock—Preferred,** and **Retained Earnings Appropriated for Treasury Stock.**

2. Record the transactions listed below in general journal form.

3. Post general journal entries only to the stockholders' equity accounts.

4. Prepare the Stockholders' Equity section of the balance sheet as of December 31, 20--.

DATE		TRANSACTIONS
Mar.	1	Reacquired 120 shares of preferred stock at $53 per share, and set up an appropriation of retained earnings equal to cost of treasury stock purchased, as required by law.
	1	Declared a 4-for-1 split of common stock and reduced the stated value to $12.50 per share. Date of record is March 20. Date of issue is April 1.
Apr.	1	Issued new shares of common stock called for by split.
June	20	Declared a cash dividend of 5 percent on preferred stock outstanding, payable July 5 to holders of record on July 1.
July	5	Paid cash dividends on preferred stock.
Nov.	10	Purchased 200 shares of the corporation's own preferred stock to be held as treasury stock, paying $51 per share. Appropriated retained earnings equal to cost of the shares.
Dec.	17	Declared the semiannual cash dividends of 5 percent on preferred stock and a $1 per share on common stock. Both are payable to stockholders of record on December 28 and are payable on January 8. Make separate entries.
	17	Received land valued at $80,000 as a gift from a neighboring city agreeing to build a new factory.
	31	The **Income Summary** account had a credit balance of $42,000 after income tax. Give the entry to close the account.

Analyze: As of December 31, what percent of total authorized preferred stock is held in treasury?

Stockholders' Equity

The Stockholders' Equity section of the balance sheets of Bass Corporation on December 31, 2004, and December 31, 2005, along with other selected account balances on the two dates is provided below. (Certain information is missing from the statements.)

In 2005 the following transactions affecting equity occurred.

a. A stock dividend was declared on common stock and issued in February. No other common stock was issued during the year.

b. A cash dividend of $2 per share was declared and paid on common stock in December.

c. The Treasury Stock—Preferred was purchased at par in January.

d. Additional preferred stock was issued for cash in March.

The yearly cash dividend of $4 per share was declared and paid on preferred stock outstanding as of December 3, 2005.

INSTRUCTIONS

Answer the following questions about transactions in 2005.

1. How many shares of preferred stock were outstanding at year-end?
2. How many common stock shares were issued as stock dividends?
3. What was the market value per share of common stock at the time the stock dividend was declared?
4. How many shares of preferred stock were purchased as treasury stock?
5. How many shares of preferred stock were issued for cash?
6. What was the sales price per share of the preferred stock issued?
7. What was the total cash dividend on preferred stock?
8. What was the total cash dividend on common stock?
9. What was the corporation's net income or loss after taxes?

	2005	2004
Stockholders' Equity		
Paid-in Capital		
Preferred Stock (8 percent, $50 par, authorized 2,000 shares)		
Issued	$ 80,000	$ 68,000
Paid-in Capital in Excess of Par		
Value—Preferred	600	–0–
Common Stock ($10 par value, 200,000 shares authorized)		
Issued	800,000	700,000
Paid-in Capital in Excess of Par		
Value—Common	20,000	
Total Paid-in Capital	$ 900,600	$ 768,000
Retained Earnings		
Appropriated for Plant Expansion	$ 250,000	$ 250,000
Appropriated for Treasury Stock	40,000	–0–
Unappropriated	640,000	600,000
Total Retained Earnings	$ 930,000	$ 850,000
	$1,830,600	$1,618,000
Less Treasury Stock—Preferred	40,000	–0–
Total Stockholders' Equity	$1,790,000	$1,618,000

Analyze: What percent of net income after taxes went to cash dividends?

Individual Investor

Virtualcom, Inc. has the following stockholders' equity on September 30, 20--.

Common Stock (200,000 shares issued)	$1,000,000
Paid-in Capital in Excess of Par	3,000,000
Retained Earnings	3,400,000
Total Stockholders' Equity	$7,400,000

For the past three years, Virtualcom, Inc. has paid dividends of $1.60 per share. On October 1, 20--, the board declared a 20 percent stock dividend instead of the $1.60 cash dividend. Before the end of the year and after the stock dividend distribution, however, the board declared a cash dividend of $1.33 per share.

In September 20-- before the stock dividend was declared, Jill Berkey purchased 10,000 shares of Virtualcom, Inc., stock for $48 per share. Now she is concerned because she purchased the stock expecting a $1.60 per share dividend, only to learn that the dividend has been reduced to $1.33 per share.

Answer the following questions concerning this investment.

1. What could have caused Virtualcom's board of directors to declare a stock dividend rather than a cash dividend in October?

2. How did the book value of Jill's stock prior to the stock dividend compare with its book value after the stock dividend?

3. Why does the market value of the stock ($48) differ from its book value?

4. How does the total amount of cash dividends differ between the $1.60 per share and the $1.33 per share?

5. Assume the market price of the stock fell to $40 after the stock dividend was announced. Does this drop represent a loss to Jill?

6. What do you think would have happened to the market price of the stock if the board had not reduced the amount of the cash dividend per share of stock?

Business Connections

Connection 1 ► **MANAGERIAL FOCUS** Shareholder's Equity

1. Three individuals are planning to form a new business. What are the five major types of entities that they can use to operate their business?

2. Assume that you are the controller of a corporation. Some members of the board of directors have asked you how the firm can have a large balance in the **Retained Earnings** account but no cash with which to pay dividends. Explain.

3. A corporation's balance sheet shows **Retained Earnings Appropriated for Plant Expansion** with a balance of $4,000,000. Does this mean that the corporation has set aside $4,000,000 in cash to expand its plant? Why would management want to establish such an account?

4. O'Neil Corporation's $50 par-value stock has a market price of $250 per share. As a result of the high price per share, finding buyers for stock that existing shareholders wish to sell has become difficult. Suggest a way for management to resolve this problem.

5. Why would the management of a corporation consider using corporate funds to purchase the firms' own outstanding stock?

6. The president of a corporation suggests to the controller that one way to convert retained earnings into permanent capital is to have a stock split. What explanation should the controller give the president?

Connection 2 ► **Ethical DILEMMA** Stock Dividend Motive Malcolm Corporation has paid substantial cash dividends in each of the past several years. However, in both 2004 and 2005, net cash flows declined considerably, in part due to rapid growth resulting in substantial increases in receivables and inventories. Dividends in both of those years were decreased. In 2006 the directors of the corporation, at the insistence of the board chairperson, declared a 20 percent stock dividend. The chairperson based this recommendation on the premise that even though there would not be a cash dividend, the shareholders would be pleased to receive more shares and that it was likely the total value of each shareholder's stock after the dividend would be slightly higher than the value before the stock dividend. As a result, the shareholders should be less upset at not receiving a cash dividend. Is this practice ethical?

Connection 3 ► **Street WISE:** Questions from the Real World Income Taxes and Dividends Refer to The Home Depot, Inc. *1999 Annual Report* in Appendix B.

1. Based on the data presented in the consolidated statements of earnings, answer the following.

   a. What approximate income tax rate does the company pay?

   b. Did the company record an accrual for current income taxes payable for the year ended January 30, 2000? If so, on which statement did you locate this data?

2. Locate the consolidated statements of stockholders' equity and comprehensive income.

   a. What per-share cash dividends were paid to common stockholders in fiscal 1999? In fiscal 1998? In fiscal 1997?

   b. What percent increase did stockholders realize in dividends from 1998 to 1999?

   c. How closely does this percent increase correlate to the percent increase in net earnings before taxes from 1998 to 1999?

FINANCIAL $TATEMENT
A N A L Y S I S **Statement of Shareholders' Equity** The following ◄ **Connection 4**
excerpt was taken from McDonald's *1999 Annual Report.*

McDonald's

Consolidated statement of shareholders' equity

(In millions except per share data)	Preferred stock issued	Common stock issued		Additional Paid-in capital	Unearned ESOP compen-sation	Retained Earnings	Accumulated Other com-prehensive income	Common stock in treasury		Total share-holders' equity
		Shares	Amount					Shares	Amount	
Balance at Dec. 31, 1998	$ 0.0	1,660.6	$16.6	$ 989.2	$(148.7)	$13,879.6	$(522.5)	(304.4)	$(4,749.5)	$9,464.7
Net income						1,947.9				1,947.9
Translation adjustments (including taxes of $53.5)							(364.3)			(364.3)
Comprehensive income										1,583.6
Common stock cash dividends ($.20 per share)						(264.7)				(264.7)
ESOP loan payment					15.8					15.8
Treasury stock purchases								(24.2)	(932.7)	(932.7)
Common equity put options issuance and expiration, net									(665.9)	(665.9)
Stock option exercises and other (including tax benefits of $185.3)				299.1	(0.4)			18.8	139.6	438.3
Balance at Dec. 31, 1999	$ 0.0	1,660.6	$16.6	$1,288.3	$(133.3)	$15,562.8	$(886.8)	(309.8)	$(6,208.5)	$9,639.1

Analyze:

1. How many shares of common stock were purchased in fiscal 1999 by the company and put into treasury?

2. What percentage of 1999 net income was used to repurchase common stock?

3. What total amount was paid by the company for dividends to common stockholders?

Analyze Online: Locate the McDonald's Web site (**www.mcdonalds.com**). Within the *Investor* section, review the consolidated statement of shareholders' equity found in the most recent annual report. Answer the following questions.

4. How many shares of common stock are outstanding? By what amount has this figure changed from fiscal 1999?

5. What is the balance of the **Treasury Stock** account?

6. What per-share dividend was paid to common stockholders?

Connection 5 ►

Extending the *Thought*   **Management Report on Internal Controls** When publicly held corporations release their annual reports, they often include a management report on internal controls. Contents of this report can include the purpose, nature and components of internal controls, the roles of internal audit, the independent auditor, and the audit committee. Management reports on internal controls are not required by any regulatory agency.

1. Why do you think corporations include this report in their annual report?

2. Which users of financial information benefit from this information?

Connection 6 ►

Business Communication   **Visual Presentation** The board of directors of Midland Medical Group Corporation is engaged in discussions to decide whether the corporation should repurchase shares of its common stock to place in treasury. As the CFO, you have been asked to speak to the group at the next board meeting to offer insight into how the decision will affect the company. The corporation has sufficient cash to repurchase 2,000 shares of its outstanding common stock (15,000 shares) at $33 per share. In your presentation, be sure to cover the following topics: advantages or disadvantages to current common stockholders, impact on the cash flow of the corporation, impact on dividends payment, advantages or disadvantages to the corporation's stock option programs, and impact on the market value of the stock.

Connection 7 ►

Team*Work*   **Cash Dividends** Corporations often declare and pay dividends quarterly. As a team, research recent dividend declarations for the corporations listed below, or select four competing corporations of interest to you. Use a search engine to locate the Web site for each company. Dividend declarations can often be found within the company's *Investor Relations* section or *Press Release* section. Record the following data for each company: amount of dividend, date of declaration, and date of payment.

Coca-Cola Co.	PepsiCo, Inc.	Nestle	Cadbury Schweppes

Connection 8 ►

inter **NET** **CONNECTION**   **Company Earnings and Dividends** Go to the Web site for Hasbro toys at **www.hasbro.com.**

1. What is the most recent stock quote?

2. What is the current dividend per share?

3. On which stock exchange is the stock traded?

Answers to Section 1 Self Review

1. Tax on first $50,000 @ 15% = $7,500; tax on next $25,000 @ 25% = $6,250; tax on next $25,000 @ 34% = $8,500; tax on next $180,000 @ 39% = $70,200, for a total of $92,450

2. The net income before taxes must be determined before the tax liability can be computed. This can be done only after all other adjustments have been entered.

3. Deferred taxes arise because the taxes actually paid during a year might not reflect the ultimate tax that will be paid on the net income reported that year for financial accounting purposes.

4. **c.** debit to **Income Tax Refund Receivable.**

5. **a.** an intangible asset.

6. Debit **Income Tax Expense,** and credit **Income Tax Payable** for $500.

Answers to Section 2 Self Review

1. If the corporation's stock is not selling well because its price is too high.

2. The date of record is the date that shareholders to receive dividends are identified. The declaration date is the date on which the board of directors formally declares a dividend.

3. No. An appropriation of retained earnings has nothing to do with cash. The appropriation merely indicates that a portion of retained earnings is not available for dividend distribution.

4. **d.** when the board passes a resolution to return the amount to unappropriated retained earnings.

5. **d.** cash dividend

6. $3,000

Answers to Section 3 Self Review

1. Donated capital arises when assets are given to the corporation, often to attract the firm to the city.

2. No. It represents assets transferred to shareholders and is a deduction from stockholders' equity.

3. **Treasury Stock** is debited and **Cash** is credited. There is no paid-in capital in excess of par value account for treasury stock.

4. **c.** a deduction from the sum of all other items in the Stockholders' Equity section.

5. **b.** Common stock.

6. $282,000

Answers to Comprehensive Self Review

1. (a) Paid-in capital, which arises from transactions involving the corporation's capital stock. (b) Retained earnings, which represent the accumulated profits less distributions to shareholders.

2. Items that do not result from routine operations, are unusual, and do not occur regularly.

3. No, they represent a part of the stockholders' equity, which is the ownership in the net assets (assets minus liabilities). A corporation can have a large balance of retained earnings but no cash. An appropriation of retained earnings is merely a restriction on dividend payments.

4. The statement of retained earnings contains all details of changes in retained earnings from the start of the year to year-end. The ending balance is included in the Shareholders' Equity section of the balance sheet.

5. None. A stock dividend does not change the total stockholders' equity in a corporation, nor does it change the ownership of any individual shareholder. In theory, the market value of the shares held by the owner would not change. However, often the total market value is higher after a stock dividend because of investors' confidence in the company.

CHAPTER 22

Learning Objectives

1. Name and define the various types of bonds.

2. Explain the advantages and disadvantages of using bonds as a method of financing.

3. Record the issuance of bonds.

4. Record the payment of interest on bonds.

5. Record the accrual of interest on bonds.

6. Compute and record the periodic amortization of a bond premium.

7. Compute and record the periodic amortization of a bond discount.

8. Record the transactions of a bond sinking fund investment.

9. Record an increase or decrease in retained earnings appropriated for bond retirement.

10. Record retirement of bonds payable.

11. Define the accounting terms new to this chapter.

Long-Term Bonds

New Terms

Bond indenture	Debentures
Bond issue costs	Discount on bonds payable
Bond retirement	Face interest rate
Bond sinking fund investment	Leveraging
Bonds payable	Market interest rate
Call price	Mortgage loan
Callable bonds	Premium on bonds payable
Carrying value of bonds	Registered bonds
Collateral trust bonds	Secured bonds
Convertible bonds	Serial bonds
Coupon bonds	Straight-line amortization
	Trading on the equity

3M

www.3m.com

*I*n its early years, 3M was first known for its innovation in abrasives and later in adhesive products like Scotch brand tapes. Over nearly 100 years, this company's technology platforms have expanded to include products like protective sheetings for highway markings, fabric protectors, multi-layer optical films for electronic displays, and antiviral medications. In 2000, the company achieved record sales, net income, and earnings per share.

In order to diversify and expand into new markets, companies often finance expansions and research and development efforts using operating cash, long-term bond issues, and additional issues of company stock. As of December 31, 2000, 3M reported approximately $971 million in long-term debt. Using financing strategies such as these, 3M will continue to pioneer new technologies and products that help make life easier, safer, and healthier.

Thinking Critically
What methods might you use to raise capital for use in research and development projects or for the expansion of your business?

For more information on 3M go to:
collegeaccounting.glencoe.com.

Section Objectives

1 **Name and define the various types of bonds.**

WHY IT'S IMPORTANT
Corporations frequently issue bonds to raise capital.

2 **Explain the advantages and disadvantages of using bonds as a method of financing.**

WHY IT'S IMPORTANT
The use of bonds as a method of financing carries certain financial obligations and tax implications.

Terms to Learn

bond indenture
bonds payable
call price
callable bonds
collateral trust bonds
convertible bonds
coupon bonds
debentures
face interest rate
leveraging
market interest rate
mortgage loan
registered bonds
secured bonds
serial bonds
trading on the equity

1 **Objective**

Name and define the various types of bonds.

Financing Through Bonds

There are many ways for corporations to raise funds. They may sell stock, or they may sign a note payable.

A long-term note may be secured by a mortgage on specific assets such as land, buildings, or equipment. A **mortgage loan** is a long-term debt created when a note is given as part of the purchase price of land or buildings.

Corporations that need long-term funds often obtain those funds by issuing bonds payable. **Bonds payable** are long-term debt instruments that are written promises to repay the principal at a future date. Interest is due at a fixed rate that is payable annually, semiannually, or quarterly over the life of the bond. Bonds are similar to notes payable, but the contract is more formal. Bonds are easily transferred from one owner (or bondholder) to another.

Types of Bonds

Bonds are classified by the following characteristics:

- Bonds can be secured by collateral, or they can be unsecured.
- Bonds can be registered or unregistered.
- Bonds can all mature on the same date, or portions can mature over a period of several years. *Mature* means to fall due or to become payable.

Secured and Unsecured Bonds

Secured bonds have property pledged to secure the claims of the bondholders. **Collateral trust bonds** involve the pledge of securities, such as stocks or bonds of other companies. A bond contract, known as a **bond indenture**, is prepared. A trustee, frequently an investment banker, is named to protect the bondholders' interests. If the bonds are not paid when due, the trustee takes legal steps to sell the pledged property and pay off the bonds.

Bonds are identified according to the nature of the property pledged and the year of maturity. Examples are as follows:

- First Mortgage 10% Real Estate Bonds Payable, 2014
- Collateral Trust 12% Bonds Payable, 2015

Unsecured bonds backed only by a corporation's general credit are called **debentures**. They involve no pledge of specific property. However, the bondholders do have some protection in case of liquidation. The claims of creditors, including bondholders, rank above those of stockholders. Creditors must be paid in full before stockholders can receive anything.

Registered and Unregistered Bonds

Registered bonds are bonds issued to a party whose name is listed in the corporation's records. Ownership is transferred by completing an assignment form and having the change of ownership entered in the corporation's records. Interest is paid by check to each registered bondholder. The corporation maintains a detailed subsidiary ledger, similar to the stockholders' ledger, for registered bonds. At all times the corporation knows who owns the bonds and who is entitled to receive interest payments.

Some bonds do not require that the names of the owners be registered. These bonds are known as **coupon bonds**. The bonds have coupons attached for each interest payment. The coupons are, in effect, checks payable to the bearer. No record of the owner's identity is kept by the corporation. On or after each interest date, the bondholder detaches the coupon from the bond and presents it to a bank for payment. Coupon bonds are often referred to as *bearer bonds* because the bearer is assumed to be the owner. Coupon bonds are rarely issued because the IRS requires corporations to report the name, tax identification number, and interest received by each bondholder. State and local governments continue to issue coupon bonds because the interest is not subject to federal income tax.

Single-Maturity and Serial-Maturity Bonds

Most bonds in an issue mature on the same day. However, **serial bonds** are payable over a period of years. For example, a corporation might issue serial bonds totaling $10 million, dated January 1, 2005, with $2,000,000 maturing each year for five years, beginning on January 1, 2015. The corporation might find it easier to retire bonds on a serial basis rather than to have all $10 million due on the same date.

Other Characteristics of Bonds Payable

Bonds are issued in various denominations. The denomination specified on the contract is called the *face value*. The typical face value is $1,000 or $10,000.

Convertible bonds give the owner the right to convert the bonds into common stock under specified conditions. For example, an indenture can give the holder of a 20-year, $1,000 bond the right to convert the bond into 50 shares of the corporation's common stock at any time. When the price of the stock reaches $20 or more ($1,000 bond ÷ 50 shares of stock), the bondholder is likely to convert it into stock.

Bonds are frequently callable. **Callable bonds** allow the issuing corporation to require the holders to surrender the bonds for payment before their maturity date. Call provisions are clearly stated on the bond. The **call price** is the amount the corporation must pay for the bond when it is called. Usually the call price is slightly above the face value. If the market interest rate declines below the face interest rate on the bonds, or if the corporation has excess cash, it might call all or part of the bonds and retire them.

Market interest rate refers to the interest rate a corporation is willing to pay and investors are willing to accept at the current time. **Face interest rate** refers to the contractual interest rate specified on the bond. Market interest rate changes constantly. Face interest rate of a bond does not change.

Accounting Textbooks
Benjamin Workman published *The American Accountant,* the earliest known accounting textbook, in 1769.

Face Value
The term "face value" also applies to notes payable and notes receivable. It is sometimes known as "face amount."

For example, assume that on October 1, 2005, SUS Corporation issues 20-year bonds with a face value of $100,000. The bonds mature on October 1, 2025. Under the terms of the indenture, SUS can call the bonds at any time after October 1, 2015, at a call price of 103 (103 percent of face value). The bonds are called by SUS on October 1, 2016. Johanson, an owner of bonds with a face value of $40,000, must surrender the bonds and will be paid $41,200 ($40,000 × 1.03).

Stock Versus Bonds as a Financing Method

② Objective

Explain the advantages and disadvantages of using bonds as a method of financing.

Corporations raise funds through various combinations of common stock, preferred stock, and bonds. Management considers several factors when deciding whether to issue stock or bonds. Table 22-1 shows some factors to consider when comparing capital stock and bonds.

TABLE 22-1 ▶
Stock and Bonds Compared

Capital Stock	Bonds Payable
Capital stock is permanent capital. There is no debt to be repaid.	Bonds payable are debt. When the bonds fall due, the debt must be repaid.
Because the stock is permanent capital, it is classified as stockholders' equity.	Because the bonds represent debt, they are classified as long-term liabilities.
Dividends are not legally required on common stock. The requirements on preferred stock depend on the contract.	Interest must be paid on the bonds.
Dividends are not deductible for income tax purposes.	Interest is deducted in arriving at the taxable income.
Preference dividends on preferred stock are usually slightly higher than interest rates on bonds because there is more risk associated with preferred stock.	Interest rates on bonds are slightly lower than dividends on preferred stock.

When deciding whether to issue bonds, a company needs to determine whether the rate of return on the assets acquired with the bond proceeds is higher than the interest rate paid on the bonds. Suppose that a newly formed corporation issued both common stock and bonds payable to provide total capital of $300,000. The owners invest $150,000 for common stock and borrow $150,000 by issuing bonds. The bonds pay 10 percent interest per year. The corporation's income before interest and taxes is $55,000. The corporate income tax rate is 20 percent. Let's compute the rate of profit on the stockholders' investment.

Amount available to stockholders:	
Net income before bond interest expense	$55,000
Bond interest expense ($150,000 × 0.10)	(15,000)
Net income before income taxes	$40,000
Income tax expense ($40,000 × 0.20)	(8,000)
Net income after taxes	$32,000

The stockholders invested $150,000 in the business, and the net income is $32,000. The stockholders earned 21.3 percent ($32,000 ÷ $150,000) profit on their equity. Let's see what happens if the owners invest $300,000 in common stock. Since there is no bond payable, there is no interest expense.

Net income before taxes	$55,000
Income tax expense ($55,000 × 0.20)	(11,000)
Net income after income taxes	$44,000

The stockholders invested $300,000, and net income is $44,000. The stockholders earned 14.7 percent ($44,000 ÷ $300,000) on their equity. With financing coming 100 percent from capital stock, the net income available to the stockholders is higher ($44,000 versus $32,000), but the rate of profit on equity is lower (14.7 percent versus 21.3 percent).

The increase in the rate of profit on stockholders' equity when bonds are used is due to the fact that the company's profits are higher than the face rate of interest (10 percent) on the bonds. Using borrowed funds to earn a profit higher than the interest that must be paid on the borrowing is called **trading on the equity**, or **leveraging**. In lean years such financing can be dangerous from the stockholders' standpoint. The bond interest expense might leave little or nothing for dividends to the stockholders. Moreover, even when the firm operates at a loss, the interest must be paid in full to the bondholders. In addition, the principal amount of the debt must also be paid when the bonds mature.

For example, if the income before interest and taxes had been only $12,000, the use of bonds payable would result in the corporation having a net loss.

Net income before bond interest expense	$12,000
Bond interest expense ($150,000 × 0.10)	(15,000)
Net loss	($ 3,000)

Holiday Observances

When working with international clients, familiarize yourself with local observances of holidays. More than 70 percent of the holidays celebrated each year change annually. Some countries have such diverse ethnic populations that they observe religious holidays for more than 10 major religions!

Section 1 Self Review

Questions

1. What is the difference between registered bonds and coupon bonds?

2. What is a convertible bond?

3. Why would a corporation issue callable bonds?

Exercises

4. Bonds that are payable over a period of years are called

   a. callable bonds.
   b. serial bonds.
   c. bearer bonds.
   d. coupon bonds.

5. Bonds backed only by the general credit of the corporation are called

   a. secured bonds.
   b. collateral trust bonds.
   c. registered bonds.
   d. debentures.

Analysis

6. A small corporation is considering a bond issue. The amount of stockholders' equity is $250,000. The corporation projects income before taxes of $45,000. The corporate income tax rate is 20 percent. If $125,000 of bonds is issued at 10 percent, what is the rate of profit on stockholders' equity?

(Answers to Section 1 Self Review are on page 840.)

Section Objectives

3 Record the issuance of bonds.

WHY IT'S IMPORTANT
The issuance of bonds creates a long-term liability that needs to be reflected in the accounting records of the issuer.

4 Record the payment of interest on bonds.

WHY IT'S IMPORTANT
Bondholders receive interest from the bond issuer as stated in the debt instrument.

5 Record the accrual of interest on bonds.

WHY IT'S IMPORTANT
At year-end expenses that have not been recorded are accrued to conform to the matching principle.

6 Compute and record the periodic amortization of a bond premium.

WHY IT'S IMPORTANT
Bond premiums reduce the overall interest expense.

7 Compute and record the periodic amortization of a bond discount.

WHY IT'S IMPORTANT
Issuing a bond at less than face value increases total interest expense.

Terms to Learn

bond issue costs
carrying value of bonds
discount on bonds payable
premium on bonds payable
straight-line amortization

Bond Issue and Interest

The board of directors of TENNAM Corporation authorized the issue of 150 registered, unsecured bonds that will mature in 10 years. The face value of each bond is $1,000. The face interest rate is 10 percent. Interest will be paid on April 1 and October 1 of each year. Interest on each bond is $100 per year ($1,000 × 0.10). Because interest is paid semiannually, each interest payment is $50 ($100 ÷ 2). Some of the authorized bonds will be sold immediately. The remainder will be held for future needs.

Bonds Issued at Face Value

On April 1, 2005, the issue date, TENNAM sells 50 bonds at face value for $50,000 ($1,000 × 50) cash. The journal entry follows.

1	2005					1
2	Apr.	1	Cash	50 000 00		2
3			10% Bonds Payable, 2015		50 000 00	3
4			Issued bonds at face value			4

After the entry is posted, the ledger account for the bonds appears as follows.

ACCOUNT 10% Bonds Payable, 2015   ACCOUNT NO. __261__
                (Authorized $150,000; Interest April 1, October 1)

DATE	DESCRIPTION	POST. REF.	DEBIT	CREDIT	BALANCE DEBIT	BALANCE CREDIT
2005						
Apr. 1		J4		50 000 00		50 000 00

Notice that the amount of bonds authorized is recorded as a memorandum on the ledger account form. On the balance sheet, the bonds payable appear as long-term liabilities. (Bonds that mature within one year from the balance sheet date appear as current liabilities.) There are three ways to report bonds on the balance sheet.

1. Show the face value of the bonds authorized, unissued, and issued.

Long-Term Liabilities
10% Bonds Payable, Due April 1, 2015
Authorized $150,000
Less Unissued   100,000
Issued $ 50,000

2. Show the face value of the bonds authorized as a parenthetical note.

Long-Term Liabilities
10% Bonds Payable, Due April 1, 2015 $50,000
(Bonds with a face value of $150,000 are
authorized, of which $100,000 are unissued.)

3. Show the face value of the bonds issued. Provide details about the bonds in a footnote to the financial statements.

Payment of Interest

On October 1, 2005, the first interest payment is due: 10 percent interest on $50,000 for six months. The interest is $2,500 ($50,000 × 0.10 × 1/2). The journal entry to record the payment is as follows.

1	2005				1
2	Oct.	1	Bond Interest Expense	2 5 0 0 00	2
3			Cash	2 5 0 0 00	3
4			Paid semiannual bond		4
5			interest		5

Corporations with many bondholders open a separate checking account for bond interest payments. A separate account makes it easier to reconcile the bank account and to keep records of interest checks that have not yet been presented for payment.

Accrual of Interest

On December 31, 2005, at the end of the fiscal year, three months (October, November, and December) of bond interest is owed but will not be paid until April 1, 2006. The accrued interest is $1,250 ($50,000 × 0.10 × 3/12). The adjusting entry is as follows.

1	2005		Adjusting Entries		1
26	Dec.	31	Bond Interest Expense	1 2 5 0 00	26
27			Bond Interest Payable	1 2 5 0 00	27
28			Accrued interest for three months		28

When the adjusting entry has been posted, the **Bond Interest Expense** account has a balance of $3,750, the correct amount of interest for the nine months the bonds have been outstanding. **Bond Interest Expense** usually appears in the Other Expenses (nonoperating expenses) section of the income statement.

ACCOUNT _Bond Interest Expense_ ACCOUNT NO. _692_

DATE		DESCRIPTION	POST. REF.	DEBIT	CREDIT	BALANCE DEBIT	BALANCE CREDIT
2005							
Oct.	1		J10	2 5 0 0 00		2 5 0 0 00	
Dec.	31	Adjusting	J12	1 2 5 0 00		3 7 5 0 00	

Entries for Second-Year Interest

Assuming that the same bonds remain outstanding during all of the second year, 2006, the following entries would be required.

- January 1: Reverse the accrued interest payable entry for $1,250 made on December 31:
  Debit **Bond Interest Payable** for $1,250.
  Credit **Bond Interest Expense** for $1,250.

❸ Objective
Record the issuance of bonds.

❹ Objective
Record the payment of interest on bonds.

❺ Objective
Record the accrual of interest on bonds.

Recall

Reversing Entries
The adjusting entry to record accrued interest is reversed on the first day of the following period.

Accounting

Government and Public Administration

Industry Overview

Federal, state, and local governments employed approximately 9 million workers in 2000. Federal government passes and enforces law, defends the United States against foreign aggression, and administers various programs. State and local governments provide vital services such as public safety, utilities, health care, and public transportation.

Career Opportunities

- Federal Tax Analyst—U.S. Dept. of Commerce
- Accounting Supervisor—Bureau of the Census
- Economic Development Advisor
- IRS Auditor
- Policy Analyst

Preparing for a Government and Public Administration Career

- Obtain a bachelor's degree for professional careers in federal, state, or local agencies.

- Complete an associate's degree or obtain two years of relevant work experience for administrative support occupations.

- Participate in community programs as a volunteer to obtain an understanding of operations and funding of public programs and services.

- Explore internship opportunities with local, state, or federal agencies.

- For a position as an accountant in the public sector, learn how to analyze financial reports and review and record revenues and expenditures. Complete audit coursework to develop an understanding of investigative techniques used to evaluate government operations and to detect fraud.

- Complete specialized coursework in tax law for a career as a tax examiner or IRS agent.

- Become familiar with government purchasing procedures and policies for a job as purchasing agent.

Thinking Critically

For-profit businesses such as Hewlett Packard and McDonald's operate to earn money for their owners. What objectives or goals do you believe are paramount to the operations of not-for-profit organizations such as governmental agencies?

Internet Application

The Fed World Web site offers federal job listings by state and region. List one job opening in the field of accounting. List two other job vacancies of interest to you. Indicate each position's salary range, major duties, and branch of government.

- April 1: Record the payment of interest for six months:
  Debit **Bond Interest Expense** for $2,500.
    Credit **Cash** for $2,500.

- October 1: Record the payment of interest for six months:
  Debit **Bond Interest Expense** for $2,500.
    Credit **Cash** for $2,500.

- December 31: Record accrued interest for three months:
  Debit **Bond Interest Expense** for $1,250.
    Credit **Bond Interest Payable** for $1,250.

After these entries have been posted, the **Bond Interest Expense** account appears as follows. Notice that on December 31, 2006, the balance in the **Bond Interest Expense** account is $5,000. This is the annual interest on the bonds ($50,000 × 0.10).

ACCOUNT	Bond Interest Expense							ACCOUNT NO.	692	
DATE	DESCRIPTION	POST. REF.	DEBIT	CREDIT	BALANCE					
					DEBIT		CREDIT			
2006										
Jan. 1	Reversing	J1		1 2 5 0 00			1 2 5 0 00			
Apr. 1		J4	2 5 0 0 00		1 2 5 0 00					
Oct. 1		J10	2 5 0 0 00		3 7 5 0 00					
Dec. 31	Adjusting	J12	1 2 5 0 00		5 0 0 0 00					

Bonds Issued at a Premium

Two years after the first bonds were sold, TENNAM issues another 20 bonds. The market interest rate is 9.5 percent. The face interest rate on the bonds remains at 10 percent. Bondholders will be attracted by the bond interest rate, which is higher than the market rate. They will be willing to pay more than the face value ($1,000) for each bond in order to earn 10 percent interest.

On April 1, 2007, $20,000 of bonds are sold at 102.4. Bond prices are quoted in terms of percent of face value. Each bond was issued for $1,024 ($1,000 × 1.024), yielding cash of $20,480 ($1,024 × 20). The issue price in excess of face value is $480 ($20,480 − $20,000). The excess of the price paid over the face value of a bond is called a **premium on bonds payable**. Investors are willing to pay a premium because the face interest rate is higher than the market interest at the time the bonds are issued. This transaction is recorded in general journal form as follows.

1	2007						1
2	Apr. 1	Cash		20 4 8 0 00			2
3		10% Bonds payable, 2015			20 0 0 0 00		3
4		Premium on Bonds Payable			4 8 0 00		4
5		Issued bonds at 102.4					5

Amortization of Bond Premium

The issuing corporation writes off, or amortizes, the premium paid by the bond purchasers over the period from the issue date to the maturity date. Amortizing the premium reduces bond interest expense shown on the income statement. In this case the bonds are 10-year bonds sold two years after their authorization date. That leaves eight years (96 months) over which to amortize the premium.

There are two ways to compute the amortization: straight-line amortization and effective interest method. The effective interest method is covered in intermediate accounting courses. This text uses the **straight-line amortization** method, which amortizes an equal amount of the premium each month. The amortization for TENNAM is $60 per year ($480 ÷ 8 years) or $5 per month ($480 ÷ 96 months).

On October 1, 2007, TENNAM records the semiannual interest on the $70,000 of bonds outstanding. The bond interest paid is $3,500 ($70,000 × 0.10 × 6/12). TENNAM also records amortization of the premium received on $20,000 of the bonds. The amortization is $30 at $5 per month. Notice how the amortization of the **Premium on Bonds Payable** reduces the amount of **Bond Interest Expense.**

Bond Prices
If the face interest rate on bonds is higher than the market interest rate, the bonds will sell at a premium.

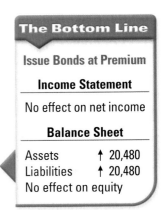

The Bottom Line

Issue Bonds at Premium

Income Statement

No effect on net income

Balance Sheet

Assets ↑ 20,480
Liabilities ↑ 20,480
No effect on equity

6 Objective
Compute and record the periodic amortization of a bond premium.

1	2007						1
2	Oct.	1	Bond Interest Expense	3 5 0 0 00			2
3			Cash		3 5 0 0 00		3
4			Payment of semiannual interest				4
5			on $70,000 of bonds				5
6							6
7		1	Premium on Bonds Payable	3 0 00			7
8			Bond Interest Expense		3 0 00		8
9			Amortization on $20,000 of				9
10			bonds for six months				10

Adjusting and Reversing Entries

On December 31, 2007, an adjusting entry is made for three months of accrued interest on the entire $70,000 of bonds outstanding. The accrued interest is $1,750 ($70,000 × 0.10 × 3/12). An adjustment is also made for the amortization of bond premium at $5 per month for three months ($15). Bond interest expense is $1,735, the interest accrued less the amount of the bond premium ($1,750 − $15). The adjustment is recorded as shown and is reversed on January 1, 2008.

			Adjusting Entries				
1	2007						1
30	Dec.	31	Bond Interest Expense	1 7 3 5 00			30
31			Premium on Bonds Payable	1 5 00			31
32			Bond Interest Payable		1 7 5 0 00		32
33			Accrue interest and amortize				33
34			premium for three months				34

Bond Prices
If the face interest rate on bonds is lower than the market interest rate, the bonds will sell at a discount.

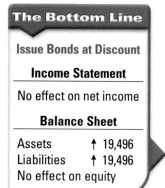

The Bottom Line

Issue Bonds at Discount

Income Statement

No effect on net income

Balance Sheet

Assets	↑ 19,496
Liabilities	↑ 19,496

No effect on equity

⑦ Objective

Compute and record the periodic amortization of a bond discount.

Bonds Issued at a Discount

TENNAM issues another 20 bonds on April 1, 2008. The market interest rate is 12 percent. The bonds' interest rate remains fixed at 10 percent. Investors will pay less than face value for a bond that pays interest at a lower rate than the market rate. The **discount on bonds payable** is the excess of the face value over the price received for a bond.

TENNAM Corporation sells 20 bonds at 97.48. Each bond is issued for $974.80 ($1,000 × 0.9748), yielding cash of $19,496 ($20,000 × 0.9748). The excess of the face value over the issue price is $504 ($20,000 − $19,496). The $504 is the discount. The entry to record issuance of the bond is shown in general journal form as follows.

1	2008						1
2	Apr.	1	Cash	19 4 9 6 00			2
3			Discount on Bonds Payable	5 0 4 00			3
4			10% Bonds payable, 2015		20 0 0 0 00		4
5			Issued bonds at 97.48				5

Amortization of Bond Discount

The issuing corporation amortizes the discount over the period from the issue date to the maturity date. Amortizing the discount increases the bond interest expense shown on the income statement. The bonds are 10-year bonds sold three years after the authorization date. That leaves seven years (84 months) over which to amortize the discount. On a straight-line basis, the amortization is $72 per year ($504 ÷ 7 years) or $6 per month ($504 ÷ 84 months).

On October 1, 2008, TENNAM Corporation records the semiannual interest on the $90,000 of bonds outstanding. The bond interest paid is $4,500 ($90,000 × 0.10 × 6/12). The company records the amortization of the premium at $5 per month for six months ($30). It records the amortization of the discount at $6 per month for six months ($36). The bond interest expense is $4,506, the interest paid ($4,500) less the amortized premium ($30) and plus the amortized discount ($36). Notice how the discount increases the actual cost of borrowing. The journal entry to record the interest payment and the amortization of the premium and the discount follows.

1	2008				1
2	Oct.	1	Bond Interest Expense	4 5 0 6 00		2
3			Premium on Bonds Payable	3 0 00		3
4			Discount on Bonds Payable		3 6 00	4
5			Cash		4 5 0 0 00	5
6			Interest payment and amortization			6
7			of premium and discount for			7
8			six months			8
9						9

Adjusting and Reversing Entries

On December 31, 2008, an adjusting entry is made to accrue interest on the bonds for the three-month period. The accrued interest is $2,250 ($90,000 × 0.10 × 3/12). An adjustment is made for the bond discount for three months at $6 per month ($18) and for the bond premium for three months at $5 per month ($15). Bond interest expense is $2,253, the interest accrued plus the discount less the premium ($2,250 + $18 − $15). The adjusting entry is recorded as follows. It is reversed on January 1, 2009.

1	2008		Adjusting Entries			1
26	Dec.	31	Bond Interest Expense	2 2 5 3 00		26
27			Premium on Bonds Payable	1 5 00		27
28			Discount on Bonds Payable		1 8 00	28
29			Bond Interest Payable		2 2 5 0 00	29
30			Accrue interest on $90,000 of bonds,			30
31			amortize premium on $20,000 of			31
32			bonds, and amortize discount on			32
33			$20,000 of bonds for three months			33
34						34

Balance Sheet Presentation of Bond Premium and Discount

The **Premium on Bonds Payable** account has a normal credit balance. It is shown as an addition to the face value of bonds payable on the balance sheet. The **Discount on Bonds Payable** account has a normal debit balance; it is subtracted from the face value of bonds payable on the balance sheet. When there are both a discount and a premium on a bond issue, the two are combined and shown on the balance sheet as a single figure. For example, on December 31, 2008, TENNAM has a net discount on bonds payable of $75 as follows:

Discount	$504	
Amortization taken (9 months at $6)	(54)	
Unamortized discount		$450
Premium	$480	
Amortization taken (21 months at $5)	(105)	
Unamortized premium		(375)
Net unamortized discount		$ 75

On December 31, 2008, TENNAM reports bonds payable on the balance sheet as follows.

Long-Term Liabilities	
10% Bonds Payable, Due April 1, 2015	
(authorized $150,000 face value, less	
$60,000 face value unissued)	$90,000
Net Discount on Bonds Payable	75
Net Liability	$89,925

The book value, or the **carrying value of bonds**, is the balance of the **Bonds Payable** account plus the **Premium on Bonds Payable** account minus the **Discount on Bonds Payable** account.

Bonds payable
+ Premium on bonds
− Discount on bonds
Carrying value or book value

Book Value
The term *book value* can apply to assets or liabilities. The book value of property, plant, and equipment is the original cost minus the accumulated depreciation.

Accounting for Bond Issue Costs

Bond issue costs are costs incurred in issuing bonds, including items such as legal and accounting fees and printing costs. Bond issue costs reduce the proceeds of borrowing. Bond issue costs may be handled in two ways:

1. Accounted for as a discount or as a reduction of premium and amortized over the period the bonds are outstanding, or

2. Debited to an expense account in the period they are incurred.

Section 2 Self Review

Questions

1. What is the straight-line method for amortizing bond discount or premium?

2. How are bond discounts shown on the balance sheet?

3. Why is amortization of a bond premium offset against interest expense?

Exercises

4. If bonds are issued for a price below their face value, the bond discount is

a. debited to expense on the date the bonds are issued.

b. amortized over the life of the bond issue.

c. shown as an addition to bonds payable in the Long-Term Liabilities section of the balance sheet.

d. shown as a deduction to bonds payable in the Current Liabilities section of the balance sheet.

5. The entry to record the issuance of bonds includes a

a. credit to **Bond Interest Payable**.

b. credit to **Bonds Payable**.

c. debit to **Bonds Payable**.

d. debit to **Bond Interest Payable**.

Analysis

6. Ten-year bonds, dated January 1, 2004, with a face value of $300,000 are issued at 102.3 on January 1, 2004. How much premium will be amortized on the interest payment date, July 1, 2004?

(Answers to Section 2 Self Review are on page 840.)

Bond Retirement

Bond retirement occurs when a bond is paid and the liability is removed from the company's balance sheet. When TENNAM'S bond issue matures, the corporation has to pay bondholders the face amount of their bonds, a total of $90,000, in cash.

Accumulating Funds to Retire Bonds

In order to ensure that the cash is available, the corporation established a bond sinking fund investment account. A **bond sinking fund investment** is a fund established to accumulate assets to pay off bonds when they mature. Some bond contracts require bond sinking funds.

Bond Sinking Fund Investment

TENNAM Corporation decides to accumulate $18,000 per year in the bond sinking fund for each of the last five years that the bonds are outstanding. The net earnings of the fund will reduce the amount that the corporation has to add each year. Suppose that the bond sinking fund investment account is started on April 1, 2010, by making an $18,000 cash deposit. The $18,000 is immediately invested. During the year $2,250 is earned on the the sinking fund investments. Expenses of $40 are incurred in operating the bond sinking fund. Net earnings for the year are $2,210. The following year only $15,790 ($18,000 − $2,210) needs to be added to the fund. This procedure is repeated each year, so that at the end of the fifth year the fund will have the $90,000 needed to retire the bonds.

The following journal entries are for the first transfer of cash to the fund, net earnings for the first year, second transfer of cash to the fund, and retirement of the bonds at the end of the fifth year.

1	2010					1
2	Apr.	1	Bond Sinking Fund Investment	18 000 00		2
3			Cash		18 000 00	3
4			First annual installment in bond			4
5			sinking fund			5

1	2011					1
2	Apr.	1	Bond Sinking Fund Investment	2 210 00		2
3			Income from Sinking Fund Investment		2 210 00	3
4			Net income earned by bond sinking			4
5			fund for year			5
6						6
7		1	Bond Sinking Fund Investment	15 790 00		7
8			Cash		15 790 00	8
9			Second annual installment in bond			9
10			sinking fund ($18,000 less $2,210			10
11			income earned for year)			11

1	2015					1
2	Apr.	1	10% Bonds Payable, 2015	90 000 00		2
3			Bond Sinking Fund Investment		90 000 00	3
4			Retirement of bonds			4

Section Objectives

8 Record the transactions of a bond sinking fund investment.

WHY IT'S IMPORTANT
Companies make plans to ensure that the required funds are available to pay off bonds on their maturity date.

9 Record an increase or decrease in retained earnings appropriated for bond retirement.

WHY IT'S IMPORTANT
Retained earnings are often restricted for specific expenditures.

10 Record retirement of bonds payable.

WHY IT'S IMPORTANT
Upon retirement of a bond, total long-term debt is adjusted to reflect the payment of the liability.

Terms to Learn

bond retirement
bond sinking fund investment

8 Objective
Record the transactions of a bond sinking fund investment.

Managerial
IMPLICATIONS

Raising Cash

- A critical management task is to ensure that cash is available to the company when it is needed.

- Managers need to know the advantages and disadvantages of raising cash through the sale of bonds and stock.

- Managers need to have a thorough understanding of bond characteristics, including the differences between registered versus bearer bonds and secured versus debenture bonds. They also need to understand convertible bonds and callable bonds.

- Bond sinking fund investments and the appropriation of retained earnings are tools that management can use to ensure that the funds are available to retire the bonds.

- Call provisions and early retirement of bonds allow for flexible financing and can reduce financing costs.

Thinking Critically
What factors would you consider in choosing between stock financing and bond financing?

This illustration assumes that an outside trustee managed the sinking fund investment account and made the necessary entries to record the fund transactions. If the corporation handled the bond sinking fund itself, additional entries would be required to show the investment of the fund's cash, the receipt of earnings, and the payment of fund expenses.

Other procedures may be used to finance the sinking fund investment. For example, an assumption may be made about the rate of earnings of the fund. A constant amount would be contributed each period, which when added to the earnings would equal the required balance. If earnings differ from the rate assumed, the contributions would be adjusted.

The bond sinking fund is reported under the heading "Investments" in the Assets section of the balance sheet. Investments are usually shown before property, plant, and equipment.

⑨ Objective

Record an increase or decrease in retained earnings appropriated for bond retirement.

Retained Earnings Appropriated for Bond Retirement

To protect bondholders and to restrict dividends, the bond contract might require that retained earnings are appropriated while the bonds are outstanding. Even if the bond contract does not require an appropriation, retained earnings may be appropriated by order of the board of directors.

Suppose that the board of directors of TENNAM Corporation decided to appropriate $18,000 of retained earnings during each of the last five years the bonds are outstanding. When the bonds are retired, the balance in the appropriated retained earnings account is returned to the **Retained Earnings** account. The **Retained Earnings Appropriated for Bond Retirement** account appears on the balance sheet under the heading "Appropriated Retained Earnings." The following entry shows an annual appropriation of retained earnings. Five such entries would be made. The next entry shows the appropriation being returned to retained earnings after the bonds are retired.

2010															
Apr.	1	Retained Earnings		18	0	0	0	00							
		Retained Earnings Appropriated for													
		Bond Retirement							18	0	0	0	00		
		Annual appropriation													

2015		Retained Earnings Appropriated for													
Apr.	1	Bond Retirement		90	0	0	0	00							
		Retained Earnings							90	0	0	0	00		
		Close appropriation account													
		upon retirement of bonds													

Retirement of Bonds

Bonds payable are usually retired at the maturity date, but some or all of the bonds can be retired prior to that date.

Retirement on Due Date

If there had been no bond sinking fund, TENNAM Corporation would have recorded the retirement on the maturity date by debiting **10% Bonds Payable, 2015,** and crediting **Cash.**

Early Retirement

A corporation may retire bonds early because it has surplus cash, or interest rates have decreased or are expected to decrease. The corporation may purchase the bonds on the open market or, if they are callable, it may require the holders to surrender their bonds for cash.

When bonds are retired prior to maturity, the bondholders are paid the agreed-upon price for the bonds plus the accrued interest to the date of purchase. There are two steps to record the retirement of bonds.

Step 1. *Amortize the discount or premium on the bonds up to the date of retirement.*

Step 2. *Remove the book value, and record the gain or loss.*
   a. Remove the book value of the bonds.
   b. Record interest up to the date of retirement.
   c. Record the cash payment for the repurchase price and interest.
   d. Record the gain or loss (book value minus the repurchase price).

Assume that on January 1, 2005, Hania Corporation issued $100,000 face value of its 10 percent, 20-year bonds, maturing January 1, 2025. Interest is payable on January 1 and July 1 of each year. The bonds were issued at 102.4, so a premium of $2,400 was recorded and is being amortized on a straight-line basis at $10 per month ($2,400 ÷ 240 months). The amortization is therefore $60 for each six-month interest payment period ($10 × 6).

On July 1, 2010, after the interest was paid and the premium was amortized, Hania had the following account balances.

10% Bonds Payable, 2025		$100,000
Premium on Bonds Payable:		
Original premium	$2,400	
Amortized January 1, 2005,		
to July 1, 2010	660	$ 1,740

Important!

Bond Retirement
The fact that retained earnings are appropriated for bond retirement does not mean that a bond retirement fund has been established.

⑩ Objective
Record retirement of bonds payable.

Important!

Gain or Loss
The gain or loss on the retirement of bonds is the book value of the bonds minus the repurchase price.

On September 1, 2010, the corporation purchased and retired $50,000 face value of the bonds—50 percent of the total outstanding. The bonds were purchased on the open market at 101 plus accrued interest.

Step 1. *Amortize the premium on the bonds up to the date of retirement. Remember to amortize only the premium of the bonds being retired, 50 percent of the bond issue.*

$10 per month $\times$ 2 months $\times$ 0.50 = $10

1	2010						1
2	Sept.	1	Premium on Bonds Payable		10 00		2
3			Bond Interest Expense			10 00	3
4			Amortize premium for two months on				4
5			retired bonds				5

Step 2. *Remove the book value, and record the gain or loss.*

    a. Remove the book value of the bonds:

        Bonds being retired: $50,000

        Premium on retired bonds:

        ($1,740 $\times$ 0.50) $-$ $10   860

    b. Record interest up to the date of retirement.

        $50,000 $\times$ 0.10 $\times$ 2/12 = $833

    c. Record the cash payment for repurchase price and interest.

        ($50,000 $\times$ 1.01) + $833 = $51,333

    d. Record the gain or loss (book value minus repurchase price).

        ($50,000 + $860) $-$ ($50,000 $\times$ 1.01) = $360

1	2010						1
2	Sept.	1	10% Bonds Payable, 2025		50 000 00		2
3			Premium on Bonds Payable		8 60 00		3
4			Bond Interest Expense		8 33 00		4
5			Cash			51 333 00	5
6			Gain on Early Retirement of Bonds			3 60 00	6

A significant gain or loss on early retirement of bonds appears on the income statement as an extraordinary gain or loss. If it is immaterial, it may appear in the Other Income or Other Expense section.

Section 3   Self Review

Questions

1. What is a bond sinking fund investment?

2. Why would a corporation purchase its own bonds and retire them?

3. How is gain or loss on early retirement of bonds shown on the income statement?

Exercises

4. The entry to record income earned by a bond sinking fund investment includes a credit to

    a. **Bonds Payable.**

    b. **Bond Sinking Fund Investment.**

    c. **Income from Sinking Fund Investment.**

    d. **Interest Income.**

5. The entry to record retirement of a bond includes a credit to

    a. **Premium on Bonds Payable.**

    b. **Retained Earnings.**

    c. **Bonds Payable.**

    d. **Retained Earnings Appropriated for Bond Retirement.**

Analysis

6. What is the entry to record $600,000 of bonds that were retired at maturity? Retained earnings were appropriated for $600,000 for bond retirement. There was no bond sinking fund.

(Answers to Section 3 Self Review are on page 840.)

Review

Chapter Summary

Corporations often use bonds to acquire funds. In this chapter, you have reviewed the types of bonds frequently issued by corporations and have learned how to record a variety of bond transactions.

Learning Objectives

❶ Name and define the various types of bonds.
- Bonds may be secured by the pledge of specific assets as security, or they may be unsecured.
- Some bonds are registered; owners are listed in corporation records. Other bonds are bearer bonds with interest coupons attached.
- Convertible bonds can be converted into common stock by the bondholder.
- Callable bonds may be recalled before their maturity date.

❷ Explain the advantages and disadvantages of using bonds as a method of financing.
- Businesses that choose to raise capital using bonds may deduct bond interest charges when computing taxable income.
- Bonds payable are debts. The face amount of the bond must be repaid at maturity. Interest must also be paid on the bonds.

❸ Record the issuance of bonds.
Bonds may be issued at face value, at a premium, or at a discount.
- If the bond's face interest rate exceeds the market interest rate when the bonds are issued, the bonds are issued at a premium.
- If the market interest rate exceeds the face interest rate on the bonds, the bonds are issued at a discount.

❹ Record the payment of interest on bonds.
A bond bears interest that is usually payable annually or semiannually at a specified rate. The amount of interest is calculated and recorded as a debit to **Bond Interest Expense** and a credit to **Cash**.

❺ Record the accrual of interest on bonds.
When bond interest dates do not coincide with the fiscal year-end, an adjustment is made for accrued bond interest at the end of the year. The adjustment is reversed at the beginning of the next year.

❻ Compute and record the periodic amortization of a bond premium.
The corporation writes off, or amortizes, a bond premium over the period from the issue date through the maturity date. The amortization is treated as a reduction of interest expense for that period.

❼ Compute and record the periodic amortization of a bond discount.
A bond discount is amortized over the period that begins on the date the bonds are issued and ends on the date of maturity. The amortization is treated as an increase to interest expense for that period.

❽ Record the transactions of a bond sinking fund investment.
A bond sinking fund accumulates cash to pay the bonds at maturity. The cash in the sinking fund is invested, earning interest to reduce the amount that the corporation will have to add in subsequent years. The establishment of the fund is recorded with a debit to **Bond Sinking Fund Investment** and a credit to **Cash**.

❾ Record an increase or decrease in retained earnings appropriated for bond retirement.
An appropriation of retained earnings for bond retirement may be established and increased by debits to **Retained Earnings** and credits to **Retained Earnings Appropriated for Bond Retirement**. An appropriation shows that some retained earnings are not available for dividends; they are needed to pay off the bonds.

❿ Record retirement of bonds payable.
Bonds are retired at maturity or, under certain circumstances, retired prior to maturity. The difference between the book value and the repurchase price is a gain or loss on retirement of bonds.

⓫ Define the accounting terms new to this chapter.

CHAPTER 22 GLOSSARY

Bond indenture (p. 812) A bond contract

Bond issue costs (p. 822) Costs incurred in issuing bonds, such as legal and accounting fees and printing costs

Bond retirement (p. 823) When a bond is paid and the liability is removed from the company's balance sheet

Bond sinking fund investment (p. 823) A fund established to accumulate assets to pay off bonds when they mature

Bonds payable (p. 812) Long-term debt instruments that are written promises to repay the principal at a future date; interest is due at a fixed rate payable over the life of the bond

Call price (p. 813) The amount the corporation must pay for the bond when it is called

Callable bonds (p. 813) Bonds that allow the issuing corporation to require the holder to surrender the bonds for payment before their maturity date

Carrying value of bonds (p. 822) The balance of the **Bonds Payable** account plus the **Premium on Bonds Payable** account minus the **Discount on Bonds Payable** account; also called *book value of bonds*

Collateral trust bonds (p. 812) Bonds secured by the pledge of securities, such as stocks or bonds of other companies

Convertible bonds (p. 813) Bonds that give the owner the right to convert the bonds into common stock under specified conditions

Coupon bonds (p. 813) Unregistered bonds that have coupons attached for each interest payment; also called *bearer bonds*

Debentures (p. 812) Unsecured bonds backed only by a corporation's general credit

Discount on bonds payable (p. 820) The excess of the face value over the price received by the corporation for a bond

Face interest rate (p. 813) The contractual interest specified on the bond

Leveraging (p. 815) Using borrowed funds to earn a profit greater than the interest that must be paid on the borrowing

Market interest rate (p. 813) The interest rate a corporation is willing to pay and investors are willing to accept at the current time

Mortgage loan (p. 812) A long-term debt created when a note is given as part of the purchase price for land or buildings

Premium on bonds payable (p. 819) The excess of the price paid over the face value of a bond

Registered bonds (p. 813) Bonds issued to a party whose name is listed in the corporation's records

Secured bonds (p. 812) Bonds for which property is pledged to secure the claims of bondholders

Serial bonds (p. 813) Bonds issued at one time but payable over a period of years

Straight-line amortization (p. 819) Amortizing the premium or discount on bonds payable in equal amounts each month over the life of the bond

Trading on the equity (p. 815) See Leveraging

Comprehensive Self Review

1. Generally, would an investor want secured bonds or debenture bonds? Why?

2. Name two disadvantages of raising capital through the issue of bonds payable rather than through the issue of preferred stock.

3. What factor or factors would cause bonds to be sold at a discount?

4. Why does a corporation use an account such as **Appropriation of Retained Earnings** for bond retirement?

5. What entry, or entries, will be made when bonds are retired at maturity?

(Answers to Comprehensive Self Review are on page 840.)

Discussion Questions

1. What is a collateral trust bond?

2. What is a bond indenture?

3. How is the **Bonds Payable** account classified on the balance sheet?

4. Are authorized, unissued bonds shown on the balance sheet? If so, where?

5. Why might a company use a special bank account for paying bond interest?

6. In a bond indenture dated January 1, 2005, Sand Corporation authorized the issuance of $500,000 face value, 11 percent, 20-year bonds payable. No bonds were issued until July 1, 2008, when bonds with a face value of $200,000 were issued. At that time, the market rate of interest on similar debt was 10 percent. Would the issue price of the bonds be more than or less than face value? Explain.

7. Why is a bond premium or discount amortized as part of the adjustment process at the end of the year?

8. Why is the year-end adjusting entry for amortization of a bond premium or discount reversed at the start of the new year?

9. How are the legal costs and other costs related to issuing bonds accounted for?

10. What is a bond sinking fund?

11. What is the relationship between a bond sinking fund and an appropriation of retained earnings for bond retirement? Explain.

12. Explain the accounting treatment necessary when bonds are retired before maturity.

Applications

Exercises 22-1 through 22-3.

CROCKETT Corporation issued $200,000 of its 10 percent bonds payable on April 1, 2004. The bonds were issued at face value. Interest is payable semiannually on October 1 and April 1.

Exercise 22-1 ►
Objective 3

Issuing bonds.

Give the general journal entry to record the April 1, 2004, bond issue.

Exercise 22-2 ►
Objective 4

Paying interest on bonds payable.

Give the entry in general journal form to record the interest payment by CROCKETT on October 1, 2004.

Exercise 22-3 ►
Objective 5

Accruing interest on bonds.

Give the entry to accrue bond interest on CROCKETT's bonds payable on December 31, 2004.

Exercises 22-4 through 22-6.

Angus Inc. was authorized to issue $1,000,000 of 11 percent bonds. On April 1, 2004, the corporation issued bonds with a face value of $90,000 at a price of 102.4. The bonds mature 10 years from the date of issue. Interest is payable semiannually on October 1 and April 1.

Exercise 22-4 ►
Objective 3

Recording issuance of bonds.

Give the general journal entry to record the April 1, 2004, bond issue.

Exercise 22-5 ►
Objective 6

Computing amortization of premium on bonds.

Using the data given above, what amount of premium will be amortized by Angus Inc. on October 1, 2004, using straight-line amortization?

Exercise 22-6 ►
Objectives 5, 6

Recording adjusting entry for bond interest and premium.

Using the data given above, give the adjusting entry that would be made by Angus Inc. on December 31, 2004, to record accrued interest and to amortize the premium.

Exercise 22-7 ►
Objective 8

Recording transactions of a bond sinking fund investment.

Give the general journal entries to record the following transactions.

a. On December 31, 2004, White Corporation established a bond sinking fund investment by depositing $40,000 with the fund trustee.

b. On December 31, 2005, White Corporation recorded $6,000 net income from its bond sinking fund investment for the year.

c. On December 31, 2005, White Corporation made a deposit of $34,000 into the bond sinking fund investment.

Exercise 22-8 ►
Objective 9

Appropriating retained earnings for bond retirement.

Record the appropriation of $100,000 of retained earnings on December 31, 2007, by Bahama Corporation to establish an appropriation for bond retirement.

Retiring bonds before maturity.

On March 1, 2004, Tank Bay, Inc., issued $100,000 of its 10 percent bonds, maturing 10 years later. Interest is payable semiannually on September 1 and March 1. The issue price was 96.4. Interest and amortization have been recorded through March 1, 2008, four years after the bonds were issued. On June 1, 2008, the corporation repurchased and retired $50,000 face value of the bonds at a purchase price of 99.8, plus accrued interest. Give the entry in general journal form to record the repurchase and retirement.

◄ **Exercise 22-9**
Objective 10

Problems

Selected problems can be completed using:
 Peachtree   QuickBooks   Spreadsheets

PROBLEM SET A

Issuing bonds; bond interest transactions.

The board of directors of Computer Services Corporation authorized the issuance of $500,000 face value, 20-year, 9 percent bonds dated March 1, 2005, and maturing on March 1, 2025. Interest is payable semiannually on March 1 and September 1. Computer Services Corporation uses the calendar year as its fiscal year. The bond transactions that occurred in 2005 and 2006 follow.

◄ **Problem 22-1A**
Objectives 3, 4, 5

Record the transactions below in general journal form. Use the account names given in the chapter.

INSTRUCTIONS

DATE		TRANSACTIONS FOR 2005
Mar.	1	Issued $300,000 of bonds at face value.
Sept.	1	Paid the semiannual interest on the bonds issued.
Dec.	31	Recorded the adjusting entry for the accrued bond interest.
	31	Closed the **Bond Interest Expense** account to the **Income Summary** account.

DATE		TRANSACTIONS FOR 2006
Jan.	1	Reversed the adjusting entry made on December 31, 2005.
Mar.	1	Issued $200,000 of bonds at face value.
	1	Paid the interest for six months on the bonds previously issued.
Sept.	1	Paid the interest for six months on the outstanding bonds.
Dec.	31	Recorded the adjusting entry for the accrued bond interest.
	31	Closed the **Bond Interest Expense** account to the **Income Summary** account.

Analyze: Based on the transactions given, what is the balance in the **Bonds Payable** account on December 31, 2005?

Problem 22-2A ►

Objectives 3, 4, 5, 6

Issuing bonds; recording interest transactions and amortization of premium.

The board of directors of Oklahoma River Shops, Inc., authorized the issuance of $1,000,000 face value, 10-year, 12 percent bonds dated April 1, 2005, and maturing on April 1, 2015. Interest is payable semiannually on April 1 and October 1. The corporation did not immediately issue the bonds because funds were not needed. The transactions that took place in 2006 and 2007 are shown below.

INSTRUCTIONS

1. Record the transactions below in general journal form. Use the account names given in the chapter.
2. Prepare the Long-Term Liabilities section of the corporation's balance sheet on December 31, 2006.

DATE		TRANSACTIONS FOR 2006
Apr.	1	Issued $500,000 face value bonds at 103.6.
Oct.	1	Paid the semiannual interest on the outstanding bonds and amortized the bond premium. (Make two entries. Use the straight-line method to compute the amortization.)
Dec.	31	Recorded the adjusting entry for accrued interest and amortization of the bond premium for three months. (Make one entry.)
	31	Closed the **Bond Interest Expense** account to the **Income Summary** account.

DATE		TRANSACTION FOR 2007
Jan.	1	Reversed the adjusting entry made on December 31, 2006.

Analyze: If the reversing entry was not recorded, what entry would be required when the interest expense is paid in April 2007?

Problem 22-3A ►

Objectives 3, 4, 5, 7

Issuing bonds; bond interest transactions and amortization of discount.

The board of directors of Blue Raider Corporation authorized the issuance of $500,000 face value, 20-year, 8 percent bonds, dated March 1, 2005, and maturing on March 1, 2025. Interest is payable semiannually on September 1 and March 1.

INSTRUCTIONS

1. Record the following transactions in general journal form. Use the account names given in the chapter.
2. Prepare the Long-Term Liabilities section of the corporation's balance sheet on December 31, 2005.

DATE		TRANSACTIONS FOR 2005
Apr.	1	Issued bonds with a face value of $100,000 at 97.61 plus accrued interest from March 1. (When bonds are issued between interest payment dates, the accrued interest is paid to the corporation by the purchaser. Credit **Bond Interest Expense**.)
Sept.	1	Paid the semiannual bond interest and amortized the discount for five months. (Make two entries. Use the straight-line method to compute the amortization.) *Continued*

DATE	(22-3A cont.) **TRANSACTIONS FOR 2005**
Dec. 31	Recorded an adjusting entry to accrue the interest and to amortize the discount. (Make one entry.)
31	Closed the **Bond Interest Expense** account to the **Income Summary** account.

DATE	**TRANSACTIONS FOR 2006**
Jan. 1	Reversed the adjusting entry made on December 31, 2005.
Mar. 1	Paid the semiannual bond interest and amortized the discount on the outstanding bonds.

Analyze: What is the balance of the **Discount on Bonds Payable** account on December 31, 2005?

Recording bond sinking fund transactions, retained earnings appropriated for bond retirement, and retirement of bonds.

◀ **Problem 22-4A**
Objectives 8, 9, 10

Low Country Technology, Inc., has outstanding $500,000 of its 10 percent bonds payable, dated January 1, 2005, and maturing on January 1, 2025, 20 years later. The corporation is required under the bond contract to transfer $25,000 to a sinking fund each year. The directors have also voted to restrict retained earnings by transferring $25,000 each year on January 1 over the life of the bond issue to a **Retained Earnings Appropriated for Bond Retirement** account.

INSTRUCTIONS

1. Prepare entries in general journal form to record the January 1, 2005, issuance of bonds, the establishment of the **Bond Sinking Fund Investment** account, and the appropriation of retained earnings.

2. Show how the **Bond Sinking Fund Investment** account and the **Retained Earnings Appropriated for Bond Retirement** account would be presented on the balance sheet as of December 31, 2010. (Assume that the ending balance of the **Bond Sinking Fund Investment** was $198,520 and the **Retained Earnings—Unappropriated** account was $248,520.)

3. Assuming that the **Bond Sinking Fund Investment** account had a balance of $500,000 on January 1, 2025, give the entry in general journal form to record the retirement of the bonds and remove the appropriation for retained earnings.

Analyze: What percentage of total retained earnings has been appropriated for bond retirement on December 31, 2010?

Retiring bonds payable prior to maturity.

◀ **Problem 22-5A**
Objective 10

On May 1, 2006, Gongola Corporation issued $200,000 face value, 8 percent bonds at 99. The bonds are dated May 1, 2006, and mature 10 years later. The discount is amortized on each interest payment date. The interest is payable semiannually on May 1 and November 1. On February 1, 2011, the corporation purchased one-half of the outstanding bonds from the bondholders and retired them. The purchase price was 98 plus accrued interest for three months.

INSTRUCTIONS

1. Give the entry in general journal form to amortize the discount on the bonds that are being retired (three months' amortization). Use the straight-line method.

2. Give the entry in general journal form to record the repurchase and retirement of the bonds. (Use the **Gain on Early Retirement of Bonds** account.)

Analyze: If Gongola Corporation did not purchase the outstanding bonds, what total bond interest would have been incurred over the life of the bond?

PROBLEM SET B

Problem 22-1B ►
Objectives 3, 4, 5

Issuing bonds; bond interest transactions.

The board of directors of National Pizza Corporation authorized the issuance of $1,000,000 face value, 10 percent bonds dated April 1, 2005. The bonds will mature on April 1, 2015. The interest is payable semiannually on April 1 and October 1. The bond transactions that occurred in 2005 and 2006 are shown below.

INSTRUCTIONS

Record the transactions below in general journal form. Use the account names given in the chapter.

DATE		TRANSACTIONS FOR 2005
April	1	Issued $500,000 of bonds at face value.
Oct.	1	Paid the semiannual bond interest on the outstanding bonds.
Dec.	31	Recorded the adjusting entry to accrue the interest on the bonds issued.
	31	Closed the **Bond Interest Expense** account to the **Income Summary** account.

DATE		TRANSACTIONS FOR 2006
Jan.	1	Reversed the adjusting entry of December 31, 2005.
April	1	Paid the semiannual bond interest.
Oct.	1	Paid the semiannual bond interest.
	1	Issued $200,000 of bonds at face value.
Dec.	31	Recorded the adjusting entry to accrue the interest on all bonds issued.
	31	Closed the **Bond Interest Expense** account to the **Income Summary** account.

Analyze: What total bond interest would have been reported on the income statement for the year ended December 31, 2005?

Problem 22-2B ►
Objectives 3, 4, 5, 6

Issuing bonds; recording interest transactions and amortization of premium.

The board of directors of Rabon Corporation authorized issuance of $2,000,000 of 10 percent bonds. Each bond has a face value of $10,000. The interest is payable semiannually on February 1 and August 1. The bonds are dated February 1, 2005, and mature 10 years later.

1. Record the transactions below in general journal form. Use the account names given in the chapter. (Round your numbers to the nearest whole dollar.)

2. Prepare the Long-Term Liabilities section of the corporation's balance sheet on December 31, 2005.

DATE		TRANSACTIONS FOR 2005
Feb.	1	Issued $1,000,000 of bonds at 112.
Aug.	1	Paid the semiannual interest on the bonds issued and recorded the amortization of the premium.
Dec.	31	Recorded the adjusting entry to accrue interest on the bonds issued and to amortize the premium for five months.
	31	Recorded the closing entry for **Bond Interest Expense.**

DATE		TRANSACTION FOR 2006
Jan.	1	Reversed the adjusting entry of December 31, 2005.

Analyze: If the reversing entry had not been recorded in January 2006, how would the payment of bond interest be recorded in February 2006?

Issuing bonds; bond interest transactions and amortization of discount.

◄ **Problem 22-3B**
Objectives 3, 4, 5, 7

The board of directors of Knox Corporation authorized the issuance of $400,000 face value, 9 percent bonds. The bonds mature 10 years from their issue date of March 1, 2005. The interest is payable semiannually on March 1 and September 1. Because the funds were not immediately needed, no bonds were issued until May 1, 2005.

1. Record the following transactions in general journal form. Use the account names given in the chapter.

2. Prepare the Long-Term Liabilities section of the corporation's balance sheet on December 31, 2005.

DATE		TRANSACTIONS FOR 2005
May	1	Issued $200,000 of bonds at 94.1 plus accrued interest from March 1. (When bonds are issued between interest payment dates, the accrued interest is paid to the corporation by the purchaser. Credit **Bond Interest Expense**.)
Sept.	1	Paid the semiannual bond interest.
	1	Amortized the discount on the bonds issued.
Dec.	31	Recorded the adjusting entry to accrue the interest on the bonds issued and to amortize the discount for four months. (Make one entry.)
Dec.	31	Closed the **Bond Interest Expense** account.

DATE		TRANSACTIONS FOR 2006
Jan.	1	Reversed the adjusting entry of December 31, 2005.
Mar.	1	Paid the semiannual bond interest and amortized the discount on the bonds issued.

Analyze: What is the balance of the **Bond Interest Expense** account at December 31, 2005, prior to closing?

Problem 22-4B ►
Objectives 8, 9, 10

Recording bond sinking fund transactions, retained earnings appropriated for bond retirement, and retirement of bonds.

Disc Products, Inc., has outstanding $100,000 face value, 10 percent bonds payable dated January 1, 2005, and maturing 10 years later. The corporation is required under the bond contract to transfer $8,500 each year to a sinking fund. The directors have also voted to restrict retained earnings by transferring $10,000 each year to a **Retained Earnings Appropriated for Bond Retirement** account.

INSTRUCTIONS

1. Prepare entries in general journal form to record the 2005 transactions.
2. Prepare the partial balance sheet for December 31, 2014, showing the presentation of the **Bond Sinking Fund Investment** and the **Retained Earnings Appropriated for Bond Retirement** (assume **Retained Earnings—Unappropriated** has a balance of $325,000).
3. Prepare the journal entries to retire the bonds and remove the appropriation of retained earnings on January 1, 2015.

DATE		TRANSACTIONS FOR 2005
Jan.	1	Sold the bonds at 100.
	1	Made the annual bond sinking fund investment deposit.
	1	Recorded the annual appropriation of retained earnings.
Dec.	31	The bond sinking fund trustee reported a net income of $900 on the sinking fund investments for the year.

On December 31, 2014, the balance in the **Bond Sinking Fund Investment** account is $100,000. The balance in the **Retained Earnings Appropriated for Bond Retirement** account is also $100,000.

Analyze: What percentage of total retained earnings had been allocated for bond retirement at December 31, 2014?

Problem 22-5B ►
Objective 10

Retiring bonds payable prior to maturity.

On April 1, 2005, Tennessee Tours Corporation issued $500,000 face value, 10 percent bonds at 99.6. The bonds were dated April 1, 2005, and will mature in 10 years. The discount is to be amortized on each interest payment date. The interest is payable semiannually on April 1 and October 1. On June 1, 2008, the corporation decided to retire the bonds. The bondholders were paid 98.5 and accrued interest for two months. Round all computations to the nearest whole dollar.

INSTRUCTIONS

1. Give the entry in general journal form to amortize the discount on the bonds on June 1, 2008.
2. Give the entry in general journal form to record the repurchase and retirement of the bonds. (Use the **Gain on Early Retirement of Bonds** account.)

Analyze: If the bond had been retired on the original due date, what credit would have been made to the **Cash** account?

Financing Decision

On December 31, 2005, the equity accounts of SEC Corporation contained the following balances.

Common stock ($10 par, 100,000 shares authorized)	
50,000 shares issued and outstanding	500,000
Retained earnings	500,000

For the year 2005, the corporation had net income before income taxes of $250,000, income taxes of $97,500, and net income after taxes of $152,500. The corporation's tax rate is 39 percent.

An expansion of the existing plant at a cost of $300,000 is planned. The corporation's president, who owns 60 percent of the corporation's common stock, estimates that the expansion would result in an increased net income of approximately $150,000 before interest and taxes. The financial vice president forecasts that the increase would be only $100,000.

Management is considering two possibilities for financing:

a. Issuance of 10,000 additional shares of common stock for $30 per share
b. Issuance of $300,000 face amount, 10-year, 10 percent bonds payable, secured by a mortgage lien on the plant

Assume that profits from existing operations will remain the same.

INSTRUCTIONS

1. Assume that the president's estimate of net income from the new plant is correct. Prepare a two-column table for each of the proposed financing plans. Show the following items: (a) total net income before interest and tax; (b) total bond interest; (c) total income tax; (d) total income after tax; (e) present income after tax; (f) increase or decrease in total income after bond interest and tax; (g) present earnings per share of common stock (compute earnings per share by dividing the net income after taxes by the number of shares of common stock outstanding); (h) estimated earnings per share of common stock.

2. Construct a similar table, assuming the financial vice president's estimate of earnings is correct.

3. Write a brief comment on the results of your analysis.

Analyze: Assume the company issued 10,000 shares of common stock and net income before taxes was $310,000. Would shareholders have realized an increase or decrease in earnings per share over fiscal 2005?

Early Retirement

On December 31, 2005, American Air Express Company has $1,000,000 of 10 percent, 15-year bonds outstanding. These bonds were issued on January 1, 2001, at par value. Interest rates have dropped to 8 percent, and the president of the company is considering buying back the outstanding 10 percent bonds and issuing new 10-year bonds with an 8 percent interest rate.

1. How much money would American Air Express save in interest payments if new, 8 percent bonds were issued?

2. Under what circumstances would this action be advantageous for American Air Express?

Business Connections

Connection 1 ► **MANAGERIAL FOCUS** Financing Through Bonds

1. What would cause corporate management to obtain cash by issuing bonds instead of selling stock?
2. Which type of bonds would give management greater flexibility in formulating and controlling a corporation's financial affairs?
3. In what situations would management be wise to issue additional common stock rather than bonds to meet long-term capital needs?
4. Why would management repurchase and retire a corporation's bonds prior to their maturity?
5. Cook Corporation's board of directors is considering authorization of a new bond issue. The controller notes that the bonds are callable at 101.6 at any time beginning five years after the date of the bond contract. What does this mean? What is the advantage of such a provision?

Ethical DILEMMA **Conflict of Interest?** ABC, Inc.'s sole stockholder

Connection 2 ► and president is also the holder of a $100,000, 10-year, 8 percent corporate unsecured bond. Interest is payable twice a year. Interest rates have begun to rise; the current market rate is close to 10 percent, although indications are that the rate will probably come down in the next six months. The president thinks that it is a good time for the company to refinance the bonds at current interest rates. Is this a conflict of interest? Why or why not?

Street WISE:
Questions from the Real World **Long-Term Debt** Refer to The Home Depot, Inc. *Annual Report* in Appendix B.

Connection 3 ►

1. Locate the notes to consolidated financial statements. Note 2 presents a detailed list of the company's long-term debt at the end of fiscal 1999 and 1998. What amount of debt is in the form of bonds? Are they secured or unsecured? What average interest rate do the bonds carry?
2. Review the letter written to The Home Depot, Inc. stockholders, customers, and associates. Based on the letter, what types of activities do you think will be funded with the bonds issued by the company?

FINANCIAL STATEMENT ANALYSIS **Bond Financing Agreements** The following excerpt is from the *2000 Annual Report* for FedEx Corporation. The company reported $1,776,253 thousand in long-term debt for the year ended May 31, 2000. A portion of this debt was a bond financing agreement.

Connection 4 ►

Note 5: Long-Term Debt and Other Financing Agreements
The components of unsecured debt were as follows:
May 31, 2000

In thousands	2000	1999
Senior debt, interest rates of 7.80% to 9.88% due through 2013	$673,970	$673,779
Bonds, interest rate of 7.60%, due in 2098	239,382	239,376
Medium term notes, interest rates of 9.95% to 10.57%, due through 2007	62,510	74,965
	$975,862	$988,120

Tax exempt bonds were issued by the Memphis-Shelby County Airport Authority ("MSCAA") and the City of Indianapolis. Lease agreements with the MSCAA and a loan agreement with the City of Indianapolis covering the facilities and equipment financed with the bond proceeds obligate FedEx to pay rentals and loan payments, respectively, equal to principal and interest due on the bonds.

Analyze:

1. If the bonds were issued in 1998, what semiannual interest payments would be due to bondholders each year until maturity?

2. What percentage of total long-term debt do bonds payable represent?

3. Why do you think FedEx, MSCAA, and the City of Indianapolis have structured financing in this way?

Analyze Online: On the FedEx Web site **(www.fedex.com)**, go to the *Investor Relations* section and click on the *Annual Report* link.

4. What total long-term debt does the most recent annual report show?

5. What portion of long-term debt is composed of bonds payable?

Extending the Thought
◄ **Connection 5**

Investing in Callable Bonds Some bonds, especially those issued by utility agencies, can be called under *maintenance and replacement* fund provisions that relate to necessary upgrades of plant and equipment. As a bond investor, you might be quoted a *yield to maturity*, the total return you will receive if you hold a bond until maturity. Yield to maturity includes all interest you will earn plus any gain or loss realized if you bought the bond below or above par. What do you think a *yield to call* is? Explain.

Business Communication
◄ **Connection 6**

Memo The board of directors of Hashimoto Nurseries, Inc., is currently reviewing the most recent financial statements. As the chief financial officer, you are responsible for ensuring that the board understands the statements. A board member assumes that since a bond sinking fund has been established, there is no need to appropriate retained earnings for bonds payable. Prepare a memo to the board explaining why retained earnings have been appropriated for bond retirement.

Team Work
◄ **Connection 7**

Investigating the Bond Market Research one of the topics listed below. Use an online business magazine such as *Business Week* **(www.businessweek.com)**, *Money* **(www.money.com)**, or *Forbes* **(www.forbes.com)**. Prepare a one-page report on the topic, and cite the sources that you use.

- Why investors buy bonds instead of stocks
- U.S. Treasury inflation-indexed securities
- Callable step-up bonds

interNET CONNECTION
◄ **Connection 8**

Standard & Poor's Bonds are rated by companies such as Standard & Poor's. Go to the Standard & Poor's Web site at **www.standardandpoors.com.** Select *Personal Wealth*; select *Basics*; select *Glossary.* What is a T-Bill? Select *Bonds.* What is the current rate on the 30-Year Bond? What is the current rate on the 3-Month T-Bill?

Answers to Section 1 Self Review

1. Registered bonds are bonds whose owners are registered in the records of the corporation. Interest is paid each payment date to the registered owner. Coupon bonds are not registered. The corporation does not know the names of owners of the bonds. To collect interest, the bondholder clips a coupon from the bond and presents it to the bank.

2. A convertible bond is one that may be converted into common stock, under specified conditions, at the option of the owner.

3. In the event of a decrease in the market interest rate, or if the corporation has extra cash, the corporation can redeem the bonds if they are callable.

4. **b.** serial bonds.

5. **d.** debentures.

6. 10.4%

Answers to Section 2 Self Review

1. An equal amount of discount or premium is amortized each month from the issue date to the maturity date.

2. Discount on bonds payable is shown on the balance sheet as a deduction from the face value of the bonds.

3. Bond premium is a device to adjust the face amount of interest to the market interest rate at the date of issuance. Thus the premium is directly related to interest expense.

4. **b.** amortized over the life of the bond issue.

5. **b.** credit to **Bonds Payable.**

6. $345

Answers to Section 3 Self Review

1. A fund used to accumulate assets to pay off bonds when they mature.

2. Bonds may be retired prior to maturity because management has surplus cash, it wants to save interest costs, or it expects interest costs to decrease.

3. Gain or loss on bond retirement is shown as an extraordinary item if the amount is significant. Otherwise, it is shown as **Other Income** or **Other Expense.**

4. **c. Income from Sinking Fund Investment.**

5. **b. Retained Earnings.**

6. Debit **Retained Earnings Appropriated for Bond Retirement** for $600,000; credit **Retained Earnings** for $600,000. Close appropriation account upon retirement of bonds.

Answers to Comprehensive Self Review

1. Secured bonds are bonds that have specific assets pledged as security. If the corporation does not pay the principal and interest, the bondholders may take possession of the assets. Debenture bonds have no specific assets pledged to secure payment. So, the secured bond is a more attractive investment.

2. Two disadvantages are (a) interest must be paid and (b) the face amount must be repaid at maturity.

3. Bonds sell at a discount when the face interest rate is less than the market rate of interest on similar investments on the date of the sale.

4. The appropriation is intended to protect the bondholders. It clearly indicates that dividends are being restricted because of a future need to pay off the bonds.

5. When bonds are retired at maturity, **Bonds Payable** is debited and **Cash** (or **Bond Sinking Fund Investment**) is credited.

MINI-PRACTICE SET 3

Corporation Accounting Cycle

Titan Corporation

This project will give you an opportunity to apply your knowledge of accounting principles and procedures to a corporation. You will handle the accounting work of Titan Corporation for 2005.

INTRODUCTION

The chart of accounts and account balances of Titan Corporation on January 1, 2005, are shown on the next page. Titan Corporation *does not use reversing entries.*

INSTRUCTIONS

Round all computations to the nearest whole dollar.

1. Open the general ledger accounts and enter the balances for January 1, 2005. Obtain the necessary figures from the chart of accounts.
2. Analyze the transactions on the pages that follow, and record them in the general journal. Use 1 as the number of the first journal page.
3. Post the journal entries to the general ledger accounts.
4. Prepare a worksheet for the year ended December 31, 2005.
5. Prepare a summary income statement for the year ended December 31, 2005.
6. Prepare a statement of retained earnings for the year ended December 31, 2005.
7. Prepare a balance sheet as of December 31, 2005.
8. Journalize and post the adjusting entries as of December 31, 2005.
9. Journalize and post the closing entries as of December 31, 2005.

Analyze: Assume that the firm declared and issued a 3:1 stock split of common stock in 2005. What is the effect on total par value?

TITAN CORPORATION
Chart of Accounts/Account Balances

Account Number	Account Name	Debit	Credit
101	Cash	$196,000	
103	Accounts Receivable	150,000	
104	Allowance for Doubtful Accounts		$ 5,000
105	Subscriptions Receivable—Common Stock		
121	Interest Receivable		
131	Merchandise Inventory	175,500	
141	Land	50,000	
151	Buildings	150,000	
152	Accumulated Depreciation—Buildings		15,000
161	Furniture and Equipment	50,000	
162	Accumulated Depreciation—Furniture and Equipment		10,000
181	Organization Costs	9,000	
202	Accounts Payable		80,000
203	Interest Payable		2,500
205	Estimated Income Taxes Payable		15,000
206	Dividends Payable—Preferred Stock		
207	Dividends Payable—Common Stock		
211	10-year, 10% Bonds Payable		100,000
212	Premium on Bonds Payable		10,500
301	8% Preferred Stock ($100 par, 10,000 shares authorized)		100,000
302	Paid-in Capital in Excess of Par—Preferred Stock		10,000
303	Common Stock ($25 par, 100,000 shares authorized)		250,000
304	Paid-in Capital in Excess of Par—Common Stock		25,000
305	Common Stock Subscribed		
306	Common Stock Dividend Distributable		
311	Retained Earnings Appropriated		10,000
312	Retained Earnings Unappropriated		147,500
343	Treasury Stock—Preferred		
399	Income Summary		
401	Sales		
501	Purchases		
601	Operating Expenses		
701	Interest Income		
711	Gain on Early Retirement of Bonds Payable		
751	Interest Expense		
753	Amortization of Organization Costs		
801	Income Tax Expense		
		$780,500	$780,500

DATE	SELECTED TRANSACTIONS FOR 2005
Jan. 4	Issued 1,500 shares of 8 percent $100 par preferred stock for $115 per share. (The corporation has been authorized to issue 10,000 shares of preferred stock.)
15	Paid estimated income taxes of $15,000 accrued at the end of 2004.
Apr. 1	Paid semiannual bond interest on the 10-year, 10 percent bonds payable and amortized the premium for the period since October 1, 2004. (The interest and premium were recorded as of December 31, 2004; the entry was not reversed.) The bonds were issued on October 1, 2003, at a price of 112, and they mature on October 1, 2013. Use straight-line amortization.
July 1	Titan Corporation's board of directors declared a cash dividend of $0.50 per share on the common stock. The dividend is payable on July 26 to stockholders of record as of July 15.
26	Paid the cash dividend on the common stock.
Aug. 12	A purchaser of 500 shares of preferred stock issued on January 4 asked the corporation to repurchase the shares. The corporation repurchased the stock for $112 per share. The stock is to be held by the corporation until it can be resold to another purchaser.
Oct. 1	Paid the semiannual bond interest and recorded amortization of the bond premium.
Dec. 1	Because of its good cash position and current bond prices, Titan Corporation repurchased and retired $20,000 par value of the 10 percent bonds that it has outstanding. The repurchase price was 98, plus accrued interest.
15	Titan Corporation's board of directors declared a cash dividend of $8 per share on the outstanding preferred stock. This dividend is payable on January 10 to stockholders of record as of December 31.
15	Titan Corporation's board of directors also declared a 10 percent stock dividend on the outstanding common stock. The new shares are to be distributed on January 10 to stockholders of record as of December 31. At the time the dividend was declared, the common stock had a fair market value of $37 per share.
30	Received a subscription for 500 shares of Titan Corporation's common stock at $30 per share from the company's president. Received cash equal to one-half the purchase price on the date of subscription. The balance of the purchase price is to be paid on January 15, 2006. (The subscriber will not be entitled to the stock dividend previously declared on the outstanding shares of common stock.)

Continued

DATE	(cont.) SELECTED TRANSACTIONS FOR 2005
Dec. 30	Because the management of Titan Corporation foresees the need to expand a warehouse the firm owns, the board of directors has restricted future dividend payments. Record the appropriation of $60,000 of retained earnings for plant expansion.

Journalize the following summary transactions using December 31, 2005, as the record date.

	SUMMARY OPERATING TRANSACTIONS FOR 2005
1.	Total sales of merchandise for the year were $2,250,000. All sales were on credit.
2.	Total collections on accounts receivable during the year were $2,245,000.
3.	Total purchases of merchandise for the year were $1,550,000. All purchases were on credit.
4.	Total operating expenses incurred during the year were $512,000. (Debit **Operating Expenses** and credit **Accounts Payable.**)
5.	Total cash payments on accounts payable during the year were $2,000,000.
6.	Total accounts receivable charged off as uncollectible during the year were $6,500. (Titan Corporation uses the allowance method to record uncollectible accounts.)

Data for Year-End Adjustments

1. The balance of **Allowance for Doubtful Accounts** should be adjusted to equal 1 percent of the balance of **Accounts Receivable.** (Debit **Operating Expenses.**)
2. Depreciation on the buildings should be recorded. (Debit **Operating Expenses.**) The firm uses the straight-line method and an estimated life of 20 years to compute this adjustment.
3. Depreciation on furniture and equipment should be recorded. The firm uses the straight-line method and an estimated life of 10 years to compute this adjustment. (Debit **Operating Expenses.**)
4. Accrued interest on the outstanding bonds payable of Titan Corporation should be recorded and the premium amortized.
5. The amortization of organization costs for the year should be recorded. Titan Corporation was formed on January 1, 2003. Organization costs of $15,000 were incurred at the time and are being amortized over a 60-month period.
6. The ending merchandise inventory is $168,500.

Other Data

Estimated federal income taxes are to be recorded using the tax rates given on page 768.

Financial Reporting and Analysis

In the spring of 2001 more than 50 security analysts toured the International Truck and Engine Corporation new cab assembly and fabrication facility in Springfield, Ohio. In order to provide accurate research and valuation reports to the public, these individuals study industries and specific companies. Analysis of a company's financial condition should include not only the review of its financial statements, but also relevant manufacturing processes, uses of resources, and potential for long-term growth.

Thinking Critically

Why do you think security analysts would be interested in a tour of a company's manufacturing facility?

CHAPTER 23

Learning Objectives

1. Use vertical analysis techniques to analyze a comparative income statement and balance sheet.

2. Use horizontal analysis techniques to analyze a comparative income statement and balance sheet.

3. Use trend analysis to evaluate financial statements.

4. Interpret the results of the statement analyses by comparison with industry averages.

5. Define the accounting terms new to this chapter.

Statement Analysis: Comparative Statements

www.dole.com

D ole Food Company, Inc. was founded by Jim Dole in 1851 with an initial investment of $1,000. Since then the company has expanded into a worldwide organization of growers, packers, processors, and shippers providing fruit, vegetables, flowers, and food products, recording revenues of $5 billion in 1999.

The financial condition of companies like Dole is often affected by a variety of market factors that can be highlighted and explained using analysis techniques. In the *Dole 1999 Annual Report,* the income statement reports revenues, expenses, and net income figures for the last three years, helping users understand increases in certain expenses and their impact on net profits.

Thinking Critically
In addition to comparing financial performance over a span of years, what other methods of analysis might be used to evaluate and identify financial trends?

For more information on Dole Food Company, Inc. go to:
collegeaccounting.glencoe.com.

New Terms

Common-size statements

Comparative statements

Horizontal analysis

Industry averages

Ratio analysis

Trend analysis

Vertical analysis

Section Objective

① **Use vertical analysis techniques to analyze a comparative income statement and balance sheet.**

WHY IT'S IMPORTANT

Analysis techniques reveal the financial strengths and weaknesses of a business.

Terms to Learn

common-size statements
comparative statements
horizontal analysis
ratio analysis
vertical analysis

① **Objective**

Use vertical analysis techniques to analyze a comparative income statement and balance sheet.

Vertical Analysis

Owners, managers, creditors, and other parties use financial statements to gather the information needed to make business decisions.

The Phases of Statement Analysis

The two phases of financial statement analysis are (1) compute differences, percentages, and ratios; and (2) interpret the results.

The Computation Phase

The first step in financial statement analysis is the *computation phase.* Three basic types of calculations are used:

- **Vertical analysis** is the relationship of each item on a financial statement to some base amount on the statement. On the income statement, each item is expressed as a percentage of net sales. On the balance sheet, each item is expressed as a percentage of total assets or total liabilities and stockholders' equity.
- **Horizontal analysis** is the percentage change for individual items in the financial statements from year to year.
- **Ratio analysis** is the relationship between various items in the financial statements. Ratio analysis can involve items on the same statement or items on different statements. Ratio analysis is discussed in Chapter 24.

The Interpretation Phase

The second step in statement analysis, the *interpretation phase,* is the more difficult and important step. Financial statement interpretation requires an understanding of financial statements and knowledge of the operations of the business and the industry. In the interpretation phase the analyst develops an understanding of the significance of the percentages and ratios computed. Analysts compare the ratios for the current year to prior years' ratios, budgeted ratios, and industry averages.

Vertical Analysis of Financial Statements

Let's learn the techniques of vertical analysis of financial statements using comparative financial statements. **Comparative statements** are financial statements presented side by side for two or more years. Figure 23-1 on page 849 shows the comparative income statement of Carolina Creations, Inc., for the years 2005 and 2004.

Vertical Analysis of the Income Statement

Notice the income statement heading. The third line indicates the periods covered by the statement. The more recent year, 2005, is in the left column. The income statement is in condensed form. In actual practice, separate schedules of the detailed Selling Expenses and General and Administrative Expenses are provided with the financial statements.

Vertical analysis of the income statement expresses each item as a percentage of the *net sales* figure. In each column the net sales figure is used

Carolina Creations, Inc.
Comparative Income Statement (Vertical Analysis)
Years Ended December 31, 2005 and 2004

	Amounts		Percent of Net Sales	
	2005	2004	2005	2004
Revenue				
Sales	3 4 8 7 6 6 5	2 9 4 0 0 2 5	106.0	105.0
Less Sales Returns and Allowances	1 9 7 4 1 5	1 3 9 5 2 5	6.0	5.0
Net Sales	3 2 9 0 2 5 0	2 8 0 0 5 0 0	100.0	100.0
Cost of Goods Sold				
Merchandise Inventory, January 1	2 2 5 0 0 0	2 7 5 0 0 0	6.8	9.8
Purchases (Net)	1 7 0 3 5 0 0	1 2 6 5 2 7 5	51.8	45.2
Freight In	2 8 5 9 8	1 9 0 0 0	0.9	0.7
Total Merchandise Available for Sale	1 9 5 7 0 9 8	1 5 5 9 2 7 5	59.5	55.7
Less Merchandise Inventory, December 31	1 9 2 5 0 0	2 2 5 0 0 0	5.9	8.0
Cost of Goods Sold	1 7 6 4 5 9 8	1 3 3 4 2 7 5	53.6	47.6
Gross Profit on Sales	1 5 2 5 6 5 2	1 4 6 6 2 2 5	46.4	52.4
Operating Expenses				
Selling Expenses	5 8 5 3 0 0	5 9 9 8 9 5	17.8	21.4
General and Administrative Expenses	7 5 2 5 0 0	7 2 5 8 7 5	22.9	25.9
Total Operating Expenses	1 3 3 7 8 0 0	1 3 2 5 7 7 0	40.7	47.4*
Net Income From Operations	1 8 7 8 5 2	1 4 0 4 5 5	5.7	5.0
Other Income				
Gain on Sale of Equipment	4 0 0 0	2 5 0 0 0	0.1	0.9
Interest Income	1 2 2 5 0	1 2 0 0 0	0.4	0.4
Total Other Income	1 6 2 5 0	3 7 0 0 0	0.5	1.3
Other Expenses				
Bond Interest Expense	5 9 0 8	5 0 0 0	0.2	0.2
Other Interest Expense	1 8 0 0	2 5 0 0	0.1	0.1
Total Other Expenses	7 7 0 8	7 5 0 0	0.2	0.3
Income Before Income Taxes	1 9 6 3 9 4	1 6 9 9 5 5	6.0	6.1
Income Tax Expense	6 7 6 5 5	5 9 4 8 4	2.1	2.1
Net Income After Income Taxes	1 2 8 7 3 9	1 1 0 4 7 1	3.9	3.9

* Rounded

▲ FIGURE 23-1
Comparative Income Statement—
Vertical Analysis

as the base, or 100 percent. Every amount in the column is expressed as a percentage of net sales. To compute an item's percentage of net sales, divide the amount of that item by the amount of net sales. For example, in 2005 the cost of goods sold is 53.6 percent of net sales.

$$\frac{\text{Cost of goods sold}}{\text{Net sales}} = \frac{\$1,764,598}{\$3,290,250} = 0.5363 = 53.63 \text{ percent}$$
(rounded to 53.6 percent)

In making these types of computations, it is customary to carry the division one place further than needed and then round off. The usual practice is to round percentages to the nearest one-tenth of a percent. The computation in the example is made to the fourth decimal (0.5363). That decimal fraction is converted to a percentage by moving the decimal point two places to the right (53.63 percent). The percentage is then rounded to the nearest one-tenth of a percent; hence, 53.63 is rounded to 53.6.

Computers in Accounting

Spreadsheets: More than Numbers

Success in accounting is more than crunching numbers. Accountants use technology to analyze and interpret financial data, and to contribute to key management decisions. Spreadsheet applications such as Lotus 1-2-3 and Microsoft® Excel are among the most powerful and widely used tools in business. Budgets, financial statements, business plans, fixed assets reports, and inventory control records are just a few uses of the electronic spreadsheet.

Spreadsheets are reference tables that arrange data in rows and columns and provide formulas for quick computations. The user can connect multiple spreadsheets, creating dependencies between reports and analyzing the relationships between financial scenarios. Voice-enabled tools help users enter and proof numbers without the keyboard. Using macros (simple programs that list a sequence of actions), the user can automate data entry tasks and routine calculations. The business community also uses spreadsheet technologies in the following ways.

Communicate and Collaborate
- Convert numbers into customized visual presentations.
- E-mail electronic spreadsheets to co-workers without leaving the spreadsheet application.
- Utilize edit tracking features to work collaboratively with co-workers on a single spreadsheet.

Analyze and Interpret
- Investigate the effects of changing key variables or assumptions in the spreadsheet.
- Forecast financial outcomes.

Exchange Data between Software Applications
- Move files between spreadsheets and accounting software modules.
- Export data to create data warehouses of financial information.

Thinking Critically
Describe how you might use an electronic spreadsheet for vertical or horizontal analysis of financial statements. What formulas would you use?

Internet Application
Locate the Web site for a commercial spreadsheet software application. Find the "Fact Sheet" or "Features List" for the current release. Prepare a report containing the application name and release date. List five new enhancements or features contained in the product. Describe potential uses for these enhancements as they relate to the preparation and presentation of financial information.

NYSE
The New York Stock Exchange (NYSE) lists more than 3,000 companies from all over the world whose collective worth is $15 trillion in global market capitalization.

In Figure 23-1 note that gross sales are more than 100 percent ($3,487,665 ÷ $3,290,250 = 106.0 percent in 2005). That is because of **Sales Returns and Allowances,** which are 6.0 percent of net sales.

The percentages are added and subtracted, giving informative subtotals and totals. Because of rounding, the individual percentages may not add up to 100 percent. In this case one or more percentages is adjusted slightly until the total equals 100 percent. If the difference is more than a small amount, it is probable that an error has been made, and all the computations should be checked before adjusting any of the amounts.

Financial statements with items expressed as percentages of a base amount are called **common-size statements**. The last two columns in the comparative income statement are referred to as a *comparative common-size statement.*

Percentages obtained by vertical analysis of the income statement are useful when compared with the company's percentages for prior years. It is helpful to make comparisons with several years to detect trends, but even year-to-year comparisons are useful. For example, the comparative

Carolina Creations, Inc.
Comparative Balance Sheet (Vertical Analysis)
December 31, 2005 and 2004

	Amounts on December 31		Percent of Total Assets	
	2005	2004	2005	2004
Assets				
Current Assets				
Cash	100 7 5 4	22 0 8 0	21.0	5.4
Accounts Receivable	92 3 0 0	73 5 0 0	19.2	18.0
Merchandise Inventory	192 5 0 0	225 0 0 0	40.1	55.3
Prepaid Expenses	6 5 0	5 0 0	0.1	0.1
Supplies	3 9 5	2 5 0	0.1	0.1
Total Current Assets	386 5 9 9	321 3 3 0	80.5	78.9
Property, Plant, and Equipment				
Land	40 0 0 0	20 0 0 0	8.3	4.9
Building and Store Equipment	71 8 0 0	77 8 0 0	15.0	19.1
Less Accumulated Depreciation—Building and Store Equipment	21 3 4 0	15 5 6 0	4.4	3.8
Net Book Value—Building and Store Equipment	50 4 6 0	62 2 4 0	10.5	15.3
Office Equipment	5 0 0 0	5 0 0 0	1.0	1.2
Less Accumulated Depreciation—Office Equipment	2 0 0 0	1 5 0 0	0.4	0.4
Net Book Value—Office Equipment	3 0 0 0	3 5 0 0	0.6	0.9
Total Property, Plant, and Equipment	93 4 6 0	85 7 4 0	19.5	21.1
Total Assets	480 0 5 9	407 0 7 0	100.0	100.0
Liabilities and Stockholders' Equity				
Current Liabilities				
Accounts Payable	35 4 0 0	93 8 5 9	7.4	23.1
Sales Tax Payable	3 5 0 0	2 5 0 0	0.7	0.6
Payroll Taxes Payable	1 1 4 5	1 0 2 5	0.2	0.3
Interest Payable	8 6 0	2 1 5	0.2	0.1
Total Current Liabilities	40 9 0 5	97 5 9 9	8.5	24.0
Long-Term Liabilities				
10% Bonds Payable, 2010	70 0 0 0	50 0 0 0	14.6	12.3
Premium on Bonds Payable	6 4 4	0	0.1	
Mortgage Payable	40 0 0 0	44 0 0 0	8.3	10.8
Total Long-Term Liabilities	110 6 4 4	94 0 0 0	23.0	23.1
Total Liabilities	151 5 4 9	191 5 9 9	31.6	47.1
Stockholders' Equity				
Preferred Stock ($100 par, 10%, 500 shares authorized, issued and outstanding)	50 0 0 0	50 0 0 0	10.4	12.3
Common Stock ($1 par, 25,000 shares authorized)				
Issued and outstanding: 4,000 shares in 2004; 4,400 shares in 2005	4 4 0 0	4 0 0 0	0.9	1.0
Paid-in Capital—Common Stock	4 9 0 0	1 0 0 0	1.0	0.2
Retained Earnings				
Retained Earnings—Unappropriated	269 2 1 0	160 4 7 1	56.1	39.4
Total Retained Earnings	269 2 1 0	160 4 7 1	56.1	39.4
Total Stockholders' Equity	328 5 1 0	215 4 7 1	68.4	52.9
Total Liabilities and Stockholders' Equity	480 0 5 9	407 0 7 0	100.0	100.0

▲ **FIGURE 23-2** Comparative Balance Sheet—Vertical Analysis

Important!

Rounding
In statement analysis, it is customary to compute percentages to the nearest one-tenth of a percent. This procedure is followed in this chapter.

Important!

Percentages
In common-size statements, percentages (of net sales on the income statement and of assets on the balance sheet) are shown instead of dollar amounts.

income statement of Carolina Creations, Inc., shows gross profit on sales of 52.4 percent in 2004 but only 46.4 percent in 2005. A comparison with the industry average might be helpful. For example, suppose that trade association publications reveal that the average gross profit for the industry is 51.7 percent. Carolina Creations, Inc.'s gross profit on sales compares unfavorably to the industry average. This could be attributed to peculiarities of its operations, local competition, or other factors. However, it indicates the need for further examination.

Vertical Analysis of the Balance Sheet

Vertical analysis of the balance sheet expresses each item as either a percentage of total assets or of total liabilities and stockholders' equity.

Figure 23-2 on page 851 shows a comparative balance sheet for Carolina Creations, Inc., with the vertical analysis results. The pair of columns on the right shows each item as a percentage of total assets for each year. The more recent year is on the left. On December 31, 2005, the cash balance was $100,754 and the total assets were $480,059. Thus the cash balance is 21.0 percent of total assets in 2005.

$$\frac{\text{Cash}}{\text{Total assets}} = \frac{\$100,754}{\$480,059} = 0.2098 = 21.0 \text{ percent}$$

In rounding off it might be necessary to adjust one or more of the figures to obtain an even 100 percent for each total.

Vertical analysis percentages of the balance sheet are very useful when they are compared with the percentages of the same company for previous years and with those of other companies in the same industry. Changes in the percentages might reveal situations that need investigation. For example, the comparative balance sheet of Carolina Creations, Inc., shows that cash has increased from 5.4 percent of total assets in 2004 to 21.0 percent of total assets in 2005. The accountant would quickly realize that this increase should be studied.

Section 1 Self Review

Questions

1. What item serves as the base for the percentage calculations in a vertical analysis of the income statement?

2. How does the computation phase of statement analysis differ from the interpretation phase?

3. What is a common-size statement?

Exercises

4. In a vertical analysis of a balance sheet, each item is expressed as a percentage of
   a. total assets or total liabilities.
   b. total assets or total stockholders' equity.
   c. total assets or total liabilities and stockholders' equity.
   d. total liabilities or total stockholders' equity.

5. Which of the following is true of vertical analysis?
   a. Each item on the balance sheet is expressed as a percentage of total liabilities.
   b. Each item in the income statement is divided by net sales.
   c. Each item in the income statement is expressed as a percentage of net income.
   d. The amount of increase or decrease for each item in the income statement is divided by net sales.

Analysis

6. The gross profit on sales for 2004 and 2005 are $346,982 and $382,891, respectively. Net sales for 2004 and 2005 are $1,287,300 and $1,165,241. Net income after income taxes for 2004 and 2005 are $123,475 and $121,875. What conclusions can you draw from these figures?

Horizontal Analysis

In this section you will learn the second type of basic calculation, horizontal analysis.

Horizontal Analysis of Financial Statements

Financial statements for two or more periods may be evaluated by means of horizontal analysis. Horizontal analysis compares the items on each line to determine the change in dollar amounts. A percentage change can be shown by using the earlier figure as the base.

Horizontal Analysis of the Income Statement

Let's learn the techniques of horizontal analysis using the comparative income statement. Figure 23-3 on page 854 shows the comparative income statement of Carolina Creations, Inc., for 2005 and 2004.

Each amount for 2005 is compared to the corresponding amount for 2004. The increase or decrease of the change and the percentage of change are shown in the right two columns. Look at the sales figures. The gross sales for 2005 are higher than those for 2004. The increase is $547,640.

Sales for 2005	$3,487,665
Sales for 2004	− 2,940,025
Increase	$ 547,640

To find the percentage of increase, divide the increase by the amount for the base year. The base year is always the earlier year. The percentage of increase for gross sales is 18.6 percent.

$$\frac{\text{Increase in sales}}{\text{Sales for base year}} = \frac{\$\ 547,640}{\$2,940,025} = 18.62 \text{ percent}$$

If the amount for the most recent year is less than that for the base year, the percentage decrease is calculated in the same manner. For example, beginning merchandise inventory decreased by $50,000 for 2005. Divide the decrease by the base year amount.

$$\frac{\text{Amount of decrease}}{\text{Amount in base year}} = \frac{(\$\ 50,000)}{\$275,000} = (18.2) \text{ percent}$$

A decrease can be expressed by using a negative sign before the number, italics, or parentheses.

All the amounts in the right two columns on the comparative statement are computed in the same manner. If the amount of change is zero, there is no percentage of change. When there is no amount for the base period, no percentage change is computed.

Interpretation of the Percentages. The amounts of increase or decrease can be added or subtracted in the column and will give correct subtotals at each point. However, the percentages cannot be added or subtracted. Each percentage relates only to the line on which it appears.

Section Objectives

2 Use horizontal analysis techniques to analyze a comparative income statement and balance sheet.

WHY IT'S IMPORTANT
Analysis techniques help managers pinpoint operational or procedural problems that require investigation.

3 Use trend analysis to evaluate financial statements.

WHY IT'S IMPORTANT
Review of several years of financial data can reveal performance trends.

4 Interpret the results of the statement analyses by comparison with industry averages.

WHY IT'S IMPORTANT
Global competition requires businesses to remain in touch with industry trends and financial conditions.

Terms to Learn

industry averages
trend analysis

2 Objective
Use horizontal analysis techniques to analyze a comparative income statement and balance sheet.

Carolina Creations, Inc.
Comparative Income Statement (Horizontal Analysis)
Years Ended December 31, 2005 and 2004

	Amounts		Increase or (Decrease)	
	2005	2004	Amount	Percent
Revenue				
Sales	3 4 8 7 6 6 5	2 9 4 0 0 2 5	5 4 7 6 4 0	18.6
Less Sales Returns and Allowances	1 9 7 4 1 5	1 3 9 5 2 5	5 7 8 9 0	41.5
Net Sales	3 2 9 0 2 5 0	2 8 0 0 5 0 0	4 8 9 7 5 0	17.5
Cost of Goods Sold				
Merchandise Inventory, January 1	2 2 5 0 0 0	2 7 5 0 0 0	(5 0 0 0 0)	(18.2)
Purchases (Net)	1 7 0 3 5 0 0	1 2 6 5 2 7 5	4 3 8 2 2 5	34.6
Freight In	2 8 5 9 8	1 9 0 0 0	9 5 9 8	50.5
Total Merchandise Available for Sale	1 9 5 7 0 9 8	1 5 5 9 2 7 5	3 9 7 8 2 3	25.5
Less Merchandise Inventory, December 31	1 9 2 5 0 0	2 2 5 0 0 0	(3 2 5 0 0)	(14.4)
Cost of Goods Sold	1 7 6 4 5 9 8	1 3 3 4 2 7 5	4 3 0 3 2 3	32.3
Gross Profit on Sales	1 5 2 5 6 5 2	1 4 6 6 2 2 5	5 9 4 2 7	4.1
Operating Expenses				
Selling Expenses	5 8 5 3 0 0	5 9 9 8 9 5	(1 4 5 9 5)	(2.4)
General and Administrative Expenses	7 5 2 5 0 0	7 2 5 8 7 5	2 6 6 2 5	3.7
Total Operating Expenses	1 3 3 7 8 0 0	1 3 2 5 7 7 0	1 2 0 3 0	0.9
Net Income from Operations	1 8 7 8 5 2	1 4 0 4 5 5	4 7 3 9 7	33.7
Other Income				
Gain on Sale of Equipment	4 0 0 0	2 5 0 0 0	(2 1 0 0 0)	(84.0)
Interest Income	1 2 2 5 0	1 2 0 0 0	2 5 0	2.1
Total Other Income	1 6 2 5 0	3 7 0 0 0	(2 0 7 5 0)	(56.1)
Other Expenses				
Bond Interest Expense	5 9 0 8	5 0 0 0	9 0 8	18.2
Other Interest Expense	1 8 0 0	2 5 0 0	(7 0 0)	(28.0)
Total Other Expenses	7 7 0 8	7 5 0 0	2 0 8	2.8
Income Before Income Taxes	1 9 6 3 9 4	1 6 9 9 5 5	2 6 4 3 9	15.6
Income Tax Expense	6 7 6 5 5	5 9 4 8 4	8 1 7 1	13.7
Net Income After Income Taxes	1 2 8 7 3 9	1 1 0 4 7 1	1 8 2 6 8	16.5

▲ **FIGURE 23-3**
Comparative Income
Statement—Horizontal Analysis

Important!

Base Year
In preparing horizontal percentage analyses, the earlier year is used as the base for computing the percentage of change.

Some important changes shown in the comparative income statement for Carolina Creations, Inc., include the following:

- Gross sales increased 18.6 percent.
- Cost of goods sold increased 32.3 percent.
- Gross profit on sales increased 4.1 percent.
- Total operating expenses increased 0.9 percent.
- Income from operations increased 33.7 percent.
- Income tax expense increased 13.7 percent.
- Net income after income taxes increased 16.5 percent.

Horizontal analysis is especially useful in identifying items that need further investigation. For example, the increase in net sales was 17.5 percent, but the increase in cost of goods sold was 32.3 percent. An alert manager would want to determine the reasons for the disproportionate increase in cost of goods sold.

Management would also be interested in learning why freight increased 50.5 percent during 2005 while purchases increased only 34.6 percent.

Keep in mind that percentages of increase or decrease can be misleading when small amounts are involved. For example, total other income decreased 56.1 percent. However, in terms of actual dollars, the amount is relatively small, from $37,000 to $16,250. On the other hand, a small percentage change is important for items involving large dollar amounts.

The process of interpretation is easier if some basis of comparison is available, such as a company budget or industry averages. Significant changes need to be investigated in detail and the reasons evaluated.

Horizontal Analysis of the Balance Sheet

A firm's balance sheets for two or more periods can be presented in comparative form to permit a detailed horizontal analysis. Figure 23-4 on page 856 shows a comparative balance sheet for Carolina Creations, Inc., for December 31 of 2005 and 2004.

The calculations are the same as those for a horizontal analysis of income statements. The amounts are compared line by line. For example, for accounts receivable the difference is an increase of $18,800 ($92,300 − $73,500). The percentage of change is 25.6 percent. It is determined by dividing the amount of the change by the base year (2004) amount: $18,800 ÷ $73,500 = 25.57, or 25.6, percent.

Trend Analysis of Financial Statements

Comparing ratio and percentage relationships of the current year with those of the immediately preceding year is a normal and helpful procedure. However, comparisons between only two years could be misleading and might not be adequate to indicate long-term trends. A better technique is **trend analysis**, which compares selected ratios and percentages over a period of time. Often the time period is five years.

Let's look at one trend. The percentage of gross profit on sales to net sales decreased from 52.4 percent in 2004 to 46.4 percent in 2005 (Figure 23-1). A higher gross profit percentage is desirable, so the decrease is unfavorable. A comparison with the several prior years follows.

	2001	2002	2003	2004	2005
Net sales	2,042,500	2,198,650	2,495,895	2,800,500	3,290,250
Cost of goods sold	878,275	1,055,352	1,198,030	1,334,275	1,764,598
Gross profit on sales	1,164,225	1,143,298	1,297,865	1,466,225	1,525,652
Percentage of gross profit to net sales	57.0	52.0	52.0	52.4	46.4

In looking at the data over five years, it is clear that the decrease in percentage from 2004 to 2005 is significant. It calls for the attention of management. Management must obtain other facts, talk with employees, and observe other trends before arriving at a solution to the problem.

Trend analysis makes it possible to ask questions about all aspects of operations of the company. The accountant makes the most valuable contribution to the success of the business when analyzing operating data.

Important!

Adding It Up
In horizontal analysis, the amounts in the Increase or Decrease columns can be added or subtracted vertically, but the percentages cannot be.

3 Objective
Use trend analysis to evaluate financial statements.

Recall

Consistency Principle
The consistency principle permits comparisons between years. Using the same methods allows meaningful comparisons.

Carolina Creations, Inc.
Comparative Balance Sheet (Horizontal Analysis)
December 31, 2005 and 2004

	Amounts		Increase or (Decrease)	
	2005	2004	Amount	Percent
Assets				
Current Assets				
Cash	100754	22080	78674	356.3
Accounts Receivable	92300	73500	18800	25.6
Merchandise Inventory	192500	225000	(32500)	(14.4)
Prepaid Expenses	650	500	150	30.0
Supplies	395	250	145	58.0
Total Current Assets	386599	321330	65269	20.3
Property, Plant, and Equipment				
Land	40000	20000	20000	100.0
Building and Store Equipment	71800	77800	(6000)	(7.7)
Less Accumulated Depreciation—Building and Store Equip.	21340	15560	5780	37.1
Net Book Value—Building and Store Equipment	50460	62240	(11780)	(18.9)
Office Equipment	5000	5000	0	0.0
Less Accumulated Depreciation—Office Equipment	2000	1500	500	33.3
Net Book Value—Office Equipment	3000	3500	(500)	(14.3)
Total Property, Plant, and Equipment	93460	85740	7720	9.0
Total Assets	480059	407070	72989	17.9
Liabilities and Stockholders' Equity				
Current Liabilities				
Accounts Payable	35400	93859	(58459)	(62.3)
Sales Tax Payable	3500	2500	1000	40.0
Payroll Taxes Payable	1145	1025	120	11.7
Interest Payable	860	215	645	300.0
Total Current Liabilities	40905	97599	(56694)	(58.1)
Long-Term Liabilities				
10% Bonds Payable, 2010	70000	50000	20000	40.0
Premium on Bonds Payable	644	0	644	
Mortgage Payable	40000	44000	(4000)	(9.1)
Total Long-Term Liabilities	110644	94000	16644	17.7
Total Liabilities	151549	191599	(40050)	(20.9)
Stockholders' Equity				
Preferred Stock ($100 par, 10%, 500 shares authorized, issued and outstanding)	50000	50000	– 0 –	0.0
Common Stock ($1 par 25,000 shares authorized)				
Issued and outstanding: 4,000 shares in 2004;				
4,400 shares in 2005	4400	4000	400	10.0
Paid-in Capital—Common Stock	4900	1000	3900	390.0
Retained Earnings				
Retained Earnings—Unappropriated	269210	160471	108739	67.8
Total Retained Earnings	269210	160471	108739	67.8
Total Stockholders' Equity	328510	215471	113039	52.5
Total Liabilities and Stockholders' Equity	480059	407070	72989	17.9

▲ **FIGURE 23-4** Comparative Balance Sheet—Horizontal Analysis

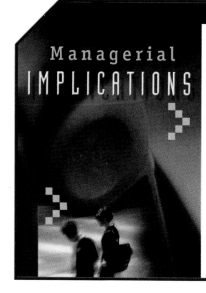

Managerial
IMPLICATIONS

Comparative Statements

- Statement analysis is extremely important to managers in detecting areas of strength and weakness in a business.

- Comparison of current data with the data of prior years indicates favorable and unfavorable trends.

- Managers compare percentages from year to year and with industry averages in order to detect variations that require prompt investigation.

- Management must consider certain factors when using industry averages.

Thinking Critically
What type of financial statement analysis would you use to assess profitability of a company for the last five years?

Comparison with Industry Averages

Trade associations survey their members to obtain financial and other data. The financial ratios and percentages that reflect averages for similar companies are called **industry averages**. This data is converted to a uniform presentation, usually in common-size statements arranged by company size (based on sales volume or total assets). It expresses income statement items as a percentage of net sales and balance sheet items as a percentage of total assets. Common-size statements can be presented for one year or for several years. Individual companies compare their results to industry averages.

Let's look at an example of how the management of Carolina Creations, Inc., might evaluate the corporation in comparison with others in the same industry. Table 23-1 on page 858 shows highly condensed data from its income statement as well as the data provided by the trade association for companies with the same general sales level. Note that income tax expense has been omitted. Because companies included in the trade averages are sole proprietorships, partnerships, and corporations, it is not appropriate to compare net income after income taxes with entities that do not pay taxes.

You can see why the comparison to industry averages would be of interest to management, owners, and others. The operations of Carolina Creations, Inc., are not as efficient or as profitable as those of its competitors. Its rate of gross profit is lower (and on a downward trend) than the industry averages. Its ratio of operating expenses to net sales is higher than that of others in the industry. In particular, its general expenses are out of line. The end result is that Carolina Creations, Inc.'s ratio of income before income tax to sales is much lower than that of its competitors. Based on this comparison, management needs to immediately determine the causes of its poor results.

In comparing to industry averages, keep in mind the following:

- Different businesses keep different types of accounts and do not classify items in the same manner.

Objective
Interpret the results of the statement analyses by comparison with industry averages.

Careers
Some of the more significant careers involving international accounting include preparing and translating financial statements, allocating home country expenses to foreign operations, analyzing foreign sales and operating income, and preparing foreign country and U.S. tax returns.

TABLE 23-1 ▶

Comparison of Trade Data

	Percentage of Net Sales			
	Carolina Creations, Inc.		Industry Average	
	2005	2004	2005	2004
Revenue				
Sales	106.0	105.0	104.0	103.5
Returns and Allowances	6.0	5.0	4.0	3.5
Net Sales	100.0	100.0	100.0	100.0
Cost of Goods Sold	53.6	47.6	50.5	47.0
Gross Profit on Sales	46.4	52.4	49.5	53.0
Operating Expenses				
Selling Expenses	17.8	21.4	18.2	20.1
General Expenses	22.9	25.9	19.5	22.0
Total Operating Expenses	40.7	47.4*	37.7	42.1
Operating Income	5.7	5.0	11.8	10.9
Other Income and Expenses				
Other Income	0.5	1.3	0.9	1.2
Other Expenses	(0.2)	(0.3)	(0.5)	(0.1)
Net Other Income or (Exp.)	0.3	1.0	0.4	1.1
Income Before Income Tax	6.0	6.1	12.2	12.0

*Rounded

- No two businesses are exactly alike. There are differences in the merchandise sold, the type of customers, and the method of financing (owners' equity versus borrowed funds). Some businesses buy fixed assets while others lease all or some of the fixed assets.
- The industry figures could include data from corporations, partnerships, and sole proprietorships. The different business entities might report salary allowances, benefits for owners, and other items in very different ways.

Despite these problems, common-size statements provided by trade associations or commercial financial service companies are important to managers in comparing their operations to other firms. They are of special value when comparing data not affected by the factors listed above.

Section 2 Self Review

Questions

1. In horizontal analysis of the balance sheet, how is the percentage of change determined?

2. In the same industry, when comparing an established company and a newer one, which company would have a higher percentage of property, plant, and equipment to total assets? Why?

3. Why is comparison with industry averages helpful when analyzing financial statements?

Exercises

4. If a comparative balance sheet shows the amount and percentage of decrease in merchandise inventory from one year to the next, the firm used
   a. vertical analysis.
   b. horizontal analysis.
   c. common-size analysis.
   d. trend analysis.

5. If current assets are $100,000 and total assets are $500,000, the percentage of current assets to total assets is

a. 2 percent.   c. 20 percent.
b. 5 percent.   d. 10 percent.

Analysis

6. Total selling expenses for 2004 and 2005 were $835,792 and $928,632, respectively. Net sales for 2004 and 2005 were $3,862,981 and $3,765,421, respectively. For each year what are total selling expenses as a percentage of net sales? What is the percentage of increase or decrease of total selling expenses?

(Answers to Section 2 Self Review are on page 877.)

Review

Chapter Summary

Financial statement analysis involves computation and interpretation. Computation includes the calculation of percentages and ratios. Interpretation means comparing one set of figures with another (prior statements, budgets, or industrial averages) and determining the financial implications of those comparisons. The comparative statement is a convenient form for the presentation of figures for analysis and appraisal.

Learning Objectives

1 **Use vertical analysis techniques to analyze a comparative income statement and balance sheet.**
Vertical analysis expresses each item as a percentage of a base amount on the statement.

- Net sales are the base for all income statement items. To compute an item's percentage of net sales, divide the amount of that item by the amount of net sales.

  Example: $\dfrac{\text{Total operating expenses}}{\text{Net sales}}$

- Total assets (or total liabilities plus owner's equity) are the base for vertical analysis items on a balance sheet. Each figure is expressed as a percentage of the base.

  Example: $\dfrac{\text{Cash}}{\text{Total assets}}$

It is customary to carry the percentage computed to one decimal place further than needed and then to round it off. The usual practice is to round percentages to the nearest one-tenth of a percent.

2 **Use horizontal analysis techniques to analyze a comparative income statement and balance sheet.**
Horizontal analysis compares items from one year to the next. The amount of change and the percentage change is computed.

- Changes to items such as gross sales, cost of goods sold, operating expenses, and net income can be studied on the income statement.

  Example: $\dfrac{\text{Increase in total operating expenses}}{\text{Total operating expenses for base year}}$

- A firm's balance sheets for two or more periods can be presented in comparative form to permit a comparison of items from year to year.

  Example: $\dfrac{\text{Increase in cash}}{\text{Cash in base year}}$

3 **Use trend analysis to evaluate financial statements.**
Comparing ratio and percentage relationships of the current year with only those of the previous year can be misleading and are not adequate to indicate long-term trends.

Using data from five or more years, trend analysis compares selected ratios and percentages to analyze operations.

Trend analysis often omits income tax expense because the companies' forms of business could be different (that is, sole proprietorships, partnerships, corporations).

4 **Interpret the results of the statement analyses by comparison with industry averages.**
Companies often compare financial statements with industry averages to determine how the company's operations stack up against other businesses in the industry. In order to make these comparisons, similar classification structures must be in place.

Varied operational procedures and accounting treatments can create inconsistency in data presentation:

- Different businesses keep different types of accounts and do not classify items in a consistent manner.

- No two businesses are exactly alike in terms of merchandise, customers, financing, asset acquisition, and other areas.

- Industry averages might include data from sole proprietorships, partnerships, and corporations. This creates inconsistency in presentation of financial information.

5 **Define the accounting terms new to this chapter.**

CHAPTER 23 GLOSSARY

Common-size statements (p. 850) Financial statements with items expressed as percentages of a base amount

Comparative statements (p. 848) Financial statements presented side by side for two or more years

Horizontal analysis (p. 848) Computing the percentage change for individual items in the financial statements from year to year

Industry averages (p. 857) Financial ratios and percentages reflecting averages for similar companies

Ratio analysis (p. 848) Computing the relationship between various items in the financial statements

Trend analysis (p. 855) Comparing selected ratios and percentages over a period of time

Vertical analysis (p. 848) Computing the relationship between each item on a financial statement to some base amount on the statement

Comprehensive Self Review

1. What is the difference between vertical analysis and horizontal analysis?

2. Why are the financial statement items of one period compared with those of the prior period?

3. Name several factors that may cause misleading results when comparing percentage figures of a specific company to industry averages.

4. The following data relates to a merchandising business over a period of five years.

   • The company's sales have increased by approximately 10 percent per year.

   • The company's gross profit has increased by about 5 percent per year.

   Is this favorable or unfavorable? Explain.

5. What is the purpose of the comparison with industry averages?

(Answers to Comprehensive Self Review are on page 877.)

Discussion Questions

1. What is horizontal analysis of the balance sheet?

2. What is meant by vertical analysis of the income statement?

3. In horizontal analysis it is common to omit a calculation of percentage change when there is no base period amount. Why?

4. Why might percentages in the Increase or Decrease column of a horizontal analysis of a comparative statement not add up to 100?

5. Would you, as an analyst, be satisfied with comparative percentages for only two years? Why?

6. Why would a short-term creditor be interested in the analysis of a company's income statement?

7. Of what use to the financial statement analyst are industry wide statements?

8. If a company's net sales and its cost of goods sold both increase by 12 percent from 2004 to 2005, would gross profit on sales also increase by 12 percent? Explain.

9. What are common-size statements?

10. The vertical analysis of Hester Corporation's balance sheets for the past five years show that the percent of inventory to total assets has increased each year. Comment on this situation.

11. In a vertical analysis of the statement of retained earnings, what is the base for comparing each item on the statement?

12. Which is more important: a large change in percentage or a large change in dollar amount? Explain.

13. What is trend analysis? How are percentages computed using trend analysis?

14. Vandos-Zeta Corporation's income statements reported the following data.

	2001	2002	2003	2004
Net sales	$300,000	$360,000	$375,000	$340,000
Gross profit on sales	12,500	15,100	17,150	14,050

Calculate the trend percentage for each year.

15. What is the base for horizontal analysis?

Applications

EXERCISES

Use the comparative income statement and the comparative balance sheet for Volunteer Corporation to solve Exercises 23-1 through 23-6.

Volunteer Corporation
Comparative Income Statement
Years Ended December 31, 2005 and 2004

	2005	2004
Sales	1 2 4 0 0 0 0	1 0 2 0 0 0 0
Less Sales Returns and Allowances	4 0 0 0 0	2 0 0 0 0
Net Sales	1 2 0 0 0 0 0	1 0 0 0 0 0 0
Cost of Goods Sold	9 0 0 0 0 0	7 0 0 0 0 0
Gross Profit on Sales	3 0 0 0 0 0	3 0 0 0 0 0
Selling Expenses	1 4 5 0 0 0	1 3 0 0 0 0
General Expenses	8 5 0 0 0	8 0 0 0 0
Total Expenses	2 3 0 0 0 0	2 1 0 0 0 0
Net Income Before Income Taxes	7 0 0 0 0	9 0 0 0 0
Income Tax Expense	1 2 5 0 0	1 8 8 5 0
Net Income After Income Taxes	5 7 5 0 0	7 1 1 5 0

Exercise 23-1 ►
Objective 1

Vertical analysis of income statement.

Using the comparative income statement, prepare a vertical analysis of all items from sales through gross profit on sales for the years 2004 and 2005.

Exercise 23-2 ►
Objective 1

Vertical analysis of balance sheet.

Prepare a vertical analysis of all asset items on the comparative balance sheet for the years 2005 and 2004.

Exercise 23-3 ►
Objective 2

Horizontal analysis of income statement.

Using the comparative income statement, prepare a horizontal analysis of all items on the income statement for 2005 and 2004.

Exercise 23-4 ►
Objective 2

Horizontal analysis of balance sheet.

Prepare a horizontal analysis of all items on the comparative balance sheet for the years 2005 and 2004.

Exercise 23-5 ►
Objective 4

Comparison with industry averages.

Suppose that you are a financial analyst who is evaluating Volunteer Corporation for a client. You have found that for similar size corporations in the same industry, the net income after income taxes averaged 7.5 percent of net sales in both years 2004 and 2005. Evaluate Volunteer's net income after taxes for both years and comment on your findings.

Volunteer Corporation
Comparative Balance Sheet
December 31, 2005 and 2004

	2005	2004
Assets		
Current Assets		
Cash	50 0 0 0	78 0 0 0
Accounts Receivable (Net)	180 0 0 0	135 0 0 0
Inventory	100 0 0 0	87 0 0 0
Total Current Assets	330 0 0 0	300 0 0 0
Property, Plant, and Equipment		
Buildings (Net)	95 0 0 0	100 0 0 0
Equipment (Net)	85 0 0 0	80 0 0 0
Land	20 0 0 0	20 0 0 0
Total Property, Plant, and Equipment	200 0 0 0	200 0 0 0
Total Assets	530 0 0 0	500 0 0 0
Liabilities and Stockholders' Equity		
Current Liabilities		
Accounts Payable	30 0 0 0	40 0 0 0
Other Current Liabilities	2 5 0 0	20 0 0 0
Total Current Liabilities	32 5 0 0	60 0 0 0
Long-Term Liabilities		
Bonds Payable	80 0 0 0	80 0 0 0
Total Long-Term Liabilities	80 0 0 0	80 0 0 0
Total Liabilities	112 5 0 0	140 0 0 0
Stockholders' Equity		
Common Stock ($20 par)	200 0 0 0	200 0 0 0
Retained Earnings	217 5 0 0	160 0 0 0
Total Stockholders' Equity	417 5 0 0	360 0 0 0
Total Liabilities and Stockholders' Equity	530 0 0 0	500 0 0 0

Vertical analysis of balance sheet; comparison with industry averages.

◄ **Exercise 23-6**
Objectives 1, 4

Assume that for companies in the same industry and of the same general size as Volunteer Corporation, stockholders' equity was 72 percent of total liabilities and stockholders' equity in 2004, and 75 percent of total liabilities and stockholders' equity in 2005. How does Volunteer compare to these industry averages?

Problems

Selected problems can be completed using:
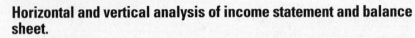
Peachtree   QuickBooks   Spreadsheets

PROBLEM SET A

Problem 23-1A ►
Objectives 1, 2

Horizontal and vertical analysis of income statement and balance sheet.

Mountainview Parts Company sells auto parts through a retail store that it operates. The firm's comparative income statement and balance sheet for the years 2005 and 2004 are shown below and on page 865.

Mountainview Parts Company
Comparative Income Statement
Years Ended December 31, 2005 and 2004

	2005	2004
Revenue		
Sales	5 6 9 7 5 0	5 1 0 9 5 0
Less Sales Returns and Allowances	1 1 4 0	1 0 2 2
Net Sales	5 6 8 6 1 0	5 0 9 9 2 8
Cost of Goods Sold		
Merchandise Inventory, January 1	4 0 9 5 5	3 9 0 4 5
Net Purchases	3 4 5 5 1 0	3 1 0 0 0 0
Total Merchandise Available for Sale	3 8 6 4 6 5	3 4 9 0 4 5
Less Merchandise Inventory, December 31	3 5 0 0 0	4 0 9 5 5
Cost of Goods Sold	3 5 1 4 6 5	3 0 8 0 9 0
Gross Profit on Sales	2 1 7 1 4 5	2 0 1 8 3 8
Operating Expenses		
Selling Expenses		
Sales Salaries Expenses	5 2 5 0 0	4 8 0 0 0
Payroll Tax Expense—Selling	5 2 5 0	4 8 0 0
Other Selling Expenses	4 8 0 0	5 2 0 0
Total Selling Expenses	6 2 5 5 0	5 8 0 0 0
General and Administrative Expenses		
Officers' Salaries Expense	1 0 0 0 0 0	7 5 0 0 0
Payroll Tax Expense—Administrative	8 5 0 0	7 5 0 0
Depreciation Expense	8 2 5 0	8 2 5 0
Other General and Administrative Expenses	5 4 5 0	5 0 0 0
Total General and Administrative Expenses	1 2 2 2 0 0	9 5 7 5 0
Total Operating Expenses	1 8 4 7 5 0	1 5 3 7 5 0
Net Income Before Income Taxes	3 2 3 9 5	4 8 0 8 8
Income Tax Expense	4 8 6 0	7 2 1 5
Net Income After Income Taxes	2 7 5 3 5	4 0 8 7 3

1. Prepare both a horizontal and a vertical analysis of the statements. Carry all calculations to two decimal places, and then round to one decimal place. (Leave all vertical analysis percentages unadjusted in this problem.)
2. Make written comments about any of the results that seem worthy of investigation.

Analyze: Based on your analysis, which expense category experienced the greatest percentage change?

Mountainview Parts Company
Comparative Balance Sheet
December 31, 2005 and 2004

	2005	2004
Assets		
Current Assets		
Cash	6 6 8 7 6	3 2 5 1 1
Accounts Receivable	6 5 5 0 0	6 2 0 0 0
Merchandise Inventory	3 5 0 0 0	4 0 9 5 5
Prepaid Expenses	5 8 0 0	5 6 0 0
Supplies	3 9 5	4 3 4
Total Current Assets	1 7 3 5 7 1	1 4 1 5 0 0
Property, Plant, and Equipment		
Land	4 0 0 0 0	4 0 0 0 0
Building and Equipment	8 2 5 0 0	8 2 5 0 0
Less Accumulated Depreciation—Building and Equipment	3 3 0 0 0	2 4 7 5 0
Net Book Value—Building and Equipment	4 9 5 0 0	5 7 7 5 0
Total Property, Plant, and Equipment	8 9 5 0 0	9 7 7 5 0
Total Assets	2 6 3 0 7 1	2 3 9 2 5 0
Liabilities and Stockholders' Equity		
Current Liabilities		
Accounts Payable	3 2 1 4 3	3 5 2 2 2
Sales Tax Payable	3 5 0 0	2 5 0 0
Payroll Taxes Payable	1 1 4 5	1 0 2 5
Income Taxes Payable	8 6 0	2 1 5
Total Current Liabilities	3 7 6 4 8	3 8 9 6 2
Long-Term Liabilities		
Mortgage Payable	4 2 6 0 0	4 5 0 0 0
Total Long-Term Liabilities	4 2 6 0 0	4 5 0 0 0
Total Liabilities	8 0 2 4 8	8 3 9 6 2
Stockholders' Equity		
Common Stock ($1 par, 25,000 shares authorized)		
Issued and outstanding, 1,000 shares	1 0 0 0	1 0 0 0
Paid-in Capital—Common Stock	1 3 4 1 5	1 3 4 1 5
Retained Earnings	1 6 8 4 0 8	1 4 0 8 7 3
Total Stockholders' Equity	1 8 2 8 2 3	1 5 5 2 8 8
Total Liabilities and Stockholders' Equity	2 6 3 0 7 1	2 3 9 2 5 0

Problem 23-2A ►
Objectives 1, 2

Horizontal and vertical analysis of balance sheet and income statement.

The Braves Merchandising Company sells sports items for youth baseball and soccer leagues. Its comparative income statement and balance sheet for the years 2004 and 2005 are shown below and on page 867.

INSTRUCTIONS

1. Prepare both a horizontal and a vertical analysis of the two statements. Carry all calculations to two decimal places, and then round to one decimal place. (Leave all vertical analysis percentages unadjusted in this problem.)

2. Make written comments about any of the results that seem worthy of investigation.

Braves Merchandising Company
Comparative Income Statement
Years Ended December 31, 2005 and 2004

	2005	2004
Revenue		
Sales	375400	325500
Less Sales Returns and Allowances	2200	1500
Net Sales	373200	324000
Cost of Goods Sold		
Merchandise Inventory, January 1	29450	32000
Net Purchases	225000	215000
Total Merchandise Available for Sale	254450	247000
Less Merchandise Inventory, December 31	35000	29450
Cost of Goods Sold	219450	217550
Gross Profit on Sales	153750	106450
Operating Expenses		
Selling Expenses		
Sales Salaries Expenses	49500	28900
Payroll Tax Expense—Selling	4950	2900
Other Selling Expenses	4800	6800
Total Selling Expenses	59250	38600
General and Administrative Expenses		
Officers' Salaries Expense	75000	45000
Payroll Tax Expense—Administrative	7500	4500
Depreciation Expense	8250	8250
Other General and Administrative Expenses	4200	2200
Total General and Administrative Expenses	94950	59950
Total Operating Expenses	154200	98550
Net Income (loss) Before Income Taxes	(450)	7900
Income Tax Expense	0	1185
Net Income (loss) After Income Taxes	(450)	6715

Braves Merchandising Company
Comparative Balance Sheet
December 31, 2005 and 2004

	2005	2004
Assets		
Current Assets		
Cash	1 9 1 2 1	2 0 6 5 6
Accounts Receivable	2 5 4 5 0	2 2 5 0 0
Merchandise Inventory	3 5 0 0 0	2 9 4 5 0
Prepaid Expenses	1 8 0 0	1 6 0 0
Supplies	2 9 5	2 3 4
Total Current Assets	8 1 6 6 6	7 4 4 4 0
Property, Plant, and Equipment		
Land	3 0 0 0 0	3 0 0 0 0
Building and Equipment	7 2 5 0 0	7 2 5 0 0
Less Accumulated Depreciation—Building and Store Equipment	2 1 7 5 0	1 4 5 0 0
Net Book Value—Building and Equipment	5 0 7 5 0	5 8 0 0 0
Store Equipment	1 5 0 0 0	1 5 0 0 0
Less Accumulated Depreciation—Store Equipment	3 0 0 0	2 0 0 0
Net Book Value—Store Equipment	1 2 0 0 0	1 3 0 0 0
Total Property, Plant, and Equipment	9 2 7 5 0	1 0 1 0 0 0
Total Assets	1 7 4 4 1 6	1 7 5 4 4 0
Liabilities and Stockholders' Equity		
Current Liabilities		
Accounts Payable	1 3 1 4 3	1 1 2 2 2
Sales Tax Payable	3 0 0 0	2 2 0 0
Payroll Taxes Payable	1 0 3 7	6 1 7
Income Taxes Payable	0	7 1 5
Total Current Liabilities	1 7 1 8 0	1 4 7 5 4
Long-Term Liabilities		
Notes Payable	1 5 0 0 0	1 8 0 0 0
Total Long-Term Liabilities	1 5 0 0 0	1 8 0 0 0
Total Liabilities	3 2 1 8 0	3 2 7 5 4
Stockholders' Equity		
Common Stock ($10 par, 25,000 shares authorized)		
Issued and outstanding: 5,000 shares	5 0 0 0 0	5 0 0 0 0
Paid-in Capital—Common Stock	3 5 9 7 1	3 5 9 7 1
Total Paid-in Capital	8 5 9 7 1	8 5 9 7 1
Retained Earnings		
Unappropriated Retained Earnings	3 1 2 6 5	5 6 7 1 5
Appropriated Retained Earnings	2 5 0 0 0	0
Total Retained Earnings	5 6 2 6 5	5 6 7 1 5
Total Stockholders' Equity	1 4 2 2 3 6	1 4 2 6 8 6
Total Liabilities and Stockholders' Equity	1 7 4 4 1 6	1 7 5 4 4 0

Analyze: Describe the changes to the line item "Unappropriated Retained Earnings" on the comparative balance sheet for fiscal 2004 and 2005.

Problem 23-1B ►
Objectives 1, 2

INSTRUCTIONS

Horizontal and vertical analysis of income statement and balance sheet.

Paperback City, Inc., sells paperback novels. The firm's comparative income statement and balance sheet for the years 2004 and 2005 follow.

1. Prepare both a horizontal and a vertical analysis of the two statements. Carry all calculations to two decimal places, and then round to one place. (Leave all vertical analysis percentages unadjusted in this problem.)

2. Make written comments about any of the results that seem worthy of investigation.

Paperback City, Inc.
Comparative Income Statement
Years Ended December 31, 2005 and 2004

	2005	2004
Revenue		
Sales	2 4 5 0 0 0	1 9 5 0 0 0
Less Sales Returns and Allowances	1 5 0 0	9 0 0
Net Sales	2 4 3 5 0 0	1 9 4 1 0 0
Cost of Goods Sold		
Merchandise Inventory, January 1	1 4 0 0 0	1 6 0 0 0
Net Purchases	1 5 5 0 0 0	9 0 0 0 0
Total Merchandise Available for Sale	1 6 9 0 0 0	1 0 6 0 0 0
Less Merchandise Inventory, December 31	5 5 0 0 0	1 4 0 0 0
Cost of Goods Sold	1 1 4 0 0 0	9 2 0 0 0
Gross Profit on Sales	1 2 9 5 0 0	1 0 2 1 0 0
Operating Expenses		
Selling Expenses		
Sales Salaries Expenses	6 0 0 0 0	5 0 0 0 0
Payroll Tax Expense—Selling	6 0 0 0	3 0 0 0
Other Selling Expenses	2 0 0 0	1 2 0 0
Total Selling Expenses	6 8 0 0 0	5 4 2 0 0
General and Administrative Expenses		
Officers' Salaries Expense	5 0 0 0 0	2 5 0 0 0
Payroll Tax Expense—Administrative	5 0 0 0	1 2 0 0
Depreciation Expense	5 0 0 0	5 0 0 0
Other General and Administrative Expenses	1 2 0 0	1 0 0 0
Total General and Administrative Expenses	6 1 2 0 0	3 2 2 0 0
Total Operating Expenses	1 2 9 2 0 0	8 6 4 0 0
Net Income Before Income Taxes	3 0 0	1 5 7 0 0
Income Tax Expense	0	2 3 5 5
Net Income After Income Taxes	3 0 0	1 3 3 4 5

Paperback City, Inc.
Comparative Balance Sheet
December 31, 2005 and 2004

	2005	2004
Assets		
Current Assets		
Cash	1 2 0 0 0	3 0 5 1 5
Accounts Receivable	2 2 8 3 1	2 5 0 0 0
Merchandise Inventory	5 5 0 0 0	1 4 0 0 0
Prepaid Expenses	6 5 0	5 0 0
Supplies	3 9 5	2 5 0
Total Current Assets	9 0 8 7 6	7 0 2 6 5
Property, Plant, and Equipment		
Land	3 5 0 0 0	3 5 0 0 0
Building and Store Equipment	5 0 0 0 0	5 0 0 0 0
Less Accumulated Depreciation—Building and Store Equipment	1 5 0 0 0	1 0 0 0 0
Net Book Value—Building and Store Equipment	3 5 0 0 0	4 0 0 0 0
Total Property, Plant, and Equipment	7 0 0 0 0	7 5 0 0 0
Total Assets	1 6 0 8 7 6	1 4 5 2 6 5
Liabilities and Stockholders' Equity		
Current Liabilities		
Accounts Payable	2 3 0 0 0	7 5 0 0
Sales Tax Payable	1 2 1 5	9 7 0
Payroll Taxes Payable	9 1 6	3 5 0
Interest Payable	6 0 0	6 0 0
Total Current Liabilities	2 5 7 3 1	9 4 2 0
Long-Term Liabilities		
Mortgage Payable	6 9 0 0 0	7 0 0 0 0
Total Long-Term Liabilities	6 9 0 0 0	7 0 0 0 0
Total Liabilities	9 4 7 3 1	7 9 4 2 0
Stockholders' Equity		
Common Stock ($1 par, 25,000 shares authorized)		
Issued and outstanding: 2,000 shares	2 0 0 0	2 0 0 0
Paid-in Capital—Common Stock	5 0 0	5 0 0
Retained Earnings	6 3 6 4 5	6 3 3 4 5
Total Stockholders' Equity	6 6 1 4 5	6 5 8 4 5
Total Liabilities and Stockholders' Equity	1 6 0 8 7 6	1 4 5 2 6 5

Analyze: If Paperback City experiences the same growth in net sales in 2006 as was reported in 2005, what net sales can be projected?

Problem 23-2B ►
Objectives 1, 2

Horizontal and vertical analysis of balance sheet and income statement.

Summer Company sells high quality summer sportswear clothing. Its comparative income statement and balance sheet for 2004 and 2005 follow.

1. Prepare both a horizontal and vertical analysis of each statement. Carry all calculations to two decimal places, and then round to one place. (Leave all vertical analysis percentages unadjusted in this problem.)

2. Make written comments about any percentages that seem worthy of further investigation.

Summer Company
Comparative Income Statement
Years Ended December 31, 2005 and 2004

	2005	2004
Revenue		
Sales	875450	825000
Less Sales Returns and Allowances	6900	7500
Net Sales	868550	817500
Cost of Goods Sold		
Merchandise Inventory, January 1	55450	49500
Net Purchases	610000	595000
Total Merchandise Available for Sale	665450	644500
Less Merchandise Inventory, December 31	51500	55450
Cost of Goods Sold	613950	589050
Gross Profit on Sales	254600	228450
Operating Expenses		
Selling Expenses		
Sales Salaries Expense	80000	65000
Payroll Tax Expense—Selling	8000	6500
Other Selling Expenses	9000	9500
Total Selling Expenses	97000	81000
General and Administrative Expenses		
Officers' Salaries Expense	100000	95000
Payroll Tax Expense—Administrative	10000	9500
Depreciation Expense	9000	9000
Other General and Administrative Expenses	2500	2200
Total General and Administrative Expenses	121500	115700
Total Operating Expenses	218500	196700
Net Income Before Income Taxes	36100	31750
Income Tax Expense	5415	4763
Net Income After Income Taxes	30685	26987

Summer Company
Comparative Balance Sheet
December 31, 2005 and 2004

	2005	2004
Assets		
Current Assets		
Cash	6 9 1 2 1	3 2 5 4 6
Accounts Receivable	6 5 0 0 0	5 6 0 0 0
Merchandise Inventory	5 1 5 0 0	5 5 4 5 0
Prepaid Expenses	1 8 0 0	1 6 0 0
Supplies	4 8 0	4 5 0
Total Current Assets	1 8 7 9 0 1	1 4 6 0 4 6
Property, Plant, and Equipment		
Land	5 3 3 1 4	5 3 3 1 4
Bulding and Equipment	9 0 0 0 0	9 0 0 0 0
Less Accumulated Depreciation—Building and Equipment	3 6 0 0 0	2 7 0 0 0
Net Book Value—Building and Equipment	5 4 0 0 0	6 3 0 0 0
Store Equipment	1 9 0 0 0	1 9 0 0 0
Less Accumulated Depreciation—Store Equipment	5 7 0 0	3 8 0 0
Net Book Value—Store Equipment	1 3 3 0 0	1 5 2 0 0
Total Property, Plant, and Equipment	1 2 0 6 1 4	1 3 1 5 1 4
Total Assets	3 0 8 5 1 5	2 7 7 5 6 0
Liabilities and Stockholders' Equity		
Current Liabilities		
Accounts Payable	5 0 4 2 0	4 7 6 2 2
Sales Tax Payable	6 5 0 0	5 6 0 0
Payroll Taxes Payable	1 0 3 7	6 1 7
Income Taxes Payable	4 1 5	7 6 3
Total Current Liabilities	5 8 3 7 2	5 4 6 0 2
Long-Term Liabilities		
Notes Payable	4 6 5 0 0	5 0 0 0 0
Total Long-Term Liabilities	4 6 5 0 0	5 0 0 0 0
Total Liabilities	1 0 4 8 7 2	1 0 4 6 0 2
Stockholders' Equity		
Common Stock ($10 par, 50,000 shares authorized)		
Issued and outstanding: 6,000 shares	6 0 0 0 0	6 0 0 0 0
Paid-in Capital—Common Stock	3 5 9 7 1	3 5 9 7 1
Total Paid-in Capital	9 5 9 7 1	9 5 9 7 1
Retained Earnings		
Unappropriated Retained Earnings	8 7 6 7 2	5 6 9 8 7
Appropriated Retained Earnings	2 0 0 0 0	2 0 0 0 0
Total Retained Earnings	1 0 7 6 7 2	7 6 9 8 7
Total Stockholders' Equity	2 0 3 6 4 3	1 7 2 9 5 8
Total Liabilities and Stockholders' Equity	3 0 8 5 1 5	2 7 7 5 6 0

Analyze: If the retail sportswear clothing industry average for cost of goods sold is 60 percent expressed as a percentage of net sales, what conclusions can you draw about Summer Company?

Analyze and Interpret

The balance sheets and condensed income statements for DWH Incorporated are shown below and on page 873.

INSTRUCTIONS

1. Prepare a combined horizontal and vertical analysis of the comparative balance sheet of DWH Incorporated.

DWH Incorporated

Comparative Balance Sheet

December 31, 2005 and 2004

	2005	2004
Assets		
Current Assets		
Cash and Cash Equivalents	5 0 7 3 7	8 9 0 0
Marketable Securities	3 5 0 0 0	2 6 5 0 0
Notes and Accounts Receivables (net)	1 7 5 0 0 0	1 7 8 0 0 0
Inventories	6 2 0 0 0	5 9 5 0 0
Prepaid Expenses	8 0 0 0	4 9 7 5
Total Current Assets	3 3 0 7 3 7	2 7 7 8 7 5
Property, Plant, and Equipment		
Land	5 0 0 0 0	5 0 0 0 0
Buildings and Equipment (Net of Accumulated Depreciation)	2 5 9 0 0 0	2 6 7 5 0 0
Total Property, Plant, and Equipment	3 0 9 0 0 0	3 1 7 5 0 0
Other Assets, including intangibles (net)	4 5 0 0 0	5 0 0 0 0
Total Assets	6 8 4 7 3 7	6 4 5 3 7 5
Liabilities and Stockholders' Equity		
Current Liabilities		
Accounts Payable and Accrued Liabilities	2 0 0 0 0	6 3 5 0 0
Notes and Loans Payable	2 5 0 0 0	3 5 0 0 0
Taxes Payable	4 5 0 0	7 0 0 0
Total Current Liabilities	4 9 5 0 0	1 0 5 5 0 0
Long-Term Liabilities		
Bonds Payable	4 8 0 0 0	4 8 0 0 0
Notes and Mortgages Payable	1 4 5 0 0 0	1 5 1 0 0 0
Other Long-Term Liabilities	6 0 0 0 0	6 8 0 0 0
Total Long-Term Liabilities	2 5 3 0 0 0	2 6 7 0 0 0
Total Liabilities	3 0 2 5 0 0	3 7 2 5 0 0
Stockholders' Equity		
Preferred Stock (authorized 1000 shares; 500 shares outstanding, $100 par, 10%)	5 0 0 0 0	5 0 0 0 0
Common Stock (authorized 100,000 shares; 10,000 shares outstanding,$1 par)	1 0 0 0 0	1 0 0 0 0
Paid-in Capital in Excess of Par—Common Stock	5 0 0 0 0	5 0 0 0 0
Total Contributed Capital	1 1 0 0 0 0	1 1 0 0 0 0
Retained Earnings	2 7 2 2 3 7	1 6 2 8 7 5
Total Stockholders' Equity	3 8 2 2 3 7	2 7 2 8 7 5
Total Liabilities and Stockholders' Equity	6 8 4 7 3 7	6 4 5 3 7 5

2. Prepare a combined horizontal and vertical analysis of the comparative income statement of DWH Incorporated.

3. DWH Incorporated is involved in selling sports equipment in Florida. It wants to expand into the remainder of the United States. What are some questions that you, as the company's accountant, would ask of the management before the business begins an expansion?

Analyze: Which asset had the highest percentage change from 2004 to 2005? What was that percentage?

DWH Incorporated Comparative Income Statement Years Ended December 31, 2005 and 2004	2005	2004
Revenue		
Sales (Net)	1 2 5 0 0 0 0	1 0 5 0 0 0 0
Cost of Goods Sold	7 7 5 0 0 0	6 5 1 0 0 0
Gross Profit on Sales	4 7 5 0 0 0	3 9 9 0 0 0
Operating Expenses	2 9 5 0 0 0	2 7 2 0 0 0
Operating Income	1 8 0 0 0 0	1 2 7 0 0 0
Other Income and Expenses		
Interest Income	3 2 0 0	3 3 0 0
Interest Expense	1 7 5 0 0	1 8 0 0 0
Taxable Income	1 6 5 7 0 0	1 1 2 3 0 0
Income Taxes	5 6 3 3 8	3 8 1 8 2
Net Income	1 0 9 3 6 2	7 4 1 1 8

Filling in the Blanks

Jackie Schmidt, the accountant for Stars Corporation, was asked to make a presentation at a Saturday meeting of the board of directors concerning the corporation's year-end financial position. While flying to the meeting, Ms. Schmidt realized she had left the income statement on her desk back at the office. Since she knew there would not be enough time for anyone to get to the office and fax her a copy of the statement, she examined the material in her briefcase to see what information was available.

A review of the statement of retained earnings revealed that net income after income taxes for the year was $124,416. From some notes she had made for the presentation, she knew that the corporation's gross profit on sales was 40 percent and net income as a percentage of net sales was 7 percent. The income tax rate for the corporation is 28 percent. She also remembered that the selling and administrative expenses were equal to each other. With this information, she was able to reconstruct the income statement before the plane reached its destination.

INSTRUCTIONS

Using the same information given above, prepare an income statement for Stars Corporation. First list the major headings for a condensed income statement. Then, starting with the net income figure, fill in the dollar amounts based on the percentage relationships given.

Business Connections

Connection 1 ►  **MANAGERIAL FOCUS** Statement Analysis

1. Suppose that a vertical analysis of the income statement shows an item to be 18 percent of net sales. How would this information be used in order to make it meaningful? With what would it be compared?

2. In 2005 the cost of goods sold was 66 percent of net sales. For 2004 the same item was 63 percent, and for 2003 it was 60 percent. What recommendations would you make about items or activities that should be investigated further?

3. In deciding whether an increase in accounts receivable during the current year is desirable or undesirable, what factors should management consider?

4. Management is concerned that over a three-year period a company's balance sheets show that the total stockholders' equity has changed from 56 percent to 51 percent to 43 percent of total equities. What factors might explain this trend?

5. A company's income statements reveal that its net income after taxes has been 4.3 percent of net sales for each of the past three years. During that time the industry average has been about 7 percent. What types of questions would management want answered in seeking an explanation for this difference?

6. A company's net sales increased by 35 percent from one year to the next year. During that period selling expenses increased by 41 percent. Is this desirable? Explain.

Connection 2 ► **Ethical DILEMMA** **Report Liability?** The bank has requested financial statements to use in evaluating your company's application for a large loan. The president of the company just recently loaned the business $100,000 but doesn't want the liability to be recorded on the corporation's books because it will dramatically increase the debt of the corporation. Will you include the president's loan on the statements that you present to the bank? Why or why not?

Connection 3 ► **Street WISE:**

Questions from the Real World **Analysis** Refer to the *1999 Annual Report* for The Home Depot, Inc. in Appendix B.

1. Locate the consolidated statements of earnings. Using vertical analysis, what is the cost of goods sold expressed as a percentage of net sales for the year ended January 30, 2000? If the industry average for this percentage is 72 percent, is The Home Depot, Inc. performing better than the industry average or worse? Why?

2. Locate the consolidated balance sheets. Using horizontal analysis, by what dollar amount have total assets increased from fiscal 1998 to 1999? What is the percentage of increase reported for total stockholders' equity?

taken from the Safeway Inc. *1999 Annual Report.*

S
SAFEWAY

Five-Year Summary Financial Information

(Dollars in millions, except per-share amounts)	52 Weeks 1999	52 Weeks 1998	52 Weeks 1997	52 Weeks 1996	52 Weeks 1995
Results of Operations					
Sales	$28,859.9	$28,484.2	$22,483.8	$17,269.0	$16,397.5
Gross Profit	$ 8,510.7	$ 7,124.5	$ 6,414.7	$ 4,774.2	$ 4,492.4
Operating and administrative expense	(6,411.4)	(5,466.5)	(5,093.2)	(3,872.1)	(3,754.6)
Net Income	$ 970.9	$ 806.7	$ 557.4	$ 460.6	$ 326.3

Analyze:

1. Compute the percentage of increase in sales for each fiscal year. Compute the percentage increase in operating and administrative expenses for each fiscal year.

2. Based on your computations, describe any figure that appears to be out of line or inconsistent with other amounts. Explain.

3. What further investigation do you think is required to understand the situation?

Analyze Online: Locate the Safeway Inc. Web site **(www.safeway.com).** Access company financials using the *Investor Relations* link.

4. Click on the *News Releases* link and select one of the financial press releases posted. Describe the type of financial information reported in the press release. What percentage increases or decreases were reported? Describe how these computations were made.

5. What reasons were given for the increased or decreased figures cited?

Extending the *Thought*   Capital Structure The methods in which a   ◄ Connection 5
company's capital is obtained from various sources are very important in analyzing the soundness of the company's financial position. Explain the differences between equity capital and debt capital. From the company's point of view, describe the risks associated with each type of capital.

Business Communication   Investigating the Numbers The balance sheet of   ◄ Connection 6
Crandall Gifts Company revealed a 25 percent increase in accounts receivable from fiscal 2004 to 2005. Net sales remained constant. As the senior accountant for the company, you are responsible for explaining this increase to upper management. Your accounting clerk will help you investigate the figure. Draft a memo to your accounting clerk with directions about the types of investigations you would like the clerk to perform. What supporting documents or schedules should be examined? What might be the cause of such an increase?

Connection 7 ► **Team***Work* **Industry Comparisons** Target Corporation and Kmart Corporation compete in the discount and variety retailing industry. As a team, compare the following financial data using any horizontal or vertical analysis techniques you have learned in this chapter. In a one-page report, discuss the data you have analyzed and what conclusions might be drawn from this information.

Consider the following issues:

- increase in sales
- cost of sales (cost of goods sold) as a percentage of net sales
- operating, selling, and administrative expenses as a percentage of net sales
- net income as a percentage of net sales

	Target Corporation (in millions)		Kmart Corporation (in millions)	
	For the Year Ended Jan. 31, 1999	For the Year Ended Jan. 31, 1998	For the Year Ended Jan. 26, 2000	For the Year Ended Jan. 27, 1999
Net Sales	$33,702	$30,662	$35,925	$33,674
Cost of Sales	23,029	21,085	28,102	26,319
Operating, Selling, and Admin. Expenses	7,490	6,843	6,523	6,245
Net Income	1,144	935	403	518

Connection 8 ► ***inter*NET CONNECTION** **Analysis of Earnings** Go to **www.lucent.com,** the Web site for Lucent Technologies.

1. How does the company's operating income this year compare with that of the previous two years?

2. Can you identify a trend? If yes, describe the trend and possible factors that created it.

3. Does the company explain the increase or decrease in net earnings? What explanation does the company provide?

Answers to Section 1 Self Review

1. Vertical analysis of the income statement is based on net sales.
2. The computation phase involves simple mathematical computations. The interpretation phase considers what caused relationships or changes and what can be done to improve the relationships or changes.
3. It is a financial statement with items expressed as a percentage of a base rather than in dollar amounts.
4. **c.** total assets (or total liabilities and stockholders' equity).
5. **b.** Each item in the income statement is divided by net sales.
6. Although sales and net income before taxes have decreased, gross profit on sales and net income after taxes have increased.

Answers to Section 2 Self Review

1. It is determined by first subtracting an amount from the base year amount and then dividing the difference by the base year amount.
2. The newer company would probably have a higher ratio because its book value is likely to be higher (less depreciation that has been charged off), and its assets are likely to be newer, which means they were acquired at higher price levels than those acquired in earlier years by the older company.
3. Such comparisons point out areas in which the business is performing either better or worse than average. The areas showing poorer performance can be investigated to determine the reason and then to address it.
4. **b.** horizontal analysis.
5. **c.** 20 percent.
6. • 2004: 21.6%
   • 2005: 24.7%
   • $92,840 increase: 11.1%

Answers to Comprehensive Self Review

1. *Vertical analysis* refers to a comparison of items on an individual financial statement. *Horizontal analysis* refers to a comparison of data for the current period with data of a prior period.
2. This comparison often reveals significant changes that need to be investigated.
3. Different accounting methods, different types of entities, different ages of assets, and different financing methods can impair comparability.
4. It is probably favorable unless management has deliberately adopted a policy of reducing prices to increase volume. The question that must be raised is whether this situation has led to increased profitability.
5. It is to indicate whether the company is operating as efficiently as others in the same industry.

CHAPTER 24

Learning Objectives

1. Compute and interpret financial ratios that measure profitability, operating results, and efficiency.

2. Compute and interpret financial ratios that measure financial strength.

3. Compute and interpret financial ratios that measure liquidity.

4. Recognize shortcomings in financial statement analysis.

5. Define the accounting terms new to this chapter.

Statement Analysis: Measuring Profitability, Financial Strength, and Liquidity

Used by permission from Disney Enterprises, Inc.

The ⒲ALT Ðɪsney Company

© Disney Enterprises, Inc.

www.disney.com

Disney is more than just a magical kingdom for Mickey and Minnie. Positioned as the third largest media conglomerate in the world, The Walt Disney Company acts as home to two cruise ships, nine theme parks, 728 Disney Stores, 36 hotels, one broadcast network, 10 television stations, and 50 radio stations. That's a lot of magic.

Disney's Broadcast Media Networks, Cable Networks, Studio Entertainment, Theme Parks and Resorts, and Consumer Products divisions contributed to net income of $1,300 million in 1999. Setting financial goals for the future, the company expresses a desire to generate more cash, consume less capital, and maximize earnings from its existing business lines.

Thinking Critically
How do you think Disney accountants can effectively evaluate whether the company has attained its stated financial goals in coming years?

For more information on Disney, go to: collegeaccounting.glencoe.com.

New Terms

Accounts receivable turnover	Liquidity
Acid-test ratio	Price-earnings ratio
Asset turnover	Quick assets
Average collection period	Return on common stockholders' equity
Current ratio	Total equities
Leveraged buyout	Working capital

① **Compute and interpret financial ratios that measure profitability, operating results, and efficiency.**

WHY IT'S IMPORTANT
Various factors, in combination with the measurement of net income, contribute to the overall prosperity of a company.

Terms to Learn

asset turnover
price-earnings ratio
return on common
 stockholders' equity

① **Objective**

Compute and interpret financial ratios that measure profitability, operating results, and efficiency.

Important!

Rate of Return on Sales
The rate of return on sales measures what part of each sales dollar remains as net income. It measures operating efficiency and profitability.

Ratios Measuring Profitability, Operating Results, and Efficiency

Ratio analysis is used to assess a company's profitability, financial strength, and liquidity. Ratio analysis investigates a relationship between two items either as a ratio (2 to 1 or 2:1) or as a rate (percentage).

Financial ratios have three classifications:

1. Profitability, operating results, and efficiency
2. Financial strength
3. Liquidity

The financial statements of Carolina Creations, Inc., will be used to illustrate ratio analysis. You will need to refer to Figures 23-3 on page 854 and 23-4 on page 856 while studying this chapter.

Profitability is measured by net income. However, a dollar amount of net income is not a sufficient yardstick. Net income of $150,000 might be excellent for a small firm but unsatisfactory for a large corporation. A number of ratios are used to determine the adequacy of a company's profit.

Rate of Return on Sales

The rate of return on sales is a measure of managerial efficiency and profitability. It is computed as follows.

$$\frac{\text{Net income}}{\text{Net sales}} = \text{Rate of return on net sales}$$

Some companies use income before taxes to calculate the percentage because income taxes depend on factors not related to sales. Carolina Creations, Inc., uses net income after income taxes to calculate the rate.

The rate of return on net sales at Carolina Creations, Inc., was 3.9 percent for 2005 and 2004 even though sales increased significantly in 2005.

2005	2004
$\frac{\$\ 128,739}{\$3,290,250} = 3.9\%$	$\frac{\$\ 110,471}{\$2,800,500} = 3.9\%$

The higher the rate of return on net sales, the more satisfactory are the business operations. Management should look for and investigate unfavorable trends.

Rate of Return on Common Stockholders' Equity

Corporations are expected to earn a profit for their shareholders. Preferred shareholders are entitled to the dividends provided for in the preferred stock contract. The remainder of the earnings is available to common shareholders. **Return on common stockholder's equity** is a key measure of how well the corporation is making a profit for its shareholders. It is computed as follows.

$$\frac{\text{Income available to common stockholders}}{\text{Common stockholders' equity}} = \begin{array}{l} \text{Return on common} \\ \text{stockholders' equity} \end{array}$$

Step 1: *Compute income available to common stockholders.* Income available to common stockholders is net income after taxes reduced by any preferred dividend requirements. Carolina Creations, Inc., has a $5,000 dividend requirement for preferred stock (500 shares at $100 par value at 10 percent). Subtract $5,000 from net income after taxes to determine the income available for common stockholders.

About Accounting

Stock Sales
From the creation of the NYSE in 1783 until 1997, stock prices were offered in increments of one-eighth of one dollar, or 12.5 cents. This changed in 1997 to one-sixteenth of a dollar, or 6.25 cents. In 2001 stock and option markets switched to the decimal system.

	2005	2004
Net income after income taxes	$128,739	$110,471
Less dividend requirements on preferred stock	5,000	5,000
Income available to common stockholders	$123,739	$105,471

Step 2: *Compute the common stockholders' equity.* There are many ways to compute common stockholders' equity: end-of-year balance, average of the beginning and ending balances, average based on quarterly balances, or average based on monthly balances. Carolina Creations, Inc., uses the end-of-year balance of total common stockholders' equity.

	2005	2004
Total stockholders' equity	$328,510	$215,471
Less preferred stock equity	50,000	50,000
Common stockholders' equity	$278,510	$165,471

Step 3: *Divide the income available to common stockholders by the common stockholders' equity.*

2005

$$\frac{\$123,739}{\$278,510} = 44.4\%$$

2004

$$\frac{\$105,471}{\$165,471} = 63.7\%$$

The decrease in the rate of return is caused by the significant increase in stockholders' equity in 2005 ($278,510 in the denominator of the above fraction). This is due to increased retained earnings. A constantly decreasing rate over a period of years would be cause for concern.

Earnings per Share of Common Stock

Earnings per share of common stock measures the profit accruing to each share of common stock owned. It is computed as follows.

$$\frac{\text{Income available to common stockholders}}{\begin{array}{c} \text{Average number of shares of common stock} \\ \text{outstanding during year} \end{array}} = \text{Earnings per share}$$

Step 1: *Compute income available to common stockholders.* Subtract the dividend requirements on preferred stock from the income after income tax.

	2005	2004
Net income after income taxes	$128,739	$110,471
Less dividend requirements on preferred stock	5,000	5,000
Income available to common stockholders	$123,739	$105,471

Step 2: *Determine the average number of shares of common stock outstanding during the year.* An analysis of the common stock account reveals that 4,000 shares were outstanding throughout 2004 and most of 2005. On October 2, 2005, 400 additional shares were issued. *The weighted average number of shares outstanding* for 2005 was 4,100, calculated as follows.

4,000 shares × 12 months = 48,000 shares
400 shares × 3 months = 1,200 shares
Total   49,200 shares

Average = 49,200 shares ÷ 12 months = 4,100 shares

Step 3: *Divide the income available to common stockholders by the average number of shares of common stock outstanding.*

2005	2004
$\dfrac{\$123,739}{4,100 \text{ shares}} = \$30.18$	$\dfrac{\$105,471}{4,000 \text{ shares}} = \$26.37$

Earnings per share were $30.18 in 2005 and $26.37 in 2004. The large increase in net income caused earnings per share to increase significantly.

Analysts, stockholders, and creditors watch the earnings per share measurement very closely. Comparing earnings per share for the same company for several years could show a trend. Keep in mind that changes in the number of shares outstanding might distort this measurement.

Price-Earnings Ratio
The price-earnings ratio depends in large part on expectations of future profitability, which cause stock prices to increase or decrease.

Price-Earnings Ratio

The **price-earnings ratio** compares the market value of common stock with the earnings per share of that stock. It is computed as follows.

$$\frac{\text{Market price per share}}{\text{Earnings per share}} = \text{Price-earnings ratio}$$

If a corporation's common stock sells for $144 per share and its earnings are $12 per share, the price-earnings ratio is 12 to 1 ($144 ÷ $12).

The price-earnings ratio is an indicator of the attractiveness of the stock as an investment at its present market value. The amount investors are willing to pay for stock is based on expectations for the future. The price-earnings ratio is not computed for privately held companies because there is no readily available market value for the shares.

Yield on Common Stock

For a publicly held corporation, the relationship between the dividends received by the stockholders and the market value of each share is important. The yield on common stock is computed as follows.

$$\frac{\text{Dividend per share}}{\text{Market price per share}} = \text{Yield on common stock}$$

Accounting
On The Job

Arts, Audio-Video Technology, and Communications

Industry Overview

Careers in the arts, audio-visual technology, and communications relate to working with multimedia content. This includes the visual and performing arts, journalism, and entertainment services.

Career Opportunities
- Film Production Accountant
- Telecommunication Systems Analyst
- Multimedia Producer
- Editorial Director
- Desktop Publishing Specialist

Preparing for an Arts, Audio-Video Technology, or Communications Career

- Complete training in concept design, video production, audio production, electronic computer imaging, or presentation technologies.

- Become proficient in the use of design software applications such as Media 100, Adobe Photoshop, Adobe Illustrator, or QuarkXpress.

- Take classes in HTML programming, Web site development, project management, and budgeting for video, Web, or audio projects.

- Gain experience with Microsoft Project and spreadsheet applications such as Excel in order to create and monitor schedules and costs.

- Obtain a bachelor's degree. Professional specialty, management, and sales occupations generally require a college degree; technical occupations often do not.

Thinking Critically
What types of activities do you think an accounts payable supervisor handles at a company such as Sony Pictures Entertainment? List the types of disbursements you think are issued from this department.

Internet Application
Research careers in communications and media at a Web site such as Media Central. What career resources are offered on the site?

For example, if the price of a share of common stock is $60 and the corporation is paying an annual dividend of $6, the yield is 10 percent ($6 ÷ $60).

Rate of Return on Total Assets

The rate of return on total assets measures the rate of return on the assets used by a company. This rate helps the analyst to judge managerial performance, measure the effectiveness of the assets used, and evaluate proposed capital expenditures. The rate is computed as follows.

$$\frac{\text{Income before interest expense and income taxes}}{\text{Total assets}} = \text{Rate of return on total assets}$$

Income before interest and taxes is used to measure how effectively management utilized the assets, regardless of how the assets were financed. If nonoperating revenue amounts (such as dividend and interest income) are large, they should not be included in income. This ensures that only income from normal business operations is considered. For Carolina Creations, Inc., income is computed by adding interest expense to income before income taxes.

	2005	2004
Income before income taxes	$196,394	$169,955
Interest expense	7,708	7,500
Income before interest and taxes	$204,102	$177,455

Analysts might average the assets at the beginning and end of the year, average the assets monthly, use the beginning assets, or use the ending assets. Carolina Creations, Inc., uses year-end total assets.

The rate of return on total assets for Carolina Creations, Inc., is as follows.

2005	2004
$\dfrac{\$204,102}{\$480,059} = 42.5\%$	$\dfrac{\$177,455}{\$407,070} = 43.6\%$

The results are meaningful only if compared with rates of prior years and with the industry average.

Asset Turnover

The ratio of net sales to total assets measures the effective use of assets in making sales. This ratio is usually called **asset turnover**. It is computed as follows.

$$\frac{\text{Net sales}}{\text{Total assets}} = \text{Asset turnover}$$

Assets that are not used in producing sales, primarily investments, are excluded. Assets may be measured as end-of-year totals, average of beginning and ending totals, or average of monthly totals. Carolina Creations, Inc., uses net sales and total assets at the end of the year.

2005	2004
$\dfrac{\$3,290,250}{\$\ 480,059} = 6.9 \text{ to } 1$	$\dfrac{\$2,800,500}{\$\ 407,070} = 6.9 \text{ to } 1$

The higher the asset turnover, the more effectively the assets of the company are being used. The trend of this ratio is important because it indicates whether asset growth is accompanied by corresponding sales growth. If sales increase proportionately more than total assets, the ratio increases, which is a favorable indicator.

Important!

Asset Turnover
A low asset turnover compared to the industry average shows that the business uses more assets to generate the same sales volume as its competitors.

Section 1 — Self Review

Questions

1. What three measurements are often used in evaluating profitability?

2. What does the rate of return on common stockholders' equity measure?

3. What does the price-earnings ratio measure?

Exercises

4. The price-earnings ratio for common stock is computed using
   a. book value.
   b. market value.
   c. par value.
   d. stated value.

5. The amount of profit accruing to each share of stock is the
   a. price-earnings ratio.
   b. yield on common stock.
   c. rate of return on common stockholders' equity.
   d. earnings per share.

Analysis

6. A corporation's stock is selling at $54 per share, and its earnings are $6 per share. The corporation is paying an annual dividend of $2.75. What is the price-earnings ratio? What is the yield on common stock?

(Answers to Section 1 Self Review are on page 909.)

Ratios Measuring Financial Strength

Section Objective

2 Compute and interpret financial ratios that measure financial strength.

WHY IT'S IMPORTANT
The long-term viability of a business depends on effective use of equity and earnings.

Terms to Learn

leveraged buyout
total equities

The next group of ratios measures the financial strength of the business.

Number of Times Bond Interest Earned

A corporation's bondholders and stockholders want to know if net income is sufficient to cover the required bond interest payments. Times bond interest earned measures this. It is computed as follows.

$$\frac{\text{Income before bond interest and income taxes}}{\text{Bond interest cash requirement}} = \text{Times bond interest earned}$$

Step 1: *Compute the income before bond interest and income taxes.* To compute the income amount, add the bond interest expense to income before income taxes. For Carolina Creations, Inc., bond interest expense was $5,000 in 2004 ($50,000 × 10 percent) and $5,908 in 2005 (interest paid on the bonds minus the amortization of bond premium). The amount is computed as follows.

	2005	2004
Income before income tax	$196,394	$169,955
Add bond interest expense	5,908	5,000
Available for bond interest	$202,302	$174,955

Step 2: *Compute the cash required to pay bond interest.* The cash interest for bonds outstanding at the end of each year is computed as follows.

2005: $70,000 × 0.10 = $7,000
2004: $50,000 × 0.10 = $5,000

Step 3: *Compute the ratio.*

2005	2004
$\frac{\$202,302}{\$\ 7,000} = 28.9 \text{ times}$	$\frac{\$174,955}{\$\ 5,000} = 35.0 \text{ times}$

Carolina Creations, Inc.'s income easily covers required bond payments.

Ratio of Stockholders' Equity to Total Equities

The sum of a corporation's liabilities and stockholders' equity is referred to as its **total equities**. The ratio of stockholders' equity to total equities measures the portion of total capital provided by the stockholders. It indicates the protection afforded creditors against possible losses. The more

Recall

Bond Premium
The excess of the price paid over the face value of a bond is known as bond premium.

capital provided by the stockholders, the greater the protection to creditors. The ratio of stockholders' equity to total equities is computed as follows.

$$\frac{\text{Stockholders' equity}}{\text{Total equities}} = \text{Ratio of stockholders' equities to total equities}$$

The ratios for Carolina Creations, Inc., follow.

2005	2004
$\frac{\$328,510}{\$480,059} = 0.68 \text{ to } 1$	$\frac{\$215,471}{\$407,070} = 0.53 \text{ to } 1$

In 2005 the stockholders of Carolina Creations, Inc., provided 68 cents of each dollar of total equities compared to 53 cents in 2004. This ratio varies widely from industry to industry. A comparison with the industry average is important in determining a desirable ratio for a particular business.

Ratio of Stockholders' Equity to Total Liabilities

The ratio of stockholders' equity to total liabilities is known as the *ratio of owned capital to borrowed capital.* It is computed as follows.

$$\frac{\text{Stockholders' equity}}{\text{Total liabilities}} = \text{Ratio of stockholders' equity to total liabilities}$$

The ratios for Carolina Creations, Inc., follow.

2005	2004
$\frac{\$328,510}{\$151,549} = 2.17 \text{ to } 1$	$\frac{\$215,471}{\$191,599} = 1.12 \text{ to } 1$

This ratio reveals a significant improvement in 2005. In 2004 stockholders provided slightly more than $1 of equity for each dollar of liability. In 2005 they provided $2.17 of equity for each dollar of debt.

In the 1980s many leveraged buyouts occurred. In a **leveraged buyout**, the purchasers of a business buy the stock, having the corporation agree to pay the sellers. The result is that the debt created by the purchase is a debt of the corporation. In many cases the debt, usually with a high interest rate, makes up a large part of the total equities of the corporation. In the mid-1980s to early 1990s, many corporations went bankrupt because they could not meet the interest and principal payments on the debts. The balance sheets of these corporations would reflect a very low ratio of stockholders' equity to total liabilities.

Book Value per Share of Stock

Book value per share measures the financial strength underlying each share of stock. It is frequently reported in financial publications. It represents the amount that each share would receive in case of liquidation if the assets were sold for book value.

When there is one class of stock outstanding, the book value of each share is total stockholders' equity divided by the number of shares outstanding. If more than one class of stock is outstanding, the rights of the various classes of stock are considered. The book value of preferred stock is computed first. Then the remaining balance of stockholders' equity is divided by the number of common shares. Special treatment is given to dividends in arrears on cumulative preferred stock. In case of liquidation, the owner of a share of preferred stock will receive its par value.

Important!

Stockholders' Equity
A low ratio of stockholders' equity to total liabilities can be risky. The corporation might not be able to make interest and principal payments on its debts.

Important!

Book Value per Share
Book value and fair market value often are quite different. Book value per share does not indicate how much the stockholder would receive if the assets were sold and the corporation liquidated.

$$\frac{\text{Common stockholders' equity}}{\text{Number of common shares}} = \text{Book value per share of common stock}$$

Follow these steps to compute the book value per share of stock for Carolina Creations, Inc.

Step 1: *Compute the claims of preferred stockholders.* There are no cumulative dividends or special liquidation provisions for the preferred stock of Carolina Creations, Inc. Therefore, the book value is the same as the par value, $100 per share. There were 500 shares of preferred stock outstanding during 2004 and 2005, so the claims of the preferred stockholders for both years are $50,000 (500 shares at $100 par value).

Step 2: *Deduct the claims of preferred stockholders from total stockholders' equity to compute the claims of common stockholders.* The common stockholders are entitled to the difference between the total stockholders' equity and the portion assigned to the preferred stock.

	2005	2004
Stockholders' equity	$328,510	$215,471
Less preferred stock equity	50,000	50,000
To common stockholders	$278,510	$165,471

Step 3: *Divide the total claims of common stockholders by the number of shares of common stock outstanding.* Carolina Creations, Inc., had 4,400 shares of common stock outstanding on December 31, 2005, and 4,000 shares outstanding on December 31, 2004. The book value of each share is computed as follows.

2005	2004

$$\frac{\$278,510}{4,400 \text{ shares}} = \$63.30 \qquad \frac{\$165,471}{4,000 \text{ shares}} = \$41.37$$

The book value of Carolina Creations, Inc.'s common stock increased from $41.37 to $63.30 per share.

Section 2 Self Review

Questions

1. What is measured by the number of times bond interest is earned?

2. How is the ratio of owned capital to borrowed capital calculated?

3. What does book value per share measure?

Exercises

4. The ratio that measures the portion of total capital provided by stockholders is the
   a. times bond interest earned.
   b. ratio of stockholders' equity to total liabilities.
   c. ratio of stockholders' equity to total equities.
   d. book value per share.

5. The ratio that measures the security afforded creditors is the
   a. price-earnings ratio.
   b. earnings per share.
   c. ratio of stockholders' equity to total liabilities.
   d. book value per share of common stock.

Analysis

6. Compute the book value per share of common stock for the following conditions:

   Common stock outstanding is 5,000 shares, total stockholders' equity is $600,000, equity of preferred stock is $450,000.

(Answers to Section 2 Self Review are on page 909.)

Section Objectives

3 Compute and interpret financial ratios that measure liquidity.

WHY IT'S IMPORTANT
To establish financial credibility, a business needs to demonstrate its ability to pay its debts when due.

4 Recognize shortcomings in financial statement analysis.

WHY IT'S IMPORTANT
The analysis of financial statements, without considering different accounting processes or operational procedures, could lead to improper conclusions.

Terms to Learn

accounts receivable turnover
acid-test ratio
average collection period
current ratio
liquidity
quick assets
working capital

3 Objective
Compute and interpret financial ratios that measure liquidity.

Recall

Current Assets
Assets are considered current if they will be converted to cash or used within one year.

Ratios Measuring Liquidity

Liquidity measures the ability of a business to pay its debts when due. Many businesses fail because they cannot pay their debts, even though they are profitable and have long-term financial strength.

Working Capital

Working capital is a measure of the ability of a company to meet its current obligations. It represents the margin of security afforded short-term creditors. Working capital, sometimes called *net working capital*, is computed as follows.

$$\text{Current assets} - \text{Current liabilities} = \text{Working capital}$$

In 2005 Carolina Creations, Inc.'s working capital increased by $121,963. This is a significant change that needs to be investigated.

	2005	2004	Increase or (Decrease)
Current assets	$386,599	$321,330	$ 65,269
Current liabilities	40,905	97,599	(56,694)
Working capital	$345,694	$223,731	$121,963

In the FedEx Corporation *2000 Annual Report,* net working capital for the period ended May 31, 2000, was computed by subtracting current liabilities of $2.8 billion from current assets of $3.2 billion.

Current Ratio

Working capital is a very important measure of liquidity. The current ratio is another way to evaluate liquidity. The **current ratio** measures the ability of a business to pay its current debts using current assets. The current ratio is computed as follows.

$$\frac{\text{Current assets}}{\text{Current liabilities}} = \text{Current ratio}$$

In 2005 Carolina Creations, Inc., had $9.45 of current assets for each dollar of current liabilities.

2005	2004
$\dfrac{\$386,599}{\$ 40,905} = 9.45{:}1$	$\dfrac{\$321,330}{\$ 97,599} = 3.29{:}1$

The current ratio varies widely among industries and even from company to company within an industry. A popular guideline is that a current ratio of at least 2 to 1 is desirable in retail and manufacturing businesses. This guideline is not applicable, however, to all businesses.

From the viewpoint of a short-term creditor, the higher the current ratio, the greater the amount of protection afforded. However, the current ratio can be too high. A very high current ratio indicates that excess current assets are on hand and are not earning income. A high current ratio could be caused by large sums of money tied up in accounts receivable that might be uncollectible. A high current ratio could also be caused by obsolete inventory or an inventory level higher than required to conduct normal operations.

Acid-Test Ratio

Although the current ratio measures a company's ability to cover current liabilities using current assets, it is not a measure of immediate liquidity. A considerable period of time might be necessary to sell the inventory and convert it into cash in the normal course of business. The **acid-test ratio** measures immediate liquidity. This ratio uses **quick assets**, which are cash, receivables, and marketable securities.

$$\frac{\text{Cash} + \text{Receivables} + \text{Marketable securities}}{\text{Current liabilities}} = \text{Acid-test ratio}$$

Carolina Creations, Inc.'s acid-test ratios follow.

2005	**2004**
$\dfrac{\$100{,}754 + \$92{,}300}{\$40{,}905} = 4.72\text{:}1$	$\dfrac{\$22{,}080 + \$73{,}500}{\$97{,}599} = 0.98\text{:}1$

The acid-test ratio shows that in 2005 Carolina Creations, Inc., had $4.72 of quick assets for each dollar of current liabilities. In 2004 the acid-test ratio was 0.98. This dramatic increase should be investigated.

Acid-test ratios vary widely from industry to industry. A general guideline is that the acid-test ratio should be at least 1 to 1. The due dates of current liabilities, composition of quick assets, and various operating factors are considered when evaluating the adequacy of the ratio. Comparisons with the industry average and with the company's ratio in prior years can be helpful.

Inventory Turnover

It is important that a business sell its inventory rapidly so that excess working capital is not tied up in merchandise. Inventory turnover measures the number of times the inventory is replaced during the period. The higher the turnover, the shorter the time between the purchase and sale of the inventory. Inventory turnover is computed as follows.

$$\frac{\text{Cost of goods sold}}{\text{Average inventory}} = \text{Inventory turnover}$$

Ideally, average inventory is computed using month-end balances. However, these amounts are not available to analysts outside the business. Therefore, year-end balances are often used, but they might not be typical of the inventory levels during the year. Inventory is often at its lowest level at year-end.

To compute the inventory turnover for Carolina Creations, Inc., follow these steps.

International INSIGHTS

Multinational Companies

True multinational companies have manufacturing plants and sales and service operations in locations around the world. Some companies create entirely new products for a foreign market. PepsiCo found that Europeans do not like the taste of U.S. colas made with artificial sweeteners, so the company developed a completely new low-caloric cola that is sold only in Europe.

Important!

Inventory Turnover
A high inventory turnover indicates tight control over the level of inventory on hand.

Step 1: *Compute the average inventory.*

	2005	2004
Inventory, Jan. 1	$225,000	$275,000
Inventory, Dec. 31	192,500	225,000
Totals	$417,500	$500,000
	÷ 2	÷ 2
Average inventory	$208,750	$250,000

Step 2: *Divide the cost of goods sold by the average inventory.*

2004	2005
$\dfrac{\$1,764,598}{\$\ 208,750} = 8.45$ times	$\dfrac{\$1,334,275}{\$\ 250,000} = 5.34$ times

The inventory turnover ratio varies widely by industry. Inventory turnover for a bakery is almost daily. A vendor of construction equipment might turn inventory just twice a year. A business must compare its inventory turnover with prior years and with the industry average.

Accounts Receivable Turnover

A company should collect accounts and notes receivable promptly. This minimizes the amount of working capital tied up in receivables and reduces the likelihood that accounts will become uncollectible. The **accounts receivable turnover** is a measure of the reasonableness of the accounts outstanding. This measurement uses net credit sales, which includes notes receivable from sales transactions. The accounts receivable turnover is computed as follows.

$$\frac{\text{Net credit sales}}{\text{Average receivables}} = \text{Accounts receivable turnover}$$

It is desirable to use monthly balances to compute the average receivables. However, since these amounts are not available to analysts outside the business, year-end balances are often used. Outside analysts normally use net sales since they cannot determine net credit sales. For Carolina Creations, Inc., accounts receivable on January 1, 2004, were $71,500. Net credit sales were $1,900,000 in 2005 and $1,500,000 in 2004.

Step 1: *Compute average accounts receivable.*

	2005	2004
Accounts receivable, Jan. 1	$ 73,500	$ 71,500
Accounts receivable, Dec. 31	92,300	73,500
Totals	$165,800	$145,000
	÷ 2	÷ 2
Average accounts receivable	$ 82,900	$ 72,500

Step 2: *Divide net credit sales by average accounts receivable.*

2005	2004
$\dfrac{\$1,900,000}{\$\ 82,900} = 22.9$ times	$\dfrac{\$1,500,000}{\$\ 72,500} = 20.7$ times

The accounts receivable turnover can be used to determine the **average collection period** of accounts receivable, or *number of days' sales in receivables.* The average collection period is computed as follows.

Managerial IMPLICATIONS

Interpreting Financial Statements

- It is important that managers understand the relationships among the items on the financial statements. Understanding these relationships will help management run the business effectively.

- Managers use statement analysis to identify areas of operations that are weak and need attention.

- It is essential that management know how to compute and interpret financial ratios. For example, a low inventory turnover compared with the industry average might reflect obsolete goods, excess merchandise, poor purchasing procedures, or other operating inefficiencies.

- Effective managers recognize the key role the accountant plays in financial statement analysis and interpretation. Accountants understand what each line on the financial statements represents and can assist management in analyzing and understanding accounting reports.

Thinking Critically
Which ratios will best measure the company's ability to meet current obligations?

$$\frac{365 \text{ days}}{\text{Accounts receivable turnover}}$$

2005	2004
$\frac{365}{22.9} = 15.9 \text{ days}$	$\frac{365}{20.7} = 17.6 \text{ days}$

Carolina Creations, Inc., collected accounts receivable in 2005 in about 16 days and about 17 days in 2004. As a general rule, the average collection period should not exceed the net credit period plus one-third. The credit terms for customers of Carolina Creations, Inc., are net 15 days. The collection period should be 20 days or less [15 + (1/3 × 15)]. For both years the collection period for Carolina Creations, Inc., is less than the guideline.

Other Ratios

The number of ratios that could be developed from financial statements is almost limitless. Analysts use their preferred ratios. Financial writers use many more ratios than those presented in this chapter. Depending on the industry, some ratios are more important than others. The ratios in this chapter are those most often used by accountants.

Some Precautionary Notes on Statement Analysis

There are limits to the benefits of financial statement analysis. Financial statements use book values. Book value depends on accounting

 Objective

Recognize shortcomings in financial statement analysis.

Cost Basis Principle
Accounts reflect historical costs, not current market values. This must be considered when analyzing financial statements. Book value rarely reflects fair market value.

procedures and policies. Different accounting policies and procedures make it difficult to compare financial results across companies. One firm, for example, might record a purchase as an asset and another firm could record it as an expense. Businesses also have many choices regarding depreciation methods, useful lives, and salvage value.

Another limitation of financial statement analysis is that financial statements are prepared assuming that the dollar is a stable monetary unit; this is far from correct. The amounts reported do not necessarily represent dollars with today's purchasing power.

Finally, it is difficult to compare financial results of businesses that use different financing methods, classify expenses differently, have different policies for paying owner-employees, and operate as different types of business entities. Financial statement analysis is useful only if these limitations are clearly understood.

Summary of Ratios

This chapter examined many ratios that are commonly used by analysts to evaluate a business. The following is a summary of the ratios.

▼ **TABLE 24-1** Summary of Ratios Used in Statement Analysis

Ratio	Equation	Performance Measured
Ratios That Measure Profitability, Operating Results, and Efficiency		
Rate of return on net sales	$\dfrac{\text{Net income after taxes}}{\text{Net sales}}$	Percentage of each sales dollar that reflects net income
Rate of return on common stockholders' equity	$\dfrac{\text{Net income after taxes} - \text{Preferred dividend requirements}}{\text{Common stockholders' equity}}$	Rate of return on book value of common stock
Earnings per share of common stock	$\dfrac{\text{Net income after taxes} - \text{Preferred dividend requirements}}{\text{Average number of shares of common stock outstanding during year}}$	Income accruing on each share of common stock
Price-earnings ratio	$\dfrac{\text{Market price per share of common stock}}{\text{Earnings per share of common stock}}$	Value of a share of common stock compared with income accruing to that share
Yield on common stock	$\dfrac{\text{Cash dividend per share of common stock}}{\text{Market value per share of common stock}}$	Cash income (dividend) from a share of common stock as a percentage of the market value of the share
Rate of return on total assets	$\dfrac{\text{Income before interest expense and income taxes}}{\text{Total assets}}$	Effectiveness of management in utilizing assets, regardless of how they were financed
Asset turnover	$\dfrac{\text{Net sales}}{\text{Total assets}}$	Effectiveness of management in using assets to generate sales
Ratios That Measure Financial Strength		
Number of times bond interest earned	$\dfrac{\text{Income before bond interest and income taxes}}{\text{Bond interest cash requirement}}$	Security afforded bondholders

Ratio of stockholders' equity to total equities	$\dfrac{\text{Stockholders' equity}}{\text{Total equities}}$	Portion of assets provided by stockholders and therefore security afforded creditors
Ratio of stockholders' equity to total liabilities	$\dfrac{\text{Stockholders' equity}}{\text{Total liabilities}}$	Owners' capital compared with liabilities; measures security afforded creditors
Book value per share of common stock	$\dfrac{\text{Total stockholders' equity} - \text{Equity of preferred stock}}{\text{Number of common shares outstanding}}$	Amount owner of each share would receive if assets were sold for their book value and the corporation was liquidated

Ratios That Measure Liquidity		
Working capital	Current assets − Current liabilities	Dollar amount of security provided short-term creditors
Current ratio	$\dfrac{\text{Current assets}}{\text{Current liabilities}}$	Ability of business to pay current debts using current assets
Acid-test ratio	$\dfrac{\text{Cash} + \text{receivables} + \text{marketable securities}}{\text{Current liabilities}}$	Immediate liquidity or short-run debt-paying ability
Inventory turnover	$\dfrac{\text{Cost of goods sold}}{\text{Average merchandise inventory}}$	Effectiveness of control of inventory for sales volume
Accounts receivable turnover	$\dfrac{\text{Net credit sales}}{\text{Average receivables}}$	Efficiency with which sales on account are collected
Average collection period	$\dfrac{\text{365 days}}{\text{Accounts receivable turnover}}$	Average number of days required to collect sales on account

▲ **TABLE 24-1 (continued)** Summary of Ratios Used in Statement Analysis

Section 3 Self Review

Questions

1. What does liquidity mean?

2. Why does working capital represent the margin of security afforded short-term creditors?

3. Why is it useful to know the inventory turnover of a company?

Exercises

4. Which of the following is not considered a quick asset?
   a. merchandise inventory
   b. marketable securities
   c. accounts receivable
   d. cash

5. The average collection period is determined by dividing
   a. 365 days by the accounts receivable turnover.

   b. net credit sales by 365 days.
   c. net credit sales by average receivables.
   d. beginning accounts receivable by ending accounts receivable.

Analysis

6. A firm has current assets of $837,372 and current liabilities of $422,155. What is the working capital and the current ratio? Are they favorable or unfavorable?

(Answers to Section 3 Self Review are on page 909.)

CHAPTER 24 — Review and Applications

Review

Chapter Summary

In the previous chapter, you learned how horizontal and vertical analysis of financial statements helps managers, creditors, and owners make informed business decisions. In this chapter, we have reviewed other financial measurements that can reveal a company's profitability, long-term financial strength, and liquidity. Ratio comparisons between items on financial statements help to measure these important factors.

Learning Objectives

1 **Compute and interpret financial ratios that measure profitability, operating results, and efficiency.**

Net income and other factors are used to evaluate profitability, operating results, and business efficiencies. Analysts review the sales of the company in relation to net income, the nature of operations, how assets are used to earn income for the business, and how successful the company has been in rewarding its stockholders.

Measures of profitability, operating results, and efficiency include
- rate of return on net sales,
- rate of return on common stockholders' equity,
- earnings per share of common stock,
- price-earnings ratio,
- yield on common stock,
- rate of return on total assets,
- asset turnover.

2 **Compute and interpret financial ratios that measure financial strength.**

The ability to satisfy long-term debt obligations and to deliver adequate dividend returns to stockholders offers key indications of a company's overall financial strength. Comparison of a company's long-term liabilities to the book value of its property, plant, and equipment can reveal the level of security afforded to long-term creditors. In addition, measurements of book value indicate the financial strength underlying each share of stock.

Measures of financial strength include
- number of times bond interest earned,
- ratio of stockholders' equity to total equities,
- ratio of stockholders' equity to total liabilities,
- book value per share of common stock.

3 **Compute and interpret financial ratios that measure liquidity.**

A company's ability to pay its currently maturing debts is of critical importance to short-term creditors, long-term creditors, and stockholders. Current assets such as cash, inventories, and accounts receivable are measured against items such as current liabilities and credit sales to establish the liquidity of the business.

Measures of liquidity include
- working capital,
- current ratio,
- acid-test ratio,
- inventory turnover,
- accounts receivable turnover,
- days' sales in receivables.

4 **Recognize shortcomings in financial statement analysis.**

The benefits of analysis are limited by a number of significant issues:
- Different companies use different accounting methods. No two companies are exactly the same: there are different mixes of products sold, different organizational structures, and different types of entities.
- Financial statements reflect historical costs, rather than current market values.
- Financial statements are prepared assuming that the dollar is a stable monetary unit.

5 **Define the accounting terms new to this chapter.**

Accounts receivable turnover (p. 890) A measure of the speed with which sales on account are collected; the ratio of net credit sales to average receivables

Acid-test ratio (p. 889) A measure of immediate liquidity; the ratio of quick assets to current liabilities

Asset turnover (p. 884) A measure of the effective use of assets in making sales; the ratio of net sales to total assets

Average collection period (p. 890) The ratio of 365 days to the accounts receivable turnover; also called the *number of days' sales in receivables*

Current ratio (p. 888) A measure of the ability of a business to pay its current debts using current assets; the ratio of current assets to current liabilities

Leveraged buyout (p. 886) Purchasing a business by acquiring the stock and obligating the business to pay the debt incurred

Liquidity (p. 888) The ability of a business to pay its debts when due

Price-earnings ratio (p. 882) The ratio of the current market value of common stock to earnings per share of that stock

Quick assets (p. 889) Cash, receivables, and marketable securities

Return on common stockholders' equity (p. 881) A measure of how well the corporation is making a profit for its shareholders; the ratio of net income available for common stockholders to common stockholders' equity

Total equities (p. 885) The sum of a corporation's liabilities and stockholders' equity

Working capital (p. 888) The measure of the ability of a company to meet its current obligations; the excess of current assets over current liabilities

Comprehensive Self Review

1. What does the ratio of net income to total assets measure?
2. In general, would it be preferable to have a higher or a lower asset turnover? Explain.
3. Explain how to compute the book value per share of common stock.
4. How is the current ratio computed?
5. How is immediate liquidity measured?

(Answers to Comprehensive Self Review are on page 909.)

Discussion Questions

1. Why is the rate of net income on stockholders' equity an important measure to stockholders?

2. What is the procedure for measuring earnings per share of common stock?

3. How does the acid-test ratio differ from the current ratio?

4. In order for the computation of earnings per share to be meaningful, with which figures must it be compared?

5. How is inventory turnover computed?

6. Why is the inventory turnover computed by an analyst outside the company likely to be higher than actual turnover? Does this distort the meaning of the computation?

7. What is the procedure for determining the average collection period of accounts receivable?

8. Why would an analyst be interested in a firm's turnover of assets?

9. What does the accounts receivable turnover measure?

10. Why is it more useful to know the number of days' sales in receivables than the turnover of receivables?

11. As a rule of thumb, what is the minimum desired current ratio?

12. Why does the fact that accounting records are kept on the basis of historical cost sometimes cause difficulties for an analyst of financial statements?

13. Does the analyst outside a company or inside a company have the advantage in analyzing financial statements? Explain.

14. In general, a higher current ratio is favorable because it reflects a greater ability to meet currently maturing obligations. However, management should become concerned if the current ratio becomes too high. Why?

15. Why would the rate of a corporation's net income on sales and the rate of net income on stockholders' equity be of interest and concern to the owners of the corporation's bonds payable?

16. What is the significance of inventory turnover?

17. What is the relationship between working capital and the current ratio?

Applications

EXERCISES

Use Volunteer Corporation's comparative financial statements below and on page 898 for Exercises 24-1 through 24-13.

Volunteer Corporation
Comparative Income Statement
Years Ended December 31, 2005 and 2004

	2005	2004
Sales	1 240 000	1 020 000
Less Sales Returns and Allowances	40 000	20 000
Net Sales	1 200 000	1 000 000
Costs of Goods Sold	900 000	700 000
Gross Profit on Sales	300 000	300 000
Selling Expenses	145 000	130 000
General Expenses	85 000	80 000
Total Expenses	230 000	210 000
Net Income Before Income Tax	70 000	90 000
Income Tax Expense	12 500	18 850
Net Income After Income Taxes	57 500	71 150

Rate of return for net income on sales.
Calculate the rate of net income on sales for 2005 and 2004.

◄ Exercise 24-1
Objective 1

Rate of net income on stockholders' equity.
Compute the rate of net income on average stockholders' equity for 2005 and 2004. Retained earnings on January 1, 2004, was $88,850.

◄ Exercise 24-2
Objective 1

Rate of net income on assets.
Compute the rate of net income before income taxes on total assets for 2005 and 2004. Base your calculation on total ending assets each year.

◄ Exercise 24-3
Objective 1

Asset turnover.
Compute the asset turnover rate for Volunteer Corporation for 2005 and 2004. Base your calculation on total ending assets each year.

◄ Exercise 24-4
Objective 1

Earnings per share.
Calculate the earnings per share of common stock for 2005 and 2004.

◄ Exercise 24-5
Objective 1

Ratio of stockholders' equity to total equities.
Compute Volunteer's ratio of stockholders' equity to total equities on December 31, 2005, and December 31, 2004.

◄ Exercise 24-6
Objective 2

Ratio of stockholders' equity to total liabilities.
Compute the ratio of stockholders' equity to total liabilities at year-end 2005.

◄ Exercise 24-7
Objective 2

Price-earnings ratio.
Calculate the price-earnings ratio for 2005 and 2004. The common stock selling price at year-end 2005 was $86.25 and for 2004 was $56.92.

◄ Exercise 24-8
Objective 1

Volunteer Corporation
Comparative Balance Sheet
December 31, 2005 and 2004

	2005	2004
Assets		
Current Assets		
Cash	5 0 0 0 0	7 8 0 0 0
Accounts Receivable (Net)	1 8 0 0 0 0	1 3 5 0 0 0
Inventory	1 0 0 0 0 0	8 7 0 0 0
Total Current Assets	3 3 0 0 0 0	3 0 0 0 0 0
Property, Plant, and Equipment		
Buildings (Net)	9 5 0 0 0	1 0 0 0 0 0
Equipment (Net)	8 5 0 0 0	8 0 0 0 0
Land	2 0 0 0 0	2 0 0 0 0
Total Property, Plant, and Equipment	2 0 0 0 0 0	2 0 0 0 0 0
Total Assets	5 3 0 0 0 0	5 0 0 0 0 0
Liabilities and Stockholders' Equity		
Current Liabilities		
Accounts Payable	3 0 0 0 0	4 0 0 0 0
Other Current Liabilities	2 5 0 0	2 0 0 0 0
Total Current Liabilities	3 2 5 0 0	6 0 0 0 0
Long-Term Liabilities	8 0 0 0 0	8 0 0 0 0
Bonds Payable	8 0 0 0 0	8 0 0 0 0
Total Long-Term Liabilities	1 1 2 5 0 0	1 4 0 0 0 0
Total Liabilities		
Stockholders' Equity		
Common Stock ($20 par value, 10,000 shares issued and outstanding)	2 0 0 0 0 0	2 0 0 0 0 0
Retained Earnings	2 1 7 5 0 0	1 6 0 0 0 0
Total Stockholders' Equity	4 1 7 5 0 0	3 6 0 0 0 0
Total Liabilities and Stockholders' Equity	5 3 0 0 0 0	5 0 0 0 0 0

Exercise 24-9 ►
Objective 2

Book value per share.

Calculate the book value per share of common stock for 2005 and 2004.

Exercise 24-10 ►
Objective 3

Current ratio.

Calculate the current ratio for 2005 and 2004.

Exercise 24-11 ►
Objective 3

Acid-test ratio.

Compute Volunteer's acid-test ratio as of December 31 for 2005 and 2004.

Exercise 24-12 ►
Objective 3

Inventory turnover.

Using the data for 2005 and 2004, calculate the inventory turnover for each year. The beginning inventory for year 2004 was $93,000.

Exercise 24-13 ►
Objective 3

Accounts receivable turnover.

Compute the accounts receivable turnover on December 31, 2005, for Volunteer Corporation. Assume that all sales were credit sales.

Problems

Selected problems can be completed using:
🍑 **Peachtree**   ⒬ **QuickBooks**   ▦ **Spreadsheets**

PROBLEM SET A

Computing financial ratios.

Part I Using the financial statements for Mountainview Parts Company from Problem 23-1A, calculate the following financial ratios. Comment on any ratio that merits additional consideration.

1. Current ratio
2. Acid-test ratio
3. Inventory turnover
4. Return on sales
5. Earnings per share of common stock
6. Book value per share of common stock
7. Return on total assets
8. Ratio of stockholders' equity to total equities
9. Rate of return on stockholders' equity
10. Asset turnover
11. Accounts receivable turnover

Assume all sales are credit sales. **Merchandise Inventory** on December 31, 2003, was $39,045. The net accounts receivable on December 31, 2003, was $22,000.

Part II Selected ratios for other common-size companies in the same industry as Mountainview Parts Company follow. Using this data and the ratios you computed in Part I, write brief comments on areas you feel are strengths, weaknesses, or require further observation for Mountainview.

1. Rate of return on stockholders' equity, 20.0 percent
2. Stockholders' equity to total equities, 0.6 to 1 (or 60%)
3. Asset turnover, 2.5 to 1
4. Merchandise inventory turnover, 7.5 times

Analyze: Mountainview experienced a 32.6 percent decrease in net income after taxes from 2004 to 2005. If the company experiences a similar pattern from 2005 to 2006, what return on sales can be anticipated if net sales increase by 5 percent in 2006?

Computing financial ratios.

Using the data from Problem 23-2A, calculate the following financial ratios for 2005 and 2004. Comment on any ratio that merits other consideration. Inventory on December 31, 2003, was $32,000.

1. Current ratio
2. Acid-test ratio
3. Inventory turnover
4. Rate of net income after taxes on net sales
5. Rate of net income after taxes on ending stockholders' equity

◀ **Problem 24-1A**
Objectives 1, 2, 3

◀ **Problem 24-2A**
Objectives 1, 2, 3

6. Earnings per share of common stock

7. Book value per share of common stock

8. Rate of net income before interest and taxes on total assets

9. Ratio of stockholders' equity to total equities

10. Asset turnover ratio

11. Ratio of stockholders' equity to total liabilities

Analyze: Assume that the industry norm for inventory turnover is 4.5. Braves Merchandising Company often receives complaints from its customers that merchandise is out of stock. Does this complaint seem consistent with the inventory turnover rate you computed for the company? Why or why not? What actions should be considered to rectify the situation?

Problem 24-3A ▶
Objectives 1, 2, 3

Compute and interpret ratios.

The following are the condensed financial statements for Vail Company and Diego Company for 2004.

Income Statements
Year Ended December 31, 2004

	Vail Company	Diego Company
Sales (Net)	5 2 5 0 0 0 0	5 5 0 0 0 0 0
Costs of Goods Sold	3 1 5 0 0 0 0	3 0 2 5 0 0 0
Gross Profit on Sales	2 1 0 0 0 0 0	2 4 7 5 0 0 0
Operating Expenses	1 7 5 0 0 0 0	2 1 5 0 0 0 0
Net Income from Operations	3 5 0 0 0 0	3 2 5 0 0 0
Interest Expense	0	1 0 0 0 0
Net Income Before Income Tax	3 5 0 0 0 0	3 1 5 0 0 0
Income Tax Expense	1 1 9 0 0 0	1 0 7 1 0 0
Net Income After Income Taxes	2 3 1 0 0 0	2 0 7 9 0 0

Balance Sheets
December 31, 2004

	Vail Company	Diego Company
Assets		
Current Assets	5 0 0 0 0 0	4 0 0 0 0 0
Property, Plant, and Equipment (Net)	5 0 0 0 0 0	6 5 0 0 0 0
Total Assets	1 0 0 0 0 0 0	1 0 5 0 0 0 0
Liabilities and Stockholders' Equity		
Liabilities		
Current Liabilities	2 5 0 0 0 0	2 7 5 0 0 0
Long-Term Liabilities (Bonds Payable)	0	1 0 0 0 0 0
Total Liabilities	2 5 0 0 0 0	3 7 5 0 0 0
Stockholders' Equity		
Common Stock ($10 par value)	1 0 0 0 0 0	1 0 0 0 0 0
Retained Earnings	6 5 0 0 0 0	5 7 5 0 0 0
Total Stockholders' Equity	7 5 0 0 0 0	6 7 5 0 0 0
Total Liabilities and Stockholders' Equity	1 0 0 0 0 0 0	1 0 5 0 0 0 0

1. Compute the following ratios for each company.

   a. Rate of net income after taxes on net sales

   b. Rate of net income before taxes and interest on total assets at year-end.

   c. Rate of net income after income taxes on stockholders' equity at year-end.

   d. Earnings per share of common stock.

   e. Ratio of stockholders' equity to total equities.

   f. Current ratio.

   g. Asset turnover.

   h. Book value per share of common stock.

2. Comment on any similarities or differences in the two companies' ratios. When possible, comment on the cause for these differences.

3. From the investor's point of view, is one company more at risk than the other?

4. Would you grant a five-year loan to either company? Explain.

Analyze: Assume that Diego Company believes that it can cut the cost of goods sold by 8 percent in 2005 while keeping net sales and operating expenses at 2004 levels. If the company met this goal, discuss the potential implications to the rate of net income after taxes on sales and earnings per share. Assume a tax rate of 34 percent.

PROBLEM SET B

Computing financial ratios.

Using the data from Problem 23-1B, Paperback City, Inc., calculate the following financial ratios. Comment on any ratio that merits further consideration. Inventory on December 31, 2003, was $16,000.

◄ **Problem 24-1B**
Objectives 1, 2, 3

Part I

1. Current ratio

2. Acid-test ratio

3. Inventory turnover

4. Return on sales

5. Earnings per share of common stock

6. Book value per share of common stock

7. Return on total assets

8. Ratio of stockholders' equity to total equities

9. Ratio of stockholders' equity to total liabilities

10. Rate of net income on ending stockholders' equity

11. The dividend yield per share of common stock. A dividend of $1.00 per share was paid in 2005 and $1.50 per share was paid in 2004. The market value per share of common stock in 2005 was $25 and in 2004 was $18.

Part II

Selected industry ratios are given below. Compare the ratios of Paperback City, Inc., with these ratios.

1. Rate of net income on sales, 5 percent

2. Return on total assets, 12 percent

3. Merchandise inventory turnover, 6 times

4. Current ratio, 2.5 to 1

Analyze: Based on the analysis you have performed, do you see a trend that could affect the market price of this company's stock during the next fiscal year?

Problem 24-2B ▶
Objectives 1, 2, 3

Computing financial ratios.

Using the data from Problem 23-2B, calculate the following financial ratios for 2005 and 2004. Comment on any ratio that merits further consideration. Inventory on December 31, 2003, was $49,500.

1. Current ratio

2. Acid-test ratio

3. Inventory turnover

4. Return on sales

5. Earnings per share of common stock

6. Book value per share of common stock

7. Return on total assets

8. Ratio of stockholders' equity to total equities

9. Rate of net income after income tax on ending stockholders' equity

Analyze: Assume that the industry norm for asset turnover is 4 to 1. Compute the asset turnover ratio for Summer Company. How is the company performing in relation to the industry norm?

Problem 24-3B ▶
Objectives 1, 2, 3

Compute and interpret various ratios.

Condensed financial statements for Candy Corporation and Dandy Corporation for 2004 follow.

INSTRUCTIONS

1. Compute the following ratios for each company.
   a. Rate of net income after taxes on net sales
   b. Rate of net income before interest and income taxes on total assets at end of year
   c. Rate of net income after taxes on stockholders' equity at end of year
   d. Earnings per share of common stock
   e. Ratio of stockholders' equity to total equities
   f. Current ratio
   g. Asset turnover
   h. Book value per share of common stock

2. Comment on the similarities and differences in the ratios computed for the two companies, pointing out the major factor that causes differences.

3. In which corporation would stock ownership be riskier? Explain.

4. Would you consider the extension of short-term credit to Candy Corporation or Dandy Corporation riskier? Explain.

Income Statements
Year Ended December 31, 2004

	Candy Corporation	Dandy Corporation
Sales (Net)	6 1 0 0 0 0 0	6 0 0 0 0 0 0
Costs of Goods Sold	3 6 6 0 0 0 0	3 3 0 0 0 0 0
Gross Profit on Sales	2 4 4 0 0 0 0	2 7 0 0 0 0 0
Operating Expenses	1 9 2 5 0 0 0	2 1 5 0 0 0 0
Net Income from Operations	5 1 5 0 0 0	5 5 0 0 0 0
Interest Expense	0	1 5 0 0 0
Net Income Before Income Tax	5 1 5 0 0 0	5 3 5 0 0 0
Income Tax Expense	1 7 5 1 0 0	1 8 1 9 0 0
Net Income After Income Tax	3 3 9 9 0 0	3 5 3 1 0 0

Balance Sheets
December 31, 2004

	Candy Corporation	Dandy Corporation
Assets		
Current Assets	3 7 5 0 0 0	3 2 5 0 0 0
Property, Plant, and Equipment (Net)	5 2 5 0 0 0	5 7 5 0 0 0
Total Assets	9 0 0 0 0 0	9 0 0 0 0 0
Liabilities and Stockholders' Equity		
Liabilities		
Current Liabilities	2 5 0 0 0 0	2 1 5 0 0 0
Long-Term Liabilities (Bonds Payable)	0	1 5 0 0 0 0
Total Liabilities	2 5 0 0 0 0	3 6 5 0 0 0
Stockholders' Equity		
Common Stock ($10 par value)	1 0 0 0 0 0	1 0 0 0 0 0
Retained Earnings	5 5 0 0 0 0	4 3 5 0 0 0
Total Stockholders' Equity	6 5 0 0 0 0	5 3 5 0 0 0
Total Liabilities and Stockholders' Equity	9 0 0 0 0 0	9 0 0 0 0 0

Analyze: What percentage of net sales was expended for operating expenses by Candy Corporation? By Dandy Corporation?

CHAPTER 24 CHALLENGE PROBLEM

Company Improvements

Mayflower Sales Company's condensed income statement and balance sheet for the years 2005 and 2004 follow.

Using the following additional information, fill in the missing values.

INSTRUCTIONS

1. The current ratio for 2005 was 2:1.
2. Accounts Receivable increased 40 percent from 2004 to 2005.

3. There were no new purchases of land, property, or equipment in 2005.
4. Accounts Payable increased 25 percent from 2004 to 2005.
5. No new shares of common stock were issued in 2005.
6. The company paid out cash dividends of $5,000 in 2005.
7. The inventory turnover ratio for 2005 was 8 times.
8. The asset turnover ratio in 2005 was 2.5 times and in 2004 was 2.2 times.
9. The earnings per share in 2005 was $3.00 and in 2004 was $2.40.
10. The income tax rate in both years was 25 percent.

Mayflower Sales Company
Condensed Comparative Income Statement
Years Ended December 31, 2005 and 2004

	AMOUNTS	
	2005	2004
Sales	?	?
Less: Cost of Goods Sold	?	600,000
Gross Profit	?	?
Operating Expenses		
Selling Expenses	300,000	284,000
General and Administrative Expenses	355,000	200,000
Total Operating Expenses	655,000	484,000
Net Income Before Income Tax	?	?
Income Tax Expense	?	?
Net Income After Income Tax	?	?

Mayflower Sales Company
Comparative Balance Sheet
December 31, 2005 and 2004

	AMOUNTS	
	2005	2004
Assets		
Current Assets		
Cash	100,000	95,000
Accounts Receivable	?	100,000
Merchandise Inventory	100,000	75,000
Total Current Assets	?	270,000
Property, Plant, and Equipment		
Land	50,000	?
Property, Plant, and Equipment	200,000	?
Less Accumulated Depreciation	(40,000)	?
Total Property, Plant, and Equipment	?	230,000
Total Assets	?	500,000

Liabilities and Stockholders' Equity		
Current Liabilities		
Accounts Payable	150,000	?
Accrued Expenses	?	?
Total Current Liabilities	170,000	130,000
Stockholders' Equity		
Common Stock ($10 par, 10,000 shares authorized)	50,000	?
Paid-in Capital in Excess of Par—Common Stock	100,000	?
Retained Earnings	?	220,000
Total Stockholders' Equity	?	?
Total Liabilities and Stockholders' Equity	?	?

Analyze: Assume that the management of Mayflower Sales Company had been given a directive by the board of directors to improve the company's current ratio in 2005. Did the company improve its standing in this regard from 2004?

CHAPTER 24 CRITICAL THINKING PROBLEM

Lending Policy

Carlos Halla, a wholesale distributor of kitchen appliances, has been approached by two general contractors who want to purchase merchandise from him on net 30-day credit terms. He shows you the following financial data about the two firms and asks for your help in evaluating their liquidity and ability to pay short-term debt.

	On-Time Construction	Easy Money Contractors
Net credit sales	$438,000	$547,500
Cost of goods sold	280,000	261,000
Cash	6,250	13,400
Accounts receivable	50,900	60,040
Inventory	56,000	45,000
Accounts payable	62,300	61,200
Salaries payable	1,200	

INSTRUCTIONS

For each company, compute the following.

1. Current ratio
2. Acid-test ratio
3. Inventory turnover
4. Accounts receivable turnover

Evaluate each company's ability to pay short-term debt and advise Halla on whether or not he should sell to these companies on credit.

Business Connections

Connection 1 ► 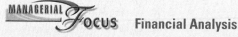 **Financial Analysis**

1. Assume that a director of a corporation where you work asks why the rate of return on assets is considered an important tool for judging managerial effectiveness. What explanation would you provide?

2. The current ratio in the company for which you work is 3 to 1. The average for other firms in the industry is 1.6 to 1. Management has asked you to evaluate this ratio. Summarize the questions that you would like to have answered before making your evaluation.

3. Management has expressed concern that you, as controller of the company, have been preparing too many ratio analyses. Management has asked you to give only three ratios that indicate profitability, three that reflect financial strength, and three that reflect liquidity. In addition, management wants to know what you would compare each ratio with in making an evaluation. In a brief summary, provide the information requested.

4. Suppose that you are the controller for a company that has an inventory turnover of eight times a year while the industry average is only six times a year. One of the officers asks you whether this is a favorable situation for the company. How would you evaluate the situation?

5. In looking at an analysis of financial statements that you have prepared for your employer, a member of the management team points out that the rate of gross profit on sales has declined in each of the past three years. Management has asked you to explain and evaluate the reasons for this situation. What other ratios might be useful in making your analysis?

Connection 2 ► **Ethical DILEMMA** **Revenue Timing** Abbott Sales, Inc., received a $125,000 telephone order on the afternoon of December 30, 2004, the last business day of the year. Susie Rogers, vice president of finance, wants the order to be recorded in December 2004 instead of January 2005. The normal procedure is that sales are recorded when the signed contract is received by Abbott Sales, Inc. The earnings per share figure at year-end is used for determining executive bonuses. Is there an ethical reason for not following normal company procedure on this year-end sale? Why or why not?

Connection 3 ► **Street WISE:**

Questions from the Real World | **Ratios** Refer to the *1999 Annual Report* for The Home Depot, Inc. in Appendix B.

1. Locate the consolidated financial statements. Calculate the rate of return on net sales and asset turnover for the years ended January 30, 2000, and January 31, 1999. Use net earnings before income tax for your computations. What conclusions might be drawn from these measurements of profitability and efficiency?

2. Calculate The Home Depot, Inc.'s working capital, current ratio, and acid-test ratio for the years ended January 30, 2000, and January 31, 1999. If you were a short-term creditor, what degree of security would you have regarding the liquidity and solvency of the company?

FINANCIAL **$TATEMENT**
A N A L Y S I S **Annual Report** The following financial data was extracted from the *1999 Annual Report* for DuPont.

◀ **Connection 4**

Consolidated Income Statement			
(Dollars in millions, except per share)	1999	1998	1997
Sales	$26,918	$24,767	$24,089
Income from Continuing Operations before Income Taxes and Minority Interests	$1,690	$2,613	$2,829
Basic Earnings (Loss) Per Share of Common Stock	$7.08	$3.96	$2.12

Consolidated Balance Sheet	
(Dollars in millions, except per share)	1999
Total Current Assets	$35,416
Total Current Liabilities	$11,228
Total Stockholders' Equity	$12,875

Analyze:

1. Calculate the rate of return on sales for 1999, 1998, and 1997. Describe the trend revealed.

2. Assume that the current market price per share of DuPont stock is $44. Calculate the price-earnings ratio.

3. How effectively do you think this company uses its assets to generate revenue? Discuss your answer. What analysis tools did you use to draw your conclusion?

Analyze Online: Locate DuPont's Web site **(www.DuPont.com).** Click on the *For Investors* link.

4. Find the most recent annual report for the company and locate the "Letter to Our Shareholders" within it. Did the letter contain any ratios or percentages describing performance or financial condition? List these references. For each ratio or percentage, describe how this figure was computed.

Extending the *Thought* **Analysis Beyond the Numbers** In the second half of 1999, The Coca-Cola Company announced plans for a major organizational realignment. Seeking to create the optimal organizational structure to serve the needs of customers, the company plans to reduce its workforce by 6,000 positions. The Coca-Cola Company projects that the realignment will reduce annual expenses by approximately $300 million

◀ **Connection 5**

once the new structure is fully implemented. As analysts review the financial performance and condition of the company, why might this information be important for a complete evaluation of The Coca-Cola Company?

Connection 6 ► **Business Communication** **Memo** Assume that you work in the investor relations department for AT&T. An investment analyst recently released a negative report regarding the current ratio for AT&T based on the data below. The analyst believes that to be acceptable, a current ratio should be at least 1 to 1 in the telecommunications industry. Write a memo to the manager of investor relations with your comments. Why do you think the analyst released this negative report? Why is this of interest to stockholders? Describe other factors you think should be considered by stockholders when reviewing this ratio.

(in billions)	December 31	
	1999	1998
Current Assets	$13.9	$14.1
Current Liabilities	$28.2	$15.4

Connection 7 ► **TeamWork** **Collecting and Interpreting Financial Data** Form teams composed of six students. As a team, you will research current financial ratios for Office Depot, Staples, and Office Max, competitors in the retail office supply industry. Assign two students to gather financial information for Office Depot. Two more students will research financial data for Staples. The other two members of the team should locate recent financial statements for Office Max. Financial statements can be found on the Web site for each company, or on the *Hoover's Online* Web site **(www.hoovers.com).**

	Rate of Return on Sales	Price-Earnings Ratio	Book Value per Share of Common Stock	Current Ratio	Asset Turnover
Office Depot					
Staples					
Office Max					

- Create the spreadsheet above using a spreadsheet software application.
- Calculate the ratios and rates listed.
- Assess the financial strength, profitability, and liquidity of these companies. Discuss your findings in a half-page summary report.

Connection 8 ► *inter*NET **CONNECTION** **Stock Analysis** Go to **www.cocacola.com.** What is the current stock price? What is the current price earnings ratio? What is the return on common equity for the two most recent years?

Answers to Section 1 Self Review

1. Rate of return on net sales, rate of return on total assets, and earnings per share of common stock are all common measures of profitability.
2. The rate of profit being earned by the corporation on the equity provided by the common stockholders.
3. The current market value of common stock to earnings per share of the stock.
4. **b.** market value.
5. **d.** earnings per share
6. • 9 to 1
   • 5 percent

Answers to Section 2 Self Review

1. The ability to make bond interest payments.
2. By dividing stockholders' equity by total liabilities.
3. The financial strength underlying each share of stock.
4. **c.** ratio of stockholders' equity to total equities.
5. **c.** ratio of stockholders' equity to total liabilities.
6. $30

Answers to Section 3 Self Review

1. The ability of a business to pay its debts when due.
2. It is a measure of the amount available to a company to pay its current obligations if the current assets can be converted into cash.
3. If the inventory turnover is too low, it suggests that the amounts tied up in the inventory are excessive for the sales volume being generated.
4. **a.** merchandise inventory
5. **a.** 365 days by the accounts receivable turnover.
6. • $415,217
   • 1.98:1
   • For most manufacturing companies, the results would be considered favorable.

Answers to Comprehensive Self Review

1. How effectively total assets are being used by management to make a profit.
2. A higher asset turnover usually suggests that assets are being used more effectively in generating sales.
3. The value is determined by dividing the common stockholders' equity (total stockholders' equity minus the book value of preferred stock) by the number of common shares outstanding.
4. The current ratio is computed by dividing the current assets by the current liabilities.
5. By the acid-test ratio.

CHAPTER 25

Learning Objectives

1. Distinguish between operating, investing, and financing activities.

2. Compute cash flows from operating activities.

3. Compute cash flows from investing activities.

4. Compute cash flows from financing activities.

5. Prepare a statement of cash flows.

6. Define the accounting terms new to this chapter.

The Statement of Cash Flows

Kodak

KODAK is a trademark of Eastman Kodak Company.

www.kodak.com

*T*echnology is the name of the game at Eastman Kodak Company—helping people take, process, and share pictures in more ways than ever before. Since the 1970s Kodak has been a leader in digital imaging techniques and has established itself as one of the top three digital camera brands in the world. Kodak products helped consumers turn 150 million of their pictures into digital files in 1999.

As they look to the future, company executives review Kodak's financial capabilities for growth. The Consolidated Statement of Cash Flows for the year ended December 31, 1999, reported more than $1.9 billion in cash flow provided by operating activities. In its *1999 Annual Report,* the company expressed its desire to use this substantial resource for growth investments.

Thinking Critically
Why do you think it is important for a company to track and report the sources and uses of cash for a given operating period?

For more information on Kodak, go to: collegeaccounting.glencoe.com.

New Terms

Cash equivalents

Direct method

Financing activities

Indirect method

Investing activities

Operating activities

Operating assets and liabilities

Schedule of operating expenses

Statement of cash flows

Section Objective

① **Distinguish between operating, investing, and financing activities.**

WHY IT'S IMPORTANT
When forecasting the cash needs of a business, accountants need to understand how cash and cash equivalents are generated as well as how the business uses its cash.

Terms to Learn

cash equivalents
financing activities
investing activities
operating activities
statement of cash flows

Sources and Uses of Cash

Corporations issue four financial statements: income statement, balance sheet, statement of retained earnings or stockholders' equity, and statement of cash flows.

The Importance of a Statement of Cash Flows

The **statement of cash flows** provides information about the cash receipts and cash payments of a business. Creditors, including bondholders, noteholders, and suppliers of goods and services, review the statement of cash flows to determine how the firm will pay interest and principal on debts. Investors examine the statement of cash flows to determine if the corporation will have the cash to pay dividends. Management is also interested in cash flows. The firm needs cash to pay employees, suppliers, and other obligations. Analyzing past cash flows is helpful because they indicate the sources and uses of cash in the future.

The Meaning of Cash

On the statement of cash flows, the term *cash* includes cash and cash equivalents. As you know cash consists of coin, currency, and bank accounts. **Cash equivalents** are easily convertible into known amounts of cash. They include certificates of deposit (CDs), U.S. Treasury bills, and money market funds. A short-term investment is a cash equivalent if it matures within three months from the date the business acquired it. Suppose a certificate of deposit acquired by a corporation on September 1, 2004, matures on March 1, 2005. The CD is not classified as a cash equivalent on the December 31, 2004, balance sheet because the maturity date is more than three months from the date the certificate was acquired.

Sources and Uses of Cash

Cash inflows are called *sources of cash. Cash outflows* are called *uses of cash.* Sources and uses of cash are classified under three headings on the statement of cash flows.

① **Objective**

Distinguish between operating, investing, and financing activities.

- **Cash Flows from Operating Activities. Operating activities** are routine business operations. Cash inflows from operating activities include the sale of merchandise or services for cash, collection of accounts receivable created by the sale of merchandise or services, and miscellaneous sources, such as interest income. Cash outflows from operations commonly result from paying operating expenses when they are incurred, paying accounts payable for merchandise purchased on account, and paying accounts payable for operating expenses incurred but not immediately paid.

- **Cash Flows from Investing Activities. Investing activities** involve the acquisition (cash outflow) or disposal (cash inflow) of long-term assets, including land, buildings, equipment, and investments in bonds and other securities.
- **Cash Flows from Financing Activities. Financing activities** involve transactions that provide cash to the business to carry on its activities. Cash inflows from financing activities include issuing bonds and capital stock for cash, borrowing cash by signing notes payable, and reselling treasury stock. Cash outflows from financing activities include paying notes or bonds payable, purchasing treasury stock, and paying cash dividends.

Table 25-1 summarizes sources (inflows) and uses (outflows) of cash.

▼ **TABLE 25-1**
Sources and Uses of
Cash in a Corporation

	Sources of Cash	Uses of Cash
Operating Activities	Sale of merchandise	Pay for merchandise
	Sale of services	Pay taxes
	Interest income	Pay salaries and wages
	Dividend income	Pay interest expense
	Miscellaneous income	Pay for other expenses
Investing Activities	Sale of land, buildings, or equipment	Pay for purchase of land, buildings, or equipment
	Principal payments collected on receivable for long-term assets	Pay for the purchase of investments in bonds or other securities
	Sale of investment in bonds or other securities	
Financing Activities	Issuance of common stock	Pay cash dividends on common stock
	Issuance of preferred stock	Pay cash dividends on preferred stock
	Issuance of bonds payable	Repay bond indebtedness
	Borrowing through signing a note payable	Repay notes payable or other borrowing
	Resale of treasury stock	Purchase treasury stock

Section 1 Self Review

Questions

1. What are cash and cash equivalents?

2. What are investing activities?

3. Is short-term borrowing by signing a note payable a financing activity? Explain.

Exercises

4. Investing activities include
   a. purchases of merchandise for cash.
   b. purchases of plant and equipment for cash.
   c. purchases of prepaid expense items such as supplies and insurance for cash.
   d. issuance of common stock.

5. An example of a financing activity is the
   a. sale of merchandise for cash.
   b. issuance of stock for cash.
   c. sale of used equipment for cash.
   d. collection of debts acquired from the sale of long-term assets.

Analysis

6. Indicate whether each account or transaction is associated with sources of cash or uses of cash.
   a. issuance of common stock
   b. interest expense
   c. taxes expense
   d. dividend income
   e. resale of treasury stock

(Answers to Section 1 Self Review are on page 945.)

2 Compute cash flows from operating activities.

WHY IT'S IMPORTANT
The income statement reports net income on an accrual basis. It does not report actual cash flows. To identify cash flows from operating activities, the financial statement reader needs to review the statement of cash flows.

Terms to Learn

operating assets and liabilities
schedule of operating
   expenses

Cash Flows from Operating Activities

To prepare the statement of cash flows, you need the income statement, schedule of operating expenses, the statement of retained earnings, and a comparative balance sheet. The **schedule of operating expenses** is a supplemental schedule showing the selling and general and administrative expenses in greater detail.

Let's use the financial statements for Carolina Creations, Inc., to explain the statement of cash flows. These statements appear in figures 25-1 through 25-4.

Carolina Creations, Inc.
Income Statement
Year Ended December 31, 2005

Revenue			
Sales	3487 665 00		
Less Sales Returns and Allowances	197 415 00		
Net Sales		3290 250 00	
Cost of Goods Sold			
Merchandise Inventory, January 1	225 000 00		
Purchases (Net)	1703 500 00		
Freight In	28 598 00		
Total Merchandise Available for Sale	1957 098 00		
Less Merchandise Inventory, December 31	192 500 00		
Cost of Goods Sold		1764 598 00	
Gross Profit on Sales		1525 652 00	
Operating Expenses			
Selling Expenses	585 300 00		
General and Administrative Expenses	752 500 00		
Total Operating Expenses		1337 800 00	
Income from Operations		187 852 00	
Other Income			
Gain on Sale of Equipment	4 000 00		
Interest Income	12 250 00		
Total Other Income		16 250 00	
Total Income for the Year		204 102 00	
Other Expenses			
Bond Interest Expense	5 908 00		
Other Interest Expense	1 800 00		
Total Other Expenses		7 708 00	
Net Income Before Income Taxes		196 394 00	
Income Tax Expense		67 655 00	
Net Income After Income Taxes		128 739 00	

FIGURE 25-1 ▶
Income Statement

Carolina Creations, Inc.
Schedule of Operating Expenses
Year Ended December 31, 2005

Selling Expenses		
Advertising	50 000 00	
Depreciation	7 780 00	
Employee Fringe Benefits	30 000 00	
Freight Out and Deliveries	35 000 00	
Insurance	2 500 00	
Miscellaneous	2 070 00	
Other Taxes	3 000 00	
Payroll Taxes—Sales Staff	33 950 00	
Rent	12 000 00	
Repairs and Maintenance	5 000 00	
Sales Commissions	164 500 00	
Sales Salaries	175 000 00	
Sales Supplies	22 500 00	
Travel and Entertainment	35 500 00	
Utilities	6 500 00	
Total Selling Expenses		585 300 00
General and Administrative Expenses		
Depreciation	500 00	
Office Employees' Salaries	150 000 00	
Office Supplies	6 500 00	
Officers' Salaries	450 000 00	
Other Taxes	16 500 00	
Payroll Taxes—Administrative Staff	60 000 00	
Postage, Copying, and Miscellaneous	10 000 00	
Rent	30 000 00	
Uncollectible Accounts Expense	16 500 00	
Utilities	12 500 00	
Total General and Administrative Expenses		752 500 00
Total Operating Expenses		1337 800 00

◀ **FIGURE 25-2**
Schedule of Operating Expenses

International Accounting

The International Accounting Standards Board treats the cash flow statement as a required financial statement *(IAS 7)*. The accounting requirements of some countries do not include a cash flow statement. Some countries require an analysis of changes in working capital referred to as the "Funds Flow Statement."

▼ **FIGURE 25-3**
Comparative Statement of Retained Earnings

Carolina Creations, Inc.
Comparative Statement of Retained Earnings
Years Ended December 31, 2005 and 2004

	Amounts		Increase or Decrease
	2005	2004	
Balance, January 1	160 471	55 000	105 471
Additions			– 0 –
Net Income After Taxes	128 739	110 471	18 268
Total	289 210	165 471	123 739
Deductions			
Dividends, Common	15 000	– 0 –	15 000
Dividends, Preferred	5 000	5 000	– 0 –
Total Deductions	20 000	5 000	15 000
Balance, December 31	269 210	160 471	108 739

Carolina Creations, Inc.
Comparative Balance Sheet
December 31, 2005 and 2004

	Amounts 2005	Amounts 2004	Increase or (Decrease)
Assets			
Current Assets			
Cash	1 0 0 7 5 4	2 2 0 8 0	7 8 6 7 4
Accounts Receivable	9 2 3 0 0	7 3 5 0 0	1 8 8 0 0
Merchandise Inventory	1 9 2 5 0 0	2 2 5 0 0 0	(3 2 5 0 0)
Prepaid Expenses	6 5 0	5 0 0	1 5 0
Supplies	3 9 5	2 5 0	1 4 5
Total Current Assets	3 8 6 5 9 9	3 2 1 3 3 0	6 5 2 6 9
Property, Plant, and Equipment			
Land	4 0 0 0 0	2 0 0 0 0	2 0 0 0 0
Building and Store Equipment	7 1 8 0 0	7 7 8 0 0	(6 0 0 0)
Less Accumulated Depreciation—Building and Store Equipment	2 1 3 4 0	1 5 5 6 0	5 7 8 0
Net Book Value—Building and Store Equipment	5 0 4 6 0	6 2 2 4 0	(1 1 7 8 0)
Office Equipment	5 0 0 0	5 0 0 0	– 0 –
Less Accumulated Depreciation—Office Equipment	2 0 0 0	1 5 0 0	5 0 0
Net Book Value—Office Equipment	3 0 0 0	3 5 0 0	(5 0 0)
Total Property, Plant, and Equipment	9 3 4 6 0	8 5 7 4 0	7 7 2 0
Total Assets	4 8 0 0 5 9	4 0 7 0 7 0	7 2 9 8 9
Liabilities and Stockholders' Equity			
Current Liabilities			
Accounts Payable	3 5 4 0 0	9 3 8 5 9	(5 8 4 5 9)
Sales Tax Payable	3 5 0 0	2 5 0 0	1 0 0 0
Payroll Taxes Payable	1 1 4 5	1 0 2 5	1 2 0
Interest Payable	8 6 0	2 1 5	6 4 5
Total Current Liabilities	4 0 9 0 5	9 7 5 9 9	(5 6 6 9 4)
Long-Term Liabilities			
Bonds Payable	7 0 0 0 0	5 0 0 0 0	2 0 0 0 0
Premium on Bonds Payable	6 4 4	– 0 –	6 4 4
Mortgage Payable	4 0 0 0 0	4 4 0 0 0	(4 0 0 0)
Total Long-Term Liabilities	1 1 0 6 4 4	9 4 0 0 0	1 6 6 4 4
Total Liabilities	1 5 1 5 4 9	1 9 1 5 9 9	(4 0 0 5 0)
Stockholders' Equity			
Preferred Stock ($100 par, 10%, 500 shares authorized, issued and outstanding)	5 0 0 0 0	5 0 0 0 0	– 0 –
Common Stock ($1 par, 25,000 shares authorized)			
Issued and outstanding: 4000 shares in 2004; 4,400 shares in 2005	4 4 0 0	4 0 0 0	4 0 0
Paid-in Capital—Common Stock	4 9 0 0	1 0 0 0	3 9 0 0
Retained Earnings—Unappropriated	2 6 9 2 1 0	1 6 0 4 7 1	1 0 8 7 3 9
Total Stockholders' Equity	3 2 8 5 1 0	2 1 5 4 7 1	1 1 3 0 3 9
Total Liabilities and Stockholders' Equity	4 8 0 0 5 9	4 0 7 0 7 0	7 2 9 8 9

▲ **FIGURE 25-4** Comparative Balance Sheet

Statement of Cash Flows

The statement of cash flows reconciles the beginning and ending cash balances. It ties together the income statement and the changes in the noncash items on the balance sheet and on the statement of retained earnings.

Figure 25-4 shows the comparative balance sheet for Carolina Creations, Inc. There are no cash equivalents on the balance sheet. In 2005 the beginning cash balance was $22,080; the ending cash balance was $100,754. Cash increased by $78,674. The statement of cash flows shows the factors that caused the increase in cash.

There are two ways to prepare the statement of cash flows: the direct method and the indirect method. Carolina Creations, Inc., uses the indirect method. The direct method will be described later in this chapter. The indirect method treats net income as the primary source of cash from operating activities and adjusts net income for changes in noncash items.

The accrual basis of accounting is used when recording transactions and preparing the balance sheet and the income statement. Net income shown on the income statement includes both cash and noncash transactions. On the statement of cash flows, net income is adjusted for the noncash items.

Figure 25-5 on page 918 shows the statement of cash flows for Carolina Creations, Inc. Let's examine it and learn how to prepare the statement of cash flows. Throughout this chapter you will need to refer to the financial statements and reports for Carolina Creations, Inc.

Recall

Accrual Basis
Under the accrual basis of accounting, revenues are recorded when earned and expenses are recorded when owed, not necessarily when the cash is received or paid.

Cash Flows from Operating Activities

The first section of the statement of cash flows shows net cash provided by operating activities. For Carolina Creations, Inc., $89,638 was provided by operating activities. Since cash flows from operating activities are closely related to net income, the starting point for the analysis of the cash flows from operating activities is the net income after income taxes, taken from the income statement in Figure 25-1. The Cash Flows from Operating Activities section of the cash flows statement explains why the net cash flows from operations ($89,638) differs from the net income after taxes ($128,739). There were several income and expense items reported on the income statement that did not involve cash inflows or outflows during that period. Let's analyze those items.

❷ **Objective**
Compute cash flows from operating activities.

Expense and Income Items Involving Long-Term Assets and Liabilities

Some items on the income statement result from adjustments related to long-term assets or long-term liabilities. They do not involve cash inflows or outflows in the current year. These adjustments are added to or subtracted from net income.

Depreciation Expense. The acquisition of property, plant, and equipment is reported in the Cash Flows from Investing Activities section of the statement of cash flows in the year acquired. Depreciation, depletion, and amortization of assets do not involve a cash outlay in the year the expense is recorded. Instead, these expenses represent a reduction in the net asset value. Figure 25-2 shows depreciation expense of $8,280 (sum of $7,780

Important!

Depreciation Expense
The depreciation expense on the income statement is not a cash outflow; therefore, it is added back to net income on the statement of cash flows.

recorded as selling expenses and $500 recorded as general and administrative expenses). The depreciation expense was recorded as follows.

1	2005						1
2	Dec.	31	Depreciation Expense (Selling)	7 7 8 0 00			2
3			Depreciation Expense (General)	5 0 0 00			3
4			Accumulated Depreciation		8 2 8 0 00		4

Note that the depreciation expense did not involve a cash outflow. Net income was reduced by a noncash expense. To obtain cash flows from operating activities, the depreciation expense is added back to net income.

FIGURE 25-5 ▶
Statement of Cash Flows

Carolina Creations, Inc.
Statement of Cash Flows
Year Ended December 31, 2005

Cash Flows from Operating Activities		
Net income after taxes (per income statement)		128 7 3 9 00
Adjustments to reconcile net income to net cash		
provided by operating activities		
Depreciation Expense	8 2 8 0 00	
Amortization of premium on bonds payable	(9 2 00)	
Gain on sale of equipment	(4 0 0 0 00)	
Changes in noncash current assets and current		
liabilities:		
Increase in accounts receivable	(18 8 0 0 00)	
Decrease in merchandise inventory	3 2 5 0 0 00	
Increase in prepaid expenses	(1 5 0 00)	
Increase in supplies	(1 4 5 00)	
Decrease in accounts payable	(58 4 5 9 00)	
Increase in sales tax payable	1 0 0 0 00	
Increase in payroll taxes payable	1 2 0 00	
Increase in interest payable	6 4 5 00	
Total adjustments		(39 1 0 1 00)
Net cash provided by operating activities		89 6 3 8 00
Cash Flows from Investing Activities		
Proceeds from sale of equipment	8 0 0 0 00	
Purchase of land	(20 0 0 0 00)	
Net cash used in investing activities		(12 0 0 0 00)
Cash Flows from Financing Activities		
Proceeds from issue of common stock	4 3 0 0 00	
Proceeds from issuance of bonds payable	20 7 3 6 00	
Payment of mortgage principal	(4 0 0 0 00)	
Payment of dividends on preferred stock	(5 0 0 0 00)	
Payment of dividends on common stock	(15 0 0 0 00)	
Net cash provided by financing activities		1 0 3 6 00
Net Increase in Cash and Cash Equivalents		78 6 7 4 00
Cash and cash equivalents, January 1, 2005		22 0 8 0 00
Cash and cash equivalents, December 31, 2005		100 7 5 4 00

Note: During the year payments for income taxes were $67,655 and payments for interest expense were $7,063.

Amortization of Premium on Bonds Payable.
The income statement shows bond interest expense of $5,908. This is not the actual cash outflow for interest. It reflects the cash paid minus $92 of bond premium amortization. The bond interest expense was recorded as follows.

11	Bond Interest Expense	5 9 0 8 00		11
12	Premium on Bonds Payable	9 2 00		12
13	Cash		6 0 0 0 00	13

The amount of bond interest expense reported on the income statement understates the actual cash outflow by $92. To obtain cash flows from operating activities, the amortization of the bond premium is deducted from net income.

Gain or Loss on Sale of Equipment.
The income statement shows a gain of $4,000 on the sale of equipment. The equipment was sold for $8,000 cash. Thus, the proceeds from the sale of the equipment was shown as a cash inflow from investing activities. At the time of sale, the following entry was made.

21	Cash	8 0 0 0 00		21
22	Accumulated Depreciation—Equipment	2 0 0 0 00		22
23	Equipment		6 0 0 0 00	23
24	Gain on Sale of Equipment		4 0 0 0 00	24

The sale of the equipment is not a part of the routine operating activities of the business. The gain of $4,000 is a part of the $8,000 in cash received from the asset sale. As we will see later, the entire $8,000 will be included in cash inflows from investing activities. It is therefore necessary to remove (deduct) the $4,000 of gain on sale of equipment from the net income figure in arriving at the net cash inflow provided by operations. A loss on sale of long-term assets would be added to net income.

Income and Expense Items Involving Changes in Current Assets and Current Liabilities

Current assets and current liabilities are often referred to as **operating assets and liabilities**. Usually, changes in current assets and current liabilities are related to routine business operations and are reflected in net income. Assume that all the changes in the current assets and current liabilities of Carolina Creations, Inc., resulted from routine operating activities.

Increases in Current Assets.
Current assets include accounts receivable, merchandise inventory, and prepaid expenses. Increases in current assets are deducted from net income to arrive at cash flows from operating activities. If a current asset, other than cash or cash equivalents, increased as a result of operations, not all of the cash flows were reflected in net income. The comparative balance sheet for Carolina Creations, Inc., Figure 25-4, shows that several current assets increased during the year.

Increase in Accounts Receivable.
Figure 25-4 shows that **Accounts Receivable** increased by $18,800. This means that more sales on account were recorded than collected. The sales were included in net income, but the cash has not been received. To obtain cash flows from operating activities, the increase in accounts receivable is subtracted from net income.

Important!

Bond Interest Expense
The bond interest expense on the income statement is less than the actual cash outflow; therefore, on the statement of cash flows, the difference is subtracted from net income.

Increase in Prepaid Expenses. Figure 25-4 shows that **Prepaid Expenses** increased by $150. This means that more was paid for prepaid expenses than was charged to expense in arriving at net income for the year. In other words, net income does not reflect the cash paid for prepaid expenses. To obtain cash flows from operating activities, the increase in prepaid expenses is subtracted from net income.

The Hasbro, Inc., consolidated statements of cash flows for the fiscal year ended December 31, 1999, reported net cash provided by operating activities of $391.5 million. Depreciation of plant and equipment, increases in accounts receivable, increases in inventories, and increases in prepaid expenses were considered when reconciling net income to net cash provided by operating activities on the statement of cash flows. These transactions affected net income, but they did not affect cash flows.

Increase in Supplies. Figure 25-4 shows that **Supplies** increased by $145. This means that more supplies were paid for than were used. Net income does not reflect all cash paid for supplies. To obtain cash flows from operating activities, the increase in supplies is subtracted from net income.

Decreases in Current Assets. Decreases in noncash current assets are added to net income to arrive at cash flows from operating activities. If current assets other than cash or cash equivalents decrease as a result of operations, some of the net income reported was not a cash flow.

Decrease in Merchandise Inventory. Figure 25-4 shows that **Merchandise Inventory** decreased by $32,500. This means that more inventory was sold than was purchased. The sale of the inventory was reflected in net income as cost of goods sold, but cash was not paid to replace the inventory. Net income reflects higher costs than actual cash outflows. To obtain cash flows from operating activities, a decrease in inventory is added to net income.

Increases in Current Liabilities. Current liabilities include accounts payable, sales tax payable, payroll taxes payable, and interest payable. Increases in current liabilities are added to net income to obtain the cash flows from operating activities.

Increase in Sales Tax Payable. Figure 25-4 shows that **Sales Tax Payable** increased by $1,000. This means that more sales tax was owed than was paid. To obtain cash flows from operating activities, the increase in sales tax payable is added to net income.

Increase in Payroll Taxes Payable. Figure 25-4 shows that **Payroll Taxes Payable** increased by $120. This means that more payroll taxes were owed than were paid. To obtain cash flow from operating activities, the increase in payroll taxes payable is added to net income.

Increase in Interest Payable. Figure 25-4 shows that **Interest Payable** increased by $645. This means that more interest was recorded as expense than was paid in cash. To obtain cash flows from operating activities, the increase in interest payable is added to net income.

Decreases in Current Liabilities. Decreases in current liabilities are subtracted from net income. If current liabilities decrease as a result of operations, some of the net income reported was not a cash flow.

Decrease in Accounts Payable. Figure 25-4 shows that **Accounts Payable** decreased $58,459. This means more cash was paid on account than purchases were recorded on account. The cash was paid out but was not reflected in net income. To obtain cash flows from operating activities, the decrease in accounts payable is subtracted from net income.

Summary of Effects of Changes in Current Assets and Current Liabilities. Let's summarize how net income is adjusted for changes in current assets and current liabilities when computing cash flows from operating activities.

	Add to Net Income	Deduct from Net Income
Increase in current asset		X
Decrease in current asset	X	
Increase in current liability	X	
Decrease in current liability		X

Figure 25-5 shows all items considered when computing net cash provided by operating activities. During the year operating activities for Carolina Creations, Inc., provided $89,638 of cash.

Effect of Net Loss on Cash Flows from Operations

If the income statement reflects a net loss, the first line of the statement of cash flows is the net loss. All adjustments for changes in current assets and current liabilities are made to the net loss figure.

Section 2 | **Self Review**

Questions

1. The income statement shows a loss of $10,000 on the sale of a building. How is the loss handled when computing net cash provided by operating activities?

2. The income statement shows depreciation expense of $34,000. How is the expense handled when computing net cash provided by operating activities?

3. During the year, the notes payable account increased from $50,000 to $85,000. How, if at all, is this reflected when computing net income from operations?

Exercises

4. The net cash provided by operating activities is affected by
   a. a change in merchandise inventory.
   b. a purchase of land for cash.
   c. the issue of bonds payable for cash.
   d. the sale of stock for cash.

5. To determine the net cash provided by operating activities, an increase in prepaid assets should be
   a. added to net income.
   b. deducted from net income.

   c. not included in the calculation.
   d. added to net cash flow.

Analysis

6. The net loss for the year was $15,000. Depreciation expense was $5,000. **Merchandise Inventory** decreased by $3,000. **Accounts Receivable** decreased by $1,500. **Accounts Payable** decreased by $2,000. **Income Tax Payable** decreased by $5,000. Calculate the net cash provided or used by operating activities for the year.

Section Objectives

3 Compute cash flows from investing activities.

WHY IT'S IMPORTANT
Cash flows from the acquisition or disposal of assets are reported separately from cash flows from operating activities.

4 Compute cash flows from financing activities.

WHY IT'S IMPORTANT
Transactions such as stock sales, securing loans, or repaying notes impact the cash balance of a business.

5 Prepare a statement of cash flows.

WHY IT'S IMPORTANT
Investors, managers, and creditors want to know the reasons for changes in a company's cash position.

Terms to Learn

direct method
indirect method

3 Objective
Compute cash flows from investing activities.

Important!

Investing Activities
Investing activities are transactions that involve the acquisition or disposal of assets that will not be used up or consumed in routine operations in a short time.

Cash Flows from Investing and Financing Activities

Investing and financing activities can produce both cash outflows and cash inflows.

Cash Flows from Investing Activities

Investing activities are transactions involving the acquisition or disposal of assets that are not consumed in routine operations within one year.

Cash Outflows from Investing Activities

The most common cash outflows from investing activities are cash payments for purchases of property, plant, and equipment and for purchases of the stocks and bonds of other corporations.

Figure 25-4 shows that the **Land** account increased by $20,000 during 2005. The increase resulted from the purchase of land for $20,000 in cash. This is a cash outflow from investing activities. It is reported on the statement of cash flows in Figure 25-5.

Cash Inflows from Investing Activities

Most cash inflows from investing activities reflect the sale of land, buildings, equipment, or investments in securities of other corporations. Payments of principal received on mortgages or notes held by the company in connection with the sale of plant and equipment are classified as cash inflows from investing activities.

In 2005 Carolina Creations, Inc., had one cash inflow from investing activities. The corporation sold equipment for $8,000 in cash.

Sales price (cash inflow)		$8,000
Asset cost	$6,000	
Accumulated depreciation	(2,000)	(4,000)
Gain on sale		$4,000

The statement of cash flows shows the $8,000 received from the sale of the equipment as a cash inflow from investing activities. Recall that the gain was subtracted from net income in the Cash Flows from Operating Activities section.

At this point it is possible to reconcile the changes in the long-term asset accounts. The net change of $6,000 (decrease) in the **Building and Store Equipment** account is reconciled as follows.

Building and store equipment, Dec. 31, 2004	$77,800
Add: Purchases during 2005	–0–
Less: Cost of equipment sold during 2005	6,000
Building and store equipment, Dec. 31, 2005	$71,800

The increase in accumulated depreciation can be reconciled to the depreciation expense for the year as follows.

Accumulated Depreciation

	Building & Store Equip.		Office Equip.		Total
2005	$21,340	+	$2,000	=	$23,340
2004	(15,560)	+	(1,500)	=	(17,060)
Increase	$ 5,780	+	$ 500	=	$ 6,280
Accumulated depreciation on equipment sold					2,000
Depreciation expense for 2005					$ 8,280

The Cash Flows from Investing Activities section of the statement of cash flows for Carolina Creations, Inc., shows that $12,000 cash was used in investing activities during 2005.

Cash Flows from Financing Activities

Financing activities include debt and equity transactions.

Cash Inflows from Financing Activities

Cash inflows from financing activities include amounts received from the original issue of preferred stock or common stock, the resale of treasury stock, and the issue of bonds and notes payable.

Proceeds of Cash Investments by Stockholders. Figure 25-4 shows that the **Common Stock** account increased by $400 and the **Paid-in Capital-Common Stock** account increased by $3,900. During 2005 Carolina Creations, Inc., issued 400 shares of common stock for $10.75 per share. This resulted in a cash inflow of $4,300 (400 × $10.75) as reported on the statement of cash flows.

Proceeds of Short-Term and Long-Term Borrowing. Figure 25-4 shows that the **Bonds Payable** account increased by $20,000 and the **Premium on Bonds Payable** increased by $644.

The company issued $20,000 of bonds payable for $20,736, which included a premium of $736. The cash inflow of $20,736 is reported as a cash flow from financing activities.

During 2005 bond premium of $92 was amortized. Remember that the amortized premium was included in the Cash Flows from Operating Activities section. The change of $644 in **Premium on Bonds Payable** is reconciled as follows.

Premium on bonds payable, Dec. 31, 2004	$–0–
Add: Premium on bonds sold in 2005	736
Less: Premium amortized in 2005	(92)
Premium on bonds payable, Dec. 31, 2005	$ 644

Cash Outflows from Financing Activities

Cash outflows from financing activities result from the repayment of debt obligations such as bonds payable, notes payable, and mortgages; the purchase of treasury stock; and the retirement of preferred stock. The payment of cash dividends is classified as a cash outflow from financing activities. Interest expense, however, is classified as an outflow of cash from operating activities.

About Accounting

Managing Cash
Large companies actively manage their own corporate cash. Smaller businesses often place their cash in money market funds due to the limited time and resources available for cash management.

❹ Objective
Compute cash flows from financing activities.

Treasury Stock
Treasury stock is a corporation's own capital stock that has been issued, fully paid for, and reacquired.

Bonds Issued at a Premium
On the day that bonds are issued, if the market rate of interest is lower than the face rate of interest, the bonds will sell at a premium.

Computers in Accounting

Presentation Software

The days of the paper flip chart and pointer are long gone. Today, accounting professionals routinely present financial matters to peers, stockholders, and company executives using presentation software. Sophisticated audiences demand presentations that deliver data in easy-to-understand formats. Color-coded pie charts, 3-D graphs, and bar charts are especially useful when presenting financial data. Presentation software offers tools for video, graphics, film, and even sound that help presenters make their points succinctly.

Presentations can be displayed using a PC screen or an overhead projection system. The software often contains templates that can be used to create very simple presentations or customized to prepare complex, interactive shows. Sound and animation can be added to highlight key points such as record earnings or the accomplishment of a financial goal.

Business professionals also use presentation software to share information across the Internet. A presentation can be published on a Web site by converting the documents to HTML format. For example, corporate executives located in Tokyo, Frankfurt, and New York can simultaneously review quarterly earnings reports and related charts and graphs that were created using presentation software and posted to a Web site.

Thinking Critically
Describe financial events that might be communicated by the accounting staff of a company to stockholders, executives, or other managers.

Internet Application
Using an Internet search engine, research three types of presentation software. Use the search term "presentation software." List the software titles, features, prices, and hardware requirements for each type of software.

Payment of Mortgage Payable. Figure 25-4 shows a decrease of $4,000 in the **Mortgage Payable** account during 2005. This decrease is a result of $4,000 of principal payments. These payments are shown on the statement of cash flows as a cash outflow from financing activities.

During 2005 Carolina Creations, Inc., did not acquire cash through short-term borrowing, nor did it repay any short-term loans. However, if it had, these short-term transactions might not appear on the balance sheet. For example, the corporation could have borrowed $5,000 by signing a three-month note payable on March 1, 2005, and repaid the note on June 1, 2005. The note would not appear on the December 31, 2005, balance sheet. However, the note would represent both an inflow and an outflow of cash. The note would be reported in the Cash Flows from Financing Activities section of the statement of cash flows.

Payment of Cash Dividends. Figure 25-3 indicates that during the year Carolina Creations, Inc., paid cash dividends of $5,000 on preferred stock and $15,000 on common stock. These amounts are included as a part of cash flows from financing activities.

The statement of cash flows shows that in 2005 cash of $1,036 was provided by the financing activities of Carolina Creations, Inc.

⑤ Objective

Prepare a statement of cash flows.

Preparing a Statement of Cash Flows

The cash flows from the three types of business activities—operating, investing, and financing—are combined to arrive at the net change in cash and cash equivalents for the year. The net change is then combined

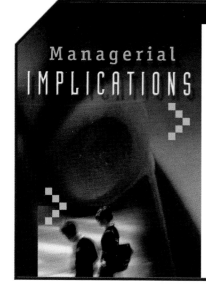

Managerial

IMPLICATIONS

Cash Flow

- Management needs to ensure that cash is available to meet operating expenses and to pay debts promptly.
- Management analyzes the statement of cash flows to evaluate the operations of the company, plan future operations, forecast cash needs, arrange proper financing, and plan dividend payments.
- Management uses the statement of cash flows to determine how well the company will be able to meet its maturing obligations.
- Management analyzes past cash flows in order to make plans that will keep the company solvent and profitable.

Thinking Critically

What effect would an unreconciled bank statement have on the statement of cash flows?

with the beginning balance of cash and cash equivalents to reconcile to the ending balance of cash and cash equivalents. Figure 25-5 shows that the net change in the cash and cash equivalents was an increase of $78,674. The cash balance was $22,080 on January 1, 2005, and $100,754 on December 31, 2005. These are the same amounts reported on the comparative balance sheet in Figure 25-4.

Direct and Indirect Methods of Preparing the Statement of Cash Flows

There are two methods of preparing the statement of cash flows: the indirect and direct methods. Figure 25-5 was prepared using the **indirect method**. Under this method, in the Cash Flows from Operating Activities section, net income is treated as the primary source of cash and is adjusted for changes in current assets and liabilities associated with net income, noncash transactions, and other items. Most corporations use the indirect method.

The Financial Accounting Standards Board allows the indirect or direct method. Under the **direct method**, all revenue and expenses reported on the income statement appear in the operating section of the statement of cash flows and show the cash received or paid out for each type of transaction. Under the direct method, a corporation reports cash flows from operating activities in two major classes: gross cash receipts and gross cash payments. The FASB suggests the following classifications for reporting cash inflows and outflows:

- cash collected from customers
- interest and dividends received
- cash paid to employees and other suppliers of goods or services, including suppliers of insurance and advertising
- interest paid
- income taxes paid

Corporations that use the direct method are encouraged to provide additional meaningful information about operating cash receipts and cash payments if feasible. The direct method is not commonly used because many businesses do not have easy access to the records of cash payments for each type of expenditure.

When the statement of cash flows is based on the direct method, it must be accompanied by a reconciliation of net income to the net cash provided by operating activities. This reconciliation shows the same information as the Cash Flows from Operating Activities section of the statement of cash flows prepared using the indirect method. The additional work is another reason that many corporations avoid the direct method of preparing the statement of cash flows. Intermediate accounting textbooks provide detailed information about the direct method.

Disclosures Required in the Statement of Cash Flows

Various disclosures are added to the statement of cash flows. If the indirect method of presentation is used, the amount of interest and income taxes paid during the period are reported in notes accompanying the statement. The note at the bottom of Figure 25-5 shows that cash payments were $67,655 for income taxes and $7,063 for interest.

In order to provide complete information to statement readers, information about noncash investing and financing activities are disclosed on the statement of cash flows. Examples of financing and investing activities not affecting cash flows include issuing bonds payable for land or converting bonds payable into common stock.

Important!

Disclosures
If the indirect method is used, the interest and income taxes paid during the period are separately disclosed.

It is possible for a company to report a net loss and a positive cash flow. Amazon.com reported a net loss of $719 million for the fiscal year ended December 31, 1999. The company's consolidated statements of cash flows for the same period revealed a substantial improvement in the cash position; cash and cash equivalents totaled $116.9 million, an increase of more than 450 percent from the beginning of the year.

Section 3 Self Review

Questions

1. During the year, equipment was sold for $100,000, and an $8,000 gain was recorded. How is this transaction reported on the statement of cash flows?

2. On the statement of cash flows, how is the payment of a cash dividend reported?

3. During the year, a corporation issued $100,000 of bonds payable in return for land with a fair market value of $100,000. How is this reported on the statement of cash flows?

Exercises

4. Most corporations prepare the statement of cash flows using the
   a. accrual method.
   b. direct method.
   c. indirect method.
   d. equivalent method.

5. The purchase of land for cash is shown on the statement of cash flows as a(n)
   a. increase in Cash Flows from Investing Activities.
   b. decrease in Cash Flows from Investing Activities.
   c. increase in Cash Flows from Financing Activities.
   d. decrease in Cash Flows from Financing Activities.

Analysis

6. A truck that originally cost $48,000 was sold for $12,000 cash. Accumulated depreciation up to the date of the sale was $34,000. A $2,000 loss was reported on the income statement. What is the effect on the statement of cash flows?

(Answers to Section 3 Self Review are on page 945.)

Review

Chapter Summary

In previous chapters, you learned about the three major financial statements prepared for corporations—the income statement, the balance sheet, and the statement of retained earnings. In addition, some corporations prepare a statement of stockholders' equity. The annually published financial statements should also include a statement of cash flows showing the sources and uses of cash.

Learning Objectives

1 **Distinguish between operating, investing, and financing activities.**

The corporation's activities are divided into three categories on the statement of cash flows: operating, investing, and financing. Cash inflows and outflows from transactions for each type of activity are shown, along with the net cash inflow or outflow.

- Cash flows from operating activities involve routine business operations: selling merchandise for cash, collecting accounts receivable, paying expenses when incurred, and paying accounts payable.
- Investing activities are transactions that involve the acquisition of assets or disposal of assets such as land, equipment, or buildings.
- Financing activities involve transactions such as issuing stocks or bonds, paying a note or bond payable, or paying cash dividends.

2 **Compute cash flows from operating activities.**

The first section of the statement of cash flows involves operating activities—buying, selling, and administrative activities. This section begins with the net income amount from the income statement.

- To arrive at the net cash flow provided by operating activities, the net income amount is adjusted for noncash items used to calculate net income.
- The most common items added to net income are (1) depreciation, (2) losses on sales of assets, (3) amortization of bond discount, (4) decreases in current assets, and (5) increases in current liabilities.
- The most common items deducted from net income are (1) gains on sales of assets, (2) amortization of bond premium, (3) increases in current assets, and (4) decreases in current liabilities.

3 **Compute cash flows from investing activities.**

The second section of the statement discloses investing activities.

- Cash inflows from investing often result from cash sales of property, plant, and equipment and cash sales of the stocks and bonds of other corporations held as investments.
- Cash outflows come from cash purchases of plant and equipment and cash purchases of the stocks and bonds of other corporations.

4 **Compute cash flows from financing activities.**

The third section of the statement concerns financing activities. These activities may reflect transactions between a corporation and its stockholders.

- Cash inflows often result from the issuing of common or preferred stock or selling treasury stock.
- Typical cash outflows are dividend payments and the purchase of treasury stock.
- Cash inflows result from issuing bonds payable for cash and from borrowing money by issuing or discounting notes payable. Cash outflows result when notes payable or bonds payable are repaid. However, interest paid on debt is seen as resulting from an operating activity.

5 **Prepare a statement of cash flows.**

There are two statement preparation methods—direct and indirect.

- Most corporations use the indirect method because the statement is easier to prepare when this method is used.
- The Financial Accounting Standards Board allows either method.
- Some major transactions that do not involve cash should be disclosed in notes to the statement of cash flows.

6 **Define the accounting terms new to this chapter.**

CHAPTER 25 GLOSSARY

Cash equivalents (p. 912) Assets that are easily convertible into known amounts of cash

Direct method (p. 925) A means of reporting sources and uses of cash under which all revenue and expenses reported on the income statement appear in the operating section of the statement of cash flows and show the cash received or paid out for each type of transaction

Financing activities (p. 913) Transactions with those who provide cash to the business to carry on its activities

Indirect method (p. 925) A means of reporting cash generated from operating activities by treating net income as the primary source of cash in the operating section of the statement of cash flows and adjusting that amount for changes in current assets and liabilities associated with net income, noncash transactions, and other items

Investing activities (p. 913) Transactions that involve the acquisition or disposal of long-term assets

Operating activities (p. 912) Routine business transactions—selling goods or services and incurring expenses

Operating assets and liabilities (p. 919) Current assets and current liabilities

Schedule of operating expenses (p. 914) A schedule that supplements the income statement, showing the selling and general and administrative expenses in greater detail

Statement of cash flows (p. 912) A financial statement that provides information about the cash receipts and cash payments of a business

Comprehensive Self Review

1. What are the three types of activities for which cash flows must be shown in a statement of cash flows?

2. What are financing activities?

3. During the year, accounts payable increased from $50,000 to $85,000. How, if at all, would this change be reflected in computing net income from operations?

4. Where on the statement of cash flows should a payment of interest expense be shown?

5. Where on the statement of cash flows should a gain on the sale of equipment be shown?

(Answers to Comprehensive Self Review are on page 945.)

Discussion Questions

1. What is the purpose of the statement of cash flows?

2. Where is information obtained for preparing the statement of cash flows?

3. Give two examples of cash inflows from investing activities.

4. Give two examples of cash outflows from investing activities.

5. Give two examples of cash outflows from financing activities.

6. Give two examples of cash inflows from financing activities.

7. What are cash and cash equivalents?

8. Is an investment in a corporate bond maturing 180 days after the purchase date a cash equivalent? Explain.

9. A corporation's income statement shows a gain of $10,000 on the sale of plant and equipment. In computing the net cash provided by operating activities, how would this $10,000 be treated?

10. A corporation's income statement shows bond interest expense of $32,500. Amortization of the discount on the bonds during the year was $1,500. What is the amount of cash outflow for bond interest expense?

11. Explain the difference between the direct method and the indirect method of preparing the statement of cash flows.

12. On January 1, 2004, the balance of the **Accounts Payable** account was $20,000. On December 31, 2004, the balance was $31,000. How, if at all, would this change be reflected in the statement of cash flows?

13. On January 1, 2004, the balance of the **Accrued Income Taxes Payable** account was $5,000. On December 31, 2004, the balance was $10,000. How, if at all, would this change be reflected in the statement of cash flows?

14. Why are cash equivalents included on the statement of cash flows?

15. Why must noncash investing and financing activities be disclosed on the statement of cash flows?

16. Identify in which of the three types of activities on the statement of cash flows the following transactions appear. Indicate whether each is a cash inflow or outflow.

   a. Cash dividends paid.

   b. Cash interest payment received.

   c. Cash on loans collected.

   d. Cash interest paid.

   e. Cash received from customers.

   f. Cash proceeds from issuing stock.

Applications

EXERCISES

Exercise 25-1 ►
Objective 1

Effects of transactions on cash flows.

What effect would each of the following transactions have on the statement of cash flows?

1. The sum of $3,500 in cash was received from the sale of used office equipment that originally cost $15,000. Depreciation of $12,700 had been taken on the asset up to the date of the sale. The resulting $1,200 gain was shown on the income statement.

2. The sum of $75,000 in cash was received from the sale of investments in the stock of another corporation. The stock had a book value of $90,000. The $15,000 loss on the sale was shown on the income statement.

Exercise 25-2 ►
Objective 2

Cash flows from operating activities.

The following data is summarized from the income statement of TVA Corporation for the year ended December 31, 2004. Using this data and ignoring changes in current assets and current liabilities, prepare a schedule of cash flows from operating activities for the year. (Use Figure 25-5 as a model for this schedule.)

TVA Corporation		
Income Statement		
Year Ended December 31, 2004		
Sales		404 5 0 0 00
Cost of Goods Sold		217 5 0 0 00
Gross Profit on Sales		187 0 0 0 00
Operating Expenses		
Depreciation	15 0 0 0 00	
Other Selling Expenses	125 0 0 0 00	
Other Administrative Expenses	50 0 0 0 00	190 0 0 0 00
Net Income/(Loss) from Operations		(3 0 0 0 00)
Bond Interest Expense		
Cash Interest	14 0 0 0 00	
Amortization of Discount on Bonds Payable	5 0 0 00	14 5 0 0 00
Net Loss for Year		(17 5 0 0 00)

Exercise 25-3 ►
Objective 2

Cash flows from operating activities.

The current assets and current liabilities of SanFran Company on December 31, 2005 and 2004, are as follows. The corporation's net income for 2005 was $60,000. Included in its expenses was depreciation of $13,000. Prepare a schedule of the cash flows from operating activities for 2005. (Use Figure 25-5 as a model for this schedule.)

	Dec. 31, 2005	Dec. 31, 2004
Cash	$ 80,000	$60,000
Accounts Receivable (Net)	107,000	85,000
Prepaid Expenses	14,000	12,000
Merchandise Inventory	68,000	65,000
Accounts Payable	94,000	95,000
Notes Payable (Borrowing)	20,000	–0–

Cash flows from operating activities.

The income statement of Rick & Sons, Inc., showed net income of $65,000 for 2004. The firm's beginning inventory was $38,000, and its ending inventory was $40,000. Accounts payable were $43,500 on January 1 and $40,500 on December 31. Compute the net cash provided by the firm's operating activities during the year.

◄ **Exercise 25-4**
Objective 2

Cash flows from operating activities.

The following information is taken from the income statement of DaMaggio Corporation for 2005.

◄ **Exercise 25-5**
Objective 2

Sales		$688,000
Cost of Goods Sold		415,000
Gross Profit on Sales		$273,000
Operating Expenses		
Depreciation	$ 13,000	
Other Operating Expenses	160,000	173,000
Net Income from Operations		$100,000

Additional information relating to account balances at the beginning and end of the year appears below.

	Jan. 1, 2005	Dec. 31, 2005
Accounts Receivable	$48,000	$46,000
Merchandise Inventory	53,000	55,000
Accrued Liabilities	4,000	1,500
Accounts Payable	31,000	21,000

Determine the cash flows from operations for 2005.

Cash flows from investing activities.

The following transactions occurred at Covenant Corporation in 2005. Use this information to compute the company's net cash flow from investing activities.

◄ **Exercise 25-6**
Objective 3

1. The company issued 5,000 shares of its own $5 par-value common stock for land with a fair market value of $25,000.

2. The company gave its president a loan of $50,000 and obtained a 10 percent note receivable, dated December 22, 2005, and maturing two years later.

3. The company sold a used truck for $5,000 in cash. The original cost of the truck was $22,000. Depreciation of $12,000 had been deducted.

Cash flows from investing activities.

The following transactions occurred at Kopp Company in 2004. Use this information to compute the company's net cash flow from investing activities.

◄ **Exercise 25-7**
Objective 3

1. The company purchased a new building for $150,000. A down payment of $50,000 was made. The balance is due in four equal annual installments (plus interest) beginning July 1, 2005.

2. The company bought 500 shares of its own preferred stock for $25,000.

3. The company purchased as an investment $10,000 par value of Download Corporation's 10 percent bonds, maturing in five years. The purchase price was $9,900.

Exercise 25-8 ►
Objective 4

Cash flows from financing activities.

The following transactions occurred at California Coupon Company in 2004. Use this information to compute the company's net cash flow from financing activities for the year.

1. Holders of $200,000 par-value 10 percent bonds surrendered the bonds for redemption and were paid $205,000 in cash. The unamortized discount on these bonds as of the date of redemption was $500.

2. Cash interest of $33,300 was paid on bonds during the year. The bond discount amortized was $300.

3. Cash dividends of $50,000 were paid on common stock during the year.

Exercise 25-9 ►
Objective 4

Cash flows from financing activities.

The following transactions occurred at Jacksonville Company in 2004. Use this information to compute the company's net cash flow from financing activities for the year.

1. The company reacquired as treasury stock 1,000 shares of its outstanding common stock, paying a total of $50,000 for the shares.

2. On December 3 the company borrowed $65,000 from the bank, signing a 90-day, 12 percent note payable.

Problems

Selected problems can be completed using:
▦ Spreadsheets

PROBLEM SET A

Problem 25-1A ►
Objectives 1, 2, 3, 4, 5

Prepare a statement of cash flows.

A comparative balance sheet for Ebeth Corporation on December 31, 2005 and 2004, follows. Additional information about the firm's financial activities during 2005 is also given below.

INSTRUCTIONS

Prepare a statement of cash flows for 2005. Additional information for 2005 follows.

a. Had a $22,000 net loss.

b. Recorded $30,000 in depreciation.

c. Issued bonds payable with a par value of $50,000 at par and received cash.

Ebeth Corporation
Comparative Balance Sheet
December 31, 2005 and 2004

Assets	2005	2004
Cash	2 9 0 0 0	2 5 0 0 0
Accounts Receivable (Net)	5 5 0 0 0	5 0 0 0 0
Merchandise Inventory	7 5 0 0 0	6 5 0 0 0
Property, Plant, and Equipment	1 3 0 0 0 0	8 0 0 0 0
Less: Accumulated Depreciation	(5 0 0 0 0)	(2 0 0 0 0)
Total Assets	2 3 9 0 0 0	2 0 0 0 0 0
Liabilities and Stockholders' Equity		
Liabilities		
Accounts Payable	4 0 0 0 0	3 2 0 0 0
Bonds Payable	6 0 0 0 0	1 0 0 0 0
Total Liabilities	1 0 0 0 0 0	4 2 0 0 0
Stockholders' Equity		
Common Stock, No Par Value	7 5 0 0 0	5 0 0 0 0
Retained Earnings	6 4 0 0 0	1 0 8 0 0 0
Total Stockholders' Equity	1 3 9 0 0 0	1 5 8 0 0 0
Total Liabilities and Stockholders' Equity	2 3 9 0 0 0	2 0 0 0 0 0

d. Received $25,000 in cash for the issue of an additional 1,000 shares of no-par-value common stock.

e. Purchased equipment for $50,000 in cash.

Analyze: Explain why an increase in accounts payable is considered an adjustment to cash flows from operating activities.

Prepare a statement of cash flows.

Postclosing trial balance data and other financial data for Sosa Company as of December 31, 2005 and 2004, follow.

◄ **Problem 25-2A**
Objectives 1, 2, 3, 4, 5

Prepare a statement of cash flows for 2005. Additional information for 2005 follows.

INSTRUCTIONS

a. Sold common stock for $50,000 in cash.

b. Had net income of $98,000 after income taxes.

c. Sold additional bonds payable for $50,000 cash at par value.

d. Completed a major addition to the building for $50,000 in cash.

e. Bought additional land for $50,000. Paid $25,000 in cash; the balance is a mortgage.

f. Paid common stock dividends of $5,000 in cash.

g. Amortized organization costs of $2,000.

Sosa Company
Postclosing Trial Balance
December 31, 2005 and 2004

Account Name	2005 Debit	2005 Credit	2004 Debit	2004 Credit
Cash	161 300 00		100 000 00	
Accounts Receivable (Net)	196 000 00		193 500 00	
Merchandise Inventory	419 525 00		410 525 00	
Prepaid Expenses	6 500 00		4 000 00	
Land	81 500 00		31 500 00	
Building	260 000 00		210 000 00	
Accumulated Depreciation—Building		76 000 00		75 000 00
Organization Costs	4 000 00		6 000 00	
Notes Payable—Trade		22 000 00		30 000 00
Accounts Payable		140 000 00		150 000 00
Payroll Taxes Payable		19 800 00		17 500 00
Income Taxes Payable		25 000 00		55 000 00
Mortgage Payable, 2009		145 000 00		120 000 00
11% Bonds Payable, 2015		230 000 00		180 000 00
Common Stock		290 000 00		240 000 00
Retained Earnings		181 025 00		88 025 00
Totals	1128 825 00	1128 825 00	955 525 00	955 525 00

Analyze: Were activities related to operations, investing, or financing responsible for the largest net inflow of cash?

Problem 25-3A ►
Objectives 1, 2, 3, 4, 5

Preparing a statement of cash flows.

The condensed income statement and comparative balance sheet of Naples Corporation as of December 31, 2005 and 2004, are provided on page 935. Other financial data is also given.

INSTRUCTIONS

Prepare a statement of cash flows for Naples Corporation for 2005. Additional information for 2005 that is pertinent to its preparation follows.

a. No items of property, plant, and equipment were disposed of during the year.

b. Paid cash for the additions to property, plant, and equipment during the year.

c. Paid $20,000 dividends on the common stock in cash during the year.

d. Issued common stock at par value for cash.

e. Paid cash to retire the mortgages when they became due.

Naples Corporation
Condensed Income Statement
Year Ended December 31, 2005

Revenues	522 2 0 0 00
Costs and Expenses	
Cost of Goods Sold	293 5 0 0 00
Salaries Expense	125 0 0 0 00
Depreciation Expense	2 5 0 0 00
Advertising Expense	32 0 0 0 00
Utilities Expense	12 0 0 0 00
Total Costs and Expenses	465 0 0 0 00
Net Income Before Income Taxes	57 2 0 0 00
Income Tax Expense	10 0 0 0 00
Net Income After Income Taxes	47 2 0 0 00

Naples Corporation
Comparative Balance Sheet
December 31, 2005 and 2004

Assets	2005	2004
Cash	7 0 0 0 0	6 0 0 0 0
Accounts Receivable (Net)	3 7 0 0 0	3 0 0 0 0
Merchandise Inventory	3 6 0 0 0	2 9 5 0 0
Prepaid Advertising	1 5 0 0	1 8 0 0
Property, Plant, and Equipment	7 5 0 0 0	5 0 0 0 0
Less: Accumulated Depreciation	(7 5 0 0)	(5 0 0 0)
Total Assets	2 1 2 0 0 0	1 6 6 3 0 0
Liabilities and Stockholders' Equity		
Liabilities		
Accounts Payable	3 5 0 0 0	2 0 0 0 0
Salaries Payable	3 0 0 0	4 0 0 0
Unearned Rental Income	1 0 0 0 0	1 5 0 0 0
Income Taxes Payable	3 0 0 0	3 5 0 0
Mortgage Payable	– 0 –	4 0 0 0 0
Total Liabilities	5 1 0 0 0	8 2 5 0 0
Stockholders' Equity		
Common Stock	7 0 0 0 0	2 0 0 0 0
Retained Earnings	9 1 0 0 0	6 3 8 0 0
Total Stockholders' Equity	1 6 1 0 0 0	8 3 8 0 0
Total Liabilities and Stockholders' Equity	2 1 2 0 0 0	1 6 6 3 0 0

Analyze: If Naples Corporation had written off an uncollectible account receivable of $3,000 during this fiscal period, what adjustment, if any, would be required on the statement of cash flows?

Prepare a statement of cash flows.

The comparative balance sheet for Salik Company as of December 31, 2005 and 2004, is shown below, followed by the condensed income statement. Other financial data for 2005 is also given.

INSTRUCTIONS

Prepare a statement of cash flows for 2005. Additional information for 2005 follows.

a. Acquired land at a cost of $50,000; paid one-half of the purchase price in cash and issued common stock for the balance.

b. Sold used equipment for $25,000 in cash. The original cost was $40,000; depreciation of $5,000 had been taken. The remaining change in the **Property, Plant, and Equipment** account represents a purchase of equipment for cash. Total depreciation expense for the year was $8,000.

c. Issued bonds payable at par value for cash.

d. Sold bond investments costing $20,000 at no gain or loss during the year; acquired other bond investments for cash.

e. Paid $25,000 cash dividends on the common stock.

Analyze: By what percentage did **Cash** increase from January 1 to December 31?

Salik Company
Comparative Balance Sheet
December 31, 2005 and 2004

Assets	2005	2004
Cash	1 2 6 2 0 0	7 6 2 0 0
Accounts Receivable (Net)	7 5 0 0 0	7 2 0 0 0
Merchandise Inventory	6 3 5 0 0	6 5 0 0 0
Prepaid Advertising	4 5 0 0	6 0 0 0
Land	7 5 0 0 0	2 5 0 0 0
Property, Plant, and Equipment	1 8 5 0 0 0	1 5 0 0 0 0
Less: Accumulated Depreciation	(1 8 0 0 0)	(1 5 0 0 0)
Investment in BOA Bonds	3 0 0 0 0	2 5 0 0 0
Total Assets	5 4 1 2 0 0	4 0 4 2 0 0
Liabilities and Stockholders' Equity		
Liabilities		
Accounts Payable	9 5 2 0 0	7 8 5 0 0
Income Taxes Payable	1 5 0 0 0	1 0 0 0 0
Bonds Payable	2 0 0 0 0 0	1 0 0 0 0 0
Total Liabilities	3 1 0 2 0 0	1 8 8 5 0 0
Stockholders' Equity		
Common Stock	1 0 0 0 0 0	7 5 0 0 0
Retained Earnings	1 3 1 0 0 0	1 4 0 7 0 0
Total Stockholders' Equity	2 3 1 0 0 0	2 1 5 7 0 0
Total Liabilities and Stockholders' Equity	5 4 1 2 0 0	4 0 4 2 0 0

Salik Company
Condensed Income Statement
Year Ended December 31, 2005

Revenues	795 0 0 0 00
Costs and Expenses	
Cost of Goods Sold	425 0 0 0 00
Depreciation Expense	8 0 0 0 00
Selling and Administrative Expenses	299 2 0 0 00
Interest Expense	22 5 0 0 00
Loss on Sale of Equipment	10 0 0 0 00
Income Tax Expense	15 0 0 0 00
Total Costs and Expenses	779 7 0 0 00
Net Income After Income Taxes	15 3 0 0 00

PROBLEM SET B

Prepare a statement of cash flows.

A comparative balance sheet for RiverCity Corporation as of December 31, 2005 and 2004, is given below.

Use this data to prepare a statement of cash flows for 2005. Additional information for 2005 follows.

a. Sold used machinery for $7,000 cash. The original cost was $25,000, and the accumulated depreciation was $20,000; included the gain of $2,000 in net income.

◄ **Problem 25-1B**
Objectives 1, 2, 3, 4, 5

SPREADSHEET

INSTRUCTIONS

RiverCity Corporation
Comparative Balance Sheet
December 31, 2005 and 2004

Assets	2005	2004
Cash	7 0 0 0 0	6 6 0 0 0
Accounts Receivable (Net)	3 7 0 0 0	3 9 0 0 0
Merchandise Inventory	3 6 0 0 0	3 5 0 0 0
Property, Plant, and Equipment	4 9 0 0 0	4 9 0 0 0
Less: Accumulated Depreciation	(3 1 0 0 0)	(3 0 0 0 0)
Total Assets	1 6 1 0 0 0	1 5 9 0 0 0
Liabilities and Stockholders' Equity		
Liabilities		
Accounts Payable	3 5 0 0 0	2 0 0 0 0
Stockholders' Equity		
Common Stock, No Par Value	8 0 0 0 0	8 0 0 0 0
Retained Earnings	4 6 0 0 0	5 9 0 0 0
Total Stockholders' Equity	1 2 6 0 0 0	1 3 9 0 0 0
Total Liabilities and Stockholders' Equity	1 6 1 0 0 0	1 5 9 0 0 0

b. Purchased new store equipment for $25,000. Paid $10,000 in cash; the balance of $15,000 is due in January 2006.

c. Had a net loss of $3,000.

d. Paid cash dividends of $10,000.

e. Recorded $6,000 in depreciation.

Analyze: List the transactions that required the greatest outlay of cash during fiscal 2005.

Problem 25-2B ►
Objectives 1, 2, 3, 4, 5

Prepare a statement of cash flows.

Postclosing trial balance data and other financial data for Music Store, Inc., as of December 31, 2005 and 2004, follow.

INSTRUCTIONS

Prepare a statement of cash flows for 2005. Additional information for 2005 follows.

a. Sold an unused lot for $45,000 in cash; it originally cost $10,000.

b. Constructed a new building for $175,000, of which $25,000 was paid in cash and $150,000 is a long-term mortgage payable.

c. Issued $50,000 of 11 percent bonds payable, maturing in 2017, for cash at par.

d. Sold common stock for $50,000 in cash.

e. Had net income of $72,000 after income taxes.

f. Paid common stock dividends of $25,000 in cash.

g. Amortized organization costs of $1,000.

Music Store, Inc.
Postclosing Trial Balance
December 31, 2005 and 2004

Account Name	2005 Debit	2005 Credit	2004 Debit	2004 Credit
Cash	211 550 00		100 000 00	
Accounts Receivable (Net)	125 000 00		123 500 00	
Merchandise Inventory	210 000 00		212 350 00	
Prepaid Expenses	4 500 00		4 800 00	
Land	65 000 00		75 000 00	
Building	275 000 00		100 000 00	
Accumulated Depreciation—Building		29 500 00		25 000 00
Organization Costs	5 000 00		6 000 00	
Notes Payable—Short Term		– 0 –		30 000 00
Accounts Payable		179 900 00		175 500 00
Payroll Taxes Payable		13 800 00		13 300 00
Income Taxes Payable		20 000 00		22 000 00
Mortgage Payable, 2009		210 000 00		60 000 00
11% Bonds Payable, 2015		200 000 00		150 000 00
Common Stock		100 000 00		50 000 00
Retained Earnings		142 850 00		95 850 00
Totals	896 050 00	896 050 00	621 650 00	621 650 00

Analyze: Did operating, investing, or financing activities generate the greatest net inflow of cash?

Prepare a statement of cash flows.

Diego Corporation's comparative balance sheet as of December 31, 2005 and 2004, and 2005 condensed income statement appear below.

Prepare a statement of cash flows for 2005. Additional information for 2005 follows.

a. Depreciation totaling $5,500 is included in expenses.

b. Sold land for $25,000 in cash; the land, which is included in plant and equipment, had a cost of $25,000.

c. Acquired a building with a fair market value of $60,000 by issuing common stock.

d. Purchased equipment for $25,000 in cash.

e. Paid dividends of $75,000. Issued common stock at par value for cash.

◄ **Problem 25-3B**
Objectives 1, 2, 3, 4, 5

_____

INSTRUCTIONS

Diego Corporation
Comparative Balance Sheet
December 31, 2005 and 2004

Assets	2005	2004
Cash	7 0 0 0 0	8 0 0 0 0
Accounts Receivable (Net)	6 2 0 0 0	6 9 0 0 0
Merchandise Inventory	4 0 0 0 0	3 8 5 0 0
Prepaid Advertising	2 2 0 0	2 4 0 0
Property, Plant, and Equipment	1 8 5 0 0 0	1 2 5 0 0 0
Less: Accumulated Depreciation	(1 8 0 0 0)	(1 2 5 0 0)
Total Assets	3 4 1 2 0 0	3 0 2 4 0 0
Liabilities and Stockholders' Equity		
Liabilities		
Accounts Payable	6 2 5 0 0	6 9 2 0 0
Accrued Liabilities	6 5 0 0	6 8 0 0
Notes Payable, due 2008	3 5 0 0 0	3 5 0 0 0
Total Liabilities	1 0 4 0 0 0	1 1 1 0 0 0
Stockholders' Equity		
Common Stock	1 6 0 0 0 0	5 0 0 0 0
Retained Earnings	7 7 2 0 0	1 4 1 4 0 0
Total Stockholders' Equity	2 3 7 2 0 0	1 9 1 4 0 0
Total Liabilities and Stockholders' Equity	3 4 1 2 0 0	3 0 2 4 0 0

Diego Corporation
Condensed Income Statement
Year Ended December 31, 2005

Sales	800 0 0 0 00
Cost of Goods Sold	(480 0 0 0 00)
Expenses	(309 2 0 0 00)
Net Income for Year	10 8 0 0 00

Analyze: If the company had purchased equipment on credit instead of using cash, what would the cash balance have been at year-end?

Problem 25-4B ►
Objectives 1, 2, 3, 4, 5

Prepare a statement of cash flows.

The comparative balance sheet for Property Rentals, Inc., as of December 31, 2005 and 2004, is shown below, followed by the condensed income statement and other financial data for 2005.

INSTRUCTIONS

Prepare a statement of cash flows for 2005. Additional information for 2005 follows.

a. Sold used equipment for $22,000 in cash that originally cost $32,000; accumulated depreciation was $8,000. The remainder of the change in **Equipment** represents equipment purchased for cash.

b. Issued notes payable with a par value of $15,000. Certain other notes were paid off during the year. Retired bonds payable at maturity.

c. Paid cash dividends of $20,000.

d. Issued common stock at par value for cash.

Property Rentals, Inc.
Comparative Balance Sheet
December 31, 2005 and 2004

Assets	2005	2004
Current Assets		
Cash	4 6 2 5 0	8 9 2 5 0
Accounts Receivable (Net)	7 2 0 0 0	6 6 7 0 0
Merchandise Inventory	2 2 4 0 0	3 2 0 0 0
Prepaid Advertising	8 0 0 0	7 5 0 0
Total Current Assets	1 4 8 6 5 0	1 9 5 4 5 0
Property, Plant, and Equipment		
Land	4 0 0 0 0	4 0 0 0 0
Property, Plant, and Equipment	1 8 5 0 0 0	1 6 0 0 0 0
Less: Accumulated Depreciation	(3 4 0 0 0)	(2 4 0 0 0)
Total Property, Plant, and Equipment	1 9 1 0 0 0	1 7 6 0 0 0
Total Assets	3 3 9 6 5 0	3 7 1 4 5 0
Liabilities and Stockholders' Equity		
Current Liabilities		
Notes Payable	4 5 0 0 0	5 0 0 0 0
Accounts Payable	3 2 5 0 0	6 2 5 0 0
Income Taxes Payable	5 0 0 0	1 0 0 0 0
Total Current Liabilities	8 2 5 0 0	1 2 2 5 0 0
Long-Term Liabilities		
Bonds Payable	– 0 –	1 0 0 0 0 0
Total Liabilities	8 2 5 0 0	2 2 2 5 0 0
Stockholders' Equity		
Common Stock	1 5 0 0 0 0	1 0 0 0 0 0
Retained Earnings	1 0 7 1 5 0	4 8 9 5 0
Total Stockholders' Equity	2 5 7 1 5 0	1 4 8 9 5 0
Total Liabilities and Stockholders' Equity	3 3 9 6 5 0	3 7 1 4 5 0

Property Rentals, Inc.
Condensed Income Statement
Year Ended December 31, 2005

Revenues		598	2 0 0	00	
Costs and Expenses					
Cost of Goods Sold		295	0 0 0	00	
Depreciation Expense		18	0 0 0	00	
Selling and Administrative Expense		175	0 0 0	00	
Interest Expense		15	0 0 0	00	
Income Tax Expense		15	0 0 0	00	
Loss on Sale of Equipment		2	0 0 0	00	
Total Costs and Expenses		520	0 0 0	00	
Net Income for Year		78	2 0 0	00	

Analyze: Was the amount of net cash provided by operating activities sufficient to cover the cash that the company required for financing activities? Explain.

CHAPTER 25 CHALLENGE PROBLEM

Adjustments

Bermuda Company was formed and began business on January 1, 2004, when Shelby Smith transferred merchandise inventory with a value of $65,000, cash of $50,000, accounts receivable of $40,000, and accounts payable of $25,000 to the corporation in exchange for common stock with a par value of $13 per share. The company's common stock was recorded at par.

Bermuda Company's statement of cash flows for 2004 is shown below and on page 942.

Based on the data supplied, prepare the December 31, 2004, balance sheet for the corporation.

INSTRUCTIONS

Bermuda Company
Statement of Cash Flows
Year Ended December 31, 2004

Cash Flow from Operations				
Net Income			55 0 0 0 00	
Adjustments:				
Depreciation of building	5 0 0 0 00			
Depreciation of equipment	2 5 0 0 00			
Increase in accounts receivable	(22 0 0 0 00)			
Increase in merchandise inventory	(11 0 0 0 00)			
Increase in prepaid insurance	(6 0 0 00)			
Increase in accounts payable	14 0 0 0 00			
Increase in income tax payable	1 0 0 0 00	(11 1 0 0 00)		
Net cash flow provided by operations			43 9 0 0 00	

Cash Flow from Investing Activities										
Purchase of land	(25	0	0	0	00)					
Purchase of building	(50	0	0	0	00)					
Purchase of equipment	(25	0	0	0	00)					
Net cash used in investing activities						(100	0	0	0	00)
Cash Flow from Financing Activities										
Issuance of common stock at $20/share	20	0	0	0	00					
Borrowing at bank by issuance of note payable	50	0	0	0	00					
Payment of principal on bank note	(5	0	0	0	00)					
Net cash provided by financing activities						65	0	0	0	00
Net increase in cash						8	9	0	0	00
Cash, January 1, 2004						50	0	0	0	00
Cash, December 31, 2004						58	9	0	0	00

Note: A building was acquired at a cost of $250,000. Cash of $50,000 was paid, and a mortgage of $200,000 was given for the balance.

Analyze: Describe five adjusting entries that were made by Bermuda Company in fiscal 2004.

CHAPTER 25 CRITICAL THINKING PROBLEM

Transactions

John Roberts, the bookkeeper for Amnicola Electric Company, asks for your help in identifying whether the following transactions should be reported on the corporation's statement of cash flows. Prepare a list for Roberts indicating whether or not each transaction should be reported on the statement. If the transaction should appear on the statement, indicate whether it should be classified as a financing activity, an investing activity, or an operating activity. If the transaction should not be part of the statement of cash flows, explain why not.

1. Prepaid three months of rent on warehouse storage facilities at the end of the year.
2. Collected on accounts receivable from a customer.
3. Paid federal income taxes due.
4. Paid suppliers amounts due on accounts payable.
5. Paid cash dividends on common stock.
6. Purchased common stock of IBM as investment for cash.
7. Borrowed cash, signing a short-term note that was repaid before the end of the year.
8. Issued preferred stock for cash.
9. Issued long-term bonds for cash; proceeds to be used to purchase new equipment for plant.
10. Used proceeds from bond issue to purchase new equipment for plant.
11. Distributed a stock dividend on common stock.
12. Received principal payments on note receivable held in connection with sale of building last year.

Business Connections

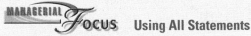 **Using All Statements**

◄ **Connection 1**

1. How can the statement of cash flows help management arrange for proper financing?

2. A corporation's income statement shows a net income of $10,000 after income taxes for the year. Its statement of cash flows shows that its cash balance increased by $150,000: net cash outflow from operating activities, $100,000; net cash inflow from financing activities, $50,000; and net cash inflow from investing activities, $200,000. The president of the corporation has commented, "Even though the company's profit is small, it is clear, based on our positive cash flow, that we are doing quite well." Do you agree with this comment? Why or why not?

3. A member of a corporation's board of directors commented that because the statement of cash flows and the income statement are so similar, there is no need to prepare the income statement. Respond.

4. Assume that you are an accountant preparing the statement of cash flows for the year. Should the cash proceeds of $100,000 from a short-term note payable discounted in May of this year be included in the statement? The note was repaid in October. Would it be preferable to simply ignore both the loan and the repayment because it might confuse management to show both? Explain.

5. A potential customer has applied for an open-account credit line with a manufacturing firm. Explain how the potential customer's statement of cash flows would help to evaluate its short-term debt-paying ability.

Ethical DILEMMA **GAAP Requirements** The majority stockholder of a small corporation tells you to "forget about preparing that cash flow statement" because he needs financial statements today to take to the bank. "Besides," he says, "we have more cash in the bank now than we did last year at this time." As a CPA, you are required to comply with GAAP. As an employee, you need to comply with the boss. What do you do?

◄ **Connection 2**

*Street***WISE:** Questions from the Real World **Sources of Cash** Refer to the *1999 Annual Report* for The Home Depot, Inc. in Appendix B.

◄ **Connection 3**

1. Locate the consolidated statements of cash flows. For the year ended January 30, 2000, what net cash was (1) provided by operations? (2) used in investing activities? (3) provided by financing activities?

2. Is the most significant source of cash generated from the company's operating, investing, or financing activities?

FINANCIAL STATEMENT ANALYSIS **Statement of Cash Flows** The following excerpt was taken from the Pier 1 Imports, Inc., *2000 Annual Report*.

◄ **Connection 4**
Pier1 imports

The Statement of Cash Flows **Chapter 25 • 943**

CONSOLIDATED STATEMENT OF CASH FLOWS

(in thousands)	Year Ended		
	2000	1999	1998
CASH FLOW FROM OPERATING ACTIVITIES			
Net Income	$74,725	$80,357	$78,047
Adjustments to reconcile net cash provided by operating activities:			
Depreciation and amortization	39,973	31,130	23,946
Deferred taxes and other	11,033	(2,575)	1,281
Change in cash from:			
Inventories	(10,133)	(24,103)	(13,617)
Accounts receivable and other current assets	586	2,500	(10,302)
Accounts payable and accrued expenses	8,962	12,826	25,031
Other assets, liabilities, and other, net	(5,528)	(4,409)	2,468
Net cash provided by operating activities	119,618	95,726	106,854
Net cash used in financing activities	(71,369)	(91,176)	(14,203)
Change in cash and cash equivalents	8,431	(38,784)	48,449
Cash and cash equivalents at beginning of year	41,945	80,729	32,280
Cash and cash equivalents at end of year	$ 50,376	$ 41,945	$ 80,729

Analyze:

1. Compute the net cash provided by investing activities for the year ended 2000.

2. On the statement of cash flows for the year ended 2001, what figure will be used for Cash and Cash Equivalents at Beginning of Year?

3. What total adjustments were made to net income to determine net cash provided by operating activities for each year presented above?

Analyze Online: Locate the Pier 1 Imports' Web site **(www.pier1.com).** Click on the *About Us* link. Use the *Investing* link to find the company's most recent annual report and consolidated statement of cash flows.

4. What net change occurred in cash and cash equivalents?

5. What activities generate the largest cash inflows for Pier 1 Imports?

Connection 5 ► *Extending the Thought* **Improving Cash Flow** Proper management of cash is imperative for a successful operation. Describe practices that would help an organization improve its cash flow. Consider credit policies, collections, pricing, and accounting processes.

Connection 6 ► **Business Communication** **Memo** Prepare a memo to Al Lee, your new staff accountant, describing the four financial statements that should be prepared at year-end. Use all the new terms in this chapter.

Connection 7 ► **TeamWork** **Understanding Cash Flow Statements** As a team, review the cash flow statements for five major corporations. Locate each company's most recent financial statements on its Web site. Create a summary page for each firm that answers the following. Was the direct or indirect method used to prepare the statement? List three types of adjustments made to reconcile net income to net cash provided by operating activities. List two types of transactions in the investing activities section and two in the financing activities section.

inter **NET**
CONNECTION   Analysis of Cash Flows Go to **www.ibm.com** and locate   ◄ **Connection 8**
IBM's statement of cash flows in its annual report. What three-year trend do you see in the net cash from operating activities? Explain the trend's significance.

Answers to Self Reviews

Answers to Section 1 Self Review

1. Currency, bank accounts, and short-term liquid investments that are easily convertible into cash.
2. Transactions that involve the acquisition or disposal of long-term assets.
3. Yes, this activity is one of financing the business.
4. **b.** purchases of plant and equipment for cash.
5. **b.** issuance of stock for cash.
6. **(a)** source, **(b)** use, **(c)** use, **(d)** source, **(e)** source

Answers to Section 2 Self Review

1. The loss does not relate to operating activities and must be added back to net income.
2. Depreciation expense does not reflect a cash outlay, so it must be added back to net income.
3. An increase in notes payable does not affect cash flow from operations, unless the notes were credited when merchandise inventory or other operating assets were purchased.
4. **a.** a change in merchandise inventory.
5. **b.** deducted from net income.
6. $12,500 used

Answers to Section 3 Self Review

1. $100,000—included as inflow from investing activities. $8,000 gain—deducted from net income.
2. As cash used in financing activities.
3. Disclosed in footnotes to the statement.
4. **c.** indirect method.
5. **b.** decrease in Cash Flows from Investing Activities.
6. $2,000 loss—added to net income. $12,000—included as inflow from investing activities.

Answers to Comprehensive Self Review

1. Operating, investing, and financing activities are shown in a statement of cash flows.
2. Financing activities are transactions between the corporation and those who provide cash.
3. The increase in accounts payable must be added to net income to arrive at cash flow from operations.
4. In a note to the statement of cash flows.
5. In the operating activities section as a deduction from net income.

MERCHANDISE
· COMPANY ·

Financial Analysis and Decision Making

Misty Mountain

This project will give you an opportunity to evaluate financial statements and to make decisions based on the information presented in the financial statements of Misty Mountain Merchandise Company.

INTRODUCTION

Misty Mountain Merchandise Company sells a variety of consumer products. The firm is organized as a corporation. The fiscal year-end is the same as the calendar year-end, December 31.

The *Study Guide & Working Papers, Chapters 14–25*, contain the following financial statements for Misty Mountain Merchandise Company:

- Comparative Income Statement (Years Ended December 31, 2005 and 2004)
- Comparative Balance Sheet (December 31, 2005 and 2004)

INSTRUCTIONS

The instructions for completing Mini-Practice Set 4 are in the *Study Guide & Working Papers, Chapters 14–25*.

Analyze: Assume that the firm declared and distributed a 5% common stock dividend in 2005. What is the effect on earnings per share in 2005? Assume that market value is equal to par value and all other information is the same.

PART 8

Responsibility and Cost Accounting

AMGEN Amgen Inc., manufactures and markets therapeutic products for oncology, hematology, and bone and inflammatory disorders. The anti-anemia drug, Epogen, and immune system stimulator, Neupogen, account for about 95 percent of the company's sales.

Thinking Critically

As the managers of Amgen make business decisions regarding the types of products to manufacture and sell, what factors do you think they consider?

CHAPTER 26

Learning Objectives

1. Explain the general principles of internal control.

2. Explain how the voucher system facilitates internal control.

3. Prepare vouchers.

4. Record vouchers in a voucher register.

5. Record payment of approved vouchers.

6. Record transactions that require special treatment in a voucher system.

7. Define the accounting terms new to this chapter.

Internal Control and the Voucher System

DELL

www.dell.com

D ell Computer Corporation ranks number 1 in the U.S. computer systems market.[1] Reporting net revenues of $31,888 million for the fiscal year ended February 2, 2001, Dell is a leading supplier of PCs and networked systems.

In addition to a focus on increasing unit sales each year, the company believes that effectiveness in managing operating expenses is an important factor in its continued success.[2] Cash payments are made for merchandise purchases; note repayments; income taxes; and selling, general, and administrative expenses. A strong system of internal controls helps companies like Dell prevent double payment of invoices, miscalculations, and losses of cash discounts.

[1] *Fortune* magazine, Most Admired Companies 1999
[2] Dell Computer Corporation *1999 Annual Report,* page 22

Thinking Critically
In what ways can companies like Dell Computer Corporation ensure that accounts payable are processed in a timely fashion and paid accurately?

For more information on Dell, go to:
collegeaccounting.glencoe.com

New Terms

Check register

Internal control system

Net of discount

Payment voucher

Schedule of vouchers payable

Tickler file

Unpaid voucher file

Voucher

Voucher register

Voucher system

Internal Control

1 Explain the general principles of internal control.

WHY IT'S IMPORTANT
Improper and careless handling of company resources can result in substantial losses to a business.

2 Explain how the voucher system facilitates internal control.

WHY IT'S IMPORTANT
Tight controls over payments ensure that the assets of the business are properly managed.

Terms to Learn

internal control system
payment voucher
voucher
voucher system

1 Objective

Explain the general principles of internal control.

Important!

Control
No one person should be in complete charge of any business transaction.

Losses to U.S. business from employee carelessness, inaccuracy, and improper handling of assets are estimated to total billions of dollars a year. No business is immune to this hazard, and to ignore it may mean the difference between a profitable operation and complete failure.

The Importance of Internal Control

Accountants recommend that all businesses, no matter their size, establish effective internal control procedures. These procedures are designed to protect the resources and financial records of the business. Internal controls also benefit employees because they limit the temptation to misuse assets. In addition, internal controls pinpoint responsibility, which prevents suspicion from falling on honest employees.

The **internal control system** has three basic purposes:

1. To safeguard assets
2. To achieve efficient processing of transactions
3. To ensure the accuracy and reliability of financial records

> A review of the annual reports of Fortune 100 companies revealed that 76 percent of the firms maintain systems of internal control. The most often cited justifications for such systems were to ensure reliable financial reporting and to safeguard assets. General Electric identified a sound, dynamic system of internal control as "a vital ingredient" for the company's quality programs.

A key element of good internal control is that the system be organized and operated so that the work of one person provides a check on the work of another, with minimum duplication of effort. If a business has enough employees to permit the necessary separation of duties, a strong system of internal control can be established. If the number of employees is small, internal control will be weaker and needs to be supplemented by more careful supervision.

The following is a list of essential internal controls:

- Do not have one person in charge of all phases of any important business transaction. One person should not be responsible for both the transaction itself and the recording of the transaction. Assign two or more employees to every major operation and have the work of one employee checked against the work of the other.
- Do not have the individuals who handle cash and other valuable assets responsible for recording the assets.
- Train employees to do their jobs. Ensure that they understand why the job or procedure is performed in the specified manner.

- Assign capable and experienced personnel of demonstrated reliability to key positions in the internal control system. Make unannounced changes in these assignments.
- Require annual vacations for all employees. Ensure that other employees perform their work during vacations.
- Support all transactions with adequate documentation. Use prenumbered forms such as numbered purchase orders, sales invoices, and checks. Account for all document numbers.
- Maintain a strong audit trail by providing references to source documents in accounting entries, cross-referencing entries that appear in different records, and keeping documents on file for a specified period of time. This ensures that every transaction can be traced through the accounting system to its origin.
- Supplement controls built into forms, records, and operating routines by electronic or mechanical devices whenever appropriate. For example, electronic cash registers and locked storerooms make theft or mishandling of assets more difficult.
- Review and evaluate the internal control system often to ensure that it operates as planned and provides adequate safeguards.
- Have the company's internal control procedures periodically reviewed by a public accounting firm to assess their effectiveness. A public accounting firm can provide an objective evaluation and, based on broad experience, is better able to locate weaknesses and design improvements. This evaluation is a routine part of the annual audit by the public accountant, who relies on internal controls to assure the integrity and accuracy of the amounts reported on the financial statements.

Important!

Vacations
Good internal control systems ensure that employees take annual vacations, during which time other employees perform their work.

The Voucher System as a Tool of Internal Control

The **voucher system** is a method of controlling liabilities and cash payments. It is based on a **voucher**, also called a **payment voucher**. A voucher is a form used to authorize payment of an obligation. In a voucher system, all payments, except for petty cash disbursements, are made by check. All checks are issued based on a properly approved voucher that is supported by suitable documentation. The voucher is the focal point for a series of tight controls built into the system.

2 Objective

Explain how the voucher system facilitates internal control.

In an audit report issued by the Louisiana Legislative Auditor in 1998, the Bossier Parish Community College was found to have an inadequate internal control system over journal vouchers. The auditor examined 140 journal vouchers prepared from July 1, 1997, through May 31, 1998, and found no written supervisory review and approval, sequential numbering, or logging for accountability. Of the 140 vouchers, 94 lacked adequate detailed support or explanation. The auditor recommended that vouchers be reviewed and approved by a supervisor or someone independent of the voucher's origination, be sequentially numbered, and be supported by detailed explanations and documentation.

Medium-sized and large businesses use the voucher system. As a business grows, the owner finds it increasingly difficult to be involved in all the firm's transactions. The owner cannot personally approve or sign all checks. That's when the internal control provided by the voucher system becomes increasingly important.

Controls Involved in a Voucher System

Controls that are built into a voucher system include the following:

- All liabilities are authorized. For example, a properly approved purchase order is required for each credit purchase of merchandise.
- All payments are made by check, except for petty cash disbursements.
- All checks are issued based on a properly approved voucher.
- Vouchers are used to set up and replenish cash funds used within the business.
- Vouchers are used to cover bills and invoices received from outside parties.
- All bills and invoices are verified before they are approved for payment.
- Only experienced and responsible employees are allowed to approve bills and invoices for payment.
- Invoices are attached to the vouchers to provide supporting documentation.
- Different employees approve the vouchers, record the vouchers and payments, and sign and mail the checks.
- All vouchers, along with the supporting documentation, are kept on file for a specified period of time.

Section 1 Self Review

Questions

1. Why do businesses need internal control systems?

2. How is the internal control principle of *division of responsibility* put into practice?

3. Is it advisable to have the accounts receivable clerk open incoming mail and prepare receipts for the checks received? Explain.

Exercises

4. A good internal control procedure is to

   a. require that only one person be responsible for the preparation and approval of vouchers.

   b. require that the person who orders goods or services authorize payment for them.

   c. require that the person who handles cash and other valuable assets is responsible for recording the assets.

   d. use prenumbered business forms.

5. Under the voucher system

   a. no liability should be incurred without prior authorization.

   b. all payments are made by check.

   c. no check is issued without a properly approved voucher.

   d. all of the above.

Analysis

6. Mia Systems is considering adopting the voucher system. Mia is a small company with ten employees. The accounting department consists of the accounting office manager and two accounting clerks. The owner of the business approves all purchases and signs all checks. Is the voucher system appropriate for Mia Systems?

  (Answers to Section 1 Self Review are on page 975.)

Using the Voucher System

Let's learn how the voucher system operates by examining the system used by Clothing Corporation, a retail merchandising corporation.

The Voucher System in Operation

In a voucher system, a voucher is prepared and approved before any obligation is paid or before a cash fund is established or replenished.

To ensure internal control, vouchers are numbered sequentially. Clothing Corporation uses a two-part number—the number to the left of the hyphen represents the month and the number to the right is the sequence within the month. For example, Voucher 3-01 identifies the first voucher (01) prepared in March (3).

Voucher 3-01 was issued on March 1 to authorize a payment of $1,000 to Business Rentals for the monthly rent on the store. Voucher 3-02 for $100 was issued to the cashier, Beth Spencer, to establish a change fund. Voucher 3-03 for $125 was issued to the office clerk, Nadia Khan, to establish a petty cash fund. The employees were named as the payees to pinpoint responsibility for the change fund and the petty cash fund.

Voucher 3-04 authorizes payment of an invoice for merchandise received on March 1 purchased on open account. The wholesaler, Gulf Shores Clothiers, offers a series of trade discounts. The following are the steps in handling the voucher.

Step 1: *Verify Receipt of the Merchandise.* The clerk who opened the mail used a rubber stamp to place a verification block on the invoice, as shown in Figure 26-1 on page 954. Then she gave the invoice to Sumay Chen, co-owner and store manager. Chen compared the quantities on the invoice with the quantities on the receiving report that was filled out when the shipment arrived. Chen placed a check mark next to each quantity on the invoice and initialed the appropriate area of the verification block.

Step 2: *Verify Prices.* Chen gave the invoice to Mike Youngblood, a co-owner. Youngblood compared it with a copy of the purchase order originally issued to the supplier. Youngblood verified that the prices on the invoice did not exceed those on the purchase order. He checked off each unit price on the invoice and entered his initials in the verification block to show that the prices charged were correct.

Step 3: *Verify Computations.* The office clerk, Nadia Khan, checked the computations on the invoice to make sure they were accurate. She verified the extensions by multiplying the quantity of each item by its unit price. She added the extensions and calculated trade discounts to verify the total. She placed a check mark next to each amount on the invoice as its accuracy was verified. Then she entered her initials in the verification block. Figure 26-1 shows the invoice after quantities, prices, and total are verified.

Section Objectives

3 **Prepare vouchers.**

WHY IT'S IMPORTANT
The verification and approval processes involved in preparing vouchers ensure that cash disbursements are authorized and accurate.

4 **Record vouchers in a voucher register.**

WHY IT'S IMPORTANT
The voucher register provides a detailed listing of business transactions that result in liabilities.

5 **Record payment of approved vendors.**

WHY IT'S IMPORTANT
Payments are made against specific vouchers that are recorded in the voucher register.

6 **Record transactions that require special treatment in a voucher system.**

WHY IT'S IMPORTANT
When a voucher system is used, the accountant needs to know how to record certain transactions that require special treatment.

Terms to Learn

check register
net of discount
schedule of vouchers payable
tickler file
unpaid voucher file
voucher register

FIGURE 26-1 ▶
Purchase Invoice

Recall

Audit Trail

In a voucher system, written approvals for each transaction provide a chain of references for tracing transactions back to the original documents.

GULF SHORES CLOTHIERS
123 Ponce De Leon Avenue
Atlanta, GA 30308

INVOICE NO. R 47651

SOLD TO CLOTHING CORPORATION
246 Summit Drive
Houston, TX 77047

Date: February 28, 20--
Customer's
Order Number 19-34
Terms: 2/10, n/30

Quantity	Description	Unit Price	Amount
✓ 10	Corduroy Suits D-4786	✓ 95.85	✓ 958.50
✓ 4	Pairs, Denim Jeans P-537	✓ 26.60	✓ 106.40
✓ 1	Denim Jacket J-34	✓ 21.35	✓ 21.35
			✓ 1,086.25
	Less 20%		✓ 217.25
			✓ 869.00
	Less 10%		✓ 86.90
			✓ 782.10

VERIFICATIONS
QUANTITIES RECIEVED — *S.C.*
PRICES CHARGED — *M.Y.*
EXTENSIONS AND TOTAL — *N.K.*

The firm uses the same verification steps for all invoices. If an error is discovered, it is immediately reported to the creditor.

Step 4: *Prepare and Approve a Voucher.* The verified invoice is the basis for preparing a voucher. Figure 26-2 shows Voucher 3-04 for the invoice from Gulf Shores Clothiers. After preparing this voucher, the accounting clerk attached the verified invoice to the voucher. The two documents were given to the store manager, who compared the invoice and the voucher and then signed the voucher to approve payment.

③ Objective

Prepare vouchers.

FIGURE 26-2 ▶
Payment Voucher

CLOTHING CORPORATION

Payment Voucher

NO. 3-04

PAYEE: Gulf Shores Clothiers
123 Ponce De Leon
Atlanta, GA 30308

Voucher Date Mar. 1, 20--
Terms 2/10, n/30
Discount Date Mar. 10, 20--
Date Due March 30, 20--

Invoice Date	Invoice Number	DESCRIPTION	AMOUNT
Feb. 28, 20--	R-47651	Suits, Jeans, and Jacket	782 10
			782 10

DISTRIBUTION	
ACCT. NO.	AMOUNT
501	$782.10

Price O.K. *M.Y.*
Material Received *S.C.*
Extensions O.K. *N.K.*
Gross Amount *782.10*
Discount _____
Net Paid _____
Approved for Pay. *Sumay Chen*
Paid by Ck. No. _____ Date _____

About Accounting

Fraud

A poll of Illinois professionals found that 72 percent said fraud is a frequent crime in the American workplace. The majority of the CPAs surveyed felt that a company's senior management should be responsible for fraud prevention and detection.

The information in the distribution box is used to make the accounting entry. It shows the account and amount to be debited (Account 501 for $782.10). The account to be credited is assumed to be **Accounts Payable.** Any additional debits and credits are entered in the distribution box.

Step 5: *Record and File the Unpaid Voucher.* After a voucher is approved, it is entered in an accounting record called the voucher register. If the voucher will be paid later, it is placed in an **unpaid voucher file**, according to due date. This file is sometimes called the **tickler file** because the file serves as a reminder of the amounts to be paid each day. The file of unpaid vouchers represents the accounts payable of the business. No formal accounts payable subsidiary ledger is maintained.

Step 6: *Pay a Voucher.* When a voucher is due for payment, a check is issued. The amount, check number, and date are recorded on the voucher. The voucher in Figure 26-2 has space for this information in the lower right corner. The voucher's payment is entered in the **check register**.

Step 7: *File a Paid Voucher.* When the check has been signed and mailed, the voucher is stamped "Paid." It is placed in a paid voucher file in numerical order. Sometimes paid vouchers are filed by the name of the payee to permit easier reference and to avoid duplication of payment.

Responsibilities must be carefully divided. Notice how division of responsibility is implemented at Clothing Corporation. The accounting clerk prepares the voucher, the store manager approves the voucher, the office clerk prepares the check, and an owner signs and mails the check.

Using the Voucher Register

After vouchers have been prepared and approved, they are entered in the voucher register in numerical order. The **voucher register** is a journal, similar to the purchases journal, used to record liabilities arising from business transactions. The voucher register provides a detailed list of the vouchers issued each month and indicates the accounts to debit and credit.

Figure 26-3 on pages 956–957 shows the voucher register of Clothing Corporation for the month of March. It has a place for entering the date and number of each voucher, the payee, and the debit and credit amounts. Separate columns are provided for accounts used frequently. These columns speed the entry of the vouchers and permit summary postings at the end of the month. Debits and credits to accounts not used frequently are recorded in the Other Accounts section. There are also columns to record the date and check number when a voucher is paid.

Usually the voucher is credited to **Accounts Payable.** However, some transactions require credits to other accounts. Refer to Voucher 3-14 in the voucher register. This voucher was issued for the net pay of Nadia Khan, the office clerk, for the semimonthly period ended March 15. Her $700 gross salary was debited to **Office Salaries Expense.** To record the taxes withheld, $43.40 was credited to **Social Security Tax Payable,** $10.15 was credited to **Medicare Tax Payable,** and $70 was credited to **Employee Income Tax Payable.** The net amount due Khan is $576.45; which was credited to **Accounts Payable.** Similar entries are made for the earnings, deductions, and net pay of other employees. Since there are several entries to the payroll accounts during each month, there are special columns for recording the payroll credits.

On March 29 Vouchers 3-27 and 3-28 were issued for payments to Mike Youngblood and Sumay Chen, the owners, for personal withdrawals. The amounts were debited to their drawing accounts.

During the month, entries in the Other Accounts section of the voucher register are posted individually to the accounts in the general ledger. At the end of the month, the voucher register is totaled, proved,

❹ Objective
Record vouchers in a voucher register.

International •••••••• **INSIGHTS**

Foreign Corrupt Practices Act of 1977

The Foreign Corrupt Practices Act of 1977 established severe penalties for companies engaged in activities such as bribes, kickbacks, illegal political contributions, and various other activities. These activities have been commonplace in many foreign countries in the past. Many companies argue that in order to compete in some countries they are almost necessary.

DATE		VOU. NO.	PAYABLE TO	PAID		ACCOUNTS PAYABLE CREDIT	SOC. SECURITY TAX PAYABLE CREDIT	MEDICARE TAX PAYABLE CREDIT	EMPLOYEE INCOME TAX PAYABLE CREDIT
				DATE	CK. NO.				
Mar.	1	3-01	Business Rentals	3/01	301	1 0 0 0 00			
	1	3-02	Beth Spencer	3/01	302	1 0 0 00			
	1	3-03	Nadia Khan	3/01	303	1 2 5 00			
	1	3-04	Gulf Shores Clothiers	3/10	304	7 8 2 10			
	3	3-05	Southern Paper Co.			2 2 5 00			
	5	3-06	P&S Office Products			7 5 00			
	9	3-07	Henry Villas, Attorney			5 0 0 00			
	9	3-08	PHB, CPAs			2 5 0 00			
	9	3-09	Blue Jean Clothing	3/19	310	5 5 0 0 00			
	10	3-10	Southern Express	3/12	305	6 5 00			
	10	3-11	Cotton Inc.	3/19	311	4 6 7 5 00			
	10	3-12	Eastern Truckers	3/13	306	7 5 00			
	10	3-13	Little Insurance Co.			5 0 0 00			
	12	3-14	Nadia Khan	3/15	307	5 7 6 45	4 3 40	1 0 15	7 0 00
	15	3-15	Beth Spencer	3/15	308	6 5 8 80	4 9 60	1 1 60	8 0 00
	15	3-16	Robert Ramirez	3/15	309	6 4 8 80	4 9 60	1 1 60	9 0 00
	18	3-17	Paper Box Company			1 9 5 00			
	25	3-18	Eastside Utilities			3 5 00			
	25	3-19	Southern Gas			1 5 5 00			
	25	3-20	Gulf Shores Clothiers			3 3 0 0 00			
	27	3-21	Public Telephone Co.			1 2 5 00			
	27	3-22	Truth Publishing Co.			4 5 0 00			
	28	3-23	On-Time Delivery			1 7 9 00			
	28	3-24	Nadia Khan	3/29	312	5 7 6 45	4 3 40	1 0 15	7 0 00
	28	3-25	Beth Spencer	3/29	313	6 5 8 80	4 9 60	1 1 60	8 0 00
	28	3-26	Robert Ramirez	3/29	314	6 4 8 80	4 9 60	1 1 60	9 0 00
	29	3-27	Mike Youngblood	3/29	315	1 0 0 0 00			
	29	3-28	Sumay Chen	3/29	316	9 5 0 00			
	30	3-29	Nadia Khan	3/29	317	6 5 00			
						24 0 9 4 20	2 8 5 20	6 6 70	4 8 0 00
						(205)	(221)	(222)	(223)

▲ **FIGURE 26-3** Voucher Register

The Purchases Journal
The voucher register replaces the purchases journal. The voucher register is posted in the same manner as the purchases journal.

⑤ Objective
Record payment of approved vouchers.

and ruled. Then the totals of all columns, except those in the Other Accounts section, are posted to the general ledger.

Businesses that use the voucher system do not need a purchases journal. The voucher register contains columns that permit the recording of merchandise purchases on credit.

Using the Check Register

Checks are recorded in the check register, which replaces the cash payments journal. If the payment is for goods purchased on credit, there may also be a credit to **Purchases Discounts.** Figure 26-4 on page 958 shows the check register for Clothing Corporation. Notice that it provides spaces for recording the date, check number, payee's name, voucher number, and amount of each payment. The checks are entered in numerical order. All of the entries involve a debit to **Accounts Payable** and a credit to **Cash.**

PURCHASES DEBIT	FREIGHT IN DEBIT	STORE SUPPLIES DEBIT	OTHER ACCOUNTS			
			ACCOUNT NAME	POST REF.	DEBIT	CREDIT
			Rent Expense	646	1 0 0 0 00	
			Change Fund	103	1 0 0 00	
			Petty Cash Fund	105	1 2 5 00	
7 8 2 10						
		2 2 5 00				
			Office Supplies	130	7 5 00	
			Professional Services Exp.	640	5 0 0 00	
			Professional Services Exp.	640	2 5 0 00	
5 5 0 0 00						
	6 5 00					
4 6 7 5 00						
	7 5 00					
			Insurance Expense	630	5 0 0 00	
			Office Salaries Expense	635	7 0 0 00	
			Office Salaries Expense	635	8 0 0 00	
			Sales Salaries Expense	645	8 0 0 00	
		1 9 5 00				
			Utilities Expense	650	3 5 00	
			Utilities Expense	650	1 5 5 00	
3 3 0 0 00						
			Misc. Office Expense	632	1 2 5 00	
			Advertising Expense	601	4 5 0 00	
			Delivery Expense	605	1 7 9 00	
			Office Salaries Expense	635	7 0 0 00	
			Office Salaries Expense	635	8 0 0 00	
			Sales Salaries Expense	645	8 0 0 00	
			Mike Youngblood, Drawing	330	1 0 0 0 00	
			Sumay Chen, Drawing	320	9 5 0 00	
	2 5 00	1 5 00	Office Supplies	130	2 5 00	
14 2 5 7 10	1 6 5 00	4 3 5 00			10 0 6 9 00	0 00
(501)	(506)	(129)			(X)	

Notice the entry on March 10. Clothing Corporation paid within the discount period and took a 2 percent discount of $15.64 ($782.10 × 0.02). Note that the debit to **Accounts Payable** is for the total amount of the voucher. The effect of the entry in the check register is shown below in general journal form for illustration purposes.

Recording Discounts
When purchases are recorded at their gross amounts, discounts are recorded when the payment is made.

20--				
Mar.	10	Accounts Payable	7 8 2 10	
		Purchases Discounts		1 5 64
		Cash		7 6 6 46

Recall that purchases discounts are shown on the income statement as a reduction in the cost of purchases. At month-end, the check register is totaled, proved, and ruled. Then the totals are posted to the general ledger.

CHECK REGISTER

	DATE	CK. NO.	PAYABLE TO	VOUCHER NUMBER	ACCOUNTS PAYABLE DEBIT	PURCHASES DISCOUNTS CREDIT	CASH CREDIT	
1	20--							1
2	Mar. 1	301	Business Rentals	3-01	1000 00		1000 00	2
3	1	302	Beth Spencer	3-02	100 00		100 00	3
4	1	303	Nadia Khan	3-03	125 00		125 00	4
5	10	304	Gulf Shores Clothiers	3-04	782 10	15 64	766 46	5
17	29	315	Mike Youngblood	3-27	1000 00		1000 00	17
18	29	316	Sumay Chen	3-28	950 00		950 00	18
19	30	317	Nadia Khan	3-29	65 00		65 00	19
20					18105 20	123 45	17981 75	20
21					(205)	(505)	(101)	21

FIGURE 26-4 ▲
Check Register

Preparing a Schedule of Vouchers Payable

Important!

Accounts Payable
When the voucher system is used, all checks written result in a debit to **Accounts Payable**.

When the voucher system is used, the file of unpaid vouchers takes the place of the accounts payable subsidiary ledger. At the end of each month, a **schedule of vouchers payable**—a list of all amounts owed for unpaid vouchers—is prepared from the items in the file. The schedule of vouchers payable is checked against the entries in the voucher register to ensure that it includes all vouchers not marked "Paid." Then the schedule's total is compared with the balance of the **Accounts Payable** control account in the general ledger to ensure that the two amounts are equal.

FIGURE 26-5 ▶
Schedule of Vouchers Payable

CLOTHING CORPORATION Schedule of Vouchers Payable March 31, 20--		
Voucher Number	Payable to	Amount
2-29	Cotton Inc.	$3,000.00
3-05	Southern Paper Company	225.00
3-06	P&S Office Products	75.00
3-07	Henry Villas, Attorney	500.00
3-08	PHB, CPAs	250.00
3-13	Little Insurance Company	500.00
3-17	Paper Box Company	195.00
3-18	Eastside Utilities	35.00
3-19	Southern Gas	155.00
3-20	Gulf Shores Clothiers	3,300.00
3-21	Public Telephone Company	125.00
3-22	Truth Publishing Company	450.00
3-23	On-Time Delivery	179.00
	Total	$8,989.00

Recall

Accounts Payable
The schedule of vouchers payable takes the place of the schedule of accounts payable. The total on the schedule of vouchers payable should equal the **Accounts Payable** control account.

On March 31 the **Accounts Payable** account of Clothing Corporation appeared as shown. The balance on March 1 was $3,000. A credit was posted from the voucher register (VR), and a debit was posted from the check register (CR). The final balance of the account, $8,989, agrees with the total of the schedule of vouchers payable.

Accounting

Health Science

Industry Overview

Professionals who plan, manage, and provide diagnostic, therapeutic, and information and environmental services in health care contribute to the growing industry of health science. More than 460,000 establishments make up the health services industry. Two-thirds of all private health services establishments are physician or dental offices. Less than 2 percent are hospitals, but they employ nearly 40 percent of all workers.

Career Opportunities
- Hospital Services—Senior Accountant
- Medical Insurance Specialist
- Family Health Administrator
- Director of Finance—Hospital Operations
- Radiological Technologist
- Clinical Project Manager

Preparing for a Health Science Career

- Become proficient in the use of basic applications, such as Word, Excel, and Access, that are used to gather, organize, and process data.

- Receive training in software applications specific to the health care industry such as Clinical Master 3.0 or Case Trakker.

- Be prepared to interpret and analyze financial information used in clinical settings.

- Develop the ability to read and create medical charts, reports, and manuals effectively using health care terminology.

- Sharpen mathematical skills, including computations of weights and measurements.

- Gain an understanding of health insurance coverage, claims processing, and claims reporting procedures and standards.

- Obtain a bachelor's degree in a specific health field for professional specialty occupations.

Thinking Critically
In September 2000 legislation was proposed to expand patients' bill of rights, seeking to increase patient choice of physicians and separate health care decisions from financial constraints. What do you think of this proposal? Explain.

Internet Application
Software developers market accounting applications customized to the needs of the health care industry. Use an Internet search engine to locate such an accounting software application. Use the search term "patient accounting." List the product name, price, and features.

ACCOUNT __Accounts Payable__   ACCOUNT NO. __205__

DATE	DESCRIPTION	POST. REF.	DEBIT	CREDIT	BALANCE DEBIT	BALANCE CREDIT
Mar. 1	Balance					3 0 0 0 00
31		VR1		24 0 9 4 20		27 0 9 4 20
31		CR1	18 1 0 5 20			8 9 8 9 00

Transactions Requiring Special Treatment

Businesses that use the voucher system can efficiently handle a large volume of transactions as long as invoices are received, verified, vouchered, and paid in the normal manner. However, the procedures are rigid, and certain infrequent transactions are awkward to record. The following are examples of transactions that require special treatment.

6 Objective

Record transactions that require special treatment in a voucher system.

Internal Control and the Voucher System **Chapter 26 • 959**

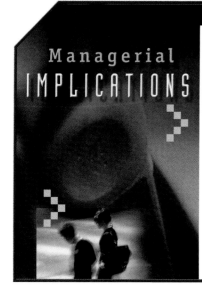

Managerial
IMPLICATIONS

Internal Control

- Management and the accountants work together to establish a well-planned system of internal control to safeguard cash and other assets.

- A good system of internal control ensures efficient transaction processing and accurate preparation of financial records, prevents liabilities from being incurred without proper authorization, and protects honest employees from suspicion by specifying responsibility.

- The voucher system is invaluable to management because of the tight control it provides over liabilities and cash payments. Every transaction is recorded, checked, and authorized. Responsibility is clearly defined throughout the process.

Thinking Critically
Why is it important to review the internal control system frequently?

Partial Payments

After a voucher has been recorded for the full invoice amount, a business can arrange to pay the invoice in installments. When this happens, the original voucher is canceled and new vouchers are issued—one voucher for each installment. The new vouchers include a credit to **Accounts Payable,** to record the new voucher, and a debit to **Accounts Payable,** to cancel the original voucher. The debit is recorded in the Other Accounts Debit column.

In the Paid section of the voucher register, on the line where the original voucher was recorded, the cancellation is noted in the Date column, and the new voucher numbers are entered in the Check Number column.

Notes Payable

A business might arrange to issue a note payable to a supplier for an unpaid invoice. In this case a general journal entry is made to debit **Accounts Payable** and credit **Notes Payable—Trade.** In the Paid section of the voucher register, the date of the note is entered in the Date column and the words *By note* are entered in the Check Number column. When the time comes for payment, a new voucher is prepared for the note and the interest expense.

Purchases Returns and Allowances

If goods are received that are for some reason unsatisfactory, either they are returned to the supplier or they are kept and an allowance is obtained from the supplier. In either case the amount finally owed to the supplier is less than the original invoice amount. In Chapter 8 you learned how to account for purchases returns and allowances. Now let's see how returns and allowances are handled if the voucher system is used.

If the original invoice has already been entered in the voucher register, the accounting records must be adjusted. For example, suppose that on February 5, Clothing Corporation receives an invoice for $900 for goods purchased from Wisconsin Wholesalers. Voucher 2-05 is prepared for the invoice. Then, on February 9, an allowance of $50 is made by the supplier to cover goods damaged in transit. The revised amount owed for the invoice is therefore $850. Either of two methods can be used to record a return or allowance.

Method 1: Issue New Voucher. On February 9 when the allowance is made, a new voucher is issued crediting **Accounts Payable** for $850, the revised amount. **Accounts Payable** is also debited for $900 to cancel the original voucher (2-05), and **Purchases Returns and Allowances** is credited for $50.

Both the new voucher (2-12) and the original voucher (2-05) appear in the voucher register. A notation is made for Voucher 2-05 indicating that it was canceled by Voucher 2-12.

Method 2: Make Notation. Some accountants use a simpler method to handle this type of adjustment. Since the voucher register for February was not closed and posted before the allowance was agreed on, the original entry can be corrected by making a notation for the $50 allowance on the same line as the original voucher entry. The notation is circled to indicate that it is a reduction in the firm's accounts payable and cost of purchases.

The adjustment is recorded on the original voucher, and when the invoice becomes due, payment is made for the net amount. At month-end the circled figures in each column of the voucher register are totaled separately from the original figures. The $50 total for returns and allowances for the month is debited to **Accounts Payable** and credited to **Purchases Returns and Allowances,** thereby accomplishing the same result as the first method. Note, however, that the second method can be used only if the revision is made *before* the voucher register has been closed for the month.

Purchases Discounts Lost

It is possible to record vouchers so that discounts not taken will stand out for investigation. To do this, record invoices in the voucher register net of discount. **Net of discount** is the invoice amount minus the cash discount offered. If the invoice is paid after the discount period, the discount is "lost" and the total invoice amount is paid. The difference is recorded in the check register by debiting an account called **Discounts Lost.** The balance of **Discounts Lost** appears on the income statement as an addition to **Purchases.**

Section 2 Self Review

Questions

1. What is the purpose of the voucher?

2. What is the purpose of the voucher register?

3. When a voucher is entered in the voucher register, what account is credited?

Exercises

4. A firm that uses a voucher register would not need a

   a. sales journal.

   b. check register.

   c. purchases journal.

   d. cash receipts journal.

5. A voucher should be prepared

   a. before a purchase order is issued.

   b. before any obligation is recorded or paid.

   c. after a check is issued to pay an invoice.

   d. after the payment is recorded.

Analysis

6. What is the journal entry to record the payment of an invoice for $734.50 with credit terms of 2/10, n/30, if payment was made in eight days? Assume the liability was already recorded in the voucher system.

CHAPTER 26 — Review and Applications

Review

Chapter Summary

Internal control is very important to the honest and efficient operation of a company. Accounting processes should be reviewed to ensure accuracy. In this chapter, you have learned about the voucher system, which is widely used to control liabilities and cash payments.

Learning Objectives

1 Explain the general principles of internal control.
Accountants use a variety of widely recognized techniques to design internal control procedures for a business.

- An essential internal control technique is to divide responsibilities. Each major accounting routine should involve at least two employees. One person's work is checked against that of another person.
- Employee training should include an understanding of why tasks are to be performed in a certain manner.
- Documentation procedures, audit trails, and management's review of tasks provide safeguards for the handling of assets and liabilities.

2 Explain how the voucher system facilitates internal control.
The voucher system is used to control liabilities and cash payments. Under the voucher system, proper authorization, written procedures for cash payments, and the division of responsibility help establish a strong system of internal control.

3 Prepare vouchers.
The voucher system requires that a voucher be prepared and authorized before any obligation is paid or before any sum is used to set up or replenish a cash fund for the business.

- Invoice prices, computations, and merchandise received should be verified.
- The voucher should be prepared and approved.
- The voucher is then placed with other approved vouchers in an unpaid vouchers file.

4 Record vouchers in a voucher register.
After vouchers are prepared and approved, they are entered in the voucher register in numerical order. The voucher is recorded in the voucher register as a credit to **Accounts Payable** and a debit to the appropriate account.

5 Record payment of approved vouchers.
The actual payment of cash is always made to settle a specific voucher that was previously recorded in the voucher register as an account payable. When a check is issued for the voucher, an entry is recorded in the check register, debiting **Accounts Payable** and crediting **Cash**. A notation is made in the voucher register showing the date paid and the check number.

6 Record transactions that require special treatment in a voucher system.

- To make partial payment of a previously recorded voucher, the original voucher is canceled and two or more new vouchers are prepared.
- When a company prepares payment for a note payable, a voucher must be prepared and authorized for the disbursement.
- If purchased items are returned or if an allowance is obtained,
  - a new voucher can be issued and the original voucher canceled, or
  - the original voucher can be adjusted by making a notation in the voucher register.
- Lost purchases discounts can be recorded so that they stand out and can be investigated.

7 Define the accounting terms new to this chapter.

Check register (p. 955) The record of cash payments of vouchers

Internal control system (p. 950) A system designed to safeguard assets, achieve efficient processing of transactions, and ensure accuracy and reliability of financial records

Net of discount (p. 961) The invoice amount minus the cash discount offered

Payment voucher (p. 951) See Voucher

Schedule of vouchers payable (p. 958) A list of all amounts owed for unpaid vouchers

Tickler file (p. 955) See Unpaid voucher file

Unpaid voucher file (p. 955) A file to hold vouchers until they are due to be paid, filed by due date

Voucher (p. 951) A form used to authorize payment of an obligation

Voucher register (p. 955) A journal used to record liabilities arising from business transactions

Voucher system (p. 951) A method of controlling liabilities and cash payments based on vouchers

Comprehensive Self Review

1. Why should all documents be prenumbered?
2. When carrying out the audit of a company's records, does the public accountant examine the system of internal control? Explain.
3. Division of responsibility is one of the most important principles of internal control. How is the principle put into practice?
4. What ledger does the unpaid vouchers file replace?
5. If a company records purchases invoices at their net amounts, after considering cash discounts, how is the cash discount taken on an invoice recorded?

(Answers to Comprehensive Self Review are on page 975.)

Discussion Questions

1. Why is there a need for internal control over business operations?

2. What is the voucher system?

3. Why is the voucher system more appropriate for medium-sized and large businesses than small businesses?

4. A number of different controls are built into the voucher system. Briefly describe five of these controls.

5. What steps are usually followed in verifying an invoice before a voucher is prepared?

6. What is the purpose of the check register?

7. What information is presented on the schedule of vouchers payable?

8. Under the voucher system, how is the balance of the **Accounts Payable** account proved at the end of each month?

9. In what order are vouchers filed in the unpaid vouchers file?

10. What types of transactions often require special treatment in the voucher system?

11. What is the purpose of recording invoices net of discount?

12. How is the **Discounts Lost** account presented on the income statement?

13. What are the steps used in a voucher system?

14. What is the relationship between the voucher register and the check register?

15. What internal control procedures are especially important in handling cash transactions?

16. Explain how each of the following unrelated procedures strengthens internal control:

    a. Dollar Delight requires its clerks to give each customer a cash register receipt.

    b. The person who collects the tickets at Coronet Cinema tears each ticket in half and gives each patron one-half of the ticket.

    c. The wait staff at Maxim's and Irina's Fine Foods use prenumbered tickets to record customers' orders. Any voided ticket must be given to the manager daily.

Applications

Record vouchers and payment of vouchers.

Record the following transactions for 20-- for Everyday.com in general journal form. On the line above each journal entry, indicate the name of the journal or register in which the transaction would actually be recorded. Omit descriptions.

◄ **Exercise 26-1**
Objectives 3, 4, 5

DATE		TRANSACTIONS
Jan.	12	Purchased merchandise from Peaches Inc. for $23,500; terms, 2/10, n/30; Voucher 1-01.
	16	Received bill for $875 from Southern Electric Company for utilities; prepared Voucher 1-02.
	21	Paid Peaches Inc. for purchase of January 12 (Voucher 1-01), less 2 percent discount.
	26	Paid Southern Electric Company for utilities (Voucher 1-02).

Record purchase and payment of invoice (discount taken).

In general journal form, record the following transactions of Hamilton Company during June 20--. Omit descriptions. On the line above the general journal entry, indicate the name of the journal or register in which the voucher would be recorded.

◄ **Exercise 26-2**
Objectives 3, 4, 5

DATE		TRANSACTIONS
June	12	Purchased merchandise for $5,000 from Metal Manufacturing Company; terms are 3/10, n/30.
	21	Paid Metal Manufacturing Company for invoice of June 12, deducting cash discount.

Record purchase and payment of invoice (discount not taken).

In general journal form, record the following transactions of Electronic Connection during October 20--. Omit descriptions. On the line above the general journal entry, indicate the name of the journal or register in which the voucher would be recorded.

◄ **Exercise 26-3**
Objectives 3, 4, 5

DATE		TRANSACTIONS
Oct.	12	Purchased merchandise for $3,500 from Cable Supply Corporation; terms are 2/10, n/30.
	30	Paid Cable Supply Corporation for invoice of October 12.

Problems

Selected problems can be completed using:
▦ **Spreadsheets**

PROBLEM SET A

Problem 26-1A ▶
Objectives 3, 4, 5

▦

INSTRUCTIONS

Recording transactions in the voucher register and the check register.

Transactions of Super Supply Company during the first two weeks of September 20-- are listed below, along with selected accounts from the firm's general ledger.

1. Record the transactions in a voucher register like the one shown in Figure 26-3 and a check register like the one shown in Figure 26-4.

2. Foot and prove the voucher register and the check register.

GENERAL LEDGER ACCOUNTS

Cash	David William, Drawing
Prepaid Insurance	Purchases
Office Supplies	Freight In
Warehouse Equipment	Purchases Discounts
Office Equipment	Rent Expense
Accounts Payable	Utilities Expense

DATE	TRANSACTIONS
Sept. 2	Prepared Voucher 9-01 for $2,600 owed to Coker Manufacturing Company for a purchase of merchandise; the terms are 3/10, n/30.
2	Prepared Voucher 9-02 for $1,500 owed to Industrial Park, Inc., for the monthly rent; paid the voucher by Check 4810.
3	Prepared Voucher 9-03 for $795 owed to Container Corporation for new storage racks for the warehouse; paid the voucher by Check 4811.
6	Prepared Voucher 9-04 for $5,000 owed to ABC Wholesalers Inc. for a purchase of merchandise; the terms are 3/10, n/30.
6	Prepared Voucher 9-05 for $195 owed to Northern Trucking Company for a freight charge on a purchase of merchandise; paid the voucher by Check 4812.
7	Prepared Voucher 9-06 for $1,600 owed to Midwest Insurance Agency for a one-year insurance policy.
9	Issued Check 4813 to pay Voucher 9-01 less the cash discount of 3 percent.
10	Prepared Voucher 9-07 for $298 owed to Valley Utilities for electricity; paid the voucher by Check 4814.
13	Prepared Voucher 9-08 for $2,773 owed to Town Distributing Company for a purchase of merchandise ($2,700) and a freight charge ($73); the terms are 1/10, n/30.
	Continued

DATE	(26-1A cont.) TRANSACTIONS
Sept. 15	Prepared Voucher 9-09 for $2,500 for a cash withdrawal by the owner for personal use; paid the voucher by Check 4815.
15	Issued Check 4816 to pay Voucher 9-04 less the cash discount of 3 percent.

Analyze: What total amount will be debited to the accounts of the general ledger for the transactions you have recorded in the voucher register for September?

Recording transactions in the voucher register and the check register.

◀ **Problem 26-2A**
Objectives 3, 4, 5

Transactions that occurred at the Weekend Worker's Hardware Company, a retail business, during April 20-- are listed below, along with selected accounts from the firm's general ledger.

INSTRUCTIONS

1. Record the transactions in a voucher register like the one shown in Figure 26-3 and a check register like the one shown in Figure 26-4.
2. Total, prove, and rule the voucher register and the check register.
3. Prepare a schedule of vouchers payable on April 30, 20--. Obtain the necessary information from the voucher register.

GENERAL LEDGER ACCOUNTS

Cash	Freight In
Store Supplies	Purchases Returns and Allowances
Office Supplies	Purchases Discounts
Store Equipment	Sales Salaries Expense
Office Equipment	Advertising Expense
Notes Payable	Rent Expense
Accounts Payable	Office Salaries Expense
Social Security Tax Payable	Sales Salaries Expense
Medicare Tax Payable	Utilities Expense
Employee Income Tax Payable	Telephone Expense
Purchases	

DATE	TRANSACTIONS
April 1	Prepared Voucher 4-01 for $1,500 owed to Backstreet Properties for the monthly rent; paid the voucher by Check 4101.
3	Prepared Voucher 4-02 for $245 owed to Office Supply Company for office supplies; the terms are n/30.
4	Prepared Voucher 4-03 for $500 owed to F&F Company for store fixtures; the terms are n/30.
5	Prepared Voucher 4-04 for $250 owed to Red Trucking Company for freight on merchandise purchased.
6	Issued Check 4102 to pay Voucher 4-04.
8	Prepared Voucher 4-05 for $2,000 to Chain Link Company for a purchase of merchandise; the terms are 2/10, n/30.
	Continued

DATE	(26-2A cont.) TRANSACTIONS
April 10	Prepared Voucher 4-06 for $6,500 to Clean Flush Company for a purchase of merchandise; terms are 2/10, n/30.
16	Issued Check 4103 to pay Voucher 4-05 less the 2 percent discount.
18	Prepared Voucher 4-07 for $500 owed to *Today's News* for advertising; paid the voucher by Check 4104.
19	Prepared Voucher 4-08 for $275 owed to Red Trucking Company for freight on merchandise purchased.
20	Issued Check 4105 to pay Voucher 4-08.
20	Issued Check 4106 to pay Voucher 4-06 less the 2 percent discount.
25	Prepared Voucher 4-09 for $5,500 owed to Straight Lumber Company for a purchase of merchandise; the terms are 2/10, n/30.
27	Prepared Voucher 4-10 for $310 owed to River City Utilities for electricity used in the store during the month; paid the voucher by Check 4107.
28	Prepared Voucher 4-11 for $100 to the River City Telephone Company for telephone service during the month; paid the voucher by Check 4108.
30	Prepared Voucher 4-12 for Joyce Smith, sales clerk, for her salary of $1,600, less $99.20 deducted for social security tax, $23.20 for Medicare tax, and $160 for income tax; paid the voucher by Check 4109. Prepared Voucher 4-13 for Becki Udall, office clerk, for her salary of $1,200, less $74.40 deducted for social security tax, $17.40 for Medicare tax, and $120 for income tax; paid the voucher by Check 4110.

Analyze: What total cash was disbursed in April?

PROBLEM SET B

Problem 26-1B ▶
Objectives 3, 4, 5

Recording transactions in the voucher register and the check register.

Transactions of Roberta Corporation during the first two weeks of May 20-- are listed on page 969, along with selected accounts from the firm's general ledger.

INSTRUCTIONS

1. Record the transactions in a voucher register like the one shown in Figure 26-3 and a check register like the one shown in Figure 26-4.
2. Foot and prove the voucher register and the check register.

GENERAL LEDGER ACCOUNTS

Cash
Store Supplies
Office Supplies
Store Equipment
Office Equipment
Accounts Payable

Marla Maple, Drawing
Purchases
Freight In
Purchases Discounts
Rent Expense
Utilities Expense

DATE		TRANSACTIONS
May	1	Prepared Voucher 5-01 for $1,000 owed to Pepper Products, Inc., for a purchase of merchandise; the terms are 3/10, n/30.
	2	Prepared Voucher 5-02 for $1,200 owed to Gap Properties, Inc., for the monthly rent on the store; paid the voucher by Check 1525.
	4	Prepared Voucher 5-03 for $799 owed to Office Products Inc. for office file cabinets; paid the voucher by Check 1526.
	5	Prepared Voucher 5-04 for $4,500 owed to Juno Inc. for a purchase of merchandise; the terms are 2/10, n/30.
	5	Prepared Voucher 5-05 for $146 owed to Covenant Trucking Inc. for a freight charge on a purchase of merchandise; paid the voucher by Check 1527.
	7	Prepared Voucher 5-06 for $450 owed to Western Products for store supplies; the terms are n/30.
	9	Issued Check 1528 to pay Voucher 5-01 less the cash discount of 3 percent.
	11	Prepared Voucher 5-07 for $349 owed to Florida Electric for electricity; paid the voucher by Check 1529.
	12	Prepared Voucher 5-08 for $1,975 owed to Illinois Products Inc. for a purchase of merchandise ($1,900) and a freight charge ($75); the terms are n/30.
	14	Issued Check 1530 to pay Voucher 5-04 less the cash discount of 2 percent.
	15	Prepared Voucher 5-09 for $1,500 for a cash withdrawal by the owner for personal use; paid the voucher by Check 1531.

Analyze: What total liabilities due to merchandise purchases were recorded in the voucher register for the month of May?

Recording transactions in the voucher register and the check register.

◄ **Problem 26-2B**
Objectives 3, 4, 5

Transactions that occurred at Eric's Books, a retail business, during July 20-- follow, along with selected accounts from the firm's general ledger.

INSTRUCTIONS

1. Record the transactions in a voucher register like the one shown in Figure 26-3 and a check register like the one shown in Figure 26-4.

2. Total, prove, and rule the voucher register and the check register.

3. Prepare a schedule of vouchers payable. Obtain the necessary information from the voucher register.

GENERAL LEDGER ACCOUNTS

Cash
Store Supplies
Office Supplies
Store Equipment
Office Equipment
Notes Payable
Accounts Payable
Social Security Tax Payable
Medicare Tax Payable
Employee Income Tax Payable
Purchases

Freight In
Purchases Returns and Allowances
Purchases Discounts
Sales Salaries Expense
Advertising Expense
Rent Expense
Office Salaries Expense
Sales Salaries Expense
Utilities Expense
Telephone Expense

DATE		TRANSACTIONS
July	1	Prepared Voucher 7-01 for $750 owed to Mickey's Properties for the monthly rent; paid the voucher by Check 7101.
	3	Prepared Voucher 7-02 for $79 owed to All Supplies for office supplies; the terms are n/30.
	5	Prepared Voucher 7-03 for $700 owed to Fixtures 'n Things for installing new fixtures in the store; the terms are n/30. (Debit **Store Equipment.**)
	5	Prepared Voucher 7-04 for $108 owed to Signal Trucking Company for freight on merchandise purchased.
	6	Issued Check 7102 to pay Voucher 7-04.
	8	Prepared Voucher 7-05 for $1,000 owed to Lookout Company for a purchase of merchandise; the terms are 2/10, n/30.
	10	Prepared Voucher 7-06 for $2,500 owed to Decatur Stores for a purchase of merchandise; the terms are 2/10, n/30.
	12	Prepared Voucher 7-07 for $150 owed to Supplies Etc. for store supplies; the terms are n/30.
	16	Issued Check 7103 to pay Voucher 7-05 less the 2 percent discount.
	18	Prepared Voucher 7-08 for $150 owed to *Everyday News* for advertising; paid the voucher by Check 7104.
	19	Prepared Voucher 7-09 for $150 owed to Lookout Trucking for freight on merchandise purchased.
	20	Issued Check 7105 to pay Voucher 7-09.
	20	Issued Check 7106 to pay Voucher 7-06 less the 2 percent discount.
	25	Prepared Voucher 7-10 for $1,900 owed to Good Stuff Inc. for a purchase of merchandise; the terms are 2/10, n/30.
		Continued

DATE	(26-2B cont.) TRANSACTIONS
27	Prepared Voucher 7-11 for $196 owed to County Utilities for electricity used in the store during the month; paid the voucher by Check 7107.
28	Prepared Voucher 7-12 for $74 owed to Century Telephone Co. for telephone service during the month; paid the voucher by Check 7108.
31	Prepared Voucher 7-13 for John Robert, the sales clerk, for his salary of $1,400, less $86.80 deducted for social security tax, $20.30 for Medicare tax, and $140 for income tax; paid the voucher by Check 7109. Prepared Voucher 7-14 for Mary Julio, the office clerk, for her salary of $1,200, less $74.40 deducted for social security tax, $17.40 for Medicare tax, and $120 for income tax; paid the voucher by Check 7110.

Analyze: List the transactions in July that increased the total assets for Eric's Books.

CHAPTER 26 CHALLENGE PROBLEM

Beginning Operations

In April of 20--, the first month of operations of Arizona Sales Corporation, the purchases of merchandise that are given below were entered in the voucher register.

INSTRUCTIONS

1. Prepare a cost of goods sold schedule for April, assuming that purchases discounts taken are treated as other income.

2. Prepare a schedule of vouchers payable on April 30, 20--. All vouchers other than those for purchases have been paid.

DATE	TRANSACTIONS
April 1	Issued Voucher 4-01, payable to Far East Electronics Corporation, for $20,000; terms, 2/10, n/30 (paid on April 9).
2	Issued Voucher 4-04, payable to Plastic Equipment Company, for $10,000; terms, 2/10, n/30 (paid on April 21).
5	Issued Voucher 4-08, payable to Keyboard Supply Company, for $16,000; terms, n/30.
20	Issued Voucher 4-15, payable to Phoenix Electronics Corporation, for $28,000; terms, 2/10, n/30 (paid on April 30).
25	Issued Voucher 4-26, payable to Signal Inc., for $12,000; terms, 2/20, n/30.
27	Issued Voucher 4-31, payable to Lite Equipment Company, for $8,000; terms, 3/10, n/30.

On April 30 an inventory was taken. The inventory consisted of all the merchandise purchased on April 27 and April 25, one-half of the merchandise purchased on April 20, and one-fourth of the merchandise purchased on April 2.

Analyze: If Arizona Sales Corporation used the account, **Discounts Lost,** what would that account's balance be at April 30, 20--?

CHAPTER 26 CRITICAL THINKING PROBLEM

Protecting the Cash

Tameka Thrower, a college accounting major, has just been hired to work part-time in the treasurer's office of the local museum. On her first day of work, her boss, Anne Brown, the treasurer, calls Tameka into her office to explain the operations and to describe her duties. The treasurer's office is small—with just two full-time employees other than Anne.

Anne explains that Nancy is in charge of all cash collections. She opens the mail, sets aside any donation checks for deposit, and distributes the rest of the mail to the appropriate persons. When the museum entrance fees are turned over to her each afternoon, she counts the money and prepares the bank deposit. It is usually too late to take the money to the bank, so Nancy locks it in her filing cabinet overnight. After returning from the bank the next morning, Nancy enters the amount of the deposit in the cash receipts journal and files the deposit slip. Once a month, Nancy prepares a summary of cash receipts for the museum's president.

Laura, the other full-time employee, handles the museum payroll. She collects the time cards at the end of the week, makes the payroll calculations, prepares the payroll checks, and enters the payroll data in the appropriate records. To save time, the office uses a machine that prints a facsimile signature on each check. The check-signing machine is kept out of sight behind a door in Anne's office, which, she explains, prevents unauthorized persons from using the machine and also eliminates the need for Laura to unlock and lock the machine each time she uses it.

As the part-timer in the office, Tameka's job will be to assist the others and fill in when they are on vacation. When Nancy goes on vacation or is absent from work, Tameka will be required to prepare the bank deposit and take it to the bank. Anne says that the last student who had the job objected to taking the deposit to the bank for fear of being robbed, a fear Anne dismisses, saying such things are usually an "inside job."

Tameka explains that she has no experience with payroll, but Anne assures her she has only to follow what Laura does and she will soon learn what she needs to know. Besides filling in for Nancy and Laura, Tameka is to help Anne prepare financial statements and close the books.

When Tameka gets home from her first day on the job, she is not sure she wants to go back. If she is robbed on the way to the bank, she will likely be accused of being involved. If she makes a mistake, how will it be discovered? This office does not seem to do anything the way Tameka learned in her accounting classes.

1. Evaluate the internal control system of the treasurer's office. Identify the strong and weak points of the system.

2. What suggestions would you make to improve it?

Business Connections

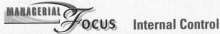
Internal Control

◀ **Connection 1**

1. Assume you are the newly hired controller of Nobar Company and have suggested that the firm adopt the voucher system. The president has asked you to provide a brief analysis of the advantages and disadvantages of this system. How would you respond?

2. The personnel manager of Nobar Company is concerned that the employees will view the installation of the voucher system as a sign of mistrust. How can this system be explained to the employees as providing benefits to them as well as to the business?

3. How can the management of a firm avoid unnecessary red tape as a by-product of its search for adequate internal controls?

4. In a small business there may be only one or two experienced and reliable employees capable of assuming key positions in an internal control system. Is it impractical to introduce internal controls in this situation? Why or why not?

5. The president of Queen Company received a letter from one of the companies from which Queen purchases merchandise. The letter expressed surprise that although Queen usually pays all invoices shortly after the due date, the company does not take advantage of all cash discounts available. The president asks you to design a system to routinely report discounts not taken. Describe the procedures you would recommend.

Ethical DILEMMA

Drawing You are one of the partners in a growing business. As part of the voucher system implementation, you each agree to sign any voucher when one of you is taking a draw. Your partner is out of town, and you need $500 today. You sign your partner's name to a voucher and withdraw the cash. When your partner comes back to town, you decided not to tell him about the withdrawal because, after all, you have a right to a share of the money. Discuss the ethical issues involved in this case.

◀ **Connection 2**

Street WISE:
Questions from the Real World

Internal Controls Refer to the *1999 Annual Report* for The Home Depot, Inc. in Appendix B.

◀ **Connection 3**

1. Refer to the letter "Management's Responsibility for Financial Statements." Describe the stated purposes for the company's system of internal controls. What steps does the company take to assess its internal control systems?

2. Locate the consolidated balance sheets. What accounts payable were outstanding on January 30, 2000? If 50 percent of these accounts payable carried cash discounts of 2/10, n/30 and were paid within the discount period, what savings did the company enjoy?

Connection 4 ►

Boise Cascade Corporation

FINANCIAL **$**TATEMENT
A N A L Y S I S   **Report of Management** The following excerpt was taken from the "Report of Management" in the Boise Cascade Corporation *1999 Annual Report*. Companies often include a Report of Management that addresses the responsibility of the corporation for the information contained in the annual report.

> "Management maintains a comprehensive system of internal controls based on written policies and procedures and the careful selection and training of employees. The system is designed to provide reasonable assurance that assets are safeguarded against loss or unauthorized use and that transactions are executed in accordance with management's authorization. The concept of reasonable assurance is based on recognition that the cost of a particular accounting control should not exceed the benefit expected to be derived."

Analyze:

1. Describe three internal control measures that Boise Cascade has taken to safeguard assets.
2. Why do you think the costs of accounting control procedures are weighed against the benefits to be gained?
3. What purposes are served by the company's maintenance of internal controls systems?

Analyze Online: Locate the company's Web site **(www.boisecascade.com).** Within the *Investor Relations* section, find the most recent annual report.

4. What references, if any, are made to internal controls in the "Report of Management"?
5. Based on the financial data found on the company's statements of income, has net income increased or decreased since the prior fiscal period? By what amount?

Connection 5 ►

Extending the *Thought*   **Components of Internal Control** Good systems of internal control are often said to contain checks and balances. What is meant by "checks and balances" in this context?

Connection 6 ►

Business **Communication**   **Establishing Internal Controls** You are the senior staff accountant for Minute Markets USA, Inc. The corporation operates 68 locations nationwide. All accounts payable and vouchers are prepared in the corporate offices in Cincinnati, Ohio. Each store employs a store manager, receiving clerk, sales clerk, and office manager. In an effort to increase internal controls within the business, you have decided to issue a memo to all store managers containing specific procedures for the receipt of goods and verification of prices and computations. Write the memo to store managers and include step-by-step instructions that will help establish good internal controls at the store level.

Team*Work*   Applying the Voucher System Alpine Ski Lodge is   ◄ Connection 7
a small vacation establishment. The lodge accountant is the only office
employee, processing approximately 60–75 disbursements per month.
The hospitality manager receives all deliveries of food and supplies. Form
two teams. One team should formulate a position in favor of the use of
the voucher system at Alpine Ski Lodge. The second team should formulate a position against the use of the voucher system for this business. Prepare written reports supporting the positions.

inter NET
CONNECTION   Market Research ACNielsen is the global leader in mar-   ◄ Connection 8
ket research. Go to its Web site at **www.acnielsen.com.** In what context
do most people hear of ACNielsen's consumer information? How does
ACNielsen collect data about consumer buying habits? How would
a retailer benefit from using ACNielsen's Retail Measurement Services?

Answers to Self Reviews

Answers to Section 1 Self Review
1. Effective internal control increases efficiency, reduces the possibility of errors, and safeguards assets.
2. By ensuring that no one individual is responsible for all phases of a transaction.
3. No. The accounts receivable clerk might be tempted to remove a check, keep it for personal use, and cover the shortage with an entry in the accounts receivable records.
4. **d.** use prenumbered business forms.
5. **d.** all of the above.
6. The voucher system is more appropriate for larger companies. Since the owner of Mia Systems approves all purchases and signs all checks, the voucher system might not be necessary.

Answers to Section 2 Self Review
1. To ensure that no check is issued without proper authorization and is backed by appropriate documentation.
2. To record every approved voucher. Entries are posted to the accounts affected.
3. **Accounts Payable.**
4. **c.** purchases journal.
5. **b.** before any obligation is recorded or paid.
6. Debit **Accounts Payable,** $734.50; credit **Purchases Discounts,** $14.69; credit **Cash,** $719.81.

Answers to Comprehensive Self Review
1. If a document is deliberately or accidentally removed and destroyed, its absence will be detected.
2. Yes. The auditor relies to a great extent on the integrity of the internal control system to help ensure that the numbers in the financial statements are reliable and correct.
3. By assigning two or more employees to every major operation.
4. The accounts payable subsidiary ledger.
5. Under this entry there is no record in the accounts of discounts taken. Only discounts lost are recorded.

CHAPTER 27

Learning Objectives

1. Explain profit centers and cost centers.

2. Prepare the Gross Profit section of a departmental income statement.

3. Explain and identify direct and indirect departmental expenses.

4. Choose the basis for allocation of indirect expenses and compute the amounts to be allocated to each department.

5. Prepare a departmental income statement showing the contribution margin and operating income for each department.

6. Use a departmental income statement in making decisions such as whether a department be closed.

7. Define the accounting terms new to this chapter.

Departmentalized Profit and Cost Centers

BARBIE and the Mattel logo are trademarks owned by and used with permission of Mattel, Inc. © 2001 Mattel, Inc. All Rights Reserved.

www.mattel.com

Mattel focuses its energy on products that work—Barbie, Hot Wheels, and Fisher-Price—just to name a few. The company first introduced Barbie in 1959 as a teenage fashion model, but she has since tackled other professions like doctor, firefighter, astronaut, and paleontologist. After 40 years, Barbie is a $1.5 billion brand.

Mattel has also participated in non-toy consumer markets, acquiring a theme park, the Ringling Bros. and Barnum & Bailey Circus, and even a motion picture company in the early 1970s. Evaluation of these ventures led Mattel to eventually sell or close all non-toy business lines. To maintain profitability, the company devotes itself to producing high-quality, imaginative toys for children.

Thinking Critically

What types of financial and non-financial data do you think Mattel considered when evaluating its non-toy divisions?

For more information on Mattel, go to: collegeaccounting.glencoe.com.

New Terms

Contribution margin

Cost center

Departmental income statement

Direct expenses

Indirect expenses

Managerial accounting

Profit center

Responsibility accounting

Semidirect expenses

Transfer price

Terms to Learn

cost center
direct expenses
indirect expenses
managerial accounting
profit center
responsibility accounting
semidirect expenses
transfer price

Profit and Cost Centers and Departmental Accounting

In previous chapters you have studied financial statements that report the results of transactions that happened in the past. This chapter shows how management can use financial data for forward-looking analysis and decision making, not just historical reporting.

Managerial Accounting

Managerial accounting is the branch of accounting that provides financial information about business segments, activities, or products. Managerial accounting supplies information about the profit made on an order or the profitability of a specific department. Management uses this information to make decisions such as when to replace a machine, whether to discontinue a product, or to determine the selling price for a new product.

> In 1998 Ford Motor Company adopted Statement of Financial Accounting Standards No. 131, Disclosures about Segments of an Enterprise and Related Information. In accordance with this standard, Ford publishes information on revenues, net income, and assets for four primary segments: Automotive, Visteon, Ford Credit, and Hertz.

Profit Centers and Cost Centers

Managerial accounting is concerned with segments of a business. The segments are often called *centers*. Accounting information is accumulated and analyzed separately for each center. There are two types of centers: cost centers and profit centers. A **cost center** is a business segment that incurs costs but does not produce revenue. A **profit center** is a business segment that produces revenue.

> DuPont operates nine strategic business units organized by product line: Agriculture & Nutrition, Nylon Enterprise, Performance Coatings & Polymers, Pharmaceuticals, Pigments & Chemicals, Pioneer, Polyester Enterprise, Specialty Fibers, and Specialty Polymers. Each segment sells products to outside customers. Some segments sell products to other business units within DuPont.

Cost centers do not directly earn revenue. Cost centers often provide services to other segments of the business. The emphasis in accounting for cost centers is on cost control. Typical cost centers include the accounting department, information systems department, maintenance department, storeroom, research laboratory, and purchasing department.

Profit centers are revenue-producing segments that sell products or services to customers outside the business. For example, a clothing store might have separate profit centers for the coat, dress, suit, and shoe departments. Sales and costs are accumulated for each department. A "profit" is computed for the department.

Sometimes it is convenient to think of a segment of a company as a profit center even though it does not sell products or services to outside customers. For example, the segment of an oil company that produces crude oil from the ground can be treated as a profit center even though the oil it produces is transferred to the company's refinery. The revenue from the segment's activities is the **transfer price** of its product—the price at which the segment's goods are transferred to another segment of the company.

① **Objective**
Explain profit centers and cost centers.

Responsibility Accounting

Responsibility accounting allows management to evaluate the performance of each segment of the business and assign responsibility for its financial results. Internal accounting reports provide detailed data for each cost and profit center so that management can determine how efficiently the individual segments are functioning.

Important!

Responsibility Accounting
Responsibility accounting provides information that helps in evaluating each segment of a business and assigning responsibility for results.

Departmentalized Operations

When a business has more than one type of sales or service activity, it is important to know what each activity is contributing to the income or loss of the business. Let's learn how accountants gather revenue and expenses for the different activities by studying the system used by Traditional Clothing, a business that sells men's clothing and shoes.

Gross Profit Section of a Departmental Income Statement

To calculate gross profit by department, Traditional Clothing gathers data by department for each transaction.

Departmental Accounts in the General Ledger. Businesses that prepare departmental financial statements maintain general ledger accounts for sales, purchases, merchandise inventory, and some operating expenses. For example, Traditional Clothing has two sales departments, clothing and shoes. The sales accounts are **Sales—Clothing** and **Sales—Shoes.**

Recording Sales and Purchases by Departments. Figure 27-1 on page 980 shows the sales journal for Traditional Clothing. Notice that there are two sales columns, one for clothing and one for shoes. Sales are recorded in the usual manner except that the sales amounts are divided between the sales columns. For example, Patrick Neuhoff purchased $100 of clothing and $50 of shoes. These amounts are reported in separate columns.

② **Objective**
Prepare the Gross Profit section of a departmental income statement.

Important!

Sales Journal
When the sales account is departmentalized, the sales journal records transactions by department.

SALES JOURNAL   PAGE _____1_____

DATE	SALES SLIP NO.	CUSTOMER'S NAME	POST. REF.	ACCOUNTS RECEIVABLE DEBIT	SALES TAX PAYABLE CREDIT	SALES— CLOTHING CREDIT	SALES— SHOES CREDIT
20--							
Jan. 2	1005	Rob Gabbin	✓	95 40	5 40	90 00	
2	1006	Patrick Neuhoff	✓	159 00	9 00	100 00	50 00
2	1007	Billy Wilson	✓	190 80	10 80	115 00	65 00
31		Totals		9 964 00	564 00	6 200 00	3 200 00
				(111)	(231)	(401)	(402)

▲ **FIGURE 27-1**
Departmental Sales Journal

Sales for all Sara Lee Corporation business segments totaled $20 billion for the year ended July 3, 1999. The company reports segment sales for Sara Lee Foods, Coffee & Tea, Household and Body Care, Foodservice, Branded Apparel, and Inter-segment divisions. In fiscal 1999 the Sara Lee Foods division accounted for almost 25 percent of all sales.

Recall

Posting
Postings are made daily from the sales journal to the individual accounts receivable subsidiary ledger accounts.

The departmental sales journal is posted in the usual manner. Transactions are posted daily in the accounts receivable subsidiary ledger. The sales journal column totals are posted to the general ledger at month-end. Similarly, the voucher register and the sales returns and allowances journal have separate columns for the two departments.

Merchandise Inventories. Merchandise inventory is counted by department so that the departmental cost of goods sold can be computed.

FIGURE 27-2 ▼
Departmental Income
Statement (Partial)

A Sample Gross Profit Section. Figure 27-2 shows the Gross Profit section of the departmental income statement for Traditional Clothing.

Traditional Clothing
Income Statement (Partial)
Year Ended December 31, 20--

	Clothing	Shoes	Total
Operating Revenue			
Sales	3 75 0 0 0	1 25 0 0 0	5 00 0 0 0
Less Sales Returns and Allowances	1 1 5 0	6 5 0	1 8 0 0
Net Sales	3 73 8 5 0	1 24 3 5 0	4 98 2 0 0
Cost of Goods Sold			
Merchandise Inventory, Jan. 1, 20--	5 9 5 0 0	1 5 0 0 0	7 4 5 0 0
Purchases	2 65 0 0 0	4 8 0 0 0	3 13 0 0 0
Freight In	4 2 0 0	5 0 0	4 7 0 0
Delivered Cost of Purchases	2 69 2 0 0	4 8 5 0 0	3 17 7 0 0
Less: Purchases Returns and Allowances	3 5 0 0	3 5 0	3 8 5 0
Purchases Discounts	6 0 0 0	4 0 0	6 4 0 0
Total Deductions	9 5 0 0	7 5 0	1 02 5 0
Net Delivered Cost of Purchases	2 59 7 0 0	4 7 7 5 0	3 07 4 5 0
Total Merchandise Available for Sale	3 19 2 0 0	6 2 7 5 0	3 81 9 5 0
Less Merchandise Inventory, Dec. 31, 20--	4 5 0 0 0	1 2 4 8 0	5 7 4 8 0
Cost of Goods Sold	2 74 2 0 0	5 0 2 7 0	3 24 4 7 0
Gross Profit on Sales	9 9 6 5 0	7 4 0 8 0	1 73 7 3 0

Operating Expenses Section of a Departmental Income Statement

There are two types of operating expenses: direct expenses and indirect (or semidirect) expenses.

Direct Expenses. Direct expenses are identified directly with a department and are recorded by department. At Traditional Clothing, sales clerks work in only one department, so it is easy to record salary expenses. Advertising costs, store supplies, cash short or over, and delivery expenses are also recorded by department.

Figure 27-3 shows the direct expenses for Traditional Clothing.

Traditional Clothing
Schedule of Direct Departmental Expenses
Year Ended December 31, 20--

	Clothing Dept.	Shoes Dept.	Total
Sales Salaries Expense	33 0 0 0	19 0 0 0	52 0 0 0
Advertising Expense	4 5 0 0	1 5 0 0	6 0 0 0
Store Supplies Expense	3 5 0	1 5 0	5 0 0
Cash Short or Over	5 2	2 5	7 7
Delivery Expense	2 7 5	0	2 7 5
Total Direct Expenses	38 1 7 7	20 6 7 5	58 8 5 2

▲ FIGURE 27-3
Schedule of Direct Departmental Expenses

Indirect and Semidirect Expenses. Not all operating costs are direct expenses. **Semidirect expenses** cannot be directly assigned to a department, but they are closely related to departmental activities. Semidirect expenses are allocated among the departments at the end of the accounting period. Semidirect expenses include depreciation on store equipment and the cost of insurance for equipment and inventory.

Indirect expenses are operating expenses that cannot be readily identified and are not closely related to activity within a department. At the end of the accounting period, indirect expenses are allocated to the departments. Examples of indirect expenses are postage and stationery.

The accountant for Traditional Clothing treats semidirect and indirect expenses as indirect expenses. The indirect expenses for Traditional Clothing follow.

Indirect Expenses	
Insurance expense	$ 6,800
Rent expense	12,000
Utilities expense	6,000
Office salaries expense	16,000
Other office expenses	1,800
Uncollectible accounts expense	1,200
Depreciation expense—furniture and fixtures	700
Depreciation expense—office equipment	500
Total indirect expenses	$45,000

Allocating Semidirect and Indirect Expense Items. After the worksheet has been completed, the accountant allocates indirect expenses to the departments. The accountant tries to find some logical relationship between the departments and each type of expense. Let's see how the

❸ Objective
Explain and identify direct and indirect departmental expenses.

About Accounting

Stress
Costs linked to stress-related mistakes and illnesses are growing, especially in U.S. businesses. This is not surprising considering that the United States surpassed even Japan in the number of hours worked in 1999.

❹ Objective
Choose the basis for allocation of indirect expenses and compute the amounts to be allocated to each department.

Computers in Accounting

Databases: Information Warehouses

The primary job of a database is to warehouse data to enable users to access and reconfigure it in a variety of ways. As accounting professionals increasingly participate in decision making in the workplace, database applications can help convert raw financial data into meaningful business information.

Although spreadsheets can help organize and present financial data, databases are designed to do many jobs that spreadsheets cannot handle:

- Data can be combined and configured in a variety of ways without affecting the underlying original data.
- Formatting filters help ensure data accuracy.
- Easy creation of customized reports gives the business user flexibility in data presentation.
- Most applications accept data imports from spreadsheet, word processing, or accounting software.

The database designer creates one or more tables where data is entered or loaded. Relationships between the tables are established and customized reports and queries are created. The design and organization of these tables and relationships is known as data modeling. Although some accountants prefer to build a database from scratch, templates are available to make the setup process fast and easy. Templates can be found in database applications such as Access, FileMaker Pro, and Paradox.

When creating a database, the accountant first considers the data's end-use. In other words, what information is needed? How is the information to be used and displayed? This provides a general guideline for how the data is stored and organized in the database. Tables within a database can be used to store information such as customer accounts, sales by product line, or expenses for various production methods.

Thinking Critically
Based on the information you have learned about departmentalized financial information, what potential uses can you identify for a database application?

Internet Application
Locate a software vender Web site. Find three database applications and review the associated product information. What types of features are offered? Is the application designed for new users, experts, or developers? What is the cost of the product? What hardware and operating system is required? As a beginning user of database applications, which product would you select?

Recall

Matching
Indirect expenses are allocated to departments to match the expenses to the revenue earned by the departments.

accountant allocates the indirect costs for Traditional Clothing. The allocated costs appear in Figure 27-4, the departmental income statement for Traditional Clothing, which appears on page 986 of this chapter. Notice that the allocated expenses are rounded to the nearest dollar.

Insurance Expense. Insurance premiums total $6,800. They are allocated based on the cost of the furniture, fixtures, and inventory used in the department's operations. As of December 31, Traditional Clothing used $49,500 in the clothing department and $14,980 in the shoes department. The accountant allocates $5,236 of insurance expense to the clothing department and $1,564 to the shoes department as shown in Table 27-1 on page 983.

Asset Item	Clothing Department	Shoes Department	Percent	Total Insurance Expense	Amount Allocated to Each Department
Merchandise inventory	$45,000	$12,480			
Furniture and fixtures	4,500	2,500			
Total clothing	$49,500	$14,980	77	× $6,800	= $5,236
Total shoes	14,980		23	× 6,800	= 1,564
Combined Totals	$64,480		100		$6,800

▲ TABLE 27-1
Allocation of Insurance Expense

Rent Expense. Rent expense was $12,000. It is allocated based on square footage. The accountant allocates $9,600 to the clothing department and $2,400 to the shoes department.

Department	Basis: Square Feet	Percent		Rent Expense		Allocation
Clothing	2,400	80	×	$12,000	=	$ 9,600
Shoes	600	20	×	12,000	=	2,400
Total	3,000	100				$12,000

Utilities Expense. Utilities expense was $6,000. It is allocated based on square footage. The accountant allocates $4,800 ($6,000 × 0.80) to the clothing department and $1,200 ($6,000 × 0.20) to the shoes department.

Office Salaries Expense. Office salaries expense was $16,000. It is allocated based on total sales for each department. The accountant allocates $12,000 to the clothing department and $4,000 to the shoes department as shown.

Department	Basis: Total Sales	Percent		Office Salaries Expense		Allocation
Clothing	$375,000	75	×	$16,000	=	$12,000
Shoes	125,000	25	×	16,000	=	4,000
Total	$500,000	100				$16,000

Other Office Expenses. Other office expenses, including postage and stationery, totaled $1,800. They are allocated based on total sales for each department. The accountant allocates $1,350 ($1,800 × 0.75) to the clothing department and $450 ($1,800 × 0.25) to the shoes department.

Uncollectible Accounts Expense. As a result of the aging of the accounts receivable balance on December 31, an adjustment of $1,200 was recorded as an expense for uncollectible accounts. The uncollectible accounts expense is allocated on the basis of credit sales, preferably on net credit sales. Sometimes it takes too much time to distinguish between returns from cash and credit sales, so gross sales on account are used to make the allocation. The accountant for Traditional Clothing uses gross credit sales. Based on the following calculations, the accountant allocates uncollectible accounts expenses of $900 to the clothing department and $300 to the shoes department.

Important!

Uncollectible Accounts Expense
If feasible, the expense for uncollectible accounts is allocated based on net credit sales.

Department	Basis: Credit Sales	Percent		Uncollectible Accounts Expense		Allocation
Clothing	$300,000	75	×	$1,200	=	$ 900
Shoes	100,000	25	×	1,200	=	300
Total	$400,000	100				$1,200

International INSIGHTS

Expansion of U.S. Businesses in Asia

Asian countries, especially China, Indonesia, and India, are developing rapidly and present growing markets for all types of products as well as opportunities for manufacturing and distribution. Many U.S. businesses have built plants that produce goods to be sold in Asia and to be imported into the United States.

Depreciation Expense—Furniture and Fixtures. The assets used to compute depreciation for furniture and fixtures are identified with specific departments. Depreciation is computed at 10 percent per year. Traditional Clothing uses $4,500 of furniture and fixtures in the clothing department and $2,500 in the shoes department. The accountant allocates $450 ($4,500 × 0.10) of depreciation to the clothing department and $250 ($2,500 × 0.10) to the shoes department.

Depreciation Expense—Office Equipment. Depreciation on the office equipment was $500. It is allocated according to total sales by department—the same basis used to allocate office salaries. The accountant allocates $375 ($500 × 0.75) to the clothing department and $125 ($500 × 0.25) to the shoes department.

Nondepartmentalized Expenses. Revenue and expenses that do not apply to operations are not allocated to the departments. Generally, all items that appear in the Other Income and Other Expenses section of the income statement are treated as nondepartmental items. For example, interest income and interest expense are not allocated to departments because they relate to the financing of the business, rather than to its operating activities.

Other income and expense accounts that are not allocated to the departments at Traditional Clothing are **Miscellaneous Income** for $610 and **Interest Expense** for $750.

Section 1 Self Review

Questions

1. How does a profit center differ from a cost center?

2. What is responsibility accounting?

3. What is a logical basis for allocating property insurance expense to departments?

Exercises

4. If a segment of a business is considered a profit center,

   a. it must sell products or services to customers outside the business.

   b. both revenue and costs are accumulated for the segment.

   c. no expenses can be allocated to the segment.

   d. it incurs costs but does not have revenues.

5. In a store with several sales departments, departmentalized accounts are used for

   a. sales only.

   b. sales, purchases, and merchandise inventory.

   c. sales and other income items only.

   d. purchases and expense items only.

Analysis

6. Department A had total sales of $120,000, and Department B had total sales of $80,000. Office salaries expense of $30,000 is allocated on the basis of total sales. How much would be allocated to Department B?

(Answers to Section 1 Self Review are on page 999.)

Departmental Income Statements

The balance sheet is prepared in the same manner whether or not a business has departmentalized operations. The income statement for a departmentalized firm, however, is expanded to highlight the individual departments' financial information.

Preparing the Departmental Income Statement

A **departmental income statement** shows each department's contribution margin and net income from operations after all expenses are allocated. Figure 27-4 on page 986 shows the departmental income statement for Traditional Clothing. Notice the amount labeled "Contribution Margin." It appears between "Total Direct Expenses" and "Indirect Expenses." **Contribution margin** is gross profit on sales minus direct expenses. It is the amount that the department has earned beyond its direct costs. The contribution margin is available to cover the semidirect and indirect expenses of running the business. A department that has a positive contribution margin is contributing toward increasing the net income (or decreasing the net loss) of the business.

Departmental Income

Income from operations by department is used to make many business decisions. However, there are limitations to using departmental operating income. For example, it is difficult to determine each department's fair share of semidirect and indirect expenses. Another limitation is that if a particular department were eliminated, many of the indirect expenses allocated to it would not be eliminated. They would have to be absorbed by the remaining departments. When making decisions knowledgeable managers rely more on contribution margin per department than on income from operations.

Contribution Margin

Departments with a positive contribution margin help to pay the semidirect and indirect costs of the business. As already mentioned, many of the indirect costs allocated to an eliminated department may have to be absorbed by the remaining departments. Departments with a negative contribution margin reduce the net income (or increase the net loss) of the business as a whole. The business would be more profitable if the department with the negative contribution margin was eliminated.

As can readily be seen, the concept of contribution margin is important to business owners and managers because it provides them with valuable assistance in making decisions. Unfortunately, contribution margin figures are not provided in traditional financial reports.

Section Objectives

5 Prepare a departmental income statement showing the contribution margin and operating income for each department.

WHY IT'S IMPORTANT
Individual departments need to cover their direct expenses and contribute toward increasing the income of the business.

6 Use a departmental income statement in making decisions such as whether a department should be closed.

WHY IT'S IMPORTANT
The viability of business segments can be evaluated based on departmental income statements.

Terms to Learn
contribution margin
departmental income statement

5 Objective
Prepare a departmental income statement showing the contribution margin and operating income for each department.

6 Objective
Use a departmental income statement in making decisions such as whether a department should be closed.

Traditional Clothing
Income Statement
Year Ended December 31, 20--

	Clothing	Shoes	Total
Operating Revenue			
Sales	375000	125000	500000
Less Sales Returns and Allowances	1150	650	1800
Net Sales	373850	124350	498200
Cost of Goods Sold			
Merchandise Inventory, Jan 1, 20--	59500	15000	74500
Purchases	265000	48000	313000
Freight In	4200	500	4700
Delivered Cost of Purchases	269200	48500	317700
Less: Purchases Returns and Allowances	3500	350	3850
Purchases Discounts	6000	400	6400
Total Deductions	9500	750	10250
Net Delivered Cost of Purchases	259700	47750	307450
Total Merchandise Available for Sale	319200	62750	381950
Less Merchandise Inventory, Dec 31, 20--	45000	12480	57480
Cost of Goods Sold	274200	50270	324470
Gross Profit on Sales	99650	74080	173730
Operating Expenses			
Direct Expenses			
Sales Salaries Expense	33000	19000	52000
Advertising Expense	4500	1500	6000
Store Supplies Expense	350	150	500
Cash Short or Over	52	25	77
Delivery Expense	275	- 0 -	275
Total Direct Expenses	38177	20675	58852
Contribution Margin	61473	53405	114878
Indirect Expenses			
Insurance Expense	5236	1564	6800
Rent Expense	9600	2400	12000
Utilities Expense	4800	1200	6000
Office Salaries Expense	12000	4000	16000
Other Office Expenses	1350	450	1800
Uncollectible Accounts Expense	900	300	1200
Depreciation Expense—Furniture and Fixtures	450	250	700
Depreciation Expense—Office Equipment	375	125	500
Total Indirect Expenses	34711	10289	45000
Net Income from Operations	26762	43116	69878
Other Income			
Miscellaneous Income			610
Other Expenses			
Interest Expense			750
Net Other Expenses			140
Net Income before Taxes			69738

▲ FIGURE 27-4
Departmental Income Statement

Managerial IMPLICATIONS

Departmental Income Statements

- Departmentalized income statements illustrate which departments are most profitable and which are losing money or have low profit margins. Once alerted, department managers can take proper steps to improve the profit picture.

- Profitable departments may be expanded. Less profitable departments may undergo policy changes or may be closed.

- Departmentalized income statements help managers evaluate and control the operations of each unit.

- The contribution margin is very important in making managerial decisions. The contribution margin is gross profit minus direct expenses. It indicates how much each department contributes toward the indirect expenses and income for the business.

- Decisions to retain, eliminate, expand, or contract a segment of the business are based on the analysis of the contribution margin of the department or product.

- Departmental income is, at best, an estimate. It should be used with great care when making decisions.

- Managers need to consider that many of the indirect expenses would not be eliminated by the decision to do away with a department.

Thinking Critically
Give two reasons why it may be improper to use departmental income to make a decision about eliminating a department.

Section 2 Self Review

Questions

1. What is contribution margin?
2. What is the difference between direct departmental expenses and indirect expenses?
3. How does the accountant choose a basis for allocating indirect expenses to sales departments?

Exercises

4. A department probably would be considered for elimination if it had a

  a. positive contribution margin and income from operations.

  b. positive contribution margin and a loss from operations.

  c. negative contribution margin and a loss from operations.

  d. positive contribution margin and no income tax expense.

5. Dept. A had gross profit of $15,000, total direct expenses of $5,000, and total indirect expenses of $4,000. What is its contribution margin?

  a. $11,000   b. $10,000
  c. $6,000   d. $9,000

Analysis

6. A department had a contribution margin of $20,000 and a loss from operations of $5,000. If the department is eliminated, the indirect expenses allocated to it will still be incurred. If the department is eliminated, how will net income for the business be affected?

(Answers to Section 2 Self Review are on page 999.) *Departmentalized Profit and Cost Centers* **Chapter 27 • 987**

Review

Chapter Summary

The basic financial statements summarize the financial operations and position of the business as a whole, but they do not provide all of the accounting information necessary in running a business. Additional information needed about individual segments and activities of the business is provided by managerial accounting. In this chapter, you have learned how departmental financial reports are prepared and how they contribute to business decision making.

Learning Objectives

1 Explain profit centers and cost centers.

Managerial accounting provides information about the operating centers of a business.

- Some operating centers are called *profit centers* because they generate both revenues and expenses.
- Other operating centers are called *cost centers* because they incur expenses in providing services but do not produce revenues.

Many retail stores refer to profit and cost centers as departments.

- Separate accounts for sales, inventory, and other elements of the cost of goods sold are established because separate information is needed for each department.
- Departmental accounts can be established in the ledger with a column for each department.
- The sales journal, voucher register, and other records of original entry gather transaction data by department.

2 Prepare the Gross Profit section of a departmental income statement.

To determine departmental gross profit, the following figures for each department must be determined:
- gross sales
- sales returns and allowances
- sales discounts
- purchases
- purchases returns and allowances
- beginning and ending inventories

3 Explain and identify direct and indirect departmental expenses.

Operating expenses that can be identified directly with a specific department are considered direct expenses. Other expenses must be allocated to departments on some predetermined basis at the end of the accounting period.

- Expenses that are allocated on a logical basis closely related to use are sometimes referred to as *semidirect expenses*.
- Expenses that must be allocated on a more arbitrary basis are called *indirect expenses*.
- Many accountants refer to both types as indirect expenses.

4 Choose the basis for allocation of indirect expenses and compute the amounts to be allocated to each department.

When selecting the basis for making the allocation of expenses, the accountant chooses a basis that
- relates the department and the expense in a logical manner,
- can be measured for each department.

5 Prepare a departmental income statement showing the contribution margin and operating income for each department.

The departmental income statement shows the contribution margin of each department as well as a final net income figure after allocation of all expenses.

6 Use a departmental income statement in making decisions such as whether a department should be closed.

The departmental income statement helps managers assess the profitability of a department. Departments with low profit margins or other operational weaknesses can be identified.

7 Define the accounting terms new to this chapter.

CHAPTER 27 GLOSSARY

Contribution margin (p. 985) Gross profit on sales minus direct expenses

Cost center (p. 978) A business segment that incurs costs but does not produce revenue

Departmental income statement (p. 985) Income statement that shows each department's contribution margin and net income from operations after all expenses are allocated

Direct expenses (p. 981) Operating expenses that are identified directly with a department and are recorded by department

Indirect expenses (p. 981) Operating expenses that cannot be readily identified and are not closely related to activity within a department

Managerial accounting (p. 978) The branch of accounting that provides financial information about business segments, activities, or products

Profit center (p. 978) A business segment that produces revenue

Responsibility accounting (p. 979) The process that allows management to evaluate the performance of each segment of the business and assign responsibility for its financial results

Semidirect expenses (p. 981) Operating expenses that cannot be directly assigned to a department but are closely related to departmental activities

Transfer price (p. 979) The price at which one segment's goods are transferred to another segment of the company

Comprehensive Self Review

1. What are the logical profit centers in a retail store?
2. How can a non-selling business segment be called a profit center?
3. Compare the recording process for direct and indirect expenses.
4. Why are indirect expenses allocated to departments?
5. Give the steps in determining a department's contribution margin.

(Answers to Comprehensive Self Review are on page 999.)

Discussion Questions

1. How does managerial accounting differ from financial accounting?
2. Why does managerial accounting focus on the future?
3. What is responsibility accounting?
4. Is departmental accounting a form of responsibility accounting? Explain.
5. Why would a retail operation departmentalize its records?
6. Define contribution margin.
7. How does a departmentalized income statement differ from one that is not departmentalized?
8. Explain the difference between semidirect and indirect expenses.
9. Suggest a logical basis for allocating these indirect expenses: heating and lighting; office equipment repairs; general institutional advertising.
10. Why is interest expense not allocated to departments?

Applications

EXERCISES

Information for Exercises 27-1 through 27-3

Selected financial data, as of December 31, 20--, for Outlet Fashions, a discount retail store, follows.

Credit sales
   Women's clothing, $502,500
   Men's clothing, $127,500
Total sales
   Women's clothing, $536,250
   Men's clothing, $288,750
Sales returns and allowances
   Women's clothing
       Credit sales, $2,500
       Cash sales, $600
   Men's clothing
       Credit sales, $2,500
       Cash sales, $500
Book value of inventory and equipment
   Women's clothing, $175,000
   Men's clothing, $75,000

Exercise 27-1 ►
Objective 4

Computing the amount of indirect expense to be allocated to a department.

Outlet Fashions' insurance expense for the year totaled $6,000 and is to be allocated on the basis of the book value of the inventory and equipment in each department. Compute the amount to be allocated to each department.

Exercise 27-2 ►
Objective 4

Computing the amount of indirect expense to be allocated to a department.

The total office expense for the year at Outlet Fashions was $45,000. Compute the amount to be allocated to each department using total sales as the basis for the allocation.

Exercise 27-3 ►
Objective 4

Computing the amount of indirect expense to be allocated to a department.

The uncollectible accounts expense at Outlet Fashions is estimated to be 1/2 of 1 percent of net credit sales. Compute the amount to be allocated to each department.

Exercise 27-4 ►
Objective 5

Preparing a departmental income statement showing contribution margin and net income for each department.

Data related to the income and expenses of Fine Gifts Company for the year ending December 31, 2006, follow.

Allocated indirect expenses
   Jewelry department $ 47,600
   China department   22,400
Interest income   800

Gross profit
    Jewelry department $211,000
    China department   92,000
Direct expenses
    Jewelry department   125,000
    China department   75,000

Prepare a partial departmental income statement showing the contribution margin and net income of each department.

Using departmental income statements in making decisions.

◄ **Exercise 27-5**
Objective 6

Data from the departmental income statement of Red Raider Company for the year ended December 31, 20--, is given below. Assuming that a department's direct expenses can be eliminated if it is closed, what factors should management consider when deciding whether to close Department 1?

	Dept. 1	Dept. 2	Total
Net sales	$280,000	$620,000	$900,000
Cost of goods sold	150,000	350,000	500,000
Gross profit on sales	$130,000	$270,000	$400,000
Direct expenses	120,000	190,000	310,000
Contribution margin	$ 10,000	$ 80,000	$ 90,000
Indirect expenses	50,000	20,000	70,000
Net income (or loss)	$(40,000)	$ 60,000	$ 20,000

Preparing a departmental income statement showing contribution margin and net income of departments.

◄ **Exercise 27-6**
Objective 5

Using the data given in Exercise 27-5, prepare an income statement for the company if Department 1 is closed.

Using a departmental income statement in making decisions.

◄ **Exercise 27-7**
Objective 6

Using the data given in Exercise 27-5, would you recommend closing Department 1? Why or why not?

Problems

Selected problems can be completed using:
    ▦ **Spreadsheets**

PROBLEM SET A

Allocating indirect expenses to departments and preparing a departmental income statement.

◄ **Problem 27-1A**
Objectives 4, 5

Selected information from the adjusted trial balance of Big Shoe Closet as of December 31, 20--, follows.

	Department A	Department B	Total
Merchandise Inventory, January 1	$ 60,000	$ 20,000	$ 80,000
Merchandise Inventory, December 31	50,000	10,000	60,000
Sales	330,000	270,000	600,000
Sales Returns and Allowances	3,300	2,700	6,000
Merchandise Purchases	152,000	138,000	290,000
Freight In	4,500	1,500	6,000
Purchases Returns and Allowances	1,500	500	2,000
Sales Salaries Expense	40,000	20,000	60,000
Advertising Expense	8,000	4,000	12,000
Store Supplies Expense	600	200	800
Cash Short or Over	40	80	120
Insurance Expense			5,000
Rent Expense			10,800
Utilities Expense			4,200
Office Salaries Expense			12,000
Other Office Expenses			1,400
Uncollectible Accounts Expense			2,500
Depr. Expense—Furniture and Fixtures			5,800
Depr. Expense—Office Equipment			200
Interest Income			300
Interest Expense			240

INSTRUCTIONS

Prepare a departmental income statement for the year ended December 31, 20--. The bases for allocating indirect expenses are given below. (**Note:** Because allocations are not precise, round each allocated amount to the nearest whole percent and dollar.) Show all allocations in a neat and orderly form.

1. **Insurance expense:** in proportion to the total of the furniture and fixtures (the gross assets before depreciation) and the ending inventory in the departments. These totals are as follows.

Department A	$108,000
Department B	12,000
Total	$120,000

2. **Rent Expense** and **Utilities Expense:** on the basis of floor space occupied, as follows.

Department A	1,400 square feet
Department B	600 square feet
Total	2,000 square feet

3. **Office Salaries Expense, Other Office Expenses,** and **Depreciation Expense—Office Equipment:** on the basis of the gross sales in each department.

4. **Uncollectible Accounts Expense:** on the basis of net sales in each department.

5. **Depreciation Expense—Furniture and Fixtures:** in proportion to cost of furniture and fixtures in each department. These costs are as follows. (Round to nearest dollar.)

Department A	$58,000
Department B	2,000
Total	$60,000

Analyze: Which department reports the highest return on net sales?

Preparing a departmental income statement and using the statement in making a business decision.

◀ **Problem 27-2A**
Objectives 5, 6

Yard 'N Stuff sells plants, fertilizers, and other garden products. The store has three departments: plants, chemicals, and tools. Certain information about the revenues and expenses of the departments for the year ended December 31, 20--, is given below. Indirect expenses have been allocated on bases similar to those discussed and illustrated in the text.

	Plants	Chemicals	Tools
Allocated indirect expenses	$ 8,500	$ 6,200	$ 7,100
Beginning merchandise inventory	4,300	6,500	8,300
Direct expenses	29,500	18,000	15,000
Ending merchandise inventory	4,600	6,400	8,100
Purchases	55,500	49,000	35,000
Purchases returns and allowances	500	400	300
Sales	105,500	95,000	56,400
Sales returns and allowances	1,500	500	400

INSTRUCTIONS

1. Prepare a departmental income statement showing the contribution margin and the net profit for each department.

2. Based solely on accounting information, would you recommend that any departments be closed? Explain.

3. What information, other than accounting data, would you suggest the owners consider in deciding whether to close any departments?

Analyze: If the indirect expenses had been allocated on the basis of net sales, what conclusions would you draw about the viability of each department? Explain.

PROBLEM SET B

Allocating indirect expenses and preparing a departmental income statement.

◀ **Problem 27-1B**
Objectives 4, 5

Selected information from the adjusted trial balance of Super Sports Store as of December 31, 20--, is shown below.

	Department A	Department B	Total
Merchandise Inventory, January 1	$ 36,900	$ 25,000	$ 61,900
Merchandise Inventory, December 31	38,000	24,000	62,000
Sales	295,000	179,000	474,000
Sales Returns and Allowances	3,500	2,800	6,300
Purchases	150,000	98,500	248,500
Freight In	5,000	1,500	6,500
Purchases Returns and Allowances	2,700	1,800	4,500
Sales Salaries Expense	45,000	26,000	71,000
Advertising Expense	12,500	600	13,100
Store Supplies Expense	850	300	1,150
Cash Short or Over	50	20	70
Insurance Expense			8,000
Rent Expense			12,000

Utilities Expense	$ 6,000
Office Salaries Expense	12,000
Other Office Expenses	1,600
Uncollectible Accounts Expense	2,500
Depr. Expense—Furniture and Fixtures	4,300
Depr. Expense—Office Equipment	200
Interest Income	510

INSTRUCTIONS

Prepare a departmental income statement for the year ended December 31, 20--. The bases for allocating indirect expenses are given below. (**Note:** Because allocations are not precise, round each allocated amount to the nearest whole percent and dollar.) Show all allocations in a neat and orderly form.

1. **Insurance Expense:** in proportion to the total of the furniture and fixtures (the gross assets before depreciation) and the ending inventory in the departments. These totals are as follows.

Department A	$ 80,000
Department B	25,000
Total	$105,000

2. **Rent Expense** and **Utilities Expense:** on the basis of floor space occupied, as follows.

Department A	1,800 square feet
Department B	1,200 square feet
Total	3,000 square feet

3. **Office Salaries Expense, Other Office Expenses,** and **Depreciation Expense—Office Equipment:** on the basis of the gross sales in each department.

4. **Uncollectible Accounts Expense:** on the basis of net sales in each department.

5. **Depreciation Expense—Furniture and Fixtures:** in proportion to cost of furniture and fixtures in each department. These costs are as follows.

Department A	$4,200
Department B	1,000
Total	$5,200

Analyze: To what degree does Department B contribute to the overall net income of the business? Express your answer as a percentage.

Preparing a departmental income statement and using the statement in making a business decision.

◀ **Problem 27-2B**
Objectives 5, 6

Your Paper Needs has three departments: office supplies, novelty items, and greeting cards. Certain information about the revenues and expenses of the departments for the year ending December 31, 20--, is given below. Indirect expenses have been allocated on bases similar to those discussed and illustrated in the text.

	Office Supplies	Novelty Items	Greeting Cards
Allocated indirect expenses	$ 1,300	$ 800	$ 1,200
Beginning merchandise inventory	4,200	1,900	800
Direct expenses	12,000	8,000	6,500
Ending merchandise inventory	4,500	1,800	500
Purchases	39,900	34,000	21,000
Purchases returns and allowances	500	400	300
Sales	54,600	38,450	29,500
Sales returns and allowances	900	450	200

INSTRUCTIONS

1. Prepare a departmental income statement showing the contribution margin and the net profit for each department.

2. Based solely on accounting information, would you recommend that any departments be closed? Explain.

3. What information, other than accounting data, would you suggest the owners consider in deciding whether to close any departments?

Analyze: What increase in net sales would be required to ensure that the novelty department would be able to cover its direct expenses? Assume that all other figures remained steady.

CHAPTER 27 CHALLENGE PROBLEM

Departmental Closure

Mountain Crafts Shop has three sales departments: wood crafts, clothing items, and toys. The store's condensed income statement for the year ended December 31, 20--, is shown below.

Mountain Crafts Shop
Condensed Income Statement
Year Ended December 31, 20--

	Wood Crafts	Clothing Items	Toys
Sales	39 0 0 0	42 0 0 0	22 0 0 0
Cost of Goods Sold	25 0 0 0	18 5 0 0	9 0 0 0
Gross Profit on Sales	14 0 0 0	23 5 0 0	13 0 0 0
Operating Expenses			
Direct Expenses	9 5 0 0	8 3 0 0	6 5 0 0
Indirect Expenses	5 5 0 0	5 2 0 0	4 0 0 0
Total Operating Expenses	15 0 0 0	13 5 0 0	10 5 0 0
Net Profit	(1 0 0 0)	10 0 0 0	2 5 0 0

Departmentalized Profit and Cost Centers **Chapter 27 • 995**

The proprietor has asked the auditor whether she should close the wood crafts and/or the toys departments. In the opinion of both the proprietor and the auditor, if the wood crafts department were discontinued, it might be possible to reduce the total indirect expenses to $12,000. If only the toys department were closed, it might be possible to reduce total indirect expenses by $2,500. In the opinion of the proprietor, if the Toys department were discontinued, sales in the clothing items department would decrease by $10,000. A decrease of $10,000 in sales in the clothing items department would result in a reduction of that department's direct expenses by $4,500. The proprietor also thinks that closing the wood crafts department would have little effect on the sales of toys.

INSTRUCTIONS

1. Based on the preceding information, what would the estimated total profit or loss be if the wood crafts department were closed?

2. What would the estimated total profit or loss be if the Toys department were closed?

3. What advice would you give the proprietor?

Analyze: What is the contribution margin for each department?

CHAPTER 27 CRITICAL THINKING PROBLEM

Indirect Costs

At the last staff meeting of the Recent Masters Art Shop, the question of how expenses are allocated to each department was raised. Since year-end bonuses are awarded to the managers on the basis of departmental net income from operations, the discussion was lively.

Jimmy Connors, manager of the framing department, said that each department should be charged only with the expenses directly related to the department. He indicated that while managers can influence the sales and direct expenses in their departments, they have little control over many of the indirect expenses such as depreciation, office salaries, and taxes.

Bill Vanders, manager of the fine art department, argued that all expenses—direct and indirect—should be allocated. "After all," he said, "all the revenue is allocated to each department, so why not allocate all the expenses? The store could not operate if it did not incur the indirect expenses." He also stated that many of the indirect expenses, such as insurance and cleaning services, could be allocated on a meaningful basis.

INSTRUCTIONS

Evaluate these comments.

Business Connections

◀ Connection 1

MANAGERIAL *FOCUS* Departmental Accounting

1. Is the identification of purchases returns and allowances by department valuable to managerial control? Explain.

2. If one department consistently has a comparatively large amount of cash short in its operations, what management action might be appropriate?

3. Why is it better for managers to use contribution margin analysis rather than net income analysis when deciding whether to retain, expand, or contract operations?

4. How does a firm's accountant determine the reasonable basis to be used in allocating a specific indirect expense? Should management be concerned about the basis used?

5. The management of a store with three sales departments plans to install a bonus system for department managers. Do you think the bonus system should be based on each department's contribution margin or on the department's net income after allocating all administrative expenses? Explain.

◀ Connection 2

Ethical DILEMMA Departmental Responsibility There are three departments in your business and you are trying to determine a reasonable basis for allocating the indirect expenses. Total sales for the business are $265,000, composed of the following departmental sales totals: $165,000, $33,000, and $67,000. Each department manager is eligible for a bonus based on net income from operations in his or her department. To simplify the allocation of indirect expenses, you decide to allocate 33 percent of indirect costs to each department. You, by the way, are the manager of the department with the $165,000 sales. Should you be making the decision on allocation of indirect costs? If you have the authority to decide, is your decision a reasonable one?

◀ Connection 3

*Street***WISE:**
Questions from the Real World   Segments Refer to the *1999 Annual Report* for The Home Depot, Inc. in Appendix B.

1. Review the Letter To Our Stockholders, Customers and Associates section called *Developing Our Capabilities.* What two companies did The Home Depot, Inc. acquire, and why did The Home Depot, Inc. acquire them?

2. Review the Letter To Our Stockholders, Customers, and Associates. If The Home Depot, Inc. decided to report on financial performance for segments within the business, what types of segments might be recommended?

Connection 4 ►

FINANCIAL $TATEMENT
A N A L Y S I S **Segment Reporting** The following excerpt was taken from the *1999 Annual Report* for Alcoa Inc., the world's leading producer of primary aluminum, fabricated aluminum, and alumina.

Segment information (in millions)	Alumina and chemicals	Primary metals	Flat-rolled products	Engineered products	Other	Total
1999						
Total sales	$2,767	$5,034	$5,164	$3,754	$3,393	$20,112
After tax operating income	$ 307	$ 535	$ 281	$ 180	$ 186	$ 1,489

Analyze:

1. List Alcoa's five operating segments.
2. Which segment yields the highest after tax operating income?
3. Which segment yields the lowest rate of return on total sales?

Analyze Online: Find the *Investor Information* section on the Alcoa Web site (**www.alcoa.com**). Click on the *Financial Data* link, and review the information presented for *Segment and Geographic Information*.

4. Describe the operations of the segment labeled *Other*.
5. Describe the items that have been excluded from segment profit computations.

Connection 5 ►

Extending 🌐 *Thought* **Inter-segment Transactions** Some corporations are organized into functional segments such as merchandising, manufacturing, and distribution divisions. Imagine that the merchandising division of a company has requested to use personnel and office supplies from the distribution division for a one-time promotion. The merchandising operation needs two clerical workers for three days and approximately $3,000 in office supplies to complete the project. The CFO decides that since the resources all come from the same corporation, he will not charge the merchandising operation for the use of the distribution division's time and supplies. Do you agree with his decision? Why or why not?

Connection 6 ►

Business Communication **Accounting for Segments** As the controller of Crown City Fashions, you have decided it would be advantageous to track financial performance for each of the company's departments: Sports Wear, Men's Wear, Kid's & Teen's Wear, and Women's Wear. Currently, the accounting records are not structured for recording department-specific transactions. Create a checklist of the types of changes that you will need to make to the general ledger in order to record transactions on a divisional basis. What types of changes will be required when preparing financial reports at month-end or year-end?

Team*Work* **Organizational Structures for Segment Reporting** ◀ **Connection 7**

As a team, research the types of organizational structures used as a basis for segment reporting. Select four large corporations that you believe might be organized into segments or business units. Locate the *Investor Relations* section of each company's Web site. The annual report contains segment information. In a summary report, include a spreadsheet that identifies the companies you have researched, their Web site addresses, the business segments they operate, and recent sales data per reporting segment.

inter NET
CONNECTION **Departmental Contributions** Berkshire Hathaway is a large ◀ **Connection 8**
company with divisions including GEICO insurance and See's Candies. Go to **www.berkshirehathaway.com.** What percentage of company revenue did each division generate? What percentage did each division contribute to the company's operating profits?

Answers to Self Reviews

Answers to Section 1 Self Review

1. A cost center incurs expenses but does not have revenues; a profit center does produce revenues.
2. It provides information for evaluating segment performance and assigning responsibility for financial results.
3. The total value of insured assets in each department.
4. **b.** both revenue and costs are accumulated for the segment.
5. **b.** sales, purchases, and merchandise inventory.
6. $12,000

Answers to Section 2 Self Review

1. Gross profit on sales minus direct expenses.
2. Direct expenses relate to a specific department. Indirect expenses must be allocated on a logical basis.
3. The accountant seeks a basis that seems to be correlated with the amount of expense and that can be measured for each department.
4. **c.** negative contribution margin and a loss from operations.
5. **b.** $10,000
6. Net income would be $20,000 lower.

Answers to Comprehensive Self Review

1. Departments that sell similar items to customers outside the business.
2. Some cost centers render services or make products that are transferred to other centers in the same company. In such cases a hypothetical revenue, or transfer price, is attributed to the goods or services transferred. This price permits measuring a "profit" for the center.
3. Direct expenses are usually charged when incurred. Indirect expenses are allocated at the end of the fiscal period.
4. Indirect expenses are allocated to departments to attempt to measure the profitability of each department.
5. Subtract the department's direct expenses from its gross profit.

CHAPTER 28

Learning Objectives

1. Prepare a statement of cost of goods manufactured.

2. Explain the basic components of manufacturing cost.

3. Prepare an income statement for a manufacturing business.

4. Prepare a balance sheet for a manufacturing business.

5. Prepare a worksheet for a manufacturing business.

6. Record the end-of-period adjusting entries for a manufacturing business.

7. Record closing entries for a manufacturing business.

8. Record reversing entries for a manufacturing business.

9. Define the accounting terms new to this chapter.

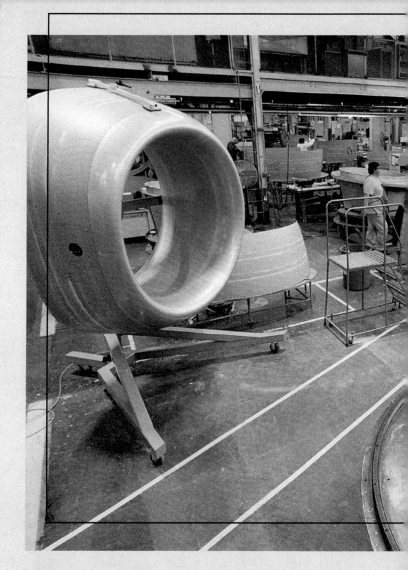

Accounting for Manufacturing Activities

GOODRICH

www.goodrich.com

*N*ext time you board an airplane and settle into your seat for a flight, take a moment to consider the manufacturers responsible for the variety of elements around you. The Goodrich Aerospace segment manufactures passenger seats, evacuation slides, brakes, lighting systems, and landing gear. New Goodrich Inflatabelt® and Inflataband® passenger restraint systems incorporate air bags into seat belts for your additional safety.

Goodrich's other operating segments, Performance Materials and Engineered Industrial Products, produce items such as large diesel engines, air compressors, ingredients for pharmaceuticals and food, and coatings for wood and metal. As a manufacturing company, Goodrich continually strives to tighten manufacturing techniques and cut costs while maintaining quality.

Thinking Critically
What types of costs do you think go into the production of passenger aircraft seats?

For more information on Goodrich Corporation, go to:
collegeaccounting.glencoe.com.

New Terms

Direct labor

Direct materials

Finished goods inventory

Indirect labor

Indirect materials and supplies

Manufacturing overhead

Manufacturing Summary account

Raw materials

Statement of cost of goods manufactured

Work in process

Terms to Learn

direct labor
direct materials
finished goods inventory
indirect labor
indirect materials and supplies
manufacturing overhead
raw materials
statement of cost of goods
    manufactured
work in process

Accounting for Manufacturing Costs

Merchandising businesses purchase merchandise to be resold in the same condition and form but at a profit. Manufacturing businesses purchase and convert raw materials into finished goods to be sold at a profit.

Cost of Goods Manufactured

The difference between merchandising and manufacturing businesses is reflected in the income statements of the two types of businesses. You can see the similarities and differences by examining the partial income statements that follow. Note that the major difference is that a manufacturing business uses "Cost of Goods Manufactured" instead of "Purchases."

Volunteer Merchandising Company
Partial Income Statement
Year Ended December 31, 20--

Revenue		
Sales (net)		550 000 00
Cost of Goods Sold		
Merchandise Inventory, Jan. 1	30 000 00	
Purchases (net)	295 500 00	
Goods Available for Sale	325 500 00	
Less Merchandise Inventory, Dec. 31	26 000 00	
Cost of Goods Sold		299 500 00
Gross Profit on Sales		250 500 00

Latin Manufacturing Inc.
Partial Income Statement
Year Ended December 31, 20--

Revenue		
Sales (net)		550 000 00
Cost of Goods Sold		
Finished Goods Inventory, Jan. 1	30 000 00	
Cost of Goods Manufactured	295 500 00	
Total Goods Available for Sale	325 500 00	
Less Finished Goods Inventory, Dec. 31	26 000 00	
Cost of Goods Sold		299 500 00
Gross Profit on Sales		250 500 00

Let's look more closely at the components that make up the cost of goods manufactured in the financial statements of a manufacturing con-

Manufacturing

Industry Overview

From picture frames to clothes, airplanes to aspirin, manufacturing activities create products used in every sector of society. The base of the U.S. economy, manufacturing contributes approximately 23 percent of the gross domestic product.

Career Opportunities

- Financial Services—Plant Operations
- Production Cost Manager
- Quality Assurance Specialist
- Inventory Manager
- Master Production Scheduler
- Raw Materials Purchasing Agent

Preparing for a Manufacturing Career

- Tour a manufacturing plant in your area for insight into operations. Corporations such as Toyota, Texas Instruments, Levi Strauss, and Nissan offer tours at select locations.

- Gain an understanding of raw materials purchasing procedures and analysis of manufacturing financial statements.

- Develop skills in electronic communications, word processing, spreadsheets, network systems, technology adaptation and transfer, problem solving, critical thinking, team building, and decision making.

- Apply for educational scholarships funded through manufacturers such as Boeing, Steinway & Sons, and Merck.

- Participate in job shadowing at a company such as Caterpillar or Boeing.

- Learn to interpret tables, graphs, and charts for manufacturing specifications and systems operations.

- Obtain a bachelor's degree in accounting, finance, marketing, or management; participate in a manufacturing management graduate program for a career in management.

Thinking Critically

If you were hired as a procurement (purchasing) agent for an airplane manufacturer such as Lockheed Martin, what skills do you think would be required? Explain.

Internet Application

Use an Internet search engine to find average salary ranges for skilled manufacturing trade workers such as pipe fitters, tool makers, and machine operators. What average salaries are paid to manufacturing engineers or managers? List 10 job titles and their corresponding salary. Include the source of your information.

---

cern. We will examine the accounts and financial statements of Latin Manufacturing Inc., a producer of wooden tables. Its manufacturing process involves the acquisition and use of raw materials such as lumber, nails, glue, paint, and varnish. These materials are cut, shaped, assembled, painted, and polished in the factory and emerge as finished products ready for sale.

Statement of Cost of Goods Manufactured

The **statement of cost of goods manufactured** shows details of the cost of goods completed for a manufacturing business. This statement supports the Cost of Goods Sold figure shown on the income statement. Figure 28-1 on page 1004 shows the statement of cost of goods manufactured for Latin Manufacturing Inc.

❶ Objective

Prepare a statement of cost of goods manufactured.

Latin Manufacturing Inc.
Statement of Cost of Goods Manufactured
Year Ended December 31, 20--

Work in Process Inventory, Jan. 1			(5) 12 0 0 0 00
Raw Materials			
Raw Materials Inventory, Jan. 1		26 0 0 0 00	
Materials Purchases	150 0 0 0 00		
Less Purchases Discounts	(3 0 0 0 00)		
Net Purchases		147 0 0 0 00	
Total Materials Available		173 0 0 0 00	
Less Raw Materials Inventory, Dec. 31		23 0 0 0 00	
Raw Materials Used		(1) 150 0 0 0 00	
Direct Labor		(2) 85 0 0 0 00	
Manufacturing Overhead			
Indirect Labor	3 0 0 0 00		
Payroll Taxes—Factory	9 0 0 0 00		
Utilities—Factory	9 0 0 0 00		
Repairs and Maintenance—Factory	6 5 0 0 00		
Indirect Materials and Supplies	7 2 0 0 00		
Depreciation—Factory Building	8 0 0 0 00		
Depreciation—Factory Equipment	5 0 0 0 00		
Insurance—Factory	4 3 0 0 00		
Property Taxes—Factory	8 0 0 0 00		
Total Manufacturing Overhead		(3) 60 0 0 0 00	
Total Manufacturing Cost			(4) 295 0 0 0 00
Total Work in Process for Year			307 0 0 0 00
Less Work in Process Inventory, Dec. 31			(6) 11 5 0 0 00
Cost of Goods Manufactured			(7) 295 5 0 0 00

FIGURE 28-1 ▲
Statement of Cost of
Goods Manufactured

② Objective

Explain the basic components
of manufacturing cost.

Components of Manufacturing Costs

The components of manufacturing cost are the raw materials used **(1),** the direct labor **(2),** and the manufacturing overhead **(3).** The numbers in parentheses refer to amounts in Figure 28-1.

Raw Materials. A major component of manufacturing cost is **raw materials**—the materials placed into production. Let's examine how data about the cost of raw materials appears on the statement of cost of goods manufactured. The beginning inventory of raw materials, $26,000, is added to net purchases of raw materials, $147,000. Net purchases is materials purchases minus purchases discounts ($150,000 − $3,000). The result is total materials available, $173,000. The ending raw materials inventory, $23,000, is subtracted to determine the raw materials used, $150,000.

In this section, all references to materials (raw materials, materials purchases, and materials available) relate to direct materials. **Direct materials** are all items that go into a product and become part of it. For example, the direct materials in a table include the wood, hardware, glue, and paint or varnish.

Indirect materials and supplies are used in manufacturing a product but do not become part of the product. Indirect materials appear in the Manufacturing Overhead section of the statement. Indirect materials include sandpaper, steel wool, cleaning materials, and lubricants. Some businesses treat insignificant direct materials, such as glue, as indirect materials.

Direct Labor. **Direct labor** costs are the costs of the personnel who work directly on the product being manufactured. Direct labor includes workers who saw and shape the lumber, assemble the pieces into tables, and finish or paint them. On the statement of cost of goods manufactured, direct labor is $85,000. This amount is obtained from the **Direct Labor** account.

Indirect labor costs are the costs of personnel who support production but are not directly involved in the manufacture of a product, such as supervisory, repair and maintenance, and janitorial staff. Supervisors are included in indirect labor because although they ensure that the work is done properly, they do not work directly on the product. Indirect labor is included in the Manufacturing Overhead section of the statement.

Manufacturing Overhead. **Manufacturing overhead** includes all manufacturing costs that are not classified as direct materials or direct labor. In addition to indirect materials and supplies and indirect labor, manufacturing overhead includes utilities, depreciation, repair and maintenance, insurance, and property taxes for factory buildings and equipment. Manufacturing overhead also includes payroll taxes on factory wages.

> Careful planning of manufacturing techniques plays a significant role in jet assemblies at The Boeing Company. The many parts of the Joint Strike Fighter X-32 jet were manufactured in different Boeing facilities thousands of miles apart. Perfect assembly of the jet was accomplished using advanced techniques such as three-dimensional solid modeling and assembly simulation, laser-guided part positioning, and minimal tooling. Overhead costs for the jet's manufacture are compiled from all involved facilities.

Work in Process

On the statement of cost of goods manufactured, the total manufacturing cost **(4)** includes all raw materials used, all direct labor costs incurred, and all manufacturing overhead applicable to the current production period. However, it does not represent the total cost of goods manufactured because some products that were finished this period were started in the previous period. **Work in process** refers to partially completed units in the production process. At the end of each period, an estimate is made of the costs of raw materials, direct labor, and manufacturing overhead for the work in process. For Latin Manufacturing Inc. the beginning inventory of work in process was $12,000 **(5),** and the ending inventory of work in process was $11,500 **(6).** The numbers in parentheses refer to amounts in Figure 28-1.

On the statement of cost of goods manufactured, the beginning work in process is added to total manufacturing cost. The result is total work in process for the year. The ending work in process is subtracted from the total work in process for the year to arrive at the cost of goods manufactured **(7).**

Benchmarking
Benchmarking involves evaluating another company's business processes and adopting them to incorporate best practices to improve performance, search for innovative ideas and gain a competitive advantage. The goal of benchmarking is to learn from others, adapt, implement, and improve.

Income Statement for a Manufacturing Concern

Notice that the cost of goods manufactured from Figure 28-1 is used to calculate the cost of goods sold in the income statement. The income statement for Latin Manufacturing Inc. appears in Figure 28-2 below.

The cost of goods sold can differ from the cost of goods manufactured because of changes in the level of **finished goods inventory**. Some finished goods that are sold in the current period were made in previous periods. Some products made during the current period will be sold in later periods. In order to prepare the income statement, a count is made of the finished goods inventory at the end of each period.

In Figure 28-2 the beginning finished goods inventory, $30,000, is added to the cost of goods manufactured, $295,500. The result is the total finished goods available for sale, $325,500. The ending finished goods inventory, $26,000, is subtracted, and the difference represents the cost of goods sold, $299,500.

Important!

Income Statement
In the income statement of a manufacturing company, the line item "Cost of Goods Manufactured" replaces "Purchases."

FIGURE 28-2 ▶
Income Statement for a Manufacturing Concern

Latin Manufacturing Inc.				
Income Statement				
Year Ended December 31, 20--				
Revenue				
Sales			553 0 0 0 00	
Less Sales Returns and Allowances			3 0 0 0 00	
Net Sales			550 0 0 0 00	
Cost of Goods Sold				
Finished Goods Inventory, Jan. 1	30 0 0 0 00			
Cost of Goods Manufactured	295 5 0 0 00			
Total Goods Available for Sale	325 5 0 0 00			
Less Finished Goods Inventory, Dec. 31	26 0 0 0 00			
Cost of Goods Sold			299 5 0 0 00	
Gross Profit on Sales			250 5 0 0 00	
Operating Expenses				
Selling Expenses (Control)	88 0 0 0 00			
Administrative Expenses (Control)	100 0 0 0 00			
Total Operating Expenses			188 0 0 0 00	
Net Income before Income Taxes			62 5 0 0 00	
Income Tax Expense			15 6 2 5 00	
Net Income after Income Taxes			46 8 7 5 00	

Important!

Cost of Goods Sold
The cost of goods sold may differ from the cost of goods manufactured because of beginning and ending inventories of finished goods.

Balance Sheet for a Manufacturing Concern

④ Objective

Prepare a balance sheet for a manufacturing business.

Figure 28-3 on page 1007 shows the balance sheet for a manufacturing business. Notice that it includes three inventory categories: raw materials, work in process, and finished goods.

Latin Manufacturing Inc.
Balance Sheet
December 31, 20--

Assets						
Current Assets						
Cash					30 5 1 8 00	
Accounts Receivable			65 3 0 0 00			
Less Allowance for Doubtful Accounts			1 3 0 0 00		64 0 0 0 00	
Inventories						
Raw Materials			23 0 0 0 00			
Work in Process			11 5 0 0 00			
Finished Goods			26 0 0 0 00		60 5 0 0 00	
Prepaid Expenses						
Prepaid Insurance			1 6 0 0 00			
Supplies on Hand			8 0 0 00		2 4 0 0 00	
Total Current Assets					157 4 1 8 00	
Property, Plant, and Equipment						
Land			10 0 0 0 00			
Factory Building	120 0 0 0 00					
Less Accumulated Depreciation	24 0 0 0 00		96 0 0 0 00			
Factory Equipment	50 0 0 0 00					
Less Accumulated Depreciation	15 0 0 0 00		35 0 0 0 00			
Office Equipment	10 0 0 0 00					
Less Accumulated Depreciation	6 0 0 0 00		4 0 0 0 00			
Total Property, Plant, and Equipment					145 0 0 0 00	
Total Assets					302 4 1 8 00	
Liabilities and Stockholders' Equity						
Current Liabilities						
Accounts Payable					17 6 0 1 75	
Salaries and Wages Payable					2 5 0 0 00	
Employee Income Tax Payable					2 5 0 00	
Social Security Tax Payable					1 5 5 00	
Medicare Tax Payable					3 6 2 5	
Total Liabilities					20 5 4 3 00	
Stockholders' Equity						
Common Stock ($10 par value, 100,000 shares authorized)						
20,000 shares issued	200 0 0 0 00					
Paid-in Capital in Excess of Par Value	20 0 0 0 00					
Total Paid-in Capital			220 0 0 0 00			
Retained Earnings			61 8 7 5 00			
Total Stockholders' Equity					281 8 7 5 00	
Total Liabilities and Stockholders' Equity					302 4 1 8 00	

▲ FIGURE 28-3
Balance Sheet for a
Manufacturing Concern

> Manufacturing businesses balance the costs of production with quality and speed to market. Quincy Compressors, a subsidiary of Goodrich Corporation, set new standards in 1999 with its 3,000 component compressors. Efficient manufacturing techniques reduced production times, eliminated excess inventories, lowered costs, and achieved 99 percent on-time delivery.

Importance of Inventory in Manufacturing Business

Managing Inventory. Chapter 17 discussed the importance of the valuation of inventory. Many businesses actually count the number of each type of goods on hand, then multiply the number of units obtained during the count by the appropriate cost per unit. This is referred to as the process of taking a *physical inventory.* It is generally performed only at the end of a period.

Managers of manufacturing businesses, however, frequently need reliable information about inventory more frequently, sometimes on a daily basis. The procedure used to obtain this information is known as keeping a *perpetual inventory.* Additions to and deletions from all inventory accounts, such as finished goods, work in process, and materials, are recorded as they occur. Although this requires additional bookkeeping, many managers justify this cost because it enables them to aggressively control costs. Perpetual inventory records are customarily verified by taking a physical count at least once a year.

> On December 31, 1999, Boise Cascade Corporation's wood products and paper manufacturing facilities held inventories of $703.9 million. This amount included finished goods, work in process, logs and other raw materials, and supplies.

Section 1 Self Review

Questions

1. What are direct materials?
2. What is work in process?
3. How does the cost of goods manufactured relate to the income statement?

Exercises

4. The components of total manufacturing cost are
   a. cost of goods manufactured, cost of goods sold, and work in process.
   b. manufacturing overhead and administrative expenses.
   c. selling expenses, administrative expenses, and manufacturing overhead.
   d. raw materials used, direct labor, and manufacturing overhead.

5. Indirect labor for a manufacturing business includes the wages of
   a. factory repair and maintenance employees.
   b. employees who assemble the product.
   c. employees who sell the product.
   d. employees who finish and paint the product.

Analysis

6. What is the cost of goods manufactured if beginning work in process was $58,000, ending work in process was $60,000, raw materials used were $25,000, direct labor was $25,000, and manufacturing overhead was $15,000?

(Answers to Section 1 Self Review are on page 1033.)

Completing the Accounting Cycle

The worksheet for a manufacturing business has a section to facilitate the preparation of the statement of cost of goods manufactured. Refer to Figure 28-4 on pages 1010–1013 as we complete the worksheet for Latin Manufacturing Inc.

The Worksheet and Financial Statements

After all transactions have been journalized and posted, the worksheet is completed. The first step is to enter the trial balance.

Entering the Trial Balance on the Worksheet

Notice that there are several accounts unique to manufacturing businesses. There are three inventory accounts: **Raw Materials Inventory, Work in Process Inventory,** and **Finished Goods Inventory.** There is a **Direct Labor** account as well as various manufacturing overhead accounts that appear on the statement of cost of goods manufactured.

The **Manufacturing Summary account** is similar to the **Income Summary** account. All of the accounts that appear on the statement of cost of goods manufactured are closed to **Manufacturing Summary.** Then the balance of **Manufacturing Summary,** which represents the cost of goods manufactured, is closed to **Income Summary.**

Entering Adjusting Entries on the Worksheet

Notice that there are some adjustments that pertain to manufacturing operations only. Carefully trace each adjustment. For the sake of simplicity, selling and administrative expenses are recorded in the control accounts.

Ending Inventories

Six adjustments are made for inventory. **Raw Materials Inventory (a)** and **(b), Work in Process Inventory (c)** and **(d),** and **Finished Goods Inventory (e)** and **(f).** The inventory accounts are credited for beginning inventory amounts and debited for the ending inventory amounts. For **Raw Materials Inventory** and **Work in Process Inventory,** the adjustment is made to **Manufacturing Summary.** For **Finished Goods Inventory** the adjustment is made to **Income Summary.**

Uncollectible Accounts

Entry **(g)** is made to record the uncollectible accounts expense, which is estimated to be 0.2 percent of net sales, or $1,100 (0.002 × $550,000).

Section Objectives

5 **Prepare a worksheet for a manufacturing business.**

WHY IT'S IMPORTANT
There are accounts on the worksheet that are specific to manufacturing businesses.

6 **Record the end-of-period adjusting entries for a manufacturing business.**

WHY IT'S IMPORTANT
Adjusting entries are made in the same way for merchandising and manufacturing businesses.

7 **Record closing entries for a manufacturing business.**

WHY IT'S IMPORTANT
All manufacturing and operating costs are closed at the end of the period.

8 **Record reversing entries for a manufacturing business.**

WHY IT'S IMPORTANT
Reversing entries save time and help to reduce errors.

Terms to Learn
Manufacturing Summary account

5 **Objective**
Prepare a worksheet for a manufacturing business.

	ACCOUNT NAME	TRIAL BALANCE DEBIT	TRIAL BALANCE CREDIT	ADJUSTMENTS DEBIT	ADJUSTMENTS CREDIT	ADJUSTED TRIAL BALANCE DEBIT	ADJUSTED TRIAL BALANCE CREDIT
1	Cash	30 5 1 8 00				30 5 1 8 00	
2	Accounts Receivable	65 3 0 0 00				65 3 0 0 00	
3	Allowance for Doubtful Accounts		2 0 0 00		(g) 1 1 0 0 00		1 3 0 0 00
4	Raw Materials Inventory	26 0 0 0 00		(b)23 0 0 0 00	(a)26 0 0 0 00	23 0 0 0 00	
5	Work in Process Inventory	12 0 0 0 00		(d)11 5 0 0 00	(c)12 0 0 0 00	11 5 0 0 00	
6	Finished Goods Inventory	30 0 0 0 00		(f)26 0 0 0 00	(e)30 0 0 0 00	26 0 0 0 00	
7	Prepaid Insurance	6 0 0 0 00			(h) 4 4 0 0 00	1 6 0 0 00	
8	Supplies on Hand			(i) 8 0 0 00		8 0 0 00	
9	Land	10 0 0 0 00				10 0 0 0 00	
10	Factory Building	120 0 0 0 00				120 0 0 0 00	
11	Accum. Depr.—Factory Bldg.		16 0 0 0 00		(j) 8 0 0 0 00		24 0 0 0 00
12	Factory Equipment	50 0 0 0 00				50 0 0 0 00	
13	Accum. Depr.—Factory Equip.		10 0 0 0 00		(j) 5 0 0 0 00		15 0 0 0 00
14	Office Equipment	10 0 0 0 00				10 0 0 0 00	
15	Accum. Depr.—Office Equip.		5 0 0 0 00		(j) 1 0 0 0 00		6 0 0 0 00
16	Accounts Payable		17 6 0 1 75				17 6 0 1 75
17	Salaries and Wages Payable				(k) 2 5 0 0 00		2 5 0 0 00
18	Income Tax Payable				(m) 2 5 0 00		2 5 0 00
19	Social Security Tax Payable				(l) 1 5 5 00		1 5 5 00
20	Medicare Tax Payable				(l) 3 6 25		3 6 25
21	Employee Income Tax Payable						
22	Common Stock, $10 Par		200 0 0 0 00				200 0 0 0 00
23	Paid-in Cap. in Exc. of Par Value		20 0 0 0 00				20 0 0 0 00
24	Retained Earnings		15 0 0 0 00				15 0 0 0 00
25	Sales		553 0 0 0 00				553 0 0 0 00
26	Sales Returns and Allowances	3 0 0 0 00				3 0 0 0 00	
27	Materials Purchases	150 0 0 0 00				150 0 0 0 00	
28	Purchases Discounts		3 0 0 0 00				3 0 0 0 00
29	Direct Labor	83 0 0 0 00		(k) 2 0 0 0 00		85 0 0 0 00	
30	Indirect Labor	2 5 0 0 00		(k) 5 0 0 00		3 0 0 0 00	
31	Payroll Taxes—Factory	8 8 0 8 75		(l) 1 9 1 25		9 0 0 0 00	
32	Utilities—Factory	9 0 0 0 00				9 0 0 0 00	
33	Repairs & Maintenance—Factory	6 5 0 0 00				6 5 0 0 00	
34	Indirect Materials and Supplies	8 0 0 0 00			(i) 8 0 0 00	7 2 0 0 00	
35	Depreciation—Factory Bldg.			(j) 8 0 0 0 00		8 0 0 0 00	
36	Depreciation—Factory Equip.			(j) 5 0 0 0 00		5 0 0 0 00	
37	Insurance—Factory			(h) 4 3 0 0 00		4 3 0 0 00	
38	Property Taxes—Factory	8 0 0 0 00				8 0 0 0 00	
39	Selling Expense (Control)	88 0 0 0 00				88 0 0 0 00	
40	Administrative Expense (Control)	97 8 0 0 00		(g) 1 1 0 0 00		100 0 0 0 00	

▲ FIGURE 28-4
Worksheet for a
Manufacturing Concern

COST OF GOODS MANUFACTURED		INCOME STATEMENT		BALANCE SHEET		
DEBIT	CREDIT	DEBIT	CREDIT	DEBIT	CREDIT	
				30 5 1 8 00		1
				65 3 0 0 00		2
					1 3 0 0 00	3
				23 0 0 0 00		4
				11 5 0 0 00		5
				26 0 0 0 00		6
				1 6 0 0 00		7
				8 0 0 00		8
				10 0 0 0 00		9
				120 0 0 0 00		10
					24 0 0 0 00	11
				50 0 0 0 00		12
					15 0 0 0 00	13
				10 0 0 0 00		14
					6 0 0 0 00	15
					17 6 0 1 75	16
					2 5 0 0 00	17
					2 5 0 00	18
					1 5 5 00	19
					3 6 25	20
						21
					200 0 0 0 00	22
					20 0 0 0 00	23
					15 0 0 0 00	24
			553 0 0 0 00			25
		3 0 0 00				26
150 0 0 0 00						27
	3 0 0 00					28
85 0 0 0 00						29
3 0 0 0 00						30
9 0 0 0 00						31
9 0 0 0 00						32
6 5 0 0 00						33
7 2 0 0 00						34
8 0 0 0 00						35
5 0 0 0 00						36
4 3 0 0 00						37
8 0 0 0 00						38
		88 0 0 0 00				39
		100 0 0 0 00				40

	ACCOUNT NAME	TRIAL BALANCE		ADJUSTMENTS		ADJUSTED TRIAL BALANCE	
		DEBIT	CREDIT	DEBIT	CREDIT	DEBIT	CREDIT
41				(h) 100 00			
42				(j) 1 000 00			
43	Income Tax Expense	15 375 00		(m) 250 00		15 625 00	
44	Manufacturing Summary			(a)26 000 00	(b)23 000 00	26 000 00	23 000 00
45				(c)12 000 00	(d)11 500 00	12 000 00	11 500 00
46	Income Summary			(e)30 000 00	(f)26 000 00	30 000 00	26 000 00
47		839 801 75	839 801 75	151 741 25	151 741 25	918 343 00	918 343 00
48	Cost of Goods Manufactured						
49							
50	Net Income						

▲ **FIGURE 28-4** (continued)
Worksheet for a
Manufacturing Concern

Important!

Manufacturing Summary
All items that appear on
the statement of cost of
goods manufactured
are transferred to the
Manufacturing Summary
account.

Expired Insurance

Entry **(h)** records insurance expired during the year. Expired insurance includes $4,300 on assets related to manufacturing (equipment, buildings, and inventories) and $100 on office equipment.

Supplies on Hand

Entry **(i)** records the adjustment for supplies on hand. At Latin Manufacturing Inc., when manufacturing supplies are purchased they are debited to the **Indirect Materials and Supplies account,** a manufacturing overhead expense account. Manufacturing companies follow this procedure because most of the supplies are consumed in a short time. Supplies used in selling and in administrative activities are debited to the **Selling Expenses Control** and **Administrative Expenses Control** accounts.

At the end of December, there was $800 of factory supplies on hand. Adjustment **(i)** debits the asset account **Supplies on Hand** for $800 and credits the overhead account **Indirect Materials and Supplies** for $800. The cost of the sales and office supplies on hand is deemed immaterial.

Depreciation

Entry **(j)** records the adjustment for depreciation on assets for the year: $8,000 on the factory building, $5,000 on the factory equipment, and $1,000 on the office equipment.

Accrued Salaries and Wages

On December 31 accrued wages are $2,000 for direct labor and $500 for indirect labor. These accruals are recorded by entry **(k).**

Payroll Taxes on Accrued Payroll

Entry **(l)** records payroll taxes on the $2,500 accrued wages of factory workers at the end of the year. All of the workers have earned the maximum amount subject to federal and state unemployment taxes. Therefore, the accrual is for $155 (0.062 × $2,500) of social security tax and $36.25 (0.0145 × $2,500) of Medicare tax.

Recall

Accruals
Adjustments are made for items that relate to the current period but that have not been paid for and do not yet appear in the accounts.

COST OF GOODS MANUFACTURED		INCOME STATEMENT		BALANCE SHEET		
DEBIT	CREDIT	DEBIT	CREDIT	DEBIT	CREDIT	
						41
						42
		15 6 2 5 00				43
26 0 0 0 00	23 0 0 0 00					44
12 0 0 0 00	11 5 0 0 00					45
		30 0 0 0 00	26 0 0 0 00			46
333 0 0 0 00	37 5 0 0 00					47
	295 5 0 0 00	295 5 0 0 00				48
333 0 0 0 00	333 0 0 0 00	532 1 2 5 00	579 0 0 0 00	348 7 1 8 00	301 8 4 3 00	49
		46 8 7 5 00			46 8 7 5 00	50
		579 0 0 0 00	579 0 0 0 00	348 7 1 8 00	348 7 1 8 00	51

Income Tax Payable

The federal income tax is estimated to be 25 percent of the taxable income. Based on the worksheet, the estimated taxable income is $62,500, and the estimated income tax for the year is $15,625 ($62,500 × 0.25). During the year $15,375 of estimated tax payments were made. As a result, $250 ($15,625 − $15,375) of additional taxes are accrued on December 31. The accrual is recorded on the worksheet as entry **(m).**

Preparing the Adjusted Trial Balance on the Worksheet

Note that for the inventory accounts both the debit and credit amounts are entered in the **Manufacturing Summary** and **Income Summary** accounts because these amounts appear on the cost of goods manufactured statement and on the income statement.

Some accountants omit the Adjusted Trial Balance columns to reduce the number of columns in the worksheet. If these columns are omitted, the adjusted balances are extended to the appropriate statement columns.

Completing the Financial Statement Columns

Accounts that appear on the statement of cost of goods manufactured are extended to Cost of Goods Manufactured columns. Accounts that appear on the income statement are transferred to the Income Statement columns. Accounts that appear on the balance sheet are extended to the Balance Sheet columns.

In the Cost of Goods Manufactured section, total debits are $333,000 and total credits are $37,500. The difference is $295,500, which is the cost of goods manufactured. The $295,500 is entered in the Credit column of the Cost of Goods Manufactured section and the Debit column of the Income Statement section.

Preparing the Financial Statements

The financial statements and the statement of cost of goods manufactured are prepared from the worksheet.

Completing the Accounting Cycle

Once the financial statements have been prepared, the accountant completes the steps in the accounting cycle: adjusting entries, closing entries, postclosing trial balance, and interpretation of the financial information.

6 Objective

Record the end-of-period adjusting entries for a manufacturing business.

Recording and Posting Adjusting Entries

Figure 28-5 shows how the adjustments recorded on the worksheet are journalized. For the sake of brevity, journal entry explanations have been omitted.

			Debit	Credit	
1	20--	(Adjustment a)			1
2	Dec. 31	Manufacturing Summary	26 0 0 0 00		2
3		Raw Materials Inventory		26 0 0 0 00	3
4					4
5		(Adjustment b)			5
6	31	Raw Materials Inventory	23 0 0 0 00		6
7		Manufacturing Summary		23 0 0 0 00	7
8					8
9		(Adjustment c)			9
10	31	Manufacturing Summary	12 0 0 0 00		10
11		Work in Process Inventory		12 0 0 0 00	11
12					12
13		(Adjustment d)			13
14	31	Work in Process Inventory	11 5 0 0 00		14
15		Manufacturing Summary		11 5 0 0 00	15
16					16
17		(Adjustment e)			17
18	31	Income Summary	30 0 0 0 00		18
19		Finished Goods Inventory		30 0 0 0 00	19
20					20
21		(Adjustment f)			21
22	31	Finished Goods Inventory	26 0 0 0 00		22
23		Income Summary		26 0 0 0 00	23
24					24
25		(Adjustment g)			25
26	31	Administrative Expense (Control)	1 1 0 0 00		26
27		Allowance for Doubtful Accounts		1 1 0 0 00	27
28					28
29		(Adjustment h)			29
30	31	Insurance—Factory	4 3 0 0 00		30
31		Administrative Expense (Control)	1 0 0 00		31
32		Prepaid Insurance		4 4 0 0 00	32
33					33
34		(Adjustment i)			34
35	31	Supplies on Hand	8 0 0 00		35
36		Indirect Materials and Supplies		8 0 0 00	36
37					37
38					38
39					39
40					40

FIGURE 28-5 ▲
Adjusting Entries

1	20--	(Adjustment j)						1
2	Dec. 31	Depreciation—Factory Building	8 0 0 0 00					2
3		Depreciation—Factory Equipment	5 0 0 0 00					3
4		Administrative Expense (Control)	1 0 0 0 00					4
5		Accumulated Depr.—Factory Building			8 0 0 0 00			5
6		Accumulated Depr.—Factory Equipment			5 0 0 0 00			6
7		Accumulated Depr.—Office Equipment			1 0 0 0 00			7
8								8
9		(Adjustment k)						9
10	31	Direct Labor	2 0 0 0 00					10
11		Indirect Labor	5 0 0 00					11
12		Salaries and Wages Payable			2 5 0 0 00			12
13								13
14		(Adjustment l)						14
15	31	Payroll Taxes—Factory	1 9 1 25					15
16		Social Security Tax Payable			1 5 5 00			16
17		Medicare Tax Payable			3 6 25			17
18								18
19		(Adjustment m)						19
20	31	Income Tax Expense	2 5 0 00					20
21		Income Tax Payable			2 5 0 00			21
22								22

Recording Closing Entries

The closing entries of a manufacturing business are done in three steps.

Closing Accounts to Manufacturing Summary. Refer to the Cost of Goods Manufactured section of the worksheet (Figure 28-4). From the Credit column, close the **Purchases Discounts** account to **Manufacturing Summary.**

1		Closing Entries			1
2	Dec. 31	Purchases Discounts	3 0 0 0 00		2
3		Manufacturing Summary		3 0 0 0 00	3
4					4

From the Debit column, close the manufacturing costs to **Manufacturing Summary.** After these entries have been posted, the balance in the **Manufacturing Summary** account is a debit of $295,500.

5	Dec. 31	Manufacturing Summary	295 0 0 0 00		5
6		Materials Purchases		150 0 0 0 00	6
7		Direct Labor		85 0 0 0 00	7
8		Indirect Labor		3 0 0 0 00	8
9		Payroll Taxes—Factory		9 0 0 0 00	9
10		Utilities—Factory		9 0 0 0 00	10
11		Repairs and Maintenance—Factory		6 5 0 0 00	11
12		Indirect Materials and Supplies		7 2 0 0 00	12
13		Depreciation—Factory Building		8 0 0 0 00	13
14		Depreciation—Factory Equipment		5 0 0 0 00	14
15		Insurance—Factory		4 3 0 0 00	15
16		Property Taxes—Factory		8 0 0 0 00	16
17					17

Managerial IMPLICATIONS

Manufacturing Costs

- Managers of manufacturing concerns must have reliable accounting data in order to plan and control operations.

- In manufacturing businesses, managers need to control the costs incurred in the production of goods.

- The cost of goods manufactured statement provides detailed information about the individual cost elements and the total cost of manufacturing. Managers use this information to evaluate past performance and to guide future operations.

- The worksheet is an efficient way to summarize and classify information so that financial statements can be prepared easily and quickly.

- Reversing entries save time and help to prevent errors in the new period.

Thinking Critically
Why does a manufacturing business have multiple inventory accounts?

ACCOUNT _Manufacturing Summary_ ACCOUNT NO. _398_

DATE		DESCRIPTION	POST. REF.	DEBIT	CREDIT	BALANCE DEBIT	BALANCE CREDIT
20--							
Dec.	31	Adj. a		26 0 0 0 00		26 0 0 0 00	
	31	Adj. b			23 0 0 0 00	3 0 0 0 00	
	31	Adj. c		12 0 0 0 00		15 0 0 0 00	
	31	Adj. d			11 5 0 0 00	3 5 0 0 00	
	31	Closing			3 0 0 0 00	5 0 0 00	
	31	Closing		295 0 0 0 00		295 5 0 0 00	

Closing Revenue and Expense Accounts into Income Summary. The entries to close the revenue and expense accounts into **Income Summary** are almost identical to those for a merchandising concern. An additional account, **Manufacturing Summary,** is closed into **Income Summary.**

17	Dec.	31	Sales	553 0 0 0 00		17
18			Income Summary		553 0 0 0 00	18
19						19
20		31	Income Summary	502 1 2 5 00		20
21			Sales Returns and Allowances		3 0 0 0 00	21
22			Selling Expense (Control)		88 0 0 0 00	22
23			Administrative Expense (Control)		100 0 0 0 00	23
24			Income Tax Expense		15 6 2 5 00	24
25			Manufacturing Summary		295 5 0 0 00	25

Closing Income Summary. At this point all revenue and expense accounts are closed. The balance in the **Income Summary** account, $46,875, represents the net income after income taxes.

Manufacturing Costs

The IASB's Standard 2, *Inventories,* provides for the same treatment of manufacturing costs as presented in this chapter. Most countries are moving toward adopting this standard.

ACCOUNT *Income Summary*   ACCOUNT NO. *399*

DATE		DESCRIPTION	POST. REF.	DEBIT	CREDIT	BALANCE	
						DEBIT	CREDIT
20--							
Dec.	31	Adj. e		30 000 00		30 000 00	
	31	Adj. f			26 000 00	4 000 00	
	31	Closing			553 000 00		549 000 00
	31	Closing		502 125 00			46 875 00

The balance of the **Income Summary** account is closed to **Retained Earnings.**

27	Dec.	31	Income Summary		46 875 00		27
28			Retained Earnings			46 875 00	28

Preparing the Postclosing Trial Balance

After adjusting and closing entries have been posted to the ledger accounts, a postclosing trial balance is prepared to prove that the adjusting and closing entries were posted correctly. The ledger account balances should match those listed in the Balance Sheet section of the worksheet.

Recording the Reversing Entries

Reversing entries are made for adjustments for accruals. Reversing entries are also made for expenditures initially debited to expense accounts and then adjusted at the end of the year.

❽ Objective

Record reversing entries for a manufacturing business.

Section 2 Self Review

Questions

1. What are the column headings on the worksheet of a manufacturing business?

2. What is the difference between the worksheet for a manufacturing and a merchandising business?

3. To what account is the **Manufacturing Summary** account closed?

Exercises

4. On the completed worksheet of a manufacturing business, the accounts related to materials purchases, direct labor, and factory overhead appear in the

   a. Income Statement section.

   b. Cost of Goods Manufactured section.

   c. Balance Sheet section.

   d. Cost of Goods Sold section.

5. On the completed worksheet of a manufacturing business, the accounts related to raw materials inventory, work in process inventory, and finished goods inventory appear in the

   a. Income Statement section.

   b. Cost of Goods Manufactured section.

   c. Balance Sheet section.

   d. Cost of Goods Sold section.

Analysis

6. What is the journal entry to adjust for accrued wages of $2,000 for direct labor and $440 for indirect labor?

CHAPTER 28 Review and Applications

Review

Chapter Summary

A manufacturing company purchases raw materials that it converts into finished goods to be sold at a profit. You have learned the differences in the preparation of financial statements for a manufacturer and a merchandiser. A different set of accounts is required to classify the costs associated with manufacturing processes.

Learning Objectives

1 Prepare a statement of cost of goods manufactured.
A statement of cost of goods manufactured is prepared to show the results of the manufacturing activities and to support the income statement.

2 Explain the basic components of manufacturing cost.
Manufacturing costs are recorded in three categories:
- Raw materials are those materials placed into production and used to create finished goods. Raw materials include direct materials and indirect materials.
- Direct labor costs are costs of personnel who work directly on the product as it is manufactured.
- Manufacturing overhead includes costs of manufacturing operations that are not classified as direct labor or direct materials. Examples are insurance, property taxes, and utilities.

3 Prepare an income statement for a manufacturing business.
One major difference distinguishes the format of an income statement of a manufacturing business from that of a merchandising company.

The cost of goods manufactured is included on the income statement as part of Cost of Goods Sold, corresponding to the merchandise purchases on the income statement of a merchandising business.

4 Prepare a balance sheet for a manufacturing business.
The balance sheet of a manufacturing business is similar to that of a merchandising business. The only new accounts required are inventory accounts for raw materials, work in process, and finished goods. The **Finished Goods Inventory** account corresponds to the **Merchandise Inventory** account of a merchandising business.

5 Prepare a worksheet for a manufacturing business.
The worksheet for a manufacturing business is similar to one for a merchandising firm, but it has an added pair of columns in which to record the figures from the cost of goods manufactured statement.
- The worksheet gives the data used for the statement of cost of goods manufactured, the income statement, and the balance sheet.
- To prepare a statement of retained earnings, accountants analyze the **Retained Earnings** account in the general ledger for the details.

6 Record the end-of-period adjusting entries for a manufacturing business.
Adjustments for inventories, expired insurance, and accruals or deferrals are entered on the worksheet and then recorded and posted in the accounting records.

7 Record closing entries for a manufacturing business.
All accounts relating to the cost of goods manufactured are closed to **Manufacturing Summary**.
- The **Manufacturing Summary** account final balance—the cost of goods manufactured—is closed to the **Income Summary** account.
- All items in the Income Statement section of the worksheet are closed to **Income Summary.**
- The final closing entry transfers net income after income taxes to the **Retained Earnings** account.

8 Record reversing entries for a manufacturing business.
After the accounting records are adjusted and closed, a postclosing trial balance is prepared. At each new period, certain adjusting entries are reversed.

9 Define the accounting terms new to this chapter.

Direct labor (p. 1005) The costs attributable to personnel who work directly on the product being manufactured

Direct materials (p.1004) All items that go into a product and become a part of it

Finished goods inventory (p. 1006) The cost of completed products ready for sale; corresponds to the **Merchandise Inventory** account of a merchandising business

Indirect labor (p. 1005) Costs attributable to personnel who support production but are not directly involved in the manufacture of a product; for example, supervisory, repair and maintenance, and janitorial staff

Indirect materials and supplies (p. 1005) Materials used in manufacturing a product that do not become a part of the product

Manufacturing overhead (p. 1005) All manufacturing costs that are not classified as direct materials or direct labor

Manufacturing Summary account (p. 1009) The account to which all items on the statement of cost of goods manufactured are closed; similar to the **Income Summary** account

Raw materials (p. 1004) The materials placed into production

Statement of cost of goods manufactured (p. 1003) A financial report showing details of the cost of goods completed for a manufacturing business

Work in process (p. 1005) Partially completed units in the production process

Comprehensive Self Review

1. What are indirect materials?
2. What is direct labor cost?
3. Explain how the following items are handled on the worksheet:
   a. beginning and ending inventories of raw materials
   b. beginning and ending inventories of work in process
   c. beginning and ending inventories of finished goods
4. Does the **Manufacturing Summary** account have a balance during the fiscal period? Explain.
5. What entries are reversed at the beginning of the accounting period?

(Answers to Comprehensive Self Review are on page 1033.)

Discussion Questions

1. How do the accounting problems of a manufacturing business differ from those of a merchandising business?

2. What procedure is used on the statement of cost of goods manufactured to arrive at the cost of raw materials used?

3. What is indirect labor?

4. It is possible that one company might consider an item, such as paint, as one of its direct materials, while another company with identical manufacturing processes might classify the item as one of its indirect materials. Why?

5. How would the wages of the employee who issues materials from the factory storeroom be classified?

6. What is manufacturing overhead?

7. Why does the figure for total manufacturing cost not equal the cost of goods manufactured?

8. Name the three inventory accounts found in the chart of accounts of a manufacturing business and explain each one.

9. How is the work in process inventory determined?

10. Give five examples of manufacturing overhead items.

11. What is the relationship between the cost of goods manufactured and the income statement?

12. What is the source of the information for preparing the journal entry to close manufacturing cost accounts to the **Manufacturing Summary** account?

13. Are the financial statements prepared after the closing entries have been posted? Explain.

14. Is the statement of cost of goods manufactured prepared before or after the income statement? Explain.

15. Describe the flow of costs through the inventory accounts of a merchandising firm.

16. Give three examples not given in the chapter of indirect labor for a manufacturing firm.

17. How is the cost of goods sold determined for a manufacturing business?

18. Explain how a manufacturing business records reversing entries and why the reversing entries are made.

Applications

Cost of goods manufactured statement (partial).

◄ Exercise 28-1
Objective 1

The following selected items appeared in the adjustments columns of the worksheet for Manning Company on December 31, 20--. From this information, prepare the section of the statement of cost of goods manufactured relating to the cost of raw materials used.

Finished Goods Inventory	$ 62,000	$65,000
Work in Process Inventory	75,000	85,000
Raw Materials Inventory	50,000	51,000
Materials Purchases	680,000	
Purchases Returns and Allowances		3,000
Freight In (on Materials Purchases)	15,000	

Adjusting entries.

◄ Exercise 28-2
Objective 6

Using the data given in Exercise 28–1, prepare the general journal entry to record adjustments for inventory accounts.

Components of manufacturing cost.

◄ Exercise 28-3
Objective 2

LEH Company's beginning raw materials inventory was $195,000. Its net purchases for the period were $898,000, and its ending raw materials inventory was $157,000. What was its cost of raw materials used?

Components of manufacturing cost.

◄ Exercise 28-4
Objective 2

Bob Company's total manufacturing cost for the year was $1,922,000. Its manufacturing overhead was $250,000, and its cost of raw materials used was $722,000. What was its direct labor cost for the year?

Components of manufacturing cost.

◄ Exercise 28-5
Objective 2

Which of the following items would not appear on the statement of cost of goods manufactured?

1. Cost of travel to national trade show
2. Depreciation of factory equipment
3. Property taxes on factory building

Components of manufacturing cost.

◄ Exercise 28-6
Objective 2

Which of the following items would not be shown on the statement of cost of goods manufactured?

1. Work in process inventory
2. Finished goods inventory
3. Raw materials inventory

Components of manufacturing cost.

◄ Exercise 28-7
Objective 2

Which of the following items would not be included in the Manufacturing Overhead section of the statement of cost of goods manufactured?

1. Payroll taxes on wages of plant guards

2. Insurance costs for factory

3. Freight in charges on purchases of raw materials

Exercise 28-8 ▶
Objective 2
Components of manufacturing cost.

Which of the following items would be included in the Manufacturing Overhead section of the statement of cost of goods manufactured?

1. Direct labor

2. Repairs to factory building

3. Raw materials used

4. Indirect materials and supplies

5. Office supplies expense

6. Advertising expense

7. Depreciation of factory equipment

Exercise 28-9 ▶
Objective 5
Worksheet for a manufacturing business.

Which of the following account balances would not be extended to the Cost of Goods Manufactured section of the worksheet?

1. Payroll taxes on outside sales salaries

2. Insurance on finished goods

3. Salary of factory shift supervisor

4. Insurance on raw materials in factory storeroom

5. Salary of accounts receivable clerk

6. Utilities for factory

7. Payroll taxes on factory wages

8. Salary of factory forklift driver

9. Freight out

10. Insurance on factory equipment

Exercise 28-10 ▶
Objectives 6, 7, 8
Adjusting, closing, and reversing entries.

Information about certain account balances in the trial balance of Cherokee Corporation on December 31, 2004, follows.

a. Balance in **Raw Materials Inventory** account that reflects the beginning balance, December 31, $38,000; physical count on December 31 that reflects the ending balance, $37,500

b. Balance in **Prepaid Insurance** account, $15,000; insurance expired, $12,000

c. Balance in **Direct Labor** account, $83,000; accrued direct labor, $3,000

d. Balance in **Factory Supplies on Hand** account, $7,500; physical count shows supplies on hand, $500

Record the following in the general journal.

1. Adjusting entries required

2. Closing entries required

3. Reversing entries on January 1, 2005

Problems

Selected problems can be completed using:
▦ **Spreadsheets**

PROBLEM SET A

Preparing a statement of cost of goods manufactured and an income statement.

Wood Manufacturing Company makes picture frames. Selected account balances on December 31, 20--, the end of its fiscal year, are given below. Data about the beginning and ending inventories are also given.

◄ **Problem 28-1A**
Objectives 1, 3

INSTRUCTIONS

1. Prepare a statement of cost of goods manufactured for 20--.
2. Prepare an income statement for 20--.

Accounts	Balances
Sales	$717,500
Sales Returns and Allowances	5,500
Materials Purchases	150,000
Direct Labor	95,000
Indirect Labor	23,000
Payroll Taxes—Factory	11,800
Utilities—Factory	10,000
Repairs and Maintenance—Factory	6,500
Indirect Materials and Supplies	6,000
Depreciation—Factory Building	5,000
Depreciation—Factory Equipment	4,500
Insurance—Factory	6,000
Property Taxes—Factory	3,400
Sales Salaries Expense	102,000
Payroll Taxes Expense—Selling	10,200
Delivery Expense	12,000
Advertising Expense	6,000
Miscellaneous Selling Expenses	24,500
Officers' Salaries Expense	95,000
Office Salaries Expense	25,000
Payroll Taxes Expense—Administrative	10,000
Other Administrative Expenses	5,000
Income Tax Expense	23,775

Inventory Data	Jan. 1, 20--	Dec. 31, 20--
Finished Goods Inventory	$30,000	$28,000
Work in Process Inventory	29,000	22,000
Raw Materials Inventory	20,000	23,000

Analyze: For every dollar earned in net sales, what portion was spent on manufacturing costs?

Preparing a statement of cost of goods manufactured, an income statement, a statement of retained earnings, and a balance sheet; completing the worksheet; recording adjusting, closing, and reversing entries.

Music Corporation manufactures parts for CD players. The Trial Balance section of its worksheet and other year-end data follow.

INSTRUCTIONS

1. Prepare a 12-column manufacturing worksheet for the year ended December 31, 2004. Enter the trial balance in the first two columns.

2. Using the data given, enter the adjustments. Then complete the worksheet. Label all inventory adjustments as (a).

3. Prepare a statement of cost of goods manufactured.

4. Prepare an income statement.

5. Prepare a statement of retained earnings. Additional data needed is as follows.

   a. Balance of **Retained Earnings** on January 1 was $180,000.

   b. Dividends declared and paid on common stock during the year amounted to $5,000.

   c. There were no changes in any other stockholders' equity accounts.

6. Prepare a balance sheet as of December 31, 2004. There are 50,000 shares of $1 par common stock outstanding, out of the 100,000 shares authorized.

7. Record the adjusting entries shown on the worksheet in general journal form. For each journal entry, use the letter that identifies the adjustment on the worksheet. Make a separate entry for each inventory adjustment. Do not give explanations.

8. Prepare the closing entries for all accounts involved in the cost of goods manufactured.

9. Prepare the closing entries for all revenue and expense accounts and the **Manufacturing Summary** account.

10. Prepare the closing entry to close the **Income Summary** account.

11. Journalize the reversing entries. Date the entries January 1, 2005.

Music Corporation
Trial Balance
December 31, 2004

ACCOUNT NAME	DEBIT	CREDIT
Cash	39 000 00	
Accounts Receivable	79 000 00	
Allowance for Doubtful Accounts		2 000 00
Raw Materials Inventory	22 000 00	
Work in Process Inventory	35 000 00	
Finished Goods Inventory	25 500 00	
Prepaid Insurance	2 400 00	
Factory Supplies	5 000 00	
Land	50 000 00	
Factory Building	150 000 00	
Accumulated Depreciation—Factory Building		45 000 00

(Continued)

(cont.)

Account	Debit	Credit
Factory Machines	50 0 0 0 00	
Accumulated Depreciation—Factory Machines		15 0 0 0 00
Office Furniture and Equipment	20 0 0 0 00	
Accumulated Depreciation—Office Furn. and Equip.		6 0 0 0 00
Accounts Payable		66 0 0 0 00
Salaries and Wages Payable		
Income Tax Payable		
Social Security Tax Payable		
Medicare Tax Payable		
Employee Income Tax Payable		
Common Stock		50 0 0 0 00
Retained Earnings		175 0 0 0 00
Sales		953 3 0 0 00
Sales Returns and Allowances	6 5 0 0 00	
Materials Purchases	295 0 0 0 00	
Purchases Returns and Allowances		5 0 0 0 00
Freight In	8 0 0 0 00	
Direct Labor	150 0 0 0 00	
Indirect Labor	39 0 0 0 00	
Payroll Taxes—Factory	17 5 0 0 00	
Utilities—Factory	25 0 0 0 00	
Repairs and Maintenance—Factory	7 5 0 0 00	
Indirect Materials and Supplies	7 9 0 0 00	
Depreciation—Factory Building		
Depreciation—Factory Machines		
Insurance—Factory		
Property Taxes—Factory	8 0 0 0 00	
Sales Salaries Expense	75 0 0 0 00	
Payroll Taxes Expense—Sales	7 5 0 0 00	
Delivery Expense	4 5 0 0 00	
Advertising Expense	2 0 0 0 00	
Uncollectible Accounts Expense		
Miscellaneous Selling Expense	8 5 0 0 00	
Officers' Salaries Expense	115 0 0 0 00	
Office Salaries Expense	35 0 0 0 00	
Payroll Taxes Expense—Administrative	15 0 0 0 00	
Depreciation Expense—Office Furn. and Equip.		
Other Administrative Expenses	2 5 0 0 00	
Income Tax Expense	10 0 0 0 00	
Manufacturing Summary		
Income Summary		
Totals	1317 3 0 0 00	1317 3 0 0 00

YEAR-END DATA

a. Physical inventories taken on December 31, 2004, show $19,000 of raw materials on hand and $23,500 of finished goods on hand. The work in process inventory is estimated to be $37,500 on the same date.

b. It is estimated that 3 percent of the outstanding accounts receivable might not be collectible.

c. Of the prepaid insurance, $1,800 covering the factory building and equipment has expired.

d. A physical inventory discloses $2,000 of factory supplies unused at the end of the period.

e. Depreciation expense for the year is as follows: $15,000 on the factory building, $5,000 on the factory machines, and $2,000 on the office furniture. (Make a compound entry.)

f. Payroll accruals at the end of the period include $2,800 of direct labor and $200 of indirect labor.

g. Payroll taxes on accrued wages are social security, 6.2 percent, and Medicare tax, 1.45 percent (round computations to nearest dollar).

h. The total income tax for the year is $24,000.

Analyze: Assume that the industry standard for direct labor costs is 20 percent of total manufacturing costs. How is Music Corporation performing as compared to this industry standard? Explain.

PROBLEM SET B

Problem 28-1B ►
Objectives 1, 3

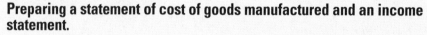

Preparing a statement of cost of goods manufactured and an income statement.

Redhot Manufacturing Company makes electric heaters. Selected account balances (listed alphabetically) for this firm on December 31, 20--, the end of its fiscal year, are given below. Data about the beginning and ending inventories is also shown.

INSTRUCTIONS

1. Prepare a statement of cost of goods manufactured for 20--.
2. Prepare an income statement for 20--.

Accounts	Balances
Depreciation—Factory Assets	$ 12,000
Depreciation Expense—Office Assets	3,200
Direct Labor	215,000
Freight In	15,000
Income Tax Expense	2,475
Indirect Labor	20,000
Indirect Materials and Supplies	6,000
Insurance—Factory	12,000
Materials Purchases	371,000
Office Salaries Expense	25,000
Officers' Salaries Expense	100,000
Other Administrative Expenses	5,000
Other Selling Expenses	15,000
Payroll Taxes Expense—Administrative	12,500
Payroll Taxes Expense—Factory	23,500
Payroll Taxes Expense—Sales Salaries	9,500
Property Taxes—Office	5,000
Property Taxes—Factory	8,000
Purchases Returns and Allowances	6,500

(Continued)

(cont.)

Repairs and Maintenance—Factory	2,000
Repairs and Maintenance—Office	1,500
Sales	978,000
Sales Returns and Allowances	9,800
Sales Salaries Expense	95,000

Inventory Data	Jan. 1, 20--	Dec. 31, 20--
Finished Goods Inventory	$35,500	$33,000
Work in Process Inventory	29,000	42,000
Raw Materials Inventory	62,000	49,500

Analyze: What percentage of total manufacturing costs did the company spend on raw materials? On direct labor costs? On overhead costs?

Preparing a statement of cost of goods manufactured, an income statement, a statement of retained earnings, and a balance sheet; completing the worksheet; recording adjusting, closing, and reversing entries.

◄ **Problem 28-2B**
Objectives 1, 3, 4, 5, 6, 7, 8

Riverboat Manufacturing Company makes boats. The Trial Balance section of its worksheet and other year-end data follow.

INSTRUCTIONS

1. Prepare a 12-column manufacturing worksheet for the fiscal year ended December 31, 2004. Enter the trial balance in the first two columns.

2. Using the data given, enter the adjustments and complete the worksheet. Label all inventory adjustments as (a).

3. Prepare a statement of cost of goods manufactured.

4. Prepare an income statement.

5. Prepare a statement of retained earnings. Additional data follows:

   a. Balance of **Retained Earnings,** January 1, was $172,375.

   b. Dividends declared and paid on common stock were $6,000.

6. Prepare a balance sheet as of December 31, 2004.

7. Record the adjusting entries shown on the worksheet in general journal form. For each journal entry, use the letter that identifies the adjustment on the worksheet. Make a separate entry for each inventory adjustment. Do not give explanations.

8. Prepare the closing entries for all accounts involved in the cost of goods manufactured.

9. Prepare the closing entries for all revenue and expense accounts and the **Manufacturing Summary** account.

10. Prepare the closing entry to close the **Income Summary** account.

11. Journalize the reversing entries. Date the entries January 1, 2005.

Riverboat Manufacturing Company
Trial Balance
December 31, 2004

ACCOUNT NAME	DEBIT	CREDIT
Cash	34 5 2 2 00	
Accounts Receivable	45 0 0 0 00	
Allowance for Doubtful Accounts		2 0 0 0 00
Raw Materials Inventory	25 5 0 0 00	
Work in Process Inventory	17 5 0 0 00	
Finished Goods Inventory	28 0 0 0 00	
Prepaid Insurance	3 2 0 0 00	
Factory Supplies	9 5 0 0 00	
Land	35 0 0 0 00	
Factory Building	150 0 0 0 00	
Accumulated Depreciation—Factory Building		10 0 0 0 00
Factory Machines	30 0 0 0 00	
Accumulated Depreciation—Factory Machines		6 0 0 0 00
Office Furniture and Equipment	20 0 0 0 00	
Accumulated Depreciation—Office Furn. and Equip.		6 0 0 0 00
Accounts Payable		66 0 0 0 00
Salaries and Wages Payable		
Income Tax Payable		
Social Security Tax Payable		
Medicare Tax Payable		
Federal Income Tax Witholding Payable		
Common Stock		60 0 0 0 00
Retained Earnings		166 3 7 5 00
Sales		899 5 0 0 00
Sales Returns and Allowances	8 5 0 0 00	
Materials Purchases	225 0 0 0 00	
Purchases Returns and Allowances		5 0 0 0 00
Freight In	8 0 0 0 00	
Direct Labor	100 0 0 0 00	
Indirect Labor	9 0 7 5 00	
Payroll Taxes—Factory	10 9 7 8 00	
Utilities—Factory	18 0 0 0 00	
Repairs and Maintenance—Factory	7 5 0 0 00	
Indirect Materials and Supplies		
Depreciation—Factory Building		
Depreciation—Factory Machines		
Insurance—Factory		
Property Taxes—Factory	8 0 0 0 00	
Sales Salaries Expense	125 0 0 0 00	
Payroll Taxes Expense—Sales	12 5 0 0 00	
Delivery Expense	25 0 0 0 00	
Advertising Expense	5 0 0 0 00	
Uncollectible Accounts Expense		
Miscellaneous Selling Expense	63 5 0 0 00	
Officers' Salaries Expense	135 0 0 0 00	
Office Salaries Expense	29 0 0 0 00	
Payroll Taxes Expense—Administrative	16 4 0 0 00	
Depreciation Expense—Office Furn. and Equip.		
Other Administrative Expenses	1 2 0 0 00	

(Continued)

(cont.)

Income Tax Expense	15 0 0 0 00			
Manufacturing Summary				
Income Summary				
Totals	1220 8 7 5 00		1220 8 7 5 00	

YEAR-END DATA

a. Ending inventories: finished goods, $29,000; work in process, $21,000; and raw materials, $21,000.

b. Estimated uncollectible accounts: increase **Allowance for Uncollectible Accounts** to 10 percent of **Accounts Receivable.**

c. Expired insurance, $2,400; debit the **Insurance—Factory** account for the amount of the necessary adjustment.

d. Factory materials and supplies on hand, $907.

e. Depreciation for the year: on factory building, $5,000; on factory machinery, $3,000; and on office equipment, $2,000.

f. Accrued factory wages: direct labor, $2,725; indirect labor, $275.

g. Accrued payroll taxes: social security, $186; Medicare tax, $43.

h. Total income tax expense for the year, $17,531.

Analyze: Assume that the industry standard for direct labor costs in the boat manufacturing industry is 31 percent of total manufacturing costs. How does this company compare to others in regard to this standard? Explain.

CHAPTER 28   CHALLENGE PROBLEM

Inventories

Certain information about the statement of cost of goods manufactured and the income statement for the year ended December 31, 20--, for Handy Production Company, a sole proprietorship, is given below.

Beginning inventory of finished goods, 95 percent of ending inventory	
Work in process inventory, January 1, 105 percent of ending inventory	
Net income (10% of net sales)	$50,000
Raw materials inventory, January 1	$30,000
Turnover of finished goods, based on ending inventory	10 times
Direct labor costs	$90,000
Manufacturing overhead, 120 percent of direct labor costs	
Work in process inventory, December 31	$18,000
Raw materials inventory, December 31	$29,000
Operating expenses, 15 percent of net sales	

INSTRUCTIONS

Prepare a statement of cost of goods manufactured and an income statement for the year.

Analyze: Did total inventories for Handy Production Company increase or decrease during the year? By what amount?

Incomplete Records

In January 20--, Jamie Wilson started LitePacks, a business manufacturing backpacks. Wilson was so busy with the manufacturing side of the business that she did not take time to set up detailed accounting records; the business checkbook was her only record of accounting transactions. When cash came in, she deposited the receipts in the bank, and when invoices were due, she wrote checks to pay them. Now it is the end of the year and Wilson would like to know how the business did during its first year of operation.

Wilson asks for your help in summarizing the first year's operations. A review of the checkbook yields the following information.

- Raw materials purchases paid for totaled $65,000.
- Wages paid to employees totaled $36,000, with payroll taxes relating to their wages of $3,600.
- Factory supplies cost $5,240.
- Utility bills paid totaled $1,260.
- Repairs to factory equipment were $900.
- Rent of $8,000 was paid on the factory building.

Discussions with Wilson disclose that $2,000 of raw materials have been received and used in the manufacturing process but have not yet been paid because the invoice for the purchase is not due until next year. Wilson has determined depreciation on the factory equipment for the year to be $900. An inventory taken on the last day of the year showed $4,600 of raw materials on hand, $5,300 of backpacks partially completed, and $3,500 of finished backpacks waiting to be sold.

INSTRUCTIONS

Prepare a statement of cost of goods manufactured for 20-- for LitePacks.

Business Connections

MANAGERIAL _FOCUS_ Manufacturing Concerns

◄ **Connection 1**

1. Why do managers need special manufacturing records and a separate statement reporting the costs involved in producing goods?

2. How can an inventory be taken if work in process items are in varying stages of completion at the end of the accounting period?

3. Why might management want to separate direct and indirect labor costs?

4. Why should the statement of cost of goods manufactured not be used alone to measure efficiency and control costs?

5. In this chapter we said that the value of sales supplies and office supplies on hand at period-end is considered too small to justify an adjusting entry. If this omission were questioned, (arguing that the accounting records should show everything), what would you say?

Ethical DILEMMA **Estimates** It is the end of the fiscal year and the vice president of production is ready to take the end-of-year physical inventory of raw materials. You have been asked to supervise this activity. The vice president calls you in and instructs you to "finish this by noon today." It is already 10 A.M., and you see no way to follow his instructions without estimating the inventories instead of counting them. You visit the materials storeroom and make your estimate without consulting any of the materials supervisors. The report is made to the vice president "confirming the inventory." No mention is made of your estimating rather than counting the inventory. Have you or the vice president violated any ethical standards?

◄ **Connection 2**

Street WISE:
Questions from the Real World **Purchases** Refer to the *1999 Annual Report* for The Home Depot, Inc. in Appendix B. Review the letter written to stockholders, customers, and associates.

◄ **Connection 3**

1. Based on this letter, what types of manufactured products does The Home Depot, Inc., purchase? What factors do you think the company weighs when purchasing items for resale in The Home Depot stores?

2. The letter describes "a commitment to leadership in addressing sustainable forestry and certification issues." What actions did the company take in 1999 toward that commitment?

FINANCIAL $TATEMENT ANALYSIS **Manufacturing Inventories** The following excerpt was taken from the Dole Food Company, Inc. *1999 Annual Report.*

◄ **Connection 4**

Note 5: Current Assets and Liabilities (in thousands)	1999	1998
Inventories		
Finished products	$175,574	$168,423
Raw materials and work in progress	181,690	156,623
Crop growing costs	55,221	47,676
Operating supplies and other	112,090	102,802
	$524,575	$475,524

Analyze:

1. What four categories does the company use to identify its inventories?

2. Which category accounts for the largest percentage of the total inventory amount in 1999?

3. How might this financial information be used by Dole Food Company, Inc. managers?

Analyze Online: Locate the company's Web site **(www.dole.com)**. Find the most recent annual report within the *Investor's Information* section of the site.

4. Review the Notes to Consolidated Financial Statements related to the company's inventories. What is the value of the ending inventory?

5. How is the total inventory categorized? What notable changes, if any, can you identify to the amounts of each inventory?

Connection 5 ► *Extending the Thought* **Manufacturing Costs and Profits** Ben & Jerry's Homemade Ice Cream merged with Unilever Corporation in 2000, but operates independently from Unilever's other ice cream producing businesses. In 1999, Ben & Jerry's manufacturing and packaging divisions introduced unbleached containers for ice cream. Using unbleached paper reduces the reliance on chlorine in the production process and thereby reduces the amount of dioxin, a carcinogen, in the environment. The company incurred increased manufacturing costs due to the pursuit of this environmental-friendly packaging option. Why do you think Ben & Jerry's management chose to incur additional manufacturing costs? What impact do you think the decision had on the company's profitability? Do you agree with the decision? Why or why not?

Connection 6 ► **Business Communication** **Letter** You have been hired as a consultant to Kevin O'Brien, a local businessman interested in purchasing the Glaze Ceramics Manufacturing Company. O'Brien has been the owner of a retail ceramics company for 12 years. He is not familiar, therefore, with manufacturing accounting practices or financial statements. Prepare a letter to O'Brien outlining the major differences between the financial statements for a merchandising business and those of a manufacturing concern. Include any other information that you feel would benefit O'Brien as he evaluates the accounting records of the manufacturing company. Remember that O'Brien will need your help in understanding terms that are unique to a manufacturing business.

Connection 7 ► **TeamWork** **Manufacturing Costs Data** The statement of cost of goods manufactured is often prepared and distributed to internal users only. Although the statement might not be available to external users of financial information, select data from the statement can be published or released in the form of a press release or quarterly earnings report. Using the Internet, search one or more of the following manufacturing industry Web sites for articles that address manufacturing costs.

- Manufacturing.net **(www.manufacturing.net)**
- Manufacturing Systems **(www.manufacturingsystems.com)**
- Manufacturing Center **(www.manufacturingcenter.com)**

inter NET
CONNECTION **Manufacturing Philosophies** Go to the Web site for The ◄ **Connection 8**
Association for Manufacturing Excellence at **www.ame.org.** Select *Con-cepts.* What is just-in-time? What is demand flow?

Answers to **Self Reviews**

Answers to Section 1 Self Review

1. Materials that go into a product and become a part of it.
2. Items that have been started into production but are not yet completed.
3. It becomes a part of the Total Goods Available for Sale in the income statement; it replaces Purchases.
4. **d.** raw materials used, direct labor, and manufacturing overhead.
5. **a.** factory repair and maintenance employees.
6. $63,000

Answers to Section 2 Self Review

1. Trial Balance, Adjustments, Adjusted Trial Balance, Cost of Goods Manufactured, Income Statement, and Balance Sheet.
2. The major way in which a manufacturing worksheet differs is in the addition of the Cost of Goods Manufactured columns.
3. The **Manufacturing Summary** account is closed into the **Income Summary** account.
4. **b.** Cost of Goods Manufactured section.
5. **c.** Balance Sheet section.
6.

Direct Labor	2,000	
Indirect Labor	440	
Salaries and Wages Payable		2,440

Answers to Comprehensive Self Review

1. Materials used in the manufacturing process that do not become part of the finished product.
2. The cost of those employees who are working directly on the product being manufactured.
3. The balances of the beginning inventories of raw materials and work in process are entered in the Adjustments columns as credits to the two inventory accounts and debits to the **Manufacturing Summary** account. The ending inventories of raw materials and work in process are entered in the Adjustments columns as debits to the inventory accounts and credits to the **Manufacturing Summary** account. The beginning inventory of finished goods is credited to **Finished Goods Inventory** and debited to **Income Summary**. The ending inventory of finished goods is debited to **Finished Goods Inventory** and credited to **Income Summary**.
4. No, the account is used only during the closing process.
5. The adjusting entries for accrued expenses and accrued income

CHAPTER 29

Learning Objectives

1. Explain how a job order cost accounting system operates.

2. Journalize the purchase and issuance of direct and indirect materials.

3. Maintain perpetual inventory records.

4. Record labor costs incurred and charge labor into production.

5. Compute overhead rates and apply overhead to jobs.

6. Compute overapplied or underapplied overhead and report it in the financial statements.

7. Maintain job order cost sheets.

8. Record the cost of jobs completed and the cost of goods sold under a perpetual inventory system.

9. Define the accounting terms new to this chapter.

Job Order Cost Accounting

New Terms

Finished goods subsidiary
ledger

Job order

Job order cost accounting

Job order cost sheet

Just-in-time system

Manufacturing overhead
ledger

Materials requisition

Overapplied overhead

Overhead application rate

Perpetual inventory
system

Process cost accounting

Production order

Raw materials ledger card

Raw materials subsidiary
ledger

Standard costs

Time tickets

Underapplied overhead

Work in process
subsidiary ledger

AVERY
DENNISON

www.averydennison.com

When you hear the name Avery
Dennison, you may think of labels
or office supplies. The California-
based company develops, manufactures, and
markets a wide range of products including
specialty tapes, chemicals, reflective highway
safety products, and adhesives.

Avery Dennison works with industrial
customers like Johnson & Johnson to develop
and manufacture custom products. A recent
Johnson & Johnson order led to the manufacture of a latex-free, non-sensitizing, emulsion
acrylic adhesive to be used in BAND-AID
brand adhesive bandages.

In 1999 and 2000, Avery Dennison produced 16 billion self-adhesive postage stamps
for another customer, the U.S. Postal Service.
Five-color printing methods were used along
with 20 percent recycled paper fiber.

Thinking Critically
**What types of raw materials inventories
do you think Avery Dennison holds?**

**For more information on Avery Dennison,
go to:**
collegeaccounting.glencoe.com.

Cost Accounting

Section Objective

1 Explain how a job order cost accounting system operates.

WHY IT'S IMPORTANT
Manufacturing businesses choose the accounting system best suited to provide detailed information about production costs.

Terms to Learn

job order
job order cost accounting
just-in-time system
perpetual inventory system
process cost accounting
production order
standard costs

1 Objective

Explain how a job order cost accounting system operates.

The statement of cost of goods manufactured provides information on manufacturing costs. However, it cannot be used to determine the cost of each unit produced and does not help in controlling costs during the accounting period. In this and subsequent chapters you will learn how to calculate the cost of producing items and track manufacturing costs.

Types of Cost Accounting Systems

There are two principal cost accounting systems:

- job order cost accounting system
- process cost accounting system

This chapter covers the job order cost accounting system. Chapter 30 introduces process cost accounting.

Standard cost accounting is described in Chapter 31. Standard cost accounting may be used with either the job order cost system or the process cost system.

Job Order Cost Accounting

The job order cost accounting system is used by businesses that produce special orders or produce more than one product in batches. Businesses that use job order cost accounting systems include custom drapery manufacturers, machine tool plants, and furniture manufacturers.

Under the **job order cost accounting** system, each "batch" of goods is produced under a **production order**, which is also known as a **job order** . Unit costs are determined for each production order. To calculate the cost per unit, divide the manufacturing costs for each order by the number of units produced.

Important!

Job Order Cost Accounting
Under a job order cost accounting system, unit costs are determined for products manufactured for each job order.

Process Cost Accounting

The **process cost accounting** system is used when standard products are manufactured using a continuous process. Businesses that use process cost accounting systems include cement plants, flour mills, and manufacturers of cake mixes.

Under the process cost accounting system, the cost of a unit of product is the sum of the unit costs in each department through which the product passes while it is being manufactured.

Important!

Process Cost Accounting
Under the process cost system, the unit cost of a product is computed by adding the unit costs from each producing department.

Standard Cost Accounting

Standard costs are a measure of what costs should be in an efficient operation. Managers can compare actual costs with standard costs to determine manufacturing efficiency. Standard cost accounting systems can be used with a job order cost accounting system or a process cost accounting system.

Cost Flows in a Job Order Cost System

Piedmont Manufacturing Corporation makes several types of tables. Customers order various tables in different quantities. Piedmont does not have a continuous manufacturing process; it produces the tables in batches. The business uses the job order cost system, which is designed to facilitate recording costs related to the following four manufacturing operations:

- Procurement (Purchasing)—obtaining materials, labor, and services necessary for the manufacturing process,
- Production—using materials, labor, and services on the factory floor,
- Warehousing—handling and storing finished goods,
- Selling—removing finished goods from the storeroom to fill orders.

Figure 29-1 summarizes the flow of costs through a job order cost accounting system.

To understand how **Raw Materials Inventory, Work in Process Inventory,** and **Finished Goods Inventory** fit into the flow of costs shown in Figure 29-1, you need to comprehend the perpetual inventory system.

The Perpetual Inventory System

The **perpetual inventory system** tracks the inventories on hand at all times. The following are typical procedures for the three types of inventory.

▼ FIGURE 29-1
Flow of Costs through Four Phases of Manufacturing

About Accounting

Survey of Manufacturers
Private industry and trade associations use results from the U.S. Census Bureau's Annual Survey of Manufacturers to plan operations, analyze markets, and make investment and production decisions.

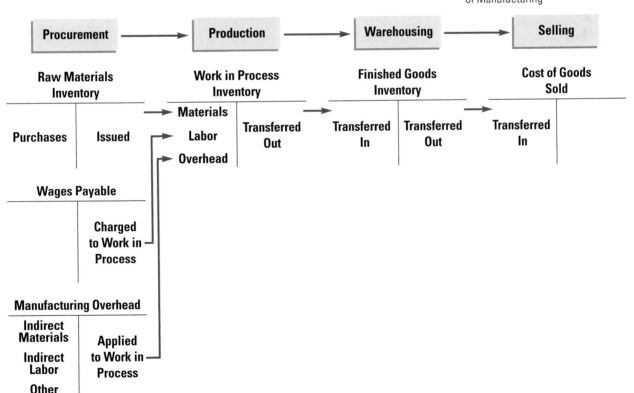

Raw Materials Inventory. Throughout the accounting period, raw materials and manufacturing supplies are recorded in the **Raw Materials Inventory** account. Purchases of raw materials and manufacturing supplies increase the **Raw Materials Inventory** account. The costs of materials used in production reduce the **Raw Materials Inventory** account. Direct materials used in production increase the **Work in Process Inventory** account. The costs of indirect materials and supplies used in production increase the **Manufacturing Overhead** account.

At the end of the accounting period, the balance of the **Raw Materials Inventory** account reflects the cost of materials and supplies on hand.

Recall

Cost Accounting System
In a manufacturing firm, managers must understand the costs of producing goods.

Beginning inventory of raw materials	XXX
Add purchases during period	XXX
Total available for use	XXX
Deduct materials used during year	XXX
Ending inventory of raw materials	XXX

At least once a year, a physical inventory count is taken to check the accuracy of the recorded inventory. In the event of a difference, the **Raw Materials Inventory** account is adjusted to agree with the physical inventory count.

> Manufacturing companies purchase raw materials in anticipation of product orders. The senior manager for raw materials purchasing at Boeing Commercial Airplanes Group told attendees at the Aluminum Outlook 2001 conference that the aerospace company anticipates airplane deliveries to increase by as much as 10 percent in the coming year. Other airplane makers such as Bombardier Inc. and Cessna are reporting record plane orders.

Work in Process Inventory. Throughout the accounting period, transactions involving production are recorded in the **Work in Process Inventory** account. All manufacturing costs placed into production during the accounting period are recorded in **Work in Process Inventory.** **Work in Process Inventory** is increased when direct materials are issued for production and for direct labor and manufacturing overhead charged into production. As production is completed, the manufacturing costs reduce **Work in Process Inventory** and increase **Finished Goods Inventory.** See Figure 29-1 for the flow of costs into and out of **Work in Process Inventory.**

The balance in the **Work in Process Inventory** account at the end of the period reflects the cost of partially completed units.

Beginning inventory of work in process	XXX
Add direct materials, direct labor, and manufacturing overhead charged to production	XXX
	XXX
Deduct cost of goods completed	XXX
Ending inventory of work in process	XXX

Finished Goods Inventory. Throughout the accounting period, transactions involving finished goods are recorded in the **Finished Goods Inventory** account. As goods are completed, the **Finished Goods Inventory** account is increased and the **Work in Process Inventory**

account is decreased. As goods are sold, **Finished Goods Inventory** is reduced, and the **Cost of Goods Sold** account is increased.

The balance of the **Finished Goods Inventory** account at the end of the period equals the cost of the finished goods on hand.

Beginning inventory of finished goods	xxx
Add cost of goods manufactured	xxx
	xxx
Deduct cost of goods sold	xxx
Ending inventory of finished goods	xxx

At least once a year, a physical inventory count is taken to check the accuracy of the recorded inventory.

Just-in-Time Inventory Systems

Some manufacturing companies attempt to eliminate raw materials inventory by using the **just-in-time system**, in which raw materials are ordered so they arrive just in time to be placed into production. When the goods arrive, they are moved immediately to the factory floor and the **Work in Process Inventory** account is increased. No entry is made in the **Raw Materials Inventory** account; in fact, there might not be a **Raw Materials Inventory** account.

The advantages of a just-in-time system are that it reduces the amount of working capital tied up in inventory, the space necessary for inventory storage, and the costs associated with storeroom personnel, insurance, and recordkeeping.

Just-in-time systems are risky unless the source of supply is highly dependable. Late deliveries or damaged materials could cause an interruption in supply that could halt manufacturing operations.

Inventory Valuation

The International Accounting Standards Board endorses average costing and FIFO (first in, first out) costing as the preferred inventory methods. It considers LIFO costing to be an acceptable, though not a preferred, method. In most countries, however, the LIFO (last in, first out) inventory method is not an acceptable inventory costing method.

Section 1 Self Review

Questions

1. What is a job order cost accounting system?

2. What is a standard cost?

3. Why are physical inventory counts made when a perpetual inventory system is used?

Exercises

4. A standard cost system can be used
   a. only with the process cost system.
   b. only with the job order cost system.
   c. in place of the job order cost system.
   d. with either the job order cost system or the process cost system.

5. Job order cost accounting is appropriate
   a. when there are continuous operations on standard types of products.
   b. when a company produces more than one product in batches rather than on a continuous basis.
   c. only for goods produced on special order.
   d. only when a company orders materials just-in-time to be placed into production.

Analysis

6. The beginning balance of **Work in Process Inventory** was $135,000. During the year direct materials of $55,000, direct labor of $35,000, and manufacturing overhead of $30,000 were charged to production. The ending inventory of work in process is $125,000. What is the cost of goods completed?

(Answers to Section 1 Self Review are on page 1061.)

Section Objectives

2 **Journalize the purchase and issuance of direct and indirect materials.**

WHY IT'S IMPORTANT
Raw materials must be accounted for.

3 **Maintain perpetual inventory records.**

WHY IT'S IMPORTANT
Physical counts are not needed for financial statements.

4 **Record labor costs incurred and charge labor into production.**

WHY IT'S IMPORTANT
Labor costs are often substantial.

5 **Compute overhead rates and apply overhead to jobs.**

WHY IT'S IMPORTANT
Businesses apply overhead to specific production jobs.

6 **Compute overapplied or underapplied overhead and report it in the financial statements.**

WHY IT'S IMPORTANT
Financial statements reflect a period's costs.

Terms to Learn

finished goods subsidiary
  ledger
mfg. overhead ledger
materials requisition
overapplied overhead
overhead application rate
raw materials ledger card
raw materials sub. ledger
time ticket
underapplied overhead
work in process sub. ledger

Job Order Cost Accounting System

Companies that use the job order cost accounting system include toy manufacturers, automobile manufacturers, and computer manufacturers.

A Job Order Cost Accounting System

The job order cost accounting system has procedures to record the costs incurred, the costs of items placed into production, and the transfer of products to finished goods.

Perpetual Inventory Accounts

The job order cost system uses three inventory accounts—**Raw Materials Inventory, Work in Process Inventory,** and **Finished Goods Inventory.** Each inventory account has a related subsidiary account. The **raw materials subsidiary ledger** contains a record for each of the different types of raw materials and manufacturing supplies used by the firm.

The **work in process subsidiary ledger** includes a job order cost sheet for each job in production. The **finished goods subsidiary ledger** contains a record for each of the different types of finished products.

Accounting for Materials

The **Raw Materials Inventory** account reflects all of the transactions related to raw materials and supplies.

Purchases of Materials. Purchases of raw materials and supplies are debited to the **Raw Materials Inventory** account. When a company uses a voucher register system, a special column is typically set up for Raw Materials Debit. All material purchases would be debited to that column. For simplicity, the raw material purchases are shown below as they would be entered in a general journal.

1	20--				1
2	June	30	Raw Materials Inventory	15 00 0 00	2
3			Accounts Payable	15 00 0 00	3
4			Cost of materials and supplies		4
5			purchased during June		5

Raw Materials Ledger. For internal control purposes, all purchases are made using prenumbered purchase orders. When the materials and supplies are received, they are checked and counted or weighed. They are sent to the storeroom with a report showing what was received. Before the invoice is approved for payment, a copy of the receiving report is compared with the supplier's invoice and with the purchase order. Prices and quantities are entered in each item's **raw materials ledger card**.

Figure 29-2 shows a raw materials ledger card. This card is for LAM02, a brace. The card shows no balance for material LAM02 at the beginning of the month. On June 3, 200 braces were purchased on Purchase Order PO-3 for $1 each. After this transaction the 200 units are reflected in the Balance section of the ledger card.

② Objective

Journalize the purchase and issuance of direct and indirect materials.

◄ **FIGURE 29-2**
Raw Materials Ledger Card

RAW MATERIALS LEDGER CARD
(FIFO Cost Method)

ITEM: *Brace* NUMBER: *LAM02*

DATE		REF.	RECEIVED			ISSUED			BALANCE		
			UNITS	PRICE	AMOUNT	UNITS	PRICE	AMOUNT	UNITS	PRICE	AMOUNT
20--		Bal									0
June	3	PO-3	200	1 00	200 00				200	1 00	200 00
	8	R-24				100	1 00	100 00	100	1 00	100 00
	12	PO-14	150	1 10	165 00				100	1 00	
									150	1 10	265 00
	17	R-51				100	1 00				
						50	1 10	155 00	100	1 10	110 00
	24	PO-32	100	1 16	116 00				100	1 10	
									100	1 16	226 00
	29	R-90				100	1 10	110 00	100	1 16	116 00

Materials Requisition. Materials or supplies are issued by the storeroom only upon presentation of a materials requisition signed by an authorized employee. The **materials requisition** describes the item and quantity needed and shows the job or purpose. Jobs are identified by a job order number, which is assigned when production on the job begins. The raw materials ledger clerk prices the items listed on the materials requisition. The storeroom clerk uses the materials requisition to record materials issued on the individual raw materials ledger cards.

Figure 29-3 illustrates a requisition for Piedmont Manufacturing Corporation issuing 100 units of material LAM02 on June 8.

Important!

Perpetual Inventory System
When a cost accounting system is used, perpetual inventory records are kept for raw materials, work in process, and finished goods.

③ Objective

Maintain perpetual inventory records.

◄ **FIGURE 29-3**
Materials Requisition Form

MATERIALS REQUISITION

No. R-24

Charged to Account No. *122*

Job No. *J-5* Date: *June 8, 20--*

Quantity	Description	Unit Cost	Total Cost
100	Braces LAM02	1 00	100 00

Authorized by: J. Sinclair

Issued by: E. Layden

Received by: T. Santos

Recall

Subsidiary Records
The job order cost sheet is a subsidiary record showing all manufacturing costs charged to a specific job. The subsidiary record supports the **Work in Process** inventory account.

Recall

Methods determining costs of inventory:
- First in, first out (FIFO)
- Last in, first out (LIFO)
- Average cost of similar items during a specified period (average cost)

Now look at the second entry on the raw materials ledger card in Figure 29-2. This entry on Requisition R-24 shows the issuance of 100 braces. The braces cost $1 each. After this transaction, 100 units are on hand at a cost of $1 per brace.

At the end of the month, the raw materials ledger clerk at Piedmont Manufacturing Corporation summarized all issued material requisitions. The summary classified the direct materials costs by jobs and listed the supplies and indirect materials issued. The summary is the basis for entries on the job order cost sheets and for a journal entry to record materials issued. The journal entry has a debit to **Work in Process Inventory** for $9,200 of direct materials placed into production, a debit to **Manufacturing Overhead** for $400 of indirect materials and supplies issued, and a credit to **Raw Materials Inventory** for the $9,600. The journal entry to record materials and supplies issued is as follows.

1	20--				1
2	June	30	Work in Process Inventory	9 2 0 0 00	2
3			Manufacturing Overhead	4 0 0 00	3
4			Raw Materials Inventory	9 6 0 0 00	4
5			Cost of materials and supplies		5
6			issued during month		6
7					7
8					8

Cost Basis. In Chapter 17 you learned that there are different methods for determining the cost of inventory including FIFO, LIFO, and average cost methods. In conformity with the consistency principle, each business chooses a cost method and follows it. Piedmont Manufacturing Corporation uses the FIFO method. Figure 29-2 shows how the FIFO method is applied to purchases and requisitions of LAM02 braces. The entry on June 12 reflects the purchase of an additional 150 units at a cost of $1.10 per unit. After this transaction there are 250 units on hand. The units are identified with specific purchases. There are 100 units from the purchase of June 3, at a cost of $1.00 per unit, and 150 units from the purchase of June 12, at a cost of $1.10 per unit. The entry on June 17 reflects the issuance of 150 units. Under the FIFO method, the units issued are assumed to be:

100 units from the purchase of June 3	
100 units × $1.00 per unit	$100.00
50 units from purchase of June 12	
50 units × $1.10 per unit	55.00
Total 150 units	$155.00

It is assumed that all units purchased on the June 3 order were issued. The 100 units on hand come from the June 12 purchase. The balance of LAM02 after the June 17 issuance is 100 units at $110 (100 × $1.10).

④ Objective

Record labor costs incurred and charge labor into production.

Accounting for Labor

Factory labor costs are identified as direct labor, which is recorded in **Work in Process Inventory,** or as indirect labor, which is recorded in **Manufacturing Overhead.** The factory labor costs incurred during June follow.

Payroll Period	Direct Labor	Indirect Labor	Total
June 8	$1,500	$ 200	$1,700
15	1,400	250	1,650
22	1,300	250	1,550
29	1,100	525	1,625
Totals	$5,300	$1,225	$6,525

The entry to record the payroll data in general journal form follows.

1	20--				1
14	June 30	Work in Process Inv. (Direct Labor)	5 3 0 0 00		14
15		Manufacturing Overhead (Indirect Labor)	1 2 2 5 00		15
16		Social Security Tax Payable		4 0 4 55	16
17		Medicare Tax Payable		9 4 61	17
18		Employee Income Tax Payable		9 7 8 75	18
19		Salaries and Wages Payable		5 0 4 7 09	19
20		Total labor costs for June			20
21					21

Employees record the time they enter and leave the plant. Workers complete a separate **time ticket** for each job indicating the job performed and the starting and stopping time. If the worker is idle for part of the day, an "idle time" time ticket is prepared so that the cost of idle time can be charged appropriately.

Usually idle time is charged to manufacturing overhead. If, however, the idle time is due solely to the specifications or peculiarities of a particular job, the idle time costs are charged to that job. Figure 29-4 shows a manual time ticket.

LABOR TIME TICKET

Name___Martin Davidson___ Date: _June 8,_ 20 _--_

Description of work	Time started ___8:00___
Assembling tables	Time stopped ___10:20___
	Hours worked___2 1/3___
	Rate of pay ___$9.00___
	Total charge ___$21.00___

Charge Job No.___J-5___

Approved by: ___J. Sinclair___

◄ FIGURE 29-4
Labor Time Ticket

Important!

Work in Process Inventory
The balance in the **Work in Process Inventory** account at the end of the period reflects the cost of work still incomplete at that time.

A cost clerk computes the total time shown on the time ticket and applies the worker's rate to obtain the cost of the labor. Labor time tickets are sorted by job and summarized at the end of each payroll period for entry on individual job order cost sheets. The total charged to all the cost sheets must agree with the direct labor debited to **Work in Process Inventory.**

Many factories use automated systems for recording the time spent by an employee on each task. Each employee has an identification card. When starting and completing work on a specific job, the employee inserts the identification card into a register or scanner. The time spent on the job is recorded electronically.

⑤ Objective

Compute overhead rates and apply overhead to jobs.

Accounting for Manufacturing Overhead

Manufacturing overhead includes all manufacturing costs except direct materials and direct labor. Common overhead items are indirect labor, indirect materials, depreciation of factory buildings and equipment, insurance, utilities, property taxes, repairs and maintenance, and payroll taxes on factory labor. There are different ways to enter overhead costs in the accounting records. Piedmont Manufacturing Corporation uses an account called **Manufacturing Overhead.** A subsidiary ledger, the **manufacturing overhead ledger**, contains a record for each overhead item. The overhead costs incurred are debited to the control account, and the details are posted to the appropriate subsidiary ledger accounts.

We have already seen that Piedmont incurred indirect materials costs (supplies) of $400 and indirect labor costs of $1,225. These amounts were debited to **Manufacturing Overhead** (see entries on pages 1042 and 1043). In addition to indirect materials and indirect labor, the company incurred overhead costs of $2,425. The entry to record these additional overhead costs in general journal form follows.

9	June	30	Manufacturing Overhead		2 4 2 5 00	9
10			Accounts Payable and other accounts		2 4 2 5 00	10
11			Overhead costs for June			11
12						12
13						13
14						14

Basing Overhead Application on Direct Labor Costs. Several methods are used to apply overhead to specific jobs, including those based on direct labor costs or direct labor hours. Piedmont Manufacturing Corporation's accountant estimates overhead and direct labor costs for the coming year. Estimated total overhead is divided by estimated total direct labor costs. The result is a predetermined **overhead application rate**. Using summaries of labor time tickets, direct labor is recorded for each job. At the same time, the direct labor costs are multiplied by the overhead rate. The result is the amount of overhead to record for each job.

Piedmont Manufacturing Corporation calculated an overhead rate of 75 percent of direct labor costs as follows.

$$\frac{\text{Estimated overhead costs}}{\text{Estimated direct labor costs}} = \frac{\$\ 90{,}000}{\$120{,}000} = 75\text{ percent}$$

In June direct labor costs charged to jobs totaled $5,300. The overhead applied to jobs was $3,975 ($5,300 × 0.75). This is recorded in general journal form as follows.

15	June	30	Work in Process Inventory		3 9 7 5 00	15
16			Manufacturing Overhead Applied		3 9 7 5 00	16
17			Overhead applied to jobs in June at			17
18			75% of direct labor costs			18
19						19
20						20
21						21

Overapplied or Underapplied Overhead. During the year the actual overhead incurred is debited to **Manufacturing Overhead.** When overhead is applied to jobs, the credit is to **Manufacturing Overhead Applied.** At the end of each month, the two accounts are compared.

○6 **Objective**

Compute overapplied or underapplied overhead and report it in the financial statements.

- If the total debits in **Manufacturing Overhead** are higher than the total credits in **Manufacturing Overhead Applied,** there is **underapplied overhead**.
- If the total debits in **Manufacturing Overhead** are less than the total credits in **Manufacturing Overhead Applied,** there is **overapplied overhead**.

In June overhead was underapplied by $75.

Manufacturing Overhead (debits)

Indirect materials and supplies	$ 400	
Indirect labor	1,225	
Other overhead costs	2,425	
Total charged to manufacturing overhead		$4,050
Manufacturing Overhead Applied (credits)		3,975
Underapplied overhead in June		$ 75

During the year underapplied or overapplied overhead occurs, in part, because the application rate is an average based on estimates for the year, and fluctuations happen from month to month.

At the end of the year, the **Manufacturing Overhead Applied** account is closed into the **Manufacturing Overhead** account. The balance in the **Manufacturing Overhead** account represents the underapplied or overapplied overhead for the year, which is closed to the **Cost of Goods Sold** account. The overapplied or underapplied amount appears as an adjustment to the Cost of Goods Sold amount on the income statement.

Section 2 Self Review

Questions

1. When direct materials are issued from the storeroom, are any entries made in the subsidiary records?

2. What entry is made for indirect materials issued from the storeroom?

3. What is overapplied overhead?

Exercises

4. The entry to record the application of overhead to jobs consists of a

   a. debit to **Manufacturing Overhead** and a credit to **Manufacturing Overhead Applied.**

   b. debit to **Manufacturing Overhead Applied** and a credit to **Manufacturing Overhead.**

   c. debit to **Work in Process Inventory** and a credit to **Manufacturing Overhead Applied.**

   d. debit to **Manufacturing Overhead Applied** and a credit to **Work in Process Inventory.**

5. At the end of the year, any underapplied overhead is shown as an adjustment to

   a. **Raw Materials Inventory.**

   b. **Cost of Goods Sold.**

   c. **Manufacturing Overhead Applied.**

   d. **Manufacturing Overhead.**

Analysis

6. A firm applies overhead based on direct labor hours. The firm estimates direct labor hours of 4,000 and overhead costs of $26,000. What is the overhead application rate?

Section Objectives

7 Maintain job order cost sheets.

WHY IT'S IMPORTANT
The job order cost sheet shows all manufacturing costs for a specific job.

8 Record the cost of jobs completed and the cost of goods sold under a perpetual inventory system.

WHY IT'S IMPORTANT
Manufacturing records need to reflect all the costs of a manufactured product.

Terms to Learn

job order cost sheet

7 Objective

Maintain job order cost sheets.

Accounting for Job Orders

Each new job started in production is assigned a number for identification and reference. A job order cost sheet is also set up at this time.

The Job Order Cost Sheet

A **job order cost sheet** is a record of all manufacturing costs charged to a specific job. It is set up when a job starts production. The cost sheets for all jobs currently in production constitute the subsidiary ledger for the **Work in Process Inventory** account.

Figure 29-5 shows the job order cost sheet for job J-5. The job was started and completed during the month of June. The information at the top of the sheet shows the job number and the product being manufactured, the start and completion dates, and the number of units ordered and produced.

- Direct materials used are entered weekly in the Materials section from summaries of materials requisitions.
- Direct labor costs are entered weekly in the Labor section from summaries of the labor time tickets.
- Overhead is computed using the predetermined overhead application rate (75 percent of direct labor costs). Overhead is entered in the Overhead Applied section.
- When the job has been completed, the costs are totaled in the Summary section. The unit cost is determined by dividing the total cost by the number of units produced.

FIGURE 29-5 ▶
Job Order Cost Sheet

JOB ORDER COST SHEET

For Stock _____X_____   Job No. ___J-5___ Date ___—___
Customer's Name _____   Started ___June 3, 20--___
Address _____   Completed ___June 15, 20--___
Item ___X123 Tables___   Quantity ___25___ (ordered)   ___25___ (completed)

MATERIALS		LABOR		OVERHEAD APPLIED			SUMMARY	
Date	Amount	Date	Amount	Date	Rate	Amount	Item	Amount
June 8	200 00	June 8	139 20	June 8	75%	104 40	Materials	$ 250 00
15	50 00	15	66 12	15	75%	49 59	Labor	205 32
							Overhead	153 99
							Total	609 31
							Unit Cost	24 372
							Comments:	
Totals	250 00		205 32			153 99		

Accounting for Work Completed

As each job is completed, the units are transferred to finished goods. The job order cost sheet contains the quantity, unit cost, and total cost

E-Procurement Systems

E-procurement (electronic procurement) systems automate the requisition and purchase of materials for a business using Internet technologies. These systems can be used to obtain raw materials and production goods needed for manufacturing processes, as well as office supplies, equipment, or maintenance and repair items. According to Forrester Research, business-to-business transactions will top $327 billion by 2002. Procurement officers, or buyers, use these electronic systems to find appropriate suppliers for materials as well as to manage inventory logistics. Purchase order creation and payment functions are often integrated within e-procurement systems.

Companies benefit from e-procurement systems in many ways. Order processing costs are reduced because the number of suppliers can be reduced. Suppliers often offer lower materials costs for orders placed via the Internet. Organizational efficiency is increased; materials being purchased are standardized and the number of authorized buyers is reduced.

Manufacturing segments—the electronics, steel, and auto industries—are often connected to large integrated procurement systems. The auto industry has developed its own e-procurement Web site known as Covisint. Auto producers such as Ford and General Motors use the site to find suppliers, create and track purchase requisitions, and log materials receipts. The online system also offers tools for production planning, demand forecasting, and payment services.

Thinking Critically
What internal control issues should be addressed when a firm is considering using an e-procurement system?

Internet Application
Research e-procurement systems using an online business magazine such as *Information Week* or *TechWeb*. Choose one article of interest on the topic, and prepare a one-page report on your findings.

---

needed to post to the inventory card in the finished goods subsidiary ledger. The finished goods ledger card is similar to the raw materials ledger card shown in Figure 29-2.

At the end of the month, a summary of completed jobs is prepared and an entry is made to transfer the total cost from the **Work in Process Inventory** account to the **Finished Goods Inventory** account.

⑧ Objective

Record the cost of jobs completed and the cost of goods sold under a perpetual inventory system.

1	20--					1
2	June	30	Finished Goods Inventory	15 00 00 0		2
3			Work in Process Inventory		15 00 00 0	3
4			Cost of jobs completed during June			4
5						5

Accounting for Cost of Goods Sold

As goods are sold, sales invoices are prepared for the customers. The cost of each order is entered on the office copy of the invoice; the cost information comes from the finished goods ledger card. Entries are made on the finished goods ledger card to record the quantities and costs of units sold. At month-end, the total cost of goods sold is determined from a summary of the information entered on the invoice copies.

6	June	30	Cost of Goods Sold	10 00 00 0		6
7			Finished Goods Inventory		10 00 00 0	7
8			Cost of goods sold during June			8

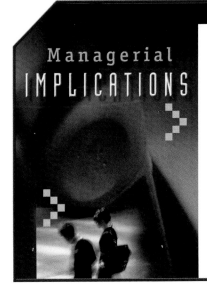

Managerial
IMPLICATIONS

Job Order Cost System

- The job order cost system keeps managers informed of the cost of manufacturing specific orders or batches of goods. It permits the computation of the cost per unit of product.
- The use of an overhead application rate helps to develop a consistent unit cost from month to month because the effects of unusual expenses or variations in monthly volume of output are averaged over the entire year.
- Unit costs help management to evaluate and maintain efficiency.
- Perpetual inventory procedures are useful tools for inventory control because they help keep management informed about inventory balances.

Thinking Critically
When is it appropriate to use a job order cost accounting system?

10	Accounts Receivable		20 00 00 00		10
11	Sales			20 00 00 00	11
12	Sales for June				12
13					13

On the June income statement, the **Cost of Goods Sold** account and adjustment for underapplied or overapplied overhead appear as follows.

Sales		$20,000
Cost of Goods Sold (per ledger account)	$10,000	
Add Underapplied Manufacturing Overhead	75	
Cost of Goods Sold (adjusted)		10,075
Gross Profit on Sales		$ 9,925

Instead of showing overapplied or underapplied overhead on the income statement, the accountant might prefer to show actual manufacturing costs on the statement of cost of goods manufactured.

Summary of Cost Flow through Inventory Accounts

The flow of costs during June is illustrated in the following three perpetual inventory accounts and the **Cost of Goods Sold** account. Piedmont Manufacturing Corporation had inventories of raw materials and finished goods on June 1 but no beginning inventory of work in process.

ACCOUNT __Raw Materials Inventory__ ACCOUNT NO. __121__

DATE		DESCRIPTION	POST. REF.	DEBIT	CREDIT	BALANCE DEBIT	BALANCE CREDIT
20--							
June	1	Balance	✓			22 3 4 0 00	
	30		J1	15 0 0 0 00		37 3 4 0 00	
	30		J1		9 6 0 0 00	27 7 4 0 00	

ACCOUNT Work in Process Inventory   ACCOUNT NO. __122__

DATE		DESCRIPTION	POST. REF.	DEBIT	CREDIT	BALANCE	
						DEBIT	CREDIT
20--							
June	30	Materials	J1	9 2 0 0 00		9 2 0 0 00	
	30	Labor	J1	5 3 0 0 00		14 5 0 0 00	
	30	Overhead					
		Applied	J1	3 9 7 5 00		18 4 7 5 00	
	30	To Finished					
		Goods	J1		15 0 0 0 00	3 4 7 5 00	

ACCOUNT Finished Goods Inventory   ACCOUNT NO. __126__

DATE		DESCRIPTION	POST. REF.	DEBIT	CREDIT	BALANCE	
						DEBIT	CREDIT
20--							
June	1	Balance	✓			16 0 0 0 00	
	30		J1	15 0 0 0 00		31 0 0 0 00	
	30		J1		10 0 0 0 00	21 0 0 0 00	

ACCOUNT Cost of Goods Sold   ACCOUNT NO. __560__

DATE		DESCRIPTION	POST. REF.	DEBIT	CREDIT	BALANCE	
						DEBIT	CREDIT
20--							
June	30		J1	10 0 0 0 00		10 0 0 0 00	

Section 3 Self Review

Questions

1. What is an overhead application rate?

2. How are job order cost sheets used?

3. Under the perpetual inventory system, what journal entries are made for sales and cost of goods sold?

Exercises

4. The entry to transfer work in process to finished goods is a

   a. debit to **Work in Process Inventory** and a credit to **Finished Goods Inventory**.

   b. debit to **Cost of Goods Sold** and a credit to **Finished Goods Inventory**.

   c. debit to **Finished Goods Inventory** and a credit to **Cost of Goods Sold.**

   d. debit to **Finished Goods Inventory** and a credit to **Work in Process Inventory.**

5. The entry to record cost of goods sold at the end of the month is a

   a. debit to **Work in Process Inventory** and a credit to **Finished Goods Inventory.**

   b. debit to **Cost of Goods Sold** and a credit to **Finished Goods Inventory.**

   c. debit to **Finished Goods Inventory** and a credit to **Cost of Goods Sold.**

   d. debit to **Finished Goods Inventory** and a credit to **Work in Process Inventory.**

Analysis

6. During the year sales were $300,000. The balance of **Cost of Goods Sold** was $250,000. Overapplied manufacturing overhead was $5,000. What is the gross profit on sales?

Review

Chapter Summary

Manufacturing companies use accounting systems that best supply detailed information about the costs of production. The job order cost system, as you learned in this chapter, provides records of costs identified to specific job orders.

Learning Objectives

1 **Explain how a job order cost accounting system operates.**

Under the job order cost accounting system, each batch of goods is produced under a production order called a job order. The job order cost system requires that inventory accounts and related subsidiary ledgers are set up for **Raw Materials, Work in Process,** and **Finished Goods.**

- The raw materials ledger is subsidiary to the **Raw Materials Inventory** account and contains a ledger card for each material.
- A job cost sheet is a subsidiary ledger for **Work in Process Inventory** in the general ledger.
- The finished goods ledger is a subsidiary to the **Finished Goods Inventory** account and has a record for each type of item.

2 **Journalize the purchase and issuance of direct and indirect materials.**

The account, **Raw Materials Inventory,** reflects all transactions related to materials and supplies.

- Purchases of raw materials are debited to the **Raw Materials Inventory** account.
- Raw materials are issued by a written requisition that shows the number of the job involved; that job is charged with the proper cost. A requisition for indirect materials or supplies is charged to the proper overhead account.

3 **Maintain perpetual inventory records.**

Materials or supplies are issued by the storeroom only upon presentation of a materials requisition describing the item and quantity needed and the job or purpose for which it is needed.

- Costs of materials placed into production are debited to **Work in Process Inventory.**
- Costs of indirect materials and supplies used are debited to **Manufacturing Overhead.**
- The total of indirect and direct materials is credited to **Raw Materials Inventory.**

4 **Record labor costs incurred and charge labor into production.**

Factory labor costs are identified as either direct labor or indirect labor. Time tickets are used for charging direct labor to specific jobs.

5 **Compute overhead rates and apply overhead to jobs.**

Manufacturing overhead is assigned to jobs based on a rate that is commonly related to direct labor costs or to direct labor hours.

6 **Compute overapplied or underapplied overhead and report it in the financial statements.**

To apply overhead to jobs, debit **Work in Process Inventory** and credit **Manufacturing Overhead Applied.** Compute the overapplied or underapplied overhead by comparing total credits recorded in **Manufacturing Overhead Applied** with total debits recorded in **Manufacturing Overhead** for the month.

- Underapplied or overapplied overhead is carried forward from month to month.
- Net underapplied or overapplied overhead is closed out each year, usually as an adjustment to **Cost of Goods Sold** on the income statement.

7 **Maintain job order cost sheets.**

The job order cost sheet shows all manufacturing costs for a specific job.

8 **Record the cost of jobs completed and the cost of goods sold under a perpetual inventory system.**

As a job is done, the cost sheet gives data needed for transferring costs from **Work in Process Inventory** to **Finished Goods Inventory.**

- Record an order's cost on the sales invoice office copy.
- Summarize the cost of goods sold each month from the invoices.
- Record the transfer entry in the general journal.

9 **Define the accounting terms new to this chapter.**

Finished goods subsidiary ledger (p. 1040) A ledger containing a record for each of the different types of finished products

Job order (p. 1036) A specific order for a specific batch of manufactured items

Job order cost accounting (p. 1036) A cost accounting system that determines the unit cost of manufactured items for each separate production order

Job order cost sheet (p.1046) A record of all manufacturing costs charged to a specific job

Just-in-time system (p. 1039) An inventory system in which raw materials are ordered so they arrive just in time to be placed into production

Manufacturing overhead ledger (p. 1044) A subsidiary ledger that contains a record for each overhead item

Materials requisition (p. 1041) A form that describes the item and quantity needed and shows the job or purpose

Overapplied overhead (p. 1045) The result of applied overhead exceeding the actual overhead costs

Overhead application rate (p. 1044) The rate at which the estimated cost of overhead is charged to each job

Perpetual inventory system (p. 1037) An inventory system that tracks the inventories on hand at all times

Process cost accounting (p. 1036) A cost accounting system whereby unit costs of manufactured items are determined by totaling unit costs in each production department

Production order (p. 1036) See Job order

Raw materials ledger card (p. 1040) A record showing details of receipts and issues for a type of raw material

Raw materials subsidiary ledger (p. 1040) A ledger containing the raw materials ledger cards

Standard costs (p. 1036) A measure of what costs should be in an efficient operation

Time ticket (p. 1043) Form used to record hours worked and jobs performed

Underapplied overhead (p. 1045) The result of actual overhead costs exceeding applied overhead

Work in process subsidiary ledger (p. 1040) A ledger containing the job order cost sheets

Comprehensive Self Review

1. Why is a cost accounting system needed?
2. What is a process cost accounting system?
3. Why is a perpetual inventory system used with a job order cost accounting system?
4. What would you find on a raw materials ledger card?
5. How is underapplied or overapplied manufacturing overhead disposed of at the end of the year?

(Answers to Comprehensive Self Review are on page 1061.)

Discussion Questions

1. What is a perpetual inventory?
2. What information does a job order cost sheet contain?
3. When direct materials are issued from the storeroom, what entries are made in the subsidiary records?
4. What is a materials requisition?
5. What does the **Raw Materials Inventory** account show?
6. What entry is made for indirect materials issued from the storeroom?
7. What is idle time? How is the cost of idle time usually accounted for?
8. Name the sources of postings to the job order cost sheet.
9. What account is debited and what account is credited when manufacturing overhead is applied?
10. Name five common manufacturing overhead costs.
11. Why is an overhead application rate used?
12. What account is debited and what account is credited when completed goods are transferred from the factory floor to the finished goods storeroom?
13. What is a time ticket? What is its relationship to an order cost sheet?
14. Name three businesses in addition to those given in the chapter that would use a process cost accounting system.
15. Discuss how costs flow through the **Raw Materials Inventory, Work in Process Inventory,** and **Finished Goods Inventory** accounts to cost of goods sold.
16. Describe a just-in-time inventory system, including its advantages and disadvantages, if any.

Applications

EXERCISES

The following data is for Exercises 29-1 through 29-4.

During November 20--, Chuck's Manufacturing Company purchased and issued the following materials and supplies. Use November 30 as the date for all entries.

Purchases		Issues from Storeroom	
Materials	$55,000	Direct materials	$47,500
Manufacturing supplies	5,000	Manufacturing supplies	4,100

Journalizing purchase of materials.

Give the entry in general journal form to record the cost of the materials purchased.

◀ **Exercise 29-1**
Objective 2

Journalizing purchase of indirect materials.

Give the entry in general journal form to record the cost of the manufacturing supplies purchased.

◀ **Exercise 29-2**
Objective 2

Journalizing the assignment of indirect materials into production.

Give the entry in general journal form to record the issuance of the manufacturing supplies into production.

◀ **Exercise 29-3**
Objective 2

Journalizing the assignment of direct materials into production.

Give the entry in general journal form to record the issuance of the direct materials into production.

◀ **Exercise 29-4**
Objective 2

Recording labor costs incurred.

A payroll summary prepared at Nash Manufacturing Company showed the following figures for January 20--.

Direct labor costs incurred	$30,000.00
Indirect labor costs incurred	3,000.00
Social security tax withheld	2,046.00
Medicare tax withheld	478.50
Income tax withheld	4,950.00

Give the January 31 entry in general journal form to record the labor costs incurred.

◀ **Exercise 29-5**
Objective 4

Computing overhead rate.

Arizona Necklace Company estimates the following manufacturing overhead costs for 20--.

Estimated direct labor hours	48,000 hours
Estimated direct labor costs	$720,000
Estimated overhead costs	$144,000

What is the overhead application rate based on direct labor costs?

◀ **Exercise 29-6**
Objective 5

Exercise 29-7 ▶
Objective 5

Applying manufacturing overhead.

Alexander Company's direct labor costs were $125,000 for June 20--.
Assuming that the company applies overhead at the rate of 75 percent of
direct labor costs, give the general journal entry for June summarizing the
overhead applied for the month.

Exercise 29-8 ▶
Objective 5

Applying overhead and cost of job.

During 20--, Mountain Manufacturing Company began and completed
Job 12-22. Costs entered on the job cost sheet for this job were $25,000
for materials and $8,000 for labor.

1. Assuming that overhead is applied at 80 percent of direct labor costs,
   compute the amount of overhead that should be applied to this job.

2. Compute the total cost of Job 12-22.

Exercise 29-9 ▶
Objective 6

Computing overapplied or underapplied overhead.

For the year 20--, Plastic Inc. had actual overhead costs of $196,500, and
its applied overhead was $192,000.

1. Did the firm have overapplied or underapplied overhead for the year?

2. What was the amount of overapplied or underapplied overhead?

Exercise 29-10 ▶
Objective 8

Recording cost of goods completed and cost of goods sold.

The records of Pacific Corporation for 20-- show that it completed goods
costing $275,000 and that it sold goods costing $295,000 for the year.
Give the entries in general journal form on December 31, 20--, to record
the cost of goods completed and the cost of goods sold for the year.

Problems

Selected problems can be completed using:
▨ **Spreadsheets**

PROBLEM SET A

Problem 29-1A ▶
Objectives 2, 4, 5, 6, 8

**Recording purchase and issuance of direct and indirect materials,
recording labor costs, applying overhead, computing overapplied
or underapplied overhead, recording cost of jobs completed and
cost of goods sold.**

In October 20--, Viking Manufacturing Co. had the following cost data.

COST DATA

a. Raw materials costing $75,000 were purchased.

b. Raw materials costing $68,000 were used: direct materials, $67,500;
   indirect materials $500.

c. Factory wages of $47,500 were incurred: direct labor $45,000; indirect
   labor $2,500. Social security tax deductions were $2,945, Medicare tax
   deductions were $689, federal income tax deductions were $7,125.

d. Other overhead costs of $28,575 were incurred. (Credit **Accounts Payable.**)

e. Estimated manufacturing overhead costs were applied to jobs in production at the rate of 75 percent of direct labor costs.

f. Finished goods costing $141,500 were transferred from production to the warehouse.

g. The cost of goods sold was $90,350.

h. Sales for the month were $139,000.

INSTRUCTIONS

1. Prepare general journal entries to record each item of cost data given. Use the account titles listed in your textbook.

2. Compute the amount of overapplied or underapplied overhead for the month.

3. Prepare a partial income statement for October. Adjust the **Cost of Goods Sold** for any overapplied or underapplied overhead.

Analyze: Based on the partial income statement you have prepared, what portion of each sales dollar is realized as gross profit?

Maintaining job order cost sheets, applying overhead to jobs, computing overapplied or underapplied overhead, recording cost of jobs completed and cost of goods sold.

◄ **Problem 29-2A**
Objectives 5, 6, 7, 8

The Finishing Company builds kitchen cabinets. On January 1, 2005, one job (0543) was in progress. The order is from Dallas Apartment Corporation and was begun on December 19, 2004. Costs accumulated to date on that job are materials, $2,000; labor, $1,000; and overhead, $500. During January the following costs were incurred in production work on Job 0543 and on Jobs 0601 and 0602, which were started on January 5, 2005.

	Materials	Labor	Overhead	Quantity
Job 0543	$ 500	$ 500	$ 250	5
Job 0601	6,000	2,000	1,000	4
Job 0602	3,000	1,000	500	2

Job 0601 is being manufactured for Texas State Furniture Outlets, and Job 0602 is for stock.

Manufacturing overhead is applied at the rate of 50 percent of direct labor costs. During January actual manufacturing overhead costs of $1,800 were incurred. Job 0543 was completed on January 18 and was delivered to the customer. The sales price was $6,500.

INSTRUCTIONS

1. Prepare job order cost sheets for the three jobs. Enter the beginning balances applicable to Job 0543.

2. Post the costs of the materials and labor for January to the job order cost sheets.

3. Compute the overhead amounts that should be applied to the three jobs worked on during the month, and enter these amounts on the job cost sheets.

4. Give the entry in general journal form to transfer the cost of the job completed from work in process to finished goods.

5. Compute the amount of underapplied or overapplied overhead for January.

Analyze: If The Finishing Company sold the five cabinets referenced in Job 0543 to Dallas Apartment Corporation for a total invoice price of $10,500, what gross profit amount was realized on the job? Assume that no overapplication or underapplication of overhead occurred on this job.

PROBLEM SET B

Problem 29-1B ▶
Objectives 2, 4, 5, 6, 8

Recording purchase and issuance of direct and indirect materials, recording labor costs, applying overhead, computing overapplied or underapplied overhead, recording cost of jobs completed and cost of goods sold.

In May 20--, Northwest Company had the following cost data.

COST DATA

a. Raw materials costing $87,500 were purchased.

b. Raw materials costing $82,500 were used: direct materials, $75,000; indirect materials, $7,500.

c. Factory wages of $73,500 were incurred: direct labor, $65,000; indirect labor, $8,500. Social security tax deductions were $4,557, Medicare tax deductions were $1,066, and income tax deductions were $11,025.

d. Other overhead costs amounting to $18,000 were incurred. (Credit **Accounts Payable.**)

e. Estimated manufacturing overhead costs were applied to jobs in production at the rate of 70 percent of direct labor costs.

f. Finished goods costing $175,000 were transferred to the warehouse.

g. Goods costing $155,000 were sold and billed to customers for $258,000.

INSTRUCTIONS

1. Prepare general journal entries to record each item of cost data given. Use the account titles in the textbook.

2. Compute the amount of overapplied or underapplied overhead for the month.

3. Prepare a partial income statement for the month of May. Adjust the cost of goods sold for any overapplied or underapplied overhead.

Analyze: What percentage of raw materials purchased during the month of May was used?

Problem 29-2B ▶
Objectives 5, 6, 7, 8

Maintaining job order cost sheets, applying overhead to jobs, computing overapplied or underapplied overhead, recording cost of jobs completed and cost of goods sold.

Quality Cabinet Company builds kitchen cabinets. On November 1, 20--, two jobs, Job O14 and Job O15, were in progress. The order is from City Apartments and was begun on October 19, 20--. The accumulated costs for each job are detailed as follows.

	Job 014	Job 015
Materials	$20,000	$10,000
Labor	15,000	6,000
Overhead	7,500	3,000

During November Job P01 was begun. Following are the November costs incurred for each of the three jobs.

	Materials	Labor	Overhead
Job 014	$2,000	$1,000	$ 500
Job 015	5,000	3,000	1,500
Job P01	6,000	2,000	1,000

Manufacturing overhead is applied at the rate of 50 percent of direct labor costs. During November actual manufacturing overhead costs of $3,200 were incurred; $1,200 to Job O14 and $1,000 each to the other two jobs. Job O14 was completed on November 18 and was delivered to the customer. The sales price was $65,000.

INSTRUCTIONS

1. Prepare job order cost sheets for the three jobs. Enter the beginning balances applicable to Jobs O14 and O15.

2. Post the costs of the materials and labor for November to the job order cost sheets.

3. Compute the overhead amounts that should be applied to the three jobs worked on during the month, and enter these amounts on the job cost sheets.

4. Give the entry in general journal form to transfer the cost of the job completed from work in process to finished goods.

5. Compute the amount of underapplied or overapplied overhead for November.

Analyze: What adjusted cost of goods sold should be reported for November manufacturing activities?

CHAPTER 29 CHALLENGE PROBLEM

Reaching Goals

Stainless Manufacturing Company manufactures one product that has several model styles. All materials are added at the beginning of production. On January 1, 20--, one job, D131, was in process, with the following accumulated costs:

Materials	$ 6,500
Direct labor	2,500
Manufacturing overhead	1,000
Total	$10,000

The beginning finished goods inventory for Stainless Manufacturing Company on January 1, 20--, was $18,000.

The following additional data is given for the month of January.

Total labor costs incurred	$23,000
Total cost of completed Job D131	14,200
Total materials costs incurred	18,000

In addition, Job J001 was begun and completed during the month. Its costs included materials of $7,000 and labor of $5,000. Job J002 was begun during the month and was in process at the end of the month. During the month sales were $60,500, and the gross profit rate was 40 percent.

INSTRUCTIONS

1. For Jobs D131, J001, and J002, calculate the cost of materials, labor, and overhead for the month of January to find the total cost of each job.

2. Prepare a schedule of cost of goods sold for the month of January.

Analyze:
On January 1, 20--, Stainless Manufacturing Company established a goal to hold raw materials costs at or below 48 percent of total job costs. Based on your computations, has the company attained this goal? Explain.

CHAPTER 29 CRITICAL THINKING PROBLEM

Gross Profit

The job order cost sheets for R&B Manufacturing Company show the following information about special orders for June and July of the current year.

| Job Number | Manufacturing Costs | | Status of Job |
	June	July	
JU–688	$7,800		Sold, 7/3
JU–689	4,050		Completed, 6/27
JU–690	2,150	$3,150	Completed, 7/8
JU–691	750	2,850	Sold, 7/10
JU–692	600	3,200	Sold, 7/16
JL–701		4,200	Sold, 7/22
JL–702		6,500	Completed, 7/20
JL–703		5,400	In process, 7/31
JL–704		2,100	In process, 7/31

The company prices its jobs to make a 40 percent gross profit on sales. Operating expenses for July totaled $6,533, and the company's income tax rate is 25 percent of net income before income taxes.

INSTRUCTIONS

1. From this data, compute the following:
   a. Work in Process Inventory, July 1
   b. Finished Goods Inventory, July 1
   c. Cost of Goods Sold for July
   d. Work in Process Inventory, July 31
   e. Finished Goods Inventory, July 31
   f. Sales for July

2. Prepare a condensed income statement for R&B Manufacturing Company for the month of July.

Business Connections

◀ Connection 1

 MANAGERIAL FOCUS **Cost Accounting Controls**

1. The president of a fairly large manufacturing company suggests that it would be more efficient to discontinue the job of storeroom clerk and to let factory workers enter the storeroom and select their own materials. Comment on this suggestion.

2. Assume that you are an accountant for a manufacturing firm. At the end of one year, there is a large overapplied overhead amount. How would you explain to management why this balance might exist?

3. Why should management insist that a physical inventory be taken once a year even though perpetual inventory records are kept?

4. From an administrative standpoint, why is direct labor cost a simple basis to use for the application of manufacturing overhead?

5. In general, would managers prefer to see overapplied or underapplied overhead? Why?

◀ Connection 2

Ethical DILEMMA **Verifiability** In the annual audit of inventories at Southside Manufacturing Company, the auditor was running late in completing her work and asks the company accountant to sign a statement verifying the amount of raw material on hand at the balance sheet date. She does not actually inspect the raw material. What do you think?

◀ Connection 3

Street WISE:
Questions from the Real World **Sales** Refer to the *1999 Annual Report* for The Home Depot, Inc. in Appendix B.

1. Read the letter written to stockholders, customers, and associates. Describe the company's mission for its e-commerce efforts. How do you think the use of an electronic ordering site for customers might benefit the buyers of merchandise within the company?

2. Locate the section "Management's Discussion and Analysis of Results of Operations and Financial Condition." Review the discussion of *Results of Operations, Fiscal year ended January 30, 2000 compared to January 31, 1999*. The Home Depot, Inc., purchases large quantities and varieties of products for resale from vendors worldwide and reports "better inventory shrink results." To what does the company attribute these results? Why do you think this is a significant measurement for the company? Explain.

◀ Connection 4

FINANCIAL STATEMENT ANALYSIS **Inventories** The excerpt on page 1060 was taken from the *1999 Annual Report* for Alcoa.

Approximately 57 percent of total inventories on December 31, 1999, were valued on a LIFO basis. If valued on an average cost basis, total inventories would have been $645 and $703 higher at the end of 1999 and 1998, respectively.

Inventories:

(in millions)

December 31	1999	1998
Finished goods	$ 363	$ 418
Work in process	550	592
Bauxite and alumina	286	347
Purchased raw materials	267	361
Operating supplies	152	163
	$1,618	$1,881

Analyze:

1. In 1999, if the average cost basis had been used to value total inventories, what would the value have been?

2. Using the LIFO basis of inventory valuation in 1999, what percentage of total inventories was composed of finished goods?

3. By what amount did total inventories decrease from 1998 to 1999?

Analyze Online: Locate the *Getting to Know Alcoa* section within the Alcoa Web site **(www.alcoa.com).**

4. Describe the premises of the "Alcoa Production System."

Connection 5 ► *Extending* the *Thought* **Cost Accounting Systems** Accounting processes and systems vary from company to company. A ship builder will employ a different costing system than a furniture builder. If you were asked to design an accounting structure and costing system for a manufacturing company, what steps would you take? How would you familiarize yourself with the processes and costs involved?

Connection 6 ► **Business Communication** **Job Order Records** Job order cost accounting systems require specific forms and ledgers used to record job-specific costs. List the ledgers, cards, sheets, or requisitions necessary to record costs using a job order cost system and create blank samples for each.

Connection 7 ► **Team***Work* **Manufacturing Processes** In groups of two or three students, interview the accounting manager or supervisor for a manufacturing business in your area. Firms that produce furniture, signs, jewelry, computer components, or cosmetics are potential organizations. Use the yellow pages of your telephone directory for ideas. Conduct your interview in person if possible. Otherwise, set up a phone interview. Prepare a list of questions before you conduct the interview. Ask for an overview of the manufacturing process and how the firm assigns costs to its products. Summarize your findings in a report to be presented to the class orally. Include the name and nature of the business operations, name and title of the person interviewed, and a description of how costs are allocated.

inter NET CONNECTION

Institute of Management Accountants Go to the Institute of Management Accountants at **www.imanet.org.** Select *About IMA.* What are the goals of the IMA? What certifications are available? Select *Ethics center.* What three standards are discussed?

◄ **Connection 8**

Answers to Self Reviews

Answers to Section 1 Self Review

1. A system in which the unit costs of production are determined for each separate production order.
2. A measure of what the cost should be in an efficient operation.
3. To check the accuracy of the recorded inventory.
4. **d.** with either the job order cost system or the process cost system.
5. **b.** when a company produces more than one product in batches rather than on a continuous basis.
6. $130,000

Answers to Section 2 Self Review

1. Direct materials issued from the storeroom are entered on the raw materials ledger card for the material. Also, a posting will be made from the summary of materials requisitions to the Materials section of the job order cost sheet.
2. Indirect materials issued are entered on the raw materials inventory cards. Periodically, based on the summary of materials requisitions, the cost of indirect materials will be charged to the **Manufacturing Overhead** account and credited to the **Raw Materials Inventory** account.
3. When the actual costs of overhead were less than the amount of overhead charged into production.
4. **c.** debit to **Work in Process Inventory** and a credit to **Manufacturing Overhead Applied.**
5. **b. Cost of Goods Sold.**
6. $6.50 per hour

Answers to Section 3 Self Review

1. A predetermined rate to assign overhead to each job, usually based on direct labor hours or direct labor cost.
2. The totals on the job order cost sheet are used as the basis of entries on the finished goods ledger sheet and to make the journal entry to transfer cost of completed jobs from **Work in Process** to **Finished Goods.**
3. Sales are recorded by debiting **Accounts Receivable** and crediting **Sales.** The cost of goods sold is recorded by debiting **Cost of Goods Sold** and crediting **Finished Goods Inventory.**
4. **d.** debit to **Finished Goods Inventory** and a credit to **Work in Process Inventory.**
5. **b.** debit to **Cost of Goods Sold** and a credit to **Finished Goods Inventory.**
6. $55,000

Answers to Comprehensive Self Review

1. To determine the cost of each manufactured unit and help managers watch cost behavior and control costs.
2. One in which the total cost of a unit of product is found by adding the unit costs in each department through which the product passes during the manufacturing process.
3. Because the firm must always know the costs of the inventory being used at each stage of production.
4. The quantities and costs of items purchased, issued, and on hand.
5. It is closed. It is usually shown in the Cost of Goods Sold section of the income statement.

CHAPTER 30

Learning Objectives

1 Compute equivalent units of production with no beginning work in process inventory.

2 Prepare a cost of production report with no beginning work in process inventory.

3 Compute the unit cost of manufacturing under the process cost accounting system.

4 Record costs incurred and the flow of costs as products move through the manufacturing process and are sold.

5 Compute equivalent production and prepare a cost of production report with a beginning work in process inventory.

6 Define the accounting terms new to this chapter.

Process Cost Accounting

New Terms

Average method of process costing

Cost of production report

Equivalent production

Process cost accounting system

CONOCO

www.conoco.com

*U*pstream ventures. Downstream opportunities. These are terms used in the conference rooms and corporate hallways of Conoco, a leading oil developer and producer. The company's exploration and production segment handles upstream ventures; it finds, develops, and produces crude oil, natural gas, and gas products. The company's downstream division takes on refining, marketing, supply, and transportation operations.

Conoco managers are keenly in touch with production processes and associated costs. In October 2000 the company's largest petroleum refinery underwent a massive facelift. Retrofits and upgrades enable the plant to receive partially refined heavy-crude oil from Venezuela and finish refining it into products such as gasoline, jet fuel, and lubricants. The upgrades also increase the plant's crude oil processing capacity.

Thinking Critically
How do you think Conoco accountants track and classify production costs as the crude oil moves through refining processes in Venezuela and Louisiana?

For more information on Conoco, go to: collegeaccounting.glencoe.com.

Section Objectives

1 Compute equivalent units of production with no beginning work in process inventory.

WHY IT'S IMPORTANT
Manufacturers estimate units completed based on labor, materials, and overhead costs.

2 Prepare a cost of production report with no beginning work in process inventory.

WHY IT'S IMPORTANT
Tracking production costs can help identify manufacturing inefficiencies or cost overruns.

3 Compute the unit cost of manufacturing under the process cost accounting system.

WHY IT'S IMPORTANT
Unit costs help management set prices.

4 Record costs incurred and the flow of costs as products move through the manufacturing process and are sold.

WHY IT'S IMPORTANT
Cumulative product costs are tracked and categorized at every point in the manufacturing process.

Terms to Learn

cost of production report
equivalent production
process cost accounting
 system

Process Cost Accounting System

A process cost accounting system is used in operations when a single product is manufactured and production is continuous. Companies that use process cost accounting systems include oil refineries, cement producers, and paint manufacturers.

The Process Cost Accounting System

In a **process cost accounting system**, costs are accumulated for each process or department and then transferred on to the next process or department. The flow of costs is similar to that shown in Figure 29-1. There are **Raw Materials Inventory** and **Finished Goods Inventory** accounts. However, job order cost sheets are not needed because products are not made in batches or by order; instead they are produced continuously. There is a separate **Work in Process** account for each department. Materials, labor, and overhead costs are identified with each department and charged to the departmental **Work in Process** accounts. At the end of the month, each departmental **Work in Process** account reflects the materials, labor, and overhead costs incurred by the department.

The process cost accounting system is like an average cost system. Total manufacturing costs are divided by the number of units worked on to obtain a cost per unit of product. As products are physically transferred from one department to the next, the related costs are also transferred.

McCallie Manufacturing Company has two production departments: laminating and finishing. All products begin in the laminating department. Trays that are to be sold in an unpainted state are moved directly to the finished goods storeroom and are recorded in the **Finished Goods Inventory** account. Other trays are moved to the finishing department. This flow of goods is shown in Figure 30-1.

▼ **FIGURE 30-1**
Flow of Goods in a Factory Operation

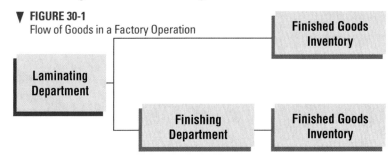

Analyzing Process Cost Data

Let's study the process cost accounting system used by McCallie Manufacturing Company. All transactions involving materials, labor, and overhead are recorded by department. The service department costs are allocated as overhead to the departments that benefit from the services. For each department there is a record of products started, completed, and in process. The stage of completion of the ending work in process is estimated. Table 30-1 summarizes the production data for June.

◀ **TABLE 30-1**
Departmental Cost Data for June 20--

	Laminating Department	Finishing Department
Costs		
Materials	$15,000.00	$ 7,900.00
Labor	24,250.00	16,875.00
Manufacturing overhead	12,100.00	11,900.00
Total costs	$51,350.00	$36,675.00
Quantities		
Started in production	5,000	–0–
Transferred in from prior department	–0–	4,000
Transferred out to next department	4,000	–0–
Transferred out to finished goods	500	3,500
Work in process—ending	500	500
Stages of Completion—Ending Work in Process		
Materials	100%	90%
Labor	70	50
Manufacturing overhead	70	50

Important!

Unit Cost
Under the process cost system, unit costs are calculated by dividing all departmental manufacturing costs by the production for the period.

In the laminating department, 5,000 units were started in production, 4,000 were transferred to the finishing department, and 500 were transferred to finished goods for sale as unpainted trays. At the end of the month, there were 500 trays in process in the laminating department. For the trays in process, all the required materials were issued, and 70 percent of the labor and overhead was added.

In the finishing department, 4,000 units were transferred in from the laminating department, and 3,500 were completed and transferred to finished goods. There were 500 trays in process at month-end, to which 90 percent of the materials and 50 percent of the labor and overhead was added.

Recall

Work in Process
Work in process refers to products that have started but have not completed the production process.

Determining Equivalent Production

Equivalent production is the estimated number of units that could have been started and completed with the same effort and costs incurred in the department during the month. Thus if two units were started during the period and only one-half of the materials were added to each, one unit could have been started and completed using those materials. Using the data in Table 30-1, let's calculate June's equivalent production.

❶ **Objective**
Compute equivalent units of production with no beginning work in process inventory.

Analyzing department costs helps managers find ways to reduce production costs. High-Tech Metal Finishing produces parts for the aerospace industry. It cleans the parts, rinsing off dirt, machine coolant, oils, and other substances left from manufacturing. The company found that foam blocked the rinsing and cleaning process, wasting time, labor, and gas for the heater. High-Tech tried a new product that reduced wastewater processing costs from 32 to 17 cents per gallon.

Important!

Equivalent Production
In computing equivalent production, accountants frequently consider labor and overhead to be at the same stage of production.

Calculating Equivalent Units for Laminating Department. Separate equivalent unit computations are made for the materials, labor, and overhead. Table 30-2 shows how to compute the equivalent units of production for the laminating department. For materials the equivalent units of production are 5,000 units (4,500 + 500). All the materials were issued for the 4,500 units transferred out and for the 500 trays in process.

For labor and manufacturing overhead, the equivalent units of production are 4,850 (4,500 + 350). All the labor and overhead were applied to the units transferred out. Of the 500 trays in ending work in process, 70 percent of the labor and overhead was applied. This is the equivalent of 350 (500 × 0.7) completed units.

TABLE 30-2 ▶
Computation of Equivalent Production, Laminating Department

Materials		
Units transferred out		
To next department: 100% × 4,000 units	4,000	
To finished goods: 100% × 500 units	500	
Total transferred out		4,500
Work in process: 100% × 500 units		500
Equivalent units of production for materials		5,000
Labor and Manufacturing Overhead		
Units transferred out		
To next department: 100% × 4,000 units	4,000	
To finished goods: 100% × 500 units	500	
Total transferred out		4,500
Work in process: 70% × 500 units		350
Equivalent units of production for labor and overhead		4,850

Manufacturing Overhead
Manufacturing overhead is all of the manufacturing costs not classified as direct materials or direct labor. Manufacturing overhead includes utilities, depreciation, maintenance, taxes, and insurance for the factory building and payroll taxes for factory wages.

Calculating Equivalent Units for Finishing Department. Table 30-3 shows the equivalent units of production for the finishing department. For materials the equivalent units are 3,950 (3,500 + 450). All the materials were issued for the 3,500 units transferred out. For the 500 trays in process, 90 percent of the materials were issued. The ending work in process for materials is 450 (500 × 0.9) equivalent units.

For labor and manufacturing overhead, the equivalent units of production are 3,750 (3,500 + 250). All the labor and overhead were applied to the units transferred out. Of the 500 trays in ending work in process, 50 percent of the labor and overhead was applied. This is the equivalent of 250 (500 × 0.5) completed units.

TABLE 30-3 ▶
Computation of Equivalent Production, Finishing Department

Materials		
Units transferred out		
To finished goods: 100% × 3,500 units	3,500	
Total transferred out		3,500
Work in process: 90% × 500 Units		450
Equivalent units of production for materials		3,950
Labor and Manufacturing Overhead		
Units transferred out		
To finished goods: 100% × 3,500 units	3,500	
Total transferred out		3,500
Work in process: 50% × 500 units		250
Equivalent units of production for labor and overhead		3,750

Preparing the Cost of Production Report

The **cost of production report** summarizes all costs charged to each department and shows the costs assigned to the goods transferred out of the department and to the goods still in process. It has separate sections to summarize quantities and costs. Each section has two parts that reconcile the total *to be accounted for* with the total *accounted for.*

Calculating Costs for the Laminating Department. Table 30-4 on page 1068 shows the cost of production report for the laminating department. The Quantity Schedule shows the units to be accounted for (a) and explains what happened to these units (b). The first part of the Cost Schedule (c) shows the total and unit cost of each element and the cumulative cost total. The unit cost is the total cost divided by the equivalent units. The unit cost for the laminating department totals $10.49.

The second part of the Cost Schedule (d) shows the cost of units completed and transferred out, $47,205. It lists the cost of the ending work in process by element, which is computed by multiplying the equivalent units by the cost per unit. For example, the ending work in process for materials is $1,500 (500 equivalent units × $3). The total work in process is the sum of the three elements plus an adjustment for rounding, $4,145. Note that the costs to account for (cumulative cost total) equal the total costs accounted for.

It is customary to round unit costs to the nearest cent. Often an adjustment is required due to rounding. The accountant for McCallie Corporation adjusts the ending work in process inventory to ensure that the cumulative cost total equals the total costs accounted for. In subsequent periods, the rounding adjustment is added to or subtracted from manufacturing overhead in work in process.

Calculating Costs for the Finishing Department. Table 30-5 on page 1069 shows the cost of production report for the finishing department. In the Quantity Schedule (a), the quantity to be accounted for consists of units transferred in from the laminating department. These units are accounted for (b) as transferred to finished goods or still in process.

In the Cost Schedule (c), there is a new item. The cost of units transferred in from the laminating department is $41,960 for 4,000 units. Costs in the finishing department are listed next, in total and per unit. The total department costs are $36,675 and the cumulative cost total is $78,635 ($41,960 + $36,675). The unit cost from the laminating department was $10.49. The unit cost for the finishing department is $9.67. The cumulative unit cost is $20.16 ($10.49 + $9.67).

The second part of the Cost Schedule (d) shows the cost of units completed and transferred out, $70,560 (3,500 units × $20.16). In addition it lists the cost of the ending work in process by element, which is computed by multiplying the equivalent units by the cost per unit. For example, the ending work in process for labor is $1,125 (250 × $4.50). The total work in process is $8,075. It includes the costs from the prior department ($5,245) and the sum of the three cost elements plus the rounding adjustment. Note that the costs to be accounted for equal the total costs accounted for.

Recording Cost Flows

The flow of costs in the accounting records follows the flow of production. Let's look at the journal entries that summarize June's operations.

2 Objective
Prepare a cost of production report with no beginning work in process inventory.

3 Objective
Compute the unit cost of manufacturing under the process cost accounting system.

Important!

Costs Accounted For
The total costs accounted for must equal the cumulative cost total for the department.

Important!

Work in Process
If there is no beginning inventory of work in process, the total cost to be accounted for is the total of (1) costs transferred in from the prior department and (2) costs incurred in the current department.

4 Objective
Record costs incurred and the flow of costs as products move through the manufacturing process and are sold.

Quantity Schedule			Units		
(a) Quantity to be accounted for					
Started in production			5,000		
Total to be accounted for			5,000		
(b) Quantity accounted for					
Transferred out to next department			4,000		
Transferred out to finished goods			500		
Work in process—ending			500		
Total accounted for			5,000		

Cost Schedule	Total Cost		E.P. Units*		Unit Cost
(c) Costs to be accounted for					
Costs in current department					
Materials	$15,000.00	÷	5,000	=	$ 3.00
Labor	24,250.00	÷	4,850	=	5.00
Manufacturing overhead	12,100.00	÷	4,850	=	2.49
Cumulative cost total	$51,350.00				$10.49
(d) Costs accounted for					
Transferred out to next department	$41,960.00	=	4,000	×	$10.49
Transferred out to finished goods	5,245.00	=	500	×	10.49
Total costs transferred out	$47,205.00				
Work in process—ending					
Materials	$ 1,500.00	=	500	×	3.00
Labor	1,750.00	=	350	×	5.00
Manufacturing overhead	871.50	=	350	×	2.49
Rounding adjustment	23.50				
Total work in process	$ 4,145.00				
Total costs accounted for	$51,350.00				* Equivalent Production Units

TABLE 30-4 ▲
Cost of Production Report,
June 20--, Laminating
Department

Charging Costs to Work in Process. Departmental **Work in Process** accounts are debited for direct materials issued to production as follows.

	20--				
1					1
2	June	30	Work in Process—Laminating Department	15 000 00	2
3			Work in Process—Finishing Department	7 900 00	3
4			Raw Materials Inventory	22 900 00	4
5			Allocation of materials to production		5

Departmental **Work in Process** accounts are debited for direct labor; various liability accounts are credited.

	20--				
1					1
2	June	30	Work in Process—Laminating Department	24 250 00	2
3			Work in Process—Finishing Department	16 875 00	3
4			Social Security Tax Payable	2 549 75	4
5			Medicare Tax Payable	596 31	5
6			Employee Income Tax Payable	6 168 75	6
7			Salaries and Wages Payable	31 810 19	7
8			Salaries and wages for June		8

When manufacturing overhead costs are incurred, they are debited to the **Manufacturing Overhead** control account. At the same time, they

Quantity Schedule			Units		
(a) Quantity to be accounted for					
Transferred in from prior department			4,000		
Total to be accounted for			4,000		
(b) Quantity accounted for					
Transferred out to finished goods			3,500		
Work in process—ending			500		
Total accounted for			4,000		

Cost Schedule	Total Cost		E.P. Units*		Unit Cost
(c) Costs to be accounted for					
Costs in prior department	$41,960.00	÷	4,000	=	$10.49
Costs in current department					
Materials	$ 7,900.00	÷	3,950	=	$ 2.00
Labor	16,875.00	÷	3,750	=	4.50
Manufacturing overhead	11,900.00	÷	3,750	=	3.17
Total current department costs	$36,675.00				$ 9.67
Cumulative cost total	$78,635.00				$20.16
(d) Costs accounted for					
Transferred out to finished goods	$70,560.00	=	3,500	×	$20.16
Work in process—ending					
Costs in prior department	$ 5,245.00	=	500	×	10.49
Costs in current department					
Materials	900.00	=	450	×	2.00
Labor	1,125.00	=	250	×	4.50
Manufacturing overhead	792.50	=	250	×	3.17
Rounding adjustment	12.50				
Total work in process	$ 8,075.00				
Total costs accounted for	$78,635.00		* Equivalent Production Units		

are entered in manufacturing overhead subsidiary ledger sheets for each department. At the end of the month, the overhead costs of all service departments are allocated to the producing departments. After this allocation the total of the overhead ledger sheets for the departments equal the total manufacturing overhead costs incurred during the month. This total also equals the balance in the **Manufacturing Overhead** control account. The **Manufacturing Overhead** control account is closed into the departmental **Work in Process** accounts.

Manufacturing overhead for June was $24,000—$12,100 for the laminating department and $11,900 for the finishing department. The following entry charges the overhead to production.

▲ TABLE 30-5
Cost of Production Report,
June 20--, Finishing Department

Important!

Costs Charged to the Department
The total of (1) the cost of products transferred out of a department and (2) the cost of ending work in process in the department must equal the cumulative cost total.

1	20--				1
2	June	30	Work in Process—Laminating Department	12 1 0 0 00	2
3			Work in Process—Finishing Department	11 9 0 0 00	3
4			Manufacturing Overhead	24 0 0 0 00	4
5			Charge overhead to work in process		5
6					6

Recording Transfers of Products out of Departments. The cost of production reports show the cost of goods transferred from the laminating department to the finishing department and to finished goods inventory,

Table 30-4, and from the finishing department to finished goods inventory, Table 30-5. Based on these reports, a journal entry is made to transfer the costs.

1	20--						1
2	June	30	Work in Process—Finishing Department	41 96 0 00			2
3			Finished Goods Inventory	5 24 5 00			3
4			Work in Process—Laminating Department		47 2 0 5 00		4
5			Cost of goods transferred out of				5
6			laminating department in June				6
7							7
8		30	Finished Goods Inventory	70 56 0 00			8
9			Work in Process—Finishing Department		70 56 0 00		9
10			Cost of goods completed in June				10

After the above entries are posted, the departmental **Work in Process** accounts appear as follows. Note that ending balances agree with the amounts shown on the departmental cost of production reports.

ACCOUNT _Work in Process—Laminating Department_   ACCOUNT NO. _122_

DATE		DESCRIPTION	POST. REF.	DEBIT	CREDIT	BALANCE DEBIT	BALANCE CREDIT
20--							
June	30	Materials	J1	15 0 0 0 00		15 0 0 0 00	
	30	Labor	J1	24 2 5 0 00		39 2 5 0 00	
	30	Overhead	J1	12 1 0 0 00		51 3 5 0 00	
	30	Transferred Out	J1		47 2 0 5 00	4 1 4 5 00	

ACCOUNT _Work in Process—Finishing Department_   ACCOUNT NO. _123_

DATE		DESCRIPTION	POST. REF.	DEBIT	CREDIT	BALANCE DEBIT	BALANCE CREDIT
20--							
June	30	Materials	J1	7 9 0 0 00		7 9 0 0 00	
	30	Labor	J1	16 8 7 5 00		24 7 7 5 00	
	30	Overhead	J1	11 9 0 0 00		36 6 7 5 00	
	30	Prior Dept.	J1	41 9 6 0 00		78 6 3 5 00	
	30	Transferred Out	J1		70 5 6 0 00	8 0 7 5 00	

Workforce Retention

To reduce unwanted turnover, employers have tried to make manufacturing jobs more attractive to employees. Of the manufacturers surveyed, 78 percent contribute to 401k and pension plans, 54 percent offer bonus plans tied to performance measures, and many publicly held companies offer stock options to employees.

H-B Instrument Company manufactures relays, thermostats, switches, and calibration instruments. Using an integrated software application called Navision Manufacturing, materials, labor, and overhead costs are recorded as products move through multiple manufacturing processes and departments. Departmental production reports, product status, costs, and materials availability data can be accessed from computerized workstations throughout the plant.

Recording Sale of Finished Goods. The final step is to record the sale of finished goods. Assume that June sales were $105,000 and the cost of the goods sold was $65,000. Note that it takes two journal entries, one to record the sales and another to record the cost of goods sold.

1	20--					1
2	June	30	Accounts Receivable	105 000 00		2
3			Sales		105 000 00	3
4			Record sales on credit for June			4
5						5
6		30	Cost of Goods Sold	65 000 00		6
7			Finished Goods		65 000 00	7
8			Cost of goods sold in June			8

After the sales and cost of goods sold are posted, the **Finished Goods Inventory** and **Cost of Goods Sold** ledger accounts appear as follows.

ACCOUNT _Finished Goods Inventory_   ACCOUNT NO. ___126___

DATE	DESCRIPTION	POST. REF.	DEBIT	CREDIT	BALANCE DEBIT	BALANCE CREDIT
20--						
June 30		J1	5 245 00		5 245 00	
30		J1	70 560 00		75 805 00	
30		J1		65 000 00	10 805 00	

ACCOUNT _Cost of Goods Sold_   ACCOUNT NO. ___560___

DATE	DESCRIPTION	POST. REF.	DEBIT	CREDIT	BALANCE DEBIT	BALANCE CREDIT
20--						
June 30		J1	65 000 00		65 000 00	

Section 1 Self Review

Questions

1. What information appears in the Quantity Schedule section of the cost of production report?

2. What journal entry is made to record the transfer of goods from the final producing department to the finished goods inventory?

3. Some of the units processed in a department are sold without further processing. Others are transferred to a second department for further processing. How will this reflect on the cost of production report?

Exercises

4. Goods are transferred from the cleaning department to the mixing department. The costs transferred in June totaled $95,000. The journal entry to record the transfer is to

a. debit **Work in Process—Mixing** for $95,000 and credit **Work in Process—Cleaning** for $95,000.

b. debit **Work in Process—Cleaning** for $95,000 and credit **Work in Process—Mixing** for $95,000.

c. debit **Cost of Goods Sold** for $95,000 and credit **Work in Process—Mixing** for $95,000.

d. debit **Cost of Goods Sold** for $95,000 and credit **Work in Process—Cleaning** for $95,000.

5. Materials issued to production are recorded by

a. debiting **Raw Materials Inventory** and crediting the departmental **Work in Process** account.

b. debiting the departmental **Work in Process** account and crediting **Raw Materials Inventory**.

c. debiting **Raw Materials Inventory** and crediting the departmental **Finished Goods** account.

d. debiting the departmental **Finished Goods** account and crediting **Raw Materials Inventory**.

Analysis

6. Compute the equivalent units of production for the finishing department assuming materials, labor, and manufacturing overhead are at the same stage of completion. The 300 units in ending work in process are two-thirds complete. There were 3,000 units transferred out.

(Answers to Section 1 Self Review are on page 1091.)

Section Objective

⑤ Compute equivalent production and prepare a cost of production report with a beginning work in process inventory.

WHY IT'S IMPORTANT
Inventories that are carried from one period to the next need to be included in cost of production computations.

Terms to Learn

average method of process costing

Work in Process Inventory

In June there was no beginning work in process for McCallie Manufacturing Company.

The Beginning Work in Process Inventory

Table 30-6 shows the production and cost data for July. It includes beginning work in process by department and by cost element. Notice that manufacturing overhead in beginning work in process is adjusted for rounding. For the laminating department at the end of June, manufacturing overhead in ending work in process was $871.50, and the rounding adjustment was $23.50 (see Table 30-4). In July the beginning work in process for manufacturing overhead was $895 ($871.50 + $23.50).

⑤ **Objective**

Compute equivalent production and prepare a cost of production report with a beginning work in process inventory.

TABLE 30-6 ▶
Departmental Production and Cost Data for July 20--

	Laminating Department	Finishing Department
Costs		
Work in process—beginning		
Costs in prior department		$ 5,245.00
Costs in current department		
Materials	$ 1,500.00	900.00
Labor	1,750.00	1,125.00
Manufacturing overhead	895.00*	805.00*
Costs transferred in from prior department		39,390.00
Current department costs—July		
Materials	16,000.00	8,000.00
Labor	25,300.00	18,000.00
Manufacturing overhead	12,000.00	13,000.00
Total costs	$57,445.00	$86,465.00
Quantities		
Work in process—beginning	500	500
Started in production	4,050	–0–
Transferred in from prior department	–0–	3,000
Transferred out to next department	3,000	–0–
Transferred out to finished goods	1,200	3,100
Work in process—ending	350	400
Stage of Completion—Ending Work in Process		
Materials	Complete	50%
Labor	30%	50
Manufacturing overhead	30	50
*Rounding adjustment included in overhead		

Determining Equivalent Production

Table 30-7 summarizes the equivalent units of production for July.

◀ **TABLE 30-7**
Computation of Equivalent
Production for July 20--

Laminating Department		
Units transferred out		
To next department	3,000	
To finished goods	1,200	4,200
Work in process—ending: 100% × 350 units		350
Equivalent production for materials		4,550
Labor and manufacturing overhead		
Units transferred out		
To next department	3,000	
To finished goods	1,200	4,200
Work in process—ending: 30% × 350 units		105
Equivalent production for labor and overhead		4,305
Finishing Department		
Prior department costs: 100% × 3,500 units		3,500
Materials, labor, and manufacturing overhead		
Units transferred out		3,100
Work in process—ending: 50% × 400 units		200
Equivalent production for materials, labor, and overhead		3,300

Preparing the Cost of Production Report

Table 30-8 on page 1074 shows the July cost of production report for both departments. McCallie Manufacturing Company uses the **average method of process costing**, which combines the cost of beginning inventory for each cost element with the costs of the current period.

Quantity Schedule. The Quantity Schedule section combines the beginning inventory of work in process plus the units started in production or received from the prior department during the period. The result is the total to be accounted for (a). These units are either transferred out or remain in process at the end of the period (b).

Cost Schedule. In the Cost Schedule, there are costs for the beginning work in process (c), (d), and (e). To determine the unit costs, the accountant adds the beginning inventory and the current period costs (f), (g), and (h) and divides the result by the equivalent units.

International INSIGHTS

Cost or Market Inventory Pricing

In the United States, *market value* is defined as what it would cost today to replace an inventory item. However, in many countries market value is defined as net realizable value, which is a product's estimated selling price less any additional costs to complete and less any selling or disposal costs.

	Materials	Labor	Overhead
Beginning	$ 1,500	$ 1,750	$ 895
Current	16,000	25,300	12,000
Total	$17,500	$27,050	$12,895
Equivalent units	4,550	4,305	4,305
Cost per unit	$3.85	$6.28	$3.00

The total unit cost for the laminating department is $13.13.

The total cost transferred out is the quantity transferred to the finishing department (i) and to finished goods inventory (j) multiplied by the total unit cost. The ending work in process inventory (k) is the equivalent production units for each cost element multiplied by the unit cost. There is a rounding adjustment of $22.90.

	Laminating Department		Finishing Department	
Quantity Schedule	Units		Units	
(a) Quantity to be accounted for				
Work in process—beginning	500		500	
Started in production	4,050		–0–	
Transferred in from prior department	–0–		3,000	
Total to be accounted for	4,550		3,500	
(b) Quantity accounted for				
Transferred out to next department	3,000		–0–	
Transferred out to finished goods	1,200		3,100	
Work in process—ending	350		400	
Total accounted for	4,550		3,500	
Cost Schedule	Total Cost	Unit Cost	Total Cost	Unit Cost
Costs to be accounted for				
Costs in prior department				
Work in process—beginning			$ 5,245.00	
Transfers in—current month			39,390.00	
Total prior department cost			$44,635.00	$12.75
Costs in current department				
Work in process—beginning				
(c) Materials	$ 1,500.00		$ 900.00	
(d) Labor	1,750.00		1,125.00	
(e) Manufacturing overhead	895.00*		805.00*	
Current period costs				
(f) Materials	16,000.00	$ 3.85	8,000.00	$ 2.70
(g) Labor	25,300.00	6.28	18,000.00	5.80
(h) Manufacturing overhead	12,000.00	3.00	13,000.00	4.18
Total current department cost	$57,445.00	$13.13	$41,830.00	$12.68
Cumulative total cost	$57,445.00	$13.13	$86,465.00	$25.43
Costs accounted for				
(i) Transferred out to next department	$39,390.00	$13.13	–0–	–0–
(j) Transferred out to finished goods	15,756.00	13.13	$78,833.00	$25.43
Total costs transferred out	$55,146.00		$78,833.00	
(k) Work in process—ending				
Costs in prior department				
Transferred in			$5,100.00	12.75
Costs in current department				
Materials	$ 1,347.50	3.85	540.00	2.70
Labor	659.40	6.28	1,160.00	5.80
Manufacturing overhead	315.00	3.00	836.00	4.18
Rounding adjustment	(22.90)		(4.00)	
Total work in process	$ 2,299.00		$ 7,632.00	
Total costs accounted for	$57,445.00		$86,465.00	

*Rounding adjustment included in overhead

▲ **TABLE 30-8**
Cost of Production Report, July 20--

Accounting

Architecture and Construction

Industry Overview

Professionals in architectural fields design structures such as homes, factories, office complexes, roads, and bridges. Those employed in the construction sector bring these designs to reality, and work on additions, repairs, and alterations to structures. The industry employs a large number of special trades workers as well as construction managers, project estimators, and financial advisors.

Career Opportunities

- Construction Contract Specialist
- Construction Funding Administrator
- Senior Cost Estimator
- General Contractor
- Project Scheduler

Preparing for an Architecture or Construction Career

- Seek training in 3D modeling and rendering, drawing and drafting, and graphics software such as AutoCAD for an architectural career.
- Complete a Bachelor of Architecture degree and practical training or internship.
- Become proficient in project scope and budgeting, specification requirements, and bid strategies. Be prepared to track project costs, pricing changes, vendor payments, and communicate with accounting and scheduling departments.
- Complete a degree in business administration, finance, or accounting for executive, administrative, and managerial careers in the construction industry. Field engineering, scheduling, and cost estimating jobs can lead to positions as construction manager, general superintendent, construction building inspector, or general manager.

Thinking Critically

If you worked as a cost estimator for an architectural firm, what team members would you collaborate with to properly assess the costs of individual projects?

Internet Application

Research the E-Architect Web site for positions that require experience or training in budgeting, project management, or cost estimation. Select two positions. List job title, responsibilities, and skills or education required.

Laminating Department

	Materials	Labor	Overhead
Equivalent units	350	105	105
Unit cost	× $3.85	× $6.28	× $3.00
Total	$1,347.50	$659.40	$315.00

For the finishing department, there are two costs from the prior department: the beginning inventory amount ($5,245) and the cost transferred in ($39,390). The total cost ($44,635) is divided by the total units (3,500) to get an average unit cost of $12.75.

Department unit costs are computed in the same manner as they were for the laminating department.

	Materials	Labor	Overhead
Beginning	$ 900.00	$ 1,125.00	$ 805.00
Current	8,000.00	18,000.00	13,000.00
Total	$8,900.00	$19,125.00	$13,805.00
Equivalent units	3,300	3,300	3,300
Cost per unit	$2.70	$5.80	$4.18

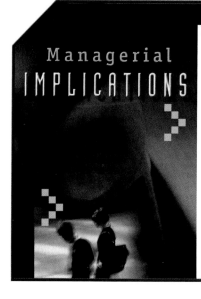

Managerial IMPLICATIONS

Process Cost Accounting

- Managers need accurate, up-to-date cost data to set prices, evaluate efficiency, and make operating decisions.

- Manufacturing firms should rely on a cost accountant to develop an accounting system that will yield the required data accurately and swiftly.

- The process cost accounting system provides a unit manufacturing cost for products that are manufactured on a continuous basis.

- The average cost method of handling beginning inventories of work in process simplifies calculation of the costs per unit.

Thinking Critically
Under what conditions would a process cost accounting system be used?

The unit cost for the current department is $12.68. The total unit cost for the finishing department is $25.43. The total cost transferred out is the quantity transferred to finished goods (j) multiplied by the total unit cost. The ending work in process inventory (k) is the equivalent production units for units transferred in and for each cost element multiplied by the unit cost. There is a $4 rounding adjustment.

Finishing Department

	Transferred In	Materials	Labor	Overhead
Equivalent units	400	200	200	200
Unit cost	× $12.75	× $2.70	× $5.80	× $4.18
Total	$5,100.00	$540.00	$1,160.00	$836.00

Recording Cost Flows

Entries to summarize the July costs and transfers, and the departmental **Work in Process** accounts after the entries are posted, appear as follows. The July beginning balances of the **Work in Process** accounts are the same as the ending balances for June. Balances in the accounts at the end of July correspond to the amounts on the July cost of production report. The two entries to record the sale of finished goods are not shown but would be recorded as described in Section 1 of this chapter.

1	20--					1
2	July	31	Work in Process—Laminating Department	16 000 00		2
3			Work in Process—Finishing Department	8 000 00		3
4			Raw Materials Inventory		24 000 00	4
5			Charge materials to production			5
6						6
7		31	Work in Process—Laminating Department	25 300 00		7
8			Work in Process—Finishing Department	18 000 00		8
9			Social Security Tax Payable		2 684 60	9
10			Medicare Tax Payable		627 85	10
11			Employee Income Tax Payable		6 388 25	11
12			Salaries and Wages Payable		33 599 30	12
13			Salaries and wages for month			13

				DEBIT	CREDIT	
15	July	31	Work in Process—Laminating Department	12 000 00		15
16			Work in Process—Finishing Department	13 000 00		16
17			Manufacturing Overhead		25 000 00	17
18			Charge overhead to work in process			18
19						19
20		31	Work in Process—Finishing Department	39 390 00		20
21			Finished Goods Inventory	15 756 00		21
22			Work in Process—Laminating Department		55 146 00	22
23			Cost of goods transferred out of			23
24			laminating department in July			24
25						25
26		31	Finished Goods Inventory	78 833 00		26
27			Work in Process—Finishing Department		78 833 00	27
28			Cost of goods completed in July			28
29			and transferred out			29

ACCOUNT Work in Process—Laminating Department   ACCOUNT NO. 122

DATE	DESCRIPTION	POST. REF.	DEBIT	CREDIT	BALANCE DEBIT	BALANCE CREDIT
20--						
July 1	Balance				4 145 00	
31	Materials	J1	16 000 00		20 145 00	
31	Labor	J1	25 300 00		45 445 00	
31	Overhead	J1	12 000 00		57 445 00	
31	Trans. Out	J1		55 146 00	2 299 00	

ACCOUNT Work in Process—Finishing Department   ACCOUNT NO. 123

DATE	DESCRIPTION	POST. REF.	DEBIT	CREDIT	BALANCE DEBIT	BALANCE CREDIT
20--						
July 1	Balance				8 075 00	
31	Materials	J1	8 000 00		16 075 00	
31	Labor	J1	18 000 00		34 075 00	
31	Overhead	J1	13 000 00		47 075 00	
31	Prior Dept.	J1	39 390 00		86 465 00	
31	Trans. Out	J1		78 833 00	7 632 00	

Section 2 Self Review

Questions

1. What is the difference between cost of production reports with and without beginning work in process inventory?

2. How is the unit cost of labor calculated when there is beginning work in process inventory?

3. In the cost of production report, how are the costs transferred in from a prior department handled?

Exercises

4. The source of the cost data in a cost of production report is
   a. **Work in Process** accounts.
   b. job order costs sheets.
   c. prior period income statement.
   d. **Raw Materials** accounts.

5. March sales are $80,000 and cost of goods sold is $50,000. What is the entry to **Finished Goods Inventory**?

a. $50,000 credit c. $80,000 debit
b. $80,000 credit d. $50,000 debit

Analysis

6. Compute the unit cost for materials when beginning work in process is $850, current period costs are $12,835, and equivalent units for the department are 4,000.

(Answers to Section 2 Self Review are on page 1091.)

Review

Chapter Summary

The process cost accounting system is commonly used when only one product is manufactured in a department and production is on a continuous basis rather than in batches or by specific job. In this chapter you have reviewed the procedures for process cost accounting systems and how they differ from a job order cost accounting system.

Learning Objectives

① Compute equivalent units of production with no beginning work in process inventory.

The equivalent production unit technique is used to convert ending work in process to equivalent finished production. Separate computations must be made for the three elements of production (materials, labor, and overhead) whenever the states of completion of the three elements in the work in process inventory are different.

② Prepare a cost of production report with no beginning work in process inventory.

The cost of production report summarizes all costs charged to each department during the month and shows how these costs are assigned to the goods transferred out of the department and those still in process.

- The equivalent production unit technique is used to convert ending work in process to equivalent finished production.
- Then the costs for each equivalent unit of materials, labor, and overhead are computed.
- The value of goods transferred out of the department, as well as of work in process inventories, is determined on the basis of the equivalent units of production for each cost element.
- The costs of the goods transferred from one department to another are charged to the receiving department and removed from the **Work in Process** account of the first department.

③ Compute the unit cost of manufacturing under the process cost accounting system.

The unit cost to manufacture a product is computed by dividing the total cost of each production element by the appropriate equivalent production units.

④ Record costs incurred and the flow of costs as products move through the manufacturing process and are sold.

- A work in process inventory account is set up for each producing department.
- Direct materials costs and direct labor costs are charged to the departmental **Work in Process** accounts.
- Overhead costs incurred are charged to the **Manufacturing Overhead** control account.
- Each producing and service department has a cost sheet in the subsidiary ledger.
- At the end of each month, the costs of the service departments are allocated to the producing departments.

⑤ Compute equivalent production and prepare a cost of production report with a beginning work in process inventory.

If there is a beginning work in process inventory, the same basic process cost accounting procedures are followed to prepare a cost of production report.

- Under the average cost system, the cost of each element in the beginning work in process is added to the cost of that element during the month.
- Equivalent units of production are computed for each element just as when there was no beginning inventory of work in process.
- The total cost of an element divided by the equivalent units of production for the element yields the unit cost for the element.
- Cost of product transferred out of the department and cost of ending work in process are then computed in the usual manner.

⑥ Define the accounting terms new to this chapter.

CHAPTER 30 GLOSSARY

Average method of process costing (p. 1073) A method of costing that combines the cost of beginning inventory for each cost element with the costs during the current period

Cost of production report (p. 1067) Summarizes all costs charged to each department and shows the costs assigned to the goods transferred out of the department and to the goods still in process

Equivalent production (p. 1065) The estimated number of units that could have been started and completed with the same effort and costs incurred in the department during the same time period

Process cost accounting system (p. 1064) A method of accounting in which costs are accumulated for each process or department and then transferred on to the next process or department

Comprehensive Self Review

1. Why can a process cost accounting system be referred to as an average cost system?

2. What is the source of the information in the Costs to Be Accounted For section of a cost of production report?

3. A company uses the process cost accounting system. It has two service departments. How will the costs of the service departments enter into the cost of an equivalent unit for the producing departments?

4. What is the purpose of the cost of production report?

5. Explain the flow of costs in the accounting records.

(Answers to Comprehensive Self Review are on page 1091.)

Discussion Questions

1. Why are job order cost sheets not used in the process cost accounting system?

2. What are equivalent units of production?

3. In a cost of production report, what items are found in the Costs to Be Accounted For section?

4. How is the ending work in process inventory computed in a process cost accounting system?

5. Will the same equivalent units always be used for materials, labor, and overhead? Explain.

6. Will the amount shown as a department's ending inventory of work in process on the cost of production report agree with the work in process for the department in the general ledger after adjusting and closing entries have been posted? Explain.

7. Why is it not necessary to use an overhead application rate when the process cost accounting system is employed?

8. Why might the process cost accounting system be unsatisfactory when several different products are being manufactured in the same department?

9. How does accounting for the raw materials inventory and the finished goods inventory differ under the process cost accounting system and the job order cost accounting system?

10. Explain what is meant by "the average method" of accounting for beginning work in process inventories in a process cost system.

11. Explain how to compute the equivalent production for labor when there is a beginning work in process inventory for the period, assuming that the average cost method is used.

Applications

EXERCISES

Data for Exercises 30-1 through 30-3.

Information about production in the fabricating department of the Metal Shop Company for March 20-- follows:

Beginning inventory	–0–
Transferred in from prior department	10,000 units
Transferred out to next department	9,500 units
Ending inventory, work in process	500 units
Stage of completion of ending work in process	
Prior department costs	100%
Materials	80%
Labor and overhead	50%

Computing equivalent production for prior department costs with no beginning inventory.

◀ **Exercise 30-1**
Objective 1

Compute the equivalent units of production for the prior department costs for the month of March for Metal Shop Company.

Computing equivalent production for materials with no beginning inventory.

◀ **Exercise 30-2**
Objective 1

Compute the equivalent units of production for materials for the month of March for Metal Shop Company.

Computing equivalent production for labor and overhead with no beginning inventory.

◀ **Exercise 30-3**
Objective 1

Compute the equivalent units of production for labor and overhead for the month of March for Metal Shop Company.

Computing equivalent production for materials and unit cost of materials with no beginning work in process.

◀ **Exercise 30-4**
Objectives 1, 3

On June 1, 20--, the assembly department of Alex Corporation had no beginning work in process. During the month, production was started on 5,000 units. The total cost of materials was $20,500. All materials were placed in production at the start of the manufacturing process in the department. During the month 4,200 units were transferred to the next department, and 800 units were still in process at the end of the month.

1. What is the cost per equivalent unit for materials?

2. What is the cost of materials in the goods transferred to the next department?

3. What is the cost of materials in the ending work in process inventory?

Data for Exercises 30-5 and 30-6.

The cutting department is the first department of the Boots R Us Manufacturing Company. On July 1, 20--, the beginning inventory in this department consisted of 500 units. Costs for the beginning work in process were as follows:

Materials (100% complete)	$5,500
Labor (80% complete)	3,500
Overhead (80% complete)	3,400

During July 20--, 2,000 units were started into production with the following costs:

Materials	$22,000
Labor	14,925
Overhead	16,608

The number of units completed and sent to the finishing department was 1,900. The ending inventory of 600 units were 100 percent complete in regard to materials, 90 percent complete with regard to labor and overhead.

Exercise 30-5 ►
Objectives 3, 5

Computing equivalent production for materials and cost per equivalent unit with beginning work in process.

1. Compute the July equivalent production for materials for Boots R Us.
2. Compute the cost per equivalent unit for materials for July.
3. Compute the cost of materials in the work transferred out of the department during the month.
4. Compute the month-end cost of materials in the ending work in process.

Exercise 30-6 ►
Objectives 3, 5

Computing equivalent production for overhead and cost per equivalent unit with beginning work in process.

1. Compute the equivalent production for overhead for July.
2. Compute the cost per equivalent unit for overhead for July.
3. Compute the cost of overhead in the goods transferred out.
4. Compute the cost of overhead in the ending work in process inventory.

Data for Exercises 30-7 through 30-9.

At SoCal Corporation production is started in the forming department. The work is then transferred to the finishing department where goods are completed and then transferred to the finished goods storeroom. Data about the company's costs during August 20-- follows.

Material costs placed into production	
Forming department	$45,500
Finishing department	4,200
Direct labor costs	
Forming department	12,000
Finishing department	16,800
Taxes withheld from employees' earnings	
Social security tax withheld	1,786
Medicare tax withheld	418
Federal income tax withheld	4,320
Overhead costs	
Forming department	12,500
Finishing department	15,500

During the month, products costing $60,000 were transferred from the forming department to the finishing department; goods costing $89,000 were transferred from the finishing department to finished goods inventory; and goods that cost $90,000 were sold on account for $150,000.

Exercise 30-7 ►
Objective 4

Recording costs incurred in production.

Give the journal entries on August 31 to summarize the following.

1. Materials placed into production

2. Labor costs charged into production

3. Overhead costs charged into production

Recording transfer of product between departments and from work in process to finished goods.

Give the general journal entries on August 31 to record the following.

1. Transfer of product from the forming department to the finishing department

2. Transfer of finished goods from the finishing department to finished goods inventory

◀ **Exercise 30-8**
Objective 4

Recording cost of goods completed.

Give general journal entries to record the following events during August.

1. Sale of goods

2. Cost of goods sold

◀ **Exercise 30-9**
Objective 4

Problems

Selected problems can be completed using:

▦ **Spreadsheets**

PROBLEM SET A

Computing equivalent production with no beginning work in process.

Outdoor Products Company manufactures a single type of garden cart. The monthly production report for February 20-- follows.

◀ **Problem 30-1A**
Objective 1

Outdoor Products Company			
Monthly Production Report for February 20--			
	Molding Department	Assembly Department	Completion Department
Quantities			
Started in production—current month	1,700	–0–	–0–
Transferred in from prior department	–0–	1,500	1,400
Transferred out to next department	1,500	1,400	–0–
Transferred out to finished goods	–0–	–0–	1,300
Work in process—ending	200	100	100
Stage of Completion—Ending Work in Process			
Materials	Complete	Complete	80%
Labor	80%	50%	80
Overhead	80	50	80

Prepare the equivalent production computations for each department.

INSTRUCTIONS

Analyze: Which department is at the lowest stage of completion in regard to labor and overhead in the month of February?

Computing equivalent production, preparing a cost of production report, computing unit costs, and recording flow of cost through manufacturing process and sale.

TV Toymakers Inc. has two producing departments—fabricating and assembly. The following data is from the firm's records for the month of July 20--. There were no beginning inventories.

	Fabricating Department	Assembly Department
Costs		
Materials	$50,000	$20,020
Labor	27,840	26,250
Manufacturing overhead	13,920	12,000
Total Costs	$91,760	$58,270
Quantities		
Beginning inventories	–0–	–0–
Started in production	10,000	–0–
Transferred in from fabricating department	–0–	8,000
Transferred out to assembly department	8,000	–0–
Transferred out to finished goods	–0–	7,000
Work in process—ending	2,000	1,000
Stage of Completion—Ending Work in Process		
Materials	100%	70%
Labor	80	50
Manufacturing overhead	80	50

INSTRUCTIONS

1. In general journal form, record the flow of costs that follow. Date all entries July 31, 20--.

   a. The issuance of materials to each department

   b. The monthly payroll for the producing departments; taxes withheld: social security, $3,353; Medicare, $784; federal income tax, $8,113

   c. The distribution of manufacturing overhead to each department

2. Prepare equivalent production computations for each department.

3. Prepare a cost of production report for each department.

4. Record the following in general journal form.

   a. The transfer of goods from the fabricating department to the assembly department

   b. The transfer of completed goods from the assembly department to the finished goods storeroom

   c. Sales on credit for $143,220; these goods cost $102,300 to manufacture

Analyze: What was the balance of the **Work in Process** account for the fabricating department on July 31?

Computing equivalent production and preparing a cost of production report with a beginning work in process.

◀ **Problem 30-3A**
Objective 5

Long-Life Liquid Corporation adds all materials at the beginning of production. On July 1, 20--, 1,000 gallons of its product were in production in the first department. During the month of July, 14,000 gallons were put into production. On July 31, 2,000 gallons were still in production. The ending inventory is estimated to be 60 percent complete as to labor and overhead. Cost data for the month follows.

	Materials	Labor	Overhead
Beginning inventory of work in process	$ 2,250	$ 620	$ 1,240
Added during July	60,000	15,000	30,000

INSTRUCTIONS

Prepare a cost of production report for the month of July, assuming that the average cost method is used.

Analyze: How many gallons of product will be held as beginning inventory of work in process on August 1 for the first department? What is the total cost for this quantity of product?

PROBLEM SET B

Computing equivalent production with no beginning work in process.

◀ **Problem 30-1B**
Objective 1

The Plastic Company manufactures plastic carts. The monthly production report for December 20-- follows.

The Plastic Company
Monthly Production Report for December 20--

	Molding Department	Assembly Department	Completion Department
Quantities			
Started in production—current month	2,000	–0–	–0–
Transferred in from prior department	–0–	1,800	1,700
Transferred out to next department	1,800	1,700	–0–
Transferred out to finished goods	–0–	–0–	1,600
Work in process—ending	200	100	100
Stage of Completion—Ending Work in Process			
Materials	100%	90%	100%
Labor	90	75	50
Overhead	90	75	50

INSTRUCTIONS

Prepare the equivalent production computations for each department.

Analyze: What portion of materials was completed in the assembly department during the month of December?

Computing equivalent production, preparing a cost of production report, computing unit costs, and recording flow of costs through manufacturing process and sale.

Best Makers Inc. has two producing departments—fabricating and assembly. The following data is from the firm's records for the month of August 20--. There were no beginning inventories.

	Fabricating Department	Assembly Department
Costs		
Materials	$ 62,500	$ 32,700
Labor	86,450	43,400
Manufacturing overhead	74,100	54,250
Total Costs	$223,050	$130,350
Quantities		
Beginning inventories	–0–	–0–
Started in production	25,000	–0–
Transferred in from fabricating department	–0–	22,000
Transferred out to assembly department	22,000	–0–
Transferred out to finished goods	–0–	21,000
Work in process—ending	3,000	1,000
Stage of Completion—Ending Work in Process		
Materials	100%	80%
Labor	90	70
Manufacturing overhead	90	70

INSTRUCTIONS

1. In general journal form, record the flow of costs that follow. Date all entries August 31, 20--.

   a. The issuance of materials to each department

   b. The producing department's monthly payroll; taxes withheld: social security, $8,050.70; Medicare, $1,882.82; federal income tax, $19,477.50

   c. The distribution of manufacturing overhead to each department

2. Prepare equivalent production computations for each department.

3. Prepare a cost of production report for each department.

4. Record the following in general journal form.

   a. The transfer of goods from fabricating to assembly

   b. The transfer of completed goods from the assembly department to the finished goods storeroom

   c. Sales on credit for $450,000; cost of goods sold, $270,000

Analyze: What is the balance of the **Work in Process** account for the fabricating department on August 31?

Computing equivalent production and preparing a cost of production report when there is beginning work in process.

Western Chemical Company manufactures a pharmaceutical chemical. All materials are put into process at the beginning of production. On

April 1, 20--, 3,000 pounds of the product were in process in the first department. During the month of April, 47,000 pounds were put into production. On April 30, 5,000 pounds were still in production. The ending inventory is estimated to be complete as to materials and 80 percent complete as to labor and overhead. Cost data for the month is as follows.

	Materials	Labor	Overhead
Beginning inventory of work in process	$ 12,500	$ 2,000	$ 1,500
Added during April	100,000	47,000	23,000

INSTRUCTIONS

Compute equivalent production, and prepare a cost of production report for the month of April, assuming that the average cost method is used.

Analyze: What total production cost is attributable to products transferred from the first department to the next department?

CHAPTER 30 CHALLENGE PROBLEM

Material Costs

Selected data about the operations of the reforming department, the first department, of Beagle Manufacturing Company for February 20-- follows.

At the beginning of the month, there were 1,000 units in process in the department, with a total cost of $33,000. Material costs of $15,000 were included in the beginning work in process inventory of $33,000. During the month, the total cost of the 23,000 units transferred to the next department was $759,000. This total included labor costs of $12 per unit and total material costs of $345,000, in addition to manufacturing overhead. Costs incurred during the month included overhead of $138,000. At the end of the month an estimated one-half of labor and overhead had been added to the 2,000 units in process. All materials are added at the start of production.

INSTRUCTIONS

1. Compute the equivalent units of production for the month.
2. Prepare a cost of production report for the department for the month.

Analyze: What percentage of total current department costs is attributable to materials costs in the reforming department?

CHAPTER 30 CRITICAL THINKING PROBLEM

Cost Flows

California Candy Company makes a chocolate candy. The continuous production operation starts in the mixing department where the chocolate, sugar, water, and other ingredients are blended. It then moves to the second department (cooking) where the ingredient mix is boiled and poured into molds. Finally, in the last department (cooling and packaging), the product is packed six boxes to a container. The containers are sealed, ready for shipping to supermarkets around the country. Prepare a diagram to show the flow of costs through California Candy Company's perpetual inventory accounts. Indicate with arrows the direction of the cost flow through the accounts.

Business Connections

Connection 1 ▶ **MANAGERIAL FOCUS** **Accurate Cost Accounting**

1. The directors of the firm where you work have asked you to explain whether the job order cost accounting system or the process cost accounting system provides the more accurate costs for each unit of product. What will you tell them?

2. What are the benefits of perpetual inventories to management?

3. How would managers use the cost of labor for each equivalent unit to help control costs?

4. Why would a comparison of the cost per equivalent unit of each cost element (materials, labor, and overhead) for the current month with that of the preceding month be useful to management?

5. A manager in the company where you work asks why it is necessary to convert production to equivalent units when determining the cost of each unit of product produced under the process cost accounting system. Explain.

Connection 2 ▶ **Ethical DILEMMA** **Estimates** The Liquid Processing Company utilizes a process cost accounting system. Suzanne Roma is the chief cost accountant. When she makes the estimate of the degree of completion of the ending work in process for each department, she always takes the approach of estimating a higher percentage complete than the cost figures may indicate. Is she violating any ethical area of accounting?

Connection 3 ▶ **StreetWISE:**
Questions from the Real World **Accounting Processes** Refer to the *1999 Annual Report* for The Home Depot, Inc. in Appendix B.

1. The Home Depot, Inc. purchases wood products such as plywood, pressed wallboard, and solid wood doors for resale in its stores. Do you think manufacturers of wood products use process or job order costing systems? Explain your answer.

2. Locate the letter written to The Home Depot, Inc. stockholders, customers, and associates in Appendix B. Describe the two store models that the company has launched. Do you think these ventures will be well received by home improvement consumers? Why or why not?

Connection 4 ▶
Kodak

FINANCIAL STATEMENT ANALYSIS **Manufacturing Operations and the Environment** The following excerpts were taken from the *Kodak 1999 Health, Safety, and Environment Annual Report.*

In the spring of 1999, Kodak publicly announced new goals designed to substantially cut not only emissions to the environment, but also the amounts of waste, energy and water used in manufacturing operations. The goals, to be achieved by January 1, 2004, address three strategic initiatives:

- greater reduction in emissions,
- preserving natural resources, and
- further strengthening of Kodak's environmental management system.

Preservation of Natural Resources
(indexed to populations)

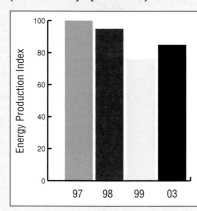

Goal: 15% reduction in energy used in manufacturing.

First-year progress: With excellent improvement at Kodak's Kirkby and Harrow plants in Great Britain, energy used in worldwide manufacturing has been reduced 24%.

Analyze

1. According to the information presented, has Kodak met its goal to reduce energy used in manufacturing in 1999?

2. Environmental goals, as previously described, impact manufacturing costs for a business such as Kodak. Describe how you think a goal such as reducing emissions might impact total manufacturing costs.

Analyze Online: Locate Kodak's current year *Health, Safety, and Environment Annual Report* on the company's Web site **(www.kodak.com).**

3. Describe current investments made by Kodak to achieve its environmental goals.

4. What results were realized in the company's film container recycling program over the past five years?

Extending the Thought **Manufacturing Standards** Corporations who compete in manufacturing environments are often faced with balancing the need to manufacture products quickly with the desire to produce quality goods. If manufacturing managers are held accountable for manufacturing costs, inventory levels, and labor variances, what types of quality standards should also be considered?

◄ **Connection 5**

Business Communication **Sharing Financial Data** Assume that you are the purchasing officer for Blazing Trails, Inc., a manufacturer of mountain bikes. You are responsible for buying all materials such as bike frames, gear systems, seats, and pedals that are used in the assembly of mountain bikes. In the past you have not been given the cost of production reports generated by the accounting department. You would like to be included on the distribution list for these monthly reports. In a memo to the accounting manager, Stan Foreman, explain why you would like to receive these reports and why you think this information will benefit you in your job.

◄ **Connection 6**

Connection 7 ►

Team_Work_ **Identifying Process Cost Accounting Systems** As a team, choose the manufacturing attributes, business types, or accounting methodologies that most appropriately align with the process cost accounting system. Explain your selections.

Business Types	Manufacturing Attributes	Accounting Methodologies
Airplane manufacturer	High standardization of production techniques	Manufacturing costs accumulated by job order
Paper manufacturer	Low production volume	Inventory accounts set up for each processing department
Baseball bat manufacturer	Repetitive production processes	Accumulated manufacturing costs transferred from department to department
Paint manufacturer	Custom product orders	Job order time cards used to collect labor costs

Connection 8 ►

inter **NET**
CONNECTION **Society for Inventory Management Benchmarking Analysis** Locate the Web site for the Society for Inventory Management **(www.simba.org).** Use the information on the Web site to answer the following.

- Name two objectives of the organization.
- Describe the types of individuals that might be interested in joining SIMBA.

Answers to Self Reviews

Answers to Section 1 Self-Review

1. The first part shows the units to be accounted for. The second part shows what happened to the units.
2. Debit **Finished Goods Inventory** and credit the **Work in Process** account of the final department.
3. The Costs Accounted For section of the cost of production report will require two lines for products transferred out of the department. One line will be Transferred Out to Next Department and the second will be Transferred Out to Finished Goods. The total of the two amounts would equal Total Costs Transferred Out.
4. **a.** debit **Work in Process—Mixing** for $95,000 and credit **Work in Process—Cleaning** for $95,000.
5. **b.** debiting the departmental **Work in Process** account and crediting **Raw Materials Inventory.**
6. 3,200 (3,000 + (300 × 2/3))

Answers to Section 2 Self Review

1. When there is a beginning work in process inventory, both the quantities and the costs for the inventory must be accounted for. The costs per equivalent unit must consider the beginning inventory of each element as well as the costs added during the current period.
2. The amount of labor cost in the beginning work in process inventory must be added to the labor costs incurred during the current period. The total is divided by the equivalent units of production to arrive at the labor cost per unit.
3. They must be treated as a "cost to be accounted for" in the department to which the product is transferred.
4. **a. Work in Process** accounts.
5. **a.** $50,000 credit (The debit is to **Cost of Goods Sold** for $50,000.)
6. $3.42

Answers to Comprehensive Self Review

1. All costs for each manufacturing element (materials, labor, and overhead) incurred during the month are added together and divided by the equivalent units of production for that element during the month. Costs incurred for each element are, in a sense, averaged.
2. The current month's costs to be accounted for in the cost of production report are taken from the departmental **Work in Process** accounts. The details of beginning inventory of work in process can be determined from the cost of production report of the prior month.
3. At the end of the month, the costs of service departments are allocated to the overhead of the producing departments.
4. It summarizes all costs charged to each department during the month and shows how these costs are assigned to the goods transferred out of the department and those still in process.
5. Direct costs are charged to the departmental **Work in Process** accounts. Overhead costs are charged to the **Manufacturing Overhead** control account, and then allocated to departmental overhead sheets for each department. At the end of the month, the costs of the service departments are allocated to the producing department. Finally, the **Manufacturing Overhead** control account is closed into the departmental **Work in Process** accounts.

CHAPTER 31

Learning Objectives

1 Explain how fixed, variable, and semivariable costs change as the level of manufacturing activity changes.

2 Use the high-low point method to determine the fixed and variable components of a semivariable cost.

3 Prepare a fixed budget for manufacturing costs.

4 Develop a flexible budget for manufacturing costs.

5 Develop standard costs per unit of product.

6 Compute the standard costs of products manufactured during the period and determine cost variances between actual costs and standard costs.

7 Compute the amounts and analyze the nature of variances from standard for raw materials, labor, and manufacturing overhead.

8 Define the accounting terms new to this chapter.

Controlling Manufacturing Costs: Standard Costs

New Terms

Budget

Budget performance
  report

Cost variance

Fixed budget

Fixed costs

Flexible budget

High-low point method

Labor efficiency variance

Labor rate variance

Labor time variance

Manufacturing cost
  budget

Materials price variance

Materials quantity
  variance

Materials usage variance

Relevant range of activity

Semivariable costs

Standard cost card

Variable costs

Variance analysis

Boise Cascade
Corporation

www.boisecascade.com

B oise Cascade operates more than
35 manufacturing facilities in the
United States, producing building
materials and wood products. In addition to
attending to environmental issues and competitive strategies, manufacturers such as
Boise Cascade are keenly aware of market
trends and product demand. In June 2000
increased interest rates, decreased demand,
and increases in imported industrial lumber
created an imbalance between supply and
demand in the wood and building materials
markets. In response Boise Cascade curtailed
production levels at several of its western
sawmills. Decreased production directives
were spread over a two-month period. Well-
timed production decisions, such as this one
made by Boise Cascade, maintain inventories
at sufficient levels while attending to overall
production costs.

Thinking Critically
**How do you think Boise Cascade accoun-
tants budget for the changing levels of
production at paper and building materials
manufacturing plants?**

**For more information on Boise Cascade
Corporation, go to:
collegeaccounting.glencoe.com.**

Cost Behavior and the Budget

Terms to Learn

budget
budget performance report
fixed budget
fixed costs
flexible budget
high-low point method
manufacturing cost budget
relevant range of activity
semivariable costs
variable costs

To control costs and make effective decisions, managers need information on the *variability of costs*—how costs change as the volume of output changes. In this chapter you will learn how cost variability is measured. You will also learn how to use cost behavior to develop budgets and standard costs.

Cost Behavior

Manufacturing costs can be classified as variable, fixed, and semivariable. It is essential to understand these terms in order to analyze costs.

Variable Costs

Variable costs are costs that vary *in total* in direct proportion to changes in the level of activity. Direct materials and direct labor are examples of variable costs. If direct materials cost $3 for one unit, then the materials cost for 1,000 units is $3,000 (1,000 × $3) and for 5,000 units is $15,000 (5,000 × $3). If direct labor cost is $5 per unit of product, the total labor cost for manufacturing 2,500 units is $12,500 (2,500 × $5) and for 4,000 units is $20,000 (4,000 units × $5).

Note that the term *variable* refers to the *total* cost. The cost *per unit* of material or labor does not change as output changes, but the total cost of material or labor changes.

Fixed Costs

Fixed costs are costs that do not change *in total* as the level of activity changes. For example, the salary of the production vice president does not vary from month to month based on the number of units produced.

Note that although fixed costs do not change in total as the level of activity changes, the cost per unit does change. For example, if factory supervisory salaries are $5,000 for the month, the cost per unit is $2.50 if 2,000 units are produced ($5,000 ÷ 2,000) and $2.00 if 2,500 units are produced ($5,000 ÷ 2,500).

Semivariable Costs

Semivariable costs, also called *mixed costs*, are costs that vary with, but not in direct proportion to, the volume of activity. A semivariable cost contains a fixed element that does not change because of changes in the level of activity. It also contains a variable component that does vary with changes in activity.

Utilities are an example of a semivariable cost. Lighting, heating, and cooling are necessary to operate the factory regardless of how many units are produced. The fixed portion of these costs ensures basic service. However, the electricity used to operate machines will vary in proportion to the level of production.

To prepare budgets, measure efficiency, develop expected costs, and analyze the differences between actual costs and expected costs, it is necessary to separate semivariable costs into their fixed and variable components. The **high-low point method** is a simple method to determine the fixed and variable components of a semivariable cost.

Let's examine how Pacific Manufacturing Company uses the high-low point method. Pacific uses the job order cost system.

1. Determine the production and cost data for the months of highest and lowest production during the past year. The data for Pacific Manufacturing Company follows. The month of June had the highest production level. January had the lowest production level.

❶ Objective

Explain how fixed, variable, and semivariable costs change as the level of manufacturing activity changes.

Month	Direct Labor Hours	Utilities Cost
January	1,600	$1,800
February	2,160	2,360
March	2,580	2,780
April	2,800	3,000
May	2,900	3,100
June	3,100	3,300
July	2,200	2,400
August	2,040	2,240
September	2,120	2,320
October	2,200	2,400
November	2,060	2,260
December	1,800	2,000

❷ Objective

Use the high-low point method to determine the fixed and variable components of a semivariable cost.

2. Compute the difference in direct labor hours in the months of highest and lowest production. Also compute the difference in utilities costs.

Month	Direct Labor Hours	Utilities Cost
June	3,100	$3,300
January	1,600	1,800
Difference	1,500	$1,500

3. Compute the variable cost per direct labor hour by dividing the difference in utilities costs by the difference in direct labor hours. The variable cost per direct labor hour is $1 ($1,500 ÷ 1,500 hours).

4. Compute the fixed cost for a month by deducting the variable cost from the total cost for that month. The variable cost is the cost per direct labor hour, computed in step 3, multiplied by the number of hours of direct labor worked during the month selected. For example, using the month of June, the total variable costs are $3,100 (3,100 hours × $1 per hour).

Important!

Fixed Costs
As the volume of output increases, the fixed cost per unit of output decreases.

Total cost	$3,300
Less variable costs	3,100
Fixed costs	$ 200

The major advantage of using the high-low point method is its simplicity. The results could be misleading, however, if the highest and lowest months are not representative of the other months. For this reason

Computers in Accounting

Data Conferencing

Face-to-face communication is considered the preferred way to conduct business meetings. Real-time exchange of ideas enables listeners and speakers to observe facial gestures and to hear vocal inflections, which help them understand decision-making styles and differences in philosophies.

In the business world today, meetings cannot always occur in person. Although technologies such as e-mail and groupware allow people to work collaboratively, sharing documents or project plans, the work does not occur in real time. These interactions are asynchronous. Synchronous meeting tools provide platforms for groups to work in real time, collaboratively developing a project or responding to questions from participants.

Data conferencing is one new form of synchronous electronic meeting. Group members share or transfer documents, participate in whiteboarding exercises (words or pictures drawn on an electronic whiteboard transmitted to remote locations), and speak to each other. Data conferencing excludes video applications that require expensive bandwidth to transmit the signal. Electronic meetings can take place via the Web, company Intranet, or networked computer system.

A data conferencing session might be conducted as follows:

- The meeting organizer launches the data conferencing application, participants log in from remote locations, and the presentation is controlled from one computer.

- Documents, drawings, designs, or financial reports are viewable and can be edited by all users.
- Participants have controls to vote on topics, type comments, or speak to the group. Users may choose to share comments with all participants or select individuals.
- Sketches can be combined with text comments and viewed by all participants simultaneously.
- Web pages can be launched on the screen and viewed by all users.
- The meeting organizer can send participants into virtual breakout sessions to tackle separate issues or brainstorm ideas.

Data conferencing cannot replace the subtle benefits of face-to-face meetings, but synchronous meeting applications can be used for training, education programs, product and service support, business decision making, and brainstorming sessions.

Thinking Critically
What experiences have you had on the job or in the classroom that have used video or data conferencing tools? Describe your impression of these tools.

Internet Application
Research some of the leading synchronous conferencing applications online. Using an Internet search engine, enter the search term "data conferencing." In a half-page report, describe the benefits to the use of a data conferencing system. List any disadvantages or impediments to the use of such a system.

some accountants also compute fixed costs using the second highest and second lowest months. They compare the results of the two calculations to ensure that they are consistent. If the results are not similar, the accountant might need to use other methods to separate fixed and variable costs; these methods are covered in cost accounting textbooks.

❸ Objective

Prepare a fixed budget for manufacturing costs.

Preparation of the Fixed Budget

A **budget** is an operating plan expressed in monetary units. Well-run companies prepare detailed budgets for each year and for each month within the year. The **manufacturing cost budget** is a budget for each manufacturing cost for the budget period.

The management of Pacific Manufacturing Company plans to produce various products during January. The budgets for direct materials and direct labor are relatively easy to compute. The unit costs of materials and unit costs of labor are multiplied by the number of units to be produced.

For example, suppose that 500 toy cars are to be produced and each car requires $1.94 of direct materials. The budgeted direct material cost for toy cars is $970.00 (500 × $1.94).

Computations are also made for all other products to be manufactured. The expected materials costs for each product are added to arrive at the materials budget for the period. Similar computations are made for direct labor costs.

The budget for manufacturing overhead costs is more complex. It is necessary to identify the cost behavior of each manufacturing overhead item as fixed, variable, or semivariable. The accountant for Pacific Manufacturing Company used the high-low point method to determine the cost behavior of each item as shown below.

	Fixed Costs per Month	Variable Costs per Direct Labor Hour
Supervision and clerical wages	$4,000	$–0–
Other indirect labor		2.00
Payroll taxes and fringe benefits	400	2.40
Manufacturing supplies	100	0.20
Depreciation	2,500	
Repairs and maintenance	500	0.50
Insurance and taxes	400	–0–
Total	$7,900	$5.10

Figure 31-1 shows the budget of manufacturing costs for Pacific Manufacturing Company for January. It is called a **fixed budget** since it shows only one level of activity—1,000 direct labor hours. Management expects that $20,000 of direct materials will be used and that 1,000 direct labor hours will be worked at $12 per hour.

Fixed overhead costs include supervision and clerical wages, depreciation, and insurance and taxes. There is one budgeted variable overhead cost—other indirect labor. It is calculated by multiplying the budgeted direct labor hours by the variable cost per hour (1,000 hours × $2).

There are three semivariable overhead costs: payroll taxes and fringe benefits, manufacturing supplies, and repairs and maintenance. The budgeted overhead for repairs and maintenance includes $500 as a fixed cost and $500 as a variable cost. The budgeted variable cost is 1,000 direct labor hours multiplied by the variable cost per hour of 50 cents (1,000 × $0.50).

Budgets serve many purposes. One key purpose is to provide a basis for measuring performance. Management needs to know how well manufacturing costs are being controlled. As soon as actual manufacturing costs have been accumulated and reported for the month, the accountant prepares a **budget performance report**, which compares actual costs and budgeted costs. Figure 31-2 shows the budget performance report for Pacific Manufacturing Company for January.

FIGURE 31-1 ▶
Fixed Budget of
Manufacturing Costs

Pacific Manufacturing Company
Budget of Manufacturing Costs
Month Ended January 31, 20--

Direct materials			20 0 0 0 00
Direct labor			12 0 0 0 00
Manufacturing overhead			
Supervision and clerical wages	4 0 0 0 00		
Other indirect labor (1,000 × $2)	2 0 0 0 00		
Payroll taxes and fringe benefits			
[$400 + (1,000 × $2.40)]	2 8 0 0 00		
Manufacturing supplies			
[$100 + (1,000 × $0.20)]	3 0 0 00		
Depreciation	2 5 0 0 00		
Repairs and maintenance			
[$500 + (1,000 × $0.50)]	1 0 0 0 00		
Insurance and taxes	4 0 0 00		
Total manufacturing overhead			13 0 0 0 00
Total manufacturing cost			45 0 0 0 00

FIGURE 31-2 ▼
Budget Performance Report

Pacific Manufacturing Company
Manufacturing Cost Budget Performance Report
Month of January 20--

	Budget	Actual	(Over) Under
Direct materials	2 0 0 0 0	1 9 1 0 0	9 0 0
Direct labor	1 2 0 0 0	1 1 8 0 0	2 0 0
Manufacturing overhead			
Supervision and clerical wages	4 0 0 0	3 0 0 0	1 0 0 0
Other indirect labor	2 0 0 0	2 1 9 0	(1 9 0)
Payroll taxes and fringe benefits	2 8 0 0	2 9 1 5	(1 1 5)
Manufacturing supplies	3 0 0	3 1 5	(1 5)
Depreciation	2 5 0 0	2 3 0 0	2 0 0
Repairs and maintenance	1 0 0 0	1 1 0 0	(1 0 0)
Insurance and taxes	4 0 0	4 0 0	—0—
Total manufacturing overhead	1 3 0 0 0	1 2 2 2 0	7 8 0
Total manufacturing cost	4 5 0 0 0	4 3 1 2 0	1 8 8 0

The budget performance report shows that there are numerous differences between the budgeted amounts and the actual costs incurred. In some cases actual costs exceeded the amounts budgeted, while in others the actual costs were less than budgeted costs. Management needs to determine why costs were over or under budget.

One of the first considerations is to determine how many hours were worked during the month. Was the actual number more or less than the hours budgeted? If the actual hours worked is close to the hours budgeted, then the fixed budget is a meaningful way to evaluate manufacturing performance. However, if the number of hours worked is materially more or less than the budgeted hours, the fixed budget is not the best tool to use to measure efficiency and cost control.

The fixed budget is based on 1,000 direct labor hours. Direct labor was budgeted at $12,000. Suppose that in January only 960 direct labor hours were worked. When management compares the actual labor costs of $11,800 to the budgeted labor costs of $12,000, the difference appears favorable. The company was under budget by $200. Actually, the difference is not favorable. Direct labor should have been $11,520 (960 hours × $12). At the level of 960 direct labor hours, the company spent $280 more than it should have ($11,800 − $11,520).

In order to provide management with a more useful tool for estimating and controlling manufacturing overhead costs, companies often prepare a budget that takes into account different levels of activity.

Preparation of the Flexible Budget

A **flexible budget** shows the budgeted costs at various levels of activity. Flexible budgets are particularly useful when the level of activity fluctuates from month to month. The flexible budget usually shows fixed and variable costs separately. The different levels of activity are called the **relevant range of activity** . For example, separate budgets might be prepared for the expected activity level as well as levels of 90 percent, 95 percent, 105 percent, and 110 percent of the expected activity level.

Figure 31-3 shows the flexible budget for Pacific Manufacturing Company for January. It has columns for the expected level of activity (1,000 direct labor hours), for 95 percent of expected activity (950 direct labor hours), and for 105 percent of expected activity (1,050 direct labor hours).

④ Objective

Develop a flexible budget for manufacturing costs.

▼ **FIGURE 31-3**
Flexible Budget of Manufacturing Costs

Pacific Manufacturing Company
Flexible Budget for Manufacturing Overhead
Month of January 20--

	Activity Level		
Number of direct labor hours	950	1000	1050
Percent of expected activity	95	100	105
Variable costs			
Other indirect labor	1900	2000	2100
Payroll taxes and fringe benefits	2280	2400	2520
Manufacturing supplies	190	200	210
Repairs and maintenance	475	500	525
Total variable costs	4845	5100	5355
Fixed costs			
Supervision and clerical wages	4000	4000	4000
Payroll taxes and fringe benefits	400	400	400
Manufacturing supplies	100	100	100
Depreciation	2500	2500	2500
Repairs and maintenance	500	500	500
Insurance and taxes	400	400	400
Total fixed costs	7900	7900	7900
Total manufacturing overhead	12745	13000	13255

Budget Performance Report
Efficiency and cost control can be evaluated by comparing actual overhead costs with the budget for the actual level of operations.

A flexible budget prepared for several activity levels is helpful for planning purposes. In addition, it allows management to see whether manufacturing overhead costs are being controlled. For example, management can compare overhead expenses at an actual activity level of 960 hours with the flexible budget for 950 hours. This will provide a reasonable indication of how well costs are being controlled. For a more precise measure of efficiency and cost control, however, a flexible budget can be prepared for the actual activity level.

Figure 31-4 shows a flexible overhead budget for an actual activity of 960 hours in February. Note that the various actual costs are both over and under the budgeted costs, although no single amount is significant.

FIGURE 31-4 ▼
Budget Performance Report

Pacific Manufacturing Company
Manufacturing Overhead Budget Performance Report
Month Ended February 28, 20--

	Budget for 960 hours	Actual	(Over) Under
Supervision and clerical wages	4 0 0 0	4 0 0 0	—0—
Other indirect labor (960 + $2)	1 9 2 0	1 9 8 0	(6 0)
Payroll taxes and fringe benefits [$400 + (960 × $2.40)]	2 7 0 4	2 6 5 0	5 4
Manufacturing supplies [$100 + (960 × $0.20)]	2 9 2	3 1 5	(2 3)
Depreciation	2 5 0 0	2 5 0 0	—0—
Repairs and maintenance [$500 + (960 × $0.50)]	9 8 0	1 0 5 0	(7 0)
Insurance and taxes	4 0 0	4 0 0	—0—
Total manufacturing overhead	1 2 7 9 6	1 2 8 9 5	(9 9)

Section 1 Self Review

Questions

1. Why is it important to analyze semi-variable costs to determine the fixed and variable components?

2. How does an increase in the level of activity affect (a) fixed costs per unit of activity, (b) total variable costs for the period, and (c) variable cost per unit?

3. What is a fixed budget?

Exercises

4. The salary of the factory supervisor is an example of a

   a. variable cost.

   b. fixed cost.

   c. semivariable cost.

   d. mixed cost.

5. A flexible budget contains

   a. fixed costs only.

   b. variable costs only.

   c. semivariable costs only.

   d. fixed, variable, and semivariable costs.

Analysis

6. The budget performance report shows the following budgeted and actual amounts. What is the total actual amount over budget or under budget?

	Budget	Actual
Wages	$7,000	$6,000
Payroll taxes	500	450
Supplies	800	900
Repairs	200	2,000

Standard Costs as a Control Tool

Recall that standard costs reflect what costs *should be* per unit manufactured under normal, efficient operating conditions. If standard costs are used to measure the efficiency and effectiveness of operations, the standards should be achievable. If they are set artificially high and cannot be attained, workers might become discouraged and demoralized, and they could make little or no attempt to achieve the standards.

There are two ways to handle standard costs. Some companies actually enter standard costs in the accounts. This procedure is discussed in cost accounting textbooks. Other companies record actual costs in the accounting system but compare these actual costs with standards in order to measure efficiency and to control manufacturing costs. This is the method used by Pacific Manufacturing Company.

Developing Standard Costs

To develop the standard cost of a specific unit of product, standards are set for each cost element, including materials, labor, and overhead.

Developing Raw Materials Standards

The *standard quantity* is the number of units of each type of raw material required to manufacture one unit of finished product. Engineers usually determine the standard quantity, although it is sometimes based on past experience in manufacturing the product. The *standard cost* is the cost of each unit of raw material required to make the product. The purchasing department determines standard cost. The *raw material standard* is the standard quantity of each raw material multiplied by its standard cost.

Developing Direct Labor Standards

The standard quantity is the number of hours of each type of labor needed to manufacture one unit of finished product. Production engineers usually determine the standard quantity by making time and motion studies. Sometimes the standard quantity is based on past experience in making the product. The standard cost is the cost of each type of labor used to make the product. The human resources department and union contracts provide wage rate information used in setting the standard cost. The *direct labor standard* is the standard quantity of each type of labor multiplied by its standard cost.

Developing Manufacturing Overhead Standards

The *standard overhead cost* per unit of product is usually based on the overhead application rate used to assign overhead costs to products. The overhead application rate can be based on direct labor cost, direct labor hours, or some other measure.

Section Objectives

5 Develop standard costs per unit of product.

WHY IT'S IMPORTANT
Manufacturing businesses need a measurement that indicates per-unit costs based on a normal, efficient operating period.

6 Compute the standard costs of products manufactured during the period and determine cost variances between actual costs and standard costs.

WHY IT'S IMPORTANT
Standard costs help managers assess efficiencies and costs.

7 Compute the amounts and analyze the nature of variances from standard for raw materials, labor, and manufacturing overhead.

WHY IT'S IMPORTANT
Labor, materials, or overhead variances help managers pinpoint inefficiencies in the manufacturing process.

Terms to Learn

cost variance
labor efficiency variance
labor rate variance
labor time variance
materials price variance
materials quantity variance
materials usage variance
standard cost card
variance analysis

Job Order Cost System
In a job order cost system, unit costs are determined for each production order.

Process Cost System
In a process cost system, unit costs are determined by totaling unit costs in each production department.

Overhead Application Rate
The overhead application rate is the rate at which overhead is applied to each job.

⑤ Objective

Develop standard costs per unit of product.

If the overhead application rate is based on direct labor hours, the standard overhead cost per unit is the standard labor *hours* for each finished unit multiplied by the overhead application rate. If the overhead application rate is based on direct labor costs, the standard overhead cost per unit is the standard labor *cost* for each finished unit multiplied by the overhead application rate.

Pacific Manufacturing Company uses a job order cost accounting system. Prior to the start of each year, the accountant prepares a manufacturing overhead budget for the year. This year's budget is based on a projection that 12,000 direct labor hours will be worked during the year.

Budgeted manufacturing overhead	
Fixed manufacturing overhead	$ 94,800
Variable manufacturing overhead,	
12,000 hours × $5.10 per hour	61,200
Total budgeted manufacturing overhead	$156,000

Pacific's manufacturing overhead application rate is based on direct labor hours. Using the budgeted manufacturing costs of $156,000 and the expectation that 12,000 direct labor hours will be used, the overhead application rate is computed as $13 per direct labor hour.

$$\frac{\text{Estimated overhead costs}}{\text{Estimated direct labor hours}} = \frac{\$156,000}{12,000 \text{ hrs.}} = \$13 \text{ per hour}$$

Using Standard Costs

Most well-managed manufacturing companies use standard costs to evaluate efficiency.

Preparing a Standard Cost Card

Standard costs are measured on a per-unit basis. A standard cost card helps facilitate the comparison of actual costs to standard costs. The **standard cost card** shows the per-unit standard costs for materials, labor, and overhead.

Figure 31-5 shows the standard cost card for product DC 24, a toy car. Each toy car requires $1.94 in direct materials and one-tenth hour of direct labor. Manufacturing overhead rate is applied at $1.30 per toy car (1/10 hour × $13.00).

FIGURE 31-5 ►
Standard Cost Card

STANDARD COST CARD	
Item: Toy Car—Product DC 24	
Materials	
Base material: 1 pound @ $1.79/lb.	$1.79
Finishing material: 3 ounces @ $0.05/oz.	0.15
Total materials	$1.94
Labor	
1/10 hour @ $12/hour	$1.20
Manufacturing Overhead	
1/10 hour @ $13/hour	$1.30
Total Standard Cost per Unit	$4.44

Comparing Actual and Standard Costs

The following is from the job order cost sheet for Job Order X2–16, for the manufacture of 1,400 decorated cars.

Job X2–16
Product: Toy Car DC 24
Number of units manufactured: 1,400
Manufacturing costs:

Materials:	
Base material, 1,425 pounds @ $1.92 per pound	$2,736.00
Finishing material, 4,300 ounces @ $.045 per ounce	193.50
Total materials	$2,929.50
Direct labor: 130 hours @ $12.10 per hour	1,573.00
Manufacturing overhead: 130 hours @ $13.00 per hour	1,690.00
Total manufacturing costs	$6,192.50

Using the standard cost card and the job order cost sheet, the accountant can compare the actual costs to the standard costs for Job X2–16. The **cost variance** is the difference between the total standard cost and the total actual cost. The cost variance is $23.50; the actual cost is $23.50 less than the standard cost.

Standard cost of 1,400 units: 1,400 units × $4.44 per unit	$6,216.00
Manufacturing costs charged to job	6,192.50
Variance	$ 23.50

Since the actual cost is less than the standard cost of the job, the variance is favorable. When the actual cost exceeds the standard cost, the variance is unfavorable.

Analyzing Variances between Standard and Actual Costs

The total variance helps measure how well costs were controlled. It is also useful to compute the variances between actual and standard cost for each cost element—materials, labor, and overhead.

Analyzing Materials Variances. The following is a summary of the materials costs for Job X2–16. The left side shows the standard costs and the right side shows the actual costs.

	Standard			Actual			Favorable (Unfavor.) Variance
	Quantity	Unit Cost	Total Cost	Quantity	Unit Cost	Total Cost	
Base material	1,400	1.79	2,506.00	1,425	1.92	2,736.00	(230.00)
Finishing material	4,200	0.05	210.00	4,300	0.045	193.50	16.50
Totals			2,716.00			2,929.50	(213.50)

Variance analysis explains the difference between standard cost and actual cost. The **materials quantity variance** (also called **materials usage variance**) is the cost of the actual quantity of raw materials used on a job minus the standard cost of the raw materials allowable for the units produced. The **materials price variance** is the actual cost of the raw materials used on a job minus the standard cost of the material used.

6 Objective

Compute the standard costs of products manufactured during the period and determine cost variances between actual costs and standard costs.

Acceptance of Accounting Standards

Some countries are reluctant to adopt accounting standards that, in the opinion of the accounting rulemakers in that country, might hinder economic growth and be contrary to the nation's economic policies.

7 Objective

Compute the amounts and analyze the nature of variances from standard for raw materials, labor, and manufacturing overhead.

Determining Materials Quantity Variance. The materials quantity variance is the difference between the actual quantity used and the standard quantity allowed multiplied by the standard cost of the material. The following are the quantity variances for the materials used on Job X2–16.

Base Material

Actual quantity	1,425 pounds
Standard quantity (1,400 units × 1 lb./unit)	1,400 pounds
Excess base material used	25 pounds
Times standard price per pound	$ 1.79
Unfavorable quantity variance	$44.75

Because the actual quantity of base material exceeded the standard quantity allowed for the job, the quantity variance for base material is unfavorable.

Finishing Material

Actual quantity	4,300 ounces
Standard quantity (1,400 units × 3 oz./unit)	4,200 ounces
Excess finishing material used	100 ounces
Times standard price per ounce	$0.05
Unfavorable quantity variance	$5.00

Because the actual quantity of finishing material exceeded the standard quantity allowed for the job, the quantity variance for finishing material is unfavorable.

The materials quantity variance measures how well the production manager and factory employees are controlling material waste. Unfavorable quantity variances often result because of defective materials or inexperienced workers.

Determining Materials Price Variance. The material price variance is the difference between the actual price and the standard cost multiplied by the actual quantity used. The following are the price variances for the materials used on Job X2–16.

Base Material

Actual price per pound	$ 1.92
Standard price per pound	1.79
Excess of actual over standard price	$ 0.13
Times actual number of pounds consumed	1,425
Unfavorable materials price variance	$185.25

Since the actual price for the base material was more than the standard price, the price variance for base material is unfavorable.

Finishing Material

Actual price per ounce	$0.045
Standard price per ounce	0.050
Excess of standard over actual price	$0.005
Times actual number of ounces consumed	4,300
Favorable material price variance	$21.50

Because the actual price of finishing material was *less than* the standard price, the price variance is *favorable*.

The purchasing department is usually responsible for the price variance. There is little that the manufacturing department can do to control the prices paid for raw materials.

Summary of Materials Variance Analysis. The materials variances for Job X2–16 are summarized as follows.

	Favorable or (Unfavorable) Variance	
Base material		
Quantity variance	$ (44.75)	
Price variance	(185.25)	$(230.00)
Finishing material		
Quantity variance	$ (5.00)	
Price variance	21.50	16.50
Total material variance		$(213.50)

Analyzing Labor Variance. The total labor variance for Job X2–16 is $107, calculated as follows.

Actual labor costs, 130 hours × $12.10 per hour	$1,573.00
Standard labor costs,	
1,400 units × 1/10 hour per unit × $12 per hour	1,680.00
Favorable labor variance	$ 107.00

The total labor variance is divided into the labor time (or efficiency) variance and the labor rate variance.

Determining Labor Time Variance. The **labor time variance** (or **labor efficiency variance**) is the difference between the actual hours worked and the standard labor hours allowed for the job multiplied by the standard cost per hour.

Actual hours worked	130
Standard hours allowed (1,400 units × 1/10 hour per unit)	140
Excess of standard over actual hours	10
Times standard rate per hour	$ 12.00
Favorable labor time variance	$120.00

Because fewer hours were worked than the numbers of hours allowed by the standard, the labor time variance is favorable.

The production manager is usually responsible for the labor time variances. Part of the time variance might be attributed to the human resources department, which hires factory employees.

Determining Labor Rate Variance. The **labor rate variance** is the difference between the actual labor rate per hour and the standard labor rate per hour multiplied by the actual number of hours worked on the job.

Actual rate per hour	$ 12.10
Standard rate per hour	12.00
Excess of actual over standard rate	$ 0.10
Times actual number of hours worked	130
Unfavorable labor rate variance	$(13.00)

Usually the human resources department is responsible for the labor rate variance. However, operating decisions also affect the labor rate variance, including whether to work overtime at one and one-half the normal rate or how to assign workers to jobs. In addition, labor market conditions and wage scales set in union contracts may make it difficult to hire workers at the standard rates.

Managerial

IMPLICATIONS

Cost Behavior

- Management needs to understand cost behavior in order to make decisions and to plan for the future.

- Budgets help in planning and controlling manufacturing costs. Fixed budgets are useful, but flexible budgets allow management to evaluate cost containment for the level of production activity.

- Standard costs reflect what costs should be when based on efficient, yet attainable, operating conditions.

- Management analyzes the difference between actual and standard costs to determine what factors caused the variances.

  - The materials price variance is the responsibility of the purchasing department.

  - The materials quantity variance is the responsibility of factory management.

  - The labor rate variance is the responsibility of the human resources department.

  - The labor time variance is the responsibility of factory management.

Thinking Critically
If you were the manager of the Purchasing Department, what steps would you take to record costs efficiently?

About
Accounting

Injuries
Musculoskeletal disorders such as carpal tunnel syndrome are common problems in the manufacturing industry. Companies that emphasize employee involvement, such as Honda, Timken, and Goodyear, tackle these problems through worker participation programs.

Summary of Direct Labor Variance Analysis. The total direct labor variance is summarized as follows.

Labor time variance, favorable	$120.00
Labor rate variance, unfavorable	(13.00)
Total labor variance, favorable	$107.00

Analyzing Manufacturing Overhead Variance. Recall that manufacturing overhead is applied to jobs using a predetermined rate, usually based on direct labor hours or direct labor costs. If the actual hours worked on a job order exceed the standard hours allowed, the job will be charged with more overhead than the standard allowed for the units produced.

Pacific Manufacturing Company applies manufacturing overhead at $13 per direct labor hour based on a standard of 12,000 direct labor hours per year. Recall that standard hours per unit are 1/10 of an hour, so standard hours for 1,400 units are 140 hours. Overhead for Job X2–16 is as follows.

Applied overhead	
Actual hours × standard rate per hour (130 hours × $13)	$1,690.00
Standard overhead	
Standard hours × standard rate per hour (140 hours × $13)	1,820.00
Favorable overhead variance	$ 130.00

The variance is favorable because fewer hours were worked than the number of standard hours allowed.

The following is a summary of the variances for Job X2–16. The variances explain the difference between actual and standard manufacturing costs.

Materials quantity variance ($44.75 + $5.00)	$ (49.75)
Materials price variance ($185.25 − $21.50)	(163.75)
Labor time variance	120.00
Labor rate variance	(13.00)
Overhead variance	130.00
Total variance	$ 23.50

Analysis of Monthly Overhead Variances. Because of the nature of overhead, businesses are unable to determine the actual overhead costs related to individual jobs. Usually overhead is analyzed based on the total actual overhead and the total standard overhead for the products manufactured.

The following is a summary of the production and cost data for September for Pacific Manufacturing Company. The company had a $920 favorable total overhead variance.

Total standard hours for goods manufactured		1,000
Total actual hours required for work completed		900
Manufacturing overhead applied to products		
1,000 hours × $13 per hour		$13,000
Actual manufacturing costs incurred:		
Fixed costs	$6,900	
Variable costs	5,180	
Total		12,080
Total overhead variance, favorable		$ 920

The variance is favorable because fewer hours were worked than the number of standard hours allowed.

Section 2 Self Review

Questions

1. What information appears on the standard cost card?

2. How is the materials quantity variance computed?

3. How is the labor rate variance computed?

Exercises

4. Which variance is controllable by the production manager?

a. labor rate variance.

b. materials price variance.

c. standard variance.

d. labor time variance.

5. The price variance is the difference between the actual price and the standard price multiplied by

a. standard quantity.

b. difference between the actual quantity and the standard quantity.

c. unused capacity.

d. actual quantity.

Analysis

6. Determine the total standard cost per unit from the following data. Budgeted production is 5,000 units. Standard materials are six yards at $3 per yard. Standard labor is two hours at $10 per hour. Manufacturing overhead is $100,000 based on production of 5,000 units of finished goods.

(Answers to Section 2 Self Review are on page 1121.)

Review

Chapter Summary

To control costs and make effective business decisions, management also needs information based on the variability of manufacturing costs. In this chapter, you have learned how cost variability is measured and how budgets are developed and evaluated for manufacturing entities.

Learning Objectives

① Explain how fixed, variable, and semivarible costs change as the level of manufacturing activity changes.

Accountants must understand cost variability—how costs behave as the volume of manufacturing activity increases or decreases.

- Total variable costs vary in direct proportion to activity level. The per-unit variable cost remains constant.
- Fixed costs remain relatively constant within the range of activity level at which the factory is likely to operate.
- Semivariable costs vary to some extent with changes in the volume of activity, but not in direct proportion. An element of these costs is fixed, while another element is variable.

② Use the high-low point method to determine the fixed and variable components of a semivariable cost.

The high-low method compares the activity and the cost of the highest month of activity in a year with the activity and cost of the lowest month of activity. The difference in cost is divided by the difference in activity to measure the variable cost per unit of activity.

③ Prepare a fixed budget for manufacturing costs.

A budget is important for planning manufacturing activities and for controlling costs. A fixed budget shows the anticipated costs for a period—a month, a quarter, or a year—for one level of production.

- At the end of the period, actual results are compared with the budget and differences are noted and investigated.
- If the production volume is significantly different from the volume assumed in preparing the budget, the budgeted figures for variable and semivariable costs will not be meaningful.

④ Develop a flexible budget for manufacturing costs.

Flexible budgets show what the budgeted costs should be at several levels within the relevant range of activity. Actual results can then be compared with more meaningful budgeted amounts.

⑤ Develop standard costs per unit of product.

Standard costs help businesses control and evaluate manufacturing efficiency. Costs of efficient, yet attainable, levels of performance are set for each element of materials, labor, and overhead. A standard cost card for each product details cost.

⑥ Compute the standard costs of products manufactured during the period and determine cost variances between actual costs and standard costs.

The difference between the total standard cost and the total actual cost is called the cost variance. At the end of the period, actual costs related to the product are compared with the standard costs allowed for each unit. Variances between standard costs and actual costs are analyzed.

⑦ Compute the amounts and analyze the nature of variances from standard for raw materials, labor, and manufacturing overhead.

- The total variance between the actual cost and standard cost of material is separated into two components: a materials quantity variance and a materials price variance.
- Similarly, the total labor cost variance is separated into two components: a labor time variance and a labor rate variance.
- Manufacturing overhead variances cannot be easily computed on a per-job or per-unit basis, especially under the job order cost accounting system. Instead, manufacturing overhead is applied to jobs using a predetermined rate often based on direct labor hours.

⑧ Define the accounting terms new to this chapter.

CHAPTER 31 GLOSSARY

Budget (p. 1096) An operating plan expressed in monetary units

Budget performance report (p. 1097) A comparison of actual costs and budgeted costs

Cost variance (p. 1103) The difference between the total standard cost and the total actual cost

Fixed budget (p. 1097) A budget representing only one level of activity

Fixed costs (p. 1094) Costs that do not change in total as the level of activity changes

Flexible budget (p. 1099) A budget that shows the budgeted costs at various levels of activity

High-low point method (p. 1095) A method to determine the fixed and variable components of a semivariable cost

Labor efficiency variance (p. 1105) See Labor time variance

Labor rate variance (p. 1105) The difference between the actual labor rate per hour and the standard labor rate per hour multiplied by the actual number of hours worked on the job

Labor time variance (p. 1105) The difference between the actual hours worked and the standard labor hours allowed for the job multiplied by the standard cost per hour

Manufacturing cost budget (p. 1096) A budget made for each manufacturing cost

Materials price variance (p. 1103) The difference between the actual price and the standard cost for materials multiplied by the actual quantity of materials used

Materials quantity variance (p. 1103) The difference between the actual quantity used and the quantity of materials allowed multiplied by the standard cost of the materials

Materials usage variance (p. 1103) See Materials quantity variance

Relevant range of activity (p. 1099) The different levels of activity at which a factory is expected to operate

Semivariable costs (p. 1094) Costs that vary with, but not in direct proportion to, the volume of activity

Standard cost card (p. 1102) A form that shows the per-unit standard costs for materials, labor, and overhead

Variable costs (p. 1094) Costs that vary in total in direct proportion to changes in the level of activity

Variance analysis (p. 1103) Explains the difference between standard cost and actual cost

Comprehensive Self Review

1. What is the primary characteristic of a fixed cost?
2. What does the following statement mean? A variable cost remains fixed per unit.
3. Is there a weakness in using a fixed budget as a cost control tool?
4. What is a flexible budget?
5. When will a job be charged more overhead than the standard allowed for the units produced?

(Answers to Comprehensive Self Review are on page 1121.)

Discussion Questions

1. Define the term *fixed cost*.
2. Explain how variable costs per unit change as the level of activity changes.
3. What are semivariable costs?
4. Briefly explain the high-low point method for analyzing semivariable costs.
5. What is the relevant range of activity as used in budgeting?
6. What is a budget?
7. What is included in a budget performance report?
8. What is a flexible budget?
9. What is the advantage of using a flexible budget?
10. What are standard costs?
11. How are standards set for materials?
12. Who provides information about wage rates in setting labor standards?
13. Explain how to compute the quantity variance for materials.
14. What does the price variance for materials show?
15. What two variances make up the total labor variance?
16. Which manager would more likely be responsible for materials quantity variances?
17. What are the possible causes of materials variances?
18. What are the possible causes of labor variances?
19. What are the possible causes of overhead variances?

Applications

EXERCISES

Using the high-low point method.

Howard Company's records show the following data for the four quarters of 20--.

Quarter	Direct Labor Hours	Utilities Cost
First	10,000	$1,600
Second	14,600	2,060
Third	12,900	1,790
Fourth	13,000	1,800

Compute the fixed and variable elements of utilities cost, using the high-low point method.

◀ **Exercise 31-1**
Objective 2

Developing a flexible budget for overhead.

In Ebeth Corporation's factory, fixed indirect labor costs are $12,000 per month. Variable indirect labor costs are $1.50 per direct labor hour. The budget for the month of July 20-- calls for employment of 10,000 direct labor hours. Compute the flexible budget amounts for indirect labor costs at the following levels of activity: 100 percent of budget, 95 percent of budget, and 105 percent of budget.

◀ **Exercise 31-2**
Objective 4

Developing standard costs per unit of product.

In preparing the standard cost for each unit of F-205, the company's only product, the accountant for Lixie Manufacturing, Ltd., has developed the following data for the year 20--.

Total budgeted production, 24,000 units

Raw material:
   Four units of raw material are required for each unit of finished goods. The cost of each unit of raw material is $5.

Labor:
   Two hours of direct labor are required for each unit of finished goods. The labor rate per hour is $12.50.

Manufacturing overhead:
   Overhead is 20 percent of direct labor.

Compute the standard cost per unit of product, showing the standard cost of materials, labor, and overhead.

◀ **Exercise 31-3**
Objective 5

Data for Exercises 31-4 through 31-11.

The standard cost card for a unit of product at Red Dog Corporation shows the following information.

Materials: 5 gallons at $3 per gallon	$15
Labor: 1/2 hour at $16 per hour	8
Overhead: 50% of direct labor	4
Total	$27

During the month of February 20--, Job 05-22 was completed. Four thousand units were produced from the job. The actual costs were as shown below.

Materials: 22,500 gallons at $2.85 per gallon	$ 64,125
Labor: 1,900 hours at $16.20 per hour	30,780
Overhead applied: 50% of direct labor	15,390
Total	$110,295

Exercise 31-4 ►
Objective 6

Computing total variance between standard costs and actual costs.

Calculate the total variance between the actual cost and the standard cost in February.

Exercise 31-5 ►
Objective 7

Computing total variance for materials.

Calculate the total variance for materials in February.

Exercise 31-6 ►
Objective 7

Computing quantity variance for materials.

Calculate the quantity variance for materials in February.

Exercise 31-7 ►
Objective 7

Computing price variance for materials.

Calculate the price variance for materials in February.

Exercise 31-8 ►
Objective 7

Computing total variance for labor.

Calculate the total variance for labor in February.

Exercise 31-9 ►
Objective 7

Computing quantity variance for labor.

Calculate the quantity variance for labor in February.

Exercise 31-10 ►
Objective 7

Computing rate variance for labor.

Calculate the rate variance for labor in February.

Exercise 31-11 ►
Objective 7

Computing total overhead variance.

Calculate the total variance for overhead in February.

Problems

Selected problems can be completed using:
▦ **Spreadsheets**

PROBLEM SET A

Problem 31-1A ►
Objective 2

▦

Analyzing semivariable costs using the high-low point method.

The accountant of Maris Manufacturing Company has compiled the following information about the direct labor hours and the indirect labor costs for each month of 20--.

INSTRUCTIONS

1. Compute the monthly fixed costs and the variable costs per hour, using the high-low point method.
2. Compute the estimated total indirect labor cost if 2,200 hours of direct labor are employed during a month.

Month	Direct Labor Hours	Indirect Labor Costs
January	2,300	$6,220
February	1,800	5,490
March	1,900	5,520
April	1,975	5,765
May	2,035	5,910
June	2,240	6,120
July	2,475	6,465
August	2,420	6,300
September	2,360	6,304
October	2,340	6,276
November	2,600	6,690
December	2,400	6,360

Analyze: What approximate percentage of total costs is attributable to variable costs?

Preparing a flexible overhead budget and an overhead performance report.

◄ **Problem 31-2A**
Objective 3

The accountant for Delay Products, Inc., has analyzed the manufacturing overhead costs for the company's assembly department. The fixed and variable costs follow.

	Variable Cost Element per Hour	Monthly Fixed Cost Element
Indirect labor	$1.00	$1,000
Payroll taxes	0.20	120
Indirect materials	0.16	100
Utilities	0.24	350
Depreciation	—	950
Taxes and insurance	—	400
Repairs	0.12	100

INSTRUCTIONS

1. Prepare a flexible budget for the department for the month of March 20--, assuming that the expected production is for 2,000 direct labor hours. Show costs for production levels of 90 percent and 110 percent of the expected production level of 2,000 hours.

2. Assume that during the month of March, actual production was 1,775 hours. Actual costs for the month were as follows.

Indirect labor	$2,800
Payroll taxes	470
Indirect materials	390
Utilities	800
Depreciation	950
Taxes and insurance	395
Repairs	300

Controlling Manufacturing Costs: Standard Costs **Chapter 31 • 1113**

Prepare a departmental monthly overhead performance report comparing actual costs with the budget allowance for the total number of hours worked.

Analyze: If Delay Products, Inc., operates at the expected production level of 2,000 direct labor hours, what total manufacturing overhead cost is projected per direct labor hour?

Problem 31-3A ►
Objective 7

Analyzing materials variances.

Chattanooga Chemical Company manufactures a product called Tectate, which requires three raw materials. Production is in batches of 1,050 gallons of raw materials that yield only 1,000 gallons of finished product. (Some evaporation of the base occurs, but the amount of evaporation varies slightly from batch to batch.) The firm uses standard costs as a control device. Its standard costs for materials for each batch of Tectate have been established as follows.

Material	Quantity	Standard Cost per Gallon	Standard Cost per Batch
Inert base	850 gal.	$ 0.26	$221.00
Acid	160 gal.	1.50	240.00
Activator	40 gal.	12.00	480.00
Total standard cost		$13.76	$941.00

The output is packaged in 50-gallon drums. During the month of June 20--, 300 drums of Tectate were produced. There was no beginning or ending inventory of work in process. The materials actually used during June are listed below.

Material	Quantity	Cost per Gallon
Inert base	12,840 gal.	$ 0.21
Acid	2,390 gal.	1.56
Activator	612 gal.	10.10

INSTRUCTIONS

1. Compute the total variance between the actual cost of the materials used during June and the standard cost of the materials. Also compute the total variance for each type of material.
2. Analyze the variances for each type of material for the month.

Analyze: Which raw materials were obtained at a price that was lower than standard cost?

Problem 31-4A ►
Objective 7

Analyzing material and labor variances.

Mountain Manufacturing Company makes a product that is processed through two departments: assembling and finishing. All materials are added in the first department. During the month of May 20--, the company made 10,000 units of the product. Standard costs and actual costs for materials and labor are given on page 1115.

STANDARD COSTS

Raw materials

Framing: 10 square feet at $0.22 per square foot	$2.20
Filler: 14 pounds at $0.05 per pound	0.70
Standard materials cost per unit	$2.90

Direct labor

Assembling dept.: 1/4 hour at $8.00 per hour	$2.00
Finishing dept.: 1/10 hour at $10.00 per hour	1.00
Standard direct labor cost per unit	$3.00

ACTUAL COSTS

Raw materials

Framing: 100,500 square feet at $0.225 per square foot	$22,612.50
Filler: 138,900 pounds at $0.053 per pound	7,361.70
Total actual materials cost	$29,974.20

Direct labor

Assembling dept.: 2,580 hours at $8.20 per hour	$21,156.00
Finishing dept.: 1,010 hours at $10.05 per hour	10,150.50
Total actual direct labor cost	$31,306.50

INSTRUCTIONS

1. Prepare a comparison of the actual cost of materials with the standard cost of materials for the 10,000 units of product. Then prepare an analysis of the materials variances.

2. Prepare a comparison of the actual cost of labor with the standard cost of labor for the 10,000 units of product. Then prepare an analysis of the labor variances.

Analyze: What total variance in labor was reported by the Finishing Department?

PROBLEM SET B

Analyzing semivariable costs using the high-low point method.

The accountant of Javier Manufacturing Company has compiled the following information about the direct labor hours and utility costs for each month of 20--.

◄ **Problem 31-1B**
Objective 2

Month	Direct Labor Hours	Utility Costs
January	2,400	$2,075
February	2,895	2,195
March	3,280	2,630
April	3,745	2,885
May	4,300	3,500
June	4,190	3,185
July	4,288	3,300
August	3,810	3,010
September	3,679	2,895
October	3,542	2,895
November	3,018	2,840
December	2,450	2,413

1. Compute the monthly fixed costs (rounded to nearest whole dollar) and the variable costs per hour (rounded to nearest whole cent) using the high-low point method.

2. Compute the estimated total indirect labor cost if 3,600 hours of direct labor are employed during the month.

Analyze: What approximate percentage of total costs is attributable to fixed costs?

Problem 31-2B ►
Objective 3

Preparing a flexible overhead budget and an overhead performance report.

MWF Manufacturing Company makes a single product that requires one hour of labor for each unit. The budgeted output for 20-- is 50,000 units. Fixed and variable overhead cost data are as follows.

	Variable Element per Hour	Yearly Fixed Cost Element
Indirect labor	$0.90	$36,000
Payroll taxes	0.09	2,000
Indirect materials	0.22	1,200
Utilities	0.60	4,000
Depreciation	—	18,000
Taxes and insurance	—	3,600
Repairs	0.15	1,200

INSTRUCTIONS

1. Prepare a flexible budget for the department for the year 20--. The flexible budget should show costs for production levels of 90 percent, 100 percent, and 110 percent of the expected production level of 50,000 units (50,000 hours).

2. Assume that during the year 20--, actual production was 45,000 hours. Actual costs for the year were as follows.

Indirect labor	$75,000
Payroll taxes	7,500
Indirect materials	11,500
Utilities	25,000
Depreciation	18,000
Taxes and insurance	3,500
Repairs	7,000

Prepare a departmental yearly overhead performance report comparing actual costs with the budget allowance for the number of hours worked.

Analyze: If MWF Manufacturing Company operates at the expected production level of 50,000 direct labor hours, what total manufacturing overhead cost can be projected per direct labor hour?

Problem 31-3B ►
Objective 7

Analyzing materials variances.

Big West Synthetics Company manufactures the product Syntex, which requires three raw materials. Production is in batches of 2,000 pounds of materials. Any waste is thrown away. The firm uses standard costs as a control device. Its standard costs for materials are as follows.

Material	Quantity	Standard Cost per Pound	Standard Cost per Batch
Plastic base	1,800 lb.	$0.18	$324
Tint	100 lb.	0.22	22
Hardener	100 lb.	0.21	21
Totals	2,000 lb.		$367

During the month of January 20--, 60,000 pounds of Syntex were produced. There was no beginning or ending inventory of work in process. The materials actually used during January are listed below.

Material	Quantity	Total Cost
Plastic base	55,300 lb.	$8,848
Tint	3,080 lb.	770
Hardener	2,950 lb.	649

INSTRUCTIONS

1. Compute the total variance between the actual cost of the materials used during January and the standard cost of the materials. Also compute the total variance for each type of material.

2. Analyze the variances for each type of material for the month.

Analyze: Which raw materials were obtained at lower-than-standard unit costs?

Analyzing material and labor variances.

◄ **Problem 31-4B**
Objective 7

North Texas Products Company makes a product that is processed through two departments: cutting and assembly. All materials are added in the first department. During the month of October 20--, 8,000 units of the product were made. Standard costs and actual costs for materials and labor are given as follows.

STANDARD COSTS

Raw materials
Panel units, 4 units at $4.50 per unit	$18.00
Assembly sets: 4 sets at $0.25 per unit	1.00
Standard materials cost per unit	$19.00

Direct labor
Cutting dept.: 1/10 hour at $16.00 per hour	$ 1.60
Assembly dept.: 1/4 hour at $18.00 per hour	4.50
Standard direct labor cost per unit	$ 6.10

ACTUAL COSTS

Raw materials
Panel units: 32,800 units at $4.46 per unit	$146,288.00
Assembly sets: 32,060 sets at $0.24 per unit	7,694.40
Total actual materials cost	$153,982.40

Direct labor
Cutting dept.: 900 hours at $16.10 per hour	$ 14,490.00
Assembly dept.: 2,100 hours at $17.75 per year	37,275.00
Total actual direct labor cost	$ 51,765.00

1. Prepare a comparison of the actual cost of materials with the standard cost of materials for the 8,000 units of product. Then prepare an analysis of the materials variances.

2. Prepare a comparison of the actual cost of labor with the standard cost of labor for the 8,000 units of product. Then prepare an analysis of the labor variances.

Analyze: Is the greatest portion of the total assembly set materials variance attributable to quantity or to price?

CHAPTER 31 CHALLENGE PROBLEM

Costs Incurred

EuroTech Corporation manufactures one product. Standard costs for each unit of the product follow.

Materials, 10 gallons @ $1.20		$12.00
Direct labor, 2 hours @ $15		30.00
Manufacturing overhead, 1 hour @ $15		15.00
Total standard costs per unit		$57.00

During the month of June 20--, 1,500 units of product were manufactured. At the end of the month, the following data was available.

a. The total materials variance was $64 favorable.

b. The materials quantity variance was $240 unfavorable.

c. The labor rate variance was $1,525 unfavorable.

d. Actual hours worked amounted to 3,050.

Answer the following questions. Show all computations.

1. What was the actual total materials cost?
2. How many units of raw material were used?
3. What was the amount of materials price variance?
4. What was the actual labor rate per hour?
5. What was the actual labor cost for the month?
6. What was the amount of labor time variance?

Analyze: What was the cost incurred per gallon of raw materials?

CHAPTER 31 CRITICAL THINKING PROBLEM

Recreating Data

BestFit Company, a manufacturer of sports shoes, uses a standard cost system. When Henre Stavros, the cost accountant for the company, started to analyze the labor variances for June, he discovered that some of the data had inadvertently been destroyed.

From a review of the data available, Henre learns that the total labor cost variance for June was $4,500 unfavorable and that the standard labor rate was $10 per hour. A cost-of-living adjustment in the workers' hourly rate caused an unfavorable labor price variance of $0.20 per hour. Total standard labor hours for June's output of shoes was 7,200 hours.

Determine the actual number of labor hours worked in June. (*Hint:* First compute the actual labor rate per hour. Then set up an equation representing the computation of the total labor variance of $4,500.)

Business Connections

◀ Connection 1

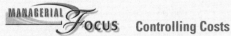 **MANAGERIAL FOCUS** **Controlling Costs**

1. How would the distinction between fixed and variable costs help management in forecasting cash needs for the business?

2. Explain how a flexible budget can be used by management to help control costs.

3. Briefly explain to management the reasons why variances between actual and standard costs of materials might exist.

4. The accountant for JRH Corporation has noticed that historically, when there have been favorable labor rate variances, there have been unfavorable labor time variances. What factors could explain this phenomenon?

5. In a large company the overall wage structure is determined by the personnel department. However, the manager of each producing department has limited control over the rates paid to individual workers. Who would be responsible for labor rate variances?

6. Explain how determination of standard costs enables managers to pinpoint responsibility for inefficient performance.

◀ Connection 2

Ethical DILEMMA **Omitting Unfavorable Reports** James, the corporate cost accountant, has a golf buddy, Henry, who is the purchasing manager for the same company. When computing the materials variance report for July, James notices that the price variance for materials is unfavorable and very high. When sending the reports to the production vice president, James does not send the price variance report. Is there a problem here?

◀ Connection 3

Street WISE: *Questions from the Real World* **Budget and Actual** Refer to the "Results of Operations" discussion in the *1999 Annual Report* for the Home Depot, Inc. in Appendix B.

1. As the company's accountants prepare budgets for the year ended January 30, 2001, what factors might be considered when forecasting net sales? (Hint: What factors affected sales in the year ended January 30, 2000?)

2. What was the change in the company's combined federal and state effective income tax rate? What caused the change?

◀ Connection 4

FINANCIAL STATEMENT ANALYSIS **Market Demand Projections** International Truck and Engine Corporation manufactures and markets mid-range diesel engines and Class 5 through 8 trucks, including school buses. The company's *1999 Annual Report* included the following information.

Millions of Dollars For the Years Ended October 31	1999	1998
Sales and Revenues	$8,647	$7,885
Net Income	$ 544	$ 299
Manufacturing gross margin	18.0%	15.3%

The company projected 2000 U.S. and Canadian Class 8 heavy truck demand to be 245,000 units, a 14 percent decrease from 1999. Class 5, 6, and 7 medium truck demand, excluding school buses, was forecasted at 128,000 units, 12 percent lower than in 1999. Demand for school buses was expected to decrease only 5 percent in 2000 to 32,000 units. Mid-range diesel engine shipments by the company to OEMs in 2000 were expected to be 324,000 units, 13 percent higher than in 1999.

Analyze:

1. Based on the demand projections, what net increase or decrease in demand did the company expect for its products in fiscal 2000?

2. Describe how company accountants can utilize these projections as they prepare manufacturing budgets for the coming year.

3. By what percentage has manufacturing gross margin improved from 1998 to 1999? What is the manufacturing gross profit amount for 1999?

Analyze Online: Locate the most recent annual report on the International Truck and Engine Corporation Web site (**www.internationaldelivers.com**).

4. What manufacturing gross margin was reported? Is this figure an improvement over the 1999 gross margin?

5. What reasons are offered for increases or decreases in the manufacturing gross margin?

Connection 5 ▶ *Extending* (the) *Thought* **Standard Costing and Service Firms** Standard costing and variance analysis techniques are most often associated with manufacturing businesses. The owner of a small graphic design company believes that standard costs should be established for the services her firm provides. Do you agree with this statement? Why or why not? How do you think such standards might be established?

Connection 6 ▶ **Business Communication** **Speech Preparation** You have been asked to speak at the Manufacturing Professionals monthly meeting on the topic "Establishing and Utilizing Standard Costs." In your company, Illuminations Lighting Manufacturing, standard costs were recently established for the production of one of your company's products, the Retro Desk Lamp, #335998. You worked with production managers, engineers, and purchasing officers to establish standard costs for materials, labor, and overhead. Prepare notes for a 10-minute speech describing how standard costs are developed and companies might use these standard costs as a control tool.

TeamWork   Motivating for Improved Productivity   Some company managers believe that using standard costing deters workers from improving their productivity. They argue that workers who achieve standards will not improve beyond these milestones. As a team, create a list of strategies that you believe will motivate employees to continually improve upon established standards within a manufacturing environment. Choose one member of your team to present your list to the class.

◄ Connection 7

*inter*NET CONNECTION   ISO 9000   The AICPA Web site contains information relevant to business managers and CPAs alike. The term *ISO 9000* is frequently heard in manufacturing companies. Go to **www.aicpa.org.** Use the search option to learn about ISO 9000. Why do companies seek ISO 9000 certification? To what extent do American manufacturers use ISO 9000 standards?

◄ Connection 8

Answers to Self Reviews

Answers to Section 1 Self Review

1. To control costs and measure efficiency it is necessary to be able to measure what costs should be at any level of activity. This requires an analysis of fixed and variable costs.
2. (a) Decrease, (b) increase, (c) no change.
3. A budget showing expected costs at only one level of production activity.
4. **b.** fixed cost.
5. **d.** fixed, variable, and semivariable costs.
6. $850 over

Answers to Section 2 Self Review

1. The per-unit standard costs of materials, labor, and overhead.
2. (1) Compute the difference between the actual number of units of a material used and the standard quantity of that material allowed for the job and (2) multiply the difference in quantity by the standard cost per unit.
3. By multiplying the difference between (1) the standard rate per hour and (2) the actual rate per hour by (3) the actual number of hours worked.
4. **d.** labor time variance.
5. **d.** actual quantity.
6. $58

Answers to Comprehensive Self Review

1. It remains constant in total during the period and does not change merely because the level of activity changes.
2. A variable cost is one whose total varies in direct proportion to the level of activity, yet the cost per unit of activity remains the same within the usual range of activity level.
3. Yes, if the level of production activity is substantially different from the level anticipated in the fixed budget, the actual and budgeted costs will not be related to comparable bases.
4. A flexible budget is a budget showing expected costs at more than one level of activity.
5. When actual hours worked exceed the standard hours allowed (assuming that the overhead application rate is based on direct labor hours).

CHAPTER 32

Learning Objectives

1. Explain the basic steps in the decision-making process.

2. Prepare income statements using the absorption costing and direct costing methods.

3. Using the contribution approach, analyze the profits of segments of a business.

4. Determine relevant cost and revenue data for decision-making purposes.

5. Apply an appropriate decision process in three situations:
   a. Pricing products in special cases
   b. Deciding whether to purchase new equipment
   c. Deciding whether to make or to buy a part

6. Define the accounting terms new to this chapter.

Cost-Revenue Analysis for Decision Making

www.dupont.com

O pen your medicine cabinet and you are likely to find a few small medi- cine containers made from clear brown resin, capped with a white safety-lock top. "Container resin" is manufactured for use in food, soft drink, cosmetics, and medicine packaging.

In 2000 DuPont and Fluor Daniel formed an alliance to design, license, and construct the world's first plants where the new Dupont processing technology, NG-3, will be used to produce polyester packaging resins. NG-3 is expected to help manufacturers produce a higher quality polyester container resin at a lower investment than is currently possible. The two partners share in research and development costs. Both will use their mar- keting and engineering expertise to maximize revenues generated from NG-3.

Thinking Critically
Why do you think companies such as DuPont partner with other corporations to achieve financial or developmental goals?

For more information on DuPont, go to: collegeaccounting.glencoe.com.

New Terms

Absorption costing	Direct costing
Capacity	Manufacturing margin
Common costs	Marginal income
Contribution margin	Opportunity cost
Controllable fixed costs	Sunk cost
Differential cost	Variable costing

Section Objectives

1. **Explain the basic steps in the decision-making process.**

   WHY IT'S IMPORTANT
   Decisions require data about feasible alternatives.

2. **Prepare income statements using the absorption costing and direct costing methods.**

   WHY IT'S IMPORTANT
   How costs are treated must be considered when decisions are made.

3. **Using the contribution approach, analyze the profits of segments of a business.**

   WHY IT'S IMPORTANT
   A business needs to assess the performance of its segments.

4. **Determine relevant cost and revenue data for decision-making purposes.**

   WHY IT'S IMPORTANT
   Decision makers need to identify relevant from nonrelevant data.

Terms to Learn

absorption costing
common costs
contribution margin
controllable fixed costs
differential cost
direct costing
manufacturing margin
marginal income
opportunity cost
sunk cost
variable costing

The Decision Process

Accountants play a key role in a company's decision-making processes. They gather, analyze, and present large amounts of financial information to decision makers.

Exploring the Decision Process

The decision-making process involves the following six steps.

Step 1. *Define the problem.*
Step 2. *Identify workable alternatives.*
Step 3. *Determine relevant cost and revenue data.*
Step 4. *Evaluate the cost and revenue data.*
Step 5. *Consider appropriate nonfinancial factors.*
Step 6. *Make a decision.*

Direct Costing versus Absorption Costing

Recall that some costs are *fixed*; they do not vary in total during a period, even though the volume of goods manufactured or sold might be higher or lower than anticipated. Examples of fixed costs are depreciation of equipment, rent on the building, and salaries and related expenses for employees. *Variable costs* vary in total directly with the volume of manufacturing or sales activity. Variable costs include sales commissions, delivery expenses, and the loss from uncollectible accounts. *Semivariable costs* have characteristics of both fixed and variable costs. Utilities expense is an example of a semivariable cost.

Under **absorption costing**, all manufacturing costs, including fixed costs, are included in the cost of goods manufactured. The value of the ending inventory includes fixed costs. Under **direct costing**, which is also known as **variable costing**, only variable costs are included in the cost of goods manufactured. Fixed manufacturing costs are written off as expenses in the period in which they are incurred. Accountants who support direct costing contend that fixed costs are not dependent on the quantity of goods produced, so they should not be allocated to specific units manufactured. They believe that fixed costs relate to the capacity to produce goods, not to the actual goods produced.

Direct costing is widely used when making business decisions; however, **direct costing is not acceptable for GAAP financial reporting purposes.**

Absorption Costing. Let's use Davis Manufacturing Corporation to illustrate the difference between absorption and direct costing. The manufacturing costs are separated into fixed and variable elements as follows.

Beginning inventory of finished goods	–0–	
Units produced (no work in process inventories)	10,000	
Units sold	8,000	
Units in ending inventory of finished goods	2,000	
Sales price for each unit	$35	
Variable manufacturing costs per unit—materials, labor, and variable manufacturing overhead	$15	
Variable selling and administrative expenses per unit sold	$3	
Fixed manufacturing costs	$60,000	
Fixed selling and administrative expenses	$60,000	

① Objective
Explain the basic steps in the decision-making process.

Figure 32-1 is a condensed income statement using absorption costing. It includes the cost of goods manufactured.

② Objective
Prepare income statements using the absorption costing and direct costing methods.

◄ **FIGURE 32-1**
Income Statement Using Absorption Costing

Davis Manufacturing Corporation
Income Statement
Year Ended December 31, 20--

Sales (8,000 units @ $35)	280	0	0	0	00
Cost of Goods Sold					
Variable Manufacturing Costs (10,000 units @ $15)	150	0	0	0	00
Fixed Manufacturing Costs	60	0	0	0	00
Total Cost of Goods Mfg. ($210,000/10,000 units = $21 per unit)	210	0	0	0	00
Less Finished Goods Inventory, December 31 (2,000 @ $21)	42	0	0	0	00
Cost of Goods Sold	168	0	0	0	00
Gross Profit on Sales	112	0	0	0	00
Selling and Admistrative Expenses					
Variable Expenses (8,000 units @ $3)	24	0	0	0	00
Fixed Expenses	60	0	0	0	00
Total Selling and Administrative Expenses	84	0	0	0	00
Net Income	28	0	0	0	00

Direct Costing. Figure 32–2 on page 1126 is a condensed income statement using direct costing. Note these differences in direct costing:

- Only variable manufacturing costs are included in the cost of goods manufactured and in the finished goods inventory.
- The **manufacturing margin** is sales minus the variable cost of goods sold.
- The **marginal income** on sales is the manufacturing margin minus variable operating expenses.
- The net income is the marginal income on sales minus fixed manufacturing costs and fixed selling and administrative expenses.
- If there is a change in the inventory level, income under absorption costing will be different from income under direct costing.

The statement in Figure 32-2 illustrates only one of several different arrangements that might be used.

When absorption costing is used, a portion of the fixed manufacturing overhead is included in finished goods inventory and is not expensed in the current period. Under absorption costing if the number of units in ending inventory increases, the amount of fixed overhead in finished goods inventory increases and the amount of fixed overhead expensed in the current period decreases. In contrast, under direct costing all fixed

About
Accounting

Problem Solving
General problem-solving skills might not be sufficient to meet the demands of a global economy. Honda of America Mfg., Inc., refined its problem-solving process. It uses a 5W, 2H process (**w**ho, **w**hat, **w**hen, **w**here, **w**hy, **h**ow, and **h**ow much) to define the root cause of a problem.

Important!

Direct Costing
Under direct costing all fixed manufacturing overhead costs are expensed in the period in which they are incurred.

FIGURE 32-2 ▶
Income Statement
Using Direct Costing

Davis Manufacturing Corporation						
Income Statement						
Year Ended December 31, 20--						
Sales (8,000 units @ $35)				280	0 0 0	00
Cost of Goods Sold						
Variable Manufacturing Costs						
(10,000 units @ $15)	150	0 0 0	00			
Less Finished Goods Inventory, December 31						
(2,000 @ $15)	30	0 0 0	00			
Cost of Goods Sold				120	0 0 0	00
Manufacturing Margin				160	0 0 0	00
Variable Selling and Administrative Expenses						
(8,000 units @ $3)				24	0 0 0	00
Marginal Income on Sales				136	0 0 0	00
Fixed Costs and Expenses						
Fixed Manufacturing Costs	60	0 0 0	00			
Fixed Selling and Administrative Expenses	60	0 0 0	00	120	0 0 0	00
Net Income				16	0 0 0	00

International
· · · • · • • • • • • **INSIGHTS**

Decision Making in International Operations

In many parts of the world there exists political and economic uncertainty. In some countries prices and costs, governments and government attitudes, and tax policies change quickly. All of these factors, and many others peculiar to the region, need to be considered when making decisions.

❸ Objective

Using the contribution approach, analyze the profits of segments of a business.

overhead is expensed in the current period. Under direct costing an increase in finished goods inventory does not affect the amount of fixed costs expensed.

When finished goods inventory increases, net income under absorption costing is higher than that under direct costing. This is the case in Figures 32-1 and 32-2. Finished goods inventory increased by 2,000 units and net income under absorption costing is $12,000 higher than net income under direct costing. When the finished goods inventory level decreases, net income under absorption costing is less than net income under direct costing.

The Concept of Contribution Margin

Contribution margin is revenues minus variable costs. Most decisions concerning segments of a business, such as branch stores, divisions, and products, also involve an analysis of the contribution margin because it avoids arbitrary allocations of common costs. **Common costs** are costs not directly traceable to a specific segment of a business. The profitability of a segment is judged by its contribution margin; that is, the amount contributed towards covering the common costs of the business and producing a profit.

The North Atlantic Islands Program Sectoral Project Studies conducted at the University of Prince Edward Island perform cost revenue analyses to help the fishing industry manage resources, set prices, and plan market development. Based on the data provided by the Project Studies, fisheries make decisions about cost-shared arrangements, contribution margin assessments, harbor-planning strategies, subsidy adoptions, salary structures, and product mix choices.

Accounting

On The Job

Scientific Research/Engineering

Industry Overview

The life and physical sciences field uses principles and theories of science and mathematics to solve problems in research and development and to help invent and improve products and processes. In turn, engineers apply these theories and principles to develop economical solutions to technical problems.

Career Opportunities

- Cost Accountant
- Biologist
- Cost Analyst
- Pharmaceutical Project Manager
- Quality Engineer
- Industrial Accountant
- Materials Engineer
- Survey Sampling Statistician

Preparing for a Scientific Research/Engineering Career

- Obtain a bachelor's degree in electrical, mechanical, or civil engineering for entry-level jobs. Specialize in a field of engineering such as 3D solid modeling.
- Complete coursework in manufacturing accounting to obtain an understanding of how manufacturing and engineering efforts affect the financial goals of a business.
- Learn basic cost-revenue analysis techniques needed to make product or process development decisions.
- Understand materials purchasing procedures.
- Develop the ability to apply scientific knowledge to specific business problems, showing consideration to product or process costs, schedules, and business objectives.

- Learn database and project management applications used to enter, track, and report on engineering processes.
- Gain proficiencies in basic software applications such as Microsoft Word, Excel, and Access, which are used to aggregate and analyze scientific data.
- Obtain a bachelor's degree in a field of science such as biology, chemistry, agriculture, physics, or geology for entry research positions. A master's or doctoral degree is required for many positions.
- Gain experience writing grant proposals and participating in budget discussions for research programs or laboratories. Learn to install and utilize software programs such as Grant Manager or Grant Tracker, which are designed to create and monitor grant budgets.

Thinking Critically
What considerations do you think a design engineer at Ford Motor Company evaluates when creating a new car design?

Internet Application
At the NASA Marshall Space Flight Center, engineers are required to possess a variety of skills. At the Marshall Flight Center Skills Code Web site, locate the skills required for Engineering/Scientific/Technical Support positions. Review the details of skill 249-00, Engineering Cost Analysis. Describe the specific tasks applicable to this skill category.

Under the contribution margin approach, the contribution margin is calculated for the business segment. Then the controllable fixed costs of the segment are deducted to determine the segment's contribution to the overall profit of the business. **Controllable fixed costs** are costs that the segment manager can control. Common costs are not allocated to specific segments when computing the contribution margin. They are deducted from the total of all segment contributions to determine the company's profit.

Cost-Revenue Analysis for Decision Making   **Chapter 32** • **1127**

The contribution margin approach allows managers to make sound decisions about adding, keeping, or eliminating a segment of the business. If a segment produces a positive contribution margin, it is helping to cover total fixed costs and to provide a profit for the business. Management would consider eliminating any segment with a negative contribution margin. Plans for adding a new segment would include a contribution margin analysis. Management would favorably consider segments with a projected positive contribution margin.

4 Objective

Determine relevant cost and revenue data for decision-making purposes.

The Concept of Relevant Costs

A **sunk cost** is a cost that has already been incurred. When making decisions, sunk costs are irrelevant. Relevant costs are future or expected costs that will change as a result of a decision. For example, when deciding whether to replace a machine, the cost of the existing machine is irrelevant. The cost of the new machine is relevant. When deciding whether to close a warehouse, a relevant cost is the salaries of the warehouse personnel. The nonrefundable prepaid rent on the warehouse is irrelevant since it has been paid and cannot be recovered.

The Concept of Differential Costs

Decision making involves comparing two or more alternatives. A **differential cost** is the difference in cost for one alternative and another. For example, the difference in cost between using a hand-operated press and an automated press is a *differential cost*. While the term *incremental cost* is often used interchangeably with differential cost, incremental cost actually means only an *increase* in cost from one alternative to another. For example, if it costs $20,000 to produce 20 units and $25,000 to produce 30 units, the incremental cost of producing the additional 10 units is $5,000 ($25,000 − $20,000).

The Concept of Opportunity Cost

Opportunity cost is the potential earnings or benefits that are given up because a certain course of action is taken. For example, assume management is deciding between purchasing equipment or investing in securities. The opportunity cost of the decision to purchase the equipment is the amount of interest or dividends that would be received on the securities if the securities had been purchased instead of the equipment.

Section 1 Self Review

Questions

1. What is the difference between absorption costing and direct costing?

2. When the finished goods inventory decreases, is net income higher under absorption costing or direct costing?

3. What is a differential cost?

Exercises

4. When direct costing is used, cost of goods sold reflects

a. both variable and fixed manufacturing costs.

b. variable manufacturing costs and variable selling and administrative expenses.

c. variable manufacturing costs only.

d. all manufacturing costs.

5. The potential earnings or benefits given up as a result of a certain course of action is a(n)

a. sunk cost.

b. incremental cost.

c. differential cost.

d. opportunity cost.

Analysis

6. Compute the contribution margin for the following case. Sales are $320,000. Variable manufacturing costs are $220,000. Finished goods inventory is $85,000. Variable selling and administrative expense are $50,000.

(Answers to Section 1 Self Review are on page 1147.)

Cost-Revenue Analysis

Section Objective

5 Apply an appropriate decision process in three situations:
a. **Pricing products in special cases**
b. **Deciding whether to purchase new equipment**
c. **Deciding whether to make or to buy a part**

WHY IT'S IMPORTANT
Differential revenues and costs are analyzed when choosing among alternatives.

Terms to Learn

capacity

In many different situations, managers analyze costs and revenues in order to make decisions. Three common cost-revenue analysis situations will be discussed in this section: (1) product pricing in special situations, (2) purchasing new equipment, and (3) making or buying a part.

---·----

The National Cost and Revenue Study is the oldest industrywide survey. It assembles and analyzes cost and revenue data for newspapers in all circulation categories. Newspaper managers use this data to compare their newspapers to other newspapers and to industry norms. Studies such as these help businesses make decisions on issues such as salary levels, product prices, and production techniques.

---·----

Product Pricing in Special Situations

Direct costing is often useful in setting prices and considering offers to buy products in special circumstances. For example, Davis Manufacturing Corporation received an offer from an overseas customer to purchase 1,000 units at $21 per unit. The units would incur the usual manufacturing and selling and administrative costs. In addition, there would be a shipping cost of $1 per unit. The company has adequate manufacturing capacity to take the special order without endangering its regular production or its ability to take care of existing customers. **Capacity** in this sense refers to a facility's power to produce or use.

5 Objective
a. Apply an appropriate decision process in pricing products in special cases.

---·----

In the semiconductor industry, improving cost effectiveness and productivity have always been high priorities. They have become more critical with increasing competition. Simulation software, the Y4 (Yield FOREcaster), helps manufacturers predict defect-related yield loss and manufacturing costs in a multiproduct fabrication line. For example, the software predicts the failure rates when foreign particles are introduced during wafer processing.

---·----

Management reviewed the information shown in Figure 32-1 on page 1125 and found the computed following average unit cost under absorption costing.

Manufacturing costs ($210,000 ÷ 10,000 units)	$21.00
Selling and administrative expenses ($84,000 ÷ 8,000 units)	10.50
Total average cost per unit	$31.50

Management also reviewed the information shown in Figure 32-2 to determine the costs under direct costing. The additional shipping expense of a $1 per unit was also considered.

Variable manufacturing costs	$15
Variable selling and administrative expenses	3
Variable costs per unit	$18
Additional shipping cost	1
Total variable cost per unit	$19

The difference between the costs ($31.50 and $19.00) is due to fixed costs, and in this situation the fixed costs are irrelevant. The fixed costs will be incurred whether or not the order is accepted. The incremental cost of making the additional 1,000 units is $19. Based on this analysis, the company would make a profit of $2 ($21 − $19) per unit if the order were accepted.

Management needs to consider carefully all relevant factors when analyzing special pricing situations. For example, management would not accept the special order if the company did not have sufficient capacity or if the special order jeopardized sales to existing customers. Also, management would need to ensure that the company does not violate federal laws that prohibit price differentials.

Purchasing New Equipment

⑤ Objective

b. Apply an appropriate decision process in deciding whether to purchase new equipment.

The management of LEH Manufacturing Company is considering the purchase of a new machine that will improve worker productivity. The machine costs $25,000 and has an estimated useful life of 10 years, with no anticipated salvage value. Table 32-1 shows the relevant data for the two alternatives.

TABLE 32-1 ▶
Cost and Revenue Data Needed for an Analysis of the Effects of Purchasing a New Machine

	If Machine Is Not Purchased	If Machine Is Purchased
Annual sales (units)	10,000	10,000
Sales price (per unit)	$ 30.00	$ 30.00
Cost of machine		$25,000.00
Other cost data:		
Materials (per unit)	$ 11.00	$ 11.00
Labor (per unit)	9.00	8.00
Variable overhead (per unit)	3.00	3.00
Fixed overhead (per year)	$18,000.00	$20,000.00*

*Includes depreciation of $2,500 a year for the new machine and the effects of certain other changes in fixed costs.

Table 32-2 shows the analysis. The left column reflects the net income under each alternative. The differential cost data is in the right column. This analysis indicates that if LEH Manufacturing Company were to purchase the machine, its net income would increase by $8,000 each year. Before making the final decision, however, management needs to consider employee morale and the quality of the product that the new machine will make.

	If Machine Is Not Purchased	If Machine Is Purchased	Differential
Annual sales	$300,000	$300,000	
Variable costs			
Materials	$110,000	$110,000	
Labor	90,000	80,000	$10,000
Manufacturing overhead	30,000	30,000	
Total variable costs	$230,000	$220,000	
Contribution margin	$ 70,000	$ 80,000	
Fixed costs	18,000	20,000	(2,000)
Net income	$ 52,000	$ 60,000	$ 8,000

◀ **TABLE 32-2**
Analysis of the Effects of Purchasing a New Machine (Based on annual income)

Making or Buying a Part

LEH Manufacturing Company purchases a part for $17 per unit. The company uses 15,000 of these parts each year. Management has determined that the part could be made in the company's molding department.

The molding department has a capacity of 20,000 direct labor hours per year. For several years it has operated at 15,000 direct labor hours per year. For the molding department, the direct labor costs are $12 per hour and variable manufacturing overhead costs are $8 per hour. Annual fixed costs for the department total $80,000. The estimated cost of materials is $7 for each part. Four parts can be produced per hour.

⑤ Objective

c. Apply an appropriate decision process in deciding whether to make or to buy a part.

Managerial IMPLICATIONS

Using Cost Revenue Analysis to Make Decisions

- Accountants gather and analyze data so that managers have the necessary information to make effective decisions between alternative courses of action.

- When making decisions managers are concerned about future costs and revenues.

- Managers use cost-revenue analysis to evaluate the financial effects of decisions before they are made.

- It is critical that managers understand cost analysis and related concepts including sunk costs, relevant costs, differential costs, opportunity costs, and contribution margin.

- Managers focus on the differential revenues and differential costs for each course of action.

- Usually, sunk costs are irrelevant in making decisions.

Thinking Critically
What factors should be considered when making financial decisions?

Table 32-3 shows the analysis of the data. If LEH Manufacturing Company decides to manufacture the part, it will realize a savings of $5 per part, which is a $75,000 savings per year.

Notice that the fixed manufacturing overhead costs are not considered because they remain the same whether the part is purchased or made.

TABLE 32-3 ▶
Analysis of the Effects of
Making or Buying a Part

Cost to purchase part		$ 17.00
Cost to manufacture part		
Variable costs only		
Materials	$7.00	
Labor (1/4 hour at $12 per hour)	3.00	
Manufacturing overhead (1/4 hour at $8 per hour)	2.00	12.00
Differential cost (savings per unit if part is manufactured)		$ 5.00
Number of parts per year		× 15,000
Total annual savings		$75,000

Every day managers must consider decisions similar to those covered in this chapter. Accountants who understand cost-revenue analysis can assist management to consider the appropriate factors to enable them to reach logical decisions that will increase the company's profitability.

In addition to the factors covered in this chapter, accountants also consider the impact of income taxes and the timing of cash receipts and expenditures. These elements have significant impact on the company's profitability.

Section 2 Self Review

Questions

1. When is direct costing helpful in special pricing situations?

2. What is the contribution margin approach to decision analysis?

3. Are fixed costs relevant when making a pricing decision for a special order if there is sufficient manufacturing capacity available?

Exercises

4. Contribution margin is calculated by deducting

  a. variable costs from revenue.

  b. variable costs and controllable fixed costs from revenue.

  c. variable costs and common costs from revenue.

  d. controllable fixed costs from revenue.

5. In deciding whether to purchase a new machine, which of the following is not relevant?

  a. depreciation

  b. labor cost savings

  c. cost of the old machine

  d. savings in materials used

Analysis

6. Wiley Corporation is considering the purchase of a new machine at a cost of $30,000. The new machine would have a life of five years and would produce 7,000 units per year (the current output). Direct labor costs would be reduced by 90 cents per unit. Variable overhead costs would be reduced by 50 cents per unit. Fixed costs, other than depreciation, would increase by $2,000 per year. Assuming all 7,000 units are sold, what is the amount of increase or decrease in net income per year if the machine is purchased?

 (Answers to Section 2 Self Review begin on page 1147.)

Review

Chapter Summary

To make decisions, management constantly requires financial data, which must be gathered and analyzed by the accountant. In this chapter, you have learned how to evaluate data when cost and revenue considerations are involved.

Learning Objectives

1 Explain the basic steps in the decision-making process.

Managers not only use financial information to help identify a problem but also to help reach decisions for solving the problem. The decision-making process involves the following steps:

- Define the problem.
- Identify workable alternatives.
- Determine relevant cost and revenue data.
- Evaluate the cost and revenue data.
- Consider appropriate nonfinancial factors.
- Make a decision.

2 Prepare income statements using the absorption costing and direct costing methods.

- In direct costing, only the variable manufacturing costs are considered as part of the cost of goods manufactured. The cost of goods sold, based solely on variable costs, is subtracted from net sales to arrive at the manufacturing margin.
- Variable selling and administrative expenses are deducted from the manufacturing margin to obtain the marginal income on sales.
- Fixed manufacturing costs and fixed operating expenses are subtracted from the marginal income on sales to obtain the net income for the period.

3 Using the contribution approach, analyze the profits of segments of a business.

The contribution margin measures the excess of revenues over variable costs. If a segment produces a contribution margin, it is helping to meet company-wide common expenses.

4 Determine relevant cost and revenue data for decision-making purposes.

- Relevant costs for making decisions are usually future costs.
- Sunk costs are historical costs and are therefore generally not relevant to business decisions.
- Determining differential costs—the differences in cost between various alternatives—is important in decision making.
- Often the contribution approach is used in evaluating the data that results from the analysis.

5 Apply an appropriate decision process in three situations:

a. Pricing products in special cases

Direct costing is often useful in setting prices, especially when special offers from potential customers to buy the company's product are being considered. Companies compare financial data to make decisions on buying or manufacturing an item used in production.

b. Deciding whether to purchase new equipment

Accountants gather relevant data to compare the proposed purchase of machine or continuing to use the old machine, estimating net income under each alternative and calculating the difference.

c. Deciding whether to make or to buy a part

When comparing alternatives to make or buy a part, data can be analyzed on the basis of unit cost or annual total costs. Fixed manufacturing costs are not considered when making this analysis, since these costs remain the same whether the part is made or bought.

6 Define the accounting terms new to this chapter.

CHAPTER 32 GLOSSARY

Absorption costing (p. 1124) The accounting procedure whereby all manufacturing costs, including fixed costs, are included in the cost of goods manufactured

Capacity (p. 1129) A facility's ability to produce or use

Common costs (p. 1126) Costs not directly traceable to a specific segment of a business

Contribution margin (p. 1126) Revenues minus variable costs

Controllable fixed costs (p. 1127) Costs that the segment manager can control

Differential cost (p. 1128) The difference in cost between one alternative and another

Direct costing (p. 1124) The accounting procedure whereby only variable costs are included in the cost of goods manufactured, and fixed manufacturing costs are written off as expenses in the period in which they are incurred

Manufacturing margin (p. 1125) Sales minus the variable cost of goods sold

Marginal income (p. 1125) The manufacturing margin minus variable operating expenses

Opportunity cost (p. 1128) Potential earnings or benefits that are given up because a certain course of action is taken

Sunk cost (p. 1128) A cost that has been incurred and will not change as a result of a decision

Variable costing (p. 1124) See Direct costing

Comprehensive Self Review

1. What are relevant costs?

2. Why are sunk costs ignored in most managerial decisions?

3. Should management automatically reject an offer by a potential customer to purchase some of the company's product at a price that is less than the company's total cost to manufacture the product? Explain.

4. Give some reasons why a company might decide to purchase a part from an outside supplier that is used in its finished product rather than manufacture the part.

5. Briefly explain incremental costs.

(Answers to Comprehensive Self Review are on page 1148.)

Discussion Questions

1. Which of the following items are subtracted from net sales to arrive at contribution margin?

   a. fixed administrative expenses

   b. variable administrative expenses

   c. fixed manufacturing costs

   d. variable manufacturing costs

   e. fixed selling expenses

   f. variable selling expenses

2. Briefly describe absorption costing.

3. What is the fundamental difference between direct costing and absorption costing?

4. Is absorption costing or direct costing more useful in making decisions? Why?

5. What is the manufacturing margin?

6. Explain the meaning of marginal income on sales.

7. What is a differential cost?

8. Explain opportunity costs.

9. What are sunk costs?

10. Suggest some nonmeasurable data that might be considered in deciding to replace existing equipment with new equipment.

11. Why might management be reluctant to accept a special order for its products at less than the normal price even though such an order would be legal and profitable?

12. Suppose that a company is considering the purchase of new equipment. The old equipment will be sold when the new equipment is acquired. How should the proceeds from the sale of the old equipment be considered in the analysis of the effects of the purchase?

13. Why do the analyses presented in this chapter focus on future costs rather than on past costs? Does this mean that historical costs are useless? Explain.

14. Why might employee morale be a factor in deciding whether to replace existing equipment with new equipment?

Applications

EXERCISES

Data for Exercises 32-1 and 32-2.

Buckeye Corporation has divided all of its costs and expenses into fixed and variable components. Data for the company's first year of operations follows.

Beginning inventory of finished goods	0
Units produced (no work in process)	12,000
Units sold	10,000
Units in ending inventory of finished goods	2,000
Sales price	$150 per unit
Variable manufacturing costs	$55 for each unit manufactured
Variable selling and administrative expenses	$25 per unit sold
Fixed manufacturing costs for year	$150,000
Fixed selling and administrative expenses for year	$125,000

Exercise 32-1 ►
Objective 2

Using the absorption method.

Using the absorption method, calculate the following:

1. Cost of goods manufactured for the year.

2. The value of the ending inventory of finished goods.

3. The cost of goods sold for the year.

4. Net income for the year.

Exercise 32-2 ►
Objective 2

Using direct costing.

Using the direct costing method, calculate the following:

1. Ending inventory of finished goods.

2. The manufacturing margin for the year.

3. Net income for the year.

Exercise 32-3 ►
Objective 4

Identifying relevant costs.

Georgia Company is considering replacing its existing computer system with new equipment. The existing system has a book value of $300,000 and a remaining useful life of three years. The new computer system would cost $800,000 and have a useful life of five years with an estimated salvage value of $50,000. The annual production of 10,000 units would not change. It would, however, reduce direct labor costs by $5 per unit. Other fixed costs would increase by $30,000 per year. Of the information just given, which items are relevant to the decision to replace the equipment?

Exercise 32-4 ►
Objectives 4, 5a

Determining relevant costs and making a pricing decision.

William Company has an opportunity to export 1,000 units of its product to a foreign country. The current selling price is $125, but the special order will be sold at a unit price of $95. This special order will not affect its current sales, all of which are domestic. Freight and shipping costs of $15 per unit would be incurred on the foreign order. Current variable manufacturing costs are $42 per unit manufactured, and variable selling and administrative costs are $23 per unit sold. Included in variable selling expenses is a sales commission of $3 per unit, which would not apply to the foreign order. Fixed manufacturing costs are $175,000 per year and fixed selling and administrative expenses are $150,000 per year. The company now manufactures and sells 6,000 units per year. What is the effect on profits if the special order is taken? Show all calculations.

◀ **Exercise 32-5**
Objectives 3, 4, 5a

Selecting relevant data, determining contribution margin of segment, and making a pricing decision.

The standard cost sheet for the leading product made by J. R. Enterprises shows the following data.

Direct materials	$ 82
Direct labor (2 hours at $18/hour)	36
Manufacturing overhead	
Variable costs (2 hours at $18/hour)	36
Fixed costs (2 hours at $27/hour)	54
Total standard cost	$208

The product normally sells for $299. The company is presently operating at only slightly over 70 percent of capacity.

1. A chain of discount stores has offered to purchase 5,000 units of the product for $229 per unit. Shipping costs would be $3 per unit. Special packaging would be needed and would cost an additional $2 per unit. There would be no other variable selling or administrative expenses. Should the order be accepted? (Show all calculations.)

2. Ignoring all factors except those given, what is the least amount that J. R. Enterprises could profitably accept for a special order of 5,000 units?

◀ **Exercise 32-6**
Objectives 4, 5b

Selecting relevant data and deciding whether to purchase equipment.

RSB Company is considering the purchase of a new factory machine at a cost of $98,000. The machine would perform a function that is now being performed by hand. The new machine would have a life of seven years and would produce 12,000 units a year (the current output). Direct labor costs would be reduced by $1.25 per unit, and variable overhead costs would be reduced by $0.75 per unit. Fixed costs other than depreciation would increase by $5,000 per year. Should the machine be purchased? What is the impact of the decision on net income?

Data for Exercises 32-7 and 32-8.

Longhorn Corporation is manufacturing a part that is used in its finished product. The costs for each unit of the part follow.

Direct materials		$21
Direct labor		16
Manufacturing overhead		
Variable costs	$5	
Fixed costs	2	7
Total cost		$44

The fixed overhead is based on $200,000 of fixed costs to manufacture 100,000 parts per year. If the part is not manufactured, fixed costs will be reduced by approximately $150,000 per year.

Exercise 32-7 ►
Objectives 3, 4, 5c

Selecting relevant data, determining contribution margin of a segment, and deciding whether to make or to buy a part.

Instead of making the part, Longhorn has an opportunity to purchase the part from an outside company for $40 per unit. Should the company accept the offer, or should it continue to manufacture the part?

Exercise 32-8 ►
Objectives 3, 4, 5c

Selecting relevant data, determining contribution margin of a segment, and deciding whether to make or buy a part.

Assume that an outside vendor has offered to sell Longhorn the part for $42 per unit. Should the company continue to manufacture the part, or should it purchase the part?

Problems

Selected problems can be completed using:
▦ **Spreadsheets**

PROBLEM SET A

Problem 32-1A ►
Objective 2

Preparing income statements based on absorption costing and direct costing.

The following data pertains to the operations of APC Corporation for the year ended December 31, 20--. It manufactures computer keyboards.

DATA FOR 20--

Sales	3,400 units @ $75/unit
Variable manufacturing costs	3,500 units @ $40/unit
Variable selling and administrative expenses	$5/unit
Fixed manufacturing costs	$63,000
Fixed selling and administrative expenses	$25,000
Finished goods inventory, January 1, 20--	400 units
Finished goods inventory, December 31, 20--	500 units

INSTRUCTIONS

1. Prepare an income statement for the year using the absorption costing approach. Assume that the 400 units in the beginning inventory of finished goods had a cost of $48 per unit.

2. Prepare an income statement for the year using the direct costing approach. Assume that the 400 units in the beginning inventory of finished goods cost $40 per unit.

3. Explain the reason for the difference between the net income or loss computed under the two methods.

Analyze: Assume that APC Corporation's manufacturing managers believe that only those costs that contribute directly to product production should be assigned to cost of goods manufactured. Which costing method would these managers prefer?

Problem 32-2A ►
Objectives 2, 3, 4, 5a

Preparing an income statement based on direct costing, choosing relevant data, determining contribution margin of a segment, and making a pricing decision.

The Flying J Corporation began operations in 20-- to manufacture a single product. There are no work in process inventories. Relevant data for the year follows.

OPERATING DATA FOR 20--

Quantities	
Beginning inventories, finished goods	–0–
Units produced during the year	3,700
Units sold during the year	3,300
Costs	
Direct materials ($25 per unit)	$92,500
Direct labor ($22 per unit)	81,400
Variable factory overhead ($9 per unit)	33,300
Fixed factory overhead	55,000
Variable selling and administrative expenses	
($8 per unit)	26,400
Fixed selling and administrative expenses	50,000
Selling price for each unit	95

INSTRUCTIONS

1. Prepare an income statement for 20--, using direct costing.

2. Assume that the company has an opportunity to sell 300 units of the product in a foreign country for $70 per unit. No fixed or variable selling and administrative expenses would be incurred in connection with these units except shipping costs of $6 per unit and miscellaneous administrative expenses of $2 per unit. The company has idle capacity, and the order would not affect present markets. Would it be profitable for the company to accept the order? Show all computations.

Analyze: What percentage of the foreign sales order would be realized as marginal income?

Choosing relevant data, determining contribution margin of a segment, and deciding whether to purchase equipment.

◄ **Problem 32-3A**
Objectives 3, 4, 5b

Baylor Company makes a single product that it sells to retail stores. The firm's polishing department uses hand labor to perform its work on all products. A proposal has been made by the company's vice president to acquire machinery that will perform most of the functions of this department. The polishing department has consistently produced 50,000 units a year, and that is the estimated production for the foreseeable future. A summary of the manufacturing costs of the department follows.

Direct materials	$ 50,000
Direct labor	1,050,000
Manufacturing overhead	
Variable costs	150,000
Fixed costs	100,000

The machinery being considered will cost $900,000 and have an estimated useful life of five years, with no salvage value. The machinery will cause the following changes in costs.

a. Direct labor will decrease by $11 per unit.

b. Direct materials will not change.

c. Variable manufacturing overhead will decrease by $5 per unit.

d. Fixed manufacturing overhead will decrease by $20,000 per year.

INSTRUCTIONS

1. Prepare an analysis showing the effect on net income of purchasing the equipment.

2. What other factors should be considered in making the decision?

Analyze: Assume that the use of the new machinery will result in a 3 percent increase in the number of imperfect products produced. These imperfect products must be reprocessed at a cost of $8 per unit, increasing variable manufacturing costs. What net annual increase or decrease in costs can be projected?

Problem 32-4A ►
Objectives 4, 5c

Choosing relevant data and deciding whether to make or buy a part.

Westwind Equipment Corporation is currently manufacturing a part that goes into its main product. Each year 3,000 of these parts are used. Cost data for the past year that relates to the 3,000 parts is given below. Fixed costs are allocated on the basis of direct labor hours. An outside company has offered to supply the part for $45 per unit, plus a shipping charge of $3 per unit. The plant now used by Westwind to manufacture the part would not be used to capacity within the foreseeable future if the part is purchased outside.

Direct materials	$72,000
Direct labor	75,000
Variable overhead costs	6,000
Fixed overhead costs	18,750

INSTRUCTIONS

1. Prepare an analysis comparing the unit cost of manufacturing the part with the unit cost of purchasing it.

2. What other factors are important in making the decision to accept or reject the offer?

Analyze: What decisions does the company face in regard to idle plant time if it purchases the part from an outside source?

PROBLEM SET B

Problem 32-1B ►
Objective 2

Preparing income statements based on absorption costing and direct costing.

The following data pertains to the operations of the CAH Manufacturing Company for the year ended December 31, 20--. The firm makes kitchen appliances.

DATA FOR 20--

Sales	3,000 units @ $65/unit
Variable manufacturing costs	2,900 units @ $30/unit
Variable selling and administrative costs	$5/unit
Fixed manufacturing costs	$50,000
Fixed selling and administrative expenses	$30,000
Finished goods inventory, January 1, 20--	300 units
Finished goods inventory, December 31, 20--	200 units

INSTRUCTIONS

1. Prepare an income statement for the year using the absorption costing approach. Assume that the 300 units in the beginning inventory of finished goods had a cost of $48 per unit.

2. Prepare an income statement for the year using the direct costing approach. Assume that the 300 units in the beginning inventory of finished goods cost $30 per unit.

3. Explain the reason for the difference between the net income or loss computed by the two different methods.

Analyze: Under the absorption costing method, what percentage of cost of goods sold is attributable to fixed manufacturing costs?

Preparing an income statement based on direct costing, choosing relevant data, determining contribution margin of a segment, and making a pricing decision.

◀ **Problem 32-2B**
Objectives 2, 3, 4, 5a

Hamilton Corporation began operations in 20-- to manufacture a single product. Relevant data for the year follows. There are no work in process inventories.

OPERATING DATA FOR 20-- Quantities

Beginning inventories, finished goods	0
Units produced during the year	5,000
Units sold during the year	4,500
Costs	
Direct materials ($22 per unit)	$110,000
Direct labor ($25 per unit)	125,000
Variable factory overhead ($8 per unit)	40,000
Fixed factory overhead	60,000
Variable selling and administrative expenses ($3 per unit)	13,500
Fixed selling and administrative expenses	25,000
Selling price for each unit	102

INSTRUCTIONS

1. Prepare an income statement for 20--, using direct costing.

2. Assume that the company has an opportunity to sell 1,000 units of the product in a foreign country for $75 per unit. No fixed or variable selling and administrative expenses would be incurred in connection with these units except a $4 shipping and handling cost per unit. The company has idle capacity, and the order would not affect present markets. Would it be profitable for the company to accept the order? Show all computations.

Analyze: If Hamilton Corporation had used the absorption costing method, would the value of beginning inventories be higher or lower than that reflected in the statement you prepared? Explain.

Choosing relevant data, determining contribution margin of a segment, and deciding whether to purchase equipment.

◀ **Problem 32-3B**
Objectives 3, 4, 5b

Brandon Manufacturing makes doors, which it sells to home builders. The firm's finishing department is not mechanized. Employees use hand tools to finish the product. The factory superintendent has proposed that the firm acquire an electric-powered machine to perform some of the finishing functions. Presently, 5,000 units per year are manufactured and sold. A summary of the manufacturing costs of the finishing department follows.

Direct materials	$50,000
Direct labor	50,000
Manufacturing overhead	
Variable costs	10,000
Fixed costs	15,000

The machine being considered will cost $50,000 and have a useful life of five years, with no salvage value. The machine will cause the following annual changes in costs.

a. Direct labor will decrease by $20,000.

b. Indirect materials will decrease by $1 per unit.

c. No change in direct materials.

d. Fixed manufacturing overhead will decrease by $5,000 per year.

INSTRUCTIONS

1. Prepare an analysis showing the effect on net income of purchasing the equipment.

2. What other factors should be considered in making the decision?

Analyze: What direct labor costs are incurred per unit for the current manual process?

Problem 32-4B ▶
Objectives 4, 5c

Choosing relevant data and deciding whether to make or buy a part.

Elan Electrical Equipment Company is currently manufacturing a part that goes into its main product. Each year 1,800 of these parts are used. Cost data for the past year that relates to the 1,800 parts is given below. Fixed costs are allocated on the basis of direct labor hours. An outside company has offered to supply the part at $88 per unit, plus a shipping charge of $3 per unit. The plant capacity now used by Elan to manufacture the part would not be used in the foreseeable future if the part is purchased outside.

Variable costs	
Direct materials	$90,000
Direct labor	45,000
Variable overhead	18,000
Fixed overhead costs	27,000

INSTRUCTIONS

1. Prepare an analysis comparing the unit cost of manufacturing the part with the unit cost of purchasing it.

2. What other factors are important in making the decision to accept or reject the offer?

Analyze: If Elan Electrical Company could negotiate a $1 shipping charge per unit for the outside supplier, what is the per-unit difference between the cost to make and the cost to purchase?

New Line of Business

Beauty Supplies distributes beauty and barber supplies to retail stores, beauty shops, and barber shops. Early in 20--, officers of the company decided to develop and market a line of shampoos and hair conditioners under their own private brand. They contracted with another company to manufacture and package the products. After the end of the first year, however, officers of Beauty Supplies became quite concerned over the profitability of the new line. An analysis of operations is shown below.

	Fixed Cost per Month	Percent of Selling Price per Unit
Average cost of products		27
Average cost of containers and packaging		8
Average freight in		2
Average delivery costs		3
Sales commissions		10
Advertising expenses		
Variable		10
Fixed	$500	
Warehousing costs		
Variable		2
Fixed	$500	
Other costs		
Variable		8
Fixed	$510	

An analysis of the fourth quarter 20-- showed sales of $5,000 for the quarter. Several officers in the company have suggested that the line of products should be discontinued.

INSTRUCTIONS

1. Based on the information above, what is the amount of income or loss for the fourth quarter?

2. Based on the information above only, should the venture be discontinued? The fixed costs are allocated costs and will not be eliminated by discontinuing the venture.

3. What questions, other than those related to the information given above, should be asked by the officers to arrive at a decision on whether or not to discontinue the product line?

4. What sales volume would be necessary to pay all variable costs and cover the allocated fixed costs?

Analyze: Assume that the sales staff has been asked to forfeit half of its sales commissions for the fourth quarter of 20--. What effect do you think this measure would have on the company's income for the period?

Making Decisions

The cost accountant for MWF Manufacturing, Inc. has prepared the analysis given below of the profitability of each of the firm's three products. All fixed costs are allocated costs and are not related to specific products.

	Item 101	Item 102	Item 103	Total
Sales	$30,000	$67,500	$80,000	$177,500
Cost of goods sold	19,500	28,500	45,500	93,500
Gross profit on sales	$10,500	$39,000	$34,500	$84,000
Operating expenses	11,000	14,000	21,000	46,000
Net income (or loss)	$ (500)	$25,000	$13,500	$38,000
Units sold	1,000	1,500	2,000	
Sales price per unit	$ 30	$ 45	$ 40	
Variable cost of goods sold per unit	$ 18	$ 18	$ 22	
Variable operating expenses per unit	$ 6	$ 6	$ 8	

Management has been considering several options concerning the company's product mix to reduce or eliminate the loss on Item 101. The company's president has asked you to prepare an analysis of the effects on the company's net income before taxes for each of the following proposals. Consider each proposal independently; no changes would occur in the other products.

PROPOSALS

1. Discontinue Item 101.

2. Increase the sales price of Item 101 to $33. Marketing analysis indicates that the increase in price will cause a decrease in sales of Item 101 to 800 units.

3. Discontinue Item 101 and use the resulting plant capacity to produce a new product, Item 104. The department's marketing studies estimate that 1,500 units could be sold at $28 each. The variable costs and expenses per unit of Item 104 are estimated to be $10 per unit manufacturing cost and $8 per unit for operating expenses.

Business Connections

◀ Connection 1

MANAGERIAL *FOCUS* **Decision Making**

1. The vice president of the manufacturing company for which you are the accountant has suggested to the president that all prices should be established on the basis of direct costing. Respond to this suggestion.

2. Assume that the company where you are employed has a substantial amount of unused plant capacity. A foreign company has offered to purchase a large quantity of your company's product, but at a price of 12 percent less than the product's normal selling price. What types of information are needed to arrive at a decision about whether to accept the order?

3. Suppose that your company is considering the purchase of a new machine for use in its production process. The cost of the machine is $295,000. If the purchase is made, an old machine currently in use will be scrapped. It has no net salvage value because its removal cost is equal to its gross salvage amount. The old machine has a book value of $150,000, and management is reluctant to take the loss that would result if this machine is scrapped. Discuss the types of information that management would need to make a decision about purchasing the new asset. Give special attention to the problem of the old asset's book value.

4. Suppose that your company has been manufacturing a part used in its finished product. The total manufacturing cost of the part is $35. An outside supplier has offered to provide the part for $32. Describe the measurable data that management would need in making a decision about whether to accept the supplier's offer.

◀ Connection 2

Ethical **DILEMMA** **Saving Money** Suppose that you could purchase a critical production part from a foreign manufacturing company at a savings of $25,000 to your company. As part of the purchase, however, there is an agreement to hire your foreign counterpart as a "consultant" for $15,000 a year. Do you agree to accept these terms? Why or why not?

◀ Connection 3

Street **WISE:**

Questions from the Real World **Cost and Revenue Decisions** Refer to the *1999 Annual Report* for The Home Depot, Inc. in Appendix B.

1. Locate "Management's Discussion and Analysis of Results of Operations and Financial Condition." Review the section *Results of Operations*. Based on this information, what cost- or revenue-based decisions are implied? What course of action is being taken on these issues?

2. Review the letter written to shareholders, customers, and associates of The Home Depot, Inc. The company expresses a directive to give preference to vendors who supply certified wood products. What cost and revenue comparisons do you think management made when arriving at this decision?

Connection 4 ▶

FINANCIAL $TATEMENT
A N A L Y S I S **Product Mix and Cost-Revenue Analysis** Following are excerpts from the Mattel, Inc., *2000 Annual Report.*

Management's Discussion and Analysis of Financial Condition and Results of Operations

2000 Financial Realignment Plan

During the third quarter of 2000, Mattel initiated a financial realignment plan designed to improve gross margin; selling, general and administrative expenses; operating profit, and cash flow. . . .

The following are the major initiatives included in the financial realignment plan:

- Reduce excess manufacturing capacity; . . .
- Eliminate product lines that do not meet required levels of profitability;
- Improve supply chain performance and economics; . . .
- Close and consolidate certain international offices.

Analyze:

1. Which major initiative could be supported by contribution margin analysis?

2. Give an example of a sunk cost that might be associated with Mattel's initiative to close and consolidate certain international offices.

3. What nonfinancial factors might be considered in Mattel's initiative to close and consolidate certain international offices?

Analyze Online: Go to the *Company* section of the Mattel, Inc. Web site **(www.mattel.com)** and find the *Investors* section. Locate the most recent annual report and answer the following questions related to *Management's Discussion and Analysis of Financial Condition and Results of Operations.*

4. What product-related decisions has the company considered in the fiscal year?

5. What nonfinancial factors might have impacted those decisions?

Connection 5 ▶

Extending the Thought **Labor and Manufacturing** Manufacturing businesses must be sensitive to market trends and product demand as they establish production levels. The manager of a steel manufacturing plant hires and fires employees frequently as a result of production activity and fluctuating product demand. Do you agree or disagree with this practice? Explain. How do you think this practice affects employee morale or productivity?

Business Communication **Costing Methods** Assume that your company has issued a directive that manufacturing managers must assume responsibility for control of both variable and direct costs. Absorption costing has been adopted toward that end. Prepare a memo to your new CEO describing why this choice has been made and how this method will help managers identify cost concerns.

◄ **Connection 6**

Team*Work* **Department Closures and Cost-Revenue Analysis** As a team, visit the floral department of your local grocery store. Imagine that this store is considering closing the floral department. Make a list of the types of costs that you think would be associated with the operation of this department. Which of these costs could be eliminated if the department were closed? Which costs might remain? Consider the effects on costs such as rent or electricity. Describe other types of financial data required to make a well-informed decision about the closure of the department.

◄ **Connection 7**

inter **NET** **CONNECTION** **Target Costing** The AICPA Web site contains information relevant to business managers and CPAs alike. Go to **www.aicpa.org.** Use the search option to find information about target costing. What is target costing? What are three of the attributes shared by target costing best practice companies?

◄ **Connection 8**

Answers to Self Reviews

Answers to Section 1 Self Review

1. Under absorption costing, all manufacturing costs, including fixed costs, are included in the cost of goods manufactured and in the ending inventory. Under direct costing, all fixed overhead is charged off as a current expense of the period when it is incurred.

2. Direct costing

3. The difference in cost between one alternative and another.

4. **c.** variable manufacturing costs only.

5. **d.** opportunity cost.

6. $135,000

Answers to Section 2 Self Review

1. It helps to determine if the company has idle capacity and has the opportunity to acquire additional business at special prices.

2. The contribution approach to analysis compares the impact of the proposed action on incremental revenues and incremental costs.

3. No, fixed costs are not relevant.

4. a. variable costs from revenue.

5. c. cost of the old machine

6. $1,800 increase

Answers to Comprehensive Self Review

1. Future or expected costs that will be incurred as a result of a specific decision.

2. Because they have already been incurred and will not change as a result of the decision being considered.

3. Acceptance of an order for less than total cost may be considered if the company has idle capacity, the price exceeds variable costs, the pricing would be legal, and the special order would not interfere with existing business.

4. It may be cheaper to purchase a part than to manufacture it; purchase may be necessary in order to assure supply; there may be a need to purchase one part in order to get favorable terms on other parts or supplies, and it may simplify the hiring of personnel or the handling of raw materials.

5. Incremental costs are the increases in total costs from one alternative to another.

Combined Journal

Most small businesses have just a few employees and can devote only a limited amount of time to the preparation of accounting records. To serve the needs of these businesses, accountants have developed certain types of record systems that have special time-saving and labor-saving features but still produce all the necessary financial information for management. One example of such a system is the combined journal discussed in this appendix.

Small firms play an important role in our economy today. In fact, almost one-half of the businesses in the United States are classified as small firms. Despite their limited size, these businesses need good accounting systems that can produce accurate and timely information.

Systems Involving the Combined Journal

The **combined journal**, also called the *combination journal*, provides the cornerstone for a simple yet effective accounting system in many small firms. As its name indicates, this journal combines features of the general journal and the special journals in a single record.

If a small business has enough transactions to make the general journal difficult to use but too few transactions to make it worthwhile to set up special journals, the combined journal offers a solution. It has many of the advantages of special journals but provides the simplicity of a single journal. Like the special journals, the combined journal contains separate money columns for the accounts used most often to record a firm's transactions. This speeds up the initial entry of transactions and permits summary postings at the end of the month. Most transactions can be recorded on a single line, and the need to write account names is minimized.

Other Accounts columns allow the recording of transactions that do not fit into any of the special columns. These columns are also used for entries that would normally appear in the general journal, such as adjusting and closing entries.

Some small firms just use a combined journal and a general ledger in their accounting systems. Others need one or more subsidiary ledgers in addition to the general ledger.

Designing a Combined Journal

To function effectively, a combined journal must be designed to meet the specific needs of a firm. For a new business, the accountant first studies the proposed operations and develops an appropriate chart of accounts. Then the accountant decides which accounts are likely to be used often enough in recording daily transactions to justify special columns in the combined journal.

	DATE	CK. NO.	DESCRIPTION	POST. REF.	CASH DEBIT	CASH CREDIT	ACCOUNTS RECEIVABLE DEBIT	ACCOUNTS RECEIVABLE CREDIT
1	2005							
2	Jan. 3	842	Rent for month			9 0 0 00		
3	5		David Levine	✓			6 0 00	
4	6		United Chemicals Inc.	✓				
5	7		Cash sales		1 1 5 0 00			
6	7	843	Payroll			5 2 0 00		
7	10		Marion Brown	✓	4 5 00			4 5 00
8	12		Pacific Products Corp.	✓				
9	13		Thomas Nolan	✓	7 0 00			7 0 00
10	14		Cash sales		1 3 8 5 00			
11	14	844	Payroll			5 2 0 00		
12	17		Joyce Miller	✓			5 5 00	
13	18		Alvarez Company	✓				
14	19	845	Telephone service			8 2 00		
15	20		Carl Janowski	✓	6 4 00			6 4 00
16	20		Dorothy Russell	✓			3 3 00	
17	21		Cash sales		1 2 7 0 00			
18	21	846	Payroll	✓		5 2 0 00		
19	24		Ace Plastic Bags	✓				
20	25		Roger DeKoven	✓			5 6 00	
21	26	847	Bell Corporation			2 3 0 00		
22	28		Cash sales		1 1 0 0 00			
23	28	848	Payroll			5 2 0 00		
24	30		Note issued for purchase					
25			of cleaning equipment					
26	31		Leslie Stewart	✓			4 1 00	
27	31		Totals		5 0 8 4 00	3 2 9 2 00	2 4 5 00	1 7 9 00
28					(101)	(101)	(111)	(111)

▲ FIGURE A-1 Combined Journal

Consider the combined journal shown above which belongs to the B & H Laundry and Dry Cleaning Services, a small business that provides laundry and dry cleaning services. In designing this journal before the firm opened, the accountant established a Cash section with Debit and Credit columns because it was known that the business would constantly be receiving cash from customers and paying out cash for expenses and other obligations. Debit and Credit columns were also set up in Accounts Receivable and Accounts Payable sections because the firm planned to offer credit to qualified customers and would make credit purchases of supplies and other items.

After further analysis it was realized that the business would have numerous entries for the sale of services, the payment of employee salaries, and the purchase of supplies. Therefore, columns were established for recording credits to **Sales,** debits to **Salaries Expense,** and debits to **Supplies.** Finally, a column was set up for an Other Accounts section to take care of transactions that cannot be entered in the special columns.

ACCOUNTS PAYABLE		SALES CREDIT	SUPPLIES EXPENSE DEBIT	SALARIES EXPENSE DEBIT	OTHER ACCOUNTS					
DEBIT	CREDIT				ACCOUNT NAME	POST REF.	DEBIT		CREDIT	
										1
					Rent expense	511	9 0 0 00			2
		6 0 00								3
	2 1 0 00		2 1 0 00							4
		1 1 5 0 00								5
				5 2 0 00						6
										7
	9 0 00		9 0 00							8
										9
		1 3 8 5 00								10
				5 2 0 00						11
		5 5 00								12
	6 0 0 00				Equipment	131	6 0 0 00			13
					Telephone exp.	514	8 2 00			14
										15
		3 3 00								16
		1 2 7 0 00								17
				5 2 0 00						18
	1 4 5 00		1 4 5 00							19
		5 6 00								20
2 3 0 00										21
		1 1 0 0 00								22
				5 2 0 00						23
										24
					Equipment	131	1 5 0 0 00			25
		4 1 00			Notes Payable	201		1 5 0 0 00		26
2 3 0 00	1 0 4 5 00	5 1 5 0 00	4 4 5 00	2 0 8 0 00			3 0 8 2 00	1 5 0 0 00		27
(202)	(202)	(401)	(121)	(517)			(X)	(X)		28

Recording Transactions in the Combined Journal

The combined journal shown in Figure A-1 contains the January 2005 transactions of B & H Laundry and Dry Cleaning Services. Notice that most of these transactions require only a single line and involve the use of just the special columns. The entries for major types of transactions are explained in the following paragraphs.

Payment of Expenses. During January, B & H Laundry and Dry Cleaning Services issued checks to pay three kinds of expenses: rent, telephone service, and employee salaries. Notice how the payment of the monthly rent on January 3 was recorded in the combined journal. Since there is no special column for rent expense, the debit part of this entry appears in the Other Accounts section. The offsetting credit appears in the Cash Credit column. The payment of the monthly telephone bill on January 19 was recorded in a similar manner. However, when employee salaries were paid on January 7, 14, 21, and 28, both parts of the entries could be made in special columns. Because the firm has a weekly payroll period, a separate column in the combined journal was set up for debits to Salaries Expense.

Sales on Credit. On January 5, 17, 20, 25, and 31, B & H Laundry and Dry Cleaning Services sold services on credit. The necessary entries were made in two special columns of the combined journal—the Accounts Receivable Debit column and the Sales Credit column.

Cash Sales. Entries for the firm's weekly cash sales were recorded on January 7, 14, 21, and 28. Again, special columns were used—the Cash Debit column and the Sales Credit column.

Cash Received on Account. When B & H Laundry and Dry Cleaning Services collected cash on account from credit customers on January 10, 13, and 20, the transactions were entered in the Cash Debit column and the Accounts Receivable Credit column.

Purchases of Supplies on Credit. Because the firm's combined journal includes a Supplies Debit column and an Accounts Payable Credit column, all purchases of supplies on credit can be recorded in special columns. Refer to the entries made on January 6, 12, and 24.

Purchases of Equipment on Credit. On January 18, B & H Laundry and Dry Cleaning Services bought some store equipment on credit. Since there is no special column for equipment, the debit part of the entry was made in the Other Accounts section. The offsetting credit appears in the Accounts Payable Credit column.

Payments on Account. Any payments made on account to creditors are recorded in two special columns—Accounts Payable Debit and Cash Credit, as shown in the entry of January 26.

Issuance of a Promissory Note. On January 30 the business purchased new cleaning equipment and issued a promissory note to the seller. Notice that both the debit to Equipment and the credit to Notes Payable had to be recorded in the Other Accounts section.

Posting from the Combined Journal

One of the advantages of the combined journal is that it simplifies the posting process. All amounts in the special columns can be posted to the general ledger on a summary basis at the end of the month. Only the figures that appear in the Other Accounts section require individual postings to the general ledger during the month. Of course, if the firm has subsidiary ledgers, individual postings must also be made to these ledgers.

Daily Postings. The procedures followed at B & H Laundry and Dry Cleaning Services will illustrate the techniques used to post from the combined journal. Each day any entries appearing in the Other Accounts section are posted to the proper accounts in the general ledger. For example, refer to the combined journal shown on pages A-2 and A-3. The five amounts listed in the Other Accounts Debit and Credit columns were posted individually during the month. The account numbers recorded in the Posting Reference column of the Other Accounts section show that the postings have been made.

Because B & H Laundry and Dry Cleaning Services has subsidiary ledgers for accounts receivable and accounts payable, individual postings were also made on a daily basis to these ledgers. As each amount was posted, a check mark was placed in the Posting Reference column of the combined journal.

End-of-Month Postings. At the end of the month, the combined journal is totaled, proved, and ruled. Then the totals of the special columns are posted to the general ledger. Proving the combined journal involves a comparison of the column totals to make sure that the debits and credits are equal. The following procedure is used:

Proof of Combined Journal	
	Debits
Cash Debit Column	$ 5,084
Accounts Receivable Debit Column	245
Accounts Payable Debit Column	230
Supplies Expense Debit Column	445
Salaries Expense Debit Column	2,080
Other Accounts Debit Column	3,082
	$11,166
	Credits
Cash Credit Column	$ 3,292
Accounts Receivable Credit Column	179
Accounts Payable Credit Column	1,045
Sales Credit Column	5,150
Other Accounts Credit Column	1,500
	$11,166

After the combined journal is proved, all column totals except those in the Other Accounts section are posted to the appropriate general ledger accounts. As each total is posted, the account number is entered beneath the column in the journal. Notice that an X is used to indicate that the column totals in the Other Accounts section are not posted, since the individual amounts were posted on a daily basis.

Typical Uses of the Combined Journal

The combined journal is used most often in small professional offices and small service businesses. It is less suitable for merchandising businesses but is sometimes used in firms of this type if they are very small and have only a limited number of transactions.

Professional Offices. The combined journal can be ideal to record the transactions that occur in a professional office, such as the office of a doctor, lawyer, accountant, or architect. However, special journals are more efficient if transactions become very numerous or are too varied.

Service Businesses. The use of the combined journal to record the transactions of B & H Laundry and Dry Cleaning Services has already been illustrated. The combined journal may be advantageous for a small service business, provided that the volume of transactions does not become excessive and the nature of the transactions does not become too complex.

Merchandising Businesses. The combined journal can be used by a merchandising business, but only if the firm is quite small and has a limited number and variety of transactions involving few accounts. However, even for a small merchandising business, the use of special journals might prove more advantageous.

Disadvantages of the Combined Journal

If the variety of transactions is so great that many different accounts are required, the combined journal will not work well. Either the business will have to set up so many columns that the journal will become unwieldy, or it will be necessary to record so many transactions in the Other Accounts columns that little efficiency will result. As a general rule, if the transactions of a business are numerous enough to merit the use of special journals, any attempt to substitute the combined journal is a mistake. Remember that each special journal can be designed for maximum efficiency in recording transactions.

Excerpts from The Home Depot, Inc. 1999 Annual Report

To Our Stockholders, Customers and Associates:

On the heels of fiscal 1998's record performance, many of our investors wondered, "What will The Home Depot do for an encore?" The encore we performed during fiscal 1999 is worthy of a "Bravo!" response. We are extremely proud of our accomplishments during fiscal 1999, particularly because they demonstrate the ongoing commitment of 201,000 associates who understand that superior customer service is the key to success for them, the Company and our investors.

We entered fiscal 1999 with confidence and a list of goals, which fit into three main categories:

1. To continue a pattern of strong and consistent sales and earnings growth.
2. To increase our ability to be a total solutions provider to do-it-yourself and professional home improvement customers.
3. To lead the marketplace to a better world.

We achieved all of our goals, exceeding most of them. As a result, we further strengthened our competitive position in the home improvement industry and solidly positioned the Company for long-term success.

Strong and Consistent Growth

Net earnings grew 44% during fiscal 1999, a key area where we exceeded our goal.

One hundred sixty-nine new stores and a 10% increase in sales at existing stores contributed to a 27% total sales gain for the year. A healthy economic environment helped, but the strength in sales was due mainly to new products and services, sharper product assortments and customer service enhancements.

We reduced product costs through efforts such as product line reviews, and imports and logistics efficiencies. These improvements gave us the financial flexibility to make further customer service-related investments in our stores, as well as invest in long-term growth initiatives, even as we recorded our 14th consecutive year of record earnings and our strongest year-over-year earnings gain since 1992.

We are firmly positioned to continue this pattern of consistent growth. New stores are planned to open at a steady rate of 21–22%. When combined with many new initiatives to enhance customer service, sales and productivity in our existing stores, we

During fiscal 1999, The Home Depot was recognized for its industry and stock market leadership by being added to the Dow Jones Industrial Average.

are confident in our ability to continue the consistent sales and earnings growth our stockholders have come to expect.

Providing Total Solutions

We reached further into our industry to find new ways to serve customers.

Our commitment to new and existing customers has expanded inside and outside the walls of Home Depot stores. As the North American home-ownership base has grown and become more diverse, so have our customers' needs. Plain vanilla is not enough – our customers want what they want, when they want it and where they want it.

In response, we added new products and services to our stores during the year. For example, we introduced a broad assortment of major appliances at nearly 150 Home Depot stores. Appliances are a natural extension of the products and services we currently offer. They also provide us with another opportunity to extend the trusting relationship we have with our customers. We expect to offer appliances in all remaining U.S. Home Depot stores during fiscal 2000.

We expanded our line of proprietary brands to include highly recognized names, such as General Electric® and Thomasville®. During fiscal 1999, we completed the introduction of GE SmartWater™ water heaters into all our stores. We also reached agreements to begin selling a new line of kitchen cabinets under the Thomasville name beginning in fiscal 2000. These new product lines are excellent examples of our merchants' creativity in developing proprietary brands that provide our customers with more choices of quality products at value prices – available only at The Home Depot.

Nearly 50,000 customers sharpened their do-it-yourself skills at Home Depot University℠, a four-week customer education program that premiered in all our stores during fiscal 1999. In addition, we added tool rental centers to 104 stores during the year, bringing the total to 150. We also further refined our test of new services for professional customers in three markets, and we added this package of services to ten additional markets.

Behind the scenes, we worked to enhance the customer service experience in our stores. We implemented new systems, tested new store formats and tweaked our staffing models, all with the mission to make our stores easier to shop and our associates more accessible to customers. We firmly believe that there is always room for improvement.

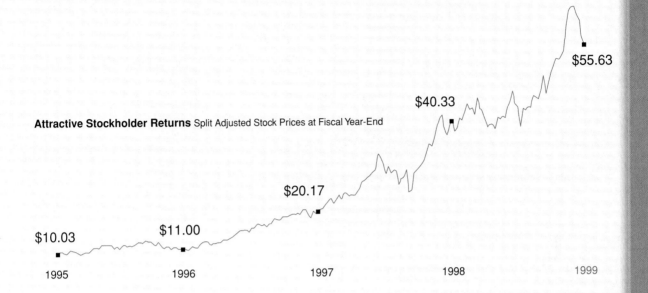

Attractive Stockholder Returns Split Adjusted Stock Prices at Fiscal Year-End

$55.63

$40.33

$20.17

$11.00

$10.03

1995   1996   1997   1998   1999

Developing Our Capabilities

We're smart enough to know what we don't know. If we don't have the expertise or experience we need, we get it. During fiscal 1999, we acquired two companies for the purpose of developing our capabilities in two important segments of the home improvement business. Georgia Lighting, purchased in June 1999, is known throughout the lighting industry for its expertise in lighting design, sourcing, merchandising and training programs. Home Depot and EXPO Design Center stores are benefiting today from this acquisition in all four areas.

In January 2000, we acquired Apex Supply Company, a wholesale distributor of plumbing, HVAC and related products. Going forward, we plan to leverage Apex's expertise and resources to better serve the needs of professional plumbers shopping in Home Depot stores.

Exploring E-Commerce

As the world watched the developments of electronic commerce, we were busy laying the foundation for our own e-commerce efforts. We view the Internet not as an *alternate* channel but as an *additional* channel to provide flexibility and convenience to our customers. Therefore, our e-commerce strategy starts with our stores.

Beginning in fiscal 2000, Home Depot customers in our initial launch markets will be able to purchase electronically all of the products available in their local Home Depot store. If they want the products delivered, we'll deliver them. If they want the to pick them up at the store, we'll have the order ready for them. With nearly 1,000 Home Depot stores spread across North America, we will have the inventory and delivery systems instantly in place to serve e-commerce customers. During this period of dot-com mania, we firmly believe that, in the long run, the most successful online retailers will be those who know how to extend to the Internet the power of their brands, the leverage of their bricks-and-mortar assets and the value of their customer service.

Launching New Ventures

Outside the walls of Home Depot, we made great progress with EXPO Design Center. We opened seven EXPO Design Center stores during fiscal 1999, and each store opening was more successful than the one before it. More customers doing remodeling and decorating projects are attracted by EXPO's ability to complete design work, product

Consistent Store Growth Number of Stores at Fiscal Year-End

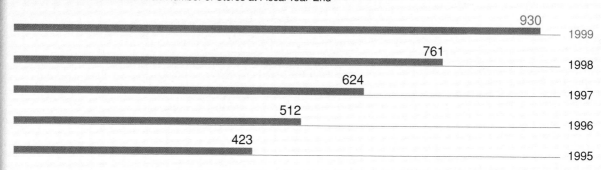

930	1999
761	1998
624	1997
512	1996
423	1995

selection and installation coordination – all under one roof. Like Home Depot 20 years ago, EXPO is poised to revolutionize this segment of the home improvement market.

We also learned more about serving the hardware convenience customer. During fiscal 1999, we opened two Villager's Hardware test stores in New Jersey. Designed primarily to serve smaller project or home enhancement customers, Villager's Hardware complements Home Depot stores with its product mix differences and a different type of shopping experience. We plan to open two more test stores in fiscal 2000. Villager's Hardware is a good example of our willingness to test new ideas and prove their success before rolling them out. By doing this, our customers and our stockholders win.

Expanding Globally

Global expansion will become a more important part of our growth plans during the next decade. Like the Internet, trends in global retailing are accelerating, as retailers consolidate, capitalize on the power of their brands throughout the world and create the scale to achieve greater operating efficiencies. The opportunities we see to serve homeowners around the world, combined with our

experiences to-date in Canada, Chile and Puerto Rico, make us excited about our long-term prospects for successful expansion outside North America. Our primary focus continues to be on growing our presence in Latin America. However, we are also exploring other opportunities around the world for further international growth.

These and many other initiatives support our goal of providing total solutions to our customers. Coupled with this goal is our objective that every initiative maintain or enhance our current return on invested capital. Given this high hurdle, for every initiative we undertake, many others have been discarded. Even so, there are still many opportunities for us to continue to widen our leadership position in the industry.

Leading the Marketplace to a Better World

Every day, we have the ability to touch millions of lives.

During fiscal 1999, we completed 797 million customer transactions. With each transaction, we had the opportunity to touch the lives of our customers by providing them with a wide assortment of low-priced home improvement products. In many cases, we also gave our do-it-yourself customers the knowledge and confidence to complete their own projects.

Career Opportunities Number of Associates at Fiscal Year-End

Year	Number of Associates
1999	201,400
1998	156,700
1997	124,400
1996	98,100
1995	80,800

At the end of fiscal 1999, we employed over 201,000 associates. We have the opportunity to touch each of their lives by building a better workplace in which every associate understands the culture and values upon which this Company was built. We have a responsibility to build an inclusive and diverse organization of the very best people, and foster an environment that supports diversity, providing the opportunity for everyone to excel.

During fiscal 1999, The Home Depot gave $15 million to support disaster relief and the building of affordable housing, to aid youth at risk and to protect the environment. We touched thousands of lives through our financial support and thousands more through our volunteer efforts.

Our actions today in protecting the environment will touch millions of lives for many years to come. Last year, we told you about our commitment to leadership in addressing sustainable forestry and certification issues. This year, we put the stake in the ground by pledging to stop selling any wood products from endangered regions by the end of 2002. Further, we will give preference to vendors that supply us with products made from certified wood. We will use the power of our purchasing dollars to promote products that do the most to preserve environmentally sensitive areas and make the most efficient use of wood.

The key to our success in this area is in the partnerships we develop with environmental groups and suppliers. I am happy to report that many environmental organizations have publicly voiced their support of our efforts, and our vendors are quickly climbing on the bandwagon. As The Home Depot expands its global presence, sustaining the environment will become an even more important issue for the Company and our vendor partners.

During fiscal 1999, The Home Depot celebrated its 20th year of business. We have achieved so much in just 20 years of history. But even more opportunity exists for us in the next 20 years. The encore performance in fiscal 1999 was outstanding – but the curtain remains wide open.

Arthur M. Blank
President & Chief Executive Officer
February 25, 2000

Management's Discussion and Analysis of Results of Operations and Financial Condition

The Home Depot, Inc. and Subsidiaries

The data below reflect selected sales data, the percentage relationship between sales and major categories in the Consolidated Statements of Earnings and the percentage change in the dollar amounts of each of the items.

Selected Consolidated Statements of Earnings Data

	Fiscal Year[1]			Percentage Increase (Decrease) in Dollar Amounts	
	1999	1998	1997	1999 vs. 1998	1998 vs. 1997
Net Sales	100.0%	100.0%	100.0%	27.2%	25.1%
Gross Profit	29.7	28.5	28.1	32.6	26.9
Operating Expenses:					
Selling and Store Operating[2]	17.8	17.7	17.8	27.9	24.1
Pre-Opening	0.3	0.3	0.3	28.4	35.4
General and Administrative	1.7	1.7	1.7	30.3	24.7
Non-Recurring Charge	–	–	0.4	NM[3]	NM[3]
Total Operating Expenses	19.8	19.7	20.2	28.1	21.7
Operating Income	9.9	8.8	7.9	42.6	40.3
Interest Income (Expense):					
Interest and Investment Income	0.1	0.1	0.2	23.3	(31.8)
Interest Expense	(0.1)	(0.1)	(0.2)	(24.3)	(11.9)
Interest, net	–	–	–	(228.6)	(450.0)
Earnings Before Income Taxes	9.9	8.8	7.9	43.3	39.8
Income Taxes	3.9	3.5	3.1	42.7	40.9
Net Earnings	6.0%	5.3%	4.8%	43.7%	39.1%
Selected Sales Data[4]					
Number of Transactions (000s)	797,229	665,125	550,226	19.9%	20.9%
Average Sale per Transaction	$ 47.87	$ 45.05	$ 43.63	6.3	3.3
Weighted Average Weekly Sales per Operating Store	$876,000	$844,000	$829,000	3.8	1.8
Weighted Average Sales per Square Foot	$ 422.53	$ 409.79	$ 405.56	3.1	1.0

[1] Fiscal years 1999, 1998 and 1997 refer to the fiscal years ended January 30, 2000; January 31, 1999; and February 1, 1998, respectively.
[2] Minority interest has been reclassified to selling and store operating expenses.
[3] Not meaningful.
[4] Excludes wholly-owned subsidiaries: Apex Supply Company, Georgia Lighting, Maintenance Warehouse, and National Blinds and Wallpaper.

Forward-Looking Statements

Certain written and oral statements made by The Home Depot, Inc. and subsidiaries (the "Company") or with the approval of an authorized executive officer of the Company may constitute "forward-looking statements" as defined under the Private Securities Litigation Reform Act of 1995. Words or phrases such as "should result," "are expected to," "we anticipate," "we estimate," "we project" or similar expressions are intended to identify forward-looking statements. These statements are subject to certain risks and uncertainties that could cause actual results to differ materially from the Company's historical experience and its present expectations or projections. These risks and uncertainties include, but are not limited to, unanticipated weather conditions; stability of costs and availability of sourcing channels; the ability to attract, train and retain highly-qualified associates; conditions affecting the availability, acquisition, development and ownership of real estate; general economic conditions; the impact of competition; and regulatory and litigation matters. Caution should be taken not to place undue reliance on any such forward-looking statements, since such statements speak only as of the date of the making of such statements. Additional information concerning these risks and uncertainties is contained in the Company's filings with the Securities and Exchange Commission, including the Company's Annual Report on Form 10-K.

Results of Operations

For an understanding of the significant factors that influenced the Company's performance during the past three fiscal years, the following discussion should be read in conjunction with the consolidated financial statements and the notes to consolidated financial statements presented in this annual report.

Fiscal year ended January 30, 2000 compared to January 31, 1999

Net sales for fiscal 1999 increased 27.2% to $38.4 billion from $30.2 billion in fiscal 1998. This increase was attributable to, among other things, full year sales from the 138 new stores opened during fiscal 1998, a 10% comparable store-for-store sales increase, and 169 new store openings and 6 store relocations during fiscal 1999.

Gross profit as a percent of sales was 29.7% for fiscal 1999 compared to 28.5% for fiscal 1998. The rate increase was primarily attributable to a lower cost of merchandise resulting from product line reviews and increased sales of imported products, other merchandising initiatives begun in prior years and continued during fiscal 1999, and sales mix shifts to higher gross margin product categories and assortments. In addition, inventory and refund systems improvements and more effective training resulted in better inventory shrink results and lower product markdowns.

Operating expenses as a percent of sales were 19.8% for fiscal 1999 compared to 19.7% for fiscal 1998. Selling and store operating expenses as a percent of sales increased to 17.8% in fiscal 1999 from 17.7% in fiscal 1998. The increase was primarily attributable to higher store selling payroll expenses resulting from market wage pressures and an increase in employee longevity, as well as to the Company's continued investment in new customer service initiatives. In addition, medical costs increased due to higher family enrollment in the Company's medical plans, increased claims and higher prescription drug costs. The Company's strong financial performance during fiscal 1999 also resulted in higher bonus expenses as a percent of sales. Credit card discounts increased as a result of higher penetrations of credit card sales and increases in non-private label discount rates. Partially offsetting these increases were lower net advertising expenses resulting from higher cooperative advertising participation by vendors and economies realized from the increased use of national advertising.

Pre-opening expenses as a percent of sales were 0.3% for both fiscal 1999 and 1998. The Company opened 169 new stores and relocated 6 stores in fiscal 1999, compared to 138 new stores and 4 store relocations in fiscal 1998. Pre-opening expenses averaged $643,000 per store in fiscal 1999 compared to $618,000 per store in fiscal 1998. The higher average expense was primarily due to the opening of more EXPO Design Center stores and expansion into certain new Home Depot markets, which involved longer pre-opening periods and higher training, travel and relocation costs.

General and administrative expenses as a percent of sales were 1.7% for both fiscal 1999 and 1998. Incremental expenses related to long-term growth and business planning initiatives, including Internet development, international operations and the opening of four new divisional offices, were offset by efficiencies realized from increased sales.

Interest and investment income as a percent of sales was 0.1% for both fiscal 1999 and 1998. Interest expense as a percent of sales was 0.1% for both comparable periods.

The Company's combined federal and state effective income tax rate decreased to 39.0% for fiscal 1999 from 39.2% for fiscal 1998. The decrease was attributable to higher tax credits in fiscal 1999 compared to fiscal 1998.

Net earnings as a percent of sales were 6.0% for fiscal 1999 compared to 5.3% for fiscal 1998, reflecting a higher gross profit rate partially offset by higher operating expenses as a percent of sales as described above. Diluted earnings per share were $1.00 for fiscal 1999 compared to $0.71 for fiscal 1998.

Consolidated Statements of Earnings

The Home Depot, Inc. and Subsidiaries

amounts in millions, except per share data

	Fiscal Year Ended		
	January 30, 2000	January 31, 1999	February 1, 1998
Net Sales	$ 38,434	$ 30,219	$ 24,156
Cost of Merchandise Sold	27,023	21,614	17,375
Gross Profit	11,411	8,605	6,781
Operating Expenses:			
Selling and Store Operating	6,832	5,341	4,303
Pre-Opening	113	88	65
General and Administrative	671	515	413
Non-Recurring Charge (note 8)	–	–	104
Total Operating Expenses	7,616	5,944	4,885
Operating Income	3,795	2,661	1,896
Interest Income (Expense):			
Interest and Investment Income	37	30	44
Interest Expense (note 2)	(28)	(37)	(42)
Interest, net	9	(7)	2
Earnings Before Income Taxes	3,804	2,654	1,898
Income Taxes (note 3)	1,484	1,040	738
Net Earnings	$ 2,320	$ 1,614	$ 1,160
Basic Earnings Per Share (note 7)	$ 1.03	$ 0.73	$ 0.53
Weighted Average Number of Common Shares Outstanding	2,244	2,206	2,188
Diluted Earnings Per Share (note 7)	$ 1.00	$ 0.71	$ 0.52
Weighted Average Number of Common Shares Outstanding Assuming Dilution	2,342	2,320	2,287

See accompanying notes to consolidated financial statements.

APPENDIX B

Consolidated Balance Sheets

The Home Depot, Inc. and Subsidiaries

amounts in millions, except per share data

	January 30, 2000	January 31, 1999
Assets		
Current Assets:		
Cash and Cash Equivalents	$ 168	$ 62
Short-Term Investments, including current maturities of long-term investments	2	–
Receivables, net	587	469
Merchandise Inventories	5,489	4,293
Other Current Assets	144	109
Total Current Assets	6,390	4,933
Property and Equipment, at cost:		
Land	3,248	2,739
Buildings	4,834	3,757
Furniture, Fixtures and Equipment	2,279	1,761
Leasehold Improvements	493	419
Construction in Progress	791	540
Capital Leases (notes 2 and 5)	245	206
	11,890	9,422
Less Accumulated Depreciation and Amortization	1,663	1,262
Net Property and Equipment	10,227	8,160
Long-Term Investments	15	15
Notes Receivable	48	26
Cost in Excess of the Fair Value of Net Assets Acquired, net of accumulated amortization of $33 at January 30, 2000 and $24 at January 31, 1999	311	268
Other	90	63
	$ 17,081	$ 13,465
Liabilities and Stockholders' Equity		
Current Liabilities:		
Accounts Payable	$ 1,993	$ 1,586
Accrued Salaries and Related Expenses	541	395
Sales Taxes Payable	269	176
Other Accrued Expenses	763	586
Income Taxes Payable	61	100
Current Installments of Long-Term Debt (notes 2 and 5)	29	14
Total Current Liabilities	3,656	2,857
Long-Term Debt, excluding current installments (notes 2 and 5)	750	1,566
Other Long-Term Liabilities	237	208
Deferred Income Taxes (note 3)	87	85
Minority Interest	10	9
Stockholders' Equity (notes 2, 4 and 6)		
Common Stock, par value $0.05. Authorized: 5,000,000,000 shares; issued and outstanding – 2,304,317,000 shares at January 30, 2000 and 2,213,178,000 shares at January 31, 1999	115	111
Paid-In Capital	4,319	2,817
Retained Earnings	7,941	5,876
Accumulated Other Comprehensive Income	(27)	(61)
	12,348	8,743
Less Shares Purchased for Compensation Plans (notes 4 and 6)	7	3
Total Stockholders' Equity	12,341	8,740
Commitments and Contingencies (notes 5 and 9)		
	$ 17,081	$ 13,465

See accompanying notes to consolidated financial statements.

Consolidated Statements of Stockholders' Equity and Comprehensive Income

The Home Depot, Inc. and Subsidiaries

amounts in millions, except per share data

	Common Stock		Paid-In Capital	Retained Earnings	Accumulated Other Comprehensive Income	Other	Total Stockholders' Equity	Comprehensive Income[1]
	Shares	Amount						
Balance, February 2, 1997	2,163	$ 108	$ 2,439	$ 3,407	$ 2	$ (1)	$ 5,955	
Shares Sold Under Employee Stock Purchase and Option Plans, net of retirements (note 4)	12	1	123	–	–	–	124	
Tax Effect of Sale of Option Shares by Employees	–	–	26	–	–	–	26	
Net Earnings	–	–	–	1,160	–	–	1,160	$1,160
Translation Adjustments	–	–	–	–	(30)	–	(30)	(30)
Immaterial Pooling of Interests	21	1	1	2	–	–	4	
Shares Purchased for Compensation Plans (notes 4 and 6)	–	–	–	–	–	(2)	(2)	
Cash Dividends ($0.063 per share)	–	–	–	(139)	–	–	(139)	
Comprehensive Income for Fiscal 1997								$ 1,130
Balance, February 1, 1998	2,196	$ 110	$ 2,589	$ 4,430	$ (28)	$ (3)	$ 7,098	
Shares Sold Under Employee Stock Purchase and Option Plans, net of retirements (note 4)	17	1	165	–	–	–	166	
Tax Effect of Sale of Option Shares by Employees	–	–	63	–	–	–	63	
Net Earnings	–	–	–	1,614	–	–	1,614	1,614
Translation Adjustments	–	–	–	–	(33)	–	(33)	(33)
Cash Dividends ($0.077 per share)	–	–	–	(168)	–	–	(168)	
Comprehensive Income for Fiscal 1998								$ 1,581
Balance, January 31, 1999	2,213	$ 111	$ 2,817	$ 5,876	$ (61)	$ (3)	$ 8,740	
Shares Sold Under Employee Stock Purchase and Option Plans, net of retirements (note 4)	19	1	273	–	–	–	274	
Tax Effect of Sale of Option Shares by Employees	–	–	132	–	–	–	132	
Conversion of $3\frac{1}{4}$% Convertible Subordinated Notes, net (note 2)	72	3	1,097	–	–	–	1,100	
Net Earnings	–	–	–	2,320	–	–	2,320	2,320
Translation Adjustments	–	–	–	–	34	–	34	34
Shares Purchased for Compensation Plans (notes 4 and 6)	–	–	–	–	–	(4)	(4)	
Cash Dividends ($0.113 per share)	–	–	–	(255)	–	–	(255)	
Comprehensive Income for Fiscal 1999								$ 2,354
Balance, January 30, 2000	2,304	$ 115	$ 4,319	$ 7,941	$ (27)	$ (7)	$ 12,341	

[1] Components of comprehensive income are reported net of related taxes.

See accompanying notes to consolidated financial statements.

APPENDIX B

Consolidated Statements of Cash Flows

The Home Depot, Inc. and Subsidiaries

amounts in millions

	Fiscal Year Ended		
	January 30, 2000	January 31, 1999	February 1, 1998
Cash Provided from Operations:			
Net Earnings	$ 2,320	$ 1,614	$ 1,160
Reconciliation of Net Earnings to Net Cash Provided by Operations:			
Depreciation and Amortization	463	373	283
(Increase) Decrease in Receivables, net	(85)	85	(166)
Increase in Merchandise Inventories	(1,142)	(698)	(885)
Increase in Accounts Payable and Accrued Expenses	820	423	577
Increase in Income Taxes Payable	93	59	83
Other	(23)	61	(23)
Net Cash Provided by Operations	2,446	1,917	1,029
Cash Flows from Investing Activities:			
Capital Expenditures, net of $37, $41 and $44 of non-cash capital expenditures in fiscal 1999, 1998 and 1997, respectively	(2,581)	(2,053)	(1,420)
Purchase of Remaining Interest in The Home Depot Canada	–	(261)	–
Payments for Businesses Acquired, net	(101)	(6)	(61)
Proceeds from Sales of Property and Equipment	87	45	85
Purchases of Investments	(32)	(2)	(194)
Proceeds from Maturities of Investments	30	4	599
Advances Secured by Real Estate, net	(25)	2	20
Net Cash Used in Investing Activities	(2,622)	(2,271)	(971)
Cash Flows from Financing Activities:			
(Repayments) Issuance of Commercial Paper Obligations, net	(246)	246	–
Proceeds from Long-Term Borrowings, net	522	–	15
Repayments of Long-Term Debt	(14)	(8)	(40)
Proceeds from Sale of Common Stock, net	267	167	122
Cash Dividends Paid to Stockholders	(255)	(168)	(139)
Minority Interest Contributions to Partnership	7	11	10
Net Cash Provided by (Used in) Financing Activities	281	248	(32)
Effect of Exchange Rate Changes on Cash and Cash Equivalents	1	(4)	–
Increase (Decrease) in Cash and Cash Equivalents	106	(110)	26
Cash and Cash Equivalents at Beginning of Year	62	172	146
Cash and Cash Equivalents at End of Year	$ 168	$ 62	$ 172
Supplemental Disclosure of Cash Payments Made for:			
Interest, net of interest capitalized	$ 26	$ 36	$ 42
Income Taxes	$ 1,396	$ 940	$ 685

See accompanying notes to consolidated financial statements.

Notes to Consolidated Financial Statements

The Home Depot, Inc. and Subsidiaries

APPENDIX B

> Note 1

Summary of Significant Accounting Policies

The Company operates Home Depot stores, which are full-service, warehouse-style stores averaging approximately 108,000 square feet in size. The stores stock approximately 40,000 to 50,000 different kinds of building materials, home improvement supplies and lawn and garden products that are sold primarily to do-it-yourselfers, but also to home improvement contractors, tradespeople and building maintenance professionals. In addition, the Company operates EXPO Design Center stores, which offer products and services primarily related to design and renovation projects, and is currently testing two Villager's Hardware stores, a convenience hardware concept that offers products and services for home enhancement and smaller project needs. At the end of fiscal 1999, the Company was operating 930 stores, including 854 Home Depot stores, 15 EXPO Design Center stores and 2 Villager's Hardware stores in the United States; 53 Home Depot stores in Canada; 4 Home Depot stores in Chile; and 2 Home Depot stores in Puerto Rico. Included in the Company's Consolidated Balance Sheets at January 30, 2000 were $707 million of net assets of the Canada, Chile and Argentina operations.

Fiscal Year

The Company's fiscal year is a 52- or 53-week period ending on the Sunday nearest to January 31. Fiscal years 1999, 1998 and 1997, which ended January 30, 2000, January 31, 1999 and February 1, 1998, respectively, consisted of 52 weeks.

Basis of Presentation

The consolidated financial statements include the accounts of the Company, its wholly-owned subsidiaries, and its majority-owned partnership. All significant intercompany transactions have been eliminated in consolidation.

Stockholders' equity, share and per share amounts for all periods presented have been adjusted for a three-for-two stock split effected in the form of a stock dividend on December 30, 1999, a two-for-one stock split effected in the form of a stock dividend on July 2, 1998, and a three-for-two stock split effected in the form of a stock dividend on July 3, 1997.

Cash Equivalents

The Company considers all highly liquid investments purchased with a maturity of three months or less to be cash equivalents. The Company's cash and cash equivalents are carried at fair market value and consist primarily of commercial paper, money market funds, U.S. government agency securities and tax-exempt notes and bonds.

Merchandise Inventories

Inventories are stated at the lower of cost (first-in, first-out) or market, as determined by the retail inventory method.

Investments

The Company's investments, consisting primarily of high-grade debt securities, are recorded at fair value and are classified as available-for-sale.

Income Taxes

The Company provides for federal, state and foreign income taxes currently payable, as well as for those deferred because of timing differences between reporting income and expenses for financial statement purposes versus tax purposes. Federal, state and foreign incentive tax credits are recorded as a reduction of income taxes. Deferred tax assets and liabilities are recognized for the future tax consequences attributable to differences between the financial statement carrying amounts of existing assets and liabilities and their respective tax bases. Deferred tax assets and liabilities are measured using enacted tax rates expected to apply to taxable income in the years in which those temporary differences are expected to be recovered or settled. The effect of a change in tax rates is recognized as income or expense in the period that includes the enactment date.

The Company and its eligible subsidiaries file a consolidated U.S. federal income tax return. Non-U.S. subsidiaries, which are consolidated for financial reporting, are not eligible to be included in consolidated U.S. federal income tax returns, and separate provisions for income taxes have been determined for these entities. The Company intends to reinvest the unremitted earnings of its non-U.S. subsidiaries and postpone their remittance. Accordingly, no provision for U.S. income taxes for non-U.S. subsidiaries was required for any year presented.

Depreciation and Amortization

The Company's buildings, furniture, fixtures and equipment are depreciated using the straight-line method over the estimated useful lives of the assets. Improvements to leased premises are amortized using the straight-line method over the life of the lease or the useful life of the improvement, whichever is shorter. The Company's property and equipment is depreciated using the following estimated useful lives:

	Life
Buildings	10–45 years
Furniture, fixtures and equipment	5–20 years
Leasehold improvements	5–30 years
Computer software	3–5 years

Advertising

Television and radio advertising production costs are amortized over the fiscal year in which the advertisements first appear. All media placement costs are expensed in the month the advertisement appears. Included in Current Assets in the Company's Consolidated Balance Sheets were $24.4 million and $22.6 million at the end of fiscal 1999 and 1998, respectively, relating to prepayments of production costs for print and broadcast advertising.

Cost in Excess of the Fair Value of Net Assets Acquired

Goodwill, which represents the excess of purchase price over fair value of net assets acquired, is amortized on a straight-line basis over 40 years. The Company assesses the recoverability of this intangible asset by determining whether the amortization of the goodwill balance over its remaining useful life can be recovered through undiscounted future operating cash flows of

the acquired operation. The amount of goodwill impairment, if any, is measured based on projected discounted future operating cash flows using a discount rate reflecting the Company's average cost of funds.

Store Pre-Opening Costs

Non-capital expenditures associated with opening new stores are expensed as incurred.

Impairment of Long-Lived Assets

The Company reviews long-lived assets for impairment when circumstances indicate the carrying amount of an asset may not be recoverable. An impairment is recognized to the extent the sum of undiscounted estimated future cash flows expected to result from the use of the asset is less than the carrying value. Accordingly, when the Company commits to relocate or close a store, the estimated unrecoverable costs are charged to selling and store operating expense. Such costs include the estimated loss on the sale of land and buildings, the book value of abandoned fixtures, equipment and leasehold improvements, and a provision for the present value of future lease obligations, less estimated sub-lease income.

Stock Compensation

Statement of Financial Accounting Standards No. 123 ("SFAS 123"), "Accounting for Stock-Based Compensation," encourages the use of a fair-value-based method of accounting. As allowed by SFAS 123, the Company has elected to account for its stock-based compensation plans under the intrinsic value-based method of accounting prescribed by Accounting Principles Board Opinion No. 25 ("APB No. 25"), "Accounting for Stock Issued to Employees." Under APB No. 25, compensation expense would be recorded on the date of grant if the current market price of the underlying stock exceeded the exercise price. The Company has adopted the disclosure requirements of SFAS 123.

Comprehensive Income

Comprehensive income includes net earnings adjusted for certain revenues, expenses, gains and losses that are excluded from net earnings under generally accepted accounting principles. Examples include foreign currency translation adjustments and unrealized gains and losses on investments.

Foreign Currency Translation

The assets and liabilities denominated in a foreign currency are translated into U.S. dollars at the current rate of exchange on the last day of the reporting period, revenues and expenses are translated at the average monthly exchange rates, and all other equity transactions are translated using the actual rate on the day of the transaction.

Use of Estimates

Management of the Company has made a number of estimates and assumptions relating to the reporting of assets and liabilities and the disclosure of contingent assets and liabilities to prepare these financial statements in conformity with generally accepted accounting principles. Actual results could differ from these estimates.

Reclassifications

Certain balances in prior fiscal years have been reclassified to conform with the presentation in the current fiscal year.

> Note 2

Long-Term Debt

The Company's long-term debt at the end of the fiscal 1999 and 1998 consisted of the following (amounts in millions):

	January 30, 2000	January 31, 1999
$3^{1}/4$% Convertible Subordinated Notes, due October 1, 2001; converted into shares of common stock of the Company at a conversion price of $15.3611 per share in October 1999	$ –	$ 1,103
$6^{1}/2$% Senior Notes, due September 15, 2004; interest payable semi-annually on March 15 and September 15 beginning in 2000	500	–
Commercial Paper; weighted average interest rate of 4.8% at January 31, 1999	–	246
Capital Lease Obligations; payable in varying installments through January 31, 2027 (see note 5)	216	180
Installment Notes Payable; interest imputed at rates between 5.2% and 10.0%; payable in varying installments through 2018	45	27
Unsecured Bank Loan; floating interest rate averaging 6.05% in fiscal 1999 and 5.90% in fiscal 1998; payable in August 2002	15	15
Variable Rate Industrial Revenue Bonds; secured by letters of credit or land; interest rates averaging 2.9% during fiscal 1999 and 3.8% during fiscal 1998; payable in varying installments through 2010	3	9
Total long-term debt	779	1,580
Less current installments	29	14
Long-term debt, excluding current installments	$ 750	$ 1,566

> # Note 8
Lawsuit Settlements

During fiscal 1997, the Company, without admitting any wrong-doing, entered into a settlement agreement with plaintiffs in the class action lawsuit *Butler et. al. v. Home Depot, Inc.*, in which the plaintiffs had asserted claims of gender discrimination. The Company subsequently reached agreements to settle three other lawsuits seeking class action status, each of which involved claims of gender discrimination.

As a result of these agreements, the Company recorded a pre-tax non-recurring charge of $104 million in fiscal 1997 and, in fiscal 1998, made payments to settle these agreements. The payments made in fiscal 1998 included $65 million to the plaintiff class members and $22.5 million to the plaintiff's attorneys in *Butler,* and approximately $8 million for other related internal costs, including implementation or enhancement of certain human resources programs, as well as the settlement terms of the three other lawsuits. Payments made in fiscal 1999 totaled $3.4 million primarily related to internal costs for human resources staffing and training for store associates. The Company expects to spend the remaining $5 million for additional training programs.

> # Note 9
Commitments and Contingencies

At January 30, 2000, the Company was contingently liable for approximately $419 million under outstanding letters of credit issued in connection with purchase commitments.

The Company is involved in litigation arising from the normal course of business. In management's opinion, this litigation is not expected to materially impact the Company's consolidated results of operations or financial condition.

> # Note 10
Acquisitions

During the first quarter of fiscal 1998, the Company purchased, for $261 million, the remaining 25% partnership interest held by The Molson Companies in The Home Depot Canada. The excess purchase price over the estimated fair value of net assets of $117 million as of the acquisition date was recorded as goodwill and is being amortized over 40 years. As a result of this transaction, the Company now owns all of The Home Depot's Canadian operations. The Home Depot Canada partnership was formed in 1994 when the Company acquired 75% of Aikenhead's Home Improvement Warehouse for approximately $162 million. The terms of the original partnership agreement provided for a put/call option, which would have resulted in the Company purchasing the remaining 25% of The Home Depot Canada at any time after the sixth anniversary of the original agreement. The companies reached a mutual agreement to complete the purchase transaction at an earlier date.

During fiscal 1999, the Company acquired Apex Supply Company, Inc. and Georgia Lighting, Inc. Both acquisitions were recorded under the purchase method of accounting.

> # Note 11
Quarterly Financial Data (unaudited)

The following is a summary of the quarterly results of operations for the fiscal years ended January 30, 2000 and January 31, 1999 (dollars in millions, except per share data):

	Net Sales	Increase In Comparable Store Sales	Gross Profit	Net Earnings	Basic Earnings Per Share	Diluted Earnings Per Share
Fiscal year ended January 30, 2000:						
First quarter	$ 8,952	9%	$ 2,566	$ 489	$ 0.22	$ 0.21
Second quarter	10,431	11%	3,029	679	0.30	0.29
Third quarter	9,877	10%	2,894	573	0.26	0.25
Fourth quarter	9,174	9%	2,922	579	0.25	0.25
Fiscal year	$ 38,434	10%	$ 11,411	$ 2,320	$ 1.03	$ 1.00
Fiscal year ended January 31, 1999:						
First quarter	$ 7,123	7%	$ 1,968	$ 337	$ 0.15	$ 0.15
Second quarter	8,139	7%	2,263	467	0.21	0.21
Third quarter	7,699	7%	2,177	392	0.18	0.17
Fourth quarter	7,258	9%	2,197	418	0.19	0.18
Fiscal year	$ 30,219	7%	$ 8,605	$ 1,614	$ 0.73	$ 0.71

APPENDIX B

Management's Responsibility for Financial Statements

The financial statements presented in this Annual Report have been prepared with integrity and objectivity and are the responsibility of the management of The Home Depot, Inc. These financial statements have been prepared in conformity with generally accepted accounting principles and properly reflect certain estimates and judgments based upon the best available information.

The Company maintains a system of internal accounting controls, which is supported by an internal audit program and is designed to provide reasonable assurance, at an appropriate cost, that the Company's assets are safeguarded and transactions are properly recorded. This system is continually reviewed and modified in response to changing business conditions and operations and as a result of recommendations by the external and internal auditors. In addition, the Company has distributed to associates its policies for conducting business affairs in a lawful and ethical manner.

The financial statements of the Company have been audited by KPMG LLP, independent auditors. Their accompanying report is based upon an audit conducted in accordance with generally accepted auditing standards, including the related review of internal accounting controls and financial reporting matters.

The Audit Committee of the Board of Directors, consisting solely of outside directors, meets quarterly with the independent auditors, the internal auditors and representatives of management to discuss auditing and financial reporting matters. The Audit Committee, acting on behalf of the stockholders, maintains an ongoing appraisal of the internal accounting controls, the activities of the outside auditors and internal auditors and the financial condition of the Company. Both the Company's independent auditors and the internal auditors have free access to the Audit Committee.

Dennis Carey
Executive Vice President and
Chief Financial Officer

Carol B. Tomé
Senior Vice President,
Finance and Accounting

Independent Auditors' Report

**The Board of Directors and Stockholders
The Home Depot, Inc.:**

We have audited the accompanying consolidated balance sheets of The Home Depot, Inc. and subsidiaries as of January 30, 2000 and January 31, 1999 and the related consolidated statements of earnings, stockholders' equity and comprehensive income, and cash flows for each of the years in the three-year period ended January 30, 2000. These consolidated financial statements are the responsibility of the Company's management. Our responsibility is to express an opinion on these consolidated financial statements based on our audits.

We conducted our audits in accordance with generally accepted auditing standards. Those standards require that we plan and perform the audit to obtain reasonable assurance about whether the financial statements are free of material misstatement. An audit includes examining, on a test basis, evidence supporting the amounts and disclosures in the financial statements. An audit also includes assessing the accounting principles used and significant estimates made by management, as well as evaluating the overall financial statement presentation. We believe that our audits provide a reasonable basis for our opinion.

In our opinion, the consolidated financial statements referred to above present fairly, in all material respects, the financial position of The Home Depot, Inc. and subsidiaries as of January 30, 2000 and January 31, 1999, and the results of their operations and their cash flows for each of the years in the three-year period ended January 30, 2000 in conformity with generally accepted accounting principles.

KPMG LLP

Atlanta, Georgia
February 25, 2000

APPENDIX B

B-15

Corporate and Stockholder Information

The Home Depot, Inc. and Subsidiaries

Store Support Center

The Home Depot, Inc.
2455 Paces Ferry Road, NW
Atlanta, GA 30339-4024
Telephone: 770-433-8211

The Home Depot Web Site

www.homedepot.com

Transfer Agent and Registrar

Fleet National Bank
c/o EquiServe Limited Partnership
P.O. Box 8040
Boston, MA 02266-8040
Telephone:
1-800-577-0177 (Voice)
1-800-952-9245 (TTY/TDD)
Internet address: www.equiserve.com

Independent Auditors

KPMG LLP
Suite 2000
303 Peachtree Street, NE
Atlanta, GA 30308

Stock Exchange Listing

New York Stock Exchange
Trading Symbol – HD

Annual Meeting

The Annual Meeting of Stockholders will be held at 10:00 a.m., May 31, 2000, at Cobb Galleria Centre, 2 Galleria Parkway, Atlanta, Georgia 30339.

Number of Stockholders

As of April 3, 2000, there were approximately 194,935 stockholders of record. This number excludes individual stockholders holding stock under nominee security position listings.

Dividends per Common Share

	First Quarter	Second Quarter	Third Quarter	Fourth Quarter
Fiscal 1999	$0.020	$0.027	$0.027	$0.040
Fiscal 1998	$0.017	$0.020	$0.020	$0.020

Direct Stock Purchase/Dividend Reinvestment Plan

New investors may make an initial investment and stockholders of record may acquire additional shares of The Home Depot common stock through the Company's direct stock purchase and dividend reinvestment plan. Subject to certain requirements, initial cash investments, quarterly cash dividends and/or additional optional cash purchases may be invested through this plan.

To obtain enrollment materials, including the prospectus, access the Company's Web site, or call 1-800-928-0380. For all other communications regarding these services, contact the Transfer Agent and Registrar.

Financial and Other Company Information

A copy of the Company's Annual Report on Form 10-K for the fiscal year ended January 30, 2000, as filed with the Securities and Exchange Commission, will be mailed upon request to:

The Home Depot, Inc.
Investor Relations
2455 Paces Ferry Road, NW
Atlanta, GA 30339-4024
Telephone: 770-384-4388

In addition, financial reports, recent filings with the Securities and Exchange Commission (including Form 10-K), store locations, news releases and other Company information are available on The Home Depot Web site.

For a copy of the 1999 Home Depot Corporate Social Responsibility Report, which also includes guidelines for applying for philanthropic grants, contact the Community Affairs department at the Store Support Center, or access the Company's Web site.

Quarterly Stock Price Range

	First Quarter	Second Quarter	Third Quarter	Fourth Quarter
Fiscal 1999				
High	$45.29	$46.63	$52.33	$69.75
Low	$35.88	$36.75	$35.75	$49.92
Fiscal 1998				
High	$24.23	$32.67	$30.63	$41.33
Low	$20.42	$22.56	$21.08	$28.75

APPENDIX B

GLOSSARY

Absorption costing (p. 1124) The accounting procedure whereby all manufacturing costs, including fixed costs, are included in the cost of goods manufactured

Accelerated method of depreciation (p. 641) A method of depreciating asset cost that allocates greater amounts of depreciation to an asset's early years of useful life

Account balance (p. 64) The difference between the amounts recorded on the two sides of an account

Account form balance sheet (p. 143) A balance sheet that lists assets on the left and liabilities and owner's equity on the right (*see also* Report form balance sheet)

Accounting (p. 4) The process by which financial information about a business is recorded, classified, summarized, interpreted, and communicated to owners, managers, and other interested parties

Accounting cycle (p. 96) A series of steps performed during each accounting period to classify, record, and summarize data for a business and to produce needed financial information

Accounting system (p. 4) A process designed to accumulate, classify, and summarize financial data

Accounts (p. 58) Written records of the assets, liabilities, and owner's equity of a business

Accounts payable (p. 26) Amounts a business must pay in the future

Accounts payable ledger (p. 262) A subsidiary ledger that contains a separate account for each creditor

Accounts receivable (p. 31) Claims for future collection from customers

Accounts receivable ledger (p. 209) A subsidiary ledger that contains credit customer accounts

Accounts receivable turnover (p. 890) A measure of the speed with which sales on account are collected; the ratio of net credit sales to average receivables

Accrual basis (p. 430) A system of accounting by which all revenues and expenses are matched and reported on financial statements for the applicable period, regardless of when the cash related to the transaction is received or paid

Accrued expenses (p. 435) Expense items that relate to the current period but have not yet been paid and do not yet appear in the accounting records

Accrued income (p. 439) Income that has been earned but not yet received and recorded

Acid-test ratio (p. 889) A measure of immediate liquidity; the ratio of quick assets to current liabilities

Adjusting entries (p. 131) Journal entries made to update accounts for items that were not recorded during the accounting period

Adjustments (p. 131) *See* Adjusting entries

Aging the accounts receivable (p. 558) Classifying accounts receivable balances according to how long they have been outstanding

Allowance method (p. 557) A method of recording uncollectible accounts that estimates losses from uncollectible accounts and charges them to expense in the period when the sales are recorded

Amortization (p. 654) The process of periodically transferring the acquisition cost of an intangible asset to an expense account

Appropriation of retained earnings (p. 782) A formal declaration of an intention to restrict dividends

Articles of partnership (p. 679) *See* Partnership agreement

Asset turnover (p. 884) A measure of the effective use of assets in making sales; the ratio of net sales to total assets

Assets (p. 28) Property owned by a business

Audit trail (p. 97) A chain of references that makes it possible to trace information, locate errors, and prevent fraud

Auditing (p. 5) The review of financial statements to assess their fairness and adherence to generally accepted accounting principles

Auditor's report (p. 13) An independent accountant's review of a firm's financial statements

Authorized capital stock (p. 729) The number of shares authorized for issue by the corporate charter

Average collection period (p. 890) The ratio of 365 days to the accounts receivable turnover; also called the number of days' sales in receivables

Average cost method (p. 613) A method of inventory costing using the average cost of units of an item available for sale during the period to arrive at cost of the ending inventory

Average method of process costing (p. 1073) A method of costing that combines the cost of beginning inventory for each cost element with the costs during the current period

Balance ledger form (p. 105) A ledger account form that shows the balance of the account after each entry is posted

Balance sheet (p. 29) A formal report of a business's financial condition on a certain date; reports the assets, liabilities, and owner's equity of the business

Bank draft (p. 596) A check written by a bank that orders another bank to pay the stated amount to a specific party

Bank reconciliation statement (p. 314) A statement that accounts for all differences between the balance on the bank statement and the book balance of cash

Banker's year (p. 584) A 360-day period used to calculate interest on a note

Bill of lading (p. 597) A business document that lists goods accepted for transportation

Blank endorsement (p. 309) A signature of the payee written on the back of the check that transfers ownership of the check without specifying to whom or for what purpose

Bond indenture (p. 812) A bond contract

Bond issue costs (p. 822) Costs incurred in issuing bonds, such as legal and accounting fees and printing costs

Bond retirement (p. 823) When a bond is paid and the liability is removed from the company's balance sheet

Bond sinking fund investment (p. 823) A fund established to accumulate assets to pay off bonds when they mature

Bonding (p. 307) The process by which employees are investigated by an insurance company that will insure the business against losses through employee theft or mishandling of funds

Bonds payable (p. 812) Long-term debt instruments that are written promises to repay the principal at a future date; interest is due at a fixed rate payable over the life of the bond

Book value (pp. 135, 780) That portion of an asset's original cost that has not yet been depreciated; the total equity applicable to a class of stock divided by the number of shares outstanding

Brand name (p. 653) *See* Trade name

Break even (p. 36) A point at which revenue equals expenses

Budget (p. 1096) An operating plan expressed in monetary units

Budget performance report (p. 1097) A comparison of actual costs and budgeted costs

Business transaction (p. 24) A financial event that changes the resources of a firm

Bylaws (p. 727) The guidelines for conducting a corporation's business affairs

Call price (p. 813) The amount the corporation must pay for the bond when it is called

Callable bonds (p. 813) Bonds that allow the issuing corporation to require the holder to surrender the bonds for payment before their maturity date

Callable preferred stock (p. 731) Stock that gives the issuing corporation the right to repurchase the preferred shares from the stockholders at a specific price

Canceled check (p. 312) A check paid by the bank on which it was drawn

Capacity (p. 1129) A facility's ability to produce or use

Capital (p. 25) Financial investment in a business; equity

Capital stock ledger (p. 745) A subsidiary ledger that contains a record of each stockholder's purchases, transfers, and current balance of shares owned; also called stockholders' ledger

Capital stock transfer journal (p. 745) A record of stock transfers used for posting to the stockholders' ledger

Capitalized costs (p. 638) All costs recorded as part of an asset's costs

Carrying value of bonds (p. 822) The balance of the Bonds Payable account plus the Premium on Bonds Payable account minus the Discount on Bonds Payable account; also called book value of bonds

Cash (p. 292) In accounting, currency, coins, checks, money orders, and funds on deposit in a bank

Cash discount (p. 259) A discount offered by suppliers for payment received within a specified period of time

Cash equivalents (p. 912) Assets that are easily convertible into known amounts of cash

Cash payments journal (p. 299) A special journal used to record transactions involving the payment of cash

Cash receipts journal (p. 292) A special journal used to record and post transactions involving the receipt of cash

Cash register proof (p. 293) A verification that the amount of currency and coins in a cash register agrees with the amount shown on the cash register audit tape

Cash Short or Over account (p. 294) An account used to record any discrepancies between the amount of currency and coins in the cash register and the amount shown on the audit tape

Cashier's check (p. 596) A draft on the issuing bank's own funds

Certified public accountant (CPA) (p. 5) An independent accountant who provides accounting services to the public for a fee

Charge-account sales (p. 221) Sales made through the use of open-account credit or one of various types of credit cards

Chart of accounts (p. 75) A list of the accounts used by a business to record its financial transactions

Check (p. 309) A written order signed by an authorized person instructing a bank to pay a specific sum of money to a designated person or business

Check register (p. 955) The record of cash payments of vouchers

Chronological order (p. 96) Organized in the order in which the events occur

Classification (p. 58) A means of identifying each account as an asset, liability, or owner's equity

Classified financial statement (p. 472) A format by which revenues and expenses on the income statement, and assets and liabilities on the balance sheet, are divided into groups of similar accounts and a subtotal is given for each group

Closing entries (p. 164) Journal entries that transfer the results of operations (net income or net loss) to owner's equity and reduce the revenue, expense, and drawing account balances to zero

Collateral trust bonds (p. 812) Bonds secured by the pledge of securities, such as stocks or bonds of other companies

Combined journal (p. A-1) A journal that combines features of the general journal and the special journals in a single record

Commercial draft (p. 596) A note issued by one party that orders another party to pay a specified sum on a specified date

Commission basis (p. 357) A method of paying employees according to a percentage of net sales

Common costs (p. 1126) Costs not directly traceable to a specific segment of a business

Common stock (p. 729) The general class of stock issued when no other class of stock is authorized; each share carries the same rights and privileges as every other share. Even if preferred stock is issued, common stock will also be issued

Common Stock Dividend Distributable account (p. 780) Equity account used to record par, or stated, value of shares to be issued as the result of the declaration of a stock dividend

Common-size statements (p. 850) Financial statements with items expressed as percentages of a base amount

Comparative statements (p. 848) Financial statements presented side by side for two or more years

Compensation record (p. 370) *See* Individual earnings record

Compound entry (p. 103) A journal entry with more than one debit or credit

Computer software (p. 653) Written programs that instruct a computer's hardware to do certain tasks

Conservatism (p. 534) The concept that revenue and assets should be understated rather than overstated if GAAP allows alternatives. Similarly, expenses and liabilities should be overstated rather than understated

Consistency principle (p. 532) The concept that requires a business to apply an accounting principle the same way from one period to the next

Contingent liability (p. 593) An item that can become a liability if certain things happen

Contra account (p. 135) An account with a normal balance that is opposite that of a related account

Contra asset account (p. 135) An asset account with a credit balance, which is contrary to the normal balance of an asset account

Contra revenue account (p. 211) An account with a debit balance, which is contrary to the normal balance for a revenue account

Contribution margin (pp. 985, 1126) Gross profit on sales minus direct expenses; revenues minus variable costs

Control account (p. 216) An account that links a subsidiary ledger and the general ledger since its balance summarizes the balances of the accounts in the subsidiary ledger

Controllable fixed costs (p. 1127) Costs that the segment manager can control

Convertible bonds (p. 813) Bonds that give the owner the right to convert the bonds into common stock under specified conditions

Convertible preferred stock (p. 730) Preferred stock that conveys the right to convert that stock to common stock after a specified date or during a period of time

Copyright (p. 653) An intangible asset; an exclusive right granted by the federal government to produce, publish, and sell a literary or artistic work for a period equal to the creator's life plus 70 years

Corporate charter (p. 724) A document issued by a state government that establishes a corporation

Corporation (p. 11) A publicly or privately owned business entity that is separate from its owners and has a legal right to own property and do business in its own name; stockholders are not responsible for the debts or taxes of the business

Correcting entry (p. 110) A journal entry made to correct an erroneous entry

Cost basis principle (p. 531) The principle that requires assets to be recorded at their cost at the time they are acquired

Cost center (p. 978) A business segment that incurs costs but does not produce revenue

Cost of goods sold (p. 256) The actual cost to the business of the merchandise sold to customers

Cost of production report (p. 1067) Summarizes all costs charged to each department and shows the costs assigned to the goods transferred out of the department and to the goods still in process

Cost variance (p. 1103) The difference between the total standard cost and the total actual cost

Coupon bonds (p. 813) Unregistered bonds that have coupons attached for each interest payment; also called bearer bonds

Credit (p. 72) An entry on the right side of an account

Credit memorandum (accounts receivable) (p. 210) A note verifying that a customer's account is being reduced by the amount of a sales return or sales allowance plus any sales tax that may have been involved

Credit memorandum (banking) (p. 312) A form that explains any addition, other than a deposit, to a checking account

Creditor (p. 9) One to whom money is owed

Cumulative preferred stock (p. 731) Stock that conveys to its owners the right to receive the preference dividend for the current year and any prior years in which the preference dividend was not paid before common stockholders receive any dividends

Current assets (p. 475) Assets consisting of cash, items that normally will be converted into cash within one year, or items that will be used up within one year

Current liabilities (p. 477) Debts that must be paid within one year

Current ratio (pp. 484, 888) A relationship between current assets and current liabilities that provides a measure of a firm's ability to pay its current debts (current ratio = current assets ÷ current liabilities)

Debentures (p. 812) Unsecured bonds backed only by a corporation's general credit

Debit (p. 72) An entry on the left side of an account

Debit memorandum (p. 313) A form that explains any deduction, other than a check, from a checking account

Declaration date (p. 779) The date on which the board of directors declares a dividend

Declining-balance method (p. 641) An accelerated method of depreciation in which an asset's book value at the beginning of a year is multiplied by a percentage to determine depreciation for the year

Deferred expenses (p. 437) *See* Prepaid expenses

Deferred income (p. 440) *See* Unearned income

Deferred income taxes (p. 770) The amount of taxes that will be payable in the future as a result of the difference between taxable income and income for financial statement purposes in the current year and in past years

Departmental income statement (p. 985) Income statement that shows each department's contribution margin and net income from operations after all expenses are allocated

Depletion (p. 652) Allocating the cost of a natural resource to expense over the period in which the resource produces revenue

Deposit in transit (p. 314) A deposit that is recorded in the cash receipts journal but that reaches the bank too late to be shown on the monthly bank statement

Deposit slip (p. 310) A form prepared to record the deposit of cash or checks to a bank account

Depreciation (p. 134) Allocation of the cost of a long-term asset to operations during its expected useful life

Differential cost (p. 1128) The difference in cost between one alternative and another

Direct charge-off method (p. 556) A method of recording uncollectible account losses as they occur

Direct costing (p. 1124) The accounting procedure whereby only variable costs are included in the cost of goods manufactured, and fixed manufacturing costs are written off as expenses in the period in which they are incurred

Direct expenses (p. 981) Operating expenses that are identified directly with a department and are recorded by department

Direct labor (p. 1005) The costs attributable to personnel who work directly on the product being manufactured

Direct materials (p. 1004) All items that go into a product and become a part of it

Direct method (p. 925) A means of reporting sources and uses of cash under which all revenue and expenses reported on the income statement appear in the operating section of the statement of cash flows and show the cash received or paid out for each type of transaction

Discount on bonds payable (p. 820) The excess of the face value over the price received by the corporation for a bond

Discounting (p. 587) Deducting the interest from the principal on a note payable or receivable in advance

Discussion memorandum (p. 12) An explanation of a topic under consideration by the Financial Accounting Standards Board

Dishonored check (p. 313) A check returned to the depositor unpaid because of insufficient funds in the drawer's account; also called an NSF check

Dissolution (p. 694) The legal termination of a partnership

Distributive share (p. 684)   The amount of net income or net loss allocated to each partner

Dividends (p. 731)   Distributions of the profits of a corporation to its shareholders

Donated capital (p. 784)   Capital resulting from the receipt of gifts by a corporation

Double-declining-balance method (p. 641)   A method of depreciation that uses a rate equal to twice the straight-line rate and applies that rate to the book value of the asset at the beginning of the year

Double-entry system (p. 72)   An accounting system that involves recording the effects of each transaction as debits and credits

Draft (p. 596)   A written order that requires one party (a person or business) to pay a stated sum of money to another party

Drawee (p. 309)   The bank on which a check is written

Drawer (p. 309)   The person or firm issuing a check

Drawing account (p. 71)   A special type of owner's equity account set up to record the owner's withdrawal of cash from the business

Economic entity (p. 9)   A business or organization whose major purpose is to produce a profit for its owners

Employee (p. 352)   A person who is hired by and works under the control and direction of the employer

Employee's Withholding Allowance Certificate, Form W-4 (p. 360)   A form used to claim exemption (withholding) allowances

Employer's Annual Federal Unemployment Tax Return, Form 940 or 940-EZ (p. 405)   Preprinted government form used by the employer to report unemployment taxes for the calendar year

Employer's Quarterly Federal Tax Return, Form 941 (p. 395)   Preprinted government form used by the employer to report payroll tax information relating to social security, Medicare, and employee income tax withholding to the Internal Revenue Service

Endorsement (p. 309)   A written authorization that transfers ownership of a check

Entity (p. 9)   Anything having its own separate identity, such as an individual, a town, a university, or a business

Equity (p. 25)   An owner's financial interest in a business

Equivalent production (p. 1065)   The estimated number of units that could have been started and completed with the same effort and costs incurred in the department during the same time period

Exempt employees (p. 364)   Salaried employees who hold supervisory or managerial positions who are not subject to the maximum hour and overtime pay provisions of the Wage and Hour Law

Expense (p. 31)   An outflow of cash, use of other assets, or incurring of a liability

Experience rating system (p. 401)   A system that rewards an employer for maintaining steady employment conditions by reducing the firm's state unemployment tax rate

Exposure draft (p. 13)   A proposed solution to a problem being considered by the Financial Accounting Standards Board

Extraordinary, nonrecurring items (p. 777)   Transactions that are highly unusual, clearly unrelated to routine operations, and that do not frequently occur

Face interest rate (p. 813)   The contractual interest specified on the bond

Face value (p. 585)   An amount of money indicated to be paid, exclusive of interest or discounts

Fair market value (p. 38)   The current worth of an asset or the price the asset would bring if sold on the open market

Fair market value method (p. 650)   A method of recording the trade-in of an asset that allows a loss to be recognized on the transaction if the book value exceeds the trade-in allowance

Federal unemployment taxes (FUTA) (p. 354)   Taxes levied by the federal government against employers to benefit unemployed workers

Financial statements (p. 4)   Periodic reports of a firm's financial position or operating results

Financing activities (p. 913)   Transactions with those who provide cash to the business to carry on its activities

Finished goods inventory (p. 1006)   The cost of completed products ready for sale; corresponds to the Merchandise Inventory account of a merchandising business

Finished goods subsidiary ledger (p. 1040)   A ledger containing a record for each of the different types of finished products

First in, first out (FIFO) method (p. 614)   A method of inventory costing that assumes the oldest merchandise is sold first

Fixed budget (p. 1097)   A budget representing only one level of activity

Fixed costs (p. 1094)   Costs that do not change in total as the level of activity changes

Flexible budget (p. 1099)   A budget that shows the budgeted costs at various levels of activity

Footing (p. 64)   A small pencil figure written at the base of an amount column showing the sum of the entries in the column

Franchise (p. 653)   An intangible asset; a right to exclusive dealership granted by a governmental unit or a business entity

Freight In account (p. 256)   An account showing transportation charges for items purchased

Full disclosure principle (p. 532)   The requirement that all information that might affect the user's interpretation of the profitability and financial position of a business be disclosed in the financial statements or in footnotes to the statements

Full endorsement (p. 310)   A signature transferring a check to a specific person, firm, or bank

Fundamental accounting equation (p. 30)   The relationship between assets and liabilities plus owner's equity

Gain (p. 646)   The disposition of an asset for more than its book value

General journal (p. 96)   A financial record for entering all types of business transactions; a record of original entry

General ledger (p. 105)   A permanent, classified record of all accounts used in a firm's operation; a record of final entry

General partner (p. 678)   A member of a partnership who has unlimited liability

Generally accepted accounting principles (GAAP) (p. 12)   Accounting standards developed and applied by professional accountants

Going concern assumption (p. 529)   The assumption that a firm will continue to operate indefinitely

Goodwill (p. 654)   An intangible asset; the value of a business in excess of the value of its identifiable assets

Governmental accounting (p. 6) Accounting work performed for a federal, state, or local governmental unit

Gross profit (p. 473) The difference between net sales and the cost of goods sold

Gross profit method (p. 619) A method of estimating inventory cost based on the assumption that the rate of gross profit on sales and the ratio of cost of goods sold to net sales are relatively constant from period to period

Gross profit percentage (p. 484) The amount of gross profit from each dollar of sales (gross profit percentage = gross profit ÷ net sales)

High-low point method (p. 1095) A method to determine the fixed and variable components of a semivariable cost

Historical cost principle (p. 531) *See* Cost basis principle

Horizontal analysis (p. 848) Computing the percentage change for individual items in the financial statements from year to year

Hourly rate basis (p. 357) A method of paying employees according to a stated rate per hour

Impairment (p. 655) A situation that occurs when the asset is determined to have a market value or a value in use less than its book value

Income statement (p. 35) A formal report of business operations covering a specific period of time; also called a profit and loss statement or a statement of income and expenses

Income Summary account (p. 164) A special owner's equity account that is used only in the closing process to summarize the results of operations

Income tax method (p. 649) A method of recording the trade-in of an asset according to tax rules that do not permit a gain or loss to be recognized on the transaction

Independent contractor (p. 352) One who is paid by a company to carry out a specific task or job but is not under the direct supervision or control of the company

Indirect expenses (p. 981) Operating expenses that cannot be readily identified and are not closely related to activity within a department

Indirect labor (p. 1005) Costs attributable to personnel who support production but are not directly involved in the manufacture of a product; for example, supervisory, repair and maintenance, and janitorial staff

Indirect materials and supplies (p. 1005) Materials used in manufacturing a product that do not become a part of the product

Indirect method (p. 925) A means of reporting cash generated from operating activities by treating net income as the primary source of cash in the operating section of the statement of cash flows and adjusting that amount for changes in current assets and liabilities associated with net income, noncash transactions, and other items

Individual earnings record (p. 370) An employee record that contains information needed to compute earnings and complete tax reports

Industry averages (p. 857) Financial ratios and percentages reflecting averages for similar companies

Intangible assets (p. 653) Assets that lack a physical substance, such as goodwill, patents, copyrights, and computer software, although software has, in a sense, a physical attribute

Interest (p. 584) The fee charged for the use of money

Internal control system (p. 950) A system designed to safeguard assets, achieve efficient processing of transactions, and ensure accuracy and reliability of financial records

International accounting (p. 13) The study of accounting principles used by different countries

Interpret (p. 174) To understand and explain the meaning and importance of something (such as financial statements)

Inventory sheet (p. 431) A form used to list the volume and type of goods a firm has in stock

Inventory turnover (p. 485) The number of times inventory is purchased and sold during the accounting period (inventory turnover = cost of goods sold ÷ average inventory)

Investing activities (p. 913) Transactions that involve the acquisition or disposal of long-term assets

Invoice (p. 219) A customer billing for merchandise bought on credit

Job order (p. 1036) A specific order for a specific batch of manufactured items

Job order cost accounting (p. 1036) A cost accounting system that determines the unit cost of manufactured items for each separate production order

Job order cost sheet (p. 1046) A record of all manufacturing costs charged to a specific job

Journal (p. 96) The record of original entry

Journalizing (p. 96) Recording transactions in a journal

Just-in-time system (p. 1039) An inventory system in which raw materials are ordered so they arrive just in time to be placed into production

Labor efficiency variance (p. 1105) *See* Labor time variance

Labor rate variance (p. 1105) The difference between the actual labor rate per hour and the standard labor rate per hour multiplied by the actual number of hours worked on the job

Labor time variance (p. 1105) The difference between the actual hours worked and the standard labor hours allowed for the job multiplied by the standard cost per hour

Last in, first out (LIFO) method (p. 614) A method of inventory costing that assumes that the most recently purchased merchandise is sold first

Ledger (p. 105) The record of final entry

Leveraged buyout (p. 886) Purchasing a business by acquiring the stock and obligating the business to pay the debt incurred

Leveraging (p. 815) Using borrowed funds to earn a profit greater than the interest that must be paid on the borrowing

Liabilities (p. 28) Debts or obligations of a business

Limited liability company (LLC) (p. 726) Provides limited liability to the owners, who can elect to have the profits taxed at the LLC level or on their individual tax returns

Limited liability partnership (LLP) (p. 725) A partnership that provides some limited liability for all partners

Limited partner (p. 678) A member of a partnership whose liability is limited to his or her investment in the partnership

Limited partnership (p. 678) A partnership having one or more limited partners

Liquidation (p. 694) Termination of a business by distributing all assets and discontinuing the business

Liquidation value (p. 730)   Value of assets to be applied to preferred stock, usually par value or an amount in excess of par value, if the corporation is liquidated

Liquidity (pp. 476, 888)   The ease with which an item can be converted into cash; the ability of a business to pay its debts when due

List price (p. 218)   An established retail price

Long-term liabilities (p. 477)   Debts of a business that are due more than one year in the future

Loss (p. 646)   The disposition of an asset for less than its book value

Lower of cost or market rule (p. 617)   The principle by which inventory is reported at either its original cost or its replacement cost, whichever is lower

Management advisory services (p. 6)   Services designed to help clients improve their information systems or their business performance

Managerial accounting (pp. 6, 978)   Accounting work carried on by an accountant employed by a single business in industry; the branch of accounting that provides financial information about business segments, activities, or products

Manufacturing business (p. 202)   A business that sells goods that it has produced

Manufacturing cost budget (p. 1096)   A budget made for each manufacturing cost

Manufacturing margin (p. 1125)   Sales minus the variable cost of goods sold

Manufacturing overhead (p. 1005)   All manufacturing costs that are not classified as direct materials or direct labor

Manufacturing overhead ledger (p. 1044)   A subsidiary ledger that contains a record for each overhead item

Manufacturing Summary account (p. 1009)   The account to which all items on the statement of cost of goods manufactured are closed; similar to the Income Summary account

Marginal income (p. 1125)   The manufacturing margin minus variable operating expenses

Markdown (p. 622)   Price reduction below the original markon

Market interest rate (p. 813)   The interest rate a corporation is willing to pay and investors are willing to accept at the current time

Market price (p. 617)   The price the business would pay to buy an item of inventory through usual channels in usual quantities

Market value (p. 729)   The price per share at which stock is bought and sold

Markon (p. 620)   The difference between the cost and the initial retail price of merchandise

Markup (p. 622)   A price increase above the original markon

Matching principle (p. 532)   The concept that revenue and the costs incurred in earning the revenue should be matched in the appropriate accounting periods

Materiality (p. 534)   The significance of an item in relation to a particular situation or set of facts

Materials price variance (p. 1103)   The difference between the actual price and the standard cost for materials multiplied by the actual quantity of materials used

Materials quantity variance (p. 1103)   The difference between the actual quantity used and the quantity of materials allowed multiplied by the standard cost of the materials

Materials requisition (p. 1041)   A form that describes the item and quantity needed and shows the job or purpose

Materials usage variance (p. 1103)   *See* Materials quantity variance

Maturity value (p. 585)   The total amount (principal plus interest) that must be paid when a note comes due

Medicare tax (p. 353)   A tax levied on employees and employers to provide medical care for the employee and the employee's spouse after each has reached age 65

Memorandum entry (p. 681)   An informational entry in the general journal

Merchandise inventory (p. 202)   The stock of goods a merchandising business keeps on hand

Merchandising business (p. 202)   A business that sells goods purchased for resale

Merit rating system (p. 401)   *See* Experience rating system

Minute book (p. 744)   A book in which accurate and complete records of all meetings of stockholders and directors are kept

Mortgage loan (p. 812)   A long-term debt created when a note is given as part of the purchase price for land or buildings

Multiple-step income statement (p. 472)   A type of income statement on which several subtotals are computed before the net income is calculated

Mutual agency (p. 678)   The characteristic of a partnership by which each partner is empowered to act as an agent for the partnership, binding the firm by his or her acts

Negotiable (p. 309)   A financial instrument whose ownership can be transferred to another person or business

Negotiable instrument (p. 584)   A financial document containing a promise or order to pay that meets all requirements of the Uniform Commercial Code in order to be transferable to another party

Net book value (p. 640)   The cost of an asset minus its accumulated depreciation, depletion, or amortization, also known as book value

Net income (p. 36)   The result of an excess of revenue over expenses

Net income line (p. 447)   The worksheet line immediately following the column totals on which net income (or net loss) is recorded in two places: the Income Statement section and the Balance Sheet section

Net loss (p. 36)   The result of an excess of expenses over revenue

Net of discount (p. 961)   The invoice amount minus the cash discount offered

Net price (p. 218)   The list price less all trade discounts

Net sales (p. 213)   The difference between the balance in the Sales account and the balance in the Sales Returns and Allowances account

Net salvage value (p. 640)   The salvage value of an asset less any costs to remove or sell the asset

Net value of accounts receivable (p. 564)   The difference between the Accounts Receivable account and the Allowance for Doubtful Accounts account

Noncumulative preferred stock (p. 731)   Stock that conveys to its owners the stated preference dividend for the current year but no rights to dividends for years in which none were declared

Nonparticipating preferred stock (p. 731)   Stock that conveys to its owners the right to only the preference dividend amount specified on the stock certificate

No-par-value stock (p. 739)   Stock that is not assigned a par value in the corporate charter

Normal balance (p. 65)   The increase side of an account

Note payable (p. 586)   A liability representing a written promise by the maker of the note (the debtor) to pay another party (the creditor) a specified amount at a specified future date

Note receivable (p. 590)   An asset representing a written promise by another party (the debtor) to pay the note holder (the creditor) a specified amount at a specified future date

Objectivity assumption (p. 530)   The idea that financial reports are unbiased and fair to all parties

On account (p. 26)   An arrangement to allow payment at a later date; also called a charge account or open-account credit

Open-account credit (p. 221)   A system that allows the sale of services or goods with the understanding that payment will be made at a later date

Operating activities (p. 912)   Routine business transactions—selling goods or services and incurring expenses

Operating assets and liabilities (p. 919)   Current assets and current liabilities

Opportunity cost (p. 1128)   Potential earnings or benefits that are given up because a certain course of action is taken

Organization costs (p. 737)   The costs associated with establishing a corporation; an intangible asset account

Outstanding checks (p. 314)   Checks that have been recorded in the cash payments journal but have not yet been paid by the bank

Overapplied overhead (p. 1045)   The result of applied overhead exceeding the actual overhead costs

Overhead application rate (p. 1044)   The rate at which the estimated cost of overhead is charged to each job

Owner's equity (p. 28)   The financial interest of the owner of a business; also called proprietorship or net worth

Paid-in capital (p. 778)   Capital acquired from capital stock transactions

Par value (p. 729)   An amount assigned by the corporate charter to each share of stock for accounting purposes

Participating preferred stock (p. 731)   Stock that conveys the right not only to the preference dividend amount but also to a share of other dividends paid

Partnership (pp. 9, 678)   A business entity owned by two or more persons who carry on a business for profit and who are legally responsible for the debts and taxes of the business

Partnership agreement (p. 679)   A legal contract forming a partnership and specifying certain details of operation

Patent (p. 653)   An intangible asset; an exclusive right given by the U.S. Patent Office to manufacture and sell an invention for a period of 17 years from the date the patent is granted

Payee (p. 309)   The person or firm to whom a check is payable

Payment date (p. 779)   The date that dividends are paid

Payment voucher (p. 951)   *See* Voucher

Payroll register (p. 365)   A record of payroll information for each employee for the pay period

Periodic inventory (p. 612)   Inventory based on a periodic count of goods on hand

Periodicity of income assumption (p. 530)   The concept that income should be reported in certain time periods

Permanent account (p. 76)   An account that is kept open from one accounting period to the next

Perpetual inventory (p. 612)   Inventory based on a running total of number of units

Perpetual inventory system (p. 1037)   An inventory system that tracks the inventories on hand at all times

Petty cash analysis sheet (p. 305)   A form used to record transactions involving petty cash

Petty cash fund (p. 292)   A special-purpose fund used to handle payments involving small amounts of money

Petty cash voucher (p. 305)   A form used to record the payments made from a petty cash fund

Physical inventory (p. 612)   An actual count of the number of units of each type of good on hand

Piece-rate basis (p. 357)   A method of paying employees according to the number of units produced

Plant and equipment (p. 477)   Property that will be used in the business for longer than one year

Postclosing trial balance (p. 173)   A statement that is prepared to prove the equality of total debits and credits after the closing process is completed

Postdated check (p. 311)   A check dated some time in the future

Posting (p. 105)   Transferring data from a journal to a ledger

Preemptive right (p. 729)   A shareholder's right to purchase a proportionate amount of any new stock issued at a later date

Preference dividend (p. 731)   A basic or stated dividend rate for preferred stock that must be paid before dividends can be paid on common stock

Preferred stock (p. 730)   A class of stock that has special claims on the corporate profits or, in case of liquidation, on corporate assets

Premium on bonds payable (p. 819)   The excess of the price paid over the face value of a bond

Prepaid expenses (pp. 131, 437)   Expense items acquired, recorded, and paid for in advance of their use

Price-earnings ratio (p. 882)   The ratio of the current market value of common stock to earnings per share of that stock

Principal (p. 585)   The amount shown on the face of a note

Private sector (p. 524)   The business sector, which is represented in developing accounting principles by the Financial Accounting Standards Board (FASB)

Process cost accounting (p. 1036)   A cost accounting system whereby unit costs of manufactured items are determined by totaling unit costs in each production department

Process cost accounting system (p. 1064)   A method of accounting in which costs are accumulated for each process or department and then transferred on to the next process or department

Production order (p. 1036)   *See* Job order

Profit center (p. 978)   A business segment that produces revenue

Promissory note (p. 294)   A written promise to pay a specified amount of money on a specific date

Property, plant, and equipment (p. 434)   Long-term assets that are used in the operation of a business and that are subject to depreciation (except for land, which is not depreciated)

Public accountants (p. 5)   Members of firms that perform accounting services for other companies

Public sector (p. 524) The government sector, which is represented in developing accounting principles by the Securities and Exchange Commission (SEC)

Purchase allowance (p. 263) A price reduction from the amount originally billed

Purchase invoice (p. 254) A bill received for goods purchased

Purchase order (p. 254) An order to the supplier of goods specifying items needed, quantity, price, and credit terms

Purchase requisition (p. 254) A list sent to the purchasing department showing the items to be ordered

Purchase return (p. 263) Return of unsatisfactory goods

Purchases account (p. 256) An account used to record cost of goods bought for resale during a period

Purchases discount (p. 259) A cash discount offered to customers for payment within a specified period

Purchases journal (p. 256) A special journal used to record the purchase of goods on credit

Qualitative characteristics (p. 528) Traits necessary for credible financial statements: usefulness, relevance, reliability, verifiability, neutrality, understandability, timeliness, comparability, and completeness

Quick assets (p. 889) Cash, receivables, and marketable securities

Ratio analysis (p. 848) Computing the relationship between various items in the financial statements

Raw materials (p. 1004) The materials placed into production

Raw materials ledger card (p. 1040) A record showing details of receipts and issues for a type of raw material

Raw materials subsidiary ledger (p. 1040) A ledger containing the raw materials ledger cards

Real property (p. 638) Assets such as land, land improvements, buildings, and other structures attached to the land

Realization principle (p. 531) The concept that revenue occurs when goods or services, merchandise, or other assets are exchanged for cash or claims to cash

Receiving report (p. 254) A form showing quantity and condition of goods received

Recognition (p. 531) The determination of the period in which to record a business transaction

Record date (p. 779) The date on which the specific stockholders to receive a dividend are determined

Recoverability test (p. 656) Test for possible impairment that compares the asset's net book value with the estimated net cash flows from future use of the asset

Registered bonds (p. 813) Bonds issued to a party whose name is listed in the corporation's records

Registrar (p. 746) A person or institution in charge of the issuance and transfer of a corporation's stock

Reinstate (p. 562) To put back or restore an accounts receivable amount that was previously written off

Relevant range of activity (p. 1099) The different levels of activity at which a factory is expected to operate

Replacement cost (p. 617) *See* Market price

Report form balance sheet (p. 143) A balance sheet that lists the asset accounts first, followed by liabilities and owner's equity

Residual value (p. 640) The estimate of the amount that could be obtained from the sale or disposition of an asset at the end of its useful life; also called salvage or scrap value

Responsibility accounting (p. 979) The process that allows management to evaluate the performance of each segment of the business and assign responsibility for its financial results

Restrictive endorsement (p. 310) A signature that transfers a check to a specific party for a stated purpose

Retail business (p. 202) A business that sells directly to individual consumers

Retail method (p. 620) A method of estimating inventory cost by applying the ratio of cost to selling price in the current accounting period to the retail price of the inventory

Retained earnings (p. 778) The cumulative profits and losses of the corporation not distributed as dividends

Return on common stockholders' equity (p. 881) A measure of how well the corporation is making a profit for its shareholders; the ratio of net income available for common stockholders to common stockholders' equity

Revenue (p. 30) An inflow of money or other assets that results from the sales of goods or services or from the use of money or property; also called income

Reversing entries (p. 485) Journal entries made to reverse the effect of certain adjusting entries involving accrued income or accrued expenses to avoid problems in recording future payments or receipts of cash in a new accounting period

Salary basis (p. 357) A method of paying employees according to an agreed-upon amount for each week or month

Sales allowance (p. 210) A reduction in the price originally charged to customers for goods or services

Sales discount (p. 259) A cash discount offered by the supplier to customers for payment within a specified period

Sales invoice (p. 254) A supplier's billing document

Sales journal (p. 203) A special journal used to record sales of merchandise on credit

Sales return (p. 210) A firm's acceptance of a return of goods from a customer

Salvage value (p. 134) An estimate of the amount that could be received by selling or disposing of an asset at the end of its useful life

Schedule of accounts payable (p. 265) A list of all balances owed to creditors

Schedule of accounts receivable (p. 216) A listing of all balances of the accounts in the accounts receivable subsidiary ledger

Schedule of operating expenses (p. 914) A schedule that supplements the income statement, showing the selling and general and administrative expenses in greater detail

Schedule of vouchers payable (p. 958) A list of all amounts owed for unpaid vouchers

Scrap value (p. 640) *See* Residual value

Secured bonds (p. 812) Bonds for which property is pledged to secure the claims of bondholders

Semidirect expenses (p. 981) Operating expenses that cannot be directly assigned to a department but are closely related to departmental activities

Semivariable costs (p. 1094) Costs that vary with, but not in direct proportion to, the volume of activity

Separate entity assumption (pp. 9, 529) The concept that a business is separate from its owners; the concept of keeping a firm's financial records separate from the owner's personal financial records

Serial bonds (p. 813) Bonds issued at one time but payable over a period of years

Service business (p. 202) A business that sells services

Service charge (p. 313) A fee charged by a bank to cover the costs of maintaining accounts and providing services

Shareholder (p. 724) A person who owns shares of stock in a corporation; also called a stockholder

Sight draft (p. 596) A commercial draft that is payable on presentation

Single-step income statement (p. 472) A type of income statement where only one computation is needed to determine the net income (total revenue − total expenses = net income)

Slide (p. 75) An accounting error involving a misplaced decimal point

Social entity (p. 9) A nonprofit organization, such as a city, public school, or public hospital

Social Security Act (p. 353) A federal act providing certain benefits for employees and their families; officially the Federal Insurance Contributions Act

Social security tax (FICA) (p. 353) A tax imposed by the Federal Insurance Contributions Act and collected on employee earnings to provide retirement and disability benefits

Sole proprietorship (p. 9) A business entity owned by one person who is legally responsible for the debts and taxes of the business

Special journal (p. 202) A journal used to record only one type of transaction

Specific identification method (p. 613) A method of inventory costing based on the actual cost of each item of merchandise

Stable monetary unit assumption (p. 529) The concept that accounting records are kept in terms of money and the assumption that the value of money is stable

Standard cost card (p. 1102) A form that shows the per-unit standard costs for materials, labor, and overhead

Standard costs (p. 1036) A measure of what costs should be in an efficient operation

State unemployment taxes (SUTA) (p. 355) Taxes levied by a state government against employers to benefit unemployed workers

Stated value (p. 729) The value that can be assigned to no-par-value stock by a board of directors for accounting purposes

Statement of account (p. 294) A form sent to a firm's customers showing transactions during the month and the balance owed

Statement of cash flows (p. 912) A financial statement that provides information about the cash receipts and cash payments of a business

Statement of cost of goods manufactured (p. 1003) A financial report showing details of the cost of goods completed for a manufacturing business

Statement of owner's equity (p. 36) A formal report of changes that occurred in the owner's financial interest during a reporting period

Statement of partners' equities (p. 693) A financial statement prepared to summarize the changes in the partners' capital accounts during an accounting period

Statement of retained earnings (p. 786) A financial statement that shows all changes that have occurred in retained earnings during the period

Statement of stockholders' equity (p. 788) A financial statement that provides an analysis reconciling the beginning and ending balance of each of the stockholders' equity accounts

Statements of Financial Accounting Standards (p. 12) Accounting principles established by the Financial Accounting Standards Board

Stock (p. 11) Certificates that represent ownership of a corporation

Stock certificate (p. 744) The form by which capital stock is issued; the certificate indicates the name of the corporation, the name of the stockholder to whom the certificate was issued, the class of stock, and the number of shares

Stock dividend (p. 779) Distribution of the corporation's own stock on a pro rata basis that results in conversion of a portion of the firm's retained earnings to permanent capital

Stock split (p. 781) When a corporation issues two or more shares of new stock to replace each share outstanding without making any changes in the capital accounts

Stockholders (p. 12) The owners of a corporation; also called shareholders

Stockholders of record (p. 779) Stockholders in whose name shares are held on date of record and who will receive a declared dividend

Stockholders' equity (p. 728) The corporate equivalent of owners' equity; also called shareholders' equity

Stockholders' ledger (p. 745) *See* Capital stock ledger

Straight-line amortization (p. 819) Amortizing the premium or discount on bonds payable in equal amounts each month over the life of the bond

Straight-line depreciation (p. 134) Allocation of an asset's cost in equal amounts to each accounting period of the asset's useful life

Subchapter S corporation (S corporation) (p. 725) An entity formed as a corporation that meets the requirements of Subchapter S of the Internal Revenue Code to be treated essentially as a partnership, so that the corporation pays no income tax

Subscribers' ledger (p. 745) A subsidiary ledger that contains an account receivable for each stock subscriber

Subscription book (p. 745) A list of the stock subscriptions received

Subsidiary ledger (p. 202) A ledger dedicated to accounts of a single type and showing details to support a general ledger account

Sum-of-the-years'-digits method (p. 642) A method of depreciating asset costs by allocating as expense each year a fractional part of the asset's depreciable cost, based on the sum of the digits of the number of years in the asset's useful life

Sunk cost (p. 1128) A cost that has been incurred and will not change as a result of a decision

T account (p. 58) A type of account, resembling a T, used to analyze the effects of a business transaction

Tangible personal property (p. 638) Assets such as machinery, equipment, furniture, and fixtures that can be removed and used elsewhere

Tax accounting (p. 5) A service that involves tax compliance and tax planning

Tax-exempt wages (p. 359) Earnings in excess of the base amount set by the Social Security Act

Temporary account (p. 77) An account whose balance is transferred to another account at the end of an accounting period

Tickler file (p. 955) *See* Unpaid voucher file

Time and a half (p. 353) Rate of pay for an employee's work in excess of 40 hours a week

Time draft (p. 597) A commercial draft that is payable during a specified period of time

Time ticket (p. 1043) Form used to record hours worked and jobs performed

Total equities (p. 885) The sum of a corporation's liabilities and stockholders' equity

Trade acceptance (p. 598) A form of commercial time draft used in transactions involving the sale of goods

Trade discount (p. 218) A reduction from list price

Trade name (p. 653) An intangible asset; an exclusive business name registered with the U.S. Patent Office; also called brand name

Trademark (p. 653) An intangible asset; an exclusive business symbol registered with the U.S. Patent Office

Trading on the equity (p. 815) *See* Leveraging

Transfer agent (p. 745) A person or institution that handles all stock transfers and transfer records for a corporation

Transfer price (p. 979) The price at which one segment's goods are transferred to another segment of the company

Transmittal of Wage and Tax Statements, Form W-3 (p. 399) Preprinted government form submitted with Forms W-2 to the Social Security Administration

Transportation In account (p. 256) *See* Freight In account

Transposition (p. 75) An accounting error involving misplaced digits in a number

Treasury stock (p. 784) A corporation's own capital stock that has been issued and reacquired; the stock must have been previously paid in full and issued to a stockholder

Trend analysis (p. 855) Comparing selected ratios and percentages over a period of time

Trial balance (p. 73) A statement to test the accuracy of total debits and credits after transactions have been recorded

Underapplied overhead (p. 1045) The result of actual overhead costs exceeding applied overhead

Unearned income (p. 440) Income received before it is earned

Unemployment insurance program (p. 401) A program that provides unemployment compensation through a tax levied on employers

Units-of-output method (p. 643) *See* Units-of-production method

Units-of-production method (p. 643) A method of depreciating asset cost at the same rate for each unit produced during each period

Unlimited liability (p. 678) The implication that a creditor can look to all partners' personal assets as well as the assets of the partnership for payment of the firm's debts

Unpaid voucher file (p. 955) A file to hold vouchers until they are due to be paid, filed by due date

Updated account balances (p. 443) The amounts entered in the Adjusted Trial Balance section of the worksheet

Valuation account (p. 557) An account, such as Allowance for Doubtful Accounts, whose balance is revalued or reappraised in light of reasonable expectations

Variable costing (p. 1124) *See* Direct costing

Variable costs (p. 1094) Costs that vary in total in direct proportion to changes in the level of activity

Variance analysis (p. 1103) Explains the difference between standard cost and actual cost

Vertical analysis (p. 848) Computing the relationship between each item on a financial statement to some base amount on the statement

Voucher (p. 951) A form used to authorize payment of an obligation

Voucher register (p. 955) A journal used to record liabilities arising from business transactions

Voucher system (p. 951) A method of controlling liabilities and cash payments based on vouchers

Wage and Tax Statement, Form W-2 (p. 398) Preprinted government form that contains information about an employee's earnings and tax withholdings for the year

Wage-bracket table method (p. 361) A simple method to determine the amount of federal income tax to be withheld using a table provided by the government

Weighted average method (p. 613) *See* Average cost method

Wholesale business (p. 218) A business that manufactures or distributes goods to retail businesses or large consumers such as hotels and hospitals

Withdrawals (p. 34) Funds taken from the business by the owner for personal use

Withholding statement (p. 398) *See* Wage and Tax Statement, Form W-2

Workers' compensation insurance (p. 356) Insurance that protects employees against losses from job-related injuries or illnesses, or compensates their families if death occurs in the course of the employment

Work in process (p. 1005) Partially completed units in the production process

Work in process subsidiary ledger (p. 1040) A ledger containing the job order cost sheets

Working capital (p. 888) The measure of the ability of a company to meet its current obligations; the excess of current assets over current liabilities

Worksheet (p. 130) A form used to gather all data needed at the end of an accounting period to prepare financial statements

INDEX

Photo Credits

3M 811(tr); Herman Agopian/Stone 521; Theodore Anderson/The Image Bank 94-95; Avery Dennison Corporation 1035(tr);

Mario Bauregard/CORBIS 291(tr); Peter Beck/CORBIS STOCK MARKET 766-767; Morton Beebe/CORBIS 523(tr);

Robert Brenner/PhotoEdit 1034-1035; Flip Chalfant/The Image Bank 846-847; Circuit City Stores, Inc. 611(tr); The Coca-Cola Company 637(tr);

CORBIS 610-611; Peter Dazely/Stone 1; Dell Computer Corporation 948-949, 949(tr); David DeLossy/The Image Bank 57(tr);

Ghislain & Marie David DeLossy/The Image Bank 429(tr); Lonnie Duka/Stone 1123(tr); Steve Dunwell/The Image Bank 162-163;

American Eagle Outfitters, Inc. 428-429; Eastman Kodak Company 911(tr); Randy Faris/CORBIS 675; FedEx Corporation 554-555, 555(tr);

Jon Feingersh/CORBIS STOCK MARKET 351(tr); Sandy Felsenphal/CORBIS 767(tr); Maria Ferrari/SuperStock 879(tr);

Allan Friedlander/SuperStock 878-879; Brett Froomer/The Image Bank 1001(tr); Galileo International Inc.163(tr);

Glencoe/McGraw-Hill 199; Goodrich Corporation 1000-1001; The Goodyear Tire & Rubber Company 522-523; Guess? Inc. 56-57;

H&R Block, Inc. 290-291; David Hanover/Stone 2-3; Walter Hodges/Stone 947; Robert Holmes/CORBIS 847(tr);

Timothy Hursley/SuperStock 636-637; International Truck and Engine Corporation 845; Zigy Kaluzny/Stone 583(tr), 1092-1093;

Vicky Kasala/The Image Bank 470-471; KB Home 582-583; Nick Koudis/PhotoDisc 2-3; Lands' End, Inc. 388-389;

John Madere/CORBIS STOCK MARKET 129(tr); James Marshall/CORBIS 200-201; Don Mason/CORBIS STOCK MARKET 350-351;

Corporate Communications/Mattel, Inc. 977(tr); Jordan Miller Photography 427; NASA 128-129;

Jose L. Pelaez/CORBIS STOCK MARKET 253(tr); Pier 1 Imports 252-253; Ed Pritchard/Stone 676-677;

Mark Richards/PhotoEdit 3(tr); Tim Right/CORBIS 095(tr); Bob Rowan; Progressive Image/CORBIS 976-977; Safeway Inc. 471(tr);

Sara Lee Corporation 723(tr); Jeff Smith/International Stock 1093(tr); Cousteau Society/The Image Bank 910-911;

Mike Eller/Southwest Airlines Co. 22-23; Southwest Airlines Co. 23(tr); SuperStock 722-723, 810-811;

Telegraph Colour Library/FPG 1122-1123; VCG/FPG International 349; Wal-Mart Stores, Inc. 201(tr); Lee White/CORBIS 389(tr);

Stephen Wilks/The Image Bank 1063(tr); Keith Wood/Stone 1062-1063; Woolpert LLP 677(tr).

SAMPLE GENERAL LEDGER ACCOUNTS

Account Name	Classification	Permanent or Temporary	Normal Balance
INCOME STATEMENT			
Fees Income	Revenue	Temporary	Credit
Sales	Revenue	Temporary	Credit
Sales Discounts	Contra Revenue	Temporary	Debit
Sales Returns and Allowances	Contra Revenue	Temporary	Debit
Purchases	Cost of Goods Sold	Temporary	Debit
Freight In	Cost of Goods Sold	Temporary	Debit
Purchases Discounts	Contra Cost of Goods Sold	Temporary	Credit
Purchases Returns and Allowances	Contra Cost of Goods Sold	Temporary	Credit
Direct Labor	Cost of Goods Manufactured	Temporary	Debit
Indirect Labor	Cost of Goods Manufactured	Temporary	Debit
Indirect Materials and Supplies	Cost of Goods Manufactured	Temporary	Debit
Payroll Taxes—Factory	Cost of Goods Manufactured	Temporary	Debit
Repairs and Maintenance—Factory	Cost of Goods Manufactured	Temporary	Debit
Depreciation—Factory	Cost of Goods Manufactured	Temporary	Debit
Insurance—Factory	Cost of Goods Manufactured	Temporary	Debit
Property Taxes—Factory	Cost of Goods Manufactured	Temporary	Debit
Advertising Expense	Operating Expense	Temporary	Debit
Amortization Expense	Operating Expense	Temporary	Debit
Bank Fees Expense	Operating Expense	Temporary	Debit
Cash Short or Over	Operating Expense	Temporary	Debit
Delivery Expense	Operating Expense	Temporary	Debit
Depreciation Expense	Operating Expense	Temporary	Debit
Insurance Expense	Operating Expense	Temporary	Debit
Payroll Taxes Expense	Operating Expense	Temporary	Debit
Property Tax Expense	Operating Expense	Temporary	Debit
Rent Expense	Operating Expense	Temporary	Debit
Research and Development Expense	Operating Expense	Temporary	Debit
Salaries Expense	Operating Expense	Temporary	Debit
Supplies Expense	Operating Expense	Temporary	Debit
Telephone Expense	Operating Expense	Temporary	Debit
Uncollectible Accounts Expense	Operating Expense	Temporary	Debit
Utilities Expense	Operating Expense	Temporary	Debit
Workers' Compensation Insurance Expense	Operating Expense	Temporary	Debit
Gain/Loss on Sale of Assets	Other Income/Expense	Temporary	—
Interest Income/Expense	Other Income/Expense	Temporary	—
Miscellaneous Income/Expense	Other Income/Expense	Temporary	—
Income Tax Expense	Other Expense	Temporary	Debit
STATEMENT OF OWNER'S EQUITY			
*(Owner's Name), Capital	Owner's Equity	Permanent	Credit
(Owner's Name), Drawing	Owner's Equity	Temporary	Debit
STATEMENT OF PARTNERS' EQUITY			
*(Partner's Name), Capital	Partners' Equity	Permanent	Credit
(Partner's Name), Drawing	Partners' Equity	Temporary	Debit
STATEMENT OF RETAINED EARNINGS			
*Retained Earnings—Appropriated	Stockholders' Equity	Permanent	Credit
*Retained Earnings	Stockholders' Equity	Permanent	Credit

*Account also appears on the balance sheet.